P9-DCM-629

Handbook of Infant Mental Health

Handbook of Infant Mental Health

Edited by
Charles H. Zeanah, Jr.

The Guilford Press

NEW YORK / LONDON

© 1993 The Guilford Press
A Division of Guilford Publications, Inc.
72 Spring Street, New York, NY 10012

Printed in the United States of America

This book is printed on acid-free paper.

Last digit is print number: 9 8 7 6 5 4 3 2 1

Library of Congress Cataloging-in-Publication Data

Handbook of infant mental health / edited by Charles H. Zeanah, Jr.
    p. cm.
   Includes bibliographical references and index.
   ISBN 0–89862-996–9
   1. Infant psychiatry. I. Zeanah, Charles H., Jr.
   [DNLM: 1. Mental Health—in infancy & childhood. 2. Mental
Disorders—in infancy & childhood. 3. Child Development Disorders.
WS 350.6 H2375 1993]
RJ502.5.H36 1993
618.92'89—dc20
DNLM/DLC
for Library of Congress
                                      93-14710
                                          CIP

Contributors

Thomas F. Anders, MD, Department of Psychiatry, University of California at Davis, Davis, California

Kathryn E. Barnard, RN, PhD, Parent–Child Nursing, Psychology, and the Center for Child Development and Mental Retardation, University of Washington, Seattle, Washington

Marianne Barton, PhD, Emma Pendleton Bradley Hospital, Providence, Rhode Island; Division of Child and Adolescent Psychiatry, Department of Psychiatry and Human Behavior, Brown University School of Medicine, Providence, Rhode Island

Diane Benoit, MD, Department of Psychiatry, The Hospital for Sick Children, Toronto, Ontario, Canada; University of Toronto, Toronto, Ontario, Canada

Richard D. Bingham, MD, Department of Psychiatry, University of Colorado Health Sciences Center, Denver, Colorado

Elizabeth R. Brown, MD, Department of Pediatrics, Boston University School of Medicine, Boston, Massachusetts; Division of Neonatology, Boston City Hospital, Boston, Massachusetts

Roseanne Clark, PhD, Department of Psychiatry, University of Wisconsin–Madison Medical School, Madison, Wisconsin

Susan Conlin, MSSW, Department of Psychiatry, University of Wisconsin, Madison, Wisconsin

Susan Crockenberg, PhD, Department of Psychology, University of Vermont, Burlington, Vermont

Judith A. Crowell, MD, Department of Psychiatry, State University of New York at Stony Brook, Stony Brook, New York

Margo Dichtelmiller, MA, School of Education, University of Michigan, Ann Arbor, Michigan

Susan Dickstein, PhD, Emma Pendleton Bradley Hospital, Providence, Rhode Island; Division of Child and Adolescent Psychiatry, Department of Psychiatry and Human Behavior, Brown University School of Medicine, Providence, Rhode Island

Martin J. Drell, MD, Division of Infant, Child, and Adolescent Psychiatry, Louisiana State University School of Medicine, New Orleans, Louisiana

Robert N. Emde, MD, Department of Psychiatry, University of Colorado Health Sciences Center, Denver, Colorado

Melissa A. Fleischmann, BA, Department of Psychology, State University of New York at Stony Brook, Stony Brook, New York

Theodore J. Gaensbauer, MD, Department of Psychiatry, University of Colorado Health Sciences Center, Denver, Colorado

Cynthia T. Garcia Coll, PhD, Department of Pediatrics, Brown University School of Medicine, Providence, Rhode Island; The Stone Center for Developmental Services and Studies, Wellesley College, Wellesley, Massachusetts

Stanley I. Greenspan, MD, Deptartment of Psychiatry, George Washington University Medical School, Washington, DC

Melvin J. Guyer, PhD, JD, Department of Psychiatry, University of Michigan, Ann Arbor, Michigan

Nancy W. Hall, MS, Department of Psychology, Yale University, New Haven, Connecticut

Robert Halpern, PhD, Erikson Institute, Chicago, Illinois

Della M. Hann, PhD, Division of Infant, Child, and Adolescent Psychiatry, Louisiana State University School of Medicine, New Orleans, Louisiana

Robert J. Harmon, MD, Department of Psychiatry, University of Colorado Health Sciences Center, Denver, Colorado

Laurence M. Hirshberg, PhD, Providence Parent–Child Center, Providence, Rhode Island; Division of Child and Adolescent Psychiatry, Department of Psychiatry and Human Behavior, Brown University School of Medicine, Providence, Rhode Island

Pauline Hopper, PhD, Department of Psychology, Yale University, New Haven, Connecticut

Thomas M. Horner, PhD, Department of Psychiatry, University of Michigan, Ann Arbor, Michigan

Fong-ruey Liaw, EdD, Teachers College, Columbia University, New York, New York

Alicia F. Lieberman, PhD, Department of Psychiatry, University of California, San Francisco, San Francisco, California; San Francisco General Hospital, San Francisco, California

Karlen Lyons-Ruth, PhD, Department of Psychiatry, Harvard Medical School at Cambridge Hospital, Cambridge, Massachusetts

Oommen K. Mammen, MD, Postpartum Disorders Service, HRI Hospital, Brookline, Massachusetts

Susan C. McDonough, PhD, School of Social Work, University of Michigan, Ann Arbor, Michigan

Samuel J. Meisels, EdD, School of Education, University of Michigan, Ann Arbor, Michigan

Elaine C. Meyer, PhD, Department of Pediatrics, Brown University School of Medicine, Providence, Rhode Island

Klaus Minde, MD, FRCP(C), Department of Psychiatry and Pediatrics, McGill University, Montreal, Quebec, Canada; Department of Psychiatry, Montreal Children's Hospital, Montreal, Quebec, Canada

Colleen E. Morisset, PhD, Parent–Child Nursing and Center for Child Development and Mental Retardation, University of Washington, Seattle, Washington

David A. Mrazek, MD, MRC Psych, Department of Psychiatry, Children's National Medical Center, Washington, DC; Department of Psychiatry, the George Washington University School of Medicine, Washington, D.C.

Patricia J. Mrazek, MSW, PhD, Institute of Medicine, National Academy of Sciences, Washington, D.C.

Joy D. Osofsky, PhD, Division of Infant, Child, and Adolescent Psychiatry, Louisiana State University Medical Center, New Orleans, Louisiana

Andrew Paulson, MA, Department of Psychiatry, University of Wisconsin–Madison Medical School, Madison, Wisconsin

Jeree H. Pawl, PhD, Department of Psychiatry, University of California San Francisco, San Francisco, California Infant–Parent Program, San Francisco General Hospital, San Francisco, California

Claire Peebles, MA, Division of Infant, Child, and Adolescent Psychiatry, Louisiana State University Medical Center, New Orleans, Louisiana

Barry M. Prizant, PhD, Division of Communication Disorders, Emerson College, Boston, Massachusetts

Joanne E. Roberts, PhD, Frank Porter Graham Child Development Center, University of North Carolina at Chapel Hill, Chapel Hill, North Carolina

Avi Sadeh, DSc, Department of Psychology, Tel Aviv University, Tel Aviv, Israel

Arnold J. Sameroff, PhD, Center for Human Growth and Development, and Department of Psychology, University of Michigan, Ann Arbor, Michigan

Ronald Seifer, PhD, Emma Pendleton Bradley Hospital, Providence, Rhode Island; Division of Child and Adolescent Psychiatry, Department of Psychiatry and Human Behavior, Brown University School of Medicine, Providence, Rhode Island

Jack P. Shonkoff, MD, Department of Pediatrics, University of Massachusetts Medical Center, Worcester, Massachusetts

Clifford H. Siegel, MD, Department of Psychiatry and Behavioral Sciences, The Children's Hospital, Denver, Colorado; Department of Psychiatry and Infant Psychiatry Clinic, University of Colorado Health Sciences Center, Denver, Colorado

Susan Spieker, PhD, Parent–Child Nursing and Center for Child Development and Mental Retardation, University of Washington, Seattle, Washington

Michael Thomasgard, MD, Department of Pediatrics, University of Massachusetts Medical Center, Worcester, Massachusetts

Fred R. Volkmar, MD, Child Study Center of Yale University, Yale University, New Haven, Connecticut

Bernice Weissbourd, MA, Family Focus and Family Resource Coalition, Chicago, Illinois; Lecturer, University of Chicago School of Social Service Administration, Chicago, Illinois

Amy M. Wetherby, PhD, Department of Communication Disorders, Florida State University, Tallahassee, Florida

Serena Wieder, PhD, Private Practice and Consulting, Washington, DC

Martha Williams, MSW, Providence Center for Counseling and Psychiatric Services, Providence, Rhode Island

Charles H. Zeanah, Jr., MD, Division of Infant, Child, and Adolescent Psychiatry, Louisiana State University School of Medicine, New Orleans, Louisiana

Edward Zigler, PhD, Department of Psychology, Yale University, New Haven, Connecticut

Barry Zuckerman, MD, Department of Pediatrics, Boston University School of Medicine, Boston, Massachusetts; Division of Developmental and Behavioral Pediatrics, Boston City Hospital, Boston, Massachusetts

Preface

A few years ago, I was finishing my training and interviewing for a "real job." The medical school I was visiting was affiliated with hospitals all over town, and my schedule included interviews at several. It so happened that the cabdriver who drove me from the hotel to the psychiatric hospital for my first several interviews also picked me up later that morning and drove me to the obstetrical hospital for other interviews. We were both surprised, I think, when he later picked me up at the obstetrical hospital and drove me this time to the child psychiatric hospital. Apparently unable to contain himself any longer, he said, "So, Doc, what's it gonna be, a baby doctor or a psychiatrist?" Feeling provocative, I said, "Well, actually, I'm a psychiatrist for babies." He gave me one of those raised-eyebrow looks and said, "For babies, huh? I don't have much use for psychiatrists myself." After a pause, he told me a story about a friend of his who had recently arrived in the United States with his wife from the "old country." She gave birth to their first child a few months after their arrival. In the few days after birth, the new mother was irritable and withdrawn, and she refused to look at her new baby. After she was discharged from the hospital, she left her husband and baby and returned to live with her extended family. The father was bewildered and heartbroken, and now was raising the baby with his extended family. "Can you believe it?" the cabdriver asked rhetorically in conclusion. After a brief pause, he said earnestly, "Hey, maybe they should have talked to you, huh? Maybe you could have helped them."

Many of us feel like the cabdriver. The image of an infant on a psychiatrist's couch seems silly, and the juxtaposition of mental illness and babyhood makes us feel uncomfortable. On further reflection, however, providing help to troubled families and trying to get infants off to a reasonable start are not such bad ideas after all. As we have made increasingly dramatic advances in our efforts to save younger, smaller, medically fragile infants, so now we must address the larger issues of the quality of life we want for babies. The challenge is for us to take mental health as seriously as we take physical health.

There is little doubt that the discipline of infant mental health is coming of age. Scientific and professional organizations, such as the World Association for Infant Mental Health (formed by a merger of the World Association for Infant Psychiatry and Allied Disciplines and the International Association for Infant Mental Health) and the International Society for Infant Studies, are both thriving in their second decade. The journals these two organizations sponsor, *Infant Mental Health Journal* and *Infant Behavior and Development*, are also over 10 years old. An ever-burgeoning literature fills these journals and many others with articles relevant to infant mental health. Demand for training in diverse disciplines concerned with the psychological development of infants and their families is increasing. Zero to Three, formerly the National Center for Clinical Infant Programs, has sponsored 12 to 16 fellowships in infant mental health for advanced trainees in a variety of disciplines each year since 1981.

Despite all this, and although it has been nearly 20 years since the first volume devoted to infant psychiatry was published (Rexford, Sander, & Shapiro, 1976), there is still no comprehensive text for the field. For this reason, the *Handbook of Infant Mental Health* was created.

No single volume can ever be comprehensive enough. Difficult decisions have had to be made, and many topics that I consider important have had to be omitted. In order to explain how some of the decisions that informed the process of developing this volume were made, I should probably describe something of my view of the scope of infant mental heath.

First, infant mental health encompasses efforts to diagnose and treat disorders in children from birth to 3 (or so) years of age. Second, efforts to develop effective prevention strategies, especially for infants in various high-risk groups, is an important aspect of infant mental health. Third, infant mental health includes the application of research on infant development to developmental psychopathology. Understanding risk, vulnerability, and protective factors as they relate to the ontogenesis of psychiatric disorders in young children, as well as disorders that become apparent in later periods of development, is one illustration of this application. Fourth, infant mental health includes efforts to revise, update, or refute our various theories of infant development. Finally, infant mental health includes applying knowledge gained from research to a number of social policy issues that affect large numbers of infants. To varying degrees, this volume is concerned with all of these issues.

Two other major guiding principles were important in developing this book. The first is an emphasis on considering the infant in context. Arnold Sameroff (1992) has recently declared the study of behavior in context to be the most important development in the last 25 years of developmental research. This emphasis is so widely accepted among clinicians and researchers (and perhaps even cabdrivers) that it has made its way into social policy, as with the explicit emphasis on families in Public Law 99-457.

The second guiding principle is an emphasis on development. The rapid pace of development in infancy is a compelling positive force that fascinates clinicians, investigators, and parents. Regarding the power of babies to enthrall us with their developmental gains, Selma Fraiberg (1980) has said that it is like having God on your side. The promise of unlimited possibilities, of a future that may be better, sustains us all in our work.

The field of infant mental health has been multidisciplinary since its inception. The contributors to this volume include many representatives of the disciplines and professions that are centrally involved in clinical infant mental health, such as child psychiatrists, clinical and developmental psychologists, communication disorder specialists, lawyers, nurses, pediatricians, special educators, and social workers. No special effort was required to include such a varied group of contributors to this volume, since each discipline has a number of individuals who have made distinguished contributions to the field. This diversity insures that we grapple with and attempt to integrate varied perspectives as we continue to grow.

In closing, I would like to acknowledge a number of individuals who made significant contributions to this effort. Despite the warnings of several colleagues about the frustrations of editing large texts, I found the contributing authors to be a pleasure to work with. I learned a great deal from them, and their enthusiasm for the effort was a significant reassurance to me throughout the process. Seymour Weingarten, the editor-in-chief of The Guilford Press, initially envisioned this volume, and he remained supportive and helpful with a number of important decisions throughout. David Lasky and Marie Sprayberry, also of The Guilford Press, were prompt, efficient, and helpful in transforming manuscript pages into a final product. Sarah Feigon was especially helpful during the editing phase, and I am grateful for the many hours she dedicated to the project. Caroline Breen and Lynne Kemp somehow managed to find time to be helpful with this, despite my repeatedly overwhelming them with other projects.

Finally, I appreciate the unflagging support of my family. My wife, Paula, manages to do it all herself and still have time and energy for me. My daughters, Emily, Katy, and Melanie, continue to inspire, delight, and amaze me. For their enduring patience and support, I am grateful.

REFERENCES

Fraiberg, S. (1980). *Clinical aspects of infant mental health: The first year of life.* New York: Basic Books.
Sameroff, A. (1992). Systems, development and early intervention. In J. P. Shonkoff, P. Hauser-Cram, M. W. Krauss, & C. C. Upshur (Eds.), Development of infants with disabilities and their families. *Monographs of the Society for Research in Child Development, 57*(6, Serial No.), 154–163.
Rexford, E. N., Sander, L. W., & Shapiro, T. (Eds.). (1976). *Infant psychiatry: A new synthesis.* New Haven, CT: Yale University Press.

Charles H. Zeanah, Jr.
New Orleans, Louisiana
January 1993

Contents

I. THE CONTEXT OF INFANT MENTAL HEALTH   1

1
Models of Development and Developmental Risk   3
     Arnold J. Sameroff

2
The Family Context of Infant Mental Health: I.   14
Affective Development in the Primary Caregiving Relationship
     Karlen Lyons-Ruth and Charles H. Zeanah, Jr.

3
The Family Context of Infant Mental Health: II.   38
Infant Development in Multiple Family Relationships
     Susan Crockenberg, Karlen Lyons-Ruth, and Susan Dickstein

4
The Sociocultural Context of Infant Development   56
     Cynthia T. Garcia Coll and Elaine C. Meyer

II. RISK CONDITIONS AND PROTECTIVE FACTORS   71

5
Poverty and Infant Development   73
     Robert Halpern

6
Prematurity and Serious Medical Illness in Infancy: 87
Implications for Development and Intervention
     Klaus Minde

7
Adolescent Parenthood: Risks and Opportunities   106
for Mothers and Infants
     Joy D. Osofsky, Della M. Hann, and Claire Peebles

8
Parental Mental Illness and Infant Development   120
   Ronald Seifer and Susan Dickstein

9
Maternal Substance Abuse and Infant Development   143
   Barry Zuckerman and Elizabeth R. Brown

10
Maltreatment and Infant Development   159
   Patricia J. Mrazek

━━━ **III. ASSESSMENT**   171

11
Clinical Interviews with Infants and their Families   173
   Laurence M. Hirshberg

12
Assessment of Developmental Status and   191
Parent–Infant Relationships: The Therapeutic
Process of Evaluation
   Roseanne Clark, Andrew Paulson, and Susan Conlin

13
Use of Structured Research Procedures in   210
Clinical Assessments of Infants
   Judith A. Crowell and Melissa A. Fleischmann

━━━ **IV. DISORDERS OF INFANCY**   223

14
Classification and the Diagnostic Process in Infancy   225
   Robert N. Emde, Richard D. Bingham,
   and Robert J. Harmon

15
Autism and the Pervasive Developmental Disorders   236
   Fred R. Volkmar

16
Mental Retardation   250
   Michael Thomasgard and Jack P. Shonkoff

17
Communication Disorders in Infants and Toddlers   260
   Barry M. Prizant, Amy M. Wetherby, and Joanne E. Roberts

18
Regulatory Disorders   280
   Stanley I. Greenspan and Serena Wieder

19
Post-Traumatic Stress Disorder 291
 Martin J. Drell, Clifford H. Siegel, and Theodore J. Gaensbauer

20
Sleep Disorders 305
 Avi Sadeh and Thomas F. Anders

21
Failure to Thrive and Feeding Disorders 317
 Diane Benoit

22
Disorders of Attachment 332
 Charles H. Zeanah, Jr., Oommen K. Mammen,
 and Alicia F. Lieberman

23
Psychosomatic Processes and Physical Illnesses 350
 David A. Mrazek

V. INTERVENTION 359

24
A Multidimensional Analysis of Early Childhood 361
Intervention Programs
 Samuel J. Meisels, Margo Dichtelmiller, and Fong-ruey Liaw

25
Preventive Interventions: Enhancing Parent–Infant Relationships 386
 Kathryn E. Barnard, Colleen E. Morisset, and Susan Spieker

26
Family Support Programs 402
 Bernice Weissbourd

27
Interaction Guidance: Understanding and Treating Early 414
Infant–Caregiver Relationship Disturbances
 Susan C. McDonough

28
Infant–Parent Psychotherapy 427
 Alicia F. Lieberman and Jeree H. Pawl

VI. SOCIAL APPLICATIONS OF INFANT 443
MENTAL HEALTH

29
Infant Day Care 445
 Marianne Barton and Martha Williams

30
Infant Placement and Custody   462
        Thomas M. Horner and Melvin J. Guyer

31
Infant Mental Health and Social Policy   480
        Edward Zigler, Pauline Hopper, and Nancy W. Hall

Index   493

I

THE CONTEXT OF
INFANT MENTAL HEALTH

The context of infant development is the context of infant mental health. Infants are so dependent upon their environments for the opportunity to develop competently that any discussion of their mental health must include a careful consideration of context. A relational view of infant development has been one of the significant trends during the past decade of research. Part I introduces the dual emphasis on context and on development that is apparent throughout the remainder of the book.

In Chapter 1, Sameroff emphasizes the importance of environment–individual transactions for models of development and developmental risk. From a systems perspective, he describes infant development as embedded within multiple layers of biological, interpersonal, and broader social influences. Continuities and discontinuities in infant development are a function of the genotype, the phenotype, and the environtype, *and* of their mutual regulatory influences on one another. The role of the clinician is to assist infants and their families to find opportunities to use their capacities adaptively or to develop new capacities necessary to negotiate challenges.

Lyons-Ruth and Zeanah (Chapter 2) introduce the family context of infant mental health by reviewing research on the importance of the primary caregiving relationship for emotional development in infancy. They argue for a relational perspective on social–emotional development, and they cite research that emphasizes both the stability of the emotional quality of the relationship and the organizational coherence of patterns of relational behavior through which affect regulation occurs. They also point out that relational stability increases the importance of understanding change—and learning how to predict and create it—a concern at the heart of clinical work. They suggest that specifying the processes leading to change is an important agenda for current research.

In Chapter 3, Crockenberg, Lyons-Ruth, and Dickstein conclude the discussion of the family context of infant mental health by reviewing research on the effects of other family members and relationships on infant development. Despite the tendency of contemporary research to focus heavily on the primary caregiving relationship, this chapter makes clear that there is already abundant research documenting the influences of other family members and relationships on infant development. The challenge for researchers and clinicians is to embrace the complexity inherent in families as we attempt to understand and serve them better.

Garcia Coll and Meyer (Chapter 4) conclude Part I with a thoughtful discussion of the belief systems and child-rearing practices that characterize different sociocultural traditions. They point out that opposite child-rearing practices are considered desirable by different cultural groups, and that in some cases they may even lead to similar outcomes. Clinicians cannot be reminded often enough to question their own culturally based assumptions, especially when dealing with families who have different assumptions. With the growing number of minority infants and families in the United States who will be seen in the future by infant mental health professionals, training in cultural diversity is essential. The authors provide a useful overview of guidelines for clinicians who undertake culturally sensitive care of infants and families.

1

Models of Development
and Developmental Risk

ARNOLD J. SAMEROFF

Recent progress in the technology of molecular genetics has led to a hope that the etiology of mental disorders will soon be revealed and that greatly improved methods for their treatment and prevention will follow. The basis for such hopes is a view of humans as determined by their biology and of development as an unfolding of predetermined lines of growth. Among these lines of development are those that produce the emotionally disturbed, such as schizophrenics and depressives; the cognitively disturbed, such as the learning-disabled and the retarded; and the undisturbed—that is, normal individuals. But does this model fit those individuals who do not stay on their predicted trajectories? For those full-term healthy infants who are predicted to have a happy course but instead end up with a variety of mental disorders later in life, one could argue that we have not yet developed the sophisticated diagnostic tools to identify their inherent deviancy at birth. On the other hand, how do we explain those infants who already show major disabilities and yet somehow do not progress to adult forms of psychiatric disturbance?

The case of Helen Keller is probably the most telling counterpoint to the maturational view of development (Keller, 1903). The story of this deaf–blind woman requires a model of development that goes beyond the maturational blueprint to incorporate the powerful effect of environments on human potential. The biographies of many individuals who were certain candidates for a life of institutionalization, but whose fate was altered to a happier end, have been fully documented (Clark & Clark, 1976).

The examples of these individuals who overcame biological adversity require explanations other than the unfolding of a maturational blueprint to explain their lives. What I present here is a model that does not grant such compelling examples a unique status. It is a developmental model arguing that all life is characterized by disturbance that is overcome, and that only through disturbance can we advance and grow. In the cognitive domain, the child must deal with a lifetime of intruding impressions that require organization and understanding. In the motor domain, burgeoning physical development presses the child to extend locomotor activity from rolling over to crawling to walking. In the social–emotional domain, the comings and goings of parenting figures pushes the child to develop models of attachment. In this view, it is the overcoming of challenge that furnishes the social, emotional, and intellectual skills that produce all forms of growth, both healthy and unhealthy. This model presumes a unity of developmental processes, both biological and behavioral, that is characterized by a dynamic relationship between the individual and the individual's context. There is an intimate connection between the capacities of the individual and the stresses and supports in the environment. Taking this model another step forward requires the appreciation that the contexts of an individual's development are not static, are not available only to be experienced; rather, they are active shapers of experience that have agendas and are organized by other individuals. In this important sense, development becomes the outcome of relationships between interacting individuals at every phase of life.

ACTIVE VERSUS PASSIVE VIEWS OF DEVELOPMENT

Theories of development have varied in the emphasis they place on contributions made by the characteristics of the person and characteristics of the environment to later behavior. Although this debate can be treated as merely an academic discussion, it has important ramifications for the distribution of vast amounts of social resources. From intervention efforts that cost millions of dollars to the educational system, which costs billions, practitioners rationalize their efforts on the basis of scientific knowledge. One of the major flaws in such knowledge is an inadequate conceptualization of the environment. Bronfenbrenner and Crouter (1983) have traced the history of empirical investigations of the environment and shown how theoretical limitations have placed limits on the sophistication of research and clinical paradigms.

The significance of nature and nurture for development can be viewed in terms of two questions. The first is whether they make a contribution at all, and the second is whether these contributions are active ones or passive ones. Riegel (1978) placed models of development into four categories reflecting various combinations of passive and active persons and environments. In the "passive person–passive environment" category, he placed mechanistic theories arising from the empiricist philosophy of Locke and Hume, in which combinations of events that occur in the environment in the presence of observers are imprinted into their minds. This view has been the basis for learning theories in which factors such as the continuity, frequency, or recency of stimuli determine how they will be coded into the receiving mind.

In a second category, the passive person is combined with an active environment. In this category are Skinnerian approaches to behavior modification, in which the conditioner actively structures the input to alter the person's behavior in particular directions, but the person is assumed to make no contribution to the outcome independent of experience. Behavioral programs for the modification of child problems fit into this category.

The third category contains the concept of the active person, but retains that of the passive environment. Into this grouping fall the cognitive theories of Piaget and the linguistic views of Chomsky. Piaget sees the person as an active constructor of knowledge based on experience with the environment. The environment is a necessary part of development, but has no active role in structuring thought or action. Similarly, Chomsky sees language development as the person's application of innate linguistic categories to linguistic experience. The organization of that experience is not a determinant of the resulting language competence.

In the fourth category are models that combine an active person and an active environment. Riegel (1978) sees these models as deriving from interpretations of the dialectical nature of development, in which the actions of the individual change reality, and then, in turn, the changes in reality effect the behavior of the individual. A colleague and I (Sameroff & Chandler, 1975) captured this process in our transactional model of development. In this view, developmental outcomes are not a product of the initial characteristics of the child or the context, or even of their combination. Outcomes are the result of the interplay between child and context across time, in which the state of one affects the next state of the other in a continuous dynamic process.

STABILITY AND CHANGE IN DEVELOPMENT

Attempts to intervene in development were initially based on stable models of child development. If a child was doing well or poorly early in life, he or she was expected to continue to do well or poorly later on. As an example, children who were identified early in life as being at developmental risk from biological circumstances, such as birth complications, were thought to have generally negative behavioral outcomes later in life. On the contrary, longitudinal research in this area has demonstrated that the majority of children suffering from such biological conditions do not have intellectual or social problems later in life (Sameroff & Chandler, 1975). On the other hand, early interventionists believed that getting children to perform well early in life would lead to their performing well throughout childhood. The early childhood education movement as exemplified in the federal Head Start program was designed to improve the learning and social competence of children during the preschool years, with the expectation that these improvements would be maintained into later life. However, follow-up research on such children has found only minimal intellectual gains being maintained into adolescence (Zigler & Trickett, 1978), although there were reduced rates of grade retention and need for participation in special education programs, as well as improved maternal attitudes toward school performance (Lazar, Darlington, Murray, Royce, & Shipper, 1982).

In both domains, early characteristics of the child are frequently overpowered by factors in the environmental context of development. Where family and cultural variables have fostered development, children with severe perinatal complications have been indistinguishable from children without complications. When these variables have hindered development, children from excellent preschool intervention programs have developed severe social and cognitive deficits. Thus, although a continuous view of developmental functioning makes intuitive sense, it has not been borne out by empirical investigations.

All developmental processes follow a similar model. In this framework, outcomes are never a function of the individual taken alone or the experiential context taken alone. Behavioral competencies are a product of the combination of an individual and his or her experience. To predict outcome, an exclusive focus on the characteristics of the individual—in this case, the child—will frequently be misleading. What need to be added are analysis and assessment of the experiences available to the child.

MODELS OF DEVELOPMENT

Ancient theorists interpreted development as an unfolding of intrinsic characteristics that either are preformed or interact epigenetically (Sameroff, 1983; see Figure 1.1). This model was countered by an environmental model of discontinuity, in which each stage of development is determined by the contemporary context, analogous to Riegel's (1978) "passive person–active environment" category. According to this model, if the context remains the same, the child remains the same; if the context changes, the child changes (see Figure 1.2).

FIGURE 1.1. Deterministic constitutional model of development. (C1–C4 represent state of the child at successive points in time.)

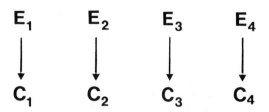

FIGURE 1.2. Deterministic environmental model of development. (E1–E4 represent experiential influences at successive points in time.)

An interactionist position combines these two, as in Figure 1.3. Here, continuity is carried by the child but moderated by possible discontinuities in experience. Anastasi (1958) is credited with the important interactionist conceptual breakthrough in pointing out that development cannot occur without an environment. There is no logical possibility of considering development of an individual independently of the environment. Continuity cannot be explained as a characteristic of the child, because each new achievement is an amalgam of characteristics of the child and his or her experience. Neither alone is predictive of later levels of functioning. If continuities are found, it is because there is a continuity in the relationship between the child and the environment, not because of continuities in either taken alone.

More recent conceptualizations of the developmental model have incorporated effects of the child on the environment, as posited by Rheingold (1966) and Bell (1968). The dynamic interactionist model (Thomas, Chess, & Birch, 1968) and the transactional model (Sameroff & Chandler, 1975) add, to the independent con-

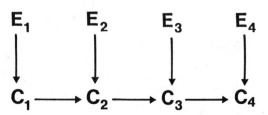

FIGURE 1.3. Interactionist model of development.

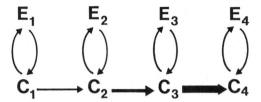

FIGURE 1.4. Reciprocal interactionist model of development.

tributions of child and environment, characteristics of the environment that are conditioned by the nature of the child. Different characteristics of the child will trigger different responses from the environment (see Figure 1.4).

Transactional Model

In the transactional model, the development of the child is seen as a product of a continuous dynamic interaction between the child and the experience provided by his or her family and social context (Sameroff & Chandler, 1975). What is innovative in the transactional model is the emphasis placed on the effect of the child on the environment, so that experiences provided by the environment are not independent of the child. The child, by his or her previous behavior, may have been a strong determinant of current experiences.

The transactions can be caused by atypical behavior of the child for which the parent has no understanding, or by normative behavior of the child that the parent understands from a distorted perspective. An example of the first case, described by Parmelee (1989), is a baby who regurgitates some of each feeding. Although this is not an unusual infant behavior, the regurgitation is upsetting to some parents, who believe that the baby is not getting enough food. The parental response may be to overfeed the infant, which increases the regurgitation, which leads the parents to believe that the baby has a disorder. A visit to the physician by the worried parents may result in a diagnosis and medication. The transaction converts parents with a normal view of their infant into parents with a disordered view, and converts a child who spits up after feedings into a medical case.

An example of the second kind of transaction is the case of Lisa, described by Brazelton and Cramer (1990). The mother brought her 14-week-old daughter for therapy because the infant cried too much. The mother interpreted the cries as anger rather than discomfort or need for discharge. The mother's fear was that her angry response to what she saw as the infant's angry cries would lead her to abuse the child. In this case, therapeutic intervention allowed a reinterpretation of the infant's cries as normal, thus interrupting the negative transaction. Unfortunately, in many disordered families the parents' inappropriate view of a young infant as angry or oppositional does lead to battering. The initial transaction in Lisa's case was that the parent changed her view from Lisa as a normal baby to Lisa as a deviant one who required angry retaliation instead of loving care.

When attempts are made to operationalize transactional processes within a specific research design, causal sequences are rarely simple. Crockenberg and Smith (1982) examined the relation of infant and mother characteristics to the development of infant temperament and mother–infant interaction during the first 3 months of life. Mothers' responsive attitudes and infants' irritability were measured during the newborn period. Three months later, the mothers who had responsive and flexible attitudes at birth responded more quickly when their infants cried, and their infants spent less time fussing and crying. On the other hand, the babies' irritability at birth was not related to the amount of crying at 3 months, but was related to the amount of time required to calm down. In other words, some aspects of the infants' crying at 3 months were the results of transactional processes, whereas other aspects could be explained more directly. Although amount of crying was a function of the subsequent caregiving experiences, time to calm down was not. From the infants' side, a transaction had occurred; the state of the children was changed as a function of the mothers' behavior.

There was also evidence in the Crockenberg and Smith (1982) study that the behavior of the mothers was changed by the specific characteristics of the children. Alert newborn infants produced mothers who spent more time in contact with them 3 months later, and mothers of irritable females responded more quickly to fussing and crying than did mothers of irritable males. In other words, mothers' behavior was sensitive to both the behavioral and physical characteristics of the children. The evidence for transactional processes in this study is an example of the multidimensional nature of both maternal and child behavior. Depending on the antecedent and outcome measures and the ages of assessment, different relations will be found, some giving strong evidence for transactions and others not.

In order for a genuine transaction to occur, the parents must be influenced by the infant's behavior to do something they would not have done if the child behaved otherwise. In many cases, parents respond with love and affection to anything the child does, and in a few cases parents respond with anger and abuse to anything the child does. These are not examples of transactions, because the parents' predominant interaction style is not changed by the behavior of the child. It is difficult to separate transactional effects from these parental effects when only one child is involved. The study of twins, however, offers a clear opportunity for observing transactional processes. A transaction will have occurred if the same parent relates differently to the two infants.

It is a common clinical observation that parents generally prefer one twin over the other. Minde, Corter, Goldberg, and Jeffers (1990) found that the majority of mothers maintained these preferences at least through the 4 years of their study. The preference was based on the infants' behavior, usually during the first 2 weeks of life, although some mothers took up to a year to establish a long-term choice. The preferred infant in a twin pair was not necessarily the one with the easier temperament. Some mothers liked the more strong-willed, independent, active twin; others preferred the more calm, easygoing twin; and still others preferred the healthier twin. The consequences of these early choices were that at 4 years the preferred twins had fewer behavior problems and higher IQ scores. In a case study, Stern (1971) reported a mother who already preferred her more active twin during pregnancy. The mother explained her bias as her identification with the more energetic twin in contrast to the calmer baby, whom she identified with her more passive husband. Minde et al. (1990) described their mothers as making similar associations between the characteristics of the preferred twin and beloved relatives or idealized developmental outcomes (e.g., a future professor or deep thinker).

In these twin studies, the same parent reacted differently to the different behavior of the two offspring. Transactions were clearly occurring in which the behavior of the preferred twin was interpreted in a different system than the behavior of the nonpreferred twin, and this difference

consequently set off a different course of development.

Observations of families in natural settings provide insights into possible causal sequences in development, but definitive evidence can only be produced by attempts to manipulate developmental variables (Bronfenbrenner, 1977). Experimental manipulations designed to illuminate transactional processes have not been frequent as yet. Bugental and Shennum (1984) assessed beliefs about causes of caregiving outcomes for a group of mothers who were then placed in interaction situations with children who had been trained to be more or less responsive and assertive. Short-term transactions were identified in some conditions, where mothers responded differently as a function of the combination of their attributions and the actual behavior of the children. Other research projects have been directed at long-term transactions resulting from massive intervention programs.

Zeskind and Ramey (1978, 1981) examined the effects of an intensive early intervention program on the development of a group of fetally malnourished infants. Intervention began at 3 months and included social work, medical, nutritional, and educational components. A control group received similar social work, medical, and nutritional services, but did not participate in the educational program. Comparisons were made in the later functioning of lower-socioeconomic-status (lower-SES) underweight infants, half of whom participated in the educational program and half of whom did not. As a group, the infants without educational intervention declined in developmental quotient (DQ) from 3 to 18 months of age and continued to score lower on tests at 36 months of age. However, within that group, the low-ponderal-index babies showed a much greater decline into the retarded range. These lower DQs were associated with lower levels of maternal involvement. In contrast, in the group of families that received educational intervention, the malnourished infants who had scored significantly lower than the rest of the group at 3 months were doing as well as the others by 18 months. Zeskind and Ramey (1981) concluded that the educational program had interrupted the negative transaction found in the control group. Whereas lower-SES mothers would usually be put off by the characteristics of fetally malnourished infants, contributing to a worsening developmental outcome (as in the control group), intervention fostered the relationship between mothers and children, thereby leading to an above-average outcome within this sample.

The transactional model in Figure 1.4 is an improvement over the interactional model in Figure 1.3 because it includes reciprocal influences between child and environment. However, another step is required to complete the picture of determinants of development. The continuity implied in the organization of the child's behavior by the series of arrows from C1 to C2 to C3 requires a parallel set of arrows indicating continuity in the organization of the environment from E1 to E2 to E3 (see Figure 1.5).

Environmental Continuity

Thousands of studies have attended to longitudinal continuities in child development, correlating early behavior with later. In contrast, very few studies have examined the consistency of environments over time. One of these is the Rochester Longitudinal Study (RLS), an examination of the development of several hundred children from birth through early adolescence, which has assessed environmental factors as well as the cognitive and social competence of the children (Sameroff, Seifer, & Zax, 1982). When the children in the RLS were 4 years old, we assessed a set of 10 environmental variables (Sameroff, Seifer, Barocas, Zax, & Greenspan, 1987). We then tested whether poor cognitive and social–emotional development in our preschool children was a function of environmental risk factors found in low-SES groups. The 10 environmental risk variables were (1) a history of maternal mental illness; (2) high maternal anxiety; (3) a parental perspectives score, derived from a combination of measures that reflected rigidity in mothers' attitudes, beliefs, and values in regard to their children's development; (4) few positive maternal interactions with the children observed during infancy; (5) heads of households in unskilled occupations; (6) minimal maternal education; (7) disadvantaged mi-

nority status; (8) reduced family support; (9) stressful life events; and (10) large family size.

When these risk factors were related to social–emotional and cognitive competence scores, major differences were found between those children with few risks and those with many. In terms of intelligence, children with no environmental risks scored more than 30 points higher than children with eight or nine risk factors.

Within the RLS, our attention has been devoted to the source of continuities and discontinuities in child performance. We have completed a new assessment of the sample when the children were 13 years of age (Sameroff, Seifer, Baldwin, & Baldwin, 1993). We were especially interested in those children from multiple-risk families who had managed to overcome early difficulties and reach normal or above-average levels of intellectual or social emotional competence. We were disappointed to find little evidence of such resilient or invulnerable children. When we recreated our multiple-risk score at age 13, we found the same powerful relationship between environmental adversity and child behavior: Those children with the most environmental risk factors had the lowest competence ratings.

The typical statistic reported in longitudinal research is the correlation between early and later performance of the children. We too found such correlations. Intelligence at 4 years correlated .72 with intelligence at 13 years, and the social competence scores at the two ages correlated .43. The usual interpretation of such numbers is that there is a continuity of competence or incompetence in the children. Such a conclusion cannot be challenged if the only assessments in a study are assessments of the children. In the RLS, environmental as well as child factors were examined. We were able to correlate environmental characteristics across time as well as child ones. We found that the correlation between environmental risk scores at the two ages was .76—as great as or greater than any continuity within the children. Those children who had poor family and social environments at 4 years of age still had them when they were 13 years old, and probably would continue to have them for the foreseeable future. Whatever a child's ability for achieving high levels of competence, it was severely undermined by the continuing paucity of environmental support. Whatever the capabilities provided to a child by individual factors, it is the environment that limits the opportunities for development.

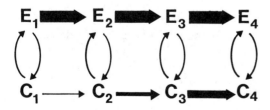

FIGURE 1.5. Social regulatory model of development.

Regulatory Systems in Development

What kind of theory is necessary to integrate the many factors that regulate development? It must explain how the individual and experience work together to produce patterns of adaptive or maladaptive functioning, and must suggest how such past or present functioning will influence the future.

The first principle to emerge in such a general theory of development is that individuals can never be removed from their contexts. Whether the goal is understanding causal connections, predicting outcomes, or designing interventions, it will not be achieved by removing an individual from the conditions that regulate development. There has been a great deal of attention given to the biological influences on development. What has now become necessary is the giving of equal attention to the environmental influences.

The development of each individual is constrained by interactions with regulatory systems acting at different levels of organization. The two most prominent of these are the biological and social regulatory systems. From conception to birth, interactions with the biological system are most prominent. In the study of embryological development, for example, there are continuous transactions between the phenotype and the genotype (Ebert & Sussex, 1970; Waddington, 1957).

A simple view of the action of genes is that they produce the parts that make up the organism. A brown eye gene, for instance, may be thought to produce a brown eye. In reality, there is a much more complex process of mutual determinism. The material in the fertilized egg cell will turn on or off specific genes in the chromosomes. The turned-on genes will initiate changes in the biochemicals in the cell. These changed biochemicals will then act back on the genetic material, turning more genes on or off in a continuous process and usually producing an adult organism.

In certain circumstances, one has the illusion of a linear relationship between a particular gene and a particular feature of the phenotype, as in the case of eye color. In reality, however, there is never a linear determinism because of the enormous complexity of biological processes. What then creates the illusion? The answer is in the regulatory system that buffers development, which Waddington (1957) described as "canali-zation." Within all the complex interactions between genotype and phenotype is a regulatory system that monitors the developmental changes to assure that they stay within defined bounds. This regulatory system and the bounds are the results of an evolutionary process that has occurred across myriad generations, and that now assures a particular outcome.

Changes in the contemporary state of the organism's embryonic phenotype trigger the genotype to provide a series of new biochemical experiences. These experiences are regulated by the turning on and off of various gene activities directed toward the production of a viable human child. These processes continue less dramatically after birth, with some exceptions—for example, the initiation of adolescence and possibly of senility.

The period from birth to adulthood, however, is dominated by interactions with the social system. Again, the state of the child triggers regulatory processes, but now the regulators are in the social environment. Examples of such coded changes are the reactions of parents to their child's ability to walk or talk, and the changes in setting provided when the child reaches preschool or school age. These regulations change the experience of the child in tune with changes in the child's physical and behavioral development.

The result of these regulatory exchanges is the expansion of each individual's capability for biological self-regulation and the development of behavioral self-regulation. Advances in motor development permit children to control their temperature and nutrition, which initially could only be regulated by caregivers. They are soon able to dress themselves and reach into the refrigerator. Despite this burgeoning independence, each individual is never freed from a relationship to an internal and external context. Should we forget this connectedness, it only takes a bout of illness or a social transgression to remind us of the physical and institutional constraints on our behavior.

THE ENVIRONTYPE

Transactional research on child development has emphasized the child's utilization of biological capacities to gain experience and the reciprocal role of experience in shaping child competencies, but there has been far less attention to how that experience is organized. Indeed, the organization of experience is explicit in the great amount of attention given by educators to curriculum development and by psychologists to behavior modification plans, but the implicit organization of experience has been left to the attention of sociologists and anthropologists. Just as there is a biological organization that regulates the physical outcome of each individual (the genotype), there is a social organization that regulates the way human beings fit into their society. This organization operates through family and cultural socialization patterns and has been postulated to constitute an "environtype" analogous to the biological genotype (Sameroff, 1985; Sameroff & Fiese, 1990).

The environtype is composed of subsystems that transact not only with the child but also with each other. Although at any point in time the environtype can be conceptualized independently of the child, changes in the abilities of the developing child are major triggers for regulatory changes, and in all likelihood are major contributors to the evolution of a developmental agenda that is each culture's timetable for developmental milestones.

For older children, the peer groups and the school are major regulators of behavior; for the period of infancy, however, I restrict the present discussion to the organization of environmental factors contained within the culture, the family, and the individual parent. These codes are hierarchically related in their evolution and in their current influence on the child. The experience of the developing child is partially determined by the beliefs, values, and personality of the parents; partially by the family's interaction patterns and transgenerational history; and partially by the socialization beliefs, controls, and supports of the culture. Developmental regulations at each of these levels are carried within codes that direct cognitive and social–emotional development, so that the child will ultimately be able to fill a role defined within society.

Cultural Code

The ingredients of the cultural code are the many different characteristics that organize a society's child–rearing system, incorporating elements of socialization and education. These processes are embedded in sets of social controls and social supports based on beliefs that differ in the amount of community consensus sustaining them, ranging from mores and norms to fads

and fashions. It is beyond the scope of this chapter to elucidate the full range of cultural regulatory processes that are relevant to development. As a consequence, only a few points are highlighted to flesh out the dimensions of the cultural code.

Although the common biological characteristics of the human species have acted to produce similar developmental agendas in most cultures, there are differences in many major features that often ignore the biological status of the individual. In most cultures formal education begins between the ages of 6 and 8 (Rogoff, 1981), when most children have reached the cognitive ability to learn from such structured experiences. On the other hand, informal education can begin at many different ages, depending on the culture's attributions to the child. The Digo and Kikuyu are two East African cultures that have different beliefs about infant capacities (deVries & Sameroff, 1984). The Digo believe that infants can learn within a few months after birth and begin socialization at that time. The Kikuyu wait until the second year of life before they believe that serious education is possible. Closer to home, a few middle-class North American parents have been convinced that prenatal experiences will enhance the cognitive development of their children. Such examples demonstrate the variability of human developmental contexts.

One of the major contemporary risk conditions toward which many programs are being directed is the elimination of adolescent pregnancies. Although for certain young mothers these pregnancies are the outcomes of individual factors, for a large proportion they are the results of a cultural code that defines maturity, family relationships, and socialization patterns with adolescent motherhood as a normative ingredient. In such instances, to focus on the problem as one that resides wholly at the individual level would be a gross misrepresentation.

Family Code

Just as cultural codes regulate the fit between individuals and the social system, family codes organize individuals within the family system. Family codes provide a source of regulation that allows a group of individuals to form a collective unit in relation to society as a whole. As the cultural code regulates development so that an individual may fill a role in society, family codes regulate development to produce members who fulfill roles within the family and ultimately are able to introduce new members into the shared system. Traditionally, new members are incorporated through birth and marriage, although remarriage has recently taken on a more frequent role in providing new family members.

The family regulates the child's development through a variety of forms that vary in their degree of explicit representation. Families have rituals that prescribe roles; stories that transmit orientations to each family member, as well as to whoever will listen; shared myths that influence individual interactions; and behavioral paradigms that change individuals' behavior when in the presence of other family members. Reiss (1989) has contrasted the degree to which these forms regulate family behavior through explicit prescriptions (i.e., the conscious knowledge of family rules that each member has) with the degree to which each family members behavior is regulated by common practice (i.e., the behavior of the family members when together. The most frequently represented regulations, according to Reiss, are exemplified by family rituals and the least by family paradigms. At intermediate levels are stories and myths. Research efforts are only beginning to explore the exact nature of how these forms are transmitted behaviorally among family members and how they are represented in cognition.

Individual Code

There is good evidence that individual behavior is influenced by the family context. When people are operating as part of a family, the behavior of each person is altered (Parke & Tinsley, 1987), frequently without awareness of the behavioral change (Reiss, 1981). However, there is also no doubt that each individual brings his or her own contribution to family interactions. The contribution of parents is much more complexly determined than that of young children, given the multiple levels that contribute to their behavior. Although the socializing regulations embodied in the cultural and family codes have been discussed, the individualized interpretations that each parenting figure imposes on these codes has not. To a large extent, these interpretations are conditioned by each parent's past participation in his or her own family's coded interactions, but they are captured uniquely by each member of the family.

These individual influences further condition each parent's responses to each child. The richness of both health and pathology embodied in these responses are well described in the clinical literature. In terms of early development, Fraiberg and her colleagues have provided descriptions of the attributions that parents bring to their parenting. These "ghosts" of unresolved childhood conflicts have been shown to "do their mischief according to a historical or topical agenda, specializing in such areas as feeding, sleep, toilet-training or discipline, depending upon the vulnerabilities of the parental past" (Fraiberg, Adelson, & Shapiro, 1975, p. 146).

Parental psychopathology has long been recognized as a contributor to the poor developmental status of children. Although we acknowledge that influence, we must also be careful to note the effects of the contexts in which parental behavior is rooted—the family and cultural codes. It is important to recognize the parents as major regulating agencies of child development, but it is equally important to recognize that parental behavior is itself embedded in regulatory contexts.

Regulation and Development

An understanding of the developmental process requires an appreciation of the transactions between and among individuals, their biological inner workings, and their social outer workings. Continuities and discontinuities are a joint function of three systems, the genotype, the phenotype, and the environtype (see Figure 1.6). The genotype is the system of biological regulation and organization. The environtype is the family and cultural code that regulates the devel-

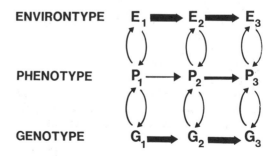

FIGURE 1.6. Transactional developmental model integrating environmental, genetic, and individual regulating systems. From Sameroff (1985).

opmental opportunities available to an individual. The phenotype, or in this case the individual person, transacts through development with both the genotype and environtype to determine individual status at any point in time. To the extent that the three systems are in a state of equilibrium, continuity of performance is to be expected. To the extent that one of the systems undergoes a reorganization, then there is a corresponding reorganization of development itself.

The definition of development as a model of adapting to disturbance is contained within the general systems theory described above. Disturbance is ubiquitous in both normal and abnormal growth processes. In normal development on the biological side, adaptive reorganizations are required in response to physical changes such as walking or adolescence. From the environmental side, such reorganizations begin with the relatively simple adaptations required when the mother leaves the room, and progress to the overcoming of more complex disturbances produced by beginning school and then graduating. It is in the individual that the inner and the outer are brought into accord with more or less success, either by seeking opportunities to use capacities or by fostering capacities to meet opportunities.

In the non–normative development of concern to the clinician, either the capacities or the opportunities are missing. The plasticity of the environtype permits compensatory regulations in the physical domain, such as providing wheelchairs for those who cannot walk; in the cognitive domain, such as teaching sign language to deaf and retarded children; and in the social–emotional domain, such as teaching parents to be responsive to their infants. On the other hand, this same environmental plasticity can prevent adaptation through abusive parents; lack of resources for child care; and denial of education to those who are of the wrong economic level, race, or sex.

From the developmental perspective described here, one must see the child's progress as embedded in relationships to contexts of the physical and social world in which clinicians can play an important role. However, to be successful in this role, interveners must understand not only the embeddedness but also the multiple sources of regulations that affect the developmental process.

REFERENCES

Anastasi, A. (1958). Heredity, environment, and the question, "How?" *Psychological Review, 75,* 81–95.

Bell, R. Q. (1968). A reinterpretation of the direction of effects in studies of socialization. *Psychological Review, 75,* 81–95.

Brazelton, T. B., & Cramer, B. G. (Eds.). (1990). *The earliest relationship.* Reading, MA: Addison-Wesley.

Bronfenbrenner, U. (1977). Toward an experimental ecology of human development. *American Psychologist, 32,* 513–531.

Bronfenbrenner, U., & Crouter, A. C. (1983). The evolution of environmental models in developmental research. In W. Kessen (Vol. Ed.), *Handbook of child psychology* (4th ed.): Vol. 1. *History, theory, and methods* (pp. 357–414). New York: Wiley.

Bugental, D. P., & Shennum, W. A. (1984). "Difficult" children as elicitors and targets of adult communication patterns: An attributional–behavioral transactional analysis. *Monographs of the Society for Research in Child Development, 49,* (1, Whole No. 205).

Clark, A. M., & Clark, A. D. B. (1976). *Early experience: Myth and evidence.* London: Open Books.

Crockenberg, S. B., & Smith, P. (1982). Antecedents of mother infant interaction and infant irritability in the first three months of life. *Infant Behavior and Development, 5,* 105–119.

deVries, M. W., & Sameroff, A. J. (1984). Culture and temperament: Influences on infant temperament in three East African societies. *American Journal of Orthopsychiatry, 54,* 83–96.

Ebert, J. D., & Sussex, I. M. (1970). *Interacting systems in development* (2nd ed.). New York: Holt, Rinehart & Winston.

Fraiberg, S., Adelson, E., & Shapiro, V. (1975). Ghosts in the nursery: A psychoanalytic approach to the problems of impaired mother–infant relationships. *Journal of the American Academy of Child Psychiatry, 14,* 387–421.

Keller, H. (1903). *The story of my life.* Garden City, NY: Doubleday, Page.

Lazar, I., Darlington, R., Murray, H., Royce, J., & Shipper, A. (1982). Lasting effects of early education: A report from the Consortium for Longitudinal Studies. *Monographs of the Society for Research in Child Development, 47,* (Nos. 2–3, Serial No. 195).

Minde, K., Corter, C., Goldberg, S., & Jeffers, D. (1990). Maternal preferences between premature twins up to age four. *Journal of the American Academy of Child and Adolescent Psychiatry, 29,* 367–374.

Parke, R. D., & Tinsley, B. J. (1987). Family interaction in infancy. In J. Osofsky (Ed.), *Handbook of infant development* (2nd ed., pp. 579–641). New York: Wiley.

Parmelee, A. H. (1989). The child's physical health and the development of relationships. In A. J. Sameroff & R. N. Emde (Eds.), *Relationship disturbances in early childhood* (pp. 145–162). New York: Basic Books.

Reiss, D. (1981). *The family's construction of reality.* Cambridge, MA: Harvard University Press.

Reiss, D. (1989). The represented and practicing family: Contrasting visions of family continuity. In A. J. Sameroff & R. N. Emde (Eds.), *Relationship disturbances in early childhood* (pp. 191–220). New York: Basic Books.

Rheingold, H. L. (1966). The development of social behavior in the human infant. In H. W. Stevenson (Ed.), Concept of development. *Monographs of the Society for Research in Child Development, 31*(5, Whole No. 107).

Riegel, K. F. (1978). *Psychology, mon amour: A countertext.* Boston: Houghton Mifflin.

Rogoff, B. (1981). Schooling and the development of cognitive skills. In H. C. Triandis & A. Heron (Eds.), *Handbook of cross-cultural psychology: Vol. 4. Developmental psychology* (pp. 233–294). Boston: Allyn & Bacon.

Sameroff, A. J. (1983). Developmental systems: Contexts and evolution. In W. Kessen (Vol. Ed.), *Handbook of child psychology* (4th ed.): *Vol. 1. History, theory, and methods* (pp. 237–294). New York: Wiley.

Sameroff, A. J. (1985). *Can development be continuous?* Paper presented at the annual meeting of the American Psychological Association, Los Angeles.

Sameroff, A. J., & Chandler, M. J. (1975). Reproductive risk and the continuum of caretaking casualty. In F. D. Horowitz, E. M. Hetherington, S. Scarr–Salapatek, & G. Siegel (Eds.), *Review of child development research* (Vol. 4, pp. 187–244). Chicago: University of Chicago.

Sameroff, A. J., & Fiese, B. H. (1990). Transactional regulation and early intervention. In S. J. Meisels & J. P. Shonkoff (Eds.), *Handbook of early childhood intervention* (pp. 119–191). New York: Cambridge University Press.

Sameroff, A. J., Seifer, R., Baldwin, C. P., & Baldwin, A. (1993). Stability of intelligence from preschool to adolescence: The influence of social and family risk factors. *Child Development, 64*, 96–105.

Sameroff, A. J., Seifer, R., Barocas, R., Zax, M., & Greenspan, S. (1987). IQ scores of 4-year-old children: Social–environmental risk factors. *Pediatrics, 79*, 343–350.

Sameroff, A. J., Seifer, R., & Zax, M. (1982). Early development of children at risk for emotional disorder. *Monographs of the Society for Research in Child Development, 47*, (No. 7, Serial No. 199).

Stern, D. (1971). A micro-analysis of mother–infant interaction: Behaviors regulating social contact between a mother and her three-and-a-half-month-old twins. *Journal of the American Academy of Child Psychiatry, 10*, 501–517.

Thomas, A., Chess, S., & Birch, H. (1968). *Temperament and behavior disorders in children*. New York: New York University Press.

Waddington, C. H. (1957). *The strategy of the genes*. London: Allen & Unwin.

Zeskind, P. S., & Ramey, C. T. (1978). Fetal malnutrition: An experimental study of its consequences for infant development in two caregiving environments. *Child Development, 49*, 1155–1162.

Zeskind, P. S., & Ramey, C. T. (1981). Preventing intellectual and interactional sequelae of fetal malnutrition: A longitudinal, transactional, and synergistic approach to development. *Child Development, 52*, 213–218.

Zigler, E., & Trickett, P. K. (1978). IQ, social competence, and evaluation of early childhood intervention programs. *American Psychologist, 33*, 789–799.

2

The Family Context of Infant Mental Health: I. Affective Development in the Primary Caregiving Relationship

KARLEN LYONS-RUTH
CHARLES H. ZEANAH, Jr.

Winnicott's (1960/1965) provocative comment that "there is no such thing as a baby" in the absence of sustaining caregiving relationships placed in dramatic relief the inseparability of infant and family context. In the current chapter, we review the most recent research relating family context and infant socioemotional development. We focus on emotional development because of its centrality to infant mental health.

Several themes emerge from this literature. In this chapter, we emphasize two major themes. The first theme is the intergenerational context of family relationships, including research support for the long-held clinical hypothesis that patterns of affect regulation, expectation, and behavior established in early relationships are likely to be carried over into later ones. This theme suggests that the "represented family" deserves attention as much as the "practicing family" (Reiss, 1989). The second theme we emphasize is the pervasive presence of mutual regulatory processes between infant and caregiver—regulatory processes that are gradually internalized as self-regulations by the infant. How affect expression and social behavior are regulated within the family thus become what Winnicott might characterize as the initial "holding environment" of the developing infant.

Two other important themes are emphasized elsewhere in this volume and are mentioned only briefly here. The first is the complexity of the system of relationships within families as they affect infant mental health (see Crockenberg, Lyons-Ruth, & Dickstein, Chapter 3, this volume). It cannot be emphasized enough that focusing on dyadic interaction alone provides only one dimension of the family context of infant development and infant mental health. As Emde (1991) has pointed out, there are increasing levels of interdependent influences within families that are far more complex than our theories or our empirical efforts to date are able to accommodate. Although many advocate moving to a systemic level to consider family context, even this bypasses a myriad of individual, dyadic, and triadic influences on development within a family. Given that our knowledge base about any of these levels is limited, continued exploration of each of them is warranted. Still, much of what we do not yet understand about infant development results from necessarily oversimplified models.

A final theme from current research is that families function as part of a larger community of social relationships, economic roles, values, and institutions (Bronfenbrenner, 1979; see Sameroff, Chapter 1, this volume, and Garcia Coll & Meyer, Chapter 4, this volume). Families exist in communities and need effective community institutions to support their functioning, particularly as family structures lose their extended, multigenerational nature. We would almost be entitled to another paradoxical claim that parents don't raise children; communities raise children. However, many of the family supports operating in communities remain invisible until social conditions erode these supports and we recognize them by their absence (Garbarino & Sherman, 1980). For example, despite intense family efforts, family structures and values are often eroded in impoverished communities by unemployment, high infant and adult mortality rates, health hazards associated with job conditions and poverty, and alternative adolescent value systems born of hopelessness. Conversely, in affluent communities, children may experience a variety of conditions that buffer the impact of family problems, including other adult role models available through friends and their families, schools that maintain their access to productive jobs, after-school programs with good adult supervision, safe neighborhoods in which lack of effective family supervision is less hazardous, and peer cultures that promote hopefulness and motivation. Thus, the family context must always be assessed in relation to the quality of family stresses and supports contributed by the community.

These four major themes are represented in the model of family context shown in Figure 2.1. As should be already clear, and as subsequent discussion reinforces, however, the model in Figure 2.1 is schematic and probably considerably underrepresents the complexity of the interrelations among the various elements of the model.

THE INTERGENERATIONAL CONTEXT OF PARENT–INFANT RELATIONSHIPS

Parental Contributions

As the first child is born and a family unit is established, one might imagine that new parents learn their parenting skills "on the job," as they become immersed in this new and all-absorbing experience. However, several lines of evidence indicate that the parent–infant relationship is not constructed *de novo* from the time of the child's birth, but is powerfully preconditioned by aspects of the parents' adaptation that are evident prior to parenthood. A number of family research teams have shown that mothers' and fathers' psychological adaptation and quality of marriage before the birth of the first child predict the quality of parenting during the early years (Belsky, Lang, & Rovine, 1985; Cowan & Cowan, 1987; Cox et al., 1985; Heinicke, Diskin, Ramsey-Klee, & Given, 1983; Lewis, Owen, & Cox, 1988). For example, Cowan, Cowan, Heming, and Miller (1991) reported that men and women who were more dissatisfied with themselves, their marriages, or their jobs before becoming parents were also more dissatisfied with their parenting roles, and experienced greater stress in connection with the parenting experience.

Other studies have documented the transmission of aspects of parental behavior across generations, using both retrospective reports and prospective designs. For example, the literature on child abuse has long reported the statistical tendency for parents who were abused in childhood to be more likely to abuse their own children (Belsky & Pensky, 1988; Herrenkohl, Herrenkohl, & Toedter, 1983; Parke & Collmer, 1975). Processes of intergenerational transmission generalize beyond abusive behaviors per se, however. In a prospective study of family interaction patterns across four generations, using the Berkeley Guidance Study archives, Elder, Caspi, and Downey (1986) found that personality, marital tension, and parenting styles tended to covary within families across generations. This correlated constellation of parental qualities was in turn related to child behavior, with conflicted, unstable parents experiencing marital tension and displaying irritable parenting behavior, which tended to produce irritable and explosive children. If unstable parental personalities and marital tension did not find expression in punitive parental behavior, however, there were few effects on children. Thus, an adult's behavior in both marital and parenting roles was foreshadowed by aspects of the adult's childhood behavior and the qualities of his or her earlier relationships with parents. Though the study of Elder and colleagues did not focus specifically on the parenting of infants, similar

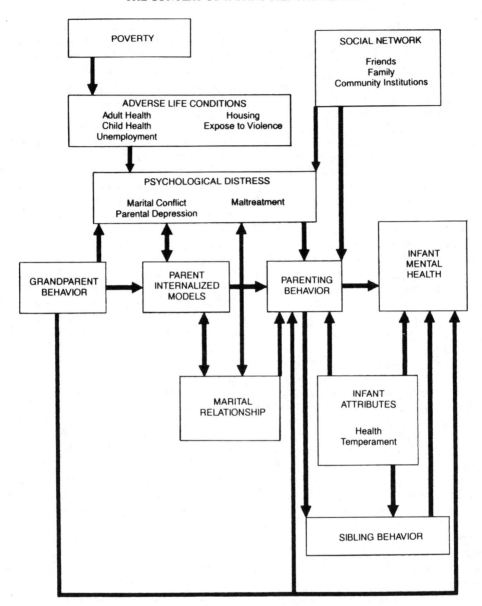

FIGURE 2.1. The family context of infant mental health.

effects of childhood family patterns on parenting behavior toward infants are also evident in a variety of studies (Cox et al., 1985; Hall, Pawlby, & Wolkind, 1979; Lyons-Ruth, Zoll, Connell, & Grunebaum, 1989; Ricks, 1985).

Recent work derived from attachment theory has further elaborated our understanding of the intergenerational transmission of relational patterns by exploring the mental representations, or internal models of attachment relationships, that accompany and may mediate these behav- ioral continuities. According to attachment theory, as patterns of interaction and affective response are repeated in close relationships over time, children build expectations about future interactions with parents and others that guide their interpretations and behaviors in new situ- ations. As these expectations and interpretations become elaborated and organized, they are termed "internal working models" of relation- ships. These working models of self and others tend to perpetuate themselves in the absence of specific influences for change, and to become incorporated as stable interpersonal tendencies that endure over time (Bowlby, 1973; Bretherton, 1985).

Main, Kaplan, and Cassidy (1985) have demonstrated that when parents' representations of attachment relationships are explored in an open-ended interview format, the degree of cognitive and affective "coherence of mind" displayed in the interview can be reliably rated. "Coherence of mind" characterizes adults who are judged to have autonomous internal models. Such coherence is judged from several factors, including open valuing of relationships; consistency between abstract interpretations and specific affective memories; absence of passivity, confusion, marked emotional oscillation, and defensive distancing from negative affects; and the ability to reflect objectively on past experiences. Autonomous internal models are in turn associated with parental sensitivity in responding to infant emotional signals and with the security of infant attachment behavior in relation to the parent (Ainsworth & Eichberg, 1991; Crowell & Feldman, 1988; Grossmann, Fremmer-Bombik, Rudolph, & Grossmann, 1988; Zeanah et al., 1993). Three recent studies have further demonstrated that autonomous adult models of attachment assessed prior to the birth of the first child are predictive of the quality of the infant–parent relationship at 1 year (Benoit & Vidovic, 1991; Fonagy, Steele, & Steele, 1991; Ward, Botyanski, Plunket, & Carlson, 1991).

Intergenerational transmission, then, involves not only organized patterns of behavior that are brought to the task of parenting, but organized ways of thinking and feeling in relationships that accompany these interaction patterns. Work on internalized models has also begun to identify a subgroup of parents whose early relationships with their own parents had been painful and conflicted, but whose adult representations and parenting behaviors were coherent and sensitively responsive. In confirmation of Fraiberg, Adelson, and Shapiro's (1975) clinical observations, these parents were characterized by an ability to reflect openly on past painful experiences and to accept the negative aspects of those experiences without marked defensiveness, while still valuing attachment relationships (Main et al., 1985; Grossmann et al., 1988). Other recent work suggests that such openness to reflect on a painful past and escape the cycle of repetition may be facilitated by the presence of one

good relationship in the parent's past (Egeland, Jacobvitz, & Sroufe, 1988) or by the presence of a supportive spouse (Quinton, Rutter, & Liddle, 1984). A new generation of intervention studies, assessing social as well as cognitive outcomes, is also beginning to confirm that a responsive therapeutic relationship increases the likelihood that a mother with a difficult family history will establish a secure attachment relationship with her infant (Beckwith & Rodning, 1991; Jacobson & Frye, 1991; Lyons-Ruth, Connell, Grunebaum, & Botein, 1990; Lieberman, Weston, & Pawl, 1991).

Infant Contributions: Temperament Models and Measurement Issues

If adults bring to the parenting relationship a set of internal models and behavioral strategies derived partly from past relationships, infants are viewed as coming with their own intrinsic tendencies for experiencing and expressing emotions, which influence how they engage with caregivers. These hypothesized biological predispositions have been studied under the concept of "infant temperament." Though few dispute that temperament is an important developmental variable, there is less consensus (and no small amount of controversy) regarding its meaning and measurement.

There are essentially four major contemporary theories of temperament. The first and best-known, proposed by Thomas, Chess, and their colleagues (Thomas, Chess, Birch, Hertzig, & Korn, 1963; Thomas, Chess, & Birch, 1968; Thomas & Chess, 1977; Chess & Thomas, 1989), is that "temperament" refers to individual differences in stylistic aspects of behavior. Although considering temperament constitutional in origin, Thomas and Chess believe that infants' temperaments are products of ongoing interaction between their endogenous characteristics and their environments.

By interviewing parents in depth about everyday behaviors in their infants, these researchers defined nine dimensions of temperament: activity level, rhythmicity of biological functions, approach–withdrawal in novel situations, adaptability to changes in routine, intensity of affective expression, predominant mood, persistence, sensory threshold, and ease of distractibility when upset. In addition, they defined three patterns of these dimensions that classified the vast majority of their sample: "Easy" infants were disposed to be rhythmic, adaptable, approaching, generally positive in mood, and mild in intensity; "difficult" infants were irregular, unadaptable, withdrawing, negative, and intense; and "slow-to-warm-up" infants were low in activity, withdrawing in new situations, slow to adapt, mild in intensity, and negative in mood.

Difficult temperament was expected to place a child at increased risk for behavioral problems, and in fact, difficult temperament at the age of 3 years was associated with concurrent and subsequent behavioral problems. Difficult temperament in infancy, however, was not associated with later behavioral problems (Thomas et al., 1968).

The major problem for those investigating Thomas and Chess's temperament dimensions has been the bias inherent in parent report instruments. Although low to moderate convergent validity has been demonstrated for parent questionnaires, they have failed tests of discriminant validity repeatedly, as many parental characteristics that ought to be orthogonal to infant temperament have been demonstrated to be related to parental ratings (Sameroff, Seifer, & Elias, 1982; Seifer, Sameroff, Barrett, & Krafchuk, 1992; Vaughn, Bradley, Joffe, Seifer, & Barglow, 1987; Wolk, Zeanah, Garcia Coll, & Carr, 1992; Zeanah, Keener, & Anders, 1986). Thus, parent ratings of infant difficult temperament reflect not only possible biological differences among infants, but also differences in personality characteristics among parents and differences among infants attributable to environmental rather than biological factors. How to separate the component of parents' ratings that reflects presumed biological contributions from the components that reflect parental perceptions and environmental influences remains a major methodological problem in the field. There has also been only moderate agreement among different measures of difficult temperament (Goldsmith, Riesser-Danner, & Briggs, 1991), although there is general agreement among investigators that the construct concerns negative emotionality (Bates, 1989). Similarly, when parents of infants are asked which infant behaviors they find most difficult, they tend to cite negative mood and unadaptability (Hubert, 1989).

The second major theory of temperament is that of Buss and Plomin (1984), who define "temperament" as the inherited aspects of personality apparent in the first year of life. They review evidence indicating that emotionality, activity, and sociability all have significant genetic contributions. According to this theory, genetic contributions do not make temperamental traits immutable, but emotionality, activity, and sociability should be among the more stable personality traits (Plomin, 1987; Goldsmith et al., 1987). Not surprisingly, this theory has inspired research that has been useful in behavioral genetics, although the insistence that temperamental attributes be genetically influenced and apparent in the first year of life has been criticized (Chess & Thomas, 1989; Hinde, 1989b; Rutter, 1989).

The third major theory is that "temperament" refers to biologically based individual differences in the reactivity of the central nervous system and in self-regulation (Rothbart & Derryberry, 1981; Rothbart, 1989). At the level of individual experience, this theory concerns differences in energy, interest and affect (Goldsmith et al., 1987). Although clearly positing biological differences at multiple levels (e.g. autonomic, cognitive, neuroendocrine), this model of temperament in infancy has again been studied primarily through a parent report questionnaire (Rothbart, 1981). Nevertheless, this theory has inspired other investigators to begin to examine the relations between behavior and physiology more directly.

Porges and colleagues (Porges & Roosevelt, in press) have developed a physiological measure of central nervous system reactivity. In this model, vagal tone and vagal reactivity are considered indices of the basic substrates of behaviors involved in movement, emotional regulation, and communication. Pathology in the physiological substrate greatly increases the risk for deviant behavior, although involvement of higher centers may modulate or exacerbate this risk. There is now preliminary evidence of vagal abnormalities in regulatory disordered infants (DeGangi, DiPietro, Greenspan, & Porges, 1991; Greenspan & Wieder, Chapter 18, this volume). Similarly, Fox and Stifter (1989) have demonstrated a relationship between vagal tone and vagal reactivity and social behavior in infants. Infants with greater vagal tone are more reactive, more facially expressive, and more responsive to the environment, and also have a broader array of attentional strategies, than infants with low vagal tone.

Kagan and colleagues have developed a more specific, physiologically based single dimension of behavioral inhibition or shyness. Kagan,

Reznick, & Snidman (1987, 1988, 1989) have developed a laboratory assessment of behavioral inhibition. They have demonstrated continuity from ages 2 to 6 years in children who are extreme on this dimension, as well as extreme on related physiological correlates (Kagan et al., 1988, 1989). The dimension of behavioral inhibition may be important in selected samples, since parents with anxiety disorders have children who are prone to behavioral inhibition (Rosenbaum et al., 1988).

The fourth theory of temperament is similar to the third, although it is distinguished by its more narrow and explicit focus on affects. Goldsmith and Campos (1986) argue that "temperament" represents individual differences in the probability of experiencing the primary emotions and emotional arousal. Temperamental dimensions are believed to form the emotional substrate of later emerging personality characteristics. For example, fearfulness is asserted to influence later shyness, and persistence to influence later achievement motivation (Goldsmith et al., 1987). Detailed longitudinal evidence from early infancy is needed to evaluate this model.

In the context of the infant–caregiver relationship, an important additional construct in studies of temperament is that of "goodness of fit" (Thomas et al., 1968). This refers to the fit between the infant's temperamental attributes and the opportunities, expectations, demands, and responses of the caregiving environment. The fit between these two determines adaptation. Seifer and Sameroff (1986) have advanced and broadened the goodness-of-fit construct by incorporating subjective relationship experiences of infant and parent as they transact over time. Essentially, they discuss temperament as a within-the-person construct, but one that in infancy is defined in the context of the primary caregiving relationship. In this model, adverse temperamental attributes have weak links with subsequent maladaptation unless contextual responses support the link. Indeed, what represents an adverse temperamental trait may vary widely across different caregiving environments, and different environments may even elicit or suppress temperamental dispositions differently. Environmental aspects of goodness of fit include factors affecting caregivers' interpretations of a particular infant in a particular context; factors defining infant behavior in the family and other caregiving contexts; and intrapsychic, interpersonal, socioeconomic, and cultural caregiver perspectives that affect child behavior.

In summary, what these approaches have in common is a focus on dispositional differences in social behavior that are rooted in the infant's central nervous system and that affect how the infant approaches, interacts in, and experiences social relationships. These dispositions are expected to be reasonably stable over time, situations, and relationships. During infancy, however, consistent evidence for stable, biologically based differences in social behavior is still largely lacking. A new generation of studies is now attempting to bring together twin study designs and physiological assessments with more objective observer ratings of infant social behavior. A fuller exploration of the ramifications of these various models for infant mental health awaits further advances in the assessment of infant temperament and physiology that can begin to separate biologically based dispositions from influences of caregiver regulation.

MUTUAL REGULATORY PROCESSES

Emotion Regulation in Infant-Parent Relationships During the First Year

Research in the 1970s and 1980s on infant–parent interaction and its relation to infant development revealed the central role of parents' responsiveness to infant signals in mediating infant cognitive and linguistic development, as well as infant sociability (e.g., Bradley & Caldwell, 1980; Cohen & Beckwith, 1979). Various investigators have also documented the tendency for maternal sensitive responsiveness to infant cues to remain stable over time, even though the infant's capacities and the specific parenting behaviors required in response to those capacities change dramatically over the first 3 years of life (Ainsworth, Blehar, Waters, & Wall, 1978; Pettit & Bates, 1984; Belsky, Taylor, & Rovine, 1984; Clarke-Stewart, 1973). Working from this central understanding, more recent researchers have attempted to broaden our understanding of responsive parent–infant relationships in two complementary directions.

One set of recent advances has come from the shift to a more molar, organizational view that social interaction is organized in enduring patterned attachment relationships (Hinde, 1989a; Bowlby, 1969). The organizational perspective represented by attachment theory (Ainsworth et al., 1978; Bowlby, 1969; Sroufe & Waters, 1977) provides one of the most integrated accounts of the functioning and development of the infant–caregiver relationship during the first 3 years, and continues to generate new knowledge critical to the understanding of infant mental health. A second and complementary shift has been to examine parent–infant interaction through a much more detailed, process-oriented lens, bringing into focus the rich fabric of emotional exchanges between parent and infant and the developmental changes affecting processes of emotion regulation during infancy and toddlerhood.

The detailed study of interactive processes between infant and caregiver during the first year is beginning to fill in our understanding of how the parent's overall organization of attachment experiences interacts with the developing capacities of the infant as a social partner. Both the more organizational and more process-oriented approaches have converged in emphasizing the importance of emotional signals as social regulators and in detailing the processes through which infant–caregiver interactions are internalized as self-regulatory patterns by the infant. These emerging emphases on emotion and self-regulation are also beginning to promise new insights into early indicators of conflict, defense, and maladaptation in early social relationships. We first review recent work describing processes of regulation in the infant–parent relationship, and then move to the more organizational level, currently represented most clearly in work on patterns of attachment relationships.

Psychobiologists remind us that biological regulation is a component of all close relationships, and that the first function of the infant–caregiver system is the physiological regulation of both members of the dyad (Hofer, 1987; Reite, Short, Seiber, & Pauley, 1981). Pipp and Harmon (1987) have further suggested that, at the most basic level, the infant's sense of security may result from adequate homeostatic regulation within the caregiving relationship, with the earliest form of "security of attachment" encoded physiologically in the experience of nondisruptive and need-satisfying regulation of early states.

One impressive experimental demonstration of the interrelations between caregiver responsiveness and infant physiological regulation in the first days of life was a study by Sander, Julia, Stechler, and Burns (1972). These investigators randomly assigned newborn infants who were waiting to be given into foster care either to the regular hospital routine for the first 10 days, or to a rooming-in relationship with a single nurse who cared for and fed the infant on demand. The regular hospital routine consisted of care in the newborn nursery by a rotating series of nurses who fed the infant on a preset schedule. The two intermediate conditions of demand feeding in the nursery and scheduled feedings by a rooming-in nurse were also evaluated. Regardless of rooming-in status, demand feeding during the first 10 days promoted earlier differentiation of day–night sleep cycles in the first days of life and greater individual stability in feeding behavior and sleep–wake cycles—stability that persisted over the first 2 months of life. Infants who had rooming-in caregivers during the first 10 days had longer awake periods and longer sleep periods by the second 10 days of life. The authors concluded that the responsiveness of the environment influences the organization of infant functioning from birth.

As the infant becomes more available for extended social exchanges after 2 months of age, investigators have documented the patterns of mutual social regulation in face-to-face play that become part of the infant's repertoire. In these process-oriented studies of early regulation of social play, researchers have found that both infant and mother tend to match the partner's direction of affective change and that the influence is bidirectional, with each partner responding to changes in the other's behavior (Beebe, Alson, Jaffe, Feldstein, & Crown, 1988; Beebe, Jaffe, Feldstein, Mays, & Alson, 1985; Cohn & Tronick, 1988). Cohn and Tronick (1988) also noted that infants were more likely to respond to changes in their mothers' behavior if the mothers were responsive to changes in their behavior. Tronick and Cohn (1989) have further found that matching of states within social play episodes increases from 3 to 9 months of age. These repeated patterns of social responsiveness come to be recognized, remembered, and anticipated by the infant in future interactions, with evidence of negative affect and disrupted behavior by the infant if the mother fails to respond as expected (Cohn & Tronick, 1983). Furthermore, evidence indicates that infants carry these patterns over to their interactions with others, at least as early as 3 months of age (Field et al., 1988). Beebe and Lachman (1988) have pointed out that the presence of such expectations constitutes evidence for very early internal representations of self and others. They have also stressed the developmental role of these early experiences of affective matching in fostering a sense of mutuality and contributing to the development of intersubjective sharing by the latter half of the first year.

However, even in the highly structured face-to-face interaction situation, more than 70% of mother–infant time is spent in unmatched states, with movement from mismatched states to matched states (and vice versa) occurring every few seconds (Tronick & Cohn, 1989). Gianino and Tronick (1988) observed that infants who experienced more of the "reparative" sequences—that is, movements from mismatched to matched states—were more likely to actively signal their mothers when the mothers were not responding contingently. Thus, Gianino and Tronick have argued that the repair of interactive errors and movement from miscoordinated states to coordinated ones may be important in refining interactive and coping skills and in providing the infant with developmental experiences of reparation and effectance. Gianino and Tronick (1988) have further described two classes of regulatory behaviors at the infant's disposal: other-directed behaviors and self-directed behaviors. If the infant is not successful in redirecting the caregiver's behavior to help the infant in regulating negative affect states, several self-regulatory behaviors are at the infant's disposal, including looking away from a disturbing event, self-soothing as seen in thumb sucking, or self-stimulating behaviors.

Several studies suggest that similar processes of affect regulation and interactive history may underlie both infant behavior in early face-to-face play and later patterns of infant attachment behavior. Both Tronick, Ricks, and Cohn (1982) and Cohn, Campbell, and Ross (1991) found that 6-month-old infants who tried, via positive expressions, to elicit a maternal response in the "still-face procedure" (a procedure where mothers are instructed to remain impassive) were more likely to be classified as securely attached at 12 months (see also Kiser, Bates, Maslin, & Bayles, 1983). Infants who showed few positive elicitations at 6 months were more likely to have parents who were overcontrolling or undercontrolling in face-to-face play, as well as more likely to be classified as insecure at 12 months (Tronick et al., 1982). Other work also suggests that intrusive, overcontrolling maternal behavior may be differentially associated with both early gaze aversion in face-to-face play and later

avoidant behavior after a brief separation (Belsky, Rovine, & Taylor, 1984; Cohn, Tronick, Matias, Connell, & Lyons-Ruth, 1986; Egeland & Farber, 1984; Isabella & Belsky, 1991; Isabella, Belsky, & von Eye, 1989; Lyons-Ruth, Connell, Zoll, & Stahl, 1987; Malatesta, Culver, Tesman, & Shepard, 1989).

Looking at developmental changes in mother–infant facial affects during face-to-face play from 2½ to 7 months, Malatesta and her colleagues (1989) found that the rate of infant smiling changed dramatically over that time. The infant's *initial* rate of smiling at 2½ months did not predict later security of attachment behavior. However, infants who increased in smiling from 2½ to 7 months relative to other infants were found at 22 months to display secure attachment behaviors, whereas infants who decreased in smiling relative to other infants displayed insecure attachment behaviors in later assessments. Presumably, affect regulation patterns becoming established in the early parent–infant relationship were responsible for the large individual changes in smiling behavior during the first half-year of life. Work by Belsky and colleagues has also shown that an infant's change from high to low negative emotionality during the first 9 months is related to favorable maternal personality characteristics and to the mother's sensitive responsiveness to her infant (Belsky, Fish, & Isabella, 1991; Fish, Stifter, & Belsky, 1991).

Early patterns of parent–infant affect regulation are also related to parental psychiatric symptomatology. Field (1984) has found that infants of mothers with high levels of depressive symptoms showed less differentiated responses to normal and still-face interactions, remaining unresponsive in both conditions. Cohn et al. (1986) found two differentiated patterns of behavior among infants of depressed mothers: Infants of withdrawn depressed mothers displayed protest and distress, whereas infants of intrusive depressed mothers showed gaze aversion. At 18 months of age, a majority of the infants of low-income depressed mothers were found to display insecure attachment patterns (Lyons-Ruth et al., 1990). More thorough reviews of patterns of early interaction among clinical populations, such as infants of depressed or maltreating parents, are available in other chapters in this volume.

These early mutual play behaviors during which facial affects are elicited and matched may be one route through which infants construct a sense of the expressive meaning of different emotional displays. It will come as no surprise to clinicians who treat infants to learn that the newborn infant is capable of producing almost all of the muscle movements that underlie facial patterns for the basic emotional displays (Oster & Ekman, 1977), and that emotions such as sadness, anger, disgust, fear, joy, interest, and surprise can be identified reliably from the facial displays of infants aged 1 to 9 months (Izard, Huebner, Risser, McGinness, & Dougherty, 1980). As Zahn-Waxler, Cummings, and Cooperman (1984) point out, however, what to infer about the affective and cognitive components of these expressions is less clear. By 6 months or later, there is clear evidence that facial displays carry specific expressive meaning for the infant (LaBarbara, Izard, Vietze, & Parisi, 1976; Nelson, Morse, & Leavitt, 1979; Oster, 1981; Stenberg, Campos, & Emde, 1983). More recently, Lewis, Alessandri, and Sullivan (1990) have studied anger expressions in 2- to 8-month-old infants; they suggest that the ability to link facial expressions both to internal states and to appropriate motivational contexts is functional by at least 2 months of age, but that an infant's cognitive level influences the infant's interpretation of whether specific environmental contexts have emotional implications.

These data, which extend downward the time of onset of the infant's ability to correctly express and interpret emotional cues, provide support for Trevarthen's (1980) long-held view that infants are preadapted from birth to interpret affective displays as information regarding subjective state and are intrinsically motivated to establish affective communication with others. In keeping with this view, Trevarthen (1980) has labeled the first several months of life as the period of "primary intersubjectivity," stressing the importance during this period of the infant's consolidating a broad sense of the potential for shared emotional experience and of the strategies for achieving, "commenting" on, and exiting from these shared affective moments. It is also important to keep in mind that affective states are communicated and regulated by many cues other than facial expressions, such as vocal tone and contour, gaze behavior, and the timing and quality of physical touch. However, the infant's discrimination and differential response to these cues have not yet received systematic study (see also Stern, 1985, for his discussion of vitality affects).

The infant's ability to differentiate and use affective information in facial and bodily cues is an important prerequisite for another important process by which infants use the affective responses of familiar caregivers to regulate their own emotional responses and behavior in situations of uncertainty. As infants move into the second 6 months of life, they increasingly look to their familiar social partners for affective cues to guide their behavior in situations of unfamiliarity or uncertainty—a process referred to as "social referencing" (Klinnert, Campos, Sorce, Emde, & Svejda, 1983). As an infant becomes more mobile, social referencing of the parent serves as an anticipatory affective guide to inform the infant about sources of danger or pleasure, and serves to regulate the infant's affect and behavior from a distance. The sense of shared emotional states and mutually regulated affective displays underlying this behavior builds on the earlier processes of affective matching in face-to-face play observed during the first 6 months of life.

Searching out and using others' affective expressions for emotional and behavioral guidance appear to be established by about 9 months of age (Campos, 1984). A majority of infants by 1 year are observed to look to adult emotional expressions in ambiguous laboratory situations that produce uncertainty, such as being faced with unfamiliar people (Feinman & Lewis, 1983), unusual moving toys or animals (Hornik, Risenhoover, & Gunnar, 1987; Walden & Ogan, 1988), or an apparent dropoff in the laboratory floor surface (Sorce, Emde, Campos, & Klinnert, 1985). Infants are less likely to approach these novel aspects of the environment when a parent displays fearful affect and are more likely to approach when positive affect is displayed. Infants also retain this information and use it to regulate their behavior in later encounters with the same objects (Hornik et al., 1987). By 1 year of age, infants look to fathers as readily as mothers, and to unfamiliar adults when mothers are not providing signals (Hirshberg & Svejda, 1990; Klinnert, Emde, Butterfield, & Campos, 1986; but see also Zarbatany & Lamb, 1985). Infants appear to become more proficient in the use of social referencing with age: Children over 1 year of age look to parents more quickly, more directly, and more often than do younger infants (Klinnert, 1984; Walden & Ogan, 1988; Hornik & Gunnar, 1988).

Individual differences in social referencing have been less systematically studied, but some evidence suggests that social referencing is more likely among infants of easy temperament (Feinman & Lewis, 1983) and that fathers who express more marital satisfaction are more likely to be referenced (Dickstein & Parke, 1988). Other work finds that by 1 year of age the frequency of an infant's social referencing of the mother is related to the overall organization of the attachment relationship between mother and infant. Infants with ambivalent attachment relationships, who tend to increase the intensity of their attachment behaviors in general, also increase their social referencing behavior compared to securely attached infants; by contrast, infants in avoidant attachment relationships, who tend to displace attention away from the attachment relationship, show decreased social referencing compared to secure infants (Dickstein, Thompson, Estes, Malkin, & Lamb, 1984).

Bretherton (1984) further relates the infant's social referencing behavior to other indicators of a broad capacity for mutual sharing of subjective states toward objects and events that emerges during the last quarter of the first year. Trevarthen and Hubley (1978) label this the period of "secondary intersubjectivity," because the focus is not on sharing affects per se but on constructing shared meanings and references to the external world. Bretherton, McNew, and Beeghly-Smith (1981) discuss this period after 9 months of age as a time when infants have acquired a "theory of mind," or an awareness that others, although separate and distinct from themselves, may be induced to share a similar psychological viewpoint. This achievement of secondary intersubjectivity, or the deliberate creation of mutually held subjective states toward aspects of the environment, is also seen in the infant's seeking to share a focus of attention with others (Murphy & Messer, 1977; Scaife & Bruner, 1975) and in the infant's deliberate communication of intentions and desires through gestures and "protolanguage" (Bates, 1979), as well as in social referencing behavior. Trevarthen (1989) has also hypothesized that 9-month-olds' stranger anxiety may be another expression of the infants' new sensitivity to the sharing of subjective meaning, with concomitant fear and distrust of unfamiliar others who may be uncomprehending.

This literature on social referencing and secondary intersubjectivity has not yet been extended to infants at social risk. However, clinical descriptions of the lack of cautious behavior among young children who have been seriously neglected point to potential disruptions in the development of normal social referencing behavior in dangerous situations (Malone, 1967). Conversely, infant social referencing behaviors provide one clear path through which parental anger or fearfulness may be monitored and used by the infant for self-guidance (see Zahn-Waxler & Kochanska, 1988).

The Attachment System: Self-Regulation of Distress and Comfort Seeking

Other insights into the caregiver's contribution to emerging patterns of infant self-regulation come from research on attachment relationships. In Bowlby's (1969) initial formulation of the importance of the infant's emotional tie to the primary caregiver, he laid out an organizational perspective on the understanding of infant and caregiver behavior that has been critical to subsequent research. This perspective emphasized the development of a goal-corrected partnership between infant and caregiver, in which a number of superficially dissimilar infant and caregiver behaviors are organized around the larger goal of maintaining the infant's sense of security.

Bowlby focused particularly on the period after 9 months of age, when the infant's active maintenance of physical access to the caregiver becomes prominent. He referred to the set of organized behaviors through which the infant self-regulates a sense of security as the "attachment behavioral system." These behaviors include the infant's actively maintaining physical proximity to a familiar caregiver and, if alarmed or distressed, retreating to the caregiver for a sense of safety and for soothing of distress. Lack of access to a familiar caregiver is capable of provoking alarm and protest in itself as the infant experiences the lack of availability of a safe haven. Since close physical contact with the caregiver is a central component of effective soothing of distress in infancy, attachment research has most vividly illuminated Winnicott's (1960/1965) central metaphor of the "holding environment." Although these attachment behaviors become increasingly visible in the infant's repertoire toward the end of the first year, striking individual differences are also seen; these reflect both temperamental differences and the pattern of affect regulation that has developed between infant and caregiver over the first year.

Bowlby's concept of a goal-corrected attachment behavioral system led Ainsworth and her colleagues to the further discovery that several patterned subtypes of infant–parent attachment behavior could be observed by the end of the first year, each characterized by a distinct strategy in relation to attachment goals. Ainsworth et al. (1978) referred to these patterns as "secure," "avoidant," and "ambivalent" attachment organizations, with a fourth subtype, termed the "disorganized/disoriented" attachment pattern, identified more recently by Main and Solomon (1990). These organized patterns are now understood to have affective as well as behavioral and representational components (Cassidy, 1993) and to be evident in parent and infant behavior throughout the first 3 years and beyond.

Infants who are secure in their attachment relationships often show some protest when being left alone or left with a stranger in an unfamiliar place by the time of the first birthday. This protest often includes obvious distress, disruption of play and exploration, and rejection of comforting from an unfamiliar adult. When the mother returns, the infant greets her warmly and often seeks to be near her or in physical contact with her, calms quickly if distressed, and returns comfortably to play and exploration (see Ainsworth et al., 1978, for additional description). Attachment research also indicates that among stable, middle-class families, secure attachment behaviors show a high level of stability over the 12- to 18-month age range (Connell, 1976; Waters, 1978). Harmonious interaction and absence of overt ambivalence during reunions remain the predominant patterns of infant behavior through 20 months of age and probably beyond, although fewer systematic studies of reunion behavior have addressed the preschool period (Cassidy, Berlin, & Belsky, 1990; Greenberg & Slough, 1991; Main et al., 1985). When observed, parents of secure infants are likely to be sensitive and responsive to the full range of infant affective signals; when interviewed, parents of secure infants are likely to display coherent and autonomous internal representations of their own earlier attachment relationships in childhood. Secure attachment relationships are viewed as organized by a stance of open emotional communication between partners.

As noted above, three alternative organizations of infant attachment behavior have been observed when caregiving conditions are less optimal. Each of these self-regulated patterns of infant behavior is, in turn, related to a particular organization of parental thinking about attachment issues. An infant who displays an "avoidant" behavioral organization does not react with protest to the mother's departure in an unfamiliar setting. Instead, the infant typically diverts attention from her exit, explores actively while she is out of the room, and is friendly to the unfamiliar adult in the room. This independent-appearing behavior often looks quite positive to an observer. However, an avoidant infant also does not immediately acknowledge the mother's return to the room, averting his or her gaze when the mother enters and initially moves away from her if she approaches.

The behavior of an avoidant infant is understood to represent a strategy for dealing with the stress of separation, rather than indicating an absence of stress per se. Main and Weston (1982) have argued that avoidant behavior represents an organized defensive strategy to avoid distress by directing attention away from information related to the mother's departure, and by displacing both anger and attention onto inanimate features of the environment. In support of this hypothesis, Malatesta et al. (1989) found that avoidant infants more frequently displayed a pressed-lips expression that is thought to index suppressed anger. Paradoxically, when observed at home, avoidant infants have been found to be more angry and distressed around their mothers than secure infants (Ainsworth et al., 1978), and their mothers have been rated as more covertly rejecting of their infants (Ainsworth et al., 1978; Lyons-Ruth et al., 1987; Main & Weston, 1982). In addition, mothers of infants who showed the pressed-lips expression under stress were more likely during the first 6 months to have shown mock surprise to infant anger and a lack of interest to infants' expressions of interest (Malatesta et al., 1989).

This affect regulation strategy on the infants' part is paralleled by analogous parental affect regulation strategies during the adult attachment interview. Parents of avoidant infants are more likely than other parents to minimize the importance of attachment relationships and of experiences of anger and distress in general, and to use idealization and inability to recall specific memories in order to avoid confronting negative affects (Cassidy & Kobak, 1988; Main et al., 1985). At the parental level, this strategy is termed a "dismissing" representational model of attachment relationships.

A second alternative attachment organization is termed "ambivalent" attachment. This behavior pattern is characterized by distress at the mother's absence and contact seeking at her return, mixed with direct or displaced anger and resistance and a failure to be fully comforted and able to return to play. The heightened distress and angry behavior often shown by ambivalent infants have been interpreted by Main and Hesse (1990) as strategies of exaggerating attachment behaviors in order to elicit a response from less responsive caregivers. When observed at home, mothers of ambivalent infants have been more disengaged and less responsive to infant crying than mothers of secure or avoidant infants (Ainsworth et al., 1978; Belsky, Rovine, & Taylor, 1984; Lyons-Ruth et al., 1987). In face-to-face play at 6 months, mothers of ambivalent infants were found to initiate the fewest interactions (Kiser et al., 1983). When mothers of ambivalent infants did respond to crying, they were less likely to comfort by tenderly holding the infants and more likely to try to calm the infants by talking or more distanced touching, such as stroking or patting (Miyake, Chen, & Campos, 1985). In other work, infants who showed sadness at reunions in the second year had mothers who were more likely to have ignored expressions of sadness in early face-to-face play, while infants who were angry at reunion had mothers who showed mock surprise to expressions of sadness (Malatesta et al., 1989). When interviewed, parents of ambivalent infants are more likely to reveal either a passive and confused stance or an openly angry stance toward their own parents, both characterized by continued internal affective overinvolvement with their parents and a pervasive sense of their inability to please their parents (Main & Hesse, 1990; Main et al., 1985). This parental stance is termed a "preoccupied" representational model of attachment relationships.

The avoidant and ambivalent patterns of infant behavior under stress occur frequently in nondisturbed family settings, and their relative rates of occurrence may also be related to cultural norms emphasizing either independence from or involvement with relationships (Grossmann et al., 1988; Miyake et al., 1985; Oppenheim, Sagi, & Lamb, 1988). The infant's propensity to experience distress in a variety of situations (a temperamental disposition) is also related to whether insecure behavior takes an avoidant or ambivalent form, but propensity toward distress is *not* related to whether the infant displays secure or insecure strategies per se (Belsky & Rovine, 1987; Vaughn, Lefever, Seifer, & Barglow, 1989). Both avoidant and ambivalent patterns are also seen as representing organized strategies of response to stress.

As noted earlier, prior to the birth of an infant, analogous organized strategies of affect regulation can be identified in parents' verbal representations of attachment relationships. Presumably, through the developing process of parent–infant affect regulation during the first year, parental regulatory strategies come to be internalized as self-regulating patterns of infant behavior. Some of the precursors of later attachment strategies seen in earlier patterns of face-to-face play and social referencing behavior have already been noted.

The consistency and organization characterizing avoidant and ambivalent (and secure) attachment patterns set them apart from the third type of less optimal attachment behavior, which is termed "disorganized/disoriented" behavior. Disorganized/disoriented attachment behavior may have special relevance to family contexts of loss, trauma, or psychopathology (Main & Hesse, 1990; Lyons-Ruth, Repacholi, McLeod, & Silva, 1991; Main & Solomon, 1990). Infants who show disorganized/disoriented behavior do not consistently manage distress and approach tendencies by avoidance and displacement, as in the avoidant attachment pattern; nor do they consistently voice their distress at separation and actively seek contact when their mothers return, as in the secure or ambivalent pattern. Instead, both approach and avoidance tendencies appear to be activated and vie for expression. The particular forms and combinations of conflict behaviors exhibited tend to be fairly idiosyncratic from child to child, but they include unpredictable alternations of approach and avoidance toward the mother, as well as other conflict behaviors (e.g., prolonged freezing or stilling, or slowed "underwater" movements). Hence the term "disorganized/disoriented" refers to the apparent lack of a consistent strategy for organizing responses to the need for comfort and security when under stress. On interview, parents of disorganized/disoriented infants tend to show indicators of lack of resolution of loss or trauma. Unresolved loss or trauma is indexed by areas of less coherent or irrational thought processes during the interview or by signs of affective flooding (Ainsworth & Eichberg, 1991; Main et al., 1985; Main & Hesse, 1990).

Although the disorganized/disoriented behaviors were initially observed by Main and colleagues among infants from middle-class families, more recent evidence indicates that infants of depressed, maltreating, or alcoholic mothers are particularly likely to show these behaviors (Carlson, Cicchetti, Barnett, & Braunwald, 1989; Lyons-Ruth et al., 1990; O'Connor, Sigman, & Brill, 1987). Infants displaying highly avoidant forms of disorganized strategies, as compared to more approach-oriented disorganized behaviors, appear to be particularly likely to have parents with serious psychosocial problems and to be at risk for later behavior problems themselves (Lyons-Ruth, Alpern, & Repacholi, 1993; Lyons-Ruth et al., 1991; Carlson et al., 1989).

Mastery Motivation in Relational Context

In addition to the attachment motivational system, another motivational system apparent during infancy is "mastery motivation." Infants in the second half of the first year increasingly direct their attention toward exploring, influencing, and controlling the environment. Although the breadth of definitions used by different investigators vary, most agree that the enthusiasm, pleasure, interest, and persistence that infants demonstrate as they explore the environment, attempt to solve problems, and approach challenging tasks reflect mastery motivation.

Because mastery behaviors are believed to be pleasurable in and of themselves, mastery is considered to be intrinsically motivated and self-reinforcing (Harter, 1978; Hunt, 1965; White, 1959). Mastery motivation has been shown to be stable over time and to be related to subsequent cognitive competence (Jennings, Yarrow, & Martin, 1984; Messer et al., 1986; Yarrow, Morgan, Jennings, Harmon, & Gaiter, 1982; Yarrow et al., 1983).

Mastery behaviors are thought to reflect early precursors of individuals' competence. Morgan and colleagues (Morgan, Harmon, & Maslin-Cole, 1990; Morgan, Maslin-Cole, & Harmon, 1991) assert that "mastery" refers to what a child is doing to increase competence and to how the child is trying to achieve greater competence. "Competence," in their model, refers to skills that the child has already mastered. Most of the research examining mastery in infancy has assessed it in relation to later cognitive rather than social competence (Jennings et al., 1984; Messer et al., 1986).

In Bowlby's (1969) organizational model, mastery (or, in his terms, "exploratory motivation") is seen as operating in a reciprocal relationship with the attachment motivational system, such that when the infant is not distressed or alarmed and the attachment system is not highly activated, the interest/exploratory system takes over, with its motivational push for the infant to examine novel features of the environment. Infants who have ready access to a familiar comforting and soothing person will then spend less time in states of distress or alarm and more time exploring and learning (see also Ainsworth et al., 1978).

Perhaps because of the emphasis on intrinsic motivation, contextual influences on mastery motivation have not received much attention, but the available research is consistent with Bowlby's model. Yarrow et al. (1984) reported that parental stimulation was associated with persistence at problem solving and practicing skills. Frodi, Bridges, and Grolnick (1985) found that mothers who supported their infants' strivings for autonomy (i.e., who were sensitive and noncontrolling during interactions), and who had more flexible child-rearing attitudes, had infants with greater persistence in mastery tasks at 12 and 20 months. Redding, Harmon, and Morgan (1990) found that depressed mood in middle-class mothers was inversely correlated with their infants' task persistence and task competence at 12 and 24 months and with their task pleasure at 24 months.

A variation on the assessment of mastery that is more relationship-based involves a tool use procedure in which mothers are available to help toddlers solve difficult problems. Matas, Arend, and Sroufe (1978) developed a procedure for 2-year-olds in which a child must enlist the caregiver's assistance to deal with challenging tasks. The investigators found that socially competent toddlers approached problem-solving tasks with flexibility, resourcefulness, and an ability to use their caregivers for assistance without being overly dependent. Caregivers of more competent toddlers were more supportive and gave assistance when needed. Behaviors of mothers and infants were predicted from the infants' attachment classifications 1 year earlier. Employing the tool use procedure, Hron-Stewart, Lefever, and Weintraub (1990) found that higher problem-solving scores were related to more maternal involvement and provision of play materials.

Crowell and Feldman (1988) modified the

tool use procedure to make it applicable across a range of ages from 24 to 54 months. They found that mothers and children's behaviors were related to the mothers' attachment classification and to the mothers' report of child behavior problems (Crowell & Feldman, 1988; Crowell, Feldman, & Ginsburg, 1988). Although the tool use task and the Crowell and Feldman modification of it comprise challenging tasks presented to a child, they do not constrain the mother's responsiveness; therefore, unlike other mastery procedures, they assess the parent–child relationship as it functions under different types of stresses.

Thus, although the original theoretical emphasis in regard to mastery was on its intrinsic motivation, there is growing evidence that mastery motivation is influenced by an infant's relationship with the primary caregiver. Caregivers who are emotionally available and who promote rather than control infants' exploratory behaviors have infants who demonstrate greater task persistence, greater pleasure in goal-directed behavior, and greater subsequent social and cognitive competence. Furthermore, Aber and Allen (1987) have presented evidence that in family situations where comfort is rarely available and infants' attachment concerns are chronically activated, the infants' exploratory activity and "secure readiness to learn" are compromised, with resultant decreases in cognitive growth and mastery. Though their initial data and theorizing concerned maltreating families, more recent evidence suggests that deficits in cognitive and linguistic development may be more broadly characteristic of infants with disorganized attachment relationships, rather than confined only to the smaller population of maltreating families (Lyons-Ruth et al., 1991; Morisset, Barnard, Greenberg, Booth, & Spieker, 1990).

The Regulation of Evaluative Standards and Affects in Toddlerhood

As infants become toddlers and move into the second half of the second year, another cognitive advance occurs with the onset of symbolic representational capacity and the associated emergence of self-awareness, evaluative standards, and the "early moral emotions" (Case, 1985; Emde, Johnson, & Easterbrooks, 1988; Kagan, 1981). The rapid emergence of language

after 18 months of age is one of the most striking signs of this advance. Other signs of new capacities that can be seen toward the end of the second year include the child's recognition of the self in mirrors and video images (Lewis & Brooks-Gunn, 1979); the emergence of "no" as an indicator of a new level of autonomy (Spitz, 1957); and the appearance of self-conscious emotions such as embarrassment (Lewis, Sullivan, Stanger, & Weiss, 1989). This cognitive advance forms one of the underpinnings of the so-called "terrible twos," in that the toddler's newly acquired capacities introduce new elements into the parent–child relationship.

In toddlerhood, children are able to keep their own goals in mind over longer sequences of activity and to judge whether they have achieved their goals. This emerging ability to self-generate standards of mastery and to monitor whether they are met forms one basis for toddlers' frequent "nos," with toddlers becoming more resistant to being distracted from their own goal-directed plans. Toddlers are also able to construct value labels or normative standards based on the evaluations of others, and are able to remember and represent their own and others' past feelings in relation to a particular event (Kagan, 1981). They begin to show distress or concern over violations of these newly constructed standards, reacting negatively to such things as broken plates, dirty clothes, or disapproved behaviors. They also are acquiring the capacity to evaluate the self as "good" or "bad," and become subject to emotions of self-consciousness, shame, or anxiety over a perceived inability to meet self-generated or normative standards.

Toddlers, in Kagan's view, once aware that standards (qualities of goodness or badness) exist, are intrinsically motivated to meet them. However, a child's own mastery standards or goals may conflict with parental goals. In addition, the moral standards of parents are often unclear to a young toddler who is just beginning to construct a cognitive domain of morally judged actions. Therefore, younger toddlers, in particular, often test to see which classes of activity are subject to evaluative judgment. Emde and Buchsbaum (1990) have described the increased rates at about 8 months of age of both parental prohibitions and infant social referencing, with the infant presumably looking more frequently to the parents to resolve newly emerging uncertainties about which acts are valued and which acts are prohibited. Both the child's need to meet self-generated standards and the need to identify those activities that violate norms may appear willfully provocative to parents.

Emde et al. (1988) hypothesize a developmental sequence in which internalization of parental "dos" and "don'ts" begins to be demonstrated in the presence of the parent by 24 months of age. Maintenance of parental standards in the parent's absence is a more complex developmental acquisition not clearly in evidence until 36 months of age or beyond (Emde & Buchsbaum, 1990; Buchsbaum & Emde, 1990). Crockenberg (Crockenberg, 1991; Crockenberg & Litman, 1990) has adopted a relational process-oriented view of parental limit setting and child compliance, arguing that the negotiation of a balance between the goals of the parent and the goals of the 2-year-old is best viewed as a two-way process of conflict resolution, rather than as a one-way process of discipline or socialization of the child by the parent. Kuczynski and Kochanska (1990) also cite evidence that parents' control strategies may provide models for their toddlers' own social behaviors, and that learning to express one's own wishes and negotiate for their inclusion in joint plans during toddlerhood may provide some of the underpinnings for effective social behavior at later ages (Dunn & Munn, 1987; Patterson, 1982; Trickett & Kuczynski, 1986). Crockenberg and Litman (1990) point out that a toddler's "no" is both conceptually and empirically distinct from angry defiance, and should be seen as a statement of the child's emerging autonomous viewpoint.

Consistent with a variety of other research is the finding that highly power-assertive behavior on the part of the parent is more likely to lead to defiant child behavior, whereas reasoning and negotiation, combined with a direct statement of the parent's needs, are more likely to result in the child's acquiescence to parental requests and internalization of parental standards (Crockenberg & Litman, 1990; Kuczynski, Kochanska, Radke-Yarrow, & Girnius-Brown, 1987; Kochanska, 1991). These researchers also point out that child compliance negotiated in an atmosphere of mutual respect for the other's needs has a very different psychological meaning and developmental trajectory than does child compliance coerced through excessive parental punishment, as seen in the compulsively compliant behavior of some maltreated children (Crittenden & DiLalla, 1988).

At the same time that toddlers are constructing an understanding of parental standards, they are also showing increasing evidence of empathy and guilt in response to others' distress (Emde Johnson, & Easterbrooks, 1988; Radke-Yarrow & Zahn-Waxler, 1984). Zahn-Waxler and colleagues have described a variety of expressions of concern, anxiety, remorse, reparation, and/or acknowledgment displayed by 2-year-olds when they have caused distress to others, as well as when they are merely bystanders; the conclusion is that empathic perceptions of others' emotions, as well as awareness of parental standards, contribute to the toddler's construction of early dos and don'ts (Cole, Barrett, & Zahn-Waxler, 1992; Zahn-Waxler, & Radke-Yarrow, 1990; Zahn-Waxler, Radke-Yarrow, & King, 1979). Emde et al. (1988) have discussed the "early moral emotions" of pride, shame, and guilt as complex emotions that do not correspond to discrete facial expressions, do not emerge until 24 to 30 months of age, and depend on the cognitive appreciation of another's evaluation of the self's performance in relation to a rule or goal. Lewis (1992) further differentiates these self-conscious evaluative emotions along a global–specific dimension: He sees a global negative self-evaluation underlying the experience of shame, but a more limited negative evaluation of a specific action or outcome underlying the toddler's experience of guilt.

Parents' regulation of interactions centering around situations of wrongdoing or others' distress has important consequences for the toddler's developing experience and internal regulation of shame and guilt. Consistent with Crockenberg's work, Chapman and Zahn-Waxler (1982) found that compared to toddlers of parents who used physical punishment or power assertion, toddlers whose parents used explanations and/or love withdrawal (disapproval or physical withdrawal) displayed higher levels of guilt and reparative behavior, as well as altruistic behavior generally. These parents who did *not* use physical coercion also tended to be empathic and sensitive in their interactions with their children generally, so that the parents' empathy for the toddlers was consistent with their demands that the toddlers be empathic toward others.

However, Chapman and Zahn-Waxler (1982) also found that more extreme forms of love withdrawal were associated both with avoidant responses and with attempts to make up with the parents, leading the authors to note that the tension and ambivalence generated for some young children by love withdrawal appeared to result in excessive guilt that was inappropriate to the situation. In contrast, more matter-of-fact parental explanations, with more moderated levels of affect, resulted in levels of toddler guilt and responsibility more in keeping with the circumstances.

In other work, Zahn-Waxler and colleagues have found that 2-year-olds exposed to repeated parental conflict at home exhibited more negative arousal to conflict than children from low-conflict homes, including increased empathic distress and comforting of the victim, and increased angry behavior toward the perceived aggressor (Cummings, Zahn-Waxler, & Radke-Yarrow, 1981; Cummings, Iannotti, & Zahn-Waxler, 1985). The authors speculated that the toddlers' assumption of responsibility during conflicts might index or lead to inappropriate guilt and a misplaced sense of personal causality for the conflict.

Zahn-Waxler, Cummings, Iannotti, and Radke-Yarrow (1984) also reported that 2- and 3-year-old children of mothers with unipolar depression were more likely than children of well mothers to become preoccupied and upset when exposed to conflict or distress, and were less aggressive and more appeasing in play with other toddlers; again, these findings suggested a heightened sensitivity and possible sense of responsibility for others' distress. The toddlers with depressed mothers also made more frequent and varied comforting responses when the mothers simulated distress. Anecdotally, the authors also observed that depressed mothers were more likely to elaborate and personalize their (simulated) expressions of sadness and to implicate the children as a cause of this distress. In addition, on interview, depressed mothers were especially likely to endorse guilt-inducing (or, in Lewis's terms, shame-inducing) strategies for regulating the toddlers' behavior and to express disappointment in their children. Thus, a toddler's exaggerated caretaking and distress may be directly responsive to a mother's disciplinary and affect regulation strategies.

Research evidence indicates that the way in which the parent and toddler traverse this period of emerging moral evaluation, increasing empathy, and increasing desire for self-regulation is conditioned by aspects of the parent-child relationship during the first year. As Zahn-Waxler and Kochanska (1988) have noted,

"Whether [feelings of guilt and responsibility] initially take healthy or maladaptive forms seems inextricably linked to the quality of the attachment relationship with the caregiver" (p. 244). In a study of 44 middle-income families, Heinecke, Diskin, Ramsey-Klee, and Oates (1986) also found that a child's modulation of aggression at age 2 was predictable from prebirth characteristics of the family, including the mother's scores on measures of adaptation, competence, and warmth, and the positive quality of the husband–wife relationship; these were, in turn, related to greater maternal responsiveness to infant need at 1 month and 24 months.

These data further support the results of studies in the attachment tradition indicating that sensitive and responsive parenting during the first 2 years of a child's life sets the stage for more flexible and cooperative assertiveness when the child is a toddler. Stayton, Hogan, and Ainsworth (1971) found that infants with sensitive and responsive caregivers were both more likely to comply with parental requests at 9 months of age and more likely to be classified as securely attached at 12 months. Other research, predicting forward from secure attachment relationships at 12 months to later toddler behavior, has found that toddlers who display secure attachment behaviors as infants are rated more highly on a variety of indicators of both autonomy and cooperation at 24 months. Toddlers with histories of secure attachment resemble all other toddlers in showing a relatively high rate of noncompliance with parental requests. However, they are more likely to be cooperative and affectionate with their mothers than are toddlers with other attachment histories. They show greater flexibility and persistence at a difficult and frustrating task, yet are also more likely to request appropriate assistance from their mothers if the task is beyond their reach (Londerville & Main, 1981; Matas et al., 1978). By contrast, toddlers who have had insecure attachment relationships as infants smile less often at their mothers, ignore them more when together, and are rated lower on the quality of affective sharing with mothers. Toddlers with insecure attachment histories also direct more anger, physical aggression, and noncompliance toward their mothers and do not use them as effectively for help with a difficult task (Londerville & Main, 1981; Matas et al., 1978).

In summary, as young children reach their third birthdays, they have constructed a sophisticated repertory of skills and strategies for communicating and negotiating in relationships—strategies that are substantially shaped by their parents' own representational models of relationships. At the age of 3, a child is on the threshold of a broadening social world of nonfamily playmates and teachers. Prospective longitudinal data confirm that the skills and strategies developing in the emotional crucible of early relationships with parents will be brought to new relationships outside the family in succeeding years. Aspects of ego resilience, sociability, warmth, and hostile aggression with peers during the preschool and early school years, and of dependence, anger, and flexible autonomy with teachers and other adults, are all predicted by aspects of attachment and adaptation observable in the infant and toddler period (Arend, Gove, & Sroufe, 1979; Lyons-Ruth et al., in press; Oppenheim et al., 1988; Sroufe, Fox, & Pancake, 1983; Waters, Wippman, & Sroufe, 1979). Thus, early affect regulation strategies and the associated representational models of self and other emerging from infant–parent relationships have consequences beyond the infant period per se. Current longitudinal research points to the relatively enduring nature of the patterns of emotional relatedness constructed during the first 3 years of life.

CONCLUSIONS

Recent developmental literature on early socioemotional development is converging on a relational perspective (e.g., Sameroff & Emde, 1989). This perspective emphasizes both the stability over time of the affective quality of the relationship, and the organizational coherence of patterns of relational behavior through which this affect regulation is accomplished. The work on relational processes in infancy reviewed here is also leading to a reconsideration and reworking of the earlier psychodynamic theories that have guided much previous clinical work with infants and adults. The discoveries that patterns of affect regulation and relational behavior are constructed and internalized by the infant from the earliest emotional dialogues with parents, and that these representational models are then brought to the task of interacting with new and unfamiliar social partners, is breathing new life into the relationally based theories of Bowlby, Sullivan, and British object relations theorists (see Bretherton, 1991), while leading to radical revisions in some of the early developmental

processes posited by theorists such as Mahler (see Lyons-Ruth, 1991; Stern, 1985) and Freud (see Emde, 1983; Emde et al., 1988; Zahn-Waxler & Kochanska, 1988).

Although stability and organization in early relationships have been clearly demonstrated, they account for only part of the developmental picture. More methodological work is needed to define aspects of infant temperament that are initially independent of relational influences, and to specify how relational and temperamental contributions to early development may moderate or potentiate one another. Other genetic and biological influences on behavior not treated here, including cognitive endowment, perinatal problems, and physical disabilities, also exert important influences on both infant and caregiver. However, the recent emergence of relational models has been partly fueled by earlier studies indicating that the influence of biological factors in early development, such as cognitive endowment or birth complications, is powerfully shaped by the early social environment (Bradley & Caldwell, 1980; Sameroff & Chandler, 1975), and conversely that positive patterns of relationship are relatively robust in the face of serious infant problems, such as marked prematurity and perinatal difficulties (Goldberg & DiVitto, 1983; Goldberg, Perrotta, Minde, & Corter, 1986).

As the evidence for relational stability accumulates, developmental researchers are also turning their attention to the complementary question of how to conceptualize and document lawful processes of relational change (Belsky et al., 1991; Egeland et al., 1988). Of particular interest are changes in relational patterns or infant behaviors associated with later maladaptive outcomes. Some evidence for the influence of marital or therapeutic relationships on a parent's relationship with an infant has already been cited, but we have much further to go in specifying the processes that lead to change. Evidence reviewed here suggests that change processes are likely to be based on the availability of additional relational partners and to involve the reorganization of complex internal representations having cognitive, affective, and behavioral components.

Finally, the subtle processes of affect communication between parent and infant, and the associated construction by the infant of internal representational models, establish a critical link between the emerging self of the infant and the social and cultural factors influencing his or her parents and grandparents. As outlined in our initial model of family factors influencing infant mental health, from the beginning of life the infant is an emotional participant in the larger world of cultural differences, life stresses, and socioeconomic inequities shaping the parents' world (McLoyd, 1990).

REFERENCES

Aber, J. L., & Allen, J. P. (1987). The effects of maltreatment on young children's socioemotional development: An attachment theory perspective. *Developmental Psychology, 23,* 406–414.

Ainsworth, M. D. S., Blehar, M., Waters, E., & Wall, S. (1978). *Patterns of attachment.* Hillsdale, NJ: Erlbaum.

Ainsworth, M. D. S., & Eichberg, C. G. (1991). Effects on infant–mother attachment of mother's unresolved loss of an attachment figure or other traumatic experience. In P. Marris, J. Stevenson-Hinde, & C. Parkes (Eds.), *Attachment across the life cycle* (pp. 160–186). London: Routledge & Kegan Paul.

Arend, R., Gove, F., & Sroufe, L. A. (1979). Continuity of individual adaptation from infancy to kindergarten: A predictive study of ego-resiliency and curiosity in preschoolers. *Child Development, 50,* 950–959.

Bates, E. (1979). Intentions, conventions and symbols. In E. Bates (Ed.), *The emergence of symbols: Cognition and communication in infancy* (pp. 33–68). New York: Academic Press.

Bates, J. E. (1989). Applications of temperament concepts. In G. A. Kohnstamm, J. E. Bates, & M. K. Rothbart (Eds.), *Temperament in childhood* (pp. 3–26). New York: Wiley.

Beckwith, L., & Rodning, C. (1991, April). Stability and correlates of attachment classifications from 13 to 36 months in a sample of preterm infants. In R. S. Marvin & J. Cassidy (Chairs), *Attachment during the preschool years: Examination of a new measure.* Symposium conducted at the biennial meeting of the Society for Research in Child Development, Seattle.

Beebe, B., Alson, D., Jaffe, J., Feldstein, S., & Crown, C. (1988). Mother–infant vocal congruence. *Journal of Psycholinguistic Research, 17*(3), 245–259.

Beebe, B., Jaffe, J., Feldstein, S., Mays, K., & Alson, D. (1985). Interpersonal timing: The application of an adult dialogue model to mother–infant vocal and kinesic interactions. In T. Field & N. Fox (Eds.), *Social perception in infants* (pp. 217–247). Norwood, NJ: Ablex.

Beebe, B., & Lachmann, F. M. (1988). The contribution of mother–infant mutual influence to the origins of self- and object representations. *Psychoanalytic Psychology, 5*(4), 305–337.

Belsky, J., Fish, M., & Isabella, R. (1991). Continuity and discontinuity in infant negative and positive emotionality: Family antecedents and attachment consequences. *Developmental Psychology, 27*(3), 421–431.

Belsky, J., Lang, M. E., & Rovine, M. (1985). Stability and change in marriage across the transition to parenthood: A second study. *Journal of Marriage and the Family, 47,* 855–865.

Belsky, J., & Pensky, E. (1988). Developmental history, personality, and family relationships: Toward an emergent family system. In R. A. Hinde & J. Stevenson-Hinde (Eds.), *Relationships within families: Mutual influences* (pp. 193–217). New York: Oxford University Press.

Belsky, J., & Rovine, M. (1987). Temperament and attachment security in the Strange Situation: An empirical rapprochement. *Child Development, 58,* 787–795.

Belsky, J., Rovine, M., & Taylor, D. (1984). The Pennsylvania Infant and Family Development Project, III: The origins of individual differences in infant–mother attachment—Maternal and infant contributions. *Child Development, 55,* 718–728.

Belsky, J., Taylor, D. G., & Rovine, M. (1984). The Pennsylvania Infant and Family Development Project, II: The development of reciprocal interaction in the mother–infant dyad. *Child Development, 55,* 706–717.

Benoit, D., & Vidovic, D. (1991, April). Transmission of attachment across three generations. In C. H. Zeanah (Chair), *Parental representations of attachment: Links across generations.* Symposium conducted at the biennial meeting of the Society for Research in Child Development, Seattle.

Bowlby, J. (1969). *Attachment and loss: Vol. 1. Attachment.* New York: Basic Books.

Bowlby, J. (1973). *Attachment and loss: Vol. 2. Separation: Anxiety and anger.* New York: Basic Books.

Bradley, R. H., & Caldwell, B. M. (1980). The relation of home environment, cognitive competence, and IQ among males and females. *Child Development, 51,* 1140–1148.

Bretherton, I. (1984). Social referencing and the interfacing of minds: A commentary on the views of Feinman and Campos. *Merrill–Palmer Quarterly, 30,* 419–427.

Bretherton, I. (1991). Pouring new wines into old wineskins: The social self as internal working model. In M. R. Gunnar & L. A. Sroufe (Eds.), *Minnesota Symposium on Child Development: Vol. 23. Self process and development* (pp. 1–41). Hillsdale, NJ: Erlbaum.

Bretherton, I. (1985). Attachment theory: Retrospect and prospect. In I. Bretherton & E. Waters (Eds.), *Growing points of attachment theory and research. Monographs of the Society for Research in Child Development, 50*(1–2, Serial No. 209), 3–35.

Bretherton, I., McNew, S., & Beeghly-Smith, M. (1981). Early person knowledge as expressed in gestural and verbal communication: When do infants acquire a "theory of mind"? In M. E. Lamb & L. R. Sherrod (Eds.), *Infant social cognition: Empirical and theoretical considerations* (pp. 333–373). Hillsdale, NJ: Lawrence Erlbaum.

Bronfenbrenner, U. (1979). *The ecology of human development.* Cambridge, MA: Harvard University Press.

Buchsbaum, H. K., & Emde, R. N. (1990). Play narratives in 36-month-old children. *Psychoanalytic Study of the Child, 45,* 129–155.

Buss, A. H., & Plomin, R. (1984). *Temperament: Early developing personality traits.* Hillsdale, NJ: Erlbaum.

Campos, J. (1984). A new perspective on emotions. *Child Abuse and Neglect, 8*(2), 147–156.

Carlson, V., Cicchetti, D., Barnett, D., & Braunwald, K. (1989). Disorganized/disoriented attachment relationships in maltreated infants. *Developmental Psychology, 25*(4), 525–531.

Case, R. (1985). *Intellectual development.* Orlando, FL: Academic Press.

Cassidy, J. (1993, March). *Emotion regulation within attachment relationships.* Paper presented at the biennial meeting of the Society for Research in Child Development, New Orleans, LA.

Cassidy, J., Berlin, L. J., & Belsky, J. (1990, April). *Attachment organization at age three: Antecedent and concurrent correlates.* Paper presented at the Seventh International Conference on Infant Studies, Montreal.

Cassidy, J., & Kobak, R. (1988). Avoidance and its relation to other defensive processes. In J. Belsky & T. Nezworski (Eds.), *Clinical implications of attachment* (pp. 300–323). Hillsdale, NJ: Erlbaum.

Chapman, M., & Zahn-Waxler, C. (1982). Young children's compliance and noncompliance to parental discipline in a natural setting. *International Journal of Behavior and Development, 5,* 81–94.

Chess, S., & Thomas, A. (1989). Issues in the clinical application of temperament. In G. A. Kohnstamm, J. E. Bates, & M. K. Rothbart (Eds.), *Temperament in childhood* (pp. 377–386). New York: Wiley.

Clarke-Stewart, K. A. (1973). Interactions between mothers and their young children: Characteristics and consequences. *Monographs of the Society for Research in Child Development, 38*(5–6, Serial No. 153).

Cohen, S. E., & Beckwith, L. (1979). Preterm infant interaction with the caregiver in the first year of life and competence at age two. *Child Development, 50,* 767–776.

Cohn, J. F., Campbell, S. B., & Ross, S. (1991). Infant response in the still-face paradigm at 6 months predicts avoidant and secure attachment at 12 months. *Development and Psychopathology, 3,* 367–376.

Cohn, J. F., & Tronick, E. (1983). Three-month-old infants' reaction to simulated maternal depression. *Child Development, 54,* 185–193.

Cohn, J. F., & Tronick, E. (1988). Mother–infant face-to-face interaction: influence is bidirectional and unrelated to periodic cycles in either partner's behavior. *Developmental Psychology, 24*(3), 386–392.

Cohn, J. F., Tronick, E., Matias, R., Connell, D., & Lyons-Ruth, K. (1986). Face-to-face interactions of depressed mothers with their infants. In E. Tronick & T. Field (Eds.), *Maternal depression and infant disturbance* (pp. 31–44). San Francisco: Jossey-Bass.

Cole, P. M., Barrett, K. C., & Zahn-Waxler, C. (1992). Emotion displays in two-year-olds during mishaps. *Child Development, 63,* 314–324.

Connell, D. B. (1976). *Individual differences in attachment: An investigation into stability, implications, and relationships to structure of early language development.* Unpublished doctoral dissertation, Syracuse University.

Cowan, C. P., & Cowan, P. A. (1987). Men's involvement in parenthood: Identifying the antecedents and understanding the barriers. In P. Berman & F. A. Pedersen (Eds.), *Men's transition to parenthood* (pp. 145–174). Hillsdale, NJ: Erlbaum.

Cowan, C. P., Cowan, P. A., Heming, G., & Miller, N. B. (1991). Becoming a family: Marriage, parenting, and child development. In P. A. Cowan & E. M. Hetherington (Eds.), *Family transitions* (pp. 79–109). Hillsdale, NJ: Erlbaum.

Cox, M. J., Owen, M. T., Lewis, J. M., Riedel, C., Scalf-McIver, L., & Suster, A. (1985). Intergenerational influences on the parent–infant relationship in the transition to parenthood. *Journal of Family Issues, 6*(4), 543–564.

Crittenden, P. M., & DiLalla, D. L. (1988). Compulsive compliance: The development of an inhibitory coping strategy in infancy. *Journal of Abnormal Child Psychology, 16,* 585–599.

Crockenberg, S. (1991, April). Conceptual issues in the study of child compliance, noncompliance and parental control. In G. Kochanska & L. Kuczynski (Chairs), *New perspectives in child compliance, noncompliance, and parental control.* Symposium conducted at the biennial meeting of the Society for Research in Child Development, Seattle, WA.

Crockenberg, S., & Litman, C. (1990). Autonomy as competence in two-year-olds: Maternal correlates of child compliance, defiance, and self-assertion. *Developmental Psychology, 26,* 961–971.

Crowell, J. A., & Feldman, S. S. (1988). Mothers' internal models of relationships and children's behavioral and developmental status: A study of mother–child interaction. *Child Development, 59,* 1273–1285.

Crowell, J. A., Feldman, S. S., & Ginsburg, N. (1988). Assessment of mother–child interaction in preschoolers with behavior problems. *Journal of the American Academy of Child and Adolescent Psychiatry, 27,* 303–311.

Cummings, E. M., Iannotti, R. J., & Zahn-Waxler, C. (1985). Influence of conflict between adults on the emotions and aggression of young children. *Developmental Psychology, 21*(93), 495–507.

Cummings, E. M., Zahn-Waxler, C., & Radke-Yarrow, M. (1981). Young children's responses to expressions of anger and affection by others in the family. *Child Development, 52,* 1274–1282.

DeGangi, G. A., DiPietro, J. A., Greenspan, S. I., & Porges, S. W. (1991). Psychophysiological characteristics of the regulatory disordered infant. *Infant Behavior and Development, 14,* 37–50.

Dickstein, S., & Parke, R. D. (1988). Social referencing in infancy: A glance at fathers and marriage. *Child Development, 59,* 506–511.

Dickstein, S., Thompson, R. A., Estes, D., Malkin, C., & Lamb, M. E. (1984). Social referencing and the security of attachment. *Infant Behavior and Development, 7,* 507–516.

Dunn, J., & Munn, P. (1987). Development of justification in disputes with mother and sibling. *Developmental Psychology, 23,* 791–798.

Egeland, B., & Farber, E. A. (1984). Infant–mother attachment: Factors related to its development and changes over time. *Child Development, 55,* 753–771.

Egeland, B., Jacobvitz, D., & Sroufe, L. A. (1988). Breaking the cycle of abuse. *Child Development, 59,* 1080–1088.

Elder, G., Caspi, A., & Downey, G. (1986). Problem behavior and family relationships: Life course and intergenerational themes. In A. Sorensen, F. Weinert, & L. Sherrod (Eds.), *Human development: Interdisciplinary perspectives* (pp. 293–340). Hillsdale, NJ: Erlbaum.

Emde, R. N. (1983). The prerepresentational self and its affective core. *Psychoanalytic Study of the Child, 38,* 165–192.

Emde, R. N. (1991). The wonder of our complex enterprise: Steps enabled by attachment and the effects of relationships on relationships. *Infant Mental Health Journal, 12,* 164–173.

Emde, R. N., & Buchsbaum, H. K. (1990). "Didn't you hear my mommy?": Autonomy with connectedness in moral self-emergence. In D. Cicchetti & M. Beeghly (Eds.), *The self in transition* (pp. 35–60). Chicago: University of Chicago Press.

Emde, R., Johnson, W. F., & Easterbrooks, A. (1988). The do's and don'ts of early moral development: Psychoanalytic tradition and current research. In J. Kagan & S. Lamb, (Eds.), *The emergence of morality* (pp. 245–277). Chicago: University of Chicago Press.

Feinman, S., & Lewis, M. (1983). Social referencing at ten months: A second-order effect on infants' responses to strangers. *Child Development, 54,* 878–887.

Field, T. (1984). Early interactions between infants and their post-partum depressed mothers. *Infant Behavior and Development, 7,* 517–523.

Field, T., Healy, B., Goldstein, S., Perry, S., Bendell, D., Schanberg, S., Zimmerman, E. A., & Kuhn, C. (1988). Infants of depressed mothers show "depressed" behavior even with nondepressed adults. *Child Development, 59,* 1569–1579.

Fish, M., Stifter, C. A., & Belsky, J. (1991). Conditions of continuity and discontinuity in infant negative emotionality: Newborn to five months. *Child Development, 62,* 1525–1537.

Fonagy, P., Steele, H., & Steele, M. (1991). Maternal representations of attachment during pregnancy predict the organization of infant–mother attachment at one year of age. *Child Development, 62,* 891–905.

Fox, N. A., & Stifter, C. A. (1989). Biological and behavioral differences in infant reactivity and regulation. In G. A. Kohnstamm, J. E. Bates, & M. K. Rothbart (Eds.), *Temperament in childhood* (pp. 169–183). New York: Wiley.

Fraiberg, S., Adelson, E., & Shapiro, V. (1975). Ghosts in the nursery. *Journal of the American Academy of Child Psychiatry, 14,* 387–421.

Frodi, A., Bridges, L., & Grolnick, W. (1985). Correlates of mastery-related behavior. *Child Development, 56,* 1291–1298.

Garbarino, J., & Sherman, D. (1980). High-risk neighborhoods and high-risk families: The human ecology of child maltreatment. *Child Development, 51,* 188–198.

Gianino, A., & Tronick, E. Z. (1988). The mutual regulation model: The infant's self and interactive regulation, coping, and defense. In T. Field, P. McCabe, & N. Schneiderman (Eds.), *Stress and coping* (pp. 47–68). Hillsdale, NJ: Erlbaum.

Goldberg, S., & DiVitto, B. (1983). *Born too soon: Preterm birth and early development.* San Francisco: W. H. Freeman.

Goldberg, S., Perrotta, M., Minde, K., & Corter, C. (1986). Maternal behavior and attachment in low birthweight twins and singletons. *Child Development, 57,* 34–46.

Goldsmith, H. H., Buss, A. H., Plomin, R., Rothbart, M. K., Thomas, A., Chess, A., Hinde, R., & McCall, R. B. (1987). Roundtable: What is temperament? Four approaches. *Child Development, 58,* 505–529.

Goldsmith, H. H., & Campos, J. J. (1986). Fundamental issues in the study of early temperament: The Denver Twin Temperament Study. In M. E. Lamb, A. L. Brown, & B. Rogoff (Eds.), *Advances in developmental psychology* (Vol. 4, pp. 231–283). Hillsdale, NJ: Erlbaum.

Goldsmith, H. H., Riesser-Danner, L. A., & Briggs, S. (1991). Evaluating convergent and discriminant validity of temperament questionnaires for preschoolers, toddlers and infants. *Developmental Psychology, 27,* 566–579.

Greenberg, M. T., & Slough, N. (1991, April). Attachment security and its correlates in preschool children: Validation of reunion assessment. In R.S. Marvin & J. Cassidy (Chairs), *Attachment during the preschool years: Examination of a new measure.* Symposium conducted at the biennial meeting of the Society for Research in Child Development, Seattle.

Grossmann, K., Fremmer-Bombik, E., Rudolph, J., & Grossmann, K. E. (1988). Maternal attachment representations as related to patterns of infant–mother attachment and maternal care during the first year. In R. A. Hinde & J. Stevenson-Hinde (Eds.), *Relationships within families: Mutual influences* (pp. 241–260). New York: Oxford University Press.

Hall, F., Pawlby, S., & Wolkind, S. (1979). Early life experiences and later mothering behavior: A study of mothers and their 20-week-old babies. In D. Shaffer & J. Dunn (Eds.), *The first year of life: Psychological and medical implications of early experiences* (pp. 153–174). New York: Wiley.

Harter, S. (1978). Effectance motivation reconsidered. *Human Development, 21,* 34–64.

Heinecke, C. M., Diskin, S. D., Ramsey-Klee, D. M., & Given, K. (1983). Pre-birth parent characteristics and family development in the first year of life. *Child Development, 54,* 194–208.

Heinecke, C. M., Diskin, S. D., Ramsey-Klee, D. M., & Oates, D. S. (1986). Pre- and postbirth antecedents of 2-year-old attention, capacity for relationships, and verbal expressiveness. *Developmental Psychology, 22*(6), 777–787.

Herrenkohl, E. C., Herrenkohl, R. C., & Toedter, L. J. (1983). Perspectives on the intergenerational transmission of abuse. In D. Finkelhor (Ed.) *The dark side of families: Current family violence research* (pp. 305–316). Beverly Hills, CA: Sage.

Hinde, R. A. (1989a). Ethological and relationships approaches. In R. Vasta (Ed.), *Annals of child development* (Vol. 6, pp. 251–285). Greenwich. CT: JAI Press.

Hinde, R. A. (1989b). Temperament as an intervening variable. In G. A. Kohnstamm, J. E. Bates, & M. K. Rothbart (Eds.), *Temperament in childhood* (pp. 27–33). New York: Wiley.

Hirshberg, L. M., & Svejda, M. (1990). When infants look to their parents: I. Infants' social referencing of mothers compared to fathers. *Child Development, 61,* 1175–1186.

Hofer, M. A. (1987). Early social relationships: A psychobiologist's view. *Child Development, 58,* 633–647.

Hornik, R., & Gunnar, M. R. (1988). A descriptive analysis of infant social referencing. *Child Development, 59,* 626–634.

Hornik, R., Risenhoover, N., & Gunnar, M. (1987). The effects of maternal positive, neutral, and negative affective communications on infant responses to new toys. *Child Development, 58,* 937–944.

Hron-Stewart, K. M., Lefever, G. B., & Weintraub, D. (1990, April). *Correlates and predictors of mastery motivation: Relations to mother–child problem-solving, temperament, attachment, and home environment.* Paper presented at the Seventh International Conference on Infant Studies, Montreal.

Hubert, N. (1989). Parental subjective reactions to perceived temperament behavior in their 6- and 24-month-old children. *Infant Behavior and Development, 12,* 185–198.

Hunt, J. McV. (1965). Intrinsic motivation and its role in psychological development. In D. Levine (Ed.), *Nebraska symposium on motivation* (Vol. 13; pp. 189–282. Lincoln, NE: University of Nebraska Press.

Isabella, R. A., & Belsky, J. (1991). Interactional synchrony and the origins of mother–infant attachment: A replication study. *Child Development, 62,* 373–384.

Isabella, R. A., Belsky, J., & von Eye, A. (1989). The origins of infant–mother attachment: An examination of interactional synchrony during the infant's first year. *Developmental Psychology, 25,* 12–21.

Izard, C. E., Huebner, R., Risser, D., McGinness, G., & Dougherty, L. (1980). The young infant's ability to produce discrete emotion expressions. *Developmental Psychology, 16,* 132–140.

Jacobson, S. W., & Frye, K. F. (1991). Effect of maternal social support on attachment: Experimental evidence. *Child Development, 62,* 572–582.

Jennings, K. D., Yarrow, L. J., & Martin, P. P. (1984). Mastery motivation and cognitive development: A longitudinal study from infancy to 3.5 years of age. *International Journal of Behavioral Development, 7,* 441–461.

Kagan, J. (1981). *The second year: The emergence of self-awareness.* Cambridge, MA: Harvard University Press.

Kagan, J., Reznick, S., & Snidman, N. (1987). The physiology and psychology of behavioral inhibition in children. *Child Development, 58,* 1459–1473.

Kagan, J., Reznick, S., & Snidman, N. (1988). Biological bases of childhood shyness. *Science, 240,* 167–171.

Kagan, J., Reznick, S., & Snidman, N. (1989). Issues in the study of temperament. In G. A. Kohnstamm, J. E. Bates, & M. K. Rothbart (Eds.), *Temperament in childhood* (pp. 133–144). New York: Wiley.

Kiser, L. J., Bates, J. E., Maslin, C. A., & Bayles, K. (1983). Mother–infant play at 6 months as a predictor of attachment security at thirteen months. *Journal of the American Academy of Child Psychiatry, 25,* 68–75.

Klinnert, M. D. (1984). The regulation of infant behavior by maternal facial expression. *Infant Behavior and Development, 7,* 447–465.

Klinnert, M. D., Campos, J. J., Sorce, J. F., Emde, R. N., & Svejda, M. (1983). Emotions as behavior regulators: Social referencing in infancy. In R. Plutchik & H. Kellerman (Eds.), *Emotion: Theory, research, and experience: Vol. 2. Emotions in early development* (pp. 57–86). New York: Academic Press.

Klinnert, M. D., Emde, R. N., Butterfield, P., & Campos, J. J. (1986). Social referencing: The infant's use of emotional signals from a friendly adult with mother present. *Developmental Psychology, 22*(4), 427–432.

Kochanska, G. (1991, April). Child compliance and noncompliance and the origins of conscience. In G. Kochanska & L. Kuczynski (Chairs), *New perspectives in child compliance, noncompliance, and parental control.* Symposium conducted at the biennial meeting of the Society for Research in Child Development, Seattle.

Kuczynski, L., & Kochanska, G. (1990). Development of children's noncompliance strategies from toddlerhood to age 5. *Developmental Psychology, 26*(3), 398–408.

Kuczynski, L., Kochanska, G., Radke-Yarrow, M., & Girnius-Brown, O. (1987). A developmental interpretation of young children's non-compliance. *Developmental Psychology, 23,* 799–806.

LaBarbera, J. D., Izard, C. E., Vietze, P., & Parisi, S. (1976). Four- and six-month-old infants' visual responses to joy, anger, and neutral expressions. *Child Development, 47,* 535–538.

Lewis, J. M., Owen, M. T., & Cox, M. J. (1988). The transition to parenthood: III. Incorporation of the child into the family. *Family Process, 27,* 411–421.

Lewis, M. (1992). *Shame: The exposed self.* New York: Free Press.

Lewis, M., Alessandri, S. M., & Sullivan, M. W. (1990). Violation of expectancy, loss of control, and anger expressions in young infants. *Developmental Psychology, 26*(5), 745–751.

Lewis, M., & Brooks-Gunn, J. (1979). *Social cognition and the acquisition of self.* New York: Plenum Press.

Lewis, M., Sullivan, M. W., Stanger, C., & Weiss, M. (1989). Self development and self-conscious emotions. *Child Development, 60,* 146–156.

Lieberman, A. F., Weston, D. R., & Pawl, J. H. (1991). Preventive intervention and outcome with anxiously attached dyads. *Child Development, 62,* 199–209.

Londerville, S., & Main, M. (1981). Security of attachment, compliance, and maternal training methods in the second year of life. *Developmental Psychology, 17*(3), 289–299.

Lyons-Ruth, K. (1991). Rapprochement or approchement: Mahler's theory reconsidered from the vantage point of recent research on early attachment relationships. *Psychoanalytic Psychology, 8*(1), 1–23.

Lyons-Ruth, K., Alpern, L., & Repacholi, B. (1993). Disorganized attachment classification and maternal psychosocial problems as predictors of hostile-aggressive behavior in the preschool classroom. *Child Development, 64,* 572–585.

Lyons-Ruth, K., Connell, D. B., Grunebaum, H., & Botein, S. (1990). Infants at social risk: Maternal depression and family support services as mediators of infant development and security of attachment. *Child Development, 61,* 85–98.

Lyons-Ruth, K., Connell, D. B., Zoll, D., & Stahl, J. (1987). Infants at social risk: Relations among infant maltreatment, maternal behavior, and infant attachment behavior. *Developmental Psychology, 23*(2), 223–232.

Lyons-Ruth, K., Repacholi, B., McLeod, S., & Silva, E. (1991). Disorganized attachment behavior in infancy: Short-term stability, maternal and infant correlates and risk-related subtypes. *Development and Psychopathology, 3,* 377–396.

Lyons-Ruth, K., Zoll, D., Connell, D., & Grunebaum, H. U. (1989). Family deviance and family disruption in childhood: Associations with maternal behavior and infant maltreatment during the first two years of life. *Development and Psychopathology, 1,* 219–236.

Main, M., & Hesse, E. (1990). Parents' unresolved traumatic experiences are related to infant disorganized attachment status: Is frightened and/or frightening parental behavior the linking mechanism? In M. Greenberg, D. Cicchetti, & E. M. Cummings (Eds.), *Attachment in the preschool years: Theory, research and intervention* (pp. 161–184). Chicago: University of Chicago Press.

Main, M., Kaplan, N., & Cassidy, J. (1985). Security in infancy, childhood and adulthood: A move to the level of representation. In I. Bretherton & E. Waters (Eds.), Growing points of attachment theory and research. *Monographs of the Society for Research in Child Development, 50*(1–2, Serial No. 209), 66–104.

Main, M., & Solomon, J. (1990). Procedures for identifying infants as disorganized/disoriented during the Ainsworth Strange Situation. In M. Greenberg, D. Cicchetti, & E.M. Cummings (Eds.), *Attachment in the preschool years: Theory, research and intervention* (pp. 121–160). Chicago: University of Chicago Press.

Main, M., & Weston, D. (1982). Avoidance of the attachment figure in infancy: Descriptions and interpretations. In C. M. Parkes & J. Stevenson-Hinde (Eds.), *The place of attachment in human behavior* (pp. 31–59). New York: Basic Books.

Malatesta, C. Z., Culver, C., Tesman, J. R., & Shepard, B. (1989). The development of emotion expression during the first two years of life. *Monographs of the Society for Research in Child Development, 54* (1–2, Serial No. 219).

Malone, C. A. (1967). Guideposts derived from normal development. In E. Pavenstedt (Ed.), *The drifters: Children of disorganized lower-class families* (pp. 85–103). Boston: Little, Brown.

Matas, L., Arend, R. A., & Sroufe, L. A. (1978). Continuity of adaptation in the second year: The relationship between quality of attachment and later competence. *Child Development, 49,* 547–556.

McLoyd, V. C. (1990). The impact of economic hardship on black families and children: Psychological distress, parenting, and socioemotional development. *Child Development, 61,* 311–346.

Messer, D. J., McCarthy, M. E., McQuiston, S., MacTurk, R. H., Yarrow, L. J., & Vietze, P. M. (1986). Relation between mastery behavior in infancy and competence in early childhood. *Developmental Psychology, 22,* 366–372.

Miyake, K., Chen, S., & Campos, J. J. (1985). Infant temperament, mother's mode of interaction, and attachment in Japan: An interim report. In I. Bretherton & E. Waters (Eds.), Growing points of attachment theory and research. *Monographs of the Society for Research in Child Development, 50*(1–2, Serial No. 209), 276–297.

Morgan, G. A., Harmon, R. J., & Maslin-Cole, C. A. (1990). Mastery motivation: definition and measurement. *Early Education and Development, 1,* 318–319.

Morgan, G. A., Harmon, R. J., & Maslin-Cole, C. A. (1991). Play assessment of mastery motivation in infants and young children. In C. E. Schaefer, K. Gitlin, & A. Sandgrund (Eds.), *Play diagnosis and assessment* (pp. 65–86). New York: Wiley.

Morisset, C. E., Barnard, K. E., Greenberg, M. T., Booth, C. L., & Spieker, S. J. (1990). Environmental influences on early language development: The context of social risk. *Development and Psychopathology, 2,* 127–149.

Murphy, C. M., & Messer, D. J. (1977). Mothers, infants and pointing: A study of a gesture. In H. R. Schaffer (Ed.), *Studies in mother–infant interaction* (pp. 325–354). London: Academic Press.

Nelson, C. A., Morse, P. A., & Leavitt, L. A. (1979). Recognition of facial expressions by seven-month-old infants. *Child Development, 50,* 1239–1242.

O'Connor, M., Sigman, M., & Brill, N. (1987). Disorganization of attachment in relation to maternal alcohol consumption. *Journal of Consulting and Clinical Psychology, 55,* 831–836.

Oppenheim, D., Sagi, A., & Lamb, M. (1988). Infant–adult attachments on the kibbutz and their relation to socioemotional development four years later. *Developmental Psychology, 24,* 427–433.

Oster, H. (1981). "Recognition" of emotional expression in infancy? In M. E. Lamb & L. R. Sherrod (Eds.), *Infant social cognition* (pp. 85–125). Hillsdale, NJ: Erlbaum.

Oster, H., & Ekman, P. (1977). Facial behavior in child development. In A. Collins (Ed.), *Minnesota Symnposium on Child Psychology* (Vol. 11, pp. 231–276). New York: Thomas A. Crowell.

Parke, R. D., & Collmer, C. W. (1975). Child abuse: An interdisciplinary analysis. In E. M. Hetherington (Ed.), *Review of child development research* (Vol. 5, pp. 509–590). Chicago: University of Chicago Press.

Patterson, G. R. (1982). *Coercive family process.* Eugene, OR: Castalia.

Pettit, G. S., & Bates, J. E. (1984). Continuity of individual differences in the mother–infant relationship from six to thirteen months. *Child Development, 555,* 729–739.

Pipp, S., & Harmon, R. J. (1987). Attachment as regulation: A commentary. *Child Development, 58,* 648–652.

Plomin, R. (1987). Developmental behavioral genetics and infancy. In J. Osofsky (Ed.), *Handbook of infant development* (pp. 363–414). New York: Wiley.

Porges, S. W., & Roosevelt, J. D. (in press). Physiological basis of temperament. In J. Noshpitz (Ed.), *Basic handbook of child psychiatry.* New York: Basic Books.

Quinton, D., Rutter, M., & Liddle, C. (1984). Institutional rearing, parenting difficulties, and marital support. *Psychological Medicine, 14,* 107–24.

Radke-Yarrow, M., & Zahn-Waxler, C. (1984). Roots, motives and patterning in children's prosocial behavior. In E. Staub, D. Bar-Tal, J. Karylowski, & J. Reykowski (Eds.), *The development and maintenance of prosocial behavior: International perspectives on positive morality* (pp. 81–99). New York: Plenum Press.

Redding, R. E., Harmon, R. J., & Morgan, G. A. (1990). Maternal depression and infants' mastery behaviors. *Infant Behavior and Development, 13,* 391–395.

Reiss, D. (1989). The represented and the practicing family. In A. J. Sameroff & R. Emde (Eds.), *Relationship disturbances in early childhood* (pp. 191–220). New York: Basic Books.

Reite, M., Short, R., Seiber, C., & Pauley, J. D. (1981). Attachment, loss, and depression. *Journal of Child Psychology and Psychiatry, 22,* 141–169.

Ricks, M. (1985). The social transmission of parental behavior: Attachment across generations. In I. Bretherton & E. Waters (Eds.), Growing points of attachment theory and research. *Monographs of the Society for Research in Child Development, 50*(1–2, Serial No. 209), 211–227.

Rosenbaum, J. F., Biederman, J., Gersten, M., Hirschfield, D. R., Meminger, S. R., Herman, J. B., Kagan, J., Reznick, S., & Snidman, N. (1988). Behavioral inhibition in children of parents with panic disorder and agorophobia. *Archives of General Psychiatry, 45,* 463–470.

Rothbart, M. (1981). Measurement of temperament in infancy. *Child Development, 52,* 569–587.

Rothbart, M. K. (1989). Temperament in childhood: A framework. In G. A. Kohnstamm, J. E. Bates, & M. K. Rothbart (Eds.), *Temperament in childhood* (pp. 59–73). New York: Wiley.

Rothbart, M., & Derryberry, D. (1981). Development of individual differences in temperament. In M. E.

Lamb & A. L. Brown (Eds.), *Advances in developmental psychology*, Vol. 1. Hillsdale, NJ: Erlbaum.

Rutter, M. (1989). Temperament: Conceptual issues and clinical implications. In G. A. Kohnstamm, J. E. Bates, & M. K. Rothbart (Eds.), *Temperament in childhood* (pp. 463–479). New York: Wiley.

Sameroff, A. J., & Chandler, M. J. (1975). Reproductive risk and the continuum of caretaking casualty. In F. D. Horowitz, E. M. Hetherington, S. Scarr-Salapatek, & G. M. Siegel (Eds.), *Review of child development research* (Vol. 4, pp. 187–244). Chicago: University of Chicago Press.

Sameroff, A. J., & Emde, R. N. (Eds.). (1989). *Relationship disturbances in early childhood*. New York: Basic Books.

Sameroff, A. J., Seifer, R., & Elias, P. K. (1982). Sociocultural variability in infant temperament ratings. *Child Development*, *53*, 164–173.

Sander, L., Julia, H., Stechler, G., & Burns, P. (1972). Continuous 24-hour interactional monitoring of infants reared in two caretaking environments. *Psychosomatic Medicine*, *34*, 270–282.

Scaife, M., & Bruner, J. S. (1975). The capacity for joint visual attention in the infant. *Nature*, *254*, 265–266.

Seifer, R., & Sameroff, A. (1986). The concept, measurement and interpretation of temperament in young children: A survey of research issues. *Advances in Developmental and Behavioral Pediatrics*, *7*, 1–43.

Seifer, R., Sameroff, A., Barrett, L. C., & Krafchuk, E. (1992). *Infant temperament measured by multiple observations and mother report*. Paper presented at the Ninth International Conference on Infant Studies, Miami.

Sorce, J. F., Emde, R. N., Campos, J. J., & Klinnert, M. D. (1985). Maternal emotional signaling: Its effect on the visual cliff behavior of one-year olds. *Developmental Psychology*, *20*, 195–200.

Spitz, R. A. (1957). *No and yes: On the genesis of human communication*. New York: International Universities Press.

Sroufe, L. A., Fox, N., & Pancake, V. (1983). Attachment and dependency in developmental perspective. *Child Development*, *54*, 1615–1627.

Sroufe, L. A., & Waters E. (1977). Attachment as an organizational construct. *Child Development*, *48*, 1184–1199.

Stayton, D. J., Hogan, R., & Ainsworth, M. D. S. (1971). Infant obedience and maternal behavior: The origins of socialization reconsidered. *Child Development*, *42*, 1057–1069.

Stenberg, C. R., Campos, J. J., & Emde, R. N. (1983). The facial expression of anger in seven-month-old infants. *Child Development*, *54*, 178–184.

Stern, D. (1985). *The interpersonal world of the infant*. New York: Basic Books.

Thomas, A., & Chess, S. (1977). *Temperament and development*. New York: Brunner/Mazel.

Thomas, A., Chess, S., & Birch, H. G. (1968). *Temperament and behavior disorders in children*. New York: New York University Press.

Thomas, A., Chess, S., Birch, H. G., Hertzig, M. E., & Korn, S. (1963). *Behavioral individuality in early childhood*. New York: New York University Press.

Trevarthen, C. (1980). The foundations of intersubjectivity: Development of interpersonal and cooperative understanding in infants. In D. R. Olson (Ed.), *The social foundations of language and thought* (pp. 1–34). New York: Norton.

Trevarthen, C. (1989). Le emozioni intuitive: L'evoluzione del loro ruollo nella communicazione tra madre e bambino [Intuitive emotions: Their changing role in communication between mother and infant]. In M. Ammaniti & N. Dazzi (Eds.), *Affetti: Natura e sviluppo dele relazione interpersonali* (pp. 97–139). Rome: La Terza.

Trevarthen, C., & Hubley, P. (1978). Secondary intersubjectivity: Confidence, confiding, and acts of meaning in the first year. In A. Locke (Ed.), *Action, gesture and symbol: The emergence of language* (pp. 183–229). London: Academic Press.

Trickett, P. K., & Kuczynski, L. (1986). Children's misbehaviors and parental discipline strategies in abusive and nonabusive families. *Developmental Psychology*, *22*, 115–123.

Tronick, E., & Cohn, J. F. (1989). Infant–mother face-to-face interaction: Age and gender differences in coordination and the occurrence of miscoordination. *Child Development*, *60*, 85–92.

Tronick, E., Ricks, M., & Cohn, J. F. (1982). Maternal and infant affective exchange: Patterns of adaptation. In T. Field & A. Fogel (Eds.), *Emotion and early interaction* (pp. 83–100). Hillsdale, NJ: Erlbaum.

Vaughn, B. E., Bradley, C. F., Joffe, L. S., Seifer, R., & Barglow, P. (1987). Maternal characteristics measured prenatally predict ratings of temperamental difficulty on the Carey Infant Temperament Questionnaire. *Developmental Psychology*, *23*, 152–161.

Vaughn, B. E., Lefever, G. B., Seifer, R., & Barglow, P. (1989). Attachment behavior, attachment security, and temperament during infancy. *Child Development*, *60*, 728–737.

Walden, T. A., & Ogan, T.A. (1988). The development of social referencing. *Child Development*, *59*, 1230–1240.

Ward, M. J., Botyanski, N. C., Plunket, S. W., & Carlson, E. A. (1991, April). The concurrent validity of the Adult Attachment Interview for adolescent mothers. In H. Steele (Chair), *Parental representations of attachment: Links across generations*. Symposium conducted at the biennial meeting of the Society for Research in Child Development, Seattle.

Waters, E. (1978). The reliability and stability of individual differences in infant–mother attachment. *Child Development*, *49*, 483–494.

Waters, E., Wippman, J., & Sroufe, L. A. (1979). Attachment, positive affect, and competence in the peer group: Two studies in construct validation. *Child Development*, *50*, 821–829.

White, R. W. (1959). Motivation reconsidered: The concept of competence. *Psychological Review*, *66*, 297–333.

Winnicott, D. W. (1965). The theory of the parent–infant relationship. In D. W. Winnicott, *The maturational processes and the facilitating environment* (pp. 37–55). New York: International Universities Press. (Original work published 1960)

Wolk, S., Zeanah, C. H., Garcia Coll, C., & Carr, S. (1992). Factors influencing parents' perceptions of temperament in early infancy. *American Journal of Orthopsychiatry*, *62*, 71–82.

Yarrow, L. J., MacTurk, R. H., Vietze, P. M., McCarthy, M. E., Klein, R. P., & McQuiston, S. (1984). Developmental course of mastery motivation during the first year of life. *Developmental Psychology*, *20*, 492–503.

Yarrow, L. J., McQuiston, S., MacTurk, R. H., McCarthy, M. E., Klein, R. P., & Vietze, P. M. (1983). Assessment of mastery motivation during the first year of life. *Developmental Psychology, 29,* 159–171.

Yarrow, L. J., Morgan, G. A., Jennings, K. D., Harmon, R. J., & Gaiter, J. L. (1982). Infants' persistence at tasks. *Infant Behavior and Development, 19,* 131–141.

Zahn-Waxler, C., Cummings, E. M., & Cooperman, G. (1984). Emotional development in childhood. *Annals of Child Development, 1,* 45–106.

Zahn-Waxler, C., Cummings, E. M., Iannotti, R. M., & Radke-Yarrow, M. (1984). Young offspring of depressed parents: A population at-risk for affective problems. In D. Cicchetti & K. Schneider-Rosen (Eds.), *New directions for child development: No. 26. Childhood depression* (pp. 81–105). San Francisco: Jossey-Bass.

Zahn-Waxler, C., & Kochanska, G. (1988). The origins of guilt. In R. Thompson (Ed.), *Nebraska Symposium on Motivation: Vol. 36. Socioemotional development* (pp. 183–258). Lincoln: University of Nebraska Press.

Zahn-Waxler, C., & Radke-Yarrow, M. (1990). The origins of concern. *Motivation and Emotion, 14,* 107–130.

Zahn-Waxler, C., Radke-Yarrow, M., & King, R. A. (1979). Child rearing and children's prosocial initiations towards victims of distress. *Child Development, 50,* 319–330.

Zarbatany, L., & Lamb, M. (1985). Social referencing as a function of information source: Mother versus strangers. *Infant Behavior and Development, 8,* 25–33.

Zeanah, C. H., Benoit, D., Barton, M., Hirshberg, L., Regan, C., & Lipsitt, L. (1993). Representations of attachment in mothers and their one year old infants. *Journal of the American Academy of Child and Adolescent Psychiatry, 32,* 278–286.

Zeanah, C. H., Keener, M. A., & Anders, T. F. (1986). Developing perceptions of temperament and their relation to mother and infant behavior. *Journal of Child Psychology and Psychiatry, 27,* 499–512.

3

The Family Context
of Infant Mental Health: II.
Infant Development in Multiple
Family Relationships

SUSAN CROCKENBERG
KARLEN LYONS-RUTH
SUSAN DICKSTEIN

INFANT–CAREGIVER RELATIONSHIPS IN THE CONTEXT OF THE FAMILY

Recent societal changes in the roles of women and in the structure of the family have invited a consideration of other family members as sources of influence on infant development. One manifestation of the look beyond mothers is the now common tendency to use the terms "parent" and "caregiver" in discussing the processes of infant development, to avoid implying that these relational functions are specific to women or even to biological relatives (see Oppenheim, Sagi, & Lamb, 1988). Another manifestation is a consideration of influences beyond the primary caregiver. Although investigators have been aware of the potential importance of this new emphasis, until relatively recently studies in which researchers have attempted to identify the family sources of differences in infant development have recruited subjects from a pool of "nuclear" families of European descent—in each of which there are two parents, a male who works outside the home and a female who does not. These are the families that have been viewed as, and indeed may have been, "normative" in U.S. culture during the early years of family-based infant research. In these families, mothers may well have had a disproportionate influence on infant development because of their almost continuous availability, and the relative lack of availability of fathers, grandparents, and others who might otherwise exert a powerful influence on the course of infant development.

Missing from studies of family influences on infant development until the middle to late 1970s were families in which fathers were absent (or at least not living with mothers and infants), and in which others (notably the mothers' mothers) were household members and available to play a central family role. The inclusion of families such as these, in which mothers were often poor, young, and nonwhite, in studies on infant development expanded our understanding of what in fact always had existed—a range of family constellations. There is now a growing research literature on such constellations, and with it a growing understanding that a mother's current family relationships affect the way she cares for her infant, and through her, the infant's development (Crockenberg, 1988a; Lewis, 1987; Parke & Tinsley, 1987).

Despite this recognition of the roles other family members may play in the life of the developing infant, the focus of many of the early studies of this genre was on the impact of family members on the mother's effectiveness as a parent. Concern with infant outcomes in this research has been limited to indirect effects—benefits accruing to the infant by virtue of the social support family members provide the mother, and the improvement in her parenting as a result of that support (see Crockenberg, 1988a, for a review). From this perspective, what differs across family contexts is the extent to which a mother requires support from others in order to exhibit the pattern of responsive, sensitive caregiving identified from normative samples as predictive of positive infant mental health (e.g., a secure attachment to the mother), as well as the source of that support. In studies of adolescent mothers, an infant's maternal grandmother has often been targeted as the major source of social support to the mother; in two-parent, middle-class families in which mothers work outside the home, the father has more frequently been identified as the mother's primary support person.

Emphasizing the mother's centrality and focusing on the indirect effect of other family members on the infant's development can neglect potentially important direct effects of other family members on infant development. Fathers, grandparents, and siblings have direct contact with infants. Sometimes the contact is brief or sporadic, as when grandparents visit once a year. Often, however, it is extensive and emotionally significant to the infant, as in the enduring relationships that develop between infants and older siblings (with whom they may, in fact, spend more time than they do with their parents). When this kind of extended, emotionally significant contact characterizes a particular infant–other relationship, it is reasonable to assume that the relationship may contribute in important ways to the infant's early experiences within the family and may account for some of the variation we observe in infant mental health. By neglecting such influences, we have missed opportunities to explain differences in infant development more accurately and completely, and to identify possible sources of both pathology and mental health in an infant's environment.

In the review that follows, we present the extant research on family contexts of infant development; describe its limitations; discuss its implications for mental health professionals; and briefly suggest research that needs to be carried out if we are to understand what experiences, with whom, are necessary for infants to develop in ways identified as competent and adjusted in modern Western culture.

THE FATHER'S ROLE IN INFANT DEVELOPMENT

The best description of contact between infants and their fathers is that it is highly variable both across families and during the course of infancy itself. Fathers' involvement is typically reported in terms of the amount of time they spend in contact with, or the frequency with which they engage in specific activities with, their infants during a week's time. Those amounts and frequencies are in most cases dramatically lower than those of mothers. In a study by Pedersen, Yarrow, Anderson, and Cain (1979) of a small sample of middle-class parents and their 5-month-old infants, mothers were responsible for the care of babies without the fathers present about 6 hours a day on average. Fathers averaged 30 minutes a day as sole caretakers of their infants.

When fathers are in contact with their infants, they are very likely to engage them in play (Kotelchuck, 1976; Nugent, Yogman, Lester, & Hoffman, 1988; Richards, Dunn, & Antonis, 1977). Caretaking by fathers is typically less frequent on average than play and is more variable across families. Moreover, these studies most often include in their samples fathers who are working full-time and mothers who are not, with the consequence that the fathers who do the most caretaking are excluded from these estimates. In studies comparing primary caregiving fathers with traditional fathers, differences favoring greater involvement or more intimate involvement of the primary caregiving father are sometimes, but not always, reported (Field, 1978; Lamb, 1982).

Father–infant interaction probably differs in quality as well, just as mother–infant interaction does, although differences in the quality of father–infant interaction have been investigated infrequently. One consequence of this variability in amount, type, and quality of interaction is that it is difficult to generalize from existing research about a father's impact on an infant's developing social competence and mental health.

Indirect Effects

Social Support

As might be anticipated in a context that views the mother as the primary caregiver of the infant, much of the research on the father's influence on infant development has focused on "indirect effects"—the influence the father has on the developing infant by virtue of his relationship with the infant's mother. One specific way the father is thought to influence the mother's care of the infant is through the "social support" (i.e., the emotional, instrumental, and informational help) he provides her. "Emotional support" refers to expressions of empathy and encouragement that convey to the mother that she is understood and capable of doing a good job in that role. When the father of the baby is also the mother's partner, the mother's sense that the relationship is secure and that she is loved, despite the inevitable decrease in time they have for each other, may be a critical aspect of emotional support.

Several recent reviews have documented the importance of social support for the quality of the care mothers provide their infants, and have identified the mothers' partners, typically the children's fathers, as the primary source of that support in families where the fathers live with the mothers and infants (Crockenberg, 1988a; Parke & Tinsley, 1987). In two studies, emotional or child care support from fathers correlated positively with observed maternal competence in the form of emotional consistency, contingent responding, and warmth and pleasure in parenting (Dickie & Matheson, 1984; Levitt, Weber, & Clark, 1986). In the latter study, more positive maternal affect was related in turn to secure infant–mother attachments. Other studies confirm that social support (especially emotional support) from the father correlates with mother and infant behavior, as well as the security of the mother–infant attachment (Crnic, Greenberg, Ragozin, Robinson, & Bashman, 1983; Durrett, Otaki, & Richards, 1984). These findings suggest a possible indirect effect of the father's support on infant emotional development mediated through the mother's behavior, but they leave open the possibility that the father may have a more direct influence on infant development.

Studies of at-risk mothers are frequently cited as providing the strongest evidence that partner support affects maternal behavior in ways that support infant development (Crockenberg, 1987a; Quinton & Rutter, 1985). In these studies, mothers with childhood histories of separation and rejection avoided negative patterns of interaction (e.g., abuse, coercion) with their toddlers when they had good social support from their partners. In the absence of such support, the "at-risk" mothers were significantly more likely to engage in dysfunctional parenting with their children. Although the possibility that the same maternal qualities that led to the selection of supportive partners also accounted for the apparent effect of partner support on maternal behavior, the research raises the possibility that the greatest impact of differences in paternal behavior on infants may occur when mothers are at risk for poor parenting by virtue of their own developmental history. How partner support affects maternal behavior under these circumstances remains obscure, however. One possibility is that the partners' stability and support reduces the stress the mothers experience in their lives or increase their ability to cope effectively with the stresses they do encounter (Cobb, 1976; Dean & Linn, 1977). Alternately, in providing mothers with ongoing emotional support, partners may compensate for or even alter mothers' "working models of relationships" in ways that allow them to be empathic and emotionally responsive toward their infants (Fraiberg, 1980).

Although the explanations offered for the observed "effect" of partner support on the maternal behavior of women at risk for poor parenting are intriguing and perhaps even compelling, the possibility remains that the pattern of influence may be considerably more complex. Fathers who provide mothers with emotional support may also participate more fully in child care. In doing so, they may encourage positive affect and competent behavior in their infants, which in turn elicits sensitive and responsive caregiving from mothers and contributes to the infants' social–emotional development (e.g., secure infant–mother attachment relationships). A systems perspective on family relationships requires that we consider the multiple ways each family member may influence the others, rather than assuming a pattern of linear influence that conforms to our assumptions about the likely direction and source of influence on development in families (Marvin & Stewart, 1990). The research on the marriage relationship in relation to parenting behavior and infant development comes closest to capturing this systems view of development with families.

The Role of Marriage in Infant Development

The role of marriage in infant development is a process involving multiple interdependent family relationship patterns. Marriage is affected by the arrival of the child; marriage has an indirect impact on infant development by influencing each parent's relationship with the child; and marriage has a direct impact on the child's development by providing an affective context within which development occurs.

There is evidence that marital satisfaction decreases with the birth of a child (Belsky & Pensky, 1988) to a relatively greater degree than the general decreases in satisfaction that occur in nonchildbearing couples (Markman & Clements, 1991). It is noteworthy, moreover, that the content of marital dissatisfaction following the child's birth generally involves finances, communication, and intimacy, rather than difficulties with the child per se. Marriage also influences child development through its impact on each parent's relationship with the infant. A supportive husband–wife relationship prior to and during the postpartum period facilitates adjustment to new parenting roles (Grossman, Eichler, & Winickoff, 1980; Russell, 1974), enhances parental feeding skill (Pedersen, 1975), and predicts interactional competence with infants (Lamb & Elster, 1985). Pedersen, Anderson, and Cain (1980) reported further that increased rates of negative behavior within marriages were related to increased rates of negative behavior directed by mothers to their infants. Marital satisfaction has been associated with security of the mother–infant, but not the father–infant, attachment relationship (Goldberg & Easterbrooks, 1984; Howes & Markman, 1989). In the latter study, the association was found between premarital assessment of the relationship and subsequent attachment, suggesting that poor marital quality precedes difficulties in the parent–infant relationship.

Marital dissatisfaction or discord may be expressed in a variety of ways, and has also been shown to predict parenting behavior and infant development. Dickstein and Parke (1988) found a pattern of distance or withdrawal by unhappily as opposed to happily married fathers, and a trend toward overinvolvement by unhappily married as opposed to happily married mothers. Moreover, although happily and unhappily married fathers displayed similar amounts of positive affect during a laboratory procedure, unhappily married fathers did not provide contingent affect displays in response to their babies' bids, and they gave less clear affective signals during referencing episodes than infants of happily married fathers. Other studies have also found that the quality of the marriage generally has a greater impact on the father–infant than on the mother–infant relationship (e.g., Belsky, Gilstrap, & Rovine, 1984; Lamb & Elster, 1985; Volling & Belsky, 1985).

Marriage further influences infant development by providing the affective climate within which development occurs. In the context of marital dissatisfaction, disruptions occur in the domains of emotional communication and regulation processes. Among other features, more negative affect is expressed and reciprocated between spouses in dissatisfied as opposed to satisfied marriages (Gottman, 1979). Although most of the research linking marital conflict with child development has focused on older children (Crockenberg & Covey, 1991), Cummings, Zahn-Waxler, and Radke-Yarrow (1981) found that even by 1 year of age infants were aware of others' anger and affectionate interactions, and had their own emotional responses to them. The more frequently the infants observed interparental anger, for example, the more distress they expressed.

In sum, these studies demonstrate the complexity of the family relationships infants enter, and lend support to the view that any "effects" on the developing infant must be viewed and studied with this complexity in mind.

Direct Effects

Attachment

Research linking the father's behavior during infancy directly to differences in infant social–emotional development has focused almost exclusively on the infant–father attachment relationship. Contrary to the view that the quality of all the infant's attachments relationships is derived from the security or insecurity of the infant–mother bond, Main and Weston (1981) reported that infants formed independent attachment relationships to mothers and fathers, based on the history of their interactions with each. In addition, infants with secure attachment relationships with both parents were more empathic during toddlerhood to an adult in distress, suggesting that secure attachments with fathers had a demonstrable effect on the infants' development. Easterbrooks and Goldberg (1990) were unable to replicate this apparent benefit of two secure infant attachments, however, in predicting ego functioning in kindergarten-age children, and in neither study did secure father–infant attachments buffer children against the apparent ill effects of insecure attachment relationships with their mothers. Thus, the contribution of the infant–father attachment relationship to the infant's current and subsequent development remains uncertain. It may be that infants in these studies spent too little time with fathers relative to mothers for the infant–father relationships to serve as a protective buffer, but with greater contact the fathers' impact on the infants' development would also be greater. If so, encouraging nurturant fathers to take on a greater share of infant care may be an effective intervention strategy in families where mothers, for whatever reason, are less able to parent effectively.

Support for greater father involvement comes from research indicating that fathers' involvement as alternate caregivers with their infants and toddlers when mothers are employed may promote healthy development in the form of secure attachments and less frequent defiant behavior. In Belsky and Rovine's (1988) study of infants who were left in alternate care during their first year, those whose mothers worked more than 20 hours a week were at significantly greater risk of developing insecure attachments with their mothers. This was not the case, however, for infants who were cared for by their fathers in their mothers' absence. There is other evidence that fathers may play an important role in a range of behaviors that reflect children's competence in relation to autonomy issues and emotional regulation during the second year of life. We turn to those studies next.

Autonomy and Regulation

By their second year, infants are increasingly aware of their own separateness from parents—an awareness that is apparent in the frequency with which they refuse, at least initially, to go along with their parents' proposed plan of action. Both mothers and fathers experience these

refusals, and it makes sense that both should play important roles in determining how their toddlers learn to balance their own needs and wishes with those of others—autonomy within a social context.

Only two research teams have studied father–toddler interaction in relation to this developmental task. Goldberg and Easterbrooks (1984) studied 72 infants aged 20 months and their parents; Belsky, Youngblade, Rovine, and Volling (1989) studied 100 children aged 3 years and their parents. In both studies, poor marital quality was associated with more negative and intrusive behavior or less emotionally supportive behavior on the part of fathers, but not mothers. Moreover, fathers' behavior was associated in turn with distinctive patterns of child behavior. At 20 months, children of fathers who provided less emotional support were more discontent (boys) or less task-oriented during a problem-solving task (girls) (Goldberg & Easterbrooks, 1984). At 3 years, children of fathers who were negative and intrusive were negative and disobedient (Belsky et al., 1989). These studies are consistent with the view that fathers probably play an important role in influencing affective development and the way autonomy issues are expressed during the second and third years of life. It is unclear, of course, whether these correlational studies reflect a father-to-child influence. We assume that this is the case, just as we assume a mother-to-child influence in studies in which mother and child behavior correlates positively. It is possible, however, that a father response to child behavior that has developed in the context of the mother–child relationship, or in direct response to marital conflict. Regardless of origin, however, the negative quality of the father–toddler relationship is noteworthy and indicates the importance of including fathers in advice/interventions offered to families in support of infant mental health.

Acknowledging that infant development occurs in response to the broader family environment that includes fathers may have an important impact on maternal mental health as well. Caplan (1989) has argued and demonstrated that there is a widespread tendency to "blame mothers" for maladjustment in their children. In nine clinical journals at three points in time (1970, 1976, and 1982), 72 types of child psychopathology were attributed to mothers; none were attributed to fathers. Moreover, the investigators reported that mothers were never described in purely positive terms, whereas this was often the case for fathers. Recognizing that fathers have a role in early social–emotional development may be an important step in the early prevention of psychopathology in children, and in protecting mothers from the grief and shame to which they may be subjected by mental health professionals who wrongly hold them solely responsible for the developmental problems of their children.

One way fathers as a group are known to differ from mothers in their interaction with their infants is their greater likelihood of engaging in physical play. In the next section, we review the data and consider the possible implications of this difference for infant development and infant emotional regulation in particular.

Physical Play

As summarized in Tinsley and Parke (1984a) and as reported above, play is the most common activity fathers engage in with their infants. Although mothers play with infants more than fathers by virtue of the greater amount of time they spend with them, fathers spend a greater proportion of their time in play with their infants than do mothers (37.5% vs. 25.8% as reported by Kotelchuck, 1976). More significantly, fathers are especially likely, and more likely than mothers, to engage in play characterized by physical movement and associated with increased infant arousal. Yogman (1982) reported, for example, that for infants between the ages of 2 weeks and 6 months, the most common types of games fathers played involved moving the infants' limbs. These limb movement games constituted 70% of all father–infant games during this age period, but only 4% of mother–infant games. These initial findings have been replicated a number of times by different investigators using infants of different ages. Power and Parke (1983) reported that fathers played more bouncing and lifting games with their 8-month-old infants than did mothers, although this difference was apparent primarily with fathers and boys. Similar differences have been reported by Lamb (1977a) between fathers and infants at 7–8 months.

As infants get older and become more motorically competent, the physical games fathers engage in with their infants change. Fathers' play remains more "physical" than mothers', however, with more "rough-and-tumble" contact and other types of gross motor activities (Lamb, 1977b, between fathers and infants at 15, 18, and 24 months; Clarke-Stewart, 1978, for infants between 15 and 30 months of age; and Teti, Bond, & Gibbs, 1988, for 18-month-old infants). The character of fathers' rough-and-tumble play with 2-year-olds also differs by child gender. As reported by McGuire (1982), with girls the play typically involved giving rides or "letting her jump on me"; for boys it was more often mock fighting or specific sports.

The evidence is consistent in suggesting that fathers provide a certain kind of physical activity for their infants, perhaps especially for their male infants, to a greater extent than do mothers. The significant question for our purpose is the effect this experience can be expected to have on the development of competence in infancy or subsequently. There are several possible effects. Because physical play is arousing, fathers may use this opportunity to help their infants learn to modulate arousal. They may take the lead both in bringing their infants' arousal level up and in bringing it down. Or, in failing to do so, they may contribute to problems of emotional regulation that occur throughout infancy. To our knowledge, there are no empirical data linking differences in fathers' behavior to infants' emotional regulation.

We may speculate also that infants exposed to physical activities will develop a greater enjoyment of and interest in such activities as they grow older. This interest and enjoyment may be an important contributor to acceptance in peer groups in which this type of play is normative, most notably boys' peer groups, and an important precursor to the development of skill in sports for both sexes. To the extent that fathers engage in less physical play with their female infants, they may be inadvertently circumscribing the opportunities girls have for experiencing success later in childhood and during adolescence, by decreasing the likelihood that they will choose a physical activity as a source of personal or professional satisfaction. From this perspective, enjoyment of physical activity would be viewed as evidence of an infant's "social competence," with potential implications for mental health at later periods of development.

Only Tinsley and Parke (1987) have examined the association between father–infant physical play and children's current or subsequent behavioral development. They reported a borderline association between fathers' physical play and infants' raw Bayley Scales of Infant Development mental scores, but no association between fathers' physical play and infants' physical development. Differences in fathers' linguistic and cognitive stimulation were similarly unrelated to differences in infant development (Hunter, McCarthy, MacTurk, & Vietze, 1987; Teti et al., 1988). Why does fathers' behavior fail to correlate with infant play and test performance? One possibility is that fathers in these studies spent much less time with their infants than mothers, and the differences in their behavior made no difference in infant development for that reason. In families where mothers and fathers share the care of their infants to a greater extent, the effect of differences in fathers' behavior on infant development may be greater. These infants should have a greater opportunity to experience their fathers' distinctive patterns of interaction and to be affected by them than would other infants.

Support for this proposition comes from Pedersen, Suwalsky, Cain, Zaslow, and Rabinovich's (1987) investigation of the impact of relatively greater amounts of time alone between fathers and infants on both the fathers' and the infants' subsequent behavior. Fathers who spent more time alone with their infants engaged in more varied activities with them at home with the mothers present, and were significantly more likely than fathers with less contact to exhibit behaviors indicative of intimacy and attachment (such as eye-to-eye contact, close holding, and positive affect). Their infants differed even more strikingly from infants who spent less time alone with their fathers: They signaled their fathers more frequently, explored objects more, and showed more reciprocal positive affect with them. These findings were not an artifact of differences in maternal behavior between the two groups, nor were they confounded by a child's gender, a mother's employment, or differences in infant–father interactions apparent at three months. The investigators note, moreover, that exploratory behavior correlates with cognitive ability in infants and toddlers, and it has also been identified as a correlate of a secure infant–mother attachment relationship (Hazen & Durrett, 1982).

It appears that the experience of caring for their young infants alters the fathers' behavior as well as that of the infants—perhaps by raising their sense of efficacy in interacting, as Pedersen et al. (1987) suggest, as well as their own feelings of attachment to their infants. Fathers who spend more time with their infants may also become more expert in developing strategies for eliciting and maintaining their infants' interest and involvement, and may facilitate their cognitive development as a consequence. Evidence from Ninio and Rinott (1988) that fathers who spent more time in infant care perceived their infants as more competent than fathers who spent less time in caregiving is consistent with this possibility. One implication of the change in father–infant interaction as a result of greater caregiving experience is that there may be long-term effects on the children's development that are not immediately apparent. Thus, the impact of differences in fathers' behavior with their 18-month-old infants documented by Teti et al. (1988) may be more apparent later in the children's development. If fathers increase their interaction with their infants during the second year of life, it may take some time before the effects of the differences fathers bring to their interaction have an impact on the infants' functioning.

Summary

As long as fathers' time with their infants can be recorded in terms of number of times or minutes a week, fathers may have relatively little impact on areas of infant development in which mothers are very actively involved. To the extent that fathers are more involved with their infants, or to the extent that they engage in behaviors or activities that mothers do not, or only minimally, engage in, we can anticipate greater paternal influences, for better or worse, on the course of infant development in general and mental health specifically. This is an important qualification of research findings that might otherwise be interpreted to mean that fathers are of no importance in understanding the development of individual differences in social competence in infancy.

In our view, clinical practice and intervention with families should be informed by research as well as by theory. If this is to occur, researchers need to identify fathers who play active roles in their infants' development, and consider how differences in their behavior contribute to differences in the way those infants develop. We need to know about fathers in a range of racially, ethnically, and economically diverse families, with mothers who are either more or less competent. We also need follow-up studies to determine the impact on infants of certain salient father behaviors (such as rough-and-tumble play), especially those that may serve to promote gender-differentiated behavior. In the absence of good research evidence, as practitioners we need to be attuned to the probability that fathers who are highly involved in their infants' care probably contribute in significant ways to their current functioning as well as to their long-term development.

GRANDPARENTS' ROLE IN INFANT DEVELOPMENT

Demographic studies of the prevalence of grandparental status and contact—there are roughly 22 million grandparents in the United States; approximately 70% of older people are grandparents; and three out of five grandparents see their grandchildren at least once a week, while nearly half see a grandchild every day— suggest that there is considerable potential for grandparents to influence development (see Tinsley & Parke, 1987, and Werner, 1984, for reviews). In non-Western cultures, this potential for grandparental influence on the course of development is even greater (Werner, 1984). Frequent babysitting help by grandparents also seems to occur, regardless of geographical location or ethnicity. According to Werner (1984), child care/babysitting assistance by grandparents has been reported among both middle-class and working-class blacks in the South (Jackson, 1971), among three-generation Mexican-American working-class families in the Midwest (Sena-Rivera, 1979), and among Native Americans in the Southwest (Red Horse, Lewis, Feit, & Decker, 1978). However, middle-class U.S. grandparents as a group are less likely to be involved in daily or weekly care of the grandchildren than are less affluent grandparents (Neugarten & Weinstein, 1964).

Although the term "grandparents" includes both grandmothers and grandfathers, in reality grandmothers typically play the more central role when their grandchildren are infants. There are some important exceptions to this generalization, however, and we consider these in the review that follows. As with fathers, the impact of grandparents on infant development is probably both indirect through the help and emotional support they provide the infants' mothers, and direct through their contact and interaction with the infants themselves. As both Crockenberg (1981) and Tinsley & Parke (1984b) point out, in providing support for mothers, grandparents also provide their grandchildren with loving care.

Indirect Effects

In families with fathers present, grandmothers are often the second most frequent source of support mentioned by mothers. In others, most notably the families of unmarried adolescent mothers, they are often the primary source of support, and in some instances better sources of support than the fathers (whose own needs may compete with the babies' for the mothers' time). In a study of English teen mothers (Crockenberg, 1988b), most of whom were married or living with the fathers of their babies, grandmothers were identified as "very frequent" source of support in roughly half the families, with only fathers more frequently so identified. When specific types of help and support were identified, grandmothers were more frequent sources of support than fathers only in the key area of "baby minding," an activity that involved caring for the infants for relatively long periods of time when the mothers were not present in their homes.

In a U.S. sample of teen mothers, fewer than 60% of whom were married or living with the babies' fathers, maternal grandmothers were identified most often as a "very frequent" source of support, with fathers in second place (Crockenberg, 1987b). Maternal grandmothers more frequently changed diapers, bathed and dressed the babies, and engaged in baby minding than any other group of support persons, including fathers. When paternal grandmothers were considered as well, grandmothers were the most frequent source of support in every category, including feeding, getting up at night with the babies, housework, and advising and encouraging the mothers. The centrality of the grandmother as a source of support for the adolescent mother and as a caregiver for the young infant suggests that her effect on the infant and the mother–infant dyad may be substantial, and that professional services directed toward support and development of both the adolescent mother and her baby should consider the grandmother as a key player in the family dynamics (Crockenberg, 1986).

There is evidence that the social support provided by grandparents is associated with "better"—that is, more nurturant or more sensitive and responsive caregiving—by the mothers who are the recipients of the support. This appears to be the case in U.S. samples, and also cross-nationally. Feiring and Taylor (1982) found that in their low-income, primarily black inner-city sample, mothers who were rated as involved and responsive also perceived a high amount of positive support from the "secondary parents," who were most frequently the mothers' mothers. In the Crockenberg (1987b, 1988b) studies cited above, family support, especially support that was provided on a daily basis, was positively associated with responsiveness to crying among mothers of 3-month-old infants in both English and U.S. samples. Moreover, the association between social support and maternal behavior remained significant after differences in responsive attitudes, ethnicity, a mother's early separation from her own family, and current life stress were taken into account statistically. These are important controls, because it is possible that while social support from a grandmother correlates with maternal behavior, the association may be an artifact of the link between the way a mother was parented as a child and the way she parents her own infant. Moreover, to the extent that we attribute the "effect" on the mother's behavior solely to the presence or lack of current social support, we may fail to provide the services or design an intervention appropriate to the specific family situation.

Other investigators have reported no salutary effect of grandmothers' social support on the maternal behavior of teen mothers, perhaps because mothers who are receiving the most support by the second year of their infants' lives may be less competent than other mothers and receive more support for that reason (Crockenberg, 1987b; Oyserman, Radin, & Saltz, 1991). Nevertheless, qualitative aspects of grandparent behavior are strongly associated with a mother's nurturant behavior toward an infant. In the Oyserman et al. (1991) study, a grandmother's nurturance toward an infant between 12 and 24 months was the best predictor of a teen mother's nurturance with her infant in families with no grandfather or father present. When both a grandmother and a grandfather were present, however, grandfather nurturance was the only significant predictor of a teen mother's nurturance. Whatever the explanation, these findings suggest that it may be premature to conclude that grandfathers are uniformly less important than grandmothers in the lives of their infant grandchildren.

Another indirect influence grandparents exercise on infants' development is through the role they play in supporting fathers, who in turn provide support for mothers, and in approving or disapproving fathers' involvement in child care (Parke & Tinsley, 1988). Tinsley and Parke (1987) reported, for example, that fathers and mothers of 7-month-old infants were similar in the extent to which they made use of grandparents as sources of support, although fathers reported greater satisfaction with contact with their own parents than with their wives' parents.

As is the case for research linking social support from fathers with infant development, a strong argument can be made for an indirect effect between grandparent contact and infant development. Providing mothers with assistance may reduce some of the stress associated with the care of an infant and may encourage sensitive, responsive, involved maternal behavior. No clear evidence of such an indirect effect on infant competence or infant mental health is available, however. Moreover, the fact that much of the assistance involves direct care of an infant argues very strongly that at least some of the "effect" on the infant's development is the result of the grandparent's direct contact and interaction with the infant. Evidence in support of a direct effect of grandparents on infant development is considered next.

Direct Effects

The likelihood that grandparents promote infant development in significant ways is consistent not just with the frequency of contact between grandparents and infants, but with the nature of the interaction that occurs when they are together. Several studies of infants of different ages suggest that grandparents interact with their grandchildren much as parents do with their children, and that infants treat their parents and their grandparents almost interchangeably in some circumstances.

Feinman and Roberts (1985) reported that 12-month-old infants behaved differently with their mothers than with most other adults with whom they interacted regularly. They did not differentiate, however, between their mothers and grandmothers. Myers, Jarvis, and Creasey (1987) reported similarly that the only difference in reaction to mothers and grandmothers, in a version of the Strange Situation, was that infants were more frequently in proximity to their mothers than to their grandmothers when both were in the room. Infants did not cry more or less at the leaving of mothers or grandmothers, nor did they show a differential change in play after mothers or grandmothers left or returned.

In contrast, their behavior to a stranger differed clearly and significantly from their behavior with mothers and grandmothers, suggesting that the similarity in their interaction with mothers and grandmothers was unique. The results of these studies are particularly impressive because, in both, none of the grandmothers lived in the same household as the grandchildren, although the grandmothers did see the grandchildren very frequently. Thus, it appears that infants who have frequent contact with grandmothers interact with them in ways that are similar to the way they relate to their parents, and that make the grandmothers potentially powerful sources of influence on infant development and infant mental health.

Similar to the influence of fathers on their children, the impact of grandparents on the development and well-being of their grandchildren undoubtedly depends on the extent and quality of the grandparent–grandchild contact, as well as on the quantity and quality of the parent–child interaction. When parents are fully engaged with their children and the interactive styles of parents and grandparents are similar, the impact of grandparents may be largely "redundant" with respect to the outcomes typically studied, as Lamb (1979) has suggested with respect to father–mother effects. Through the overlap in their behavior with the experiences parents provide their infants, grandparents may create a more efficient learning system for the grandchildren. The impact of grandparental involvement and interaction may be most apparent in infant development, however, when the parents are relatively uninvolved or unskillful and the greater involvement and skill of the grandparents may compensate for this lack.

Evidence that grandparents serve as backup socialization agents and contribute in significant ways to the development and mental health of their grandchildren comes from several sources. Rutter (1985) has reported evidence that a child with a psychiatrically disturbed parent is less likely to show psychological disturbance in turn if a "supportive adult," who is usually a relative and most often a grandmother, has played an active role in the child's care. Werner and Smith (1982) identified children from their longitudinal study on Kauai who were at risk for poor development, but who by age 18 showed no sign of deviant outcomes. During infancy, one protective factor was the absence of prolonged separations from the mother, including separations due to maternal employment, *without adequate child care*. Many of these resilient children experienced long separations from their mothers, but were cared for by other family members—typically grandmothers who provided them with consistency and love. This involvement of grandmothers and grandfathers usually continued throughout childhood and adolescence, and in interviews at age 18, many of the resilient children "gave credit to their grandparents for the nurturance they had received in childhood and the structure and guidance they had provided for them in adolescence" (Werner, 1984, p. 98).

Further evidence that grandmothers' involvement in the care of their grandchildren during infancy may foster their social–emotional adjustment comes from a study by Benn and Saltz (1989) of adolescent mothers and their infants. All grandmothers lived with their daughters and grandchildren, but they varied in the extent to which they were involved in the care of the infants. Infants of grandmothers who were most directly involved in their care were more likely to be securely attached to their mothers than were other infants. The inference that this effect was a direct one is based on other evidence from the study, which indicated that the mothers themselves were not, by their own report, particularly good caregivers to their infants. The investigators suggest, however, that because not much was required of the mothers, they may have been playful and nurturant during the times they were together with their infants (much like fathers in two-parent families), fostering a secure attachment thereby. From this perspective, the grandmothers' role was primarily to limit the infants' demands to a level that was manageable for the mothers. Another intriguing possibility, which is consistent with a systems approach to infant mental health, is that the grandmothers may also have nurtured the infants in a way that promoted secure attachments with themselves and the positive affect and confident exploratory behavior that accompany such attachments. These infant behaviors may have elicited a degree of engagement and responsiveness from the adolescent mothers that in turn contributed to the secure attachment between mothers and infants. These data confirm Bronfenbrenner's (1979) thesis that a critical factor in a child's development is the active involvement of at least one adult who is simply crazy about the child. Clearly, a grandparent can be that person, and facilitating such grandparent–grandchild relationships may be an important preventative measure in fostering children's mental health.

Grandparents as Primary Caregivers

In many contexts, grandparents take on the primary role of nurturing and socializing children, which is typically allocated to parents in middle-class Caucasian families. Werner (1984) reports, for example, that fosterage or informal adoption by grandparents has been common in Polynesian island societies, and that in modern Hawaii grandparents continue to "*hanai*" grandchildren, especially if a daughter bears an out-of-wedlock child. Not only is the practice of surrogate parenting not diminishing; in certain groups (most notably in some poor black communities), it appears to be increasing as male unemployment, the number of out-of-wedlock births not placed for adoption, and the incidence of drug addiction among young black parents rise (Burton & Dilworth-Anderson, 1991). Burton (1990) reports that in one black community in which economic circumstances have undermined the ability of black males to contribute to the support of their families, teenage childbearing combined with grandmother surrogate parenting has become an acceptable and highly functional life course strategy. Early childbearing is encouraged to give grandmothers the "opportunity to experience the parent role" while they still have the energy to care for young children; young mothers contribute to the family by caring for the great-grandmother generation.

Emphasis on the beneficial effects to infants of grandparent care should not lead us to overlook the possibility of undesirable consequences for infants and grandmothers alike. Not all grandmothers wish to take on the role of surrogate parent to an infant or young child, and this is particularly likely to be the case when grandmotherhood occurs "too early." In an interview study of black grandmothers, Burton (1985) found that women who became grandmothers before the age of 38 were unhappy with the role because it interfered with other activities and relationships. From the infants' point of view, such reluctant grandmothers often rejected the role themselves, leaving the great-grandmothers to take on the responsibility of caring for the new babies. From the great-grandmothers' own accounts, this was a daunting task for women in their 60s or early 70s, often in poor health,

and frequently caring for several grandchildren and great-grandchildren (Burton, 1989). By the second year of life, if not sooner, caregivers must create safe environments for increasingly mobile infants, and they must be able to set limits on behavior in kind but firm ways. In many cases, aging grandparents may not be up to the task, at least in the absence of extensive support from professionals and from other family members.

To our knowledge, there has been no research on adverse effects of grandparent care on infants; however, this may become available in the not too distant future, given the prevalence of relative care of infants and children while mothers are employed outside the home (Klein, 1985). A child may also suffer emotionally as a result of such informal arrangements if a falling out between the grandmother and mother, or a change in the mother's life, results in the abrupt removal of the infant from an important attachment figure. Differences between mothers and grandmothers with respect to expectations for behavior and implementation of routines may also be problematic for children where caregiving is shared, especially if the adults criticize each other publicly.

None of these potential pitfalls of grandparental care argues against the involvement of grandmothers as supplementary or surrogate parents. They suggest, however, that assistance in anticipating and resolving potential conflicts between the caregiving adults may be critical to the success of this venture. In one study of adolescent mothers, young mothers spoke forthrightly about their conflicts with their mothers (and partners) over child care, and endorsed a plan that would include those with whom they shared caregiving responsibility in the delivery of advice on child care (Crockenberg, 1986). Social welfare professionals are often in a position to legitimate grandparents as alternate or supportive caregivers of infants and young children and to arrange for the financial and other resources that will make this caregiving economically feasible. Werner (1984), citing Red Horse et al. (1978), reports, however, that welfare case workers are often reluctant to place children (especially infants) with grandparents who are themselves poor and members of an ethnic or racial group stigmatized in our predominantly Anglo-American culture, despite a history of extended family involvement within such groups (Hill, 1977; Martin & Martin, 1978; Red Horse et al., 1978).

Grandfathers

Parke and Tinsley's (1988) chapter on the role of grandfathers in the context of the family summarizes the relatively limited information available on grandfathers and their infant grandchildren. Although grandfathers were more behaviorally responsive to unfamiliar infants in a waiting room then men at any other stage of life except fathers of young children, and although they approach and touched unfamiliar infants more often than other men (Feldman & Nash, 1978, 1979; Feldman, Biringen, & Nash, 1981; Feldman, Nash, & Curtrona, 1977), other evidence suggests that their direct involvement in the care of their own infant grandchildren is relatively limited in comparison with that of grandmothers (McGreal, 1985). In Crockenberg's (1987b, 1988a) studies of U.S. and English adolescent mothers, grandfathers were never identified as frequent or very frequent sources of social support by the young mothers when the infants were 3 months old. Like the grandfathers in Tinsley and Parke's (1984b) research, however, the grandfathers in these studies often provided financial support to their adult/teenage children that was meant to benefit their grandchildren as well.

Tinsley and Parke's (1987) and Parke and Tinsley's (1988) reports of their research on grandfathers confirm that grandfathers are less competent than grandmothers and parents when they are instructed to play with their infant grandchildren, and that this lack is apparent in the infants' behavior. When infants were with their grandfathers, they laughed and smiled less and fussed more than when they were with parents or grandmothers. Presumably, the relatively lower interactive competence of grandfathers is a function of experience, and grandfathers who interact more with their infant grandchildren will be more skilled than those who interact less.

There are some exceptions, moreover, to what appears to be low grandfather involvement and likely low grandfather influence on development during infancy. In a study by Radin, Oyserman, and Benn (1989), grandfathers and grandchildren who lived in the same home were studied. The mothers in these families were all adolescents, and the fathers of the infants were absent from the households. The level and quality of a grandfather's involvement, rather than his presence per se, were associated with infant emotional development and behavior at 12 and 24 months. When grandfathers were highly nurturant, infants, especially females, showed less negative affect in potentially stressful situations—less fear during administration of the Bayley, and less anger, fear, or distress during the Strange Situation. High grandfather nurturance was also associated at 24 months with less compliance with the teen mothers. High grandfather restrictiveness was similarly associated with less cooperation with the teen mothers at both ages.

This is the clearest evidence to date of the possible impact of grandfather involvement in infant development, and indicates the importance of considering qualitative differences in grandfather behavior. As the investigators suggest, however, the impact of even "positive" grandfather behavior may not be entirely beneficial when considered from the viewpoint of the family system as a whole. For example, a nurturant grandfather may inadvertently undermine a teen mother's attempt to exercise control over her 2-year-old. Alternatively, the grandfather may be compensating for an overcontrolling mother whose own overcontrol accounts for the infant's lack of compliance. Because collinearity (correlations between the behavior of grandfathers and other family members) was not controlled for in the Radin et al. study, it is also possible that some of the influence attributed to grandfathers was an artifact of the influence of the mothers and grandmothers on infant development.

Summary

Infants and grandparents who regularly see each other interact in much the same way as infants and parents, suggesting that some grandmothers and grandfathers may be important sources of influence on infant development. Benefits of grandparental contact are most apparent when infants are otherwise at risk for poor development by virtue of their parents' characteristics or the context of their lives, and grandparents provide the consistent loving care associated with good development outcome.

The available research is consistent with the view that grandparents are an extremely valuable resource in promoting infant mental health. It suggests that one way professionals can address the mental health needs of infants is by providing grandparents with information about child care and by creating opportunities for them to develop skills for being effective support persons to their children, the infant's parents. In discussing what they valued in the way their mothers gave support, English adolescent mothers focused on their mothers' respect for their autonomy as a key feature (Crockenberg, 1988b). "She tells me what she thinks," they would say, "but she lets me make my own decisions because I am the baby's mother."

SIBLING INFLUENCES ON INFANT DEVELOPMENT

Indirect Effects

Like research on fathers, early research on the effect of siblings on infant development focused on how the presence of an older sibling or siblings altered the infant's relationship with the mother. In contrast, however, the emphasis with siblings has been on possible negative effects on infants of having older siblings because of the demands older siblings place on mothers, which in turn may affect their ability to engage with the infants. More recently, interest in the possible effects of siblings on infant development has shifted to effects that occur by virtue of an infant's direct contact with a sibling or siblings.

Direct Effects

Dunn wrote in her 1983 review that "little is known about the behavior of very young infants with their older siblings" p. 792, in part because studies have focused on the impact of an infant on an older sibling, rather than the reverse. That infants have very frequent contact with older siblings has been well documented, however, both in diary studies and in observational studies carried out in many cultures. In Lawson and Ingleby's (1974) study of second children, for example, by 1 year of age infants spent almost as much time in interaction with their siblings as they did with their mothers, and far more time than with their fathers. Although no current data are available, we would speculate that among the families of employed mothers in the United States, infants may frequently spend more time with older siblings than they do with either parent. It behooves us, therefore, to consider what the impact of that contact might be on an infant.

Sibling Caretaking

In cultures where older siblings serve as alternate caregivers for their infant siblings, infants appear to form similar attachments to mothers and siblings. Nearly all the infants in Ainsworth's (1967) Ugandan study became attached both to their mothers and to others who shared in their care, typically older sisters. Gussi infants, who were also cared for by both mothers and siblings, showed a similar pattern of attachment to both. And Kikiyu infants in Kenya showed positive affective responses to both mothers and their sibling caregivers as early as 7 months of age (Leiderman & Leiderman, 1974).

Although it is likely to be less extensive and more supervised, and therefore, potentially less helpful to mothers than the care provided by fathers or grandparents, older siblings in modern Western cultures do care for their infant siblings or attempt to do so (Dunn, 1983). There is evidence, moreover, that this care may be effective in providing comfort and security to infants in potentially frightening or stressful circumstances. In Stewart's (1983) study of infants and older siblings in the Strange Situation, more than half of the 4-year-olds attempted to reassure their infant siblings during separation from the mothers, and the infants for their part were calmed by the siblings' intervention. When a stranger entered the room, most of the infants moved closer to the siblings, using them as a "secure base," and only then began to respond to the stranger in a friendly manner. Evidence from an earlier study of infant attachment by Schaffer and Emerson (1964) indicated that infants became attached to older siblings as indicated by the distress at the siblings' absence, pleasure at their return, and preference for them as playmates. In Dunn and Kendrick's (1982) study, 50% of 14-month-old infants with older siblings were reported to miss them in their absence.

Findings of attachment and separation distress raise the possibility that infants abruptly separated from older siblings who have served as attachment figures and comforters may experience a significant loss, accompanied by depressed affect and inhibited play. Such separations may occur, for example, when an older child enters school, when both children are placed in different child care programs, or when siblings are placed with different parents as the result of a divorce or in different foster settings.

Siblings also appear to serve as a secure base for the exploration of infant siblings, and in the role of comforter in the course of longer separations of infants from parents. In the natural setting of a yard at a private home, 16 infants aged 22 months moved farther away from their mothers and stayed away longer when older siblings were present (Samuels, 1980). Heinicke and Westheimer (1966) reported that infants showed less distress at admission to a residential nursery when they were admitted with siblings. These findings suggest that placing infants in child care with older siblings when both parents work outside the home may have a similar effect of reducing any distress associated with the separation, as well as providing parents with another perspective on the infants' experience in their absence. This prediction is consistent with our earlier discussions of father and grandparent effects on infant development; like them, siblings may play a greater role in shaping the infants' experience and hence their development when parents are not available to the infants, or for whatever reason do not provide nurturant, responsive care.

Imitation and Interaction

Older siblings offer infants the opportunity to learn specific behaviors through imitation, through reciprocal interaction, and sometimes through direct teaching. Studies reviewed by Dunn (1983) of both Canadian (Pepler, Corter, & Abramovitch, 1982) and British (Dunn & Kendrick, 1982) families indicated that more than 25% of all interactions between infants between 12 and 24 months of age and their older siblings were imitative, with most of these involving imitation of the older by the younger siblings. Presumably this means that older siblings are potentially powerful models for younger siblings for all kinds of behavior, including those that parents would prefer they did not learn. The study by Dunn and Kendrick (1982) indicated that infant siblings became increasingly aggressive over time, presumably as a result of their exposure to older siblings, although comparison with infants without siblings were not made. Infants may also develop behavioral repertoires or cognitive skills by virtue of interacting with their siblings, who not only perform the behavior themselves, but also create the affective or material context that leads to the adoption of specific behaviors. Dunn and Kendrick (1982)

reported anecdotally, for example, that by 14 months of age, younger siblings demonstrated behavior indicating some understanding of what would annoy the older siblings. In one instance, an infant sibling took on the identity of the older sibling's imaginary playmate in a move that could not have been the result of simple imitation. They also reported demonstrations of prosocial behaviors by infant siblings during the second year of life—behaviors that were attuned to the affective needs of their older siblings.

Turn taking is another skill infants develop in interaction with others. To investigate the role older siblings might play in the development of turn-taking competence, Vandell and Wilson (1987) observed 26 second-born infant boys and girls interacting with their mothers, with their 3- to 6-year-old siblings, and with an unfamiliar peer. In contrast to their interactions with mothers, infants' interactions with siblings involved less turn taking and less contingent responsiveness. Nevertheless, infants with more turn-taking experience with either mothers or older siblings subsequently engaged in more turn taking with peers. Apparently, infants learn more about turn taking through their interaction with their mothers, but skillful siblings may also encourage the development of turn taking skills. Whether the association between sibling turn taking involves a causal influence is unclear, however, because mother and sibling behavior covary.

Sibling-created play experiences may also facilitate infant cognitive and linguistic development, especially when the age space between older and younger siblings is relatively large, although the extant research fails to demonstrate such an effect (Teti, Bond, & Gibbs, 1986; Gibbs, Teti, & Bond, 1987). Although infants in more widely spaced infant dyads experienced a more intellectually and socially stimulating environment than infants where spacing between siblings was closer, there were no associations between any measure of infant–sibling interaction and the infants' cognitive level as assessed on the Bayley Mental Development Index, as observed in the infants' solitary play, or as observed in their linguistic development. In contrast, several aspects of mothers' interaction with infants significantly predicted infant Bayley Mental scores and their level of solitary play, both concurrently and between 12 and 18 months (Teti, Bond, & Gibbs, 1988). The investigators propose that the more limited time widely spaced siblings spend together may account for the lack of association between more sophisticated sibling play and linguistic interactions and infant cognitive development. Another possibility is that just as fathers and grandparents may have the greatest impact on infant development when mothers are less involved or less competently involved with their infants, so also may older siblings have a greater impact on their infant siblings under such circumstances.

Summary

The potential for siblings to influence the development of their younger siblings is great in view of the amount of time they typically spend together. The clearest evidence to date of such an influence is in the role older siblings play in providing comfort and security to infant siblings in times of distress and separation from parents. It is also clear that infants imitate older siblings, and we need to know more specifically how this tendency may contribute to the development of competent or incompetent infant behavior, especially in circumstances where parents are less available either as models or as interactive partners for their infants than is typical. For example, do sibling interaction and the positive affect that occurs in the course of that interaction serve as protective factors for infants being cared for by depressed mothers? Or, alternatively, does extensive contact with an angry, aggressive older sibling increase the likelihood that an infant will develop similar behavior? One implication of older sibling influence on infant development, through both modeling and condition setting, is that behavior that has a certain origin for an older child may have an entirely different origin for a younger child.

CONCLUSION

As this chapter reflects, research delineating the subtle processes of early emotion regulation and research documenting the complexity of family systems have largely proceeded independently. One emerging research frontier exists at the interface of these two areas. How are the regulatory influences of multiple social partners integrated in an infant's emerging construction of social and subjective reality? How do we properly conceptualize both the dyadic and systemic nature of family relationships? What developmental and contextual factors influence

the salience of different relationships or different levels of family process at particular points during the first 3 years of life? The questions become particularly pressing in relation to families with negative, dysregulated patterns of interaction and caregiving, especially where conflicting patterns of regulation may be experienced during early development. These complex questions are now motivating new analytic approaches and new conceptual frameworks (Hinde, 1989), with substantial progress on these questions likely to be evident in succeeding editions of this handbook.

REFERENCES

Ainsworth, M. D. S. (1967). *Infancy in Uganda: Infant care and the growth of love.* Baltimore: Johns Hopkins University Press.

Belsky, J., Gilstrap, B., & Rovine, M. (1984). The Pennsylvania Infant and Family Development Project I: Stability and change in mother–infant and father–infant interaction in a family setting at one, three, and nine months. *Child Development, 55,* 692–705.

Belsky, J., & Pensky, E. (1988). Marital change across the transition to parenthood. *Marriage and Family Review, 12,* 133–156.

Belsky, J., & Rovine, M. J. (1988). Nonmaternal care in the first year of life and the security of infant–parent attachment. *Child Development, 59,* 157–167.

Belsky, J., Youngblade, L., Rovine, M. J., & Volling, B. (1989). *Patterns of marital change and parent–child interaction.* Paper presented at the biennial meeting of the Society for Research in Child Development, Kansas City, MO.

Benn, R., & Saltz, E. (1989). The effect of grandmother support on teen parenting and infant attachment patterns within the family. In N. Radin (Chair), *Teen mothers: Their fathers, their mothers, their boyfriends and their babies.* Symposium presented at the biennial meeting of the Society for Research in Child Development, Kansas City, MO.

Bronfenbrenner, U. (1979). *The ecology of human development.* Cambridge, MA: Harvard University Press.

Burton, L. (1985). *Early and on-time grandmotherhood in multigeneration black families.* Unpublished doctoral dissertation, University of Southern California.

Burton, L. (1989). *Black grandmothers as a family resource: Perspectives on social service needs.* Paper presented at the National Conference on Mental Health and Aging, University of California at Los Angeles.

Burton, L. (1990). Teenage childbearing as an alternative life-course strategy in multigenerational black families. *Human Nature, 2,* 123–143.

Burton, L., & Dilworth-Anderson, P. (1991). The intergenerational family roles of aged black Americans. *Marriage and Family Review, 16,* 311–330.

Caplan, P. (1989). *Don't blame mother: Mending the mother–daughter relationship.* New York: Harper & Row.

Clarke-Stewart, K. A. (1978). And daddy makes three: The

father's impact on mother and young child. *Child Development, 49,* 466-478.

Cobb, S. (1976). Social support as a moderator of life stress. *Psychosomatic Medicine, 38*(5), 300–314.

Crnic, K. A., Greenberg, M. T., Ragozin, A. A., Robinson, N. M., & Basham, R. B. (1983). Effects of stress and social support on mothers and premature and full-term infants. *Child Development, 54,* 209–217.

Crockenberg, S. (1981). Infant irritability, mother responsiveness, and social influences on the security of infant–mother attachment. *Child Development, 52,* 857–865.

Crockenberg, S. (1986). Professional support for adolescent mothers: Who gives it, how adolescent mothers evaluate it, what they would prefer. *Infant Mental Health Journal, 7*(1), 49–58.

Crockenberg, S. (1987a). Predictors and correlates of anger toward and punitive control of toddlers by adolescent mothers. *Child Development, 58,* 964–975.

Crockenberg, S. (1987b). Support for adolescent mothers during the postnatal period: Theory and research. In C. F. Zachariah Boukydis (Ed.), *Research on support for parents and infants in the postnatal period* (pp. 3–24). Norwood, NJ: Ablex.

Crockenberg, S. (1988a). Social support and parenting. In H. Fitzgerald, B. Lester, & M. Yogman (Eds.), *Theory and research in behavioral pediatrics* (pp. 141–174). New York: Plenum Press.

Crockenberg, S. (1988b). English teenage mothers: Attitudes, behavior and social support. In E. J. Anthony, C. Koupernik, & C. Chiland (Eds.), *The child in his family: Vol. 8. Perilous development: Child raising and identity formation under stress* (pp. 93–103). New York: Wiley.

Crockenberg, S., & Covey, S. L. (1991). Marital conflict and externalizing behavior in children. In D. Cicchetti (Ed.), *Rochester Symposium on Developmental Psychopathology: Vol. 3. Research and clinical contributions to a theory of developmental psychopathology* (pp. 235–260). Rochester, NY: University of Rochester Press.

Cummings, E. M., Zahn-Waxler, C., & Radke-Yarrow, M. (1981). Young children's responses to expressions of anger and affection by others in the family. *Child Development, 52,* 1274–1282.

Dean, A., & Lin, N. (1977). The stress-buffering role of social support. *Journal of Nervous and Mental Disease, 165*(6), 403–417.

Dickie, J. R., & Matheson, P. (1984). *Mother–father–infant: Who needs support?* Paper presented at the meeting of the American Psychological Association, Toronto.

Dickstein, S., & Parke, R. D. (1988). Social referencing: A glance at fathers and marriage. *Child Development, 59,* 506–511.

Dunn, J. (1983). Sibling relationships in early childhood. *Child Development, 54,* 787–811.

Dunn, J., & Kendrick, C. (1982). *Siblings: Love, envy and understanding.* Cambridge, MA: Harvard University Press.

Durrett, M. E., Otaki, M., & Richards, P. (1984). Attachment and the mother's perception of support from the father. *International Journal of Behavioral Development, 7,* 167–176.

Easterbrooks, M. A., & Goldberg, W. A. (1990). Toddler-parent attachment: Relation to children's sociopersonality functioning during kindergarten. In M. T. Greenberg, D. Cicchetti, & E. M. Cummings (Eds.),

Attachment in the Preschool Years: Theory, research, and intervention (pp. 221–244). Chicago: University of Chicago Press.

Feinman, S., & Roberts, D. (1985, April). *Infant's interaction with grandparents, relatives, and adult friends of the family.* Paper presented at the biennial meeting of the Society for Research in Child Development, Toronto.

Feiring, C., & Taylor, J. (1982). *The influence of the infant and secondary parent on maternal behaviors.* Unpublished manuscript, Educational Testing Service.

Feldman, S. S., Biringen, Z. C., & Nash, S. C. (1981). Fluctuations of sex-related self-attributions as a function of stage of family life cycle. *Developmental Psychology, 17,* 24–35.

Feldman, S. S., & Nash, S. C. (1978). Interest in babies during young adulthood. *Child Development, 49,* 617–622.

Feldman, S. S., & Nash, S. C. (1979). Sex differences in responsiveness to babies among mature adults. *Developmental Psychology, 15,* 430–436.

Feldman, S. S., Nash, S. C., & Cutrona, C. (1977). The influence of age and sex on responsiveness to babies. *Developmental Psychology, 13,* 675–676.

Field, T. M. (1978). Interaction behaviors of primary versus secondary caretaker fathers. *Developmental Psychology, 14,* 183–185.

Fraiberg, S. (Ed.). (1980). *Clinical studies in infant mental health: The first year of life.* New York: Basic Books.

Gibbs, E. D., Teti, D. M., & Bond, L. A. (1987). Infant-sibling communication: Relationships to birth-spacing and cognitive and linguistic development. *Infant Behavior and Development, 10,* 307–323.

Goldberg, W. A., & Easterbrooks, M. A. (1984). The role of marital quality in toddler development. *Child Development, 20,* 504–515.

Gottman, J. (1979). *Marital interaction: Experimental investigations.* New York: Academic Press.

Grossman, F. K., Eichler, L. S., & Winickoff, S. A. (1980). *Pregnancy, birth, and parenthood.* San Francisco: Jossey-Bass.

Hazen, N., & Durrett, M. (1982). Relationship of security of attachment to exploration and cognitive mapping ability in two-year-olds. *Developmental Psychology, 18,* 751–759.

Heinicke, C. M., & Westheimer, I. J. (1966). *Brief separations.* New York: International Universities Press.

Hill, R. (1977). *Informal adoption among black families.* New York: National Urban League.

Hinde, R. A. (1989). Ethological and relationships approaches. In R. Vasta (Ed.), *Annals of Child Development* (Vol. 6, pp. 251–285). Greenwich, CT: JAI Press.

Howes, P. W., & Markman, H. J. (1989). Marital quality and child attachment: A longitudinal investigation. *Child Development, 60,* 1044–1051.

Hunter, F. T., McCarthy, M. E., MacTurk, R. H., & Vietze, P. M. (1987). Infants' social-constructive interactions with mothers and fathers. *Developmental Psychology, 23,* 249–254.

Jackson, J. J. (1971). Sex and social class variations in black aged parent–adult child relationships. *Aging Human Development, 2,* 96–107.

Klein, R. P. (1985). Caregiving arrangements by employed women with children under 1 year of age. *Developmental Psychology, 21,* 403–406.

Kotelchuck, M. (1976). The infant's relationship to the

father: Experimental evidence. In M. E. Lamb (Ed.), *The role of the father in child development* (pp. 329–344). New York: Wiley.

Lamb, M. E. (1977a). Father–infant and mother–infant interaction in the first year of life. *Child Development*, *48*, 167–181.

Lamb, M. E. (1977b). The development of mother–infant and father–infant attachments in the second year of life. *Developmental Psychology*, *13*, 639–649.

Lamb, M. E. (1979). Parental influences and the father's role: A personal perspective. *American Psychologist*, *34*, 938–943.

Lamb, M. E. (1982). *Nontraditional families: Parenting and child development.* Hillsdale, NJ: Erlbaum.

Lamb, M. E., & Elster, A. B. (1985). Adolescent mother–infant–father relationships. *Developmental Psychology*, *21*, 768–773.

Lawson, A., & Ingleby, J. D. (1974). Daily routines of preschool children: Effects of age, birth order, sex and social class, and developmental correlates. *Psychological Medicine*, *4*, 399–415.

Leiderman, P., & Leiderman, G. (1974). Familial influences on infant development in an East African agricultural community. In E. J. Anthony & C. Koupernik (Eds.), *The child in his family:* (Vol. 3, pp. 305–330). New York: Wiley.

Levitt, M. J., Weber, R. A., & Clark, M. C. (1986). Social network relationships as sources of maternal support and well-being. *Development Psychology*, *22*(3), 310–316.

Lewis, M. (1987). Social development in infancy and early childhood. In J. D. Osofsky (Ed.), *Handbook of infant development* (2nd ed., pp. 419–493). New York: Wiley.

Main, M., & Weston, D. R. (1981). The quality of the toddler's relationship to mother and to father: Related to conflict behavior and the readiness to establish new relationships. *Child Development*, *52*, 932–940.

Markman, H. J., & Clements, M. (1991). *Why fathers' prebirth negativity and a first-born daughter predict marital problems: Results from a ten year investigation.* Paper presented at the biennial meeting of the Society for Research in Child Development, Seattle.

Martin, E. P., & Martin, J. M. (1978). *The black extended family.* Chicago: University of Chicago Press.

Marvin, R., & Stewart, R. (1990). A family systems framework for the study of attachment. In M. T. Greenberg, D. Cicchetti, & E. M. Cummings (Eds.), *Attachment in the preschool years: Theory, research, and intervention* (pp. 51–86). Chicago: University of Chicago Press.

McGreal, C. E. (1985). *The grandparent–grandchild relationship during the neonatal period.* Paper presented at the biennial meeting of the Society for Research in Child Development, Toronto.

McGuire, J. (1982). Gender-specific differences in early childhood: The impact of the father. In N. Beail & J. McGuire (Eds.), *Fathers: Psychological Perspectives.* London: Junction Books.

Myers, B. J., Jarvis, P. A., & Creasey, G. L. (1987). Infants' behavior with their mothers and grandmothers. *Infant Behavior and Development*, *10*, 245–259.

Neugarten, B., & Weinstein, K. (1964). The changing American grandparent. *Journal of Marriage and the Family*, *26*, 197–205.

Ninio, A., & Rinott, N. (1988). Fathers' involvement in the care of their infants and their attributions of cogni-

tive competence to infants. *Child Development*, *59*, 652–663.

Nugent, J. K., Yogman, M., Lester, B., & Hoffman, J. (1988). The father's impact on infant development in the first critical year of life. In E. J. Anthony, C. Koupernik, & C. Chiland (Eds.), *The child in his family: Vol. 8. Perilous development: Child raising and identity formation under stress* (pp. 117–142). New York: Wiley.

Oppenheim, D., Sagi, A., & Lamb, M. (1988). Infant–adult attachments on the kibbutz and their relation to socioemotional development four years later. *Developmental Psychology*, *24*, 427–433.

Oyserman, D., Radin, N., & Saltz, E. (1991). *Determinants of nurturant parenting in teen mothers living at home.* Unpublished manuscript, University of Michigan.

Parke, R. D., & Tinsley, B. J. (1987). Family interaction in infancy. In J. D. Osofsky (Ed.), *Handbook of infant development* (2nd ed., pp. 579–641). New York: Wiley.

Parke, R. D., & Tinsley, B. J. (1988). The role of grandfathers in the context of the family. In P. Bronstein & C. P. Cowan (Eds.), *Fatherhood today: Men's changing role in the family* (pp. 236–250). New York: Wiley.

Pedersen, F. A. (1975, September). *Mother, father and infant interactive system.* Paper presented at the annual convention of the American Psychological Association, Chicago.

Pedersen, F. A., Anderson, B. T., & Cain, R. L. (1980). Parent–infant and husband–wife interactions observed at age five months. In F. A. Pedersen (Ed.), *The father–infant relationship* (pp. 71–86). New York: Praeger.

Pedersen, F. A., Suwalsky, J. T. D., Cain, R. L., Zaslow, M. J., & Rabinovich, B. A. (1987). Paternal care of infants during maternal separations: Associations with father–infant interaction at one year. *Psychiatry*, *50*, 193–205.

Pedersen, F. A., Yarrow, L. J., Anderson, B. J., & Cain, R. L. (1979). Conceptualization of father influences in the infancy period. In M. Lewis & L. A. Rosenblum (Eds.), *The child and its family* (pp. 45–66). New York: Plenum Press.

Pepler, D., Corter, C., & Abramovitch, R. (1982). Social relations among children: Siblings and peers. In K. Rubin & H. Ross (Eds.), *Peer relationships and social skills in childhood* (pp. 209–227). New York: Springer-Verlag.

Power, T. G., & Parke, R. D. (1983). Patterns of mother and father play with their 8 month old infant: A multiple analyses approach. *Infant Behavior and Development*, *6*, 453–459.

Quinton, D., & Rutter, M. (1985). Parenting behavior of mothers raised "in care." In R. Nicol (Ed.), *Longitudinal studies in child psychology and psychiatry* (pp. 157–201). Chichester, England: Wiley.

Radin, N., Oyserman, D., & Benn, R. (1989). *The influence of grandfathers on the young children of teen mothers.* Paper presented at the biennial meeting of the Society for Research in Child Development, Kansas City, MO.

Red Horse, J. C., Lewis, R., Feit, H., & Decker, M. (1978). Family behavior of urban American Indians. *Social Casework*, *59*, 67–72.

Richards, M. P. M., Dunn, J. F., & Antonis, B. (1977). Caretaking in the first year of life: The role of fathers' and mothers' social isolation. *Child: Care, Health and Development*, *3*, 23–26.

Russell, C. S. (1974). Transition to parenthood: Problems and gratifications. *Journal of Marriage and the Family, 36,* 294–301.

Rutter, M. (1985). Resilience in the face of adversity. *British Journal of Psychiatry, 147,* 598–611.

Samuels, H. R. (1980). The effect of an older sibling on infant locomotor exploration of a new environment. *Child Development, 51,* 607–609.

Schaffer, H. R., & Emerson, P. E. (1964). The development of social attachments in infancy. *Monographs of the Society for Research in Child Development, 29*(3, Serial No. 94).

Sena-Rivera, J. (1979). La familia Chicano. In E. Corfman (Ed.), *Families today* (Vol. 1, pp. 67–128). Washington, DC.: U.S. Government Printing Office.

Stewart, R. B. (1983). Sibling attachment relationships: Child–infant interactions in the Strange Situation. *Developmental Psychology, 19*(2), 192–199.

Teti, D. M., Bond, L. A., & Gibbs, E. D. (1986). Sibling-created experiences: Relationships to birth-spacing and infant cognitive development. *Infant Behavior and Development, 9,* 27–42.

Teti, D. M., Bond, L. A., & Gibbs, E. D. (1988). Mothers, fathers, and siblings: A comparison of play styles and their influence upon infant cognitive level. *International Journal of Behavioral Development, 11*(4), 415–432.

Tinsley, B. J., & Parke, R. D. (1984a). Fatherhood: Historical and contemporary perspectives. In K. McCluskey & H. Reese (Eds.), *Life span development: Historical and generational effects* (pp. 203–248). New York: Academic Press.

Tinsley, B. J., & Parke, R. D. (1984b). The contemporary impact of the extended family on the nuclear family: Grandparents as support and socialization agents. In M. Lewis (Ed.), *Beyond the dyad* (pp. 161–194). New York: Plenum Press.

Tinsley, B. J., & Parke, R. D. (1987). Grandparents as interactive and social support agents for families with young infants. *International Journal of Aging and Human Development, 25*(4), 259–277.

Vandell, D. L., & Wilson, K. S. (1987). Infants' interactions with mother, sibling, and peer: Contrasts and relations between interaction systems. *Child Development, 58,* 176–186.

Volling, B., & Belsky, J. (1985, April). *The interaction of marriage and parenting.* Paper presented at the biennial meetings of the Society for Research in Child Development, Toronto.

Werner, E. E. (1984). *Child care: Kith, kin, and hired hands.* Baltimore: University Park Press.

Werner, E. E., & Smith, R. S. (1982). *Vulnerable but invincible: A longitudinal study of resilient children and youth.* New York: McGraw-Hill.

Yogman, M. W. (1982). Development of the father–infant relationship. In H. Fitzgerald, B. Lester, & M. W. Yogman (Eds.), *Theory and research in behavioral pediatrics* (Vol. 1, pp. 221–279). New York: Plenum Press.

4

The Sociocultural Context of Infant Development

CYNTHIA T. GARCIA COLL
ELAINE C. MEYER

Infants are born into a social world, and their ultimate success in survival depends on their successful integration into a larger societal and cultural context. Most parents are interested in having their children acquire the necessary skills to become successful members of the society at large. Through the child-rearing process, parents transmit the rights and wrongs of the society, and other knowledge they consider to be important for their children. This process begins at birth and is transmitted through a family system that is imbedded in a larger societal and cultural context. Parents are influenced by their own developmental histories, as well as by past and present cultural influences. No two families are identical; however, within major societal and cultural systems, families tend to be more similar than different. That is to say, cultural systems provide various family environments that are considered within normative parameters (LeVine, 1977). Where a family falls within this normative range may be conceptualized as a function of the family members' past developmental histories; the present family dynamics; and extrafamilial social, economic, and cultural pressures.

The purpose of this chapter is to examine the impact of the sociocultural context of infants and families, and to postulate how these influences can affect infants' mental health. Several theoretical models are reviewed that incorporate the sociocultural context as one of many sources

of environmental influences to which parents and infants are subjected. In addition, several major generalizations are made from the empirical literature. The special situation of ethnic minorities in the United States is addressed, since their situation as "minority" groups permeates their sociocultural context. The clinical implications derived from this discussion address such basic concepts as the definition of mental health problems, attributions regarding infant mental health problems, expectations for appropriate interventions, and responsibility for implementation of these interventions.

THEORETICAL MODELS

Several theoretical models have been postulated that are useful in understanding the sociocultural context of infants and their caregiving environments. Whiting (1977) developed one of the first social-anthropological models that can provide a framework for infant development. Within this framework, physical environment and historical circumstances are seen as determinants of a society's maintenance systems, which include the social structure, economy, and household type. These maintenance systems, in conjunction with historically shaped value systems, influence the number and identity of caregivers, feeding schedules, children's tasks, techniques of discipline, and other aspects of the

56

children's environment (Super, 1981). Whiting's work led the way to the conceptualization of infant caregiving practices as a reflection of the overall cultural milieu.

LeVine (1977) has provided another useful theoretical framework within which to understand the development of caregiving environments in different cultures. He posits that child-rearing techniques depend to some extent on the nature of the instrumental competencies that adults are expected to master in a given population. Adults, consciously or unconsciously, try to inculcate through various child-rearing techniques the cognitive, linguistic, motivational, and social competencies that are considered relevant to their cultural milieu.

Another important notion introduced by LeVine is that a universal hierarchy of parental goals exists. These goals are as follows:

1. The physical survival and health of the child.
2. The development of the child's behavioral capacity for economic self-maintenance in maturity.
3. The development of the child's behavioral capacities for maximizing other cultural values (e.g., morality).

According to LeVine (1977), if the survival and health of the child are threatened (goal 1), these become the foremost concern of the parents, since achieving this goal is a prerequisite for attaining goals 2 and 3. There is also a rough developmental sequence implied in these goals. In all human populations, physical survival and health are of greatest concern during the first years of a child's life, whereas attention to the other two goals can be postponed until the child's survival seems assured. This framework suggests that cultures differing in the rate of infant mortality or economic resources (or in their perception of these) will hold different goals for their infants even at the earliest stages of development.

Two other prevalent models of human development emphasize the importance of the sociocultural context. Bronfenbrenner (1986) has provided the most detailed theoretical elaboration of how the ecological context influences a child's development. The child's environment is organized into settings that vary in the amount of direct contact with the child. Among the external systems affecting the family (and as a consequence the child), Bronfenbrenner (1986) discusses the mesosystem (other environments

where the child spends time, such as school or day care), the exosystem (other settings in which the parents live their lives, such as employment), and the chronosystem (changes and continuities over time in the environments in which a person is living, such as school entry or entering the labor force). Thus, the sociocultural context is operationalized in terms of settings and the interrelations among these settings.

In the latest version of the transactional model, Sameroff and Fiese (1990) introduce the notion of "cultural code" as "the complex of characteristics that organize a society's child-rearing system, incorporating elements of socialization and education" (p. 34). Developmental outcome is viewed as the product of the cultural, family, and individual (members') codes. Macroregulations (or the cultural "developmental agenda") are the model forms of regulations operating in the cultural code. Areas in which cultural influences are expected, or where the environment is structured to provide different experiences to the child in different cultures, include age of weaning, toilet training, schooling, initiation rites, and marriage.

In sum, several theoretical models postulate mechanisms by which the sociocultural context influences the family, their child-rearing techniques, and their developmental goals and value systems. Because the family is the primary mediator of environmental influences on the infant, the family world view is an important consideration for any mental health professional.

EMPIRICAL EVIDENCE

It is beyond the scope of this chapter to present a comprehensive review of the literature on the sociocultural influences on infant development (for comprehensive chapters and reviews, see Leiderman, Tulkin, & Rosenfeld, 1977; Nugent, Lester, & Brazelton, 1989; Triandis & Heron, 1981; Wagner & Stevenson, 1982). However, various basic generalizations can be made from this literature that are relevant for understanding infant mental health (see Garcia Coll, 1992).

1. Regardless of the child-rearing technique under examination, most patterns of behaviors displayed by parents around the world are thought by those parents to be for the benefit of their children. For example, North American society values freedom of action. As an illustration of how this value is translated in early

infancy, we now consider playpens as restrictive and unnecessary for early motor and exploratory behavior. Our belief is that by allowing children to explore, we stimulate them and create a "better" environment for them to develop in. A contrasting view is provided by a mother from the Peruvian highlands. When asked about the reasons for keeping infants and toddlers tied up and swaddled on cradleboards until the age of 18–24 months (a custom, by the way, that is still observed among some Native American groups in the United States, but that would be considered unacceptable within the mainstream culture), the mother explained that the main reason was that it made the children stronger. Thus, boys were kept on cradleboards longer than girls, in preparation for the harder work that boys would be expected to do in the fields. It is interesting to consider the psychological consequences of being strapped and unable to move for the first 18–24 months of one's life, and to wonder how a tradition like this might contribute to the passivity and humility that characterize these children and adults. Among parents in different parts of Africa, LeVine (1977) also describes the practices of mothers' carrying toddlers on their backs and restricting the mobility of children who can walk as adaptive responses to and recognitions of the hazards of cooking fires to small children. Thus, we conclude from the literature that even opposite child-rearing techniques can be thought by the parents to be beneficial (and sometimes even to provide the same benefits) for the children.

2. Another set of conclusions that we can derive from the extant literature is that in spite of wide variations in child-rearing techniques around the world, most human beings show remarkable consistency in some areas of development. As an example, even if we speak different languages or differ in our reliance on verbal or nonverbal cues, most human beings ultimately learn to communicate effectively in their immediate surroundings. The rate of language acquisition may differ; the content or mode of communication may vary; but the great majority of children learn to speak or become competent communicators. The same can be said about basic cognitive, intellectual, and social skills. From the literature on the development of attachments, we have learned that most infants, even if exposed to multiple caregivers, form primary attachments, and that the quality of these attachments is predictive of the quality of the interactions between the children

and other adults and peers (see Bretherton & Waters, 1985). However, what may differ from one culture to another is how affection is expressed, how growth is fostered within the relationship(s), or how much separation versus enmeshment is valued. For example, if the ideal for adult relationships is relative enmeshment (or relative lack of ego boundaries), such as that described for Puerto Rican families by Canino and Canino (1980), we would expect that the attachment and separation processes would foster interpersonal dependency (rather than autonomy) in these children and their families.

3. The literature also suggests that some aspects of development vary in timing, content, or expression in different cultures. Some aspects of human development seem more susceptible to environmental influences than others, and some are actually specific to some cultural contexts and not to others. There are numerous examples of so-called "cognitive skills" that are present in some cultures and not others (see Wagner & Stevenson, 1982). Memory or conservation skills are very much a function of the stimuli used to be tested. Similarly, abstract reasoning or hypothetical–deductive thinking seems to be more prevalent in some societies than in others (e.g., Dasen & Heron, 1981).

Another example comes from the literature on the definition of the self. Numerous studies have documented how cultures vary in their emphasis on autonomy and individualism versus interdependence and collectivity (Brinton Lykes, 1985). It has been suggested that Western civilizations emphasize the self as autonomous and individual, whereas other cultures emphasize the collectivity, often to the point of dissolution of any notion of individuality (Shweder & Bourne, 1984). Scholars working with very diverse cultures (e.g., Puerto Rico, Japan, India) have all come to similar conclusions of the prevalence of a collective sense of self; terms as "symbiotic reciprocity," "sociocentric–organic organization," and "normal enmeshment" have been used to describe the normative relational developmental processes observed in these cultures (Canino & Canino, 1980; Shweder & Bourne, 1984; Roland, 1987).

Child-rearing practices will mediate the learning or acquisition of these modes of social interaction. For fostering the development of a more collectivist sense of self (in contrast to a more individualistic sense of self), immediate, all-gratifying mothering of the child is continued far beyond what theorists such as Mahler

(Mahler, Pine, & Bergman, 1975), would consider optimal for normal development (Roland, 1987). This parenting style is accompanied by greater physical closeness (frequently being carried, closer sleeping arrangements), less sensitivity to the child's individual needs and feelings, and discouragement to a much greater extent of separation and individualization. The collectivity is emphasized by the presence of multiple caregivers or significant others, who may include grandmothers, aunts, older siblings or cousins. Members of the extended family are an integral part of the collectivity where the child grows up, as well as an integral part of the adults' social life.

4. A final conclusion from the literature is that gender differences seem to be universal. Boys and girls tend to be treated, responded to, and socialized differently; their developmental pathways differ in some areas; and the status of adult women in most societies differs from that of men. Pioneer work by Beatrice and John Whiting (1975) described similar sex differences in children across six quite diverse cultures, including New England, Africa, Mexico, India, and the South Pacific:

> Girls are more intimate-dependent (touched and sought help) than boys, but these differences are significant only in the 3–6 age group; girls are also more nurturing, significantly so at 7 to 11 years of age (they helped and offered support); boys tend to be more dominant–dependent and are significantly more aggressive. These findings are remarkably consistent in all six societies. (pp. 147–148)

Gender differences in behavior from birth have been documented in a variety of cultures (Horowitz et al., 1977; Leijon & Finnstrom, 1981; Fricker, Hindermann, & Bruppacher, 1989). But more important than actual sex differences in behavior may be the caregivers' interpretations of an infant's behavior, development, and needs as a function of the infant's gender. The more sex-stereotyped the adult roles are in a society, the stronger the gender differences in child-rearing practices that we should expect.

ETHNIC GROUPS IN THE UNITED STATES

It is much easier to appreciate the impact of cultural diversity on human development when we talk about cultures and countries other than the United States. It seems much harder to understand, accept, incorporate, or even tolerate cultural diversity at home (Garcia Coll, 1992). Child-rearing practices that might be seen as interesting in another culture may seem intolerable when practiced in our neighborhood. The complex interaction between social class and culture comes into play when we react to differences in child-rearing patterns and expectation in ethnic groups in the United States.

Developmental processes for so-called "minority" or "ethnic" groups in the United States are influenced not only by cultural beliefs and caregiving practices, but by other important influences as well. Developmental goals, instrumental competencies, and child-rearing techniques are different in these groups (Ogbu, 1981), and these differences are important enough to be clearly recognized. There are studies documenting that from the infancy of offspring, parental beliefs, goals, and behavior differ between minority and Anglo families in the United States (see Garcia Coll, 1990, for a review).

As the word "minority" implies, these groups occupy different resource environments, which affect other sources of influence in their development (Ogbu, 1981). Most members of minority groups in the United States have lower socioeconomic status than the population at large, with some few exceptions (e.g., Cuban-Americans and some subgroups of Asian-Americans). Unemployment and lower educational attainment are more prevalent among such minority populations as Native Americans, African-Americans, and Hispanics (U.S. Senate Select Committee on Indian Affairs, 1985; National Commission on Children, 1990). From conception, minority individuals are directly or indirectly exposed to a host of problems associated with socioeconomic disadvantage, including differential access to medical care, residential segregation, substandard housing, and unemployment or underemployment. As a result, these individuals may experience poor health (mental as well as physical), loss of civil rights, prejudice, discrimination, and poor self-image (LeMasters, 1970). For example, there is a striking difference in health status between many minority populations and the Caucasian population throughout the lifespan (U.S. Department of Health and Human Services, 1986). These problems are compounded by the underutilization of health services, especially general preventive care, because of socioeconomic, linguistic, and cultural barriers (Anderson, Giachello, & Aday, 1986; Boyce et al., 1986; Chavez, Cornelius, & Jones, 1986).

The family contexts of minority infants are different as well; they tend to be characterized by younger mothers, a higher percentage of single mothers, and large extended families. Studies have also shown that although a high percentage of African-American families are single-parent households (U.S. Bureau of the Census, 1990), kin residence sharing has long been acknowledged as characteristic of the African-American family (Gutman, 1976; Martin & Martin, 1978; Staples & Miranda, 1980). Despite these observations, however, there is a paucity of research concerning the impact of kinship on child rearing, parent–child interaction, or developmental processes throughout the lifespan (Wilson, 1984). Nevertheless, if we recognize that these minority and ethnic families experience different cultural expectations, family constellations, and access to economic and social resources, in addition to being subjected to prejudice, racism, classism, sexism, and segregation, we would expect that their world view and their infants' developmental outcome would be profoundly affected by these life experiences.

CLINICAL IMPLICATIONS

Increasingly, mental health clinicians will be called upon to serve infants and their families from these diverse cultural backgrounds. It is estimated that by the year 2000, minority children will account for nearly one-third of all children in the United States (National Commission on Children, 1990). The growth of Hispanic and Asian populations in the United States has been especially rapid as a result of higher birth rates, a greater number of women of child-bearing age within these groups, and the continued influx of documented and undocumented immigrants.

Beyond the growing numbers of minority infants and their families, the implementation of Public Law 99-457, which mandates services for developmentally delayed and at-risk infants and children from birth to 3 years of age, represents a legal imperative to serve many minority infants and their families. The law embraces a family-focused approach to early intervention services rather than a child-focused approach, thus requiring consideration of the sociocultural context of the family in assessment and inter-vention. Specifically, the Individualized Family Service Plan (IFSP) must include, in addition to goals and services for the child, a statement of family needs and strengths, goals and services for the family, and case management services designed to help families gain access to services across multiple agencies. Clearly, the sociocultural characteristics of the family figure prominently in the successful planning and implementation of early intervention services.

Both theoretical models and empirical evidence provided by studies conducted with various culturally diverse populations suggest the need to address the relevance of sociocultural aspects of care. Sociocultural characteristics of infants and their families determine, in part, what issues will be viewed as problems warranting intervention and what kinds of clinical interventions will be acceptable. Sociocultural factors can also mediate the effectiveness of various clinical interventions. As a result of these increasing demands, there is growing awareness among clinicians that assessments and interventions need to be both culturally sensitive and culturally relevant.

Currently, there is a strong emphasis on the importance of integrating of sociocultural aspects of family life into service delivery. Earlier perspectives, which viewed minority cultures as deviant rather than different (the "cultural deviant" perspective) or viewed majority and minority cultures as nondistinct from each other (the "cultural equivalent" perspective), have been gradually replaced by the "cultural variant" perspective (Thomas, 1992). The cultural variant perspective recognizes and preserves cultural diversity; with respect to clinical service delivery, it sanctions and promotes culturally sensitive and culturally relevant intervention strategies.

In striving to develop culturally sensitive and relevant interventions that meet any given family's needs, it is important to assess the family's adjustment to migration and degree of acculturation to the dominant culture, and to integrate the findings into treatment plans. Arredondo-Dowd (1981) and Espin (1987) have provided frameworks for assessing the impact of migration and acculturation on the individual and family system. The culturally competent clinician refrains from making cultural assumptions, even though they may be well-intentioned, without direct assessment of the family's degree of acculturation (Cohen, 1972; Cuellar, Harris, & Jasso, 1980; Thomas, 1992).

"Acculturation" may be conceptualized as a process of learning about a new culture, and deciding what is to be saved or sacrificed from the old culture (Lin, Masuda, & Tazuma, 1982). Acculturation and adaptation to a new culture may include several stages: initial joy, relief, and idealization of the new culture; disillusionment associated with adjustment; and gradual acceptance of the good and bad aspects of the new culture (Arredondo-Dowd, 1981). Research and instrument development in the area of acculturation have progressed from the use of single indicators (e.g., language or number of years in the country) to include multiple sociocultural characteristics, such as nationality, occupational status, attitudes, personal identity, food and activity preferences, and social group preferences (Cuellar et al., 1980). The degree of acculturation occurs on a continuum in which a family's ethnic identity ranges from, for example, very Mexican to bicultural to very Anglicized.

Szapocznik and colleagues (Szapocznik, Kurtines, & Fernandez, 1980; Szapocznik et al., 1986) have elaborated on the process of acculturation and its impact on psychological well-being. They propose that in order to minimize the detrimental efforts of adaptation to a new culture, individuals must strive to become *bicultural*. In their framework, the traditional view of acculturation as adoption of the host culture and rejection of the culture of origin leads to psychosocial maladjustment. Szapocznik and colleagues assert that it is not adaptive to discard those skills that effectively allow individuals to interact with the culture of origin, such as language or relationship style:

> Effective adjustment requires an acceptance of both worlds as well as skills to live amongst and interact with both cultural groups. Bicultural individuals must be aware of these differences and need to develop the flexibility to implement different survival skills according to the cultural context in which they function. (Szapocznik et al., 1980, pp. 3–4)

The role of the clinician is to facilitate an effective bicultural adjustment not only for the individual, but for all family members, in order to reduce intergenerational–intercultural conflict. In devising culturally sensitive intervention plans for infants and children, it is important to assess and to integrate the degree of acculturation of their primary caregivers and extended families.

In the interest of fostering culturally sensitive assessment and intervention strategies, clinicians are also encouraged to consider the following fundamental questions from each family's perspective: Is there a problem that requires intervention? Why is there a problem? What can be done? Who can help with the problem? Exploration of these questions can elucidate the family's sociocultural perspective about the need for clinical intervention and expectations for services. Early exploration of these issues helps to set the stage for culturally sensitive work, establishes the clinician as someone who is interested in the family perspective, and fosters the therapeutic working relationship.

Is There A Problem?

One basic issue is the definition of a developmental or socioemotional problem in infancy. As mental health clinicians, we have certain preconceived standards about what constitute normative processes for infant development, parent–infant relationships, child-rearing practices, and parenting abilities. In general, the normative parameters that clinicians utilize to identify problems reflect the dominant Anglo culture. To put it another way, the yardstick by which we measure and identify problems is largely majority-culture-bound.

The tradition of such comparative paradigms, in which minority children and their families are compared to children belonging to the dominant culture, has had serious shortcomings and consequences. At issue most often has been the invidiousness of interpreting differences as deficits, and of utilizing instruments normed on Anglo children to assess the development of minority children (Myers, Rana, & Harris, 1979; Washington & McLoyd, 1982). This approach has contributed to misidentification of children and their relative strengths and weaknesses, and has resulted in some misguided early intervention efforts. In addition, such comparative paradigms have hindered the development of meaningful, culturally anchored assessment and intervention approaches (McLoyd, 1990).

Thus, it is important to begin the clinical relationship by establishing whether the family perceives a problem, as well as determining the circumstances surrounding the referral. To what degree do the clinician and family agree on the nature and scope of the problem? It is possible that clinicians may identify a problem requiring intervention, but that parents, according to their world view and sociocultural context, may not perceive the same phenomena as a problem. For example, the use of physical punishment may be an integral part of child care practices in some cultures; however, it is not acceptable in the dominant culture and, according to child protective legislation, warrants intervention. Or it may be that parents do perceive there is a problem, but they may not agree regarding the severity of the problem or the need for immediate intervention. In contrast, the parents may identify concerns that they believe are worthy of intervention but that are not viewed as problematic or worthy of intervention by clinicians. Parents from diverse cultures vary widely in their views regarding the kind of problems that warrant seeking intervention, views on what it means to acknowledge the need for help (e.g., failure, punishment), ways in which getting help is initiated, and previous experiences with health care providers and authority figures.

To address the issue of whether a problem exists, thorough assessment is essential. It is crucial to ask the primary caregiver(s) (in some cases, not only the mother) about their perspectives of how the infant is doing across several developmental areas, including the area of concern to the clinician. Especially when multiple caregivers are involved, the clinician should encourage the family to decide who should be present for the assessment (e.g., grandmother, church member), rather than assuming that the parents (or only the mother) should be the only members in attendance. Clinicians also need to be respectful of the hierarchical structure of the family, and to address questions and facilitate decision making accordingly. For example, in many Asian cultures the father is appointed family spokesperson, even though he may not be the one who knows the most about the infant's presenting problems. It is important for the clinician to convey the message that he or she is genuinely interested in listening to and understanding the family's perspective, with an appreciation of the role that culture may play. The assessment serves as a forum not only for gathering concrete descriptions about behavior and observing parent–child interactions, but also for learning about the family's perspectives about the reasons for referral. Thus, the assessment process becomes a dialogue in which the clinician may begin where the family is, rather than making preliminary assumptions.

To illustrate the process, here is an example. A young black inner-city mother reluctantly brought her 14-month-old son to a mental health clinic following a warning from his day care center. She feared that he would no longer be able to attend his day care center, as the staff described him as "overactive" and "aggressive" with other children. From the mother's perspective, her son's energy and ability to "stand up for himself" were positive attributes, which she felt would serve him well in "the real world." She shared her frustration over what she viewed as the staff's negative appraisal of her son and her parenting abilities. When given the opportunity, she described her commitment to her son's best interests, and her worries about raising him in an unsafe environment. The clinician acknowledged the mother's perspective and affirmed her capacity to parent her son and to make decisions in his behalf. The clinician joined the mother in the common goal of wanting the best for her son, including a stable, supportive day care setting as well as opportunities to learn how to survive in the real world. Intervention efforts included basic child behavior management strategies that enabled him to "succeed" in the day care setting without "breaking his spirit"; dialogue between the mother and the day care staff; and affirmation of the mother's parenting goal to nurture her son's judgment, in order to ensure his safety and survival.

Why Is There A Problem?

Aside from recognition of a problem, the family and clinician may differ regarding the attributions or explanations for why the problem occurred. Families adhere to different conceptions of how infant developmental outcome is determined and the degree to which outcome may be modified (Gutierrez, Sameroff, & Karrer, 1988). Variance in the expected infant developmental trajectory, uneven development, or delayed development may be understood differently by families of various sociocultural backgrounds. This question gets at a family's search for meaning of why an infant is not developing as expected—a search that is typically influenced by the family's sociocultural and religious characteristics. Indeed, when a family is faced with the stress inherent in grappling with why a problem has occurred, turning to familiar cultural and religious roots may provide some comfort and order out of chaos (Comoroff & McGuire, 1981).

There are, of course, many different attributions and explanations that families may base in part upon their sociocultural backgrounds.

There may be minimal contemplation about an infant's problem, with the belief that it is due to fate or God's will. In this case, there may be little additional questioning or action on the part of the family. Other families may actively express concern and seek information as a means to regain control, to understand the problem, and to cope with the problem. Some families may interpret the problem as a form of punishment or retribution for wrongdoing that they or their ancestors may have committed. The problem may also be understood in the context of various cultural folk beliefs. For example, people from Puerto Rico may attribute an infant's respiratory infection to fluctuations in body temperature, referred to as "hot and cold," with little integration of the prevailing biological models of disease (Poma, 1983). In still other situations, an infant's problem might be viewed as one that is meant to challenge the family members, or to test their religious faith or courage. Clearly, the family's interpretation of why the infant has the problem bears directly on what will be considered an appropriate intervention. If the clinician fails to incorporate these aspects into care, the family is likely to decline or resist treatment.

It is imperative that the clinician assess the family's explanatory model of why the problem is occurring, as a means of enhancing communication, facilitating rapport, designing socioculturally compatible treatment plans, and reducing the likelihood of family–clinician conflict (Kleinman, Eisenberg, & Good, 1978; Korbin & Johnston, 1982). As has been elucidated by medical anthropological and cross-cultural research, it is important to recognize that clinician–family interactions are transactions between explanatory models. In some cases, these transactions may involve major discrepancies in cognitive content, therapeutic values, expectations, and goals (Freidson, 1961; King, 1962; Kleinman, 1977). In the interest of delivering culturally sensitive and relevant care to infants and young children, clinicians must not assume that their explanatory model is the same as, or even compatible with, that of the families they see. Importantly, clinicians also need to recognize the variability within various cultural groups and the degree of acculturation endorsed by families, in order to further refine their clinical service delivery (Cohen, 1972; Cuellar et al., 1980; Rogler, Malgady, Costantino, & Blumenthal, 1987).

Kleinman et al. (1978) offer useful clinical strategies to elicit a medical client's explanatory model of illness. Several of the assessment questions they propose are easily adapted for use with families and their infants and young children who present with socioemotional, behavioral, or developmental problems. The questions may be adapted as follows:

1. What do you think has caused your child's problem?
2. Why do you think it started when it did?
3. What do you think the problem does to your child? How does it work?
4. How severe is your child's problem? Do you expect that it will have a short- or long-term course?
5. What kind of treatment do you think your child should receive?
6. What are the most important results that you hope to have your child receive from treatment?
7. What are the main things that the problem has caused for you and your child?
8. What do you fear most about your child's problem?

Such questions enable the family members to share their perspective on the problem and how it affects the family system, while informing the clinician about the family's expectations for treatment and outcome. Devoting time to understanding important sociocultural aspects early in the clinical process is time well spent, because mismatches between the clinician and family regarding problem definition and causation can derail even the best-intended clinical interventions. It should be noted that this approach is consistent with the spirit of current early intervention legislation and with the principles of family-centered care (Shelton, Jeppson, & Johnson, 1987). Family-centered care recognizes the family as the constant in the child's life; incorporates family strengths and individuality; respects different methods of coping; and honors the racial, ethnic, cultural, and socioeconomic diversity of families (National Center for Family-Centered Care, 1990).

What Can Be Done?

Even if the family agrees that there is a problem and that intervention is appropriate, underlying cultural assumptions about the nature of the problem and expectations for change may influence the family's expectations regarding the course of action to be taken. For example, in a case of hyperactivity, colic, or sleep problems, some families may expect the clinician to prescribe medication to remedy the problem. Just as it is important for the clinician to take time to understand the family's perspective on why the problem occurred, it is equally important to explore the family's perspective on what kinds of interventions would be appropriate. This includes discussion about any actions the family may have already taken prior to referral; the ideas and opinions of various extended family members about what should be done; the degree to which parents and other family members believe the problem is amenable to treatment; their own motivation to address the problem; and the expectations for treatment effectiveness. This process can facilitate the development of individualized, culturally relevant treatment approaches that are more likely to be successful.

Although it behooves the clinician to understand the general cultural assumptions and characteristics of different minority populations as a group, adequate care must be taken to appreciate the variability within different groups. A general understanding of a given minority population can equip the clinician to select and offer treatments that are theoretically better suited to the culture (Inclan & Hernandez, 1992). However, issues related to the family's degree of acculturation and individual needs must also be reflected in treatment planning. These issues are well addressed in an article by Rogler et al. (1987) exploring the planning and delivery of culturally sensitive mental health services with the Hispanic population.

Cuento therapy, or folktale therapy, serves as an illustration of how mental health service delivery may be culturally adapted for children (Costantino, Malgady, & Rogler, 1985; Rogler et al., 1987). *Cuento* therapy incorporates the traditional Puerto Rican medium of telling folktales that serves to transmit cultural values, to foster pride in Puerto Rican heritage, and to reinforce adaptive behavior. The folktales have been adapted to convey the knowledge, values, and skills useful in coping with the demands of being raised in inner-city neighborhoods. The medium of telling folktales to address problems of childhood may represent a more culturally familiar and acceptable treatment approach for serving Puerto Rican children and their families.

Treatment approaches that are typically available for infants and young children and their families may or may not be acceptable to, or deemed appropriate by, various culturally diverse populations. Discussion of child and family problems with a mental health professional who is outside of the family system may be considered inappropriate, or possibly something to be avoided. In many Asian cultures, for example, the need to seek intervention services carries with it considerable reluctance and may engender a sense of shame, loss of respect, and failure on the part of the parents (Cleveland, 1983).

Recommendations for play therapy, or for working with parents to facilitate parent–infant play interactions, may similarly be regarded as inappropriate by some cultural groups. Whereas middle-class North American mothers consider it part of their role to play with their children, mothers from other cultures may laugh with embarrassment at the idea of playing with their children or being their children's conversational partners, because these are the roles relegated traditionally to siblings, other children, and occasionally grandparents (Rogoff, 1990). Similarly, recommendations in which parents are encouraged to teach their children certain skills may also be differentially acceptable to families, in part because of their perceptions about the role of parents as teachers (Laosa, 1978). In a study examining the relative importance of parental roles among different ethnic groups, Asian-American parents placed a very high emphasis on their role as teachers to their children (Steward & Steward, 1973). Thus, in designing intervention plans, it is culturally congruent to include some opportunities for parental teaching among the recommendations for some groups, but not for others.

Who Can Help with the Problem?

Families from culturally diverse backgrounds may vary regarding who should implement the intervention, and what the role of the clinician should be. Some families may expect the clinician to provide treatment directly, rather than directing or coordinating treatment. The concept of case management in early intervention, and the involvement of multiple health care providers from various disciplines, may be unfamiliar and overwhelming to families. Several issues are implicit in the "Who can help?" question, including parental and professional role expectations, accountability, entrustment of care for the child, and confidentiality.

Intervention plans that assign specific intervention responsibilities to parents, or that require modification of typical family routines, may not be what families generally expect from treatment. Specifically, following through on recommendations, such as daily physical therapy exercises, may be viewed as optional and not critical to the parental role. For instance, as noted above, how parents conceptualize themselves as teachers varies as a function of cultural background (Steward & Steward, 1973), and influences whether and to what degree parents will support these aspects of the intervention plan. Thus, the development of culturally relevant treatment approaches requires consideration of what roles are familiar and acceptable to parents; how intervention strategies may be reasonably shared between family members and clinicians; what the expectations are regarding the responsibility for implementation; and how the family is socialized to the therapeutic process. In the interest of developing workable intervention plans, the clinician needs to balance the family's sociocultural expectations for treatment and its resources with the realities of service delivery possibilities.

Families of diverse cultural backgrounds may also vary regarding available formal and informal social support networks, as well as persons who may be considered as possible resources to engage in intervention efforts. Assumptions need to be clarified regarding the traditional roles of mothers and fathers, and their availability and motivation to fulfill primary responsibility for intervention. For example, Thomas (1992) suggests the utility of assessing the father's role in child rearing as a continuous variable, rather than merely documenting his absence or presence. When multiple caregivers and authority figures are present in a family, there may be additional people who may be successfully integrated into intervention plans.

In some cases, it may be most effective to teach several family members the skills necessary to handle the special needs of the infant, while supporting the hierarchical structure embraced by the family. Clinicians are encouraged to collaborate with parents and other identified authority figures, not only to arrive at a mutual problem definition, but also to utilize available family resources and to assign intervention roles that fit with cultural expectations. In some cases, families turn to familiar cultural folk healers, elders, or religious leaders for advice and strategies to remedy problems with their infants and children. These members of the community may be enlisted by a family prior to involvement with the clinician, or in addition to the clinician's intervention efforts. The clinician is well advised to ask the family directly about other people and traditional approaches that the family considers relevant to addressing the child's problem and to understanding the family's perspective. Stafford (1978) suggests that when there is a strong family commitment to folk practices, clinicians will be most successful if they accept that belief and work with it, including the simultaneous use of traditional approaches with intervention efforts. These may include the use of herbal teas and remedies, massage, prayer, and consultation with culturally ordained authority figures and advisors. Rather than immediately discouraging these efforts, the clinician is encouraged to consider whether such efforts may result in potential benefits, may have no effect, or may pose dangers to the child. It is important to remember that family members initially employ these efforts because they have been culturally sanctioned, and because they have their child's best interests in mind. In many cases, these traditional approaches may be combined with standard practices for a culturally tailored intervention plan. However, if there is indication that the traditional aspects of care may be harmful to the child or incompatible with the recommended intervention efforts, the clinician must address these issues with the family.

Regarding the issue of "ethnic match" between family and clinician, Thomas (1992) points out that securing the best services is of primary interest to most families, with the clinician's specific ethnic background generally a less important factor. However, the issue of cultural mistrust—that is a lack of trust by members of minority groups in members of a dominant group—should also be considered. In general, studies with African-Americans (and more recently with Hispanics and Native Americans) have found cultural mistrust to explain high dropout rates from counseling with white clinicians, lower expectations for the counseling process, and lower performance on intelligence tests (Terrell & Terrell, 1981; Thompson, Neville, Weathers, Posten, & Atkinson, 1990; Watkins & Terrell, 1988). Thus, in determining whether an ethnic match between family and clinician would be preferable for any given family, it is important to assess the family's degree of trust toward members of the dominant culture, as well as the family's preference. It may also be possible that families would prefer a clinician from the dominant culture, depending upon their degree of acculturation, personal preference, and developmental agenda for their children. In any case, the clinician is well advised to explore these issues early, in order to develop treatment plans that will be acceptable to families.

IMPLICATIONS FOR MENTAL HEALTH CARE PROVIDERS

Although mental health clinicians may acknowledge the importance of integrating sociocultural aspects into care, the actual "how to" may present quite a challenge. Clinicians may be unsure of how sociocultural sensitivity should be translated into clinical care practices. Clinicians vary in the amount of formal coursework and training that they may have had to prepare them; the amount of emphasis their training has placed on the importance of sociocultural aspects of care; and opportunities to serve ethnically diverse populations. Perhaps the most important commitment clinicians can make is to "cultivate a culturally sensitive perspective" (Thomas, 1992). This commitment moves well beyond mere good intentions to deliver culturally sensitive care. It involves a willingness on the part of clinicians to explore their own cultural background, to recognize how it influences their view of the world, and to be able to take the perspectives of others who come from different cultural backgrounds.

Becoming a culturally competent clinician may be thought of as a developmental process in which there is always room for personal and professional growth (Cross, 1988). Thomas (1985) asserts:

Counselors need to begin with an honest self-appraisal of their own identity, their view of their own cultural group, their view of others of similar and different status, and their views of the dominant culture. They must ask themselves where do they fall in their own ethnic/racial identity, how they presently behave toward those who happen to be at various stages of development, and whether they are functioning in hindering or support[ive] ways. (p. 126)

Clinicians, and the institutions in which they practice, may respond to cultural differences along a continuum that ranges from cultural proficiency to cultural destructiveness. Basic cultural competence is characterized by an acceptance and respect for cultural differences; ongoing self-assessment regarding culture; vigilance toward the dynamics that result from cultural differences; continuous expansion of cultural knowledge and resources; and adaptations to service delivery in order to better meet the needs of minority populations (Cross, 1988). Thus, cultural competence may be thought of as a congruent set of behaviors, attitudes, and institutional policies that together enable the clinician to work effectively in cross-cultural contexts.

Various disciplines have recommended training prerequisites, and some disciplines have delineated professional competencies and practice guidelines, to better meet the needs of culturally diverse populations (American Psychological Association, 1991; Christensen, 1992). For example, a diverse group of early intervention professionals ranked multicultural competency training needs in the following order: gaining general understanding of specific cultures; child-rearing practices; family patterns; views of exceptionality; availability and use of community resources; linguistic differences; acknowledging one's own cultural and biases; belief about professionals; nonverbal communication styles; views of medical practices; sex roles; and religion (Christensen, 1992). As can be readily gleaned from this list, the process of becoming a culturally competent clinician requires didactic and experimental learning opportunities, in addition to personal exploration of one's own ethnic and cultural identity. The many aspects of understanding cultural diversity, and of being able to provide clinically sensitive and relevant services, require that clinicians think complexly, tolerate difference and ambiguity, and intervene creatively with minority populations.

The American Psychological Association (1991) has recently issued guidelines for providers of psychological services to ethnic, linguistic, and culturally diverse populations. In light of impressive evidence that the issues of culture and language do have an impact upon the utilization and provision of appropriate mental health services (Cheung & Snowden, 1990; Comas-Diaz & Griffith, 1988; Dauphinais, Dauphinais, & Rowe, 1981; Lorion, 1974; McGoldrick, Pearce, & Giordano, 1982; Snowden & Cheung, 1990; Everett, Proctor, & Cartmell, 1983), these guidelines prompt psychologists to follow several general principles. Among the guidelines are suggestions to consider the validity of instruments and procedures with given ethnic populations; to recognize ethnicity and culture as significant parameters in understanding psychological processes; to respect the ideas of family members and community structures, hierarchies, values, and beliefs within the culture; to respect the family's religion and/or spiritual beliefs and values, since these affect world view, psychosocial functioning, and expressions of distress; and to document culturally and sociopolitically relevant factors in the records (e.g., number of years in this country, change in social status as a result of coming to this country). Regarding language, it is recommended that psychologists interact in the language requested by their clients and, if this is not feasible, to make referrals if possible.

The culturally competent clinician thus adopts a framework of cultural diversity and recognizes the central role that sociocultural characteristics may play in the assessment and therapeutic processes with infants and their families, as well as in evaluation outcomes. Spiegel (cited in Canino & Canino, 1980, p. 535) explains that when the therapist incorporates social class and cultural aspects into the therapeutic process, he or she becomes somewhat of an anthropologist. Clinicians need to familiarize themselves with the child-rearing customs and family relationship dynamics of those culturally different groups they will be called upon to serve. Such efforts provide a cultural introduction and serve as a foundation to tailoring culturally relevant treatment. Through readings about sociocultural characteristics and issues of various groups, clinical case conferences and discussions, consultations with ethnic minority resource people and clinicians, and clinical experiences, the clinician cultivates a better understanding of culturally anchored "goalposts" and improves his or her ability to evaluate and treat infants and their families. This includes the ability to perceive the degree to which a behavior may deviate from or conform to not only North American middle-class standards, but also the values of the clients' social class, ethnic group, and geographical setting.

In summary, clinicians are encouraged to explore several fundamental questions from the clients' perspective to foster culturally sensitive work with infants and their families: Is there a problem? Why is there a problem? What can be done? And who should intervene to address the problem? These broad inquiries have utility in clarifying the basic issues; initiating a meaningful dialogue between clinician and caregivers; and facilitating the production of culturally relevant, individualized treatment plans. The importance of thorough assessment is underscored, including assessment of a family's degree of acculturation. Clinicians are encouraged to explore each family's definition of the problem and opinions regarding appropriate intervention approaches, with particular emphasis on the influence of sociocultural aspects. Beyond issues of adapting service delivery models, clinicians are urged to commit themselves to the lifelong process of refining their cultural sensitivity and competence, in order to better serve the growing population of minority infants and their families.

REFERENCES

American Psychological Association, Board of Ethnic Minority Affairs, Task Force on the Delivery of Services to Ethnic Minority Populations. (1991). *Guidelines for providers of psychological services to ethnic, linguistic, and culturally diverse populations.* Washington, DC: American Psychological Association.

Anderson, R. M., Giachello, A. L., & Aday, L. A. (1986). Access of Hispanics to health care and cuts in services: A state-of-the-art overview. *Public Health Reports, 101,* 238–252.

Arredondo-Dowd, P. (1981). Personal loss and grief as a result of immigration. *Personnel and Guidance Journal, 59,* 376–378.

Boyce, W. T., Schaefer, C., Harrison, H. R., Haffner, W. H. J., Lewis, M., & Wright, A. L. (1986). Social and cultural factors in pregnancy complications among Navajo women. *American Journal of Epidemiology, 124,* 242–253.

Bretherton, I., & Waters, E. (Eds.). (1985). Growing points of attachment theory and research. *Monographs of the Society for Research in Child Development, 50*(1–2, Serial No. 209).

Brinton Lykes, M. (1985). Gender and individualistic vs. collectivist bases for notions about the self. *Journal of Personality, 53*(2), 356–383.

Bronfenbrenner, U. (1986). Ecology of the family as a context for human development: Research perspectives. *Developmental Psychology, 22,* 723–742.

Canino, I. & Canino, G. (1980). Impact of stress on the Puerto Rican family: Treatment considerations. *American Journal of Orthopsychiatry, 50*(3), 535–541.

Chavez, L. R., Cornelius, W. A., & Jones, O. W. (1986). Utilization of health services by Mexican immigrant women in San Diego. *Women and Health, 11,* 3–20.

Cheung, F. K., & Snowden, L. R. (1990). Community mental health and ethnic minority populations. *Community Mental Health Journal, 26,* 277–291.

Christensen, C. M. (1992). Multicultural competencies in early intervention: Training professionals for a pluralistic society. *Infants and Young Children, 4*(3), 49–63.

Cleveland, T. (1983). The family—A critical factor in prevention. In W. Hall, G. St. Denis, & C. Young (Eds.), *Proceedings The family: A critical factor in prevention* (p. 17). Washington, DC: U.S. Department of Health and Human Services.

Cohen, R. (1972). Principles of preventive mental health programs for ethnic minority populations: The acculturation of Puerto Ricans to the United States. *American Journal of Psychiatry, 128*(12), 79–83.

Comas-Diaz, L., & Griffith, E. H. (1988). *Clinical guidelines in cross-cultural mental health.* New York: Wiley.

Comoroff, J., & McGuire, P. (1981). Ambiguity and the search for meaning: Childhood leukaemia in the modern clinical context. *Social Science and Medicine, 1513,* 115–123.

Costantino, G., Malgady, R., & Rogler, L. (1985). *Cuento therapy: Folktales as a culturally sensitive psychotherapy for Puerto Rican children* (Hispanic Research Center Monograph No. 12). Maplewood, NJ: Waterfront Press.

Cross, T. L. (1988). Services to minority populations: Cultural competence continuum. *Focal Point: Bulletin of the Research and Training Center to Improve Services for Seriously Emotionally Handicapped Children and Their Families,* (Portland State University, Portland, OR), 3(1), 1–4.

Cuellar, I., Harris, L. C., & Jasso, R. (1980). An acculturation scale for Mexican American normal and clinical populations. *Hispanic Journal of Behavioral Sciences, 2*(3), 199–217.

Dasen, P. & Heron, A. (1981). Cross-cultural tests of Piaget's theory. In H. Triandis & A. Heron (Eds.), *Handbook of cross-cultural psychology: Vol. 4. Developmental psychology.* Boston: Allyn & Bacon.

Dauphinais, P., Dauphinais, L., & Rowe, W. (1981). Effects of race and communication style on Indian perceptions of counselor effectiveness. *Counselor Education and Supervision, 20,* 37–46.

Espin, O. (1987). Psychological impact of migration on Latinas: Implications for psychotherapeutic practice. *Psychology of Women Quarterly, 11,* 489–503.

Everett, F., Proctor, N., & Cartmell, B. (1983). Providing psychological services to American Indian children and families. *Professional Psychology: Research and Practice, 14*(5), 588–603.

Freidson, E. (1961). *Patients' views of medical practice.* New York: Russell Sage Foundation.

Fricker, H. S., Hindermann, R., & Bruppacher, R. (1989). The Aaru study on pregnancy and the newborn. In J. K. Nugent, B. M. Lester, & T. B. Brazelton (Eds.), *The cultural context of infancy: Vol. 1. Biology, culture, and infant development.* Norwood, NJ: Ablex.

Garcia Coll, C. T. (1990). Developmental outcome of minority infants: A process-oriented look into our beginnings. *Child Development, 61,* 270–289.

Garcia Coll, C. T. (1992). *Cultural diversity: Implications for theory and practice* (Stone Center Work in Progress No. 59). Wellesley, MA: Stone Center for Developmental Services and Studies, Wellesley College.

Gutierrez, J., Sameroff, A., & Karrer, B. (1988). Acculturation and SES effects on Mexican-American parents' concepts of development. *Child Development, 59,* 250–255.

Gutman, H. G. (1976). *The black family in slavery and freedom: 1750–1925.* New York: Vintage.

Horowitz, F., Ashton, L., Culp, R., Gaddis, E., Levin, S., & Reichman, B. (1977). The effects of obstretrical medication on the behavior of Israeli newborn infants and some comparisons with Uruguayan and American infants. *Child Development, 48,* 1607–1623.

Inclan, J., & Hernandez, M. (1992). Cross-cultural perspectives and codependence: The case of poor Hispanics. *American Journal of Orthopsychiatry, 62,* 245–255.

King, S. (1962). *Perceptions of illness in medical practice.* New York: Russell Sage Foundation.

Kleinman, A. M. (1978). Comparisons of patient–practitioner transactions in Taiwan: The cultural construction of clinical reality. In A. M. Kleinman, P. Kunstadter, E. R. Alexander, & J. L. Gale (Eds.), *Culture and healing in Asian societies: Anthropological Psychiatric and Public Health Studies* (pp. 329–374). Cambridge, MA: Schenkman.

Kleinman, A. M., Eisenberg, L., & Good, B. (1978). Culture, illness, and care: Clinical lessons from anthropologic and cross-cultural research. *Annals of Internal Medicine, 88*(2), 251–258.

Korbin, J. E., & Johnston, M. (1982). Steps toward resolving cultural conflict in a pediatric hospital. *Clinical Pediatrics, 21*(5), 259-263.

Laosa, L. M. (1978). Maternal teaching strategies in Chicano families of varied educational and socioeconomic levels. *Child Development, 49,* 1129–1135.

Leiderman, P. H., Tulkin, S. R., & Rosenfeld, A. (Eds.). (1977). *Culture and infancy: Variations in the human experience.* New York: Academic Press.

Leijon, I., & Finnstrom, O. (1981). Studies on the Brazelton Neonatal Behavioral Assessment Scale. *Neuropediatrics, 12,* 242–253.

LeMasters, E. (1970). *Parents in modern America* (Vol. 4). Homewood, IL: Dorsey Press.

LeVine, R. (1977). Child rearing as cultural adaptation. In P. H. Leiderman, S. R. Tulkin, & A. Rosenfeld (Eds.), *Culture and infancy: Variations in the human experience* (pp. 15–27). New York: Academic Press.

Lin, K. M., Masuda, M., & Tazuma, L. (1982). Adaptational problems of Vietnamese refugees: III. Case studies in clinic and field: Adaptive and maladaptive. *Psychiatry Journal of the University of Ottawa, 7,* 173–183.

Lorion, R. P. (1974). Patient and therapist variables in the treatment of low income patients. *Psychological Bulletin, 81,* 344–354.

Mahler, M., Pine, F., & Bergman, A. (1975). *The psychological birth of the human infant: Symbiosis and individuation.* New York: Basic Books.

Martin, E. P., & Martin, J. M. (1978). *The black extended family.* Chicago: University of Chicago Press.

McGoldrick, M., Pearce, J. K., & Giordano, J. (Eds.). (1982). *Ethnicity and family therapy.* New York: Guilford Press.

McLoyd, V. C. (1990). Minority children: Introduction to special issue. *Child Development, 61*(2), 263–266.

Myers, H. F., Rana, P. G., & Harris, M. (1979). *Black child development in America, 1927–1977.* Westport, CT: Greenwood.

National Center for Family-Centered Care. (1990). *What is family-centered care?* Washington, DC: Association for the Care of Children's Health.

National Commission on Children. (1990). *Beyond rhetoric—A new American agenda for children and families.* Washington, DC: U.S. Government Printing Office.

Nugent, J. K., Lester, B. M., & Brazelton, T. B. (Eds.). (1989). *The cultural context of infancy: Vol. 1. Biology, culture, and infant development.* Norwood, NJ: Ablex.

Ogbu, J. (1981). Origins of human competence: A cultural–ecological perspective. *Child Development, 52,* 413–429.

Poma, P. A. (1983). Hispanic cultural influences on medical practice. *Journal of the National Medical Association, 75*(10), 21–26.

Rogler, L. H., Malgady, R. G., Costantino, G., & Blumenthal, R. (1987). What do culturally sensitive mental health services mean? The case of Hispanics. *American Psychologist, 42*(6), 565–570.

Rogoff, B. (1990). *Apprenticeship in thinking: Cognitive development in social context.* New York: Oxford University Press.

Roland, A. (1987). The familial self, the individualized self, and the transcendent self: Psychoanalytic reflections of India and America. *Psychoanalytic Review, 74*(2), 237–250.

Sameroff, A. J., & Fiese, B. H. (1990). Transactional regulation and early intervention. In S. J. Meisels & J. P. Shonkoff (Eds.), *Handbook of early childhood intervention.* New York: Cambridge University Press.

Shelton, T. L., Jeppson, E. S., & Johnson, B. H. (1987). *Family-centered care for children with special health care needs.* Washington, DC: Association for the Care of Children's Health.

Shweder, R., & Bourne, E. (1984). Does the concept of the person vary cross-culturally? In R. Shweder & R. LeVine (Eds.), *Culture theory: Essays on mind, self, and emotion* (pp. 158–199). Cambridge, England: Cambridge University Press.

Snowden, L. R., & Cheung, F. K. (1990). Use of inpatient mental health services by members of ethnic minority groups. *American Psychologist, 45,* 347–355.

Stafford, A. (1978). The application of clinical anthropology to medical practice: A case study of recurrent abdominal pain in a preadolescent Mexican-American female. In E. Bauwens (Ed.), *The anthropology of health* (pp. 12–22). St. Louis: C. V. Mosby.

Staples, R., & Miranda, A. (1980). Racial and cultural variations among American families: A decennial review of the literature on minority families. *Journal of Marriage and the Family, 42,* 157–173.

Steward, M. S., & Steward, D. S. (1973). The observation of Anglo, Mexican, and Chinese-American mothers teaching their young sons. *Child Development, 44,* 329–337.

Super, C. M. (1981). Cross-cultural research on infancy. In H. C. Triandis & A. Heron (Eds.), *Handbook of cross-cultural psychology: Vol. 4. Developmental psychology* (pp. 17–53). Boston: Allyn & Bacon.

Szapocznik, J., Kurtines, W., & Fernandez, T. (1980). Bicultural involvement and adjustment in Hispanic American youths. *International Journal of Intercultural Relations, 4,* 353–365.

Szapocznik, J., Rio, A., Perez-Vidal, A., Kurtines, W., Hervis, O., & Santistebun, D. (1986). Bi-cultural effectiveness training (BET): An experimental test of an intervention modality for families experiencing intergenerational/intercultural conflict. *Hispanic Journal of Behavioral Sciences, 4,* 303–330.

Terrell, F., & Terrell, S. (1981). An inventory to measure cultural mistrust among blacks. *Western Journal of Black Studies, 5*(3), 180–185.

Thomas, D. D. (1992). *Cultural diversity: Understanding the variability within.* Paper presented at the Eighth National Conference of Parent Care, Inc., New Orleans.

Thomas, R. (1985, September). Considering the identity of minority adults. *Journal of Employment Counseling,* pp. 126–127.

Thompson, C., Neville, H., Weathers, P., Posten, W. C., & Atkinson, D. (1990). Cultural mistrust and racism reaction among African-American students. *Journal of College Student Development, 31,* 162–168.

Triandis, H. C., & Heron, A. (Eds.). (1981). *Handbook of cross-cultural psychology: Vol. 4. Developmental psychology.* Boston: Allyn & Bacon.

U.S. Bureau of the Census. (1990). *Marital status and living arrangements, March, 1989* (Current Population Reports, Series P-20, No. 445). Washington, DC: U.S. Government Printing Office.

U.S. Department of Health and Human Services. (1986). *Report of the Secretary's Task Force on Black and Minority Health.* Washington, DC: U.S. Government Printing Office.

U.S. Senate Select Committee on Indian Affairs. (1985). *Indian juvenile alcoholism and eligibility for BIA schools* (Senate Hearing No. 99-286). Washington, DC: U.S. Government Printing Office.

Watkins, C. E., & Terrell, F. (1988). Mistrust level and its effects on counseling expectations in black client–white counselor relationships: An analogue study. *Journal of Counseling Psychology, 35*(2), 194–197.

Wagner, D. A., & Stevenson, H. W. (Eds.). (1982). *Cultural perspectives on child development.* San Francisco: W. H. Freeman.

Washington, E., & McLoyd, V. C. (1982). The external validity of research involving American minorities. *Human Development, 25,* 324–339.

Whiting, B., & Whiting, J. W. M. (1975). *Children of six cultures: A psycho-cultural analysis.* Cambridge, MA: Harvard University Press.

Whiting, J. W. M. (1977). A model for psychocultural research. In P. H. Leiderman, S. R. Tulkin, & A. Rosenfeld (Eds.), *Culture and infancy: Variations in the human experience.* New York: Academic Press.

Wilson, M. N. (1984). Mothers' and grandmothers' perceptions of parental behavior in three generational black families. *Child Development, 55,* 1333–1339.

II

RISK CONDITIONS
AND PROTECTIVE FACTORS

Prevention and clinical work with infants and families have always been closely linked. A desire on the part of clinicians to intervene before problems become severe and entrenched—indeed, if possible, before problems arise—has led to a focus on risk and protective factors in development. Determining which risk factors are salient makes possible the identification of groups at high risk for psychopathology and maladaptation, and it enables interventions to be targeted more specifically. Determining which protective factors are operative and how they operate enables us to understand individual differences in adaptation, contributes to the design of interventions, and assists in the refinement and further characterization of high-risk groups.

In Part II, specific risk conditions are described with regard to their implications for infant development. Individual differences within broad risk conditions are also considered. The specific risk factors chosen are well known, with large bodies of literature devoted to each. Nevertheless, they have also been (of necessity) arbitrarily chosen, and it is important to bear in mind that they rarely occur in isolation. Furthermore, there are considerable data already available suggesting that with regard to broad outcomes, the nature of the specific risk factors is less important than the sheer number of risk factors affecting an infant and family.

In Chapter 5, Halpern begins with a discussion of the daunting potential implications of poverty for infant development and adaptation. He challenges us, in part through his own struggle with the topic, to consider the meaning of being a poor infant in the United States, and at the same time to recognize that global risk factors such as poverty actually tell us little of what we really want to know about a particular baby and family. What look like similar situations or events to an investigator may have vastly different meanings for each poor child and family; this requires us to appreciate as best we can the subjective experience of infants and their caregivers.

Minde, in Chapter 6, considers the biological risk conditions of prematurity and other serious medical illnesses in infancy. A complex interplay of intrinsic biological abnormalities and extrinsic contextual variables affect the development of premature and seriously ill infants. Minde cites data documenting that the scope of the problem is broader than has been previously realized. Reviewing the experience of both premature and other chronically hospitalized infants, Minde also considers the parental and environmental characteristics that either facilitate recovery or lead to undesirable outcomes. He concludes by describing how the infant mental health clinician can ameliorate the outcome of these infants and families.

Osofsky, Hann, and Peebles (Chapter 7) review what is known about the enormous social problem of adolescent parenthood. They document the numerous associated variables that contribute to adverse outcomes of infants of adolescent parents. At the same time, they suggest a redirection of research efforts toward a more complete understanding of protective factors that enable adolescent mothers to overcome adversity. An appreciation of these factors is needed to improve our intervention efforts. Importantly, the chapter includes a section on the often-forgotten adolescent father.

Seifer and Dickstein, in Chapter 8, review and critique studies that have addressed the implications of parental mental illness for infant development, concentrating on schizophrenia and depression. They also describe and evaluate proposed models that might account for the better-established findings. They conclude by summarizing a broad range of adverse outcomes in infants of parents with major mental illnesses.

In Chapter 9, Zuckerman and Brown review what is known about maternal substance abuse and infant development. They consider potential mechanisms of influence that may impinge on the infant directly (prenatally) and indirectly (postnatally), and they outline the complex potential interactions of thse varaiables in a particular infant. They also consider the effects of specific substances. In conclusion, they propose collaboration between infant mental health professionals and addiction specialists to provide integrated services to these infants and families.

Patricia J. Mrazek (Chapter 10) concludes Part II with a review of maltreatment in infancy. Despite the unique developmental characteristics of this age group, and data documenting the serious nature of the problem for young children, it is clear that the special features of maltreatment in infancy have not often been considered. She reviews the severe short-term and long-term sequelae that have been documented following maltreatment in infancy.

5

Poverty and Infant Development

ROBERT HALPERN

Child development practitioners and researchers have long recognized that where a child is situated socially and economically in society has a profound influence on the nature of that child's experiences. Yet in spite of this recognition, we still do not understand adequately how broad situational factors, such as the character of a family's neighborhood or a family's dependence on the state for its subsistence, influence specific processes in very young children's lives. Infancy researchers especially have tended to view contextual factors as additional sources of explanation, rather than as central in interpreting what is observed in an infant and his or her family.

In this chapter, I focus on what it means for a child to be born and spend his or her earliest years in poverty. My focus is on those families that experience chronic poverty—in part because they represent a growing proportion of all poor families with young children, in part because the meaning of poverty is more coherent and predictable for such families. I should note at the outset that this chapter has proven both straightforward and surprisingly difficult to write. At one level, it is not difficult to describe the meaning of being poor in U.S. society, even for infants. The influence of poverty is evident both in material hardship and in a variety of social dimensions of experience. Poverty denies infants and their mothers adequate health care. It places infants and their families in physically

neglected, and often geographically and socially isolated, communities; indeed, it sometimes denies infants homes and communities. Poverty stigmatizes people, first requiring them to prove their worthiness for the most basic supports, and then defining them by the fact that they need such supports. The constant difficulties and social depredation associated with being poor in U.S. society undermine the physical energy and psychological well-being of caregivers, and thus the capacity of those caregivers to provide attentive and nurturant care. Not least, poverty is relentless. It acts on infants and their caregivers day in and day out, month in and month out, providing little respite or opportunity for recovery.

At a different level, though, poverty seems too global a variable for explaining specific processes in infants' and families' lives. The influence of poverty and its correlates on infants is mediated by such factors as an infant's birth order, physical integrity, and temperament; parents' age, nurturance history, and social supports; and degree of material hardship. Infants in economically disadvantaged families, like their more advantaged peers, differ widely in their ability to evoke what they need from the environment. Caregivers also differ widely in their ability to buffer children from the effects of environmental stresses. Furthermore, as Cohler (1987, pp. 364–365) reminds us, "little is known about the manner in which persons create a narrative

that renders adversity coherent in terms of experienced life history . . . too often it is assumed
that such circumstances as poverty and family
disorganization lead to increased suffering and
turmoil." For some persons adversity represents
a challenge to be overcome, rather than an indicator of personal failure. In this light, it can be
argued that even seemingly identical situations
and events have a unique psychological meaning for each poor child and family. The only way
to understand that meaning is to come to know
how that individual—or, in the case of an infant,
his or her caregiver—experiences and interprets
those situations and events.

I am not sure which level of discussion, if
either, is the more essential one: the shared
meaning of being poor, or the individuality of
each child's and family's experience of poverty.
By focusing on the common injuries of poverty,
one underemphasizes the adaptiveness and
courage many families demonstrate in the face
of adversity. Defining a group of families by
their economic disadvantage, even for purposes
of advocacy, is an inherently uncomfortable
task. Constructing groups or assigning labels to
human beings leads to a kind of reification in
which the group or the label eventually takes on
a life of its own. Nonetheless, whether they are
well endowed and cared for or not, poor infants
have to cope with and adapt to a variety of common stresses—lack of food or other necessities,
unexpected crises such as eviction, or the situationally rooted frustration that periodically
erupts from a caregiver who is usually protective and nurturant.

A PRELIMINARY PORTRAIT OF INFANCY UNDER CONDITIONS OF POVERTY

Demographics, Health, and Social Risks

Some 1.75 million children under 2 years of
age (900,000 children under 1 year of age, and
850,000 children between 1 and 2 years of age)
live in poverty in the United States—about
a quarter of all children under 2. The official
poverty level is about $13,000 for a family of
four. There are a number of correlates of poverty in families with young children, and these
form the broad context for infancy in such families (National Center for Children in Poverty,
1990). Almost two-thirds of poor infants live in
mother-only families, and slightly more than

two-thirds live in families supported by welfare.
Over half of poor infants live in households in
which parents have not completed high school.
About half live in families in which the mother
began childbearing in her teens. Some 40% of
all poor children under 2 (about 700,000 infants
and toddlers) live in neighborhoods of concentrated poverty in urban areas; 30% live in rural
areas; and the remainder live mostly in suburban areas or in neighborhoods contiguous to
high-poverty central city neighborhoods.

Each contextual or situational correlate of
poverty by itself has a significant impact on an
infant's life. But individual correlates of poverty
are rarely present by themselves. To be born to a
family that is on welfare brings with it a host of
stresses and strains, beginning with the chronic
strain of never having enough money and ranging to the limited choice of where one's family
might live. Limitations on where one's family lives
in turn limit the supports available to one's family, including health, education, and other services.
It places one's family in a context in which others
are preoccupied with their own survival. The
young family on welfare, living in a socially isolated community, is often headed by a young
woman who is in her teens or who began
childbearing as a teenager, and so on. When
present together, the correlates of poverty create
an overall context for infant well-being and development that is exceedingly powerful.

Poverty and its correlates directly affect infants' well-being from the moment they are conceived. Poor women are significantly more likely
than their more economically advantaged peers
to have poor health histories before becoming
pregnant; to receive inadequate prenatal care (in
its broadest sense); to experience high levels of
stress throughout their pregnancy; and to engage
in harmful health behavior during pregnancy. It
is estimated that as many as one in four poor
infants are now born to mothers who abused
drugs during their pregnancy (S. Hans, University of Chicago, Department of Psychiatry, personal communication, 1991). As a result of all
these factors, their unborn babies are more likely
to experience severe and/or chronic intrauterine stress. Such stress not only contributes to
premature labor and delivery but undermines
intrauterine growth, leading to small size for
gestational age. Chronic or severe intrauterine
stress may also contribute to subtle neurological damage in infants. In other words, under
conditions of poverty, an infant is significantly
more likely to be born constitutionally vulnerable and to be a difficult-to-care-for baby.

The same factors that contribute to poor birth outcomes among economically disadvantaged families continue to operate during infancy and early childhood, undermining infants' capacity to compensate for that vulnerability and the capacity of parents to respond (Birch & Gussow, 1970). A fussy, disorganized, low-birthweight infant is likely to overtax the limited physical and emotional resources of an already overstressed mother. She in turn responds to that infant "in ways counterproductive to his recovery"—for example, leaving him or her alone when he provides inadequate feedback (Brazelton, 1983, p. 353). Once set in motion, this negative pattern of interaction becomes increasingly difficult to redirect (Beckwith, 1988).

Poor infants are not only much more likely than more economically advantaged peers to be born constitutionally vulnerable, but when not born so are much more likely to become vulnerable. Poor infants and toddlers are much more likely than economically advantaged peers to lack adequate nutrition—in particular, to have inadequate iron status. Fewer than half of income-eligible infants, young children, and nursing women receive Women, Infants, and Children (WIC) food supplements (National Center for Children in Poverty, 1990). Poor infants and toddlers are much more likely than their more economically advantaged peers to have toxic blood lead levels (National Commission to Prevent Infant Mortality, 1991). Some 70% of Chicago's preschool-age children live in buildings built before 1950, when paint contained up to 50% lead (Griffin, 1988). There is also growing evidence of high lead concentrations in the environment surrounding poor children's homes. Poor infants and toddlers have a higher incidence of both minor and more serious health problems (including recurring middle-ear infections, asthma, and pneumonia), and of such injuries as arm or leg fractures and poisonings (Zeitel, 1989; Klerman, 1991). At the same time, poor infants have less access to non-hospital-based medical care than their more economically advantaged peers. Because they have more serious health problems (including complications from lack of treatment of easily treatable problems), and because they have less access to primary care, poor infants and toddlers have much higher rates of hospitalization and longer average hospital stays than more economically advantaged peers (Klerman, 1991, p. 40). In addition to the inherent trauma of hospital procedures for very young children, there is evidence that separations from parents

during the first 2 years due to hospitalization can have enduring effects on children, especially if the parent–infant relationship is not a secure one at the time of separation (Garmezy, 1983, p. 58).

In the extreme, poor infants experience much higher rates of postneonatal mortality, which is more closely tied than neonatal mortality to inadequate living conditions, as well as to constitutional vulnerability and specific parental behaviors (National Commission to Prevent Infant Mortality, 1988). In one study in Washington, D.C., postneonatal mortality was found to be 1.4 per 1000 live births in census tracts with the lowest percentage of welfare-dependent families, and 10.1 per 1000 live births in census tracts with highest percentage of such families (Eberstadt, 1988).

There is little information available on the percentage of poor infants and toddlers who experience problems of care requiring intervention by child welfare authorities. The best data available come from work being done by Goerge and colleagues at the Chapin Hall Center for Children, University of Chicago (R. Goerge, personal communication, 1991). These data suggest that about 1 in 10 poor infants and toddlers live in families that come into contact with the child welfare system, and that the proportion is increasing. The majority of these cases involve one or another form of neglect. A number of observers have questioned whether child welfare authorities are failing in some cases to distinguish between impaired parent–child relationships and effects of poverty, including the inability to shelter, feed, and clothe children (Pelton, 1989). Increasingly, though, findings of neglect are associated with parental drug abuse. When neglect or abuse is confirmed, poor infants and toddlers are much more likely to be removed from their homes and placed in foster care than their more economically advantaged peers (Lindsey, 1991), and once in care are more likely to remain there longer. Data collected by the American Public Welfare Association indicate that there about 50,000 children under 2 years of age in foster care in the United States (T. Tatara, personal communication, 1991). The great majority of these children, perhaps 70%, are from poor families.

The Worsening Situation of Poor Families

Worsening social and economic conditions among poor families are heightening the inherent health and developmental risks faced by poor infants. The real dollar value of Aid to Families with Dependent Children (AFDC), food stamps, and housing subsidies has declined dramatically over the past decade. A recent study of families on welfare in New York City found that over 60% were forced to put off paying for rent or utilities in order to pay for even more immediate necessities, such as food, clothing, and bedding for children (Simpson, 1990). In the same study, the average family exhausted its monthly food stamp allotment in 19 days. One respondent noted, "Every month I have to decide which bill to pay, which doesn't give you a clear mind. You're always depressed" (Simpson, 1990, p. 15). More and more families are only one or two crises away from homelessness. For example, not being able to pay the rent one month can be the first step toward homelessness, especially if a family has any unexpected financial demands the following months, pushing it further and further behind.

The risk of homelessness for young families has been exacerbated by a decline in federally subsidized housing starts for low-income families, from 180,000 units per year in 1980 to 20,000 units per year today (*New York Times*, 1991, p. A14). Although data are imprecise, it is estimated that perhaps 10% of poor families with infants and young children now experience homelessness at some point in time (L. Mihally, Children's Defense Fund, personal communication, 1991). There is even evidence that pregnancy and birth of a child may be causal factors in homelessness. One recent study in New York City found that 35% of homeless women were pregnant and 26% had given birth within the past year (Weitzman, 1989).

Not surprisingly, homeless infants and young children appear to be at the highest risk of any group of poor children for all the health and developmental problems noted above (Molnar, Roth, & Klein, 1990). The circumstances of homeless families' lives make the care and nurturance of infants and young children almost impossible. Take as just one example the difficulty that families living in welfare hotels have in keeping infant formula sanitary: "Lack of refrigeration is particularly problematic for mothers with infants who must devise other methods for keeping milk or formula cold, such as using toilet tanks as coolers" (Gallagher, cited in Institute of Medicine, 1988, p. 67). Homelessness often brings with it a variety of feelings—loss, shame, anger, total depletion, an "end-of-

the-road feeling"—that undermine the capacity to function in the parental role (M. Erickson, University of Minnesota, personal communication, 1991). The effects of these debilitating feelings are exacerbated by the loss of privacy and the "pressures of public mothering" (Molnar et al., 1990, p. 115).

A growing proportion of poor families with young children now live in urban neighborhoods characterized by high concentrations of poverty, profound isolation from the larger society, and the disintegration of all the elements that hold a community together and sustain its residents. Such neighborhoods are experiencing the breakdown of social, religious, and economic institutions that are critical to daily living and that often provide paths out of poverty for people. Members of young families' informal support systems are likely to have significant difficulties of their own, and thus to be unavailable to provide guidance, nurturance, and practical assistance. Together, these trends not only are leaving families with fewer resources to draw on, but are contributing to survival-oriented patterns of coping and relating to others. Such patterns include wariness and mistrust of one's neighbors, friends, and even family; in some cases, they extend to deliberate withdrawal from community life.

With its competitive ethos, its emphasis on individual responsibility, and its reluctant structure of public supports, U.S. society has never been hospitable to poor families. Such families have always had to fight their way into the social and economic mainstream by making constant sacrifices and using a variety of informal paths of mobility. A growing proportion of poor infants now live in families in which parents may no longer see their way out of poverty. For these families, paths of mobility are closed out, and sacrifice no longer seems to pay off (Wacquant & Wilson, 1989). The lives and experiences of infants in such families are likely to be very different from those in families where parents are still striving.

THE FAMILY LIFE OF POOR INFANTS

The Broad Pattern of Early Care of Poor Infants

In addition to affecting the larger social ecology of infants' lives, poverty may be expected to influence infants' immediate ecology, including daily routines, caregiving roles and responsibilities, and the general interpersonal environment of the home. There is only a relatively modest literature on these features of poor infants' lives, in spite of their importance to infants' well-being and development. There has been little research on such issues as the pattern of daily life of poor infants; the role that nonresident biological fathers and father surrogates play in infant care, and the factors that shape that role; the ways in which extended family networks negotiate and enact caregiving roles and responsibilities; and the effects of all these patterns on mother–infant relationships.

Available literature suggests that the temporal structure and daily routines of poor infants and toddlers, especially those from chronically poor families, are often somewhat variable and in some cases erratic. Two recent studies describe daily routines characterized by irregular times for waking up, meals, and sleep, and by irregular sleep places (Escalona, 1987; Norton, 1990). There is some evidence of greater fluctuation in household composition and people present on a regular basis in the homes of poor infants than in those of their more advantaged peers. Not surprisingly, there is also evidence of overcrowding in the homes of poor families with young children (Simpson, 1990). In a study of an inner-city housing project in Chicago, Norton (1990, p. 6) found households "so crowded with adults and other children that our target babies wander around in a welter of adults, almost like little nonpersons, spoken to curtly, only if they get in the way." Her description may or may not be unique to the context of public inner-city housing projects.

In a study of premature infants from families experiencing different degrees of economic disadvantage, Escalona (1987, p. 35) found that poor infants and toddlers in her sample spent more time in the care of secondary and ancillary caregivers than did their more economically advantaged peers: "They were fed, dressed, put to bed, and taken on outings by many different people and in a good many different locations." An infant or toddler might go to bed in his or her own bed one night, the mother's bed on another, and her grandmother's bed on still another night. Particularly among black families, it has been observed that primary responsibility for care of an infant can be shared by more than one maternal figure and can shift over time. In her study of "The Flats," a black community in southern Illinois, Stack (1974, pp. 62–63) notes that child rearing was regarded "as part of the flux and elasticity" of existence. As households shifted, so did rights and responsibilities for children. At the same time, a male or female relative who did not live in the household might be a regular part of a young child's life, becoming someone he or she could learn to count on.

Approximately 80% of unwed fathers do not live with their children (Smollar & Ooms, 1987). The little available literature on the caregiving role of such fathers is somewhat contradictory. In a study in New York City that included this group of fathers, Sullivan (1989, p. 54) found that most seemed committed to their children, providing as much direct child care and support as they were able (even using proceeds from criminal activity at times). The fathers "visited regularly, and frequently took the children to their own homes, for weekends or even longer periods of time." Anderson (1989) provides a different picture: He found only a few young inner-city fathers willing or able to take on the responsibility of fatherhood. This group included those with long-term relationships with the mothers prior to the pregnancies, and/or those who were only "marginally related to their peer groups." Involved fathers also "tend to emerge from nurturing families, and religious observance plays an important role in their lives" (p. 67). The majority of nonresident fathers appeared to be unwilling, unable, or physically unavailable to assume the responsibilities implied by fatherhood. When they admitted paternity at all, they wanted it to be on their own terms, which were often largely symbolic: "In theory the part-time father is able to retain his freedom while having limited commitment to the woman and the little ones 'calling me daddy'" (p. 75).

An increasingly noted (although certainly not new) caregiving pattern among poor families, especially black families, is for the mother's (or, less commonly, the father's) own mother to take primary responsibility for care of an infant. The meaning of this pattern for the infant obviously depends on the situation—whether it is something that both mother and grandmother want, the grandmother's other responsibilities, the grandmother's own capacity for nurturant parenting, and not least the characteristics of the infant. Many grandmothers reportedly take on this responsibility willingly, and some may even use it (consciously or unconsciously) as an opportunity to make up for the inadequate parenting they provided their own daughters (Burton, 1990). For other grandmothers, it may be an unwelcome and overwhelming responsibility, ambivalently assumed. As one grandmother noted in a recent newspaper article on this subject, "Sometimes I wished I never had children" (Martin, 1991, p. E6). Finally, there is reason to believe that a disproportionate percentage of the young children involved in these situations are likely to be difficult to care for, especially if they were born to substance-abusing mothers.

The Quality of Early Parenting under Conditions of Poverty

Just as the effects of poverty on infants are both mediated by individual differences and in many ways predictable, so are the effects of poverty on the quality of parenting poor infants receive. Poor parents, like others, differ in their personal histories, and thus in their basic capacity to parent and their understanding of what parenting is all about. They differ in their current life situation, including age, marital status, and social supports. They differ in their current mental and physical health. Infants also differ in the demands they make on parents' capacities and personal resources. Ornstein and Ornstein (1985) note that with each child the parent's empathic capacities are tested anew. Each child "creates" his or her own mother and father. A child who is easy to care for can contribute to adequate parenting even in parents with few emotional and physical reserves to draw on. A difficult-to-care-for infant can erode such reserves even in parents in whom they are plentiful.

Although many factors influence the quality and experience of parenting, the presence of poverty increases the likelihood that each of these factors will act to increase the odds of compromised parenting. Poverty increases the likelihood that infants will be born difficult to care for. Poverty uncovers and magnifies the effects of vulnerabilities in parents, whether adversity in their own childhoods (Solnit, 1983) or a history of psychiatric illness in their families (Stott, Musick, & Cohler, 1984). Poverty produces its own stressors, such as dangerous and unpleasant neighborhood environments; dilapidated, overcrowded housing; and the dehumanization and loss of control that often accompany welfare dependency in U.S. society. Poor parents' lives are marked by constant financial strain and by unattractive and often limited choices. In order to secure necessities for her children, a poor parent may have to put up with an intrusive, disdainful caseworker who makes her feel that by seeking support she is doing something shameful. Even then she may have to decide between paying the rent and feeding her children. For her children to succeed, she may have to devote her life to protecting them from a toxic environment, pushing her own aspirations into the distance. In the majority of poor families, the father is not present in the home to provide care for the infant (and, just as important, support to the mother). Other potential sources of support are themselves likely to be struggling with poverty-related stresses. Indeed, in some cases, those close to a young mother may actively undermine her efforts to care for her children (Musick, 1993).

Together, the correlates of poverty preoccupy parents in ways that undermine their preoccupation with their infants. These correlates sap parents' physical energy, try their patience, undermine their sense of competence, and reduce their sense of control over their lives. They contribute to immobilizing feelings of exhaustion, irritability, anger, and in some cases futility. Lack of energy, combined with such immobilizing feelings, can undermine the attentiveness that is a key to interpreting and responding appropriately to infants' moods and immediate needs. These feelings inhibit caregivers' availability to share and acknowledge infants' feelings, including the expressions of pleasure and joy that validate the effort needed to attend to infants' needs (Eldridge & Schmidt, 1990). For those parents who have poor nurturance histories, the realities of poverty complicate the enormous effort needed to break the cycle, to parent differently than one's parents did (Musick, 1993).

Reduced, or in some cases less consistent, attentiveness to infants has been observed in a number of studies of families living in chronic poverty (Bromwich, 1978; Escalona, 1987; Jeffers, 1967; Norton, 1990; Rainwater, 1970). Nonetheless, it has been described and interpreted quite differently in these studies. In a ground-breaking participant observation study of patterns of early caregiving in a Washington, D.C., public housing project, Jeffers (1967) observed significant mood swings in the mothers she came to know. These mood swings were attributable in part to specific precipitating events and difficulties—a family crisis; a fight with a spouse, friend, or family member; running out of money or food. In some cases there was no obvious precipitating cause, beyond the debilitating effects of constant stress. The mood swings contributed to inconsistency in the affected women's day-to-day care of their infants and young children. The same infant behavior might evoke anger one day, pleasure the next, and no response at all on another day.

In a study of the same era, involving black inner-city mothers in St. Louis, Rainwater (1970) observed that they did not show

> deep psychological involvement with infants and young children . . . They rarely manifest the anxious attention to children, the sense of awesome responsibility, along with the pleasure, that is characteristic of many working class women . . . taking care of babies is regarded as a routine activity which is not at all problematic. (p. 218)

At the same time, echoing Jeffers, Rainwater noted a tendency for poor infants and toddlers in this community to be alternatively enjoyed or ignored, depending on what else was preoccupying adult caretakers at any particular moment. In general, there was an expectation that it was young children's job to fit into the household, rather than adults' responsibility to adjust to young children's needs.

In an intervention study with premature infants and their families, Bromwich (1978) found that it was very difficult for many of the poor parents in the sample to sustain an adequate level of attention to their infants, even though their intentions were good. Infants' needs were often pushed into the background by problems of family members or relatives, or by crises or unexpected events. Bromwich noted that some infants of preoccupied or depleted parents were able to assert themselves strongly and persistently enough to get their parents to pay attention, especially when they really needed them. For example, she related one incident in which an infant repeatedly rolled a ball back to his mother, all the while watching her face for some sign of interest and pleasure: "He does this until the mother begins to smile, look at him, and almost affectionately (without touching him) tilt her head; she finally smiles with him and returns the ball again" (p. 141). But not all infants in Bromwich's study had the resources that this one did.

In the study noted earlier, Escalona (1987) found that the majority of poor infants in the sample received plentiful love from parents, grandparents, and other relatives, but that the expression of such love was idiosyncratic, occurring when an adult happened to be available to provide it. In a study whose primary focus was acquisition of time concepts by inner-city infants and toddlers in Chicago, Norton (1990) did extended home observations of patterns of parent–infant interaction. She found that many of the mothers she observed were "too needy and too anxious to note and respond to their children sensitively enough to provide the reciprocal patterns of alternating synchrony . . . as necessary foundations for early time concepts" (p. 6).

In addition to undermining parents' ability to be consistently attentive, poverty and its correlates may also contribute to parental preoccupation with particular aspects of caregiving (e.g., those related to protection and physical care) at the expense of other aspects (e.g., those related to play and empathic responsiveness). Jeffers (1967) found that patterns of early child rearing in the community she studied were strongly influenced by mothers' own frequent histories of childhood poverty and material deprivation. Memories of this deprivation, which typically involved lack of food or clothing, were often on women's minds, consciously and unconsciously affecting their goals and behavior. For some mothers, "caring" for an infant or young child meant providing good physical care rather than emotional closeness. When asked to name the things she thought were most important to children, one mother replied, "Food, clothes, medical care, a mama and a daddy" (p. 91). Of another mother, Jeffers noted: "Mrs. Queene's emphasis on physical care showed itself early in her children's upbringing. One of her reasons for wanting another child was the satisfaction she got caring for babies: she loved to 'keep their clothes clean and see nice white diapers hanging on the line'" (p. 82). For some mothers, childhood deprivation was not limited to the lack of material necessities: "Just as some spoke of not having any childhood, some spoke of not having any fun, either as children or adults" (p. 96). For these mothers especially, having fun with their young children often seemed an unaffordable luxury.

Jeffers's early findings are echoed in a more recent study by Crittendon and Bonvillian (1984), in which they found that poor mothers seemed to get less enjoyment from playing with their infants than did their more economically advantaged peers. Crittendon and Bonvillian also found a tendency for poor parents to try to be in control during their interactions with their babies, rather than to respond flexibly and contingently. They report that "control of the immediate situation was a pervasive problem for the low SES mothers; the effect was that of a caring mother who saw herself as being in charge of directing the play rather than jointly interacting with her infant" (1984, p. 259). Jeffers (1967), and more recently Zelkowitz (1982), noted that mothers experiencing stress were sometimes conscious of the limited effectiveness of their interactions with their babies, but lacked the physical and psychological energy to behave more effectively.

Beyond such conscious explanations, efforts to control infants' behavior may in some cases be a function of factors of which parents are less aware. For some parents, efforts to control infants' behavior may serve unconsciously to compensate for feelings of powerlessness or emptiness in other areas of their lives, including their adult relationships. Ornstein and Ornstein (1985) have argued that problems in parenting are most likely to occur when parents use their children (albeit unconsciously) to fill a sense of inner emptiness or to bolster shaky self-esteem. A parent may approach an infant with a genuine intent to care for him or her, but underneath is "a yearning for the infant to respond in a highly specific way," one that meets whatever particular need the parent has (Ornstein & Ornstein, 1985, p. 204). Emde and Sameroff (1989, p. 10) note that the infant is sometimes seen as "a way to overcome social disappointments and fulfill dreams of success." The problem is that the infant cannot compensate for what a young parent has not received throughout life.

Anderson (1991, pp. 390–391) provides an example of the process through which very young inner-city women use their infants to fulfill an unmet need to feel competent and special. Babies, both in their presence and in their physical attractiveness, become "the cornerstone of status" within the peer group:

> When the babies arrive, the street groups become informal baby clubs. The girls support one another, taking care to praise one another and the babies. But they also use their babies to compete with each other for status. In this context the baby is viewed as an extension of the mother and reflects directly upon her . . . mother and child must look good to negate the generalized notion that the mother has messed up her life. (pp. 390–391)

Anderson observed that parenting problems often began to develop in this population when

an infant's increasingly complex demands began to outweigh the personal benefits to the mother associated with parenthood. The older infant, no longer viewed as an extension of the mother, becomes a burden, and in some cases the target of a young mother's frustration and disappointment.

Childhood Adversity and Parenting under Conditions of Poverty

A growing proportion of young adults living in poverty are embarking on parenthood with personal histories marked not just by material deprivation, but by disruptions in caregiving, inadequate nurturance and/or rejection, family violence (including sexual abuse), and often a sense of failure in most areas outside family life as well. The residue of such a life, compounded by continuing hardship, may leave parents unprepared or unable to spare their children this life as well (Egeland, Jacobvitz, & Sroufe, 1988; Meers, 1973; Musick & Halpern, 1988). Among this highest-risk group of parents, lessened sensitivity and responsiveness to their infants are more likely to be general and pervasive, although they may be expressed very differently in different parents—for example, as chronic unavailability, or conversely in consistently misattuned (or even angry) responses to the infant.

Personal histories filled with adversity affect parenting capacities and orientations through many routes. Parents' own nurturance histories, and how parents interpret those histories to themselves, contribute to what have been called their "internal representational models"—what they are like as people, what can be expected from other people, and what parent–child and other relationships are like (Main, Kaplan, & Cassidy, 1985; Stern-Bruschweiler & Stern, 1989). Parents with a pervasively negative nurturance history are likely, in the absence of help in exploring the pain of that history and becoming aware of its continuing effects, to reproduce this pattern in their relationships with their children (Egeland et al., 1988).

Fraiberg, Shapiro, and Cherniss (1983, p. 59) note that the birth of a baby "evokes profound memories and feelings in his parents which normally lie deep in personality." If these are memories and feelings of abandonment, rejection, or being unprotected by one's own parents, they are likely to be activated by the infant's profound need to be "heard," responded to, and protected by his or her mother. A mother who was hurt in some way as a child, and whose own mother failed to protect her from that hurt, may be unable to identify with her young children's need for protection, and may believe that there is nothing she as a parent can do to protect her children from being hurt. A mother who was not loved and nurtured as a child may find it difficult and painful to identify with, and therefore respond to, a baby's need for love and nurturance. She may not feel that she has anything to give the baby. One way a mother may avoid painful memories and feelings is to avoid what appears to be their source—the infant. The effect, of course, is to repeat the past in the present.

As part of their larger intervention–research study of low-income infants at heightened risk of inattentive parenting, Lyons-Ruth, Zoll, Connell, and Grunebaum (1989) examined the long-term effects of different kinds and amounts of childhood adversity on mothers' parenting capacity and behaviors. They found different patterns of effects resulting from different kinds of adversity—traumatic events such as separation from, divorce of, or death of parents; family moves; family conflict; parental rejection or lack of warmth; severe punishment; quality of peer relations; and degree of supervision. For example, persistently non-nurturant and rejecting childhood care contributed strongly to "negative affect conveyed toward the infant," but did not reduce a mother's "overall level of involvement with her infant." Indeed, "rather than withdrawing from involvement, mothers with the most difficult histories are likely to become involved in hostile and intrusive interactions by the time their infants reach toddlerhood" (Lyons-Ruth et al., 1989, p. 230). When adversity was related more to disruptive or traumatic events in a mother's childhood, it tended to undermine expression of positive affective responses rather than to produce negative ones. For example, this pattern of adversity undermined such aspects of parenting as positive monitoring and supervising, comforting, and praise (Lyons-Ruth et al., 1989).

Adverse childhood experience affects parenting through indirect routes, in addition to directly undermining feelings about and capacities for parenting. It can undermine mothers' basic feelings of worth and competence, which provide the foundation for their specific sense of worth and competence as caregivers. A fragile sense of competence is particularly problematic with difficult-to-care-for babies, whose behaviors undermine feelings of adequacy

(Brazelton, 1983). A history of adversity, particularly of broken or disrupted attachments, can affect mothers' ability to form supportive adult relationships. For instance, such a history can contribute to adult behavioral patterns that "make it difficult for others to respond in a caring, supportive way" (Egeland & Erickson, 1990, p. 31). In a study of adolescent parents and their toddlers, Crockenberg (1987) found that childhood experience marked by disrupted and/or non-nurturant mothering undermined not only parenting capacities, but the full range of a young mother's relationships. Mothers with poor nurturance histories were less likely to have supportive relationships with their families and partners, and therefore were less likely to recieve support in their parenting efforts.

A history of adversity creates vulnerabilities that are activated by both normative and unexpected challenges and changes. The birth of an infant is one such challenge, and can trigger anxiety, depression, and worsening well-being in already vulnerable women. These responses can be attributed to the added demands placed on women who already feel overwhelmed, the distressing memories and feelings activated by the presence of the infant, or both in some cases. The effect is a kind of downward spiral. When the infant responds anxiously to his or her mother's anxiety, she in turn becomes more anxious at his or her behavior. When the infant reacts to the mother's depression-related withdrawal by trying harder to evoke what he or she needs, this response further overwhelms or distresses the mother, who then reacts by withdrawing further or by becoming angry, and so on in an escalating cycle. Eventually the infant himself or herself may begin to withdraw, not only from interactions with the mother but from other social interactions as well. The infant eventually may also internalize his or her mother's psychological state. Field, Heal, Goldstein, Perry, and Bendell (1988) found that 3- to 6-month-olds with chronically depressed mothers appeared depressed, even when interacting with animated strangers.

BEYOND PARENT AND INFANT: RELATIONSHIP ISSUES

In recent years there has been growing attention to the parent–infant relationship as a distinct phenomenon, both shaped by and subsequently shaping what the infant and the parent bring to it. The preceding discussion has touched on relationship issues at many points. As argued above, poverty and its correlates clearly affect what each of the participants bring to the parent–infant relationship: in the infant's case, constitutional integrity, self-regulation abilities, and so forth; in the parent's case, basic parenting capacities, maturity, current well-being, child-rearing goals, general proccupations, and the like.

In keeping with the preceding pages, it is plausible to argue that under conditions of poverty both the infant and the parent are at heightened risk of contributing to relationship difficulties. At the same time, the parent–infant relationship does not exist in a vacuum. It is important to ask how the broader context associated with poverty affects the meaning and import of the parent–infant relationship. For example, as described earlier, many poor infants have more than one primary caregiver, and may have shifting primary caregivers over time. In a different vein, many poor infants start life with very young and therefore immature mothers. Such mothers may traverse more developmental ground than older mothers during the infants' first year or two of life.

I focus first on mother–infant relationships. There are few normative data comparing non-clinical samples of mothers and infants from different socioeconomic backgrounds. There is some evidence of less stability in attachment patterns among poor mothers and infants than among their more advantaged peers. Sroufe (1979, p. 840) reports on a study in which he found that "while 48 of 50 middle class infants had the same attachment classifications at 12 and 18 months, only 62 of 100 poor children were classified similarly." Egeland and Farber (1984) found that maternal characteristics, infant characteristics, and family circumstances interacted in complex ways in a low-income sample to predict both security of attachment at either 12 or 18 months, and stability in attachment patterns across time. The maturation of mothers who had begun child rearing very young, the status at any point in time of mothers' relationships with men, and the evolving role of grandmothers all influenced the mothers' interest in and availability to their infants. In some cases young mothers (often with little support) began to "mature" their way out of the personal preoccupations of adolescence, and for some out of depression, anxiety, and interpersonal conflict as well. A young mother might resolve conflicts with her own

mother about who was responsible for her baby by moving out, leading to gradual improvement in the mother–infant relationship. Conversely, a change at home for the worse or a deteriorating relationship with a boyfriend could contribute to a change from secure to anxious attachment between the two time points.

There is little research on the question of whether the mother–infant relationship has the same meaning for poor infants as for their more economically advantaged peers. For example, attachment research has focused almost exclusively on mother–infant attachment, assuming that the mother is always the primary attachment figure. This is an increasingly tenuous assumption. There is almost no literature on grandmother–infant attachment—either the pattern or the purposes it serves for the infant. Nor is there literature on the effects of multiple, diffuse attachments.

Multiple caregivers, and the multiple attachments that often result, can be adaptive to the unpredictability that many poor families experience. In the St. Louis study, Rainwater (1970, p. 218) reported that "seldom is there not at least one person in the household who enjoys handling and caring for the baby and who attends to him in an interested and enthusiastic way." Infants can probably "extract" what they need from more than one caring figure (Ornstein & Ornstein, 1985). Bettelheim (1967, p. 48) has argued that the important thing is that the infant and young child "have a star to steer by . . . a constellation can replace the individual star provided what is lost in intensity is made up for in the definiteness of the direction by which to navigate."

Nonetheless, it is not known whether an infant can gain the same sense of "confident expectation" that his or her needs will be met from a collective of caregivers as from one consistent caregiving figure. Nor is it known whether an infant can take "the crucial developmental step from prime interest in need fulfillment to interest in the need fulfilling person" under these circumstances (Furman, 1987, p. 20). A degree of continuity would seem critical to at least some of the qualities that define good parent–infant relationships—for example, dependability and predictability, and the gradual process of establishing reciprocity. The degree of continuity and reliability in parent–infant relationships may also set the pattern of expectations regarding future relationships. Indeed, Silverstein and Krate (1975) found that many elementary-age inner-city children viewed adults as unreliable sources of nurturance and protection, and speculated that this was in part a long-term effect of multiple, diffuse early attachments.

IMPLICATIONS FOR INFANT WELL-BEING AND DEVELOPMENT

Kagan, Kearsley, and Zelazo (1978, p. 147) note that infants' and toddlers' day-in, day-out environmental experiences most strongly predict later well-being and competence. In that sense, infants are both uniquely vulnerable and remarkably resilient. For most infants, healthy early childhood development is likely to be thwarted only when opportunities for healthy coping and adaptation are continuously thwarted, day in and day out. Such pervasive developmental "blockage" in turn is most likely to occur when multiple hindrances to healthy development are present simultaneously, and when multiple hindrances remain present over time.

Ever greater numbers of poor infants are experiencing both these conditions, and thus the conditions for compromised early childhood development. In fact, what has served in the literature as the paradigmatic example of highest-risk infancy—a constitutionally vulnerable infant, a vulnerable and overwhelmed caregiver, and an unsupportive social and community context—is rapidly becoming the norm for poor infants.

Still, there is much we need to learn about the consequences of specific patterns of experience among poor infants. What, for example, happens to an infant who sometimes gets plentiful protection, feedback, and validation, but at other times may get none, depending on caregivers' moods and levels of stress in the environment? What happens to an infant who must constantly work to gain and sustain his or her mother's attention? What is the effect of the unpredictability and even randomness in the daily lives of some poor infants? What happens to an infant who repeatedly observes and senses his or her mother's feelings of powerlessness? What specifically are poor infants learning in their first relationships that carry over to their later relationships and their approach to life challenges? How do infants come to internalize the chronic stresses associated with poverty? Questions such as these are relevant to a sizable and growing proportion of infants in U.S. society.

There is not much literature on the effects of erratic (as opposed to consistently attentive or inattentive) nurturance, or on the effects of the more general unpredictability that characterizes some poor infants' lives. There is some evidence that the lessened predictability and consistency in maternal responsiveness found in poor families may undermine babies' ability to master cause and effect (Clarke-Stewart, 1977). Minuchin (1967) suggests that erratic nurturance, especially in the context of an unstable family life, can lead to a sense of an unstable and unpredictable world, and can hinder developmental movement from a diffuse to a more focused sense of self. It has been argued that erratic early parenting contributes to an unsolidified parent–infant relationship, and later to excessive concern for and preoccupation with the mother by the young child (Khan, 1963). Finally, Norton (1990) argues that as a result of unpredictability and randomness in daily life, some inner-city infants and toddlers are not socialized into the kinds of temporal understandings that provide a foundation for later adjustment to school. She argues that these infants are "robbed [by their early experience] of the sense of efficacy and control so necessary to sequence behavior through time, to develop a sense of self, and to learn" (p. 6).

It is not fully clear whether and how situationally related feelings of powerlessness in caregivers come to be internalized by infants. This depends in part on the extent to which such feelings affect caregivers' responsiveness to their infants. If a parent fails to respond to an infant's bids for attention and care, then that infant may come to feel powerless himself or herself at some level. Less directly, infants develop a sense of loyalty to and identification with their parents' expectations and wishes, in part because such identification helps them feel connected to their parents. If parents' past and present experience leads them to believe that they have little control over the world, this belief is likely to be communicated to their infants or toddlers in many different ways. Eventually, parents' ways of coping with adversity, as well as with normal life challenges, are adopted by their young children as their own (Massie, Bronstein, Afterman, & Campbell, 1988).

As children gain language and greater representational capacities in the second year, how parents "formulate" and explain events and experiences to them becomes increasingly important (Emde & Buchsbaum, 1990, p. 40).

For example, in her discussion of father-absent families, Siegler (1982, p. 67) notes that mothers "can keep the image of the father alive for the child, in both positive and negative ways, by constructing a narrative about the father's absence. This family tale organizes the child's thoughts and feelings." Siegler goes on to note, however, that in some situations, such as abandonment by the father, "this narrative may not be able to have a satisfactory beginning, middle, and end." Poor parents may often be in a dilemma in this regard, wanting to reassure their young children that things are fine, but not feeling reassuring or reassured themselves. In that sense the reality of such families' life situation, and parents' own personal situation, intrude on the parents' efforts to foster and nurture positive expectations in their children. What begins as the parents' legacy often becomes the children's as well.

Older infancy and toddlerhood, with their greater focus on exploration, language, and autonomy, may be especially challenging periods for some parents. Parents who feel generally powerless may have less sense that they can play a positive role in helping their infants and toddlers achieve their goals. Parents who themselves have a fragile sense of worth may respond more to their very young children's failure than to their success (Escalona, 1987). Parents who are preoccupied in various ways with their own lack of well-being may be unable to recognize and validate infants' and toddlers' achievements. The effect for young children of a lack of positive feedback and encouragement is a gradual loss of the desire to please parents and other adults—a desire that serves as a motivation for acquiring impulse control, and an engine for future efforts at mastery and achievement. This pattern may explain in part Escalona's (1987) finding that young children in the poorest families in her sample tended to avoid or not to persevere with the most difficult tasks presented to them.

What is the outlook for the growing proportion of poor infants being reared by parents who experienced significant disruption or lack of nurturance as children? I have noted earlier that histories marked by rejection and/or disruption, often compounded by continuing relationship difficulties, can seriously undermine parents' emotional availability to their infants. Emde (1989, p. 49) argues that one enduring effect of diminished emotional availability in parents is a "restriction of experience" needed by the infant to develop such qualities as "a sense of reciproc-

ity with others and of rules for social interchange . . . a sense of empathy for another's distress or joy." In the extreme, when the caregiver is chronically unavailable, the infant or young child may come to feel "unworthy of care" (Sroufe, 1990, p. 298).

In summary, the later course of poor infants' lives is powerfully shaped by the contexts that define their early lives, and by the adaptations made to those contexts. The patterns of interaction and emotions associated with early relationships reverberate over a long period of time, influencing later relationships, sense of self-worth, and approaches to both normative and unexpected challenges. The overall context of scarcity and depredation associated with poverty stands as an inherent contradiction to the nurturance, protection, and validation that build a foundation for embracing and mastering later developmental tasks. In a study of early-elementary-age children in central Harlem, Silverstein and Krate (1975) found that children's early adaptations to the stresses of life in that community, especially lessened adult support, necessitated

> ways of perceiving and coping with life that are effective in reducing anxiety, avoiding danger, and obtaining scarce material and social rewards. However, in the process of adapting, children may forfeit much of the plasticity of mind and attitude necessary for continuing differentiation and expansion of the self. (p. 33)

Poor children may learn early on to survive with lessened protection, support, and validation from caregivers and the broader environment. But the cost is in their trust of and beliefs about the world; in their ability to form healthy, reciprocal relationships; and in their capacity to use these relationships as a foundation for their own development.

In the introduction to this chapter, I have suggested that there are two different perspectives on the meaning of poverty for infants. One emphasizes the shared and very real hardships and injuries associated with poverty in U.S. society; the other the distinctness of each child's and family's experience and interpretation of those hardships. These two perspectives are in many respects contradictory. Yet both are necessary to the challenge of improving the well-being and life chances of poor infants. The former perspective raises the question of why U.S. society allows its most vulnerable members to experience hardship, injury, and loss to such an extent.

We as a society have to face this question if the lives of poor infants and their families are to improve to any meaningful degree. The latter perspective is critical to the more particular, discrete tasks of those working in helping relationships with individual infants and their families. Poverty constrains human beings, but it does not define them.

REFERENCES

Anderson, E. (1989). Sex codes and family life among poor inner-city youth. *Annals of the American Academy of Political and Social Science, 501,* 59–77.

Anderson, E. (1991). Neighborhood effects on teenage pregnancy. In C. Jencks & P. Peterson (Eds.), *The urban underclass.* Washington, DC: Brookings Institution Press.

Beckwith, L. (1988). Intervention with disadvantaged parents of sick preterm infants. *Psychiatry, 51,* 242–247.

Bettelheim, B. (1967). *The empty fortress.* New York: Free Press.

Birch, H. & Gussow, J. (1970). Disadvantaged children: Health, nutrition, and school failure. New York: Harcourt, Brace and Jovanovich.

Brazelton, T. B. (1983). Assessment techniques for enhancing infant development. In J. Call, E. Galenson, & R. Tyson (Eds.), *Frontiers of infant psychiatry.* New York: Basic Books.

Bromwich, R. (1978). *Working with parents and infants.* Austin, TX: Pro-Ed.

Burton, L. (1990). Teenage childbearing as an alternative life course strategy in multigeneration black families. *Human Nature, 1*(2), 123–143.

Clarke-Stewart, A. (1977). *Child care in the family.* New York: Academic Press.

Cohler, B. J. (1987). Adversity, resilience, and the study of lives. In E. J. Anthony & B. J. Cohler (Eds.), *The invulnerable child.* New York: Guilford Press.

Crittendon, P., & Bonvillian, J. (1984). The relationship between maternal risk status and maternal sensitivity. *American Journal of Orthopsychiatry, 54*(2), 250–262.

Crockenberg, S. (1987). Predictors and correlates of anger toward and punitive control of toddlers by adolescent mothers. *Child Development, 58,* 964–975.

Eberstadt, N. (1988, Winter). Economic and material poverty in the U.S. *The Public Interest, 90,* 50–65.

Egeland, B., & Erickson, M. (1990). Rising above the past: Strategies for helping new mothers break the cycle of abuse and neglect. *Zero to Three, 11*(2), 29–35.

Egeland, B., & Farber, E. (1984). Infant–mother attachment: Factors related to its development and change over time. *Child Development, 53*(3), 753–771.

Egeland, B., Jacobvitz, D., & Sroufe, L. (1988). Breaking the cycle of abuse. *Child Development, 59*(4), 1080–1088.

Eldridge, A., & Schmidt, E. (1990). The capacity to parent: A self psychological approach to parent–child psychotherapy. *Clinical Social Work Journal, 18*(4), 339–351.

Emde, R. (1989). The infant's relationship experience: Developmental and affective aspects. In A. Sameroff &

R. Emde (Eds.), *Relationship disturbances in early childhood.* New York: Basic Books.

Emde, R., & Buchsbaum, H. (1990). "Didn't you hear my mommy?": Autonomy with connectedness in moral self-emergence. In D. Cichetti & M. Beeghly (Eds.), *The self in transition: Infancy to childhood.* Chicago: University of Chicago Press.

Emde, R., & Sameroff, A. (1989). Understanding early relationship disturbances. In A. Sameroff & R. Emde (Eds.), *Relationship disturbances in early childhood.* New York: Basic Books.

Escalona, S. (1987). *Critical issues in the early development of premature infants.* New Haven, CT: Yale University Press.

Field, T., Heal, B., Goldstein, S., Perry, D., & Bendell, D. (1988). Depressed behavior even with nondepressed adults. *Child Development, 59,* 1569–1579.

Fraiberg, S., Shapiro, V., & Cherniss, D. (1983). Treatment modalities. In J. Call, E. Galenson, & R. Tyson (Eds.), *Frontiers of infant psychiatry.* New York: Basic Books.

Furman, E. (1987). *Helping children grow.* Madison, CT: International Universities Press.

Garmezy, N. (1983). Stressors of childhood. In N. Garmezy & M. Rutter (Eds.), *Stress, coping and development in children.* New York: McGraw-Hill.

Griffin, J. (1988, October 16). Prison of the past cripples poor kids. *Chicago Tribune,* section 2, p. 1.

Institute of Medicine. (1988). *Health, homelessness and human needs.* Washington, DC: National Academy of Sciences.

Jeffers, C. (1967). *Living poor.* Ann Arbor, MI: Ann Arbor Press.

Kagan, J., Kearsley, R., & Zelazo, P. (1978). *Infancy.* Cambridge, MA: Harvard University Press.

Khan, M. (1963). The concept of cumulative trauma. *Psychoanalytic Study of the Child, 18,* 286–306.

Klerman, L. (1991). *Alive and well?* New York: National Center for Children in Poverty.

Lindsey, D. (1991). Factors affecting the foster care placement decision: An analysis of national survey data. *American Journal of Orthopsychiatry, 61*(2), 273–282.

Lyons-Ruth, K., Zoll, D., Connell, D., & Grunebaum, H. (1989). Family deviance and family disruption in childhood: Associations with maternal behavior and infant maltreatment during the first two years of life. *Development and Psychopathology, 1,* 219–236.

Main, M., Kaplan, N., & Cassidy, J. (1985). Security in infancy, childhood, and adulthood: A move to the level of representation. In I. Bretherton & E. Waters (Eds.), *Growing points of attachment theory and research. Monographs of the Society for Research in Child Development, 50*(1–2, Serial No. 209), 66–104.

Martin, D. (1991, May 12). Now the work that's never done is grandmother's. *New York Times,* p. E6.

Massie, H., Bronstein, A., Afterman, K., & Campbell, B. (1988). Inner themes and outer behaviors in early childhood development: A longitudinal study. *Psychoanalytic Study of the Child, 43,* 213–242.

Meers, D. (1973). Psychoanalytic research and intellectual functioning of ghetto-reared black children. *Psychoanalytic Study of the Child, 28,* 395–418.

Minuchin, S. (1967). *Families of the slums.* New York: Basic Books.

Molnar, J., Roth, W., & Klein, T. (1990). Constantly compromised: The impact of homelessness on children. *Journal of Social Issues, 46*(4), 109–124.

Musick, J. (1993). Poor, hungry and pregnant: The psychology of high-risk adolescence. New Haven, CT: Yale University Press.

Musick, J., & Halpern, R. (1988). Giving children a chance: What role community-based early parenting interventions? In M. Steinbruner (Ed.), *Giving children a chance: The case for more effective national policy.* Washington, DC: Center for National Policy Press.

National Center for Children in Poverty. (1990). *Five million children.* New York: Author.

National Commission to Prevent Infant Mortality. (1988). *Death before life: The tragedy of infant mortality.* Washington, DC: Author.

National Commission to Prevent Infant Mortality. (1991). *Healthy brain development: Precursors to learning.* Washington, DC: Author.

New York Times. (1991). Editorial. New York: Author.

Norton, D. (1990). Understanding the early experience of black children in high-risk environments: Culturally and ecologically relevant research in regard to support for families. *Zero to Three, 10*(4), 1–7.

Ornstein, A., & Ornstein, P. (1985). Parenting as a function of the adult self: A psychoanalytic developmental perspective. In E. J. Anthony & G. Pollock (Eds.), *Parental influences in health and disease.* Boston: Little, Brown.

Pelton, L. (1989). *For reasons of poverty.* New York: Praeger.

Rainwater, L. (1970). *Behind ghetto walls: Black life in a federal slum.* Chicago: Aldine.

Siegler, A. (1982). Changing aspects of the family: A psychoanalytic perspective on early intervention. In E. Zigler & E. Gordon (Eds.), *Day care: Scientific and social policy issues.* Boston: Auburn House.

Silverstein, B., & Krate, R. (1975). *Children of the dark ghetto.* New York: Praeger.

Simpson, P. (1990). *Living in poverty: Coping on the welfare grant.* New York: Community Service Society.

Smollar, J., & Ooms, T. (1987). *Young unwed fathers.* Washington, DC: U.S. Department of Health and Human Services, Office of the Assistant Secretary for Planning and Evaluation.

Solnit, A. (1983). Foreword. In S. Provence & A. Naylor, *Working with disadvantaged parents and their children.* New Haven, CT: Yale University Press.

Sroufe, L. (1979). The coherence of individual development: Early care, attachment and subsequent developmental issues. *American Psychologist, 34*(10), 834–841.

Sroufe, L. (1990). An organizational perspective on the self. In D. Cicchetti & M. Beeghly (Eds.), *The self in transition: Infancy to childhood.* Chicago: University of Chicago Press.

Stack, C. (1974). *All our kin: Strategies for survival in a black community.* New York: Harper & Row.

Stern-Bruschweiler, N., & Stern, D. (1989). A model for conceptualizing the role of the mother's representational world in various mother–infant therapies. *Infant Mental Health Journal, 10*(3), 142–156.

Stott, F., Musick, J., & Cohler, B. (1984). Intervention for the severely disturbed mother. In B. Cohler & J. Musick (Eds.), *New directions in mental health: No. 24. Intervention for psychiatrically impaired parents.* San Francisco: Jossey-Bass.

Sullivan, M. (1989). Absent fathers in the inner city. *Annals of the American Academy of Political and Social Science, 501,* 48–57.

Wacquant, L., & Wilson, W. (1989). The cost of racial and class exclusion in the inner-city. *Annals of the American Academy of Political and Social Science, 501,* 8–25.

Weitzman, B. (1989). Pregnancy and childbirth: Risk factors for homelessness? *Family Planning Perspectives, 21*(4), 175–178.

Zeitel, L. (1989). Infant illness among New York City's disadvantaged. In M. Krasner (Ed.), *Poverty and health in New York City.* New York: United Hospital Fund of New York.

Zelkowitz, P. (1982). Parenting philosophies and practices. In D. Belle (Ed.), *Lives in stress.* Beverly Hills, CA: Sage.

6

Prematurity and Serious Medical Illness in Infancy: Implications for Development and Intervention

KLAUS MINDE

Prematurity and serious medical illnesses that occur during infancy have long provided an opportunity to assess the potential role that biological adversities and parenting behaviors can play in the development of children. At the same time, such conditions also represent very complex variables. To take prematurity as an example, we know that despite the objective criteria defining this condition, prematurity is associated with other factors such as multiple births, lower socioeconomic status, and particular emotional responses by parents. At the same time, the experience of the premature infant and his or her family in the hospital, as well as the final outcome, will vary with the technology available in differing settings. Likewise, medical conditions caused by genetic defects or postnatal infections that require long or frequent hospitalizations in infancy can be precursors of lifelong handicaps or may reflect treatable abnormalities. Such a prognosis, together with many other variables, will influence the future development of children who have experienced medical illnesses during infancy.

In the present chapter, I first delineate the scope of the problem; that is, I examine the number of children who spend a significant amount of time in hospitals during their first 3 years of life and explore the reasons for these hospitalizations. Because published studies here are limited, a good many of these data are based on specific government and hospital statistics.

I then summarize data from a variety of studies as they relate to the biological and emotional risks premature and other hospitalized infants experience during their hospitalization and later in life. From the extensive literature on this topic, I select only those studies that have looked at small premature infants (i.e., children born weighing less than 1500 grams) and others who have spent at least 2 months in hospital before their third birthday. To eliminate potentially transient findings, I only discuss work where validated instruments have been used, and report on outcome as well as process studies. Finally, I discuss the practical implications of these data for the infant mental health practitioner, and outline intervention strategies or programs that have demonstrated practical value for the development of these vulnerable infants and their families.

PREVALENCE AND SURVIVAL

About 1.1% of all annual live births in the United States and Canada are children weighing less than 1500 grams (Pharoah & Alberman,

1990). This means that there are about 35,000 such births per year in the United States and 3800 in Canada (Statistics Canada, personal communication, 1991). Infants weighing less than 1500 grams at birth are at least 8 weeks premature and will normally remain hospitalized until they have reached their expected date of birth. Survival of these babies has increased remarkably during the past 10 years. Although recent reports are based mainly on well-equipped regional centers, findings show that survival is generally more than 25% in infants weighing between 500 and 750 grams, more than 50% for those weighing 751 to 1000 grams (Bauchner, Brown, & Peskin, 1988), and 90% for babies with a birthweight between 1001 and 1500 grams (Pharoah & Alberman, 1990). These data, which document the improved overall outcome for these infants, also suggest that more premature infants remain in hospitals for a longer time now than ever before.

Data for infants suffering from other illnesses requiring long-term hospitalization are less clear. In the Canadian census of 1986–1987, 4% of all children under age 4 were described as handicapped (defined as needing a prosthesis, as having health conditions limiting activities normal for age and other long-term health conditions, or as having to attend special schools or classes). How many children were so diagnosed during their first year of life is not clear from these figures. Likewise, there are no published data on the total length of hospitalization children experienced during their first 3 years of life, although data from the above-mentioned Canadian census indicate that 110,000 infants under 1 year of age were hospitalized in this country in 1986. Of these children, some 2500 had at least one hospital admission that lasted longer than 3 months during the first and second years of life (Statistics Canada, personal communication, 1991).

At the Montreal Children's Hospital, the pediatric teaching hospital of McGill University, 3025 children under the age of 2 were admitted between April 1990 and March 1991. Of these, 101 stayed between 30 and 60 days; 33 between 61 and 90 days; 28 between 91 and 180 days; and 11 for more than 180 days (mean 349 days). This means that a total of 173, or 5.7% of all admissions for the age group, remained in the hospital for longer than one month. If one subtracts all of those children who were discharged by 6 months of age, and hence did not remain in the hospital during the most sensitive ages of 6

to 24 months, the number of long-staying children decreases from 173 to 71 (Direction Générale du Budget et de l'Administration Québecoise, 1992). As about 35% of the total admissions of infants in this age group occurred before the age of 6 months, these 71 children still make up about 3.5% of all the children hospitalized after 6 months of age. Furthermore, it should be pointed out that 96 of all the 173 long-staying children had more than one admission during this 1 year (mean = 4.4, SD = 3.0, range = 2–18) and may have had admissions in the preceding year as well. The clinical conditions of the older infants were primarily related to cardiovascular disease (10%), congenital abnormalities (25%), central nervous system (CNS) problems (9%), and infections (25%). However, there were also two children with failure to thrive, two who were abused, and two who were waiting for placement.

In summary, then, there is clear evidence that a substantial number of young children spend a significant part of their very early life in hospitals. These children generally have serious physical disorders, and their families must adjust to parenting their infants away from their homes. It is important for them to receive practical assistance and sensitive support.

DEVELOPMENTAL SEQUELAE

Biological Risk Factors

Small premature infants continue to suffer more often from cerebral disorders than do full-term infants (Kopp, 1987). Although the overall incidence of major neurodevelopmental disorders in this population has decreased in recent years, some 10–15% still show intellectual and/or neurological abnormalities (Costello et al., 1988; Hoy, Bill, & Sykes, 1988; Minde, Perrotta, & Hellmann, 1988). In the group of infants with birthweights under 1000 grams, recent reports quote rates of 17–27% with cerebral palsy and IQ's below 70 or other neurosensory impediments (Brothwood, Wolke, Gamsu, & Cooper, 1988; Lefebvre, Bard, Veilleux, & Martel, 1988), and identify an additional 10–20% who are affected with less severe neurological problems, such as epilepsy or an IQ between 70 and 85 (Orgill, Astbury, Bajuk, & Yu, 1982). This means that despite the overall decrease in complications we see in these infants, they still show a prevalence of cerebral palsy that is 10 to 40 times higher than in full-term babies (Hagberg, Hagberg, & Zetterstrom, 1989).

The biological sequelae of full-term infants who have experienced repeated early hospitalizations are far more difficult to estimate, as we have no valid literature on the range of diagnoses of these children. In the above-mentioned major pediatric teaching hospital, 45% of all the involved children were hospitalized because of genetic abnormalities such as severe cystic fibrosis; of these children, 80% had a poor prognosis. The others suffered from conditions such as orthopedic or cardiac anomalies, immune deficiencies, or chronic respiratory diseases (e.g., Ondine's curse) (Montreal Children's Hospital, personal communication, 1991).

Finally, there was a small group of children who were hospitalized because of malignancies and congenital abnormalities such as biliary atresia, and who needed multiple or complicated operations or organ transplants. Although only a few of these conditions are associated with neurological and intellectual impairments, many of these children certainly suffered from conditions that could mark their future development.

Behavioral Risk Factors

In addition to the biological consequences of prematurity, many factors surrounding the birth of the low-birthweight infant can potentially influence the quality of this infant's later life. On the one hand, such an infant may have characteristics that can make parenting difficult. An example here would be the comparatively high incidence of brain damage these children suffer, even in present-day high-technology nurseries. Children with neurological damage, in turn, show an incidence of behavior disorders two to three times higher than that of control populations (Rutter, 1989; Seidel, Chadwick, & Rutter, 1975; Minde, 1984). On the other hand, the long-term outcome of prematurity is to a significant degree also influenced by the particular responses each individual caretaker has to the early birth of such an infant, and by the effect this can have on the developing child's transaction with his or her family (Sameroff & Chandler, 1975; Sigman & Parmelee, 1979; Minde, 1980; Stern & Karraker, 1990).

Although details are discussed in the next section, the literature on very-low-birthweight infants later in life has long suggested that these children are at an increased risk for a variety of behavioral difficulties, including major and minor psychiatric disorders (Drillien, 1964). Half a century ago, prematurely born children were already described as suffering from "restlessness, nervousness, fatigueability which resulted in distractibility and disturbed concentration" (Benton, 1940, p. 737). However, research on this population has been rather unsystematic and decidedly atheoretical (Kopp, 1983).

Early hospitalization for nonpremature children has also been associated with adverse later emotional consequences (Douglas, 1975; Quinton & Rutter, 1976). However, here again it is not clear whether children with specific illnesses or particular family patterns are more vulnerable to later disorders.

Although such factors make comparisons of studies difficult, one can nevertheless distinguish between two general types of investigations that have examined these issues, best labeled the "outcome" and the "process" approaches.

Outcome Studies

Premature Infants

Most studies of premature infants are using the outcome approach. They focus on short- or long-term benefits of specific neonatal intensive care unit (NICU) treatment techniques or institutionalized psychosocial support programs such as liberal visiting hours. Percentages of disturbed children are tabulated, and the children are categorized according to their particular neonatal complications or specific treatments they received. Recent studies using the outcome approach have come from Field, Dempsey, and Shuman (1983); Silva, MaGee, and Williams (1984); Dunn et al. (1986); Minde et al. (1989); and Goldberg, Corter, Lojkasek, and Minde (1990).

Field et al. (1983) followed 57 premature infants who had an average birthweight of 1597 grams and compared them to a group of normal, full-term, and postmature infants. On average, her preterms had experienced 3 days of mechanical ventilation. At 2 and 5 years of age, the premature children were rated significantly worse on the Behavior Problem Checklist devised by Quay and Pederson (1975).

Silva et al. (1984), in a follow-up study of 31 preterm, 71 small-for-gestational-age, and 750 full-term infants born in one New Zealand hospital, found the preterm group at ages 5 and 9 years to have been rated by their parents and

teachers as showing significantly more symptoms on the Rutter Child Scale (Rutter, 1967)
than the normal controls. However, these scores,
though statistically higher in the preterm group,
ranged only between 7.1 at age 5 and 9.7 at age
9—that is, well below the cutoff point of 13,
which according to Rutter suggests the possible
presence of a psychological disorder.

In a follow-up study of premature infants
born in the 1960s, Dunn et al. (1986) looked at
40 out of 61 preterm survivors aged 12 to 15
years, who had showed signs of "minimal brain
dysfunction" at 6 years. As young adolescents,
40.5% of these survivors were given a psychiatric diagnosis by a child psychiatrist. This diagnosis was based on a report from a social worker
who made a home visit and saw each child together with his or her parents. The parents also
filled in a questionnaire and the Devreux Adolescent Behavior Rating Scale. Unfortunately, the
authors give no information about these ratings,
and since the 40 children of this study made up
a particularly high-risk subsample from among
335 low-birthweight children enrolled in this follow-up study, this percentage figure is of little
direct value. It merely confirms the well-established observation that children who show signs
of cerebral dysfunction also often tend to fail in
their social relationships.

Our own group followed 77 children, of
whom 46 were twins, for 4 years (Minde et al.,
1989). Youngsters in our study all had weighed
less than 1500 grams at birth and been assessed
at various times during their first year of life. At
48 months, the children and their families all
received a comprehensive evaluation; this included a clinical psychiatric interview, as well as
information on behavioral and cognitive functioning obtained from teachers, parents, and clinicians. Children with serious CNS damage were
excluded from the evaluation.

All of the children showed normal intelligence
and good physical health at 4 years. However,
43% of the youngsters scored within the abnormal range on the Richman–Graham Behavior
Questionnaire (Richman & Graham, 1971)
completed by the parents, which indicated a likelihood of a behavior disorder. This was four
times higher than the rate among a nonclinical
preschool group examined by us earlier (Minde
& Minde, 1977). The high-scoring children did
not differ in their sex distribution, neonatal illness scores, or intellectual assessment at 12 and
48 months; however, more high scorers were reported by their mothers to have a difficult tem-

perament than children with low scores, both at
1 year (55% vs. 14%) and at 4 years (42% vs.
7%). Teacher ratings on the Preschool Behavior Questionnaire (PBQ; Behar & Stringfield,
1977) showed that 24% of the children scored
in the abnormal range. This was higher than reported in previous investigations, but correlated
poorly with the maternal ratings ($r = .17$).

It is interesting that an analysis of the individual items of the Richman–Graham Behavior
Questionnaire scored by the parents indicated
that the most frequently appearing problems
(i.e., those occurring in more than 40% of all
children) were associated with eating difficulties,
settling, and overactivity, as well as with temper
tantrums, demanding attention, and general difficulties of control. Likewise, the PBQ items
noted to be present most often by teachers were
"restless," "solitary," "inattentive," and "poor
concentration." One could conceptualize these
symptoms as representing a general immaturity,
possible hyperactivity, or an overall poor behavioral organization. This interpretation is supported by the results of our psychiatric evaluation of these children and their families. Here
only seven children (10.9%) warranted a psychiatric diagnosis according to the criteria of the
*Diagnostic and Statistical Manual of Mental Dis-
orders*, third edition (DSM-III). This is compatible with findings in other nonclinical populations (Offord et al., 1987).

Goldberg and colleagues (1990) tried to examine specific socioemotional factors predictive
of high scores on the behavior questionnaire
filled out by parents and teachers. Traditional
attachment ratings obtained at age 12 months
did not differentiate between high- and low-scor-
ing children at 4 years of age on either questionnaire. However 75% of the children who were
given a D-rating (Main & Solomon, 1986),
which assesses the coherence of strategies children use in coping with separations and reunions, were given a psychiatric diagnosis three
years later. This suggests that the D category may
assess children's emotional disturbance.

Most predictive for teacher behavior ratings
were scores on maternal responsiveness derived
during mother–child observations, and on a
Family Rating Scale which assessed the emotional functioning of the family, both at 12
months and 48 months. Specifically, the observed mother–child relationship and family
rating at age 12 months accounted for 31% of
the variance, and in year four they entered the
stepwise regression analysis accounting for 55%

of the variance of the behavioral problems score as rated by the teachers. As teachers are generally more objective in their assessment of emotional problems of children, this suggests that family and interactional variables will significantly determine the emotional outcome even of medically highly compromised infants.

In summary, then, there is evidence from outcome studies that a substantial number of premature infants score high on various behavioral checklists, primarily on symptoms denoting attentional factors and impulsivity. However, there is no convincing evidence that these children have a higher rate of psychiatric disturbances.

Other Hospitalized Infants

The behavioral outcomes of children who were repeatedly hospitalized during their first 3 years of life were studied by Douglas (1975) and Quinton and Rutter (1976). Both investigations revealed that a single hospital admission of less than 1 week did not lead to later difficulties in children. However, multiple admissions, of which at least one had taken place between 6 and 60 months of age, were associated with a very significant increase in both psychiatric disorder and delinquency at ages 12 to 14. These findings suggest that young children are "sensitized" by their initial hospitalization. Because they are unable to conceptualize the nonpermanence of this experience, a second hospitalization and associated separation from their caretakers are then experienced as very serious stress. However, Quinton and Rutter (1976) also pointed out in their study that the children with multiple hospital admissions came more often from disadvantaged homes. This underlines the complexity of factors that contribute to seemingly basic health data such as hospital admissions.

It is of interest that only two investigations have examined the long-term effects of a hospital stay on children born with an abnormality that could be permanently treated but required extensive hospitalization early in life. Beavers (1974) tested a group of 22 boys aged 7 to 14, who had undergone surgery for esophageal atresia as infants, against normal controls on academic and psychological norms. Although the clinical group did not differ in intelligence or academic achievement, they were found to have a lower self-concept and to be more anxious. Similar findings were reported by Shapiro

(1978) on 26 children who had undergone heart surgery in infancy but had remained well since.

When we look at outcome studies of specific populations of chronically ill children who could be expected to have been hospitalized early in life, the literature provides little guidance. Although many studies have examined the long-term psychological sequelae of specific medical conditions such as asthma, diabetes, or cancer, authors do not specify the age of onset of the diseases in these children and never mention the number or length of hospitalizations these children experienced. Recent reviews (Eiser, 1990; Pless & Nolan, 1991) nevertheless confirm that compared to physically well children, those with any type of chronic disorder have about twice the risk of developing a secondary emotional handicap. This is true for population-based studies (Cadman, Doyle, Szatmari, & Offord, 1987) as well as those referring to single disease groups. The exceptions here again are children who suffered CNS damage, of whom 35% showed psychiatric disturbances (Breslau, 1985). Younger children seem to do much worse than older ones. Dowd, Novak, and Ray (1977) observed 29 infants who had to be immobilized for a variety of reasons. During periods of immobilization, infants less than 18 months cried and fought their restraints, while older infants displayed more passive behavior. Even when the restraints were removed, the older infants remained immobile, as if they were unaware of their ability to move their limbs again.

Some years before Dowd et al.'s work was published, Holt (1968) obtained some follow-up data on early hospital experiences from school-age youngsters that confirm some of the observations above. Holt examined 30 children aged 8 to 12 who had been hospitalized during their toddler years (ages 2 to 5) for a variety of illnesses. The children were interviewed and allowed to play with a medical play kit as well as with family figures. Their single worst recollections about their hospital stays were related to restraints and painful procedures, although none were associated with particular individuals. Some children repeatedly went over their experiences 6 to 7 years earlier. Interestingly, in their drawings they did not include their mothers, as if they had felt abandoned by them during their hospitalization.

In summary, then, the hospitalization of young children is clearly upsetting to them. Although long-term detrimental effects have not been documented in children hospitalized during the last decade, when parents were actively encouraged to help with caring for their children in hospitals, we should remain cautious in our assessment until we can identify those aspects of hospitalization that determine later emotional well-being in such populations. Process studies may be helpful, because they attempt to discover the pathways that lead from event A to outcome B.

Process Studies

In the process approach, investigators focus on small premature infants or hospitalized children as a prototype for studying how specific events and interactions may lead to normal or compromised psychosocial functioning. As will be appreciated, developmental pathways are generally complex and multifaceted. Process studies therefore do not always follow the rigorous criteria of traditional scientific inquiry, but also include clinical data or individuals' reflections on how they have experienced specific events.

To understand an individual's development, we have to recognize that his or her pathway encompasses a wide range of interrelated factors that may have functioned as stressful or supportive biological or environmental events. Few theoretical models are sufficiently detailed to allow the testing of hypotheses linking specific precursors and outcomes of development in a prospective fashion. As any clinician knows, it is often possible to understand the complexity of an individual's present strengths and difficulties by examining his or her past life history. However, continuities apparent in retrospect do not automatically allow us to make assumptions about the effects of a specific event or handicap on later psychosocial functioning, although they can help us identify important determinants of overall development, such as a child's temperament or particular socioeconomic condition.

The model most commonly used to understand the complex interchanges between an infant and its caretakers is the transactional model, first described by Sameroff and Chandler (1975). These investigators saw the behavior of a child as primarily the result of the ongoing changes and reassessments of behavior that take place between each child and those interacting with him or her, within the context of their biological and social limitations. They also documented that the final intellectual and behavioral outcome of children who have experienced a biological in-

sult early in life depends far more on the care these children receive than on the severity of their injury. Their theoretical model is thus an open one, suggesting that change can occur at any time and that long-term predictions are difficult to make.

Another model that has been used to examine these issues is based on the idea that children pass through specific "way stations," which can either ameliorate or compromise further development (Rutter, 1989). Rutter stresses that these way stations may be developmentally determined (e.g., they may include influences that come to bear when the child learns to talk or enters adolescence) or can have primarily social or interpersonal determinants (e.g., an infant may make the mother feel depressed, which in turn will lead her to become emotionally unavailable, leading to insecure attachment on the part of the infant).

It should be stressed that both these models encompass the notion that the interpretation of an individual's behavior can be based on observable interactions between the individual and others, as well as on the more or less idiosyncratic attributions the interactional partners may make about each other's behavior. They are therefore compatible with the increasing literature suggesting that our thoughts and fantasies about our children form an important matrix of the children's early emotional experiences as they determine much of our early interactions with them (Lebovici, 1983; Stern, 1985).

Premature Infants

What do we know about the impact prematurity may have on the transactional system of an infant? A substantial body of descriptive research suggests that mothers of premature infants show continuing anxiety and low confidence in their caregiving competence, at least during the first year of their infants' lives (Crnic, Greenberg, Ragozin, Robinson, & Basham, 1983; Brooten et al., 1988; Corter & Minde, 1987). These parental concerns are thought to be related to specific interaction patterns that have been observed between premature infants and their caretakers. Briefly, it has been suggested that preterm infants have problems with information processing and are therefore easily disorganized in their overall behavior (Brazelton, Koslowski, & Main, 1974; Field, 1977). Because this disorganization often makes them appear hyporeactive to everyday stimuli or handling, mothers initially tend to compensate for this perceived deficit through excessive stimulation. This often has the unintended effect of derailing the infants' behavior even further. Consequently, they may abruptly shift from hypo- to hyperreactivity, leaving the caretakers unsure of how to stimulate these infants appropriately (Beckwith & Cohen, 1983; Barnard, Bee, & Hammond, 1984).

Als (1992) has developed this thinking further. She has analyzed the NICU environment and its effect on infants who have suddenly been displaced from the econiche of the maternal womb which is adapted to provide support and nurture their neurodevelopmental progress, and developed the concept of "synaction." This concept incorporates a number of developmental principles (i.e., the principle of continuous organism–environment interaction) and explains many of the neurodevelopmental and parenting problems these infants experience.

Another suggested pathway to compromised parenting is thought to be the generally lower socioeconomic status of the parents of premature infants (Crnic et al., 1983). Poverty, among other things, is associated with limited emotional support services for mothers and subsequent maternal insensitivity (Sameroff, 1986; see also Halpern, Chapter 5, this volume).

Some authors also believe that an important aspect of our approach to these infants is based on stereotyped concepts we hold about prematurity. According to Stern and Karraker (1990), premature infants are generally seen as less physically developed, less cognitively competent, less behaviorally active, less sociable, and less likable than full-term infants. Interestingly, this does not only apply to women who have no personal experience in caring for a premature infant, but also to actual mothers of premature infants (Stern & Karraker, 1990). However, it should be stressed that mothers vary substantially in the extent to which they stereotype their infants, and there are no data showing that these early misperceptions have a significant effect on the later development of these infants (Stern & Karraker, 1990).

Still another set of events that typically affects the early interaction between caretakers and their small premature infants is linked to the disruption of some basic biological and social parameters associated with the pregnancy and delivery of such infants. Premature infants may be born only 3 to 4 weeks after their mothers have first felt the babies' movements. Experiencing a

moving infant is an important step in the ongoing process of prenatal maternal preoccupation and attachment of the mother to her infant (Minde & Stewart, 1988; Brazelton & Cramer, 1990). If this process is suddenly interrupted, giving birth changes from being the crowning event of a clearly marked preparation and waiting time to a crisis associated with anxiety and fear of losing this baby. In addition, mothers of premature infants have usually not yet attended childbirth classes, and therefore are often relatively poorly informed about the demands of early parenting. Often they also experience a sense of failure and loss for having given birth to less than perfect babies under difficult circumstances. Added to this is the often overwhelming technical environment of an NICU, the initial home of these tiny infants, and the mothers' fear that their infants may grow up with a developmental handicap.

Yet, after a premature delivery, there is little time to mourn the loss of the perfect baby before the demands of the new sick infant must be met. Because it is often difficult for parents to obtain or comprehend appropriate information about their infant early on, because they are so preoccupied with their own adjustment to this unforeseen event, unreasonable expectations of the baby's future may develop. For example, many parents worry that their children will not be sufficiently attached to them because of the anomaly of their neonatal experience. In addition, mothers even today are frequently criticized by their relatives for having "failed" their families by giving birth to such tiny infants (Minde, 1984). The ensuing feelings of guilt, anger, and despair are exacerbated when mothers have given birth in an outside hospital (i.e., a hospital other than the one with an NICU, to which the infants have been transferred) and are separated from their infants during the first days of their lives. The acute yearning for their infants that many mothers in outside hospitals experience during this time was one of the reasons why some 10% of our mothers signed themselves out of these hospitals before their obstetricians felt this to be appropriate (Minde, 1987). A premature infant's father is often the only parent readily available to NICU staff, as well as the conveyor of information to the mother. He therefore becomes a special source of comfort to the mother during this period. Nevertheless, a substantial number of fathers become so protective of their wives or partners at that time that they screen out information they feel the infants' mothers should not hear yet (Marton, Minde, & Ogilvie, 1981).

These clinical data have recently been supplemented by a study that has shown that a mother's representation and fantasy of her baby increase in richness between the fourth and seventh months of pregnancy. After that time, maternal thoughts about the growing infant become more vague. This is seen as a normal defensive phenomenon that allows the child to be born into a less predetermined set of expectations, and thus to have a better chance to establish his or her unique characteristics within a more neutral environment (Ammaniti, 1989). These observations suggest a greater potential discordance between the imagined baby and real baby following a premature birth. This may add to the difficulties a mother may have in developing an easy and positive relationship with her newborn.

Another potential obstacle parents have to deal with is the NICU as an institution. As stated above, an NICU is invariably a busy and highly technical space. However, such a unit also has a unique culture, based on myths and belief systems. For example, parents will usually be exposed to an ongoing split between the intimacy suggested by personalized namecards for their infants ("It is a boy") and the routine aspects of the almost robot-like care suggested by a respirator. There are also the ever-present statistics ("In this unit on average we lose six infants per month") versus the fate of their own infants, and the reputation of specific nurses ("Nurse A. is a sweetheart, but Nurse B. can be a dragon") to whom parents have to entrust their infants. Finally, there is the sudden termination of this intense emotional experience following the babies' discharge, and the strong resulting tendency to seal off the whole experience (Brody & Klein, 1980). Yet all through the hospital stay a truly intimate contact between a parent and baby is impossible, and parents can make few decisions about their infants because even many routine caretaking tasks, such as feeding times, are determined by the medical establishment. Because many mothers who give birth to premature babies have had previous miscarriages and other serious obstetrical complications, they are especially sensitized to the potential loss of their infants. It is no wonder, therefore, that parents of premature infants often feel like visitors rather than parents to their newborns, which prevents them from gaining confidence in their parenting skills (Freud, 1988; Minde & Stewart, 1988).

Concerns for the psychosocial welfare of infants and parents have lead to many changes in the NICU scene in the last 25 years, best exemplified by the liberalization of visiting hours. Yet parents continue to show differential behaviors toward their infants, and clinicians have long searched for explanations of such caretaking patterns. In our own studies, where we continuously recorded 10 discrete parent behaviors and 8 infant behaviors for 45 minutes twice per week, we found that mothers generally became more engaged with their infants during each successive visit. However, some mothers were consistently more engaged than others (Minde, Marton, Manning, & Hines, 1980). Not unexpectedly, we found that the quantity of interaction a mother showed during her visits was related to the frequency of her visits; mothers who showed little activity with their children visited infrequently. More significantly, we also found that the level of engagement with the infants in the hospital predicted the numbers of interactions mothers showed toward these infants in the home at 3 months corrected age (i.e., the time at which the infants would have been 3 months of age if they had been carried to term).

To determine what might contribute to these relatively stable differences in engagement, we examined background data taken from the psychiatric interview with each mother during the hospital period. Although we assumed that complications during pregnancy or delivery and the social class of the family would give us important clues, the factor that in reality most clearly distinguished between the high- and low-engagement groups was the strength of the relationships a mother reported with her own mother and with her husband. Factors such as the length of time a mother could see her infant after birth or the initial prognosis given her by the physician also did not correlate with her later style of interaction. This strongly suggests that early maternal behavior with premature infants is subject to second-order effects of the mothers' other relationships, and that it does not reflect events occurring at the time of delivery.

Having established that the family system affects an infant's social environment during the early days of life, we considered the infant's contribution to parenting behavior. This was done by examining sequences of mother–infant interaction for evidence of mutual influence in which one partner responds to the immediately preceding behavior of the other (Minde, Marton, et al., 1980). Among low-engagement mothers and their infants, there was little evidence that either partner was responding to the other. In contrast, mothers in the high-engagement group often responded to their infants' behavior (i.e., "infant stretches" was followed by "mother smiles").

The medical complications experienced by premature infants also appear to have a substantial impact on their parents' perceptions. Using an objective scale for measuring the 20 most common diseases or pathophysiological states encountered in premature infants every day, we reported on 20 infants with very few complications and 20 infants with serious complications during their hospital stay (Minde, Whitelaw, Brown, & Fitzhardinge, 1983). The two groups did not differ on variables such as weight, gestational age, or socioeconomic status, but there was a clear association between illness and mother–infant interaction. In a dyad with a sicker baby, the baby's level of motor activity and alertness and the mother's levels of smiling and touching were consistently lower, both during nursery visits and during observations 6 and 12 weeks after discharge home. In a companion study that involved 14 infants with a long perinatal illness (more than 35 days) and 17 with a short perinatal illness (fewer than 17 days), we also found significant differences in infant and parental behaviors. In the case of an infant who was sick for fewer than 17 days, both motor and social behaviors of the infant and mother rebounded quickly following recovery from the illness. However, in the case of an infant who was sick for more than 35 days, the recovery of maternal behavior lagged behind the infant's recovery, and this could still be noted 3 months after discharge home. This means that even after the sick infant had recovered physically and reached healthy levels of activity with no sign of CNS damage, maternal behavior remained at a lower level. These associations permit different interpretations:

1. Illness may act on maternal behavior via the infant's behavior. This interpretation requires some additional features to account for effects that persist after the infant's behavior has recovered.

2. Illness may act independently on the infant's behavior and on the mother's behavior—for example, by causing the mother to view the child as fragile. Our data provide support for this later possibility. The low level of maternal interaction following the apparent recovery of an infant seems to reflect the mother's worries about possible brain damage or other later difficulties of the infant.

The discussion up to now has primarily dealt with the effects of prematurity on mother–child interaction. Although mothers remain the primary caretakers for most infants even today, the influence of fathers and siblings on the mothers and their own responses to the ecology of the NICU have recently been more readily appreciated. In our own studies, we found that fathers on average visited their infants as much as mothers did (Marton et al., 1981). Furthermore, there was no difference in engagement levels of mothers and fathers, and very little difference in the particular ways they interacted with the babies. Even following discharge home, fathers remained active and involved with their infants. For example, during seven continuous 24-hour periods 3 months after discharge, fathers fed their infants in 17% of the feeding instances, changed diapers in 13% of the instances, and gave a bath in 10% of the observed bathing episodes. These were three times higher than the rates reported for fathers of full-term infants (Marton et al., 1981).

Our finding of similarities in mothers' and fathers' interactions with their infants in the hospital and following discharge is supported by Parke's research on fathers (Tinsley & Parke, 1983). In addition to demonstrating that both parents do the same sorts of things with a premature baby, Parke showed that the mother as well as the father explored more and smiled more at the baby when the other parent was present than when either parent visited the baby alone. This suggests that parents draw support from each other while interacting with their baby.

Siblings have also been recently introduced to the NICU scene (Ballard, Maloney, Shank, & Hollister, 1984; Maloney, Ballard, Hollister, & Shank, 1983). In these programs, siblings ranging in age from 2 to 19 years were allowed to visit their newborn siblings once. Parent and child interviews and questionnaires were used to compare the visiting group with a control group before and after the visit. The few differences that were found favored the visiting group. For example, more parents in the visiting group reported that their older children "were doing better" following the visit. The siblings who visited generally said that they enjoyed the visit and did not seem disturbed by the experience. In fact, clinical observations suggested that children, being less conscious of the association between high technology and illness/disease, may provide much direct and indirect support to parents who are mourning the illness of their newborn infant.

In summary, then, there is good evidence from process studies that the interactional difficulties between premature infants and their mothers are reflections of the mothers' insecurity and low self-esteem. These characteristics in turn may be related to the early relationships a mother had with her own mother, reinforced by the ecology of the NICU, an infant's initial medical status, and the support available from the spouse and the rest of the family.

Other Hospitalized Infants

When we look for data-based process studies to explain how early hospitalizations in non-premature infants are translated into compromised behavior in later life, few such studies are available. There are multiple reasons for this. Authors studying the process of hospitalization have traditionally examined older children or looked at samples that included a wide age range of patients. They have also tried to substantiate associations between specific sociodemographic or personal factors and children's psychological upsets. However, very young children's concepts of hospitals or their prior personalities are of little relevance in predicting the effects of hospitalization on them. Likewise, there is little evidence that specific procedures such as an injection or a rectal temperature, which are frequently examined variables, will differentially affect young children.

In fact, our knowledge about development would indicate that the emotional stress experienced by a hospitalized infant can be primarily attributed both to the rupture of the infant's developing attachment with his or her caregivers and to the parallel loss of habits or routines that help the young child organize his or her day-to-day life experiences. Young children's need to be secure and concretely assured about those ministering to them is clearly violated in a hospital. To give just some examples, a normal 36-month-old child on average has contacts with 6.6 different individuals per day and 8.4 individuals per week (Lewis, 1987). Hospitalized infants, on the other hand, have to cope with 40 or more different faces every day (Pinard & Minde, 1991). Young children require continu-

ous and sensitive caretaking experiences as they develop patterns of trust to those important to them. However, nurses tend to have a more stereotyped way of acting than do parents, and are involved in painful procedures as well as nurturing activities. This is confusing and upsetting to young children, as they cannot yet differentiate the various roles of a nurse, and it may explain why orderlies or other nonmedical staff not associated with pain and hurt are often seen as more caring.

Children also need routines to give them a sense of predictability and control over their lives, yet hospitals provide few such helpful structures. Thus beds are used for playing as well as sleeping; lights may be on all through the night; comforting toys may not qualify for hygienic reasons; and the ever-changing scene of newly admitted or discharged patients does not allow easily for adaptation and the development of new structures.

Following the concerns of some early psychoanalysts such as Anna Freud and John Bowlby, as well as pediatricians interested in children's mental health, the British government in 1959 formed a commission headed by Sir Harry Platt (Ministry of Health, 1959); this group defined the needs of hospitalized children and their families, and developed guidelines for implementing them. In 1980, the Consumers Association set up an independent study to check how far the suggestions made in the Platt Report had become routines during the intervening 21 years (Consumers Association, 1980). This second report was based on visits to 12 pediatric hospital departments and interviews with almost 300 parents and 250 hospital staff members. The verdict was that changes in hospital care practices had indeed occurred but had not led to sufficient improvements. Mothers in most hospitals were still not permitted to stay overnight with their sick infants, even though they could stay with their older children. Fifty percent of all hospitals still did not permit visits by siblings, and 30% had no continuous services for parents (e.g., providing food in the cafeteria at night or during the weekend). Similarly, nurses still did not ask for special likes or dislikes of children and did not routinely tell parents about the behavior problems of their children. Although these data reflect the situation in Great Britain in 1980, North American studies confirm these observations.

The most extensive evaluation of the pediatric milieu for toddlers and preschool children was done by Knafl, Cavallari, and Dixon (1988). In this study, 62 families whose young children were hospitalized for up to 3 weeks were repeatedly interviewed. Among other things, parents were classified in terms of their participation in their children's day-to-day activities in the hospital as level I or level II parents. Level I parents were more compliant toward the medical system and tried to look after their children by "being nice" to the hospital staff. They had less education and had experienced fewer hospitalizations within their families. Level II mothers more often brought along a sibling and were generally more critical of the nursing care (42% vs. 0%) and overall medical care (29% vs. 3%) their infants received. Although all parents perceived themselves as "workers" who participated in their children's care, level II mothers did not accept traditional decisions about medical and nursing roles, and actively negotiated their own standing with each group of professionals.

The authors do not provide follow-up data on the infants, but suggest that the more active behavior of level II parents, though creating more conflicts within the ward milieu, seemed to have been beneficial to the infants. No reason is offered for this conclusion. However, one may speculate that the 24 level II mothers (30% of the total sample) were generally more secure and autonomous in their mothering roles, and for that reason could model a more active form of support for their infants. Fathers of level II infants were also more involved with their infants; that is, they played and visited more often with them than did level I fathers.

Another study examined the process of admitting sixteen 11- to 48-month-old infants to a hospital (Roskies, Bedard, Gavreau-Guilbault, & LaFortune, 1975). The authors of this study followed these infants during the first 6 hours of their hospitalization, recording every contact the children had, each procedure they were exposed to, and the ways in which various groups of individuals (e.g., nurses, physicians, parents, and infants) interacted with each other. Furthermore, the 16 children were divided into eight emergency admissions (mean age = 25 months) and eight elective admissions (mean age = 26 months).

The results paint a worrisome picture of our caretaking practices. Roskies and her colleagues, among other data, reported that the emergency admissions affected children who had primarily chronic diseases and had all been hospitalized before. Interestingly, their admissions were more

often triggered by the mothers' feeling that they "couldn't take it any more" than by a true medical emergency. Yet neither group of children was told by their parents about the admission before they arrived at the hospital. Children experiencing an emergency admission had more painful procedures (eight vs. three), but in only 35% were the children warned or informed about them. The emergency admission children also experienced more action in less time, saw more white-clad people, and witnessed less positive interactions between their parents and the medical staff (50% vs. 85%). Six of the eight parents of the emergency admissions left the hospital within 1 hour after admission, while none of the parents of elective admissions did so. The former group also did not bring along toys or other objects that might have helped the infants in their adjustment to the hospital. This work suggests that even in a modern pediatric university hospital, the process of admitting children is still carried out with little awareness of its possible emotional consequences, which may easily cause the children to feel abandoned and misunderstood.

Another area examined in the most recent literature review on pediatric hospitalization (Thompson, 1985) suggests that mothers of young infants are much more committed to their infants if they had them home for 2 or more weeks during the first 3 months of life. In a study involving some 30 infants, Lampe, Trause, and Kennell (1977) found that only 16% of infants who had never been home were visited daily by their caretakers, whereas 70% of those who had been home had daily visits. As samples were matched for social class and illness, Lampe et al. suggested that a relationship has to be sealed through total care provided at home before a mother can truly commit herself to her infant.

Some confirmation of this assumption comes from a more recent study, where parental visits for 80 infants with a mean age of 16 months were observed (Blitzer, Zuckerman, Pozen, & Blitzer, 1983). Results indicate that the medium length of visit per day was 5 hours and that 29% of parents stayed 24 hours. Mothers of children who had been breast-fed stayed the longest. Blitzer and colleagues suggest that this is a reflection of the special sense of intimacy both children and their mothers gain from the act of breast feeding. One could equally well speculate that mothers who breast-feed may have a somewhat stronger commitment to their children, and therefore also tend to visit them for longer periods.

To summarize these data, much evidence suggests that a hospital stay is highly stressful for young children as well as their families. Although no recent studies have delineated the possible consequences different durations of hospitalizations may have on the later psychosocial functioning of children, the present review indicates that hospital traditions are difficult to modify and require close monitoring by mental health professionals. Thus the mission of hospitals even today is based on priorities other than those suggested by mental health principles. In effect, professionals in hospitals see themselves as diagnosticians and treaters of illness and disease, and not as therapists for the psychosocial development of infants. In addition, hospitals have the task of catering to their long-staying employees, whereas individual patients stay for comparatively brief periods. As a result, hospital organizations are serving two very different populations. This does not always lead to practices that are sensitive to children's developmental needs. Finally, we have to recognize that many young hospitalized children suffer from chronic illnesses that require further medical interventions, and that these illnesses may be associated with disruptions in the children's normal developmental pathway. Thus, behavioral abnormalities in such populations may be based on both biological and psychological difficulties (Benoit, Zeanah, Boucher, & Minde, 1992).

THE ROLES OF THE INFANT MENTAL HEALTH WORKER IN HOSPITAL SETTINGS

Infant psychiatrists and other infant mental health specialists can have a significant role in providing "early intervention" to infants and their families (Zeanah & McDonough, 1989; Bromwich, 1990). This term refers to the concept that the infant specialist "intervenes" (i.e., "comes between") the components of a system early, in order to help those involved in the system to achieve a developmentally more appropriate functioning.

Using Bronfenbrenner's (1979) integrated approach to sources of social influence as a model, I postulate that such an intervention can take place on three distinct levels. Thus the infant specialist can play a role in the assessment and treatment of emotional disturbances in infants and their families. This would reflect on Bronfenbrenner's "microsystem." However, a family also exists in the context of a "mesosystem," in which there are links between the child's microsystem settings. A good example here would be the effect a ward milieu might have on a child's behavior in hospital and later at home. Furthermore, policies and regulations on levels where a child does not directly participate will also influence the child's behavior. Bronfenbrenner calls this the "exosystem." Relevant examples here would be the overall philosophy or ecology of an institution vis-à-vis parental involvement in the care of an infant and the actual support given to a family.

In this section, I discuss the overall parameters of such interventions and provide some clinical examples to emphasize specific points.

Influencing the Hospital Ecology

Although the last 20 years have seen great changes in the awareness administrators and clinicians have shown toward the needs of infants and their families, much can still be done to assist young children and their families in coping with the hospital experience. For example, our own studies, which took place in a 65-bed NICU, showed that infants who stayed an average of 49 days in the hospital were cared for by 72 different nurses (Minde, Marton, et al., 1980).

Infant mental health practitioners should attempt to participate actively, and to consult with hospital administrators and other interested groups, in creating a hospital milieu that furthers both the physical and psychological well-being of their infant patients. Although the approaches individual clinicians may take in influencing their respective institutions should respect local conditions, I present the following recommendations for making the NICU and the infant ward a more normal and therapeutic environment. In particular, these recommendations are intended to promote the attachment of parents to their infants through facilitating parental visiting.

1. A neonatal intensive care nursery should be limited to 30 beds, because larger units require so much personnel that meaningful personal interactions among staff, patients, and their families become very difficult.

2. Each intensive care nursery should have preventive intervention programs. In a recent

annotation, Wolke (1991) points out that small and inexpensive changes in the physical and social environment and nursing care pattern can help reduce unnecessary suffering of the smallest infants. These changes include the way small infants are handled (regular massages increase food intake and decrease apneas), the noise and light they are exposed to, and the way they are positioned in their incubators (they do better if they are put into a hammock). Als (1992) in her very recent chapter also outlines methods by which these infants can be shielded against untoward stimulation. This includes a review of the advisability of suctioning or chest physical therapy schedules as well as vital sign taking and other routine medical procedures. Suggestions also deal with positioning of the infants, specific holding techniques and generally providing specific state regulatory and neurodevelopmentally supportive practices.

3. Each intensive care nursery should have facilities that make visiting a comfortable task for parents. For example, there should be rocking chairs, facilities for breast feeding or pumping, and areas where parents can be alone with their infants.

4. The physician who provides care to a premature infant should be identified to the parents, and he or she should actively approach the parents and tell them of their infant's progress. This is especially important for disadvantaged caregivers, who often find it hard to advocate for their infants. Parents should also be told how to get in touch with the physician in charge of their infant (i.e., they should be given times of ward rounds or regular conferences).

5. Each infant should have a key nurse assigned to him or her for the entire hospitalization. This nurse would then be in a position to monitor the parents' visiting patterns and to find out details of their personal and social backgrounds. This knowledge may give important clues about the individuals' parenting abilities, and may be used to alert other professionals if additional support is needed.

6. The parents should be given every opportunity to partake in the care of their infants. Thus, there should be no limits to parental and sibling visits, and parents should be encouraged to get involved early in the routine infant care. Breast feeding should be encouraged and facilitated, and all parents should receive literature on prematurity as well as ward routines.

7. Parents of a premature infant should have the opportunity to sleep at least one night with their infant in one room prior to the infant's discharge from the hospital. This will familiarize the parents with the infant quite dramatically, and should alleviate parental fears associated with the infant's transfer from hospital to home. Similar policies should be adopted on the regular infant ward. In addition, infants hospitalized for any length of time need ongoing stimulation and care to an extent not usually provided by nurses. Child life programs can be of great assistance, as can well-trained volunteers. Parents should also have the opportunity to stay with their infants for 24 hours a day. Such parents need "adult" services, such as showers, a place to put their clothes, or a place to get a snack on Sunday night.

The infant psychiatrist or mental health specialist, because of his or her intimate knowledge of child development and the psychosocial conditions necessary for optimizing the developmental process, can document the need for such services or assist others who attempt to obtain them.

Case 1

The NICU in a major teaching hospital admitted 1-week-old infant K., who suffered from an immune deficiency disorder that would require the baby to remain in total isolation (i.e., be handled by fully masked staff members) for approximately 12 months. An older sibling had died of the same condition 2½ years earlier at 3 weeks of age. The parents lived 500 kilometers away in a small town; the father had been unemployed for 8 years. There was a 4-year-old sister who was well. Financial constraints made visiting difficult. The infant psychiatrist was consulted to help with planning for infant K.'s development in the hospital 4 weeks after admission. After a detailed assessment of the family and discussions with the ward staff, the following suggestions were made and put into effect:

1. The family was provided with funds to have them visit baby K. two times per month for 5 days each.

2. The infant was assigned two key nurses who spent all their shifts with him and who met with the infant psychiatrist every week to discuss the overall care plan.

3. Because K. only had contact with masked staff members, which deprived him of seeing human smiles and laughter, and because his family visited on only 10 out of 30 days per month, the

family was encouraged to make a 3-minute video-tape for K. On the tape, family members sang and talked to K. This tape was shown to K. after each meal, coupling satiety and the mother's soothing voice, and helping to keep the infant in touch with his family.

4. When K. was 4 months old, a second bed was put in his isolation room. In this bed he played and ate. The first bed remained his "sleeping bed."

K. clearly recognized his family on the video by 8 weeks; despite many medical complications, he attached well to his mother and showed a normal developmental progression all through his hospital stay. K. underwent two bone marrow transplants during his first 6 months of life. The second transplant took well, and the infant was sent home at 11 months.

Providing Consultation and Support for the Staff and the Families of Hospitalized Infants

In addition to helping create and maintain institutional developmental support structures for infants and their families, the infant psychiatrist or infant mental health specialist can also take part in the day-to-day activities of an NICU or regular infant ward. This may include participating in regular staff ward rounds, psychosocial rounds, staff meetings, and/or in-service conferences. Joining members of the medical staff at their rounds is often especially beneficial, because medical problems can be linked with psychosocial concerns as they come up and possible interventions be discussed immediately. The roles of the infant specialist in these situations may be as follows:

1. Helping parents and staff members to understand their different roles and needs vis-à-vis the infant and each other.

2. Serving as an advocate who is able to explain specific behaviors of a parent or staff person to others, and thus facilitating communication between individuals or groups.

3. Assisting parents in understanding their feelings or actions, and thus helping them regain control over their lives (Minde & Stewart, 1988).

4. Teaching principles of child and family development. This may include lecturing about the possible detrimental consequences of hospitalization—developmental aberrations associated with repeated separation from primary caretakers, and Post-Traumatic Stress Disorder caused by specific traumatic medical or nursing procedures. It may also include discussions about ways the hospital staff can monitor the internal representations parents have of their children (i.e., pick out those who see their infants as perpetually helpless, vulnerable, ill, or handicapped).

It is obvious that interventions by the infant specialist in any of these areas must be geared to the specific hospital milieu, the characteristics of parents and children, and the medical condition of each child in question. The roles of the infant specialist can also include encouraging specific remedial or supportive activities:

5. Helping to set up a hospital-wide program that identifies infants who may have to remain in hospital for more than 3 to 4 weeks. Staff members can then be educated to provide an environment for these infants that approximates their normal developmental needs as closely as possible. For example, the infant specialist may want to insure that such children (a) are cared for by only three to four key nurses, so as to maintain their sense of having primary caretakers; (b) have painful laboratory or other investigative procedures scheduled within one specific hour during the day, so as to free the children from the ongoing fear of being hurt during the rest of the day; and (c) have a schedule set up that details daily activities (e.g., 8 A.M., breakfast; 8:30, bath; 9 A.M., occupational therapy; 9:30, play with key nurse; etc.). Such a schedule can assure the routines that are necessary to give young children a sense of mastery over their lives.

6. Encouraging members of the nursing staff to include parents in their team. This can be helped by assessing the parents' strengths and limitations, after which their individual care commitment is negotiated. However, parental involvement can also be increased by giving parents exclusive caretaking tasks (e.g., bathing the child), which they must perform every day and are required to delegate to someone else such as a nurse if they cannot be present on a particular day. Such a task will often give the parents the sense that they are vital members of the treatment team, and will increase their visits and general involvement with their infant.

7. Helping to set up group meetings for parents of premature infants. Such meetings are an effective way to increase these parents' feelings

of competence. One way to structure such groups is to ask a mother or father who has had such a small infant within the last 12 months to be the leader. Such "veteran" parents invariably establish an intense relationship with the new parents very quickly, and allow them to work through some of their grief quite rapidly. Once this has been achieved, the new parents will feel that they are more active participants in the caretaking process, which leaves them in a better state to assimilate information on the treatment and care of their infants (Minde, Shosenberg, et al., 1980).

In my experience, 8 to 10 such meetings are indicated. During later group meetings, specific resource people can speak on infant stimulation, the hospital's neonatal follow-up program, or the general philosophy of neonatal intensive care. Films and slides highlighting the developmental needs of premature infants can also be provided. In addition, attempts can be made to help parents with concrete problems, such as getting babysitters, a better apartment, or improved unemployment benefits. Finally, parents can learn how to negotiate the administrative complexities associated with an NICU and can provide practical and emotional support to each other.

8. Encouraging the staff to provide flexible hospital arrangements for young children who stay in the hospital for longer periods. An example here may be to provide a child with two beds or a clearly divided crib where one side is the "sleeping" side and the other the "play" or "eating" side. Such an arrangement will support the child's need for clearly demarcated structures in his or her day-to-day life. Parents may be encouraged to bring some special foods from home. It is also important to have the child sleep in a darkened room and to provide sufficient space for parental rooming-in.

Case 2

A 13-month-old infant girl, D., was admitted with secondary burns to her legs and stomach, the result of an accidental placement by her father in an overheated bathtub. Fifteen percent of her body was affected. The infant's 18-year-old mother, who came from a Caribbean island and did not live with the father, visited only two times per week for 3 hours. To prevent infection, the infant was tied to the bed for 18 hours per day, because staff members feared she might scratch her open wounds. There was a debate as to whether or not to graft the burn wounds. The mother opposed any operation, fearing the actual death of her infant. Infant D. received morphine regularly for pain control.

After 3 weeks, the baby had virtually stopped eating, lost all her speech, and pulled out about 20% of her hair. She also slept about 17 hours per day. A consultation was sought. After three visits with the infant, and individual meetings with both parents and one grandmother, the infant psychiatrist arrived at and implemented the following plan:

1. The medical staff was persuaded that the father was not neglectful and that his story of accidentally placing the baby in the hot tub could be believed.

2. Once this was accomplished, each parent was persuaded to visit the infant for 4 hours per day. This allowed for less tying of D.'s hands and feet.

3. The mother was shown how to soothe her baby and to be more receptive to her needs. She was also permitted to bring the baby Caribbean food. This increased parental contact, made D. less fearful, allowing for a decrease of morphine. It also helped D. to become more active and to provide more pleasure to her parents.

4. The infant psychiatrist now played with the baby three times a week for 20 minutes, while the mother watched. After a few sessions, the mother was encouraged to use the same toys with her infant and to develop some special games with her.

Three weeks later, D. had stopped pulling her hair, her appetite had increased, and she cried far less. She was also tied for only 4 to 8 hours now. Three days later, both parents consented to the skin graft operation, which D. survived without any complications.

Providing Direct Treatment Services for Young Children and Their Parents

There is increasing evidence that the direct treatment of infants within the context of their families or other caretaking systems can have a significant impact on the infants' psychological functioning (Minde & Minde, 1981; Cramer et al., 1990; Lieberman, Weston, & Pawl, 1991; Pinard & Minde, 1991).

The principles of such treatment are to allow a hospitalized infant to experience the world as predictable, and to give the infant an opportunity to interact with an adult who permits him or her to experience some autonomy and mastery. This can be done by arranging a specific play time with the infant for 30 minutes at the same time every day in a private designated space. The therapist may use a small number of toys that are of interest to the child. During these sessions the therapist has the infant choose the activity or game and follows his or her interactive lead. Infants will rapidly understand and appreciate the specialness of these time periods, as they provide them with an opportunity to experience a relationship whose intensity they can significantly modulate. As much as a hospitalized child's day-to-day activities are controlled from without, these islands of interactional mastery provide important nuclei for growing security and competence. After the infant has become familiar with the therapist, parents can be brought in to observe the interactions and to discuss their observations. This furthers their sensitive perception of the infant's behavior, including reciprocal communications and an awareness of the infant's sources of competence or stress. It can also demonstrate ways in which a particular behavior problem may be solved. It is obvious that such a therapeutic regimen can only work within the context of a mutually supportive partnership among different hospital professionals, because both a private space and a regular, uninterrupted time period must be assured to allow treatment to proceed.

Case 3

A 34-month-old girl, M., had had seriously compromised kidney functions since the age of 4 months and had received dialysis five times a week for 18 months. She was hospitalized 3 months earlier for a renal transplant, but rejected the kidney and was now again on dialysis in the ICU. Her family lived 100 kilometers away and was devastated, as the parents very much wished for M. to be a normal girl again. Yet both parents visited daily for many hours and were interested in M.'s thoughts and feelings.

M., who was a highly intelligent girl, appeared furious at the world in general. She often screamed at nurses and her parents without any obvious provocation, opposed every demand made on her, and had the staff divided between those who wanted to "teach her a lesson" and those who felt that "one has to give in to her." A psychiatric consultation was sought.

After several meetings with the staff members involved in M.'s care as well as her family, the in-

fant psychiatrist felt that M.'s anger was primarily a reflection of her sense of powerlessness and her repeated disappointments in her elusive health. He decided to see M. five times weekly for 20 to 30 minutes alone in her room at the same time of day. To these meetings he brought a limited number of toys (including a syringe and a female doll in a special bag), and offered to be with M. and play with her to learn more about her.

M. rapidly engaged in active play, reflecting many of her thoughts and feelings. The therapist followed her suggestions and at times also reflected on M.'s feelings. Within 3 weeks, M. was much calmer; she decided that only doctors in green uniforms were bad (the surgeons), and began to participate more actively in her dialysis. A change to a home dialysis program eventually became possible.

SUMMARY AND CONCLUSIONS

The present chapter gives a review of investigations examining the impact that prematurity and hospitalizations early in life may have on the emotional development and behavior of children up to school age. It furthermore summarizes ways in which infant mental health workers can assist hospital staff in modifying hospital practices and administrative routines to help children and their families in achieving and maintaining an optimal developmental progression. Finally, the reader is given some practical suggestions about how to deliver clinically relevant interventions to hospitalized infants and their families.

The data reviewed in this chapter document that the parenting of very small premature infants is a highly complex process that defies easy generalization. However, they also suggest that these infants pass through specific "way stations," which may serve as important markers for their later development. For example, premature infants do show specific behavioral characteristics during their first year of life that make parenting more difficult and stressful. Mothers who rapidly engage themselves with their newborn infants in the hospital nursery also seem to be more sensitive to their behavioral cues and to have a better relationship with these children during the ensuing years. There is also good evidence that interventions during the first months of life can modify the interactional patterns of the mother–child dyad quite significantly. Such interventions seem especially useful when they combine a supportive and educational component, and when they include other parents who have recently lived through the experience of having a premature infant.

A further important theme of the studies reviewed is the repeated finding that children who are hospitalized early in life, even within the context of present-day liberal visiting practices, are profoundly affected by this experience. In fact, it appears that the ecology of a hospital, which demands that the young child cope with many unfamiliar individuals and unpredictable challenges to his or her body, by its very nature does not foster normal development. As recent medical technology has made survival of many children with serious medical illnesses possible now, we see a parallel increase in the hospitalization rates of young children in our tertiary care institutions. This requires us to think about new ways of empowering families to participate in the care of their infants in hospitals. It also makes a reassessment of routine hospital practices desirable.

The infant psychiatrist, who has an appreciation of the biological aspects of disease because of his or her training in medicine, is also an expert on the developmental needs of infants; following a systems approach he or she can provide a helpful role in sensitizing the many players in this field to the best interest of the infant. Nevertheless, the present chapter also shows that the work of establishing the developmental pathways that can guide the growth and development of these special infants has only begun and will provide many challenges for future generations of researchers and clinicians.

REFERENCES

Als, H. (1992). Individualized, family-focused developmental care for the very low-birthweight preterm infant in the NICU. In S. L. Friedman & M. D. Sigman (Eds.), The psychological development of low birthweight children (pp. 341–388). Norwood, NJ: Ablex.

Ammaniti, M. (Chair). (1989). Symposium on maternal representations. Symposium conducted at the Fourth World Congress of Infant Psychiatry and Allied Disciplines, Lugano, Switzerland.

Ballard, J. L., Maloney, M., Shank, M., & Hollister, L. (1984). Sibling visits to a newborn intensive care unit: Implications for siblings, parents, and infants. Child Psychiatry and Human Development, 14, 203–215.

Barnard, K., Bee, H., & Hammond, M. (1984). Developmental changes in maternal interactions with term and preterm infants. Infant Behavior and Development, 7, 101–113.

Bauchner, H., Brown, E., & Peskin, J. (1988). Premature graduates of the newborn intensive care unit: A guide to follow-up. Pediatric Clinics of North America, 35, 1207–1225.

Beavers, B. C. (1974). An exploratory study of the psychological sequelae of surgery and hospitalization in male children. Dissertation Abstracts International, 34, 5160B.

Beckwith, L., & Cohen, S. (1983, April). Continuity of caregiving with preterm infants. Paper presented at the biennial meeting of the Society for Research in Child Development, Detroit.

Behar, L., & Stringfield, S. (1977). The Preschool Behavior Questionnaire. Journal of Abnormal Child Psychology, 5, 265–275.

Benoit, D., Zeanah, C. H., Boucher, C., & Minde, K. (1992). Sleep disturbances in early childhood: Association with insecure maternal attachment. Journal of the American Academy of Child and Adolescent Psychiatry, 31, 86–93.

Benton, A. L. (1940). Mental development of prematurely born children. American Journal of Orthopsychiatry, 10, 719–746.

Blitzer, E. C., Zuckerman, B., Pozen, J. T., & Blitzer, P. H. (1983). Another myth: Reduced hospital visiting by inner-city mothers. Pediatrics, 71, 504–509.

Brazelton, T. B., & Cramer, B. G. (1990). The earliest relationship. Reading, MA: Addison-Wesley.

Brazelton, T. B., Koslowski, B., & Main, M. (1974). The origins of reciprocity: The early mother–infant interaction. In M. Lewis & L. Rosenblum (Eds.), The effect of the infant on its caregiver (pp. 49–76). New York: Wiley.

Breslau, N. (1985). Psychiatric disorder in children with physical disabilities. Journal of the American Academy of Child Psychiatry, 24, 87–94.

Brody, E. B., & Klein, K. (1980). The intensive care nursery as a small society: Its contribution to the socialization and learning of the paediatric intern. Paediatrician, 9, 169–181.

Bromwich, R. M. (1990). The interaction approach to early intervention. Infant Mental Health Journal, 11, 66–79.

Bronfenbrenner, U. (1979). The ecology of human development. Cambridge, MA: Harvard University Press.

Brooten, D., Gennaro, S., Brown, L., Butts, P., Gibbons, A., Bakewill-Sachs, S., & Kumar, S. (1988). Anxiety, depression, and hostility in mothers of preterm infants. Nursing Research, 37, 213–216.

Brothwood, M., Wolke, D., Gamsu, H., & Cooper, D. (1988). Mortality, morbidity, growth and development of babies weighing 501–1000 grams and 1001–1500 grams at birth. Acta Paediatrica Scandinavica, 77, 10–18.

Cadman, D., Doyle, M., Szatmari, P., & Offord, D. R. (1987). Chronic illness, disability, and mental and social well-being: Findings of the Ontario Child Health Study. Pediatrics, 79, 805–813.

Consumers Association. (1980, May). Children in hospital: A report on the extent to which hospitals have implemented DHSS recommendations since the Platt Report. London: Author.

Corter, C., & Minde, K. (1987). Impact of infant prematurity on family systems. In M. Wolraich (Ed.), Advances in developmental and behavioral pediatrics (pp. 1–48). Greenwich, CT: JAI Press.

Costello, A. M. L., Hamilton, P. A., Baudin, J., Townsend,

J., Bradford, B. C., Stewart, A. L., & Reynolds, E.O.R. (1988). Prediction of neurodevelopmental impairment at four years from brain ultrasound appearance of very preterm infants. *Developmental Medicine and Child Neurology, 30,* 711–722.

Cramer, B., Robert-Tissot, C., Stern, D. N., Serpa-Rusconi, S., De Muralt, M., Besson, G., Palacio-Espasa, F., Bachmann, J. P., Knauer, D., Berney, C., & D'Arcis, U. (1990). Outcome evaluation in brief mother–infant psychotherapy: A brief report. *Infant Mental Health Journal, 11,* 278–300.

Crnic, K. A., Greenberg, M. T., Ragozin, A. S., Robinson, N. M., & Basham, R. B. (1983). Effects of stress and social support on mothers and premature and full-term infants. *Child Development, 54,* 209–217.

Direction Générale du Budget et de l'Administration Québecoise. (1992). [Unpublished raw data]. Quebec City: Author. Service de la Gestion et de la Diffusion de l'Information Québec.

Douglas, J. W. B. (1975). Early hospital admissions and later disturbances of behavior and learning. *Developmental Medicine and Child Neurology, 17,* 456–480.

Dowd, E. L., Novak, J. C., & Ray, E. J. (1977). Releasing the hospitalized child from restraints. *MCN: American Journal of Maternal Child Nursing, 2,* 370–373.

Drillien, C. M. (1964). *The growth and development of the prematurely born infant.* Edinburgh: Livingstone.

Dunn, H. G., Ho, H. H., Crichton, J. U., Robertson, A. M., McBurney, A. K., Grunau, R. V., & Penfold, P. S (1986). Evolution of minimal brain dysfunctions to the age of 12 to 15 years. In H. G. Dunn (Ed.), *Clinics in developmental medicine: No. 95–96. Sequelae of low birthweight: The Vancouver study* (pp. 249–272). Oxford: MacKeith Press.

Eiser, C. (1990). Psychological effects of chronic disease. *Journal of Child Psychology and Psychiatry, 31,* 85–98.

Field, T. M. (1977). Effects of early separation, interactive deficits and experimental manipulations on mother–infant face-to-face interaction. *Child Development, 48,* 763–771.

Field, T. M., Dempsey, J., & Shuman, H. H. (1983). Five-year follow-up of preterm respiratory distress syndrome and post-term postmaturity syndrome infants. In T. M. Field & A. Sostek (Eds.), *Infants born at risk: Physiological, perceptual and cognitive processes* (pp. 317–335). New York: Grune & Stratton.

Freud, W. E. (1988). Prenatal attachment, the perinatal continuum and the psychological side of neonatal intensive care. In P. Fedor-Freybergh & V. M. Vogel (Eds.), *Prenatal and perinatal psychology and medicine* (pp. 217–234). Park-Ridge, NJ: Parthenon.

Goldberg, S., Corter, C., Lojkasek. M., & Minde, K. (1990). Prediction of behavior problems in 4-year-olds born prematurely. *Development and Psychopathology, 2,* 15–30.

Hagberg, B., Hagberg, G., & Zetterstrom, R. (1989). Decreasing perinatal mortality—increase in cerebral morbidity? *Acta Paediatrica Scandinavica, 78,* 664–670.

Holt, J. L. (1968). Discussion of the method and the clinical implications from the study "Children's recall of a preschool age hospital experience after an interval of five years." *Communications in Nursing Research, 1,* 56–72.

Hoy, E. A., Bill, J. M., & Sykes, D. H. (1988). Very low birthweight: A long term developmental impairment? *International Journal of Behavior Development, 11,* 37–67.

Knafl, K. A., Cavallari, K. A., & Dixon, D. M. (1988). *Pediatric hospitalization: Family and nurse perspectives.* Glenview, IL: Scott, Foresman.

Kopp, C. B. (1983). Risk factors in development. In M. Haith & J. J. Campos (Vol. Eds.), *Handbook of child psychology* (4th ed.): *Vol. 2. Infancy and developmental psychobiology* (pp. 1081–1188). New York: Wiley.

Kopp, C. B. (1987). Developmental risk: Historical reflections. In J. D. Osofsky (Ed.), *Handbook of infant development* (2nd ed., pp. 881–912). New York: Wiley.

Lampe, J., Trause, M. A., & Kennell, J. (1977). Parental visiting of sick infants: The effect of living at home prior to hospitalization. *Pediatrics, 59,* 294–296.

Lebovici, S. (1983). Le nourrison, la mère et la psychanalyse. In *Collection Paidos.* Paris: Le Centurion.

Lefebvre, F., Bard, H., Veilleux, A., & Martel, C. (1988). Outcome at school age of children with birthweights of 1000 grams or less. *Developmental Medicine and Child Neurology, 30,* 170–180.

Lewis, M. (1987). Social development in infancy and early childhood. In J. D. Osofsky (Ed.), *Handbook of infant development* (2nd ed., pp. 419–493). New York: Wiley.

Lieberman, A. F., Weston, D., & Pawl, J. H. (1991). Preventive intervention and outcome with anxiously attached dyads. *Child Development, 62,* 199–209.

Maloney, M. J., Ballard, J., Hollister, L., & Shank, M. (1983). A prospective, controlled study of scheduled sibling visits to a newborn intensive care unit. *Journal of the American Academy of Child Psychiatry, 22,* 565–570.

Main, M., Solomon, J. (1986). Discovery of an insecure–disorganized/disoriented attachment pattern. In T. B. Brazelton & N. W. Yogman (Eds.) *Affective development in infancy.* Norwood, NJ: Ablex.

Marton, P., Minde, K., & Ogilvie, J. (1981). Mother–infant interactions in the premature nursery: A sequential analysis. In S. Friedman & M. Sigman (Eds.), *Birth and psychological development* (pp. 179–205). New York: Academic Press.

Minde, K. (1980). Bonding of parents to premature infants: Theory and practice. In P. Taylor (Ed.), *Monographs in neonatology series: Parent–Infant relationships* (pp. 291–313). New York: Grune & Stratton.

Minde, K. (1984). The impact of prematurity on the later behavior of children and on their families. *Clinics in Perinatology, 11,* 227–244.

Minde, K. (1987). Parenting the premature infant: Problems and opportunities. In H. W. Taeusch & M. W. Yogman (Eds.), *Follow-up management of the high-risk infant* (pp. 315–322). Boston: Little, Brown.

Minde, K., Goldberg, S., Perrotta, M., Washington, J., Lojkasek, M., Corter, C., & Parker, K. (1989). Continuities and discontinuities in the development of 64 very small premature infants to 4 years of age. *Journal of Child Psychology and Psychiatry, 30,* 391–404.

Minde, K., Marton, P., Manning, P., & Hines, B. (1980). Some determinants of mother–infant interaction in the premature nursery. *Journal of the American Academy of Child Psychiatry, 19,* 139–164.

Minde, K., & Minde, R. (1977). Behavioural screening of preschool children: A new approach to mental health? In P. J. Graham (Ed.), *Epidemiological ap-*

proaches in child psychiatry (pp. 139–164). London: Academic Press.

Minde, K., & Minde, R. (1981). Psychiatric intervention in infancy. Journal of the American Academy of Child Psychiatry, 20, 217–238.

Minde, K., Perrotta, M., & Hellmann, J. (1988). The impact of delayed development in premature infants on mother–infant interaction: A prospective investigation. Journal of Pediatrics, 112, 136–142.

Minde, K., Shosenberg, N., Marton, P., Thompson, J., Ripley, J., & Burns, S. (1980). Self-help groups in a premature nursery: A controlled evaluation. Journal of Pediatrics, 96, 933–940.

Minde, K., & Stewart, D. (1988). Psychiatric services in the neonatal intensive care unit. In R. Cohen (Ed.), Psychiatric consultation in childbirth settings (pp. 151–164). New York: Plenum Press.

Minde, K., Whitelaw, H., Brown, J., & Fitzhardinge, P. (1983). Effect of neonatal complications in premature infants on early parent–infant interaction. Developmental Medicine and Child Neurology, 25, 763–777.

Ministry of Health. (1959). Welfare of children in hospitals (Platt Report). London: Her Majesty's Stationery Office.

Offord, D. R., Boyle, M. H., Szatmari, P., Rae-Grant, N., Links, P., Cadman, D. T., Byles, J. A., Crawford, J. W., Munroe-Blum, H., Bynne, C., Thomas, H., & Woodward, C. A. (1987). The Ontario Child Health Study: Prevalence of disorder and rates of service utilization. Archives of General Psychiatry, 44, 832–836.

Orgill, A. A., Astbury, J., Bajuk, B., & Yu, V. Y. H. (1982). Early development of infants 1000 g or less at birth. Archives of Disease in Childhood, 57, 823–827.

Pharoah, P. O. D., & Alberman, E. D. (1990). Annual statistical review. Archives of Disease in Childhood, 65, 147–151.

Pless, B., & Nolan, T. (1991). Revision, replication and neglect: Research on maladjustment in chronic illness. Journal of Child Psychology and Psychiatry, 32, 347–365.

Pinard, L., & Minde, K. (1991). The infant psychiatrist and the transplant team. Canadian Journal of Psychiatry, 36, 442–446.

Quay, H., & Pederson, D. W. (1975). Manual for the Behavior Problem Checklist. Unpublished manuscript.

Quinton, D., & Rutter, M. (1976). Early hospital admissions and later disturbances of behaviors: An attempted replication of Douglas' findings. Developmental Medicine and Child Neurology, 18, 447–459.

Richman, N., & Graham, P. (1971). A behavioural screening questionnaire for use with three-year-old children: Preliminary findings. Journal of Child Psychology and Psychiatry, 16, 277–287.

Roskies, E., Bedard, P., Gavreau-Guilbault, H., & LaFortune, D. (1975). Emergency hospitalization of young children: Some neglected psychological considerations. Medical Care, 13, 570–581.

Rutter, M. (1967). A children's behaviour questionnaire for completion by teachers: Preliminary findings. Journal of Child Psychology and Psychiatry, 8, 1–11.

Rutter, M. (1989). Psychological sequelae of brain damage in children. American Journal of Psychiatry, 138, 1533–1544.

Sameroff, A. J. (1986). Environmental context of child development. Journal of Pediatrics, 109, 192–200.

Sameroff, A., & Chandler, M. (1975). Reproductive risk and the continuum of caretaking casualty. In F. D. Horowitz, E. M. Hetherington, S. Scarr-Salapatek, & G. Siegel (Eds.), Review of child development research (Vol. 4, pp. 187–244). Chicago: University of Chicago Press.

Seidel, U. P., Chadwick, O., & Rutter, M. (1975). Psychological disorder in crippled children: A comparative study of children with and without brain damage. Developmental Medicine and Child Neurology, 17, 563–573.

Shapiro, R. (1978). Psychological sequelae of childhood cancer and heart surgery. Dissertation Abstracts International, 38, 5549B.

Sigman, M., & Parmelee, A. H. (1979). Longitudinal evaluation of the preterm infant. In T. M. Field, A. M. Sostek, S. Goldberg, & H. H. Shuman (Eds.), Infants born at risk: Behavior and development (pp. 193–217). Jamaica, NY: Spectrum.

Silva, P. A., MaGee, R., & Williams, S. (1984). A longitudinal study of the intelligence and behavior of preterm and small for gestational age children. Journal of Developmental and Behavioral Pediatrics, 5, 1–5.

Stern, D. (1985). The interpersonal world of the infant. New York: Basic Books.

Stern, M., & Karraker, K. H. (1990). The prematurity stereotype: Empirical evidence and implications for practice. Infant Mental Health Journal, 11, 3–11.

Thompson, R. H. (1985). Psychosocial research on pediatric hospitalization and health care. Springfield, IL: Charles C Thomas.

Tinsley, B., & Parke, R. (1983). The person–environment relationship: Lessons from families with preterm infants. In D. Magnusson & V. Allen (Eds.), Human development: An interactional perspective (pp. 93–110). New York: Academic Press.

Wolke, D. (1991). Annotation: Supporting the development of low birthweight infants. Journal of Child Psychology and Psychiatry, 32, 723–741.

Zeanah, C. H., & McDonough, S. (1989). Clinical approaches to families in early intervention. Seminars in Perinatology, 13, 513–522.

7

Adolescent Parenthood: Risks and Opportunities for Mothers and Infants

JOY D. OSOFSKY
DELLA M. HANN
CLAIRE PEEBLES

Adolescent pregnancy is one of the major social problems facing our country today. With about 480,000 births each year to young women under the age of 19, or one-quarter of the adolescent young women in the 1980s becoming pregnant (21% of whites and 41% of blacks), the impact on our society is enormous (Brooks-Gunn & Chase-Landsdale, 1991). The latest National Center for Health Statistics (1991) report on teenage pregnancy is even more alarming. The rate of births to young black women under the age of 15 has been increasing since 1983, and the rate to teenagers in general, which had declined somewhat in the early 1980s, has again increased. According to Tomkins (1989) and Ladner and Gourdine (1985), recent studies as compared with those done 10 years ago indicate a much greater sense of hopelessness and helplessness today. The young women and their families feel that they have little control over their lives and few options available to them. With adolescent pregnancy comes early parenthood—forcing many young women, who are still children themselves, into the position of having to take on enormous responsibilities.

The purpose of this chapter is to review the risks and opportunities, or resiliency, resulting from adolescent pregnancy and parenthood.

Risks include those that affect the adolescent mother, as well as her child. Risks that relate to mental health and socioemotional development are emphasized because of the focus of this handbook. After reviewing both general risks for mother and infant and those specific to socioemotional outcomes, we discuss protective factors, including characteristics of the mother, the child, the dyad, and the family that lead to more positive outcomes. A section on the less often studied father follows, reviewing both risks and protective factors. Finally, the concluding section focuses on intervention with adolescent mothers and their infants.

THEORETICAL FRAMEWORK FOR UNDERSTANDING ADOLESCENT MOTHERS AND THEIR FAMILIES

Earlier considerations of adolescent mothers frequently used a psychodynamic framework to understand some of the motivating and conflictual factors that may have contributed to a young woman's becoming pregnant in her adolescence (Bibring, Dwyer, Huntington, & Valenstein, 1961; Benedek, 1970). This early perspective seemed unsatisfactory, and the work moved in somewhat atheoretical directions. The situation of adolescent mothers and their families was often complicated by overwhelming environmental factors, such as poverty, family instability, educational, and economic issues. In recent years, however, several investigators have proposed theoretical frameworks that can help to explain the complex factors that may contribute to a young woman's becoming pregnant as a teenager (Sameroff & Chandler, 1975; Bronfenbrenner, 1988; Belsky, 1984; Chase-Landsdale, Brooks-Gunn, & Palkoff, 1991; Elder, Caspi, & Burton, 1987; Kahn & Antonucci, 1980; Reiss, 1989). We discuss the relevance of these frameworks in this section, and add a further perspective that integrates the more recent theoretical ideas with the earlier psychodynamic explanations.

The lifespan developmental approach is important for understanding intergenerational issues and ways in which they may contribute to adolescent pregnancy. Geertz (1973) has proposed that culture is best understood not as complexes of discrete behavioral patterns and customs, but as a set of integrating recipes, rules, and even control mechanisms that assure the survival of a particular society. One important control mechanism is the relationship between adults and children within a society. Kahn and Antonucci (1980) have suggested that social relationships be considered within a lifespan developmental framework, and that individuals move through life influenced, protected, and sometimes placed at risk by their social relationships. Families (or, for many teenage mothers, their single mothers) try to raise their children to become competent adults within their own social group. However, it may be that mothers of teenage mothers are limiting their children's goals to those within their own views and experiences.

The situation of adolescent mothers may also be reconsidered from a psychodynamic developmental perspective—specifically, an object relations point of view (Greenberg & Mitchell, 1983; Mahler, Pine, & Bergman, 1975). From this perspective, it may be that adolescents, especially poor adolescents, struggle with adolescent identity issues, separation/individuation issues, and lack of opportunities. As a teenager tries to separate from her family (especially her mother) and find her own way, she may be severely hampered by lack of opportunity. Therefore, she may try to resolve these psychological and prac-

tical struggles by becoming pregnant—an option that confirms her femininity and identity as a woman, and allows her to have a newly defined and (frequently) integrated role within the family system. Thus, the young woman resolves her identity dilemma by developing a new rapprochement (Mahler et al., 1975) with her mother and within the family. Although to some this option may seem maladaptive, for many the solution may be viewed as a positive one, based on traditions within the family (Ladner & Gourdine, 1985; Burton & Bengtson, 1985).

In order to understand more about the social-ecological perspective (Bronfenbrenner, 1985, 1986, 1988; Brooks-Gunn & Chase-Landsdale, 1991; Chase-Landsdale et al., 1991) within which teenage pregnancy occurs, the *context* of development for the family and the individual needs to be investigated. The ecological perspective (Bronfenbrenner, 1988) proposes that interactions between the person and the environment must be examined in order to understand development and adaptation. With adolescent pregnancy for the individual come also a family of origin, a network of relationships, a neighborhood, and school and/or work environments. The ecology of her environment, in addition to her individual characteristics and prior experiences, will have a strong impact on how she adjusts both to the pregnancy and to young motherhood.

An additional perspective is that of family systems theory (Hinde & Stevenson-Hinde, 1988)—that is, how the family is understood as an organized system made up of interdependent relationships and subsystems. Examples of many of the different relationships within families that make up the subsystems have been explicated recently by Stevenson-Hinde (1990) and by Emde (1991). A focus on the family system allows one to assess the emotional quality of the family as a whole; considering that most adolescent mothers do not live in isolation, this probably represents a more realistic understanding of the family environment of such a mother.

Reiss (1981) has proposed the "community frame" as a locally based belief system that provides an interpretative model for defining a stressful situation and developing appropriate adaptive strategies. Thus, in attempting to understand both individual and family adaptation to teenage pregnancy, we need to study community-based ideologies of the context of adolescent pregnancy, including the reality of poverty; individual and family capacities to cope with the pressures and stresses; and the messages and expectations, both spoken and unspoken (transmitted through behaviors and affective reactions), that are communicated.

Each of these theoretical frameworks provides alternative, but related, perspectives for understanding and interpreting adolescent pregnancy, including both the individuals involved and the environment in which they live. Chase-Landsdale et al. (1991) have emphasized in a recent paper that both the developmental and the ecological perspectives take into account changes in behavior in terms of the individual, the family, and the environmental structure that influences the family. These issues are extremely important in understanding teenage pregnancy, which creates a situation that most strongly affects one individual (the pregnant teenager), but also has an impact on the family and the broader environment at both individual and structural levels. Furthermore, environmental intervention is often needed to effect positive change through interventions with the individuals and the family.

OVERALL RISK FACTORS

Teenage mothers and their children suffer from both short-term and longer-term psychological, social, and economic difficulties. Brooks-Gunn and Furstenberg (1986) have provided a comprehensive description of some of the known outcomes in their excellent review article. Poverty contributes enormously to the problems faced by teenage mothers. It increases their risk for a number of environmental difficulties, including living in high-crime, high-violence areas; moving frequently; having difficulty coping with the day-to-day responsibilities and demands of raising a child; and having less social and emotional support than is usually available to older mothers. Because of our extensive knowledge about the adverse effects of poverty on psychological, social, emotional, and cognitive development, it can be assumed that adolescent mothers themselves as well as their children are at significant risk. Living in a single-parent, impoverished environment alone can lead to higher rates of behavior problems and problems in school, as well as mental health risks (Turner, Grindstaff, & Phillips, 1990; Kellam, Ensminger, & Turner, 1977; Spivak & Weitzman, 1987; Halpern, Chapter 5, this volume).

Many adolescent mothers are less well equipped and less able than older mothers to provide a positive socioemotional environment for their infants and children. Reasons include developmental conflicts specific to adolescence that interfere with their parenting ability, as well as problematic psychosocial factors. From the perspective of adolescent personality issues, our recent studies (Osofsky, Peebles, Fick, & Hann, 1992; Fick, Peebles, Osofsky, & Hann, 1992; Peebles, Fick, & Osofsky, 1992) point to several adolescent developmental factors that may interfere with parenting abilities. For example, adolescent mothers show more identity diffusion, less autonomy, more difficulties with trust, more depression, and lower self-esteem than nonpregnant adolescents. At times, it seems as if there is a mismatch between adolescent development and infant developmental needs that interferes with teenagers' parenting abilities (Osofsky & Eberhart-Wright, 1992). As for psychosocial issues that contribute to risk, adolescent mothers are less likely than older mothers to complete high school, attend college, find stable employment, marry, or be self-supporting (Chilman, 1983; Furstenberg, 1976, 1987).

MENTAL HEALTH RISKS

The extreme risk factors in the environment in which adolescent mothers live with their children lead not only to negative psychosocial consequences, but also significant mental health risks that may have previously been overlooked. In a recent study carried out in New Orleans on the effects of chronic community violence on 58 children aged 9–12 years (Osofsky, Wewers, Fick, Hann, & Richters, 1993), we found that almost half of the children included in the sample were born to mothers who became parents as teenagers. Furthermore, there was a significant relationship between reported behavior problems in these children on the Child Behavior Checklist (Achenbach, 1979) and their having been born to adolescent mothers. Informal reports from mental health clinics indicate that children of adolescent mothers are frequently seen with significant behavioral and personality problems. Thus, being born and raised in the family of an adolescent mother may increase a child's exposure to environmental and family factors that increase mental health risks.

Recent evidence has shown that adolescent mothers are more likely to be depressed than older mothers (Garrison, Schluchter, Schoenbach, & Kaplan, 1989; Carter, Osofsky, & Hann, 1991a; Hann, Osofsky, Barnard, & Leonard, 1992; Osofsky & Eberhart-Wright, 1988). There are sufficient data indicating that depressed mothers are more emotionally unavailable to their infants and children, generally providing both a less empathic and a less responsive environment. In a recent study, Zuravin (1989) has emphasized the link between maternal depression and mother-to-child aggression, finding that moderately (but not severely) depressed low-income mothers are at increased risk for child abuse and physical aggression. Several caveats are necessary in interpreting the results of this study, including the method used to measure depression and the sample studied. However, the possibility that maternal depression may affect the quality of the interactive relationship between mother and child should not be underestimated. For low-income, already stressed dyads, maternal depression may place the infants and children at greater risk for less emotional availability and other problems in the relationship. Our work (Osofsky & Eberhart-Wright, 1988; Carter et al, 1991a; Hann, Castino, Jarosinski, & Britton, 1991) and the work of others (Radke-Yarrow, Cummings, Kuczynski, & Chapman, 1985; Field, Healy, Goldstein, & Guthertz, 1990; Tronick & Gianino, 1986; Zahn-Waxler, Kochanska, Krupnick, & McKnew, 1990) also indicate that the children of depressed mothers are at higher risk for problems in affect regulation, including both increased depression (or subdued affect) and inappropriate aggression. According to Tronick and Gianino (1986), if the infant is able to cope with a nonresponsive environment and maintain self- and interactive regulation simultaneously, then the result is likely to be a positive mental health outcome. On the other hand, if the infant cannot maintain interactive regulation, then self-regulation will be the primary means of coping, and the outcome is likely to be problematic. The combination of depression in the mothers and difficulty in affect regulation, resulting in less emotional availability, increases the risk of these infants and children for the development of problematic behaviors or psychopathology.

BIOLOGICAL RISKS

Although it has been assumed for many years that there is significant biological risk in teenage pregnancy—with a higher incidence of obstetrical complications such as toxemia, anemia, and hypertension, and prenatal complications such as low birthweight, prematurity, and infant mortality (Dwyer, 1974; Fielding, 1978; Klein, 1974)—more recent studies have indicated that with good prenatal care this risk can be greatly reduced (Broman, 1981; McCormick, 1985; Roosa, 1984; Zuckerman et al., 1983). When factors that contribute to low birthweight and increased mortality risk (such as poverty, inadequate nutrition, race, maternal education, maternal age at the extremes, and prior obstetrical history) are controlled for, adolescent motherhood does not contribute differentially to outcome (Hollingsworth, Kotchen, & Felice, 1983). With very young mothers under the age of 15, there may be increased risk; however, no systematic studies have been conducted (McCormick, 1985).

A major factor contributing to risk is the lack of adequate nutrition and prenatal care during pregnancy. A combination of gynecological age, socioeconomic difficulties, poor nutrition, late diagnosis of pregnancy, and fragmented services available to pregnant teenagers operates against good prenatal care and optimal pregnancy outcome. Adolescents are more likely to avoid or deny that they are having problems, which, in addition to limited community resources in urban centers, contributes to their not obtaining health care (Osofsky, Osofsky, & Diamond, 1988).

Furstenberg (1976, 1987), in one of the most extensive follow-up studies of teenage mothers and their children from a social and psychological perspective, emphasizes the importance of these psychosocial factors in evaluating outcomes for adolescent mothers and their infants. Thus, even though there may be greater physiological risk for some adolescent mothers and their infants, the overriding concerns affecting outcomes appear to be more in the psychosocial area (Furstenberg, 1976; Turner et al., 1990).

PARENTING RISKS FOR THE INFANTS AND CHILDREN

Beyond the high-risk socioemotional environment that adolescent mothers provide for their infants and children, there is consistent evidence for problems in the cognitive environment, including both the mothers' initiation of verbal interaction and responsiveness to their offspring

(Osofsky, Culp, Eberhart-Wright, Ware, & Hann, 1988; Furstenberg, Brooks-Gunn, & Morgan, 1987; Brooks-Gunn & Furstenberg, 1986; Chase-Landsdale et al., 1991; Culp, Appelbaum, Osofsky, & Levy, 1988; Crockenberg, 1987; Field, 1980; Osofsky, 1991; Osofsky & Eberhart-Wright, 1992). When observing interactions between adolescent mothers and their infants, one is frequently struck with the quietness of the interaction. Many of the mothers talk very little to their infants and young children, and, as might be expected, the children verbalize relatively little. When the mothers do talk, they often merely give short commands or discipline the children, rather than providing elaborated responses or statements. Thus, many of these children grow up in impoverished cognitive environments as well as economic and socioemotional environments. The increased risk when they enter the organized school environment is obvious.

In terms of their knowledge of child development and developmental milestones for their children, adolescent mothers as compared with adult mothers in several studies have been characterized by a lack of knowledge of developmental milestones, more punitive child-rearing attitudes, and perceptions of their own infants' temperament as more difficult (Field, Widmayer, Stringer, & Ignatoff, 1980; Frodi, 1983). In a more recent investigation, Frodi, Grolnick, Bridges, and Berko (1990) reported that mothers' more realistic expectations about developmental milestones, nonpunitive child-rearing attitudes, and ratings of their infants' temperament as easy were significantly related to the quality of infant–mother attachment. Both an early study (de Lissovoy, 1973) and a later study of teenage mothers with preterm infants (Field, 1980) reported that teenage mothers expect their children to reach developmental milestones earlier—data that are consistent with findings from our studies on teenage mothers (Osofsky, Peebles, & Fick, 1992). Epstein (1979) reported in a study of 98 pregnant adolescents attending health clinics and parent education programs that many of them underestimated infants' abilities in social, cognitive, and language functioning, but had more accurate ideas about their abilities in areas in which they were being educated. Brooks-Gunn and Furstenberg (1986) conclude in their review article that even when socioeconomic status is controlled for, teenage mothers appear to have less knowledge about developmental milestones than do older mothers.

In addition to the less realistic and more punitive child-rearing attitudes associated with adolescent mothers (Field et al., 1980; Baranowski, Schilmoeller, & Higgins, 1990; Brooks-Gunn & Furstenberg, 1986), recent research examining adolescent mother–child interactions has indicated that the parenting practices of adolescent mothers may increase their children's risk for less adaptive developmental outcomes. When compared to the interactions of adult mothers and their children, interactions between adolescent mothers and their children differ in terms of both the amount and quality of behaviors displayed. As alluded to above, studies of mother–child interactions conducted in the home as well as in home-like laboratory situations have found that adolescent mothers are likely to be less verbal and more physical when interacting with their infants (Garcia Coll, Hoffman, & Oh, 1987; Culp et al., 1988; Osofsky & Osofsky, 1970). The paucity of talking between adolescent mothers and their infants, combined with the less descriptive and articulate verbal interactions of adolescent mothers and their toddlers (Osofsky, Barnard, et al., 1991), may contribute to the poorer cognitive and linguistic outcomes associated with the children of adolescent mothers (East & Felice, 1990; Furstenberg, Brooks-Gunn, & Chase-Landsdale, 1989).

Recent research examining more qualitative aspects of mother–child interactions has also found less optimal patterns of interactions between adolescent mothers and their children. In a study examining interactions of adolescent versus adult mothers with their 4-month-old infants, Ragozin, Basham, Crnic, Greenberg, and Robinson (1982) found maternal age to be a strong predictor of sensitivity among primiparous women, with younger mothers displaying less sensitive behavior than older mothers. Similarly, Garcia Coll et al. (1987) found adolescent mothers to be less involved, responsive, and positive with their 4-month-old infants, in comparison to a group of socially disadvantaged adult mothers and their infants.

The less sensitive and less emotionally positive patterns of interactions associated with adolescent mothers and their young infants have also been observed between adolescent mothers and their toddlers (Hann, Osofsky, et al., 1992; Hann, Robinson, Osofsky, & Little, 1991). When compared to the interactions observed between adult mothers and their toddlers, adolescent mother–toddler interactions were found to be less sensitive, more intrusive, less positive, and more negative. In addition, adolescent mothers and their toddlers were more likely to engage in dysregulated patterns of affective inter-action—that is, ones in which either negative affects were emphasized (e.g., child cried and mother yelled) or affective cues were misread by the dyad (e.g., child became angry and mother laughed). Participation in dysregulated patterns of affect was more characteristic of adolescent mothers and toddlers than of either socially advantaged or socially disadvantaged adult mothers and toddlers (Hann, Osofsky, et al., 1991).

The developmental ramifications of the less optimal interaction patterns associated with adolescent mothers and their children may be detected early in the socioemotional develop-ment of these children. Lamb, Hopps, and Elster (1987) found the distribution of infant attach-ment classifications to differ between infants of adolescent and adult mothers. Infants of adolescent mothers showed significantly more avoidant behavior and were more likely to be classified as avoidantly attached. More recent attachment research, which has included disor-ganized patterns of attachment in addition to se-cure and insecure patterns (Main & Solomon, 1990), has indicated that the infants of adoles-cent mothers may be at high risk for develop-ing disorganized attachments to their mothers (Hann, Castino, et al., 1991; Spieker, 1989). The suggestion that children of adolescent mothers are at higher risk for developing insecure attach-ment relationships is consistent with previous research concerning the etiology of avoidant and disorganized attachment. Both avoidant and disorganized attachment patterns have been associated with earlier insensitive, negative, and emotionally unavailable caregiving (Main & Hesse, 1990; Londerville & Main, 1981)—patterns that have been observed frequently with adolescent mothers and their children. Adolescent mothers and their children's in-creased risk for developing less optimal pat-terns of interaction, and the children's increased risk for developing insecure and disorganized attachment relationships, may contribute to the poorer social and emotional outcomes seen in these children (Furstenberg et al., 1989; Brooks-Gunn & Furstenberg, 1986; Osofsky & Eberhart-Wright, 1988; Osofsky, Eberhart-Wright, Ware, & Hann, 1992). Further research, however, is needed to establish the links between early patterns of mother–child interaction and infant attachment to later socioemotional outcomes with adolescent mothers and their children.

INDIVIDUAL DIFFERENCES IN INFANTS AFFECTING OUTCOMES

Adolescent mother–child interaction may be af-fected by individual characteristics of the child. Temperament as an individual-difference factor has been studied extensively recently. Depend-ing on how it manifests itself, temperament may be either a risk or a protective factor. In this section, the potential risks associated with tem-perament are discussed. There is some evidence that temperamental characteristics differ in chil-dren born to teenage as compared to older mothers, based on ratings on a parent report temperament scale (Field, 1980; Broman, 1981; Maracek, 1985). However, more studies and comparative behavioral measures of tempera-ment would be helpful in clarifying whether the infants are perceived differently or whether they also have behavioral differences. More distract-ibility and less adaptive behaviors have been reported in more active babies; however, envi-ronmental factors (e.g., less contingent respon-siveness and less talking to the infants as com-pared to physical stimulation) also might contribute to distractibility and less adaptive behaviors.

Risks related to the children's sex may be important for outcomes for infants of teenage mothers, although, again, more data are needed before the potential complexity of different find-ings can be fully understood. In our ongoing studies, we have found sex differences in pat-terns of interactions and displays of affect in the first year of life, although these are mediated to some extent by individual characteristics of the mothers, such as maternal depression. At 13 months of age, female infants of depressed mothers display less intense negative affect than male infants of depressed mothers (Carter et al., 1991a). Also, male infants receive more affec-tionate contact and more verbal expressiveness from their mothers than female infants. In gen-eral, mothers appear to provide more bound-aries with their little boys and are more likely to be less involved with their little girls. How-ever, several observers of young mothers and their infants have also commented that moth-ers' reactions to their little boys may vary more, depending on their own life situation at that time.

PROTECTIVE FACTORS

It has already been discussed that many adolescent mothers and their children live under conditions of chronic stress, including poverty, limited educational resources, and family instability (Brooks-Gunn & Furstenberg, 1986; Dubow & Luster, 1990; Osofsky, Culp, et al., 1988). Yet, in the face of such adversities, some adolescent mothers and their children seem to do relatively well. Some young mothers go on to lead highly productive lives and are able to facilitate their children's development. The reasons for these successes under adverse circumstances are not understood completely. The majority of the literature focuses on why individuals who are at risk fail. A better question to ask might be why some do not fail. What has gone right with these individuals? There is as much to be learned from studying the reasons for success as there is from studying failure, if not more.

In any examination of risk factors, it becomes apparent that there are also "protective factors" that serve as buffers against the risks. These protective factors sometimes lead to relative invulnerability or resiliency for adolescent mothers and their children. "Resiliency" refers to a marked ability to recover from or adjust easily to misfortune or chronic life stress—that is, adaptation despite challenging or threatening circumstances (Masten, Best, & Garmezy, 1990; Werner & Smith, 1982). Identifying protective factors can help us to create interventions to foster the development of resiliency in those individuals who are considered most vulnerable.

Several protective factors seem to be extremely important in terms of mediating outcomes for both adolescent mothers and their infants and children. One that comes up repeatedly in study after study is the role of support for a young mother, whether it comes from her family, extended family, friends, the father of the child, or outside agencies. Social support is generally defined as the factors leading individuals to believe that they are cared for, are esteemed, and have people on whom they can depend in times of need (Cobb, 1976). Conceptually, social support is viewed as a buffer, facilitating an individual's ability to handle stress. Brooks-Gunn and Furstenberg (1986) emphasize that the availability and use of social support may buffer the individual from the possible deleterious effects of negative life events. Furstenberg (1976) and Kellam et al. (1977) have reported that children of teenage mothers tend to have better developmental outcomes if there is alternative supportive child care by another person in the home. Brooks-Gunn and Furstenberg (1986) have posited several mechanisms to explain the impact of another person in the home for a teenage mother:

> [This person may] (1) act as a buffer, in lessening the psychological or economic impact of negative events upon the family; (2) act as a source of socioemotional support for the mother (which results in indirect benefits to the child); increased maternal well-being due to support may result in more interest in or responsivity to the child (Lewis & Feiring, 1981); and/or (3) act as a direct source of support for the child. (p. 235)

In our studies with adolescent mothers in Topeka, Kansas and New Orleans, Louisiana, we have found that both social support in general, particularly the young mothers' perception of support (as compared with the reported actual support), and specific support from the grandmothers had a significant impact on life outcomes for both the infants and young mothers (Osofsky, Culp, et al., 1988; Osofsky, 1991). Perceived support was also found to enhance the interactive relationship between the young mothers and their infants. The amount of support available to young mothers has been related to depression and self-esteem. In the New Orleans study, we found that the greater the number of people available for support to a young mother, the lower her level of reported depression and the higher her level of self-esteem. Grandmothers have also been found to act as a source of social support and as socializing agents for their grandchildren by Pearson, Hunter, Ensminger, and Kellam (1990). Similar findings by Stevens (1984) offer more evidence that the presence of a responsive grandmother appears to act as a buffer and as a positive influence on a child's development. Perception of social support has likewise been reported by others as an important mediator of the young mother's capacity to utilize available support in her environment (Kissman & Shapiro, 1990). These findings have strong implications for intervention: They suggest that strengthening social support systems in teenage mothers' and their infants' caregiving environment may result in reducing risk and facilitating resiliency.

In the Furstenberg et al. (1987) follow-up of a sample of teenage mothers and their children in Baltimore after 17 years, several factors were found to be extremely important for more successful outcomes. The young mothers' being able to continue with educational goals affected outcomes for both them and their children in terms of their feelings about themselves and their economic opportunities. Limiting their fertility was a second factor that positively influenced outcomes. A third major factor that seemed to have a great impact on their economic situation was whether they were married and stayed married before or after the birth of their children. Marriage provided both psychological support and a steady income to allow a family to be self-supporting. Furstenberg et al. (1987) pointed out, however, that this latter factor may have played a more significant role for a cohort growing up in the 1960s than it would today. In terms of outcomes for the children of teen mothers, "no single model described the impact of maternal career contingencies on the course of the children's development" (p. 145). However, several factors were predictive of poor outcomes, including welfare dependency, high fertility, and (at different developmental periods) marital status and family support. The authors emphasized that the usual assumption that failure is inevitable may not be valid, since they found that many of the mothers they studied were doing better than expected, and much better than they had been doing for the first 5 years after they had the children.

In our 5-year follow-up of adolescent mothers and children in Topeka, we found that self-esteem was another important mediator of outcomes for both the young mothers and their infants (Osofsky, Culp, et al., 1988). The relationships between child outcomes at 44 months, with particular emphasis on child behavioral conduct, and earlier indices of maternal functioning indicated that self-esteem and depression may be important mediators of outcomes; more problematic development was related to higher levels of depression and lower levels of self-esteem. At 54 months, earlier problems in maternal self-esteem and depression were associated with more problematic forms of child internalizing behavior as measured by the Child Behavior Checklist (Achenbach, 1979). In our ongoing studies of adolescent mothers and their children in New Orleans, preliminary results point in a similar direction: Problems in self-esteem and depression appear to be associated with more problematic personality patterns for the adolescent mothers themselves, as well as poorer outcomes for their infants in socio-emotional domains. In an attempt to learn more about personality factors that may contribute to adolescent pregnancy, we are studying a sample of young mothers and a matched nonpregnant adolescent sample at high psychosocial risk. On personality measures of identity and psychosocial development, preliminary findings suggest differences between these groups. The pregnant adolescents report higher levels of identity diffusion than their nonpregnant counterparts; the nonpregnant adolescents report higher levels of identity achievement than the pregnant adolescents. On measures of psychosocial development, the pregnant group reports lower levels of trust than the nonpregnant group. This is an important area to pursue further in relation to risk factors that may contribute to early pregnancy, as well as protective factors that may help an at-risk adolescent avoid early pregnancy.

In several studies, infant intelligence has emerged as a protective factor that appears to contribute to resiliency. Problem-solving skills increase the number of alternatives available to infants for problem-focused coping. Infants with more advanced problem-solving skills should have more effective coping skills when responding to environmental demands (Karraker & Lake, 1991). Low IQ has been associated with behavioral maladjustment, social incompetence, and academic failure, whereas high IQ has been shown to be a protective factor predictive of more successful adjustment and achievement (Werner & Smith, 1982; Madge & Tizard, 1981). Pellegrini, Masten, Garmezy, and Ferrarese (1987) have reported a "social comprehension" component that is associated with competence under stress. Strongly correlated with IQ, this component contributes significantly to both social and academic competence. In our studies of adolescent mothers, we have found child intelligence to be a strength leading to more positive outcomes in the mothers as well as the children (Osofsky & Eberhart-Wright, 1992).

Although temperament has been mentioned in the section on risk, temperament can also be a protective factor. Resilient children tend to have the ability, beginning in infancy, to gain other people's positive attention. They often possess personality characteristics, such as positive mood and friendliness, that elicit positive responses from family members as well as strangers (Garmezy, 1983; Rutter, 1978). We have observed that similar characteristics have similar results for children of adolescent mothers (Osofsky & Eberhart-Wright, 1992). Infants who are active and socially responsive are most likely to show resistance to stress in childhood and adulthood (Werner & Smith, 1982). Lerner and East (1984) suggested that infants with easier temperaments can more readily obtain suitable care and help with coping from their environments. Cowen, Wyman, Work, and Parker (1990), using self-report and behavioral measures of temperament, found resilient outcomes in children with easy temperaments. These infants were easier to manage, more outgoing, and more relaxed. In our work with adolescent mothers in Topeka and New Orleans, several positive temperamental characteristics in infants and children were found that contributed to invulnerability and/or resiliency. These included a social nature apparent from birth, the ability to charm others, and a zest for living (Osofsky & Eberhart-Wright, 1992).

Examining the relationships among risk factors, protective factors, and resiliency can provide a better understanding of developmental outcomes for both adolescent mothers and their children. Understanding resiliency in members of a high-risk population can enhance intervention efforts directed at those members who are less successful. Knowing which individuals are at greater risk, as well as which protective factors facilitate resiliency, is crucial to developing effective intervention programs.

ADOLESCENT FATHERHOOD

This review has focused on adolescent motherhood, in an attempt to understand the young mother and her child in the context of her family and environment. For most adolescents who became mothers in the 1980s, the fathers of the children have not played a significant role in either the mothers' lives or the socialization of the children. We have seen a shift in the involvement of young fathers, with their increasing absence from cohorts of young mothers studied in the 1980s as compared to those followed in the 1960s (Furstenberg et al., 1987). Many factors have probably contributed to the lesser involvement of young fathers. First, marriage is much less likely at present than it was in the 1960s (Chase-Landsdale & Vinovskis, 1987; Furstenberg, 1987), and acceptance of single-parent families is greater. Second, there has been an increase in poverty, with economic factors strongly affecting the lack of consistent presence of young males in the lives of adolescent moth-

ers and their children. Third, there is increased pressure for the young mothers to finish school themselves in order to be self-supporting, which discourages early marriage. For the interested reader, Chase-Landsdale and Vinovskis (1987) and Furstenberg (1987) have contributed articles reviewing different perspectives on teenage marriage to a recent issue of The Public Interest.

Parke and Neville (1987), in their review of teenage fatherhood, maintain that prior neglect of adolescent fathers has also resulted from the general lack of concern in our society with the male role in infancy and childhood. Contributing factors to this situation include theoretical models of infant development that have placed primary emphasis on the mother–infant relationship; the unfounded issue of biological preparedness of mothers in contrast with fathers; and support of traditional models of father involvement and sex-role allocation that have not changed dramatically in recent years.

It must be emphasized, in attempting to understand the issue of adolescent fatherhood and the role of the young men who impregnate teenage women, that the majority of such men are not teenagers. Although it is very difficult to obtain accurate figures on the numbers of teenage males who impregnate teenage women, because some fathers deny paternity and demographic data about fathers are not consistently available, the studies that have been done indicate that at least half of adolescent mothers are impregnated by older men (Furstenberg et al., 1989). Because of this fact, the issues may be quite different in trying to understand the personal dynamics and family structure of adolescent mothers as compared with the young men who are involved with them.

In terms of sexual knowledge, teenage fathers are generally uninformed about sexuality and reproduction (Barret & Robinson, 1982; Brown, 1983). Teenage fathers either do not use contraception or use it inconsistently (Alan Guttmacher Institute, 1981). Their knowledge about child development and expectations for their children are likely to be unrealistic (de Lissovoy, 1973; Rivara, Sweeney, & Henderson, 1986). Although a young father tends to be less adversely affected by early parenthood than a young mother, his educational future is negatively influenced by the occurrence of an early birth even if he does not marry the mother (Card & Wise, 1978; Marsiglio, 1987; Parke & Neville, 1987). It is not clear, however, whether dropping out of school precedes or follows early fatherhood. Most young men who become fathers as teenagers are at very high psychosocial risk in other ways.

There are conflicting data about the degree of involvement that the males desire and maintain with the young mothers (see Elster & Panzarine, 1983; Chase-Landsdale & Vinovskis, 1987; Furstenberg, 1987). Whereas some studies have reported that fathers want to maintain involvement with the mothers of their children and with the children, other studies report discrepant findings. There is general agreement, however, that if a father maintains positive involvement with a mother and child over a period of time, he serves as an important source of support that affects outcomes for both the mother and child in positive ways.

Although few services are available specifically for young fathers, educational assistance and job skills programs frequently deal with young fathers. Unfortunately, unless such perspectives are built into the programs, little attention is given to the issue of the young men as fathers and the role they may be playing. In proposing a family perspective to understand teenage motherhood, it is important to take into account the role and involvement of both the natural father and other men in the young mother's life who may play an important supportive role for both her and her child.

INTERVENTIONS WITH ADOLESCENT MOTHERS AND THEIR INFANTS

On the basis of research to date, as well as earlier and ongoing intervention efforts, there is little question that a comprehensive approach to intervention is needed with adolescent mothers and their infants. It is important to recognize and design programs to take into account the needs of the individuals, who are both children—the adolescent mother and her child—going through their own developmental struggles. The interventions should also be directed at the dyad and the broader family context of the adolescent mother. For a comprehensive review of intervention programs and strategies, see Meisels and Shonkoff (1990). In this section, rather than reviewing programs that have been implemented with adolescent mothers and their infants, we emphasize important issues and areas emerging from our discussion of protective factors for both mothers and infants. Our reason-

ing is that if individuals and programs address these issues and areas for adolescent mothers, the interventions will be more effective. The issues we see as vital include support, education, personality issues, self-esteem, depression, match between infant and mother, and the invulnerability of the individual under stress.

Support for individuals can be conceptualized in many different ways. As compared with earlier approaches to therapeutic issues that focused exclusively on the individual, more recent emphasis has been placed on relationships (Sameroff & Emde, 1989). Taking a relationships perspective is important for developing effective interventions for adolescent mothers, their children, and their families. Many adolescent mothers come from families that have lacked consistency and stable relationships. Thus, building a relationship first is necessary, in order to develop the trust to be able to provide effective intervention for the mother and child. In our ongoing studies of adolescent mothers and a matched high-risk group of nonpregnant adolescents, one of the personality dimensions that appears to discriminate between the two groups is trust as conceptualized from Erikson's (1968) developmental perspective. Without trust, which is basic for psychological development, it is difficult to build other aspects of healthy development and relationships. Thus, an intervention program for adolescent mothers must address their needs first at a basic level—the level of having a trusting relationship.

Taking a relationships approach to intervention will help to accomplish several other important tasks. We know that self-esteem is an important intervening factor contributing to more positive outcomes for a young mother and her child (Osofsky, Culp, et al., 1988; Furstenberg et al., 1987). The mother's being able to form a meaningful relationship, including trust in another person who has confidence in her, raises her self-esteem. If the adolescent feels better about herself, she will be better equipped to parent her infant effectively.

In our experience in developing interventions with adolescent mothers, we have found that it is most helpful to use strategies that assist the mothers in empathizing with their babies. Adolescence is a developmental period when individuals tend to focus mainly on themselves rather than other persons. Thus, a baby or child may threaten the egocentricity of a teenager. For a teenager, her own feelings are crucial, not those of others. Even if a young woman is already a mother, she will continue with her struggle to determine "Who am I?" Thus, helping the mother tune into her baby's feelings is difficult, but crucial, for both the baby and the relationship. We have found that using video cameras and other techniques help young mothers to focus playfully on their babies' feelings (Carter, Osofsky, & Hann, 1991b) and to recognize the impact of their behaviors on the babies.

Finally, it is important to recognize the issue of "the match" in developing intervention efforts. Each baby and each mother are different, and sometimes the most helpful information that can be imparted to a mother, either younger or older, is just that message. When a mother recognizes the individuality of her baby, the match may become less important as a test of her mothering ability. This issue is particularly important for adolescent mothers and other mothers at high psychosocial risk who may be focusing more on their own needs than on those of the babies. It is very reassuring for a mother to hear that she may not always be responsible for the difficult behaviors manifested by her baby. Encouraging the recognition and acceptance of the child's individuality will increase the mother's acceptance of the child.

Adolescent pregnancy and parenthood are times of significant risk for both the young mother and her infant. In this chapter, some of the factors that contribute to risk, as well as protective factors that influence resiliency within individuals and dyads, have been reviewed. We feel that an emphasis on positive mental health—that is, a focus on what may go right rather than wrong with adolescent mothers and their infants—will lead us forward toward the development of more effective preventive interventions.

REFERENCES

Achenbach, T. M. (1979). The Child Behavior Profile: An empirically based system for assessing children's behavioral problems and competencies. *International Journal of Mental Health, 7,* 24–42.

Alan Guttmacher Institute. (1981). *Teenage pregnancy: The problem that hasn't gone away.* New York: Author.

Baranowski, M. D., Schilmoeller, G. L., & Higgins, B. S. (1990). Parenting attitudes of adolescent and older mothers. *Adolescence, 25,* 781–790.

Barret, R. L., & Robinson, B. E. (1982). A descriptive study of teenage expectant fathers. *Family Relations, 31,* 349–352.

Belsky, J. (1984). The determinants of parenting. *Child Development, 55,* 83–96.

Benedek, T. (1970). The psychobiology of pregnancy. In E. J. Anthony & T. Benedek (Eds.), *Parenthood: Its psychology and psychopathology* (pp. 137–152). Boston: Little, Brown.

Bibring, G. L., Dwyer, T. F., Huntington, D. S., & Valenstein, A. F. (1961). A study of the psychological processes in pregnancy and of the earliest mother–child relationship: I. Some propositions and comments. *Psychoanalytic Study of the Child, 16,* 9–24.

Broman, S. H. (1981). Long-term development of children born to teenagers. In K. Scott, T. Field, & E. G. Robertson (Eds.), *Teenage parents and their offspring* (pp. 195–224). New York: Grune & Stratton.

Bronfenbrenner, U. (1985, May). *Interacting systems in human development. Research paradigms: Present and future.* Paper presented at the meeting of the Society for Research in Child Development Study Group, Cornell University, Ithaca, NY.

Bronfenbrenner, U. (1986). Ecology of the family as a context for human development. *Development Psychology, 22,* 723–742.

Bronfenbrenner, U. (1988). Ecological systems theory. *Annals of Child Development, 6,* 187–249.

Brooks-Gunn, J., & Chase-Landsdale, L. (1991). Teenage childbearing: Effects on children. In R. M. Lerner, A. C. Peterson, & J. Brooks-Gunn (Eds.). *Encyclopedia of adolescence* (pp. 103–106). New York: Garland.

Brooks-Gunn, J., & Furstenberg, F. F. (1986). The children of adolescent mothers: Physical, academic, and psychological outcomes. *Developmental Review, 6,* 224–251.

Brown, S. V. (1983). The commitment and concerns of black adolescent parents. *Social Work Research and Abstracts, 19,* 27–34.

Burton, L. M., & Bengtson, V. L. (1985). Black grandmothers: Issues of timing and continuity of roles. In V. L. Bengtson & J. F. Robertson (Eds.), *Grandparenthood: Research and policy perspectives* (pp. 61–77). Beverly Hills, CA: Sage.

Card, J. J., & Wise, L. L. (1978). Teenage mothers and teenage fathers: The impact of early childbearing on the parents' personal and professional lives. *Family Planning Perspectives, 10,* 199–205.

Carter, S., Osofsky, J. D., & Hann, D. M. (1991a, April). *Maternal depression and affect in adolescent mothers and their infants.* Paper presented at the biennial meeting of the Society for Research in Child Development, Seattle.

Carter, S., Osofsky, J. D., & Hann, D. M. (1991b). Speaking for baby: Therapeutic interventions with adolescent mothers and their infants. *Infant Mental Health Journal, 12,* 291–301.

Chase-Landsdale, L., Brooks-Gunn, J., & Palkoff, R. L. (1991). Research programs for adolescent mothers: Missing links and future promises. *Family Relations, 40,* 1–8.

Chase-Landsdale, L., & Vinovskis, M. (1987). Should we discourage teenage marriage? *The Public Interest, 87,* 23–37.

Chilman, C. (1983). *Adolescent sexuality in a changing American society: Social and psychological perspectives for the human services professions* (2nd ed.). New York: Wiley.

Cobb, S. (1976). Social support as a moderator of life stress. *Psychosomatic Medicine, 38,* 300–314.

Cowen, E. L., Wyman, P. A., Work, W. C., & Parker, G. R. (1990). The Rochester Child Resilience Project: Overview and summary of first year findings. *Development and Psychopathology, 2,* 193–212.

Crockenberg, S. (1987). Support for adolescent mothers during the postnatal period: Theory and research. In C. F. Z. Boukydis (Ed.) *Research on support for parents and infants in the postnatal period* (pp. 3–24). Hillsdale, NJ: Erlbaum.

Culp, R. E., Appelbaum, M. I., Osofsky, J. D., & Levy, J. A. (1988). Adolescent and older mothers: Comparison between prenatal maternal variables and newborn interaction measures. *Infant Behavior and Development, 11,* 353–362.

de Lissovoy, V. (1973). Child care by adolescent parents. *Children Today, 2,* 22–25.

Dubow, E. F., & Luster, T. (1990). Adjustment of children born to teenage mothers: The contribution of risk and protective factors. *Journal of Marriage and the Family, 52,* 393–405.

Dwyer, J. (1974). Teenage pregnancy. *American Journal of Obstetrics and Gynecology, 118,* 373–376.

East, P. L., & Felice, M. E. (1990). Outcomes and parent–child relationships of former adolescent mothers and their 12-year-old children. *Developmental and Behavioral Pediatrics, 11,* 175–183.

Elder, G. H., Jr., Caspi, A., & Burton, L. M. (1987). Adolescent transitions in developmental perspective: Sociological and historical insights. In M. Gunnar (Ed.), *Minnesota Symposium on Child Development* (Vol. 21, pp. 151–179). Hillsdale, NJ: Erlbaum.

Elster, A. B., & Panzarine, S. (1983). Teenage fathers: Stresses during gestation and early parenthood. *Clinical Pediatrics, 22,* 700–703.

Emde, R. N. (1991). The wonder of our complex enterprise: Steps enabled by attachment and the effects of relationships on relationships. *Infant Mental Health Journal, 12,* 164–173.

Epstein, A. S. (1979, March). *Pregnant teenagers' knowledge of infant development.* Paper presented at the biennial meeting of the Society for Research in Child Development, San Francisco.

Erikson, E. H. (1968). *Identity: Youth and crisis.* New York: Norton.

Fick, A., Peebles, C., Osofsky, J. D., & Hann, D. M. (1992, March). *Relationships among identity development, depression and self-esteem in pregnant and non-pregnant adolescents.* Poster presented at the meeting of the Society for Adolescent Research, Washington, DC.

Field, T. M. (1980). Interactions of preterm and term infants with their lower and middle class teenage and adult mothers. In T. M. Field, S. Goldberg, D. Stern, & A. Sostek (Eds), *High risk infants and children: Adult and peer interactions* (pp. 113–130). New York: Academic Press.

Field, T. M., Healy, B., Goldstein, S., & Guthertz, M. (1990). Behavior–state matching and synchrony in mother–infant interactions of nondepressed versus depressed dyads. *Developmental Psychology, 26,* 7–14.

Field, T. M., Widmayer, S. M., Stringer, S., & Ignatoff, E. (1980). Teenage, lower class, black mothers and their pre-term infants: An intervention and developmental follow-up study. *Child Development, 51,* 426–436.

Fielding, J. (1978). Adolescent pregnancy revisited. *New England Journal of Medicine, 299,* 893–896.

Frodi, A. (1983). Attachment behavior and sociability with strangers in premature and full-term infants. *Infant Mental Health Journal, 4,* 13–22.

Frodi, A., Grolnick, W., Bridges, L., & Berko, J. (1990). Infants of adolescent and adult mothers: Two indices

of socioemotional development. *Adolescence, 25,* 363–374.

Furstenberg, F. F., Jr. (1976). The social consequences of teenage parenthood. *Family Planning Perspectives, 8,* 148–164.

Furstenberg, F. F., Jr. (1987). Bringing back the shotgun wedding. *The Public Interest, 87,* 121–127.

Furstenberg, F. F., Jr., Brooks-Gunn, J., & Chase-Landsdale, L. (1989). Teenaged pregnancy and childbearing. *American Psychologist, 44,* 313–320.

Furstenberg, F. F., Jr., Brooks-Gunn, J., & Morgan, P. (1987). *Adolescent mothers in later life.* New York: Cambridge University Press.

Garcia Coll, C. T., Hoffman, J., & Oh, W. (1987). The social ecology and early parenting of Caucasian adolescent mothers. *Child Development, 58,* 955–962.

Garmezy, N. (1983). Stressors of childhood. In N. Garmezy & M. Rutter (Eds.), *Stress, coping and development* (pp. 43–85). New York: McGraw-Hill.

Garrison, C. Z., Schluchter, M. D., Schoenbach, V. J., & Kaplan, B. K. (1989). Epidemiology of depressive symptoms in young adolescents. *Journal of the American Academy of Child and Adolescent Psychiatry, 28,* 343–351.

Geertz, C. (1973). *The interpretation of cultures.* New York: Basic Books.

Greenberg, J. R., & Mitchell, S. A. (1983). *Object relations in psychoanalytic theory.* Cambridge, MA: Harvard University Press.

Hann, D. M., Castino, R. J., Jarosinski, J., & Britton, H. (1991, April). Relating mother–toddler negotiation patterns to infant attachment and maternal depression with an adolescent mother sample. In J. D. Osofsky & L. Hubbs-Tait (Chairs), *Consequences of adolescent parenting: Predicting behavior problems in toddlers and preschoolers.* Symposium conducted at the biennial meeting of the Society for Research in Child Development, Seattle.

Hann, D. M., Osofsky, J. D., Barnard, K., & Leonard, G. (1992). *Dyadic affect regulation in three caregiving environments.* Manuscript submitted for publication.

Hann, D. M., Robinson, J. L., Osofsky, J. D., & Little, C. (1991). *Emotional availability in two caregiving environments: Low-risk adult mothers and socially at-risk adolescent mothers.* Paper presented at the biennial meeting of Society for Research in Child Development, Seattle.

Hinde, R., & Stevenson-Hinde, J. (1988). *Relationships within families: Mutual influences.* Oxford: Clarendon Press.

Hollingsworth, D. R., Kotchen, J. M., & Felice, M. E. (1983). Impact of gynecologic age on outcome of adolescent pregnancy. In E.R. McAnarney (Ed.), *Premature adolescent pregnancy and parenthood* (pp. 169–194). New York: Grune & Stratton.

Kahn, R. L., & Antonucci, T. C. (1980). Convoys over the life course: Attachment, roles and social support. In P. B. Baltes & O. G. Brim (Eds.), *Life-span development and behavior* (pp. 253–286). New York: Academic Press.

Karraker, K. H., & Lake, M. (1991). Normative stress and coping processes in infancy. In M. Cummings, A. Greene, & K. Karraker (Eds.), *Life-span developmental psychology: Perspectives on stress and coping* (Vol. 1, pp. 85–108). Hillsdale, NJ: Erlbaum.

Kellam, S. G., Ensminger, M. E., & Turner, R. J. (1977). Family structure and the mental health of children. *Archives of General Psychiatry, 34,* 1012–1022.

Klein, L. (1974). Early teenage pregnancy, contraception and repeat pregnancy. *American Journal of Obstetrics and Gynecology, 120,* 249–256.

Kissman, K., & Shapiro, J. (1990). The composites of social support and well-being among adolescent mothers. *International Journal of Adolescence and Youth, 2,* 165–173.

Ladner, J., & Gourdine, R. M. (1985). Black mothers and daughters: Some preliminary findings. In V. L. Bengtson & J. F. Robertson (Eds.), *Grandparenthood: Research and policy perspectives.* Beverly Hills, CA: Sage.

Lamb, M. E., Hopps, K., & Elster, A. B. (1987). Strange situation behavior of infants with adolescent mothers. *Infant Behavior and Development, 10,* 39–48.

Lerner, R. M., & East, P. L. (1984). The role of infant temperament in stress, coping, and socioemotional functioning in early development. *Infant Mental Health Journal, 5,* 148–159.

Lewis, M., & Feiring, C. (1981). Direct and indirect interactions in social relationships. In L. Lipsitt (Ed.), *Advances in infancy research* (Vol. 1, pp. 129–161). Norwood, NJ: Ablex.

Londerville, S., & Main, M. (1981). Security of attachment, compliance, and maternal training methods in the second year of life. *Developmental Psychology, 17,* 289–299.

Madge, N., & Tizard, J. (1981). Intelligence. In M. Rutter (Ed.), *Developmental psychiatry* (pp. 245–265). Baltimore: University Park Press.

Mahler, M., Pine, F., & Bergman, A. (1975). *The psychological birth of the human infant.* New York: Basic Books.

Main, M., & Hesse, E. (1990). Parents' unresolved traumatic experiences are related to infant disorganized attachment status: Is frightened and/or frightening parental behavior the linking mechanism? In M. Greenberg, D. Cicchetti, & E. M. Cummings (Eds.), *Attachment in the preschool years: Theory, research and intervention* (pp. 161–184). Chicago: University of Chicago Press.

Main, M., & Solomon, J. (1990). Procedures for identifying infants as disorganized–disoriented during the Ainsworth Strange Situation. In M. Greenberg, D. Cicchetti, & E. M. Cummings (Eds.), *Attachment in the preschool years: Theory, research and intervention* (pp. 121–160). Chicago: University of Chicago Press.

Maracek, J. (1985). *The effects of adolescent childbearing on childrens' cognitive and psychosocial development.* Unpublished manuscript.

Marsiglio, W. (1987). Adolescent fathers in the United States: Their initial living arrangements, marital experience and educational outcomes. *Family Planning Perspectives, 19,* 240–251.

Masten, A. S., Best, K. M., & Garmezy, N. (1990). Resilience and development: Contributions from the study of children who overcome adversity. *Developmental Psychopathology, 2,* 425–444.

McCormick, M. C. (1985). The contribution of low birth weight to infant mortality and child morbidity. *New England Journal of Medicine, 312,* 82–90.

Meisels, S. J., & Shonkoff, J. P. (1990). *Handbook of early childhood intervention.* New York: Cambridge University Press.

National Center for Health Statistics. (1991). *Monthly Vital Statistics Report, 40*(8), Supplement, December 12, 1991.

Osofsky, H. J., & Osofsky, J. D. (1970). Adolescents as mothers: Results of a program for low-income pregnant teenagers with some emphasis upon infants' development. *American Journal of Orthopsychiatry, 40,* 825–834.

Osofsky, J. D. (1991). *A preventive intervention program for adolescent mothers and their infants.* Final report to the Institute of Mental Hygiene, New Orleans.

Osofsky, J. D., Barnard, K. B., Beckwith, L., Appelbaum, M., Morrisett, C., Hann, D. M., & Osofsky, J. D. (1993). *Early emotional development: Results of collaborative intervention project.* Paper presented at biennial meeting of Society for Research in Child Development, New Orleans.

Osofsky, J. D., Culp, A. W., Eberhart-Wright, A., Ware, L. M., & Hann, D. M. (1988). Final report to Kenworthy Foundation, Menninger Clinic, Topeka, KS, and Louisiana State University Medical Center, New Orleans.

Osofsky, J. D., & Eberhart-Wright, A. (1988). Affective exchanges between high risk mothers and infants. *International Journal of Psycho-Analysis, 69,* 221–231.

Osofsky, J. D., & Eberhart-Wright, A. (1992). Risk and protective factors for parents and infants. In G. Suci & S. Robertson (Eds.), *Human development: Future directions in infant development research* (pp. 25–39). New York: Springer-Verlag.

Osofsky, J. D., Eberhart-Wright, A., Ware, L. M., & Hann, D. M. (1992). Children of adolescent mothers: A group at risk for psychopathology. *Infant Mental Health Journal, 13,* 119–131.

Osofsky, J. D., Osofsky, H. J., & Diamond, M. O. (1988). The transition to parenthood: Special tasks and risk factors for adolescent mothers. In G. Y. Michaels & W. A. Goldberg (Eds.), *The transition to parenthood* (pp. 209–234). New York: Cambridge University Press.

Osofsky, J. D., Peebles, C., Fick, A., & Hann, D. M. (1992). *Relationships between personality development and affective development in African-American adolescent mothers and their infants.* Manuscript submitted for publication.

Osofsky, J. D., Wewers, S., Fick, A., Hann, D. M., & Richters, J. (1993). Children's exposure to chronic community violence: What are we doing to our children? *Psychiatry, 56,* 36–45.

Parke, R. D., & Neville, B. (1987). Teenage fatherhood. In S. L. Hofferth & C. D. Hayes (Eds.) *Risking the future: Adolescent sexuality, pregnancy, and childbearing* (pp. 145–173). Washington, DC: National Academy Press.

Pearson, J. L., Hunter, A. G., Ensminger, M. E., & Kellam, S. G. (1990). Black grandmothers in multigenerational households: Diversity in family structure and parenting involvement in the Woodlawn Community. *Child Development, 61,* 434–442.

Peebles, C. D., Fick, A., & Osofsky, J. D. (1992). *Relationship between adolescent pregnancy, depression, self esteem and psychosocial development.* Poster presented at the meeting of the Society for Adolescent Research, Washington, DC.

Pellegrini, D. S., Mastin, A. S., Garmezy, N., & Ferrarese, M. J. (1987). Correlates of social and academic competence in middle childhood. *Journal of Child Psychology and Psychiatry, 28*(5), 699–714.

Radke-Yarrow, M., Cummings, E. M., Kuczynski, L., & Chapman, M. (1985). Patterns of attachment in two and three-year-olds in normal families and families with parental depression. *Child Development, 56,* 884–893.

Ragozin, A. S., Basham, R. B., Crnic, K. A., Greenberg, M. T., & Robinson, N. M. (1982). Effects of maternal age on parenting role. *Developmental Psychology, 18,* 627–634.

Reiss, D. (1981). *The family's construction of reality.* Cambridge, MA: Harvard University Press.

Reiss, D. (1989). The represented and practicing family: Contrasting visions of family continuity. In A. J. Sameroff & R. N. Emde (Eds.), *Relationship disturbances in early childhood* (pp. 191–220). New York: Basic Books.

Rivara, F. P., Sweeney, P. J., & Henderson, B. F. (1986). Black teenage fathers: What happens when the child is born? *Pediatrics, 78,* 151–158.

Roosa, M. (1984). Short-term effects of teenage parenting program on knowledge and attitudes. *Adolescence, 18,* 348–360.

Rutter, M. (1978). Early sources of security and competence. In J. Bruner & A. Gordon (Eds.), *Human growth and development* (pp. 33–61). New York: Oxford University Press.

Sameroff, A. J., & Chandler, M. J. (1975). Reproductive risk and continuum of caretaking casualty. In F. D. Horowitz, E. M. Hetherington, S. Scarr-Salapatek, & G. Siegel (Eds.), *Review of child development research* (Vol. 4, pp. 187–243). Chicago: University of Chicago Press.

Sameroff, A. J., & Emde, R. N. (Eds.). (1989). *Relationship disturbances in early childhood.* New York: Basic Books.

Spieker, S. (1989). *Mothering in adolescence: Factors related to infant security* (Grant No. MC-J-50535). Washing-ton, DC: Maternal and Child Health and Crippled Children's Services.

Spivak, H., & Weitzman, M. (1987). Social barriers faced by adolescent parents and their children. *Journal of the American Medical Association, 258,* 1500–1504.

Stevens, J. H., Jr. (1984). Child development knowledge and parenting skill. *Family Relations, 33,* 237–244.

Stevenson-Hinde, J. (1990). Attachment within family systems: An overview. *Infant Mental Health Journal, 11,* 218–227.

Tomkins, C. (1989, March 27). Profiles: A sense of urgency. *The New Yorker,* pp. 48–72.

Tronick, E. Z., & Gianino, A. F., Jr. (1986). The transmission of maternal disturbance to the infant. In E. Z. Tronick & T. M. Field (Eds.), *New directions for child development: No. 34. Maternal depression and infant disturbance* (pp. 47–68). San Francisco: Jossey-Bass.

Turner, R. J., Grindstaff, C. F., & Phillips, N. (1990). Social support and outcome in teenage pregnancy. *Journal of Health and Social Behavior, 31,* 43–57.

Werner, E. E., & Smith, R. S. (1982). *Vulnerable but invincible: A study of resilient children.* New York: McGraw-Hill.

Zahn-Waxler, C., Kochanska, G., Krupnick, J., & McKnew, D. (1990). Patterns of guilt in children of depressed and well mothers. *Developmental Psychology, 26,* 51–59.

Zuckerman, B. S., Alpert, J. J., Dooling, E., Hingson, R., Kaye, H., Morelock, S., & Openheim, E. (1983). Neonatal outcome: Is adolescent pregnancy a risk factor? *Pediatrics, 71,* 489–493.

Zuravin, S. J. (1989). Severity of maternal depression and three types of mother-to-child aggression. *American Journal of Orthopsychiatry, 59,* 377–389.

8

Parental Mental Illness and Infant Development

RONALD SEIFER
SUSAN DICKSTEIN

The original motivation for studying children of parents with mental illness was to gather evidence regarding the etiology of serious mental disorders. It has long been known that children born to parents with mental illness are at increased risk themselves for a variety of disorders (Garmezy & Streitman, 1974). In addition, researchers recognized methodological difficulties for the study of etiology when examining individuals who already manifested the disorders (Mednick & McNeil, 1968). From these realizations grew the "high-risk" method for studying the etiology of mental disorders, particularly schizophrenia.

The earliest high-risk studies concentrated on older children and adolescents, so that the researchers might be able to observe the subjects as they grew through the risk period for the disorder (about 45 years of age for schizophrenia). One notable exception to this pattern was the work of Fish (1977) on a small cohort of infants born in the early 1950s.

As research on etiology, the initial work was not satisfying to some developmentalists. To the extent that one purpose of high-risk studies was to disentangle influences of constitution and context, beginning the examination of children after several years of developing in potentially disordered family contexts was not desirable. By the late 1960s and 1970s, several more studies were begun that examined children born to parents with mental illness (particularly schizo-

phrenia) from the infancy period onward (Cohler & Musick, 1983; Goodman, 1987; Marcus, Auerbach, Wilkinson, & Burack, 1981; McNeil & Kaij, 1987; Sameroff, Seifer, & Zax, 1982). Following these initial studies, there have been many more projects, primarily targeted at children born to depressed mothers (Beardslee, Bemporad, Keller, & Klerman, 1983; Field, Healy, Goldstein, & Guthertz, 1990; Radke-Yarrow, Nottelmann, Martinez, Fox, & Blemont, 1992; Sameroff, 1989; Cohn, Matias, Tronick, Connell, & Lyons-Ruth, 1986).

As the initial burst of enthusiasm for uncovering etiological factors in mental illness has waned, attention has turned more and more to the interesting developmental processes that high-risk studies might reveal. It has become clear that there will be no simple solutions to the problems of understanding the etiology of mental disorder, because high-risk studies have probably raised more questions than they have answered (Watt, Anthony, Wynne, & Rolf, 1984). However, a body of knowledge about differences in development associated with parental mental illness is emerging, and this may be of significance for understanding normative development as well as the development of pathology (Cicchetti, 1984; Sroufe & Rutter, 1984).

In this chapter, we review existing knowledge about the development of infants whose parents have some form of mental illness. This is a topic of immense importance to infant mental health clinicians. We begin with a brief review of the general long-term consequences of having a parent with mental disorder. Included in this discussion are theoretical models of intergenerational transmission of illness, identification of parents, and general methodological issues in this area of research. The main sections of the chapter are integrated reviews of major developmental processes in infancy, with findings specific to children born to mentally ill women. A summary and integration conclude the chapter.

EXAMINING THE CONSEQUENCES OF PARENTAL MENTAL DISORDER FOR INFANT DEVELOPMENT

The most straightforward hypothesis regarding mental illness in parents is that it results in mental illness in their children. There is ample epidemiological evidence to suggest that mental illness does indeed run in families (Weissman, Leckman, Merikangas, Gammon, & Prusoff, 1984; Weissman, Wickramaratne, et al., 1984; Weissman et al., 1987; Beardslee et al., 1983). In addition, there is also substantial evidence that parental mental illness is related to other types of negative outcomes in offspring, such as delinquency, poor social adaptations, or cognitive deficits (Watt et al., 1984).

Given this range of potential outcomes, researchers are faced with the task of identifying these conditions, or their precursors, during the first years of life. Application of diagnoses from the *Diagnostic and Statistical Manual of Mental Disorders,* third edition, revised (DSM-III-R; American Psychiatric Association, 1987) is not useful with infants, because perhaps only a few diagnoses can be made in this age range. Similarly, assessing cognitive status that is predictive of later development is difficult until the end of the second year of life; delinquency will not be manifested until much later in development; social relationships with peers are incipient rather than developed. Thus, when studying the effects of parental mental illness in infants, one is left with the need to study interim outcomes that may be predictive of later dysfunction. Such interim outcomes include parent–child interaction, attachment relationships, developmental quotient (DQ), language achievements, temperament, developmental milestones, and biobehavioral regulation (e.g., eating, sleeping).

Unfortunately, little is known about the relation of such interim status variables and the development of later dysfunctional behavior. Most importantly, it is not clear whether there are specific developmental paths from single interim markers to individual outcomes—for instance, whether non-secure attachment is related to a diagnosis of depression later in life. Alternatively, developmental relations may be nonspecific and predictive of many possible negative outcomes. For example, non-secure attachment may predict later problems in a variety of domains, such as mental health, peer relations, and family functioning.

The result of this uncertainty has been to study the development of at-risk infants by means of state-of-the-art assessments of infant status that researchers believe have the best chance of producing longitudinal prediction of later developmental problems. Researchers have hoped that by demonstrating associations between parental status and patterns of infant development, they may also identify key constructs that illuminate the processes of intergenerational transmission of illness and incompetence.

Models of Transmission

Evidence of familial clustering of mental disorder has inevitably led to genetic hypotheses regarding the mechanism of intergenerational transmission (Rosenthal, Wender, Kety, Welner, & Schulsinger, 1971; Egeland et al., 1987). Epidemiological studies routinely demonstrate that mental illness runs in families, with demonstrable clustering according to specific diagnoses or groups of diagnoses, such as depressive disorders or schizophrenic spectrum disorders (Watt, 1984). Furthermore, adoption and cross-fostering studies show that the rates of disorder among adopted-away offspring of ill parents and adopted children reared by ill parents relate more to biological parentage than to the context in which the children are reared (Rosenthal et al., 1971; Wender, Rosenthal, Kety, Schulsinger, & Welner, 1974; Kety, Rosenthal, Wender, Schulsinger, & Jacobsen, 1975; Mendelewicz & Rainer, 1977).

Despite the wealth of evidence supporting genetic models, it is also clear that these models may explain only a small portion of variance in the development of mental illness. Although a full critique of the genetic literature is beyond the scope of this chapter, several points can be made. The genetics of mental illness, by any investigator's assessment, are not simple—the presumed genetic action is polygenic with complex patterns of inheritance. Even where single-gene sites are being investigated, as in the case of bipolar illness, the genetic models are still presumed to be complex in nature (Rosenthal et al., 1971). To date, any specific markers identified by DNA-sequencing studies for mental disorders have not withstood the test of replication (Hodgkinson et al., 1987; Holden, 1991).

Although many more children with a family history of mental disorder than expected will themselves develop mental illness, the vast majority of individuals with mental disorder (including the serious disorders of depression and schizophrenia) do not have a demonstrable family history of the illness. Furthermore, even though there is some tendency for particular disorders to run in families, many if not most of the offspring of ill parents have disorders different from those of their parents (Downey & Coyne, 1990).

Adoption studies have also been criticized. Issues such as selective placement, contact with biological parents and other family members after placement, generalizability beyond the homogeneous Scandinavian cultures where the bulk of this work has been done, and the magnitude of the effects have all been noted. In sum, despite some impressive evidence for genetic influence in intergenerational transmission, the ultimate importance of genetic factors in the development of mental disorder is still an open question.

There are also constitutional models of intergenerational transmission that do not presuppose genetic components. The most prominent of these models involves the effects of perinatal insult, which may be more frequent in mothers with mental illness. McNeil and Kaij (1987) have reviewed an extensive literature on pregnancy and birth complications in mothers with mental illness and have concluded, despite the often contradictory findings in the literature, that there is indeed an increased incidence in mothers with schizophrenia. However, these effects are clearly small in magnitude, and there is little evidence to suggest that these perinatal complications are implicated in the developmental progress of these children. Other indirect evidence for constitutional models of transmission comes from the large literature that attempts to identify structural and functional deficits or differences in individuals with diagnosed disorders (e.g., Fish, Marcus, Hans, Auerbach, & Perdue, 1992).

Environmental models posit that differences in the developmental context of children account for the incidence of mental disorder later in life. Factors such as parental disparagement or abuse, family composition, parenting behavior, and social networks have been invoked as explanations (e.g., Downey & Coyne, 1990). Related models identify specific environmental risk factors, but indicate that the number of risks is the operative factor, rather than the specific type of risk (Sameroff, Seifer, Barocas, Zax, & Greenspan, 1987; Walker, Downey, & Bergman, 1989).

The developmental psychopathology model attempts to integrate constitutional and environmental models (Sroufe & Rutter, 1984; Cicchetti, 1984). Children are viewed as one aspect of a developing system that can be examined at different levels of complexity (biological, individual, social, cultural). In addition, the system is assumed to be dynamic and developing, so that change may be found at any of these levels of analysis. This approach attempts to encompass findings consistent with other models discussed above, and yet to reconcile the fact than none of those models account for large portions of variance in predicting the incidence of mental disorders.

Maternal Diagnosis

The vast majority of studies examining infant development in relation to parental mental illness have focused on mothers identified with disorders. This reflects the traditional economies associated with studying mothers, as opposed to fathers, in developmental research. Most children from non-nuclear families live with their mothers. Mothers are usually responsible for caregiving (especially during the first years of life); they are more accessible to researchers than fathers are; and they are perhaps more influential in determining the development of their children. Because the existing literature has focused on mothers, this provides an important reference for replication. An additional factor in the field of transmission of mental illness is also an issue: When genetic models are important to consider, identifying with certainty the biological parentage of mothers is easier than with fathers. Although this list of reasons explains *why* mothers are routinely the focus of these studies, it is not an *endorsement* of that bias.

Whatever position one holds about the emphasis on mothers in this area of research, the fact remains that a review of the literature must perforce focus on maternal diagnosis. It should be noted that two areas where fathers have received attention in the literature on parental mental illness are alcohol abuse and delinquency. However, little effort has been devoted to studying infant offspring of these men, and the topic is therefore not a focus in this chapter.

One clear pattern in existing studies is that two diagnoses have dominated the field: schizophrenia and depression. This state of affairs is understandable. Schizophrenia, although affecting only 1% of the population, is an enormous public health problem in terms of the suffering of affected individuals, cost to the health care system, and other social implications (e.g., homelessness). Likewise, depression, with its growing incidence, is also a major public health concern with devastating impact on affected individuals. Of particular importance in the infancy period is the issue of postpartum depression. Although this diagnosis (or any discussion of the issue) does not appear in DSM-III-R, there is much active research on the phenomenon as well as its effects on young infants (O'Hara, Schlechte, Lewis, & Wright, 1991).

An emerging diagnosis of interest is maternal substance use disorder, although the focus is as much on prenatal exposure to a presumed teratogen as on the development of substance use in offspring of these women. Since this topic is covered in Chapter 9 of this volume, it is not discussed further in this chapter.

Generic Methodological Issues

Before we review specific research, it is important to note methodological issues that greatly influence the interpretation of data from these high-risk studies. Unfortunately, because of the difficulty of identifying and studying these families, many cross-sectional and longitudinal studies suffer from methodological shortcomings that limit the interpretation of results. Some of these problems are discussed below.

Identification of Disorders

The first choice one must make in this research area is the identification of families who will participate in studies. One often-used method is to obtain names of patients in clinical settings so that they may be invited to participate in research projects. This has the advantage of identifying people who have sought treatment and have been previously diagnosed by mental health professionals. Unfortunately, those diagnoses are most often unreliable, and are often driven by forces antithetical to the research enterprise (e.g., the need to gain reimbursement from third parties). Strict reliance on hospital or clinic records, with no independent diagnosis by research personnel, raises serious questions about the validity of that study. From a practical standpoint, obtaining referrals from clinical settings makes it difficult to find families who have children of the right age to satisfy the needs of large studies.

Another strategy is to advertise for parents who have (1) the required mental disorder and (2) children with the right characteristics. However, this approach may provide samples of parents who have never sought treatment for their disorders. Simply meeting diagnostic criteria without the history of seeking treatment for a disorder may be an insufficient selection criterion.

A final issue is whether diagnosis should be the key identifier in these high-risk studies. The use of diagnosis as the marker for parental illness presupposes a model of specifically transmitted disorders. Studies that have examined categorical diagnostic descriptions of illness with dimensional symptom-based or severity assessments have found the categorical factors to be least useful in predicting child development (Sameroff et al., 1982; Watt, 1984). Also, from a theoretical perspective, the experience of the infant with a specific symptom expression may be more important than whether specific syndromal criteria have been met. Thus, some studies of depression have employed the strategy of sampling parents on the basis of high degrees of symptom expression.

Age of Children

Since it is difficult to identify large numbers of families for these high-risk studies, it is sometimes useful to examine children in a wider age range as opposed to children at a single fixed point in development. The obvious advantage of this approach is to maximize the available samples for study. The disadvantage, especially as the age of the children decreases, is that level of development will be a covariate that must be consistently examined and may qualify interpretations. There is also difficulty in generalizing information gained at one assessment age to other ages of interest.

Control Groups

Many studies examine only a group of families where parents have mental illness. Alternatively, studies may have a single control group of families with no illness. Both of these strategies are flawed. In the first case, there is no good way to compare rates of problems found in an identified group with any particular reference. Since researchers are aware of the nature of their population, thresholds for identifying disorder are often set very low, and rates appear high. However, when a no-illness control group is employed, comparably elevated rates are generally found among the control families as well (e.g., Beardslee et al., 1983).

No-illness control groups do not solve all design problems, however. There are many factors associated with specific mental illness diagnoses—chronicity of illness, severity of illness, and specific symptom dimensions (Sameroff et al., 1982). There is evidence that the nonspecific illness factors have as much influence on development as specific diagnostic factors, if not actually more. Finally, in addition to confounded factors of mental illness, there are many nonillness factors that are confounded, such as socioeconomic status (SES), social support, stability of family life, or neighborhood quality. These contextual factors must also be considered (see the discussion of multiple-risk models in the concluding section).

Longitudinal designs

Many high-risk studies follow families over extended periods of time. This brings up two important interpretation issues. The first involves the analysis and understanding of change or developmental growth. There is increasing realization that models of change over time are relatively primitive in human development research, and that research design and data analysis have not kept pace with theory and model building (Burchinal & Appelbaum, 1991; Willett, 1988). Thus, statements about change over time or causal relations must be accepted with the highest degree of caution. The second issue involves replication of findings. In many instances, replication of a phenomenon occurs in the same study using the same sample at different points in development. Although this evidence is important, it must be interpreted with the understanding that sample-specific characteristics may be driving the finding at both time points, and that these may not generalize to other samples.

STUDIES OF CHILDREN BORN TO MENTALLY ILL PARENTS

In the last two decades, the impact of parental psychopathology on child outcome has received much attention from researchers in a variety of disciplines. Two recent thorough reviews (Goodman, in press; Downey & Coyne, 1990) provide evidence for the increased risk of child disturbance and parenting difficulty associated with parental psychopathology, especially focusing on maternal depression. These reviews highlight the need to attend to contextual factors (such as psychosocial stress and family relationships) and to assess diagnostic criteria carefully, given the heterogeneity of expression of depressive disorder. In this section of the chapter, we focus on the impact of maternal psychopathology during *infancy and* early *childhood*, emphasizing (1) the impact of pathology on normative developmental processes within the first year of life; and (2) its effects in the context of the unique transitions faced by families during this time (i.e., transition to parenthood, change in parental role functioning, and marital relationship changes).

Our bias in organizing the material in this section is consistent with a developmental systems perspective on the origins and maintenance of individual pathology. Two basic assumptions are operative. First, early parent–infant interactions are social in nature and provide the primary context in which generalized social skills are learned. Second, infants maintain affective interactions from their earliest contacts with caregivers, which foster component skills necessary for later, more externally oriented social interactions (Sroufe & Waters, 1977). Four broad domains are reviewed: individual functioning, dyadic interaction, social interaction beyond the dyad, and family context.

Individual Functioning

Although relatively little can be discerned about very young children that is independent of their social contexts, two major domains of individual functioning addressed in the high-risk literature have been developmental status and temperament. In older children, developmental status is typically measured using IQ tests. With younger children, DQ is often assessed, even though the correlation with later IQ is relatively low. Temperament is also a widely used measure of individual behavior in infants and young children. Poor functioning on DQ tests and difficult temperament are both related to adjustment difficulties later in life, although there is little evidence that either is related in important etiological ways to serious mental disorder (Thomas & Chess, 1977; Worland, Edenhart-Pepe, Weeks, & Konnen, 1984).

There is little evidence that children of ill parents are remarkable in their performance on DQ exams. General DQ scores may be slightly lower in children whose parents have some form of mental disorder, but there is little indication that DQ is being differentially related to specific diagnoses (e.g., Sameroff et al., 1982). Factors such as severity of parental illness, or associated factors such as SES, probably account for the small effects that are found.

One recent study has attempted to disentangle some of these factors. Lyons-Ruth, Connell, and Grunebaum (1990) examined three groups of families with multiple risks (treated, untreated but had sought services, and community comparison), which were further subdivided on whether the mother had depressive symptoms. Child IQ scores in the treated group did not differ as a function of maternal depression, and averaged slightly over 100 (i.e., well within normal limits). However, in the untreated and community groups, there were decreases of 10 to 15 IQ points in the subgroups of children whose mothers were depressed.

There is more support for the notion that there are temperamental differences in young children of ill parents. Studies examining schizophrenic and depressed mothers' reports of their children's temperament have consistently found that ill mothers rate their children as more difficult than well mothers do (Sameroff, Barocas, & Seifer, 1984; Hans, Marcus, & Auerbach, 1987; Goodman & Van Buskirk, 1986; D'Angelo, Krock, O'Neill, & Boyle, 1983), although it is unclear which of the clinical groups accounts for the effects. These studies all suffer from a common confound: The ill mother is the informant about the child's temperament, and no independent assessment of the child is included. In stud-

ies where one aspect of temperament—behavioral inhibition—has been directly observed, children whose mothers have an anxiety disorder show increased levels of inhibition (Rosenbaum et al., 1988; Biederman et al., 1990; Hirshfeld et al., 1992), as do children of depressed mothers (Kochanska, 1991).

Dyadic Interaction

Human infants engage in species-typical behavior that involves communication with others (Newson, 1977). From birth, infants demonstrate perceptual sensitivities especially oriented toward human stimulation and response organization designed to facilitate contact with people (Schaffer, 1984). From very early on, parents and infants interact in ways that not only serve to regulate biological functions (e.g., state regulation, feeding), but support social and emotional learning as well (Brazelton, 1979). By the first year of life, organized attachment relationships are an integral part of the dyadic developmental process.

Individual State and Developmental Regulation

One of the fundamental qualities of social interactions is that each participant must be available for social discourse. For infants, an important component of this availability is their ability to regulate their own states of arousal and attention. When developmental milestones occur, there is often an expectation (usually implicit) that whole complexes of behaviors will emerge. For example, organization of increased periods of wakeful/alert states, social smiles, gaze maintenance, and interest in extended social interaction emerge at about 3 to 4 months of age. Parents' interactive behaviors will often be predicated on these expectations.

However, if an infant has particular difficulty with internal state regulation, there may be serious consequences for social interaction if the parent–child dyad does not adapt well to these state changes. Furthermore, when there is a lack of synchrony in developmental achievements, a parent's expectations may be disconfirmed, again resulting in interaction difficulties if the dyad does not adapt well.

Fish (1957, 1971), studying children of schizophrenic mothers, found disturbances of timing and integration of neurological maturation during the infancy period, as well as shifts in periods of acceleration and retardation of motor skills. Some infants of schizophrenic mothers were found to maintain abnormally quiet, inactive states with little or no crying, which were evident from birth and continued to 18 months of age; other infants were initially active and then became inactive, apathetic, and toneless. Marcus et al. (1981) found that infants born to schizophrenic mothers (as compared with mothers with affective disorders, mothers with personality disorders, and controls) showed neurointegrative deficits, rendering them especially vulnerable to external insults.

These infant findings may best be understood when placed in the context of research with older children. When assessed during childhood, offspring of schizophrenics were found to be more impaired by distraction and to have more difficulty paying attention (Asarnow & MacCrimmon, 1981; Harvey, Weintraub, & Neale, 1985; MacCrimmon, Cleghorn, Asarnow, & Steffy, 1980; Werner & Smith, 1982); they were also found to have hyperlabile and hypersensitive autonomic functioning (Mednick, 1973; Mednick & Schulsinger, 1968, 1974; Mednick, Schulsinger, & Venables, 1981). This was suggested to reflect a necessary protective avoidance of potentially distressing internal and external stimuli. However, emotional preoccupation hinders a child's ability to attend, observe, understand, and become an active participant in his or her social environment (Bettelheim, 1967). Taken together, these studies have shown the offspring of schizophrenic parents to have vulnerabilities (which may be biological and/or environmental), affecting their ability to attend to, control, and regulate their social surroundings.

Interaction Style

Most infants engage in face-to-face interaction by about 6 weeks of age (Trevarthen, 1984). By this time, the infant is able to fixate gaze on a social partner. Parents typically capitalize on this increased attention to perpetuate more connected, responsive interactions (Stern, 1977). For example, parents' exchanges become more repetitive and dramatic, with greater importance placed on temporal contiguity (Fogel, 1977; Kaye & Fogel, 1980). Even though an infant is by no means a passive participant, a parent has more flexibility of response, and thus assumes greater responsibility for directing and maintaining these early interactions. Parents can vary in their sensitivity to the format and rules of the script, and can regulate their rhythm of movement so it is contingent upon the infant's own temporal patterning, repeat activity to sustain infant gaze, and present information at levels commensurate with the infant's capacities (Fogel, 1977; Schaffer, 1984; Trevarthen, 1984; Tronick, Als, & Brazelton, 1980).

Disruptions in early distress–relief interactions have important consequences for infant development. For example, in Spitz's (1965) classic studies of infants reared in residential placements with minimal human contact or contingent stimulation, these infants were lethargic, depressed in appearance, and resistant to social interaction. It is becoming increasingly clear that deprivation need not be as extensive as that described by Spitz to affect infant development. As discussed below, numerous studies have documented interaction differences in mother–child dyads where the mothers are ill or symptomatic on the depression spectrum. They converge on the finding that depressed mothers are less contingently responsive, more disengaged, and more negative during dyadic interactions with their infants. In turn, the infants are also less positive and more negative. However, studies vary in their confirmation of this general pattern. There is also some evidence that schizophrenic mothers may have even more distorted interaction patterns.

Many studies with depressed mothers have used the face-to-face paradigm (Tronick, Als, Adamson, Wise, & Brazelton, 1978). This structured interaction involves several 2-minute episodes where the child is in an infant seat and the mother is seated directly facing her child. One typical protocol is to have 2 minutes of free play, 2 minutes of "still-face" behavior by the mothers, followed by a 2-minute free-play "reunion." Infants are quite sensitive to perturbations within these brief interactive sequences. When mothers' behavior was systematically altered by having them maintain a still-face pose, withhold communication, or present only their profiles, infants evidenced distress by looking to their mothers less often and for shorter intervals, frowning, grimacing, pouting, gaze averting, and/or making strong bids for mothers' attention (Cohn & Tronick, 1983; Tronick, Als, & Adamson, 1979; Tronick et al., 1978).

Infants whose mothers scored high on the Beck Depression Inventory had uniformly lower rates of positive behavior (and higher rates of negative behavior) in face-to-face interaction with their 3- to 6-month-old infants (Field et al., 1988; Field, 1984). The range of behavior included physical activity, head orientation, gaze, facial expression, vocalization, and fussiness. Mothers' physical activity, vocalization, responsivity, and game playing were also different. Of particular interest is that the infants' behavioral differences generalized to episodes of interaction with an unfamiliar adult, indicating development of behavior patterns in these young infants that extended beyond the caregiving dyad. In other studies, depressed mothers and their infants spent more time in matched negative behavior states, and less time in matched positive behavior states, compared with dyads where the mothers were not depressed (Field et al., 1990). Cohn, Campbell, Matias, and Hopkins (1990) confirmed only some of these results. Specifically, depressed mothers had higher rates of negative behavior overall. However, lower rates of positive maternal behaviors were found with sons only; no differences in infant behavior were found. In studying the contour of mother vocalization (i.e., the adaptation for young children commonly called "motherese"), Bettes (1988) found that depressed mothers were less able to adapt their interaction style according to this cultural norm.

In more free-ranging interactions, the impact of maternal depression is less clear. Seifer, Sameroff, Anagnostopolou, and Elias (in press) did not find differences among schizophrenic, depressed, personality-disordered, and well mothers on many indices of mother and infant behavior—including spontaneous, responsive, and negative—at both 4 and 12 months of age. In contrast to the lack of mental health effects, SES produced large group effects, and large differences in behavior were observed depending on the situation in which the behavior occurred (caretaking, close, or distant). The reports of McNeil, Persson-Blennow, and colleagues (McNeil, Naslund, Persson-Blennow, & Kaij, 1985; Persson-Blennow, Naslund, McNeil, Kaij, & Malmquist-Larsson, 1984; Persson-Blennow, Naslund, McNeil, & Kaij, 1986) describe many comparisons of schizophrenic, affect-disordered, and well mothers at six points across the first year of life. Variables examined included positive and negative behaviors, amount of contact, and responsiveness to infant needs. Although many significant findings were reported for the large variable sets, the number of such findings was about at levels expected by

chance. There was little consistency in which variables were significant at different points during the first year. The only consistency was that the schizophrenic group differed from controls more often than other diagnostic groups (bipolar, affective, atypical psychosis). Goodman and Brumley (1990), in contrast, found significant differences between schizophrenic and well groups (with depressed generally midway between), indicating less affection, greater anger/hostility, and poorer home environment (as measured by the Home Observation for Measurement of the Environment inventory) for the schizophrenic group. In sum, when nonstructured observations are employed, there is only sporadic evidence that children of ill parents have substantially different interaction experiences compared with children of well parents during the early years of life.

Attachment Relationships

One of the results of parent–child interaction during the first year of life is the development of attachment relationships. Sroufe and Waters (1977) characterize this as a set of behaviors that serve an infant's organized working model of the availability and utility of caregivers in the resolution of distress. In research using the Strange Situation procedure, which includes a series of separations and reunions to activate the attachment system (Ainsworth, Blehar, Waters, & Wall, 1978), attachments are characterized as "secure" (the parent is a secure base for exploration and provides comfort and organization in the face of distress) or "insecure," with subtypes of "avoidant" (infants actively avoid parents when stressed) and "resistant" (infants display active resistance to physical and social contact when stressed). Also, "disorganized" patterns of attachment have been noted (Main & Solomon, 1990). Insecure attachment has been found to be a precursor to later developmental problems in social competence and school performance (Sroufe, 1990; Egeland, 1989; Radke-Yarrow et al., 1992).

Two studies completed by Naslund, Persson-Blennow, McNeil, Kaij, and Malmquist-Larsson (1984a, 1984b) found that infants and their schizophrenic mothers maintained insecure attachment relationships (characterized by avoidance and/or ambivalence); in addition, these infants demonstrated virtually no fear of strangers (a usual reaction demonstrated by 8- to 12-month-olds, indicating selective preference for certain persons over others, and an emerging capacity to separate psychologically from mother when involved in social encounters). These findings suggest that infants of schizophrenics indeed demonstrate disrupted patterns of interaction with significant and social others. Given the disrupted environment into which these infants are born, it is possible to consider their dysregulated interactive patterns as an adaptive means of existing within their family situation. However, these behaviors serve to limit the babies' ability to interact adequately with significant social others (e.g., grandparents, babysitters, etc.), who might otherwise serve as important buffers for these vulnerable infants.

In several studies, maternal depression has been related to higher rates of insecure attachment (Radke-Yarrow, Cummings, Kuczynski, & Chapman, 1985; Donovan & Leavitt, 1989; Gaensbauer, Harmon, Cytryn, & McKnew, 1984). Perhaps more striking are the data available for children of bipolar parents. Seven children of bipolar inpatients (four mothers, three fathers) were studied at 12, 15, and 18 months of age and compared with matched no-illness controls. At 12 months the groups were indistinguishable (71% in each group had secure attachment), but by 18 months only one of the seven (or 14%) of the bipolar offspring had secure attachment versus four of the seven (57%) in the control group (Gaensbauer et al., 1984). DeMulder and Radke-Yarrow (1991) also found high rates (67%) of insecure attachment in children of bipolar mothers compared with children of unipolar and well mothers (42%). About half of the children in the bipolar group met criteria for disorganized attachment. Insecure attachment classification was significantly related to downcast and negative mother behaviors.

More recently, attachment status was evaluated in the Lyons-Ruth et al. (1990) study, where three groups of multiple-risk families (treated, untreated, community) were subdivided on whether or not mothers were depressed. Children in the untreated/depressed group had the highest rates of insecure disorganized behavior. However, overall rates on insecure attachments were not markedly different among the groups.

Parenting Perceptions and Beliefs

Closely related to how parents and infants behave with each other is how parents understand the meaning of those interactions. Early research on parental beliefs about child difficulties found

that depressed mothers tended to overinterpret or distort child behavior as problematic (Rickard, Forehand, Wells, Griest, & McMahon, 1981). General parenting attitudes were also more negative in ill parents (i.e., more authoritarian, more hostile, and less democratic), although diagnostic groups of schizophrenia, depression, and personality disorder could not be distinguished (Sameroff et al., 1982). This study also found that ill mothers (but no specific diagnostic group) had lower expectations for their children's life course achievement.

More recent work (with older children) has attempted to examine the interplay between maternal illness and child behavior. For example, Brody and Forehand (1986) replicated previous work, finding a main effect for parental illness in parents' ratings of their children's maladjustment. However, they also found an interaction effect indicating that this phenomenon was limited to those children who evidenced high levels of noncompliance. In a similar vein, Conrad and Hammen (1989) found that teacher- and child-reported child symptoms interacted with maternal symptoms in the prediction of maternal rated child maladjustment. That is, ill mothers with symptomatic children provided more negative assessments than did well mothers with equally problematic children. It is interesting to note that the well mothers did not differentiate between children with and without symptoms as rated by the children and the teachers. Richters and Pellegrini (1989) compared maternal and teacher report of children in groups of well, depressed, and depressed/remitted mothers. They found differences between well and ill mothers in reports of child maladjustment, but this corresponded with teacher reports. Richters and Pelligrini argue that depressed mothers do indeed report more child problems, but that most evidence supports the idea that these are appropriate (not distorted) reports (see also Richters, 1992).

From the perspective of maternal satisfaction and control in the role of parent, there are interesting differences among well and affect-disordered mothers. Kochanska, Radke-Yarrow, Kuczynski, and Friedman (1987) found that overall satisfaction was equivalent among well, unipolar, and bipolar mothers, but that the unipolar mothers had a more selective pattern: They were more satisfied with cognitive development and less satisfied in the affective and social domains. When beliefs about control were examined, bipolar mothers more often endorsed notions of genetic control of their children's behavior. Also, both bipolar and unipolar mothers attributed uncontrollable causes to their children's behavior more often than well mothers.

Despite these many findings, some investigators have indicated that maternal psychopathology is not important in determining links to maternal behavior at all, finding more association with demographic variables. For example, Sameroff et al. (1982) found no effects remaining for either diagnosis or severity of illness after SES was partialed out. Teti, Gelfand, and Pompa (1990) examined parenting behaviors, mental health status, demographic factors, and psychosocial measures (including stress and self-esteem); they found no evidence that mental health variables in mothers with Major Depression, Dysthymia, and adjustment disorders had any predictive value. (It should be noted that there were no well mothers in this study.) Conger, McCarty, Yang, Lahey, and Kropp (1984) also concluded that demographic factors played the dominant role in explaining parenting variables when emotional distress was indexed in abusive and nonabusive parents. Given the diversity of findings, it seems clear that there are no simple associations between maternal depression and parenting styles or beliefs; rather, it is likely that a variety of factors interact to produce outcomes. It is further likely that the nature (and number) of these factors will vary according to the developmental stage of the child and family, as well as the context within which particular behaviors are observed.

Conflict in Interactions

As infants grow older, one of the important social-developmental processes is that of separation/individuation (Sander, 1980; Mahler, Pine, & Bergman, 1975; Erikson, 1950). A common feature of this period, as the children assert their independence, is the development of conflict interactions between parents and their children during which issues of parental control strategies are highlighted (Patterson, 1982). The extent to which these issues are negotiated between parents and their children relates to the development of patterns of social interaction, empathy, and aggression (Kochanska, Kuczynski, & Radke-Yarrow, 1989). It is hypothesized that infants and affect-disordered parents may have special difficulty in regulating these interactions, because of decreased parental consistency in demands, expectations, and contingencies for behavior.

Kochanska et al. (1987) studied naturally occurring episodes of mother–child conflict in groups of well, unipolar depressed, and bipolar mothers. They found that affectively ill mothers tended to avoid confrontation and did not use compromise resolution strategies. Also, severity of the disorder was a critical factor within the unipolar group: More seriously ill mothers were less likely to achieve compromise resolutions with their infants. On the other hand, more seriously impaired bipolar mothers were more likely to be nonconfrontational, to ultimately use enforcement rather than negotiated resolution strategies, to have less immediate success, and to initiate unresolvable conflict episodes. They also noted normative trends when the children were between 2 and 4 years of age, when mothers generally become increasingly successful, compromise more, and resort less to the use of power and control. Finally, Kuczynski and colleagues (e.g., Kuczynski, Kochanska, Radke-Yarrow, & Girnius-Brown, 1987; Kuczynski & Kochanska, 1990) have studied children through the preschool years and found trends suggesting that girls are generally more compliant and less defiant than boys, with maternal psychopathology not contributing significantly to group differences. Despite the lack of main effects for the diagnosis of depression, higher severity of depression was related to more child passive noncompliance (Kuczynski & Kochanska, 1990).

Expressed emotion (Hooley & Teasdale, 1989) is another manifestation of conflict in family communication. Children who were identified during preschool years as having multiple risk conditions (including parental mental illness) were more likely to have poor social–emotional outcomes at 13 years when their mothers had high levels of negative expressed emotion (Seifer, Sameroff, Baldwin, & Baldwin, 1992).

Beyond the Dyad

During the first few months of life, infants learn the contingent relationship between instrumentality and affect within dyadic (i.e., parent–infant) interactions. Soon infants become interested in objects and people outside the dyad. By 6 months of age, infants become more aware of objects in the external environment, and the nature of their social interactions changes to include third parties (Schaffer, 1984). Thus, a baby may attend to an attractive object, and the parent follows the baby's gaze toward that object. The parent then typically elaborates upon the interaction by pointing to, labeling, and/or commenting upon the object. This phenomenon, termed "visual co-orientation" (Collis, 1977), provides significant interpersonal learning opportunities for the infant. Through the parent's behavior, the baby learns that dyadic interactions can be expanded to include other objects of interest, is exposed to elaborations through various affective channels, and experiences contingencies between his or her own attentive behavior and predictable consequences in the behavior of others (Schaffer, 1984). Similar developments occur in activity centered around an object, where babies learn (1) the discriminative value of affective cues in relation to external objects; (2) the regulation of their social behavior on the basis of affective information; and (3) the fact that parents are valuable sources of affective information, helping to determine which objects are to be approached and avoided.

"Social referencing" is a related phenomenon, which involves the tendency of an infant to seek out emotional and instrumental information from a caregiver in an ambiguous or stressful situation (Campos & Stenberg, 1981; Feinman, 1982); this reflects a culmination of abilities learned within the context of early parent–infant interactions discussed above. Infants begin to learn that their own affective involvement (1) influences other's behavior in predictable and desirable ways; (2) makes them effective interactive partners; and (3) facilitates the flow of communication by highlighting contingencies and change points within the interaction. The phenomenon of social referencing illustrates an infant's knowledge that affective signals have social significance beyond the dyad.

Among the major symptoms of schizophrenia are egocentricity and a concomitant lack of ego boundaries, often resulting in attribution of one's own feelings and thoughts to others. The child of a schizophrenic parent may therefore be left with unmet needs, given the parent's preoccupation with his or her own needs and problems (Lidz, 1968). During the child's infancy, such egocentrism may be manifested as failure to provide the social referencing cues that are essential to developing rules about to social and object contexts.

In older children, Jones (1977) and Singer and Wynne (1965) found that communication

between schizophrenic parents and their children was problematic, in that the focus of attention was not shared; there were many distractions and intrusions of a personally meaningful yet contextually irrelevant nature; and descriptions of important aspects of stimuli were distorted and/or misperceived. Chandler (1978) found that the children of schizophrenics performed more poorly on perspective-taking tasks (i.e., were more likely to maintain egocentric assumptions) and evidenced less independent attitudes and beliefs (i.e., had a poorly developed sense of self). These parents' failure to acknowledge their children's perspectives may lead to decreased levels of parent–child interaction, as well as lower levels of children's competent behaviors (Harder, Cokes, Fisher, Cole, & Perkins, 1982). Given early disruptions in parent–infant relationships, the framework for the children's subsequent social interactions becomes skewed, so that they minimize their own needs and learn that they have little control of and no unique role in social interactions. Although a full discussion is beyond the scope of this chapter, research addressing the social competence of children of schizophrenic parents during school-age years has shown that these children do indeed demonstrate maladaptive patterns of social interaction (e.g., Baldwin, Cole, & Baldwin, 1982; Rolf, 1972).

Children born to bipolar parents have more difficulty with social interactions (Zahn-Waxler, Cummings, McKnew, & Radke-Yarrow, 1984; Zahn-Waxler, McKnew, Cummings, Davenport, & Radke-Yarrow, 1984). Early studies on problem behavior and peer relations, although limited by small sample size (i.e., 7 children with bipolar parents compared with 20 controls), found that 2-year-old index children were more shy, dependent, and hyperactive, as well as having more temper tantrums and less impulse control. These index children also demonstrated less altruism and more inappropriate or displaced aggression with peers (especially when separated from their mothers). Finally, the index children had more difficulty regulating their emotional response to anger and distress, often exhibiting intense or persistent aggression in this context.

Family Context

Thus far, we have reviewed developmental changes during the first year of life, organized primarily around the milestones achieved by the infant. We now review the context within which this development occurs—namely, the family. Recent reports (e.g., Radke-Yarrow et al., 1992) have stressed the need to be sensitive to factors that covary with a diagnosis of depression (e.g., marital discord, low SES, and increased psychosocial stress) that may contribute to poor child outcomes. Thus, when one is studying the effects of depression on young children's development, it is also necessary to consider the context in which this development occurs.

The phase of development in which the couple becomes a family—namely, the transition to parenthood—involves many changes in functioning to accommodate the new infant. For example, research on this transition-to-parenthood phase indicates that functional aspects of the couple's day-to-day activities change to incorporate the new role as parents. In the postpartum period, couples tend to behave in more sex-role-stereotyped ways regarding household tasks, child care responsibilities, and employment activities outside the home (e.g., Cowan, Cowan, Coie, & Coie, 1978). Several aspects of this transition are discussed as they illuminate the course of infant development: the marital relationship, postpartum depression in mothers, and the general level of psychosocial stress affecting the family.

Marital Quality

A significant source of stress during the transition to parenthood, found to be especially true for mothers, is a decrease in the quality and salience of the marriage (Goldberg, Michaels, & Lamb, 1985; Glenn & McLanahan, 1982; Rollins & Feldman, 1970; Lewis, Owen, & Cox, 1988). Recent findings suggest that difficulties within the marriage often involve issues regarding finances, marital intimacy, and time constraints, rather than difficulties pertaining to the infant per se (Hoffman & Manis, 1978; Markman & Clements, 1991). Overall, the postpartum period is a time of significant challenge to the marital relationship.

Marital quality during this period is important, because a supportive husband–wife relationship prior to and during the postpartum period enhances adjustment to new parenting roles (Brody, Pillegrini, & Sigel, 1986; Grossman, Eichler, & Winickoff, 1980; Russell, 1974), feeding skill (Pedersen, 1978), interactional competence (Lamb & Elster, 1985), and quality of attachment (Goldberg & Easterbrooks, 1984; see also Parke & Tinsley, 1987). The extent to which the parents feel supported within their marriage is also related to the nature of their emotional involvement with their baby (Lamb, 1979). Pedersen, Zaslow, Cain, and Anderson (1981) found that increased rates of negative behavior within the marriage were related to increased rates of negative behavior directed by mothers to their infants. Finally, marital harmony has important consequences for the socialization of emotions within the family unit as a whole (Winnicott, 1964/1987).

Marital dissatisfaction affects infant development in many ways. First, dissatisfied (as opposed to satisfied) parents communicate more negative affect between themselves, demonstrate more reciprocity of this negative affect, and engage in more persistent negative patterns (Gottman & Levenson, 1986; Krokoff, 1987; Markman, 1981). This atmosphere of negative affect affects young children, in that it is manifested as lower levels of concern for others, more interest in self, less compliance, and more defiance (Crockenberg, 1985; Cummings, Pellegrini, Notarius, & Cummings, 1989).

Marital discord may also influence children in the form of negative interactions that occur in their presence, but in which they are not directly involved (Cummings, Zahn-Waxler, & Radke-Yarrow, 1981). Marital discord, however, does not necessarily involve either displays of overt interparental anger or anger directed toward a child. Instead, there may be disruptions in instrumental behavior that preclude attention and sensitive responsiveness to the child (Goldberg & Easterbrooks, 1984), and/or overcompensation on the part of a parent in his or her relationship with the child to "make up" for the poor relationship with the spouse (Brody et al., 1986). Within this context, children develop insecure attachment relationships with their parents (Goldberg & Easterbrooks, 1984; Howes & Markman, 1989; Cox, Owen, Lewis, & Henderson, 1989) and manifest disruptions in social referencing behavior (Dickstein & Parke, 1988).

The quality of the marriage not only has implications for normative parent–child interaction and developmental child outcomes; it has also been linked to etiology and maintenance of major affective disorder (Barnett & Gotlib, 1988; Waring & Patton, 1984), has been emphasized in treatment approaches to depression (Jacobson, Dobson, Fruzetti, Schmaling, & Salusky, 1991; Jacobson, Holtzworth-Munroe, & Schmaling, 1989), and has been considered predictive of relapse of the depressive disorder (Hooley & Teasdale, 1989). Difficulties in interpersonal interaction processes in couples with a depressed spouse include increased negative affect, inequality in decision making, and increased negative perceptions (e.g., Kowalik & Gotlib, 1987; Whisman & Jacobson, 1989; Gotlib & Whiffen, 1989). Although these are behaviors typical of maritally distressed couples, whether or not depression is involved, research has begun to study the unique contribution of depression to difficulty in marital interaction (Schmaling & Jacobson, 1990; Fincham, Beach, & Bradbury, 1989).

Recent studies have focused on the concomitant impact of depression and poor marital quality on children. Fendrich, Warner, and Weissman (1990) simultaneously assessed parental depression, family interaction factors, and child outcomes, and found that family risk factors including marital discord were more prevalent among children of depressed as compared to nondepressed parents.

In a related vein, Rogler (1968) studied the nature of the marital relationship when one spouse was schizophrenic. Couples from a lower-SES Puerto Rican area were assessed. Families with a schizophrenic husband were similar to well families in terms of family functioning and marital satisfaction. However, families with a schizophrenic wife were significantly more disorganized and displayed more marital difficulty. Rogler (1968) suggested a cultural explanation, in that the wife's illness prevented her from fulfilling customary social functions. However, when the husband was ill, the wife assumed increased responsibilities and "took over" for her husband within the bounds of the wife's role within this culture. Unfortunately, Rogler did not study the affective and/or communicative processes between these husbands and wives, nor the impact of the parental conflicts and role changes on the children (Clausen, 1968). Nonetheless, the study makes clear the need to assess the impact of parental illness on the marital relationship, and in turn, the influences on roles and expectations within the family as a whole.

Although there is relatively little empirical confirmation of the links between marital quality and infant development in families with ill parents, there is much circumstantial evidence to indicate that this is an important domain for further research. The clear connections between marital quality and illness and between marital quality and early development suggest that illness, marital quality, and early development are related in ways that will be important to uncover.

Postpartum Depression

Normative change associated with the postpartum period, and the challenges faced by families at this time (including marital discord), may produce difficulty in negotiating the transition to parenthood. Within this context, many families face the additional risk of postpartum depression. Depression in the postpartum period is controversial; researchers disagree as to whether it is distinct in any way from Major Depression that may coincidentally occur following the birth of the child (e.g., O'Hara & Zekoski, 1988). Recent studies have suggested that the point prevalence of Major Depression during any 2- to 3-month period is similar (i.e., approximately 10%) in postpartum and non-childbearing women (O'Hara, Zekoski, Philipps, & Wright, 1990; Campbell & Cohn, 1991). (This prevalence rate has been found to be higher in adolescent mothers [Troutman & Cutrona, 1990]; the issues regarding this are interesting, yet beyond the scope of this chapter.) There has been increasing evidence that postpartum depression can be considered within the spectrum of major affective disorders (O'Hara et al., 1991). For example, O'Hara et al. (1990) found that, independent of a diagnosis of Major Depression, childbearing women reported increased depressive symptomatology at all assessment times up to 6 weeks postpartum, and reported increased marital difficulty early in the postpartum period. The researchers compared women who met criteria for Major Depression, and found that marital dissatisfaction remained stable over the 6-week postpartum period for depressed childbearing women, whereas marital difficulties improved during the same 6-week period for the depressed nonchildbearing women.

Increased attention has been focused on differentiating "maternity blues" from Major Depression in the postpartum period (i.e., postpartum depression), by assessing the intensity, duration, and number of depressive symptoms (e.g., loss of energy, appetite changes, and sleep disturbances) as they cluster to meet psychiatric diagnostic criteria for Major Depression (Hopkins, Campbell, & Marcus, 1989). Postpartum depression has been distinguished from "maternity blues," in that it is associated with different types of psychosocial and obstetrical stressors (Iles, Gath, & Kennerley, 1989; Kennerley & Gath, 1989a, 1989b), although studies exploring these correlates of postpartum depression have produced varied results (Gotlib, Whiffen, Mount, Milne, & Cordy, 1989; Hopkins, Campbell, & Marcus, 1987; O'Hara et al., 1991; Campbell & Cohn, 1991).

In the postpartum period, mothers with depressive symptoms have been found to exhibit difficulties in interaction with their newborns, including decreased eye gaze during feeding (Livingood, Daen, & Smith, 1983) and less playfulness and reciprocity (Field, 1984; Field et al., 1985). Whiffen and Gotlib (1989) found that postpartum depressed mothers perceived their 2-month-old infants as more bothersome and had more trouble with infant care.

Finally, it is important to mention that no studies have focused on fathers' internal experiences during the postpartum transition. It is possible that in typical families in which fathers do not significantly alter work schedules, they may experience feelings of exclusion from the initial bonding process, inadequacy regarding caregiving, and distractibility at the workplace. Pruett (1987), in fact, anecdotally described "paternity blues" occurring in the first 3 months postpartum, involving feelings ranging from inadequacy to frustration related to the new paternal role.

Psychosocial Stress

The postpartum period is a time in the family's life during which the parents generally experience increased financial as well as other psychosocial stress, which may play a major role in the experience of depression (e.g., Coyne & Downey, 1991). Higher rates of negative events characterized the social environment of families with a depressed parent (Billings & Moos, 1983; Hammen, 1991). Depressed women had confidants who displayed more negative speech content (Belsher & Costello, 1991). They also had ruminative styles of responding to their depression, which perhaps prolonged the duration of episodes (Nolen-Hoeksema, 1991).

Thus, compared to families without a depressed parent, these families' relationships were less cohesive, less expressive, and more conflicted; had less emphasis on independence, joint recreational activities, and moral/religious values; and were less organized in planning family activities. In general, the impact of family stressors on child health was similar in depressed and nondepressed families (i.e., more stress was related to more problems for the children).

As families with depression have more external stresses, these external stresses may in turn lead to the onset of depressive symptoms. For example, mothers who preferred to be employed but in fact remained at home as primary caregivers reported high rates of depressive symptoms (Hock & DeMeis, 1990). There is also evidence to suggest that women who have more parenting and marital stressors have increasing depressive symptoms during the first 6 months postpartum (Boyce, Hickie, & Parker, 1991). Cutrona and Troutman (1986) have presented a model to integrate family stressors, infant behavior, and postpartum depressive symptoms.

In reviewing the work on family context and transmission of mental disorder, we find it ironic to note the relatively small number of studies that have been conducted explicitly from a family perspective. It is, of course, the familial rates of disorder that have driven the field of high-risk mental disorders research. Yet few studies have explicitly examined whole families and their functioning, even though there is ample evidence that family processes support illness in individuals as well as disturbances in parent–child relations. Future work in this area is sorely needed.

SUMMARY AND INTEGRATION

The empirical literature on infants of mentally ill parents has provided many interesting clues to aid our understanding of the intergenerational transmission of illness. However, few domains of functioning have been systematically studied in a manner that yields firm conclusions. Perhaps the most thoroughly covered topic is the area of mother–infant interaction, yet many fundamental questions remain unanswered even here. Nevertheless, the data that have been accumulated suggest that different models of family regulation are useful to consider. Models of affect attunement, goodness of fit, mutual regulation, and family transactions are useful in organizing the diversity of findings.

Goodness-of-Fit Model

The "goodness-of-fit" model (Thomas & Chess, 1977) stresses the nature of the temperament–environment interactive process (Radke-Yarrow,

1986). Goodness of fit involves concordance between the expectations of the environment (in this case, the parent) and the infant's abilities, characteristics, and style of behaving. Demands, stresses, and conflicts are inevitable concomitants of the developmental process that occur as new expectations and demands for change accompany progressively higher levels of functioning (Thomas & Chess, 1977). Childhood behavior disturbance is viewed as resulting from excessive stress or conflict involving dissonance between the environment and the child's capacities. Thus, deviations within the environment (e.g., low SES, parental psychopathology) and/or the person (e.g., mental illness, physical handicap, mental retardation) do not necessarily lead to distorted interactions; the style of interaction between the two can be adjusted for these differences.

Early parent–infant interaction typically involves parental attempts to expand the infant's exposure to the social world. In this view, the infant comes to the world with his or her own level and range of tolerance for stimulation and arousal mechanisms. Thus the parent (directed by his or her own beliefs, values, expectations, and behavior) "matches" his or her behavior to the infant's state of arousal. Stern (1985) has importantly pointed out that a temperamental mismatch between parent and infant facilitates the broadening of the infant's experience, as long as it falls within a level that the infant can tolerate. More extreme mismatches are detrimental to infant social and emotional learning. For example, the parent may be intrusive and/or overcontrolling. When overstimulated, the infant initially responds by using coping and defensive mechanisms (e.g., averting eye gaze, orienting body away)—responses that often escalate to more overt negative behavior.

As we have reviewed above, many of these disruptions in interactive sequences are manifested in a dyad where the mother is depressed or otherwise ill. An infant who must consistently deal with social and emotional overstimulation by aversion and crying may, over time, learn a more extreme form of coping involving avoidance, withdrawal, and affective muting. Alternatively, when understimulated, an infant must seek out experience and regulate the social–emotional world without requisite developmental skills. Stern (1985) has proposed that this results in narrowing of the infant's core self because of the decreased input from others.

The goodness-of-fit model does not propose an all-or-nothing match between parents and infants. Rather, a parent may be unsympathetic to certain infant characteristics, restrictive about certain activities, and/or unsure with respect to certain child care responsibilities. On the other hand, the same parent may be accepting, nonrestrictive, and self-confident with respect to other activities and characteristics of the child (Thomas & Chess, 1977). However, parents and infants whose temperamental patterns are very discrepant are suspected to have more difficulty in reaching and maintaining a common ground. What is crucial in this formulation is the degree to which family systems adapt to the unique characteristics of individual children, and the degree to which flexible resources are appropriately applied to the many difficult developmental tasks.

Affect Attunement Model

The "affect attunement" model (e.g., Stern, 1985) builds upon the goodness-of-fit model with more emphasis on the details of specific interactions. Attunement involves (1) parental matching (not necessarily imitating) of the infant's internal feeling state; (2) cross-modal affective expression between parent and infant; and (3) demonstration of behaviors that express the quality of the shared affect state (Stern, Hofer, Haft, & Dore, 1985). In order for attunement to occur, the parent must be able to interpret the infant's feeling state from his or her overt behavior, and then respond in such a way as to convey emotional resonance with the baby's feelings without directly imitating the baby's behaviors. The infant must be able to understand that the parental response is related to the infant's original feeling experience.

Attunement involves intermodal resonance between parent and infant. For example, if the baby is playing vigorously with a toy by banging the pieces together, his or her parent may express attunement by clapping hands in rhythm with the infant, or making verbal exclamations in a tonal quality that matches the intensity of the child's actions. Stern (1985) has suggested that when the parent is attuned to the baby, the baby continues his or her behavior without disruption. However, if the parent's expressions are above or below the infant's level of intensity or rhythm, the infant will notice the discrepancy and briefly curtail activity. Interpersonal communication, as created by attunement, promotes the infant's coming to recognize shared internal feeling states. The converse is also true: Feeling states that are never attuned will not become part of the infant's developing repertoire.

The studies reviewed above indicate that these qualities promoting affect attunement are apparently deficient in children with ill parents. Dyadic interaction is distorted; conflicts in interactions are more common; parenting attitudes may be distorted; marital discord or psychosocial stressors may create a negative affective climate in which this attunement occurs. One especially intriguing finding was that the cultural norm of communicating with infants in "motherese" was less apparent in ill mothers.

Mutual Regulation Model

The "mutual regulation" model (e.g., Tronick, Cohn, & Shea, 1986) emphasizes infant initiation and regulation of the social interaction. The affect attunement and mutual regulation models are similar in the assumption that the infant's emotions serve to coordinate social communication; however, whereas the affect attunement model stresses parental matching of the infant's inner subjective state (independent of the infant's overt behavior), the mutual regulation model conceptualizes the infant's activity and affect as interdependent, with the infant as much in control of the social exchange as the parent. This model involves the infant's acting to deploy emotional signals in an attempt to control the social environment. If the infant successfully controls the situation (i.e., gets the parent to interact reciprocally), positive emotions are generated, and the infant gains a sense of effectance; if, however, the infant fails to control the situation, negative emotions are generated, and the infant experiences a sense of helplessness. The infant's success or failure depends, in part, on the cooperation, sensitivity, and responsiveness of the parent.

Both parents and infants experience social successes and failures. Whereas infants' reactions are largely affected by immediate external and internal stimuli, parents' reactions are more affected by historical and social factors that modify the parents' self-esteem and thus their interactions with the infants. When parents come to the interactions with positive historical social experiences, their sensitivity to the infants will likely be increased; when parents have had negative historical experiences, their behavior is likely to be disorganized and less sensitive. Thus the parents' reactions to the infants contribute to the infants' sense of effectance.

Similar to the goodness-of-fit model, the mutual regulation model of effectance (1) highlights the interdependence of the temperamental or personality factors of a parent and an infant; and (2) predicts positive consequences for some amount of interactive mismatch between the parent and infant—that is, the infant is provided with an opportunity to renegotiate the interaction, from which renewed feelings of effectance can emerge.

We have reviewed several studies indicating that infants and young children of ill parents are compromised in their ability to regulate their own activity and regulate social interactions. Furthermore, their developmental trajectories may not be as well regulated as those of children from families without mental illness. These deficits in regulatory processes in children with ill parents may serve as risks for less than optimal development. This lack of infant regulatory abilities may place extra, unrecognized burdens on the very parents who may be least able to adapt effectively to those needs.

Transactional Model

The transactional model provides a broader framework within which to place the previously described family regulation models. A transactional model posits infants who actively work to regulate their social and emotional world, an environment in which these infants perform this work, and relationships of mutual influence and change between infants and their environments. Successful predictions regarding long-range (and more immediate) developmental outcomes cannot be made on the basis of a continuum of reproductive casualty alone (e.g., birth complications or potential genetic contributions of parental mental illness). An equally important continuum of caretaking casualty exists that moderates the reproductive casualty (Sameroff & Chandler, 1975). Thus, important aspects include (1) the degree of match between the infant and environment, in which the infant can restrict and/or expand his or her own boundaries; and (2) the extent to which interactions within the environment reflect versus contradict the infant's internal experiences.

Wynne (1968) stressed three important issues regarding the transactional viewpoint (see also

Sameroff, 1980). First, behavior must be considered within the context in which it occurs. Second, internal change (within both infant and parent) results from interchange with others; thus, both parent and infant exhibit behavioral and emotional responses that have emerged as adaptations to their environment. Finally, the family system strives for homeostasis; if the transactions at any given developmental phase are distorted or omitted, all subsequent developmental phases will be altered. The (mal)adaptive specificity of particular events or behaviors will vary with each individual developmental course (Wynne, 1968).

Multiple-Risk Models

An offshoot of the transactional approach is a model of risk that simultaneously considers multiple sources of risk and attends to number, rather than specificity, of risk factors (Sameroff et al., 1987; Seifer, Sameroff, Baldwin, & Baldwin 1992). In the absence of the ability to actively trace the individual developments within dyads that a full implementation of the transactional model would involve, interim predictions are that (1) more risk factors should increase the probability of the establishment of negative transactional processes and the inability to self-correct the developing system; (2) the nature of the risk is relatively unimportant, because perturbation in relationships may be caused by many different events; (3) specific outcomes should be related to general (not specific) risk, because families may adapt well to some perturbations but not to others; and (4) specific risks may be related to many different types of negative outcomes, because of the individuality of transactional processes.

This model is consistent with the many qualifications attached to the research findings we have reviewed on children of ill parents. Only small portions of variance in child behavior or outcome are explained by any single risk factor. Instead, we propose that many risks must be considered simultaneously with the risk of parental illness. Such risks include, among others, interaction disturbances, parenting beliefs, marital conflict, and poverty. The cumulative nature of the risk will best explain the developmental outcomes of children who are at risk because of parental illness (Sameroff et al., 1987; Seifer, Sameroff, Baldwin, & Baldwin 1992; Teti et al., 1990).

What Can We Say with Certainty?

To conclude, we summarize important findings that (1) have been established in high-quality studies and (2) have been replicated to some degree:

- Children whose parents have mental illness are themselves at increased risk for mental health problems.
- Maternal depression and schizophrenia are associated with other risk factors (such as psychosocial stress, poverty, or marital difficulty); such associations heighten poor outcomes.
- Depressed mothers are less positive and more negative when interacting with their infants (at least in structured laboratory situations).
- Infants of depressed mothers are likewise less positive and more negative when interacting with their mothers in these laboratory protocols, and perhaps when interacting with other adults.
- Insecure attachment is more common in children of ill parents.
- Conflict between parents and children is more prevalent in families where a parent is ill.
- Young children of depressed mothers tend to be more impulsive and to have more difficult peer interactions.
- Depressed mothers view their children's behavior more negatively than well mothers do, but this may result from having children who in fact demonstrate more difficult behavior.

ACKNOWLEDGMENT

This work was supported by grants from the National Institute of Mental Health and the W. T. Grant Foundation.

REFERENCES

Ainsworth, M. D. S., Blehar, M. C., Waters, E., & Wall, S. (1978). *Patterns of attachment.* Hillsdale, NJ: Erlbaum.

American Psychiatric Association. (1987). *Diagnostic and statistical manual of mental disorders* (3rd ed., rev.). Washington, DC: Author.

Asarnow, R. F., & MacCrimmon, D. J. (1981). Span of apprehension deficits during the post-psychotic stages of schizophrenia: A replication and extension. *Archives of General Psychiatry, 38,* 1006–1011.

Baldwin, A. L., Cole, R. E., & Baldwin, C. P. (1982). Parental pathology, family interaction, and the competence of the child in school. *Monographs of the Society for Research in Child Development, 47*(5, Serial No. 197).

Barnett, P. A., & Gotlib, I. H. (1988). Psychosocial functioning and depression: Distinguishing among antecedents, concomitants, and consequences. *Psychological Bulletin, 104,* 97–126.

Beardslee, W. R., Bemporad, J., Keller, M. B., & Klerman, G. L. (1983). Children of parents with major affective disorder: A review. *American Journal of Psychiatry, 140,* 825-832.

Belsher, G., & Costello, C. G. (1991). Do confidants of depressed women provide less social support than confidants of nondepressed women? *Journal of Abnormal Psychology, 100,* 516–525.

Bettelheim, B. (1967). *The empty fortress: Infantile autism and the birth of the self.* New York: Free Press.

Bettes, B. A. (1988). Maternal depression and motherese: Temporal and intonational features. *Child Development, 59,* 1089–1096.

Biederman, J., Rosenbaum, J. F., Hirshfeld, D. R., Faraone, S. V., Bolduc, E. A., Gersten, M., Meminger, S. R., Kagan, J., Snidman, N., & Reznick, J. S. (1990). Psychiatric correlates of behavioral inhibition in young children of parents with and without psychiatric disorder. *Archives of General Psychiatry, 47,* 21–26.

Billings, A. G., & Moos, R. H. (1983). Comparisons of children of depressed and nondepressed parents: A social–environmental perspective. *Journal of Abnormal Child Psychology, 11,* 463–486.

Boyce, P., Hickie, I., & Parker, G. (1991). Parents, partners or personality? Risk factors for post-natal depression. *Journal of Affective Disorders, 21,* 245–255.

Brazelton, T. B. (1979). Evidence of communication in neonatal behavioral assessment. In M. Bullowa (Ed.), *Before speech: The beginning of interpersonal communication* (pp. 79–88). Cambridge, England: Cambridge University Press.

Brody, G. H., & Forehand, R. (1986). Maternal perceptions of child maladjustment as a function of the combined influence of child behavior and maternal depression. *Journal of Consulting and Clinical Psychology, 54,* 237–240.

Brody, G. H., Pillegrini, A. D., & Sigel, I. E. (1986). Marital quality and mother–child and father–child interactions with school-aged children. *Developmental Psychology, 22,* 291–296.

Burchinal, M., & Appelbaum, M. I. (1991). Estimating individual developmental functions: Methods and their assumptions. *Child Development, 62,* 23–43.

Campbell, S. B., & Cohn, J. F. (1991). Prevalence and correlates of postpartum depression in first-time mothers. *Journal of Abnormal Psychology, 100,* 594–599.

Campos, J. J., & Stenberg, C. (1981). Perception, appraisal, and emotion: The onset of social referencing. In M. E. Lamb & L. Sherrod (Eds.), *Infant social cognition* (pp. 273–314). Hillsdale, NJ: Erlbaum.

Chandler, M. J. (1978). Role taking, referential communication, and egocentric intrusions in mother–child interactions of children vulnerable to risk of parental psychosis. In E. J. Anthony, C. Koupernik, & C. Chiland (Eds.), *The child in his family: Vol. 4. Vulnerable children* (pp. 347–357). New York: Wiley.

Cicchetti, D. (1984). The emergence of developmental psychopathology. *Child Development, 55,* 1–8.

Clausen, J. A. (1968). Interpersonal factors in the transmission of schizophrenia. In D. Rosenthal & S. S.

Kety (Eds.), *The transmission of schizophrenia* (pp. 251–263). Oxford: Pergamon Press.

Cohler, B. J., & Musick, J. S. (1983). Psychopathology of parenthood: Implications for mental health of children. *Infant Mental Health Journal, 4,* 140-164.

Cohn, J. F., Campbell, S. B., Matias, R., & Hopkins, J. (1990). Face-to-face interactions of postpartum depressed and nondepressed mother–infant pairs at 2 months. *Developmental Psychology, 26,* 15–23.

Cohn, J. F., Matias, R., Tronick, E. Z., Connell, D., & Lyons-Ruth, K. (1986). Face-to-face interactions of depressed mothers and their infants. In E. Z. Tronick & T. Field (Eds.), *New directions for child development: No. 34. Maternal depression and infant disturbance* (pp. 31–47). San Francisco: Jossey-Bass.

Cohn, J. F., & Tronick, E. Z. (1983). Three-month-old infants' reaction to simulated maternal depression. *Child Development, 54,* 185–193.

Collis, G. M. (1977). Visual co-orientation and maternal speech. In H. R. Schaffer (Ed.), *Studies in mother–infant interaction* (pp. 355–375). London: Academic Press.

Conger, R. D., McCarty, J. A., Yang, R. K., Lahey, B. B., & Kropp, J. P. (1984). Perception of child, child-rearing values, and emotional distress as mediating links between environmental stressors and observed maternal behavior. *Child Development, 55,* 2234–2247.

Conrad, M., & Hammen, C. (1989). Role of maternal depression in perceptions of child maladjustment. *Journal of Consulting and Clinical Psychology, 57,* 663–667.

Cowan, C. P., Cowan, P. A., Coie, L., & Coie, J. D. (1978). The impact of a first child's birth on the couple's relationship. In W. B. Miller & L. F. Newman (Eds.), *The first child and family formation* (pp. 296–324). Chapel Hill: Carolina Population Center, University of North Carolina.

Cox, M. J., Owen, M. T., Lewis, J. M., & Henderson, V. K. (1989). Marriage, adult adjustment, and early parenting. *Child Development, 60,* 1015–1024.

Coyne, J. C., & Downey, G. (1991). Social factors and psychopathology: Stress, social support, and coping processes. *Annual Review of Psychology, 42,* 401–425.

Crockenberg, S. (1985). Toddlers' reaction to maternal anger. *Merrill–Palmer Quarterly, 31,* 857–865.

Cummings, J. S., Pellegrini, D. S., Notarius, C. I., & Cummings, E. M. (1989). Children's responses to angry adult behavior as a function of marital distress and history of interparent hostility. *Child Development, 60,* 1035–1043.

Cummings, E. M., Zahn-Waxler, C., & Radke-Yarrow, M. (1981). Young children's responses to expressions of anger and affection by others in the family. *Child Development, 52,* 1274–1282.

Cutrona, C. E., & Troutman, C. R. (1986). Social support, infant temperament, and parenting self-efficacy: A mediational model of postpartum depression. *Child Development, 57,* 1507–1518.

D'Angelo, E. J., Krock, L. A., O'Neill, L. D., & Boyle, M. P. (1983). Developmental and temperamental characteristics of infants at risk for serious psychopathology. In J. D. Call, E. Galenson, & R. L. Tyson (Eds.), *Frontiers of infant psychiatry* (Vol. 11, pp. 190–200). New York: Basic Books.

DeMulder, E. K., & Radke-Yarrow, M. (1991). Attachment with affectively ill and well mothers: Concurrent behavioral correlates. *Development and Psychopathology*, *3*, 227–242.

Dickstein, S., & Parke, R. D. (1988). Social referencing: A glance at fathers and marriage. *Child Development*, *59*, 506–511.

Donovan, W. L., & Leavitt, L. A. (1989). Maternal self-efficacy and infant attachment: Integrating physiology, perceptions, and behavior. *Child Development*, *60*, 460–472.

Downey, G., & Coyne, J. C. (1990). Children of depressed parents: An integrative review. *Psychological Bulletin*, *108*, 50–76.

Egeland, B. (1989). Relation between mother–infant attachment and later social–emotional functioning. In T. J. Tighe (Chair), *Continuity in development from infancy*. Symposium presented at the meeting of the American Association for the Advancement of Science, San Francisco.

Egeland, J. A., Gerhard, D. S., Pauls, D. L., Sussex, J. N., Kidd, K. K., Allen, C. R., Hostetter, A. M., & Housman, D. E. (1987). Bipolar affective disorders linked to DNA markers on chromosome 11. *Nature*, *325*, 783–787.

Erikson, E. H. (1950). *Childhood and society*. New York: Norton.

Feinman, S. (1982). Social referencing in infancy. *Merrill–Palmer Quarterly*, *28*, 445–470.

Fendrich, M., Warner, V., & Weissman, M. M. (1990). Family risk factors, parental depression, and psychopathology in offspring. *Developmental Psychology*, *26*(1), 40–50.

Field, T. M. (1984). Early interactions between infants and their postpartum depressed mothers. *Infant Behavior and Development*, *7*, 517–522.

Field, T. M., Healy, B., Goldstein, S., & Guthertz, M. (1990). Behavior-state matching and synchrony in mother–infant interactions of nondepressed versus depressed dyads. *Developmental Psychology*, *26*, 7–14.

Field, T. M., Healy, B., Goldstein, S., Perry, S., Bendell, D., Schanberg, S., Zimmerman, E. A., & Kuhn, C. (1988). Infants of depressed mothers show "depressed" behavior even with nondepressed adults. *Child Development*, *59*, 1569–1579.

Field, T. M., Sandberg, D., Garcia, R., Vega-Lahr, N., Goldstein, S., & Guy, L. (1985). Pregnancy problems, postpartum depression, and early mother–infant interactions. *Developmental Psychology*, *21*, 1152–1156.

Fincham, F. D., Beach, S. R. H., & Bradbury, T. N. (1989). Marital distress, depression, and attributions: Is the marital distress–attribution association an artifact of depression? *Journal of Consulting and Clinical Psychology*, *57*, 768–771.

Fish, B. (1957). The detection of schizophrenia in infancy. *Journal of Nervous and Mental Disease*, *125*, 1–24.

Fish, B. (1971). Contributions of developmental research to a theory of schizophrenia. In J. Hellmuth (Ed.), *Exceptional infant: Studies in abnormalities* (pp. 473–483). New York: Brunner/Mazel.

Fish, B. (1977). Neurobiologic antecedents of schizophrenia in children: Evidence for an inherited, congenital neurointegrative deficit. *Archives of General Psychiatry*, *34*, 1297–1313.

Fish, B., Marcus, J., Hans, S. L., Auerbach, J. G., & Perdue, S. (1992). Infants at risk for schizophrenia: Sequelae of a genetic neurointegrative defect. *Archives of General Psychiatry*, *49*, 221–235.

Fogel, A. (1977). Temporal organization in mother–infant face-to-face interaction. In H. R. Schaffer (Ed.), *Studies in mother–infant interaction* (pp. 119–152). New York: Academic Press.

Gaensbauer, T. J., Harmon, R. J., Cytryn, L., & McKnew, D. H. (1984). Social and affective development in infants with a manic-depressive parent. *American Journal of Psychiatry*, *141*, 223–229.

Garmezy, N., & Streitmen, S. (1974). Children at risk: The search for the antecedents of schizophrenia. Part 1: Conceptual models and research methods. *Schizophrenia Bulletin*, *8*, 14–90.

Glenn, N. D., & McLanahan, S. (1982). Children and marital happiness: A further specification of the relationship. *Journal of Marriage and the Family*, 63–72.

Goldberg, W. A., & Easterbrooks, M. A. (1984). The role of marital quality in toddler development. *Child Development*, *20*, 504–515.

Goldberg, W. A., Michaels, G. Y., & Lamb, M. E. (1985). Husbands' and wives' adjustments to pregnancy and first parenthood. *Journal of Family Issues*, *6*, 483–503.

Goodman, S. H. (1987). Emory University project on children of disturbed parents. *Schizophrenia Bulletin*, *13*, 411–423.

Goodman, S. H. (in press). Understanding the effects of depressed mothers on their children. In E. F. Walker, B. Cornblatt, & R. Dworkin (Eds.), *Progress in experimental psychopathology research*. New York: Springer.

Goodman, S. H., & Brumley, H. E. (1990). Schizophrenic and depressed mothers: Relational deficits in parenting. *Developmental Psychology*, *26*, 31–39.

Goodman, S. H., & Van Buskirk, A. (1986). *Schizophrenic and depressed mothers ratings of their children's temperament*. Unpublished manuscript, Emory University.

Gotlib, I. H., & Whiffen, V. E. (1989). Depression and marital functioning: An examination of specificity and gender differences. *Journal of Abnormal Psychology*, *98*, 23–30.

Gotlib, I. H., Whiffen, V. E., Mount, J. H., Milne, K., & Cordy, N. I. (1989). Prevalence rates and demographic characteristics associated with depression in pregnancy and the postpartum. *Journal of Consulting and Clinical Psychology*, *57*, 269–274.

Gottman, J. M., & Levenson, R. W. (1986). Assessing the role of emotion in marriage. *Behavioral Assessment*, *8*, 31–48.

Grossman, F. K., Eichler, L. S., & Winickoff, S. A. (1980). *Pregnancy, birth, and parenthood*. San Francisco: Jossey-Bass.

Hammen, C. (1991). Generalization of stress in the course of unipolar depression. *Journal of Abnormal Psychology*, *100*, 555–561.

Hans, S., Marcus, J., & Auerbach, J. (1987). *Jerusalem Infant Development Study*. Paper presented at the Schizophrenia Consortium Conference on Risk in Infancy, Newport, RI.

Harder, D., Kokes, R. F., Fisher, L., Cole, R. E., & Perkins, P. (1982). Parent psychopathology and child functioning among sons at risk for psychological disorder. In A. L. Baldwin, R. E. Cole, & C. P. Baldwin (Eds.), Parental pathology, family interaction, and the competence of the child in school. *Monographs of the Society for Research in Child Development*, *47*(5, Serial No. 197).

Harvey, P. D., Weintraub, S., & Neale, J. M. (1985). Short report: Span of apprehension deficits in children vulnerable to psychopathology: A failure to replicate. *Journal of Abnormal Psychology, 94*, 410–413.

Hirshfeld, D. R., Rosenbaum, J. F., Biederman, J., Bolduc, E. A., Faraone, S. V., Snidman, N., Reznick, J. S., & Kagan, J. (1992). Stable behavioral inhibition and its association with anxiety disorder. *Journal of the American Academy of Child and Adolescent Psychiatry, 31*, 103–111.

Hock, E., & DeMeis, D. K. (1990). Depression in mothers of infants: The role of maternal employment. *Developmental Psychology, 26*, 285–291.

Hodgkinson, S., Sherrington, R., Gurling, H., Marchbanks, R., Peeders, S., Mallet, J., McInnis, M., Petursson, H., & Brynjolfsson, J. (1987). Molecular genetic evidence for heterogeneity in manic depression. *Nature, 325*, 805–806.

Hoffman, L. W., & Manis, J. D. (1978). Parental satisfactions and dissatisfactions. In R. M. Lerner & G. B. Spanier (Eds.), *Child influences on maternal and family interaction: A life span perspective* (pp. 165–212). New York: Academic Press.

Holden, C. (1991). Probing the complex genetics of alcoholism. *Science, 251*, 163–164.

Hooley, J. M., & Teasdale, J. D. (1989). Predictors of relapse in unipolar depressives: Expressed emotion, marital distress, and perceived criticism. *Journal of Abnormal Psychology, 98*, 229–235.

Hopkins, J., Campbell, S. B., & Marcus, M. (1987). Role of infant-related stressors in postpartum depression. *Journal of Abnormal Psychology, 96*, 237–241.

Hopkins, J., Campbell, S. B., & Marcus, M. (1989). Postpartum depression and postpartum adaptation: Overlapping constructs? *Journal of Affective Disorders, 17*, 251–254.

Howes, P. W., & Markman, H. J. (1989). Marital quality and child attachment: A longitudinal investigation. *Child Development, 60*, 1044–1051.

Iles, S., Gath, D., & Kennerley, H. (1989). Maternity blues: II. A comparison between post-operative women and post-natal women. *British Journal of Psychiatry, 155*, 363–366.

Jacobson, N. S., Dobson, K., Fruzzetti, A. E., Schmaling, K. B., & Salusky, S. (1991). Marital therapy as a treatment for depression. *Journal of Consulting and Clinical Psychology, 59*, 547–557.

Jacobson, N. S., Holtzworth-Munroe, A., & Schmaling, K. B. (1989). Marital therapy and spouse involvement in the treatment of depression, agoraphobia, and alcoholism. *Journal of Consulting and Clinical Psychology, 57*, 5–10.

Jones, J. E. (1977). Patterns of transactional style deviance in the TAT's of parents of schizophrenics. *Family Process, 16*, 327–337.

Kaye, K., & Fogel, A. (1980). The temporal structure of face-to-face communication between mothers and infants. *Developmental Psychology, 16*, 454–464.

Kennerley, H., & Gath, D. (1989a). Maternity blues: I. Detection and measurement by questionnaire. *British Journal of Psychiatry, 155*, 356–362.

Kennerley, H., & Gath, D. (1989b). Maternity blues: III. Associations with obstetric, psychological, and psychiatric factors. *British Journal of Psychiatry, 155*, 367–373.

Kety, S. S., Rosenthal, D., Wender, P. H., Schulsinger, F., & Jacobsen, B. (1975). Mental illness in the biological and adoptive families of adopted individuals who have become schizophrenic: A preliminary report based on psychiatric interviews. In R. R. Fieve, D. Rosenthal, & H. Brill (Eds.), *Genetic research in psychiatry* (pp. 147–165). Baltimore: Johns Hopkins University Press.

Kochanska, G. (1991). Patterns of inhibition to the unfamiliar in children of normal and affectively ill mothers. *Child Development, 62*, 250–263.

Kochanska, G., Kuczynski, L., & Radke-Yarrow, M. (1989). Correspondence between mothers' self-reported and observed child-rearing practices. *Child Development, 60*, 56–63.

Kochanska, G., Radke-Yarrow, M., Kuczynski, L., & Friedman, S. L. (1987). Normal and affectively ill mothers' beliefs about their children. *American Journal of Orthopsychiatry, 57*, 345–350.

Kowalik, D. L., & Gotlib, I. H. (1987). Depression and marital interaction: Concordance between intent and perception of communication. *Journal of Abnormal Psychology, 96*, 127–134.

Krokoff, L. J. (1987). The correlates of negative affect in marriage: An exploratory study of gender differences. *Journal of Family Issues, 8*, 111–135.

Kuczynski, L., & Kochanska, G. (1990). Development of children's noncompliance strategies from toddlerhood to age 5. *Developmental Psychology, 26*, 398–408.

Kuczynski, L., Kochanska, G., Radke-Yarrow, M., & Girnius-Brown, O. (1987). A developmental interpretation of young children's noncompliance. *Developmental Psychology, 23*, 799–806.

Lamb, M. E. (1979). The effects of social context on dyadic social interaction. In M. E. Lamb, S. T. Suomi, & G. R. Stephenson (Eds.), *Social interaction analysis: Methodological issues* (pp. 253–268). Madison: University of Wisconsin Press.

Lamb, M. E., & Elster, A. B. (1985). Adolescent mother–infant–father relationships. *Developmental Psychology, 21*, 768–773.

Lewis, J. M., Owen, M. T., & Cox, M. J. (1988). The transition to parenthood: III. Incorporation of the child into the family. *Family Process, 27*, 411–421.

Lidz, T. (1968). The family, language, and the transmission of schizophrenia. In D. Rosenthal & S. S. Kety (Eds.), *The transmission of schizophrenia* (pp. 175–184). Oxford: Pergamon Press.

Livingood, A. B., Daen, P., & Smith, B. D. (1983). The depressed mother as a source of stimulation for her infant. *Journal of Clinical Psychology, 39*, 369–375.

Lyons-Ruth, K., Connell, D. B., & Grunebaum, H. U. (1990). Infants at social risk: Maternal depression and family support services as mediators of infant development and security of attachment. *Child Development, 61*, 85–98.

MacCrimmon, D. J., Cleghorn, L. M., Asarnow, R. F., & Steffy, R. A. (1980). Children at risk for schizophrenia: Clinical and attentional characteristics. *Archives of General Psychiatry, 37*, 671–674.

Mahler, M. S., Pine, F., & Bergman, A. (1975). *The psychological birth of the human infant.* New York: Basic Books.

Main, M., & Solomon, J. (1990). Procedures for identifying infants as disorganized/disoriented during the Ainsworth Strange Situation. In M. T. Greenburg, D. Cicchetti, & E. M. Cummings (Eds.), *Attachment in the preschool years: Theory, research, and intervention* (pp. 121–160). Chicago: University of Chicago Press.

Marcus, J., Auerbach, J., Wilkinson, L., & Burack, C. M. (1981). Infants at risk for schizophrenia. *Archives of General Psychiatry, 38*, 703–713.

Markman, H. J. (1981). Prediction of marital distress: A five-year follow-up. *Journal of Consulting and Clinical Psychology, 49*, 760–762.

Markman, H. J., & Clements, M. (1991). *Why fathers' prebirth negativity and a first-born daughter predict marital problems: Results from a ten year investigation.* Paper presented at the biennial meeting of the Society for Research in Child Development, Seattle.

McNeil, T. F., & Kaij, L. (1987). Offspring of women with non-organic psychosis: Early sample characteristics at six years of age. *Schizophrenia Bulletin, 13*, 373–382.

McNeil, T. F., Naslund, B., Persson-Blennow, I., & Kaij, L. (1985). Offspring of women with nonorganic psychosis: Mother–infant interaction at three-and-a-half and six months of age. *Acta Psychiatrica Scandinavica, 71*, 551–558.

Mednick, S. A. (1973). Breakdown in high-risk subjects: Familial and early environmental factors. *Journal of Abnormal Psychology, 82*, 469–475.

Mednick, S. A., & McNeil, T. F. (1968). Current methodology in research on the etiology of schizophrenia: Serious difficulties which suggest the use of the high-risk group method. *Psychological Bulletin, 70*, 681–693.

Mednick, S. A., & Schulsinger, F. (1968). Some premorbid characteristics related to breakdown in children with schizophrenic mothers. In D. Rosenthal & S. S. Kety (Eds.), *The transmission of schizophrenia* (pp. 267–291). Oxford: Pergamon Press.

Mednick, S. A., & Schulsinger, F. (1974). Studies of children at high risk for schizophrenia. In S. A. Mednick, F. Schulsinger, J. Higgins, & B. Bell (Eds.), *Genetics, environment and psychopathology.* New York: North-Holland.

Mednick, S. A., Schulsinger, F., & Venables, P. H. (1981). A fifteen-year follow-up of children with schizophrenic mothers (Denmark). In S. A. Mednick & A. E. Baert (Eds.), *Prospective longitudinal research: An empirical basis for the primary prevention of psychosocial disorders* (pp. 286–295). Oxford: Oxford University Press.

Mendlewicz, J., & Rainer, J. D. (1977). Adoption study supporting genetic transmission in manic–depressive illness. *Nature, 268*, 327–329.

Naslund, B., Persson-Blennow, I., McNeil, T., Kaij, L., & Malmquist-Larsson, A. (1984a). Offspring of women with nonorganic psychosis: Infant attachment to the mother at one year of age. *Acta Psychiatrica Scandinavica, 69*, 231–241.

Naslund, B., Persson-Blennow, I., McNeil, T., Kaij, L., & Malmquist-Larsson, A. (1984b). Offspring of women with nonorganic psychosis: Fear of strangers during the first year of life. *Acta Psychiatrica Scandinavica, 69*, 435–444.

Newson, J. (1977). An inter-subjective approach to the description of mother–infant interaction. In H. R. Schaffer (Ed.), *Studies in mother–infant interaction* (pp. 47–61). London: Academic Press.

Nolen-Hoeksema, S. (1991). Responses to depression and their effects on the duration of depressive episodes. *Journal of Abnormal Psychology, 100*, 569–582.

O'Hara, M. W., Schlechte, J. A., Lewis, D. A., & Wright, E. J. (1991). Prospective study of postpartum blues. *Archives of General Psychiatry, 48*, 801–806.

O'Hara, M. W., & Zekoski, E. M. (1988). Postpartum depression: A comprehensive review. In R. Kumar & I. F. Brockington (Eds.), *Motherhood and mental illness: Vol. 2. Causes and consequences* (pp. 17–63). London, England: Wright.

O'Hara, M. W., Zekoski, E. M., Philipps, L. H., & Wright, E. J. (1990). Controlled prospective study of postpartum mood disorders: Comparison of childbearing and nonchildbearing women. *Journal of Abnormal Psychology, 99*, 3–15.

Parke, R. D., & Tinsley, B. R. (1987). Family interaction in infancy. In J. D. Osofsky (Ed.), *Handbook of infant development* (2nd ed., pp. 579–641). New York: Wiley.

Patterson, G. R. (1982). *A social learning approach to family intervention: Vol. 3. Coercive family process.* Eugene, OR: Castalia.

Pedersen, F. A. (1978). Father influence viewed in a family context. In M. E. Lamb (Ed.), *The role of the father in child development* (pp. 295–317). New York: Wiley.

Pedersen, F. A., Zaslow, M. J., Cain, R. L., & Anderson, B. J. (1981). Caesarean childbirth: Psychological implications for mothers and fathers. *Infant Mental Health Journal, 2*, 257–263.

Persson-Blennow, I., Naslund, B., McNeil, T. F., & Kaij, L. (1986). Offspring of women with nonorganic psychosis: Mother–infant interaction at one year of age. *Acta Psychiatrica Scandinavica, 73*, 207–213.

Persson-Blennow, I., Naslund, B., McNeil, T. F., Kaij, L., & Malmquist-Larsson, A. (1984). Offspring of women with nonorganic psychosis: Mother–infant interaction at three days of age. *Acta Psychiatrica Scandinavica, 70*, 149–159.

Pruett, K. D. (1987). *The nurturing father.* New York: Warner.

Radke-Yarrow, M. (1986). Affective development in young children. In T. B. Brazelton & M. W. Yogman (Eds.), *Affective development in infancy* (pp. 145–152). Norwood, NJ: Ablex.

Radke-Yarrow, M., Cummings, E. M., Kuczynski, L., & Chapman, M. (1985). Patterns of attachment in two- and three-year-olds in normal families and families with parental depression. *Child Development, 56*, 884–893.

Radke-Yarrow, M., Nottelmann, E., Martinez, P., Fox, M. B., & Blemont, B. (1992). Young children of affectively ill parents: A longitudinal study of psychosocial development. *Journal of the American Academy of Child and Adolescent Psychiatry, 31*, 68–77.

Richters, J. (1992). Depressed mothers as informants about their children: A critical review of the evidence for distortion. *Psychological Bulletin, 112*(3), 485–499.

Richters, J., & Pellegrini, D. (1989). Depressed mothers' judgments about their children: An examination of the depression–distortion hypothesis. *Child Development, 60*, 1068–1075.

Rickard, K. M., Forehand, R., Wells, K. C., Griest, D. L., & McMahon, R. J. (1981). A comparison of mothers of clinic-referred deviant, clinic-referred nondeviant, and nonclinic children. *Behaviour Research and Therapy, 19*, 201–205.

Rogler, L. (1968). Does schizophrenia disorganize the family? The modification of an hypothesis. In D. Rosenthal & S. S. Kety (Eds.), *The transmission of schizophrenia* (pp. 129–136). Oxford: Pergamon Press.

Rolf, J. E. (1972). The social and academic competence of children vulnerable to schizophrenia and other behavior pathologies. *Journal of Abnormal Psychology, 80,* 225–243.

Rollins, B. C., & Feldman, H. (1970). Marital satisfaction over the family life cycle. *Journal of Marriage and the Family,* 20–27.

Rosenbaum, J. F., Biederman, J., Gersten, M., Hirshfeld, D. R., Meminger, S. R., Herman, J. B., Kagan, J., Reznick, J. S., & Snidman, N. (1988). Behavioral inhibition in children of parents with panic disorder and agoraphobia. *Archives of General Psychiatry, 45,* 463–470.

Rosenthal, D., Wender, P. H., Kety, S. S., Welner, J., & Schulsinger, F. (1971). The adopted-away offspring of schizophrenics. *American Journal of Psychiatry, 123,* 307–311.

Russell, C. S. (1974). Transition to parenthood: Problems and gratifications. *Journal of Marriage and the Family, 36,* 294–301.

Sameroff, A. J. (1980). Issues in early reproductive and caretaking risk: Review and current status. In D. B. Sawin, R. C. Hawkins, L. O. Walker, & J. H. Penticuff (Eds.), *Exceptional infant: Psychosocial risks in infant–environment transactions* (Vol. 4, pp. 343–359). New York: Brunner/Mazel.

Sameroff, A. J. (1989, September 1). *Family–child study of affective and anxiety disorders* (Grant No. MH44755). National Institute of Mental Health, Washington, DC.

Sameroff, A. J., Barocas, R., & Seifer, R. (1984). The early development of children born to mentally-ill women. In N. F. Watt, E. J. Anthony, L. C. Wynne, & J. Rolf (Eds.), *Children at risk for schizophrenia: A longitudinal perspective* (pp. 482–514). Cambridge, England: Cambridge University Press.

Sameroff, A. J., & Chandler, M. (1975). Reproductive risk and the continuum of caretaking casualty. In F. D. Horowitz, E. M. Hetherington, S. Scarr-Salapatek, & G. Siegel (Eds.), *Review of child development research* (Vol. 4, pp. 187–244). Chicago: University of Chicago Press.

Sameroff, A. J., Seifer, R., Barocas, R., Zax, M., & Greenspan, S. (1987). IQ scores of 4-year-old children: Social–environmental risk factors. *Pediatrics, 79,* 343–350.

Sameroff, A. J., Seifer, R., & Zax, M. (1982). Early development of children at risk for emotional disorder. *Monographs of the Society for Research in Child Development, 47*(7, Serial No. 199).

Sander, L. W. (1980). New knowledge about the infant from current research: Implications for psychoanalysis. *Journal of the American Psychoanalytic Association, 28,* 181–192.

Schaffer, H. R. (1984). *The child's entry into a social world.* London: Academic Press.

Schmaling, K. B., & Jacobson, N. S. (1990). Marital interaction and depression. *Journal of Abnormal Psychology, 99,* 229–236.

Seifer, R., Sameroff, A. J., Anagnostopolou, R., & Elias, P. K. (1992). Mother–infant interaction during the first year: Effects of situation, maternal mental illness and demographic factors. *Infant Behavior and Development, 15,* 405–426.

Seifer, R., Sameroff, A. J., Baldwin, C. P., & Baldwin, A. (1992). Child and family factors that ameliorate risk between 4 and 13 years of age. *Journal of the Ameri-*
can Academy of Child and Adolescent Psychiatry, 31, 893–903.

Singer, M., & Wynne, L. (1965). Thought disorder and family relations of schizophrenics: III. Methodology using projective techniques. *Archives of General Psychiatry, 12,* 187–200.

Spitz, R. A. (1965). *The first year of life: A psychoanalytic study of normal and deviant development of object relations.* New York: International Universities Press.

Sroufe, L. A. (1990). Considering normal and abnormal together: The essence of developmental psychopathology. *Development and Psychopathology, 2,* 335–347.

Sroufe, L. A., & Rutter, M. (1984). The domain of developmental psychopathology. *Child Development, 55,* 17–29.

Sroufe, L. A., & Waters, E. (1977). Attachment as an organizational construct. *Child Development, 48,* 1184–1199.

Stern, D. N. (1977). *The first relationship: Mother and infant.* Cambridge, MA: Harvard University Press.

Stern, D. N. (1985). *The interpersonal world of the infant.* New York: Basic Books.

Stern, D. N., Hofer, L., Haft, W., & Dore, J. (1985). Affect attunement: The sharing of feeling states between mother and infant by means of inter-modal fluency. In T. M. Field & N. A. Fox (Eds.), *Social perception in infants* (pp. 249–268). Norwood, NJ: Ablex.

Teti, D. M., Gelfand, D. M., & Pompa, J. (1990, April). *Differences in depressed mothers' ability to parent: Maternal, infant, and environmental correlates.* Poster presented at the Seventh International Conference on Infant Studies, Montreal.

Thomas, A., & Chess, S. (1977). *Temperament and development.* New York: Brunner/Mazel.

Trevarthen, C. (1984). Emotions in infancy: Regulators of contact and relationships with persons. In K. R. Scherer & P. Ekman (Eds.), *Approaches to emotion* (pp. 129–157). Hillsdale, NJ: Lawrence Erlbaum.

Tronick, E. Z., Als, H., & Adamson, L. (1979). Structure of early face-to-face communicative interactions. In M. Bullowa (Ed.), *Before speech: The beginning of interpersonal communication* (pp. 349–372). Cambridge, England: Cambridge University Press.

Tronick, E. Z., Als, H., Adamson, L., Wise, S., & Brazelton, T. B. (1978). The infant's response to entrapment between contradictory messages in face-to-face interaction. *Journal of the American Academy of Child Psychiatry, 17,* 1–13.

Tronick, E. Z., Als, H., & Brazelton, T. B. (1980). Monadic phases: A structural descriptive analysis of infant–mother face-to-face interaction. *Merrill–Palmer Quarterly, 26,* 3–24.

Tronick, E. Z., Cohn, J., & Shea, E. (1986). The transfer of affect between mothers and infants. In T. B. Brazelton & M. Yogman (Eds.), *Affective development in infancy* (pp. 11–25). Norwood, NJ: Ablex.

Troutman, B. R., & Cutrona, C. E. (1990). Nonpsychotic postpartum depression among adolescent mothers. *Journal of Abnormal Psychology, 99,* 69–78.

Walker, E., Downey, G., & Bergman, A. (1989). The effects of parental psychopathology and maltreatment on child behavior: A test of the diathesis–stress model. *Child Development, 60,* 15–24.

Waring, E. M., & Patton, D. (1984). Marital intimacy and depression. *British Journal of Psychiatry, 145,* 641–644.

Watt, N. F. (1984). In a nutshell: The first two decades of high-risk research in schizophrenia. In N. F. Watt, E. J. Anthony, L. C. Wynne, & J. Rolf (Eds.), *Children at risk for schizophrenia: A longitudinal perspective* (pp. 572–595). Cambridge, England: Cambridge University Press.

Watt, N. F., Anthony, E. J., Wynne, L. C. & Rolf, J. (Eds.). (1984). *Children at risk for schizophrenia: A longitudinal perspective.* Cambridge, England: Cambridge University Press.

Weissman, M. M., Gammon, G. D., John, K., Merikangas, K. R., Warner, V., Prusoff, B. A., & Sholomskas, D. (1987). Children of depressed parents. *Archives of General Psychiatry, 44,* 847–853.

Weissman, M. M., Leckman, J. F., Merikangas, K. R., Gammon, G. D., & Prusoff, B. A. (1984). Depression and anxiety disorders in parents and children: Results from the Yale Family Study. *Archives of General Psychiatry, 41,* 845–852.

Weissman, M. M., Wickramaratne, P., Merikangas, K. R., Leckman, J. F., Prusoff, B. A., Caruso, K. A., Kidd, K. K., & Gammon, G. D. (1984). Onset of major depression in early adulthood: Increased familial loading and specificity. *Archives of General Psychiatry, 41,* 1136–1143.

Wender, P. H., Rosenthal, D., Kety, S. S., Schulsinger, F., & Welner, J. (1974). Crossfostering. *Archives of General Psychiatry, 30,* 121–128.

Werner, E. E., & Smith, R. S. (1982). *Vulnerable but invincible: A study of resilient children.* New York: McGraw-Hill.

Whiffen, V. E., & Gottlib, I. H. (1989). Infants of postpartum depressed mothers: Temperament and cognitive status. *Journal of Abnormal Psychology, 98,* 274–279.

Whisman, M. A., & Jacobson, N. S. (1989). Depression, marital satisfaction, and marital and personality measures of sex roles. *Journal of Marital and Family Therapy, 15,* 177–186.

Willett, J. B. (1988). Questions and answers in the measurement of change. In E. Z. Rothkopf (Ed.), *Review of research in education* (Vol. 15, pp. 345–422). Washington, DC: American Education Research Association.

Winnicott, D. W. (1987). *The child, the family, and the outside world.* Reading, MA: Addison-Wesley. (Original work published 1964)

Worland, J., Edenhart-Pepe, R., Weeks, D. G., & Konnen, P. M. (1984). Cognitive evaluation of children at risk: IQ, differentiation, and egocentricity. In N. F. Watt, E. J. Anthony, L. C. Wynne, & J. Rolf (Eds.), *Children at risk for schizophrenia: A longitudinal perspective* (pp. 148–159). Cambridge, England: Cambridge University Press.

Wynne, L. C. (1968). Methodologic and conceptual issues in the study of schizophrenics and their families. In D. Rosenthal & S. S. Kety (Eds.), *The transmission of schizophrenia* (pp. 185–199). Oxford: Pergamon Press.

Zahn-Waxler, C., Cummings, E. M., McKnew, D. H., & Radke-Yarrow, M. (1984). Altruism, aggression, and social interactions in young children with a manic–depressive parent. *Child Development, 55,* 112–122.

Zahn-Waxler, C., McKnew, D. H., Cummings, E. M., Davenport, Y. B., & Radke-Yarrow, M. (1984). Problem behaviors and peer interactions of young children with a manic–depressive parent. *American Journal of Psychiatry, 141,* 236–240.

9

Maternal Substance Abuse and Infant Development

BARRY ZUCKERMAN
ELIZABETH R. BROWN

Substance abuse has become a major public health problem. As many as 20–30 million people in the United States abuse illicit substances, and about 5 million are regular users. With the increased overall drug abuse in the population, the number of women of childbearing age using drugs while pregnant has also increased. A U.S. General Accounting Office (1990) report to Congress suggests that somewhere between 100,000 and 375,000 women each year give birth after exposing their unborn children to illicit drugs, including marijuana. When alcohol and nicotine are included, the number of exposed children is even higher.

Structural damage, such as that to the limbs of children affected by thalidomide or alteration of the faces of children with severe fetal alcohol syndrome, is a rare consequence of prenatal drug exposure. Intrauterine growth retardation and neonatal behavioral dysfunction (e.g., difficulty maintaining an alert state, irritability, etc.) are more sensitive indicators of the prenatal effect of a drug, especially a psychoactive drug. Nevertheless, the tendency of a pregnant woman to use more than one drug and the usual presence of other risk factors (especially poor nutrition) make it difficult to isolate the effects of one drug.

Long-term developmental and behavioral effects are even harder to determine, because the difficulty of controlling for prenatal variables is compounded by the contributions of the often adverse postnatal environment. For this reason, the development of a child affected by exposure to drugs is best understood by considering the interrelated pre- and postnatal factors. The prenatal effects of drugs on the central nervous system (CNS) are seen as creating biological vulnerability—that is, dysfunction that may be completely or partly compensated for by postnatal brain growth and development and/or by competent caregiving. This vulnerability, however, renders the child more susceptible to the effects of poor caregiving.

PRENATAL INFLUENCES

Psychoactive substances cross the placenta and the blood–brain barrier, potentially affecting the developing CNS directly. Some drugs affect the fetus indirectly via decreasing maternal nutrition and/or vasoconstriction (which results in hypoxia and decreased nutrient transfer). A consistent, specific insult to the fetal CNS from prenatal exposure to drugs and alcohol has not been well documented, however. Prenatal cocaine use, excessive alcohol consumption, and narcotic use are all associated with smaller head circumference, indicating a potential significant structural effect on the brain. Other specific effects have been described, frequently in single studies, but their clinical implications are unknown (Zuckerman & Bresnahan, 1991). Neonatal neurobehavioral disturbances that may reflect direct CNS effects are consistently found only in heroin- and methadone-exposed newborns (Finnegan, 1990).

The consequences to the newborn of prenatal drug exposure depend on many factors, including the type of drug; the timing, dose, and frequency of exposure; and other adverse health habits associated with a drug-using lifestyle. For example, infants whose mothers had a positive urine assay for cocaine during pregnancy were 400 grams smaller than infants whose mothers did not use cocaine, but only 25% of this weight decrement could be attributed directly to cocaine; statistical analysis indicated that the remainder was due to other factors, such as cigarette smoking, poor nutrition, and marijuana use (Zuckerman, Frank, et al., 1989).

POSTNATAL INFLUENCES

The newborn brain has a significant capacity for adaptation. Animal studies show that even though damaged nerve cells are not replaced, new synaptic connections are made and/or certain areas of the brain develop new functions to replace ones lost from the damaged area (Anastasiow, 1990). Recovery, or plasticity, is greater in the newborn than in the adult and is facilitated by a favorable caretaking environment. Consistent with this animal research, research on humans during the past 20 years confirms the importance of the social environment and responsive caregiving in determining the developmental outcome of biologically vulnerable newborns (Hunt, Cooper, & Tooley, 1988; Beckwith & Parmalee, 1986; Werner, 1989).

Outcome of infants exposed prenatally to narcotics also appears to depend at least in part on their environment, especially as they get older. Compared with unexposed infants, methadone-exposed infants had poor motor coordination at 4 months; however, this difference almost disappeared by 12 months except among infants from families at high social risk (Marcus, Hans, & Jeremy, 1982). At 2 years, these same infants demonstrated impaired development compared with a control group only when prenatal methadone exposure was combined with low socioeconomic status (SES) (Hans, 1989). Finally, Lifschitz, Wilson, Smith, and Desmond (1985) showed that among infants exposed to opiates *in utero*, the quality of the postnatal environment and not the amount of maternal opiate use appeared to be the more important determinant of outcome.

The developmental outcome of an infant exposed to drugs is determined by the dynamic interaction of the child and the social environment. Infants prenatally exposed to drugs are in double jeopardy. They suffer a biological vulnerability as a result of prenatal physiological effects, which is then compounded by parenting dysfunction associated with and caused by prenatal addiction.

Not all women who use alcohol or illegal drugs are addicted. Addiction to alcohol may take 15 years of use, and addiction to heroin or cocaine up to 5 years of use. Nevertheless, the highly rewarding properties of crack cocaine have accelerated the progression from recreational use to addiction to within weeks to months of first use for some individuals. Crucial to the understanding of addiction are the ideas of loss of control over the use of a substance and compulsive preoccupation with drug use despite its consequences. Addiction may be associated with other comorbidities, including Major Depression and Post-Traumatic Stress Disorder. Drug or alcohol dependency is best understood as a chronic and progressive disorder that affects a woman's ability to care for herself and her children.

Interactions between drug-using mothers and their infants affect the infants' developmental functioning (Bernstein, Jeremy, & Marcus, 1986). Dysfunctional interactions may interfere with an infant's ability to recover from a biological vulnerability caused by prenatal drug exposure. The difficulty may lie not only with parental dysfunction secondary to addiction, but also with drug-induced behavioral changes in the infant that interfere with maternal–infant interactions. A common problem of infants exposed to drugs *in utero* is difficulty in regulating arousal. During infancy, a caregiver is motivated to provide stimulation when an infant is underaroused and to reduce it when the infant is overexcited. This is believed to facilitate the child's capacity to regulate arousal. Among non-drug-using mothers, those who are intrusive at 6 months and overstimulating at 3½ years are more likely to have hyperactive children than mothers who are not intrusive or overstimulating (Jacobvitz & Sroufe, 1987). Examples of these behaviors are seen in mothers who tickle their infants or try to get the infants' attention when they are turning away, or in other ways disrupt the infants' ongoing activity, possibly impairing the infants' ability to control arousal. Such behavior seems more likely to have adverse effects on biologically vulnerable, drug-exposed infants, contributing to impulsivity, distractibility, and restlessness. On the other hand, infants who have difficulty regulating themselves because of prenatal drug exposure are helped to regulate arousal by caregivers who respond to their needs in an appropriate manner.

Infants with poor arousal may not elicit sufficient caregiving from their mothers. If a mother has a drug problem, the effects of drugs, drug-seeking behavior, and withdrawal from drugs are likely to render her less sensitive to her infant's signals for stimulation and nutrition. This combination of poor arousal as a direct effect of prenatal drugs with less sensitive caregiving may result in a cycle of neglect that leads to failure to thrive. Thus, dysfunctional parenting as a result of addiction impairs an infant's ability to recover from biological vulnerability associated with prenatal drug use. Among the problems associated with drug and alcohol use, violence and depression are important and deserve special attention. Drug and alcohol use by a pregnant woman and the father of her infant provide a context that increases the likelihood that the woman will be the victim of violence during pregnancy (Amaro, Fried, Cabral, & Zuckerman, 1990). Her children are likely to witness violence in their home and/or be the victims of violence (Bays, 1990; Black & Mayer, 1980). Depression frequently occurs among drug-using and addicted women (Zuckerman, Amaro, Bauchner, & Cabral, 1989); other studies have found children of depressed mothers to show greater irritability at birth (Zuckerman, Bauchner, Parker, & Cabral, 1990), and to have more behavior problems, accidents, learning problems, and affective disease at older ages, than children raised by nondepressed mothers (Zuckerman & Beardslee, 1987). Thus, depression among drug-using mothers may also play an important role in contributing to adverse child outcomes.

COCAINE

Pharmacology

Cocaine is a tropane alkaloid derived from the leaves of the erthroxylon coca plant, found on the mountain slopes of Central and South America. It is a stimulant, similar to the amphetamines in structure and function. Cocaine is soluble in water or lipid and has a wide volume of distribution. It crosses the placenta by simple diffusion and readily crosses the blood–brain barrier. Cocaine has been found in brain concentrations four times higher than the peak plasma concentration (Fiks, Johnson, & Rosen, 1985). Cocaine affects multiple neurotransmitter systems in the CNS, including the dopamine (DA) and norepinephrine (NE) systems. It blocks presynaptic reuptake of these neurotransmitters, resulting in an exaggerated signal because of the excess of these agents at the postsynaptic membrane.

By blocking the presynaptic reuptake of DA in the CNS, increasing DA synthesis, and upregulating DA receptors on the postsynaptic nerve, cocaine produces a neurochemical magnification of the pleasure response (Spitz & Rosecan, 1987); this creates a heightened sense of power, euphoria, and sexual excitement. This augmented pleasure response initiates drug-seeking behavior that is so persistent that rats press levers to obtain cocaine until they die of overdose (Geary, 1987). With chronic use, cocaine results in a depletion of DA in the CNS, which is thought to cause depressive symptoms and is considered an important component of cocaine withdrawal and addiction (Gawin & Kleber, 1984).

The alertness, hypervigilance, and peripheral sympathetic arousal induced by cocaine use result from cocaine's effect on the NE transmitter system. In the CNS, NE modulates global alertness and vigilance; in the peripheral nervous system, it increases heart rate and contractility, blood pressure, peripheral muscle contractility, and blood glucose, while stimulating behavioral arousal associated with the "fight-or-flight" response. Cocaine blocks reuptake of NE at the presynaptic terminal, increases NE synthesis, and upregulates NE receptors on the postsynaptic nerve, resulting in an accumulation of NE in the nerve synapse and propagation of NE-mediated signals.

Newborn Outcome

Cocaine's vasoactive effects have been implicted in the etiology of such complications as abruptio placentae, preterm labor and delivery, poor fetal growth, congenital abnormalities, and hemorrhagic and cystic lesions in the CNS. Although maternal cocaine use has been associated with prematurity in some studies, this finding is not universal (Zuckerman & Bresnahan, 1991). Cocaine constricts placental vessels, leading to fetal hypoxemia and decreased nutrient transfer (Woods, Plessinger, & Clark, 1987).

Consistent with this finding, numerous studies have shown an association between cocaine use during pregnancy and a decrease in birthweight and head circumference (Zuckerman & Bresnahan, 1991). Nevertheless, this effect on growth is probably compounded by maternal undernutrition and polydrug abuse (Frank et al., 1988; Zuckerman, Frank, et al., 1989). Only one of the studies demonstrating poor fetal growth and small head circumference controlled for these potentially confounding variables (Zuckerman, Frank, et al., 1989). Infants exposed to cocaine showed a symmetrical pattern of growth retardation, suggesting a chronic influence or one starting early in gestation. These infants also showed suppressed fat stores and lean body mass, a pattern commonly associated with maternal malnutrition. Since maternal nutritional markers such as maternal weight for height and pregnancy weight gain were statistically controlled for, the finding suggests decreased nutrient transfer (Frank et al., 1990).

Only one case report of a significant cerebral infarction associated with prenatal cocaine exposure has been published (Chasnoff, Bussey, Savich, & Stack, 1986), but a systematic study reported that 35% of stimulant-exposed (cocaine, methamphetamine) asymptomatic infants undergoing cranial ultrasound in the first 3 days of life showed either echodensities or echolucencies indicating CNS vascular injury (Dixon & Bejar, 1989). This rate of abnormal findings was comparable to that in full-term infants with perinatal illness (e.g., meconium aspiration), and much greater than in healthy full-term newborns. However, this finding was not replicated in a subsequent study that showed the same rate of findings by sonogram between cocaine-exposed and unexposed infants (Frank, McCarten, Cabral, Levenson, & Zuckerman, 1992).

Rare but serious congenital abnormalities such as urogenital anomalies (Chavez, Mulinare, & Cordero, 1989) and distal limb deformities (Hoyme et al., 1990), have also been reported. Decreased uterine blood flow can result in disruption of existing structures or altered morphogenesis of developing structures, leading to these anatomical abnormalities. Single studies show

minor electroencephalographic (EEG), auditory evoked potential, and eye ground changes, all of which return to normal within the first few months of life (Zuckerman & Bresnahan, 1991).

Neurobehavioral abnormalities have been reported in some but not all studies. Firm conclusions cannot be drawn because of the inconsistency of the findings. Methodological problems associated with the research raise important questions regarding the validity of findings. The most important of these is the inability to control for confounding factors, including use of other drugs and risk factors. Also, most studies rely on one postpartum urine test and/or self-report of cocaine use to identify users. This can result in misclassification of users as nonusers, and can either obscure differences between groups or elevate the magnitude of effect of the cocaine group.

Assuming that cocaine would result in a withdrawal syndrome, many studies have assessed cocaine-exposed infants with the Neonatal Abstinence Scale (NAS), which was developed by Finnegan (1990) to describe withdrawal among opiate-exposed infants. One study found opiate-exposed infants to have higher NAS scores than cocaine/methamphetamine-exposed infants (Oro & Dixon, 1987). Another study showed higher NAS scores for cocaine/opiate-exposed infants than either cocaine- or opiate-exposed infants alone, suggesting a possible synergistic effect between cocaine and opiates (Fulroth, Phillips, & Durand, 1989). Nevertheless, this was not confirmed in a subsequent study (Doberczak, Kandall, & Wiletts, 1991). Two other studies (Ryan, Ehrlich, & Finnegan, 1987; Hadeed & Siegel, 1989) found no differences in NAS scores between cocaine-exposed and unexposed groups.

It is possible that the NAS is not sensitive enough to determine prenatal cocaine effects. It was developed to measure opiate withdrawal and measures signs such as irritability, sweating, jitteriness, and vomiting, which are not commonly seen in newborns exposed to cocaine but not opiates. Clinically, cocaine-exposed newborns are poorly responsive and sleepy. When alert, they are easily overstimulated; they therefore become irritable and quickly return to sleep.

A number of studies have evaluated the neurobehavioral functioning of cocaine-exposed infants with the Brazelton Neonatal Behavioral Assessment Scale (NBAS), which is a much more sensitive assessment of newborn behavior that the NAS. Results of these studies are inconsistent regarding both the presence of an association between prenatal cocaine use and neurobehavioral dysfunction, and the type of dysfunction identified. Chasnoff and colleagues, in two different studies (Chasnoff, Burns, Schnoll, & Burns, 1985; Chasnoff, Burns, Burns, & Schnoll, 1986), found cocaine-exposed newborns to have increased tremulousness and startles, decreased interactive behaviors, and increased state lability. Women for these studies were drawn from a special prenatal drug treatment program, and the effects of other drugs (especially opiates), as well as other risk factors, probably contributed to the findings. In a third report, Chasnoff, Griffith, MacGregor, Dirkes, and Burns (1989) showed that even infants whose mothers had stopped using drugs in the first trimester showed impaired orientation, motor function, reflexes, and state regulation compared to infants whose mothers used no drugs. A study conducted by another research team (Eisen et al., 1991) found impaired habituation on the NBAS and more stress behaviors among cocaine-exposed infants compared to controls. Multivariate analysis demonstrated that other factors (obstetric complications and maternal alcohol use), and not cocaine, were associated with stress behaviors; nevertheless, prenatal cocaine continued to be associated with poor habituation when these and other factors were controlled analytically. A final study (Neuspiel, Hamel, Hochberg, Greene, & Campbell, 1991) showed no differences on NBAS scores between cocaine-exposed and unexposed newborns in the first 3 days of life. Although a second examination between 11 and 30 days of life showed that cocaine-exposed infants had significantly lower scores in motor functioning, the magnitude of the effect decreased by over 50% and the association was no longer statistically significant when confounding variables were controlled for.

Factors other than drugs, especially poor nutrition, that can lead to neurobehavioral dysfunction may contribute to the variability in outcomes. One study (Lester et al., 1991), using cry characteristics, has supported this possibility by identifying two neurobehavioral profiles among cocaine-exposed newborns. One profile, characterized as "excitable," is hypothesized to be due to the direct effect of cocaine exposure. The other profile, characterized as "depressed," is thought to be due to a secondary effect of intrauterine growth retardation. Possible "opposite" effects of cocaine and undernutrition may help explain the variability in newborn behavior seen clinically in the above-cited studies.

Whether alterations in behavior are attributable to withdrawal or to a direct effect of cocaine on the brain's neurotransmitters is unknown. A role for neurotransmitter changes was suggested by a pilot study (Mirochnick, Meyer, Cole, Herren, & Zuckerman, 1991) showing that blood levels of the NE precursor dihydroxyphenylalanine were higher in cocaine- exposed than in unexposed newborns. Among the cocaine-exposed newborns, high NE concentrations in blood were associated with poor responsivity to auditory and visual stimuli as measured by the NBAS (Orientation subscale). Nevertheless, blood NE levels do not necessarily indicate levels in the CNS. The neurotransmitter changes shown in this preliminary study may have been entirely attributable to chronic stress associated with cocaine-induced vasoconstriction and hypoxia *in utero*.

Developmental Outcome

In the fetal brain, neurotransmitters contribute to brain development by influencing neuronal migration and differentiation as well as synaptic proliferation (Lauder, 1988). During the prenatal period, neurotransmitters also affect the development of receptor sites (Miller & Friedhoff, 1988). For example, an induced prenatal decrease in DA results in a significant postnatal decrease in the number of DA receptors. Following birth, these receptors do not appear to have the normal capacity to up-regulate or increase in number in response to decreases in DA. Timing of cocaine use may be critical in determining which aspects of the brain are altered; different alterations lead to different functional and behavioral difficulties. Only one developmental study of children prenatally exposed to cocaine and not opiates has been published to date. This study shows no mean differences on the Bayley Scales of Infant Mental Development. At 2-years of age, the cocaine exposed children were compared to socially matched controls (Chasnoff, Griffith, Freier, & Murray, 1992).

Global outcome measures, such as developmental quotients and behavior problem scales, may not identify the specific impact of prenatal cocaine exposure. Since prenatal alterations of neurotransmitters impair the postnatal ability of the receptors to make adaptive responses to changes in neurotransmitters, the adaptive capacity of the organism to maintain physiological and behavioral homeostasis in response to stress may also be impaired. This can lead to difficulty with the regulation of activity, emotional responsivity, and attentional regulation. Thus, a complete assessment of these specific functions should include both stress and nonstress situations. In one study, drug-exposed (cocaine, opiates, and other drugs) toddlers had significantly greater difficulty than nonexposed toddlers in unstructured tasks—that is, tasks that required the children's initiation, goal setting, and follow-through (Rodning, Beckwith, & Howard, 1990). This type of dysfunction represents a behavioral disorganization that may not be identified in the structured settings of traditional developmental assessment tests. On the other hand, the newborn brain may be able to adapt and to compensate for at least some of these biological changes. If behavior and developmental problems are identified, the extent to which these problems are the results of caregiver dysfunction versus biological vulnerability created by prenatal cocaine exposure will need to be determined.

OPIATES

Pharmacology

Opiates are a group of opium-derived alkaloids obtained by drying the milky white sap of the unripe seed of *Papaver somniferum*, a poppy plant that is indigenous to Asia Minor. At least 20 alkaloids are found in opium powder, including the naturally occurring opiates (morphine, codeine, opium) that have been in use for millennia. Narcotic addiction was first described in Western world in 1822 by Thomas De Quincey in *Confessions of an English Opium-Eater*.

Semisynthetic narcotics, made by simple biochemical modifications of morphine, include heroin (diacetylmorphine), hydromorphone (Dilaudid), oxycodone (present in Percocet, Percodan, and Tylox), and hydrocodone (Vicodin). Heroin was first manufactured in the last quarter of the 19th century. Totally synthetic narcotics, whose chemical structure is unrelated to morphine, include methadone, fentanyl, meperidine (Demerol), and propoxyphene (Darvon). Methadone, which has physiological effects identical to those of morphine, was first manufactured in Germany in the 1940s. Both semisynthetic and synthetic narcotics are termed "opioids," whereas naturally occurring compounds derived from opium are termed "opiates." Narcotics include both opioids and opiates.

Opioids produce analgesia, lowered anxiety, improved mood, drowsiness, and a clouding of the sensorium. In sufficient dose, they also cause respiratory depression, peripheral vasodilatation, and decreased intestinal peristalsis. Although it is possible to use opioid drugs in a sporadic fashion, continued use tends to lead to drug dependency. "Dependency" is usually defined when drug tolerance exists (an increased dose is needed to obtain the same effect) and when a withdrawal syndrome results from the sudden cessation of drug use. "Addiction" is usually defined as compulsive drug-seeking behavior in the face of adverse consequences to the drug user.

As early as 1888, C. E. Ruth published an article questioning the use of opium in pregnant women, and described increased *in utero* activity and associated seizures associated with maternal administration of opium. Current estimates are that about 225,000 U.S. women of childbearing age are using intravenous drugs and about 9000 narcotic-exposed infants are born each year (about 2–3 per 1000 live births). This rate will be much higher in areas of increased drug use. At the Boston City Hospital, the rate of narcotic addiction is 20 per 1000 live-born infants.

Newborn Outcome

There is no convincing evidence that exposure to narcotics *in utero* results in an increased rate of congenital malformations in either animal or human pregnancies. Some animal studies have shown teratogenic effects, but only at extremely large doses. Many of these studies did not control for the effects of anorexia and decreased caloric intake seen in most animals given narcotics (Hutchings, 1982). Studies that have used smaller doses more closely approximating human usage, and that have taken nutritional intake into account, have not demonstrated an increased rate of malformations. In humans, no consistent pattern of anomalies has been described in infants, nor has the rate of malformations been increased over that seen in the general population (Ostrea & Chavez, 1979;

Naeye, Blanc, Leblanc, & Khatamee, 1973; Stimmel & Adamson, 1976; Kandall et al., 1977).

The primary effects on the fetus of maternal narcotic use are intrauterine growth retardation and neurobehavioral dysfunction. Numerous studies have documented low birthweight for gestational age in infants exposed to narcotics *in utero* (Hans, 1989; Lifschitz et al., 1985; Wilson, Desmond, & Wait, 1981; Kaltenbach & Finnegan, 1989b). Although participation in a methadone maintenance program in pregnancy improves birthweight, the infants are still significantly growth-retarded relative to drug-free controls (Kandall et al., 1976; Wilson et al., 1981). However, other confounding factors among narcotic-using pregnant women complicate drawing a firm conclusion regarding a causal relationship between opiate use and low birthweight. When outcomes were controlled for differences in race, adequacy of prenatal care, weight gain during pregnancy, prenatal risk score, maternal education, and maternal smoking, no differences in birthweight were seen between drug-exposed (heroin or methadone) and drug-free infants (Lifshitz et al., 1985). Follow-up of these infants at 3 years of age showed that the growth of the drug-exposed infants was no more impaired than that of the control group of similar SES, although means for height, weight, and head circumference were below the 50th percentile. The multiple risk factors in the lifestyle of drug-abusing pregnant women appear to be major factors in the growth retardation reported both prenatally and postnatally for this group of infants.

There is growing evidence that *in utero* exposure to narcotic drugs may result in abnormal structural organization of the fetal brain (Smith, Hui, & Crofford, 1977; Zagon & McLaughlin, 1984, Sakellaridis, Mangoura, & Veradakis, 1986). Morphine decreases the packing density of neurons in the medial and lateral preoptic areas of the hypothalamus, and in all layers of the cerebral cortex (Hammer, Ricalde, & Seatriz, 1989). Since receptors affect dentritic growth and mature at different rates in different parts of the brain, prenatal exposure could produce different effects, depending on timing of the exposure. Thus, the neurobehavioral abnormalities seen in narcotic-exposed infants may be attributable in part to underlying structural changes in brain development.

Neurochemical alterations resulting from prenatal opiate exposure may be expressed either as neurological dysfunction or as neurobehav-ioral abnormalities. Herzlinger, Kandall, and Vaughan (1977) reported an incidence of seizures of 1.2% for heroin-exposed infants and 7.8% for methadone-exposed infants. A 1-year follow-up study of infants with abstinence-related seizures showed that most early EEG and neurological abnormalities associated with abstinence-related seizures were transient (Doberczak, Shanzer, Senie, and Kandall, 1988). By 8 to 16 months of age, results of all neurological exams were normal; none of the infants developed a seizure disorder. It is possible that the cause of abstinence-related seizures may be the depletion of neurotransmitters (Smith et al., 1977; McGinty & Ford, 1980; Rosenman & Smith, 1972), which if restored over time would result in improved synaptic function, leading to improved neurological function.

The most immediate neurological complication seen in narcotic-exposed infants is the presence of a neonatal abstinence syndrome. During *in utero* exposure to narcotics, a fetus develops drug dependency, including tolerance for narcotics. After delivery, the infant develops symptoms of irritability, tremulousness, sweating, stuffy nose, difficulty in feeding (due to an uncoordinated and inefficient suck; Kron, Litt, & Phoenix, 1976), diarrhea, and vomiting. The neurochemical pathways underlying drug withdrawal symptoms are poorly understood. As noted above, Finnegan (1990) developed the NAS, a scoring system commonly used to quantify the severity of withdrawal symptoms, to determine when pharmacotherapy is indicated, and to guide therapy once it is begun.

The onset of symptoms depends on the type of narcotic. Heroin has a short half-life (4 hours), so that withdrawal symptoms are apparent on the first day of life. Methadone, on the other hand, has a very long half-life (32 hours in the newborn), so that the drug stays in the newborn's system for days. Therefore, withdrawal symptoms seldom occur before 24–48 hours of life and can occur as late as 7 to 10 days after birth. Methadone is excreted in the infant's urine for 10–14 days after birth (Kreek, 1979), which may account for the very prolonged withdrawal period seen with methadone-exposed infants. In addition, a subacute withdrawal syndrome characterized by restlessness, agitation, tremors, and sleep disturbance may last up to 3–6 months after birth and may be a reflection of the prolonged metabolism and excretion of methadone (Hutchings, 1982).

The severity of withdrawal is related to the

maternal methadone dose. Mothers maintained on a dose of less than 20 mg/day most often have infants who can be managed with the "tender loving care" approach to treatment, including swaddling, use of a pacifier, feeding on demand with hypercaloric formula, and decreased environmental stimuli (low lighting levels, decreased noise levels, and minimal handling) (Madden, 1978; Ostrea, Chavez, & Strauss, 1976; Strauss, Starr, Ostrea, Chavez, & Stryker, 1976; Connaughton, Reeser, Shut, & Finnegan, 1977; Green, Silverman, Suffet, Taleporos, & Turkel, 1979). For those infants whose symptoms cannot be controlled with this approach, pharmacotherapy is indicated.

About 60% of narcotic-exposed infants (heroin 40–50%, methadone 70–90%) will exhibit sufficiently severe withdrawal to require pharmacotherapy. The need for drug treatment is determined by using the Finnegan (1990) NAS scoring system. Infants are scored at 4 hours of age and then every 2 hours for 24 hours if heroin-exposed, and for 48 hours if methadone-exposed. If three consecutive scores are greater than 8 or two consecutive scores are greater than 12, drug treatment should be begun. Several drugs have been used to treat these infants, including opium (paregoric or denatured tincture of opium [DTO]), phenobarbital, diazepam, and chlorpromazine. Chlorpromazine has multiple untoward side effects (including cerebellar dysfunction, decreased seizure threshold, and hematological problems) that make it an undesirable drug for use with the newborn, even though it is quite effective in managing symptoms. Diazepam has been shown in many studies to lack efficacy when used as single-drug therapy and is thus not the first drug of choice. The major drugs used to treat narcotic withdrawal are phenobarbital, which is most useful for infants with polydrug exposure (opioid and nonopioid illicit drugs), and opium, in the form of either paregoric or DTO.

Paregoric is the drug of choice for women using narcotics alone. Finnegan (1990) has shown that 93% of such infants will respond well to single-drug therapy with paregoric, which controls the CNS and gastrointestinal symptoms and allows the newborn to maintain normal sucking activity, so that feeding ability is improved. The disadvantages of paregoric are longer duration of therapy and a possible continued suppression of catecholamine synthesis. Phenobarbital controls the CNS symptoms

extremely well, but is not effective in controlling diarrhea. It has a longer duration of time between treatment and symptom control, but results in a shorter total duration of treatment. It is the drug of choice in non-narcotic-related neonatal abstinence syndrome and for narcotic withdrawal in infants exposed to multiple drugs *in utero*. Once a maintenance dose has been established for either drug, the dose is decreased by about 10% per day, so that the mean duration of therapy is about 2–3 weeks.

Behavioral abnormalities have been described for these infants in studies using the Brazelton NBAS. The problems include increased irritability, tremors, and muscle tone; infants also have decreased consolability and are less responsive to visual stimuli (Strauss et al., 1976; Ostrea et al., 1976). Treatment with DTO or phenobarbital results in improved neuromotor function, but neurobehavioral abnormalities persist (Brown et al., 1989). This suggests that the neurological and neurobehavioral dysfunction may have different etiologies.

Developmental Outcome

There is no convincing evidence that exposure to narcotics *in utero* results in abnormal cognitive or developmental delay in infants when exposed infants are compared to appropriate controls of similar SES. The major studies of children 2 years or older are reviewed in Table 9.1. Only one study showed any significant differences in global developmental cognitive function between narcotic-exposed and control infants. Hans (1989) found no overall differences in cognitive function; however, methadone-exposed children raised at the lowest SES level fared worse than control infants at the same low SES, suggesting that *in utero* methadone exposure may produce injury to which is added the insult of being raised in a disadvantaged social environment. This would provide support for the concept of early prevention and intervention strategies to improve the quality of home care for this group of infants.

Nevertheless, in one preliminary study of school performance of a small number of heroin-exposed children, a different picture emerged. As many as 40% will require special educational classes, and 25% will need to repeat one or more grades (Wilson, 1989). Behavioral dysfunction in the classroom was reported by

TABLE 9.1. Cognitive Function in Narcotic-Exposed Infants and Children

Author	Study age (years)	Methadone/ heroin-exposed group		Control group	
		Mental Development Index	(SD)	Mental Development Index	(SD)
Chasnoff et al. (1986)	2.00	98.7	(16.0)	96.2	(15.9)
Kaltenbach et al. (1979)	2.00	91.0	(8.26)	95.0	(11.93)
Hans (1989)	2.00	92.0	(13.1)	95.8	(12.4)
Wilson (1989)	3–5	90.4	(13)	89.4	(13)
Kaltenbach & Finnegan (1989a)	4.50	106.51	(12.96)	106.05	(13.10)
Strauss et al. (1979)	5.00	86.8	(13.3)	86.2	(16.3)

teachers of 75% of the school-age children. Teachers reported inattention and poor self-discipline in half the students. This preliminary observation, if replicated, suggests at least two possibilities. First, prenatal narcotic exposure may impair specific CNS-associated learning functions or autonomic-system-regulating mechanisms, with the subsequent results of impulsivity and emotional lability. Global developmental or even cognitive scores in structured assessment situations may not identify these problems. Alternatively, child rearing by addicted or recovering mothers may be more dysfunctional than that of SES-matched mothers, and this may also impair children's learning and behavior. It is also possible that both mechanisms play a role; this again illustrates the potential "double jeopardy" experienced by drug-exposed infants if intervention is not available.

ALCOHOL

Pharmacology

Alcohol is quickly absorbed from the gastrointestinal tract by passive diffusion; since it is water-soluble, it is rapidly distributed throughout the body. Alcohol is primarily metabolized to acetaldehyde in the liver. Both alcohol and acetaldehyde cross the placenta.

Newborn Outcome

A specific pattern of malformations, first described by Jones, Smith, Ulleland, and Streiss-guth (1973), is called the "fetal alcohol syndrome" (FAS). A child must have signs in each of three categories to conform to the diagnosis of FAS: (1) prenatal and/or postnatal growth retardation; (2) CNS involvement (jitteriness, developmental delay, hyperactivity); and (3) at least two of three characteristic forms of facial dysmorphology (microcephaly, short palpebral fissures, poorly developed philtrum, thin upper lip, and/or flattening of the maxillary area) (Zuckerman, Parker, Hingson, Alpert, & Mitchel, 1986).

Of 1000 alcoholic women, approximately 10 to 20 will bear children affected by FAS (Abel & Sokol, 1987). The mother of a child with FAS typically has about 14 drinks per day (Abel & Sokol, 1990). The mechanism by which alcohol adversely affects the fetus is unknown. Although excessive drinking during pregnancy is harmful, fewer than two drinks per day do not appear to have an adverse effect on birthweight, provided the that mother is well nourished and healthy (Alpert & Zuckerman, 1991). The effects of poor nutrition, cigarette smoking, and other inter-related risk factors among alcoholic women contribute additively, or perhaps synergistically, to the detriment of fetal growth and development (Zuckerman et al., 1986).

Case studies of neurobehavioral functioning of infants with FAS, and a small number of studies of nondysmorphic infants of women who consumed alcohol during pregnancy, have been reported. In one study with nonblinded examinations and no comparison group, six infants with FAS showed neurobehavioral dysfunction categorized as withdrawal from alcohol (Pierog, Chandavasu, & Wexler, 1977). It would be difficult to attribute these findings solely to alcohol, since five of the infants were small for gestational age and the sixth was premature. Urine testing to detect abuse of other drugs was conducted for one infant. In a study with a comparison group, infants of mothers who consumed an average of six drinks per day were more likely to have behaviors characterized as a withdrawal syndrome (Coles, Smith, Fernhoff, & Falek, 1984). However, these infants weighed, on average, almost 1 pound less than infants in the comparison group, indicating other possible causes of the findings. Except for marijuana, use of illegal drugs was not assessed. In studies that controlled better for confounding variables, maternal alcohol consumption was associated with poorer habituation (Streissguth, Martin, & Barr, 1983), poorer arousal (Streissguth et al., 1983; Jacobson, Fien, Jacobson, Schwartz, & Dowler, 1984), and EEG sleep disturbances (Scher, Richardson, Coble, Day, & Stuffer, 1988). Other investigators have failed to find an association between alcohol consumption and neonatal neurobehavioral dysfunction (Ernhardt et al., 1985; Fried & Makin, 1987; Tennes & Blackard, 1980). The inconsistent findings of neurobehavioral dysfunction among infants exposed prenatally to alcohol prevent firm conclusions.

Developmental Outcome

The most consistent developmental characteristics described for children with FAS are developmental delay, hyperactivity, and poor or delayed motor development. Specific signs of motor dysfunction are tremors, motor incoordination, weak grasp, difficulty with eye–hand coordination, and slow motor performance time (Aronson, Kyllerman, Sabel, Sandin, & Olegard, 1985; Kyllerman, Aronson, Sabel, Karlberg, & Sandin, 1985). One study of children of alcoholic mothers, not all of whom had FAS, showed that visual perceptual ability was even more affected than overall IQ (Aronson et al., 1985). Developmental problems among children with FAS may remain over time. Among 61 adolescents and adults suffering from FAS, the average IQ was 68 (with wide variations). Academic functioning was at the second- to fourth-grade level, and the individuals demonstrated poor judgment, distractibility, and difficulty in perceiving social cues. Unfortunately, the evaluations were not blinded; the subjects represent a convenience sample; and the family environ-

ments were remarkably unstable. These factors threaten the validity of conclusions regarding the independent prenatal effect of alcohol in contributing to these findings (Streissguth et al., 1991).

In a clinically referred sample of children with learning problems, retrospective identification of maternal use of alcohol during pregnancy was obtained among children with normal intelligence, but mild dysmorphic features of FAS and Attention Deficit Disorder (Shaywitz, Cohen, & Shaywitz, 1980). Another study showed that as children with FAS got older, their cognitive functioning and mental health status improved, although their hyperactivity did not (Steinhausen, 1984). It is likely that other prenatal factors associated with alcoholic mothers, such as poor nutrition, cigarette smoking, other drug use, and medical illnesses, contribute to these developmental problems. In the postnatal period, parenting dysfunction, whether in the form of specific interactive styles (such as overstimulation or intrusiveness) or in the form of more significant problems (such as abuse and neglect resulting in injuries or failure to thrive), contributes to these poor outcomes. Unfortunately, the roles of these other factors have not been adequately investigated in the developmental outcome of children with FAS.

The impact of low levels of alcohol consumption during pregnancy remains an important question. Only one prospective study evaluating alcohol consumption during pregnancy and developmental outcome beyond 3 years has been conducted. At 8 months of age, infants of mothers who drank two or more drinks per day had lower Bayley Scales of Infant Development scores than did infants of mothers who had no or one drink per day, when other confounding variables were controlled for (Streissguth, Barr, Martin, & Herman, 1980). However, women who consumed more than eight drinks per day were grouped with those who drank two or more. A reanalysis of these data showed that only the developmental scores of the infants exposed to higher amounts (eight or more drinks per day) were significantly lower (Abel & Sokol, 1990). In a follow-up evaluation of this sample at 4 years of age, prenatal consumption of three or more drinks per day was associated with a decrement of 5 IQ points (Streissguth, Sampson, & Barr, 1989). Although some confounding variables were controlled for, this study has been critiqued for not controlling for race, which may be a factor in susceptibility to prenatal alcohol effects (Abel & Sokol, 1990). Incomplete control for confounding variables is especially important when the magnitude of effect is relatively small. When the children in this same sample were 7 years old, a pattern of maternal binge drinking, especially prior to the recognition of pregnancy, were correlated with intelligence and achievement scores after selected confounding variables were controlled for (Sampson, Streissguth, Barr, & Bookstein, 1989). Average daily consumption during pregnancy was correlated to a lesser degree. Thus, binge drinking (which involves high-dose exposure in a short time frame) appears to be potentially more harmful than a nonbinge pattern of drinking, even though its impact in this form is small.

Another analysis by the same research group showed that prenatal alcohol consumption bore a linear relationship to fine and gross motor functioning at 4 years of age (Barr, Darby, Streissguth, & Sampson, 1990) and attentional factors (distractibility and reaction time) at 7 years of age (Streissguth et al., 1986). Children exposed to as little as one drink (0.5 ounce of absolute alcohol per day) prenatally had poor scores on numerous gross and fine motor tasks (Barr et al., 1990). No threshold effect was identified, suggesting that even small amounts of alcohol may contribute to these findings at a later age. Although these studies did control for many confounding variables, important variables such as mother–child interaction, birthweight, and gestational age were not controlled for. The magnitude of effect on both attentional and motor scores was small, and this fact, coupled with the incomplete control for confounding variables, makes impossible any firm conclusion about the impact of lower levels of drinking on subsequent developmental functioning.

MARIJUANA

Pharmacology

Marijuana use is most common among individuals in their late teens and early 20s. The range of women reported to use marijuana during pregnancy varies from 5% to 34%. The principal psychoactive chemical of marijuana is 1-delta-9-tetrahydrocannabinol (THC). Approximately one-half of the THC present in a marijuana cigarette is absorbed following inhalation (Renault, Shuster, & Heinrich, 1971). Following hydroxylation in the liver, most metabolites of THC are eliminated in the feces and urine (Abel, 1983). Because it has a strong affinity for lipids, THC is stored in fatty tissues of the body (Kruez & Axelrod, 1973). A single dose of cannabis has a tissue half-life in humans of 7 days and may take up to 30 days to be completely excreted (Nahas, 1976). For this reason, marijuana accumulates in the body during chronic use.

Like all psychoactive drugs, marijuana crosses the placenta. Placental transfer is highest early in gestation and diminishes as pregnancy progresses (Indanpaan-Heikkila, Fritchie, Englert, Ho, & McIsaac, 1969). In addition to its potential direct effect, marijuana has the indirect effect of decreasing fetal oxygenation. Inhalation of marijuana smoke by animals has been shown to produce maternal ventilation/perfusion abnormalities, with subsequent fetal hypoxia lasting approximately 60 minutes (Clapp, Wesley & Cooke, 1986). Hypoxia also results from inhalation of carbon monoxide, which is present at higher levels than that in cigarette smoke (Wu, Tashkin, & Djahed, 1988).

Newborn Outcome

Only seven studies with large enough sample sizes to control for confounding variables have investigated the effects of marijuana on human fetal growth, and their results are conflicting (Zuckerman, 1988). Only one study used both self-report and urine assay for marijuana during pregnancy. Women who had a positive urine assay for marijuana during pregnancy bore infants with lower birthweight and shorter length when confounding variables were controlled for. Had urine tests for marijuana not been performed, the significant association between prenatal marijuana use and decreased fetal growth would have been missed (Zuckerman, Frank, et al., 1989). Prenatal marijuana use was also associated with decreased arm muscle mass and decreased body nonfat mass; fat stores were normal (Frank et al., 1990). This pattern is consistent with hypoxia or other non-nutritional causes of impaired fetal growth, and is similar to that seen in infants exposed to maternal cigarette smoking.

Studies of neurobehavioral functions of newborns exposed prenatally to marijuana have been few. One research group showed that moderate and heavy maternal marijuana use during pregnancy was associated with infants who had increased tremors, decreased responsiveness to visual stimuli during sleep, and a higher-pitched cry (Fried & Makin, 1987). Another research group found no such correlation (Tennes et al., 1985). Heavy marijuana smoking during pregnancy altered the computer-measured acoustic characteristics of the newborn cry, in a manner consistent with patterns that in other studies had been related to perinatal risk factors and to later poor developmental outcome (Lester & Dreher, 1989). Another study, which assessed neonatal sleep cycling and arousal, showed that marijuana use during pregnancy was associated with a decrease in the amount of trace alternans quiet sleep (Scher et al., 1988). These findings suggest that heavy marijuana use may affect the neurophysiological integrity of the newborn.

Developmental Outcome

Only two studies have evaluated developmental and behavioral functioning among children exposed prenatally to marijuana. No independent association was seen between prenatal marijuana use and developmental scores at 12 and 24 months (Fried & Watkinson, 1988). However, when these children were 4 years old, heavy prenatal marijuana use (more than six joints per week) during pregnancy was associated with poor scores on the Memory and Verbal subscales of the McCarthy Test, compared with scores of children of mothers who did not smoke marijuana. This finding remained after confounding variables, including the home environment, were controlled for (Fried & Watkinson, 1990). Another study found no effects of IQ at age 4 (Streissguth et al., 1989). Thus, firm conclusions are difficult to draw.

CLINICAL IMPLICATIONS

Infants born to drug- and alcohol-abusing mothers are at risk for developmental and behavioral problems resulting from both prenatal exposure and dysfunctional parenting. However, no studies have consistently shown that an individual drug causes a specific developmental dysfunction.

These children need comprehensive assessment, including evaluation of their motor, cognitive, language, social, and emotional functioning. Following an assessment, a comprehensive intervention program addressing a child's developmental, nutritional, and health needs should be developed. Comprehensive services, including drug treatment, health care, and family support services, are needed for the mother. An important problem for substance-abusing women is the lack of appropriate treatment programs to meet their needs and their children's needs. Traditionally, treatment programs were designed by men to treat male alcoholics and addicts. Since these men were often alone, treatment focused only on the individuals and not on the significant others in their lives. Special issues for women have not been adequately taken into account. Mothers may be reluctant to give up their children to go into a treatment program, or they may fear losing them altogether. Programs need to be developed that treat women within the context of their families.

Consistent with recommendations of the National Commission on Infant Mortality (1988) and with our own experience, the provision of services in a model of "one-stop shopping" may be most effective, because keeping multiple appointments in different sites is difficult for all mothers (especially those using drugs). Providing key services such as pediatric health care, drug treatment, child development, and family planning in one location with one appointment system and the same staff promotes compliance with these services and ultimate effectiveness. Addiction specialists and infant mental health specialists need to work closely together to help addicted parents and their children. The infant mental health specialists can help the addiction specialists understand the mothers' interest in their children, and thus provide a special window of opportunity to reach the mothers. Addiction treatment programs need to learn how to balance addiction treatment with the needs of children and the mothers' need to be good parents. Addiction specialists can help infant mental health professionals understand enabling behavior and hold mothers to an appropriate level of accountability.

ACKNOWLEDGMENTS

This work was supported by grants from the Harris Foundation, Bureau of Health Care Delivery and Assistance, Maternal and Child Health Branch (No.

MCJ 009094), and the National Institute for Drug Abuse (Nos. RO1-DA 06532-01 and RO1-DA 04099). We thank Jeanne McCarthy and Nancy Coyne for their help in preparing the manuscript.

REFERENCES

Abel, E. L. (1983). *Marijuana, tobacco, alcohol and reproduction*. Boca Raton, FL: CRC Press.

Abel, E. L., & Sokol, R. J. (1987). Incidence of fetal alcohol syndrome and ecomonic impact of FAS-related anomalies. *Alcohol and Drug Dependence, 19*, 51–70.

Abel, E. L., & Sokol, R. J. (1990). Is occasional light drinking during pregnancy harmful? In R. C. Engs (Ed.), *Controversy in the addiction field* (pp. 158–163). Dubuque, IA: Kendall-Hunt.

Alpert, J., & Zuckerman, B. (1991). Alcohol use during pregnancy: what is the risk? *Pediatrics in Review, 12*, 375–379.

Amaro, H., Fried, L. E., Cabral, H., & Zuckerman, B. (1990). Violence during pregnancy and substance use. *American Journal of Public Health, 80*, 575–579.

Anastasiow, N. J. (1990). Implications of the neurological model for early intervention. In S. J. Meisels & J. P. Shonkoff (Eds.), *Handbook of early childhood intervention* (pp. 196–216). New York: Cambridge University Press.

Aronson, M., Kyllerman, M., Sabel, K. G., Sandin, B., & Olegard, R. (1985). Children of alcoholic mothers: Developmental, perceptual and behavioral characteristics as compared to matched controls. *Acta Paediatrica Scandinavica, 74*, 27–35.

Barr, H. M., Darby, B. L., Streissguth, A. P., & Sampson, P. D. (1990). Prenatal exposure to alcohol, caffeine, tobacco, and aspirin: Effects on fine and gross motor performance in 4-year-old children. *Developmental Psychology, 26*, 339–348.

Bays, J. (1990). Substance abuse and child abuse: Impact of addiction on the child. *Pediatric Clinics of North America, 37*, 881–904.

Beckwith, K., & Parmalee, A. (1986). EEG patterns in preterm infants, home environment, and later I.Q. *Child Development, 57*, 777–789.

Bernstein, V. J., Jeremy, R. J., & Marcus, J. (1986). Mother–infant interaction in multiproblem families: Finding those at risk. *Journal of the American Academy of Child Psychiatry, 5*, 631–640.

Black, R., & Mayer, J. (1980). Parents with special problems: Alcoholism and opiate addiction. *Child Abuse and Neglect, 4*, 45–51.

Brown, E. R., Cole, J., Parker, S., Coulter, D., Corwin, M., & Abozgyne, K. (1989). Treatment of newborn narcotic abstinence fails to normalize infant behavior. *Pediatric Research, 25*, 12A.

Chasnoff, I. J., Burns, K. A., Burns, W. J., & Schnoll, S. H. (1986). Prenatal drug exposure: Effects on neonatal and infant growth and development. *Neurobehavioral Toxicology and Teratology, 8*, 357–362.

Chasnoff, I. J., Burns, W. J., Schnoll, S. H., & Burns, K. A. (1985). cocaine use in pregnancy. *New England Journal of Medicine, 313*, 666–669.

Chasnoff, I. J., Bussey, M. E., Savich, R., & Stack, C. (1986). Perinatal cerebral infarction and maternal cocaine use. *Journal of Pediatrics, 108*, 456–459.

Chasnoff, I. J., Griffith, D. R. Freier, C., Murray, J. (1992). Cocaine/polydrug use and pregnancy: Two year follow-up. *Pediatrics, 89*, 284–289.

Chasnoff, I. J., Griffith, D. R., MacGregor, S., Dirkes, K., & Burns, K.A. (1989). Temporal patterns of cocaine use in pregnancy. *Journal of the American Medical Association, 261*, 1741–44.

Chavez, G. F., Mulinare, J., & Cordero, J. F. (1989). Maternal cocaine use during early pregnancy as a risk factor for congenital urogenital anomalies. *Journal of the American Medical Association, 262*, 795–798.

Clapp, J., Wesley, M., & Cooke, R. (1986). The effects of marijuana smoke on gas exchange in bovine pregnancy. *Alcohol and Drug Research, 7*, 85.

Coles, C. D., Smith, I. E., Fernhoff, P. M., & Falek, A. (1984). Neonatal ethanol withdrawal: Characteristics in clinically normal, nondysmorphic neonates. *Journal of Pediatrics, 105*, 445–451.

Connaughton, J. F., Reeser, D., Shut, J., & Finnegan, L. P. (1977). Perinatal addiction: Outcome and management. *American Journal of Obstetrics and Gynecology, 129*, 679–686.

De Quincey, T. (1822). *Confessions of an English opium-eater*. London.

Dixon, S. D., & Bejar, R. (1989). Echoncephalographic findings in neonates associated with maternal cocaine and methamphetamine use: Incidence and clinical correlates. *Journal of Pediatrics, 115*, 77–79.

Doberczak, T. M., Kandall, S. A., & Wiletts, I. (1991). Neonatal opiate abstinence syndrome in term and preterm infants. *Journal of Pediatrics, 118*, 933–937.

Doberczak, T. M., Shanzer, S., Senie, R. T., & Kandall, S. A. (1988). Neonatal neurologic and electroencephalographic effects of intrauterine cocaine exposure. *Journal of Pediatrics, 113*, 354–358.

Eisen, L. N., Field, T. M., Bandstra, E. S., Roberts, J. P., Morrow, C., & Larson, S. K. (1991). Perinatal cocaine effects on neonatal stress behavior and performance on the Brazelton Scale. *Pediatrics, 88*, 477–480.

Ernhardt, C. B., Wolf, A. W., Linn, P. C., Sokol, R. J., Kennard, M. J., & Filipovich, M. A. (1985). Alcohol-related birth defects: Syndromal anomalies, intrauterine growth retardation and neonatal behavioral assessment. *Alcoholism: Clinical and Experimental Research, 9*, 447–453.

Fiks, K., Johnson, H., & Rosen, T. (1985). Methadone-maintained mothers: Three year follow-up of parental functioning. *International Journal of the Addictions, 20*, 651–660.

Finnegan, L. P. (1990). Neonatal abstinence. In N. M. Nelson (Ed.), *Current therapy in neonatal–perinatal medicine* (Vol. 2, pp. 314–320). Philadelphia: B.C. Decker.

Frank, D. A., Bauchner, H., Parker, S., Huber, A., Kyei-Aboagye, K., Cabral, H., & Zuckerman, B. (1990). Neonatal body proportionality and body composition after in utero exposure to cocaine and marijuana. *Journal of Pediatrics, 117*, 622–626.

Frank, D. A., McCarten, K., Cabral, H., Levenson, S., & Zuckerman, B. (1992). Cranial ultrasound in term newborns: Failure to replicate excess abnormalities in cocaine exposed newborns. *Pediatric Research, 31*, 247A.

Frank, D. A., Zuckerman, B., Reece, H., Amaro, H., Hingson, R., Fried, L., Cabral, H., Levenson, S., Kayne, H., Vinci, R., Bauchner, H., & Parker, S. (1988). Cocaine use during pregnancy: Prevalence and correlates. *Pediatrics, 82,* 888–895.

Fried, P. A., & Makin, J. E. (1987). Neonatal behavioral correlates of prenatal exposure to marijuana, cigarettes, and alcohol in a low risk population. *Neurobehavioral Toxicology and Teratology, 9,* 1–7.

Fried, P. A., & Watkinson, B. (1988). 12- and 24-month neurobehavioral follow-up of children prenatally exposed to marijuana, cigarettes and alcohol. *Neurobehavioral Toxicology and Teratology, 10,* 305–313.

Fried, P. A., & Watkinson, B. (1990). 36- and 48-month neurobehavioral follow-up of children prenatally exposed to marijuana, cigarettes, and alcohol. *Journal of Developmental and Behavioral Pediatrics, 11,* 49–58.

Fulroth, R., Phillips, B., & Durand, D. J. (1989). Perinatal outcome of infants exposed to cocaine and/or heroin in utero. *American Journal of Diseases of Children, 143,* 905–910.

Gawin, F. H., & Kleber, H. D. (1984). Cocaine abuse treatment. *Archives of General Psychiatry, 41,* 903–909.

Geary, N. (1987). Cocaine animal research studies. In H. I. Spitz & J. S. Rosecan (Eds.), *Cocaine abuse: New directions in treatment and research* (pp. 19–47). New York: Brunner/Mazel.

Green, M., Silverman, I., Suffet, F., Taleporos, E., & Turkel, W. V. (1979). Outcomes of pregnancy for addicts receiving comprehensive care. *American Journal of Drug and Alcohol Abuse, 6,* 413–429.

Hadeed, A. J., & Siegel, S. R. (1989). Maternal cocaine use during pregnancy: Effect on the newborn infant. *Pediatrics, 84,* 205–210.

Hammer, R. P., Ricalde, A. A., & Seatriz, J. V. (1989). Effects of opiates on brain development. *Neurotoxicology, 10,* 475–484.

Hans, S. L. (1989). Developmental consequences of prenatal exposure to methadone. *Annals of the New York Academy of Sciences, 562,* 195–207.

Herzlinger, R. A., Kandall, S. R., & Vaughan, H. G. (1977). Neonatal seizures associated with narcotic withdrawal. *Journal of Pediatrics, 91,* 638–641.

Hoyme, H. E., Jones, K. L., Dixon, S. D., Jewett, T., Hanson, J. W., Robinson, K. L., Msall, M. E., & Allanson, J. E. (1990). Prenatal cocaine exposure and fetal vascular disruption. *Pediatrics, 85,* 743–747.

Hoyme, H. E., Jones, K. L., Van Allen, M. I., Saunders, B. J., & Benirschke, K. (1982). Vascular pathogenesis of transverse limb reduction defects. *Journal of Pediatrics, 101,* 839–844.

Hunt, J. V., Cooper, B. A. B., & Tooley, W. H. (1988). Very low birth weight infants at 8 and 11 years of age: Role of neonatal illness and family status. *Pediatrics, 82,* 596–603.

Hutchings, D. E. (1982). Methadone and heroin during pregnancy: A review of behavioral effects in human and animal offspring. *Neurobehavioral Toxicology and Teratology, 4,* 429–434.

Indanpaan-Heikkila, J., Fritchie, G., Englert, L., Ho, B. T., & McIsaac, W. M. (1969). Placental transfer of tritiated I tetrahydrocannabinol. *New England Journal of Medicine, 281,* 330–335.

Jacobson, S. W., Fien, G. G., Jacobson, J. L., Schwartz, P. M., & Dowler, J. K. (1984). Neonatal correlates of prenatal exposure to smoking, caffeine, and alcohol. *Infant Behavior and Development, 7,* 253–265.

Jacobvitz, D., & Sroufe, L. A. (1987). The early caregiver–child relationship and attention–deficit disorder with hyperactivity in kindergarten: A prospective study. *Child Development, 58,* 1488–1495.

Jones, K. L., Smith, D. W., Ulleland, C. N., & Streissguth, A. P. (1973). Pattern of malformation in offspring of chronic alcoholic women. *Lancet, i,* 1267–1271.

Kaltenbach, K. A., & Finnegan, L. P. (1989a). Children exposed to methadone in utero: Assesment of developmental and cognitive ability. *Annals of the New York Academy of Sciences, 562,* 360–362.

Kaltenbach, K. A., & Finnegan, L. P. (1989b). Prenatal narcotic exposure: Perinatal and developmental effects. *Neurotoxicology, 10,* 567–604.

Kaltenbach, K. A., Graziani, L. & Finnegan, L. P. (1979). Methadone exposure in utero: Developmental status at one and two years of age. *Pharmacology, Biochemistry and Behavior, 11*(Suppl.), 15–17.

Kandall, S. R., Albin, S., Gartner, L. M., Lee, K. S., Eidelman, A., & Lowinson, J. (1977). The narcotic dependent mother: Fetal and neonatal consequences. *Early Human Development, 1–2,* 159–166.

Kandall, S. R., Albin, S., Lowinson, J., Berle, B., Eidelman, A. I., & Gartner, L. M. (1976). Differential effects of maternal heroin and methadone use on birthweight. *Pediatrics, 58,* 681–685.

Kreek, M. J. (1979). Methadone disposition during the perinatal period in humans. *Pharmacology, Biochemistry and Behavior, 11,* 7–13.

Kron, R. E. M., Litt, M., & Phoenix, M. D. (1976). Neonatal narcotic abstinence: Effects of pharmacotherapeutic agents and maternal drug usage on nutritive sucking behavior. *Journal of Pediatrics, 88,* 637–641.

Kruez, D., & Axelrod, J. (1973). Delta-9-tetrahydrocannabinol: Localization in body fat. *Science, 179,* 391–392.

Kyllerman, M., Aronson, M., Sabel, K. G., Karlberg, E., & Sandin, B. (1985). Children of alcoholic mothers: Growth and motor performance compared to matched controls. *Acta Paediatrica Scandinavica, 74,* 20–26.

Lauder, J. M. (1988). Neurotransmitters as morphogens. *Progress in Brain Research, 73,* 365.

Lester, B. M., Corwin, M. J., Sepkoski, C., Seifer, R., Peucker, M., McLaughlin, S., & Golub, H. (1991). Neurobehavioral syndromes in cocaine exposed newborn infants. *Child Development, 62,* 694–705.

Lester, B. M., & Dreher, M. (1989). Effects of marijuana use during pregnancy on newborn cry. *Child Development, 60,* 765–771.

Lifschitz, M. H., Wilson, G. S., Smith, E. O. & Desmond, M. M. (1985). Factors affecting head growth and intellectual function in children of drug addicts. *Pediatrics, 75,* 269–274.

Madden, J. D. (1978). Problems pertaining to the care of newborn infants of drug addicted mothers. *Journal of Reproductive Medicine, 20,* 303–310.

Marcus, J., Hans, S. L., & Jeremy, R. J. (1982). Differential motor and state functioning in newborns of women on methadone. *Neurobehavioral Toxicology and Teratology, 4,* 459–462.

McGinty, J. F., & Ford, D. H. (1980). Effects of prenatal methadone on rat brain catecholamines. *Developmental Neuroscience, 3,* 224–234.

Miller, J. C., & Friedhoff, A. J. (1988). Prenatal neurotransmitter programming of postnatal receptor function. *Progress in Brain Research, 73,* 509.

Mirochnick, M., Meyer, J., Cole, J., Herren, T., & Zuckerman, B. (1991). Circulating catecholamine in cocaine-exposed neonates: A pilot study. *Pediatrics.*

Naeye, R. L., Blanc, W., Leblanc, W., & Khatamee, M. A. (1973). Fetal complications of maternal heroin addiction: Abnormal growth, infections and episodes of stress. *Journal of Pediatrics, 83,* 1055–1060.

Nahas, G. (1976). *Marijuana: Chemistry, biochemistry and cellular effects.* New York: Springer-Verlag.

National Commission to Prevent Infant Mortality. (1988). *Infant mortality: Caring for our future.* Washington, DC: Author.

Neuspiel, D. R., Hamel, E., Hochberg, E., Greene, J., & Campbell, D. (1991). Maternal cocaine use and infant behavior. *Neurobehavioral Toxicology and Teratology, 13,* 229–233.

Oro, A. & Dixon, S. (1987). Perinatal cocaine and methamphetamine exposure: Maternal and neonatal correlates. *Journal of Pediatrics, 111,* 571–578.

Ostrea, E. M., & Chavez, C. J. (1979). Perinatal problems (excluding neonatal withdrawal) in maternal drug addictions: A study of 830 cases. *Journal of Pediatrics, 94,* 292–296.

Ostrea, E. M., Chavez, C. J., & Strauss, M. E. (1976). A study of factors that influence the severity of neonatal narcotic withdrawal. *Journal of Pediatrics, 88,* 642–645.

Pierog, S., Chandavasu, S., & Wexler, I. (1977). Withdrawal symptoms in infants with the fetal alcohol syndrome. *Journal of Pediatrics, 90,* 630–633.

Renault, P., Shuster, C., & Heinrich, R. (1971). Marijuana: Standardized smoke administration and dose–effect curves on heart rate in humans. *Science, 174,* 589–592.

Rodning, C., Beckwith, L., & Howard, J. (1990). Characteristics of attachment organization and play organization in prenatally drug-exposed toddlers. *Development and Psychopathology, 1,* 277–289.

Rosenman, S. J., & Smith, C. B. (1972). ¹⁴C-Catecholamine synthesis in mouse brain during morphine withdrawal. *Nature, 240,* 153–155.

Ruth, C. E. (1888). The effect of opium on the unborn child. *Journal of the American Medical Association, 10,* 292–295.

Ryan, L., Ehrlich, S., & Finnegan, L. (1987). Cocaine abuse in pregnancy: Effects on the fetus and newborn. *Neurobehavioral Toxicology and Teratology, 9,* 295–299.

Sakellaridis, N., Mangoura, D., & Veradakis, A. (1986). Effects of opiates on the growth of neuron-enriched cultures from chick embryonic brain. *International Journal of Developmental Neuroscience, 4,* 293–302.

Sampson, P. D., Streissguth, A. P., Barr, H. M., & Bookstein, F. L. (1989). Neurobehavioral effects of prenatal alcohol: Part II. Partial least squares analysis. *Neurobehavioral Toxicology and Teratology, 11,* 477–491.

Scher, M. S., Richardson, G. A., Coble, P. A., Day, N. L., & Stuffer, D. S. (1988). The effects of prenatal alcohol and marijuana exposure: Disturbances in neonatal sleepcycling and arousal. *Pediatric Research, 24,* 101–105.

Shaywitz, S. E., Cohen, D. J., & Shaywitz, B. (1980). Behavior and learning difficulties in children of normal intelligence born to alcoholic mothers. *Journal of Pediatrics, 96,* 978–982.

Smith, A. A., Hui, F. W., & Crofford, H. J. (1977). Inhibition of growth in young mice treated with d,l-methadone. *European Journal of Pharmacology, 43,* 307–309.

Spitz, H. I., & Rosecan, J. S. (Eds.). (1987). *Cocaine abuse: New directions in treatment and research.* New York: Brunner/Mazel.

Steinhausen, H. C. (1984). Psychopathology in the offspring of alcoholic parents. *Journal of the American Academy of Child Psychiatry, 23,* 465–471.

Stimmel, B., & Adamson, K. (1976). Narcotic dependency in pregnancy: Methadone maintenance compared to use of street drugs. *Journal of the American Medical Association, 235,* 1121–1125.

Strauss, M. E., Lessen-Firestone, J. K., Chavez, C. J., & Stryker, J. C. (1979). Children of methadone-treated women at five years of age. *Pharmacology, Biochemistry and Behavior, 11*(Suppl.), 3–6.

Strauss, M. E., Starr, R. H., Ostrea, E. M., Chavez, C. J., & Stryker, J. C. (1976). Behavioral concomitants of prenatal addiction to narcotics. *Journal of Pediatrics, 89,* 842–846.

Streissguth, A. P., Aase, J. M., Clarren, S. K., Randel, S. P., LaRue, R. A., & Smith, D. F. (1991). Fetal alcohol syndrome in adolescents and adults. *Journal of the American Medical Association, 265,* 1961–1967.

Streissguth, A. P., Barr, H. M., Martin, D. C., Herman C. S. (1980). Effects of maternal alcohol, nicotine and caffeine use during pregnancy on infant mental and motor development at eight months. *Alcoholism (NY), 4,* 152–164.

Streissguth, A. P., Barr, H. M., Sampson, P. D., Parrish-Johnson, J. C., Kirchner, G. L., & Martin, D. C. (1986). Attention, distraction and reaction time at age 7 years and prenatal alcohol exposure. *Neurobehavioral Toxicology and Teratology, 8,* 717–725.

Streissguth, A. P., Martin, D. C., & Barr, H. M. (1983). Maternal alcohol use and neonatal habituation assessed with the Brazelton Scale. *Child Development, 54,* 1109–1118.

Streissguth, A. P., Sampson, P. D., & Barr, H. M. (1989). IQ at age 4 in relation to maternal alcohol use and smoking during pregnancy. *Developmental Psychology, 25,* 3–11.

Tennes, K., Avitable, N., Blackard, C., Boyles, C., Hassoun, B., Holmes, L., & Kreye, M. (1985). Marijuana: Prenatal and postnatal exposure in the human infant. In T. M. Pinkert (Ed.), *Current research on the Consequences of maternal drug abuse* (NIDA Research Monograph No. 59, pp. 48–60). Rockville, MD: National Institute on Drug Abuse.

Tennes, K., & Blackard, C. (1980). Maternal alcohol consumption, birth weight, and minor physical anomalies. *American Journal of Obstetrics and Gynecology, 138,* 774–780.

U.S. General Accounting Office. (1990, June 28). *Drug-exposed infants: A generation at risk* (Report to the Chairman, Committee on Finance, U.S. Senate). Washington, DC: U.S. Government Printing Office.

Werner, E. (1989). Children of the Garden Island. *Scientific American,* 106–111.

Wilson, G. S. (1989). Clinical studies of infants and children exposed prenatally to heroin. *Annals of the New York Academy of Sciences, 562,* 183–194.

Wilson, G. S., Desmond, M. M., & Wait, R. B. (1981). Follow up of methadone-treated and untreated narcotic-dependent women and their infants: Health, developmental, and social implications. *Journal of Pediatrics, 98,* 716–722.

Woods, J. R., Jr., Plessinger, M. A., & Clark, K. E. (1987).

Effect of cocaine on uterine blood flow and fetal oxygenation. *Journal of the American Medical Association, 257,* 957–961.

Wu, T., Tashkin, D., & Djahed, B. (1988). Pulmonary hazards of smoking marijuana as compared to tobacco. *New England Journal of Medicine, 318,* 347.

Zagon, I. S., & McLaughlin, P. J. (1984). Naltrexone regulates body and brain development in rats: A role for endogenous opioids in growth. *Life Science, 35,* 2057–2064.

Zuckerman, B. (1988). Marijuana and cigarette smoking during pregnancy: Neonatal effects. In I. Chasnoff (Ed.), *Drugs, alcohol, pregnancy and parenting* (p. 73–89). Dordrecht, The Netherlands: Kluwer.

Zuckerman, B., Amaro, H., Bauchner, H., & Cabral, H. (1989). Depressive symptoms during pregnancy: Relationship to poor health behavior. *American Journal of Obstetrics and Gynecology, 160,* 1107–1111.

Zuckerman, B., Bauchner, H., Paker, S., Cabral H. (1990). Maternal depressive symptoms during pregnancy and newborn irritability. *Journal of Developmental and Behavioral Pediatrics, 11,* 190–194.

Zuckerman, B., & Beardslee, W. (1987). Maternal depression: An issue for pediatricians. *Pediatrics, 79,* 110–117.

Zuckerman, B., & Bresnahan, K. (1991). Developmental and behavioral consequences of prenatal drug and alcohol exposure. *Pediatric Clinics of North America, 83,* 1387–1407.

Zuckerman, B., Frank, D., Hingson R., Amaro, H., Levenson, S. M., Kayne, H., Parker, S., Vinci, R., Aboagye, K., Fried, L. E., Cabral, H., Timperi, R., & Bauchner, H. (1989). Effects of maternal marijuana and cocaine use on fetal growth. *New England Journal of Medicine, 320,* 762–768.

Zuckerman, B., Parker, S. J., Hingson, R., Alpert, J. J., & Mitchel, J. (1986). Maternal psychoactive substance use and its effect on the neonate. In A. Milunsky, E. A. Friedman, & L. Gluck (Eds.), *Maternal psychoactive substance use and its effect on the neonate* (pp. 125–170). New York: Plenum Press.

10

Maltreatment and Infant Development

PATRICIA J. MRAZEK

Child maltreatment, in all its forms, is a dramatic contradiction to the usual care, nurturing, and love that parents give their children (Mrazek & Mrazek, 1985). Maltreatment of children under 3 years of age is a major social problem in the United States and throughout the world. Despite the current professional and public focus on sexual abuse of older children and adolescents, abuse and neglect of infants and toddlers are the most serious forms of maltreatment because they frequently result in death or permanent injury. This chapter describes the nature and scope of the problem, the risk and protective factors associated with maltreatment at this age, immediate and long-term sequelae, the status of assessment of risk factors, and primary preventive programs.

NATURE AND SCOPE OF THE PROBLEM

"Child maltreatment" is not easily defined. Generally, it refers to the child caretaking practices of certain individuals that are seen as unacceptable by the majority of a population at a given period in history and in a particular culture. Usually the term is directed at uncaring parents and parents in absentia, but it can also be applied to a society as a whole. Although this chapter focuses on child maltreatment by individuals, it would be an oversight not to put such maltreatment into the context of our society's current attitude toward children.

The status of U.S. children has clearly deteriorated over the last 20 years (Fuchs & Reklis, 1992). Infant mortality, fetal addiction, poor health care, poverty, inadequate housing, violent neighborhoods, homelessness, and inadequate preparation for learning are but a short list of the problems that confront a surprisingly large number of young children in the United States.

In 1989, the Annie E. Casey Foundation and the Center for the Study of Social Policy launched Kids Count, a project that profiles the condition of America's children at the national, state, and community levels. Their 1992 report, the *Kids Count Data Book*, profiles a nation failing to keep pace with the needs of its children. The national trends over the 1980s show that the United States made no progress or lost former gains in seven of nine measures of well-being: percentage of low-birthweight babies (3% worse); teen violent death rate, ages 15–19 (11% worse); percentage of all births to single teens (14% worse); juvenile custody rate, ages 10–15 (10% worse); percentage graduating from high school (no change); percentage of children in poverty (22% worse); and percentage of children in single-parent families (13% worse). Although two measures of well-being did improve—the infant mortality rate by 22%, and the child death rate for ages 1–14 by 18%—that progress was not shared equally by all children. African-American children were at greatest risk for infant mortality and teen death.

Child advocacy organizations are harsh in their criticism of public policies that have allowed such conditions not only to exist but to increase. Inadequate funding of preventive services such as subsidized medical care, Aid to Families with Dependent Children, Head Start, food programs, and subsidized day care have contributed to the problem. There has also been considerable neglect of the emotional needs of many young children and their families in the United States. Many parents struggle with the problems emanating from substance abuse (including alcoholism) and from other mental disorders. Mothers at home full-time with young children are particularly at risk for depression. Services to such families are often unavailable, or if available are not evaluated as to their effectiveness. The mental health needs of very young children are frequently overlooked by those in the medical care system, which often provides the only care available to children at such an early age.

Set against this background of the societal neglect of children, child maltreatment by family members and individual caretakers may seem to pale in its importance. Indeed, this is the view of some who favor broad social reforms as the remedy for the rising number of child abuse cases. This chapter has a different perspective, which is based much more in a clinical tradition of viewing maltreatment in multiple contextual layers. The premise here is that every maltreated child must be seen as a failure of the expected, "good enough" parenting within an individual family, as well as a failure of the society to provide an environment that will lessen risk and provide built-in safety nets when the child's primary family fails in its parenting functions.

The National Center on Child Abuse and Neglect recently released incidence data for 1990 (U.S. Department of Health and Human Services [DHHS], 1992). During that year, 160,392 children under the age of 3 were reported to child protective services or social service agencies in the United States as suspected child maltreatment cases, and these cases were investigated and substantiated. Of all child victims through age 18 more children under 1 year of age were maltreated than at any other year; there were 55,241 of these children. Of all child abuse victims, 6.5% were under 1 year of age; 19% were under 3 years of age.

Approximately 1200 children died from abuse and neglect in 1990. Even though the government has not as yet reported this figure by age groups, it is widely recognized that a majority of maltreatment deaths occur among children under 3 years of age. In children younger than 1 year of age, physical abuse is the leading cause of death, and in children between the ages of 1 and 4 years, homicide accounts for 10% of all deaths (Waller, Baker, & Szocka, 1989).

TYPES OF MALTREATMENT

The spectrum of child maltreatment includes physical abuse, neglect, sexual abuse, Munchausen syndrome by proxy, fetal abuse, and emotional abuse. Neglect is the most frequent form of maltreatment experienced by children (45%), with physical abuse as the second (25%) and sexual abuse as the third (16%) (U.S. DHHS, 1992). Although these are discussed separately for heuristic purposes, there is a growing recognition that maltreatment generally occurs in mixed forms. In addition to the types of maltreatment experienced by a child, effects differ depending on a child's age and developmental stage.

Physical Abuse

Of child victims of physical abuse, one-third are estimated to be under 1 year of age and another one-third from 1 to 6 years of age. (Schmitt & Krugman, 1992). Infants with intractable crying are especially vulnerable to head injuries. Negativism, wetting, soiling, and spilling may make a slightly older infant more vulnerable.

The external signs of physical abuse are bruises, lacerations, scars, and burns (from hot water or cigarettes). Subdural hematomas are the most dangerous inflicted injury; more than 95% of serious intracranial injuries during the first year of life are the result of abuse (Schmitt & Krugman, 1992). These cases result from violent shakings or slamming the head against a hard object. Intra-abdominal injuries, especially a ruptured liver or spleen, are the second most common cause of death in battered children (Schmitt & Krugman, 1992). Many young abused children receive multiple bone fractures that go unrecognized until a thorough roentgenological bone survey is made. Sixty percent of femur fractures in infants younger than 1 year of age, but only 20% in 1- and 2-year olds, are attributable to abuse (Thomas, Rosenfield, Leventhal, & Markowitz, 1991).

Sexual Abuse

Approximately one-third of all sexual abuse cases involve children under 6 years of age (Schmitt & Krugman, 1992). Even children under 3 can be victims. Sexual abuse at this age typically involves genital fondling and oral intercourse. These cases are often difficult to evaluate and diagnose because the children cannot communicate clearly what has happened. Some children present with idiosyncratic trauma to the genitals, such as a string tied around a boy's penis to prevent urination. Such cases may be better conceptualized as physical abuse to the genitals than as sexual abuse.

Failure to Thrive

Children under the age of 2 are particularly vulnerable to a form of maltreatment known as "failure to thrive." In approximately 70% of cases of failure to thrive, no organic contributors can be identified; 50% of these are cases of neglect, while the other 20% are accidental (e.g., errors in formula preparation) (Schmitt & Krugman, 1992). The main cause of failure to thrive in infants is that the children are not fed enough; hence, with hospitalization, such children often begin gaining weight. The parents of such children may be so psychologically unavailable that they are unaware of the children's condition. As soon as children are able to walk, and especially after age 2, the situation improves because the children can obtain food for themselves. But when such children are younger and the failure to thrive remains undetected, a small percentage of them do die from starvation. Schmitt and Krugman (1992) report that 5–10% of children with failure to thrive are also physically abused. In those who are detected, the weight loss and understature from malnutrition are reversible; however, if severe malnutrition has persisted beyond 6 months of age, normal head circumference and brain growth may not be achieved (Schmitt & Krugman, 1992). (See Benoit, Chapter 21, this volume, for a more detailed review of failure to thrive.)

Munchausen Syndrome by Proxy

In cases of Munchausen syndrome by proxy, a parent, usually the mother, fabricates symptoms

for the child and may actually cause an illness that results in unnecessary medical evaluation and treatment. Methods of inducement are often bizarre, such as coating a newborn with povidone–iodine to mimic jaundice, and sometimes dangerous, such as administering ipecac to induce vomiting (Mrazek, 1990). Indeed, an unusually high rate of death has been reported among victims and their siblings (Rosenberg, 1987).

Drowning and Near-Drowning

Child maltreatment by drowning or near-drowning is an underdiagnosed and under-reported problem (Griest & Zumwalt, 1989). The highest incidence of drownings (in those younger than 25 years) occurs in children aged 1 to 4 years, and the bathtub is the site in about 20% of cases. Tub drownings most often occur to 10- to 12-month-olds who are the youngest or next-to-youngest members of large families. Swimming pools are the sites of the highest death rates for children 1 to 3 years old (Conn, 1992). Most of these drownings and the similar near-drownings occur when the children are unsupervised. The Centers for Disease Control and Prevention refer to such incidents as "nonintentional injuries/deaths" (Brown, Foege, Bender & Axnick, 1990) rather than as accidents, but they may also constitute neglect.

Fetal Abuse

Fetal abuse or neglect occurs when a pregnant women knowingly fails to provide a "good enough" environment for her developing fetal child. The most dramatic example is substance abuse by a woman during pregnancy. Maternal addiction to heroine, methadone, phenobarbitals, cocaine, and alcohol can result in stillbirths, low birth rate, congenital anomalies, physiological addiction, and severe developmental and mental deficiencies (Behrman, 1992).

Other maternal behaviors, although markedly less serious than substance abuse/addiction, can also be considered within the maltreatment spectrum: nicotine addiction, failure to obtain adequate prenatal care, refusal to gain weight, and exposure to high-risk situations such as spouse abuse (Condon, 1986). All of these can have detrimental effects on the developing fetus.

Complex legal and ethical questions are involved in determining what constitutes fetal abuse.

Co-Occurring Forms of Maltreatment

Even though child maltreatment is a spectrum of different kinds of abusive and neglectful behaviors, rarely does a single incident or type occur in isolation. Just as having one psychiatric disorder places an individual at high risk of having a second or even a third diagnosis, having one type of maltreatment (particularly under the age of 3) puts the child at risk for other forms of maltreatment, co-occurring or occurring in succession throughout his or her childhood.

Increasingly, data are reported documenting multiple forms of abuse in the same individual. For example, Westen, Ludolph, Misle, Ruffins, and Block (1990) found that 80% of girls who were sexually assaulted by their fathers were also physically abused by them. Of girls abused by their fathers, 70% were also abused by someone else. A history of physical and sexual abuse similarly predicted a history of neglect. Although these data concern adolescents, there is some evidence that multiple forms of abuse also occur under the age of 3 (Pianta, Egeland, & Erickson, 1989).

Moreover, the recurrence of maltreatment after intervention is alarmingly frequent. Cohn (1979) found that abuse recurred in one-third of families under treatment. When the initial abuse had been serious, over one-half of the parents abused their child again within 1 year.

RISK FACTORS

Considerable attention and effort have been devoted to the identification of risk factors for child maltreatment in infancy and young childhood. Unfortunately, many research efforts have been seriously flawed. Most maltreatment studies have not differentiated between correlated and causal risk factors, for instance. There has been a lack of appreciation that correlation does not necessarily imply etiology and that one way of determining whether correlated risk factors are causal is with a methodologically sound preventive intervention study.

The following categorization, based in part on work by Holden, Willis, and Corcoran (1992),

identifies risk factors along with the levels of empirical evidence for each factor. There are a few risk factors associated with child maltreatment that are supported by strong evidence. These factors are highly correlated with child maltreatment:

• *Negative maternal attitude toward the pregnancy* (either unwanted or unplanned) (Altemeir, O'Conner, Vietze, Sandler, & Sherrod, 1982). These attitudes may be more predictive of neglect than of abuse (Zuravin, 1987).

• *High levels of perceived social stress.* Perceived stress is highly individualized, but frequent stressors include poor health, inadequate finances, and unhappy life events (which may include large family size and close spacing of children) Altemeier et al, 1982; Friedrich & Wheeler, 1982.

• *Low socioeconomic status.* This factor is implicated as increasing the risk for a variety of adverse experiences for young children, including maltreatment. (See Halpern, Chapter 5, this volume, for a full discussion of poverty and infant development.)

The following risk factors have some empirical evidence to support them, but further investigation is required before they can be seen as clearly related to maltreatment:

• *Lack of financial resources.*

• *Low intelligence* (Hansen, Pallotta, Tishelman, Conaway, & MacMillan, 1989).

• *Parent's criminal record* (Caplan, Watters, White, Parry, & Bates, 1984)

• *Loss of previous child* (Altemeier et al. 1982).

• *History of child maltreatment.* The theory of the intergenerational transmission of child abuse has long been accepted, although empirical support supplies important caveats (Hunter, Kilstrom, Kraybill, & Loda, 1978; Egeland, Jacobvitz, & Papatola, 1987). Kaufman and Zigler (1987) conservatively estimate a rate of intergenerational transmission to be about 30%, or roughly five times the rate in the population at large. From the perspective of the internal organization of experience, Zeanah and Zeanah (1989) have suggested that there is better evidence for intergenerational transmission of attachment relationship patterns than of abuse or neglect per se. Reviewing preliminary findings of concordance between attachment classifications in parents and infants, they speculate about how infants may internalize adverse relationship experiences and then re-enact them in subsequent caregiving relationships. They suggest that whether maltreatment occurs in these relationships may depend more on current contextual factors.

• *Negative maternal traits.* Examples include poor self-esteem, anger/aggression, impulsivity, emotional difficulties, lack of knowledge of parenting, and psychiatric difficulties.

• *Absence of social support and social isolation.* These are more strongly associated with neglect than with abuse (Egeland & Brunnewell, 1979; Seagull, 1987).

• *Substance abuse.* Substance abuse, especially parental alcoholism, has long been shown to be associated with child maltreatment, but much less has been known about the relationship of parental cocaine use and child abuse. Famularo, Kinscherff, and Fenton (1992) have recently shown specific associations between alcohol abuse and physical maltreatment and between cocaine use and sexual maltreatment in a sample of parents who had significantly maltreated their children. Ages of the children were not reported.

There are many long-standing clinical beliefs about risk factors for which there is little or only conflicting empirical evidence. These "clinical hunches" may have some validity, but until this is demonstrated, the following probably should not be identified as risk factors:

• *Young maternal age and single marital status.* Only retrospective designs have found these to be associated risk factors; prospective designs have not. Also, when socioeconomic status is controlled for, age does not appear as a factor. Connelly and Straus (1992), in a retrospective study of a nationally representative sample, examined the relationship between mother's age and physical abuse (measured by a self-report questionnaire). When other factors were controlled for, mother's age at the time of birth of the abused child was significantly correlated with the rate of child abuse, whereas mother's age at the time of abuse was not.

• *Racial status.* This has not been found to be a significant predictor of subsequent child maltreatment.

• *Medical problems with pregnancy and/or complications at birth.* These were implicated by early retrospective investigations (Lynch & Roberts, 1977), but more recent prospective studies have not found this association. There is little reliable evidence that low birthweight or birth defects increase a child's risk for abuse, even though it seems that a parent (especially one who is already at risk because of other factors)

may feel like a failure and take out his or her frustrations on the infant or young child.

• *Failure to bond with infant soon after delivery.* Failure to bond has received a lot of attention, but it has not stood up to empirical verification. It lends itself to overly simplistic notions of parent–child relationships, such as that parents either are or are not bonded, rather than to recognition of the range and complexity of normal and disordered attachment relationships between parents and infants.

• *Difficult infant temperament.* Research has not clearly demonstrated an association between difficult temperament and child maltreatment (Sroufe & Waters, 1982); however, no research investigation has been reported that has assessed temperament measures just following birth and rates of subsequent maltreatment. Despite the lack of evidence, some clinicians continue to see difficult temperament as a major risk factor. Infants with difficult temperaments include those who are irritable, who are unpredictable in their sleeping and eating patterns, who are difficult to console, who cry for long periods of time, and who remain stiff rather than relaxing when held. It is not difficult to postulate an association between such behavior and child abuse, especially episodes of shaking and blows directed to the head. Difficult temperament in a toddler is manifested by irritability to tolerate frustration, very poor responses to changes in environment or routine, extremely short attention span coupled with frequent demands for attention, and difficulty with being soothed or distracted. Such a child may be at increased risk for abuse, especially when the caregiver wants the child to eat, sleep, or cooperate with toileting. Despite clinical wisdom and the realization that some children with difficult temperaments do get abused, the association lacks empirical support, perhaps because of difficulties in measuring difficult temperament. If stressed parents experience an infant as irritable, difficult to soothe, or hard to manage, and ascribe to him or her hostile intent and malevolent characteristics, then the infant may be at increased risk regardless of whether or not he or she satisfies criteria for temperamental difficulty.

Too little attention has been paid to the interaction among different risk factors. It may be that a particular factor only becomes predictive when it is associated with another factor or cluster of factors. One factor may potentiate the power of another factor that has remained dormant.

PROTECTIVE FACTORS

Much of what is known about protective factors does not come from studies of child maltreatment, but rather from related areas of child and family development. Protective factors can exist within the individual, family, or community. If they are missing from one domain, it is more critical that they occur amply in another. In some ways protective factors are the polar opposites of risk factors. However, it may be that the protective factors do not operate as such unless needed. If risk levels are low, the importance of health, intelligence, and social networks may not be recognized.

The Kauai Longitudinal Study (Werner & Smith, 1992) is one of the most comprehensive prospective studies of risk and resiliency. The study followed a 1955 birth cohort of 505 individuals from the prenatal period to adulthood. It monitored the impact of a variety of biological and psychosocial risk factors, stressful life events, and protective factors on the development of these individuals. Werner and Smith (1992) found that constitutional factors (health and temperamental characteristics) discriminated most clearly between resilient children and their high-risk peers in infancy and early childhood. At first glance, this finding seems to contradict the evidence that health and temperament do not appear to be predictors of child maltreatment. But Werner and Smith's finding is related to how the *children* coped with their environment, not how their parents coped (i.e., failed to cope and maltreated their children). Werner and Smith also found that the support of alternate caregivers, such as grandparents or siblings, was a protective factor that gained importance as the children got older.

SEQUELAE OF INFANT MALTREATMENT

Maltreatment can be expected to have different effects on different children for a multitude of reasons: the type of maltreatment, the frequency of the abuse, the existence of co-occurring forms of abuse and neglect, the psychiatric status of the parents, the age of the parents (and therefore the developmental tasks that the parents must negotiate), the child's pre-existing physical and emotional health, and the age of the child. The abusive environment itself, often including social isolation, poverty, deteriorating neighborhoods, and inadequate access to medical care, becomes the organizing and adverse context in which the infant must develop.

The age of the child is important in two regards: Maltreatment can have different effects depending upon the salient biological/maturational tasks, as well as upon the relevant psychological/developmental tasks of the age period.

The biological status of a child under the age of 3 years is very fragile, and an assault on the child will have more impact at this age than at any other age. Also, the biological maturation of a child under 3 years of age is so rapid and so sequenced that an assault on the organism, such as severe nutritional neglect or a blow to the head, may cause irreparable harm to the developing brain. Follow-up studies to document the short-term biological consequences have to date been inadequate. Unlike some types of abuse with older children, the most critical issue facing a maltreated child under 3 years of age is physical survival. As mentioned earlier, most child maltreatment fatalities occur with this age group. Many of the children who do survive have sustained multiple injuries to all parts of their bodies, necessitating lengthy hospitalization (and in many cases surgeries and rehabilitation). Injuries to the brain from hitting and shaking are common and can result in personal damage, including reduced intelligence, seizures, motor problems, language problems, and neurological "soft signs." Sometimes the physical sequelae are more subtle. These include weight loss, inability to fight infection, and hearing loss; the last of these is often a result of untreated otitis media.

One of the biological effects of maltreatment can be sustained poor physical growth. Although a severe case of nonorganic failure to thrive is likely to be recognized and provided with medical care, persistent but less severe neglect through the early years may result in poor growth—in terms not only of height and weight, but also of head circumference. Such cases have been referred to as "psychosocial dwarfism." Sometimes these children go unrecognized until another form of maltreatment, such as physical abuse, brings them to medical attention. When such children are placed in alternative environments, such as hospitals or foster homes, their rate of statural growth is accelerated, and they tend to catch up with their normal trajectory.

Skuse (1992) has recently reviewed the relationship among deprivation, physical growth, and the impaired development of language. Those children whose growth is impaired tend also to have delayed language; conversely, children with impaired cognitive skills secondary to an impoverished upbringing do seem to be rather small for their age. This association may be attributable to their shared dependency on a common cause—that is, the neglectful environment has failed to provide nutrition or language stimulation. Or perhaps an environment that can interfere so severely with learning can also interfere with the production of growth hormone secretion. Whatever the etiology, such associations between biological and cognitive–emotional development need further exploration.

As yet there are no prospective data regarding the long-term biological outcomes of battered children as adults, but it is conceivable that there are such effects of maltreatment. Perpetrator variables associated with physical child abuse include neurological and neuropsychological characteristics, physiological reactivity, and physical health problems (Milner & Chilamkurti, 1991). Whether these variables are in fact results of childhood maltreatment remain to be seen.

Lewis (1992), in a review of the psychophysiological literature related to violent behaviors, postulates that maltreatment not only has psychodynamic consequences but also modifies the neurophysiology of the individual. She asserts:

> It is reasonable to hypothesize that abusive, neglectful treatment diminishes concentrations in the brain of substances such as serotonin that ordinarily help to modulate feelings; maltreatment seems to increase the outpouring of substances such as dopamine and testosterone that enhance competitive and retaliatory aggression. These same substances also contribute to hypervigilance, and thus increase the fearfulness and paranoia that give rise to violent acts. p. 388

Testosterone and other hormones also affect the structure of the brain. The special difficulties that abused toddlers have expressing feelings in words may reflect neuroanatomical and neurophysiological changes induced by abuse, rather than merely psychological intimidation. Furthermore, the apparent lack of empathy observed in abused, aggressive children may be a manifestation of a centrally mediated expressive deficit coupled with a conditioned imperviousness to certain painful stimuli, and not simply a reflection of nastiness or character pathology. In an already vulnerable child, the biological impact of the maltreatment may be so considerable that the child grows into an impulsive, irritable, paranoid adult with impaired judgment and inability to recognize and experience his or her own pain or the pain of others.

The interference of maltreatment with the psychological development of the child has received more attention, but detailed prospective studies have been limited. Gaensbauer, Mrazek, and Harmon (1980) were among the first investigators to examine the specific patterns of infant response to maltreatment. Part of what had delayed the investigation of emotional development of these children had been the lack of an adequate methodology for systematic assessment. Using a methodology for assessing emotional expression in nonmaltreated children (Gaensbauer, Mrazek, & Emde, 1979), Gaensbauer et al. (1980) studied 30 maltreated children who had come to the attention of social service agencies. The infants ranged in age from 12 to 26 months, with a mean age of 20 months. Most of them had experienced severe problems in parenting, including varying combinations of physical and emotional abuse and/or neglect, chaotic home environments, separations from parents, foster placements, and inconsistent caretaking experiences. Given that the parents of these abused/neglected children were aware that the laboratory evaluation might affect administrative decisions regarding their families' future, it was noted that they made strong efforts to demonstrate positive interactions with the children.

The investigators reported differences between the maltreated children and the normative samples they had seen. First, the Mental scale scores from the Bayley Scales of Infant Development varied widely, but overall scores were somewhat below normal. The lower scores were thought to be related to the infants' lack of abilities and to temperamental characteristics that interfered with their performance under test conditions. Second, the maltreated infants' reaction to their mothers' departure and reunion during a separation paradigm reflected insecure infant attachments. These infants showed relatively little distress when their mothers left the room. When distress was evident, it included an angry component that persisted long after the mothers' return. Whereas no infants in the normal sample showed more attachment to the stranger as compared to their mothers, in the maltreated group six infants showed more attachment behavior to the experimenter. Third, the maltreated children showed distinctive affective behavior patterns, which the investigators believed were the essential elements of the developmental disturbance in these infants.

Gaensbauer and Mrazek (1981) characterized four categories of abused infants:

1. *Developmentally and affectively retarded* (40%). These children had endured significant stimulus deprivation and tended to be emotionally blunted, socially underpassive, inattentive to their environment, and retarded in all spheres—cognitive, emotional, and motoric. They had perhaps suffered the most devastating form of neglect, similar to the "hospitalism" cases Rene Spitz (1945) described.

2. *Depressed* (20%). These children showed predominant elements of sadness and depression, but with considerable encouragement they could brighten up and perform at their age levels. They were extremely sensitive to rebuffs of whatever nature, as though they were re-experiencing a sense of having "loved and lost."

3. *Ambivalent, affectively labile* (25%). Although these children were quite capable of functioning at their age levels, they showed ambivalent reactions in a consistent and marked fashion. They showed pleasure at times, but withdrawal or anger could quickly emerge under stress. They did not, however, appear to be overtly depressed. These infants seemed to have experienced inconsistent mothering, alternating between periods of sensitivity and reciprocally rewarding interaction on the one hand and periods of maltreatment on the other.

4. *Angry* (somewhat less than 20%). These infants showed very high arousal, low amounts of frustration tolerance, and extreme amounts of anger. They were extremely active and showed disorganization in their play. They had been exposed to chaotic, highly charged environments with frequent, harsh punishments from caretakers.

George and Main (1979) studied the social-interactive behaviors of abused toddlers and compared them to those of disadvantaged, non-abused toddlers. The abused toddlers were much more angry, and they directed their anger toward their peers and caregivers. They hit, slapped, kicked, displayed unprovoked, out-of-context hostility, and avoided friendly overtures from others. Such children are not ampathic (Sroufe, 1983), but rather, they show anger and aggression in response to distress in peers (Main & George, 1985). Such behavior is likely to elicit patterns of rejection from others in subsequent relationships of these children.

Cicchetti and colleagues have linked the premises of developmental psychopathology to the field of child abuse and neglect. They have called attention to the need for a lessened focus on psychopathology and an increased focus on developmental and ecological perspectives. Schneider-Rosen and Cicchetti (1984) evaluated the quality of attachment in maltreated infants to their caretakers. Their sample, drawn from the Harvard Child Maltreatment Project, consisted of 18 maltreated infants and 19 comparison infants. These children ranged in age from 17 to 20 months, and the maltreated children had experienced emotional maltreatment, physical abuse, physical neglect, or some combination of these forms. The maltreated group had a higher percentage of insecurely attached infants (67%) than did the non-maltreated group (26%). Subsequent research has demonstrated that the proportion of maltreated infants who are securely attached is probably much smaller, in the range of 5–10% (Carlson, Cicchetti, Barnett & Braunwald, 1989). Still it is unclear why any infant who has been maltreated would be securely attached to his or her caregiver. What other factors might account for this? Are there positive attributes of the caregiver that can override the maltreatment? Can social supports within the environment or temperamental characteristics or level of intelligence account for the difference? Further research is needed about this interesting subgroup.

In an expansion of their original work, Schneider-Rosen, Braunwald, Carlson, and Cicchetti (1985) reported on the classification of attachments of maltreated and comparison infants at 12, 18, and 24 months. A greater proportion of maltreated infants in each of the three age groups was insecurely attached. However, no clear relationships between the quality of attachment and the types of maltreatment emerged within any of the age groups. What did emerge was an increase in the percentage of maltreated infants who manifested anxious–avoidant (group A) attachments when observed cross-sectionally from 12 to 24 months of age. At 12 months, 29% of the maltreated infants were classified avoidant, but at 18 months and 24 months 46% were classified avoidant. This may reflect the young child's efforts to cope with a dangerous and inconsistent environment. As a group, the insecurely attached maltreated children tended to remain insecurely attached, whereas the securely attached infants tended to shift to insecure attachments.

A significant breakthrough in this area has been the discovery of a heterogenous group of infants now classified as disorganized/disoriented with respect to attachment (Main & Solomon,

1986). Using this new classification, Carlson, Cicchetti, Barnett & Braunwald (1989) found that 82% of their maltreated sample fulfilled criteria for that classification.

Egeland and colleagues have provided the field with an excellent prospective and methodologically sound examination of the effects of child maltreatment (Pianta et al., 1989). The Minnesota Mother–Child Project identified 267 mothers at risk for parenting problems due to low socioeconomic status, young age, unmarried status, and unplanned pregnancy. Of these families, 44 children were identified as abused and subgrouped into four overlapping types: (1) physically abusive (n = 24); (2) neglectful (n = 24), (3) hostile–rejecting (n = 19), and (4) psychologically unavailable (n = 19). The maltreated and well-cared-for infants did not differ (or at least could not be observed to differ) until 18 months of age when maltreated infants were more likely to exhibit an anxious pattern of attachment to their mothers. Infants of "psychologically unavailable" mothers declined dramatically in performance on the Bayley Scales from 9 to 18 months, and continued to show more severe and varied problems than infants from the three other maltreated groups. Egeland & Erickson (1987) described the psychologically unavailable caregivers as unresponsive, detached, depressed and uninvolved, displaying no pleasure in interaction, and failing to comfort their children in times of distress. Speculation can be made whether such unresponsive caregivers remain in such a passive state when crises and tensions escalate. Anecdotal evidence suggests that these same caregivers can become explosive at such times. This is one of the problems with research regarding maltreatment: the worst behavior of caregivers is rarely seen in the experimental situation. Egeland concluded that the earlier the abuse to the developing child, the more severe the consequences. Maternal sensitivity and lack of support resulted in a failure to develop trust as infants and failure to negotiate autonomy as toddlers.

ASSESSMENT OF RISK FACTORS

The emphasis in prediction and prevention has been on the occurrence of maltreatment, that is, which parent might abuse his or her child and how can that be prevented? One strategy for the prevention of child maltreatment is to identify high-risk groups and provide interventions which are known to be effective. The movement toward prediction of individuals who are at risk for becoming abusive or neglectful began in the early 1970s in Denver, Colorado. Early predictive questionnaires yielded many false positives, and observations of mother-child bonding at the time of delivery are no longer believed to have an essential role in forecasting later parenting behavior.

Some prediction efforts have met with more success however, such as the work of Leventhal, Garber, and Brady (1989) who identified a sample of infants during the neonatal period who were at high risk for abuse and neglect and matched them with a comparison group. Four years later when medical records were reviewed, the high risk group had significantly more occurrences of maltreatment and poor weight gain from nonorganic causes. However, overall, the identification of high-risk infants or high-risk parents have met with mixed results.

Targeting high-risk populations rather than individuals may yield better results. Also, one way of determining whether correlated risk factors are indeed causal is with methodologically-sound preventive intervention studies. Nevertheless, most of the research on the effectiveness of different prevention efforts have yielded mixed results. In the most comprehensive review to date of the effectiveness of interventions aimed at the primary prevention of child maltreatment, MacMillan, MacMillan, and Offord (1992) have reached these conclusions:

1. There is evidence that extended home visitation can prevent physical abuse and neglect among families with single parents, teenage parents and/or poverty.
2. The evidence regarding intensive pediatric contact, use of a drop-in center, short-term home visitation, early and extended postpartum contact, and parent training programs remains inconclusive.
3. No study has produced direct data indicating that education actually reduces the occurrence of sexual abuse.

PRIMARY PREVENTION

Even though most of the research results are equivocal, two research programs employing home visitation met with significant success and demonstrated a reduction in child maltreatment. The first of these was the Prenatal/Early Infancy Project in Elmira, New York, conducted by Olds and colleagues (Olds, Henderson, Chamberlin, & Tatelbaum, 1986; Olds, Henderson, Tatelbaum, & Chamberlin, 1986, 1988); the second was the Children and Youth Program conducted by Hardy and Streett (1989). Both research programs utilized rigorous designs and targeted home visitation interventions to high-risk groups. The Olds et al. program began prenatally, and positive effects regarding length of gestation (for children born to very young, adolesents) and birthweight (for children born to women who smoked) were found. Among the women at highest risk for caregiving dysfunction (poor unmarried teens), those who were visited by a nurse had fewer instances of verified child abuse and neglect during the first 2 years of their children's lives than the comparison group. Four years after the delivery of their first children, nurse-visited white women who had not graduated from high school when they registered in the study returned to school more rapidly than the comparison group. They also showed an 82% increase in the months they were employed, had 43% fewer subsequent pregnancies, and postponed the birth of second children an average of 12 months longer. When Olds and colleagues' demonstration grant was finished, the local health department continued the project. As the U.S. General Accounting Office (1990) has reported, however, the research methodology and the target group were altered significantly, and the results were no longer so successful.

The second successful prevention study was the Children and Youth Program (Hardy & Streett, 1989), which targeted poor, inner-city black women 18 years of age or older. The study children, compared to the control children, were more likely to have received complete immunizations; less likely to have had head trauma, chronic or recurrent otitis media, or severe diaper rash; less likely to have been admitted to a hospital; and less likely to have been suspected or confirmed victims of child abuse or neglect.

TREATMENT

The first priority of a clinician must be the physical protection of a child. If the maltreatment has already occurred and the etiology is clear, the local child protective service agency must be informed. If the situation is life-threatening, the child must be removed from the parental home. A developmental evaluation of the child with close attention to his or her affective style may be invaluable in the treatment planning. Whether the child is placed with a foster family or remains with his or her biological parents, interventions regarding parenting can be helpful.

CONCLUSIONS

Infant and child maltreatment continues to be a pervasive social problem. Abuse and neglect of infants and toddlers always involve suffering and can result in death or permanent negative sequelae for the children. More research is needed to understand how to design and implement effective primary prevention programs. This will require a more thorough understanding of risk and protective factors, as well as an increased appreciation of how to deliver service programs that improve outcomes and minimize adverse consequences for infants and their families.

REFERENCES

Altemeier, W. A., O'Conner, S., Vietze, P. M., Sandler, H. M., & Sherrod, K. B. (1982). Antecedents of child abuse. *Journal of Pediatrics, 100,* 823–829.

Annie E. Casey Foundation, & the Center for the Study of Social Policy (1992). *Kids count data book: State profiles of child well-being.* Greenwich, Ct, and Washington, DC: Authors.

Behrman, R. E. (Ed). (1992). Substance abuse and withdrawals. In R. E. Behrman (Ed.), *Nelson textbook of pediatrics* (14th ed., pp. 490–492). Philadelphia: W. B. Saunders.

Benedict, M. I., White, R. B., & Cornely, D. A. (1985). Maternal perinatal risk factors and child abuse. *Child Abuse and Neglect, 9,* 217–224.

Brown, S. T., Foege, W. H., Bender, T. R., & N. Axnick (1990). Injury prevention and control. *Annual review of Public Health, 11,* 251–266.

Caplan, P. J., Watters, J., White, G., Parry, R., & Bates, R. (1984). Toronto Multiagency Child Abuse Research Project: The abused and the abuser. *Child Abuse and Neglect, 8,* 343–351.

Carlson, V., Cicchetti, D., Barnett, D., & Braunwald, K. G. (1989). Finding order in disorganization: Lessons from research on maltreated infants' attachments to their caregivers. In D. Cicchetti & V. Carlson (Eds.), *Child maltreatment: Theory and research on the causes and consequences of child abuse and neglect* (pp. 494–528). New York: Cambridge University Press.

Cohn, A. H. (1979). Essential elements of successful child abuse and neglect treatment. *Child Abuse and Neglect, 3,* 491–496.

Condon, J. T. (1986). The spectrum of fetal abuse in pregnant women. *Journal of Nervous and Mental Disease, 174*(9), 509–516.

Conn, A. W. (1992). Drowning and near–drowning. In R. E. Behrman (Ed.), *Nelson textbook of pediatrics.* (14th ed., pp. 230–233). Philadelphia: W. B. Saunders.

Connelly, C. D., & Straus, M. A. (1992). Mother's age and risk for physical abuse. *Child Abuse and Neglect, 16,* 709–718.

Egeland, B., & Brunnquell, D. (1979). An at-risk approach to the study of child abuse: Some Preliminary Findings. *Journal of the American Academy of Child and Adolescent Psychiatry, 18,* 219–235.

Egeland, B., & Erickson, M. F. (1987). Psychologically unavailable caregiving. In M. R. Brassard, R. Germain, & S. N. Hart (Eds.), *Psychological maltreatment of children and youth* (pp. 110–120). Elmsford, NY: Pergamon Press.

Egeland, B., Jacobvitz, D., & Papatola, K. (1987). Intergenerational continuity of parental abuse. In R. Gelles and J. Lancaster (Eds.), *Biosocial aspects of child abuse* (pp. 255–276). New York: Aldine.

Famularo, R., Kinscherff, R., & Fenton, T. (1992). Parental substance abuse and the nature of child maltreatment. *Child Abuse and Neglect, 16,* 475–483.

Friedrich, W. N., & Wheeler, K. K. (1982). The abusing parent revisited: A decade of psychological research. *Journal of Nervous and Mental Disease, 170,* 577–587.

Fuchs, V., & Reklis, D. (1992). America's children: Economic perspectives and policy options. *Science, 255,* 41–46.

Gaensbauer, T. J., & Mrazek, D. A. (1981). Differences in the patterning of affective expression in infants. *Journal of the American Academy of Child and Adolescent Psychiatry, 20,* 673–691.

Gaensbauer, T. J., Mrazek, D. A., & Emde, R. N. (1979). Patterning of emotional response in a playroom laboratory situation. *Infant Behavior and Development, 2,* 163–178.

Gaensbauer, T. J., Mrazek, D. A., & Harmon, R. J. (1980). Emotional expression in abused and/or neglected infants. In N. Frude (Ed.), *Psychological approaches to child abuse.* (pp. 120–135). London: Batsford.

George, C., & Main, M. (1979). Social interactions of young abused children: Approach, avoidance, and aggression. *Child Development, 50,* 306–318.

Griest, K. I., & Zumwalt, R. E. (1989). Child abuse by drowning. *Pediatrics, 83,* 41–46.

Hansen, D. J., Pallotta, G. M., Tishelman, A. C., Conaway, L. P., & MacMillan, V. M. (1989). Parental problem-solving skills and child behavior problems: A comparison of physically abusive, neglectful, clinic, and community families. *Journal of Family Violence, 4,* 353–368.

Hardy, J. B., & Streett, R. (1989). Family support and parenting education in the home: An effective extension of clinic-based preventive health care services for poor children. *Journal of Pediatrics, 115*(6), 927–931.

Holden, E. W., Willis, D. J., & Corcoran, M. M. (1992). Preventing child maltreatment during the prenatal/perinatal period. In D. Willis, E. W. Holden, & M. Rosenberg (Eds.), *Prevention of child maltreatment: Developmental and ecological perspectives* (pp. 17–46). New York: Wiley–Interscience.

Hunter, R., Kilstrom, N., Kraybill, E., & Loda, F. (1978). Antecedents of child abuse and neglect in premature infants: A prospective study in a newborn intensive care unit. *Pediatrics, 61,* 629–635.

Kaufman, J., & Zigler, E. (1987). Do abused children become abusive parents? *American Journal of Orthopsychiatry, 57,* 186–192.

Leventhal, J. M., Garber, R. B., & Brady, C. A. (1989). Identification during the postpartum period of infants who are at high risk of child maltreatment. *Journal of Pediatrics, 114,* 481–487.

Lewis, D. O. (1992). From abuse to violence: Psychological consequences of maltreatment. *Journal of the American Academy of Child and Adolescent Psychiatry, 31*(3), 383–391.

Lynch, M. A., & Roberts, J. (1977). Predicting child abuse: Signs of bonding failure in the maternity hospital. *British Medical Journal, i,* 624–626.

MacMillan, H. L., MacMillan, J. H., & Offord, D. R., (1993). Periodic health examination, 1993 update: 1. Primary prevention of child maltreatment. *Canadian Medical Association Journal, 148*(2): 151–163.

Main, M., & George, C. (1985). Responses of abused and disadvantaged toddlers to distress in agemates: A study in the daycare setting. *Developmental Psychology, 21*(3), 407–412.

Main, M., & Solomon, J. (1986). Discovery of an insecure disorganized/disoriented attachment pattern. In T. B. Brazelton & M. W. Yogman (Eds.), *Affective development in infancy.* Norwood, NJ: Ablex.

Milner, J. S., & Chilamkurti, C. (1991). Physical child abuse perpetrator characteristics: A review of the literature. *Journal of Interpersonal Violence, 6*(3), 345–366.

Mrazek, D. A. & Mrazek, P. J. (1985). Child maltreatment. In M. Rutter & L. Hersov (Eds.), *Child and adolescent psychiatry: Modern approaches,* (2nd ed., pp. 679–697). Oxford: Blackwell.

Mrazek, P. J. (1990). Child maltreatment. *Current Opinion in Pediatrics, 2,* 715–718.

Olds, D. L., Henderson, C. R., Chamberlin, R., & Tatelbaum, R. (1986). Preventing child abuse and neglect: A randomized trial of nurse home visitation. *Pediatrics, 78*(1), 65–78.

Olds, D. L., Henderson, C. R., Tatelbaum, R., & Chamberlin, R. (1986). Improving the delivery of prenatal care and outcomes of pregnancy: A randomized trial of nurse home visitation. *Pediatrics, 77*(1), 16–28.

Olds, D. L., Henderson, C. R., Tatelbaum, R., & Chamberlin, R. (1988). Improving the life-course development of socially disadvantaged mothers: A randomized trial of nurse home visitation. *American Journal of Public Health, 78*(11), 1436–1445.

Pianta, R., Egeland, B., & Erickson, M. F. (1989). The antecedents of maltreatment: Results of the mother–child interaction research project. In D. Cicchetti & V. Carlson (Eds.). *Child maltreatment: Theory and research on the causes and consequences of child abuse and neglect* (pp. 203–253) New York: Cambridge University Press.

Rosenberg, D. A. (1987). Web of deceit: A literature review of Munchausen syndrome by proxy. *Child Abuse and Neglect, 11,* 547–563.

Schmitt, B. D., & Krugman, R. D. (1992). Abuse and neglect of children. In R. E. Behrman (Ed.), *Nelson textbook of pediatrics* (14th ed., pp. 78–83). Philadelphia: W. B. Saunders.

Schneider-Rosen, K., Braunwald, K. G., Carlson, V., &

Cicchetti, D. (1985). Current perspectives in attachment theory: Illustration from the study of maltreated infants. In I. Bretherton & E. Waters (Eds.), *Growing points of attachment theory and research. Monographs of the Society for Research in Child Development, 50*(1–2, Serial No. 209), 194–210.

Schneider-Rosen, K., & Cicchetti, D. (1984). The relationship between affect and cognition in maltreated infants: Quality of attachment and the development of visual self-recognition. *Child Development, 55,* 648–658.

Seagull, E. A. W. (1987). Social support and child maltreatment: A review of the evidence. *Child Abuse and Neglect, 11,* 41–52.

Skuse, D. (1992). *The relationship between deprivation, physical growth and the impaired development of language.* Unpublished manuscript, Institute of Child Health, London.

Spitz, R. (1945). Hospitalism: An inquiry into the genesis of psychiatric conditions in early childhood. *Psychoanalytic Study of the Child, 1,* 53–74.

Sroufe, L. A. (1983). Infant–caregiver attachment and patterns of adaptation in preschool: The roots of maladaptation and competence. In M. Perlmutter (Ed.), *Minnesota Symposium on Child Development* (Vol. 16, pp. 41–83). Hillsdale, NJ: Erlbaum.

Sroufe, L. A., & Waters, E. (1982). Issues of temperament and attachment. *American Journal of Orthopsychiatry, 52,* 743–747.

Thomas, S. A., Rosenfield, N. S., Leventhal, J. M., & Markowitz, R. I. (1991). Long-bone fractures in young children: Distinguishing accidental injuries from child abuse. *Pediatrics, 88*(3), 471–476.

U.S. Department of Health and Human Services (1992). *National child abuse and neglect data system: Working paper 1, 1990 summary data component.* DHHS Publication No. (ACF) 92-30361.

U.S. General Accounting Office. (1990). *Home visiting: A promising early intervention strategy for at-risk families.* (Publication No. GAO/HRD-90–83). Washington, DC: U.S. General Accounting Office.

Waller, A. E., Baker, S. P., & Szocka, A. (1989). Childhood injury deaths: National analysis and geographic variations. *American Journal of Public Health, 79,* 310–315.

Werner, E. E., & Smith, R. S. (1992). *Overcoming the odds: High risk children from birth to adulthood.* Ithaca, NY: Cornell University Press.

Westen, D., Ludolph, P., Misle, B., Ruffins, S., & Block, J. (1990). Physical and sexual abuse in adolescent girls with borderline personality disorders. *American Journal of Orthopsychiatry, 60,* 55–66.

Zeanah, C. H., & Zeanah, P. D. (1989). Intergenerational transmission of maltreatment: Insights from attachment theory and research. *Psychiatry, 52,* 177–196.

Zuravin, S.J. (1987). Unplanned pregnancies, family planning problems and child maltreatment. *Family Relations, 36,* 135–139.

III

ASSESSMENT

Clinicians involved in infant mental health come from a variety of professional disciplines, which have different philosophies about assessment and strategies for assessment. The recent emphasis on assessing infants in their family contexts in early intervention has narrowed some of the traditional differences, but they still exist to varying degrees. Part III attempts to capture a range of approaches to assessment, from unstructured clinical interviews to traditional infant tests to the use of structured research paradigms in clinical work with infants and families.

Hirshberg, in Chapter 11, describes the process and content of the clinical interview with the family of an infant referred for evaluation. He emphasizes that gathering specific facts about the family may be less useful than careful analysis of a particular moment or experience that embodies the essence of the central problem. He also suggests understanding the family members' responses to their infant, to one another, and to the clinician as shaped in part by the nature of the therapeutic relationship as it develops during the process of the interview. Therefore, the primary goal of the interview is to form a personal relationship with the family members, in order to construct with them a way of understanding the problem and to work on developing a plan to resolve it. Hirshberg also recommends attending to the strengths and weaknesses evident in a number of specific domains of the infant–parent relationship. In the course of the interview, the clinician evaluates what the infant and the parents bring to the relationship, as well as specific precipitants of the current problem and the wider social context in which the problem occurs.

Clark, Paulson, and Conlin emphasize the importance of assessing the infant in context in Chapter 12. Infant assessment is a process that involves determining developmental status, functioning in different settings, and the quality of relationships with primary caregivers. They describe the "what," "when," and "how" of conducting developmental assessments of infants, emphasizing that structured assessment of the infant's developmental status should be used as a foundation for a more comprehensive understanding of the infant's functioning in context. As they review specific approaches, they stress the close involvement of parents in the developmental process and the fact that assessment often functions as a preliminary intervention.

In Chapter 13, Crowell and Fleischmann consider the potential and problems in using structured research paradigms in clinical infant mental health. They emphasize that in order for structured paradigms to be useful, they must yield information about an individual child that assists the clinician in understanding factors that have initiated or maintained problem behaviors; in predicting the child's developmental trajectory; and/or in planning interventions that might change this trajectory. They propose six standards that structured paradigms should meet in order to be clinically meaningful.

11

Clinical Interviews with Infants and their Families

LAURENCE M. HIRSHBERG

The conduct of the clinical interview of the infant and family, like all clinical work, is more craft than science. Much depends on the individual style of the interviewer; clearly, differing styles may be equally effective, or differentially effective with different families. Nevertheless, certain practices and techniques are basic or essential to this craft, as to any other, and this chapter outlines and discusses these.

The approach to the interview described below has emerged out of a clinic-based rather than a home-based approach to assessment and treatment, and out of work with both socially advantaged families and multiply disadvantaged families. It is clear that the context of a home visit changes the ecology of the interview substantially and alters its rhythm and feel. Some of the recommendations made here will need substantial modification in a home-visit-based assessment. The sociocultural context also has a marked impact on the interview process, and interviewers may need to modify their approach in the light of what is culturally fitting (see Garcia Coll & Meyer, Chapter 4, this volume).

This chapter is not intended to describe the conduct of the comprehensive evaluation as a whole, but more narrowly addresses the process of the family interview, which is frequently only one part of the complete comprehensive evaluation. In many cases, specialized assessments such as cognitive-developmental testing, a speech and language evaluation, or an electroencephalogram (EEG) will be necessary to com-

plete a comprehensive evaluation. The goal of the clinical interview as conceived here is to consider carefully whether such specialized assessments may be necessary, and if so, to elaborate specific referral questions for them.

Although much can be observed about the functioning and nature of the infant–parent relationship in the course of the interview as it unfolds, it may also be necessary or useful to conduct a structured interaction assessment procedure designed to elicit or tap relationship functioning in a variety of domains of the relationship—including, for example, free-play situations, structured learning tasks at a variety of levels of difficulty, feeding, and separation and reunion. A number of formats are used for these assessments, and they can be employed for both research and clinical purposes. The assessments are often videotaped and used subsequently for exploration of issues with the parents (see Crowell & Fleischmann, Chapter 13, this volume).

Generally a number of interviews will be necessary in order to complete the evaluation, and it is useful to let the parents know this in the initial contact. Although individual clinicians may differ in this regard, it is usually best to see infants together with their primary caregivers in the initial interview. If a mother initially reports that the father cannot attend the session, persistent indications from the clinician that his presence is important usually suffice. In the case of a single mother living with her parent or parents, the baby's grandparents should also be present for some portion of the initial interview, unless they do not provide a significant amount of care to the infant. When grandparents are present, it is important for the clinician to communicate to the mother through the conduct of the interview that she is recognized as the child's primary caregiver, even while acknowledging to the grandparents their significant role and contribution.

In the case of a very active or older toddler, it may be useful to hold subsequent sessions without the toddler's being present, to allow for a more sustained focus on the parents and/or to allow the parents to address issues about which they may not be comfortable talking in the presence of a linguistically competent toddler.

It is important to have on hand the essential baby supplies—diapers, wipes, toys suited to a variety of developmental stages, and food for a snack—should the need arise.

In this chapter, I first discuss some basic theoretical and practical principles with important implications for the process of the clinical interview. I then go on to outline the essential areas of investigation to be covered during the interview, and offer some suggestions as to how to cover them in the context of the interview.

THE INTERVIEW PROCESS

The Goal of the Interviews

In the view of the assessment process advocated here, the goal of the clinical interviews is conceived as the mutual development (together with the parents) of a clear and focused understanding of the core of the problem—a formulation of the central organizing conflict or dynamic. Although gathering information is often an important adjunctive activity in the process of arriving at such a formulation of the problem, it is just that—adjunctive. It is critical that the information be gathered in the service of an active ongoing effort, together with the parents, to organize the experience of the family and to construct an account of the family's experience with the baby. This account is then continually modified or elaborated throughout the interviews and the subsequent treatment.

The gathering together of a number of disjointed facts about the family is often much less productive to this process of actively making sense of the central organizing family problem

than the careful analysis of some small detail or single experience that embodies or instantiates the core problem or difficulty. In some comments about the process of historiography, Walter Benjamin, a German social philosopher, made the same point more eloquently by quoting his favorite Jewish aphorism: "The Lord God dwells in detail." (Benjamin, 1968) I take this aphorism to mean that the essence or spirit of the whole resides within the smallest parts, and that the details of experience offer a sort of privileged access to a complete understanding of the essence or whole. I find this to be a useful guide in the process of the clinical interview. Any of the background "facts" may well be superfluous to a focused understanding of the core of the case. I believe that Selma Fraiberg was referring to this phenomenon in her comment that parents often repeat with their infants their own childhood traumas "in terrible and exacting detail" (Fraiberg, 1980, p. 165). The repetition is frequently especially evident in the terrible and exacting detail.

The Clinical Relational Matrix

In the approach to the clinical interview with infants and families advanced here, it is assumed as a basic principle that when parents come to see a clinician with a problem with an infant, their response in every respect—to their infant, to each other, and to the clinician—is shaped by the nature of their relationship to the clinician as it continually unfolds in the interview process. As a result, the goal of the interview process is not to gather objective data, but *to form a personal relationship through which the assessor can elicit and observe in the family a range of psychological functioning on the basis of which the problem can be understood and a plan made cooperatively to resolve it* (Shevrin & Shechtman, 1973).

There are practical reasons why the clinician must focus on the emerging relationship with the family. Most importantly, with many families, no in-depth evaluation can be conducted at all without efforts to facilitate the development of a working alliance. Unless the parents can develop some degree of trust for the interviewer and experience empathic concern on his or her part, as well as a strong sense of respect for their wishes as parents and their needs as individuals, they are not likely to cooperate fully in the evaluation and disclose their painful experiences with the baby. Such parental "characteristics" as extreme emotional distance, coldness, or flatness in the interview, or a resolute failure to acknowledge any responsibility for the baby's problem and insistence on blaming the baby, may be as much a sign of distrust for the interviewer (who is often seen as an agent of some program or social service agency) as it is a product of a fixed character structure or psychopathology.

One mother described her 12-month-old baby as impossible to soothe or regulate, constantly crying, and often having tantrums. After being seen months earlier by another infant clinician, Mrs. M. was wary in her initial appointments, expecting a repeat of what she had perceived as mistreatment at the hands of the previous clinician. She reported that she had been told after a 1-hour observation that there was "nothing wrong" with the baby. She was furious about this outcome, feeling that it amounted to a dismissal of her concerns. She insisted heatedly that this was really a bad child; in fact, she said, she frequently found herself calling this, her second daughter, her "vile child."

Mrs. M. had recently been left by her husband, in part because he could no longer tolerate the baby's screaming. Initially, she was entirely unable to acknowledge any difficulties within herself in relation to the baby. Her denial persisted until she and the interviewer had talked about her frustration with the baby; her anguish, anger, and fear at being left by her husband; and her pride and pleasure in her older daughter. In the context of these explorations, she began to describe her own history of extreme emotional and physical abuse. In this context, she mentioned that she had always been called "the problem child" and was clearly the scapegoat, subject to frank and brutal abuse in her family of origin.

Having formed some trust with the interviewer in the course of these sessions, Mrs. M. could then make use of a connection with her own troubled past when the "vile child" and "problem child" phrases were linked by the evaluator. Only then could she begin to describe her difficulties in soothing and calming her distressed infant, her lack of tolerance for her daughter's insistent demandingness, her extremely intense feelings of hatred when her baby so insistently signaled her need, and her placing this baby in the all-too-familiar position of the family scapegoat.

Another practical reason for focusing on the nature of the relationship in assessment relates to treatment compliance. The likelihood that recommendations for treatment made as an outcome of the assessment will be favorably received and carried out by the parents depends in part on their relationship to the clinician. If parents feel blamed or criticized, intruded upon, unheard or unappreciated, or even rejected, they will be much less likely to follow through on treatment than if they feel understood, accepted, respected, and appreciated.

But beyond these pragmatic grounds, there are epistemological and theoretical reasons for this emphasis on the centrality of the relationship of parents and clinician. Contemporary epistemology calls into question the long-held theory (and common-sense view) that "the facts" or data may properly be thought of as objective, external, as existing in some sense apart from the knowing activity of the subject. According to this superseded epistemology, knowledge is attained by accurately uncovering or discovering "the facts" and their interrelationships. By contrast, contemporary epistemologists argue that all knowledge is a process by which the knower actively organizes, orders, or shapes what is given to perception or thought, and thereby constructs or constitutes what is known (Hirshberg, 1989). Knowledge then represents an outcome of a dynamic interaction of knower and known, subject and object.

In the context of the clinical interview, the critical point is that *what is learned about the infant and family is a picture or account that is constructed in the course of an active, dynamic exchange between family members and evaluator.* Recognition of the knowledge-constitutive status of the clinical relationship entails that the interviewer carefully attend to how he or she is being experienced by the family, how he or she is experiencing them, and how the interpersonal or relational matrix in the clinical setting (including cultural, class, race, and other factors) shapes the interview as it unfolds and the story as it emerges. As Fraiberg (1980) emphasizes, this attention to the nature of the emerging relationship should begin, if possible, with the referral itself or the first phone contact.

Transference

This view of the assessment process carries with it another implication: If the account one receives is necessarily a product of the current relational matrix, then the diagnostic importance of the history that is given in an interview recedes somewhat in significance by comparison with a careful examination of the interview process, since the history itself is a product of the current process. The factors that count most are how an account is being organized or construed in the interview, and what is happening with this family and baby now.

This view is in marked contrast to a history-taking or medical-model-based approach to the assessment interview, according to which the purpose of the interview is to obtain "the facts" about the course of the symptoms or problems over time and about any other phenomena causally related to the symptoms or problem, in order to diagnose the problem and prescribe a treatment. The view propounded above is also quite similar to the emphasis on the importance of transference phenomena in psychoanalytic clinical theory and practice.

In the history of psychoanalytic thinking, the concept of "transference" has been used to refer to the patient's imposing or transferring onto his or her experience of the therapist expectations, wishes, and fears that derive not primarily from the context of the real patient-therapist relationship, but from childhood relationships (Freud, 1912/1958). Thus, transference represents the repetition of childhood relational experiences in the relationship with the therapist.

More recently, this construct has been generalized to explain how all experience in relationships is organized, structured, and interpreted (Greenberg & Mitchell, 1983; Mitchell, 1988; Stern, 1985). The notion is that we create mental representations of ourselves and emotionally important others in affectively organized or patterned interactions or relationships—representations that may vary across different domains of experience or interaction. These "representations," "schemas," "internal working models," or "object relations paradigms," as they are variously called, are based on our early experiences in relationships, and are then subject to modification and change based on ongoing relational experience. It is on the basis of these organized sets of expectations about relationships that we perceive, structure, construe, and interpret all experience in interaction and relationship with others. In this view, all social experience involves what psychoanalysts have called "transference."

With regard to the implications for psychoanalytic technique of the phenomenon of transference, the technical recommendation is to pay more attention to what the patient is doing in saying something than to what he or she is saying; the idea is to attend to how the patient's responses reflect his or her functioning in the relationship to the therapist. The same qualified recommendation holds true for the clinical interview of the infant and family: The clinician should pay at least as much attention to what the parents and infant are doing during the interview as to what they are saying. This includes not just how the parents and infant interact and relate to each other and to the clinician during the interview, but also what the parents are doing interactively (with the interviewer and within the family) by saying what they are saying and how they are saying it. A parent's account of the infant's troubles may be organized as much to persuade the interviewer of the infant's inherent badness, or to castigate and punish a spouse for perceived irresponsibility, or to recruit the interviewer as a nurturant caregiver for and ally of the parent, as it is to convey "the facts" about the problem.

Clinical work with the infant in the family is a setting in many ways ideally suited to the analysis of transference. However, in the context of the assessment of the infant and family, the patient-to-therapist transference is supplemented, or sometimes supplanted, as the primary arena for exploration and interpretation by the parent-to-infant and/or parent-to-parent transference. To translate this into contemporary terms, the focus in this context is on how each parent organizes and interprets his or her experience of the infant (and the spouse), and therefore on the set of expectations, wishes, needs, fears, and fantasies that shape each parent's view of the baby (and spouse) and the parents' view of themselves in relationship to the baby (and each other).

The parent-to-infant relationship organization has several advantages over the patient-to-therapist transference as a field for early exploration and interpretation. The most important of these are its affective intensity and availability. Very little evokes as much intense emotion in most people as troubles with a baby. Moreover, the affect is often quite intense during the interviews, since the baby is present. The parents' imposition onto the baby of expectations, needs, wishes, and fears inappropriate to that relationship or from their own past can be more accessible to exploration; often, a clinician can almost see it happening in front of him or her. A pointed, detailed exploration of some emotionally laden or significant interaction or experience during the interview can reveal much that is significant in the organization of the parents' relationships to the baby.

Another advantage is the fact that for most people it is more readily sensible and seems more reasonable that important psychological conflicts will be expressed in relation to their children than to a therapist they have just met. Early explorations regarding the parent-to-infant relationship can then often be much closer to common sense in work with infants and families than transference interpretations in psychoanalytic psychotherapy with adults. In addition, the motivation to change the disturbed way of relating is also often much more intense when infants are involved than in psychotherapy of adults. As Fraiberg (1980) points out, most parents want desperately to do well by their babies, to make a better life for them. There is thus frequently ample ground on which to build an early working alliance, and to use this to support a quite challenging assessment style.

History Making Rather than History Taking

Although it is important to learn basic background information—such as the history of the pregnancy, of any medical complications, and of the parental marriage or relationship, as well as data on other influences in the life of the family (day care, work situations, extended family, cultural contexts, etc.)—such information is much better learned as an integral part of the process of exploring together with the parents, that is through their account of the baby and the family, than by going through a list of routine questions in different areas.

This is perhaps most important with regard to potentially sensitive and troubling information about the parents' own early childhood experiences and their effect on them as parents. Many parents are quite naturally on the defensive when this line of inquiry comes up; often, they are gritting their teeth in the expectation of criticism and blame for the baby's problem. Those who are most emphatic in their overt blame of the baby frequently blame themselves secretly and severely; the severity of their angry accusations about the "bad" baby reflects their own less overt but often quite intense self-criticism. And, after all, the parents have come for help because the baby has a problem, not to chat

about their own childhoods. The goal, therefore, is to explore and discover together with the parents *the past as it is active in the present.*

There are a number of advantages of this method of "getting the history" through the parents' narrative. First, the evaluator's interest in this information is naturally linked to the parents' own concerns and motives, and so it is more sensible to them and perhaps less threatening. Second, the history naturally becomes organized or focused around the problem, especially in the parents' experience of the interview. This often facilitates the recognition and emotional acknowledgment of dynamically important connections. It is also more likely that any important determinants of the problem that may become apparent in such a baby-focused exploration are more readily comprehensible to the parents, and again are perhaps more easily worked with, since the disclosure of the information often indicates an ability and readiness to come to terms with it.

The example given above illustrates this point. The evaluator did ask about the phrase "vile child" when it was first used, but the mother was so angry and mistrustful that the question was not productive. Once she had formed an alliance with the evaluator and had explored some of the consequences of her own extremely troubled early experience, the significance of the phrase as an indicator of a "repetition of a childhood tragedy" (Fraiberg, 1980) could be understood and used. In this case, it led to a startled recognition by the mother of her experience of her baby as an unwanted, disavowed aspect of self. As she put it then, her baby was her "mirror image"—giving loud voice to the angry neediness that she had always forcibly suppressed and had come to pride herself in not having.

It is rare that an important area of inquiry cannot be linked to the immediate account that the parents are giving. For instance, expressions of disappointment or frustration about difficulties with the baby can be used to explore the parents' expectations about the baby and about parenthood during the pregnancy, and earlier—even during childhood: "The way things have turned out is frustrating to you, maybe different from your image of what it is to be a parent [or to have a baby]. How did you imagine it would be before the baby was born?" Similarly, questions about the parents' marital functioning can be followed in the context of accounts of the problem with the baby and how it is being handled in the family. Functioning in other areas of the marriage can similarly be linked: "So you have some serious conflicts about how to handle this problem with the baby. How do you get along otherwise?"

After one or two initial interviews conducted in this manner, the clinician is in a position to compile the information gained and determine whether any important areas of inquiry have been omitted. If so, direct inquiry can be made subsequently to fill in the complete picture.

Experience in Dynamic Detail

Perhaps most important in the assessment of the infant–parent relationship is the selection of some emotionally critical or nodal interactions that occur during the interview to explore in very fine detail with the parents. The interviewer should look for critical dynamic chains or sequences of response of one partner to the other, in which an initial emotional response is subject to continuous influence and change as a result of the ongoing feedback from the partner. Such sequences can contain and disclose important determinants of the infant's and parents' behavior that cannot be captured on the basis of general descriptive features of interactions or relationships (intrusiveness, noncontingency, disengagement, etc.).

For example, M., an 18-month-old boy referred because of severe head banging, was playing with a small wooden hammer while his mother, Mrs. A., talked with the interviewer. He was banging a variety of objects, not with any particular aggressiveness or anger, but playfully, experimentally, and with vigorousness and interest. M. approached his mother and gave her chair a rather gentle bang on the leg. Mrs. A. stiffened immediately, and with noticeable suppressed anger but little forcefulness or assertiveness asked him to stop it. M. in turn stiffened, paused, and then banged the chair again repeatedly, this time in a genuinely aggressive manner. Mrs. A. responded more angrily this time, but again somewhat ineffectually, by telling her son to stop. More angrily this time, M. hit her chair again, whereupon she got out of her chair, grabbed him by the arm, and told him he was being bad and would have to cut it out. The toddler fell limp to the ground, so that he was hanging by his arm, and began to cry loudly. His mother looked quite exasperated, hurt, and confused; she let go of his

arm and returned to her seat, leaving him crying more loudly in a heap on the floor. Then he began to bang his head repeatedly on the floor. Mrs. A. yelled at him several times to stop while watching him, then stood up and grabbed him by the arm again. She looked quite withdrawn and cold; he appeared absolutely forlorn, bereft of support and contact, without any solution, lost. At this point, the interviewer intervened.

In this sequence, the initial emotional response of each partner was profoundly transformed by that of the other. An initial experience of curious assertiveness and interest in sharing was transformed into an angry, painful interaction, culminating in a distant, hopeless sense of impasse and despair in both partners.

It is usually best to select such an experience after an overall sense of the problem and the functioning of the relationships in the family has emerged, so that the interviewer knows which areas of difficulty are most important, dynamically live, and likely to be fruitfully explored, and so that the interviewer has a feel for the parents' willingness and ability to explore their experiences in detail. Having selected such an interaction or experience, the interviewer should ask the parents to describe what they were thinking and feeling at each point of the interaction; what they felt like doing or saying; and what they thought the infant was thinking, feeling, and trying to accomplish or communicate at each point in the interaction. Together, the interviewer and parents should explore how what occurred is similar to or different from interactions when at home, from the infant's interactions with other people, and from the parents' interactions with other children and adults. The interviewer should ask how the parents imagine others (including their spouse, parents, in-laws, etc.) would think and feel about such interactions.

It may be necessary to be quite active in the process of this exploration. Parents may need to be provided with a slow pace by being walked through the interaction, especially if they initially produce a very simple or global account of the experience. It may be helpful to ask about the fine details, often beginning with unthreatening aspects of the interaction. The interviewer should emphasize that people usually have numerous thoughts and feelings all at once or in a very short time, and that he or she is interested in *all* of those thoughts and feelings, even if they might seem irrelevant or even silly. Initial attempts by the parents to disavow the significance or complexity of the interaction should be gently confronted—by saying, for instance, that these are the kinds of things that parents often "don't pay much attention to" or "seem unimportant," but such details are often helpful in understanding how the troubles with the baby affect them. Much can be gained by resolutely "playing dumb."

In the example given above of the interaction between the head-banging toddler and his mother, the interviewer proceeded by settling the toddler down to a snack and using this time to explore the interaction that had just occurred between M. and Mrs. A. in detail.

In a previous session, Mrs. A. had described her very intense and troubled relationship with her father in some detail. She was the older of two girls. Her father had desperately wanted a son, and the younger daughter's gender was a regular subject of heated argument between her parents. Mrs. A. filled in the gap after her sister's birth (which occurred when she was 5) by becoming a tomboy and a "buddy" to her father—spending her time fishing, hunting, target shooting, and working around the farm with him. She cherished the closeness with him that she gained with her masculinization, and delighted in the renown resulting from her success in boyish activities.

Her father was an extremely short-tempered, impatient, strict, protoabusive man. He had a drinking problem that, according to her report, remained in control until the family moved to Florida. He could not find work there, so the family was supported by his wife; he then began to drink heavily. He also lost his "buddy" at the same time, as his daughter reached adolescence and discovered boys as objects of desire rather than competition. Her father reportedly became intensely preoccupied with her budding sexuality, extremely jealous of her dating, and regularly physically abusive. Because of the unabated physical abuse, Mrs. A. moved away to live with her grandparents at the age of 15.

In the course of the exploration, it quickly became clear that Mrs. A. had experienced M.'s banging as an aggressive attack on her. Almost instantly, she had become furiously angry, confused, paralyzed, and withdrawn: angry because she felt he was attacking her; confused because she couldn't understand why he was hitting her (he was supposed to love her and she tried so hard to love him); paralyzed and withdrawn because she was afraid that otherwise she would hit him and hurt him. With

detailed questioning, Mrs. A. was able to describe the sequence of these feelings in this interaction with her son. When the interviewer then asked the obvious question about what she had felt when her father attacked her, the identification of father and son was evident, palpable, and alive. She talked about wanting to kill her father at these times—aching to strike him back, but afraid that if she did, his abuse would only grow more fierce. She also described her feelings of helplessness and despair, since she wanted so badly for him to cherish her again as he had when she was a child and could not understand his present dissatisfaction with her.

Provoking Anxiety

Of course, as in any clinical encounter, the interviewer must be aware of the effect of these interventions on the parents. If this type of encouragement of self-reflection meets with stiffened resistance or a negative response, it is important to note and inquire about that, and take time to work with and respectfully challenge the resistance. Although it is critical not to alienate the parents with an intrusive style, many parents are able to use an empathic nudge from a clinician to explore further.

Some clinicians may worry about alienating parents with such a sustained and methodical focus on anxiety-provoking areas of their experience; the concern is that the anxiety will be so high that these parents may subsequently withdraw from the evaluation process or resist the recommendation for treatment. Although these considerations should certainly be borne in mind, the converse danger is the more serious and probably far more common one—that the parents feel as if the interviewer has "missed the boat" because he or she has failed to explore and hence failed to understand the truly painful and worrisome experiences in their lives with the baby. In contrast to and often together with the expected anxiety at having painful conflicts disclosed and explored in this sort of focused interview, parents often feel a profound relief that finally someone else understands, and therefore begin to hope that help is possible. In this view, *it is the very anxiety that such exploration evokes that tells the interviewer he or she is on the right track and should move carefully ahead, and signals to the parents that previously incomprehensible problems can be understood.* Throughout the course of the interview, the clinician should be alert to the signs of anxiety that betoken significant areas of conflict in the infant–parent relationship, and should either make a mental note for later detailed exploration, or zero in and explore the conflict in fine-grained detail as it emerges. Problems with a baby almost invariably involve the most basic and most intensely experienced emotions and conflicts in a parent's life. A clinical interview that does not explore these in the degree of depth that the parents can make use of, and does not illuminate their significance for the parent and the baby, has simply failed in its dual task—failed to understand the infant's problem, and failed to form a therapeutic relationship on the basis of which the problem can be solved.

The parents' form of response to these efforts during the evaluation to overcome anxieties and resistance and to explore personal meanings and experiences related to the problem with the baby is a crucial index for the assessment, especially when the clinician is considering treatment recommendations. Does the parents' initial wariness or defensiveness give way to more open exchange as a consequence of the interviewer's respectful but active approach? How do the parents respond to any careful challenges to defenses? Do the parents respond to the invitation to explore in detail their experience with the baby and what it means to them with deepened interest, richer and more revealing material, and a heightened level of relatedness to the interviewer, or with distance, hostility, superficiality, or vagueness?

If a parent or parents cannot make use of this fairly assertive mode of help at self-understanding, the interviewer will need to "back off," take a somewhat less active and assertive stance, and perhaps turn to less threatening areas of the evaluation. This should be noted for the purposes of making a recommendation for treatment.

Having outlined an active, anxiety-provoking strategy for conduct of the clinical interview with infants and parents, I must emphasize that this kind of persistence in actively exploring areas of anxiety and dysfunction does not in any way entail that the interviewer be perceived or experienced by the parents as critical or blaming. Such *shared* recognition of the effect of inner conflict on a parent's behavior, which has emerged from an emotionally charged interaction and exchange with the interviewer, is quite different in the parent's experience from being told by a distant expert that he or she is to blame for the child's problems. The experience of being

understood in a rich, complex, and deep way by another person is felt to be a supportive one, and often elicits considerable energy and hope alongside the anxiety.

In this regard, it is also important that the interviewer recognize with the parents the areas of strength in the functioning of the infant and parents, and in the infant–parent relationship, in addition to areas of difficulty. It is particularly important to single out for comment and exploration with the parents experiences with the infant during the interview that signal positive functioning and attachment. For many and varying reasons, parents may have trouble recognizing in themselves and hence utilizing in the service of the baby's development yearnings for closeness and love that they have repudiated or suppressed in the past. Positive feelings and wishes may be expressed only in a tentative or restrained way, and exploration of the details of these experiences is as important as exploration of negative experiences.

For example, one young mother had four children, the two older of whom (ages 3 and 5) had been temporarily placed in foster care by child protective services and had multiple psychiatric hospitalizations since then. She retained custody of her 2-year-old daughter and a newborn son, and was being interviewed while holding the newborn. Although she showed absolutely no tenderness or affection with the older boys, and she was describing their difficulties to the interviewer in a markedly flat and disengaged manner, she was observed at the same time to be gently stroking the newborn's head and rubbing his back and chest, seemingly without awareness. When asked how she felt in holding and stroking the baby that way, she replied in a distant, matter-of-fact tone that she felt nothing in particular; she was just holding him. When the interviewer commented that her hands were communicating her loving feelings even as her voice and words denied them, she responded by reflecting on the differences in her feelings of closeness to the children, and on her sense of alienation from the two children who had been taken from her. These explorations led her to memories of her own lifelong history of disrupted and chaotic attachment and caregiving in her family of origin and in the numerous foster care arrangements that had followed her removal from her mother's care in the first year of her life. She described these, in the context of this exchange, in a richer and more meaningful way than she had in an earlier interview.

Here the positive affectionate feelings and yearnings were verbally repudiated or disavowed. However, through the interviewer's active encouragement and attention to the details of the positive interaction as it unfolded, the mother was able to acknowledge her loving feelings, recognize important aspects of her relationship to her children, and deepen her understanding of her troubles with her children and their relationship to her own prior experience. As a consequence, she could begin to perceive and experience herself as a mother who was striving to be a warm and affectionate parent, against psychological barriers within herself that had been erected over the course of her own development, instead of her dominant view of herself as someone beset by "bad" or "evil" kids.

Quite apart from the importance of recognizing and working therapeutically with split-off or disavowed positive feelings and wishes, it is important to keep in mind that parental self-esteem and confidence can be given an important boost through the interviewer's recognition of the positive effects on the baby of the parents' efforts and care. Sustained and persistent focus on areas of difficulty should not be pursued at the cost of attention to and acknowledgment of parental strengths, and vice versa.

INFORMATION GATHERING

The goal of the information-gathering component of the clinical interview is to develop as complete and comprehensive a view as possible of *the infant in context*, in order to facilitate a shared understanding of the infant's problem and to develop a plan for treatment. This includes information about individual characteristics of the infant; characteristics of the parents and other important people in the infant's life; characteristics of the cultural and social world in which the infant is developing; and information about the relationship between the infant and each of the significant figures in his or her life.

As emphasized above, it is preferable to learn as much as possible about all of these aspects of the case from observations during the interviews and from the account given by the parents, rather than in response to a fixed or routine series of questions to "get the history." However, what is learned through observation during the interviews and through the parents' story must often be supplemented with some degree of direct inquiry. Again, it is best when possible to link this inquiry to experiences in the interview. With regard to all the areas of information mentioned below, it is also critical to evaluate in detail their emotional or dynamic meaning to the parents.

In some cases, it will be necessary to seek a specialized assessment, such as a cognitive, neurological, or speech and language evaluation, to supplement the interview process. If such a specialized assessment is warranted, it is important to prepare the parents for the referral by explaining clearly and carefully the concerns that lead the interviewer to seek such an evaluation and the questions the interviewer is seeking to have answered, as well as by taking time to answer any questions the parents may have and to probe for any concerns about the referral they may have trouble expressing or acknowledging. It is also critical to formulate clear and specific referral questions for the clinician to whom the interviewer is making the referral, and to carefully integrate the findings of such specialized assessments into the final formulation communicated to the parents.

Parent–Infant Interaction and Relationship

First, and most obviously, the family interview process presents an opportunity to attend carefully to the sample of interaction between each parent and the baby. In order to reduce the possible impact on the parents' interaction with their baby of their being on the interviewer's "turf" in an office-based practice, it is advisable to let them know at the outset that they should do whatever they need to do in order to care for the baby during the course of the interview. The interviewer should be careful not to take the initiative to resume the interview too quickly after an interruption by the parent to attend to the baby; it is important to allow the parent to pace the alternation of attention to interviewer and baby, and to manage the competing demands as he or she sees fit. This is an important aspect of parental functioning that can be observed in process in the interview, and the interviewer should take precautions to interfere as little as possible in the unfolding of this process.

There are a number of important interdependent areas or domains of functioning to observe and assess in the infant–parent relationship. Although these are described and categorized by different theorists and clinicians in varying ways (see, e.g., Clark, 1985; Emde, 1989; Greenspan, 1981; Sander, 1975), there appears to be general agreement about the most important areas of observation. Emde (1989) proposes seven domains of functioning: (1) attachment and the organization of the experience in the relationship of emotional and physical closeness or availability, as well as separation, distance, and individuation; (2) vigilance and protection, or the organization of experience in the relationship related to maintaining the safety of the infant; (3) physiological regulation of food intake, warmth, stimulation, and mental states (sleep, alertness); (4) play, symbolism, and communication of meanings; (5) teaching and learning; (6) power and control, discipline; and (7) regulation of emotion or affect, including the expression and communication of emotion.

About the functioning of the dyad in each domain, it is important to assess relative strengths and weaknesses, the importance of stressors in the origin and maintenance of any disturbance, the duration of any disturbance, its relative rigidity or responsiveness to change, its impact on the development of infant and parent, and the level of perceived discomfort or distress experienced in relation to the disturbance. Across domains, it is important to assess the pervasiveness or specificity of the strengths and weakness noted in each area.

The Attachment Relationship

The assessment of the infant–parent attachment relationship requires careful observation of how the partners in each dyad organize the interaction and relationship to balance the need for felt security or comfort through closeness with that for exploration and mastery of the surround. (For a detailed description of normative and pathological development in the attachment relationship, see Zeanah Mammen, & Lieberman, Chapter 22, this volume.) Most important is to attend to the infant's use of each parent as a secure base (Ainsworth & Wittig, 1969) for supporting exploration of the room, including the toys available to him or her, and for supporting interaction with the interviewer. Does the infant use contact or proximity with the parents, or perhaps distal communication and eye contact, in order to reassure himself or herself about the safety of the environment and to facilitate moving away from the parent to explore? Does he or she do this initially upon entering the room or upon being exposed to a new stimulus? Does the infant seek physical contact and proximity or visual contact in an ongoing way during exploration, and how does this work?

If and when the infant seeks comfort through physical contact with or proximity to his or her parents, is it effective in reassuring and comforting the infant? Is it pleasurable for the infant? Does it lead to the infant's return to exploration and play? How is this contact or proximity seeking on the infant's part experienced by the parents? What do the parents communicate to the infant (overtly as well as implicitly) about the experience of closeness through their responses? What does the infant communicate to the parents about this experience? Perhaps most importantly, what do this communication and this experience mean to the parents and to the baby?

The quality of the infant's physical and social exploration is of interest in the assessment of the attachment relationship. Does the infant show pleasure, interest, or exuberance in the exploration, or is he or she cautious, wary, sober, or perhaps listless, indifferent, or mechanical? Does the quality of the exploration evolve with the infant's familiarity with the situation? Does the quality of the infant's exploration differ on the basis of the parental response he or she is getting?

The interviewer should look at a process closely related to attachment, called "social referencing" in the developmental literature (Campos & Stenberg, 1981; Hirshberg & Svedja, 1990; Hirshberg, 1990; Sorce, Emde, Campos, & Klinnert, 1985). Does the infant actively use the parents as a source of information about the unfamiliar situation through non-verbal communication, checking to see how they feel about the situation, and making use of their response in regulating their exploratory or social behavior? Are the parents responsive to this referencing of them by their infant, providing feedback without unduly imposing themselves on the baby? How does the infant respond to the parental signals received?

Because the interview process rarely provides for a natural separation of infant and parent, it is usually necessary to inquire about how the infant and the parents respond to routine separations. How does the baby respond to the immediate separation when left with other caregivers? How does this change over time during such a separation? Does the baby adapt and settle and become comfortable, or remain overtly distressed or perhaps low-key (Mahler, Pine, & Bergman, 1975)? Are these responses different when the baby is separated from the mother as compared to the father, and different when he or she is left in the care of different people (say, with relatives vs. babysitters)? How has the baby's response to separation changed over the course of his development?

Similarly, it is important to inquire in detail about all the thoughts and feelings each parent has when he or she separates from the infant. What do the parents think and feel if the baby clings or protests against separation, or if he or she fails to do so? What do they want to do? What do they actually do? What do they imagine the baby is thinking and feeling? What do they believe to be developmentally appropriate? A related area of inquiry is how the parents respond now and responded in the past to those important developmental accomplishments by the baby (such as his or her first steps or weaning) that signify the infant's emerging autonomy and individuation. Are the parents able to foster the child's autonomy, or do they find it threatening and hence compromise or undermine it?

Safety and Protection

Other important aspects of the infant–parent relationship to observe are the parents' vigilance about and provision of protection of the infant's physical safety, as well as the infant's response to this input from each parent and his or her self-regulation regarding physical safety. Is the parent continuously monitoring the infant's safety and taking action to protect him or her when necessary? Is the parent appropriately vigilant and protective, or either overprotective and highly anxious about the baby's safety on the one hand, or careless and lacking in awareness or concern on the other? Does the infant or toddler show either excessive caution and timidity, or recklessness?

Again here, observations regarding this area of parent–infant functioning should be combined with inquiry if there are indications of difficulties—for example, a history of "accident proneness" on the part of the infant or evidence of or complaints about recklessness, especially about a toddler. Unless this area is part of the presenting problem as defined by the parents, it is best to link the inquiry to an observation. For example, the interviewer may note when a

toddler climbs onto a table that the child seems quite adventurous, and wonder how this goes at home. It is usually best to begin with an open-ended and either neutrally or positively connoted question, rather than a series of specific questions, since the former allows the parents to reveal how they organize this area of experience—what seems important, relevant, and appropriate to them. Coupled with inquiry into the kinds of experiences a family may have had should be exploration of what these experiences mean and have meant to the parents. How do they experience the baby's physical strivings and adventurousness? How do they feel when the child hurts himself or herself or is in a dangerous situation? What sorts of things do they imagine might happen? What are they afraid of if they are afraid, and how does that relate to their own history? What do they want to do, and what do they actually do?

Physiological Regulation

A third domain of infant–parent relationship functioning is that of the physiological regulation of food intake, warmth, stimulation, elimination, and mental states such as sleep and alertness. The developmental task of the dyad is to facilitate through reciprocal regulation the emergence and consolidation of basic consistent rhythms of somatic experience, so that organized patterns of functioning are achieved—patterns that then allow for the pursuit of developmentally facilitating activities by the infant in the wider world.

Likely areas of observation in the consulting room or clinic include the regulation of stimulation and of food intake. The interviewer should note how aware the parents are of the infant's level of stimulation and arousal, and how willing and able they are to mediate this as necessary. Can a parent intervene to organize the infant or reduce stimulation if the infant becomes overstimulated or disorganized? Can the parent provide an interesting focus of activity for the infant if he or she becomes bored or restless? On the infant's part, how does he or she respond to regulating input from the parent? Does the infant seem to seek this input and respond favorably to it, or to shun and resist it?

Do the parents seem to keep track of the infant's hunger states and their likely effect on his or her affect and behavior? It is important to note whether, as many do, the parents have brought with them a snack to provide to the baby as necessary. In any case, a snack may be provided to the parents to afford an opportunity to observe how the family organizes the infant's eating experience, and what the infant's eating may mean to the parents and is coming to mean to the infant.

Again, inquiry will be necessary to supplement observation. Questions concerning the infant's physiological patterns are again best posed initially in an open-ended fashion. If the response to this line of inquiry is vague or nonspecific, it may be necessary to ask very detailed questions in order to construct a sense of how the dyad functions in this area. It is often helpful to ask a parent to describe the previous day from moment to moment, starting at the baby's awakening and going until bedtime, in order to obtain this information.

Play

The clinical interview may also afford the clinician opportunity to observe the functioning of the infant–parent dyad at play. If this does not occur spontaneously in the unfolding of the interview, it may be advisable for the interviewer to tell the parents that the interviewer would like to take some time to see how the baby plays with them. The interviewer should observe whether the parents are able to relax and be comfortable in playing with the infant; to comprehend the infant's level of understanding or perspective; to follow the infant's lead when he or she is leading; and to provide organization, structure, or stimulation as necessary. Does the play seem pleasurable for the parents? Are they able—even in the context of a formal interview and in the presence of a stranger—to "loosen up," regress temporarily, and enjoy the "free space" of the play? Do they experience delight in the baby's play? Is the play pleasurable to the infant? The interviewer should also note with which parent the infant is more comfortable or joyful in play. Do the parents notice any differences? How do they understand these differences? Finally, it is important to inquire how the parents' perception of the quality of their play during the interview compares to that of their usual play at home.

Teaching and Learning

Related to play is the area of teaching and learning. Again, there may be spontaneous opportunities to observe the functioning of each dyad in this area, or it may be necessary to provide the parents with a simple task appropriate to the infant's developmental level and ask them to "help the baby to learn" how to do it. The interviewer should observe the parents' manner of introducing or explaining the task, the clarity of any cues or instructions, the contingency of the timing of cues, and the speed or pacing of the cues. Do the parents show flexibility in helping the child, and can they keep the child focused on the task? Are the parents able to provide only the help necessary for the child to remain involved in and positively motivated to complete the task, and to provide input that begins at the child's level and leads him or her to the next step, thus reflecting an understanding of the child's perspective on and experience in the task? The interviewer should consider also the parents' willingness and ability to support the child's own efforts at exploration and mastery through such responses as verbal encouragement or physical support when necessary, expression of pleasure in success, and general communication of interest and positive involvement in the child's experience while learning. Finally, what is the infant's response to parental "teaching" input? Does it appear to be a familiar and comfortable activity? Is the infant responsive to the parent in this context? Does he or she seek for and use parental help in learning?

Power and Control

Still another dimension of relationship functioning to attend to in the assessment is that of the exercise of power and control. Do the parents present themselves to the infant as calm, confident, and in control—of themselves, of the infant, and of the situation they are in? Or, by contrast, do they appear as passive, overwhelmed, disorganized, or confused, or perhaps tense, even potentially explosive? How do they manage the challenges the infant may present to them during the interviews (e.g., a refusal to clean up, constant interruptions, some aggressive acting out, or even simply mounting distress)?

On the infant's part, does he or she basically acknowledge and appear confident of parental organization and control, or does he or she instead attempt to take charge, with manipulative or controlling behavior? Such controlling behavior may be caregiving and solicitous, or may be angry, critical, or provocative. Although current research is documenting the emergence of empathic responses in infants (Radke-Yarrow & Zahn-Waxler, 1984), a role-reversed relationship pattern in which the baby bears the emotional burden of the relationship with the parent betokens an attachment disorder that warrants careful assessment in the clinical interview (Bowlby, 1973; Zeanah, Mammen, & Lieberman, Chapter 22, this volume; Zeanah & Klitzke, 1991).

For example, one mother was being interviewed while her toddler was busily involved in playing on the other side of the room. When she began to cry quite softly upon discussing her feelings about the death of her mother several years prior to the birth of her baby, the toddler immediately and abruptly interrupted his play to rush over to his mother and pat her on the back consolingly. This same mother later described an occasion in which she put her son in his crib for a "time out," and then sat in a rocker in his room to wait till it was over. Witnessing his intense distress over the confinement, she began to cry out of guilt and confusion, whereupon her toddler quickly ceased his crying, stood up in the crib, and called out to her, telling her not to cry.

The interviewer should attend also to how the parents manage together the function of providing control to the infant. Do the parents subtly or overtly undermine each other, or does one use the child to provoke the other? Are there alliances between infant and one parent against the other?

Regulation of Emotion

Finally, the interviewer should observe carefully the functioning of the parent–infant relationships in the mutual regulation of emotion or affect, including the expression and communication of emotion. This is probably the most important area of relationship functioning, since the emotions or affects experienced in any interaction are critical in determining its psychological significance or meaning in the infant–parent relationship. For example, two feeding interactions, both of which may be similarly competent from the point of view of the regulation of food intake, may nevertheless be quite disparate in their emotional significance to the partners and hence to the relationship. One may be emotionally empty and mechanical, or perhaps tense or cold and distant, while the other, by contrast, is relaxed, joyful, and warm. The emotional quality of the feeding is most salient for the organization of the infant–parent relationship. More generally, a number of clinical

theoreticians from varying points of view argue that the affect experienced in an interaction provides the core element around which the experience is organized psychologically, and hence becomes effective in shaping later interactions and relationships (Kernberg, 1976; Emde, 1989; Horowitz, 1989; Mitchell, 1988).

A number of aspects of the emotional functioning of the infant–parent relationship are worthy of note. What is the overall affective tone of the infant–parent interactions observed? Does it differ greatly from moment to moment, activity to activity, parent to parent, session to session? For each partner, are affects expressed openly or in a guarded, muted, or restrained way? Again, for each partner, are they expressed congruently across different channels of expression, such as tone of voice, facial expression, gesture, and body language? The interviewer should observe also whether a full range of emotion is experienced in the interactions, and whether emotions are experienced at varying levels of intensity. These are standard clinical dimensions for assessing affect in individuals; however, research and clinical experience suggest that many of these aspects of emotion regulation and functioning may show continuity within and variability across specific relationships, especially for infants and younger children, but probably also to some degree for adults.

The interviewer should attend also to the particular emotional responses each partner has in response to the emotions and behavior of the other. He or she should look for the kinds of critical sequences in emotional exchanges described above, in which the emotional response of each partner continually modifies and is modified by that of the other.

Finally, it is important to recognize that infant–parent interaction can vary significantly in different relational contexts. For example, a mother and toddler may relate quite differently in the father's presence than when they are alone together. The interviewer should consider also the place of the infant's relationship with each parent in the network of relationships within the family, including the baby's siblings, grandparents, and so on.

What the Infant Brings to Relationships

Winnicott's (1960/1965) dictum that "There is no such thing as a baby" may perfectly well be stood on its head: There is no such thing as a parent, but only parents of particular children. Parental functioning can be impeded or facilitated, conflicts smoothed out or powerfully elicited, and needs met or denied by particular characteristics of the infant, such as regulatory capacity or style, developmental strengths or weaknesses, gender or appearance, or other dimensions along which individual infants differ. The example of Mrs. M., given earlier in this chapter, illustrates this point. This mother had a 4-year-old daughter with no significant behavioral problems. Their relationship was much less overtly conflicted, as the first child had successfully adopted a role-reversed relationship with her mother, in which she adapted to her mother's intolerance or disavowal of neediness.

In the course of the interview, the clinician will have opportunity to make observations concerning the infant's individual characteristics and how they contribute to the presenting problem. The interviewer should attend to the baby's physical appearance: Is the baby particularly appealing or unattractive, thin or heavy, frail or robust in appearance, small or large for age? What do the parents make of this? Whom do family members think the baby looks like in the family? The clinician should also take into account the baby's medical history, including the course of the pregnancy and the infant's perinatal status, as well as his or her cognitive development and other important areas of development and maturation. These include the rapidity and vigor of the infant's motor development; the timeliness of the infant's development of social interest and social relatedness, and of communicative and linguistic competence; and the infant's developmental level of play and symbolization. Any significant questions regarding these latter areas warrant a full-scale cognitive and developmental evaluation (see Clark, Chapter 12, this volume).

Another important area of observation is that of the infant's capacities and patterns in regulating physiological, sensory, attentional, motor, and affective processes, and in organizing, maintaining, and shifting states of alertness and arousal (see Greenspan & Wieder, Chapter 18, this volume). Although there is ongoing debate among clinicians and researchers about the extent to which such characteristics are biologically or constitutionally based, and differences among individual clinicians regarding this issue are influential in shaping approaches to diagnosis and treatment, an important first step in the assessment is the construction of a descriptive account of the infant's regulatory capacities and temperamental style, without assumptions as to its origin. The interviewer should observe and inquire about any signs of unusual responsiveness (under- or overreactivity) to auditory, visual, or tactile stimuli, as well as any unusual temporal patterns in self-regulation (e.g., an unusually rapid or slow rise time in reactivity, or a low threshold of arousal). Is the process by which the infant attempts to modulate and regulate arousal smooth and integrated, or disorganized? Does he or she gradually signal distress, or do overload and distress seem precipitous and unpredictable? The interviewer should attend both to the infant's attempts at self-regulation and to his or her elicitation of regulatory input from his caregivers. Significant also is how the infant adapts to changes in routine and to transitions in activities. This can be observed in the course of the interview by seeing how the infant settles into the consultation or play room, responds to the end of the interview, and handles such shifts as when the interviewer asks the parents to play with him or her, or when the interviewer begins or ends playing with him or her. Inquiry concerning the baby's coping with change and transitions should also be made.

What the Parents Bring to Relationships

In a manner similar to that described above for the infant's individual characteristics, the interviewer should observe and inquire about characteristics of each parent that may be contributing to the infant's problem. The goal is not by any means a complete psychological or psychiatric evaluation of the parents, but an assessment of how parental strengths and weaknesses are involved in the problem and may best be worked with to contribute to the solution. It is important to assess parental factors with regard to general aspects of parental personality and functioning, as well as with regard to specific aspects of their functioning as parents and as parents of this baby.

One area of consideration is that of the parents' personality and the degree of "fit" between the infant and each parent. The interviewer should observe the parents' mood and characteristic style or manner in expressing and regulating such emotions as anger, anxiety, sadness, love or affection, joy, guilt, and so on, and their response to these emotions in others, particularly the infant. Which emotions are easily tolerated or accepted in the self and in others, and which must be disavowed, suppressed, or otherwise defended against? The interviewer should also observe how the parents function with regard to control and self-control, and to power and assertiveness or passivity in relationships. What is their level of defensiveness or openness? Are they able to acknowledge and tolerate emotional conflict, and to accept weaknesses, imperfections, or failures in themselves and others? To what extent are they psychologically minded and empathic, able to observe themselves and others, suspend judgment, take another perspective, and consider others' needs, motives, wishes? In which areas of experience can they do this, and in which can they not? To what extent do they have awareness or appreciation of their own psychological richness, complexity, and depth, and that of others? Again, the interviewer should attend to these areas of functioning with particular reference to the infant.

Attention to each parent's self-image is also important. How do they perceive themselves? How do they wish to be perceived, feel they are perceived, and fear being perceived, both in a general sense, and more specifically as parents? Important here as well is the question of how the parents are similar to and different from their own parents, both with regard to child-rearing attitudes and practices, and with regard to the kind of relationship they are developing with their child. Assessment should also cover how the parents seem to be experiencing or perceiving others in relation to or interaction with them, (again, especially the infant). The interviewer should observe each parent's defensive style and other areas of ego functioning, again attending to areas of strength and weakness.

This information is especially important in developing a treatment plan. It is advisable to begin considering the various possible treatment options available and to take some time to actively assess the parents' ability to use the different treatment modalities successfully. The relevant parental characteristics depend on the specific treatment modalities under consideration.

Perhaps most importantly, the interviewer should assess how the parents perceive, experience, and interpret the infant. How have they organized or constructed their view or representation of the baby and of their relationship to him or her, in relation to a variety of salient

dimensions? How do they view the baby's personality? How is he or she like and unlike other children in the family? What had they imagined the baby would be like during the pregnancy, and how is he or she like or unlike that image? How is the baby like and unlike each parent, both with respect to the parent's personality now and to the kind of baby he or she was? This last question usually opens up for exploration the parents' own early experiences and how they may be involved in the problems with the baby. Again here, it is crucial not to pass by or gloss over any areas of anxiety or conflict that may emerge, but instead to focus incisively on them in a persistent but respectful manner.

The interviewer should inquire also as to how the parents' view of the infant has changed over time as the baby has developed. It is often useful to inquire about the parents' experience of the baby at the common important periods of developmental transition. Are the parents flexible and open in their view of the infant, allowing it to change with the baby's changes, or are they closed and rigid in their attitude?

The interviewer should inquire also about the parents' images or fantasies about the baby prior to and during the pregnancy—what they had been expecting, hoping for, fearing or dreading, and so on—and about their experience of the baby at birth. It is often important to inquire whether the parents had wanted a boy or a girl, why, and how they responded initially and respond now if their wishes were unfulfilled. It is also often useful to inquire about how the baby was named and why.

In general, a stance of principled ignorance is usually best; the interviewer should operate on the assumption that he or she only understands fully what the parents communicate fully and in detail. It is important to address any inconsistencies in the parents' account, or ways in which the baby as represented by the parents may diverge from the baby as observed in the interview. Asking the parents whether some behavior or characteristic observed in the session is what they had in mind can also be helpful.

Finally, it is useful to inquire about how the parents view the infant and themselves when in a variety of different affective states. What is the baby like when he or she is joyful, angry, sad, afraid, or frustrated? How do the parents feel when the baby is feeling these ways? And how does the baby feel and respond when the parents are joyful, angry, sad, afraid, or frustrated?

The goal of this general area of inquiry is to develop with the parents an understanding of how they have created or organized a way of experiencing the infant; how this is affected by their own history and inner experience (thoughts, feelings, wishes, dreams, fears); and how this view of the baby affects their response to the baby and hence the baby's experience.

Specific Precipitant

One critical area for exploration that invariably emerges with the parents' first account of the problem is that of the specific precipitant for the appearance of the problem. Precipitants may be external events or developmental events. It is often important to be very detailed in this inquiry, as parents not infrequently overlook important precipitants of the baby's troubles. The interviewer should inquire as well about the specific precipitant for the decision to seek help: "So the problem had been going on for a while. Why did you call or decide to call on that particular day, rather than any day prior?"

The Wider Context

Finally, it is critical to obtain information about the infants wider life context—social, cultural, economic. What other adults does the infant have significant contact with, and what are these relationships like? Is the infant in day care, and if so, with whom, where, and for how long? Are there any salient cultural attitudes about or practices regarding infants or infant–parent relationships that may have an effect on the problem? What is the family's financial and work situation, and what other stressors for the family might there be?

FORMULATION AND TERMINATION

Ideally, the course of the interviews carries with it its own conclusions. The experience of the parents and the clinician is that *they have come to some new understanding together about the nature of the problem*. In this circumstance, the diagnostic "formulation" is neither produced by the clinician nor experienced by the parents as some abstract or arcane intellectual concoction. Instead, it is a summary of what has been coop-

eratively learned, and should be communicated in terms that the parents can readily understand and will respond to emotionally.

It is best to avoid organizing such a formulation around higher-level or abstract clinical concepts, such as character dynamics, diagnostic entities, or psychodynamic speculations, that have not been well verified by the experiential data of the interview. Instead, the interviewer should focus on material related to present life issues that are relatively close to the parents' experience, that have been disclosed in or revealed by the interview process, and that can be acknowledged on some level by the parents. In summarizing and communicating this understanding to the parents, it is useful to refer to experiences during the evaluation that have already been explored and at least partially understood.

Like this organized understanding of the baby, the family, and the problem, it is crucial that the recommendations for treatment be experienced by the family as being developed cooperatively. It is important to consider with the parents again at the end of the interview what they want help with, and what kind of help they want. The interviewer should consider also what kind of help the parents can make use of, as well as what impediments to help may be posed by sociocultural, economic, and psychological factors.

It is often useful to consider available treatment modalities and assess for the fit of family and modality prior to a final session in which results are communicated. The optimal way to assess this is to make a trial intervention in the modality under consideration and observe how the family responds. One example has already been discussed—that of assessing the parents' response to those interventions from the interviewer that encourage exploration and understanding in psychological depth of the infant–parent relationship, with regard to the appropriateness of focused infant–parent psychotherapy for the family. The interviewer will have made a number of trial interventions in accord with this model and will have noted the parents' response. If the parents have been able to use the interviewer's help to understand more fully the nature of their relationship to each other and to the baby (and how this influences the baby's problems specifically and his or her development more generally), and/or to develop a greater level of relatedness or closeness with the interviewer, then an active, focused course of infant–parent psychotherapy may be appropriate; the interviewer can describe the treatment to the parents by making reference to the therapeutic work already begun in the evaluation. If, by contrast, the parents have not been able to use this sort of active, focused help in understanding, then infant–parent psychotherapy may still be the treatment of choice, but a somewhat slower-paced, less anxiety-provoking approach may be indicated (see Lieberman & Pawl, Chapter 27, this volume).

Another example of trial intervention might be with regard to the possibility of interaction guidance or coaching (see McDonough, Chapter 26, this volume). The interviewer considering this as a treatment option might intervene in the course of an observed interaction to provide a representative intervention in this modality, and observe the parents' response.

In formulating treatment recommendations, careful consideration should also be given to how parents have responded to interventions made by other clinicians, such as pediatricians or social workers, prior to the evaluation. This is often a fruitful area for detailed exploration of how the parents have experienced prior contacts with those aiming to help them and their family.

It is preferable when treatment can be provided by the assessing clinician, although clearly this cannot always be the case. When it is not, the end of the evaluation represents a "termination" as that process is understood in the literature on psychotherapy. This is perhaps especially true when the kind of active, anxiety-provoking techniques described above are successful in the interview and lead to a fruitful collaborative understanding of the problem. Despite the relatively small amount of contact, the parents may experience the interviewer as someone who has helped them in a very important way. Although it is generally not feasible to treat the end of the evaluation as a full-fledged termination, the interviewer should be attuned to these meanings of the situation. Some postevaluation follow-up contact may be helpful to aid the family in the transition to a new clinician.

REFERENCES

Ainsworth, M. D. S., & Wittig, B. (1969). Attachment and exploratory behavior in one year olds in a strange situation. In B. M. Foss (Ed.), *Determinants of infant behavior* (Vol. 4, pp. 111–136). New York: Wiley.

Benjamin, W. (1968). *Illuminations, essays and reflections.* New York, Schocken Books.

Bowlby, J. (1973). *Attachment and loss: Vol. 2. Separation: Anxiety and anger.* New York: Basic Books.

Campos, J. J., & Stenberg, C. (1981). Perception, appraisal, and emotion: The onset of social referencing. In M. Lamb & L. R. Sherrod (Eds.), *Infant social cognition* (pp. 273–314). Hillsdale, NJ: Erlbaum.

Clark, R. (1985). *The parent–child early relational assessment.* Unpublished manuscript, University of Wisconsin.

Emde, R. N. (1989). The infant's relationship experience: Developmental and affective aspects. In A. J. Sameroff & R. N. Emde (Eds.), *Relationship disturbances in early childhood* (pp. 33–51). New York: Basic Books.

Fraiberg, S. (1980). *Clinical studies in infant mental health.* New York: Basic Books.

Freud, S. (1958). The dynamics of transference. In J. Strachey (Ed. and Trans.), *The standard edition of the complete psychological works of Sigmund Freud* (Vol. 12, pp. 97–108). London: Hogarth Press. (Original work published 1912)

Greenberg, J. R., & Mitchell, S. (1983). *Object relations in psychoanalytic theory.* Cambridge, MA: Harvard University Press.

Greenspan, S. (1981). Developmental structuralist approach to the classification of adaptive and pathologic personality organizations: Infancy and early childhood. *American Journal of Psychiatry, 138,* 725–735.

Hirshberg, L. M. (1989). Remembering: Reproduction or construction? *Psychoanalysis and Contemporary Thought, 12,* 343–381.

Hirshberg, L. M. (1990). When infants look to their parents: Part II. Twelve month olds' response to conflicting parental emotional signals. *Child Development, 61,* 1187–1191.

Hirshberg, L. M., & Svejda, M. (1990). When infants look to their parents: Part I. Infants' emotional referencing of mothers and fathers: A comparative study. *Child Development, 61,* 1175–1186.

Horowitz, M. J. (1989). Relationship schema formation: Role relationship models and intrapsychic conflict. *Psychiatry, 52*(3), 260–274.

Kernberg, O. (1976). *Object relations theory and clinical psychoanalysis.* New York: Jason Aronson.

Mahler, M. S., Pine, F., & Bergman, A. (1975). *The psychological birth of the human infant: Symbiosis and individuation.* New York: Basic Books.

Mitchell, S. A. (1988). *Relational concepts in psychoanalysis: An integration.* Cambridge, MA: Harvard University Press.

Radke-Yarrow, M., & Zahn-Waxler, C. (1984). Roots, motives, and patterning in children's prosocial behavior. In E. Staub, D. Bar-Tal, J. Karylowski, & J. Reykowski (Eds.), *The development and maintenance of prosocial behavior: International perspectives on positive morality* (pp. 155–176). New York: Plenum Press.

Sander, L. (1975). Infant and caretaking environment: Investigation and conceptualization of adaptive behavior in a system of increasing complexity. In E. J. Anthony (Ed.), *Explorations in child psychiatry* (pp. 129–166). New York: Plenum Press.

Shevrin, H., & Shechtman, F. (1973). *Bulletin of the Menninger Clinic, 37,* 451–494.

Sorce, J. F., Emde, R. N., Campos, J. J., & Klinnert, M. D.

(1985). Maternal emotional signalling: Its effect on the visual cliff behavior of one year olds. *Developmental Psychology, 21*, 195–200.

Stern, D. (1985). *The Interpersonal world of the infant.* New York: Basic Books.

Winnicott, D. W. (1965). The theory of the parent–infant relationship. In D. W. Winnicott, *The maturational processes and the facilitating environment* (pp. 37–55). New York: International Universities Press. (Original work published 1960.)

Zeanah, C. H., & Klitzke, M. (1991). Role reversal and the self-effacing solution: Observations from infant parent psychotherapy. *Psychiatry, 54*, 346–357.

12

Assessment of Developmental Status and Parent-Infant Relationships: The Therapeutic Process of Evaluation

ROSEANNE CLARK
ANDREW PAULSON
SUSAN CONLIN

Infancy has been recognized as a period of rapid growth and change. Historically, development during this dynamic period was felt to be biologically determined. However, developmental researchers have demonstrated that development has multiple determinants and that the transaction between these determinants is what contributes most significantly to the developmental process (Sameroff & Chandler, 1975). Infant assessment according to this model considers ecological and cultural validity as significant in evaluating the developmental status of the individual (Bronfenbrenner, 1986; Sameroff, Chapter 1, this volume; Garcia Coll & Meyer, Chapter 4, this volume). A critical determinant that we emphasize in this chapter is the social matrix within which the child is developing—that is, family relationships, particularly the parent–child relationship. This chapter will outline the importance of both including the parents in the assessment process and of evaluating the infant's strengths and areas of concern in the context of the family. The process of infant assessment must include not only a measure of the infant's developmental status, but also an evaluation of the quality of his or her relation-

ship with primary caregivers. It is through these relationships that development is supported and enhanced, and familial and cultural norms, values, and issues are transmitted and understood. When the parents are involved in the assessment, the assessment can have therapeutic value for the infant and his or her family as well.

Recent research supports and recommends evaluation of the parent–infant relationship as a significant source of information regarding the infant's current and future functioning (Barnard & Kelly, 1990). When both strengths and concerns are identified with family members, their capacity to support their infant's development can be strengthened. The research regarding parent–child interactions has shown that children with mothers who are socially responsive, who use elaborated and precise verbal teaching strategies, and who encourage representational thinking tend to perform better on standardized measures of intelligence (Bornstein, 1989; Clarke-Stewart, 1973; Lewis & Coates, 1980). Papousek and Papousek (1987) have found that most interactions between parents and alert infants are of a didactic nature and that these interactions support the development of social and cognitive competence in infancy. This research is based in a Vygotskian framework, which postulates that parents facilitate a child's development by (1) providing social support and interest in the social environment, (2) translating the requirements of daily tasks so that they are understandable for the young child, and (3) helping the child move from dependence on others to autonomous functioning in completing daily tasks (Johnson, 1990). This process is completed within the "zone of proximal development" (Vygotsky, 1979), or the distance between the child's independent functioning and the skills and capacities the child displays with social support. This concept is similar to and consistent with the concepts of "scaffolding" and "joint attention" proposed by Bruner (1985), as well as the quality of assistance described by Sroufe (1979). Scaffolding is a process by which an adult provides the support necessary for a child to complete a task successfully, but also extends the child's current skills and knowledge to a higher level.

Scaffolding can be provided on an affective level as well, and the parents' capacity to recognize their child's emotional as well as cognitive, communicative, or problem-solving needs may be as important in supporting a child's developing capacities and sense of competence. This emotional scaffolding has been described in the developmental psychoanalytic literature as the parent functioning in the role of the child's auxiliary ego (Freud, 1977; Sandler, Kennedy & Tyson, 1980). D.W. Winnicott (1965) suggested that the parents' predictability and capacity to provide a "holding environment" for the child should allow the child to be free to explore and see what he or she can make happen, rather than anxiously reacting to possible impingements from the environment. The concepts of "sensitivity" and "responsivity" (Ainsworth, Blehar, Waters, & Wall, 1978), "emotional availability" (Emde, 1980), "mirroring" (Kohut, 1971; Stern, 1985), "structuring and mediating the environment," and "connectedness" (Clark, 1985) all describe important aspects of optimal parental care that support a child's growing capacities and sense of self.

Studies have shown that children of parents who demonstrate sensitivity, responsivity, and flexibility in adjusting their strategies to the needs of their children have children who perform better on a number of problem-solving tasks (Ninio & Bruner, 1978; Pellegrini, Brody, & Sigel, 1985; Wertsch, 1985). As theory and research have indicated, the process of teaching children includes emotional as well as cognitive scaffolding. Information regarding the parents' use of or lack of these supportive strategies is critical to a comprehensive assessment, because it provides a basis not only for hypotheses about the child's current developmental functioning, but for useful recommendations for therapeutic intervention as well.

THE PROCESS OF INFANT ASSESSMENT

In infant mental health settings, the developmental status of the infant is an integral component of a comprehensive assessment. Often the primary reason why a child is brought in to the clinic is a caregiver's concern regarding delays or disturbances in the infant's development. The child may have participated in a preliminary developmental screening in a pediatric or day care setting, or may have been evaluated in an early intervention program. At times a family is referred because of parenting difficulties or concerns. This may especially be the case when a referral is from social services or a child welfare agency, a mental health program and/or a professional who may be treating a mother who is depressed or has another psychiatric disorder. Infants and young children of parents who are depressed have been found to evidence delays in cognitive, language and attentional skills as well as sober or a constricted range of affect (Clark, 1986; Cogill, Caplan, Alexandra, Robson, & Kumar, 1986; Lyons-Ruth, Zoll, Connell, & Grunebaum, 1986). The goal of the infant mental health professional is to build a more comprehensive picture of the child's developmental functioning which includes assessment of the child's primary relationships (i.e., with family members, teachers, health care providers, the examiner/therapist) and across different environments (e.g., home and school). A comprehensive assessment can assist the therapist in focusing intervention efforts as well as in evaluating progress during the therapeutic process.

We have found that comprehensive assessments are best conducted with the parents' collaborative participation. To begin with the parents should be asked what it is that they expect and what it is that they are interested in finding out from this assessment. Also, what are their feelings as they enter into the assessment process? Who is this child to them and what do the developmental delays or behaviors of concern mean to them. Parents have a wealth of information regarding their children, which frequently is not given the weight it deserves. Parents' observations and contributions are particularly salient with infants, whose development can vary from day to day and even hour to hour. Infant functioning is very state-dependent; because of this, assessments should be done on a regular and periodic basis (Meisels & Provence, 1989).

There is important information to be gathered from parents prior to and while assessing an infant or young child's developmental status. This includes developmental history, including the pregnancy, labor, and delivery experiences, and occurrence of any pre- or postnatal trauma; health history, especially acute or chronic illnesses that may affect sensory functioning or skill acquisition (e.g., meningitis or recurrent/severe otitis media, both of which can result in mild to severe hearing losses that can affect learning in many areas, especially linguistic and social–emotional functioning); and family/social history, including psychiatric history, psychological functioning and developmental and relationship history of parents, and the meaning of the child and the child's behavior or condition to the parents. The process of gathering information should be more than just gathering facts; it should allow parents the opportunity to wonder and reflect about past events and memories. This process of "wondering along" is particularly helpful in understanding the internal working model each parent has of the child and of their relationship.

In an infant or young child, developmental disturbances are often manifested as delays in speech or language, cognitive functioning, or motor functioning. In addition, delays and disturbances in the quality of communication and motor functioning may be observed in the young child with emotional disturbances. Often delays in development appear scattered over the various discrete areas of functioning. This may be a function of poorly developed attentional or communicative skills, such as those seen in children with multisystem delays, regulatory difficulties, or processing/learning problems (Greenspan, 1992) or in children in high-risk environments (e.g., families with parental psychiatric disturbances) (Clark, 1983).

The developmental status evaluation remains the foundation of a comprehensive assessment. The developmental assessment can provide the parent, clinician(s), and teachers with an understanding of the infant's current skills across various developmental domains, and can provide a preliminary picture of the infant's behavioral style. The developmental assessment is also an opportunity to observe an infant's social and emotional functioning in a structured or set situation (Gaensbauer & Harmon, 1981; Winnicott, 1975). The infant's skills can be compared with those of peers, and a pattern of strengths and areas of concern can be developed. Once identified, these concerns may form the basis of referrals for more in-depth evaluations in one or more of the following areas: occupational therapy, speech and language, hearing, and/or pediatric neurology.

A structured assessment of a young child's developmental status with a parent present can provide important observations regarding the young child's behavioral capacities to focus and sustain attention, retain and follow instructions, persist and solve problems, and make use of environmental facilitation. The presence of one or both parents in the room during the developmental assessment is recommended in two instances: (1) if an infant is young enough to require holding; (2) if an infant would function at a more optimal level with the parent(s) present.

In the case of a young child in a disturbed or conflictual relationship with a parent, it may be advisable to conduct a structured assessment, with the parents and another therapist observing from behind a one-way mirror. The parents can then report on how the child's performance and behavior are similar to or differ from his or her typical behavior. The second therapist's joining and facilitating the parents in observing and assessing the child's development can help to expand the parents' perceptions of their child, involve the parents in identifying areas of concern as well as emerging skills, and provide an opportunity to assess the meaning of the child's behavior and developmental functioning for the parents (Clark & Milner, 1989).

An evaluation of the quality of the parent–child interaction should be an integral component of the comprehensive evaluation. This can include direct observations and/or videotaping to assess the parents' capacities across different situations to provide both emotional and cognitive scaffolding for their young child. Video-taping can be made both safe and therapeutic as the parents are encouraged to describe how these interactions may be alike or different from how things usually are, and therapists and parents together can assess what each member of the dyad may contribute to the quality of the interactions. The parents' participation in both a subjective assessment of their relationship with their child and an objective evaluation of the quality of the parent–child interaction may assist him or her in developing strategies for supporting the child's development and in strengthening the emergence of delayed skills according to the child's unique needs.

We have introduced the important aspects of a developmental assessment for the infant mental health professional to consider: the *how*, *what*, and *when* of conducting a developmental assessment of an infant or young child. These can be summarized as follows.

- *How* does one conduct a developmental assessment? These are the important elements of the process or approach:

  1. Asking parents what information they would like to receive from this assessment.
  2. Providing a safe, comfortable environment for the child.
  3. Assessing the infant's optimal level of functioning and/or what he or she can do with environmental facilitation.
  4. Involving one or both parents in the process, in the room or behind a one-way mirror, of assessing their child's skills, interests, behavior, and adaptive capacities.
  5. Engaging parents in assessing their relationship with their child through use of a video replay interview focused on helping them to identify strengths and difficulties they may have in supporting their child's emerging skills and sense of self in relation to others.
  6. Being aware of and sensitive to cultural differences, and respecting and appreciating these when interacting with and assessing children and their families.

- *What* is a developmental assessment? It should include these components:

  1. Gathering information about the child's developmental, health, and family/social history with the parents.

  2. Engaging the young child in the structured or semistructured assessment of developmental skills and emerging capacities along various developmental lines.
  3. Assessing the child's behavior and coping abilities during testing and play sessions.
  4. Observing the child across different settings (i.e., home, office, day care).
  5. Evaluating the quality of parent–child relationships/interactions, including identification of strengths and areas of concern.

- *When* and how often should one conduct a developmental assessment?

  1. Reassessing if there are concerns about the infant's state, health, or performance.
  2. Assessing on a periodic basis, with at least informal assessment and involvement of parents throughout the therapeutic process.

INFANT ASSESSMENT: RELIABILITY AND VALIDITY

Having established what a developmental assessment is in infancy and early childhood, it is important to consider how and on what basis one will measure a central aspect of it (i.e., the infant's developmental status). Although tools for measuring an infant's developmental status have existed since the early part of the century (Gesell, 1929), the last 20 years have witnessed a dramatic increase in the types of measures available for assessing infants. With the advent of Public Law 99–457, additional infant assessment measures have been developed or revised. Even currently used infant assessment tools have moved from predominantly global measures of gross functioning, such as the Bayley Scales of Infant Development (Bayley, 1969) and the Stanford–Binet Intelligence Test (Thorndike, Hagen, & Sattler, 1986), to more domain- and context-specific measures, such as the Connecticut Infant–Toddler Developmental Assessment Program (IDA; Erikson & Vater, 1988) and the Infant Mullen Scales of Early Learning (Infant MSEL; Infant Mullen, 1991). As the tools for assessing infants increase in numbers and become more refined and sophisticated, the psychometric properties of reliability and validity continue to be the standards by which to appraise the quality of any measure.

The issues of reliability and validity have been challenging ones for developers of infant assessment tools. As stated earlier, the developmental process within infancy and early childhood is complex and involves rapid change. To establish reliability and validity (particularly predictive validity) within such a context is difficult. A basic tenet of reliability commonly reported is that the results produced or observed by one examiner will be the same when the same measure is used by another independent examiner at approximately the same point in time (interrater reliability), and that the results will be similar when the child is tested at two relatively close points in time (test–retest reliability). These are minimum standards that developers of assessment tools must meet. However, with new federal legislation (Public Law 99–457) mandating that infants who have or who are at risk for developmental delays be identified, more clinicians are being asked to assess infants, often without specific training in infant assessment. It is critical that those individuals who administer infant tests have specialized training in infant assessment as well as infant development; without this specialized training, the reliability of any measure is seriously compromised.

In Wisconsin, the Birth-3 Interagency Coordinating Council's Screening and Assessment Task Committee recently developed a list of competencies needed for personnel who evaluate infants and young children, including (1) knowledge of all areas of child development, including the range of developmental functioning in normal, atypical, and high-risk populations; (2) ability to establish rapport to elicit optimal level of functioning with infants/toddlers, including those with special needs; (3) ability to effectively assess a child's developmental functioning through observation, interviews, nonstandardized checklists, and questionnaires; and (4) ability to administer and interpret formal screening, evaluation, and assessment tools for children from birth to 3 years of age (Clark, Lange, and the Screening and Assessment Task Committee, 1992). These competencies stress the importance of acquiring specialized training and direct experience with infants, young children, and their families.

Issues regarding validity have been equally challenging and complex. It is commonly understood that a measure is valid if it accurately describes an individual's current functioning (content and construct validity) and predicts that individual's future functioning (criterion validity). The question regarding the continuity of infant development has been particularly salient to questions regarding validity. The belief of some developers of infant assessment tools is that development is continuous and linear. This continuous model of development has been challenged, particularly within infancy. Infancy and early childhood may be more accurately described developmentally by individual differences and discontinuity (Emde, 1981). Thus the process of creating developmentally valid measures is complex and requires a multifaceted approach.

An infant assessment measure is generally able to establish construct and content validity when it describes the current functioning of the infant. However, these measures have not been successful in predicting future outcomes on the basis of current functioning (Kopp & McCall, 1982). The poor predicative capacities may be a function of both inadequate assessment tools and inferior assessment procedures. Recent developments in infant assessment have supported the premise that the traditional manner of assessing infants (e.g., administration of the Bayley Scales of Infant Development) is not the best method of providing an accurate measure of developmental status. Gibbs (1990, p. 85), in a review of why infant tests are not reliable predictors of future performance, highlighted three possible explanations: (1) development may not be as continuous as we may have assumed; (2) intelligence in infancy is qualitatively different from intelligence in childhood; and (3) development is influenced by social and environmental factors that may preclude good prediction from infancy to later ages.

Recent developments in the assessment of attention, memory, and perceptual skills in infancy have led to more promising results regarding predictive validity (Drotar, 1987; Fagan, 1982; Ruff, Lawson, Parrinello, & Weissberg, 1990). Fagan (1987) has reported that an infant's visual processing skills are strongly associated with later measures of cognitive capabilities. Ruff et al. (1990) have also demonstrated that focused attention is predictive of later cognitive competencies. Ruff has developed a system to code focused attention during free play. Although the technique is still experimental, her findings have been quite promising. Ruff's model of assessing infants' attention is particularly appealing because it can be easily integrated into the traditional infant assessment process. Both Fagan (1987) and Ruff et al. (1990) recommend that measures of attention, memory, and visual processing be incorporated within other modes of assessment.

Recent reviews have also indicated that the social competence of infants may be the best predictor of their later functioning (Bernstein, Hans, & Percansky, 1991). The development of social competence, according to Bernstein and colleagues, is often dependent on the quality of the parent–child relationship. Attachment researchers have demonstrated that those infants who have developed secure attachments within the first year of life tend to have more positive developmental outcomes later in childhood (Matas, Arend, & Sroufe, 1978). These findings, coupled with the research previously presented on parent–child interactions, suggest that we rethink the content and constructs that guide our assessments of infants. In regard to improving the validity of infant assessment measures, transactional theory (Sameroff & Chandler, 1975) again underlies the recommendation that clinicians utilize a more comprehensive, integrative approach that includes measures of the infant, of the parent–infant relationship, and of the environmental context within which the infant is developing.

INFANT ASSESSMENT MEASURES

This section highlights selected measures of developmental and psychological functioning useful in providing individual assessments of infants and young children. It is beyond the scope of this chapter to include developmental screening tools, such as the Denver II (Frankenburg et al., 1990), the Early Screening Inventory (Meisels, 1985), the Minnesota Child Development Inventory (Ireton & Thwing, 1974), or the Early Language Milestone Screener (Capute & Accardo, 1978). For reviews of such tools, see Meisels (1985) and Meisels and Wasik (1990).

Brazelton Neonatal Behavioral Assessment Scale

The Brazelton Neonatal Behavioral Assessment Scale (NBAS; Brazelton, 1984) was designed to assess the infant's available responses to his or her environment, and thus, indirectly, the infant's effect on the environment. The NBAS was originally devised for use with the normal full-term newborn, and it samples a broad range of neonatal behaviors, including reflexive/elicited responses and behavioral items (Francis, Self, & Horowitz, 1987). Specifically, the NBAS records the pattern of state change in the infant over the course of the examination, as well as the infant's lability and direction in response to external and internal stimuli. In all but a few items, the infant's score is based on his or her best, not average, performance (Brazelton, 1984).

The NBAS usually takes 20–30 minutes to administer, and more than one administration is recommended—usually on the 3rd day and again on the 9th or 10th day after birth (Als, Tronick, Lester, & Brazelton, 1979; Brazelton, 1984). If only one behavioral assessment is to be made, Brazelton (1984) suggests that a later test (after the 3rd day of life) may be a more valid predictor of cognitive and social assets, because of the effects that trauma associated with birth is likely to have on infants during their first few days of life. The test items may be performed in the order listed in the scale, but after the initial response decrement (holding a flashlight 10–12 inches from the infant, shining the light directly into the infant's eyes for 1–2 seconds), it is important to follow the infant's cues (Brazelton, 1984).

The basic scoresheet includes 28 behavioral items, each of which is scored on a 9-point scale, and 18 elicited responses, each of which is scored on a 4-point scale (Brazelton, 1984). For premature or fragile infants, nine supplementary items (also on a 9-point scale) have been devised; Brazelton (1984) states that these are intended to capture some of the more general characteristics of the infant's behavior (i.e., robustness and endurance, regulatory capacity, quality of alert responsiveness) as well as the response of the examiner to the infant (i.e., examiner persistence, reinforcement value of infant). It is suggested that the examiner write a descriptive paragraph in order to record evidence of the infant's maturity, as well as his or her subjective impressions regarding the infant's reactions, appearance, behavior, and predictions about the kind of responses these characteristics will produce in the mother (Brazelton, 1984). Modest evidence of predictive validity is available from studies linking NBAS scores to later performance on the Bayley Scales of Infant Development.

Although the NBAS was originally developed for use with healthy full-term infants, it has also been used for the study of high-risk infants (Als et al., 1979; Brazelton, 1984; Brazelton, Nugent, & Lester, 1987). Brazelton (1984) claims that studies of infants born to diabetic, alcoholic, narcotic-addicted, and malnourished mothers have shown that the NBAS is a useful tool in describing the differences between the behavioral repertoires of these high-risk infants and those of normal full-term infants. A process for involving parents in the administration of parts of the NBAS has been developed by Cardone and Gilkerson (1990) (see the discussion of Family Administered Neonatal Activities in a later section of this chapter).

Bayley Scales of Infant Development

The Bayley Scales of Infant Development (Bayley, 1969) constitute one of the most widely used diagnostic instruments for children from 2 to 30 months of age. The primary value of the Bayley is that it provides the basis for establishing a child's current developmental status and the extent of any deviation from normal expectancy.

The Bayley consists of three components: the Mental scale, the Psychomotor scale, and the Infant Behavior Record. The Mental scale assesses perceptual, memory, problem-solving, communicative, and verbal skills. The Psychomotor scale is intended to measure gross and fine motor abilities. The Infant Behavior Record provides a behavioral profile consisting of a number of items on which the infant's affective and behavioral responses to the examiner and the testing environment is rated.

The Bayley takes approximately 45 minutes to 1 hour to administer, depending on the age and interest of the child and the proficiency of the examiner. The Bayley is described by McCune, Kalmanson, Fleck, Glazewski, and Sillari (1990) as a structured play session that should be enjoyed by parents, child, and examiner alike. The manual suggests that the caregiver be present during the testing, and items may be presented by him or her when the examiner thinks it indicated. The 163 items on the Mental scale and the 81 items on the Psychomotor

scale are arranged in order of the age at which 50% of the children at each age in the norm group passed the item (Bayley, 1969).

Studies have demonstrated that the Bayley has adequate predictive validity within the first 3 years of life and with infants who have significant delays. However, the long-term predictive validity of the Bayley is quite poor for children who are within the average range or who exhibit only slight delays in their development (Gibbs, 1990; Sigel, 1981; Whatley, 1987).

Because the Bayley was standardized on a sample of normal, noninstitutionalized, English-speaking children, it must be used cautiously with high-risk children and may not be usable at all with some groups of handicapped children. Whatley (1987) states that items on the Mental scale often require visual and auditory abilities that many handicapped children do not have, and no standardized version of the Bayley has yet been developed for use with physically challenged, hearing or visually impaired children (although individual researchers and clinicians have employed modifications of the Bayley procedure).

For most clinicians, the Bayley is more useful as a way to examine an infants' current strengths and weaknesses than as a measure of intelligence or as a predictive measure. A revision of the Bayley, the BSID-II, is currently being field-tested and normed by the Psychological Corporation (J. Mitchell, personal communication, 1993). This revision was begun in 1988, with the goals of updating the norms, expanding the age range to include children from 1 month to 42 months, to updating and expanding the content of the scale (e.g., social behavior, visual and auditory habituation, problem solving, and language items) and to make the infant behavior record an integral part of the administration of the Bayley. Improved sampling techniques and testing of clinical populations will both increase the reliability of the scale and make it possible to develop profiles and modifications for use with special populations.

Griffiths Mental Development Scales

The Griffiths Mental Development Scales constitute a standardized intelligence test that measures trends of development indicative of mental growth in young children from birth to 8 years of age (Griffiths, 1954). It is used more widely in Europe than in the United States. The Griffiths is divided into five subscales: Locomotor, Personal–Social, Hearing–Speech, Eye–Hand Coordination, and Performance. A sixth scale, Practical Reasoning, is added for children ages 3 to 8 years. The time required for administration is between 20 and 40 minutes. Examiners are trained to complete the questionnaire and to pose problems using a standardized phraseology by following the infant's or young child's lead (Griffiths, 1954).

The Griffiths is divided into two levels: (1) birth to 2 years of age, and (2) 3 to 8 years of age. Although there is no special order for scale administration, it is suggested that the examiner try to complete the subscales one by one. However, when the infant or young child indicates that he or she is no longer interested in participating in the contents of a particular scale, the examiner may switch to another scale.

Scoring for the Griffiths consists of computing a developmental age and quotient for each scale, as well as an overall mental age and intelligence quotient. The Griffiths has been shown to be useful for evaluating very young and/or handicapped children. However, the standardization on the instrument was done in the mid-1950s and thus is outdated for current use. The Griffiths are useful however in clinical research work with infants because of its capacity to describe functioning in specific areas of development. A recently reported study found three of the Griffiths subscales (Locomotor, Personal–Social, and Performance) to be inversely related to the amount of stress in mothers' lives (Parks, Lenz, & Jenkins, 1992).

Stanford–Binet Intelligence Scale, Fourth Edition

The Stanford–Binet Intelligence Scale is designed to assess the general intellectual abilities of persons ages 2 through 23 years (Thorndike et al., 1986). The Stanford–Binet contains 15 subtests that are organized into four cognitive ability sections: Verbal Reasoning, Abstract/Visual Reasoning, Quantitative Reasoning, and Short-Term Memory. The Stanford–Binet is administered by a trained professional such as a psychologist, and takes 45 to 90 minutes to complete. Scoring involves converting raw scores into three types of standard scores (scaled, area, and a composite); the computation of area and composite scores is suggested when less than the entire scale is administered (Thorndike et al., 1986).

Validity studies comparing the Stanford–Binet with other intelligence tests, such as the Wechsler Intelligence Scale for Children—Revised and the Mental Processing Composite score of the Kaufman Assessment Battery for Children, indicate satisfactory concurrent validity (range from .81 to .91; Thorndike et al., 1986). Lower concurrent validity scores have been found among special populations such as gifted or mentally retarded populations, indicating that scores on other intelligence tests may not be comparable to scores on the Stanford–Binet with these populations. The Stanford–Binet has been criticized with respect to its standardization, specifically the overrepresentation of high-socioeconomic-status subjects (Spruill, 1987). Although weighting techniques have been incorporated to account for this bias, the validity of these techniques is unclear. In addition, simply evaluating a young child's IQ without additional information regarding his or her developmental progress in areas such as physical health, motoric functioning, or social interaction does not allow appropriate identification of aspects of functioning that may be of concern to infant mental health professionals.

Infant Mullen Scales of Early Learning

The Infant MSEL is one of the most recently developed infant measures; it attempts to assess an infant's specific abilities in terms of domains of functioning. Based theoretically on a neurodevelopmental model, the Infant MSEL is divided into five subscales within the domains of motor, visual, and language abilities: Gross Motor Base, Visual Receptive Organization, Visual Expressive Organization, Language Receptive Organization, and Language Expressive Organization. The clinician is provided with T-scores and age equivalent scores for each of the domains, which facilitate an understanding of a particular child's strengths and areas of concern.

The Infant MSEL has undergone a national standardization ($n = 1231$), which included representation based on stratified variables of sex, race, parental occupation, and urban–rural residence (based on census projection data of 1989) of children from birth to 38 months of age. Validity data have supported the five factors of the Infant MSEL. These data indicated that each of the subscales was poorly correlated with the more global Mental Development Index of the Bayley, providing further support for the construct of separate skills in infancy. Reliability coefficients have ranged from .70 to .99 and have included both test–retest and interscorer reliability studies.

The five subscales of the Infant MSEL are particularly useful with infants who have delays in specific domains, such as motoric delays. Because of the stand-alone quality of the subscales, clinicians are better able to assess strengths and weaknesses and to make specific recommendations regarding intervention goals. Research is currently assessing the Infant MSEL's utility with a variety of at-risk infant populations (Mullen, 1991). An area of needed research is the predictive validity of the Infant MSEL. Although relatively new, the Infant MSEL is an important addition to the infant assessment field.

Early Coping Inventory

The Early Coping Inventory is an observation instrument for assessing the coping-related behaviors that a child uses to manage the routines, opportunities, challenges, and frustrations encountered in daily living (Zeitlin, Williamson, & Szczepanski, 1988). It is designed for use with children who function developmentally from 4 to 36 months of age. The Early Coping Inventory has 48 items divided into three categories that describe a child's coping style (Zeitlin et al., 1988). The first category, Sensorimotor Organization, includes behaviors used to regulate psychophysiological functions and to integrate sensory and motor processes. The second, Reactive Behaviors, includes actions used to respond to demands of the physical and social environments. The third category, Self-Initiated Behaviors, includes autonomously generated, self-directed actions that are used to meet personal needs and to interact with objects and people.

Ratings are based on a 5-point scale of effectiveness (from "not effective" to "consistently effective across situations") of the child's behavior. Effective behavior is defined as (1) appropriate for the situations; (2) appropriate for the child's developmental age; and (3) successfully used by the child (Zeitlin et al., 1988). The Early Coping Inventory is especially valuable in clinical settings in that it provides assessment of results that translate well into specific therapeutic goals and approaches.

Transdisciplinary Play-Based Assessment

The Transdisciplinary Play-Based Assessment (TPBA) is both an assessment and an intervention process to help parents and professionals better understand a child's level of social–emotional, cognitive, language/communication, and sensorimotor development (Linder, 1990). The TPBA can be conducted by any number and combination of professionals in conjunction with parents, and is appropriate for children who function between the ages of 6 months and 6 years of age. Structured and unstructured play situations are organized around information provided by the parents prior to the play session on developmental checklists about their child.

The TPBA is intended for use in any creative play environment, whether it be the child's home or a play room at the child's preschool, or day care center. If the TPBA takes place in the child's home, Linder (1990) suggests that novel toys (which are age-appropriate) be brought by the assessment team, to insure that the child will be stimulated and intrigued by the choice of toys to play with. It is important that the session take place in a natural environment for the child, one that is conducive to eliciting the child's highest skill level. The TPBA has six phases, each of which usually lasts for an amount of time suggested by Linder (1990); the entire assessment takes 60–90 minutes.

The TPBA is a creative new process of infant/child assessment and intervention that supports a child in attaining his or her highest level of achievement in a play setting. Although Linder (1990) states that parents may find more meaning in the results of traditional assessment procedures that include their child's adaptive abilities, the TPBA has a number of advantages over more traditional assessments. For example, the TPBA allows for flexibility through its individualized approach, provides parents with a holistic assessment by an entire team of trained professionals who work together, involves parents in both the information collecting and in the intervention, focuses on "process" by collecting qualitative data, and insures that every child is testable by proceeding from whatever point the child is capable of beginning at (Linder, 1990).

Connecticut Infant-Toddler Developmental Assessment Program

The IDA is a family-centered team assessment approach that addresses the health and development of children from birth to 3 years of age (Erikson & Vater, 1988). The IDA was designed to improve early identification of handicapped and at-risk children, and it can be used in all situations where there is any concern about a child. Parents are involved in all aspects of the assessment process, which consists of five major domains: Gross Motor, Fine Motor, Relationship to Inanimate Objects, Language, and Self-Help. Three subdomains include Relationship to Persons, Emotions and Feeling States, and Coping. A developmental profile of the child results from the IDA, together with a summary of other health and family findings (Provence, Erikson, Vater, & Palmeri, 1986, 1990).

The IDA differs from other developmental assessments in its level of comprehension, integration, ability to facilitate decision making, and regard for emotional development and interpersonal relationships; it is also distinguished by the fact that it is conducted by a team of practitioners who are credentialed in one of the developmental disciplines (Erikson & Vater, 1988). The IDA is comprehensive in that it is designed to assess health, family/social, and developmental dimensions of the child, and integrated to the degree that it provides a framework for the integration and review of data from multiple sources, including observation, self-report, medical records, and clinical consultations (Erikson & Vater, 1988). Information from the IDA is used to aid practitioners in making service referrals that are needed by the child and his or her family; the IDA is particularly oriented toward assessing children who have mild to moderate developmental problems. The IDA is unique in that it values developmental aspects of children that are not related to traditional skill areas, such as emotions, coping style and relationships with people. Finally, by incorporating an interdisciplinary team of IDA-trained and certified professionals, the IDA insures a developmental assessment of the child based on multiple professional perspectives.

Evaluation studies designed to evaluate the content validity of the IDA have noted its comparability to other scales with respect to skills and abilities expected of infants and toddlers at various ages. Exact item agreement between the IDA and other scales—such as the Bayley Scales of Infant Development, the Hawaiian Early Learning Profile, the Learning Age Profile, the language scales of Schiefelbush, Sullivan, and Ganz (1980), and the language scale of Oller—ranged between 84% and 100%. Agencies that received referrals as a result of an assessment based on the IDA further demonstrate the assessment ability of this instrument, in that a great majority (83%) of those agencies considered the referral appropriate (Anastasiow, 1988).

The IDA is a comprehensive assessment tool that incorporates parental input and regards emotional development and a child's relationships with people as central to the assessment process thus making it a valuable addition to infant assessments available to the infant mental health professional.

PARENT-INFANT INTERACTION/ RELATIONSHIP MEASURES

The quality of parent–infant interaction and parent–infant relationships is a critical source for assessing a young child's current developmental functioning. The earliest and primary relationships provide a social matrix within which development in all areas of functioning occurs, including cognitive, social–emotional, communicative, and motoric capabilities. The infant learns from, responds to, and copes with the vicissitudes of that social matrix (Stern, 1985). The infant's or young child's primary relationships contribute to the development of his or her beliefs regarding what may be expected in relationships with others, as well as of his or her coping abilities and personality. Social and emotional functioning are best assessed within the context of relationships.

This section highlights selected measures showing the quality of parent–infant interactions and relationships that are useful in providing a more comprehensive and valid assessment of infants and young children.

Family Administered Neonatal Activities

The Family Administered Neonatal Activities (FANA) constitute a specialized application of the NBAS. The FANA was introduced in 1987 as a new component of a hospital-based family support program. Its purposes include (1) providing family support to promote competence and adaptation; (2) serving as an intervention for functioning families experiencing situational stresses, such as an unusually long labor and delivery process, or previous experience with perinatal loss; and (3) serving as a preliminary assessment in families where there is concern about the ability to care for infants at home (Cardone & Gilkerson, 1990).

Two distinctive features of the FANA are (1) that it is based on a model of parent competence; and (2) that it is clinical rather than educational in nature (i.e., the facilitator is trained to guide and respond to the parents' interpretations of the baby, rather than interpreting the baby to the parents) (Cardone & Gilkerson, 1990). In other words, the facilitator is in a role to support and empower parental perceptions, efforts, and competencies, and parents are provided a structure within which to interpret their child's behavior themselves. Direct interpretations of the baby are not provided by the facilitator.

The FANA takes approximately 35–40 minutes to administer and is typically conducted on the second postpartum day in the mother's room at the hospital, with the mother, father, and infant present. The four phases of a FANA session are a chart review, a parent perception interview, application of the NBAS, and an integrative summary. A chart review is conducted first to obtain information about the mother's pregnancy history, the labor and delivery, and the infant's status, so as to provide the facilitator with background information on the mother–infant dyad. In the parent perception interview, the facilitator inquires about each parent's personal well-being, the mother's labor and delivery experience, and the baby's name and its historical significance (Cardone & Gilkerson, 1990). Although facilitators are trained to listen to and acknowledge parental observations, perceptions, and concerns, they are also trained *not* to normalize, reassure, or teach new information to parents during this interview.

During the FANA, the administration of the NBAS takes 15–20 minutes, and parents are guided by the facilitator to elicit 28 selected items from their infant. These items are seen as particularly engaging to parents, and the order of these items is ultimately determined by the infant's state at the time of administration (Brazelton, 1984). The final phase of the FANA is the integrative summary: The facilitator guides a discussion in which parents are encouraged to integrate their initial observations and perceptions of their infant with the behaviors displayed during the NBAS (Cardone & Gilkerson, 1990). Some joint observations by the parents and facilitator may challenge earlier parental perceptions that resulted from unrealistic expectations. With this information, the infant's behavior can then be used as a vehicle through which parents can affirm or challenge their initial perceptions, guided by the facilitator's expertise and knowledge.

Formal evaluation of the FANA is not yet available. Specialized training is required for clinicians interested in facilitating this clinical assessment process.

Nursing Child Assessment Satellite Training Teaching and Feeding Scales

The Nursing Child Assessment Satellite Training (NCAST) Teaching and Feeding Scales rate mother and child behaviors on a total of 149 variables (Barnard, 1979). The NCAST Scales are intended primarily for use with mothers who are at medical risk during pregnancy, during delivery, or postnatally; with mothers whose infants are premature or fail to thrive; or in situations where a child is at risk for neglect and/or abuse (Farran, Clark, & Ray, 1990). Teaching and feeding behaviors of the mother are rated for the occurrence–nonoccurrence of sensitivity to the child's cues, responding to the child's distress, and fostering social–emotional as well as cognitive growth in the child. Behaviors of the child (ages 6–36 months) are rated on both scales for clarity of cues and responsiveness to the mother.

The feeding aspect of this assessment is intended to involve a natural feeding situation for the dyad; the teaching part is set up as a structured session in which the mother is first asked to teach a task to her child at his or her age level, and then to teach a task at a more advanced level (Barnard, 1979; Barnard et al., 1989).

The Feeding Scale has been found to have moderate to high correlations with the Home Observation for Measurement of the Environment (HOME; Caldwell & Bradley, 1978) concurrently and across time, and the Teaching Scale has been found to be moderately correlated with developmental outcomes when the child is 36 months old (Bee et al., 1982).

The Teaching Scale has been found to be more strongly correlated with cognitive development than the Feeding Scale. Feeding observations may be especially useful in infant mental health settings and in situations where an infant has a specific feeding disorder and a mother needs help in learning how to help her infant through this difficulty (Farran et al., 1990). A limitation of the NCAST Scales is that only the absence or presence of behaviors is rated; this limits the capacity of the instrument to document increments of change with intervention. It is a very usable instrument for public health nurses or other professionals working with families with young children. Extensive training is required.

Home Observation for Measurement of the Environment

Two versions of the HOME (Caldwell & Bradley, 1978) exist: one for infants (birth to 3 years) and one for preschoolers (3 to 6 years; Bradley, Caldwell, & Elardo, 1977). The HOME is designed to measure factors related to the infant's home environment, such as the mother's responsivity and acceptance, her organization of the infant's physical environment and provision of appropriate play materials, her involvement with the infant, and opportunities for variety in the infant's daily stimulation (e.g., the father provides some caretaking for the infant every day; Bradley et al., 1977). The HOME is administered in the child's home at a time when the child is awake and present, and it takes approximately 1 hour to complete. The items in the HOME (45 for the infant version and 55 for the preschool version) are scored on a yes–no basis, and information is collected through a combination of observation and interview techniques.

The HOME has been found to be more strongly correlated with the Stanford–Binet at 3 years of age than scores from the Bayley Mental Development Index (r's = .59 and .32, respectively; Elardo, Bradley, & Caldwell, 1977). In a study of possible linkages between the quality of the home environment and language competence, correlations between HOME scores at 2 years and Illinois Test of Psycholinguistic Abilities scores at 3 years were .57 for black children and .74 for white children (Elardo et al., 1977). Strengths of the HOME are that it is administered in the natural environment of the child and it elicits parental input. A limitation is that only absence or presence of behaviors is rated, rather than the quality of the behaviors observed. Clinical decisions based on information derived from the HOME may benefit from qualitative information that is not included in this instrument, particularly if the person who conducted the interview is not present during the clinical intervention process to provide this input.

Greenspan–Lieberman Observation System for Assessment of Caregiver–Infant Interaction during Semi-Structured Play

The Greenspan–Lieberman Observation System for Assessment of Caregiver–Infant Interaction during Semi-Structured Play (GLOS) consists of 53 parent and 43 child variables that are rated every 15 seconds from a 10–minute videotape of a semistructured mother–child free-play situation. The purpose of the GLOS is to define observable and measurable indicator behaviors that can be used clinically when observing and assessing mother–infant interactions (Greenspan & Lieberman, 1980).

Parent and child behaviors are listed separately and in alphabetical order. Parental variables include the parent's interaction with his or her infant, including the number of pleasurable, neutral, or aversive tactile experiences exhibited, and the number of contingent responses to the infant's behavior (Greenspan & Lieberman, 1980). Infants aged 2–12 months (adaptations have been made for newborns and toddlers) are rated on their proximity or avoidance of physical contact with their caregivers and responses to caregiver behaviors (Greenspan & Lieberman, 1980). Dyadic behaviors are not recorded with the GLOS, and all ratings are objective in nature; no subjective perceptions of the parent are elicited.

Compared to young adult mothers, adolescent mothers rated with the GLOS were less vocal, more detached, and more negative with their 6–month-old infants, and less vocal with their 24–month-old infants (Hofheimer & O'Grady, 1986). Farran et al. (1990) have pointed out problems in using the GLOS because of the alphabetical ordering (instead of categorical ordering) of variables, as well as difficulties in interpreting results because positive and negative behaviors exist beside each other. The variables to be observed, however, are quite clinically relevant (e.g., parental anticontingent behavior) and can be useful in focusing intervention efforts with high-risk dyads.

Parent Behavior Progression

The Parent Behavior Progression (PBP) is a checklist of 17 reported or observed parent behaviors that occur at each of six levels (Bromwich, 1981, 1983). The purpose of the PBP is to assess parental behaviors and to aid in formulating short-term goals (Bromwich, 1981, 1983) focused on improving the quality of parent–child interactions. Physical and social behaviors of the infant (birth to 36 months) are provided in a checklist supplement to the PBP (Bromwich, 1983). The first three parental behavior levels are comprised of affective behaviors believed to facilitate attachment; the last three levels consist of behaviors that are important for facilitating cognitive growth (Bromwich, 1981, 1983). Observations are done during two to three home visits. Although the PBP is quasi-hierarchical in design, lower-level behaviors do not need to exist for upper-level behaviors to occur (Bromwich, 1981, 1983).

Correlations between the HOME at 9 months and the PBP at 4, 8, and 12 months have been found to be moderate (r's = .47, .69, and .75, respectively; Allen, Affleck, McQueeny, & McGrade, 1982). PBP scores at 12 and 18 months were also correlated with HOME scores at 18 months (r's = .42 and .60, respectively). These correlations suggest that the PBP and the HOME may be more strongly correlated when the infant's age is similar for each test. A strength of the PBP is that it elicits parental perceptions and helps guide information efforts.

The Parent-Child Early Relational Assessment

The Parent–Child Early Relational Assessment (PCERA; Clark, 1985) is an assessment of the quality of parent–child relationships, with both objective and subjective components. It comprises 65 parental, child, and dyadic variables. The purpose of the PCERA is to provide a phenomenological assessment of the affective and behavioral quality of interactions between the parent and child, for both research and clinical purposes (i.e., clinical assessment, formulation of intervention goals, and documentation of therapeutic progress) in families at risk for or evidencing early relational disturbances. The major premise is that parental affect and behavior provide a regulatory or organizing function for the infant's development and functioning (Clark, Musick, Stott, Klehr, & Cohler, 1984). Twenty minutes of interaction of the infant or young child are taped with each parent during four 5-minute segments (free play, structured task, feeding, and a separation–reunion period). Segments are rated for parent, child, and dyadic variables using 5-point Likert scales with behavioral anchors. The PCERA is an expansion and modification of an earlier-developed instrument, the Rating Scales of Mother–Child Interaction (Clark, Musick, Stott, & Klehr, 1980). Variables were developed on the basis of psychodynamic and Soviet cognitive linguistic theory and developmental studies. Parent–child interactions are assessed across different situations in order to tap areas of conflict and parental competencies that a feeding/nurturing situation as compared to a teaching/limit-setting or free-play situation may elicit.

Parent–child interactions may be videotaped in an office or home setting. Parents are told that this is a snapshot of one point in time and that they will be asked after the videotaping how it is similar or different from how things usually are. An initial warmup is included prior to taping interaction segments, to enhance comfort and to minimize deviations from what is typical for the dyad.

In the objective component of the assessment the parent is rated on the amount, duration, and intensity of positive affective and behavioral involvement (e.g., sensitivity and responsiveness to the infant's cues, structuring and mediating of the environment, genuine visual regard and mirroring of the child's feeling states) and negative affect and behavior toward the infant/young child (e.g., angry/hostile tone of voice, displeasure, criticism, intrusiveness, and, inconsistency). The infant is rated on the amount, duration, and intensity of positive affect and interactive behavior (e.g., mood, attentional, motoric and communicative skills, social initiative and responsiveness and negative affect and behavior (e.g., averting gaze, irritability, sober mood, emotional lability, etc.) Each dyad is rated on the quality of mutual involvement and joint attention to the task and the amount of reciprocity, enjoyment, or tension that exists within the dyad.

The subjective aspect of the assessment involves a video replay interview with the parent. Sections of tape are selected and replayed and parents are engaged in "wondering" about their relationship with their child, the meaning of the child's behavior to them, who the child looks like or reminds them of, their sense of competence in the parenting role, and what is difficult or enjoyable in the interaction with their child.

Discriminant validity has been established through demonstrated differences between various groups of high risk and well-functioning parent–infant dyads including mothers diagnosed with psychiatric illnesses and well mothers on variables related to maternal affective involvement and responsiveness and consistency (Clark, 1983; Musick, Clark, & Cohler, 1981). In addition, scales adapted from the PCERA have been found to be statistically related to security of an infant's attachment to the mother at the same age, as defined by the Ainsworth Strange Situation. With good mother–infant relations, mothers' demonstrate more sensitivity to infants' cues, structuring of the environment, less anxious or depressed affect and the securely attached infants evidence significantly less irritability, less avoidance and less aggressiveness than in insecurely attached infants (Teti, Nakagawa, Das, Wirth, & Ablard, 1989). Norming, reliability, and additional validity studies are currently being conducted. The PCERA provides a comprehensive evaluation of parent–child interactions and the quality of the dyadic relationship. Parents are involved in assessing their relationship with their child. The parental perceptions elicited following the videotaping provide useful information for both clinicians and parents in collaborating on goals for therapeutic intervention. The PCERA manual must be supplemented by clinical experience and specific training, especially when the PCERA is being used for research.

ASSESSMENT AS A THERAPEUTIC PROCESS

The assessment process can have tremendous therapeutic value if the parents are integrally involved in it (Brazelton, 1981; Clark & Milner, 1989; Cardone & Gilkerson, 1990; Parker & Zuckerman, 1990). In our clinical experience, the assessment provides a unique opportunity to provide preliminary intervention.

We conclude our chapter by sharing a comprehensive assessment process used in the Parent–Infant Development Program and Clinic, Department of Psychiatry, University of Wisconsin Hospital and Clinics. The program provides screening, evaluation, and therapeutic intervention services to families with infants and young children (from birth to 3 years of age) when disturbances in parenting and/or developmental or psychosocial disturbances in the infant/child are identified. The focus of the clinic is on assessing and treating developmental and early relational disturbances.

The diagnostic evaluation consists of six to eight sessions and includes assessment of the psychosocial and developmental status of the infant, the parent–child relationship, and parental and family functioning via clinical interviews, relationship histories, and structured self-report questionnaires. Throughout the evaluation, trial interventions based on the understandings developed from the interviews, the questionnaires, and the PCERA, as well as the subjective experiences of the parent(s) during the evaluation process, are implemented. The interventions themselves focus on the parents' expressed concerns, the jointly assessed quality of the parent–infant relationship, and the child's developmental and emotional needs. The parents' own conflicts and difficulties are explored. They are encouraged to explore how their own experiences of being parented may affect how they perceive and relate to their child. As the evaluation progresses, the parents are helped to read and respond to the child's cues more empathically (Bromwich, 1981), as well as to provide structure or limits for their child. The concept of a therapeutic evaluation is illustrated in the following case.

Case Example

Michael E., an 11–month-old white male, was referred to the clinic by the Perinatal Follow-Up Service in hopes that we could suggest "new ways for Michael's mother to relate to this hypersensitive infant." Michael had been born to a 30-year-old mother and weighed 5 pounds, 1 ounce at birth. The pregnancy was complicated by pre-eclampsia, resulting in induction after 37 weeks. Michael displayed significant respiratory problems at birth (requiring ventilatory assistance for 2 weeks), as well as suspected sepsis requiring a 10-day course of antibiotics. The neonatologist did not assure his parents of his survival. However, his mother and father recounted that when he was ready to be discharged, the neonatal intensive care nurse, on observing Michael's activity level and alertness, told them that they were "going to have their hands full in a few months." The parents felt that her prediction had proven true. As a young baby, Michael was colicky, "not cuddly," and difficult to soothe. Four formula changes were required before his parents found a formula that he could tolerate without projectile vomiting. Difficulties with sleep continued up until the time of the Parent–Infant Clinic intake at 11 months of age, with Michael waking two to four times a night and requiring a bottle to settle. Michael's mother said that they "couldn't keep him in a car seat," that he was aggressive to his older sister (age 3), that he continually crawled away from them, and that they could no longer find a babysitter to stay with him because of his activity level. Mrs. E. was considering quitting work and wanted to know whether we felt she should do so to care for him. At the time of intake, Michael's parents were quite concerned that he may be hyperactive, that his aggressive behavior would lead to his being labeled a "bully" in the future, as well as about possible learning difficulties.

In observing Michael with his parents, it quickly became apparent that he was not hyperactive. He was able to attend to what was happening around him and to sustain attention in play activities. In fact, on the Bayley Scales of Infant Development Michael was able to complete a number of tasks requiring focused attention, with an overall performance on the Mental Development Index in the high average range. He was persistent and focused during the formal testing, attempting repeatedly to build a tower with three blocks. He performed best when the tasks had materials he could manipulate and did not require much interaction with the examiner. When required to interact, he became reticent and appeared anxious. This was particularly evident during the play session: He was obviously interested in the appealing toys placed before him, but it was not until the therapist created more distance between the toys and herself that Michael actively began to explore. Michael tolerated and then actively enjoyed interacting with the therapist, who slowly and then more actively engaged with Michael in a sensitive and responsive manner.

In the administration of the PCERA, it was observed that Michael did appear hypersensitive (Greenspan & Lourie, 1981) and responded to his parents' anxious behavior and affect by displaying withdrawal and anxiety in interactions (e.g., squirming to get off his mother's lap). In the video replay interview, Michael's parents shared that they felt ambivalent about their son;

they wanted to feel close to him, but felt rejected by his tactile defensiveness and environmental exploration. It appeared difficult for them to recognize their negative feelings about him because of their sense of gratitude that he had survived his first month of life. With the help of the clinicians, they came to realize that although Michael's high activity level seemed continually burdensome and exhausting to them, it also reassured them that he was alive and motorically competent. Their fears that Michael was going to become a "bully" became more understandable during the video replay interview. Mrs. E. remarked that Michael reminded her of her side of the family in both looks and temperament—particularly her father, whom she experienced as "hot-headed" with a quick temper, and who was on the "go, go, go" all the time. She noted that she also had a temper. Mrs. E. added that she experienced Michael as "demanding."

This view of Michael repeated Mrs. E.'s experience of her father. In the interview focused on her own developmental and relationship history, she shared that her father expected that all his children would go to college and that she, the oldest child, would be a doctor—an expectation that she may have experienced as a demand. She attended college, but she did not reach her father's goal for her. Instead, she married Mr. E., who did not attend college. Both Mr. and Mrs. E. stated that they worked all the time, and revealed feelings of inadequacy at work. Mrs. E. shared that she would like not to work as much and that her nurturing role model was her mother, who stayed home to care for the children.

Mr. E. was the second child in his family; he experienced his father, who was alcoholic, as also having a temper and being unpredictable. His father had been badly beaten up by a gang of "bullies" 2 or 3 years previously—an experience that had left the father quite paranoid and ill. This had in turn deprived both Mr. and Mrs. E. of the support and companionship of Mr. E.'s mother when she became depressed and preoccupied with her husband's health. Thus this usual generational source of information and support regarding parenting was removed.

In spite of some increased awareness of what their son's behavior and temperament meant to them and how it might relate to family-of-origin issues, the parents' interaction with Michael still proved unsatisfactory to them. It was only as they were able to view him through a one-way mirror, in the context of a diagnostic play session, that they were truly able to divest Michael of their own fears of incompetence and rejection. This evolved as the therapist provided a kind of joint attention, watching their child with them from behind the mirror. Although they viewed him as delayed in development, unpredictable, inattentive, and rejecting, they watched him relate attentively and responsively to the therapist. They wondered why he was so much more interactive with her. Their feelings of inadequacy and of thankfulness that he survived his very tentative first month of life emerged with the help of the therapist. Mr. E. remarked, "Yeah, we don't play with him like that—it looks like he really likes that—he's smiling." They discussed with each other whether he would respond to them that way.

Mrs. E.'s eyes filled with tears as she remembered Michael as so ill, how depressed she was, and how afraid they had been that he would not survive. The therapist wondered with them whether it might be difficult to really engage with him, to let themselves become attached, if they still feared for his health and survival. The therapist asked whether they had ever been told that he would survive, and they responded quietly, "No, not really." The therapist encouraged them to ask their pediatrician in the Perinatal Follow-Up Clinic in order to be reassured. The therapist who conducted the play session noted that Michael responded more when she used several modalities—affect, deep rather than light touch, and gaze, as well as verbal interaction—and wondered with the parents about a possible hearing problem. Mr. and Mrs. E. said that he had had several ear infections and agreed to have an audiological exam performed. Their own feelings of inadequacy, fears of becoming attached to Michael lest he die, and resultant depressive feelings appeared to prevent them from being playful and involved with him (Anthony, 1983; Pound, 1982).

With support from the therapist for their competence in accurately reading his cues, provision of nonjudgmental developmental guidance (Fraiberg, 1980) regarding the approaches that their child with special sensitivities might respond to, and some interpretation of the transference with the therapist related to their feelings of inadequacy and competence, the parents found that they were more able to engage Michael in play and to encourage and enjoy his developmental advances. They became aware that their interaction with Michael was very much affected by how they perceived him and themselves, by how ill he had been, and by whom he reminded them of (i.e., what he meant to them). Follow-up 1 year later indicated that Michael's parents felt he was doing well, as were they. Because he continued to have ear infections and some hearing loss during those times had been noted, tubes were placed in his ears. They felt he was more responsive. They reflected on the opportunity to look carefully along with a therapist at their feelings toward and about Michael, and felt that it had been significant in allowing them to join more fully with him and to negotiate a fit. They were now assured that he would survive, and understood differently what they had perceived as pushing-away, "rejecting behavior"; now they were able to see it as age-appropriate efforts toward autonomy (Clark & Milner, 1989).

Comment

The work with this family illustrates how engaging parents as participants in the evaluation process, valuing their subjective perceptions of their infant, and gaining an empathic understanding of how their relationship and family-of-origin issues influence their perceptions of and interactions with their infant can be therapeutic in itself. Just presenting Michael's parents with results of the Bayley may have eased their concerns somewhat regarding his current developmental status, but would not have sufficiently addressed the complex internal model they had developed of their son. With some families, as in this case, a therapeutic evaluation may obviate the need for further treatment; with others, this experience can prepare parents for and engage them in the process of parent–infant psychotherapy.

CONCLUSION

We have presented a therapeutic model of infant assessment that focuses on the process as well as the content of evaluations. The traditional model for obtaining developmental assessments —that is, a structured assessment of the child's developmental status or functioning—is the cornerstone from which a more comprehensive approach is developed. Assessments during infancy are unique, in that parents are so closely tied to the developmental process. Infant mental health professionals cannot ignore the importance of this relationship for the current and future functioning of the infant or young child. Thus, we have focused on providing a model that carefully and comprehensively includes parents, both in evaluating the parent–child relationship and in observing, reflecting upon, and participating in all aspects of the assessment process. The assessment process as discussed in this chapter lends itself readily to therapeutic interventions. The case presented represents how data from multiple sources can be communicated in a manner that facilitates change both in the beliefs parents have about their child and in how they interact with him or her. It is our premise that a comprehensive approach to infant assessment not only provides a more valid picture of an infant or young child's current developmental status, but also provides an avenue for change.

REFERENCES

Ainsworth, M. D. S., Blehar, M. C., Waters, E., & Wall, S. (1978). *Patterns of attachment.* Hillsdale, NJ: Erlbaum.

Allen, D., Affleck, G., McQueeny, M., & McGrade, B. (1982). Validation of the parent behavior progression in early intervention programs. *Mental Retardation, 20,* 159–163.

Als, H., Tronick, E., Lester, B., & Brazelton, T. (1979). Specific neonatal measures: The Brazelton Neonatal Behavioral Assessment Scale. In J. D. Osofsky (Ed.), *Handbook of infant development* (pp. 185–215). New York: Wiley.

Anastasiow, N. (1988). IDA technical report. New Haven, CT: Author.

Anthony, E. J. (1983). An overview of the effects of maternal depression on the infant and child. In H. Morrison (Ed.), *Children of depressed parents: Risk, identification and intervention* (pp. 1–16). New York: Grune & Stratton.

Barnard, K. E. (1979). *Instructor's learning resource manual.* Seattle: NCAST, University of Washington.

Barnard, K. E., Hammond, M. A., Booth, H. L., Mitchell, S. K., & Spieker, S. J. (1989). Measurement and meaning of parent–child interaction. In F. J. Morrison, C. E. Lord, & D. P. Keating (Eds.), *Applied development psychology,* Vol. III, New York: Academic Press.

Barnard, K. E., & Kelly, J. (1990). Assessment of parent–child interaction. In S. J. Meisels & J. P. Shonkoff (Eds.), *Handbook of early childhood intervention* (pp. 278–302). New York: Cambridge University Press.

Bayley, N. (1969). *Bayley Scales of Infant Development.* New York: Psychological Corporation.

Bee, H., Barnard, K. E., Eyres, S., Gray, C., Hammond, M., Spietz, A., Snyder, C., & Clark, B. (1982). Prediction of IQ and language skill from child performance,

family characteristics, and mother–infant interaction. *Child Development, 53,* 1134–1156.

Bernstein, V. J., Hans, S. L., & Percansky, C. (1991). Advocating for the young child in need through strengthening the parent–child relationship. *Journal of Clinical Child Psychology, 20,* 28–41.

Bornstein, M. H. (1989). Between caretakers and their young: Two modes of interaction and their consequences for cognitive growth. In M.H. Bornstein & J.S. Bruner (Eds.), *Interaction in human development* (pp. 197–214). Hillsdale, NJ: Erlbaum.

Bradley, R., Caldwell, B., & Elardo, R. (1977). Home environment, social status and mental test performance. *Journal of Educational Psychology, 69,* 697–701.

Brazelton, T. B. (1981). Assessment as a method for enhancing infant development. *Zero to Three: Bulletin of the National Center for Clinical Infant Programs, 2*(1), 1–8.

Brazelton, T. B. (1984). *Neonatal Behavioral Assessment Scale.* Philadelphia: J.B. Lippincott.

Brazelton, T. B., Nugent, K., & Lester, B. (1987). Neonatal Behavioral Assessment Scale. In J. D. Osofsky (Ed.), *Handbook of infant development* (2nd ed., pp. 780–817). New York: Wiley.

Bromwich, R. (1981). *Working with parents and infants: An interactional approach.* Baltimore: University Park Press.

Bromwich, R. (1983). *Parent Behavior Progression: Manual and 1983 supplement.* Northridge, CA: Center for Research Development and Services, Department of Educational Psychology, California State University.

Bronfenbrenner, U. (1986). Ecology of the family as a context for human development research perspectives. *Developmental Psychology, 22,* 723–742.

Bruner, J. S. (1985). Vygotsky: A historical and conceptual perspective. In J.V. Wertsch (Ed.), *Culture, communication and cognition: Vygotskian perspectives,* (pp. 21–34). New York: Cambridge University Press.

Caldwell, B., & Bradley, R. (1978). *Manual for the Home Observation for Measurement of the Environment.* Little Rock: University of Arkansas.

Capute, A. J., & Accardo, P. J. (1978). Linguistic and auditory milestones during the first two years of life. *Clinical Pediatrics, 17,* 847–853.

Cardone, I. A., & Gilkerson, L. (1990). Family Administered Neonatal Activities: An exploratory method for the integration of parental perceptions and newborn behavior. *Infant Mental Health Journal, 11,* 127–141.

Clark, R. (1983). *Interactions of psychiatrically ill and well mothers and their young children: Quality of maternal care and child competence.* Unpublished Doctoral dissertation, Northwestern University.

Clark, R. (1985). *The Parent–Child Early Relational Assessment.* Madison: Department of Psychiatry, University of Wisconsin Medical School.

Clark, R. (1986). *Maternal Affective Disturbances and Child Competence.* Paper Presented at the International Conference on Infant Studies: Los Angeles.

Clark, R., Lange, J., & the Screening and Assessment Task Committee of the Birth-3 Interagency Coordinating Council. (1992). In J. Haglund, M. Hanley, J. Lange, & P. Rosin (Eds.), *Evaluation and assessment of infants and toddlers within a family centered approach: A resource guide* (p. 12). Madison: Wisconsin Department of Health and Social Services Birth to Three Program and the Wisconsin Department of Public Instruction.

Clark, R., & Milner, K. (1989). *Assessment of parent–child early relational disturbances: The therapeutic process of evaluation.* Paper presented at the Fourth World Congress on Infant Psychiatry and Allied Disciplines, Luguno, Switzerland.

Clark, R., Musick, J. S., Stott, F. M., and Klehr, K. B. (1980). *Rating Scales of Mother–Child Interaction.* Unpublished.

Clark, R., Musick, J. S., Stott, F. M., Klehr, K. B., & Cohler, B. J. (1984). Mother–child dyads at risk: Development of rating scales for early identification of disturbances in affect and behavior. *Infant Behavior and Development, 7,* 72. (Abstract).

Clarke-Stewart, K. A. (1973). Interactions between mothers and their young children: Characteristics and consequences. *Monographs of the Society for Research in Child Development, 38* (6–7, Serial No. 153).

Cogill, S., Caplan, H., Alexandra, H., Robson, K., & Kumar, R. (1986). Impact of maternal postnatal depression on cognitive development of young children. *British Medical Journal, 292,* 1165–1167.

Drotar, D. (1987). Implications of recent advances in neonatal and infant behavioral assessment. *Journal of Developmental and Behavioral Pediatrics, 8,* 51–53.

Elardo, R., Bradley, R., & Caldwell, B. (1977). A longitudinal study of the relation of infants' home environments to language development at age three. *Child Development, 48,* 595–603.

Emde, R. N. (1980). Emotional Availability: A reciprocal reward system for infants and parents with implications for prevention of psychosocial disorders. In P. Taylor (Ed.), *Parent–infant relationships* (87–115). New York: Grune & Stratton.

Emde, R. N. (1981). Searching for perspectives: Systems sensitivity and opportunities in studying the infancy of the organizing child of the universe. In K. Bloom (Ed.), *Prospective issues in infancy research* (pp. 1–24). Hillsdale, NJ: Erlbaum.

Erikson, J., & Vater, S. (1988, June). *Connecticut Infant–Toddler Developmental Assessment Program (IDA): Report of a four year demonstration project.* New Haven, CT: Child Study Center, Yale University.

Fagan, J. (1982). New evidence for the prediction of intelligence from infancy. *Infant Mental Health Journal, 3*(4), 219–228.

Fagan, J. (1987), *The Fagan Test of Infant Intelligence.* Cleveland, OH: Infantest Corporation.

Farran, D., Clark, K., & Ray, A. (1990). Measures of parent–child interaction. In E. D. Gibbs & D. Teti (Eds.), *Interdisciplinary assessment of infants: A guide for early intervention professionals* (pp. 227–248). Baltimore: Paul H. Brookes.

Fraiberg, S. (Ed.). (1980). *Clinical studies in infant mental health: The first year of life.* New York: Basic Books.

Francis, P., Self, P., & Horowitz, F. (1987). The behavioral assessment of the neonate: An overview. In J. D. Osofsky (Ed.), *Handbook of infant development* (2nd ed., pp. 723–779). New York: Wiley.

Frankenburg, W. K., Dodds, J., Archer, P., Bresnick, B., Maschka, P., Edelman, N., & Shapiro, H. (1990). *Screening manual for the Denver II.* Denver, CO: Denver Developmental Materials.

Freud, A. (1965). *Normality and pathology in childhood: Assessments of development.* New York: International Universities Press.

Freud, W. E. (1977). The baby profile. In R. S. Eissler, A. Freud, M. Kris, & A. J. Solnit (Eds.), An anthology of the psychoanalytic study of the child. *Psychoanalytic assessment: The diagnostic profile* (pp. 115–138). New Haven: Yale University Press.

Gaensbauer, T., & Harmon, R. (1981). Clinical assessment in infancy utilizing structured playroom situations. *Journal of the American Academy of Child Psychiatry, 20,* 264–280.

Gesell, A. (1929). *Infancy and human growth.* New York: Macmillan.

Gibbs, E.D. (1990). Assessment of infant mental ability: Conventional tests and issues of prediction. In E. D. Gibbs & D. Teti (Eds.), *Interdisciplinary assessment of infants: A guide for early intervention professionals* (pp. 77–90). Baltimore: Paul H. Brookes.

Greenspan, S. I. (1992). *Infancy and early childhood: The practice of clinical assessment and intervention with emotional and developmental challenges.* Madison, CT: International Universities Press.

Greenspan, S. I., & Lieberman, A. (1980). Infants, mothers and their interactions: A quantitative clinical approach to developmental assessment. In S. I. Greenspan & G. H. Pollock (Eds.), *The course of life: Psychoanalytic contributions toward understanding personality development. Vol. 1. Infancy and early childhood* (pp. 271–312). (DHHS Publication No. ADM 80–786). Washington, DC: U.S. Government Printing Office.

Greenspan, S.I., & Lourie, R.S. (1981). Developmental structuralist approach to the classification of adaptive and pathologic personality organization: Application to infancy and early childhood. *American Journal of Psychiatry, 136*(6), 725–735.

Griffiths, R. (1954). *The abilities of babies: A study in mental measurement.* London, England: Lowe and Brydon.

Hofheimer, J. A., & O'Grady, K. E. (1986, April). *Early interactions between adolescents and their infants as predictors of development at two years.* Paper presented at the International Conference on Infant Studies, Los Angeles.

Ireton, H., & Thwing, E. (1974). *The Minnesota Child Development Inventory.* Minneapolis: Behavioral Science Systems.

Johnson, E.J. (1990). *Maternal beliefs as predictors of parenting behavior of adolescent and young adult single mothers.* Unpublished doctoral dissertation, University of Wisconsin–Madison.

Kohut, H. (1971). *The analysis of the self: A systematic approach to the psychoanalytic treatment of narcissistic personality disorders.* New York: International Universities Press.

Kopp, C. B., & McCall, R. B. (1982). Predicting later mental performance for normal, at-risk, and handicapped infants. In P.B. Baltes & O.G. Brim (Eds.), *Life-span development and behavior* (Vol. 4, pp. 33–61). New York: Academic Press.

Linder, T. (1990). *Transdisciplinary Play-Based Assessment: A functional approach to working with young children.* Baltimore: Paul H. Brookes.

Lewis, M., & Coates, D. (1980). Mother–infant interaction and infant cognitive performance. *Infant Behavior and Development, 3,* 95–105.

Lyons-Ruth, K., Zoll, D., Connell, D., & Grunebaum, H. (1986). The depressed mother and her one-year-old infant: Environment, interaction, attachment, and infant development. In E. Tronick and T. Field (Eds.), *Maternal depression and infant disturbance: New directions for child development* (pp. 61–82). San Francisco: Jossey-Bass.

Matas, L., Arend, R. A., & Sroufe, L. A. (1978). Continuity of adaptation in the second year: The relationship between quality of attachment and later competence. *Child Development, 49,* 547–556.

McCune, L., Kalmanson, B., Fleck, M., Glazewski, B., & Sillari, J. (1990). An interdisciplinary model of infant assessment. In S. J. Meisels & J. P. Shonkoff (Eds.), *Handbook of early childhood intervention* (pp. 219–245). New York: Cambridge University Press.

Meisels, S. J. (1985). *Developmental screening in early childhood: A guide* (rev. ed.). Washington, DC: National Association for the Education of Young Children.

Meisels, S. J., & Provence, S. (1989). *Screening and assessment: Guidelines for identifying young disabled and developmentally vulnerable children and their families.* Washington, DC: National Center for Clinical Infant Programs.

Meisels, S. J., & Wasik, B. A. (1990). Who should be served? Identifying children in need of early intervention. In S. J. Meisels & J. P. Shonkoff (Eds.), *Handbook of early childhood intervention* (pp. 605–632). New York: Cambridge University Press.

Mullen, E. M. (1991). *The Infant Mullen Scales of Early Learning: Instrument descriptions.* Cranston, RI: T.O.T.A.L. Child.

Musick, J., Clark, R., & Cohler, B. (1981). The Mother's Project: A program for mentally ill mothers of young children. In B. Weissbourd & J. S. Musick (Eds.), *Infants: Their social environments* (pp. 111–127). Washington, DC: National Association for the Education of Young Children.

Ninio, A., & Bruner, J. S. (1978). The achievement and antecedents of labelling. *Journal of Child Language, 5,* 1–15.

Oller, D. K. (1985). Infant vocalizations: Traditional beliefs and current evidence. In S. Harel & N. Anastasiow (Eds.), *The at-risk infant: Psycho/Social/Medical aspects* (pp. 323–332). Baltimore, MD: P. H. Brooks.

Papousek, H., & Papousek, M. (1987). Intuitive parenting: A dialectic counterpart to the infant's integrative competence. In J. D. Osofsky (Ed.), *Handbook of infant development* (2nd ed., pp. 669–720). New York: Wiley.

Parker, S., & Zuckerman, B. (1990). Therapeutic aspects of the assessment process. In S. J. Meisels & J. P. Shonkoff (Eds.), *Handbook of early childhood intervention* (pp. 350–370). New York: Cambridge University Press.

Parks, P. L., Lenz, E. R., & Jenkins, L. S. (1992). The role of social support and stressors for mothers and infants. *Child: Care, Health and Development, 18,* 151–171.

Pellegrini, A. D., Brody, G. H., & Sigel, I. E. (1985). Parents' teaching strategies with their children: The effects of parental and child status variables. *Journal of Psycholinguistic Research, 14,* 509–521.

Pound, A. (1982). Attachment and maternal depression. In C. M. Parkes & J. Stevenson-Hinde (Eds.), *The place of attachment in human behavior* (pp. 118–130). New York: Basic Books.

Provence, S., Erikson, J., Vater, S., & Palmeri, S. (1985). *The Connecticut infant–toddler developmental assessment program: The procedures manual for the IDA assessment.* New Haven: Unpublished Manual.

Ruff, H., Lawson, K., Parrinello, R., & Weissberg, R. (1990). Long-Term stability of individual differences in sustained attention in the early years. *Child Development, 61,* 60–75.

Sameroff, A., & Chandler, M. (1975). Reproductive risk and the continuum of caretaking casualty. In F. D. Horowitz, E. M. Hetherington, S. Scarr-Salapetek, & G. M. Siegel (Eds.), *Review of child development research* (Vol. 4, pp. 187–244). Chicago: University of Chicago Press.

Sandler, J., Kennedy, H., & Tyson, R. (1980). *The technique of child psychoanalysis: Discussions with Anna Freud.* Cambridge, MA: Harvard University Press.

Schiefelbush, R. L., Sullivan, J. W., & Ganz, V. K. (1980). Assessing children who are at risk for speech. In S. Harel (Ed.), *The at-risk infant: A practical interdisciplinary approach to the prevention, discovery, assessment, and management of developmental disabilities* (pp. 277–284). Amsterdam: Excerpta Medica.

Sigel, L. (1981). Infant tests as predictors of cognitive and language development at two years. *Child Development, 52,* 545–557.

Spruill, J. (1987). Stanford–Binet Intelligence Scale, fourth edition. In D. Keyser & R. Sweetland (Eds.), *Test critiques* (Vol. 8, pp. 544–559). Austin, TX: Pro-Ed.

Sroufe, L. A. (1979). Socioemotional development. In J.D. Osofsky (Ed.), *Handbook of infant development* (pp. 462–516). New York: Wiley.

Stern, D. (1985). *The interpersonal world of the infant: A view from psychoanalysis and developmental psychology.* New York: Basic Books.

Teti, D., Nakagawa, M., Das, R., Wirth, O., & Ablard, K. (1989, April). *Behavioral correlates of child–mother attachment and attachment concordance among infants and older siblings.* Paper presented at the biennial meeting of the Society for Research in Child Development, Kansas City, MO.

Thorndike, R., Hagen, E., & Sattler, J. (1986). *Stanford-Binet Intelligence Scale* (4th ed.). Chicago: Riverside.

Vygotsky, L. S. (1979). *Mind in society: The development of higher psychological processes.* Cambridge, MA: Harvard University Press.

Wertsch, J. V. (1985). Adult–child interaction as a source of self-regulation in children. In S. Yussen (Ed.), *The growth of reflection in children* (pp. 69–97). New York: Academic Press.

Whatley, J. (1987). Bayley Scales of Infant Development. In D. Keyser & R. Sweetland (Eds.), *Test critiques* (Vol. 6, pp. 38–47). Kansas City, MO: Westport.

Winnicott, D. W. (1965). *The maturational process and the facilitating environment.* New York: International Universities Press.

Winnicott, D. W. (1975). The observation of infants in a set situation. In D. W. Winnicott (Ed.), *Through pediatrics to psycho-analysis* (pp. 52–69). New York: Basic Books.

Zeitlin, S., Williamson, G. G., & Szczepanski, M. (1988). *Manual for the Early Coping Inventory: A measure of adaptive behavior.* Bensenville, IL: Scholastic Testing Service.

13

Use of Structured Research Procedures in Clinical Assessments of Infants

JUDITH A. CROWELL
MELISSA A. FLEISCHMANN

CAN RESEARCH PROCEDURE BE USED IN THE CLINIC?

Various structured and semistructured assessment procedures for infants and toddlers have been developed over the past two decades. The majority of structured assessments have their origins in the study of normal development, and are intended to capture some aspect of infant behavior within a laboratory situation. Laboratory assessments have also been used to examine developmental processes in deviant or clinical populations (children with autism, children with Down syndrome, abused children, etc.). Comparing and contrasting "normal" samples of children with "clinical" samples illuminates processes in normal and abnormal development. Such research is very useful in understanding how and why groups of children behave as they do, and what this behavior may suggest for future developmental pathways. To be useful in such a setting, a structured assessment procedure must give a clinician information about an *individual* child—information that will assist the clinician in understanding the processes that have initiated or that maintain problem behaviors in the child, in predicting the child's developmental trajectory, and in planning interventions that might alter this trajectory. Can structured research procedures be reasonably employed by clinicians in their work with infants and their families?

The particular nature of clinical work with infants makes it an area where clinical assessments and research procedures can and do merge quite effectively. In part this is due to the theoretical stance of developmental psychopathology, which has exerted an increasingly important influence on infant psychiatry in the past decade. Within this framework, with the exceptions of the Pervasive Developmental Disorders and mental retardation, problems in infancy cannot be understood as discrete symptom-based disorders that reside solely within the infant (Cicchetti, 1984, 1987; Garber, 1984; Greenspan & Porges, 1984; Sroufe & Rutter, 1984). Rather, psychopathology in an infant is conceived of as disorganization or maladaptation in the interrelationship between the infant and its environment (in particular, its caretakers). Pathology is viewed as a lack of integration of the social, emotional, and cognitive competencies necessary for adaptation at each particular developmental level (Cicchetti, 1984, 1987).

The theoretical framework of developmental psychopathology illuminates the limitations of or problems with assessment of pathology in infants. Cicchetti (1987) outlines several areas of difficulty. First, there are currently few empirical data on normal development and evolution of behavioral problems or deviations in nonclinical populations. Thus it is difficult to find the border between normative behavioral difficulties and true pathology, and to identify specific factors that initiate and maintain significant problems. Second, the period of infancy is a time of rapid developmental change. For example, the child whose language is developing normally sounds markedly different at 1 year than at 3 years of age. Similarly, pathological processes may show a lack of "symptomatic isomorphism" across substages of development. Third, there is a lack of pathognomonic signs of psychopathology in infancy. In other words, the behaviors of infants are not very specific. The repertoire of pathological signs and symptoms is limited, and signs and symptoms do not point to particular processes or problems. Individual infants must then be examined within a general context of what is "normal" in various developmental domains. A fourth problem, as noted above, is that problems are rarely found "within the infant." Thus assessment must include the behavior, interactions, and input of the infant's caregivers (Crowell, Feldman, & Ginsberg, 1988), and this adds greater complexity to the evaluation and its interpretation.

Research in infant development and the procedures developed to study the normative behavior of both infants and their parents are thus potentially of great use to the clinician. Although pathognomonic signs of psychopathology are lacking, patterns of certain normative behaviors have been delineated for groups of parents and children across the first 3 years of life. The behavior of a particular child and parent can thus be compared systematically with the group patterns, and the comparison can focus on a particular developmental domain. Given the importance of parent–child interaction in understanding child problem behaviors (Baumrind, 1971; Crittenden, 1985; Erickson, Sroufe, & Egeland, 1985; Fraiberg, 1980; Main, Kaplan, & Cassidy, 1985; Matas, Arend, & Sroufe, 1978), it can be clinically useful to assess interaction in a standardized way—one that is comparable across individuals and groups (Crowell et al., 1988).

What are the criteria for structured clinical assessments of infants that most effectively allow for comparisons between "normative behavior" and an individual child's behavior? The clinical assessment has some particular requirements that are not always necessary, and therefore not always present, in research procedures. The following list points out some of the key aspects needed for an assessment procedure to be useful to clinicians (Crowell et al., 1988; Gaensbauer & Harmon, 1981).

1. Direct observation of the infant, and of the parent(s), is a key aspect of assessment.

2. The assessment should usually examine several facets of development, and its structure and content should be appropriate for the age and development of the child. It should take into account the fact that children do not come to clinics at set ages; therefore, to be optimally useful, the procedure should serve an age span.

3. Optimally, a parent should be assessed for the appropriateness or matching of his or her behavior to the child's developmental level.

4. The assessment needs to be efficient in terms of time, and should not be highly complex in its structure or materials.

5. The method of evaluating behavior should be understandable and sensible to a clinician who may not have the time or opportunity to learn a complex scoring system. The clinician can and should record events and behaviors, whether or not a formal scoring system is used.

6. The infant and parent should have an opportunity to be natural and spontaneous. The situation should not be so structured, complicated, and/or restrictive that it is difficult for an intelligent observer to draw a parallel between the assessment and "real life." The clinician's interventions take place in real life, and they must make sense and have their impact there, not in a laboratory.

Specific research procedures that have been used to varying degrees in clinical research and/or clinical assessments are discussed below. It can be seen that the first three criteria are relatively easily met by most methods, but research procedures do not often fulfill the last three criteria.

SPECIFIC STRUCTURED ASSESSMENTS

Assessment procedures that have potential clinical applications are described below, as are their clinical advantages and disadvantages. Procedures for young infants are presented first, fol-

lowed by those used for older infants and toddlers up to 3 years of age, and then by two procedures used with parents only.

Procedures for Young Infants

The Neonatal Behavioral Assessment Scale

The Neonatal Behavioral Assessment Scale
(NBAS; Brazelton, 1984) was developed for use
with infants of 36–44 weeks gestational age (full-
term infants are 38–40 weeks gestational age).
Although it is widely used in research, it can be
used as a clinical tool with individual infants and
their parents. The first part of the exam focuses
on basic reflexes, and the second part consists
of behavioral items (e.g., response decrements
to light and sound, and orientation to visual
stimuli). Overall, the scale detects or assesses (1)
mild dysfunction of the central nervous system,
(2) temperamental variations in normal infants,
and (3) neonatal capacity to organize the autonomic and central nervous systems to respond
to stimuli.

Infant performance on the NBAS appears to
be more predictive of later neurological status
than is a standard neurological examination of
the infant (Tronick & Brazelton, 1975). The
NBAS relates to Bayley Scales of Infant Development scores at 10 weeks (Sostek & Anders,
1977) and 9 months (Vaughn, Taraldson, Crichton, & Egeland, 1980). It assists in predictions
of quality of maternal caregiving at both 3 and
6 months (Vaughn et al., 1980). NBAS scores
also have been associated with infant attachment.
Infants classified as resistant at 1 year in the Strange
Situation (Ainsworth, Blehar, Waters, & Wall,
1978; see below) show less optimal NBAS scores
on the Orientation, Motor Maturity, and Physiological Regulation clusters than other infants
(Waters, Vaughn, & Egeland, 1980).

Clinically, the NBAS has been used successfully as a learning device for both nursing staff
and new parents. Mothers who have observed
or carried out the examination on their infants
have been found to be more responsive and
attuned to their infants 1 month later (Widmayer & Field, 1980; Worobey & Belsky, 1982).
Observing the administration of the NBAS allows a mother to observe her infant's ability to
respond to stimuli and the infant's capabilities
for quieting itself. Thus mothers can be helped
to attune to the special needs of their individual
infants.

The NBAS has two major limitations in clinical practice. First, the age range for which it is
appropriate is limited to the first weeks of life
of full-term or nearly full-term infants. Thus it
is most useful for predicting potential problems
in such infants and pointing to the need for preventive action and/or intervention, rather than
assessing the nature of current problem behaviors. Second, specific and extensive training is
necessary for the examination to be administered
and interpreted. Such training is available
through workshops given typically at medical
centers that specialize in neonatal and infant
treatment and research. Training films and materials are also available. Examiners need to be
trained to an interobserver agreement level of
.90, and a practitioner must use the examination regularly to maintain an acceptable skill
level (Brazelton, 1984). It is possible that similar clinical benefits could accrue from an evaluation that is not so difficult to learn, but this has
not been explored.

The Face-to-Face Procedure

The "face-to-face" procedure (Tronick, Als,
Adamson, Wise, & Brazelton, 1978) is designed
to assess the synchronicity of infant–mother
interactions for infants under 9 months. Theoretically, when an infant attempts to elicit responses from the mother, and is successful in
receiving appropriate, contingent, and sensitive
responses, he or she will develop a sense of self-
efficacy. Inappropriate responses by the mother,
such as a blank face or turning away, lead to
infant confusion, irritability, and (theoretically)
a sense of being ineffectual (Cohn & Tronick,
1983).

The mother and infant engage in a face-to-
face interaction, with videocameras focused on
each partner. The dyad is then viewed together
by means of split-screen technology. The infant
is scored for vocalizations, direction of gaze,
head orientation and position, facial expression,
amount of movement, blinks, specific hand and
foot movements, and tongue placement. The
mother is scored on vocalization, head and body
position, handling of the infant, direction of
gaze, and facial expressions (Tronick, Als, &
Brazelton, 1980).

The units of analysis of the face-to-face procedure are called "monadic phases" (Tronick
et al., 1980). Monadic phases are segments of
interactive behavior that provide information
about who is acting, what he or she is doing, and

when he or she is doing it. Theoretically, there is a hierarchy of goals in such interactions; these include initiation of the interaction, mutual orientation of the partners, greetings, cyclical exchange of affective information (as in play dialogues and games), and mutual disengagement (Tronick et al., 1978). The ability of the mother-child dyad to engage in rule-consistent turn-taking interactions in early infancy has been shown to predict a child's later style of interacting (Stern, 1971; Tronick et al., 1978; Tronick, Cohn, & Shea, 1986). Infants who successfully elicit their mothers at 6 months of age are more likely to be securely attached at 1 year than infants who fail to elicit responsive maternal behaviors.

The face-to-face procedure requires expensive and elaborate videotaping equipment and knowledge of microcoding techniques, and therefore is not of immediate use to a practitioner. However, on a "simple" level, a parent and child can be observed for such things as turn-taking behavior, eye contact versus gaze avoidance, and maternal responsiveness. The assessment allows for natural and spontaneous behavior in the interaction. Although the interaction does not cover a spectrum of developmental tasks, it does assess a core element of all parent–child interactions. The quality of interaction may indicate potential problems and it can also suggest intervention techniques to an experienced clinician.

Procedures for Older Infants and Toddlers

The Strange Situation

The Strange Situation (Ainsworth et al., 1978; Ainsworth & Wittig, 1969) is a laboratory procedure designed to activate a child's attachment system and elicit attachment behaviors. It was one of the first structured assessment procedures for infants developed, and has been among the most enduring. Attachment theory is based on observations of human infants and infants of other species, and posits an "attachment system" that acts to keep the young within the proximity of its caretakers for reasons of security and protection (Bowlby, 1969). The Strange Situation was designed to assess a child's attachment classification in a laboratory, in part to reduce the time and effort required for extensive naturalistic observations of parents and infants. It has been validated against home observations of 23 infants and their mothers over the course of the

first year of life (Ainsworth et al., 1978). It is used in the study of infants 12–18+ months old.

The Strange Situation consists of eight episodes that gradually increase the stress placed on the infant. The stress activates the pattern of attachment behavior of the infant with the attachment figure participating in the procedure. The first episode is only 30 seconds in duration; all the others are 3 minutes unless the infant is distressed, in which case the episode is abbreviated. The episodes are as follows (for the sake of simplicity, the attachment figure is referred to as the "mother").

1. The mother and child are introduced to the experimental room, which is provided with two chairs and a number of infant toys on the floor.
2. The mother sits in the chair while the infant is allowed to explore the room.
3. A "stranger," always female, enters the room and sits on the chair next to the mother. She is silent for the first minute, talks to the mother for the second minute, and engages the infant in the third minute.
4. The mother leaves the room, leaving her purse on her chair as a sign to the child that she will return. The child and the stranger remain together in the room.
5. The mother returns to the room, and the stranger leaves unobtrusively so as not to hamper the reunion period.
6. The mother leaves again, and this time the child is alone in the room.
7. The stranger joins the infant and tries to console/interact with the child.
8. The mother returns and picks up the infant, and the stranger leaves.

The child's attachment classification is based primarily on the reunion behaviors of the child in episodes 5 and 8. The child's behavior during the separations is not indicative of the child's attachment behavior or classification. Initially, three attachment patterns were observed in the Strange Situation: "insecure/avoidant," "secure," and "insecure/resistant." The percentages of each type in a normal middle-class sample are as follows: About 70% are classified as secure with their caregivers, about 5–15% are in the insecure/resistant group, and about 10–25% of children are in the insecure/avoidant group.

The prototypic secure behavior of an infant in this situation includes use of the caregiver as a secure base to explore and play with the novel toys, the active seeking of the caregiver when distressed by separation, and the ability to be comforted by the caregiver upon reunion. Infants classified as insecure are observed to be avoidant of their caregivers in reunion and appear to focus on the environment as a distraction from distress, or may be resistant to the efforts of the caregivers to comfort them on reunion, maintaining an irritable and agitated stance.

In the past decade, research using the Strange Situation has expanded to the study of children of high-risk families. In these high-risk populations, a fourth classification of children has been described (Crittenden, 1988; Main & Solomon, 1986). These children demonstrate "disorganized/disoriented" behaviors toward their caregivers in the Strange Situation. The disorganized behaviors include freezing or stilling, stereotypies, incomplete approaches, fear reactions to the caregivers, and/or combined avoidant and resistant strategies. The behavior of these children has led to the sense that the children do not have a "plan of action" to activate in the case of attachment-related events, and thus are simply at a loss as to how to behave (Main & Solomon, 1986). These behaviors have been observed in situations where the children are afraid of the parents (e.g., abused infants), or when the parents seem fearful or disorganized in reaction to some traumatic event (e.g., abuse or death) (Main & Solomon, 1986). As yet there are no subclassifications within the disorganized/disoriented classification that point to specific behavior problems or to specific pathogenic events.

Research with Down syndrome infants have shown patterns of attachment similar to those of mental-age-matched nonhandicapped infants (Thompson, Cicchetti, Lamb, & Malkin, 1985). Studies of infants with a history of nonorganic failure to thrive, infants with affective disorders, and children with a history of maltreatment all report a higher incidence of insecure attachment (Drotar, Malone, & Nowak, 1985; Egeland & Sroufe, 1981; Gordon & Jameson, 1979; Radke-Yarrow, Cummings, Kuczynski, & Chapman, 1985; Schneider-Rosen, Braunwald, Carlson, & Cicchetti, 1985).

Despite its extensive correlates with child functioning in a variety of domains (Bretherton, 1985; Sroufe & Fleeson, 1986), the Strange Situation is not a useful clinical procedure. It is intentionally artificial in its episodic structure and the constraint of the caregiver's behavior,

in order to create increasing stress that will elicit a pattern of infant attachment behavior. Although there are correlates with home behavior of dyads (Ainsworth et al., 1978), it is not a procedure that captures "real life" (i.e., is naturalistic). It is therefore not possible for an untrained observer to draw meaningful conclusions from the behavior of either participant. Training to code the Strange Situation is lengthy and technical, and requires training to reliability from an approved researcher. The situation itself requires a room set aside for this purpose, videotape equipment, toys, and a stranger.

Nevertheless, the procedure has served as a foundation for a clinical assessment paradigm (Gaensbauer & Harmon, 1981), and also as a prototype for the development of methods that extend the age range for assessing attachment behaviors. A modified Strange Situation for 3- to 4-year-olds (Cassidy & Marvin with the Attachment Working Group, 1989), and an Attachment Q-sort that assesses attachment behaviors in children from 2 to 5 years of age, have been developed (Waters & Deane, 1985). The Q-sort can be done either by a trained observer or by the child's mother. In addition, other semistructured observations have been developed to assess domains of child functioning that correlate with attachment behavior.

The Structured Playroom

The Structured Playroom (Gaensbauer & Harmon, 1981) is derived from certain aspects of the Strange Situation in its format, but uses four episodes of longer duration from the age of approximately 12–18 months. There is a free-play period, which is used to assess the infant's exploration and use of the mother in playing and exploring a new environment. The second episode involves both the mother and a stranger, and assesses the infant's differential responses to approach and contact with the two adults. The third episode is a structured developmental examination with the Bayley Scales of Infant Development, and includes assessment of the infant's interaction with the examiner. The fourth episode is a a separation–reunion sequence, which compares the infant's response to the mother's departure with the infant's response to the stranger's departure.

The clinician assesses the following areas: the infant's emotional responsiveness, the infant's ability to organize social behaviors and cooperate in play, the interaction between mother and infant, and the infant's competence in the environment. The behaviors of both parents and infants are assessed. A significant difference has been found between the differential responses of infants to mothers and strangers in groups of normal versus abused infants, and negative infant responses to mothers' approaches are associated with low infant competence in play and low Bayley Scale scores (Gaensbauer & Harmon, 1981). Training in the specific aspects of the procedure is important for interpreting the dyadic behaviors, as is clinical experience with this age group.

The Parent–Child Early Relational Assessment

The Parent–Child Early Relational Assessment (Clark, 1985) is a semistructured interaction for assessing the experience of a dyad and the quality or tone of the relationship in infants and toddlers. It is a modification of The Mother's Project Rating Scales of Mother–Child Interaction (Clark, Musick, Stott, & Klehr, 1980). The parent and infant are observed and videotaped in four 5-minute segments: (1) feeding, (2) structured task, (3) free play, and (4) separation–reunion.

During feeding, the parent's capacity for nurturing, social interaction, and sensitivity to cues are assessed. The child is observed for the clarity of his or her cues, affect regulation, social initiative, and responsivity. Comfort, tension, and regulation within the dyad are also observed in this situation. In the structured task, the parent's capacity to structure the environment according to the child's needs is observed. The child is assessed for attention, persistence, and interest in complying with parental expectations, and the dyad is observed for joint attention, reciprocity in negotiations, and mutuality. The play situation allows for assessment of the parent's playfulness and enjoyment of the child, and ability to facilitate the child's exploration and representational play; the dyad is rated for social interaction, mutuality, and reciprocity. In the final segment, the parent's ability and comfort in preparing the child for a brief separation are observed. The child is assessed for capacity for self-regulation and for quality of mood and play during the parent's absence. The dyad is assessed in reunion for quality of affect and re-engagement. At the end of the entire videotaped ses-

sion, the parent is given a chance to review portions of the tape. A semistructured interview is also administered to assess the parent's thoughts and feelings about both the session and the child, as well as how representative the parent feels the session was of the dyad's normal interactive style.

For scoring the session, it is recommended that the videotape be viewed at least five times, and each segment is scored separately on 5-point scales. The parent is scored for tone of voice, affect, characteristic mood, expressed attitude toward child, affective and behavioral involvement, and style. The child is assessed for expressed affect and characteristic mood, behavior/adaptive abilities, focus on parent's emotional state, activity level, and communication. The dyad is rated on affective quality of interaction and mutuality. Six factor-analytic scales have been derived: (1) Maternal Affective Involvement and Responsiveness; (2) Maternal Negative Affect and Behavior; (3) Infant Organization, Attentional and Social Skills; (4) Infant Disregulation, Irritability, and Negative Behavior; (5) Dyadic Mutuality and Reciprocity; and (6) Dyadic Tension.

Clinical research using this assessment has shown significant differences in mother–child interaction between dyads in which the mothers were mentally ill and matched dyads with well mothers (Stott, Musick, Clark, & Cohler, 1983). Mentally ill mothers were less involved with feeding, were less able to read their children's cues, and responded with less empathy to the children. They also initiated fewer social interactions, and there was less reciprocity. During play, the mentally ill mothers provided less structuring, had less contact (both physical and vocal) with the children, and were less consistent than the well mothers. Children of mentally ill mothers showed more negative affect and less communicative competence than did the children of well mothers. In a related study, affectively mentally ill mothers were significantly different from well mothers in involvement and consistency (Clark, 1986). Their children exhibited more difficulty in tasks; were less able to modulate their aggressive impulses and use language to express their needs; expressed little positive affect; and often engaged in non-compliant or aggressive behaviors, apparently in an effort to elicit maternal responses.

This assessment procedure offers the opportunity to observe a dyad interacting in a variety of activities. The scoring system itself is complex and time-consuming, however. The procedure does include a review of the videotaped session with the parent; this can be a very useful way to engage a parent in discussion about parenting and the meaning of his or her own behavior and that of the child, and is a valuable clinical addition to any interaction procedure.

The Tool Use Task

The tool use task (Matas et al., 1978) was designed to assess the continuing development of stage-salient competencies in young toddlers. It was hypothesized that an autonomous toddler would deal with problem-solving tasks with flexibility, resourcefulness, and an ability to make use of adult assistance without needing to be overly dependent on this assistance. The tool use task was intended to assess the link between early competence in attachment and later competence in working cooperatively with the caregiver on a task. The task involves the use of tools in increasingly difficult problem solving. As is true for the Strange Situation, this procedure is designed to tax the child's capacity for coordinating affect, cognition, and behavior, and for drawing upon personal and environmental resources (Matas et al., 1978).

The procedure is designed for 24-month-old children and consists of a free-play period, a cleanup period, and four problem-solving tasks. During the free-play period, the child's symbolic play is coded. During cleanup, the child is scored for oppositionality. The child is then rated on the four problem-solving tasks for compliance, active noncompliance and ignoring, verbal negativism, frustration behavior, aggressive behavior, whining or crying, help seeking, and non-task-related behavior. Rating scales are also used to assess enthusiasm and positive and negative affect.

Maternal behavior is assessed on two dimensions: supportive presence and quality of assistance. "Supportive presence" is the extent to which the mother appears available to the child and supportive of his or her efforts. "Quality of assistance" refers to helping the child see the relationship between actions required to solve the task, and giving minimal assistance needed to keep the child working at solving the problem.

Dyadic behaviors in this situation have been related to attachment status 1 year earlier (Matas et al., 1978). Children classified as securely attached in infancy subsequently showed a greater amount of symbolic play, although they did not differ in developmental level from children classified as insecure. In the tasks they were more enthusiastic, affectively positive, and persistent; they exhibited less off-task behavior, ignoring of their mothers, and noncompliance. The mothers of children classified as secure in infancy were more supportive and better at giving assistance. There was almost no overlap in the scores of securely versus insecurely attached children.

A Clinical Problem-Solving Procedure

A clinical problem-solving procedure for assessment of toddlers and preschoolers has been developed from the tool use task (Crowell & Feldman, 1988; Crowell et al., 1988). Changes in the original research procedure have been made for clinical research and practical clinical purposes. First, the assessment has been broadened to apply to children aged 24–54 months (or within this developmental range), as children do not present to clinics at set ages. Second, the specially designed tool tasks have been changed to tasks involving common toys and activities. These tasks are ranked by difficulty, so that a child of any age and developmental level within the age span noted above can be given a series of increasingly difficult tasks. As in the tool use task, the last two tasks are too difficult for the child to complete independently. Third, the mothers are given more control over the session by not having an experimenter in the room. This places an increased demand on the mothers to be organized. Fourth, the session includes a separation–reunion sequence in addition to the free play, cleanup time, and the four tasks.

For scoring the procedure, the session is videotaped. The behavioral ratings of the mother and child in free play, cleanup, and the four tasks are based upon the scoring described above for the tool use task (Matas et al., 1978). Mother and child behaviors in the separation–reunion sequence are scored separately from the other portions of the session. For the separation–reunion, the mother is rated on her preparation of the child for separation, her ease of separation, and her emotional responsiveness, particularly in reunion. The child is rated for anxiety manifested before the mother's departure, level of protest and active coping during separation, and avoidance of and negativity toward the mother on reunion.

The behavior of dyads in interaction was assessed across three groups: two clinic samples (children with intact and delayed development), and a matched nonclinic group (Crowell et al., 1988). Differences in behavior of mothers and children in the three groups were found during the tasks and in the separation–reunion sequence. Clinic mothers scored more poorly than comparison mothers in help and support, as well as in pre- and postseparation behavior; the mothers of delayed clinic children were rated as less supportive and helpful than the mothers of intact clinic children. In comparison to the nonclinic sample, clinic children were less affectionate with their mothers in the task session, but not more negative or noncompliant. They were more avoidant on reunion. Intact and delayed clinic children differed from each other predominantly in task behavior, but not in separation behavior or in relationship with their mothers. Patterns of maternal and child behavior in the tasks and during separation–reunion were also related to the mothers' attachment classifications as determined by the Adult Attachment Interview (Crowell & Feldman, 1988, 1991).

Although there is a scoring system for this procedure that requires training, the procedure was adapted from the tool use tasks (Matas et al., 1978) with the intention of creating a useful and usable clinical assessment procedure. The session attempts to assess the realm of activities that mothers and children ordinarily engage in together, and the mothers have some flexibility to organize the session. Therefore the session has a "real-life" quality within the imposed structure. A clinician who is familiar with this age group, but untrained in the specifics of scoring, can make direct observations of dyadic interaction and of parent and child behavior that are clinically useful.

The Parental Acceptance Procedure

The Parental Acceptance Procedure (Rothbaum & Schneider-Rosen, 1988; Schneider-Rosen, 1990) is used to assess sensitivity and contingency of a parent's responses to a toddler or preschool child. The underlying assumption is that sensitive and contingent parenting allows the child to learn trust and use the caretaker as a secure base from which to explore. Behaviors of *both* the parent and the child are evaluated, although the focus is on the parent's behavior (Schneider-Rosen, 1990). Twenty minutes of interaction are videotaped, and the dyad may be engaged in any activity (free play, tasks, book reading, cleanup, etc.). However, three different situations should be assessed for at least 5 minutes each.

The procedure is videotaped, and is scored using a minute-by-minute analysis that assesses the parent's ability to integrate the child's needs for evaluation, availability, and structure with both the parent's needs and the constraints of reality. Scoring of evaluation assesses the parent's affective tone, encouragement of efforts, and focus on acceptable versus unacceptable behavior. Scoring of availability includes parental receptivity to the child's seeking contact or proximity, sensitivity to the child's feelings and needs, willingness to engage with the child, and allowing independent action. The scoring of structure includes the parent's helpfulness, induction of positive mood and/or motivation, consistency and smoothness of transitions, and management options given to the child. Each need is scored, and the scores are averaged to give a parental acceptance score. At the low end of acceptance, the parent views the child's need for control in opposition to the parent's need for control, and thus attempts to oppose the child's goals. In the midrange, the child's need for control is viewed as partially in opposition to the parent's need for control, and the parent bargains with the child. A highly accepting parent sees no conflict between his or her own need for control and the child's need for control, and allows control to be shared.

The relationship between parental acceptance and self-control in children at 18, 24, and 30 months of age is currently being assessed (Schneider-Rosen, Rothbaum, & Wenz-Gross, 1989). A recent study has evaluated the relationship between parental acceptance and the capacity to display empathy toward the parent, and competence in interacting with same-sex peers, in a sample of 2-year-olds (Schneider-Rosen, Spada, & DeVirgilio, 1992). The stability of parental acceptance across time, and the association between early acceptance and later child functioning (compliance, perceived competence, and empathy), are being assessed in a sample of 50 children seen at 2 and 4 years of age (Schneider-Rosen, Beatty, & Rothbaum, 1992).

The lack of a specific protocol for parent–child interaction lends itself readily to a clinic setting, as it is always helpful to observe parents and their children in several situations. However, the minute-by-minute analysis used to score this procedure for research purposes make it difficult and time-consuming for clinicians.

Procedures for Parents

The Adult Attachment Interview

The Adult Attachment Interview (George, Kaplan, & Main, 1985) is a structured assessment that presents a "special case" in the clinical evaluation of the child, as the child is not directly observed. The interview is administered to adults and is designed to assess an adult's "state of mind" with respect to attachment relationships. Subjects are asked to describe their childhood experiences with their own parents, and how they feel the experiences have affected their adult personality and their behavior with their children. On the basis of the experiences described, and the ways in which the subject discusses them and derives meaning from them, the adult is classified into one of three groups (secure/autonomous, insecure/dismissing, or insecure/preoccupied) that best characterizes his or her state of mind regarding attachment relationships (Main & Goldwyn, 1984). The interview has been used to assess parents' working models in clinical and nonclinical populations of infants, young children, and school-age children. Patterns of infant and child behavior, and of parental behavior in interaction with preschoolers, have been found to correspond with Adult Attachment Interview classifications (Crowell & Feldman, 1991; Crowell et al., 1988; Crowell, O'Connor, Wollmers, Sprafkin, & Rao, 1991; Eichberg, 1987; Main et al., 1985).

The Adult Attachment Interview itself is not difficult for an experienced interviewer to learn. In contrast, the scoring system of the interview is complex, requires special training, and is very time-consuming and expensive (Main & Goldwyn, 1984); therefore, it is not particularly useful to a clinician. However, the interview itself resembles a clinical interview in content and style, but is more intense and structured. Even for a clinician untrained in the specifics of scoring, it offers a rich and valuable glimpse into an adult's view of his or her early life. Thus the interview can give insight into the behavior of parents in interactions with their own children.

The Working Model of the Child Interview

The Working Model of the Child Interview (Zeanah, Benoit, & Barton, 1986) is a structured interview for parents of infants. The questions are intended to assess a parent's working model of his or her relationship to a particular child. It is a parallel interview to the Adult Attachment Interview. The questions cover a wide range of topics, including the child's development from pregnancy to the present; the parent's impression of the child's personality and uniqueness; behavioral problems perceived by the parent; the relationship with the child; concerns about the child; and hopes for the future. The interviews are scored on a variety of scales addressing the parent's coherence when discussing the child, the richness of perceptions, flexibility with respect to the child's growth and development, intensity of involvement with and sensitivity to the child, perception of how difficult the child is to care for, and acceptance of the child. The parental narrative is then classified into one of three groups: "balanced," "disengaged," and "distorted." A balanced narrative gives a full impression of the child's personality and the relationship with the parent. The parent seems highly involved with the child and values the relationship as having meaning for the child's development. A disengaged narrative reflects the parent's emotional distance or aloofness from the infant, as seen in relatively flat descriptions and low emotional intensity. A distorted narrative is incoherent (i.e., internally inconsistent) and reveals unrealistic viewpoints. Although the parent's involvement with the child may be intense, it seems confused or overwhelmed in nature.

This interview is a relatively new instrument that appears to have both research and clinical value. Infants' attachment security was found to be associated with the scale ratings and classifications of their parents' interviews, in that infants classified as secure had parents who showed greater richness in their perceptions of the infants, were more sensitive to the infants were more flexible in the face of the infants' change and development, and were more coherent in their narratives (Zeanah, Benoit, Hirshberg, Barton, & Regan, 1991). Clinically, the interview provides a fascinating look into how a parent thinks about his or her child and the relationship with the child; it has the potential to provide an excellent foundation for intensive therapy with the parent and infant.

OVERALL CONSIDERATIONS IN USING RESEARCH PROCEDURES FOR CLINICAL PURPOSES

Traditionally in medicine, and to the extent possible in psychiatry, assessment of signs and symptoms leads to specific diagnoses. There is a clear implication of pathology that is located within an individual. In contrast, research paradigms assess behavior and affect, out of which patterns may be identified and classified. Classifications are more fluid than diagnoses, and do not necessarily describe an individual; rather, they may characterize a relationship pattern. Although classifications or behavioral ratings may have correlates with certain problems or later psychopathology (Cicchetti, 1984, 1987; Sroufe, 1989), they do not indicate pathology in and of themselves. It can be argued that deviant behavior in infants is described better by patterns or classifications, because of rapid developmental change and the impact of the caregiving environment on infant behavior. Nevertheless, this is not reflected in the current diagnostic system in psychiatry (American Psychiatric Association, 1987). Currently, there are no structured observational assessments used to diagnose infants. Nevertheless, it is clear that semistructured assessment procedures for infants and parents are potentially useful in characterizing processes or patterns of behavior, in making predictions, and in planning interventions.

Information obtained from research on groups of infants should be applied to individual infants with some caution. As just noted, none of the procedures described above yields a diagnosis, in the sense of providing a clear indicator or sign of pathology. However, as noted above, there is a lack of pathognomonic signs of psychopathology in infancy. Because individual infants must be examined within a general context of what is normal, it is not such a problem to compare and contrast their behavior with that of those infants characterized in careful study of normal development. The clinician may use this information in a general or statistical sense, drawing upon knowledge of correlates of the assessment to predict potential future problems, in much the same way that knowledge of other risk factors informs treatment planning and prognosis.

Physical and logistical issues are important considerations in using research protocols for clinical purposes. Laboratory procedures often require just that—a laboratory. This means that a particular location or space with particular features is needed (a room of a certain size, one-way mirrors, etc.). Special equipment is often necessary, such as a videotaping system and particular toys or tasks. Structured assessments take time, and clinicians and multidisciplinary infant teams are usually busy. If a clinician does not have the time to do the procedure himself or herself, then other assistance is necessary, as the sessions must be videotaped and/or observed and rated by someone.

The training of observers or raters is also a practical issue. Obviously, if the results of the assessment are to be used for research purposes as well as clinical purposes, then training is vitally important. However, even if the clinician only intends the procedure to be used clinically, a knowledge of scoring and of the meaning of different behaviors is vital for understanding many procedures and useful for most others. Specific training to reliably score semistructured assessments is time-consuming, and requires input from those who developed the assessment or individuals who are well and reliably trained themselves. Many of these scoring systems are sophisticated and involve microanalytic techniques, or are qualitative and may rely on knowledge of theory and behavior. The clinician or the clinician/researcher should keep these factors and his or her own needs and questions in mind when selecting a procedure.

Despite these many considerations, structured assessments of infants and children are useful procedures for clinicians. A clinician who routinely incorporates a structured assessment that meets the criteria outlined above into his or her overall diagnostic evaluation will gain interesting and valuable insights into the behavior of parents and children, even if he or she is not specifically trained in the research protocol or scoring. Over time, the clinician will come to learn what behaviors are typical or atypical in the situation. He or she will see interesting interactions that address strengths and weaknesses in infants and parents. In particular, the clinician will have a window on "real life" that is not obtainable through parental history, questionnaires, or even his or her own interactions with individual infants.

REFERENCES

Ainsworth, M. D. S., Blehar, M., Waters, E., & Wall, S. (1978). *Patterns of attachment: A psychological study of the strange situation.* Hillsdale, NJ: Erlbaum.

Ainsworth, M. D. S., & Wittig, B. A. (1969). Attachment and exploratory behavior of one-year-olds in a strange situation. In B. M. Foss (Ed.), *Determinants of infant behavior* (Vol. 4, pp. 113–136). London: Methuen.

American Psychiatric Association (1987). *Diagnostic and statistical manual of mental disorders* (3rd ed., rev.). Washington, DC: Author.

Baumrind, D. (1971). Current patterns of parental authority. *Developmental Psychopathology Monograph, 4,* 1–103.

Bowlby, J. (1969). *Attachment and loss: Vol. 1. Attachment.* New York: Basic Books.

Brazelton, T. B. (1984). *Neonatal Behavioral Assessment Scale.* London: Spastics International.

Bretherton, I. (1985). Attachment theory: Retrospect and prospect. In I. Bretherton & E. Waters (Eds.), *Growing points of attachmnent theory and research. Monographs of the Society for Research in Child Development, 50* (1–2, Serial No. 209), 3–35.

Cassidy, J., & Marvin, R., with the Attachment Working Group of the John D. and Catherine T. MacArthur Network on the Transition from Infancy to Early Childhood. (1989). *A system for coding the organization of attachment behavior in 3- and 4-year-old children.* Paper presented at the Sixth International Conference on Infant Studies, Washington, DC.

Cicchetti, D. (1984). The emergence of developmental psychopathology. *Child Development, 55,* 1–7.

Cicchetti, D. (1987). Developmental psychopathology in infancy: Illustration from the study of maltreated youngsters. *Journal of Consulting and Clinical Psychology, 55,* 837–845.

Clark, R. (1985). *The Parent–Child Early Relational Assessment.* Unpublished manuscript, University of Wisconsin–Madison.

Clark, R. (1986). *Maternal affective disturbance and child competence.* Paper presented at the Third International Conference on Infant Studies, Los Angeles.

Clark, R., Musick, J., Stott, F., & Klehr, K. (1980). *The Mother's Project Rating Scales of Mother–Child Interaction.* Unpublished manuscript, University of Wisconsin–Madison.

Cohn, J. F., & Tronick, E. Z. (1983). Three-month-old infants' reaction to simulated maternal depression. *Child Development, 54,* 185–193.

Crittenden, P. M. (1985). Social networks, quality of child-rearing and child development. *Child Development, 56,* 1299–1313.

Crittenden, P. M. (1988). Relationships at risk. In J. Belsky & T. Nezworski (Eds.), *Clinical implications of attachment* (pp. 136–174). Hillsdale, NJ: Erlbaum.

Crowell, J. A., & Feldman, S. S. (1988). Mothers' internal working models of relationships and children's behavioral and developmental status: A study of mother–child interaction. *Child Development, 59,* 1273–1285.

Crowell, J. A., & Feldman, S. S. (1991). Mothers' working models of attachment relationships and mother and child behavior during separation and reunion. *Developmental Psychology, 27,* 597–605.

Crowell, J. A., Feldman, S. S., & Ginsberg, N. (1988). Assessment of mother–child interaction in preschoolers with behavior problems. *Journal of the American Academy of Child and Adolescent Psychiatry, 27,* 303–311.

Crowell, J. A., O'Connor, E., Wollmers, G., Sprafkin, J.,

& Rao, U. (1991). *Mothers' conceptualizations of parent–child relationships: Relation to mother–child interaction and child behavior problems.* Development and Psychopathology, 3, 431–444.

Drotar, D., Malone, C. A., & Nowak, M. (1985). *Early outcome in failure to thrive: Correlates of security of attachment.* Paper presented at the biennial meeting of the Society for Research in Child Development, Toronto.

Egeland, B., & Sroufe, L. A. (1981). Developmental sequelae of maltreatment in infancy. In R. Rizley & D. Cicchetti (Eds.), *Developmental perspectives on child maltreatment* (pp. 77–92). San Francisco: Jossey-Bass.

Eichberg, C. (1987). *Quality of infant–parent attachment: Related to mother's representation of her own relationship history.* Paper presented at the biennial meeting of the Society for Research in Child Development, Baltimore.

Erickson, M. F., Sroufe, L. A., & Egeland, B. (1985). The relationship between quality of attachment and behavior problems in preschool in a high risk sample. In I. Bretherton & E. Waters (Eds.), *Growing points of attachment theory and research. Monographs of the Society for Research in Child Development, 50*(1–2, Serial No. 209), 110–135.

Fraiberg, S. H. (1980). *Clinical studies in infant mental health: The first year of life.* New York: Basic Books.

Gaensbauer, T. J., & Harmon, R. J. (1981). Clincal assessment in infancy utilizing structured playroom situations. *Journal of the American Academy of Child Psychiatry, 20,* 264–280.

Garber, J. (1984). Classification of childhood psychopathology: A developmental perspective. *Child Development, 55,* 30–48.

George, C., Kaplan, N., & Main, M. (1985). *Adult Attachment Interview.* Unpublished manuscript, University of California at Berkeley.

Gordon, A. H., & Jameson, J. C. (1979). Infant–mother attachment in infants with non-organic failure to thrive syndrome. *Journal of the American Academy of Child Psychiatry, 18,* 96–99.

Greenspan, S. I., & Porges, S. W. (1984). Psychopathology in infancy and early childhood: Clinical perspectives on the organization of sensory and affective-thematic experiences. *Child Development, 55,* 49–70.

Main, M., & Goldwyn, R. (1984). *Adult Attachment Interview scoring system.* Unpublished manuscript, University of California at Berkeley.

Main, M., Kaplan, N., & Cassidy, J. (1985). Security in infancy, childhood, and adulthood: A move to the level of representation. In I. Bretherton & E. Waters (Eds.), Growing points of attachment theory and research. *Monographs of the Society for Research in Child Development, 50*(1–2, Serial No. 209), 66–104.

Main, M., & Solomon, J. (1986). Discovery of an insecure-disorganized/disoriented attachment pattern: Procedures, findings and implications for the classification of behavior. In T. B. Brazelton & M. Yogman (Eds.), *Affective development in infancy.* Norwood, NJ: Ablex.

Matas, L., Arend, R. A., & Sroufe, L. A. (1978). Continuity of adaptation in the second year: The relationship between quality of attachment and later competence. *Child Development, 49,* 547–556.

Radke-Yarrow, M., Cummings, E. M., Kuczynski, L., & Chapman, M. (1985). Patterns of attachment in two-

and three-year-olds in normal families and families with depression. *Child Development, 56,* 884–893.

Rothbaum, F., & Schneider-Rosen, K. (1988). *Parental acceptance scoring manual: A system for assessing interactions between parents and their young children.* Unpublished manuscript, Tufts University and Boston College.

Schneider-Rosen, K. (1990). The developmental reorganization of attachment relationships: Guidelines for classifications beyond infancy. In M. T. Greenberg, D. Cicchetti, & E. M. Cummings (Eds.), *Attachment in the preschool years: Theory, research and intervention* (pp. 185–220). Chicago: University of Chicago Press.

Schneider-Rosen, K., Beatty, M., & Rothbaum, F. (1992). [The stability and predictive value of parental acceptance: A two year longitudinal analysis]. Manuscript in preparation.

Schneider-Rosen, K., Braunwald, K., Carlson, V., & Cicchetti, D. (1985). Current perspectives in attachment theory: Illustration from the study of maltreated infants. In I. Bretherton & E. Waters (Eds.), Growing points of attachment theory and research. *Monographs of the Society for Research in Child Development, 50*(1–2, Serial No. 209), 194–210.

Schneider-Rosen, K., Rothbaum, F., & Wenz-Gross, M. (1989). *Parental acceptance and the development of self-control for 18 to 30 months of age.* Unpublished manuscript, Boston College.

Schneider-Rosen, K., Spada, K., & DeVirgilio, C. (1992). *Parental acceptance and its relation to empathy and peer interactions at two years of age.* Manuscript in preparation.

Sostek, A. M., & Anders, T. (1977). Relationships among the Brazelton Neonatal Scale, Bayley Infant Scales, and early temperament. *Child Development, 48,* 320–323.

Sroufe, L. A., & Fleeson, J. (1986). Attachment and the construction of relationships. In W. Hartup & Z. Rubin (Eds.), *Relationships and development* (pp. 51–71). Hillsdale, NJ: Erlbaum.

Sroufe, L. A., & Rutter, M. (1984). The domain of developmental psychopathology. *Child Development, 55,* 17–29.

Stern, D. D. (1971). A microanalysis of mother–infant play. *Journal of the American Academy of Child Psychiatry, 13,* 402–421.

Stott, F. M., Musick, J. S., Clark, R., & Cohler, B. J. (1983). Developmental patterns in the infants and young children of mentally ill mothers. *Infant Mental Health Journal, 4,* 217–235.

Thompson, R., Cicchetti, D., Lamb, M. E., & Malkin, C. (1985). The emotional responses of Down syndrome and normal infants in the Strange Situation: The organization of affective behavior in infants. *Developmental Psychopathology, 21,* 828–841.

Tronick, E. Z., Als, H., Adamson, L., Wise, S., & Brazelton, T. B. (1978). The infant's response to entrapment between contradictory messages in face-to-face interaction. *Journal of the American Academy of Child Psychiatry, 17,* 1–13.

Tronick, E. Z., Als, H., & Brazelton, T. B. (1980). Monadic phases: A structural descriptive analysis of infant–mother face-to-face interaction. *Merrill–Palmer Quarterly, 26,* 3–24.

Tronick, E. Z., & Brazelton, T. B. (1975). Clinical uses of the Brazelton Neonatal Behavioral Assessment Scale. In B. Z. Friedlander & L. Rosenblum (Eds.), *Exceptional infant.* New York: Brunner/Mazel.

Tronick, E. Z., Cohn, J., & Shea, E. (1986). The transfer of affect between mothers and infants. In T. B. Brazelton & M. Yogman (Eds.), *Affective development in infancy* (pp. 11–25). Norwood, NJ: Ablex.

Vaughn, E. E., Taraldson, B., Crichton, L., & Egeland, B. (1980). Relationships between neonatal behavioral organization and infant behavior in the first year of life. *Infant Behavior and Development, 3,* 47–66.

Waters, E., & Deane, K. (1985). Defining and assessing individual differences in attachment relationships: Q-onetuodology and the organization of behavior in infancy and early childhood. In I. Bretherton & E. Waters (Eds.) Growing points of attachment theory and research. *Monographs of the Society for Research in Child Development 50* (1–2, Serial No. 209), 41–65.

Waters, E., Vaughn, B. E., & Egeland, B. (1980). Individual differences in infant–mother attachment relationships at age one: Antecedents in neonatal behavior in an urban economically disadvantaged sample. *Child Development, 51,* 208–216.

Widmayer, S., & Field, T. (1980). Effects of Brazelton demonstrations on early interactions of preterm infants. *Infant Behavior and Development, 3,* 78–89.

Worobey, J., & Belsky, J. (1982). Employing the Brazelton scale to influence mothering: An experimental comparison of three strategies. *Developmental Psychology, 18,* 736–743.

Zeanah, C., Benoit, D., & Barton, M. (1986). *Working model of the child interview.* Unpublished manuscript, Brown University.

Zeanah, C., Benoit, D., Hirshberg, L., Barton, M., & Regan, C. (1991, October). *Classifying mothers' representations of their infants: Results from structured interviews.* Paper presented at the annual meeting of the American Academy of Child and Adolescent Psychiatry, San Francisco.

IV

DISORDERS OF INFANCY

Why are there so few disorders of infancy in the official nosologies such as DSM-IV and ICD-10? Several possible reasons must be considered. First, it is not clear that systems of classification designed to describe adult disorders are applicable to an age group in which developmental change is rapid and contextual variables are integral. In other words, the disorders may exist but may not be well described. Some have suggested that clinical disturbances in infants are best described as relationship disorders rather than within-the-individual disorders, for example. Second, development is relatively less differentiated in infancy, so that signs and symptoms of disorder may be less specific. Thus it may be possible to identify disordered infants categorically, but not to specify clearly the nature of the disorder. Third, some may find the idea of infants with disorders politically objectionable; they may be offended by the idea of giving potentially stigmatizing labels to young children. Others, more comfortable with notions of risk and resilience, will object to the lack of validation of categorical disorders in young children. Beyond mental retardation and the Pervasive Developmental Disorders, in which known or presumed central nervous system abnormalities are believed to explain an infant's symptoms and signs, there has been little validation of other disorders.

As the chapters in Part IV make clear, this volume takes a clear stance that disorders of infancy do exist, and it makes a preliminary effort to describe them. The many complicated issues involved in such an undertaking are thoughtfully considered by Emde, Bingham, and Harmon in Chapter 14, which provides a helpful overview to the entire section. They enumerate reasons why disorders of infancy challenge the traditional systems of psychiatric diagnosis. They also underscore the important distinction of classifying disorders but assessing individuals.

The next three chapters review several of the better-validated disorders encountered in infant mental health. Volkmar (Chapter 15) thoroughly reviews autism and the autistic spectrum, including other disorders that involve delays and deviance in social, cognitive, and communicative domains. In Chapter 16, Thomasgard and Shonkoff review the topic of mental retardation as it affects children younger than 3 years of age. Their chapter includes an important section on family context that questions the adequacy and accuracy of pathological models of family adaptation.

Prizant, Wetherby, and Roberts (Chapter 17) provide an overview of communication disorders in young children, including early communication development, risk factors associated with communication disorders, diagnostic schemes, assessment of infants, and intervention with children and parents. They conclude with a discussion of implications for infant mental health professionals.

Continuing the description of central nervous system abnormalities, Greenspan and Weider describe regulatory disorders in Chapter 18. This group of disorders involves irregularities in sensory reactivity, self-regulation, and behavioral organization. Greenspan and Weider describe the clinical features of different types of regulatory disorders, and they mention some of the indirect validity data underlying their description. Further research must attempt to delineate clearly the boundaries of these disorders.

Drell, Siegel, and Gaensbauer (Chapter 19) review what is known about Post-Traumatic Stress Disorder in infancy. This is an example of a disorder whose criteria for adults are well described, but unsatisfactory for children because developmental differences in childhood are not taken into account. The situation is even more problematic in infancy. In an important section, the authors review research on infant development as it applies to considering when and whether infants are capable of experiencing post-traumatic symptoms. Case examples illustrate typical clinical pictures.

Symptom-based disorders are considered in Chapters 20 and 21. Complaints about sleep problems are among the most common that parents of infants make to pediatricians. Sadeh and Anders (Chapter 20) review the development of sleep–wake states and describe the signs, symptoms, etiology, assessment, and treatment of sleep disorders in infancy. They emphasize the psychological issues of separation and autonomy as they relate to sleep and parent–infant relationships. Benoit (Chapter 21) describes failure to thrive and feeding disorders in infancy. She points out that despite considerable overlap, not all infants who are failing to thrive have feeding disorders, and not all infants with feeding disorders are failing to thrive. After reviewing physiological, developmental, and environmental factors believed to affect eating and growth, she considers the more common clinical syndromes in this area.

In Chapter 22, Zeanah, Mammen, and Lieberman describe disorders of attachment from the standpoint of developmental research. Critical of descriptions of disorders of attachment in current nosologies, they propose criteria for five types of attachment disorders that are grounded in clinical observations and in knowledge about parent–infant relationships gained from attachment research. They illustrate each type with case examples, and they call for efforts to validate the construct of attachment disorders.

In the concluding chapter of the section, David A. Mrazek (Chapter 23) describes recent advances in conceptualizing psychosomatic disorders. He explicates the intricate interactions of psychological and physical processes in infants, illustrating them with discussions of obesity and asthma. He concludes with a new model that can guide psychological interventions for medical illnesses expressing themselves in infancy.

14

Classification and the Diagnostic Process in Infancy

ROBERT N. EMDE
RICHARD D. BINGHAM
ROBERT J. HARMON

Classification schemes in infancy are in the process of rapid evolution, reflecting changing perspectives from clinical experience, advancing knowledge, and new directions in research. The clinical field of infant mental health, moreover, has a number of features that have made standard approaches to classification challenging and difficult. We therefore believe that it is important for the student of the field to consider these features and why they challenge medical and adult-oriented traditions in diagnosis. It will then be possible to appreciate what is useful in current classification schemes.

FEATURES OF THE INFANT MENTAL HEALTH FIELD THAT CHALLENGE THE MEDICAL TRADITION OF DIAGNOSIS

The infant mental health field has from its inception been *multidisciplinary*. This feature has led to various contributions to clinical classification that have represented a variety of conceptual and taxonomic paradigms. Another feature of the field that challenges the task of classification is its *developmental orientation*. This orientation goes beyond the understanding of changes within individuals across age; it also

requires an understanding of dynamic processes of exchange between organism and environment. Thus, change over time and developmental transformations in behavior are characteristic of the phenomena to be classified, as opposed to a fixity of symptom clusters, often thought to characterize disorders of later life. The field of infant mental health is also *multigenerational*, and, from the point of view of child advocacy, it is necessarily relationship- and family-oriented—a feature that often makes the locus of diagnostic emphasis uncertain. Finally, diagnostic classification in infancy has been difficult because the infant mental health field has been *prevention-oriented* from its beginnings, and the identification of risk as well as disorder has been viewed as crucial. A central feature of practice in the field has been an orientation to potential problems prior to the appearance of disorder. Practitioners use early intervention in order to prevent disorder at later ages.

Let us now consider the traditional concerns of medical diagnosis as they apply to infancy. These provide a historical background for the perplexing challenges of classification in infant mental health.

Since the ancient Greek times of Hippocrates, diagnosis has been linked to prognosis and the clinician's desire to make predictive statements about outcomes. Infancy, however, is a time of rapid change, and the clinician's activity at every turn is geared to facilitate favorable developmental change. This presents a formidable challenge to the task of discerning continuities in disorder across time. Traditional diagnostic classification has not been developmentally based, and therefore has not directly confronted this challenge.

The emphasis of the infant mental health field on prevention makes strong demands of a diagnostic system. As with prognosis, classification of risk conditions (without overt disorder) must identify meaningful predictive relationships. In other words, *preceding* conditions of family environment, infant disability, or risk in some other area must be shown to be linked to later infant and childhood mental health problems. In order to guide efforts at preventive intervention, the classification for infancy must capture both the presence of disorder and the presence of conditions that lead to disorder.

Another traditional concern of medical diagnosis has to do with the inclusion of etiologic factors in classification, even though etiological relationships are not necessary for a system of classification (Rutter & Gould, 1985). Moreover, systems of classification often reflect assumptions about the nature of the etiologic processes involved. The application of medical nosology to mental disorders was first strengthened by medical research in the 19th century; more recently, dramatic progress in the neurosciences has fostered a model of searching for mental disease in the form of biologically based disturbances of the brain. Such a model often tends to encourage the search for single etiologic factors, but simple, direct lines of causation seem rare in infant mental health problems. Rather, most such problems result from multiple etiologic factors that involve interactions of environmental and intrinsic elements in varying combinations and degrees.

The medical view of mental disorder as arising from disturbances of the brain has also led to a tendency of designating disorder in categorical terms (i.e., viewing disorder as either present or absent). In this view, abnormality is assumed to be discontinuous from and of a different class than normality (Pennington, 1991), and the distinction between the two is considered to be clear-cut. Still, as has recently been pointed out, evidence regarding many of the common emotional and behavioral disorders throughout childhood suggests that they are often better conceptualized as dimensional (i.e., as existing on a continuum with normality) than as categorical (Rutter & Tuma, 1988; Achenbach, 1988). A related aspect of the categorical view is that disorders will occur in distinct syndromes without overlap. A challenge to this view occurs when two or more different psychiatric syndromes are present in the same child. In current psychiatric literature, the presence of two or more syndromes in the same person is referred to as "comorbidity." Since complex interrelations are commonly found among various childhood emotional and behavioral problems (e.g., anxiety and depression or Conduct Disorder and Attention-Deficit Hyperactivity Disorder), underlying processes seem to be shared across various disorders. The prominence of comorbidity challenges any classification system to validate the boundaries that define its categories, and infancy disorders share these challenges with later childhood disorders.

Another assumption that is closely related to the categorical organization of current medically based classification schemes is that disorder is presumed to reside within individuals. Yet, as we have mentioned, the family relationship context must be considered central and in many ways indispensable in evaluating infant behavior and functioning. This presents a special problem to infancy clinicians: When disturbances are embedded in caregiving relationships, and may be specific to such relationships, how are they to be classified? Many infancy clinicians believe that the inclusion of functioning within the context of specific relationships is necessary for a classification to be useful in guiding treatment. Accepted classification systems, however, have yet to venture beyond a focus on the individual.

There is another issue that deserves mention at this point. This is generally referred to as the concern about "labeling"—a concern about potentially negative impacts accruing to individual children when diagnostic labels for emotional and behavioral disorders are applied. To the extent that such a process is associated with negative expectations or social stigmatization, untoward influences may limit individual potential, generate shame, and perpetuate problems. Some may thus consider the risk of such influences from labeling to be greater in early development, when expectations are being formed and internalized.

All of these issues illustrate the challenge that the field of infant mental health presents for the application of traditional classification schemes.

Infancy clinicians have realized that modifications must be made in traditional approaches to classification in order to address such issues. The diverse roots of the infant mental health field provide opportunities for integrating multiple conceptual paradigms. This integration is likely to yield innovative approaches to classification, which are needed.

We next review the purposes of classification. This leads us to consider the importance of multiple dimensions of assessment in infancy. Assessment, in our view, must precede the clinician's use of a classification scheme. We then provide a brief review of how existing classification schemes address infant mental health problems. A discussion of some illustrative disorders allows us to make some points about differential diagnosis, as well as to indicate some areas where research is needed. In concluding, we summarize what we believe is important about the diagnostic process and suggest future directions.

PURPOSES OF CLASSIFICATION AND THE NEED FOR ASSESSMENT

Considering the many challenges and concerns about classification in infancy, many may wonder why it should be essential. It seems useful, therefore, to review the positive purposes of classification.

Classification is a basic human activity, a way of ordering our knowledge and generating hypotheses. Clinical classification, simply put, is a way of communicating knowledge among professionals for the purposes of helping people and advancing knowledge. The direct clinical purpose of this kind of communication is to tap existing knowledge in order to make decisions about treatment or prevention. There is also a research purpose: Meaningful classification schemes and reliable methods of applying them are crucial tools in determining the etiology of specific disorders, their course, and the efficacy of treatment.

There are various approaches to classification. Rutter and Gould (1985) have reviewed criteria for advanced diagnostic schemes. These include clear definitions of terms with established reliability of usage; differentiation among disorders that have established validity concerning etiology, course, and treatment with respect to symptom clusters; and clear decision rules for making judgments. These are demanding criteria and are not met in new clinical areas such as infant mental health. Nonetheless, the classification schemes we review below reflect the current knowledge of the field and provide a basis for future changes.

We believe it important to remind ourselves that an important principle, seldom made explicit, underlies clinical classification—namely, that we classify disorders, not individuals. As Rutter and Gould (1985) have pointed out, to classify individuals is not only scientifically inappropriate, but demeaning. Still, the clinician is faced with the necessity of evaluating individuals prior to the classification of disorder. We therefore move next to the process of assessment.

Through assessment, the particular distinguishing features of an individual infant and family are identified. Assessment schemes guide our evaluation of individuals and their families, whereas classification schemes apply to disorders. Our focus in this chapter is on classification, but it is necessary to consider some aspects of assessment. One reason is that clinicians begin the diagnostic process with assessment and subsequently arrive at diagnostic classification. Another reason is that several of the perplexing and challenging issues enumerated earlier concerning classification in the field of infant mental health may be partly addressed through assessing multiple domains and incorporating these into classification.

Precisely because of its multidisciplinary nature, the field of infant mental health has great potential to provide a major contribution to other areas of mental health in the realm of integrating multiple domains of assessment. The diverse background of infant mental health practitioners provides multiple paradigms and multiple methods of assessment. At its historical roots is the psychodynamic paradigm, which has been powerfully applied to understanding infant–parent difficulties (Fraiberg, 1980; Brazelton & Cramer, 1990; Cramer et al., 1990). Although the psychodynamic paradigm has provided a useful clinical framework, it has not provided a classification system with demonstrated reliability or validity. However, analytic concepts and sensitivity have contributed to the creation of observational ratings by developmentalists, which can, with modifications, be of use in assessment and have potential for integration into classification (Gaensbauer & Harmon, 1981). A similar valuable contribution to clinical work comes from family systems theory (Minuchin, 1974; Scharff & Scharff, 1987), but its direct use in classification is similarly limited by inadequate reliability and validity, although important efforts at improving this may soon yield useful schemes (Jacob & Tennenbaum, 1988; Reiss & Klein, 1987). Assessments by speech and language therapists will clearly be important in some circumstances. It seems likely that the nature of the associations between communication deficits and psychiatric disorders (Cantwell & Baker, 1988) may be further elucidated by characterizing these associations in infancy and early childhood, in addition to the research done in middle childhood. Special areas of health assessment from physical and occupational therapy should also be incorporated. The importance of these domains is emphasized by important relationships now being discovered between sensorimotor functioning and emotional regulation or infant mental health (Greenspan, 1992; Poisson & DeGangi, 1991).

The approach of including multiple domains or axes in the formal diagnostic system has been accepted to varying degrees in both of the major current classification schemes: the revised third edition of the *Diagnostic and Statistical Manual of Mental Disorders* (DSM-III-R; American Psychiatric Association, 1987), and the draft 10th revision of the *International Classification of Diseases* (ICD-10; World Health Organization, 1988). The multiaxial approach that has been applauded by many in general psychiatry is equally important, if not more so, in evaluating infancy problems. An individual's functioning is assessed in a multidimensional way in order to determine prognosis, plan intervention, and monitor outcomes. The five axes of the DSM-III-R system assess (I) major psychiatric syndromes; (II) personality disorders/traits and developmental/learning disorders (including mental retardation); (III) contributing physical/medical problems; (IV) psychosocial stressors; and (V) level of functioning.

Here is a brief list of some areas of assessment that are considered crucial in clinical infant mental health and should be familiar to clinicians:

Child developmental level
Child health (DSM-III-R, Axis III)
Psychosocial stressors for child (DSM-III-R, Axis IV)
Adequacy of environment for child
Level and quality of relating
Infant–parent relationship
Caregiver characteristics

Some of these aspects of assessment, as noted, map onto current axes of DSM-III-R. We have included other areas of assessment that deserve particular emphasis for infant mental health work. From the point of view of assessment, we emphasize that each child needs to be characterized individually, according to his or her level of development, health, and adaptation, and according to his or her unique relationships and environmental context. The clinician must attend to these areas, as well as the specific criteria for the syndrome categories that are evolving.

CLASSIFICATION SCHEMES

The categories of DSM-III-R and the provisional version of ICD-10 that are specific childhood diagnoses relevant to the classification of disorder in the first 3 postnatal years are presented in Table 14.1 (diagnoses as listed in Rapoport & Ismond, 1990; specific developmental disorders are excluded). Other psychiatric disorders that are not specific to childhood, but are relevant to infancy, include depression and Post-Traumatic Stress Disorder. The categories of these schemes, however, do not cover some of

TABLE 14.1. DSM-III-R and ICD-10 (Draft) Diagnostic Categories of Childhood Disorders Applicable to Infancy

DSM-III-R	ICD-10(draft)
Autistic Disorder	Childhood Autism
Pervasive Developmental Disorder NOS	Atypical Autism
Childhood Disintegrative Disorder	
Overactive Disorder Associated with Stereotyped Movements	
Oppositional Defiant Disorder	
Separation Anxiety Disorder	Separation Anxiety Disorder
Rumination Disorder of Infancy	
Reactive Attachment Disorder of Infancy or Early Childhood	Reactive Attachment Disorder of Childhood

the major symptom groupings and phenomena relevant for infancy.

The first known textbook for infant psychiatry contains a classificatory scheme that attempts to follow the DSM-III-R approach insofar as possible while extending it. The following disorders are arrayed by Minde and Minde (1986): (1) Autistic Disorder; (2) Reactive Attachment Disorder; (3) Disorder of Behavioral Organization; (4) Disorder of Sleep; and (5) Disorder of Eating. As elaborated in the textbook, this classificatory scheme goes beyond the DSM approach in considering developmental processes as central. Behavioral organization and behavioral regulation are given particular emphasis. As a beginning, this scheme has been considered useful, but it is also limited in scope and detail. Additional classification is needed in infancy, with criteria that cover different forms of problems related to this early age and take account of the fact that some adult-devised symptoms cannot be expressed.

A more recent classification scheme results from a current working task group of the National Center for Clinical Infant Programs (NCCIP). This group, chaired initially by Stanley Greenspan and later by Serena Weider, includes many active practitioners of infant psychiatry in North America, including Klaus Minde. We give particular emphasis to this scheme and its criteria, since it represents the efforts of the first task force of leading infant mental health practitioners that has been assembled for such a purpose. The major diagnostic categories of what we refer to as the NCCIP scheme include (1) Disorders of Social Development and Communication; (2) Psychic Trauma Disorders; (3) Regulatory Disorders; (4) Disorders of Affect; and (5) Adjustment Reaction Disorders.

We briefly discuss the defining characteristics of each of the NCCIP diagnostic categories, which are listed in Table 14.2 along with their subcategories. Disorders of Social Development and Communication are organized in a manner very similar to that of the DSM-III-R, with the subcategories of Autism and Atypical Pervasive Developmental Disorder. The diagnostic criteria for Autism have received much more attention and empirical work than those for other infancy disorders; therefore, the criteria in this scheme differ little from those in DSM-III-R. Psychic Trauma Disorders are subcategorized according to those resulting from a single event or connected series of traumatic events and

TABLE 14.2. NCCIP Classification Scheme

Disorders of Social Development and Communication
    Autism
    Atypical Pervasive Developmental Disorder

Psychic Trauma Disorders
    Acute, Single Event
    Chronic, Repeated

Regulatory Disorders
    Hypersensitivity Type
    Underreactive Type
    Active–Aggressive Type
    Mixed Type
    Regulatory Based Sleep Disorder
    Regulatory Based Eating Disorder

Disorders of Affect
    Anxiety Disorder
    Mood Disorders
        Prolonged Bereavement
        Depression
        Labile Mood Disorder
    Mixed Disorder of Emotional Expressiveness
    Deprivation Syndrome

Adjustment Reaction Disorders

those resulting from repeated or enduring traumatic events. The criteria for these disorders are similar to the core symptoms given for Post-Traumatic Stress Disorder in DSM-III-R, but also bring in symptoms tailored to the developmental capacities of infants (see the first case vignette below). The creation of a separate category associated with chronic trauma is valuable in giving emphasis to the problems of abuse and neglect, which are common in infant mental health practice. Regulatory Disorders are marked by disturbances in sensory, sensorimotor, or organizational processing. The creation of this category represents the first major attempt at classification of constitutional/maturational difficulties. Previously these children have simply been referred to in various ways as "fussy," "overly sensitive," or "reactive," without systematic attempts to delineate the specific nature of the difficulty or make specific categorizations. An important aspect of the subcategories provided in this system is the requirement that the type of sensory, sensorimotor, or organizational problems be specified. Sleep and eating/feeding problems are common clinical concerns in infancy, and particular subtypes of Regulatory Disorders are provided for these problems. The fourth class, Disorders of Affect, encompasses a range of disorders found under several different subheadings in DSM-III-R. Both Anxiety Disorder and Mood Disorders are included, as well as disorders that are related to specific environmental circumstances—namely, Prolonged (pathological) Bereavement and Deprivation Syndrome. The latter is analogous to Reactive Attachment Disorder, but the disorder name places greater emphasis on the relationship to inadequate care. Deprivation Syndrome may be associated with a growth disturbance (e.g., failure to thrive), but is considered to be a separate entity. The last category, Adjustment Reaction Disorders, is not much different from DSM-III-R, except that the duration is less than 4 months (not 6 months).

A particularly valuable aspect of the work by the task force is the development of a standard set of assessment scales, which are to be completed as part of a diagnostic evaluation (NCCIP, 1991). The aspects of assessment we have listed earlier in this chapter are covered by the various scales in the manual, which have detailed anchor points to guide the ratings. One of the values of systematically completing these scales for a large number of infants is to determine how useful they might be for broadening data used in classification.

Now we turn to an area of assessment that we view as having special importance for infant mental health work, and that therefore needs to be formally brought into classification systems. As we have mentioned at the beginning of the chapter, emotional and behavioral problems of infancy are embedded in problems of caregiving relationships. Moreover, it seems essential to identify unhealthy or maladaptive relationships as contrasted with healthy relationships and to understand their determinants. If this is done, we can build a knowledge base for understanding how much a child's individual characteristics contribute to the quality of the relationship and how much the nature of experience with the caregiving environment contributes. By doing this, we can also determine how problematic early relationships can be remedied through improved social interactions.

Early steps toward classification of relationship disorders resulted from a recent collaborative effort to compose a developmental model for relationship disturbances (Sameroff & Emde, 1989). Two schemes have been derived from this work. The first scheme classifies problematic relationships into these categories: "overregulated," "underregulated," "inappropriate," "irregular," or "chaotic" (Anders, 1989). Although these categories are descriptively and theoretically appealing, clinicians have experienced difficulty in using them to achieve reliable judgments. The second scheme, the Parent–Infant Relationship Global Assessment Scale (a basic version of which has been adopted as part of the NCCIP manual), categorizes the severity of the relationship disturbance as shown in Table 14.3. Specific criteria have been developed for the severity levels of perturbation, disturbance, and disorder. In its initial application, the scale shows promise of reliability among clinicians (C. H. Zeanah, personal communication, 1991).

These efforts converge with the belief of many clinicians that an axis for classification of relationship disorders should regularly be used to supplement an axis for the classification of individual-based disorders in children under 3 years of age. The use of such an axis would reflect the fact that infancy problems are embedded in caregiving relationship problems. The NCCIP diagnostic classification system expects to move toward such an axis designation in the near future. Consideration of relationship problems adds a new level of analysis to the diagnostic process, yet at this new level the same issues of reliability and validity still apply. It also remains to be seen whether either the severity or the specific nature of relationship problems will be systematically related to important clinical variables, such as etiology, treatment, and outcome.

Another domain of diagnosis that is related to relationship disorders and is worth considering in more detail is that of "psychosocial stressors," or Axis IV in the DSM system. For infants and young children this becomes roughly equivalent to the quality of the home environment. The NCCIP diagnostic manual also includes the assessment of this domain, with scales for Psychosocial Stressors and Adequacy of the Environment. The Adequacy of the Envi-

TABLE 14.3. Parent–Infant Relationship Global Assessment Scale

Score range	Classification
90–81	Well adapted
80–71	Adapted
70–61	Perturbed
60–51	Significantly perturbed
50–41	Disturbed
40–31	Significantly disturbed
30–21	Disordered
20–11	Significantly disordered
10–0	Imminent danger

ronment Scale covers relationships within the family and the familial emotional climate; it also assesses whether the physical environment meets the basic needs for shelter, health care, nutrition, stimulation, and safety. Ratings on the scale are made with consideration of the appropriateness of the environment to the individual child. The importance of improving the classification of psychosocial stressors is reflected in attempts by others to develop a psychosocial scale for use with children. Early tests of reliability and validity are encouraging (Shaffer, Gould, Rutter, & Sturge, 1991).

THREE CASE VIGNETTES ILLUSTRATING CLASSIFICATION IN INFANCY

We now provide several case vignettes to illustrate disorders or clinical problems that involve some of the classification issues we have discussed. The vignettes illustrate the usefulness of the NCCIP classification scheme with three very different types of clinical problems.

Case 1: Psychic Trauma Disorder

The first case vignette is chosen to illustrate a disorder wherein most of the key features pertaining to older children and adults can be applied in infancy—Psychic Trauma Disorder. As in adulthood, this syndrome is unusual in having its etiology clearly based on an experience of an overwhelmingly frightening event. Throughout life, it is a disorder that involves the dysregulated emotional processing of a terrifying experience with both underregulation (e.g., intrusions of fright in nightmares and upon exposure to reminders of the event, and irritability with outbursts of anger) and overregulation (e.g., avoidance of reminders, psychic numbing, and withdrawal of interest with decreased exploration). But there are areas that are different for infants and young children. These concern a more limited capacity for coping and defense, as well as a variety of confusing causal inferences that the young child may construct.

Joan, aged 2 years and 2 months, was riding with her father and pregnant mother when they were involved in a severe car accident. The driver of the other car made an illegal left turn in front of her father. The father was hospitalized for several weeks because of injuries; the girl was taken to an emer-

gency room for removal of glass fragments in her face; and her pregnant mother was unhurt. The little girl developed nightmares, became extremely fearful and hypervigilant, was difficult to soothe, and (quite surprisingly to the parents) was very angry toward her father and refused to ride in the car. Unfortunately, the parents purchased a new car that was almost identical to the one involved in the accident. Although both they and their daughter were eventually able to deal with most of the issues from the accident, Joan continued to exhibit nightmares and anger toward her father, and refused to ride in the new car. She was quite fearful of riding in any car, but specifically the new car, which her parents had to admit in retrospect obviously reminded her and them of the "crash"— Joan's word for describing the accident.

The family was referred for evaluation and treatment, which focused on the obvious post-traumatic symptomatology; the displacement of Joan's anger about the experience onto her father, whom she held responsible; and the understanding of her symptoms as post-traumatic. With brief therapy, Joan's symptoms abated.

Case 2: Regulatory Disorder

In contrast to the disorder just discussed, the category of Regulatory Disorders in infancy is not paralleled by any class of disorders in other childhood or adult classification schemes. Most clinicians would view the concept of regulation as an important framework from which to view many kinds of mental health disorders. Clinicians working with infants, however, not only find it essential to assess the contribution of intrinsic regulatory factors, but also find it useful to designate primary syndromes of regulatory disorders in order to direct intervention strategies (Minde & Minde, 1986; Greenspan, 1992). In the current state of our knowledge, there are many questions of predictive and discriminant validity regarding regulatory syndromes that need exploration. To what extent do these syndromes relate in any systematic fashion to later known childhood disorders that may involve similar "regulatory" problems (e.g., Attention-Deficit Hyperactivity Disorder and Atypical Pervasive Developmental Disorder)? To what extent do such disorders overlap with the abnormalities in social relatedness considered primary in the Disorders of Social Development and Communication? Perhaps as future research is able to identify primary impairments involved in the infant's sensory, motor, and executive functioning (organizational processing), a more specific terminology may evolve. Our second case illustrates an infant's difficulty in achieving effective state regulation, control over sensory input, and smooth motor functioning. The infant also showed some associated difficulty in social relatedness.

Karen had been a very difficult child since birth: She was colicky, had difficulties both in going to sleep and in sleeping for more than a few hours at a time, and evidenced extreme state regulation difficulties. She tolerated separations from her parents (particularly her mother) poorly, in spite of very good care by the parents. She did not seem to soothe herself, was easily overstimulated, and was fearful of most situations that would usually result in exploration and interaction. In addition, she made poor eye contact with adults and had a tendency to withdraw from social interaction with anyone but her parents. Her expressive language was delayed; there were occasional instances of echolalia; and she was quite clumsy and poorly coordinated.

At the time she was referred for evaluation, she had been diagnosed as having Pervasive Developmental Disorder NOS. However, her play and her interaction with both her mother and the evaluator suggested a degree of social relatedness inconsistent with an autistic spectrum disorder. From both observation and a more detailed history, it became clear that she had a Regulatory Disorder, Mixed Type (see Greenspan & Wieder, Chapter 18, this volume). As might be expected, Karen's mother was overwhelmed in taking care of such a difficult child, but was also relieved that the diagnosis and prognosis were less severe than what she was originally told. Treatment focused on Karen's speech and language delays, on her motor difficulties, and on the mother–child interaction. Individual therapy was also provided for the mother, to help her deal with having such a constitutionally difficult child.

Case 3: Adjustment Disorder versus Mood Disorder with a Relationship Disorder Axis Designation

Most instances of clinically disordered relationships involve an infant's relationship with the primary caregiver, the mother or father. We would remind the reader that disordered relationships can also involve other meaningful caregivers in the infant's life. The assessment leading to the designation of clinically disordered relationships on a separate axis necessarily involves the evaluation of multiple relationships within the family. Our third vignette illustrates the usefulness of having relationship disturbances highlighted by a separate axis, which in this case would be applied to Sarah's relationship with her day care provider. The influence of other family relationships is also apparent.

Sarah was a 3-month-old infant whose professional parents became concerned about her after she was placed in day care so that her mother could return to work part-time. Sarah had been planned, and her parents had postponed childbearing to finish their professional training. She was very much wanted and loved, and both parents spent a great deal of time with her. The mother's decision to go back to work part-time was based on her contract with her employer, but was also something that she felt was important for her to do. The parents had begun to look for day care prior to Sarah's birth, and had chosen a home day care setting run by a middle-aged, "grandmotherly" woman who looked after a small number of children under the age of 5 years.

Both parents adjusted their schedules so that Sarah would be in day care the shortest possible amount of time each day. The mother would drop her off at day care and the father would pick her up. The first day Sarah was picked up, the father felt that she had a "glazed" facial expression and seemed quite somber. His initial response was that he was overreacting to her mood, a result of his own guilt about her being in day care. Over the next several days, however, he became convinced that she was having a difficult adjustment, and it seemed to him that it took longer and longer for her to warm up after their return home. In the following week, because of scheduling problems, Sarah's mother picked her up and confirmed the observation that Sarah had a glazed look, seemed sad and depressed, was motorically inactive, and took several hours to smile at either parent. Their concern resulted in an infant mental health consultation.

After a review of the pertinent historical information, the father brought Sarah in for a session, and the parents' concerns were confirmed. Sarah appeared very withdrawn, looked depressed, did not make eye contact with either her father or the infant therapist, and was motorically quite inactive. This compared dramatically to a second visit several days later when she had not been in day care; on this occasion, she was an active, smiling, and very engaged and developmentally appropriate

3-month-old. The parents also described the on-set of sleep disturbance (difficulties in falling asleep and waking up crying more often than usual) and problems with feeding. They felt that after 2 weeks in day care these problems should probably be getting better, but instead they seemed to be getting worse.

A visit was made to the day care setting, which was exactly as described. A very warm middle-aged woman kept a neat but developmentally appropriate house, with children actively engaged in play. Sarah, on the other hand, was lying passively in her crib, seemingly depressed and withdrawn. In discussion with the day care provider, it became clear that she was someone who relied on infants' cues for her to respond to them. She described Sarah as a very quiet child who seemed to eat well and spend most of her time in the crib or in a playpen. She did not see her as unhappy or depressed, but rather a child who "needed time to herself." This was in sharp contrast to the parents, who were active in initiating interaction with Sarah; in fact, their interactive style might be described by some as "intrusive." What seemed clear was that there were difficulties in the "match" between Sarah's experience with her very attentive and stimulating parents, and that with an equally warm but less interactive day care provider. Although at this point, from a diagnostic view, the clinical picture would seem to indicate an Adjustment Disorder, the depth of the child's depression, withdrawal, and developing symptoms certainly would indicate the potential for a Mood Disorder. Of particular importance was the "poor fit" in the relationship with her new caregiver.

Intervention consisted of a change in day care providers, since the original caregiver did not seem to understand the issues that Sarah's parents felt were so important. A younger day care provider who was more like the parents was chosen, and the change resulted in a gradual abatement of the symptoms over the next several weeks. Since it took some time for Sarah to become "herself" again, the parents were afraid that they had irreparably damaged her mental health—an issue that was also worked through as part of the consultation.

CONCLUSION: THE DIAGNOSTIC PROCESS AND FUTURE DIRECTIONS

The diagnostic process, in our view, is a superordinate one that necessarily makes use of two activities: (1) assessing individuals, and (2) locating patterns of observations in a classificatory scheme that will allow linkage to knowledge about syndromes that are found in many individuals. Moreover, the diagnostic process is a dynamic one. It is ongoing rather than a one-time feature of clinical work. It goes beyond "labeling," and, as we have seen in this chapter, it becomes challenging and complex when we take into account relationship disorders and the contexts of development.

This chapter has aimed at providing the reader with an approach to the diagnostic process by presenting the classification of disorders within the framework of individual assessment. We have also emphasized that classification schemes for disorders in infancy are recent and can be expected to evolve rapidly. A focus of current thinking about classification is provided by the scheme from the NCCIP task group, which makes use of multiple approaches. These approaches take into account the contexts of caregiving relationships, rapid developmental change, and the need to gather a broad array of data as classification categories are clarified. This system has been designed to move beyond a classification system derived from clinical consensus to a system that allows for testing of hypotheses about the scheme itself. The scheme we recommend is multiaxial, involving ratings of dimensions of functioning in addition to categorizations of disorder. There are many pathways to health and adaptation, as well as to illness and maladaptive outcomes, and a combined approach is necessary to delimit pathways both for the clinician working with a case and for the researcher testing hypotheses across cases.

Two further points are important for our conclusion. First, we emphasize again that it is useful for the clinician to consider relationship disorders as well as individual-based infancy disorders. In many cases, the source of pathology can be found in a disordered or disorganized family or social context that has prevented the adaptations found in normal development, and it seems inappropriate to locate the behavioral deviance in the young child. Whether or not we classify relationship disorders, we must recognize that the disordered family or social context often contributes in a critical way to the emotional and behavioral problems of infancy. Although studies from developmental psychology have portrayed the complex, embedded nature of infant functioning within relationships, diagnostic formulations about mental health problems have yet to achieve the level of sophistication that takes such knowledge fully into account. Many family therapy approaches, on the other hand, offer a sophisticated way of understanding mental health problems as embedded in relationships, but eschew individual conceptualizations of emotional and behavioral problems. The latter approach seems equally limiting, just as does the exclusive focus on the individual child. What is needed in the diagnostic process is attention to both individual characteristics and important relationships, as well as to their important interactions.

Second, we emphasize that it is important to anchor classifications within a thorough knowledge of the context of development. The behavioral manifestations of both disordered individuals and disordered relationships may change over time. Feeding disturbances may become sleep disturbances, and attachment problems may become exploration problems (Emde & Sameroff, 1989); consequently, clinicians must have a clear sense of the normative dynamic transformations in child behavior in order to make use of any classification scheme.

What about the future? Cantwell and Baker (1988) note that classification schemes can be evaluated in terms of reliability, validity, coverage, and feasibility. Schemes for classifying infancy disorders are very recent, and the one we have focused on will surely change as these sources of evaluation are considered. Attempts to provide better coverage and usefulness with respect to clinical problems in infancy have led to improvements contained in recent classification schemes that go beyond the DSM and ICD systems. Still, studies of reliability and validity are just beginning for these newer schemes. Most of this kind of work lies ahead of us. We believe that future changes in classification will increasingly incorporate data from multiaxial assessments into our taxonomy, and thereby provide a more differentiated picture of the many factors that converge to yield the clinical syndromes of infancy. Whatever the changes yet to come may be, it is clear that the clinician involved in prevention and treatment activities in infant mental health must rely heavily on individual assessment while the classification of disorders continues to progress.

REFERENCES

Achenbach, T. M. (1988). Integrating assessment and taxonomy. In M. Rutter, A. H. Tuma, & I. S. Lann (Eds.), *Assessment and diagnosis in child psychopathology* (pp. 300–346). New York: Guilford Press.

American Psychiatric Association. (1987). *Diagnostic and statistical manual of mental disorders* (3rd ed., rev.). Washington, DC: Author.

Anders, T. F. (1989). Clinical syndromes, relationship disturbances, and their assessment. In A. J. Sameroff & R. N. Emde (Eds.), *Relationship disturbances in early childhood: A developmental approach* (pp. 125–144). New York: Basic Books.

Brazelton, T. B., & Cramer, B. G. (1990). *The earliest relationship: Parents, infants, and the drama of early attachment.* Reading, MA: Addison-Wesley.

Cantwell, D. P., & Baker, T. (1988). Issues in the classification of child and adolescent psychiatry. *Journal of the American Academy of Child and Adolescent Psychiatry, 27*(5), 521–533.

Cramer, B., Robert-Tissot, C., Stern, D. N., Serpa-Rusconi, S., De Muralt, M., Besson, G., Palacio-Espasa, F., Bachmann, J.-P., Knauer, D., Berney, C., & D'Arcis, U. (1990). Outcome evaluation in brief mother–infant psychotherapy: A preliminary report. *Infant Mental Health Journal, 11*(3), 278–300.

Emde, R. N., & Sameroff, A. J. (1989). Understanding early relationship disturbances. In A. J. Sameroff & R. N. Emde (Eds.), *Relationship disturbances in early childhood: A developmental approach* (pp. 1–267). New York: Basic Books.

Fraiberg, S. (1980). *Clinical studies in infant mental health.* New York: Basic Books.

Gaensbauer, T. J., & Harmon, R. J. (1981). Clinical assessment in infancy utilizing structured playroom situations. *Journal of the American Academy of Child Psychiatry, 20,* 264–280.

Greenspan, S. I. (1992). *Infancy and early childhood.* Madison, CT: International Universities Press.

Jacob, T., & Tennenbaum, D. L. (1988). Family assessment methods. In M. Rutter, A. H. Tuma, & I. S. Lann (Eds.), *Assessment and diagnosis in child psychopathology* (pp. 196–231). New York: Guilford Press.

Minde, K., & Minde, R. (1986). *Infant psychiatry: An introductory textbook.* Beverly Hills, CA: Sage.

Minuchin, S. (1974). *Families and family therapy.* Cambridge, MA: Harvard University Press.

National Center for Clinical Infant Programs (NCCIP). (1991). *Diagnostic classification study manual.* Arlington, VA: Author.

Pennington, B. F. (1991). *Diagnosing learning disorders: A neuropsychological framework.* New York: Guilford Press.

Poisson, S. S., & DeGangi, G. A. (1991). *Emotional and sensory processing problems: Assessment and treatment approaches for young children and their families.* Rockville, MD: Reginald S. Lourie Center for Infants and Young Children.

Rapoport, J. L., & Ismond, D. R. (1990). *DSM-III-R training guide for diagnosis of childhood disorders.* New York: Brunner/Mazel.

Reiss, D., & Klein, D. (1987). Paradigm and pathogenesis: A family-centered approach to problems of etiology and treatment of psychiatric disorders. In T. Jacob (Ed.), *Family interaction and psychopathology: Theory, methods, and findings.* New York: Plenum Press.

Rutter, M., & Gould, M. (1985). Classification. In M. Rutter & L. Hersov (Eds.), *Child and adolescent psychiatry: Modern approaches* (pp. 304–321). Oxford: Blackwell Scientific.

Rutter, M., & Tuma, A. H. (1988). Diagnosis and classification: Some outstanding issues. In M. Rutter, A. H. Tuma, & I. S. Lann (Eds.), *Assessment and diagnosis in child psychopathology* (pp. 437–452). New York: Guilford Press.

Sameroff, A. J., & Emde, R. N. (Eds.). (1989). *Relationship disturbances in early childhood: A developmental approach.* New York: Basic Books.

Scharff, D. E., & Scharff, J. S. (1987). *Object relations family therapy.* Northvale, NJ: Jason Aronson.

Shaffer, D., Gould, M. S., Rutter, M., & Sturge, C. (1991). Reliability and validity of a psychosocial axis in patients with child psychiatric disorder. *Journal of the American Academy of Child and Adolescent Psychiatry, 30*(1), 109–115.

World Health Organization. (1988). *International classification of diseases* (10th ed., draft). Geneva: Author.

15

Autism and the Pervasive Developmental Disorders

FRED R. VOLKMAR

The Pervasive Developmental Disorders (PDDs) are a group of conditions that share some general clinical features but that probably reflect diverse etiologies. The conditions have their onset in infancy or early childhood, and are associated with characteristic patterns of delay and deviance in the development of basic social, communicative, and cognitive skills. Of the various conditions that are sometimes included within the overarching PDD class, Infantile Autism—or Autistic Disorder, as it more recently has been termed in the revised third edition of the *Diagnostic and Statistical Manual of Mental Disorders* (DSM-III-R; American Psychiatric Association [APA], 1987)—has been the most intensively studied and is discussed in greatest detail in this chapter. Different diagnostic systems variably include other conditions within the PDD class. These "nonautistic PDDs" have been less commonly studied than autism, and their validity, apart from that of autism, remains somewhat controversial. In general the PDDs are associated with some degree of mental retardation, although the pattern of developmental and behavioral features differs from that seen in children with primary mental retardation. The term "Pervasive Developmental Disorder" rightly emphasizes the pervasiveness of difficulties across various domains of development, as well as the important developmental aspects of these conditions.

DIAGNOSTIC CONCEPTS

Historical Background

Over the past century, a major point of debate has been the relationship of the severe psychiatric disturbances of childhood to adult psychoses. In 1867, Maudsley suggested that children could exhibit "insanity," and by the early 1900s Kraepelin's concept of "dementia praecox" had been extended to children ("dementia praecoxissima"). Despite the efforts of some investigators, the concept of "childhood psychosis" became more or less synonymous with the term "childhood schizophrenia"; in many ways the assumption of continuity between child and adult forms of "psychosis" was based on the severity of the conditions (Volkmar & Cohen, 1988). However, various lines of evidence now suggest that autism differs from schizophrenia in a number of ways, and the term "psychosis" has seemed increasingly less appropriate to apply to children, particularly to younger and lower-functioning children.

Of the various forms of "childhood psychosis" that have been proposed, some are now essentially only of historical interest, such as Mahler's (1952) notion of "symbiotic psychosis" or the DSM-III (APA, 1980) diagnosis of Childhood Onset PDD. Other disorders have proven more enduring.

DSM-III-R includes only one condition apart from autism—PDD Not Otherwise Specified (PDD NOS), By contrast, the 10th revision of the *International Classification of Diseases* (ICD-10; World Health Organization, 1992) will likely include various syndromes (Asperger syndrome, Rett syndrome), Childhood Disintegrative Disorder, and Atypical Autism, in addition to the "subthreshold" PDD NOS category. It is likely that some of these conditions will be included in DSM-IV as well. In many instances, modifications in the original description of the concept have been based on subsequent research.

Autism

Of all the diagnostic concepts proposed, Leo Kanner's (1943) description of the syndrome of early infantile autism has proven to be remarkably enduring. Kanner described 11 children who apparently exhibited a congenital inability to relate to other people ("autism"), which was in striking contrast to the relatedness to aspects of the inanimate environment. These children also exhibited a number of unusual developmental and behavioral features, such as insistence on sameness and resistance to change; stereotyped mannerisms; and, when language developed at all, unusual language (echolalia, pronoun reversal, and extreme literalness). Kanner initially felt that infantile autism was not the earliest manifestation of schizophrenia, but his use of the term "autism" suggested a possible point of similarity.

Although Kanner's phenomenological description of the condition has held up remarkably well, certain aspects of his original report provided false leads for subsequent research. For example, his initial report suggested that autism was not associated with mental retardation; that autistic children were more likely to come from more educated families; and that the condition was not associated with other, "organic" conditions. It is now clear that most autistic children are also mentally retarded and that the condition can be observed in association with a host of medical conditions, including congenital rubella and fragile-X syndrome (Coleman, 1987). Also, autistic children commonly develop seizure disorders (Volkmar & Nelson, 1990). Other neurobiological abnormalities are also frequently observed and consistent with an as-yet-unspecified underlying "organic" etiology (Golden, 1987). Kanner's observation of deviance in parent–child interaction was taken by some

(e.g., Bettelheim, 1967) to suggest a potential role of parental psychopathology in syndrome pathogenesis; at the time of his initial report there was, of course, less appreciation of the contribution of the child to deviant parent–child interaction (Bell & Harper, 1977). Even then, the notion of a "congenital" disturbance seemed difficult to reconcile with the notion that parents contributed to the development of the syndrome. It now appears that deviant patterns of parent–child interaction stem primarily from the disturbance in the child, and that parental psychopathology is no more frequent in parents of autistic children than in those of children with other developmental disorders (DeMyer, Hingtgen, & Jackson, 1981).

The validity of the syndrome described by Kanner has been suggested by various lines of evidence. A series of studies (e.g., Kolvin, 1971; Rutter, 1972; Volkmar, Cohen, Hoshino, Rende, & Paul, 1988) have consistently revealed that autism differs from childhood schizophrenia in clinical features (e.g., age at onset, absence of delusions/hallucinations, social and communicative abilities), in course, and in family history.

Nonautistic PDDs

Childhood Disintegrative Disorder

In 1908, Theodor Heller, a Viennese educator, proposed the term "dementia infantilis" (now usually referred to as Childhood Disintegrative Disorder or as "Heller syndrome") to describe a condition in which young children who had previously developed normally exhibited marked developmental and behavioral deterioration with only minimal subsequent recovery (Heller, 1908/1969). In the years subsequent to Heller's description, perhaps 100 cases of the condition have appeared in the world literature (see Volkmar, 1992, for a review). Generally, early development is entirely normal and the child progresses to the point of using language prior to the onset of a profound developmental regression; once established, the condition behaviorally resembles autism, although the prognosis may be somewhat worse (Volkmar & Cohen, 1989). In some instances, the condition has been reported in association with a specific disease process—for example, a progressive neurological condition (Corbett, 1987). The disorder was not included in either DSM-III (APA, 1980) or DSM-III-R (APA, 1987), on the presumption that such cases invariably reflected some other medical condition. It is now clear, however, that such a medical condition is observed only in a minority of cases. It is likely that the condition will be included in DSM-IV.

Asperger Syndrome

In the year following Kanner's report, Hans Asperger (1944), a Viennese medical student unaware of Kanner's work, proposed another diagnostic category, "autistic psychopathy." As described by Asperger, this condition (now known as "Asperger syndrome") differed from autism in that only males were thought to be affected; language skills were more preserved and motor skills less preserved than in autism; and the condition was believed to run in families (particularly in fathers). Asperger's report received relatively little attention in the English literature until the 1980s (Wing, 1981). The condition has more commonly been regarded in the United States as "high-functioning autism," and the validity of the condition, as distinct from high-functioning autism, remains to be clearly established (Gillberg, 1989). As with Kanner's description of autism, some modifications of the diagnostic concept have been made (Wing, 1981). The disorder will be included in ICD-10, however, and is of interest, particularly for research purposes.

Rett Syndrome

Andreas Rett (1966) described the syndrome now commonly referred to as "Rett syndrome." Rett had observed two girls in a waiting room who exhibited remarkably similar patterns of deviant behavior and early development; he subsequently identified a series of cases. Although it includes some "autistic-like" features, particularly during the preschool years, this syndrome appears to differ from autism in several ways: It is reported only in females; the "autistic-like" phase is relatively brief; and it is associated with characteristic motor behaviors (stereotyped "washing" or "wringing" hand movements), abnormalities in gait or trunk movement (e.g., apraxia or gait, scoliosis), and breath-holding spells. Associated mental retardation is even more severe than in autism, and the early history is remarkable for normal early growth and development followed (in the first months of life) by developmental regression, relative failure of head growth, and loss of purposeful hand movements. As with autism, the

initial description of the condition has been somewhat modified and aspects of the natural history clarified (Moeschler, Charman, Berg, & Graham, 1988). The condition will be included in ICD-10 in the PDD class; inclusion in DSM-IV is less certain.

Atypical PDD or PDD NOS

The category PDD NOS was used in DSM-III-R (APA, 1987) to replace the earlier category Atypical PDD; this latter concept had been unintentionally, although probably correctly, suggestive of Rank's (1949) earlier diagnostic concept of "atypical personality development"—a term also used to describe children with some, but not all, features of autism. Such children exhibit patterns of unusual sensitivities, difficulties in social interaction, and other problems suggestive of autism without meeting full criteria for the latter condition.

The diagnosis PDD NOS is problematic in several respects. The category is poorly defined since the definition is essentially a negative one, and although the condition is probably much more common than strictly defined autism, research on it has been rare. The lack of an explicit definition (or definitions) also means that the concept is used rather inconsistently. Some investigators equate it with Asperger syndrome; others view it as part of an underlying spectrum with autism; and still others have attempted to define explicit subtypes (Cohen, Paul, & Volkmar, 1987). The use of the term for very low-functioning "autistic-like" children is a further complication. More commonly, the PDD NOS category has been used for children with better cognitive and communicative skills; the most common reasons for referral in such cases are parents' concerns about the children's emotional and social development, rather than, as in autism, concerns about the failure to develop language. The attempt, as in ICD-10, to distinguish between Atypical Autism and Atypical PDD may facilitate research in this area.

AUTISM: CLINICAL DESCRIPTION

Onset and Characteristics of Early Development

Kanner (1943) originally suggested that autism is present from birth. Subsequent research has suggested that the condition is usually apparent within the first year of life, but sometimes appears to have its onset within the second or third year of life (Short & Schopler, 1988; Volkmar, Stier, & Cohen, 1985). Very rarely, an "autistic-like" condition may have its onset after the third birthday. Age and type of onset have some value in the differential diagnosis of autism, although various extraneous factors may act to delay case detection (e.g., parental sophistication or denial, level of associated mental retardation in the child).

In some sense, infants and very young autistic children may be thought to exhibit the "purest" form of the disorder (Volkmar & Cohen, 1988). Studies of this age group are, however, uncommon. Most studies of early development in autism rely on parental retrospection (e.g., Ornitz, Guthrie, & Farley, 1977) or, less frequently, on contemporaneous videotapes or movies of the children (e.g., Massie, 1978). Both these methods have their limitations. Although parents often have concerns from the first months of life, usually their concern increases markedly as language fails to develop. They seek guidance from health professionals, most often when a child is 18–24 months old and still not speaking. The parents may report concern that the child might be deaf, although they paradoxically often note that the child is exquisitely sensitive to certain sounds in the inanimate environment (e.g., the noise of the vacuum cleaner).

Similarly, a child may not respond differentially to parents, but may be particularly attached to an unusual object. The young autistic child may also be interested in nonfunctional aspects of objects, such as their smell or taste, and normal use of materials for play is typically absent. Younger autistic children often exhibit unusual stereotyped behaviors or motor mannerisms (including hand flapping and toe walking) and seem to prefer such activities to those involving social interaction, although such behaviors become more prominent as the children become older. Bizarre affective responses may be observed. A child may become highly agitated if the same route or routine is not precisely followed.

Unfortunately, delays in case recognition by primary care providers remain common. For example, Siegel, Pliner, Eschler, and Elliot (1988) noted that typically 3 years elapsed between the time parents expressed concern to a child's physician and the time when a definitive diagnosis was made, usually at about age 5. To some extent, delays in case detection and referral in autism appear to reflect primary care providers' general unawareness of mental health problems in childhood (e.g., Costello & Pantino, 1987), as well as lack of familiarity with autism, difficulties in the use of categorical diagnostic criteria, and the lack of readily applied screening instruments. These delays are unfortunate, since there is some suggestion that early intervention may reduce subsequent morbidity (Lovass, 1987), and it is clear that developmental skills at age 5 predict subsequent outcome (Lotter, 1978). The issue of early case detection and intervention has assumed increasing importance, in light of recent federal mandates for extension of services to young children.

Initial studies of the early development of autistic children suggested that their development is erratic and characterized by lags and spurts, uneven development across domains of functioning, "splinter skills," and the loss of previously acquired skills. Some diagnostic systems (e.g., Ritvo & Freeman, 1978) have included unusual rates and sequences of development as criteria for the condition. Recent research confirms that there may be either islets of special ability or domains in which levels of functioning are relatively higher (Burack & Volkmar, 1992). This apparent developmental unevenness becomes more pronounced past the sensorimotor period (Losche, 1990). In general, however, development within a given domain follows expected developmental sequences.

Social Development

Autism was initially described as a disturbance of affective contact (Kanner, 1943). Social deviance remains one of the primary features, if not *the* major defining feature, of the condition. Until recently, however, it has been the focus of comparatively little systematic investigation (Fein, Pennington, Markowitz, Braverman, & Waterhouse, 1986). The lack of research in this area has reflected an awareness that some differential social responsiveness in affected children typically develops over time, as well as the tendency to view social aspects of development as "secondary" to other disturbances, such as those in cognition or communication (the "cognitive primacy hypothesis") (Cairns, 1979).

The social development of young autistic children is qualitatively different from that seen in even very young infants and also differs from that observed in mental retardation not associated with autism (Volkmar, 1987). For normally developing infants, social stimuli are particularly interesting; the usual predisposition to form social relationships appears to be an important foundation for the development of other skills (Bruner, 1975; Stern, 1985). In contrast, for autistic infants and young children, the human face holds little interest; lack of eye contact, poor or absent attachments, and a general lack of social interest are typical (Volkmar, 1987). Although some evidence of differentiated social responsiveness may be observed in young autistic children (Sigman & Ungerer, 1984), the usual robust patterns of attachment do not develop. Autistic children may not respond differentially to their parents until the elementary school years. Deficits in social interaction remain a source of marked disability even for autistic adults with highest intellectual functioning (Volkmar, 1987).

Communicative Development

Autistic children exhibit profound problems in communication that are not simply limited to linguistic functioning (Paul, 1987). About half of autistic individuals never gain useful communicative speech, and those individuals who do speak exhibit language that is distinctive in numerous ways (Paul, 1987), including immediate and delayed echolalia, pronoun reversal, failure to use appropriate intonation, impaired semantic development, extreme literalness, and failures in the pragmatic uses of language. It is important to note that echolalia per se is observed in normally developing children who are acquiring language. Adaptive functions of echolalia in autistic children have been noted (Fay & Schuler, 1980). The language and communicative deficits in autism differ from those seen in the developmentally language-disordered child (Paul, 1987). The early communicative development of individuals with apparent Asperger syndrome appears to be less impaired than that observed in more classically autistic individuals (Wing, 1981).

Cognitive Development

For many years, there was a presumption that autistic children were not also mentally retarded. This presumption was based on several factors:

(1) the observation that on certain parts of traditional IQ tests (e.g., subtests involving rote memory), autistic children would often score in the normal or near-normal range; (2) the notion that the otherwise generally poor performance on IQ tests was a function of negativism and poor "testability"; and (3) the observation that some autistic children exhibited unusual "splinter skills" or islets of special ability. It is now clear that when tests appropriate to the individuals' developmental level are used, most individuals with autism score in the mentally retarded range, and that IQ is a potent predictor of ultimate outcome (DeMyer et al., 1981). Older autistic children exhibit persistent deficits in abstract thinking and in sequencing and processing information; their performance on nonverbal or performance scales is typically much higher than their verbal performance.

Developmental and psychological testing of infants and young autistic children is sometimes difficult, but often reveals difficulties with tasks that require more verbal language (either receptive or expressive), symbolic thinking, or social interaction (e.g., tasks that involve imitation). Often nonverbal problem-solving abilities (e.g., matching shapes, solving simple inset puzzles) are closer to age-expected levels (Sigman, Ungerer, Mundy, & Sherman, 1987). Deficits in sensorimotor skills, as opposed to more symbolic or verbal skills, are more variably noted (Curcio, 1976; Morgan, Curtrer, Coplin, & Rodrique, 1989); deficits in early gestural and verbal imitative skills have been noted (Sigman & Ungerer, 1984).

A recent line of research has suggested that autistic children exhibit deficits in the capacity to attribute mental states to others (the "theory-of-mind hypothesis") (Baron-Cohen, 1989). This line of research has been based on studies suggesting that autistic children fail to make appropriate attributions about the beliefs, feelings, and intentions of others, as observed in various experimental situations. This research is of considerable interest to the extent that it more parsimoniously accounts for observed deficits in social interaction and play in autistic children. Nevertheless, the theory is limited in several important respects. The theory is highly cognitive, in the sense that the social deficits in autism are viewed as secondary to an essentially cognitive deficit. Because "theory-of-mind" capacities are not apparently exhibited much before 1 year of age, the theory does not account for the very early onset of the condition. Moreover, experimental work using the theory has tended to focus on verbal subjects, and it is unclear how or whether the theory has applicability to lower-functioning subjects, especially mute subjects (Klin & Volkmar, 1992). At least some work has suggested that apparent "theory-of-mind" problems are more a function of developmental level than of diagnostic category (Prior, Dahlstrom, & Squires, 1990; Klin & Volkmar, 1992).

Neurobiological Studies

Considerable evidence suggests the operation of some as-yet-unspecified, neurobiological factor or factors in the pathogenesis of autism. For example, autistic children are more likely to exhibit physical anomalies, persistent primitive reflexes, various neurological "soft signs," abnormalities on electroencephalogram (EEG) or on computerized tomographic (CT) or magnetic resonance imaging (MRI) scan, and an increased incidence of seizures (Golden, 1987). As many as 25% of autistic individuals develop seizure disorders; recent work suggests that the risk of seizure is significantly increased throughout the developmental period, including infancy and early childhood (Volkmar & Nelson, 1990). There is some suggestion of reduced obstetrical and neonatal optimality (Tsai, 1987). Autism is also observed in association with a host of other medical conditions, such as phenylketonuria, congenital rubella, tuberous sclerosis, and fragile-X syndrome (Coleman, 1987); on the other hand, it is much less commonly associated with other conditions, notably Down syndrome.

There is now evidence suggesting the operation of genetic mechanisms in at least some cases (Pauls, 1987). The early impression that there were no genetic aspects of the syndrome failed to take into account that cases do not reproduce, that parents may stop having children after the birth of an autistic child, and that the base rate of autism in the population is low (Pauls, 1987). Recent research suggests that siblings of autistic children are at significantly greater risk for also exhibiting autism and other developmental difficulties, and that monozygotic twins are more likely than fraternal twins to be concordant for the disorder (Folstein & Rutter, 1977).

Despite the considerable evidence favoring some neurobiological factor or factors in the pathogenesis of autism, precise and testable mechanisms have yet to be identified. Neurobiological findings vary considerably, and findings are often subtle. Neuroanatomical models of the disorder have placed the "site" of the lesion at various points on the neuraxis, from the brainstem to the cerebellum to the cortex. Although it is clear that as a group, autistic children exhibit elevated peripheral levels of serotonin (a central nervous system [CNS] neurotransmitter), the significance of this observation is unclear, since the relationship of peripheral to CNS serotonin levels is not clearly established and since individuals with other conditions also exhibit elevated serotonin levels (Anderson & Hoshino, 1987).

Epidemiology

Various problems pose complications for epidemiological studies—for instance, the relative infrequency of the conditions, difficulties in case identification, changes in diagnostic criteria, and the nature of definitions used. However, most studies of autism have suggested prevalence rates of between 2 and 5 cases per 10,000 children (Zahner & Pauls, 1987). Most studies suggest that autism is usually four or five times as common in males as in females, but when girls are affected they are more severely affected, particularly in terms of lower IQ. The significance of the observed sex difference is unclear, but it may reflect the operation of underlying genetic mechanisms (Lord & Schopler, 1987). Although Kanner initially (1943) suggested a preponderance of autism in families of higher socioeconomic status (SES), subsequent research controlling for factors that might bias case detection have not confirmed his assertion (Schopler, Andrews, & Strupp, 1980). Autistic children come from families of all SES groups.

Epidemiological information on other, nonautistic PDDs is more limited. It does, however, appear that Atypical PDD or PDD NOS is much more common than more strictly defined autism. The other PPDs are apparently less common than autism. For example, Childhood Disintegrative Disorder is perhaps 10 times less common than more strictly defined autism.

Psychosocial Factors

Studies of parents of autistic children have suggested that they do not differ from parents of other developmentally disordered children in interactional style, in exhibiting unusual personality characteristics, or in exhibiting deviant caretaking practices (DeMyer et al., 1981). The observation that autism is rarely observed in other siblings is also inconsistent with the notion that parents somehow "cause" autism.

On the other hand, the experience of having an autistic child may have a profound influence on the family (Schopler & Mesibov, 1984). In addition to the impact of mental retardation usually associated with autism, parents and siblings must cope with the autistic child's lack of social responsiveness and with a host of unusual behaviors. Stresses on parents and other family members vary over the course of the autistic child's development. Different patterns of adaptation are noted, depending on such factors as personal and community resources, pre-existing patterns of adaptation, and so forth (Morgan, 1988).

Course and Prognosis

Younger children more typically display the "pervasive" unrelatedness alluded to in the DSM-III (APA, 1980) criteria for the condition. Although some evidence of differentiated responsiveness to parents may be observed as a child reaches the elementary school years, patterns of social interaction remain quite deviant, and the child's behavior can be quite problematic. Often some gains in communicative and social skills are observed during the elementary school years. During adolescence, some autistic children exhibit behavioral deterioration, and a smaller number improve (Rutter, 1970). As adults, even the highest-functioning individuals exhibit marked difficulties in social interaction (Volkmar & Cohen, 1988). Various interactional styles can be observed in the autistic child, ranging from aloof to passive to eccentric (Wing & Atwood, 1987); these styles appear to be closely related to developmental level (Volkmar, Bregman, Cohen, Hooks, & Stevenson, 1989).

Available data suggest that the outcome for autistic children is quite poor; perhaps only one-third are able to achieve some degree of personal independence and self-sufficiency as adults (DeMyer et al., 1981). In general, two major factors appear predictive of ultimate outcome: the acquisition of truly communicative speech by age 5, and IQ. IQ can be difficult to assess, but when assessed with tests appropriate to a person's developmental level, it is reasonably stable and predictive (Lotter, 1978). It is important to realize that much of the available outcome information is based on samples collected during the 1960s and 1970s. During this period fewer services were available, and services provided were often not provided until the school years. There is some reason to hope that in the 1980s and 1990s the mandates for earlier intervention, earlier recognition of the disorder, and more intensive interventions (Lovass, 1987) will have improved the long-term outcome for the disorder. Research in this area is critically needed.

DIAGNOSIS OF AUTISM

Categorical Definitions

Categorical definitions of autism have typically emphasized four features essential for diagnosis: (1) early onset: (2) social dysfunction; (3) communicative dysfunction; and (4) various unusual behaviors, such as stereotypies and resistance to change, which are typically subsumed under the term "insistence on sameness." Other features, such as discrepancies in rates and sequences of development, have less commonly been viewed as central for purposes of definition. Consistent with Rutter's (1978) influential synthesis of Kanner's (1943) original description of the condition and of subsequent research, most categorical definitions emphasize that deviance in social and communicative development is not just a function of developmental level. On the other hand, precise metrics for operationalizing this construct have not proven easy to develop. Other factors, such as the range in syndrome expression, changes with age, and the frequency of "autistic-like" behaviors in individuals with severe mental retardation, have complicated the development of categorical definitions. Precise diagnosis of affected infants and young children is often complicated.

The DSM-III (APA, 1980) definition of Infantile Autism was largely consistent with that of Rutter (1978). It emphasized the early onset (<30 months) of "pervasive" social impairment, gross deficits in language development when speech was present, and bizarre responses to the environment. This definition proved unsatisfactory in several ways: It was most appropriate to younger and lower-functioning individuals; it failed to encompass developmental changes in syndrome expression; and it failed to address broader aspects of problems in communication beyond language (Volkmar & Cohen, 1988). Major revisions were made in DSM-III-R (APA, 1987).

The DSM-III-R definition of Autistic Disorder was intended to be more developmentally oriented and "ahistorical" in nature (i.e., a diagnosis could be made on the basis of present examination only). The DSM-III-R definition consists of a set of 16 detailed criteria grouped into three categories (deviance in social development, deviance in communication/play/ imagination, and restricted range of interests and activities). To achieve a diagnosis of Autistic Disorder, an individual must exhibit at least 8 of the 16 criteria, with a minimum number of criteria specified from each category. Although age of onset is no longer a diagnostic criterion, it can be specified as before or after 36 months. Unfortunately, it appears that the attempt to provide a greater developmental orientation has resulted in a broadened definition, so that many children, particularly young children, may be incorrectly classified as autistic (Volkmar, Bregman, Cohen, & Cicchetti, 1988).

In contrast to DSM-III-R, the ICD-10 definition of the disorder will be more similar to that used in DSM-III (Volkmar, Bregman, Cohen, & Cicchetti, 1992). As part of the DSM-IV revision process a large, multisite field trial is currently underway. For purposes of both service and research, it will be helpful if the DSM-IV and ICD-10 research definitions are largely convergent.

Dimensional Definitions

Dimensional approaches have also been used in the diagnosis of autism. In contrast to the categorical approach, these methods attempt to assess dimensions of function–dysfunction that are relevant to the diagnosis. Most dimensional assessment instruments are designed for school-age children and adolescents. In a few instances, early development and behaviors are assessed, although usually retrospectively (Parks, 1983). These instruments rely either on parental or teacher report or on direct observation in structured settings; in most instances, highly deviant behaviors are rated or sampled. Reliance on parental retrospection brings attendant issues of reliability, but direct observational procedures may prove less useful for sampling low-frequency behaviors. Assessment of highly deviant

behavior similarly raises problems for instrument development and standardization (Parks, 1983). In infants and young children, the frequency of apparently "autistic-like" behaviors raises particular problems for most "deviance model" assessment instruments.

Another approach relies on dimensional assessment instruments that are more truly developmental in nature. The usefulness of normative assessments of cognitive and communicative ability is well established (Cohen et al., 1987; Watson & Marcus, 1988). The availability of an instrument that normatively assesses social skills, the Revised Vineland Adaptive Behavior Scales (Sparrow, Balla, & Cicchetti, 1984), offers considerable potential in this regard. In contrast to most standardized assessments of cognitive or communicative behavior, the Revised Vineland assesses adaptive behavior (i.e., use of behaviors to meet the demands of daily life) from birth to adulthood, based on a semistructured interview with parents or caregivers. Relative to developmentally disordered, non-PDD comparison groups, the social development of autistic children as assessed by the Vineland is lower than expected, given the children's overall developmental level (Volkmar et al., 1987).

CLINICAL ASSESSMENT

The clinical assessment of a child with autism or some other PDD is most effectively conducted by an experienced interdisciplinary team. By definition, children with autism and other PDDs have delays in multiple areas of functioning that often require professionals with different areas of expertise, including the assessment of communication, overall developmental functioning, and behavioral status. Two fundamental considerations should guide the assessment process: (1) an awareness of the challenges that autistic children pose for usual assessment methods (Cohen et al., 1987), and (2) an awareness that some modifications in more usual assessment procedures may be helpful to parents (Morgan, 1988). For example, to the extent possible, parents should be encouraged to observe the evaluation of their child. This procedure both helps to demystify assessment procedures and provides a common set of observations for subsequent discussion; the rationale for specific tests and procedures and the meaning of specific observations can be reviewed with parents more efficiently.

A careful history should be obtained, including information related to the pregnancy and neonatal period, early development and characteristics of development, and medical and family history. For example, was the baby very "easy" and content to be left alone? Was it hard to get a response from the child? Did the child smile responsively? Was it hard to feed the baby? Information on the nature and age at apparent onset of the condition can provide important information relevant to differential diagnosis. Questions about development can sometimes be helpfully framed for parents around a specific time or well-remembered event (e.g., the first birthday). The history should include information about normally expected skills (early social interest, babbling and early communicative behaviors, motor development, etc.), followed by a discussion of more deviant behaviors (avoidance of eye contact, failures to anticipate being picked up or to adapt to a parent's body when picked up, resistance to change, idiosyncratic interests or attachments, etc.). The process of taking the history should convey to parents a sense that information they provide is both helpful and welcome; the process of taking the history can help the clinician establish a collaborative relationship with parents.

Assessment of the child should include both psychological and communication assessments that aim to establish levels of functioning in various areas of development. Assessment instruments should be selected with consideration of the child's apparent developmental levels. For cognitive assessment, tests that are not highly dependent on verbal abilities should be used, such as the Bayley Scales of Infant Development (Bayley, 1969), the Merrill–Palmer Scale (Stutsman, 1948), or the Uzgiris–Hunt Scales (Uzgiris & Hunt, 1975; Dunst, 1980). For children with nonverbal mental ages over 2 years, several nonverbal tests are available (see Cohen et al., 1987, and Watson & Marcus, 1988, for discussions of assessment instruments). For young or low-functioning children, several communication scales are available: the Receptive–Expressive Emergent Language Scale (Bzoch & League, 1971); the Sequenced Inventory of Communicative Development (Hedrick, Prather, & Tobin, 1975); the Reynell Developmental Language Scales (Reynell, 1969); and the Communication and Symbolic Behavior Scales (Wetherby & Prizant, 1990). As noted previously, the Revised Vineland (Sparrow et al., 1984) can be used with infants and young children, and provides estimates of adaptive skills in communication, daily living, socialization, and motor areas.

Modifications in usual procedures for administering specific tests are sometimes clinically indicated, although the results obtained must then be viewed with even greater caution. Parents may tend to overestimate levels of functioning if, for example, their impression is based on certain isolated skills or skills that are routinized and highly context-dependent. If practical, measures of social and communicative skills can be evaluated relative to estimates of overall developmental level. Information derived from these assessments is also helpful in guiding intervention programs.

Psychiatric examination of the child should include observation during more and less structured periods (e.g., while interacting with parents and while engaged in assessment procedures by other members of the evaluating team). Areas for assessment, observation, and/or inquiry with parents include social development (interest in social interaction, patterns of gaze and eye contact, differential attachments, style of social interaction), communication (receptive and expressive language, nonverbal and pragmatic communication, communicative intents, echolalia), responses to the environment (motor stereotypies, idiosyncratic responses, resistance to change), and play skills (nonfunctional or idiosyncratic uses of play materials, developmental level of play). The child's capacities for self-awareness (interest in mirror image, awareness of his or her own body) and motor skills should be observed. Problem behaviors that are likely to interfere with remedial programming should also be noted (marked aggression or problems in attention). Given the difficulties in assessing infants and younger children, several assessment sessions may be required.

Depending on the nature of a child's individual strengths and weaknesses, the services of various professionals may be needed, including child psychiatrists, psychologists, communication specialists, occupational and physical therapists, and so forth. If a multidisciplinary treatment team is providing the evaluation, it is important that team members maintain close communication with each other to avoid fragmentation and duplication of effort. When possible, the evaluation should be sufficiently integrated that parents receive a single coherent picture of the child and his or her difficulties. A plethora of individual reports is less helpful than a longer report with input from all members of the evaluating team; such a report also has the practical advantage of facilitating discussion among team members, who must be able to understand and reconcile apparent discrepancies in the results.

For younger children, consultations with other medical professionals, such as pediatric neurologists or geneticists, may be indicated. History or examination may suggest the need for specific laboratory studies or medical procedures. For example, a family history of mental retardation, or severe mental retardation or dysmorphic features in the child, would suggest the need for a genetic screen and chromosome analysis (including screening for fragile-X syndrome); symptoms suggestive of seizures (apparent periodic unresponsiveness) would suggest the need for an EEG and possible neurological consultation; and so forth. CT or MRI scan may be indicated and sometimes reveal such disorders as tuberous sclerosis or degenerative CNS disease. A careful history of the pregnancy and neonatal period should be obtained to ascertain possible pre- or postnatal infections (e.g., congenital rubella).

Usually the child's hearing has been tested prior to comprehensive evaluation. If this has not been done or it was not possible to elicit the child's cooperation, brainstem auditory evoked response procedures should be used. Although autism is associated with a number of other medical conditions, in most instances even extensive medical evaluations fail to reveal an associated medical condition. This suggests exercising reasonable care in obtaining additional assessments. On the other hand, certain features may indicate the importance of extensive medical investigations—for example, the abrupt behavioral and developmental deterioration of a child who was previously developing normally.

The differential diagnosis of autism and other PDDs includes language and other specific developmental disorders, mental retardation, sensory impairments (particularly deafness), and Reactive Attachment Disorders. Usually children with language disorders do not exhibit the pattern of serious social deviance and deficit exhibited in autism; often nonverbal communicative abilities are an area of evident strength. In mental retardation, social and communicative skills are usually on a par with overall cognitive skills. Deaf children may exhibit some difficulties in social interaction and repetitive activities; however, they are usually interested in social interaction and may make use of gestures for com-

municative purposes. Children with Reactive Attachment Disorders have, by definition, experienced marked psychosocial deprivation that results in deficits in social interaction (most notably in attachment). However, the quality of social deficit is different from that in autism, and the disturbance tends to remit relatively quickly after an appropriately responsive psychosocial environment is provided.

In young children the task of differential diagnosis is complicated by the inherent difficulties in child assessment; the frequency of "autistic-like" behaviors in other conditions; and the fact that autism can be associated with deafness and with mental retardation, as well as with other medical conditions. Differential diagnosis is often most complicated in young children who lack expressive language, exhibit odd social behavior, and have some apparent degree of cognitive delay. Consideration of the pattern of developmental deviance is often help in such instances (e.g., assessment of levels of sensorimotor and cognitive skills relative to communicative and social skills). When direct assessment of a child is difficult, results of the Revised Vineland (Sparrow et al., 1984) may be helpful in this regard. In general, the presence of some communicative functions and of some evidence of differential social responsiveness argues against the diagnosis of autism. It must, however, be emphasized that often the issue of diagnosis in such cases is clarified with certainty only over time. It is appropriate to share with parents a sense of the clinician's degree of confidence in the diagnosis. It is also important to realize that the diagnosis may have important (if not necessarily intended) implications for other purposes, such as educational programming, special services in the community, and so forth. It is critical that the importance of educational and other interventions be emphasized, regardless of how "classically" autistic the child appears to be.

INTERVENTIONS

In the absence of a definitive cure, there are a thousand treatments. Virtually every conceivable treatment has been applied to autism, including somatic treatments (electroshock therapy and "patterning"), behavior modification, drug therapy, psychotherapy, nutritional treatments, and educational intervention (DeMyer et al., 1981). With the exception of a few areas (notably behavior modification and pharmacological intervention, and to a lesser extent educational interventions), most proposed interventions have not been rigorously studied, and it has been difficult to assess treatment effects systematically. Unfortunately, short-term changes readily occur when treaters and/or evaluators are not blind to the hypothesis under study; such changes may be neither sustained nor clinically meaningful. In other instances, particularly with single-case reports, it is unclear whether the individual was actually autistic and which factor or factors may have been responsible for improvement. The observation that a few autistic individuals achieve relatively good outcomes is gratifying, but also complicates the interpretation of single-case studies. Further compounding the problem is that there is usually no such thing as an "untreated" autistic child; that is, even by the time the diagnosis is definitively made, parents have often tried multiple interventions.

At present the available evidence suggests the importance of appropriate, intensive educational interventions to foster the acquisition of basic social, cognitive, and communicative skills (Prizant & Schuler, 1987; Olley & Stevenson, 1989), which are in turn related to outcome. Behavior modification techniques can be quite helpful. Early and continuous intervention is highly desirable; some reports (e.g., Lovass, 1987) have suggested marked improvement following early, intensive intervention. Educational programs should be highly structured (Rutter & Bartak, 1973) and oriented to the individual needs of the child. Intervention programs should be comprehensive and include the services of various professionals (e.g., special educators, speech pathologists, occupational therapists, etc.). Parental involvement should be encouraged to enhance consistency in approaches at home and in school, as well as to facilitate generalization of skills across settings. Professionals should work with parents to obtain appropriate educational placement and to help parents become aware of other community resources, such as respite care. Recent federal mandates for provision of remedial services from birth will, it is hoped, increase the availability of services.

During the 1950s it was common for professionals to recommend that parents consider institutionalization for severely disabled children. This practice led to the isolation and segregation of children with severe developmental disabilities; as a result, many such individuals were prevented from reaching their full potential. An awareness of these issues has produced a marked shift in social policy, with most state agencies now attempting to maintain children in their families and communities. Unfortunately, many necessary services may not be provided. A similar issue has arisen with regard to the integration of autistic children into regular classroom settings. The rationale for this approach is based on a strongly held philosophical position that "special" educational settings are inferior and discriminatory by their nature, as well as on a small body of empirical research (e.g., Charlop, Schreiman, & Tyron, 1983) suggesting that autistic children can indeed learn from normal peers. Given the nature of social deficits in autism, there is considerable reason to worry that autistic children may not be as able as mentally retarded but nonautistic children to profit from such an approach. In considerations of alternative educational placements, the individual needs of the child should be paramount.

In general, pharmacological interventions with infants and young autistic children are best avoided. The best-studied agents (i.e., the major tranquilizers) have some limited uses in selected cases, but their many side effects (particularly sedation) may prove problematic (Campbell, Anderson, Green, & Deutsch, 1987). These agents may be indicated in some situations, but are typically used with older children, and even then at the lowest effective dose for the shortest period of time. The efficacy of other pharmacological agents has not been clearly established.

Many nontraditional treatments are presently available. In discussing such treatments with parents, the clinician should explore the rationale for the proposed treatment, the evidence (if any) of efficacy, and its potential costs (in both financial and human terms) to the child and family. Treatments that are minimally disruptive of the child's educational program and that hold little apparent risk to the child for the child are of less concern than those entailing considerable disruption of the child's educational program and/or the family's life.

In the clinical management of the autistic child, it is important not to lose sight of the needs of the family (Morgan, 1988). The adaptation of parents, siblings, and other family members often varies over time, both as a result of the normative stress and transitions inherent in family life and as a result of the special needs of the autistic child. Patterns of coping can take various forms, with various degrees of positive and negative adaptation. Parental and family isolation, "burnout," and marital disharmony may be observed, and the increased demands on parents may be experienced negatively by siblings. On the other hand, many families cope well. Support for the family may take various forms, depending on the specific needs of the family and the special characteristics of the autistic child; such support is best delivered in the context of an ongoing relationship. It should be reemphasized that the need for intervention in the family does not imply that parents are responsible for the affected child's autism.

SUMMARY

Considerable progress in understanding the nature of autism and related disorders has been made over the past 50 years. Given the early onset of the condition, it is somewhat paradoxical that our knowledge of autism in infants and very young children remains limited in important respects. Our knowledge of the other PDDs in infancy and early childhood is even more limited. Mental health professionals have important roles to play in evaluation and provision of remedial programming. Although it now appears that these conditions arise as the result of some insult to the developing CNS, precise and testable pathophysiological mechanisms remain to be identified. The study of infants and young children with autism may have important implications for both clinical service and our understanding of the structure of early child development.

REFERENCES

American Psychiatric Association (APA). (1980). *Diagnostic and statistical manual of mental disorders* (3rd ed.). Washington, DC: Author.

American Psychiatric Association (APA). (1987). *Diagnostic and statistical manual of mental disorders* (3rd ed., rev.). Washington, DC: Author.

Anderson, G. M., & Hosino, Y. (1987). Neurochemical studies of autism. In D. Cohen & A. Donnellan (Eds.), *Handbook of autism and pervasive developmental disorders* (pp. 166–191). New York: Wiley.

Asperger, H. (1944). Die 'autistichen psychopathen' im kindersalter. *Archiv für psychiatrie und Nervenkrankheiten, 117*, 76–136.

Baron-Cohen, S. (1989). The autistic child's theory of mind: A case of specific developmental delay. *Journal of Child Psychology and Psychiatry, 30*, 285–297.

Bayley, N. (1969). *Bayley Scales of Infant Development.* New York: Psychological Corporation.

Bell, R. Q., & Harper, L. V. (1977). *Child effects on adults.* Hillsdale, NJ: Erlbaum.

Bettelheim, B. (1967). *The empty fortress.* New York: Free Press.

Bruner, J. (1975). The ontogenesis of speech acts. *Journal of Child Language, 1*, 1–20.

Burack, J., & Volkmar, F. R. (1992). Development of low- and high-functioning autistic children. *Journal of Child Psychology and Psychiatry, 33*, 606–617.

Bzoch, K., & League, R. (1971). *Receptive–Expressive Emergent Language Scale.* Gainesville, FL: Language Educational Division, Computer Management Corporation.

Cairns, R. B. (1979). *Social development: The origins and plasticity of interchanges.* San Francisco: W. H. Freeman.

Campbell, M., Anderson, L. T., Green, W. H., & Deutsch, S. I. (1987). Psychopharmacology. In D. Cohen & A. Donnellan (Eds.), *Handbook of autism and pervasive developmental disorders* (pp. 545–565). New York: Wiley.

Charlop, M. J., Schreiman, L., & Tryon, A. D. (1983). Learning though observation: The effects of peer modeling on acquisition and generalization in autistic children. *Journal of Abnormal Child Psychology, 11*, 355–366.

Cohen, D. J., Paul, R., & Volkmar, F. R. (1987). Issues in the classification of pervasive developmental disorders and associated conditions. In D. Cohen & A. Donnellan (Eds.), *Handbook of autism and pervasive developmental disorders* (pp. 20–40). New York: Wiley.

Coleman, M. (1987). The search for neurobiological subgroups in autism. In E. Schopler & G. Mesibov (Eds.), *Neurobiological issues in autism* (pp. 163–179). New York: Plenum.

Corbett, J. (1987). Development, disintegration, and dementia. *Journal of Mental Deficiency Research, 31*, 349–356.

Costello, E. J., & Pantino, T. (1987). The new morbidity: Who should treat it? *Journal of Developmental and Behavioral Pediatrics, 8*, 288–291.

Curcio, F. (1976). Sensorimotor functioning and communication in mute autistic children. *Journal of Autism and Childhood Schizophrenia, 8*, 281–292.

DeMyer, M. K., Hingtgen, J. N., & Jackson, R. K. (1981). Infantile autism reviewed: A decade of research. *Schizophrenia Bulletin, 7*, 388–451.

Dunst, C. (1980). *A clinical and educational manual for use with the Uzgiris and Hunt Scales.* Baltimore: University Park Press.

Fay, W., & Schuler, A. L. (1980). *Emerging language in autistic children.* Baltimore: University Park Press.

Fein, D., Pennington, B., Markowitz, P., Braverman, M., & Waterhouse, L. (1986). Towards a neuropsychological model of infantile autism: Are the social deficits primary? *Journal of the American Academy of Child Psychiatry, 25*, 198–212.

Folstein, S., & Rutter, M. (1977). Infantile autism: A genetic study of 21 twin pairs. *Journal of Child Psychology and Psychiatry, 18*, 297–321.

Gillberg, C. (1989). Asperger's syndrome in 23 Swedish children. *Developmental Medicine and Child Neurology, 31*, 520–521.

Golden, G. (1987). Neurological functioning. In D. Cohen & A. Donnellan (Eds.), *Handbook of autism and pervasive developmental disorders* (pp. 133–147). New York: Wiley.

Hedrick, D., Prather, F., & Tobin, A. (1975). *Sequenced*

Inventory of Communicative Development. Seattle: University of Washington Press.

Heller, T. (1969). Uber Dementia infantalis. In J. G. Howells (Ed.), *Modern perspectives in international child psychiatry.* Edinburgh: Oliver & Boyd. (Original work published 1908)

Kanner, L. (1943). Autistic disturbances of affective contact. *Nervous Child, 2,* 217–250.

Klin, A., & Volkmar, F. R. (1992). The development of individuals with autism. Some implications for the theory of mind hypothesis. *Journal of Child Psychology and Psychiatry, 15,* 317–331.

Kolvin, I. (1971). Studies in the childhood psychoses: I. Diagnostic criteria and classification. *British Journal of Psychiatry, 118,* 381–384.

Lord, C., & Schopler, E. (1987). Neurobiological implications of sex differences in autism. In E. Schopler & G. Mesibov (Eds.), *Neurobiological issues in autism* (pp. 192–212). New York: Plenum.

Losche, G. (1990). Sensorimotor and action development in autistic children from infancy to early childhood. *Journal of Child Psychology and Psychiatry, 31,* 749–762.

Lotter, V. (1978). Follow-up studies. In M. Rutter & E. Schopler (Eds.), *Autism: A reappraisal of concepts and treatment* (pp. 475–496). New York: Plenum Press.

Lovass, O. I. (1987). Behavioral treatment and normal educational and intellectual functioning in young autistic children. *Journal of Consulting and Clinical Psychology, 55,* 3–9.

Mahler, M. (1952). On child psychoses and schizophrenia: Autistic and symbiotic infantile psychoses. *Psychoanalytic Study of the Child, 7,* 286–305.

Massie, H. N. (1978). Blind ratings of mother–infant interaction in home movies of prepsychotic and normal infants. *American Journal of Psychiatry, 135,* 1271–1374.

Moeschler, J. B., Charman, C. E., Berg, S. Z., & Graham, J. H. (1988). Rett syndrome: Natural history and management. *Pediatrics, 82,* 1–10.

Morgan, S. (1988). The autistic child and family functioning: A developmental–family systems perspective. *Journal of Autism and Developmental Disorders, 18,* 263–280.

Morgan, S., Curtrer, P. S., Coplin, J. W., & Rodrique, J. R. (1989). Do autistic children differ from retarded and normal children in Piagetian sensorimotor functioning? *Journal of Child Psychology and Psychiatry, 30,* 857–864.

Olley, J.G., & Stevenson, S.E. (1989). Preschool curriculum for children with autism: Addressing early social skills. In G. Dawson (Ed.), *Autism: Nature, diagnosis, and treatment* (pp. 346–366). New York: Guilford Press.

Ornitz, E. M., Guthrie, D., & Farley, A. H. (1977). The early development of autistic children. *Journal of Autism and Childhood Schizophrenia, 7,* 207–229.

Parks, S. L. (1983). The assessment of autistic children: A selective review of available instruments. *Journal of Autism and Developmental Disorders, 13,* 255–267.

Paul, R. (1987). Communication in autism. In D. Cohen & A. Donnellan (Eds.), *Handbook of autism and pervasive developmental disorders* (pp. 61–84). New York: Wiley.

Pauls, D. (1987). The familiarity of autism and related disorders: A review of the evidence. In D. Cohen & A. Donnellan (Eds.), *Handbook of autism and perva-*sive developmental disorders (pp. 192–198). New York: Wiley.

Prior, M., Dahlstrom, B., & Squires, T. (1990). Autistic children's knowledge of thinking and feeling states in other people. *Journal of Child Psychology and Psychiatry, 31,* 587–601.

Prizant, B. M., & Schuler, A. L. (1987). Facilitating communication–pre-language approaches. In D. Cohen & A. Donnelan (Eds.), *Handbook of autism and pervasive developmental disorders* (pp. 301–315). New York: Wiley.

Rank, B. (1949). Adaptation of the psychoanalytic technique for the treatment of young children with atypical development. *American Journal of Orthopsychiatry, 19,* 130–139.

Rett, A. (1966). Uber ein eigenartiges hirntophisces syndrome bei hyperammonie im kindersalter. *Wein Medizinische Wochenschrift, 118,* 723–726.

Reynell, J. (1969). *Reynell Developmental Language Scales.* Windsor, England: National Foundation for Educational Research.

Ritvo, E. R., & Freeman, B. J. (1978). National Society for Autistic Children definition of the syndrome of autism. *Journal of Autism and Developmental Disorders, 8,* 162–169.

Rutter M. (1970). Autistic children: Infancy to adulthood. *Seminars in Psychiatry, 2,* 435–450.

Rutter, M. (1972). Childhood schizophrenia reconsidered. *Journal of Autism and Childhood Schizophrenia, 2,* 315–338.

Rutter, M. (1978). Diagnosis and definition. In M. Rutter & E. Schopler (Eds.), *Autism: A reappraisal of concepts and treatment* (pp. 1–25). New York: Plenum Press.

Rutter, M., & Bartak, L. (1973). Special educational treatment of autistic children: A comparative study. II. Follow-up findings and implications for services. *Journal of Child Psychology and Psychiatry, 14,* 241–270.

Schopler, E., Andrews, C. E., & Strupp, K. (1980). Do autistic children come from upper-middle-class parents? *Journal of Autism and Developmental Disorders, 10,* 91–103.

Schopler, E., & Mesibov, G. (Eds.). (1984). *The effects of autism on the family.* New York: Plenum Press.

Short, A. B., & Schopler, E. (1988). Factors relating to age of onset in autism. *Journal of Autism and Developmental Disorders, 18,* 207–216.

Siegel, B., Pliner, C., Eschler, J., & Elliot, G. R. (1988). How autistic children are diagnosed: Difficulties in identification of children with multiple developmental delays. *Journal of Developmental and Behavioral Pediatrics, 9,* 199–204.

Sigman, M., & Ungerer, J. N. (1984). Attachment behaviors in autistic children. *Journal of Autism and Developmental Disorders, 14,* 231–244.

Sigman, M., Ungerer, J., Mundy, P., & Sherman, T. (1987). Cognition in autistic children. In D. Cohen & A. Donnellan (Eds.), *Handbook of autism and pervasive developmental disorders* (pp. 103–120). New York: Wiley.

Sparrow, S., Balla, D., & Cicchetti, D. (1984). *Revised Vineland Adaptive Behavior Scales.* Circle Pines, MN: American Guidance Service.

Stern, D. (1985). *The interpersonal world of the human infant.* New York: Basic Books.

Stutsman, R. (1948). *Merrill–Palmer Scale.* Los Angeles: Western Psychological Services.

Tsai, L. Y. (1987). Pre-, peri-, and neonatal factors in autism. In E. Schopler & G.B. Mesibov (Eds.), *Neurobiological issues in autism* (pp. 180–187). New York: Plenum Press.

Uzgiris, I. C., & Hunt, J. M. (1975). *Assessment in infancy: Ordinal scales of psychological development.* Urbana: University of Illinois Press.

Volkmar, F. R. (1987). Social development. In D. Cohen & A. Donnellan (Eds.), *Handbook of autism and pervasive developmental disorders* (pp. 41–60). New York: Wiley.

Volkmar, F. R. (1992). Childhood disintegrative disorder: Issues for DSM-IV. *Journal of Autism and Developmental Disorders, 22,* 625–642.

Volkmar, F. R., Bregman, J., Cohen D. J., & Cicchetti D. V. (1988). DSM-III and DSM-III-R diagnoses of autism. *American Journal of Psychiatry, 145,* 1404–1408.

Volkmar, F. R., Bregman, J., Cohen D. J., & Cicchetti D. V. (1992). Three diagnostic systems for autism. *Journal of Autism and Developmental Disorders, 22,* 483–492.

Volkmar, F. R., Bregman, J., Cohen, D. J., Hooks, M., & Stevenson, J. (1989). An examination of social typologies in autism. *Journal of the American Academy of Child and Adolescent Psychiatry, 28,* 82–86.

Volkmar, F. R., & Cohen, D. J. (1988). Diagnosis of pervasive developmental disorders. In B. Lahey & A. Kazdin (Eds.), *Advances in clinical child psychology* (Vol. 11, pp. 249–284). New York: Plenum Press.

Volkmar, F. R., & Cohen, D. J. (1989). Disintegrative disorder or "late onset" autism. *Journal of Child Psychology and Psychiatry, 30,* 717–724.

Volkmar, F. R., Cohen, D. J., Hoshino, Y., Rende, R., & Paul, R. (1988). Phenomenology and classification of the childhood psychoses. *Psychological Medicine, 18,* 191–201.

Volkmar, F. R., & Nelson, D. (1990). Seizure disorders in autism. *Journal of the American Academy of Child and Adolescent Psychiatry, 29,* 127–129.

Volkmar, F. R., Sparrow, S., Goudreau, D., Cicchetti, D. V., Paul, R., & Cohen, D. J. (1987). Social deficits in autism: An operational approach using the Vineland Adaptive Behavior Scales. *Journal of the American Academy of Child and Adolescent Psychiatry, 26,* 156–161.

Volkmar, F. R., Stier, D. M., & Cohen, D. J. (1985). Age of recognition of pervasive developmental disorder. *American Journal of Psychiatry, 142,* 1450–1452.

Watson, L. R., & Marcus, L. M. (1988). Diagnosis and assessment of preschool children. In E. Schopler & G. Mesibov (Eds.), *Diagnosis and assessment in autism* (pp. 271–301). New York: Plenum Press

Wetherby, A. M., & Prizant, B. M. (1990). *Communication and Symbolic Behavior Scales* (research ed.). Chicago: Riverside.

Wing, L. (1981). Asperger's syndrome: A clinical account. *Psychological Medicine, 11,* 115–129.

Wing, L., & Atwood, A. (1987). Syndromes of autism and atypical development. In D. J. Cohen & A. M. Donnellan (Eds.), *Handbook of autism and pervasive developmental disorders* (pp. 3–19). New York: Wiley.

World Health Organization. (1992). *International classification of diseases* (10th ed.). Geneva: Author.

Zahner, G. E. P., & Pauls, D. L. (1987). Epidemiological surveys of infantile autism. In D. Cohen & A. Donnellan (Eds.), *Handbook of autism and pervasive developmental disorders* (pp. 199–210). New York: Wiley.

16

Mental Retardation

MICHAEL THOMASGARD
JACK P. SHONKOFF

Mental retardation is a condition with important implications that extend over the entire life-span. During the early years, it may be identified suddenly as one feature of a diagnosable disorder, or it may emerge gradually in the context of the anxiety and uncertainty that accompany a slower developmental pace. For the professional who works in the field of infant mental health, the phenomenon of mental retardation poses many different clinical challenges, which demand considerable diagnostic and therapeutic expertise.

A sophisticated and sensitive approach to the early identification of mental retardation requires a recognition that the term itself implies both a clinical entity and a social status. As such, it may be viewed as an intrinsic characteristic of an individual, as well as a social category that is defined and assigned by society. The distinction between these two definitions goes far beyond a simple matter of semantics. This is especially important in the case of mild mental retardation, which characterizes the majority of the population of individuals with intellectual impairment, and is particularly difficult to delineate in the infant–toddler period.

According to conventional standards promulgated by the American Association on Mental Retardation, a clinical diagnosis of mental retardation is based upon the documentation of "significantly subaverage general intellectual functioning" (defined as greater than two standard deviations below the mean on a standardized intelligence test), "existing concurrently with deficits in adaptive behavior" (Grossman, 1983). Thus, a low intelligence quotient (IQ) is a necessary but not sufficient prerequisite to a confirmed diagnosis. Furthermore, the criteria used to assess adaptive behaviors are influenced to a great extent by the specific expectations and demands of a particular sociocultural milieu. In fact, some observers have argued that although the concept of mental retardation implies inherent limits to one's abilities, the degree to which an individual is "handicapped" by this condition is determined to a great extent by the relative stigmatization that accompanies his or her assigned social status (e.g., Mercer, 1973). In this context, the sociopolitical revolution in attitudes toward individuals with developmental disabilities that has transpired in the United States over the past two decades has resulted in significant advances in the quality of life for many children with a wide variety of special needs (Scheerenberger, 1987). Notwithstanding these dramatic gains, the suspicion or confirmation of a diagnosis of mental retardation in early childhood remains a delicate family issue that requires highly skilled professional assistance.

EPIDEMIOLOGY

The epidemiology of mental retardation is complex, and is influenced by socioeconomic status, age, and the diagnostic criteria used to establish the diagnosis. Because conventional psychometric practice sets the lower limit of the normal range for measured intelligence at two standard deviations below the mean, just under 3% of any randomly selected population should meet the criterion for "significantly subaverage general intellectual functioning." However, since performance on a standardized intelligence test after 18–24 months of age is correlated with socioeconomic status, the rate of retardation based solely on IQ is higher among children who are poor and particularly among those who are also from a minority ethnic group. Such differences are determined by multiple factors that are associated with the interplay between poverty and ethnic status, including culturally based test bias, the developmental impacts of the social disorganization that often accompanies economic stress, and the greater prevalence of biological vulnerability associated with such risk factors as inadequate prenatal care and poor nutrition. This complex interaction between socioeconomic status and measured intelligence is further complicated by the relative subjectivity of the concept of "deficits in adaptive behavior," since the criteria for judging adaptive behavior rely on culturally determined standards to define the parameters of "normal."

Beyond the confounding influences of culture and social class, numerous cross-cultural studies have converged in the finding that the prevalence of mental retardation also changes in a predictable fashion with age (Gruenberg, 1964; Lapouse & Weitzner, 1970). Typically, the numbers of children who are diagnosed as mentally retarded are relatively low in the infant–toddler period, rise gradually in the preschool years, increase sharply in the early elementary grades, and then decline in late adolescence and early adulthood. To a large extent, this consistent pattern underscores the social context of the diagnostic label, as it reflects the greater scrutiny and more restricted range of performance expectations that characterize a formal education system. Indeed, many children who receive a clinical diagnosis of mild mental retardation shed the stigma of their label when they leave school and are able to find a functional niche that meets reasonable criteria for adaptive behavior in adult society.

The epidemiology of mental retardation in the infant and toddler years is particularly problematic. For the relatively small number of young children who demonstrate severe to profound delays in their cognitive skills, an early diagnosis is feasible and most appropriate. This is also true when a child has a specific, recognizable condition (such as Down syndrome) that implies inevitable cognitive impairment. However, it has been estimated that only 5% of individuals with mental retardation have severe intellectual deficits. Furthermore, IQ scores generally do not begin to achieve reasonable levels of stability before 3 years of age. Consequently, it is difficult to identify mental retardation definitively during the first 3 years of life. In many suspected cases, a preferred alternative diagnosis is "developmental delay." When a slow timetable for early skill acquisition is transient and secondary to maturational variation, this diagnostic category proves to be useful. However, when a young child's rate of development continues to lag significantly behind that of his or her chronological peers, a persistent diagnosis of developmental delay eventually becomes misleading in its implication that the child will, at some point in the future, "catch up." Because the stability of developmental quotients in the borderline range is so low during the early years of life, the epidemiology of mental retardation in the infant–toddler period remains imprecise (Kopp, 1983; McCall, Appelbaum, & Hogarty, 1973).

PATHOGENESIS

An understanding of the pathogenesis of mental retardation can best be achieved within the framework of a transactional/ecological model of human development (Bronfenbrenner, 1979; Sameroff & Chandler, 1975; Sameroff & Fiese, 1990). Ultimately, all intellectual activity relies upon brain function. However, how well the brain is able to do its job is dependent upon a complex interplay between the integrity and maturational status of the central nervous system and the influences of the environment in which the individual lives (Shonkoff & Marshall, 1990). The task of the clinician is to elucidate the interacting contributions of biology and experience to explain the wide range of observed differences in human abilities.

Although recent research has resulted in a dramatic expansion in our understanding of brain development, the specific etiology or underlying pathophysiology of mental retardation is often obscure (Lemire, Leoser, Leech, & Alvord, 1985). Even when a specific causal agent can be identified (e.g., a chromosomal abnormality or a documented congenital infection), it is still generally unclear how an extra piece of a chromosome or a specific central nervous system infection can produce such a wide range of functional outcomes. Most commonly, the specific etiology of mental retardation is unknown. This section provides a selected overview of broad categories of conditions or circumstances that have been associated with significant intellectual impairment.

Genetic causes of retardation represent a relatively small percentage of this population, but their identification offers the benefit of a specific answer to the question of why a child is impaired. Several different mechanisms of genetic transmission of mental retardation have been identified. Chromosomal disorders include Down syndrome and X-linked conditions, one-third of which are believed to be manifested in the fragile-X syndrome (Lubs, 1983). Many well-described single-gene abnormalities result in varying degrees of risk for intellectual disability. These include inborn errors of metabolism (e.g., phenylketonuria and Tay–Sachs disease) and neurocutaneous disorders (e.g., tuberous sclerosis and neurofibromatosis). A large number of poorly defined familial syndromes with polygenic inheritance patterns have also been described.

Early embryonic disruptions in the first trimester of pregnancy represent another important category of causes of mental retardation. In some circumstances, chromosomal abnormalities (e.g., trisomies or mosaics) may be induced by external, nongenetic influences. Intrauterine infections (e.g., cytomegalovirus, rubella, toxoplasmosis, human immunodeficiency virus) can have adverse impacts on early brain development, with serious postnatal sequelae. Abused substances such as alcohol may affect neuronal cell migration and produce significant neurological deficits. Exposures to ionizing radiation or teratogenic medications also warrant careful consideration. Recent concerns about illicit drug use, particularly with respect to cocaine, have fueled alarming and frequently exaggerated presentations in the popular media and have raised serious questions for investigators (Neuspiel & Hamel, 1991). Further research in this area is needed.

The association between a variety of well-described perinatal difficulties and subsequent mental retardation is well known. Among the more common central nervous system insults that occur at or near the time of delivery or in the immediate neonatal period are substantial hypoxic–ischemic injury (i.e., oxygen deprivation), moderate to severe intracranial hemorrhage, and metabolic disorders such as severe hypoglycemia and extreme hyperbilirubinemia. Newborns with prematurity have a higher incidence of such insults, although full-term neonates are also vulnerable.

Postnatal brain injuries that result in mental retardation represent a relatively small but important percentage of this special population. Insults to the central nervous system may be secondary to infection (e.g., encephalitis or meningitis), trauma (e.g., severe head injury), asphyxia (e.g., near drowning or suffocation), metabolic disorders (e.g., hypoglycemia or hypernatremia), toxins (e.g., lead), intracranial hemorrhage, or severe malnutrition.

Notwithstanding the long list of intrinsic malformations or secondary injuries to the developing nervous system that can result in later mental retardation, the largest number of "explained" cases of intellectual impairment are believed to be secondary to disruptive life experiences. Specifically, the adverse developmental effects of family disorganization, parental psychopathology, parental substance abuse, and severely dysfunctional infant–caregiver interactions can all result in significant cognitive compromise (Kopp, 1983). Children living in poverty often bear the compound burden of biological and environmental vulnerability (Shonkoff, 1982).

Finally, despite extensive diagnostic evaluations, it is frequently not possible to identify a specific etiology for mental retardation in a given individual. In most of these cases, a presumption is made that the etiology is of prenatal origin. In some circumstances, the possibility of multiple contributing factors is likely.

A search for the cause of mental retardation requires considerable tolerance for ambiguity and uncertainty. The range of potential etiological factors is broad, as summarized in Table 16.1. In a practical sense, the goal of a diagnostic evaluation should be to identify all possible contributing influences, and to evaluate each in terms of its relevance for designing an appropriate strategy of intervention.

NATURAL HISTORY

The natural history of mental retardation varies with its level of severity, the presence or absence

TABLE 16.1. Potential Risk Factors for Mental Retardation

Prenatal

Hereditary Disorders (present before conception)
 Chromosomal abnormalities (e.g., translocations, Down Syndrome, fragile-X syndrome)
 Inborn errors of metabolism (e.g., Tay–Sachs disease, Hurler syndrome, phenylketonuria)
 Other single-gene abnormalities (e.g., neurofibromatosis, tuberous sclerosis)
 Polygenic familial syndromes

Early embryonic alterations (often with associated physical findings)
 Chromosomal disorders (e.g., trisomies)
 Infections (e.g., cytomegalovirus, rubella, toxoplasmosis, syphilis, human immunodeficiency virus)
 Teratogens (e.g., alcohol, radiation)
 Toxins (e.g., cocaine, lead, maternal phenylketonuria)
 Placental dysfunction

Perinatal

Central nervous system insults (increased risk with extreme prematurity)
 Hypoxic–ischemic injury
 Intracranial hemorrhage
 Metabolic disorders (e.g., hypoglycemia, severe hyperbilirubinemia)
 Infections (e.g., meningitis, encephalitis)

Postnatal

Central nervous system insults
 Infections (e.g., meningitis, encephalitis)
 Trauma (e.g., severe head injury)
 Asphyxia (e.g., near-drowning, prolonged apnea)
 Metabolic disorders (e.g., hypoglycemia, hypernatremia)
 Toxins (e.g., lead)
 Malnutrition

Environmental disruptions
 Poverty and family disorganization
 Dysfunctional caregiver–infant interaction
 Parental psychopathology
 Parental substance abuse

Unknown

of associated disabilities, the quality of the caregiving environment, and the extent to which supportive educational and therapeutic resources are mobilized to enhance developmental outcomes. Concurrent motor impairments, sensory deficits, or chronic health conditions may pose significant additional developmental burdens. Relationships with nurturant caregivers can serve as potent developmental promoters. Ultimately, all outcomes reflect the influences of both nature and nurture.

Almost 90% of children who are classified as mentally retarded fall within the mild range. Children with mild mental retardation (IQ = 52–67) are rarely suspected in the first year of life and often are not identified before the later preschool period. Typically, such youngsters are first suspected of having a problem when they demonstrate lags in the development of their language skills. The achievement of motor milestones in this subgroup is usually within normal limits. During middle childhood, most children with mild retardation require special education, although the balance between special class placement and mainstreamed experiences in integrated settings is highly variable. Some youngsters with mild mental retardation are able to read at a fourth- to sixth-grade level. Adults with mild retardation are often able to lead independent lives, which can include regular employment (in a "semiskilled" or "unskilled" job), marriage, and parenthood.

Children with moderate mental retardation (IQ = 36–51) are often identified in middle to late infancy, when their slow rate of developmental progress becomes apparent. Some youngsters with moderate retardation are able to master academic tasks up to a second-grade level. Generally speaking, however, their formal education is directed toward the facilitation of self-care skills. Many adults with moderate mental retardation are capable of living semiindependently, and are able to function successfully in supervised community homes and sheltered workshops.

Children with severe mental retardation (IQ = 20–35) and those who are profoundly impaired (IQ below 20) should be identified early in the first year of life. Severe to profound retardation is associated with substantial neurological impairment whose etiology remains unknown in more than half of the cases. Children with IQ scores above 20 are capable of learning simple self-care and rudimentary communication skills. Those with IQ scores below 20 develop minimal language abilities and require total supervision throughout their lives.

With the exception of a relatively small but important subgroup of children who have progressive neurological disorders characterized by gradual or rapid deterioration in functioning over time, individuals with mental retardation continue to develop new skills throughout their lives. However, extreme variability in developmental trajectories, and the vagaries of the transactional process, make specific long-term predictions for individual children tenuous.

PRESENTING SIGNS AND SYMPTOMS

The possibility of a diagnosis of mental retardation arises during the infant–toddler period in one of two ways: as part of a suspected congenital disorder, or as manifested by the delayed achievement of early developmental milestones. A classic example of the first type of presentation is a child with Down syndrome. In this case, distinctive physical features suggest a condition that is recognizable at birth and that can be confirmed by chromosomal analysis. However, such circumstances represent a relatively small percentage of all children who will ultimately meet the criteria for a diagnosis of mental retardation.

Many children with cognitive impairments are not identified easily in the first year or two of life. Their physical examination may be completely unremarkable, and the absence of atypical phenotypic features may provide false reassurance when early developmental delays are found in children who "look normal." Because considerable variability in the rate of mastery of developmental milestones is a characteristic feature of the normative population, a suspected diagnosis of mental retardation is best confirmed over time. Although evidence of significant delay at any single evaluation is certainly worrisome, it is the longitudinal pattern of developmental progress that provides the most useful information needed to confirm or rule out the diagnosis. An overview of developmental skills and their timetable for accomplishment in the first 30 months of life is provided in Table 16.2. Failure to meet these milestones ("red flags") does not necessarily imply a firm diagnosis, but it should prompt a closer evaluation of the child's abilities.

Infants who will exhibit moderate to severe retardation in later childhood typically demonstrate delayed psychomotor development in the first year of life. Those who will function in the range of mild retardation often exhibit a normal rate of acquisition of gross motor skills, but show evidence of cognitive impairment through their slower acquisition of language abilities and delayed imitative behavior in the second year. Immature play skills (e.g., persistent mouthing, delayed onset of functional or representational use of toys, etc.) provide another useful marker of a slower timetable for cognitive achievement. A careful observer may also become concerned about a young child who requires excessive repetitions before learning new tasks, or a toddler who shows diminished curiosity or an inability to generalize newly learned skills.

The central theme that underlies a suspicion of mental retardation in any young child is the failure to demonstrate new skills at a rate commensurate with that of his or her chronological peers. Children whose abilities reflect marked atypicality rather than simple delay suggest the possibility of other diagnostic considerations. A significant impairment in social interaction, for example, may indicate a diagnosis of Pervasive Developmental Disorder or autism. Persistent failure to follow directions may reflect a significant hearing impairment or a specific disorder of language. Increasing frustration and externalizing behavior problems in a child with limited speech production may be a manifestation of oral–motor dyspraxia. Children who demonstrate evidence of regression and loss of previously attained skills require systematic assessment to evaluate the possibility of a progressive neurological disorder. Various inborn errors of metabolism and congenital infection with human immunodeficiency virus are examples of such conditions.

EVALUATION AND DIFFERENTIAL DIAGNOSIS

Evidence of significant developmental delay, or of persistent lags over time, in any young child demands a timely, comprehensive evaluation. Multiple assessment perspectives must be addressed, and professionals with expertise in the examination of young children are required. The completion of a formal psychological evaluation, using a well-standardized diagnostic measure, is a necessary prerequisite to considering a diagnosis of mental retardation (see Clark, Chapter 12, this volume). In complex cases, a multidisciplinary assessment process may be essential to elucidate the child's skills and difficulties across a variety of developmental domains, including speech and language, perceptual–motor, and sensory function. As children approach 3

TABLE 16.2. Milestones of Cognitive Development ("Red Flags")

Age	Object permanence/causality	Exploration/play	Language
By 6 months	Staring at place from which object is dropped	Ability to console self	Cooing
	Repetition of pleasurable activities (e.g., thumb sucking)	Mouthing of object placed in hand	Reciprocal vocalizations
By 12 months	Watching dropped object	Nonspecific manipulation (banging, shaking, mouthing, dropping)	Babbling
	Searching for object while hidden in view	Nonspecific exploration (fingering, turning, examining)	Use of word-like vocalizations
	Simple means–ends action (e.g., using string to attain a toy)	Ability to play peek-a-boo	Response to verbal requests
By 18 months	Finding object after multiple visible displacements	Ability to place objects into a container (filling/ dumping)	Use of intelligible single words to express needs
		Functional use of objects on own body (e.g., brushing hair)	Recognition of objects when named
By 24 months	Finding object after multiple invisible displacements	Ability to group/stack toys in a meaningful way	Ability to follow two-step command
	Handing toys to adult to make them work (e.g., pushing car, but not using wind-up key)	Ability to perform action on a doll (e.g., feeding doll)	Use of 2-word phrases
By 30 months	Discovering causal mechanisms without seeing them work (e.g., turning wind-up key on toy to activate)	Ability to perform actions in meaningful sequence (e.g., pretending to cook, bring pan to table, put food on plate, and eat)	Ability to point to and name body parts

years of age, IQ measures become increasingly reliable and have reasonable predictive validity. Although their prognostic value is limited in early infancy for children who are not severely delayed, standardized measures of mental and psychomotor development can provide objective, concurrent data on emerging abilities in the early years. Ultimately, however, their greatest utility is derived from their documentation of developmental progress over an extended period of time.

Once significant intellectual impairment has been confirmed, a thorough medical evaluation is mandatory. The pediatric history should include a detailed review of pre- and perinatal events, a search for possible sources of injury to the central nervous system after the newborn period, and an extended family pedigree to identify potential familial causes of mental retarda-

tion. Extensive information must also be collected about the child's caregiving milieu and life experiences. When completed, a comprehensive history generates an inventory of all relevant factors within the child's past and present environment that may either facilitate or impede normal developmental progress. Moreover, when conducted properly, the interview process itself provides an opportunity for the clinician to establish a trusting relationship with the parents, and to elicit information about their fears and fantasies regarding the etiology, nature, and prognosis of their child's developmental problems.

A thorough physical examination is also essential, in order to identify features that may suggest a specific diagnosis or a treatable medical condition. Several references are available to facilitate the identification of discrete syndromes characterized by intellectual impairment and distinctive physical characteristics (e.g., Bergsma, 1979; Holmes et al., 1972; Jones, 1988). Finally, *appropriate* laboratory studies (e.g., chromosomal analysis, blood and urine screens for metabolic disorders, audiological evaluation, etc.) should be conducted. Greater detail on the indications for specific medical studies is provided elsewhere (e.g., Shonkoff, 1992). Although the medical assessment of a child with suspected mental retardation is often best conducted by a developmental pediatrician or a pediatric neurologist, a knowledgeable and motivated primary care physician can coordinate an appropriate diagnostic evaluation.

THE FAMILY CONTEXT OF MENTAL RETARDATION

The literature on parental responses and adaptation to the birth and early rearing of a child with developmental disabilities includes both theoretical and empirical contributions. Solnit and Stark (1961) conceptualized the birth of a "defective child" as a severe narcissistic injury. Grounded in psychoanalytic theory, they described a necessary mourning process in which parents must grieve over the loss of the child they expected and adapt to the realities and responsibility of caring for the child they have. Olshansky (1962) postulated that the parents of a "mentally defective child" experience a chronic state of "sorrow" that can never be resolved. This fundamental theme of parental grief has been a major influence on professional attitudes toward work with parents of young children with disabilities over the past several decades.

Empirical investigations of parental adaptation to the birth and care of a child with a disability have discerned an evolving process characterized by three predictable stages (e.g., Drotar, Baskiewicz, Irvin, Kennell, & Klaus, 1975). The first stage involves a sense of shock and frequent denial in response to the initial confirmation of the diagnosis. The second stage is typically a tumultuous period during which parents may experience a variety of powerful feelings, including anger, guilt, depression, and/ or shame. The third and final stage is generally characterized by a sense of acceptance and adaptive adjustment that is reflected in an ability to deal constructively with the realities of the child's disability. Although these postulated stages of parental adjustment can serve as a use-

ful framework to guide clinical management, it is important to acknowledge that individual variability is common and that the applicability of the model can have important limitations. Some parents move quickly toward positive adaptation; others persist in a state of chronic emotional disequilibrium. Some parents may appear to achieve acceptance and positive adaptation, and then experience "regression" characterized by a re-emergence of potent feelings of guilt and anger. Such periods of disequilibrium may be particularly problematic at times of transition, such as school entry.

A wise clinician uses the model of adaptive stages as a flexible framework for ongoing management. Hasty conclusions that individual parents are progressing too slowly or too rapidly can be inappropriate and counterproductive. Generally speaking, it is more useful to question whether an atypical pattern of parental adjustment is interfering with family functioning or with the parents' ability to meet their children's needs, rather than to assume that deviance from the expected pattern is necessarily pathological or that it requires therapeutic intervention.

In recent years, both researchers and parent advocates have increasingly questioned the traditional "pathological model" of family adaptation (Gallagher, 1990; Pizzo, 1990). Indeed, some studies have indicated that many parents of young children with significant disabilities are quite resilient and experience rates of depression or family discord that are often not very different from those found among parents of young children without special needs (Gallagher & Vietze, 1986; Shonkoff, Hauser-Cram, Krauss, & Upshur, 1992). These findings may simply reflect a shift in professional perceptions, or they may be related to the impact of greater availability of potent social supports for families of children with disabilities (Krauss, 1986).

Current knowledge suggests that the process of parental adjustment to the realization of having a child with mental retardation is complex and multidimensional. Although the concepts of narcissistic injury and grief are salient and of considerable theoretical benefit in the clinical setting, parental resilience is clearly much greater in many cases than has been acknowledged in the past. In this context, the wise professional engaged in the field of infant mental health avoids a stereotypic approach to families, and seeks a constructive balance between support for positive adaptation and targeted intervention for dysfunctional behavior.

TREATMENT

The treatment of young children with mental retardation must be family-focused. Indeed, the shift from a child-oriented educational/therapeutic model to a broad-based ecological approach to the child in the context of his or her family represents an important aspect of the revolution in early childhood intervention that has characterized the past decade (Shonkoff & Meisels, 1990).

Professional support for young children with mental retardation and their families begins with the process of sharing diagnostic information with the parents. When handled poorly, the initial diagnostic phase will remain as a bitter memory whose details linger in the minds of the parents for many years thereafter. When handled with sensitivity and technical skill, this experience can contribute to a strong foundation for productive family adaptation and for constructive parent–professional collaboration. In either case, the process through which parents are informed that their child has mental retardation is a defining moment in a family's life (Featherstone, 1980; Turnbull & Turnbull, 1985).

Sharing difficult information with parents about their child is conducted best when it is a respectful and truly interactive experience. Thus, it is the responsibility of the informing professional to focus simultaneously on the content of what he or she has to convey and on the manner and extent to which the parents are "listening to" and "hearing" what is being said. A mechanical and insensitive presentation of a diagnostic label is the most frequently cited example of poor professional performance. Beyond the need for respect and compassion, however, a thoughtful communication strategy must appreciate the wide range of individual differences among families in their cognitive and affective styles, as well as in the coping strategies they use to deal with stressful events.

The challenge of sharing difficult information with parents demands adequate time, in terms of both the initial session and the availability of opportunities for subsequent discussion. When conducted well, the process of presenting a serious diagnosis involves an ongoing dialogue that focuses on both information and affect within an evolving relationship. Before beginning the initial feedback discussion, the clinician must determine the most important thing he or she has to say. This message should be presented at the very beginning of the interview in a brief, carefully worded statement. It is then critical to stop, elicit a reaction from the parents, and proceed to answer all questions as honestly and completely as possible. If there is very little parental response, it is helpful to continue the interview by inviting an affective reaction or by inquiring about whether the shared information was expected or a surprise. After this initial period, during which the central message is presented and digested, a more detailed discussion of related issues and concerns can ensue.

The critical aspect of the initial sharing of a diagnosis of mental retardation is not what the clinician says, but what the parents hear and absorb. Unanswerable questions regarding etiology and prognosis must be addressed in a straightforward manner. It is important and helpful to clarify the distinctions among what is known after the evaluation is completed (e.g., the nature of the child's *current* abilities and difficulties), what will be understood better over time (e.g., the child's *future* performance and the types of services that will be needed later in life), and what may never be answered definitively (e.g., the etiology of the disability). The presentation of a plan of intervention and a sense of the "next steps" is most helpful. Finally, asking parents what they will tell relatives and friends who are waiting to hear about the results of the evaluation is a useful way to assess what they themselves have heard and retained.

The process of sharing diagnostic information must be viewed flexibly and must accommodate a wide range of coping styles. Some parents are helped by a large volume of information. Others become overwhelmed quite easily and are served better through the delivery of information in "installments" over time. A sensitive and competent clinician will tailor his or her interaction to the individual styles and preferences of the parents. In all cases, however, the initial diagnostic session must end with a clear sense of open information sharing, a plan for the initiation of a service program, and an identified time for a follow-up consultation. It is essential that every effort be made to include both parents (if available) in this process. Invitations to meet with other important persons (e.g., grandparents and/or siblings) can be helpful.

Beyond the completion of a comprehensive diagnostic evaluation, the essence of constructive clinical management in the care of a child with mental retardation is the establishment of a collaborative partnership between the family and the helping professionals. At the time of its initiation, this relationship is inherently asymmetrical, as parents come to professionals because they need what they have to offer. Over time, however, shared responsibility for decision making is the preferred model of clinical care. When the contributions of multiple professionals are needed, clarification of specific responsibilities and coordination of efforts are essential.

Increasing emphasis on the central role of parents in the care of their children with developmental disabilities is a critical feature of an ongoing revolution that has taken place in the United States with regard to attitudes about children with special needs and their families. Within this framework, the parent is viewed as the most invested and enduring adult resource for the child. Thus, early intervention programs (described more fully by Meisels, Dichtelmiller, & Liaw, Chapter 23, this volume) are designed to support the family's ability to nurture their child's development.

Beyond the need for a sophisticated medical evaluation for any child with mental retardation, further pediatric care should be determined by each child's individual needs. Although all children with mental retardation should have a regular source of primary care for routine health maintenance, subspecialty medical services are indicated selectively only for those children with specific medical conditions requiring such care. Seizure disorders, orthopedic problems, and vision and hearing deficits are some of the associated medical conditions that require subspecialty management. Most children with mental retardation, however, are physically healthy and should not be viewed as having a chronic "medical" problem. For such children, routine health care by a responsive pediatrician is sufficient medical supervision.

Appropriate, state-of-the-art "treatment" for children with mental retardation is dependent upon constructive collaboration between a supportive family environment and an individualized education program. As for any child, long-term goals should focus on the facilitation of positive self-esteem, independence, social competence, and the development of a broad range of skills. All children need a supportive caregiving environment in order to achieve these fundamental goals. Children with mental retardation need more active help in order to reach the same objectives. As the vital context within which this process begins to unfold in infancy and during the early preschool years, the caregiving environment must be the focus of

early "treatment." When that environment is disrupted by dysfunctional relationships, the role of the infant mental health specialist can be particularly important.

REFERENCES

Bergsma, D. (1979). *Birth defects compendium* (2nd ed.). New York: Alan R. Liss.

Bronfenbrenner, U. (1979). *The ecology of human development: Experiments by nature and design.* Cambridge, MA: Harvard University Press.

Drotar, D., Baskiewicz, B., Irvin, N., Kennell, J., & Klaus, M. (1975). The adaptation of parents to the birth of an infant with a congenital malformation: A hypothetical model. *Pediatrics, 56,* 710–717.

Featherstone, H. (1980). *A difference in the family.* New York: Basic Books.

Gallagher, J. (1990). The family as a focus for intervention. In S. J. Meisels & J. P. Shonkoff (Eds.), *Handbook of early childhood intervention.* New York: Cambridge University Press.

Gallagher, J., & Vietze, P. (Eds.). (1986). *Families of handicapped persons.* Baltimore: Paul H. Brookes.

Grossman, H. (Ed.). (1983). *Manual on terminology and classification in mental retardation.* Washington, DC: American Association on Mental Deficiency.

Gruenberg, E. (1964). Epidemiology. In H. Stevens & R. Heber (Eds.), *Mental retardation—A review of research.* Chicago: University of Chicago Press.

Holmes, L., Moser, H., Halldorsson, S., Mack, C., Pant, S., & Matzilevich, B. (1972). *Mental retardation: An atlas of diseases with associated physical abnormalities.* New York: Macmillan.

Jones, K. (1988). *Smith's recognizable patterns of human malformation* (4th ed.). Philadelphia: W. B. Saunders.

Kopp, C. (1983). Risk factors in development. In W. Kessen (Vol. Ed.), *Handbook of child psychology* (4th ed.): Vol. 1. History, theory, and methods. New York: Wiley.

Krauss, M. W. (1986). Patterns and trends in public services to families with a mentally retarded member. In J. Gallagher & P. Vietze (Eds.), *Families of handicapped persons.* Baltimore: Paul H. Brookes.

Lapouse, R., & Weitzner, M. (1970). Epidemiology. In J. Wortis (Ed.), *Mental retardation: An annual review* (Vol. 1). New York: Grune & Strutton.

Lemire, P., Leoser, J., Leech, R., & Alvord, E. (1985). *Normal and abnormal development of the human nervous system.* New York: Harper & Row.

Lubs, H. (1983). X-linked mental retardation and the marker X. In A. Enery & D. Rimoin (Eds.), *Principles and practice of medical genetics.* Edinburgh: Churchill Livingstone.

McCall, R., Appelbaum, M., & Hogarty, P. (1973). Developmental changes in mental performance. *Monographs of the Society for Research in Child Development, 38*(3, Serial No. 150).

Mercer, J. (1973). *Labeling the mentally retarded.* Berkeley: University of California Press.

Neuspiel, D., & Hamel, S. (1991). Cocaine and infant behavior. *Journal of Developmental and Behavioral Pediatrics, 12,* 55–64.

Olshansky, S. (1962). Chronic sorrow: A response to having a mentally defective child. *Social Casework, 43,* 190–193.

Pizzo, P. (1990). Parent advocacy: A resource for early intervention. In S. J. Meisels & J. P. Shonkoff (Eds.), *Handbook of early childhood intervention.* New York: Cambridge University Press.

Sameroff, A., & Chandler, M. (1975). Reproductive risk and the continuum of caretaking casualty. In F. D. Horowitz, E. M. Hetherington, S. Scarr-Salapatek, & G. Siegel (Eds.), *Review of child development research* (Vol. 4). Chicago: University of Chicago Press.

Sameroff, A., & Fiese, B. (1990). Transactional regulation and early intervention. In S. J. Meisels & J. P. Shonkoff (Eds.), *Handbook of early childhood intervention.* New York: Cambridge University Press.

Scheerenberger, R. (1987). *A history of mental retardation: A quarter century of promise.* Baltimore: Paul H. Brookes.

Shonkoff, J. P. (1982). Biological and social factors contributing to mild mental retardation. In K. Heller, W. Holtzman, & S. Messick (Eds.), *Placing children in special education: A strategy for equity.* Washington, DC: National Academy Press.

Shonkoff, J. P. (1992). Mental retardation. In R. Behrman (Ed.), *Nelson textbook of pediatrics* (14th ed.). Philadelphia: W. B. Saunders.

Shonkoff, J. P., Hauser-Cram, P., Krauss, M., & Upshur, C. (1992). Development of infants with disabilities and their families: Implications for theory and service delivery. *Monographs of the Society for Research in Child Development, 57*(6, Serial No. 230).

Shonkoff, J. P., & Marshall, P. (1990). Biological bases of developmental dysfunction. In S. J. Meisels & J. P. Shonkoff (Eds.), *Handbook of early childhood intervention.* New York: Cambridge University Press.

Shonkoff, J. P., & Meisels, S. J. (1990). Early childhood intervention: The evolution of a concept. In S. J. Meisels & J. P. Shonkoff (Eds.), *Handbook of early childhood intervention.* New York: Cambridge University Press.

Solnit, A., & Stark, M. (1961). Mourning and the birth of a defective child. *Psychoanalytic Study of the Child, 16,* 523–537.

Turnbull, H.R., & Turnbull, A. (1985). *Parents speak out: Then and now.* Columbus, OH: Charles E. Merrill.

17

Communication Disorders in Infants and Toddlers

BARRY M. PRIZANT
AMY M. WETHERBY
JOANNE E. ROBERTS

After 3 years of marriage, Scott and Lisa were looking forward to the birth of their first child. The pregnancy was uneventful, and at 41 weeks Lisa gave birth to a boy. There was some initial concern at delivery because of a nuchal cord and the baby's blue skin color. Scott observed the nurses' efforts to resuscitate the baby. After a few minutes, a pink and healthy skin color was apparent, and the baby boy, named Timothy, was given to Lisa. The physician and nurses reassured Scott that everything was fine. Tim was a difficult baby during the first 6 months; he did not sleep well, and he was colicky and difficult to console. Scott and Lisa, irritable from sleep deprivation, often quarreled as to how to divide the responsibility for Tim's care and how to deal with his crying and irritability. In the second 6 months, there was some improvement in sleep regulation, but Lisa developed concerns about Tim's high level of activity, as well as his fleeting attention to her when she tried to cuddle him or engage him in face-to-face interaction. She also noted that Tim babbled very little. Their pediatrician told them that Tim was a healthy baby, and they had nothing to be concerned about. This satisfied Scott, but Lisa remained concerned.

Tim began to walk at 13 months, and became somewhat easier to engage socially, which allayed some of Lisa's concerns. However, these concerns were rekindled when Lisa began to seek day care and had the opportunity to observe many children

of about Tim's age who were socially engaging, attentive, playful, and very communicative through gesture and vocalizations (and even words in some cases). Lisa reflected on the fact that Tim never pointed at a distance for things he wanted, and communicated primarily through reaching and vocalizing. Scott vehemently denied that anything was wrong, citing Tim's good health and saying that Tim was the "strong, silent type."

The situation worsened. Between 14 and 20 months, Tim gradually became more irritable and had frequent tantrums, sometimes hitting his head on the floor. This occurred when Lisa attempted to set limits on his exploratory activities, but also occurred for no apparent reason. Of greatest distress to Lisa was her feeling that her relationship with Tim was limited, and she worried whether she was doing anything wrong. Scott continued to deny that there was any reason for concern. During this period, he had minimal contact with Tim and spent longer periods at work, often coming home after Tim was asleep. Lisa became increasingly concerned about Tim's lack of speech, and she hoped that when he began to talk everything would be fine. On the advice of a friend, she began to attempt to engage him in short "teaching sessions," which often resulted in Tim's struggling to get away, and sometimes in tantrums.

By 24 months Tim had improved little, and Scott and Lisa argued regularly about whether there was any cause for concern and whether professional help should be sought. In another 2 months, Scott agreed with some reluctance to Lisa's request to ask the pediatrician about having a hearing evaluation performed. The pediatrician made the referral to an audiologist, and Tim's hearing was found to be within normal limits. An additional referral was made to an early childhood developmental team, because of Tim's limited attention and delayed language. Tim was finally seen for an evaluation at 30 months; indeed, significant communication delays and attentional problems were detected. The team made a provisional *Diagnostic and Statistical Manual of Mental Disorders,* third edition, revised (DSM-III-R; American Psychiatric Association [APA], 1987) diagnosis of Developmental Receptive Language Disorder with Attention-Deficit Hyperactivity Disorder, although there was some discussion of Pervasive Developmental Disorder Not Otherwise Specified (NOS). The plan was to refer Tim to an early intervention program, to develop an Individualized Family Service Plan (IFSP), and to follow Tim's development in the preschool years. The team also recommended marital counseling for Scott and Lisa, who openly shared their anger and loss of faith in each other, but were still committed to the marriage and were interested in receiving professional assistance.

This is only one of many possible case scenarios involving a young child who presents a complex behavioral picture highlighted by delays in communication and language development. In this example, biological risk factors were most prominent; however, the transactional impact on the caregivers and the family unit was clear. The associated behavioral disturbances and caregiver–child relationship problems added to the complexity of the picture, and clearly indicated that an intervention strategy would have to go beyond the child and address family issues. Other possible scenarios related to communication disorders in children associated with more pervasive biological (e.g., Down syndrome, *in utero* drug exposure), environmental (e.g., poverty, neglect/abuse), and transactional risk conditions can pose even greater challenges to professionals.

In this chapter, we provide an overview of issues related to communication disorders in young children, including currently used terminology and diagnostic schemes, early communication development, and risk factors associated with communication disorders. Information about assessment and intervention for young children and

their families is also provided. We conclude with a discussion of implications for mental health professionals.

TERMINOLOGY AND DEFINITIONS

In any consideration of communication problems in young children, distinctions have to be made among the terms "communication," "language," and "speech." "Communication" is the broadest construct; it includes any behavioral act, whether intentional or unintentional, that influences the behavior, ideas, or attitudes of another person. "Language" is a complex, conventional system of arbitrary symbols that are combined and used in a rule-governed manner for communication (Lahey, 1988). The acquisition of language involves learning rules for four dimensions of language: (1) "pragmatics," the rules governing language use in social contexts; (2) "semantics," the rules governing the meanings of words and word classes; (3) "morphology" and "syntax," the rules for combining morphemes (i.e., units of meaning) and words into sentences; and (4) "phonology," the rules governing the allowable sounds and sound combinations within a specific language system. "Speech" is one mode for the expression of language, involving production and reception of vocal signals. A second important distinction is between "expressive communication" (the ability to produce vocalizations, gestures, and/or speech) and "receptive communication" (the ability to receive and/or comprehend the communicative signals of others). Competence in both receptive and expressive skills is essential for successful communication.

A "communication disorder" is an impairment in the ability to (1) receive and/or process a symbol system; (2) represent concepts or symbol systems; and/or (3) transmit or use symbol systems (American Speech–Language–Hearing Association [ASHA], 1982). Communication disorders are typically diagnosed and treated by speech–language pathologists and audiologists. For children from birth to 3 years of age, Public Law 99–457 requires that concerns about a child's development, including communication development, be addressed through a multidisciplinary process, and that an IFSP be developed to address child and family needs (McGonigel, Kaufmann, & Johnson, 1991).

Children's language disorders have been classified as "primary" or "secondary" on the basis of contributory factors (Ludlow, 1980). A primary language disorder is present when the language impairment cannot be accounted for by a sensory deficit (e.g., visual or hearing impairment) or motor deficit (e.g., cerebral palsy), a cognitive and/or social impairment, or adverse environmental conditions, and is often presumed to be the result of a dysfunction or impaired development in the central nervous system. Secondary language disorders include language impairments associated with and presumed to be caused by other factors, such as a sensory deficit, a cognitive impairment, or adverse environmental conditions.

Childhood communication disorders have traditionally been classified into mutually exclusive categories according to a diagnostic model based on etiological factors, including biologically determined sensory, cognitive, and social impairments, as well as adverse environmental conditions. The etiological diagnostic model has several limitations when applied to childhood communication disorders, however (Wetherby, 1985). These limitations include the high frequency of problems associated with idiopathic (i.e., unknown) or multiple etiologies; the difficulty in classifying childhood communication disorders into mutually exclusive categories on the basis of etiological factors; and the great variability in behavioral presentation even when a common etiological factor is known. For example, children with Down syndrome show great variability in speech and language abilities, ranging from mild to severe impairments. A diagnostic model based primarily on etiology also does not account for the interaction of biological and environmental influences on language development (Wetherby, 1985), and does not provide specific implications for intervention planning (Lahey, 1988).

Impairments of communication, language, or speech development are best understood by considering a child's profile of abilities and disabilities across communicative, linguistic, cognitive, and social–affective domains of development. It is useful to conceive of the spectrum of childhood disorders as ranging along a continuum from specific speech and language delays to more pervasive social–communicative and/or cognitive impairments. Profiling a child's language, cognitive, and social abilities and disabilities provides direct information for intervention planning and may contribute to early identification (Wetherby & Prizant, 1992).

Different categorical frameworks for diagnosing speech, language, and communication disorders have been developed by the ASHA (1982) and the APA (1987). These frameworks have been developed for older children and adults; currently, there is a paucity of information regarding the validity of applying these frameworks to very young children.

Speech, language, and communication disorders in young children are relatively common, with reported prevalence rates of 8% in preschoolers (Ludlow, 1980) and 11% in kindergartners (Beitchman, Nair, Clegg, & Patel, 1986). Of all identified handicapped preschool children in the 3- to 5-year-old range, 70% have speech and language impairments (U.S. Department of Education, 1987). Although communication disorders are among the most prevalent disabilities in early childhood, they are typically not identified until after 3 years of age except when associated with severe developmental disabilities or other impairments that can be identified early in life (e.g., severe to profound cognitive impairments, physical disabilities, and sensory impairments) (Wetherby & Prizant, 1992). The early identification of a primary language and communication impairment has traditionally posed a dilemma. The first evident symptom of a communication impairment attended to by parents and most professionals is a delay in language development when other significant disabilities do not co-occur with the communication problem. Since the typical range of first-word acquisition is between 12 and 20 months of age (Bates, O'Connell, & Shore, 1987), a child is typically not referred for a language delay until at best 20–24 months, but more commonly after 36 months.

LANGUAGE AND COMMUNICATION DEVELOPMENT: AN OVERVIEW

A large body of research has described the sequences through which children acquire various communication skills (see Bates et al., 1987; Lahey, 1988; and McLean, 1990, for reviews). This research has documented that communication development is closely related to social and cognitive development; that communication abilities are first expressed in nonverbal behavior and then in verbal (symbolic) behavior; and that the complexity and variety of communicative behavior increases as children grow older.

The social–affective exchange occurring between infants and caregivers provides the foundation for the social or pragmatic aspects of communication (McLean, 1990). Interrelationships between communication and socioemotional development have received increased attention in recent years (see Prizant & Wetherby, 1990b; Prizant & Meyer, in press, for further discussion).

The roots of receptive communication development are apparent from birth. Very early in development, infants orient to sounds and speech in the environment and recognize familiar voices, and by approximately 4 months, they become proficient at localizing auditory stimulation. There is increasing evidence that the infant's auditory system is especially attuned to perceive acoustic features of oral language, particularly intonational patterns that aid in recognition of familiar voices (Leonard, 1991). By the last few months of the first year, children respond to many nonlinguistic cues such as gestures and situational routines, as well as commonly used ritualized language (e.g., "peek-a-boo") and single words in familiar routines that may give the appearance of fairly sophisticated comprehension.

From birth, and in the first few months of life, an infant's facial expressions, body posture, vocalizations, and even skin color communicate a great deal of information to caregivers. The information communicated includes a child's state of comfort, discomfort or distress, readiness to engage in interaction, and interest in objects or events. In these early months, caregivers respond to infant cues to help regulate the child's level of physiological and emotional arousal (Tronick, 1989). Thus, an infant's behavior comes to serve communicative functions when adults interpret and respond to the behavior. Responses may include efforts to comfort the child, to provide appropriate levels of stimulation, and to provide for tangible needs such as feeding or changing the child. Caregivers speak in a tone of voice that serves to heighten the child's attention and to elicit sustained face-to-face contact. An infant may quiet in response to a caregiver's voice and touch, and may focus on the caregiver's face, creating early joint attentional states and a transactional pattern of cycles of affective engagement and disengagement (Brazelton & Cramer, 1990).

Between 3 and 8 months of age, a child makes significant social, cognitive, and motoric gains that provide the foundation for further communicative growth. Social–affective development is characterized by increased engagement with caregivers, production of more varied and readable behavioral signals, and increased ability to participate in reciprocal vocal and action-based turn-taking sequences, which are thought to be precursory to later communicative reciprocity (Bruner, 1981). With a child's increased mobility and interest in exploration of the immediate environment, many opportunities are provided for adults to engage in teaching interactions involving language modeling and mutual engagement with toys. During this period, caregivers continue to respond to their child's behavior as if it were intentionally communicative, and such contingent responding leads to the child's intentional use of signals to affect the behavior of others (McLean, 1990).

The last 3 months of the first year are characterized by a major shift in communication development: the intentional use of communicative signals to have specific preplanned effects on the behavior of others (Bates, 1979). Initially, primitive gestures and vocalizations are used to communicate intentions, but by 12 months and continuing into the second year, prelinguistic communicative means or behaviors become more sophisticated and conventionalized. Stern (1985) has noted, however, that infants are far more adept at communicating emotions than specific intentions by the end of the first year. These communicative intentions are initially expressed through preverbal means, and later are expressed through language as it emerges. Bruner (1981) has noted that children communicate for three major purposes by the end of the first year:

1. Behavioral regulation—signals to regulate another person's behavior for purposes of requesting objects or actions, rejecting objects, or protesting another person's behavior (e.g., pointing to request food, pushing bottle away to reject it).

2. Social interaction—signals to attract and maintain another's attention to oneself for affiliative purposes, such as greeting, calling, requesting social routines, and requesting comfort (e.g., waving "bye-bye," reaching to be comforted).

3. Joint attention—signals used to direct another person's attention to interesting objects and events, for the purpose of sharing the experience with that person (e.g., showing interesting toys to others, pointing at an object to bring it to someone's attention). Later in development,

children share information about topics through providing and requesting information through language.

The second year is marked by the acquisition of language, and children's communicative signaling becomes more consistent, explicit, readable, and sophisticated in form, resulting in greater success in communicating intentions and in regulating interactions. There is also a dramatic increase in rate of communication (Wetherby, Cain, Yonclas, & Walker, 1988) between 12 and 24 months. Early in the single-word stage, between 12 and 18 months, acquisition of new words is very slow and unstable; words may be used very inconsistently, and may drop out of a child's vocabulary as new words are acquired. Gestures and vocalization still comprise a large proportion of communicative behaviors. Vocabulary increases slowly and steadily until about 18 months, when two major shifts begin to occur. First, vocabulary begins to expand at a dramatic rate; this period is known as the "vocabulary explosion." Second, children begin to combine two or more words that express more complex meanings. Throughout this period, there is much continuity in the meanings that children communicate in the transition from prelinguistic to linguistic communication. Children's emerging words, which begin to appear during the first half of the second year, express meanings similar to those that were initially expressed through nonverbal behavior. These include recognition of the existence, disappearance, and recurrence of objects and events, and statements of desire and rejection. During this period, language use still refers primarily to immediately observable events.

In the second year, children's receptive development is characterized by more consistent responding to language directed to them, with less need for contextual or environmental support. By about 1 year, consistent responses to inhibitions (i.e., "no") and simple familiar actions are observed. By 18 months, children can locate familiar objects, identify body parts, and follow simple directions. By 24 months, comprehension of vocabulary has expanded greatly, and children are able to respond to words referring to objects or persons not in the immediate environment. Throughout this period, children typically comprehend more language than they can produce.

Between 24 and 36 months, the basics of sentence grammar, including morphology (word organization) and syntax (sentence organization), are acquired by children. Children move from a semantic or meaning base to sentence grammar. Grammatical knowledge and forms that serve to fine-tune and modulate meanings are acquired. An ever-expanding vocabulary makes the use of language more precise, explicit, and descriptive. A variety of sentence modalities appear, allowing for more conventional grammatical means for asking questions and expressing negation. Communication about future and past events and about emotional states increases substantially throughout this period, and connected narrative discourse (e.g., stories) emerges as children begin to relate logical sequences of events across many utterances. Advances in comprehension typically predate achievements in production. Children are increasingly able to understand language pertaining to past and future events, and are capable of responding to a much wider range of vocabulary. Children's greater comprehension and increased ability to follow meaning in narrative discourse plays a major role in their emergence as conversational partners.

RISK FACTORS ASSOCIATED WITH COMMUNICATION DISORDERS

Both biological conditions and environmental circumstances are believed to put children at risk for the development of communication disorders. Biological conditions affecting communication disorders can be categorized as genetic (hereditary), congenital (attributable to insults during the prenatal or perinatal periods that are not hereditary), or postnatal. Genetic conditions include chromosomal disorders (e.g., Down syndrome), sex-linked chromosomal disorders (e.g., fragile-X syndrome), and metabolic disorders (e.g., phenylketonuria [PKU]). Congenital conditions include infections (e.g., rubella), birth trauma, exposure of the fetus to teratogens (e.g., drugs and alcohol), anoxia, and prematurity/low birthweight. Examples of postnatal factors are exposure to meningitis, lead poisoning, and chronic ear infections. Factors in the environment that have been shown to influence communication development include the quality of the child-rearing environment, responsiveness and involvement of caregivers, and presence of neglect and child abuse.

Neural bases of communication development

are vulnerable to both biological and environmental influences during early childhood (Pennington & Smith, 1983). Although the following discussion isolates these factors, the developmental outcome of young children is clearly influenced by an interaction of biological and environmental factors (Sameroff & Fiese, 1990).

Biological Factors

Genetic and Metabolic Disorders

Many genetic syndromes (e.g., Down syndrome, fragile-X syndrome, *cri du chat* syndrome) are commonly associated with communication disorders, although both the severity and the nature of the disorders vary greatly (see Jung, 1987, and Sparks, 1984, for descriptions of genetic syndromes associated with communication disorders). For many years, all children with mental retardation, regardless of etiology, were believed to be delayed in their speech and language development, and to function similarly to children of commensurate developmental age (Stoel-Gammon, 1990). However, recent studies of preschool children with Down syndrome have documented a specific deficit in language learning affecting language production but not necessarily comprehension, and affecting syntax more than vocabulary. Other common characteristics of the speech and language of children with Down syndrome include differences in phonology, in voice quality (breathy, low-pitched voice), and in pragmatics. Fragile-X syndrome is another genetic disorder commonly associated with communication disorders, although speech and language skills vary greatly. Males often display perseverative speech and show deficits in expressive language, voice quality, speech intelligibility, and language use (e.g., difficulty maintaining the topic of a conversation, reduced eye contact) (Scharfenaker, 1990). Females often do not have speech and language difficulties, except in pragmatics. Several studies also have associated speech and language problems with specific metabolic disorders (e.g., PKU, galactosemia, histidinemia), despite attempts at early metabolic treatment in infancy (Melnick, Michals, & Matalon, 1981).

Congenital Factors

Prenatal infection and exposure to toxins may lead to varying degrees of neurological damage. Children prenatally exposed to rubella often exhibit speech and language problems, which may be attributed to the hearing loss commonly associated with rubella (Jung, 1987). Studies of speech and language of children with fetal alcohol syndrome show that they display reduced comprehension and production, as well as difficulties with the semantic, syntactic, and pragmatic dimensions of language (Jung, 1987). Other congenital factors that may have a significant impact on a child's communication development include prenatal exposure to crack and cocaine, and complications related to human immunodeficiency virus. Ongoing research will contribute much information about the long-term effects of these and other congenital factors on children's communication abilities.

Anoxia or asphyxia is a perinatal factor that has been linked to later communication difficulties (Sparks, 1984). Except for cases of extreme anoxia, most children who survive anoxic insults at birth do not have severe mental or physical handicaps, although the role of such insults in speech and language problems is unclear. The presence of anoxia alone has been found not to predict later developmental outcomes reliably until the effects of environmental factors (e.g. poverty) and perinatal factors (low birthweight) are factored in (Sameroff, 1986).

Low-birthweight and premature infants, as compared to full-term infants, have also been reported to experience delays in receptive and expressive language development (Vohr, Coll, & Oh, 1988; Siegel, 1982). Other studies have reported that these early differences appear to disappear at 2–3 years of age (Greenberg & Crnic, 1988; Menyuk, Liebergott, Schultz, Chesnick, & Ferrier, 1991), although language disorders and learning disabilities are more prevalent among low-birthweight children once they reach school age. Differences in reported results may reflect the use of measures that may not be sensitive to language differences in the later preschool years. However, most of the studies reporting significant findings have also shown that the etiology of language delay in low-birthweight children is multifactorial, with a child's gestational age, socioeconomic status, and neurological status contributing to later language performance (Vohr et al., 1988). Furthermore, the quality of the home environment, independent of socioeconomic status, has been shown to relate to language abilities at 3 years of age for premature infants, although not for full-term infants (Siegel, 1982).

Postnatal Factors

An association between recurrent and persistent otitis media with effusion (OME), or middle-ear disease, during early childhood and later communication disorders has been reported (Teele et al., 1990). OME is one of the most common early childhood illnesses and is problematic because fluid present within the middle-ear cavity impairs the normal transmission of acoustic information. A mild to moderate conductive hearing loss often results, which may persist for up to 6 months beyond an acute episode of OME (Bluestone & Klein, 1990). It is the fluctuating hearing loss associated with OME that has been assumed to be responsible for later developmental problems. Although many studies have reported that children with a history of early OME have poorer scores on language measures than do children with few episodes (Teele et al., 1990; Friel-Patti & Finitzo-Hieber, 1990), other studies have not reported significant findings (Roberts, Burchinal, Davis, Collier, & Henderson, 1991; Wright et al., 1988).

Environmental Factors

Poverty

Environmental factors such as socioeconomic status and the nature of caregiver–infant interactions are believed to play a significant role in language development. For example, preschool and school-age children from families of lower socioeconomic status have been reported to be less responsive in conversations, to give less precise and relevant responses, and to use the abstract functions of language for reasoning, predicting, and imagining less frequently than more advantaged children (Tizard, Hughes, Carmichael, & Pinkerton, 1983; Tough, 1977). Yet, Wells (1985), in a longitudinal study of British children from middle- and lower-class families, did not find differences in language development at 5 years of age. According to Snow (1983), children reared in poverty compared to middle-class children differ in their use of decontextualized language, the middle-class children being more skilled at using language that is abstract and distant (rather than tied to the present context and concrete) than the children from low-income families. However, the factors often associated with poverty (e.g., poor maternal health during pregnancy, untreated child illnesses), along with less than optimal child-rearing practices, are what put some children at risk for developmental problems, not simply socioeconomic class in and of itself.

Interactional Disturbances

Interactional disturbances have been identified in a wide range of conditions and situations. Such disturbances have been associated with problematic child-rearing practices, including under- or overstimulation; limited synchrony, reciprocity, and contingent responding; and developmentally inappropriate expectations. Thormann (1985) indicated that children of adolescent mothers are at developmental risk because of many of these problems in child-rearing practices. Tronick (1989) found that mothers with depression showed flatter affect and fewer contingent responses than control mothers. In turn, the depressed mothers' infants were less responsive in interactions. Field (1987) and Beckwith (1990) noted that interactional disturbances have been documented in mothers with bipolar disorders and with cognitive impairments. Although these situations differ greatly, these experiences are believed to place children at risk for developmental as well as emotional problems. Given that supportive caregiver–child interactions and relationships are believed to underlie communication development, a disturbance in communication development might well be an outcome of such compromised early experience. Clearly, more conclusive data are needed to determine the specific impact of early abnormal interactional experiences, apart from other biological and environmental factors, on later language and communication development.

Child Abuse/Neglect

Children experiencing abuse and neglect have been shown to have later difficulties in receptive and expressive language (particularly after 2 years of age), compared to children who have not been maltreated (Cicchetti, 1989; Allen & Oliver, 1982; Fox, Long, & Langlois, 1988). There is also some indication that abused and neglected children may show less initiative, be less responsive, and avert their gaze during interactions (Cicchetti, 1989). Severely neglected children have been shown to be at even greater risk for communication problems than abused children (Fox et al., 1988; Allen & Oliver, 1982).

The interaction styles of maltreating and non-maltreating mothers consistently show differences in behaviors critical to facilitating communicative competence in young children. Mothers of abused children have been shown to talk less, to initiate fewer interactions, to be more controlling and negative, and to be less positive (Cicchetti, 1989). Sparks (1989) has recommended cautious interpretation of the findings associating maltreatment and communication problems, because definitions of "maltreatment," "abuse," and "neglect" vary, as do subject selection criteria.

In summary, both biological and environmental risk factors are associated with communication disorders. However, there are no simple equations to predict extent or severity of communication problems from knowledge of risk factors. General conclusions that can be drawn from this literature are as follows:

1. Except at the extremes of biological dysfunction, the number rather than the nature of risk factors is the best determinant of outcomes. Sameroff and Fiese (1990) noted that the number of risk factors is a prime determinant of developmental outcome within each socioeconomic level. Furthermore, similar outcomes result from different combinations of risk factors. Moreover, although communication problems are often associated with the presence of risk conditions, these associations do not imply direct causality.

2. Children with a particular etiology do not represent a homogeneous group in their communication difficulties. There is great variability in developmental outcome, ranging from severe communication impairments to no adverse effects.

3. It is often difficult, if not impossible, to determine the direction of causation between childhood communication problems and caregiver behavior. For example, by definition, children with communication problems use signals that are less easy to interpret, and they may be less responsive to caregiver initiations. During early interactions with these children, their mothers have been found to be more directive and to talk more than mothers of typically developing children, leading some to attribute the children's difficulties to caregiver interaction style. However, in some cases, more directive styles have been found to be adaptive in fostering successful interactions (Marfo, 1990).

SEQUELAE OF EARLY CHILDHOOD LANGUAGE AND COMMUNICATION DISORDERS

The far-reaching effects of early childhood communication disorders are apparent in the problems experienced by children and their families. First, a significant body of research has demonstrated a high co-occurrence of communication and emotional and behavioral disorders in preschool and school-age children. From 50% to 60% of children and adolescents with communication disorders have been reported to have concomitant emotional and behavioral disorders (Prizant et al., 1990). Stevenson and Richman (1976) found that 59% of 3-year-olds with expressive language delays were reported to have significant behavioral disturbances. Baker and Cantwell (1987) reported that 50% of 600 preschool and school-age children referred to a community speech and language clinic for speech and language problems were found to have diagnosable psychiatric problems, and the rate increased to 60% 5 years later. Baltaxe and Simmons (1988) found that 82% of preschoolers referred to a psychiatric clinic for emotional and behavioral disorders had co-occurring communication disorders. There are differing opinions regarding causal relationships between communication and emotional–behavioral disorders. For example, it is not clear whether early communication disorders can lead to emotional and behavioral disorders, whether the reverse relationship may hold, or whether transactional complexities in development may limit the usefulness of unidirectional models (Prizant et al., 1990). There is general agreement, however, that intervention programs must address young children's communication problems. Baker and Cantwell (1987) suggested that "early intervention in the speech and language area may prevent the development of psychiatric disorders" (p. 509).

Second, a significant relationship has been found between a history of preschool language disorders and later learning problems. Howlin and Rutter (1987) have noted that learning disorders and educational problems are highly prevalent among children with speech and language disorders. Aram and Hall (1989) found that 60% of children who displayed language disorders at a preschool level required special education during later childhood. It has been suggested that language intervention at an early age may prevent learning problems at school age

(Guralnick & Bennett, 1987). Third, it has also been suggested that children with communication disorders may be more likely to experience problems in peer relationships than other children (Howlin & Rutter, 1987; Guralnick, 1990). They have been shown to have difficulties in engaging in group interactions and having their requests responded to (Guralnick, 1990). Communication difficulties may place a child at a disadvantage in participating in the social exchange and negotiation inherent in play. Furthermore, because of the important role played by language in behavioral and emotional self-regulation (Prizant & Wetherby, 1990b; Prizant & Meyer, in press), children with language disorders may behave in inappropriate or impulsive ways, and thus may be less desirable as playmates.

Finally, families of children with communication problems may experience stress related to problems in early identification and management of their children's behavior. Difficulties in early identification of communication disorders may arise from the lack of clearly defined criteria for determining communication problems in young children, and the resulting lack of appropriate referrals when a problem is suspected by caregivers (Prizant & Wetherby, 1993). Thus, parents of children with communication disorders may experience significant stress because of spousal conflict over whether a problem exists, and whether professional guidance should be sought (Gottlieb, 1988). This problem is more likely to occur when communication and language delays do not coexist with significant physical, sensory, or cognitive disabilities, any of which may lead to earlier identification and more definitive diagnosis. The behavior of young children with communication difficulties may also pose significant challenges for parents. From extensive family interviews, Bristol and Schopler (1984) identified major sources of stress in the preschool years reported by parents of children with social and communication disorders. These sources included the children's lack of effective communication, lack of response to family members, and behavior management problems.

Although conclusive data are not yet available, early identification and intervention that addresses family concerns about a child's communication difficulties may serve to alleviate some degree of stress for caregivers, and may prevent or mitigate later learning problems and emotional or behavioral disturbances (Baker & Cantwell, 1987; Guralnick & Bennett, 1987).

Therefore, efforts directed toward family issues may have far-reaching positive and preventive effects for both children and families (Prizant et al., 1990); this underscores the need for early referral.

PRINCIPLES OF ASSESSMENT

Communication assessment should be guided by a number of basic principles or underlying assumptions (Prizant & Bailey, 1992). Communication development is also closely related to other aspects of development, including cognitive, motor, and socioemotional development. Thus, assessment should address these relationships. Some basic assessment principles are as follows:

1. Assessment involves gathering information about a child's communicative behavior across situational contexts over time; it is an ongoing process, not a one-time episodic event. A child's communicative abilities vary greatly as a function of many factors, including (but not limited to) the environment or setting in which a child is observed, the persons interacting with the child, and the familiarity of the situation (Lund & Duchan, 1993).

2. A variety of strategies should be used for collecting information, including direct assessment, naturalistic observation, and interviewing significant others (Prizant & Wetherby, 1985; Schuler, Peck, Willard, & Theimer, 1989).

3. A variety of instruments or tools may be used in assessment, and should be selected on the basis of a child's developmental level, purpose of the assessment, and assessment strategies used. Both formal and informal approaches to assessment are relevant for young children. Formal assessment may involve administration of standardized assessment protocols or developmental checklists; informal assessment may involve observing children during typical interactions with caregivers (see Roberts & Crais, 1989, and Rossetti, 1990, for reviews). Formal communication assessment instruments designed for children from birth through 3 years of age have been criticized for their focus on developmental milestones and measurement of isolated skills, rather than measurement of children's ability to regulate and participate in communicative exchanges (Prizant & Wetherby, 1990a). A recently developed instrument, the Communication and Symbolic Behavior Scales

(Wetherby & Prizant, 1992), was designed to profile young children's abilities across social–affective, communicative, and symbolic domains, in order to document their capacity to regulate communicative and social interactions.

4. Communication assessment must account for conventional as well as unconventional communicative behavior. For some young children, the acquisition of conventional verbal or nonverbal means of communication is especially difficult. Because of their disability, some children may develop idiosyncratic and even socially unacceptable means to communicate their intentions. Idiosyncratic means may include subtle or difficult-to-read behaviors that can only be understood by those who know a child well. Such behavior has been documented in children with multiple handicaps (Yoder, 1987) and children with social–communicative disorders such as autism (Prizant & Wetherby, 1985).

5. The parents or primary caregivers should be considered expert informants about their child's communicative competence. As noted earlier, communication development and competence are naturally variable across contexts, and caregivers have opportunities to observe and interact with their child far more frequently, and in far more familiar and emotionally secure situations for the child, than do professionals. Professionals must refine their interviewing skills (see Winton & Bailey, 1992) and use appropriate communication assessment interview tools and strategies to tap into such knowledge (see Schuler et al., 1989). Of course, in situations where caregivers' behavior has placed a child at developmental risk (e.g., child abuse or neglect), special strategies may have to be used for both assessment and intervention (Bromwich, 1990).

6. Developmental research on the sequence and processes of language and communication development should provide the framework for assessing a child's communicative abilities. Familiarity with this information is essential for a number of reasons. First, although clear individual differences exist in some aspects of language acquisition, nearly 30 years' worth of research has documented relatively invariant sequences and stages of development (Bates et al., 1987), and thus can provide an organizational framework for documenting a child's abilities and progress in development (Lahey, 1988). Second, an intervention plan should be based on a child's current level of ability, with developmentally appropriate skills targeted in setting short- and long-term goals. Of course,

goal setting is greatly influenced by a child's functional needs and caregiver priorities; however, unless these factors are cast within a developmental framework, goals and expectations may be unrealistic, and in the short term are likely to be unattainable.

7. Assessment should always provide direct implications and directions for intervention. Ongoing assessment that documents changes in a child's communication and language behavior can be used to evaluate the effectiveness of intervention approaches. Alternative strategies, if needed, can be developed to address a child's emerging communicative needs within the context of the child's developmental strengths and weaknesses.

8. Caregivers' active involvement and participation in assessment activities should be viewed as potential forms of intervention; they may contribute significantly to the caregivers' understanding of their child's communicative strengths and needs, and thus may ultimately benefit the child. Positive effects of caregiver observation and participation have been documented in early neurobehavioral assessment (Brazelton & Cramer, 1990), and such participation is now being advocated for early communication assessment (Prizant & Wetherby, 1990a).

DOMAINS OF ASSESSMENT

Appropriate communication assessment is an essential component of providing intervention for a child and his or her family. A referral to a speech–language pathologist for a complete communication assessment is warranted when expected communicative behaviors are not observed (see Table 17.1), or when a child is deemed at risk for communication problems because of biological or environmental factors. A comprehensive communication assessment involves assessment of the child's abilities, the behavior of communicative partners, and the quality of learning contexts.

Assessing the Child's Abilities

Expressive Language and Communication

The first assessment domain includes documentation of (1) communicative means, or the be-

TABLE 17.1. Checklist of Expected Communicative Behaviors*

Expressive	Receptive
By 6 months	
1. Vocalizes any sounds	1. Turns towards voice
2. Produces a range of vocalizations (e.g., crying, cooing)	2. Startles at loud sounds
3. Produces a variety of facial expressions	3. Can be comforted by caregiver's voice
By 12 months	
1. Babbles with variety of consonant-like sounds (e.g., ba-ba, ga-ga)	1. Ceases activity when told "no"
2. Takes turns vocalizing	2. Can participate in familiar social games (e.g., peek-a-boo)
3. Imitates vocalizations or gestures	3. Consistently locates source of sound in environment
4. Uses conventional gestures (e.g., points) and vocalizations	4. Looks at or acts on objects mentioned or pointed to by adults
5. Communicates for behavioral regulation, social interaction, and joint attention	
By 18 months	
1. Produces a variety of sounds that may sound like words or short sentences	1. Responds to his or her name
2. Uses variety of gestures and vocalizations to request objects, and direct attention	2. Responds to names of objects within sight
3. Produces a few meaningful words	3. Responds to simple requests (e.g., come here, sit down, stand up)
By 24 months	
1. Uses at least 10–15 words meaningfully	1. Responds consistently to many names of objects in immediate environment
2. Uses 2 word sentences meaningfully, including simple questions	2. Retrieves some objects out of sight upon request
3. Speech is present and at least 50% intelligible to caregivers	3. Responds to 2-step requests (e.g., "get the ball" and "bounce it")
By 36 months	
1. Produces sentences of 3–5 words	1. Responds to "what," "who," or "where" questions
2. Talks about past and future events	2. Points to many different pictures in a book on request
3. Asks questions using "what," "who," and "where"	3. Responds to questions or comments about objects/events outside of immediate context
4. Has vocabulary of 100–200 words Speech is greater than 75% intelligible to caregivers	4. Shows interest in other person's conversations

*Child should be referred for evaluation if most behaviors have not been observed by specific age (based on direct observation or caregiver report).

haviors by which information is communicated (e.g., gestures, vocalizations, words); and (2) communicative functions, or the purposes for which a child communicates (Prizant & Schuler, 1987a). Of overriding concern is the readability of a child's behavior (Dunst, Lowe, & Bartholomew, 1990). As children advance developmentally and are better able to regulate interactions, the purposes for which they communicate may change. Such changes are reflected in the variety of pragmatic coding systems for docu-

menting communicative intentions and functions (see Chapman, 1981, for a review).

Receptive Language and Communication

A child's ability to receive and respond to others' communicative signals is the second domain that should be addressed in assessment. Initially, a full audiological assessment relevant to a child's chronological age and developmental level should be conducted by an audiologist to assess hearing status (Roush, 1991). Even a mild hearing impairment can result in a loss of acoustic information needed for accurate speech reception, which may affect a child's ability to learn language.

Audiometric assessment of young children is accomplished with behavioral and electrophysiological test procedures. Children at a developmental age of 5–6 months can be tested by means of behavioral procedures of "visual reinforcement audiometry" (VRA). In VRA, a child is conditioned to turn his or her head in the direction of a sound, and is then reinforced for each head turn by a toy that moves and lights up. Children who are suspected of hearing loss, and who are less than 6 months of developmental age or for whom VRA was not successful, can be tested with an electrophysiological method known as "auditory brainstem response" (ABR). However, ABR provides limited information about hearing sensitivity and may require sedation before testing. (See Northern & Downs, 1989, for further description of hearing testing.) Children's ability to respond to communicative signals in the natural environment, such as communicative gestures, vocalizations, words, and multiword utterances, should also be documented.

Speech Production

At-risk or developmentally delayed children may develop speech of limited intelligibility, or may not be able to acquire and use speech as a primary mode of communication. Assessment should address the intelligibility and quality of speech and vocal production, the variety of sounds produced, and the status of a child's oral–motor function to determine whether an augmentative or nonspeech mode of communication may be beneficial (e.g., communication board, sign language) (see Blackstone, 1986).

Language-Related Cognitive Abilities

Communication and language abilities should always be considered in the context of a child's cognitive abilities, including attentional capacities, symbolic play development, and understanding of cause–effect relations (Bates, 1979). Profiling a young child's communicative abilities, relative to his or her nonverbal cognitive abilities and capacities, provides information about the nature of a communication or language delay. Westby (1988) and Linder (1990) provide guidelines for assessing language-related cognitive abilities in young children.

Social-Affective Behavior

Social–affective signals include facial expression and displays of affect, gaze behavior, vocalizations, and other behavior reflecting emotional and physiological states. Some children with communicative impairments may demonstrate limited use of gaze shifts to regulate interactions, and their emotional states may be difficult to read because of a limited range of affect expression (Prizant & Wetherby, 1990a).

Assessing the Behavior of Communicative Partners and the Quality of Learning Contexts

Communicative partners include persons who interact with a child on a regular basis. Partners demonstrate a wide range of strategies that may serve to support a child's communicative growth, or that in some cases may hinder communicative transactions and possibly constrain growth. In extreme cases, partners may develop maladaptive interactive styles that are detrimental to a child's communicative and socioemotional development (Field, 1987). The purposes of assessing partners' styles are to help the partners develop an awareness of the strategies they use that facilitate successful interactions, and to help them recognize and modify interactive styles that may limit successful communicative exchange. Dimensions of a partner's style that may be documented include degree of acceptance of a child's communicative attempts (Duchan, 1989); use of directive versus facilitative styles of interaction (Marfo, 1990); and use of specific interactive strategies, such as responding contingently to child behavior, providing developmentally appropriate communicative models, maintaining the topic of child initiations, and expanding or elaborating on communicative attempts. Comfort (1988), MacDonald (1989), Peck (1989), and Duchan (1989) review approaches for assessing dimensions of partner–child interaction.

In addition to the interactive factors noted above, other contextual factors play an important role in communication development, and therefore should be considered in assessment.

Peck (1989) has noted that social contexts should be assessed for opportunities for young children to participate in communicative interactions, in developmentally appropriate activities, and in predictable and consistent caregiving and play routines.

The following recent resources provide more in-depth information on language and communication assessment for infants, toddlers, and preschool children: Lahey (1988); Lund and Duchan (1993); Rossetti (1990); Schuler (1989); and Roberts and Crais (1989).

PRINCIPLES OF INTERVENTION

Strategies and procedures to enhance communication and language abilities will vary greatly, depending on a child's chronological age; developmental status in areas of communicative, social, and cognitive functioning; motor abilities; and unique learning style. Other significant factors include family priorities and routines, family supports, and caregivers' motivation and ability to make any necessary modifications to support their child's communicative growth. Service delivery options available (e.g., home- or center-based services) will also influence the types of services provided, and the frequency and duration of these services.

Despite this wide range of factors affecting intervention practices, current literature suggests some generic "best practices" in communication enhancement for all young children and their families, grounded in a number of underlying principles. The following general principles have been drawn from Bricker (1989), Bromwich (1990), MacDonald (1989), and Prizant and Bailey (1992):

1. Communication enhancement is one dimension of an integrated intervention plan for a child and his or her family. Communication enhancement efforts can be targeted in a wide variety of daily routines, as well as in the context of activities addressing other developmental needs of a child. The importance of communicative growth should not be underestimated. The degree of successful communication and interaction between a child and his or her caregivers, peers, and siblings probably has a significant impact on the parents' sense of competence, the well-being of the family, and the social and emotional well-being of the child (Theadore, Maher, & Prizant, 1990).

2. Successful approaches to communication enhancement are achieved through caregiver–professional partnerships. Coordination is needed in (a) the use of an interactive style most conducive to a child's active participation and communicative growth; (b) the development of strategies for arranging learning environments; and (c) the use of specific approaches to help a child develop more sophisticated means of communication. In some cases, caregivers' perceptions of their child's communication abilities may be skewed toward attributing lesser or greater competence than is observed by a clinician. In these situations, an important goal is helping caregivers to develop more accurate perceptions or to redefine their perceptions of their child's abilities in a supportive and collaborative problem-solving climate (Theadore et al., 1990).

3. Caregivers should be viewed as primary intervention agents. Whether services are provided in a home- or center-based program, caregivers possess the greatest potential for actuating positive change in their child's communicative abilities (MacDonald, 1989). However, caregivers must be willing participants; this requires that they be respected and supported in setting communication priorities and goals that they value.

4. Communication enhancement efforts should be embedded in naturally occurring events and routines. The value of using naturally occurring events for communication enhancement has been demonstrated repeatedly (Warren & Kaiser, 1986). Warren and Kaiser (1986) reviewed the research literature on "milieu approaches," a category of intervention strategies that use naturally occurring events as contexts for communication enhancement. Milieu approaches are characterized by (a) following the child's attentional focus and interests, and encouraging child-initiated communication; (b) providing and seizing upon naturally occurring opportunities to communicate; (c) teaching within the context of social interaction and conversational exchange; and (d) using language facilitation strategies that are observed to occur naturally in early caregiver–child interactions.

5. Augmentative means of communication should be introduced for children who are at risk for limited speech development. Because of neuromotor problems, some children may not be able to acquire and use speech as a primary communication mode. A thorough assessment should result in a plan to introduce a nonspeech mode of communication (e.g., communica-

tion board, sign language, electronic system) to enable a child to communicate as effectively as possible. It is essential that such efforts be closely coordinated with caregivers. (See Blackstone, 1986, for further information.)

6. Communicative partners' style is a major intervention consideration. As communication enhancement approaches have become more focused on interactional and relationship variables, rather than child variables alone, the modification of partners' interactive style may become a primary intervention goal (Bromwich, 1990; MacDonald, 1989; Wilcox, 1989). However, when a facilitative and responsive style is observed to be used, the caregiver should be supported and encouraged to continue his or her efforts.

FACILITATIVE INTERACTIVE STRATEGIES

"Interactive strategies" are ways in which communicative partners spontaneously interact with and respond to young children that are supportive of their communicative growth. The importance of this area of intervention is underscored by (1) the fact that opportunities for supporting communicative growth occur naturally throughout the day; (2) research demonstrating that caregivers' style of interaction has an important influence on language and communication development (Mahoney, 1988); and (3) the transactional nature of communication development, which suggests that when caregivers use a more facilitative interactive style, children develop a greater sense of efficacy and competence in communication. This growing sense of efficacy results in greater active participation in social exchange, which in turn reinforces caregivers' sense of efficacy and competence (Dunst et al., 1990). Recent literature provides guidelines for developing interactive strategies to facilitate communicative growth. The following interactive strategies are drawn from Duchan (1986, 1989), MacDonald (1989), and MacDonald and Gillette (1988).

Acceptance of Children's Communicative Bids

Communicative partners provide young children with differential feedback regarding their communicative attempts or bids. Duchan (1989)

has discussed three categories of feedback along a continuum of acceptance of communicative attempts: rejection, conditional acceptance, and unqualified acceptance. In general, conditional and unqualified acceptance are more facilitative of communicative success and growth. Conditional acceptance includes both acknowledging a child's intentions and meanings, and providing positive corrective feedback. Unqualified acceptance includes various forms of positive feedback, such as attention, verbal and nonverbal expressions of acceptance (e.g., head nods, "yeah," "uh-huh," exact imitations), and expressions of positive affect. The degree and nature of acceptance of children's communicative attempts naturally depend on the content of the interaction and on an individual child's needs. However, this literature suggests that (1) direct and indirect rejection of children's communicative attempts should be avoided; (2) unconditional acceptance may be most effective at early communicative stages to increase reciprocity in interactions, to build upon early emerging intentional communication, and to encourage interactions with withdrawn and reticent children; and (3) conditional acceptance is most supportive of communication development for children at early language stages.

Facilitative versus Directive Style

The degree of directiveness or facilitativeness of partner style has received much attention (Duchan, 1989; Marfo, 1990). A directive style is characterized by adult-selected topics and activities, excessive use of imperatives (commands) and test questions (i.e., asking questions when the answer is known to test a child's knowledge), and intrusiveness or imposition on the child's behavior through excessive physical prompting or forcing appropriate responses (Clark & Seifer, 1985). A directive style has been found to result in fewer child initiations, less elaborate responses, a limited range of communicative functions expressed, and even conversational reticence or passivity (Duchan, 1989). A facilitative style, which is currently advocated by much of the literature in early communicative intervention, is characterized by following a child's attentional focus, offering choices and alternatives within activities, responding to and acknowledging a child's intent, modeling a variety of communicative functions (including commenting on a child's activities), and expanding and elaborating upon the topic of a child's verbal and nonverbal communication.

Adjusting Language and Social Input

The timing and complexity of language and social input to a young child may have a dramatic impact on the child's ability to sustain attention to others, to take turns in interactions, and to comprehend others' intentions expressed through language and gestures. Features of language input that support children's communicative growth have been documented in literature on mother–child interaction (Snow & Ferguson, 1977). Several specific adjustments have been shown to facilitate and support interactions and communicative growth.

Simple Vocabulary and Reduced Sentence Length

Young children learn word meanings by associating language they hear with persons, objects, and actions in the environment around them. Children also better attend to and are able to process language at or slightly above their level of comprehension.

Exaggerated Intonation, Slower Rate, and Clear Segmentation of Speech

Exaggerated intonation has been shown to be perceptually salient for young children and infants, and serves to heighten attention to speech, as well as to communicate affective information (Fernald, 1985). A slower rate, clearer segmentation of speech, and pauses to give a child time to respond provide children at early language levels with greater processing time and clearer cues for perceiving word boundaries, and relating language they hear to events they observe or are involved in (Prizant & Schuler, 1987b).

Contingent Responding

Responses that are semantically contingent, or focused on what a child is doing or attending to, have also been found to support language growth. Expansions (i.e., providing a slightly more grammatically complete utterance) and extensions or expatiations (i.e., providing additional information or extending a topic while incorporating information from the child's utterance) are forms of semantic contingency.

APPROACHES TO WORKING WITH CAREGIVERS IN COMMUNICATION ENHANCEMENT

Approaches to working with caregivers draw heavily from the developmental research literature on mother–child interaction and communication development. They involve attempts to have caregivers provide more intensive learning experiences, using styles and strategies that have been found to be most highly correlated with optimal communication development (MacDonald, 1989; Mahoney, 1988; Manolson, 1992). One underlying assumption of these approaches is that caregivers of at-risk and disabled children need to be supported in their positive efforts to facilitate their children's development. However, some caregivers may also need to modify their interactive styles to be more conducive of their children's communication development (Barnard & Kelly, 1990; Marfo, 1990).

Most caregiver-directed approaches concerned with communication development address the following goals: (1) sensitizing caregivers to their children's level of communication, their specific strategies in communicating, and specific difficulties their children face; (2) informing caregivers about the sequences and processes of language and communication development; (3) helping caregivers to develop interactive styles that are responsive to their children and supportive of successful communicative interactions; (4) helping caregivers modify daily activities and routines, and develop new activities, to support communication development; and (5) improving relationships between caregivers and their young children by helping caregivers to redefine their perceptions of their children's abilities. Different models for providing services to caregivers have been reviewed for caregivers of at-risk infants and toddlers (Seitz & Provence, 1990) and for caregivers of developmentally disabled children (Marfo, 1990). Examples of two models are presented, with representative approaches that focus on communication issues.

Direct Individual Caregiver–Child Therapy

In the first model, a professional works directly with a caregiver and his or her child. A teacher or clinician often interacts directly with a child, and asks the caregiver to observe and eventually to emulate the style modeled. The work of MacDonald (MacDonald, 1989; MacDonald & Gillette, 1988) and Mahoney (1988) is exemplary of this model, which has been shown to be effective in home- and clinic-based settings. These programs are based on the concepts of balanced turn taking and developmental matching. In MacDonald's approach, clinicians or educators work directly with caregivers and their children during play interactions, with the goals of identifying (1) communication skills needed by the children, (2) problems that interfere with successful interaction, and (3) strategies that caregivers can learn to support their children's development and to resolve interactional problems. Caregivers are taught to follow their children's attentional focus, and to take turns that are "progressively matched" to their children's behavior. The concept of "progressive matching", which is central to this approach, refers to imitating a child's behavior and then providing slightly more advanced models.

Mahoney's (1988) Transactional Intervention Program was based upon research indicating that caregivers of developmentally delayed children tended to dominate interactions and make requests that were inappropriate for their children's communication levels. The program involved home visits and videotaping with 34 handicapped children 2–32 months of age. Parents were taught strategies of child-centered communication approaches (e.g., turn taking, interactive matching, reducing numbers of requests, reading and interpreting a child's behavior, providing developmentally more advanced models, etc.). Results of the program indicated that all caregivers made significant changes in interactive style (i.e., to less directive styles), and that outcome levels of child communication and cognitive development were related to the degree of directiveness in caregiver interaction style. That is, children of the least directive parents made the greatest gains. Mahoney's work clearly demonstrates the potential for affecting change in caregiver behavior, as well as the relationship of such change to children's development.

Interactive coaching (Field, 1982) and interactive guidance (see McDonough, Chapter 26, this volume) are additional strategies used in a caregiver–child therapy context. These approaches are typically less direct in teaching caregivers strategies, and may not involve direct interaction between a child and a professional. Professionals may observe caregiver–child interactions during regular routines or play activities

and make suggestions for improving communicative and caregiving interactions that caregivers can implement immediately. Such indirect approaches focus on building a therapeutic alliance, so that a caregiver and professional work together in the best interests of a child.

Caregiver Educational Programs

Educational approaches provide information and support to caregivers, often in a group format, without direct involvement between a professional and a child. Educational programs may focus on helping caregivers to understand principles of communication development, as well as the caregivers' role in facilitating their children's development of communicative competence.

The Hanen Early Language Parent Program (Manolson, 1992) is a program that uses a group format and adult learning principles (i.e., active involvement and participation, negotiated agenda) to help caregivers modify their interactive styles and develop strategies to support their children's development. The program typically involves evening meetings with caregivers from five to eight families and periodic home visits over a 3-month period. The content of the program is divided into two parts. The first part focuses on identifying children's communicative abilities and on caregivers' patterns of responses to their children's communicative attempts, with an emphasis on the importance of caregivers' recognizing, acknowledging, and expanding on their children's attempts to communicate. The second part assists caregivers in increasing opportunities for communication within daily routines. Caregivers are asked to keep home diaries and to discuss issues openly with the group. A mutually supportive atmosphere is crucial for caregivers to share their successes and challenges with others. To create such an atmosphere, the Hanen approach uses parent "graduates" from previous programs to cofacilitate programs. Modifications of the Hanen program have been developed to meet the needs of high-risk infants and their caregivers (e.g., Girolometto, Ushycky, & Hellman, 1988).

IMPLICATIONS FOR MENTAL HEALTH PROFESSIONALS

Mental health professionals working with very young children and their families need to be aware of issues related to early identification, assessment, and intervention for communication disorders for a number of reasons. First, communication disorders are associated with biological and environmental risk factors similar to those for emotional and behavioral disorders; therefore, it is likely that young children first seen by mental health professionals will either have or be at risk for communication disorders. The research documenting a high co-occurrence of communication disorders and emotional–behavioral disorders clearly supports this contention. If indicators of communication problems are observed, a referral can then be made for a communication assessment as part of a team approach.

Second, early detection of communication disorders is important because of the likelihood that such difficulties have a significant transactional impact on developing relationships between children and caregivers (Greenspan, 1988). Screening instruments are available for early detection of communication problems (Coplan, 1987). Intervention studies have documented the beneficial effects of early intervention for children under 3 years of age (Shonkoff & Hauser-Cram, 1987). In addition, early identification, differential diagnosis, and provision of appropriate services may significantly reduce stress on families (Theadore et al., 1990), and may thus be an important measure to prevent the development of secondary emotional, behavioral, and learning problems. Intervention based on helping caregivers to develop supportive interactive and caregiving styles, and appropriate perceptions of their children, may also play an important role in the prevention of relationship disturbances.

Finally, speech–language pathologists and mental health professionals have traditionally had limited opportunities to work together on issues related to communication disorders and their impact on children and families. Different diagnostic frameworks and terminology, different models of development, and relatively isolated training at preservice levels have perpetuated this lack of integration. Thus, most mental health professionals are limited in their knowledge of communication disorders, and most professionals in communication disorders have limited knowledge of psychosocial and family issues (Prizant et al., 1990; Prizant & Meyer, in press). Public Law 99–457 and its mandate for interdisciplinary cooperation within a family-centered framework hold great promise for making this fragmentation a thing of the past, and such a development can only serve to benefit young children and their families.

REFERENCES

Allen, R., & Oliver, J. (1982). The effects of child maltreatment on language development. *Child Abuse and Neglect, 5,* 299–305.

American Psychiatric Association (APA). (1987). *Diagnostic and statistical manual of mental disorders* (3rd ed., rev.). Washington, DC: Author.

American Speech–Language–Hearing Association (ASHA). (1982). Definitions: Communicative disorders and variations. *American Speech–Language–Hearing Association Journal, 24,* 949–950.

Aram, D., & Hall, N. (1989). Longitudinal follow-up of children with preschool communication disorders. *School Psychology Review, 18,* 457–501.

Baker, L., & Cantwell, D. (1987). A prospective psychiatric follow-up of children with speech/language disorders. *Journal of the American Academy of Child and Adolescent Psychiatry, 26,* 546–553.

Baltaxe, C.A.M., & Simmons, J.Q. (1988). Communication deficits in preschool children with psychiatric disorders. *Seminars in Speech and Language, 8,* 81–90.

Barnard, K., & Kelly, J. (1990). Assessment of parent–child interaction. In S. J. Meisels & J. P. Shonkoff (Eds.), *Handbook of early childhood intervention.* New York: Cambridge University Press.

Bates, E. (1979). On the evolution and development of symbols. In E. Bates, T. Benigni, I. Bretherton, L. Camaioni, & V. Volterra, (Eds.), *The emergence of symbols: Cognition and communication in infancy.* New York: Academic Press.

Bates, E., O'Connell, B., & Shore, C. (1987). Language and communication in infancy. In J. D. Osofsky (Ed.), *Handbook of infant development* (2nd ed.). New York: Wiley.

Beckwith, L. (1990). Adaptive and maladaptive parenting: Implications for intervention. In S. J. Meisels & J. P. Shonkoff (Eds.), *Handbook of early childhood intervention.* New York: Cambridge University Press.

Beitchman, J., Nair, R., Clegg, M., & Patel, P. (1986). Prevalence of speech and language disorders in five year old kindergarten children in the Ottawa–Carleton region. *Journal of Speech and Hearing Disorders, 51,* 98–110.

Blackstone, S. (1986). *Augmentative communication: An introduction.* Rockville, MD: American Speech–Language–Hearing Association.

Bluestone, C., & Klein, J. (1990). Intratemporal complications and sequelae of otitis media. In C. Bluestone, S. Stool, & M. Scheetz (Eds.), *Pediatric otolaryngology.* Philadelphia: W. B. Saunders.

Brazelton, T. B., & Cramer, B. (1990). *The earliest relationship.* New York: Addison-Wesley.

Bricker, D. (1989). *Early intervention for at-risk infants, toddlers and preschool children.* Palo Alto, CA: VORT.

Bromwich, R. (1990). The interaction approach to early intervention. *Infant Mental Health Journal, 11,* 66–79.

Bristol, M., & Schopler, E. (1984). A developmental perspective on stress and coping in families of autistic children. In J. Blacher (Ed.), *Families of severely handicapped children*. New York: Academic Press.

Bruner, J. (1981). The social context of language acquisition. *Language and Communication, 1,* 155–178.

Chapman, R. (1981). Exploring children's communicative intents. In J. Miller, (Ed.), *Assessing language production in children*. Baltimore: University Park Press.

Cicchetti, D. (1989). How research on child maltreatment has informed the study of child development: Perspectives from developmental psychology. In D. Cicchetti & V. Carlson (Eds.), *Handbook of child maltreatment*. New York: Cambridge University Press.

Clark, G., & Seifer, R. (1985). Assessment of parents' interactions with their developmentally delayed infants. *Infant Mental Health Journal, 6,* 214–225.

Comfort, M. (1988). Assessing parent–child interaction. In D. Bailey & R. Simeonsson (Eds.), *Family assessment in early intervention*. Columbus, OH: Charles E. Merrill.

Coplan, J. (1987). *Early language milestone scale* (rev. ed.). Austin, TX: Pro-Ed.

Duchan, J. (1986). Language intervention through sense-making and fine tuning. In R. Schiefelbusch (Ed.), *Language competence: Assessment and intervention*. Austin, TX: Pro-Ed.

Duchan, J. (1989). Evaluating adults' talk to children: Assessing adult attunement. *Seminars in Speech and Language, 10,* 17–27.

Dunst, C., Lowe, L., & Bartholomew, P. (1990). Contingent social responsiveness, family ecology, and infant communicative competence. *National Student Speech, Language, and Hearing Association Journal, 17,* 39–49.

Fernald, A. (1985). Four-month-old infants prefer to listen to motherese. *Infant Behavior and Development, 10,* 181–195.

Field, T. (1982). Interaction coaching for high-risk infants and their parents. In H. Moss, R. Hess, & C. Swift (Eds.), *Early intervention programs for infants*. Binghamton, NY: Haworth Press.

Field, T. (1987). Affective and interactive disturbances in infants. In J. D. Osofsky (Ed.), *Handbook of infant development* (2nd ed.). New York: Wiley.

Fox, L., Long, S., & Langlois, A. (1988). Patterns of language comprehension deficit in abused and neglected children. *Journal of Speech and Hearing Disorders, 53,* 239–244.

Friel-Patti, S., & Finitzo-Hieber, T. (1990). Language learning in a prospective study of otitis media with effusion in the first two years of life. *Journal of Speech and Hearing Research, 33,* 188–194.

Girolometto, L., Ushycky, I., & Hellman, J. (1988). Hanen training program for parents of high risk infants. In *Proceedings of the symposium High Risk Infants: Facilitating Interaction and Communication*. Toronto: Hanen Early Language Resource Centre.

Gottlieb, M. (1988). The response of families to language disorders in the young child. *Seminars in Speech and Language, 9,* 47–53.

Greenberg, M., & Crnic, K. (1988). Longitudinal predictors of developmental status and social interaction in premature and full-term infants at age two. *Child Development, 59,* 554–570.

Greenspan, S. (1988). Fostering emotional and social development in infants with disabilities. *Zero to Three, 8,* 8–18.

Guralnick, M. (1990). Social competence and early intervention. *Journal of Early Intervention, 14,* 3–14.

Guralnick, M., & Bennett, F. (1987). *The effectiveness of early intervention for at-risk and handicapped children*. New York: Academic Press.

Howlin, P., & Rutter, M. (1987). The consequences of language delay for other aspects of development. In W. Yule & M. Rutter (Eds.), *Language development and language disorders*. Philadelphia: J. B. Lippincott.

Jung, J. (1987). *Genetic syndromes in communication disorders*. London, Ontario: College-Hill Press.

Lahey, M. (1988). *Language disorders and language development*. New York: Macmillan.

Leonard, L. (1991). New trends in the study of early language acquisition. *American Speech–Language–Hearing Association Journal, 33,* 43–44.

Linder, T. (1990). *Transdisciplinary play-based assessment*. Baltimore: Paul H. Brookes.

Ludlow, C. (1980). Children's language disorders: Recent research advances. *Annals of Neurology, 7,* 497–507.

Lund, N., & Duchan, J. (1993). *Assessing children's language in naturalistic contexts* (3rd ed.). Englewood Cliffs, NJ: Prentice-Hall.

MacDonald, J. (1989). *Becoming partners with children*. San Antonio, TX: Special Press.

MacDonald, J., & Gillette, Y. (1988). Communicating partners: A conversational model for building parent–child relationships with handicapped children. In K. Marfo (Ed.), *Parent–child interaction and developmental disabilities*. New York: Praeger.

Mahoney, G. (1988). Enhancing the developmental competence of handicapped infants. In K. Marfo (Ed.), *Parent–child interaction and developmental disabilities*. New York: Praeger.

Manolson, A. (1992). *It takes two to talk* (2nd ed.). Toronto: Hanen Early Language Resource Centre.

Marfo, K. (1990). Maternal directiveness in interactions with mentally handicapped children: An analytical commentary. *Journal of Child Psychology and Psychiatry, 31,* 531–549.

McGonigel, M., Kaufmann, B., & Johnson, B. (1991). *Guidelines and recommended practices for the individualized family service plan* (2nd ed.). Bethesda, MD: Association for the Care of Children's Health.

McLean, L. (1990). Communication development in the first two years of life: A transactional process. *Zero to Three, 11,* 13–19.

Melnick, C., Michals, K., & Matalon, R. (1981). Linguistic development of children with phenylketonuria and normal intelligence. *Journal of Pediatrics, 98,* 269–272.

Menyuk, P., Liebergott, J., Schultz, M., Chesnick, M., & Ferrier, L. (1991). Patterns of early lexical and cognitive development in premature and full-term infants. *Journal of Speech and Hearing Research, 34,* 88–94.

Northern, J., & Downs, M. (1989). *Hearing in children* (3rd ed.). Baltimore: Williams & Wilkins.

Peck, C. (1989). Assessment of social communicative competence: Evaluating environments. *Seminars in Speech and Language, 10,* 1–15.

Pennington, B., & Smith, S. (1983). Genetic influences on learning disabilities and speech and language disorders. *Child Development, 54,* 369–387.

Prizant, B. M., Audet, L., Burke, G., Hummel, L., Maher, S., & Theadore, G. (1990). Communication disorders and emotional/behavioral disorders in children. *Journal of Speech and Hearing Disorders, 55*, 179–192.

Prizant, B. M., & Bailey, D. (1992). Facilitating acquisition and use of communication skills. In D. Bailey & M. Wolery (Eds.), *Teaching infants and preschoolers with handicaps*. Columbus, OH: Charles E. Merrill.

Prizant, B. M., & Meyer, E. C. (in press). Socioemotional aspects of communication disorders in young children and their families. *American Journal of Speech-Language Pathology*.

Prizant, B. M., & Schuler, A. (1987a). Facilitating communication: Theoretical foundations. In D. Cohen & A. Donnellan (Eds.), *Handbook of autism and pervasive developmental disorders*. New York: Wiley.

Prizant, B. M., & Schuler, A. (1987b). Facilitating communication: Language approaches. In D. Cohen & A. Donnellan (Eds.), *Handbook of autism and pervasive developmental disorders*. New York: Wiley.

Prizant, B. M., & Wetherby, A. M. (1985). Intentional communicative behavior of children with autism: Theoretical and practical issues. *Australian Journal of Human Communication Disorders, 13*, 21–59.

Prizant, B. M., & Wetherby, A. M. (1990a). Assessing the communication of infants and toddlers: Integrating a socioemotional perspective. *Zero to Three, 11*, 1–12.

Prizant, B. M., & Wetherby, A. M. (1990b). Toward an integrated view of language and socioemotional development in children. *Topics in Language Disorders, 10*, 1–16.

Prizant, B. M., & Wetherby, A. M. (1993). Communication in preschool autistic children. In E. Schopler, M. VanBourgondien, & M. Bristol (Eds.), *Preschool issues in autism*. New York: Plenum Press.

Roberts, J. E., & Crais, E. (1989). Assessing communication skills. In D. Bailey & M. Wolery (Eds.), *Assessing infants and children with handicaps*. Columbus, OH: Charles E. Merrill.

Roberts, J. E., Burchinal, M., Davis, B., Collier, A., & Henderson, F. (1991). Otitis media in early childhood and later language development. *Journal of Speech and Hearing Research*.

Rossetti, L. (1990). *Infant–toddler assessment: An interdisciplinary approach*. Boston: College-Hill Press.

Roush, J. (1991). Early intervention: Expanding the audiologist's role. *American Speech–Hearing–Language Association Journal, 33*, 47–49.

Sameroff, A. J. (1986). Environmental context of development. *Journal of Pediatrics, 109*, 192–200.

Sameroff, A. J., & Fiese, B. (1990). Transactional regulation and early intervention. In S. J. Meisels & J. P. Shonkoff (Eds.), *Handbook of early childhood intervention*. New York: Cambridge University Press.

Scharfenaker, S. (1990). The fragile X syndrome. *American Speech–Hearing–Language Association Journal, 9*, 45–47.

Schuler, A. (1989). Assessing communicative competence. *Seminars in Speech and Language, 10*.

Schuler, A., Peck, C., Willard, C., & Theimer, K. (1989). Assessment of communicative means and functions through interview: Assessing the communicative capabilities of individuals with limited language. *Seminars in Speech and Language, 10*, 51–61.

Seitz, V., & Provence, S. (1990). Caregiver-focused models of early intervention. In S. J. Meisels & J. P. Shonkoff (Eds.), *Handbook of early childhood intervention*. New York: Cambridge University Press.

Shonkoff, J. P., & Hauser-Cram, P. (1987). Early intervention for disabled infants and their families: A quantitative analysis. *Pediatrics, 80*, 650–658.

Siegel, L. (1982). Reproductive, perinatal, and environmental factors as predictors of the cognitive and language development of preterm and full-term infants. *Child Development, 53*, 963–973.

Snow, C. (1983). Literacy and language: Relationships during the preschool years. *Harvard Educational Review, 53*, 165–189.

Snow, C., & Ferguson, C. (1977). *Talking to children: Language input and acquisition*. Cambridge, England: Cambridge University Press.

Sparks, S. (1984). *Birth defects and speech and language disorders*. San Diego: College-Hill Press.

Sparks, S. (1989). Speech and language in maltreated children: Response to McCauley and Swisher (1987). *Journal of Speech and Hearing Disorders, 54*, 124–125.

Stern, D. (1985). *The interpersonal world of the infant*. New York: Basic Books.

Stevenson, J., & Richman, N. (1976). The prevalence of language delay in a population of three-year-old children and its association with general retardation. *Developmental Medicine and Child Neurology, 18*, 431–441.

Stoel-Gammon, C. (1990). Down syndrome: Effects on language development. *American Speech–Hearing–Language Association Journal, 32*, 42–44.

Teele, D., Klein, J., Chase, C., Menyuk, P., Rosner, B., & The Greater Boston Otitis Media Group. (1990). Otitis media in infancy and intellectual ability, school achievement, speech, and language at age 7 years. *Journal of Infectious Diseases, 162*, 685–694.

Theadore, G., Maher, S., & Prizant, B. (1990). Early assessment and intervention with emotional and behavioral disorders and communication disorders. *Topics in Language Disorders, 10*, 42–56.

Thormann, M. (1985). Attitudes of adolescents toward infants and young children. In S. Harel & N. Anastasiow (Eds.), *The at-risk infant: Psycho/socio/medical aspects*. Baltimore: Paul H. Brookes.

Tizard, B., Hughes, M., Carmichael, H., & Pinkerton, G. (1983). Language and social class: Is verbal deprivation a myth? *Journal of Child Psychology and Psychiatry, 24*, 533–542.

Tough, J. (1977). *The development of meaning: A study of children's use of language*. London: George Allen & Unwin.

Tronick, E. (1989). Emotions and emotional communication in infancy. *American Psychologist, 44*, 112–119.

U.S. Department of Education. (1987). *Ninth annual report to Congress on the implementation of the Education of the Handicapped Act*. Washington, DC: U.S. Government Printing Office.

Vohr, B., Coll, C., & Oh, W. (1988). Language development of low-birth weight infants at two years. *Developmental Medicine and Child Neurology, 30*, 608–615.

Warren, S., & Kaiser, A. (1986). Incidental language teaching: A critical review. *Journal of Speech and Hearing Disorders, 51*, 291–299.

Wells, G. (1985). *Language development in the preschool years*. Cambridge: Cambridge University Press.

Westby, C. (1988). Children's play: Reflections of social competence. *Seminars in Speech and Language, 9*, 1–13.

Wetherby, A. M. (1985). Speech and language disorders in children: An overview. In J. K. Darby (Ed.), *Speech and language evaluation in neurology: Childhood disorders.* New York: Grune & Stratton.

Wetherby, A. M., Cain, D., Yonclas, D., & Walker, V. (1988). Analysis of intentional communication of normal children from the prelinguistic to the multiword stage. *Journal of Speech and Hearing Research, 31,* 240–252.

Wetherby, A. M., & Prizant, B. M. (1992). *Communication and Symbolic Behavior Scales* Chicago: Riverside.

Wetherby, A. M., & Prizant, B. M. (1992). Profiling young children's communicative competence. In S. Warren & J. Reichle (Eds.), *Causes and effects in communication disorders.* Baltimore: Paul H. Brookes.

Wilcox, M. J. (1989). Delivering communication-based services to infants, toddlers, and their families: Approaches and models. *Topics in Language Disorders, 10,* 68–79.

Winton, P., & Bailey, D. (1992). Communicating with families: Examining practices and facilitating change. In R. Fewell, D. Sexton, & M. Lobman (Eds.), *Families of young children with special needs: A primer for services.* Austin, TX: Pro-Ed.

Wright, P., Sell, S., McConnell, K., Sitton, A., Thompson, J., Vaughn, B., & Bess, F. (1988). Impact of recurrent otitis media on middle ear function, hearing, and language. *Pediatrics, 113,* 581–587.

Yoder, P. (1987). Relationship between degree of infant handicap and clarity of infant cues. *American Journal of Mental Deficiency, 91,* 639–641.

18

Regulatory Disorders

STANLEY I. GREENSPAN
SERENA WIEDER

A NEW CONSTRUCT OF REGULATORY DISORDERS

Easy babies, fussy babies, quiet babies, self-scheduled babies, sensitive babies, "don't change the routine" babies, "pick up and go" babies—these are just a few examples of individual differences in self-regulation that reflect constitutional and maturational variations. Individual differences in sensory reactivity, self-regulation, and behavioral organization in infants have been recognized during the last two to three decades (Escalona, 1968; Greenspan, 1992; DeGangi, Porges, & Greenspan, in press; DeGangi, DiPietro, Greenspan, & Porges, 1991; Doussard-Roosevelt, Walker, Portales, Greenspan, & Porges, 1990).

Still, the work describing individual differences in self-regulation has not been integrated into our understanding of behavioral manifestations, symptoms, and problems in adaptation. Because an infant has a limited number of responses or behavioral patterns in relationship to various stresses or difficulties, there has always been considerable overlap in the behavioral symptoms signaling such difficulties. The purpose of this chapter is to present a new diagnostic construct of regulatory disorders (Greenspan, 1992; NCCIP, 1991) that considers distinct behavioral patterns, coupled with specific difficulties in sensory, sensorimotor, or processing capacities.

According to the present construct, infants and young children with regulatory disorders present challenging variations in their constitutional and maturational patterns, as well as in their interactive and family patterns. These variations in turn affect how the children perceive and organize experience. The construct of regulatory disorders emerged from clinical work with a variety of infants and families, where it appeared that some infants had significant constitutional and maturational variations that were contributing to their symptoms. Difficulties with either processing sensation (inflow) or motor planning (outflow)—that is, being able to take in or respond back to the world—compromised the infants' ability to negotiate with and adjust to their caregivers and environment (see Greenspan, 1989, for a discussion of constitutional variables).

Emerging research supports the initial clinical impressions. For example, 8-month-olds with a range of behavioral control difficulties (e.g., in sleeping, eating, self-calming, attention, etc.) evidenced sensory reactivity and motor differences (as assessed via reliable rating scales), as well as measurable psychological and physiological differences. These differences persisted at 18 months and 4 years of age. At 4 years of age, there were also behavioral and learning difficulties (DeGangi et al., in press).

The early regulatory patterns can be viewed either as distinct disorders at early developmental stages, in the sense that they constitute maladaptive and often disruptive behavioral patterns, or as intermediary risk patterns for later symptoms and disorders. Whenever one is considering a developmental pattern, one can view early behavior in these two ways, particularly when the early pattern is part of the ongoing interaction with the environment and when this early interaction has later consequences. It may be tempting to view early regulatory differences as simply variations in temperament. The regulatory patterns, however, are determined by "hands-on" assessment (not by parental reports, as with temperament), and are related to specific sensory processing and motor patterns (not simply to general adaptive characteristics, as with temperament). Moreover, as we hope to demonstrate in future research, these regulatory patterns can be altered with proper interventions.

Consider these two infants as illustrations of this construct:

David, who is 5 months old, sleeps quietly in a darkened room. The phone is turned off. His parents do not vacuum, play the stereo, or talk loudly. Several months of crying, fussiness, endless rocking sessions, and disrupted sleep have led to this. Every effort is made to make sure that David never misses his nap in his own crib. He cringes when his diaper is changed and cries when he must get dressed, arching away. Although he likes to look around, he is slow to move or turn over. David is also startled by unexpected loud sounds and begins to cry, unable to turn to the sound readily. His parents often feel exhausted and puzzled, trying hard to hide their feelings of disappointment and self-doubt, even from each other. It is not even clear to them that he recognizes they are different from others, since he shows such little pleasure when they approach; yet he clings to them.

In contrast, Mark is 5 months old too. His mother is about to whisk him off to meet a friend at a cafe, even though it is his naptime. He can always nap there; the noise, lights, and commotion of the cafe do not bother him. He loves to look around and follow people and sounds, turning eagerly in every direction. When upset, he calmed himself quickly as a newborn by sucking on his fist, and now seems to quiet just in response to looking at his mother's face and hearing her voice. In fact, last night he stayed up while his parents had dinner with friends; he joyfully entertained everyone with coos and smiles as he went from hand to hand, while his parents glowed.

These two infants are strikingly different. From birth, each infant must suddenly take in and organize the myriad of sensations of touch, lights, movement, sight, sounds, pain, temperature, and smells of his or her new world. The infant's capacity to take in and organize these sensations, as well as the crucial relationships being offered, is evident. Some infants, such as Mark, adapt easily and stay calm and alert, available for bonding and attachment, as evidenced by a quiet, alert state with eye contact and listening. Mark can use vision, hearing, touch, and movement to regulate himself and take an interest in the world. When upset, just looking at his mother helps him become calm and happy, and so do her soothing voice and touch. In fact, he brightens and takes in the world with great confidence and security, able to organize the various sensations and information coming at him at the same time. In contrast, little David needs to shut out sounds and vision; he is calmed more by the slow, steady rocking movements of his mother in the quiet, darkened room. When alert he can take in his parents by looking or listening to one at a time, but too many people or too much stimulation in the environment overwhelms him, and he becomes disorganized and fusses terribly. Neither David nor his parents are enjoying this crucial period of life.

Infants organize themselves in different ways. Clinical observations indicate that to stay calm, some infants suck their fists, gaze at a mobile or face, listen to a soothing voice, or enjoy rocking. Some use one or two sensory modalities, such as vision and movement (rocking), but may become overwhelmed or seem unresponsive to auditory stimuli. Other infants prefer vision and hearing to self-regulate and take an interest in the world, but do not like touch and movement. In contrast to those infants who are hypersensitive and tend to overreact, other infants seem to underreact to what is going on around them, as their parents work harder and harder to get their attention or even a small smile. They tend to be easy and undemanding as babies, not bothered by very much. Later, they may wander around, holding onto a familiar object to focus on when too much is going on. These infants appear to be underreactive, hardly noticing the sensations until they become very vigorous and intense, and then overreacting as they insist on restoring a hands-off quiet state.

A baby who is excessively needy and demanding, fussy or finicky, intermittently angry, labile in his or her moods, or underresponsive and slow to warm up and adapt to new situations has an impact—on the family, on the nature of interactions between the child and family members, and on the way the child perceives himself or herself and integrates experience. Sometimes one sensory pathway, or sometimes two or more, are involved.

When regulatory disorders are evident, they are characterized by difficulties in regulating physiological, sensory, attentional, and motor or affective processes, and in organizing a calm, alert, or affectively positive state. Although the causes of these disorders are unclear, these infants have difficulties in organizing adaptive functions involving feelings, behaviors, and learning. Difficulties can range from mild to severe; may affect one or more areas of development; and will be evident in one or more of the following ways:

1. The physiological or state repertoire (e.g., irregular breathing, startles, gagging, etc.).
2. Gross and fine motor activity (e.g., poor tonus, jerky or limp movements, poor posture, poor motor planning, etc.).
3. Attentional organization (e.g., driven and "hyper" versus perseverating on small or repetitive details).
4. Affective organization, including predominant affective tone, range of affects, and degree of modulation (e.g., affect may vary from flat to screaming, but predominantly sober or unhappy).
5. Sleep, eating, or elimination patterns.

To be considered a regulatory disorder, a distinct behavioral pattern must be coupled with difficulty in sensory, sensorimotor, or processing capacities that affects daily adaptation and relationships. When both behavioral and constitutional maturational elements are not present, other diagnoses may be more appropriate. For example, an infant who is irritable and withdrawn after being abandoned may be evidencing an expectable type of attachment difficulty. An infant who is irritable and overly reactive to routine interpersonal experiences, in the absence of clearly identified sensory, sensorimotor, or processing difficulty, may be evidencing an anxiety or mood disorder.

The specific sensory, sensorimotor, and processing difficulties involved in regulatory disorders include the following:

1. The child is over- or underreactive to loud, high- or low-pitched noises.

2. The child is over- or underreactive to bright lights or new and striking visual images (e.g., colors, shapes, complex fields).
3. Tactile defensiveness is apparent (e.g., overreactivity to changing clothes, bathing, or stroking of arms, legs, or trunk; avoidance of touching "messy" textures; etc.), and/or the child is underreactive to touch or pain.
4. The child is under- or overreactive to movement in space (e.g., brisk horizontal or vertical movements, such as those involved in tossing a child in the air, playing merry-go-round, jumping, etc.).
5. The child is under- or overreactive to odors.
6. The child is under- or overreactive to temperature.
7. Poor motor tone is apparent (e.g., gravitational or postural insecurity, oral–motor difficulties).
8. The child has less than age-appropriate motor planning skills (e.g., complex motor patterns, such as alternating hand banging).
9. The child has less than age-appropriate fine motor skills.
10. The child has less than age-appropriate auditory–verbal discrimination or integration capacity (e.g., an 8-month-old should be able to imitate distinct sounds; a 2½-year-old should be able to follow or repeat requests; a 3-year-old should be able to put together words and actions).
11. Less than age-appropriate visual–spatial discrimination or integration capacity is apparent (e.g., an 8-month-old should recognize different facial configurations; a 2½-year-old should know where to turn to get to a friend's house; a 3-year-old should be able to put together certain spaces, such as a room, with activities).

TYPES OF REGULATORY DISORDERS

Six types of regulatory disorders have been proposed; the criteria for each are described in this section.

Type I: Hypersensitive Type

1. The child is often overly reactive to routine sensory experiences, such as light touch, loud noises, or bright lights.

2. The child also has at least one of the following characteristics:

a. The child tends to be easily upset (e.g., irritable, often crying or unhappy), cannot soothe self, and finds it difficult to return to sleep and/or recover from frustration or disappointment.

b. The child may also be negative and controlling ("the fearful little dictator").

c. The child can be fearful, cautious, and clinging (e.g., at 4 months, even when sitting in the mother's lap, may take more than 15 minutes to "flirt" with a new person, looking serious and worried; or at 8 months, may pull away and squirm intensely when a new person tries to pick him or her up, even after 15 minutes of gentle wooing).

d. The child dislikes changes in routine or new experiences, including visiting other people's homes, school, and so on. When frightened of new experiences, he or she clings to the mother or father (e.g., wants to be picked up and held). The child will not explore new surroundings even for a few minutes.

e. The child tends to shy away from new peers even after 18 months of age.

f. Night wakings tend to be associated with a strong desire to be held by the mother until the child sleeps again or for entire night.

g. In school settings, the child tends to be overwhelmed by a large group (circle times tend to be difficult) and seeks a one-on-one relationship with the teacher.

Type II: Underreactive Type

1. The child is often underreactive to and has difficulty processing auditory–verbal experiences. In addition, he or she may be either over- or underreactive to tactile and visual–spatial experiences, and may also have motor tone and motor planning difficulties.

2. At least one of the following also applies:

a. The child tends to be unfocused or inattentive, "tuned out."

b. The child tends to be withdrawn, but responds (to some degree) to wooing.

c. The child will intermittently stare off into space or at distant objects.

d. The child is preoccupied with inner sensations (or at later ages, with his or her own thoughts or feelings for private pretend play), and/or is withdrawn. For example, at 4 months of age the infant tends to scan the environment but not to focus in on the mother's or father's face and/or voice with intentional affect (e.g., focused smiling); at 8 months of age the infant may play with a block or seem to focus on an object for an inordinate amount of time, excluding his parents' inviting overtures; at 2 years of age, the child may wander about aimlessly; at 3½ years of age, the child may play with building blocks or a special dollhouse, lost in private "thoughts" or fantasy games. Note that none of these characteristics is so pervasive as to constitute an autistic pattern.

Type III: Active/Aggressive Type

1. The infant often has a mixed pattern of sensory over- or underreactivity, motor planning difficulties, and sometimes fine motor lags. Also, this child tends toward poor motor modulation and motor discharge patterns, particularly when frustrated, angry, or vulnerable (e.g., crawling or running into things or people, making loud noises or sounds). He or she seems to be looking at or listening fleetingly to each sound or sight, so that attention and study of any one thing is lacking; the child is unable to attend in an age-expected manner. For example, by 4 months, an infant should be able to attend for 5 or more seconds; by 8 months, for 20 or more seconds; and by 18 months, for a few minutes at a time. By 9 to 12 months, however, this infant seems to be looking at or listening fleetingly to each sound or sight so that attention and study of any one thing is lacking.

2. The child also has at least one of the following characteristics:

a. He or she tends to be overly active.

b. He or she tends to be destructive and/or aggressive. For example, by 9 to 12 months, the child may already be pulling other children's hair deliberately; by 18 months, he or she may be hurting others with biting and kicking, and may break toys and hurt animals.

c. He or she tends to find it difficult to inhibit excitement (i.e., gets carried away) or to shift "states" (e.g., to go to sleep).

Type IV: Mixed Type

1. The child tends to have mixed features of mild to moderate severity of types I through III, with no one set of characteristics predominating. For example, he or she may be fearful but also aggressive. The child must have at least one

physical characteristic from category 1 and one from category 2.

2. The child tends to have some mixed features of types I through III, though one or another may predominate, with at least one significant sensory processing difficulty—auditory-verbal, visual–spatial, and/or perceptual–motor —contributing to the behavioral difficulties. When social withdrawal or aimless idiosyncratic behavior is a significant symptom, it is not so severe as to constitute an autistic pattern, because the child either shows intermittent or ongoing reciprocal social relating or can be socially engaged by a skilled therapist sensitive to both the underlying processing difficulties and their associated emotional patterns. The child must have at least one serious difficulty and one or more somewhat problematic behaviors from category 2 in type I, II, or III.

Sleeping Difficulties[1]

When a sleep disturbance is the only presenting problem in an infant under 1 year of age, the diagnosis of a primary regulatory-based sleep disorder should be considered. These difficulties in going to sleep, or waking and returning to sleep, appear related to general difficulties with self-calming and dealing with transitions, but do not have clearly associated sensory reactivity, sensory processing, and/or motor difficulties. This type of diagnosis should only be used when the problem is not primarily attributable to anxiety, relationship, or mood disturbances; transient adjustment problems; psychic trauma disorder; or other types of regulatory disorders.

Eating Difficulties[2]

When an eating/feeding disturbance, manifested by difficulties establishing regular feeding patterns with adequate or appropriate intake, is the only presenting problem in an infant under 1 year of age, the diagnosis of a primary regulatory-based eating disorder should be considered. This disturbance is part of an overall pattern of poor self-regulation related to difficulties with self-calming and transitions; again, however, this diagnosis only applies when eating difficulties do not have clearly associated sensory reactivity, sensory or processing, and/or motor difficulties.

[1]Formulated in collaboration with Klaus Minde.
[2]Formulated in collaboration with Irene Chatoor.

If the difficulties are accompanied by notable sensorimotor problems, such as tactile hypersensitivity (e.g., the child rejects certain food textures) and/or low oral–motor tone (e.g., the child will only eat soft foods), then the specific regulatory subtypes should be considered instead. If organic/structural problems affect the ability to eat or digest food (e.g., cleft palate, reflux, etc.), this type of diagnosis also does not apply. However, sometimes an eating disturbance may originate in organic or structural difficulties, but continues after these initial difficulties have been resolved, in the presence of ongoing finicky or fussy behavior; in such a case, this type may still apply.

When eating disturbances are part of a larger symptom picture, associated with other affective or behavioral disturbances related to primary relationships, trauma, or other adjustment difficulties, one of the other disorders may be a more appropriate diagnosis. If irregular eating patterns or severely constricted food choices are part of multisystem developmental delays and patterns of rigidity and inability to take in new experiences, as in autism or Pervasive Developmental Disorder, this type does not apply.

THERAPEUTIC APPROACHES FOR REGULATORY DISORDERS

In a sense, the unusual constitutional and maturational variations evidenced by infants and young children with regulatory problems color all of their experience. In contrast to children whose major difficulties emanate from challenges in the interactional or family patterns, regulatory-disordered infants or young children require major efforts to help them overcome their own constitutional and maturational difficulties with self-regulation; however, the focus on fostering better regulatory capacities cannot and should not occur in isolation from the interactive and family patterns. Three brief case illustrations represent this complex interaction and the therapeutic approaches needed.

The Story of Julie: Regulatory Disorder, Hypersensitive Type (Type I)

Julie finally fell asleep at her mother's breast as they both lay on the large mattress on the floor. It was after midnight, and the previous hours had been spent pacing, rocking, and finally nursing Julie to sleep. Julie was 13 months old. Her crib had been abandoned 6 or 7 months earlier, when her mother could no longer bear the persistent crying of her first long-awaited baby. She seemed so helpless, so like a rag doll, so needy, that even the father's anger and dismay could not sway the mother from trying her best to assure her daughter that she could be cared for and would not be abandoned to crying herself to sleep.

Everyone blamed the mother for overprotecting her child. Her pediatrician told her to let the baby cry so that she would learn to go to sleep. The mother's own psychotherapist explored her symbiotic/parasitic needs, fears of separation, or perhaps fears of her daughter's anger if she was not totally there for her. Her husband accused her of rejection as he became more competitive, jealous, and depressed.

Julie was born after a planned, healthy pregnancy and an uneventful delivery. She appeared alert and responsive, quick to look around, and quick to be held so that she felt secure and trusting that someone was always there for her. Although Julie enjoyed being held when dressed, she was sensitive to light touch when stroked and did not like the initial contact with water when bathed, but seemed to adapt. She became vigilant to loud or sudden noises, quickly seeking their source. Frequent feedings and night wakings were routine, and nursing became the way to calm her during early periods of fussy and colicky behavior. Nevertheless, the first 6 months of Julie's life were a pleasure for all. It was not yet apparent that her poor self-regulation of sleeping and eating patterns or her sensitivities or reactivity should be of concern. Her good looking, listening, and vocal responsiveness became the sensory pathways through which she was also able to begin conveying her intentions. Early communication was rich and intense.

At about six months, the family moved to a new house; Julie reacted to a DPT shot; and she started waking more frequently. This continued over the next half year, and worsened whenever she got ill. The parents also noticed that Julie was the last to sit among her peers in the mother's parent group, and was not quite crawling at 10 months. Even at 13 months her sitting was still not stable, and the mother recalled that she was slow to hold her head up. It was not apparent to anyone that this pattern indicated low motor tone and motor planning difficulties. Poor postural security and motor delays, however, delayed the active distancing and approach behaviors, and Julie in fact stayed in her mother's symbiotic orbit longer than usual. This was attributed to the overprotective nature of her relationship with the mother.

But Julie vocalized all the time, began speaking by 8 months, and seemed to understand much of what was said to her, following directions and repeating the words. Although she certainly cried to protest, she would not throw objects lest she lose her balance, and had few ways to express anger safely. Nor did she become attached to any transitional objects, preferring to have her mother at her side day and night. Her separation anxiety actually worsened at 1 year of age when the family housekeeper, whom she knew well, left. After that no one else was acceptable, and her parents stopped going out during the day and in the evenings, since no one else could get her to sleep. Without mobility either early or later, practicing, individuation, and separation were compromised. Instead, Julie used her precocious verbal abilities to keep her mother close. There was no need to guess what she wanted. Tension, however, began to mount between her parents, and Julie became more intense and verbally demanding, especially at any indication of separation.

The mother did not recognize how quick she was to move in on her baby, offering help before Julie needed it and leading her in activities. This was not done in an intrusive or controlling manner, but in a subdued and rather passive fashion with long pauses. She was an anxious parent who was worried about what to do next, lest she make a mistake. A pattern developed wherein Julie also became passive and permitted herself to be controlled by the mother's overtures and gestures, and the mother looked anxious and hesitant and then became overprotective. In this pattern they were highly reciprocal. The father could encourage more assertiveness and activity, putting implicit demands on Julie to respond to him. He tended to retreat, however, in response to his wife's anxiety and began to doubt himself; still, he kept insisting that Julie be allowed to cry at night so that she would finally learn to fall asleep, and yearned for his wife's return.

Thus, when Julie began her second year of life, she was a very bright, verbal child, with strong attachments and relatedness, who appeared happy and responsive to those she knew. However, she was only beginning to stand and walk; her crawling was poor; and she still had difficulty keeping her body upright even for sitting, where she would stretch her legs out far apart and fix her shoulders to stiffen her back, in order to maintain her upright posture. She was also quite sensitive to touch and was hesitant to explore unknown objects or spaces. Julie still could not fall asleep without her mother lying with her and would not be left with anyone.

The parents brought Julie in for an evaluation at 13 months. Observations and parental reports indicated the need for an occupational therapist with expertise in sensory reactivity and processing to examine her poor motor tone, tactile hypersensitivity, and other constitutional variations. Difficulties were indeed confirmed and found to be quite significant, with therapy recommended twice a week. Julie had not been able to establish adequate self-regulation, but did develop a warm and strong attachment in her early months. This attachment became increasingly anxious as she had difficulty with intentional and assertive interactions and with separation. She was able to communicate purposefully and was speaking long before her peers, but it did not help her to negotiate the developmental tasks at hand.

Why wasn't Julie diagnosed earlier? Because Julie partially attained motor milestones (which have considerable range in infancy) and adapted at least to the familiar "hands-on" care of her mother, the impact of low tone and tactile hypersensitivity was not fully recognized, as it might have been in a high-risk child with expectable motor problems. Similarly, since Julie was beginning to get up on her feet, it was not so evident that she did not experience the security of strong posture, which could support more active and assertive behavior. She took steps gingerly and did not run off, eager to climb or push. She asked others to do things for her, becoming more verbally controlling, rather than physically experiencing her shakiness and insecurity. When she did walk, the effort appeared so great that she did not notice things underfoot and would quickly lose her balance and fall. Along with this, she had one parent sending a signal to be careful, and another urging her on but then blaming her for her shortcomings. Thus when she would have ordinarily been dealing with separation and moving out into the world, she was clinging tightly day and night, even though she was individuating on cognitive and symbolic levels.

If separation anxiety were her only diagnosis and Julie's regulatory difficulties were not ad-

dressed, she would not have obtained the treatment she needed to negotiate the next steps of development, and might thus have become a highly anxious child with major personality constrictions. Simultaneously considering Julie's regulatory difficulties, parental issues, and the specific tasks of each stage of development made it possible to guide Julie's development through the specific challenges this combination presented. At first, treatment responded to the presenting problems by (1) focusing on encouraging mastery through interactive play centered on Julie's assertiveness; and (2) focusing on the sleep/separation process and helping the mother see that Julie indeed had the capacities to cope and take charge of her own security at night. More autonomy and assertiveness were also encouraged in day-to-day routines and especially play, making use of Julie's excellent emerging representational capacities. Meanwhile Julie responded well to occupational therapy, which treated the low motor tone, postural insecurities, tactile defensiveness, and motor planning difficulties. The parents also explored the different meanings this problem had for them and tried to support each other, realizing that their relationship was at least as important as that with Julie. As the next steps were anticipated, it was possible to ameliorate and support the ego functions needed to allow Julie the room to keep growing.

By 2½ years of age Julie was an assertive, independent toddler, able to separate and go to sleep on her own, fighting her own turf battles with peers, and enjoying her new physical competence. She was a delightful and happy little girl who was taking in more and more of the world in a self-regulated fashion, finding solutions to difficulties when they arose, and happy with her parents and herself. She appeared to welcome new situations, learned and imitated quickly, and when anxious helped herself by reasoning and thinking. She told others how she felt, using her language and symbolic play capacities to share feelings, to solve problems, and to negotiate her world and relationships.

The Story of Ben: Regulatory Disorder, Active/Aggressive Type (Type III)

Ben's nursery school teacher called his parents again. Ben was continuing to hit and bite, and the other children were frightened of him. He was only calm in the paint corner, where he worked by himself and created wonderful, colorful images he could describe in detail even at age 2. As a first child, his parents perceived him as "just fine" until he started nursery school. This occurred shortly after his sister was born, and perhaps this contributed to his outbursts of aggression. As she became more active, so did he, directing his frustration and anger at her by pushing, knocking her over, and even biting. With his parents Ben could recite all the rules and say what he would do next time, but in reality he was impulsive and appeared unremorseful, making others feel anxious and angry. Lots of "Sorry's" and time outs later, Ben's parents sought help.

When first seen, this cute blond little boy appeared terribly anxious. He was clearly very bright, but also intense and defensive. Ben was curious and asked lots of questions about the toys, trying each out but not organizing any themes. With more support he could elaborate with the doctor kit, cutting off the doll's hurt foot. He then noticed the animals and reported that the zebra was angry and bit because the mother and father hit; he then proceeded to line up all the "biting" animals in one place and the "good" animals in another. Ben could easily elaborate representationally. His characters were always angry, hitting, retaliating, and in trouble unless they could be alone. He was always anxious and could not convey any emotions related to warmth, closeness, or dependency.

More careful observation of Ben over the next few sessions indicated that he would usually respond to questions related to his play, but did not interact spontaneously, missing cues and gestures unless they were verbalized. He would have alligators eating people and missiles exploding everywhere. This would alternate with picking safe little figures, such as the Berenstain Bear family, whom he used to re-enact his real-life situations as he struggled to be good and find safety in a world fraught with danger and trouble.

Ben's conflicts and anxieties seemed obvious. The initial treatment approach focused on parent guidance, especially since the mother was depressed and the father had withdrawn. The parents were encouraged to get down on the floor every day for "floor time" to play—that is, to interact in a way that followed their child's lead, encouraged symbolic representation, provided cues to support self-regulation, and strengthened their interactive relationship (see the detailed description of "floor time" in Greenspan, 1987). Appropriate limits were defined, and individual psychotherapy and teacher consultation were provided. Ben responded quickly as everyone important in his life mobilized to support him and restore his self-esteem. He did especially well in an outdoor summer camp program, where there were few demands and plenty of space and activity. He began to show increased warmth and comfort with closeness and to enjoy life more.

A few months later, when school resumed, severe difficulties began again in Ben's preschool. His new teacher reported hitting, pushing, and flinging behavior that seemed unprovoked and was again frightening his classmates. Ben was again isolated and everyone was anxious. In his play sessions he seemed unusually alarmed by any unexpected movement, and even objected to the therapist's moving a figure without his saying so. Although he could now organize a more complex "good guy, bad guy" scene, he insisted on holding both figures and only one could attack (i.e., his). He was always the bad guy and the victor. Ben struggled to find motives for his figures' actions, but unsuccessfully. If threatened, he would turn red and seem to jump out of his skin, ready to "kill."

Ben's extreme efforts to control everyone in his environment, and the degree of panic he exhibited when anything happened that he did not expect (including his own impulsiveness), made it imperative to re-examine the underlying nature of his difficulties. The explanations used so far were not sufficient, although the problems defined to date contributed significantly to his difficulties: He was anxious, aggressive, and impulsive; his family was distressed, with a depressed mother and a distant and blaming father; and his teacher had already "marked" him as a "bad kid." Because he was so bright and verbal, and promised to be good, rewards and punishments should have gotten him in shape but had not.

Considering Ben's actions more carefully now suggested several possible underlying processing difficulties. His protection from the outside world was overly fragile. Ben showed alarm when anyone came too close unexpectedly, but when he initiated physical contact he was sufficiently comfortable that he could reach out to be cuddled in the early hours of the morning. Even when someone he knew very well made a casual friendly gesture toward him, he would pull back and ask the person not to touch him.

When he played with figures, he had to hold one in each hand and be the only one to move. If he was in the middle of an action and something was said, he appeared not to attend. He was sensitive to sounds around him, easily distracted but slow to orient himself. He had difficulty recognizing "personal space" and would poke, bump, and seek inappropriate contact with other children. He was also small for his age, tended to toe in, and had low motor tone.

His early history was again reviewed, and the mother now reported early regulatory difficulties. Ben had always been a poor sleeper and an erratic eater; as a baby, he had a short fuse and was quick to scream. He hated being picked up or experiencing high or sudden movements; however, he walked early at 10 months after a very brief crawling period. Once he was on his feet, these earlier difficulties were less apparent and seemed to be set aside. Further observations (e.g., the difficulty he had manipulating two toy figures in different hands at the same time) confirmed moderate to severe delays in Ben's visual system, resulting in tremendous stress, since Ben received conflicting messages from his two eyes. He could not use vision efficiently to direct his movements or to interpret other people's actions correctly. Difficulties with motor planning, perceptual–motor coordination, and laterality resulted. Reduced motor tone and tactile defensiveness completed this regulatory disorder.

Ben began an intensive therapy program of vision therapy, occupational therapy, and perceptual–motor therapy, in addition to psychotherapy and parent guidance. It was clear that Ben needed to learn how to anticipate and practice in areas where his regulatory system was challenged. Problem-solving discussions (Greenspan, 1987) between parents and child were begun to anticipate what would happen the next day at school, focusing on the feelings he would have and the behaviors he would exhibit in response to these feelings. Helping Ben figure out what to expect reduced his sense of surprise and shock, and prepared him for even uncomfortable situations. Psychotherapy also helped Ben experience empathy for his difficulty and get a sense of his assumptions about life, especially how he wanted everything done his way but at the same time was frightened of others' competing or being angry with him.

Within several months Ben appeared more organized, oriented and focused. He was quick to develop relationships with his additional new therapists (developmental optometrist, occupa-

tional therapist, and perceptual–motor therapist) and worked quite hard. He became happier, and not only did better with his sister but made his first friends. In psychotherapy he continued to struggle with whether he was good or bad, frequently and suddenly changing roles within minutes of each other. When his fears and wishes for power were interpreted, he seemed relieved but also very sad, because he also wanted friends. As psychotherapy continued to address his confusion and self-doubt regarding his ability to stay in control, it became apparent that Ben wanted to kill off all the other "good guys" in order to have a second chance to become a "good guy" himself.

The Story of Mark: Regulatory Disorder, Underreactive Type (Type II)

Mark was an easy, undemanding baby who would smile and respond if approached quietly, but did not initiate or seek much contact. In a busy household with tense working parents and a very demanding 3-year-old sister, it was not readily apparent how underreactive he was. At 18 months he brightened when his parents sang nursery rhymes, danced, and moved with him, but left on his own he would watch his little cars moving back and forth, spin little objects, and often rub a little toy back and forth across his belly. He was also very sensitive to sounds, reacting with alarm to sirens and unexpected noises, and had everyone speaking to him in a near-whisper. Yet, when he could be engaged, he was related and warm and clearly a bright child. Thus, although he responded to wooing and would reach out when he wanted something specific, he tended to tune out and overfocus on his own little activities, conveying a sense of fragility and constant apprehension as to how the world would impinge on him.

As Mark's second year of life progressed, he appeared to understand what was said when he was listening, but his listening was inconsistent. Noisy and crowded restaurants or shopping malls were distressing, but he sought out vibrating noises. He continued to enjoy swinging, running, chase games, and jumping; these activities made him smile and laugh with pleasure. His motor planning was more uncertain, but he would persist in climbing and getting in and out of small places. Mark had always tended to scan his environment and then overfocus on something small in front of him. Further examination indicated that his eyes did not converge very well, and as a result of developmental immaturities he employed fragmented visual skills such as fixation, locking in, and tuning out. Activities were started to encourage him to track and use vision to guide his movements.

At 2 years of age, Mark continued to be withdrawn and unfocused. Sensitive and persistent wooing would engage him briefly, but then he would retreat into simple repetitive behaviors with his toys, which kept the world away. Pleasure was only evident when strong sensorimotor actions gave him a clearer sense of where his body was in space and allowed him to organize and become aware of his experience. His language and symbolic gestures remained very simple, but Mark started to speak and carry out symbolic acts with dolls. His overall affective quality was still very guarded and subdued. Being with him always meant asking, "Will he respond or not?" Anything appeared to overwhelm him as his anxiety interacted with the anxiety of those around him. This little boy lived in a field of tension and fear, selecting bits and pieces of experience he could tolerate.

Living with Mark required exquisite sensitivity to his regulatory difficulties to engage and help him from being overwhelmed. His good cognition and receptive language enabled his parents to anticipate and practice the activities that would be difficult for him. Trial runs in new or challenging situations were helpful. The noise and the likelihood of being touched in his nursery school classroom kept him at the edges of the room, but he could still learn from a distance when not pressured. Having him play with one child exposed him, in the safety of his own house with his mother present, to situations where he might bump shoulders, deal with aggression, and hear loud noises.

Being empathic was especially difficult, because it was not always clear whether he understood, and when he did respond it was often through rejection. Mark did respond to empathy expressed through facial expressions and gestures, which picked up the child's mood states and conveyed an expectable understanding of them. He especially responded to sources of anxiety (toys breaking, dolls getting hurt or falling, things getting lost or messy, etc.). Mark could engage in conversations centering around these issues, as well as vocally object to any interference with the rituals he established to stay safe, such as leaving the door open "just a crack."

Mark continued to constrict his world, preferring *Sesame Street* figures to people. He was like a "fearful dictator" who wanted everything done his way, but at the same time he was frightened and did not want others to compete with or get angry at him. Setting limits on some of his behavior helped create a sense of security—that his environment could not be totally manipulated or intimidated by him, but also that he would not be at the mercy of everything affecting him.

Mark progressed slowly, showing increased adaptation at nursery school and at home. He also received speech and occupational therapy, and attended a speech and language preschool program. His parents included him in all family activities, going many places and arranging many play dates; still, he could not interact readily with other children, preferring the stereotyped world of *Sesame Street* characters who lent him affect and predictability. Parent–child therapy essentially supported more direct and consistent interaction—gently requiring Mark to respond, and challenging him to deal with his anxieties and experiment with aggression. He began with just tentatively throwing a puppet behind the couch and rushing to retrieve it, but eventually progressed to throwing it with great delight, knowing he was in charge. He also started to express complex feelings, particularly his anger and distress. He became able to verbalize such abstract feelings as "A terrible thing happened. My grandparents went back to New York," or "I wish I could have it, but I know I can't have it." Once he could express himself and determine what was negotiable and what wasn't, he became happier and more energetic. New symbolic doors began to open as he felt more secure and could begin to be representational; he was no longer as anxious and defensive.

General Therapeutic Principles for Regulatory Disorders

The foregoing cases suggest a number of therapeutic principles, including the following:

1. Strengthen the sensory, sensorimotor, or processing vulnerabilities.
2. Work with the way in which the maturational variables influence stage-specific affects, behaviors, and interaction.
3. Help parents correct distortions and projections that are in part based on the child's maturational challenges.

4. Facilitate stage-specific, individual-difference-oriented caregiver–child interaction patterns.

5. Foster higher developmental levels.

6. Foster, as the child becomes representational, understanding of his or her maturational patterns through pretend play and discussions (e.g., "Loud noises make me feel like jumping out of my skin").

7. Foster flexible coping strategies for new challenges.

CONCLUSION

The new diagnostic concept of regulatory disorders provides a way to assess the individual differences in each child and suggests how these differences may underlie problems in adaptation and learning. This perspective enhances understanding of the other factors influencing the child's life, such as the environment and family dynamics. It also points to the specific intervention approaches needed to support healthier adaptation and development (see Greenspan, 1992). As can be seen in all three of the cases described above, children with regulatory disorders may seem so overwhelmed, helpless, and unhappy most of the time that clinicians, educators, and parents are at a loss as to how to help them. These children require many tiny steps, one toe in the water at a time—whether the problems involve sleeping or eating, joining in group time, learning to be more assertive, having fewer tantrums, improving focus and concentration, or learning to use words rather than behaviors. Parents, educators, and clinicians need to develop a hierarchy of manageable steps for each child. The critical challenge for children with regulatory disorders is to overcome their sense of standing still or even moving backwards, and to help them get some forward momentum so that they can feel a sense of mastery. It doesn't make a difference how small the steps are, as long as they can move forward.

REFERENCES

DeGangi, G. A., DiPietro, J. A., Greenspan, S. I., & Porges, S. W. (1991). Psychophysiological characteristics of the regulatory disordered infant. *Infant Behavior and Development, 14*, 37–50.

DeGangi, G. A., Porges, S. W., & Greenspan, S. I. (in press). The longitudinal outcomes of regulatory disordered infants. *Infant Behavior and Development.*

Doussard-Roosevelt, J. A., Walker, P. S., Portales, A. J., Greenspan, S. I., & Porges, S. W. (1990). Vagal tone and the fussy infant: Atypical vagal reactivity in the difficult infant. *Infant Behavior and Development, 13,* 352. (Abstract)

Escalona, S. (1968). *The roots of individuality.* Chicago: Aldine.

Greenspan, S. I. (1987). *The essential partnership.* New York: Viking.

Greenspan, S. I. (1989). *The development of the ego.* Madison, CT: International Universities Press.

Greenspan, S. I. (1992). *Infancy and early childhood: The practice of clinical assessment and intervention with emotional and developmental challenges.* Madison, CT: International Universities Press.

Zero to Three National Center for Clinical Infant Programs. (1993). *Diagnostic classification study manual.* Arlington, VA: Author.

19

Post-Traumatic Stress Disorder

MARTIN J. DRELL
CLIFFORD H. SIEGEL
THEODORE J. GAENSBAUER

The idea that Post-Traumatic Stress Disorder (PTSD) occurs in infants and toddlers is a relatively new concept. We are unaware of any previous literature reviews on this subject. In this chapter, we assert that the disorder occurs in infants and toddlers; that it can be identified reliably with some modifications in existing criteria; and that it can be treated, although no data about treatment efficacy are yet available. We believe that identification will contribute to improved care of infants and toddlers who experience traumatic events.

In order to explore the concept of PTSD in infants and toddlers, we briefly review the history of PTSD in children, and describe links between the existing literature on PTSD with major focuses on developmental considerations and the caregiving environment. We illustrate the problem with two case vignettes and then explore issues of assessment and treatment, as well as questions for future research.

HISTORICAL OVERVIEW

PTSD, under this specific name, first appeared as a diagnosis in the *Diagnostic and Statistical Manual of Mental Disorders*, third edition (DSM-III; American Psychiatric Association, 1980). In this form, it represented "a syndrome with unique constellations of symptoms and a course characterized by biphasic clusters of re-experi-

encing and avoidant symptoms and a variety of miscellaneous symptoms, including arousal" (Schwarz & Kowalski, 1991, p. 592). DSM-III made no specific mention of children, a deficiency that was modified in DSM-III-R (American Psychiatric Association, 1987). This revision "expanded the definition of the concept of stressor and altered and rearranged symptoms in all clusters. Major modifications expanded the ranges of items in the re-experiencing and avoidance clusters, required an increase in the number of avoidant symptoms from one to three . . . and included items to represent PTSD in children" (Schwarz & Kowalski, 1991, p. 592).

The idea that extreme life stressors may cause psychological problems is certainly not a new concept. Its modern origins date back to the 19th century. Trimble (1985) points out that the horrors of the U.S. Civil War, as well as the development of workers' compensation, focused interest on the impact of trauma. From the start, there were debates concerning organic versus "functional" etiologies of trauma-related syndromes. These etiological debates can be traced throughout the history of this disorder and continue to the present (van der Kolk, 1988; Kolb, 1987; Giller, 1990), with an upsurge in studies following each major war and traumatic events.

As would be expected, World War I brought a resurgence of interest; it introduced the terms "shell shock" and "traumatic neurosis." The former term, coined by Mott (1919), referred to a syndrome caused by microstructural lesions in the central nervous system. The latter term was influenced heavily by Freudian theory, which was gaining prominence at the time. Freud proposed that events are traumatic if the ego is overwhelmed, and he introduced the idea that ego defenses are brought into play to help cope with and master traumatic stimuli. In *Moses and Monotheism*, Freud (1939/1964) elaborated a theory that included "positive effects" of trauma, which tend to repeat the trauma, and "negative effects," which tend to defensively avoid the trauma. He felt that both of these effects are part of a traumatic fixation.

After World War I, there was a substantial growth of interest in child and adolescent mental health issues. Several of the early pioneers in child mental health, such as Levy (1945), Spitz (1946), and Bowlby (1969, 1973, 1980), looked specifically at the impact of traumatic environments on children and laid the foundations for later work in this area. World War II brought with it more studies of traumatized children. Anna Freud and her colleagues studied various groups of children affected by the war (Freud & Burlingham, 1943; Freud & Dann, 1951). They concluded that the reactions of these children were largely a function of the reactions of their caretakers.

Beginning in the 1950s, there were increasing numbers of studies on children's reactions to natural disasters and other stressful events. Gradually increasing methodological sophistication in these studies included direct observations, the use of multiple informants, standardized interviewing formats, longitudinal designs, control groups, increased numbers of data points, and epidemiological studies of normals.

In 1976, Lenore Terr began what was to become a nodal study. In the "Chowchilla study," she followed 26 school-age (ages 5–14 years) children who were kidnapped from their school bus by three armed men. The kidnappers drove the children for 11 hours in vans with blackened windows before placing them in a buried truck trailer. After 16–17 hours underground, the children managed to escape. All of the children developed PTSD symptoms. This prospective study with controls demonstrated, according to Terr, that regardless of the contributions "of the child's prior developmental, psychiatric, and medical history, his or her parental relationships, the relationships of his or her parents to the community, his or her past psychic trauma, and/

or stressful events inside the family, the child would suffer from psychic trauma if the traumatic event was extreme enough and was directly experienced" (Terr, 1991, p. 756). The study highlighted not only the incidence of psychic trauma (100%) in the Chowchilla group, but the high prevalence of psychic trauma in the "normal" control group (40%).

Numerous studies recounting the impact of various traumatic events on children followed this seminal study. These have been reviewed and summarized by Pynoos (1990). He categorized the extreme stressors that have been associated with PTSD in children as follows: (1) kidnapping and hostage situations (e.g., Terr, 1981); (2) exposure to violence, including terrorism, gang violence, sniper attacks, and war atrocities (e.g., Eth & Pynoos, 1985); (3) witnessing rape, murder, and suicidal behavior (e.g., Frederick, 1985); (4) sexual or physical abuse (e.g., Deblinger, McLeer, Atkins, Ralphe, & Foa, 1989); (5) severe accidental injury, including burns and hit-and-run accidents (e.g., Stoddard, Normal, & Murphy, 1989); (6) life-threatening illnesses and life-endangering medical procedures (e.g., Nir, 1985); (7) train, airplane, ship, and automobile accidents (e.g., Martini, Ryan, Nakayama, & Ramenofsky, 1990); and (8) major natural disasters (e.g., Galante & Foa, 1986).

At this point, much is known about the symptoms that children over 3 years of age suffer following a traumatic event. Pynoos (1990) proposed criteria for PTSD in children; these include experiencing an event that would be distressing for almost anyone, re-experiencing the trauma in various ways, psychological numbing/avoidance, and increased arousal. These symptoms are similar in enough respects to those of adults to allow for the use of the same criteria with only modest modifications. Still, much is left unknown concerning the response of children under 3 years of age to traumatic events.

DEVELOPMENTAL CONSIDERATIONS

Extraordinarily rapid and complex changes in development during the first 3 years of life suggest that traumatic effects may have particularly far-reaching effects through their influence on basic developmental processes. In addition, we may expect differences not only in the experience of and reaction to trauma between infants and older children and adults, but also across the course of infancy.

Given that some of the symptoms of PTSD require sophisticated perceptual and cognitive abilities (e.g., avoidance of thoughts associated with the trauma, distressing recollections of the event), one may ask whether infants are capable of having PTSD. We believe that infants may have both a narrower and a broader range of reactions to trauma than do older children and adults. That infants can have enduring, disruptive reactions to traumatic events seems unequivocal; a more pressing question is which events become traumatic. Developmental processes of perception, memory, cognition, and emotions are crucial in determining the answer.

In considering which events will be traumatic for infants, the requirement of DSM-III-R that the traumatic event be "outside the range of normal human experience" and "distressing to almost anyone" (American Psychiatric Association, 1987, p. 247) requires modification. For instance, a 10-month-old infant developed a long-lasting avoidance of the outdoors following being in the front lawn when a lawn mower was started nearby. Although "usual" experiences may traumatize some infants, this should not imply that infants are generally more easily traumatized by negative or startling experiences. Negative emotional experience itself can actually aid in the development of self-regulation of self-knowledge (Kopp, 1989), and novelty itself can produce negative reactions without any discernible lasting effects (Lamb, Morrison, & Malkin, 1987). Whether any experience will be so overwhelming as to be traumatic depends in part on the nature of the experience itself (physical intensity, intensity of presentation in other realms, suddenness) (Kopp, 1989), as well as on the nature of the receiver of the experience (threshold for various stimuli, state of alertness, capacities for defense and adaptation). A working definition of PTSD in infancy might be "a lasting dysfunction in intra- or interpersonal life that follows from and is related to overwhelming experience(s)," without further specifying the nature of this experience.

Whether and which symptoms will develop is necessarily related to the capacities of infants for perceiving and "remembering" experience. Since newborns have visual acuity on the order of 20/200, and since they progress to visual acuity of 20/20 by 12 months, infants during most of their first year are quite capable of discerning many visual particulars around them. In the auditory sphere, infants show not only the ability to distinguish particular voices early on, but also the ability to distinguish particular phonemes of speech (Haith, 1990). Emotional distinctions may be limited to general positive or negative valences in the early stages of reciprocity with caregivers, but by the second half of the first year, fear and anger are distinguishable from general distress (Campos, Barrett, Lamb, Goldsmith, & Stenberg, 1983). Although much research on infant perception hinges on demonstration of infant preferences and reactions, it seems apparent that infants are in fact not just choosing and reacting, but actively organizing their experiences (Campos et al., 1983).

These capacities probably contribute to infants' abilities to remember. Infants' limited declarative abilities can only hint at what they recall (Mandler, 1983). During the first 18 months, infants are generalizing experiences to some extent (Nelson, 1986; Mandler, 1983), although the sensorimotor nature of their mental life and of their enactive representations suggest that early representations will be quite "real"— that is, based on raw perceptions and emotional experiences, without the benefit of or interference from greater reasoning ability or more "symbolic" representation. Event sequencing is a difficult memory task for very young children (Price & Goodman, 1990; Nelson & Gruendel, 1986), but memory of important or "nodal" events, often defined by the contingent actions involved and/or by their salience to the individual, is apparent in infancy (Price & Goodman, 1990; Younger & Cohen, 1986; Slackman, Hudson, & Fivush, 1986). The memory for the relations between perceptual experiences can include surprising degrees of subtle distinction by the end of the first year (Younger, 1990). Even though children's memory and perceptual skills become more complex with age, the capacity for perceiving and remembering events, including traumatic ones, clearly exists from the earliest months of life.

The first stage of a traumatic event that causes a disorder is the perception of the event or a series of events. The state of alertness of the infant during such occurrence(s) is important, just as it is for older children. In a family recently involved in an auto accident, the children who were asleep at the onset of the accident had less of a traumatic reaction than those who were awake. However, the state of alertness is an important factor throughout the occurrence of a traumatic episode, not just at its onset, as being jolted out of an unalert state may add to the suddenness and intensity and contribute to the subsequent overwhelming nature of an experience for the infant. There will also be individual differences in the threshold for various perceptual stimuli (Greenspan, 1987). Infants with unusually high sensitivity to intrusions in their auditory, visual, tactile, or emotional perceptions, without the cognitive ability to understand this sensitivity and to modulate the reception, will be at greater risk for being overwhelmed by particular experiences. The role of such internal thresholds or "stimulus barriers" has been long noted for infants (Freud, 1920/1950), as has the role of the parent or caregiver in providing an external stimulus barrier.

Research further indicates that the amount of distress experienced by young children may depend more upon the meaning to the child of the caretaker's affect than on the intensity of the affect per se (Eisenberg et al., 1988). As such, the traumatic nature of an event for an infant may be colored by intense excitement or a sudden burst of positive emotion on the part of the caregiver.

Infants also need help from others in maintaining their physiological regulation. Less internal control of physiological excitation in infancy adds to the potential for perceptual experience to "feel" overwhelming. Infants in adequate caretaking environments will more rapidly develop internal physiological regulation (Greenspan, 1987; Sander, 1975). Nevertheless, given that such regulation matures only gradually (Emde, Gaensbauer, & Harmon, 1976), infants may be more vulnerable as a group than older children to such physiological stresses.

Overwhelming events can also lead to distortions in the coding of the event. This observation has been made in the study of multiple perceptual realms in traumatized children (Terr, 1990). Admittedly, these distortions may involve representational abilities beyond those of an infant (such as those involved in substituting one person for another or changing time relations that depend upon some organized sense of time), but it is not unlikely that overwhelming experience in infancy may lead to "distortions" in the associations between the perceptions that infants do form. The nature of these distortions will shift with the capacity for various defensive processes within the child. How

much we can know about the actual internal coding of any experience is further confounded by the probable gap between what is shown to us by the child (verbally or otherwise) and what is actually internal (Nelson, 1986).

The management of perceptual input is biological as well as cognitive–emotional. Some forms of overstimulation are so terrible as to be damaging to developing neurons, raising the question of whether emotional trauma may damage neurons in the limbic system (Kolb, 1988).

The external management of such input, including after it has occurred, returns us again to the infant's environment. Soothing can help the infant's physiological regulation. Immediately supplanting possible traumatic events with positive experiences attuned to the infant's ability to accept new stimulation may de-emphasize the centrality of the possible trauma; not avoiding the infant's or toddler's evoked or initiated associations via affect or action to an overwhelming experience may communicate that the reactions are manageable. By the second year, talking to the infant about the experience may be an important indication of this acceptance, especially since infants' understanding of language precedes their expressive abilities. Toddlers more specifically seek out external help from caregivers in regard to aversive stimuli than do infants (Kopp, 1989), so that parental interactions with infants may mediate between traumatic events and outcomes for infants. In some cases (including Case 2, below), the parents' own traumatic response to the trauma endured by their child creates a complicated transaction or "PTSD à deux" that may maintain or contribute to dysfunctions in both parties.

Having delineated some of the possible attributes of intake and management of potentially traumatic experience, we now propose some hypotheses about sequelae. Dysfunctional outcomes are potentially quite broad. If an association is formed for the infant between attention to external stimuli and overwhelming results, than a generalized withdrawal may occur (Fraiberg, 1982), including an avoidance of feeding, of exploration, and of interpersonal interaction. General dysfunctions may include physiological ones, such as the lack of brainstem habituation to auditory stimuli observed in sexually abused children (Ornitz & Pynoos, 1989), and may lead to an overreactivity to multiple perceptions (with or without a parallel withdrawal). To the extent that emotions are not only reactions but organizers of experience (Mandler, 1983; Campos, Campos, & Barrett, 1989), the enduring upset from overwhelming experience may inculcate ongoing physiological changes in hormonal, autonomic, or even immunological functions. An enduring negative emotional tone may take the form of ongoing irritability (Fraiberg, 1982), or may organize a very different (probably more distant) interpersonal field for the infant (Campos et al., 1989), which then may have further negative sequelae of its own. Any or all of these outcomes may limit the infant's ability to continue organizing and regulating experience, leading to more general dysregulation in the child (Rieder & Cicchetti, 1989).

The dysfunctional outcomes mentioned thus far are all similar in that they depend on the recurrence of some perception "reminiscent" of trauma(s), even if that perception is a frequent part of everyday life. Although children are known to evoke memories of and reactions to trauma without any reminders (Terr, 1990), it is unlikely that this will occur during the first 15–18 months, when infants are still operating with "recognition memory" (Fraiberg, 1969). Nevertheless, such evocative memories will operate in dreams, fantasy play, and behavior in slightly older children.

The discussion of possible dysfunctional outcomes or disorders may now be summarized in the form of those symptoms proposed to be the concrete manifestations of dysfunction during different periods of infant development:

Age 0–6 months: Hypervigilance; exaggerated startle; various forms of dysregulation; irritability; and/or withdrawal in generalized form or in response to specific perceptions or states.

Age 6–12 months: Any of the preceding and/or markedly increased anxiety in strange situations; more specific angry reactions in particular situations; more active attempts to avoid (given increased mobility) specific situations; developmental regressions; sleep disorders in the form of night terrors or other Stage 4 phenomena.

Age 12–18 months: Any of the preceding and/or unusual proximity to or "clinginess" with caregivers; relative avoidance of particular affects or situations that might evoke such affects; language focus via over- or underusage of words associated with the trauma.

Age 18–24 months: Any of the preceding and/or preoccupations with symbols of the traumatic event(s); nightmares; more enlarged verbal preoccupations.

Age 24–36 months: Any of the preceding and/or symptoms as in older children (as specified in DSM-III-R).

This tentative list of symptoms indicates that infants "grow into" those dysfunctions common to older children and adults, but also that earlier forms are not necessarily abandoned with age, given the additive nature of our delineation. This is consistent with views of development suggesting that new and more complex capacities do not replace those that came previously, but are added to them, leaving "older" forms of functioning still available in the repertoire of the individual and/or relationship (Stern, 1985).

Just as with other processes of early development, where the outcomes of PTSD begin and where they end are less distinct in infancy. The importance of early life for long-lasting personality functioning suggests that outcomes such as those described above may have far-reaching consequences above and beyond pure "symptoms" of a particular disorder. The possible permutations of the fabric of personality are too numerous to permit an exhaustive discussion, but a few possible examples are in order. Given the prominent role of activity of the infant in learning in all spheres (Haith, 1990; Harris, 1983), infants who become generally or specifically withdrawn will have limitations placed on the amount and complexity of information they can obtain; this in turn will lead to rigidities in cognitive style, fewer mastery experiences, and probably a more negative self-concept. Infants who are hypervigilant will have less energy for many developmental processes, including "emotional" learning, and may form a hypercathexis to reality (Khan, 1945) that obviates the development of richer forms of internal life, including more complex representational maps of self, other, and relationships. If self-distraction or irritability and anger are prominent symptoms, there may be significant shifts in the attachment relationship, which in turn has been shown to be related to future peer relationships (Sroufe, 1983) and future self-concept (Main, Kaplan, & Cassidy, 1985; Pipp & Easterbrooks, 1992) or general mental health (Bowlby, 1988). Lastly, the need to avoid certain affects in oneself or the environment may lead to the development of a "false self," from which will ensue other significant personality disruptions (Khan, 1945; Winnicott, 1958, Winnicott, 1965).

CASE ILLUSTRATIONS

In order to illustrate the clinical phenomenology of PTSD symptoms in children under 3 years of age, we present two case illustrations.

Case 1

Beth, aged 22 months, had been involved in an auto accident approximately 13 months prior to evaluation. At 9 months of age, she was in an infant seat in the back of a car driven by her grandmother, with her mother in the front passenger seat. A large truck hit their car as two lanes converged, causing their car to roll over completely and then to crash down a river embankment 20 feet below. The car landed on its front end in the dry river bed, then fell right side up. Miraculously, none of the passengers were seriously injured.

Beth received a number of bruises on her head and body, and was quite emotionally distraught. She screamed and was able to be calmed only when her mother nursed her. At the hospital where all of the women were taken, she screamed for 2 hours straight. Her mother received a fractured wrist, as well as numerous contusions. Beth's grandmother was the most seriously injured, with significant back pain and marked bruising of her extremities.

Following the accident, Beth experienced a number of significant symptoms. She was not able to sleep through the night, and her mother had to go into her room between two and eight times a night to console her. Nightmares in which she woke up screaming occurred once or twice a week initially, though these diminished in frequency over the period of 13 months prior to the first meeting with the examiner. There was also a significant change in her personality from happy and outgoing to clingy, whiny, and insecure. Over time, this fussiness diminished and was replaced by a subdued, serious demeanor, which continued to the time of the evaluation. Also, there were specific symptoms of anxiety when she was exposed to situations that reminded her of the accident. In particular, she was very frightened of going in the car and appeared frightened of another accident occurring. She would, for example, scream whenever she saw a truck nearby, warning her mother, "Truck, Mommy, truck!" She refused to sit in the back seat of the car, where she had been sitting at the time of the accident.

There had been significant effects on her physical health as well. Since the accident, she had required hospitalization on two occasions for dehydration following what appeared to be a viral illness with marked vomiting. She demonstrated a marked fear of doctors; her mother recalled that during one hospitalization, the medical team attempted to separate Beth from her mother in order to conduct an examination, and Beth screamed so intensely that this was impossible. The most alarming symptom was the apparent impact of the stress on her appetite and physical growth. Prior to the accident, she had been growing at a healthy rate and was in the 75th percentile for height and weight. Following the accident, she lost 1 pound and then remained at the same weight for the next 9 months. She lost her appetite, refused to eat, and would remain in her high chair for only a brief period of time before becoming restless and wanting to get down. Between the age of 18 months and the time of evaluation, she had gained 3 pounds, but she was still below the 3rd percentile in weight. Her head circumference had remained in the 50th percentile, consistent with the diagnosis of nonorganic failure to thrive.

During the first evaluative session with Beth, she was very subdued and somewhat fearful of the examiner, though she was comfortable coming into the playroom with her mother. Most remarkable was the specificity of her memory of the accident. Using some small dolls to represent Beth, her mother, and her grandmother in a play automobile, plus a toy truck and a couple of flat pieces of plastic to represent the river bed, the examiner laid the car and truck out in the positions alongside the "river" as they existed prior to the accident. He then asked Beth to show what happened. She proceeded to carry out an almost exact demonstration of what had occurred. Her mother was stunned by the accuracy of the portrayal. Beth did not show a great deal of affect during this session, maintaining a state of what appeared to be subdued detachment. She was quite attentive to the play during periods when the examiner demonstrated some phase of the accident, and then moved away to explore other toys, moving back and forth as her tolerance permitted. She needed frequent visual contact with her mother for reassurance, but showed no evidence of active distress.

The degree to which Beth was struggling with PTSD symptoms was perhaps best indicated by the marked recrudescence of symptoms that followed this relatively brief recreation of the accident. On the evening after the session, she woke up twice screaming and wanted to go to her mother's bed. She woke up four times the next night and awakened at least once per night for the next three weeks leading up to the second session. This was in marked contrast to the relative absence of nightmares immediately prior to the first session. Her awakening at night seemed clearly connected to nightmares of being injured, in that she repeated the word "owies" to her mother—a clear reference to the injuries that she, her mother, and her grandmother had experienced from the accident. She did not eat dinner that night and did not eat normally for the next 3 days. She was also somewhat more withdrawn than usual.

Interestingly, after approximately a week (according to her mother), there appeared to be a rebound effect in that Beth showed evidence of being much more aggressive than usual. For example, she struck her mother, something she had never done previously. Another indication of her remarkable memory for the accident was evidenced by the fact that 4 days following this first session, when she and her mother were driving down the same street past the area where the accident had occurred, she called out to her mother, "Car in there." When her mother stated that there was not a car in the river, Beth became quite angry. In retrospect, her mother realized that Beth had been referring to the accident. In the second evaluative session, Beth returned to the play materials used in the first session and spontaneously carried out a number of play actions related to the accident. These included a recreation of the accident itself; the ambulance trip to the hospital; and medical treatment of her grandmother and mother, involving putting Band-Aids on the exact locations of the injuries they had sustained.

Beth's symptomatology and play were consistent with classic PTSD in a number of respects. Memories of the traumatic event were clearly intruding upon her consciousness, both in situations which reminded her of the accident. Intrusive thoughts and memories were reflected in her need to spontaneously re-enact the situation in the play session, as well as in specific nightmares about "owies." There was also evidence of attempts to avoid situations that reminded her of the accident, such as refusing to sit in the back seat of the car, and even fearfulness of getting in a car. She also showed evidence of what would be described as psychic "numbing." Her subdued, withdrawn personality style, which was quite different from her preaccident outgoing nature, appeared to reflect this defensive numbing, as well as a considerable degree of depressive affect. She showed a number of other more general symptoms commonly seen in PTSD, including marked separation anxiety and clinginess, markedly increased fearfulness, difficulty sleeping, regressed behavior with difficulties in modulation of anger, and a very severe eating disturbance. The degree of trauma was thus reflected not only in psychological effects, but by a loss of appetite that severely impaired her ability to gain weight. In observing Beth, particularly in the second session, the examiner had a strong sense of a fearful tension that encompassed her entire body at certain moments during the session. Further evidence for the specificity of her PTSD symptoms was the marked recrudescence of all her symptoms following the initial session in which memories of the accident were evoked—symptoms that duplicated responses seen in the immediate postaccident period.

Case 2

Molly was 21 months old when she was playing in the backyard and was bitten by a neighbor's dog. Her mother painfully related how the subsequent experience at the hospital was as traumatic as the dog bite and resultant eye injury. Molly was frightened and uncooperative in the emergency room. Delays occurred because of problems with anesthesia and the wait for a plastic surgeon. The entire process took an exhausting 5 hours.

The mother reported being consumed by guilt over her failure to protect her child. She remembered the scene frequently in what she called "walking nightmares." She reported becoming more protective and trying to keep busy to avoid thinking of the incident. The mother missed work for a week in order to tend to her child after the dog bite. It was a difficult time for Molly, as she did not like the patch she had to wear over her eye. The doctor's appointment to remove the stitches proved another trauma for Molly and her mother. Since Molly refused to stay still and her mother was unable to hold her, general anesthesia was used. The mother felt further guilt about her failure to calm her daughter.

Shortly after this episode, Molly saw the offending dog in the neighbor's front yard. Molly became terrified and clingy for hours. As she clung she repeated over and over, "Bad dog, bad dog. Got me. My eye."

There were no major difficulties for the next 2 months, even though Molly saw the dog on occasion. However, there was a slow tendency for Molly to overgeneralize and see all dogs, and then all animals, as bad. This upset the mother, who loved and owned dogs and considered them among her "best friends."

Approximately 2 months after the dog bite, Molly (now aged 23 months) began to have nightmares about every 5 days. During the nightmares, she would hold her eye and scream, "Mamma, Mamma, bad dog got me." These cries were associated with thrashing behavior. After each episode, Molly would calm and restlessly go back to sleep for the remainder of the night. Having never asked her daughter, the mother was unable to say whether Molly remembered the nightmares when she woke up. These nightmares lasted 6 weeks.

Approximately 14 weeks after the dog bite, the mother called the therapist. When asked why she had selected this time to seek help, the mother stated that the "final straw" had come a week before when her daughter screamed for her mother at bedtime, held her pillow tightly over her head, and repeated over and over, "Big dog got me." The mother could think of no precipitant to the episode, which lasted 3 hours, except for a dog barking faintly in the distance. The mother reported feeling overwhelmed.

The mother emphasized how close she and her daughter were. She stated that people were always saying that they were "too enmeshed." To such comments, the mother would respond, "She's everything to me. She's all I have except two dogs." More specific questioning concerning issues of attachment elicited the fact that the mother had been overprotective since early infancy and that this may have been contributed to by some difficulties during the pregnancy. Mother related that there had been very few "strangers" and only one babysitter throughout Molly's life. She described other members of her family as unsupportive, even though they lived close by.

The mother's relationship with her husband had deteriorated almost from Molly's birth. The mother disliked the father's lack of participation in the family and the fact that he could not tolerate Molly's crying and normal oppositional behavior. The mother had initiated a marital separation 4 months prior to the dog bite incident. The father had reluctantly left, and at the time of the evaluation was actively trying to reconcile with his wife. She vowed at the time of the psychiatric evaluation to get a divorce and wondered why she was delaying initiation of this process. The mother refused to have the father involved in the evaluation.

Molly was a bright-eyed yet subdued child who had only a slight problem separating from her mother for the initial play interview. She walked slowly to the therapist's office and methodically acquainted herself with the office toys. She was attracted to all the toy dogs in the room, and especially to a very toothy dinosaur doll. After lengthy explorations, she settled on playing with a "doggie" doll, although any attempts to carry out a theme in play with the dog failed. She appeared to want to play with the dog, but was unable to do so. The longest sequence involved her repeatedly trying to find a place for the dog in each room of the dollhouse, which she had converted into a doghouse. When the therapist asked about the dogs, Molly turned to play with something else and then later returned to playing with the dog. After a question concerning the dog that bit her, Molly said, "Bad doggie didn't bite," and returned to her efforts to figure out which room the doggie went into.

Molly's simultaneous fascination with and reluctance to play with toy dogs continued throughout the sessions. In fact, she had extreme difficulty continuing and finishing any play sequence. The mother reported that this was similar to her behavior at home.

Extraneous noises scared Molly. When these occurred, she would run to get her mother and would refuse to continue the session without her mother's being in the room. With the mother present, Molly would share with her some of the events of the therapy. These events included her fascination with a lovable doll named "Fruf" that had a "boo-boo" on his bottom (where the felt was worn thin). Half of the time, however, "boo-boo" seemed to sound more like "poo-poo." She also showed her mom the toothy dinosaur, which was now proclaimed a "good dinosaur." As she showed off the dinosaur, Molly bit it and smiled.

The therapist shared with the mother his tentative formulation. It centered on Molly's difficulties with aggression. The therapist felt that Molly's attempts at dealing with aggression—an inevitable and normal aspect of separation/individuation—had been complicated by the dog bite incident. Molly was portrayed as desperately and unsuccessfully trying to deal with anxieties subsequent to the dog bite through the use of several defensive strategies, such as splitting and displacement. The therapist added that the mother's related difficulties with anger and separation/individuation might complicate her abilities to facilitate her child's development in these areas.

The therapist proposed a flexible treatment format that included a combination of individual sessions with Molly, joint sessions with Molly and her mother, and sessions with the mother alone. Throughout the treatment, the therapist gave developmental guidance to the mother, based specifically on the formulation. They discussed in many sessions and in many ways the mother's and daughter's difficulties dealing with anger. As recommended, the mother purchased a dollhouse and other salient toys to "open up" the issue of feelings in general and the biting incident in particular. Molly became more verbal with everyone, and she was reported to be more loving and more aggressive with the "good" dogs at home.

Nevertheless, Molly's initial improvement was followed by the development of new symptoms. She looked sadder than before, and although her nightmares had resolved, she continued to experience difficulties at bedtime. She also expressed a new fear of the "coo-koo man." These symptoms appeared to be related to Molly's reaction to the loss of her father and to her continuing underlying fears of hurting her mother. Molly's play was full of references to the mother's being hurt and needing to go to the hospital. Molly also often left the playroom and went to check on her mother in the waiting room. In one joint session, she showed the mother a toy dog and then grinned as she threw it to the ground. The therapist interpreted this as Molly's trying to see whether it was OK to become angry with the dog and even with Mommy. This interpretation seemed to hit a responsive note in Molly and her mother.

The remainder of the treatment involved periods of improvement in Molly, interspersed with periods of symptom recrudescence. Each setback eventually led to a new understanding of the relationship among Molly's symptoms, her struggle with aggression and dependence–independence, and a similar struggle in her mother. Treatment ended after Molly's mother filed for divorce, and Molly was described as being her "spunky old self" once again.

ASSESSMENT

In the evaluation of a traumatized infant, general principles relevant to assessment of the infant's overall social, emotional, and cognitive functioning, as outlined in previous chapters, apply. However, the evaluation of the effects of trauma in infancy has some unique aspects that should be emphasized.

The first area requiring particular attention relates to the history obtained from the parents. In addition to the typical developmental history, a detailed review of the child's trauma is necessary. This exploration should encompass not only the trauma itself but all of the associated events, including treatment interventions. Often, collateral events and interventions can be as traumatic to a child as the trauma itself. A second area of emphasis is careful history gathering concerning the whole range of the infant's symptoms. Typical PTSD symptomatology in this age group may involve intrusive imagery and nightmares; experiences of reliving and reenactment in response to stimuli reminding the child of the trauma; and avoidance of situations and stimuli associated with the trauma. Associated symptoms—including restricted range of affect, detachment, decreased interest in significant activities and/or loss of recently acquired developmental skills, and more generalized psychophysiological disturbances (such as sleep difficulties and autonomic hypersensitivity)—are also likely to be identified. A third area of exploration concerns the specific impact that the trauma may have on larger developmental issues. A fourth area of assessment involves the reactions of the parents to the trauma, particularly their ability to respond to the infant's needs and their own need for treatment.

During direct observations, one should pay special attention to specific behavioral features typically associated with trauma, such as evidence of intrusive imagery, repetitive play enactments, avoidance of certain play materials or themes, constriction of mood, and the like. We also recommend careful recreation of the traumatic scenes, either directly or through play, as an integral part of the direct clinical assessment of the traumatized child. The infant's emotional reactions to such exposure will have diagnostic implications. Close observation of the infant's emotional reactions, coping mechanisms, and behavioral responses, as well as the specific stimulus situations that elicit the various reactions will provide important information about the nature and severity of the PTSD symptoms and their accessibility to therapeutic intervention.

TREATMENT

Given the limitations in our understanding of PTSD in infancy, approaches to treatment must be considered tentative. Well-established treatment principles in the infant mental health field, based on developmental needs for nurturance and stimulation, stability of caregivers, contingent responsivity, and affective attunement (as described in other chapters in this volume), are fundamental to helping children suffering from PTSD symptoms. The reinstitution of a stable and nurturant environment for an infant immediately following a traumatic experience is a crucial precondition for therapeutic work. However, a key question is how to move beyond the more generally applicable therapeutic approaches in order to identify specific psychotherapeutic interventions that can help the infant master traumatic experience.

As a starting point for considering specific therapeutic approaches to PTSD reactions in infants, it is appropriate to look to treatment principles derived from therapeutic experiences with adults and older children. There is general consensus that the cornerstone of treatment involves helping the individual re-experience the trauma and its meaning in affectively tolerable doses in the context of a safe environment (Pynoos, 1990). Only in this way, it seems, can the overwhelming traumatic experiences be mastered and integrated into the person's personality and emotional life. How might this principle apply in infancy? What would constitute developmentally appropriate techniques for facilitating the re-experiencing of trauma in affectively tolerable doses in the context of a safe environment? In this section, we put forth some ideas as to how this might be accomplished, taking into account the major developmental changes occurring during the infancy period (as summarized earlier), and bearing in mind that growing experience in this area will no doubt significantly add to or modify the ideas presented here.

A major impact of trauma during infancy, particularly in the early months of life, will be on basic patterns of psychophysiological regulation and action sequences of reciprocal social exchange. The infant's heightened needs for se-

curity, regressive behavioral and physiological functioning, and/or increased vulnerability to states of hypervigilance and arousal will require heightened sensitivity on the part of caregivers. The clinician can help parents monitor the infant's capacity to handle stimulation, can identify particular stimuli likely to elicit hyperarousal, and can aid in developing effective soothing strategies. The general approach may be conceptually modeled after the strategies used in working with premature or "hypersensitive" infants (see Greenspan & Wieder, Chapter 18, this volume; Field et al., 1986).

In early infancy, the need for specific interventions related to the trauma itself will depend on the degree to which crucial caregiving routines have been disrupted as a result of the trauma. For example, if a trauma has been associated with feeding or sleeping, recognition of cues associated with the trauma may be sufficient to cause affective distress and functional disturbance in these crucial activities. To help an infant to "recreate" and assimilate trauma in this instance, an interactionally based behavioral desensitization program can be used. The infant can be exposed to anxiety-generating cues and/or situations in small, graduated doses in closer and closer approximation to whatever the noxious situation and associated cues may be (e.g., feeding, being held or touched, sitting in a high chair, or tolerating being in a crib).

The case of a 4-month-old infant girl provided a naturalistic example of this desensitization process (Gaensbauer, 1982). Having been abused by her father during feedings, she reacted with distress to close approaches and holding by males. She was sensitive not only to a general gestalt indicating an adult male, but also to specific cues involving voice and length of hair. After 3 weeks of care in a supportive foster home with a concerned and involved foster father, this negative reaction to men—at least as reflected in her responses to a male stranger's approach in the playroom laboratory—had disappeared.

For infants less than 6 months old, desensitization approaches should emphasize concrete interactional encounters involving the specific distress situation, with the caregiver or therapist as the primary stimulus. In the second half of the first year, as the infant's perceptual capacities and awareness of his or her surroundings expand, experiences of trauma (and, correspondingly, the cues that can elicit memories of trauma) can become more complex and generalized. A classic example of the kind of expansion of fear that can be seen in the 6- to12-month-period is J. B. Watson's well-known report that conditioned fears of rabbits in 9- to 11-month-old infants generalized to other furry objects, including fur coats, Santa Claus masks, and even rugs (Watson, 1928). In this period, desensitization techniques still apply, but the techniques used to recreate the trauma should have more specific reference to the objects or contexts associated with the trauma, over and above the interactive elements.

In Beth's case (see Case 1 above), if treatment had been provided immediately following the accident, a stepwise desensitization could have been prescribed. One could imagine involving Beth in the following sequence: playing with the car seat in the house; playing in the car in the driveway; playing with the car seat in the car; sitting in the car seat in the front seat without driving; driving around the block; and so on. Watson (1928) noted that without deconditioning, such fears would last for months with the same intensity, providing early witness to the sustained effects of traumatic experience and the need for specific intervention.

By the second year, as causal chains and associative links become more extended and indirect, and as perceptions and memory become more internally based, cues eliciting PTSD reactions will correspondingly become more varied and representational in nature. It is at this stage that therapeutic techniques utilizing a child's tendencies to re-enact his or her experience through play materials and through sensorimotor activity becomes appropriate both developmentally and therapeutically. As early as 1 year of age, play materials can represent and recreate traumatic situations in sensorimotor or "functional play" terms. The type of approach we envision would be similar to the "structured play therapy" techniques originally described by David Levy (1939), in which the infant or child is presented with play situations reconstructing as closely as possible the anxiety-evoking events. Of course, the child's comfort with the therapist and readiness to handle the situations presented must be taken into account.

In conceptualizing how to use structured play, it is important to keep in mind that most traumatic events have a number of different elements, and that to help the child resolve the trauma fully, all of the elements should be addressed. These elements include not only the direct impact of the traumatic event itself, but also various associated elements—for example,

the context in which the trauma has occurred; the associated meanings assigned to the trauma (guilt, having been bad, anger at caregivers for not preventing the trauma, etc.); the impact of the trauma on the accomplishment of phase-specific developmental tasks; and the impact of the trauma on the caregiver and subsequent caregiver–infant interaction. Molly (see Case 2, above) developed typical PTSD symptoms, but these symptoms also interfered with the accomplishment of developmental tasks and had profound effects on the mother–infant relationship. Structured situations that reproduce aspects of the trauma situation, and then allow the child to play out "what happens next," encourage the child to reveal his or her emotional reactions, defensive operations, reparative fantasies, and personalized understanding of the trauma.

In order to establish a therapeutic environment within which children can tolerate such re-experiencing, we have found it helpful to meet intensively with the children, sometimes as frequently as two to three times per week. At times an extended treatment is required, although in our experience most PTSD symptoms can be resolved within 3–6 months.

In keeping with traditional approaches to trauma, the important reference points for interpretive and supportive focus must be the specific affects elicited during the play. Bringing out, identifying, and helping a child to integrate these strong affects are aspects crucial to therapeutic progress. For infants in the first year, empathic understanding will most effectively be conveyed physically through holding and comforting. As an infant grows older and representational play emerges, the therapist can use responsive play scenarios as a means of conveying empathy and making interpretations. For example, the child's feelings may be revealed through the actions of the characters in the play and the introduction of new elements that open up possibilities for mastery. A particular challenge in working with preverbal infants is to facilitate a later integration of the preverbal traumatic experience into the verbal arena. Preverbal memories and feelings must be made accessible to verbal channels of expression so that continuing processing of the trauma can occur. Terr (1988) has provided a number of poignant and compelling case examples in which preverbal trauma remains out of conscious verbal awareness but is clearly present in memory in the form of behavior. By the second half of the second year, the therapist can utilize verbal communication as an important channel for interpretation. These will evolve from the initially very direct labeling of affects (sad, mad, scared) or concepts (dog bites, "Mommy, gone," or "owies") to more elaborate forms connecting important ideas and conveying empathy with the more complex meaning given by the child to the traumatic experience (e.g., a little girl thinks it is her fault because she was angry at Daddy).

We have found it quite helpful for parents to participate in sessions with their infant for a number of reasons. These include their knowledge of the infant's symptoms; their helpfulness in providing the details that allow the recreation of the events; and especially the fact that their presence as the traumatic feelings are re-awakened provides an opportunity for them to be present for the child in the midst of the trauma in ways that may not have been possible at the time of the trauma. The parents' presence during therapeutic sessions may also help them understand the infant's internalization of the traumatic experience and allow them to appreciate the process of treatment. In particular, the therapist can provide a model for how the parents can communicate with their child about his or her feelings as they come up at home. The therapist can also shift as necessary to the parents' needs by providing support to them as they share their own reactions and concerns.

As illustrated in the case examples, PTSD symptoms are often exacerbated by therapeutic work and carried over into the home setting. It is important for parents to be prepared for the degree of symptomatology that may be evoked. Through their availability and understanding at these moments of traumatic re-experiencing (both in the office and at home), parents can be an integral part of the resolution process and can also help their child to rework the issues of abandonment and loss of trust that are so often present. At times, we have found it helpful for parents to set up relevant play materials at home, so that the child can play out traumatic events with the parents participating and empathizing. These special materials should be kept separate from the child's other toys, but should be accessible to the child so that he or she can return spontaneously to re-enact various elements of the experience as desired.

A useful rule of thumb is that any symptoms or behaviors that appear or are intensified in the midst of the therapeutic work should be interpreted as deriving from the traumatic event until proven otherwise. This generalization provides parents a useful tool for communicating their empathy with the various forms of reliving and re-enacting expressed by the child. We encourage parents, as they are responding to various symptoms or behaviors (e.g., nightmares, fearfulness, aggressiveness, or regression), to help the child interpret these symptomatic reactions as occurring because the child is remembering, in some fashion, the feelings associated with the trauma. In our experience, the identification of the affect, the connection of the current feeling to the original trauma, and the parents' comforting are all helpful in relieving the pressure involved in such acting out. Providing parents with such a model may reduce a tendency of many parents to react to the outward symptoms punitively rather than empathically. Negative cycles engendered by punitive responses can take on a life of their own and lead to more lasting characterological and interactive distortions.

CONCLUSION

Case studies such as those presented in this chapter indicate that infants and toddlers do develop PTSD, with many symptoms similar to those of older children and adults. Specific current knowledge about development in infants and toddlers and about principles of treatment for them has guided clinical work with cases of PTSD, but much work remains to be done. Larger numbers of cases need to be identified and assessed in systematic ways. Future work will need to include early identification of cases, identification of developmental processes involved, and extended follow-up. Emphasis on the outcome of various existing treatment approaches and establishment of newer, more effective approaches will be necessary. Special focus should be placed on treatments that take the nodal role of parents into account and sensitively involve them.

At this point, there are many extant specific questions concerning PTSD in infants and toddlers. There is little firm knowledge about the distinctions in outcome between children who suffer single traumas and those who suffer repeated traumas. Similarly, much needs to be learned about the impact of different sorts of trauma, such as whether trauma suffered at the hands of one's caretakers leads to specific symptoms with profiles of defenses and adaptive behaviors different from those following trauma inflicted by a noncaretaker. What, if any, are the differences between the traumatic-like effects of loss and separation and the effects of the more discrete events usually associated with PTSD? Discerning such points of intersection and variance is what lies ahead for research on PTSD in infants and toddlers as we attempt to construct a developmentally informed biopsychosocial model for this disorder.

REFERENCES

American Psychiatric Association. (1980). *Diagnostic and statistical manual of mental disorders* (3rd ed.). Washington, DC: Author.

American Psychiatric Association. (1987). *Diagnostic and statistical manual of mental disorders* (3rd ed., rev.). Washington, DC: Author.

Bowlby, J. (1969). *Attachment and loss: Vol. 1. Attachment.* New York: Basic Books.

Bowlby, J. (1973). *Attachment and loss: Vol. 2. Separation: Anxiety and anger.* New York: Basic Books.

Bowlby, J. (1980). *Attachment and loss: Vol. 3. Loss: Sadness and depression.* New York: Basic Books.

Bowlby, J. (1988). Developmental psychiatry comes of age. *American Journal of Psychiatry, 145*, 1–10.

Campos, J. J., Barrett, K. C., Lamb, M. E., Goldsmith, H. H., & Stenberg, C. (1983). Socioemotional development. In M. M. Haith & J. J. Campos (Vol. Eds.), *Handbook of child psychology* (4th ed.): *Vol. 2. Infancy and developmental psychobiology* (pp. 783–915). New York: Wiley.

Campos, J. J., Campos, R. G., & Barrett, K. C. (1989). Emergent themes in the study of emotional development and emotion regulation. *Developmental Psychology, 25*, 394–402.

Deblinger, E., McLeer, S. V., Atkins, M. S., Ralphe, D., & Foa, E. (1989). Post-traumatic stress in sexually abused, physically abused, and non-abused children. *Child Abuse and Neglect, 13*, 403–408.

Eisenberg, N., Fabes, R. A., Bustamante, D., Mathy, R. M., Miller, P. A., & Lindholm, E. (1988). Differentiation of vicariously induced emotional reactions in children. *Developmental Psychology, 24*, 237–246.

Emde, R. N., Gaensbauer, T. J., & Harmon, R. J. (1976). *Emotional expression in infancy: A biobehavioral study.* New York: International Universities Press.

Eth, S., & Pynoos, R. S. (Eds.). (1985). *Post-traumatic stress disorder in children.* Washington, DC: American Psychiatric Press.

Field, T., Schanberg, S., Scafidi, F., Bauer, C., Vega-Lahr, N., Garcia, R., Nystrom, J., & Kuhn, C. (1986). Tactile/kinesthetic stimulation effects on pre-term neonates. *Pediatrics, 77*, 654–658.

Fraiberg, S. (1969). Libidinal object constancy and mental representation. *Psychoanalytic Study of the Child, 24*, 9–47.

Fraiberg, S. (1982). Pathological defenses in infancy. *Psychoanalytic Quarterly, 51*, 612–635.

Frederick, C. J. (1985). Children traumatized by catastrophic situations. In S. Eth & R. Pynoos (Eds.), *Post-traumatic stress disorder in children* (pp. 73–99). Washington, DC: American Psychiatric Press.

Freud, A., & Burlingham, D. (1943). *War and Children.* London: Medical War Books.

Freud, A., & Dann, S. (1951). An experiment in group upbringing. *Psychoanalytic Study of the Child, 6*, 127–168.

Freud, S. (1950). *Beyond the pleasure principle* (J. Strachey, Trans.). New York: Liveright. (Original work published 1920)

Freud, S. (1964). Moses and monotheism. In J. Strachey (Ed.), *The standard edition of the complete psychological works of Sigmund Freud* (Vol. 23, pp. 1–137). London: Hogarth Press. (Original work published 1939)

Gaensbauer, T. J. (1982). The differentiation of discrete affects: A case report. *Psychoanalytic Study of the Child, 37*, 29–66.

Galante, R., & Foa, D. (1986). An epidemiological study of psychic trauma and treatment effectiveness after a natural disaster. *Journal of the American Academy of Child and Adolescent Psychiatry, 25*, 357–363.

Giller, E. L. (Ed.). (1990). *Biological assessment and treatment of post traumatic stress disorder.* Washington, DC: American Psychiatric Press.

Greenspan, S. I. (1987). *Psychopathology and adaptation in infancy and early childhood: Principles of clinical diagnosis and preventive intervention.* New York: International Universities Press.

Haith, M. M. (1990). Progress in the understanding of sensory and perceptual processes in early infancy. *Merrill–Palmer Quarterly, 36*(1), 1–26.

Harris, P. L. (1983). Infant cognition. In J. H. Flavell & E. M. Markman (Vol. Eds.). *Handbook of child psychology* (4th ed.): *Vol. 3. Cognitive development* (pp. 689–782). New York: Wiley.

Khan, M. (1945). The concept of cumulative trauma. *Psychoanalytic Study of the Child, 18*, 54–88.

Kolb, L. C. (1987). A neuropsychological hypothesis explaining post-traumatic stress disorders. *American Journal of Psychiatry, 144*, 989–995.

Kolb, L. C. (1988). A critical survey of hypotheses regarding post-traumatic stress disorders in light of recent research findings. *Journal of Traumatic Stress, 1*(3), 291–304.

Kopp, C. B. (1989). Regulation of distress and negative emotions: A developmental view. *Developmental Psychology, 25*(3), 343–354.

Lamb, M. E., Morrison, D. C., & Malkin, C. M. (1987). The development of infant social expectations in face to face interactions: A longitudinal study. *Merrill–Palmer Quarterly, 33*(2), 241–254.

Levy, D. (1939). Release therapy. *American Journal of Orthopsychiatry, 9*, 713–736.

Levy, D. (1945). Psychic trauma of operations in children. *American Journal of Diseases of Children, 69*, 7–25.

Main, M., Kaplan, K., & Cassidy, J. (1985). Security in infancy, childhood, and adulthood: A move to the level of representation. In I. Bretherton & E. Waters (Eds.), Growing points of attachment theory and research. *Monographs of the Society for Research in Child Development, 50*(1–2, Serial No. 209), 66–104.

Mandler, J. M. (1983). Representation. In J. H. Flavell & E. M. Markman (Vol. Eds.), *Handbook of child psychology* (4th ed.): *Vol. 3. Cognitive development* (pp. 420–494). New York: Wiley.

Martini, D. R., Ryan, C., Nakayama, D., & Ramenofsky, M. (1990). Psychiatric sequelae after traumatic injury: The Pittsburg regatta accident. *Journal of the*

American Academy of Child and Adolescent Psychiatry, 29(1), 70–75.

Mott, F. W. (1919). *War neuroses and shell shock.* London: Oxford Medical.

Nelson, K. (1986). Event knowledge and cognitive development. In K. Nelson (Ed.), *Event knowledge: Structure and function in development* (pp. 1–19). Hillsdale, NJ: Erlbaum.

Nelson, K., & Gruendel, J. (1986). Children's scripts. In K. Nelson (Ed.), *Event knowledge: Structure and function in development* (pp. 21–46). Hillsdale, NJ: Erlbaum.

Nir, Y. (1985). Post-traumatic stress disorder in children with cancer. In S. Eth & R. S. Pynoos (Eds.), *Post-traumatic stress disorder in children* (pp. 121–132). Washington, DC: American Psychiatric Press.

Ornitz, E. M., & Pynoos, R. S. (1989). Startle modulation in children with post-traumatic stress disorder. *American Journal of Psychiatry, 146,* 866–870.

Pipp, S. L., Easterbrooks, M. A., & Harmon, R. J. (1992). Relation between attachment and knowledge of self and mother in 1–3 year old infants. *Child Development, 63,* 738–750.

Price, D. W. W., & Goodman, G. S. (1990). Visiting the wizard: Children's memory for a recurring event. *Child Development, 61,* 664–680.

Pynoos, R. S. (1990). Post-traumatic stress disorder in children and adolescents. In B. Garfinkel, G. Carlson, & E. Weller (Eds.), *Psychiatric disorders in children and adolescents* (pp. 48–63). Philadelphia: W. B. Saunders.

Rieder, C., & Cicchetti, D. (1989). Organizational perspective on cognitive control functioning and cognitive–affective balance in maltreated children. *Developmental Psychology, 25,* 382–393.

Sander, L. W. (1975). Infant and caretaking environment: Investigation and conceptualization of adaptive behavior in systems of increasing complexity. In E. J. Anthony (Ed.), *Explorations in child psychiatry* (pp. 129–166). New York: Plenum Press.

Schwarz, E. D., & Kowalski, J. M. (1991). Post-traumatic stress disorder after a school shooting: Effects of symptoms threshold section and diagnosis by DSM-III, DSM-III-R, or proposed DSM-IV. *American Journal of Psychiatry, 148,* 592–597.

Slackman, E. A., Hudson, J. A., & Fivush, R. (1986). Actions, actors, links, and goals: The structure of children's event representations. In K. Nelson (Ed.), *Event knowledge: Structure and function in development* (pp. 47–69). Hillsdale, NJ: Erlbaum.

Spitz, R. A. (1946). Hospitalism: A follow-up report. *Psychoanalytic Study of the Child, 2,* 113–117.

Sroufe, L. (1983). Infant caregiver attachment and adaptation in the preschool: The roots of competence and maladaption. In M. Perlmutter (Ed.), *Minnesota Symposium on Developmental Psychology.* Hillsdale, NJ: Erlbaum.

Stern, D. N. (1985). *The interpersonal world of the infant.* New York: Basic Books.

Stoddard, F. J., Normal, D. K., & Murphy, J. M. (1989). A diagnostic outcome study of children and adolescents with severe burns. *Journal of Trauma, 29,* 471–477.

Terr, L. (1981). Forbidden games: Post-traumatic child's play. *Journal of the American Academy of Child Psychiatry, 20,* 741–759.

Terr, L. (1988). What happens to the memories of early childhood trauma? *Journal of the American Academy of Child and Adolescent Psychiatry, 27,* 96–104.

Terr, L. (1990). *Too scared to cry.* New York: Harper & Row.

Terr, L. (1991). Acute responses to external events and post-traumatic stress disorders. In M. Lewis (Ed.), *Child and adolescent psychiatry: A comprehensive textbook* (pp. 755–763). Baltimore: Williams & Wilkins.

Trimble, M. (1985). Post-traumatic stress disorder: History of a concept. In C. Figley (Ed.), *Trauma and its wake* (pp. 5–14). New York: Brunner/Mazel.

van der Kolk, B. A. (1988). The trauma spectrum: The interaction of biological and social events in the genesis of the trauma response. *Journal of Traumatic Stress, 1,* 273–290.

Watson, J. B. (1928). *Psychological care of infant and child.* New York: Norton.

Winnicott, D. W. (1958). Birth memories, birth trauma, and anxiety. In D. W. Winnicott, *Through pediatrics to psychoanalysis* (pp. 174–193). London: Hogarth Press.

Winnicott, D. W. (1965). Ego distortion in terms of true and false self. In D. W. Winnicott, *The maturational processes and the facilitating environment* (pp. 140– 152). New York: International Universities Press.

Younger, B. A. (1990). Infants' detection of correlations among feature categories. *Child Development, 61,* 614–620.

Younger, B. A., & Cohen, L. B. (1986). Developmental change in infant's perception of correlations among attributes. *Child Development, 57,* 803–815.

20

Sleep Disorders

AVI SADEH
THOMAS F. ANDERS

This chapter first reviews the development of sleep–wake states in human infants and young children (less than 3 years of age), and then describes the clinical presentation of sleep disorders in this age group. Since sleep states and their relationship to wakefulness undergo prominent developmental changes, an understanding of these processes is essential for the assessment of specific disturbances. We describe the signs, symptoms, possible etiological mechanisms, assessment methods, and appropriate interventions for both the psychological and biological syndromes.

DEVELOPMENTAL ASPECTS OF SLEEP-WAKE ORGANIZATION

The first year of life requires major adaptations for the human infant in physiological, perceptual, and motor functioning, as well as in the establishment of primary, regulating social relationships. In all these domains, the early development of sleep–wake state organization is key. Neurobehavioral development coordinates internal biological "clocks" with recurring body signals, such as hunger, anxiety, pain, and periodic environmental cues (e.g., the light–dark cycle, ambient temperature/noise changes, and regularly scheduled periods of social interaction).

Two interrelated chronobiological processes mature during the early stages of sleep–wake state organization in human infants. "Diurnal organization" refers to the circadian (about 24-hour) periodicity of the sleep–wake cycle that is associated with the light–dark cycle. "Ultradian organization" refers to the ultradian (60- to 90-minute) periodicity that regulates the rapid-eye-movement and non-rapid-eye-movement (REM-NREM) sleep cycle and the sleep stages associated with NREM sleep.

Diurnal Organization: The Sleep-Wake Cycle

At birth, normal, full-term newborns spend two-thirds of the 24 hours asleep. At this age sleep is polyphasic, so that sleep–wake states alternate in 3- to 4-hour cycles. There is as much wakefulness at night as sleep during the day (Coons & Guilleminault, 1982). Within the first month following birth, sleep–wake state organization begins to adapt to the light–dark cycle and to social cues. By 6 months of age, the longest continuous sleep period has lengthened from 4 to 6 hours; several long periods make up the night, interrupted by brief awakenings. Sleep has shifted from polyphasic expression to predominant nighttime expression. The wakeful periods similarly consolidate, lengthen, and shift to the daytime, interrupted by brief periods of sleep. Gradually the total number of sleep–wake cycles in a 24-hour period decreases as periods of sleep and wakefulness coalesce and shift to a diurnal pattern of expression.

Six-month old infants sleep 50% of the 24-hour period. Most of their sleep occurs during one or two episodes at night; at this age, they usually have two additional short naps. In subsequent months, one of the daytime naps disappears and sleep becomes restricted to two clock times—one long episode during the night and one brief nap during the afternoon. In the preschool years, depending on social expectations, many children give up the remaining daytime nap and sleep becomes truly monotonic, although a tendency for afternoon naps remains throughout the life cycle (Lavie, 1986). Failures in the process of nighttime sleep consolidation constitute a major source of sleep disorders in infants and adults.

Ultradian Organization: The REM-NREM Cycle

During the first 3 months of life, when asleep, infants spend 50% of their sleep time in REM sleep (also known as "dream sleep," "active sleep," and "paradoxical sleep") and 50% of their sleeping time in NREM sleep (also known as "quiet sleep" and "slow-wave sleep"). REM sleep in newborns is characterized by bilaterally synchronous REMs under closed lids; an electrically activated, low-voltage, fast electroencephalogram (EEG) pattern; phasic movements of peripheral muscles characterized by small twitches of the extremities; and facial grimaces. When the young infant falls asleep, the initial sleep episode is typically a sleep onset REM period.

By 3 months of age, the proportion of REM sleep begins to diminish, and sleep onset REM periods begin to be replaced by sleep onset NREM periods. The intensity of body motility during REM sleep decreases with increased peripheral muscle atonia. During NREM sleep, the EEG pattern begins to differentiate, so that by 6 months of age four stages of NREM EEG patterns can be distinguished. The EEG of Stage 1 NREM sleep resembles the low-voltage, fast pattern of REM sleep, but muscle atonia and REMs are absent. High-voltage, slow, synchronized delta waves define Stages 3 and 4 NREM sleep, and sleep spindles and K-complexes define Stage 2 NREM sleep.

These changes in the organization of sleep state architecture occur simultaneously with changes in the temporal organization of the REM-NREM cycle. In the neonatal period, REM and NREM sleep periods alternate with each other in 50 to 60 minute sleep cycles. In each sleep cycle during the sleep period, there is as much REM sleep as NREM sleep; that is, temporal regulation of the REM-NREM cycle has not begun. After 3 months of age, although REM periods continue to recur with a periodicity of 50–60 minutes, the amount of REM sleep in each cycle begins to shift. REM sleep predominates in the later sleep cycles of the night, and NREM Stage 4 sleep predominates during the earlier cycles.

By 3 years of age, the temporal organization of sleep of toddlers resembles adult sleep except for the sleep cycle periodicity. The longer adult sleep cycle periodicity of 90 minutes is not observed until adolescence. The expected maturational changes in diurnal and ultradian organization are often not fully achieved by all infants in the same way, however, and sleep problems become a prevalent source of concern for parents during infancy and early childhood.

ASSESSMENT OF SLEEP IN INFANCY

In well-baby pediatric visits, parental concerns about infant sleep problems are common. Parents report that they often do not receive an appropriate evaluation and that the advice they receive is not helpful. Moreover, some older children suffer from primary sleep problems that either are not diagnosed or may be misdiagnosed as psychiatric conditions (e.g., depression or hyperactivity).

Since there are close ties between psychopathology and sleep problems, and since the relationship between psychopathology and sleep disruption may be interactive and reinforcing, it is important that routine inquiries about sleep and a structured evaluation of sleep disturbances be an integral part of every infant–toddler mental health assessment. The inquiry and evaluation should be organized according to a developmental framework. A clinician should screen for possible sleep problems that can be either a cause or a complication of the child's mental health problem.

In the general assessment of infants and toddlers, when sleep has not been a problem, clinicians should screen for difficulties in sleep–wake schedules. Does an infant's schedule conform to the family's schedule in a socially appropriate way, and does it meet the infant's need for sleep? How many hours of sleep does the child get each day? How regular is this pattern? Screening should also inquire about any potential sleep problems (difficulties in falling asleep, night waking, parasomnias, etc.). Are there breathing difficulties and snoring during sleep? And finally, screening should assess daytime functioning in regard to sleep. Does the infant appear to be too sleepy or weary during the day? How regular are daytime naps? Is there any evidence of daytime sleepiness?

When a sleep problem exists, a more careful and detailed history needs to be obtained. Specific diaries of sleep schedules, bedtime routines, sleeping arrangements, family history of sleep problems, sibling relationships, and current environmental stresses need to be reviewed. For persistent problems, still more objective and technical methods are available. Polysomnography provides detailed information regarding the EEG, the electro-oculogram (eye movements), the electromyogram (muscle tone), and respiratory patterns from multiple electrodes during sleep. Such instrumentation requires certified clinical polysomnographers and a sleep laboratory for all-night study, although ambulatory polysomnography is becoming more popular in assessment of young infants and children. The data are useful in examining sleep stage architecture and diagnosing a number of specific sleep problems such as sleep apnea. Polysomnography is recommended for clinicians whenever they have reason to suspect an organic cause for a sleep problem, or when severe daytime sleepiness occurs with no reasonable explanation.

Alternative ambulatory methods for objectively recording infant sleep in the home include direct observation by specially trained technicians (Thoman, 1975), time-lapse video recording (Anders & Sostek, 1976), pressure-sensitive mattress recording of motility and respiration (Thoman & Glazier, 1987), and limb actigraph recording (Sadeh, Alster, Urbach, & Lavie, 1989; Sadeh, Lavie, Scher, Tirosh, & Epstein, 1991). Each of these methods has advantages and limitations, but each generally provides clinicians with objective and reliable information, derived from algorithms that approximate polysomnographic sleep–wake state scoring regarding sleep quality, sleep efficiency, and level of sleep–wake state maturation. Such methods can facilitate an understanding of the nature of the sleep problem and can be used for follow-up after treatment to provide information regarding the efficacy of the intervention.

COMMON SLEEP PROBLEMS OF INFANCY AND EARLY CHILDHOOD

The International Classification of Sleep Disorders, published by the American Sleep Disorders Association (1990), defines three major categories of disordered sleep: (1) Dysomnias; (2) Parasomnias; and (3) Sleep Disorders Associated with Medical/Psychiatric Conditions. Since the most common sleep problems of infants and young children are characterized by night waking, difficulty in falling asleep, or both, they are classified in the new nosology as Dysomnias. More specific subclasses suggested in the nosology, such as Limit-Setting Sleep Disorder, Sleep-Onset Association Disorder, or Food Allergy Insomnia, point to the possible etiologies of these problems. In this chapter, we use the more traditional terminology and focus on possible extrinsic and intrinsic concomitants of the problems that often become the focus of intervention.

Night Waking Problems

Descriptions of night waking in infants have mostly been provided by parental reports, although recently time-lapse video recordings, pressure-sensitive mattress recordings, and actigraph studies have contributed more objective data. Significant differences have been reported, as might be expected, between parental reports and the monitoring methods.

Night waking problems are the first to appear developmentally. During early infancy, when polyphasic sleep is normative, recurring periods of nighttime wakefulness are typical. As consolidation of nighttime sleep occurs, persistent night waking begins to be labeled as a disturbance. Still, brief awakenings during the night are typical through the first 18 months of life.

Both the frequency and length of nighttime awakenings tend to decrease with age. Moore and Ucko (1957), surveying maternal reports, noted that 70% of 3-month-olds in their sample "slept" through the night (from midnight to 5 A.M.), whereas 83% of the 6-month-olds and 90% of the 9-month-olds were reported to sleep through the night. These proportions fail to account for brief awakenings of which a parent is unaware. Moore and Ucko defined night waking as a "problem" when a child awakened and cried one or more times between midnight and 5 A.M. on at least four of seven nights, for at least 4 consecutive weeks. By 1 year of age, 50% of infants who had slept through the night were reported as night wakers. During the second year of life, a further transient increase in problematic night awakenings was reported. In other studies using parental reports, nearly 20% of toddlers were described as night wakers (Bernal, 1973; Jenkins, Owen, Bax, & Hart, 1984). The prevalence decreases to 1–5% in school-age children (Richman, Stevenson, & Graham, 1982; Gass & Strauch, 1984). There are indications, however, that this may be an underestimation, since school-age children do not necessarily report sleep problems to their parents (Anders, Carskadon, Dement, & Harvey, 1978).

Videosomnography and actigraphy strongly suggest that nighttime awakenings in early childhood are more prevalent than parental reports indicate (Anders, 1978; Paret, 1983; Sadeh et al., 1991). These methods indicate that most infants wake up one or more times briefly for 1 to 5 minutes every night. Parents are unaware of these awakenings because the child does not cry out. For example, studies using the activity monitor have reported that in the age range of 9–24 months, nonproblem sleepers woke up twice nightly on average. Most of these infants were able to soothe themselves and return to sleep without signaling (Sadeh et al., 1991).

What differentiates problematic nighttime awakenings from normative awakenings? It appears that it is an infant's inability versus ability to return to sleep—in other words, the infant's "signaling" rather than "self-soothing" response to the awakening. During the first few months of life, 95% of infants cry (signal) after a nighttime awakening and require a parental response before returning to sleep. By 1 year of age, 60–70% of infants are able to self-soothe and return to sleep on their own. Thus, night waking as a problem is more appropriately defined as the infant's response following an awakening rather than as the awakening per se.

Sleep Onset Disorders
(Sleep Onset Insomnia)

Problems at bedtime are associated with both going to bed and falling asleep. From a developmental perspective, problems with falling asleep precede problems with going to bed. Feeding, rocking, and being held often co-occur with sleep onset at young ages, even though newborns are able to fall asleep on their own and do not need these soothing maternal interventions to help them. Some infants experience difficulty when these habitual interaction patterns are changed, especially when the change is attempted after 9 months of age.

During the second year of life, such children may protest vigorously or cry at bedtime and refuse to remain in bed in a recumbent position. A child may demand to be rocked, to be nursed, or to lie next to a parent while falling asleep. In extreme cases, a child is unable to fall asleep unless he or she engages in a more complex bedtime ritual, such as being taken for a car ride.

Bedtime and falling asleep represent a separation from the parent and from the "world" for the infant. As older infants and toddlers strive for psychological autonomy, being without a parent is often associated with anxiety. Primary caregivers or attachment figures seem especially needed for some infants, in order to provide a sense of security at this recurrent time of separation. Separation anxiety may be experienced by a parent as well. In some families, separation may be more difficult for an infant who is temperamentally disposed to have difficulty shutting out external social activity and settling into sleep. In other cases, the parent may need the infant's presence to prevent the manifestations of anxiety or guilt in regard to separation. Clearly, separation problems are dyadic, and evaluation of both partners in the relationship is necessary. Studies that have addressed separation problems at bedtime report increasing difficulties with age. Beltramini and Hertzig (1983) reported that 26% of 1-year-olds needed more than 30 minutes to fall asleep on at least three nights a week, compared to 66% of 5-year-olds.

In families in which both parents work all day, the evening may be the primary time for family relaxation and socialization. For 3- and 4-year-old children, going to bed means missing out on opportunities for play and engaging in their world. Often both the children and their parents need this family time. They stay up later, encouraged by their family's schedule. Finally, young children are easily overstimulated and frightened by novel or incomprehensible daytime experiences. Being alone in the dark may rekindle anxiety in these youngsters. The differential diagnosis of a phase delay syndrome secondary to progressively later sleep onsets also needs to be considered.

Thus, problems of initiating sleep and problems of night waking appear to originate from different developmental stages. Night waking is normal during the first 6 months of life. By 1 year of age, night waking followed by crying (signaling) may be problematic and needs to be differentiated from night waking followed by a return to sleep without crying (self-soothing). Signaling infants have not learned to fall asleep on their own. In contrast, the problem of falling asleep, originates in most cases from issues related to separation during the second year of life and possibly from social demands or nighttime fears at older ages. It is likely that a high proportion of infants with night waking have problems that persist and generalize to include difficulties in going to bed and falling asleep during toddlerhood. Thus, signalers at 1 year of age are likely to have sleep onset problems at bedtime by 2 years of age.

Returning-to-Sleep Problems (Middle-of-the-Night Insomnia)

Difficulty in returning to sleep following a nighttime awakening may resemble the difficulty in falling asleep at bedtime. The child may exhibit nonspecific anxiety; may show specific fears of the dark or of being alone; or may be in a good mood, fully awake and alert as if the morning had come. At young ages, the wakeful infant does not return to sleep for a prolonged period, demanding the same pattern of habitual parental soothing that was used when he or she was put to bed. At older ages, the toddler may leave the bed and seek out the parents. At even older ages, the child may find some other ways of inducing sleep, such as reading or watching television. In most of the recurrent and persistent cases of difficulty in returning to sleep, the middle-of-the-night routine for returning to sleep needs to be similar to the routine of falling asleep at the beginning of the night. Less commonly, the problem may be related to other sleep-related causes (e.g., irregular day–night schedule problems, nightmares, or a disruptive and chaotic sleep environment).

THE ORIGINS OF SLEEP PROBLEMS IN INFANCY AND EARLY CHILDHOOD

A number of investigators have attempted to study the causes of these common problems in infancy and early childhood. Since age-related factors contribute differentially to their etiology and classification, major factors in understanding possible causes are the age and developmental stage of the child, as well as his or her relationship with primary caregivers.

In the first 3 months of life, night awakenings have been associated with nutritional factors and states of physical discomfort (Moore & Ucko, 1957). It is reasonable to assume that since at this age infants need physiological regulation by their caregivers for maintenance of homeostasis, sleep difficulties may arise from insufficient or inadequate regulation. Whereas Wright, Macleod, and Cooper (1983) and Eaton-Evans and Dugdale (1988) reported a relationship between breast feeding and prolongation of night awakenings, other research has failed to find such a relationship (Beal, 1969; Jones, Ferreira, Brown, & Macdonald, 1978). Kahn, Mozin, Rebuffat, Sottiaux, and Muller (1989) identified allergy to cow's milk in a group of infants with persistent sleep problems who did not benefit from behavioral interventions. Kahn et al. (1991) have also demonstrated that proximal esophageal reflux can induce arousals in infants.

The amount of food consumption prior to sleep, a common parental concern, has not been found to be related to sleep disruption. Sleep patterns of 4-week-old and 4-month-old infants who were fed an enriched diet did not differ from those of infants on a regular diet (Macknin, Medendorp, & Maier, 1989). Feeding styles (demand vs. schedule) also were not found to be related to nighttime awakenings (Moore & Ucko, 1957). Inconsistent and unsatisfying feedings, however, were associated with more sleep problems. It is possible that inconsistent feedings may be reflective of general inconsistency in parenting, which in turn influences the consolidation of sleep–wake patterns.

Specific infant characteristics such as sensitivity, activity, responsivity, and persistence, referred to in the aggregate as infant "temperament" or "behavioral style," may also affect sleep–wake organization. Carey (1974) found in a pediatric clinic sample that according to parental report, infants with sleep problems had lower sensory thresholds than infants in the clinic without sleep problems. Carey concluded that too much emphasis has been placed on parental characteristics, and that sleep problems are more likely to result from factors associated with infant temperament in interaction with the environmental context. Thus, according to Carey, overreactivity to external stimuli may predispose an infant to multiple night awakenings and settling difficulties. In support of this hypothesis, Weissbluth and Liu (1983) found that children with "difficult" temperaments slept less than children with "easy" temperaments, and Schaefer (1990) found a higher-than-expected incidence of "difficult" temperament in young children referred for night awakenings. The possibility of reporter bias flaws all of these studies, however. Keener, Zeanah, and Anders (1988), in a sample of nonreferred, normal infants, did not find any temperament differences (as judged by mothers) between infants who cried when they woke up during the night, scored independently from time-lapse videotapes, and those who did not.

The relationship between other common physiological conditions and sleep problems during early infancy has not been examined adequately. Infants with colic have been reported to sleep less than infants without colic (Weissbluth, 1987). Ear infections, airway congestion and teething may cause temporary discomfort, and have been anecdotally reported to disrupt sleep.

"Cosleeping" (i.e., a parent's sleeping with an infant) at an early age has been reported to affect sleep–wake state regulation and organization. The age of the infant again seems to be related to whether or not cosleeping is associated with sleep problems. In the first 6 months of life, the physiological adaptation of infants may benefit from cosleeping as the best approximation to prenatal mother–infant physiological unity (McKenna, Mosko, Dungy, & McAninch, 1990). Newborns who cosleep with their mothers spend more time in quiet sleep and less time in crying and indeterminate sleep than newborns who sleep in a separate room (Keffe, 1987). McKenna et al. (1990) have suggested that cosleeping at an early age increases the number of brief, spontaneous arousals from sleep, which may in turn reduce the opportunity for the occurrence of sudden infant death syndrome (SIDS). He reports that SIDS is rare or nonexistent in cultures where cosleeping at young ages is common.

Lozoff, Wolf, and Davis (1984, 1985), on the other hand, found a fourfold increase in sleep problems in older children who were cosleeping with their parents. Zuckerman, Stevenson, and Baily (1987) reported an even higher ratio in respect to the cosleeping partner's sleep problems. Other studies in Western cultures also suggest relationships between cosleeping and sleep problems (Kataria, Swanson, & Trevathan, 1987; Schacter, Fuchs, Bijur, & Stone, 1989). Cultural practices may determine whether cosleeping is associated with sleep problems. Studies conducted in other cultures report conflicting results. The important dimension may not be cosleeping per se, but rather the psychosocial meaning of (and cultural sanctions in regard to) cosleeping.

Parental conflict, maternal personality, and maternal psychopathology have also been identified as contributing factors in infants' sleep problems. Richman (1981) reported that mothers of 1- to 2-year-old sleep disturbed infants exhibited more psychopathology than mothers of control infants. These mothers tended to be nervous, to lose control more often, and to have less trusting, supportive relationships with their husbands. Zuckerman et al. (1987) reported that maternal depression was the only measure of maternal psychopathology that was significantly more common in children with persistent sleep problems from the age of 8 months to 3 years. Guedeney and Kreisler (1987) also reported a relationship between sleep problems in the first 18 months of life and traumatic events, maternal depression, and maternal anxiety during the pregnancy. Because all of these studies were correlational and cross-sectional in design, it is difficult to ascribe causality to maternal factors with any certainty.

Finally, sleep problems in early childhood have frequently been associated with other behavior problems. Richman (1981) reported that in her 1- to 2-year-old sample, sleep problems were correlated with such problem behaviors as problem eating, lowered physical resilience, and accident proneness.

Perhaps the most consistent research finding regarding sleep problems in early childhood is the association of sleep problems with parent–infant bedtime interaction. For example, Van Tassel (1985) studied the relative influence of child and environmental factors on sleep disturbances in the first and second years of life and found that bedtime interactions (e.g., nighttime feeding) were the best predictors of sleep problems in both early and late infancy. Adair, Bauchner, Philipp, Levenson, and Zuckerman (1991) found that infants whose parents were present while the infants were falling asleep were significantly more likely to wake at night than infants whose parents were not present. Johnson (1991), in a telephone survey of parents of 12- to 35-month-old children, found highly significant differences between night wakers and good sleepers in bedtime routines. Infants who were actively soothed by their parents (nursed, rocked, or comforted) were more likely to be night wakers. Eighty percent of infants who were self-soothers were sleeping through the night, compared to fewer than one-third of the infants who were soothed to sleep by their parents.

These recent findings replicate and support clinical experience that associates bedtime practices and sleep problems in infancy (Ferber, 1985; Douglas & Richman, 1984). Behavioral analysis suggests that parental attention is sufficiently rewarding to maintain night waking. In addition, parental involvement may inhibit the emergence of self-soothing strategies. However, since most of these studies and earlier ones have been correlational in design, causal relationships should be interpreted cautiously. It is equally plausible to assume that infants who have difficulty in falling asleep or who have a propensity for night waking "push" their parents to become more involved at bedtime, compared to infants who "teach" their parents that their presence is not necessary. The sleep-disturbed infants may, in turn, "reward" (in the short run) such activities as feeding and rocking by falling asleep relatively quickly.

PERSISTENCE OF INFANT SLEEP PROBLEMS

Although normal development favors sleep consolidation and a decrease in nighttime awakenings, studies aimed at examining this process have noted that frequent night awakenings often persist and that sleep problems continue during the preschool years. Zuckerman et al. (1987) followed up 8-month-old infants with sleep problems and found that 41% of them still had problems when they were 3 years old. Only 26% of the children with sleep problems at 3 years did not manifest them when they were 8-month-olds. In a 3-year follow-up study of 2-year-olds, Kataria et al. (1987) found that 84% of the children still suffered from their sleep problems. Similarly, Richman et al. (1982) found that almost half of 3-year-old night wakers had had their problem from birth, and that 40% of the children who had sleep problems at 8 years had had problems at least from the time they were 3 years old. These reports emphasize that sleep problems in infancy are often persistent and may lead to chronic sleep problems, as some retrospective studies of adults with sleep problems have suggested (Monroe, 1967; Salzarulo & Chevalier, 1983; Hauri & Olmstead, 1980).

INTERVENTION IN INFANT AND EARLY CHILDHOOD SLEEP PROBLEMS

Approaches to Treatment

The relationship between sleep problems in early childhood and parent–infant interaction style has been repeatedly demonstrated in the literature (e.g., Bernal, 1973; Moore & Ucko, 1957; Paret, 1983; Sander, Stechler, Julia, & Burns, 1970). Several approaches to treatment have been attempted in managing nonorganic sleep disturbances of infants. They have included pharmacological, behavioral, and psychotherapeutic regimens, alone or in combination.

For example, sleep-inducing medications are prescribed most often for young infants who present with night waking by pediatricians and family physicians. Ounsted and Hendrick (1977) summarized survey data indicating that 25% of children had received a sleep medication by the age of 18 months. The widespread use of medication in infants persists, despite the fact that research conducted to test efficacy has been limited, and that support for the therapeutic benefit of such medication is marginal.

Russo, Gururaj, and Allen (1976) reported statistically significant improvement of sleep problems in children between 2 and 12 years of age following treatment with diphenhydramine in comparison to placebo. Richman (1985), in a double-blind study of children aged 1–2 years using Vallergan Forte, also found significant improvement on medication; however, the amount of improvement was limited from a clinical perspective and was not long-lasting. In another controlled study, Simonoff and Stores (1987) found that trimeprazine tartrate was more effective than placebo in the short-term treatment of multiple nighttime awakenings in children aged 1 to 3 years. It is important to note that many parents refuse the use of sleep medication for their children. Moreover, evidence from studies, especially with adults, show significant negative effects from long-term use of sleep medication.

The central hypothesis that underlies most behavioral interventions in early childhood is that sleep problems result from habitual, learned interactional patterns of a child and caregiver. The links among parent–child interaction, parenting styles, and sleep problems have been empirically demonstrated (Moore & Ucko, 1957; Bernal, 1973; Paret, 1983; Sander et al., 1970).

Behavioral techniques usually focus on teaching children to fall asleep by themselves in their own beds with minimal parental interaction. Various techniques have been described in the clinical and research literature (Douglas & Richman, 1982, 1984; Ferber, 1985; Weissbluth, 1987). The "cold-turkey" approach instructs parents to ignore the crying and protestations of their children until the children fall asleep in the absence of any intervention. This treatment is based on the behavioral principle of extinction and attempts to eliminate the positive reinforcement of the parents' presence. It may be difficult for some parents to tolerate, and many young children do not return to sleep even after they are significantly exhausted.

A less abrupt variant of rapid, total extinction prescribes graduated withdrawal of parental involvement. A parent may initially stop rocking a child to sleep, but puts the child in his or her bed and remains in close proximity for a while until the child falls asleep. In the next step, the parent leaves the child's bedroom once the child has been put to bed.

A variant of graduated withdrawal incorporates "checking" (Douglas & Richman, 1984). The child is put to sleep in his or her own bed. If the child protests or cries, the parent responds after a wait of 5 minutes. Then the parent goes into the room to restore the child to a sleeping position. These checks are repeated at 5-minute intervals as long as the child protests. This method again aims to teach the child a routine of falling asleep without any external interactional support. The child is repeatedly reassured by the parental presence, but he or she is also repeatedly exposed to the routine of falling asleep in bed with minimal parental involvement. A modification of checking, suggested by Ferber (1985), recommends a gradual, progressive lengthening of the period between approaches to the child.

Sleep aids have been considered to function as parent substitutes while children are falling asleep. At young ages, infants use fingers or pacifiers and other soft objects. Gradually, as they mature, they either continue to use such objects or stop. At the point when an infant selects a "special" object, the sleep aid becomes imbued with the particular properties of an attachment object. That is, the sleep aid provides comfort and security during separation and in the absence of the primary attachment figure. Winnicott (1965) has described this process in terms of the developing capacity to be alone and

the attainment of a "transitional object." Since sleep is a lengthy period of separation, the transitional object serves to comfort the infant during wake–sleep transitions. Research on the relationship between sleep and transitional objects has provided some support for their utility. Paret (1983), using time-lapse video recordings, found that 9-month-old infants who slept uninterruptedly without signaling were more likely to suck their fingers or use transitional objects then infants who were night wakers. Wolf and Lozoff (1989) found a negative correlation between the presence of parents while falling asleep and the use of transitional objects: Children who fell asleep in the absence of their parents were more likely to use transitional objects than children who tended to fall asleep in the presence of the parents. These findings support the theory that a possible function for the transitional sleep aid is as a soothing parent substitute during the transition from wakefulness to sleep when a parent is not present. Interestingly, in a sample of older children (aged 4 to 14 years), no significant relationships were found between the use of transitional objects and sleep problems (Klackenberg, 1987).

A somewhat different approach for treating night waking is that of scheduled awakenings prior to the time of the expected, spontaneous awakening (McGarr & Hovel, 1980). This approach is aimed at preventing the rewarding association among night waking, crying, and parental intervention. The method has been difficult for parents to follow.

Still another approach to treatment is derived from a cross-cultural perspective. Cosleeping provides the continuous presence of a parent in the child's bedroom for a few nights while the child is taught to fall asleep without parental active involvement (Sadeh, 1990). This method is based on the same assumptions as the use of a transitional object—namely, that such problems as nightly awakenings and difficulties in falling asleep result from separation fears and the child's need to be reassured by the parent's presence. Cosleeping or temporary parental presence is often a solution initiated spontaneously by the child or by the parent.

Finally, in contrast to the focused behavioral interventions that attempt to redirect parent–child bedtime interactions, unstructured, psychodynamically oriented approaches have been used in order to focus on the meanings and motivations of parents' behavior in the context of their children's sleep behavior (Daws, 1989).

The Efficacy
of Behavioral Interventions

Many case reports demonstrate the efficacy of behavioral interventions in treating sleep problems. Williams (1959) described the treatment of a 4-year-old boy who suffered from nightly temper tantrums. The tantrums disappeared after the parents consistently ignored them and reappeared when the parents resumed their previous response.

Behavioral interventions have been reported to be effective in treating sleep problems, even in severe cases of mental retardation and autism (Howlin, 1984). Weissbluth (1981) used gradual shaping of sleep onset time to effect the relationship between sleep schedule and multiple night awakenings. Jones and Verduyn (1983) reported an 84% success rate in 19 children with sleep problems treated with behavioral methods. These results were maintained at a 6-month follow-up. Graziano and Mooney (1982) have been successful in using behavioral methods with children who have nighttime fears.

The clinical case reports of childhood sleep problems (e.g., Douglas & Richman, 1984; Ferber, 1985) have stimulated more systematic research on the efficacy of behavioral treatments. One of the first studies, conducted by Richman, Douglas, Hunt, Lansdown, and Levene (1985), reported a 77% improvement in 35 children aged 1 to 5 years. Treatment consisted of training the parents in the use of behavioral techniques tailored specifically to the individual needs and problems of their children. Rickert and Johnson (1988) compared two techniques for treating night waking and crying. The first technique was completely ignoring a child's crying and protests; the second was the use of scheduled awakenings prior to the expected spontaneous night awakenings. The two techniques were both effective, but there was more noncompliance in parents who could not tolerate ignoring their children's persistent protestations.

A few studies have raised questions about the specificity of particular behavioral interventions. Seymour, Brock, During, and Poole (1989) compared the effectiveness of behavioral guidance with and without therapist support; they found that written information and standard behavioral guidance by therapists were equally effective, and that both were more effective than no treatment in a waiting-list control group. Weir and Dinnick (1988) found that children whose parents were trained by health visitors in behavior modification showed marked improvement compared to children in a control group at a 6- month follow-up. Finally, Sadeh (1990) used an activity monitor to measure changes in sleep patterns of sleep-disturbed infants during behavior intervention, and found that the checking procedure (Richman et al., 1985) and cosleeping for a defined period were equally effective in producing a marked improvement of sleep.

The relative paucity of studies in this area is related to a number of issues. First, the classification of sleep problems in infants and toddlers has not been standardized. Second, as described above, signs and symptoms are age-related; that is, what is a normal pattern of waking at one age becomes deviant at another. Furthermore, the natural history of sleep problems in this population has not been adequately studied, so that the prognosis and developmental outcome of any pattern are virtually unknown. Most sleep problems are transient, related to environmental perturbations or physical disruptions. Finally, relying on parental reports has not been satisfactory. Both in describing the initial presenting problem and in reporting on the efficacy of treatment, parents often tell professionals what the professionals expect to hear. Careful studies that control for developmental, environmental, and family circumstances, and that monitor the course of the sleep disturbance from baseline through treatment and follow-up periods, are necessary.

PARASOMNIAS IN
EARLY CHILDHOOD

In general, the Parasomnias are associated with age groups that are beyond the scope of this chapter and this volume; nevertheless, some are relevant to infants and young children. All Parasomnias are more common in males than in females, and children with attacks often have a positive family history for Parasomnias. Night terrors begin to appear in 2-year-olds. The attacks are usually frightening to parents, who may seek professional help. During a night terror attack, the child "wakes up" screaming and appears extremely frightened and agitated. In fact, the child is not awake, but deep in Stage 4 NREM sleep. The child is difficult to soothe, is unaware of his or her surroundings, and may fight with the person who is trying to console him or her. Night terrors are considered to be atypical arousals from these deep sleep stages. Unless the problem is intractable in terms of frequency and persistence, there is no need for special intervention; children normally "outgrow" their attacks as they mature.

Other common bedtime behaviors that concern parents of toddlers are the repetitive rhythmic behaviors at sleep onset, which may include self-rocking and head banging. These behaviors, usually observed while an infant is trying to fall asleep, have been classified as Parasomnias in the new nosology (American Sleep Disorders Association, 1990). Klackenberg (1987) reported that at 9 months of age, 58% of infants exhibited at least one of these repetitive behaviors (head turning, head banging, or rocking). The prevalence of these activities decreased to 33% by 18 months of age and to 22% by 2 years of age. When intense rocking or head banging persists and is disruptive, parents may view the behavior as a problem. Most often, guidance and support for the parents suffice; the only concern should be in assuring the child's safety from self-injury.

SLEEP APNEA SYNDROME

The most common organic sleep disorder in young children is sleep apnea, the failure to breathe during sleep. Two distinct central nervous system mechanisms control breathing in humans. A voluntary cortical mechanism functions during wakefulness and provides control of breathing during speech; an involuntary subcortical mechanism maintains oxygen saturation during sleep. When the involuntary system fails during sleep, blood and brain oxygen saturation falls to dangerous levels. Self-preservation is achieved by a brief awakening, which is sufficient to return control of breathing to the voluntary system. Once the sleep apnea episode has ended with an awakening, the subject returns to sleep. The awakening during sleep is most often a microarousal unknown to the sleeper. This sequence may recur many times during the night if the involuntary respiratory control mechanisms are dysfunctional. One explanation that has been offered for SIDS—which peaks in frequency from the third to ninth months of life, and in which airway obstruction and obesity are not found—is immaturity of the central arousal mechanism, even though there are no empirical findings linking sleep apnea and SIDS.

There are several possible causes of sleep apnea in young children. Sleep apnea may result from mechanical obstruction of the upper airway secondary to anatomical factors, such as enlarged tonsils and adenoids or excessive obesity; or from medical and neurological conditions of the lungs and the control systems in the central nervous system; or from combinations of central and peripheral mechanisms.

Sleep apnea syndrome can produce chronic sleep loss. Consequently, such children usually present with symptoms of daytime sleepiness and chronic fatigue. If the awakenings also interrupt the secretion of growth hormone, which normally occurs during NREM Stage 4 sleep, the child may present with mild growth retardation (or, in extreme cases, a full-blown failure-to-thrive syndrome).

Sleep apnea should be investigated by polysomnographic technology in a sleep laboratory, in order to identify its specific cause and prescribe the appropriate intervention. In light of the risk of SIDS, infants with a history of severe apneic episodes that require resuscitation, or apneas with bradycardia or transient hypoxia of unknown etiology, should be monitored with cardiorespiratory home monitoring. This enables the parents to intervene by waking the infant immediately upon the signaling of an apneic episode (Guilleminault, 1987).

SUMMARY AND CONCLUSIONS

This chapter has reviewed sleep–wake state development and sleep disorders in human infants and young children through the first 3 years of life. We have emphasized the importance of taking a developmental perspective in assessing and diagnosing sleep problems in this age group. We have reviewed a diverse set of treatments and have recommended that treatment strategies be individualized to match the child's age and developmental needs, as well as the family circumstances that appear to be related to the sleep problem. We have particularly focused on the psychological issues of separation and autonomy as they relate to sleep and parent–infant relationships.

There is much more research that needs to be done, although progress has been made in that we are gathering data more objectively and systematically. We need better explanations about the origins, natural history, and long-term sequelae of sleep problems in infancy. We need to understand the behavioral and personality concomitants of "morning types" and "evening types," and of long sleepers and short sleepers. Application of the transactional model (Sameroff & Emde, 1989) to sleep problems of infancy suggests that we also need a better understanding of the origins and role of internal clocks and pacemakers, synchronization, and other constitutional contributors, and that we need to integrate with this an understanding of the changing demands of the environment and the needs of the infant during early development.

REFERENCES

Adair, R., Bauchner, H., Philipp, B., Levenson, S., & Zuckerman, B. (1991). Night waking during infancy: Role of parental presence at bedtime. *Pediatrics*, *87*(4), 500–504.

American Sleep Disorders Association. (1990). *The international classification of sleep disorders: Diagnostic and coding manual*. Kansas City, KS: Allen Press.

Anders, T. F. (1978). Home recorded sleep in two and nine month old infants. *Journal of the American Academy of Child Psychiatry*, *17*, 421–432.

Anders, T. F., Carskadon, M. A., Dement, W. C., & Harvey, K. (1978). Sleep habits of children and the identification of pathologically sleepy children. *Child Psychiatry and Human Development*, *9*, 56–63.

Anders, T. F., & Sostek, A. M. (1976). The use of time lapse video recording of sleep–wake behavior in human infants. *Psychophysiology*, *13*(2), 155–158.

Beltramini, A. V., & Herzig, M. E. (1983). Sleep and bedtime behavior in pre-school aged children. *Pediatrics*, *71*, 153–158.

Bernal, J. (1973). Night waking in infants during the first 14 months. *Developmental Medicine and Child Neurology*, *14*, 362–372.

Beal, V. A. (1969). Termination of night feeding in infancy. *Journal of Pediatrics*, *75*, 690–692.

Carey, W. B. (1974). Night waking and temperament in infancy. *Journal of Pediatrics*, *84*, 756–758.

Coons, S., & Guilleminault, C. (1982). Development of sleep–wake patterns and non-rapid eye movement sleep stages during the first six months of life in normal infants. *Pediatrics*, *69*(6), 793–798.

Daws, D. (1989). *Through the night: Helping parents and sleepless infants*. London: Free Association Books.

Douglas, J., & Richman, N. (1982). *Sleep management manual*. London: Department of Psychological Medicine, Great Ormond Street Children's Hospital.

Douglas, J., & Richman, N. (1984). *My child won't sleep*. Harmondsworth, England: Penguin Books.

Eaton-Evans, J., & Dugdale, A. E. (1988). Sleep patterns of infants in the first year of life. *Archives of Disease in Childhood*, *63*, 647–649.

Ferber, R. (1985). *Solve your child's sleep problems*. New York: Simon & Schuster.

Gass, E., & Strauch, I. (1984). *The development of sleep behavior between 3 and 11 years*. Paper presented at the Seventh European Sleep Congress, Munich.

Graziano, A. M., & Mooney, K. C. (1982). Behavioral treatment of "nightfears" in children: Maintenance

of improvement at 2½- to 3-year follow-up. *Journal of Consulting and Clinical Psychology*, *50*, 598–599.

Guedeney, A., & Kreisler, L. (1987). Sleep disorders in the first 18 months of life: Hypothesis on the role of mother–child emotional exchanges. *Infant Mental Health Journal*, *8*(3), 307–318.

Guilleminault, C. (1987). Disorders of excessive daytime sleepiness. In C. Guilleminault (Ed.), *Sleep and its disorders in children*. New York: Raven Press.

Hauri, P., & Olmstead, E. (1980). Childhood-onset insomnia. *Sleep*, *3*, 59–65.

Howlin, P. (1984). A brief report on the elimination of long-term sleeping problems in a 6 year old autistic boy. *Behavioral Psychotherapy*, *12*, 257–260.

Jenkins, S., Owen, C., Bax, M., & Hart, H. (1984). Continuities of common behavior problems in pre-school children. *Journal of Child Psychology and Psychiatry*, *25*, 75–89.

Johnson, M. C. (1991). Infant and toddler sleep: A telephone survey of parents in one community. *Journal of Developmental and Behavioral Pediatrics*, *12*(2), 108–114.

Jones, B. N., Ferreira, M. C. R., Brown, M. F., & Macdonald, L. (1978). The association between perinatal factors and night waking. *Developmental Medicine and Child Neurology*, *20*, 427–434.

Jones, D. P., & Verduyn, C. M. (1983). Behavioural management of sleep problems. *Archives of Disease in Childhood*, *58*(6), 442–444.

Kahn, A., Mozin, M. J., Rebuffat, E., Sottiaux, M., & Muller, M. F. (1989). Milk intolerance in children with persistent sleeplessness: A prospective double-blind crossover evaluation. *Pediatrics*, *84*, 595–603.

Kahn, A., Rebuffat, E., Sottiaux, M., Dufour, D., Cadranel, S., & Reiterer, F. (1991). Arousals induced by proximal esophageal reflux in infants. *Sleep*, *14*(1), 39–42.

Kataria, S., Swanson, M. S., & Trevathan, G. E. (1987). Persistence of sleep disturbances in preschool children. *Journal of Pediatrics*, *110*, 642–646.

Keffe, M. R. (1987). Comparison of neonatal nighttime sleep–wake patterns in nursery versus rooming-in environments. *Nursery Research*, *36*, 140–144.

Keener, M. A., Zeanah, C. H., & Anders, T. F. (1988). Infant temperament, sleep organization, and nighttime parental interventions. *Pediatrics*, *81*, 762–771.

Klackenberg, G. (1987). Incidence of parasomnias in children in a general population. In C. Guilleminault (Ed.), *Sleep and its disorders in children*. New York: Raven Press.

Lavie, P. (1986). Ultrashort sleep–waking schedule: III. "Gates" and "forbidden zones" for sleep. *Electroencephalography and Clinical Neurophysiology*, *63*, 414–425.

Lozoff, B., Wolf, A. W., & Davis, N. S. (1984). Cosleeping in urban families with young children in the United States. *Pediatrics*, *74*, 171–182.

Lozoff, B., Wolf, A. W., & Davis, N. S. (1985). Sleep problems seen in pediatric practice. *Pediatrics*, *75*, 477–483.

Macknin, M. L., Medendorp, S. V., & Maier, M. C. (1989). Infant sleep and bedtime cereal. *American Journal of Diseases of Children*, *143*, 1066–1068.

McGarr, R. J., & Hovel, M. F. (1980). In search of the sandman: Shaping an infant to sleep. *Education and Treatment of Children*, *3*, 173–182.

McKenna, J. J., Mosko, S., Dungy, C., & McAninch, J. (1990). Sleep and arousal patterns of co-sleeping human mother/infant pairs: A preliminary physiological study with implication for the study of sudden infant death syndrome (SIDS). *American Journal of Physical Anthropology, 83,* 331–347.

Monroe, L. J. (1967). Psychological and physiological differences between good and poor sleepers. *Journal of Abnormal Psychology, 72,* 255–264.

Moore, T., & Ucko, L. E. (1957). Night waking in early infancy. *Archives of Disease in Childhood, 32,* 333–342.

Ounsted, M., & Hendrick, A. M. (1977). The first-born child: Patterns of development. *Developmental Medicine and Child Neurology, 19,* 446–453.

Paret, I. (1983). Night waking and its relation to mother–infant interaction in nine month old infants. In J. D. Call, E. Galenson, & R. L. Tyson (Eds.), *Frontiers of infant psychiatry.* New York: Basic Books.

Richman, N. (1981). A community survey of characteristics of one to two year olds with sleep disruptions. *Journal of the American Academy of Child Psychiatry, 20,* 281–291.

Richman, N. (1985). A double-blind drug trial of sleep problems in young children. *Journal of Child Psychology and Psychiatry, 26,* 591–598.

Richman, N., Douglas, J., Hunt, H., Lansdown, R., & Levene, R. (1985). Behavioural methods in the treatment of sleep disorders: A pilot study. *Journal of Child Psychology and Psychiatry, 26,* 581–590.

Richman, N., Stevenson, J., & Graham, P. (1982). *Preschool to school: A behavioral study.* London: Academic Press.

Rickert, V. I., & Johnson, C. M. (1988). Reducing nocturnal awakening and crying episodes in infants and young children: A comparison between scheduled awakenings and systematic ignoring. *Pediatrics, 81,* 203–212.

Russo, R., Gururaj, V., & Allen, J. (1976). The effectiveness of diphenhydramine HCl in pediatric sleep disorders. *Journal of Clinical Pharmacology, 16,* 284–288.

Sadeh, A. (1990). Actigraphic home-monitoring of sleep-disturbed infants: Comparison to controls and assessment of intervention. In J. Horne (Ed.), *Sleep '90.* Bochum, Germany: Pontenagal Press.

Sadeh, A., Alster, J., Urbach, D., & Lavie, P. (1989). Actigraphically based automatic bedtime sleep–wake scoring: Validity and clinical applications. *Journal of Ambulatory Monitoring, 2*(3), 209–216.

Sadeh, A., Lavie, P., Scher, A., Tirosh, E., & Epstein, R. (1991). Actigraphic home monitoring of sleep-disturbed and control infants and young children: A new method for pediatric assessment of sleep–wake patterns. *Pediatrics, 87*(4), 494–499.

Salzarulo, P., & Chevalier, A. (1983). Sleep problems in children and their relationships with early disturbances of the waking–sleeping rhythms. *Sleep, 6*(1), 47–51.

Sameroff, A. J., & Emde, R. N. (Eds.). (1989). *Relationship disturbances in early childhood: A developmental approach.* New York: Basic Books.

Sander, L., Stechler, G., Julia, H., & Burns, P. (1970). Early mother–infant interaction and 24-hour patterns of activity and sleep. *Journal of the American Academy of Child Psychiatry, 9,* 103–123.

Schaefer, C. E. (1990). Night waking and temperament in early childhood. *Psychological Report, 67,* 192–194.

Schacter, F. F., Fuchs, M. L., Bijur, P. E., & Stone, R. K. (1989). Cosleeping and sleep problems in Hispanic American urban young children. *Pediatrics, 84,* 522–530.

Seymour, F. W., Brock, P., During, M., & Poole, G. (1989). Reducing sleep disruption in young children: Evaluation of therapist-guided and written information approaches. A brief report. *Journal of Child Psychology and Psychiatry, 30*(6), 913–918.

Simonoff, E. A., & Stores, G. (1987). Controlled trial of trimeprazine tartrate for night waking. *Archives of Disease in Childhood, 62*(3), 253–257.

Thoman, E. B. (1975). Sleep and wake behaviors in neonates: Consistencies and consequences. *Merrill–Palmer Quarterly, 21,* 295–314.

Thoman, E. B., & Glazier, R. C. (1987). Computer scoring of motility patterns for states of sleep and wakefuleness: Human infants. *Sleep, 10,* 122–129.

Van Tassel, E. B. (1985). The relative influence of child and environmental characteristics on sleep disturbances in the first and second year of life. *Journal of Developmental and Behavioral Pediatrics, 6,* 81–86.

Weir, I. K., & Dinnick, S. (1988). Behaviour modification in the treatment of sleep problems occuring in young children: A controlled trial using health visitors as therapists. *Child: Care, Health and Development, 14,* 355–367.

Weissbluth, M. (1981). Modification of sleep schedule with reduction of night waking: A case report. *Sleep, 5*(3), 262–266.

Weissbluth, M. (1987). *Sleep well: Peaceful nights for your child and you.* London: Unwin Hyman.

Weissbluth, M., & Liu, K. (1983). Sleep patterns, attention span and infant temperament. *Journal of Developmental and Behavioral Pediatrics, 4,* 34–36.

Williams, C. D. (1959). The elimination of tantrum behavior by extinction proceures. *Journal of Abnormal and Social Psychology, 59,* 269.

Winnicott, D. W. (1965). The capacity to be alone. In D. W. Winnicott, *The maturational processes and the facilitating environment.* New York: International Universities Press.

Wolf, A. W., & Lozoff, B. (1989). Object attachment, thumbsucking, and the passage to sleep. *Journal of the American Academy of Child and Adolescent Psychiatry, 28*(2), 287–292.

Wright, P., Macleod, H. A., & Cooper, M. J. (1983). Waking at night: The effect of early feeding experience. *Child: Care, Health and Development, 9,* 309–319.

Zuckerman, B., Stevenson, J., & Baily, V. (1987). Sleep problems in early childhood: Continuities, predictive factors, and behavioral correlates. *Pediatrics, 80,* 664–671.

21

Failure to Thrive and Feeding Disorders

DIANE BENOIT

Failure to thrive (FTT) and feeding disorders are relatively common problems encountered during infancy and early childhood. Specifically, FTT is estimated to represent 1–5% of all pediatric hospital admissions of infants (Berwick, 1980; Hannaway, 1976) and affects 3.5–14% of infants in ambulatory care settings (Altemeier, O'Connor, Sherrod, Yeager, & Vietze, 1985; Mitchell, Gorrell, & Greenberg, 1980). On the other hand, feeding disorders affect 6–35% of young children (Jenkins, Bax, & Hart, 1980; Palmer & Horn, 1978; Richman, 1981). Although FTT and feeding disorders may coexist, the frequency of association has not yet been established (Drotar, 1985).

This chapter is divided into three sections. The first section reviews various physiological, developmental, and environmental factors that are believed to affect eating and growth patterns. The second and third sections focus on FTT and specific infant feeding disorders, respectively.

DEVELOPMENTAL CONSIDERATIONS

Physiological Factors

Healthy, full-term infants have an innate capacity to suck and swallow, and can regulate their oral intake by adjusting the volume of intake to the caloric density of the feed. "Hunger–satiety cycles" allow the infant to learn that ingesting fluids or solids can replace physical sensations of discomfort (i.e., hunger) with feelings of comfort and contentment (i.e., satiety). Although physical sensations of hunger and satiety (and associated feelings of discomfort and well-being) are rather undifferentiated in the first few months of life, infants progressively learn to discriminate between these emotional and physical sensations during the latter part of the first year of life. This process of "somato-psychological differentiation" and the hunger–satiety cycles have major implications for the treatment of certain types of feeding disorders (Benoit, 1990; Chatoor, 1989).

Illingworth and Lister (1964) suggested that failure to introduce fluids and solids during "critical or sensitive periods," in conjunction with factors such as infant personality and environment, may result in later feeding difficulties. For instance, if an infant is not given the opportunity to suck in the first few weeks of life, the ability to suck and drink may be jeopardized or even lost. Similar long-term sequelae may be found in children who are not given solids when the ability to chew first appears, on average at about 6 months of age.

Normal Growth and Eating Patterns

A detailed description of various anthropometric methods used to assess nutritional status and growth parameters is beyond the scope of this chapter. However, it must be emphasized that the physical growth standards most frequently used are the National Center for Health Statistics (NCHS) growth charts (Hamill et al., 1979), and the weight-for-height percentage obtained from these charts provides an objective assessment of current nutritional status. A low weight-for-height percentage provides an estimate of wasting, which is used to determine the severity of an infant's growth failure. On the other hand, the height-for-age percentage gives an index of past nutritional history.

Infants gain weight at different rates, depending on constitutional and health factors, their level of physical activity, and the caloric content of their diets. Emotional stress has been documented to cause cortisol secretion levels that are higher than normal and have a growth-retarding effect (Brasel, 1980). Thus, emotional stress and malnutrition may have similar effects on metabolism and on ponderal and linear growth.

Several factors seem to contribute to the development of adaptive eating behaviors in a healthy and neurologically intact infant: comfortable and developmentally appropriate positioning of the child and distraction-free surroundings at mealtimes; developmentally appropriate feeding schedule and diet; and contingent and sensitive responses of the caregiver. When these conditions are met, most healthy infants are likely to develop adaptive eating behaviors. However, when problems in one or more of these areas occur, a child is at risk for developing a variety of maladaptive eating behaviors, such as persistent food refusal (e.g., turning the head away from the source of food, pushing spoon/bottle away, tightening lips/gums/teeth to refuse entry of spoon/nipple into the mouth, engaging in escape behaviors, gagging and vomiting, refusing to swallow, spitting out, having tantrums). Such behaviors may generate feelings of anxiety, frustration, and inadequacy in the caregiver, who may then respond by ignoring, coaxing, or force-feeding the child, thus establishing mutually unsatisfying feeding interactions.

Individual Differences

It is well known that infants begin to show food likes and dislikes during the first year of life. Indeed, in a large British study, Jenkins et al. (1980) found that 12–23% of mothers reported food selectivity in their infants.

Infants may have genetic and constitutional characteristics affecting their growth (e.g., constitutional short stature) and their ability to ingest, metabolize, or digest food. In addition, a wide variety of medical problems—ranging from acute infections to life-threatening/chronic conditions—may interfere with the body's capacity to use nutrients efficiently, and may be responsible for transient and chronic feeding difficulties and/or growth failure.

"Environmental" Factors

Studies of various populations of different racial and ethnic backgrounds have shown that environment, by far, exerts the most powerful influence over the physical size in young children (Habicht, Martorell, Yarborough, Malina, & Klein, 1974). The next sections describe such factors in more detail in the context of clinical disorders.

FAILURE TO THRIVE

Definition and Classification

FTT is not a diagnosis in itself; rather, it is a symptom associated with varying degrees of malnutrition and developmental delays (Frank & Zeisel, 1988; Woolston, 1985). There is still no universally accepted definition of FTT, but recently some criteria have been used more frequently, such as (1) weight below the 5th percentile on NCHS growth charts, and/or (2) deceleration in the rate of weight gain from birth to the present (weight decrease of at least two standard deviations on NCHS growth charts). Given that FTT is not a diagnosis, it is not surprising that it is not included in the revised third edition of the *Diagnostic and Statistical Manual of Mental Disorders* (DSM-III-R; American Psychiatric Association [APA], 1987) or the ninth revision of the *International Classification of Diseases and its Clinical Modification* (ICD-9-CM; World Health Organization [WHO], 1978).

The traditional "organic" versus "nonorganic" etiological dichotomy for FTT has been misleading (Berwick, Levy, & Kleinerman, 1982; Casey, 1988; Woolston, 1985). In fact, it is estimated that between 15% and 35% of FTT infants have both organic and nonorganic (i.e., "mixed") contributors (Berwick et al., 1982; Casey, Wortham, & Nelson, 1984; Singer, 1986), whereas only 16–30% of FTT children have organic diseases severe enough to explain their growth failure (Berwick et al., 1982). Moreover, given that inadequate caloric intake seems to be the immediate precipitant of growth failure (Bell & Woolston, 1985; Whitten, Pettit, & Fischoff, 1969), one could argue that all FTT infants suffer from the serious medical problem of malnutrition. Recent approaches have emphasized the importance of viewing FTT as a continuum and simultaneously examining both organic and nonorganic factors that might contribute to an infant's growth failure (Bithoney & Dubowitz, 1985; Casey, 1988). In this section, the term "FTT" refers to cases that have psychosocial contributors.

Several clinicians and researchers have developed classification systems and used "FTT" interchangeably with "feeding disorder." This is unfortunate, because FTT infants do not necessarily have a feeding disorder and infants with a feeding disorder do not necessarily fail to thrive (Benoit, 1992).

Anna Freud (1946) was the first to develop a classification system based on the presumed theoretical etiology of the feeding disorder. Her system included (1) organic feeding disturbances, (2) nonorganic disturbances of the instinctive process, and (3) neurotic feeding disturbances.

Woolston's (1983) phenomenological classification includes three types of FTT and eating disorders: (1) Type I, or Reactive Attachment Disorder of Infancy; (2) Type II, or Simple Calorie–Protein Malnutrition; and (3) Type III, or Pathological Food Refusal. Each type is reported to have specific infant, maternal, and mother–infant interactional characteristics. Only Type III refers specifically to an eating disorder.

Woolston (1985) has also described a multiaxial classification of FTT that includes assessments of physical illness, growth failure, development delays, caretaker–infant interaction, feeding, age of onset, and cognitive and financial disability of caretakers. Such a multiaxial classification system reflects the variety of factors that have been implicated as etiological contributors to FTT, including infant, mother, family, social, and mother–infant relationship characteristics.

Finally, Chatoor's developmental classification of FTT and feeding disorders (Chatoor, Dickson, Schaefer, & Egan, 1985; Chatoor & Egan, 1987) includes three types of FTT/feeding disorders: (1) disorders of homeostasis (for infants 0–2 months old); (2) disorders of attachment (for infants 2–6 months old); and (3) disorders of separation and individuation, or "infantile anorexia nervosa" (for children 6 months to 3 years old). Each of Chatoor's developmental feeding disorders is said to create, exacerbate, or result from FTT.

These classification systems have not been extensively evaluated empirically, and have failed to provide a conceptual framework from which to understand a variety of behavioral feeding problems and disorders not associated with FTT.

Clinical Manifestations

Infant Characteristics

Considerable heterogeneity has been reported in the characteristics of FTT infants. Boys and girls appear to be equally affected. Even though low birthweight (defined as birthweight below 2500 grams) and prematurity are generally believed to constitute biological risk factors for FTT (Frank, 1985), studies examining differences between FTT infants and controls have shown conflicting results (Benoit, Zeanah, & Barton, 1989; Mitchell et al., 1980; Sherrod, O'Connor, Altemeier, & Vietze, 1985; Vietze et al., 1980). These studies also have yielded conflicting results about whether FTT infants have, on average, lower birthweights than controls. Children with FTT are prone to recurrent infections (Mitchell et al., 1980) and show a decreased ability to recover from these (Frank, 1985). Most FTT children are developmentally delayed (Drotar, Malone, & Negray, 1980; Powell & Low, 1983). It is not yet clear whether these developmental delays result from malnutrition or reflect suboptimal stimulation provided to these children, or both.

Physically, most FTT infants are cachectic. Motorically, they may exhibit unusual postures such as "strap hanging" (arms held up, elbows bent, and fists clenched) and "scissoring," and may be listless or hypertonic (see Berkowitz & Senter, 1987, for a review). Affectively, they may look sad, depressed, withdrawn, and irritable (Chatoor, 1989; Drotar et al., 1980; Powell & Low, 1983), or may be apathetic, wary, or watchful (Leonard, Rhymes, & Solnit, 1966). Some may exhibit the "radar gaze" (Barbero & Shaheen, 1967). Other FTT children have been described as rigid, difficult, hyperactive, and angry (Evans, Reinhart, & Succop, 1972; Powell & Low, 1983; Rosenn, Loeb, & Jura, 1980). Some prefer interacting with inanimate objects (Rosenn et al., 1980), make little eye contact, rarely vocalize, seem to dislike cuddling, and may engage in self-stimulatory activities (Berkowitz & Senter, 1987; Powell & Low, 1983). Some parents report voracious appetite despite persistent weight loss (Glaser, Heagarty, Bullard, & Pivchik, 1968; Powell, Brasel, & Blizzard, 1967; Silver & Finkelstein, 1967). The implication of these characteristics is that genetic or constitutional characteristics in the context of certain environmental conditions may place infants at increased risk for subsequent development of FTT.

Maternal Characteristics

Personality disturbances and other forms of psychopathology in the mothers of FTT children have been frequently described in clinical observations (Coleman & Provence, 1957; Fischoff, Whitten, & Pettit, 1971; Hufton & Oates, 1977; Woolston, 1983). Specifically, mothers of FTT infants have been described as having depression and anger (Evans et al., 1972; Fosson & Wilson, 1987); impaired coping abilities, withdrawal, and inability to stimulate their babies (Casey et al., 1984; Hess, Hess, & Hard, 1977; Vietze et al., 1980); low self-esteem (Leonard et al., 1966); feelings of inadequacy in their own mothering (Elmer, Gregg, & Ellison, 1969; Whitten et al., 1969), and the need to be mothered themselves (Kerr, Bogues, & Kerr, 1978; Stewart, 1973).

Controlled studies show a trend toward increased rates of suicide attempts, addictions, anxiety, depression, and social isolation in mothers of FTT infants (Polan, Kaplan, et al., 1991; Pollitt, Eichler, & Chan, 1975). Crittenden (1987) found that, compared to maltreating and adequate mothers, mothers of FTT children were more often "mentally and emotionally handicapped." Several other controlled studies have failed to show significant differences in the rate of maternal psychopathology (Benoit et al., 1989; Kotelchuck & Newberger, 1983; Newberger, Reed, Daniel, Hyde, & Kotelchuck, 1977). Polan, Kaplan, and their colleagues (1991) were the first to use both a control group and operationalized diagnostic criteria—the Structured Clinical Interview for DSM-III-R (the nonpatient version for personality disorders; Spitzer & Williams, 1986). They found that, compared to controls, mothers of FTT children had higher rates of affective disorders, substance abuse, and personality disorders. Nevertheless, controlled studies examining the association of maternal psychopathology and FTT have been conducted on small samples and on populations of various socioeconomic backgrounds, making comparison and generalization difficult at this point.

Family Characteristics

Mother–Infant Relationship. FTT has long been attributed to deviant caregiver–infant relationships (Berkowitz & Senter, 1987; Chatoor, Egan, Getson, Menvielle, & O'Donnell, 1987; Fraiberg, Adelson, & Shapiro, 1975; Leonard et al., 1966; Powell & Low, 1983; Rosenn et al., 1980). This is illustrated in numerous clinical reports referring to FTT as "maternal deprivation" (Patton & Gardner, 1963), "deprivation dwarfism" (Silver & Finkelstein, 1967), "psychosocial deprivation" (Caldwell, 1971), and "environmental retardation" (Coleman & Provence, 1957). FTT continues to be considered part of a continuum of child maltreatment (Newberger et al., 1977). In fact, an association between abuse and FTT has been documented in both noncontrolled and controlled studies (Crittenden, 1987; Hufton & Oates, 1977; Krieger, 1973), and reports of death secondary to FTT, although rare, seem to relate to physical abuse (Hufton & Oates, 1977).

Compared to mothers of thriving children, mothers of FTT infants make fewer positive vocalizations (praise, approval, laughter) and more negative vocalizations (criticism, threats) when interacting with their FTT infants; they are also less responsive to their infants' distress and nondistress signals, generally spending more time ignoring the children (Berkowitz & Senter, 1987). Similarly, mutual gazing, mutual interactions, and contingent behaviors occur rarely during interactions between mothers and their FTT infants (Berkowitz, 1985; Berkowitz & Senter, 1987; Pollitt & Eichler, 1976; Powell & Low, 1983; Vietze et al., 1980). When interacting with their mothers, FTT children have been found to inhibit their own feelings and desires and to be uncooperative (Crittenden, 1987). In addition, they exhibit more negative affect than controls when interacting with their mothers in feeding and non-feeding situations (Chatoor, 1989; Polan, Leon, et al., 1991), and the negative affect seems to relate to their malnutrition (Polan, Leon, et al., 1991).

There are marked individual differences in the quality of interactions between FTT infants and their mothers (Finlon & Drotar, 1983). Some mothers provide intrusively high stimulation

(Chatoor & Egan, 1983; Crittenden, 1987), are angry and hostile (Evans et al., 1972), are neglectful and abusive (Crittenden, 1987), are reluctant to caress or praise (Pollitt & Eichler, 1976), or lack knowledge about infants (Elmer et al., 1969; Whitten et al., 1969).

Several studies have used the Strange Situation procedure (Ainsworth, Blehar, Waters, & Wall, 1978) to assess the quality of the infant–mother attachment relationship in FTT. In noncontrolled studies that have not used the "disorganized" infant classification, Gordon and Jameson (1979) and Drotar, Malone, et al. (1985) found that 50% and 45% of FTT infants were classified as insecurely attached, respectively. However, in two controlled studies using the "A/C" category (i.e., a subgroup of the "disorganized" classification), Crittenden (1987) and Valenzuela (1990), respectively, found that 45% and 32% of FTT children were classified A/C; in both studies, over 90% of FTT children were insecurely attached to their mothers, compared to fewer than 50% of controls. These findings suggest that high levels of anger, ambivalence, fear, and emotional suppression exist in FTT children's relationship with their mothers. The 45% and 32% A/C classifications in these studies support the idea that FTT may be viewed as a continuum of child maltreatment, since other studies of child maltreatment have documented a large proportion of such disorganized patterns during the reunion episodes of the Strange Situation. In addition, my colleagues and I (Benoit et al., 1989) found that mothers of FTT infants were more likely than control mothers to be classified as insecurely attached, as measured by the Adult Attachment Interview (George, Kaplan, & Main, 1985). This finding suggests that mothers of FTT infants are passive, confused, or intensely angry about attachment relationships, or tend to dismiss the importance of attachment relationships and their effects altogether. These mothers may show insensitivity to their infants' cues and signals by either rejecting the children's bids for attention and comfort, or responding to their infants' distress in confused, confusing, and unpredictable ways.

Family Situation. Family problems (Mitchell et al., 1980; Glaser et al., 1968) and distressed marital relationships have been documented in noncontrolled and controlled studies of FTT (Benoit et al., 1989; Crittenden, 1987; Drotar, Woychik, et al., 1985; Glaser et al., 1968; Hufton & Oates, 1977; Kerr et al., 1978; Pollitt et al.,

1975; Shaheen, Alexander, Truskowsky, & Barbero, 1968; Stewart, 1973). In addition, Crittenden (1987) found that FTT children were more likely than maltreated and "normal" children to have a low position in the birth order in a family of three to four children (see also Benoit et al., 1989; Drotar, Malone, et al., 1985; Shaheen et al., 1968). Crittenden also found that mothers of FTT infants were more often abused by their partners than were maltreating and adequate mothers. Families of FTT infants are notoriously difficult to treat and follow (Drotar, Malone, et al., 1985; Drotar, Woychik, et al., 1985; Rathbun, 1985).

Although some studies suggest that FTT infants may come from intact, two-parent families (Crittenden, 1987; Shaheen et al., 1968), socially adverse conditions such as substandard living conditions (Hufton & Oates, 1977), poverty, unemployment, alcoholism (Altemeier et al., 1985; Elmer et al., 1969), and isolation (Leonard et al., 1966) characterize many of these families (Drotar & Malone, 1982; Drotar, Woychik, et al., 1985; Glaser et al., 1968).

Characteristics of Siblings. Siblings are usually close in age (Crittenden, 1987; Drotar, Woychik, et al., 1985; Hufton & Oates, 1977), may also have FTT (Elmer et al., 1969; Glaser et al., 1968), and may suffer from serious and chronic illnesses (Glaser et al., 1968; Kerr et al., 1978; Pollitt et al., 1975; Shaheen et al., 1968; Stewart, 1973). In addition, Crittenden (1987) found that a significant number of siblings of FTT infants were abused and/or neglected themselves. She also reported that compared to siblings of children who were abused and/or neglected but not failing to thrive, siblings of FTT children had more adjustment problems. These included passivity, withdrawal, aggression, academic difficulties and learning disabilities, adult-like caretaking of a parent, mental retardation, enuresis, stuttering, and accident proneness. These findings suggest that in these families the inadequate caregiving may not be limited to the FTT infant.

Given the frequency of association between "organic" and "nonorganic" contributors; the wide variety of adverse infant, caregiver, parent–child relationship, and family characteristics; and the seriousness of the problem, it is essential to simultaneously assess psychosocial and medical factors that may be contributing to FTT. The range and severity of problems associated with FTT infants and their families suggest strongly that a comprehensive, multidisciplinary team approach is essential to assess and treat the condition.

Treatment

Various treatment approaches have been described, including behavioral (Linscheid & Rasnake, 1985), interactional or developmental (Chatoor et al., 1985; Chatoor, Kerzner, et al., 1987; Lieberman & Birch, 1985; McDonough, 1990; Shapiro, Fraiberg, & Adelson, 1976), and family-oriented (Drotar, Malone, et al., 1985) approaches. Polan, Kaplan, and their colleagues (1991) suggest that treatment should be aimed at treating the affective disorder or preventing a depressive episode in mood-disordered mothers of FTT infants, and/or supporting the adaptive coping strategies of mothers with personality disorders. Most clinicians and researchers emphasize that the treatment of FTT is a complex process and may require multiple and specific problem-oriented interventions (Rathbun, 1985). In their intervention study, which compared three approaches (short-term advocacy, family-centered intervention, and parent–infant intervention), Drotar, Malone, and their colleagues (1985) found that no treatment method was superior in predicting outcome.

In his meta-analysis of eight follow-up studies examining the efficacy of hospitalization of FTT infants, Fryer (1988) found that hospitalization significantly enhanced the probability of sustained catch-up physical growth, but did not significantly enhance psychosocial outcome of the children. Sturm and Drotar (1989) emphasized the importance of closely monitoring FTT infants' nutritional status and growth parameters following hospitalization. It should be stressed that a substantial percentage of FTT children actually lose weight in hospitals (Glaser et al., 1968; Shaheen et al., 1968).

Controlled investigations of treatment outcome are lacking; this represents one of the areas most in need of empirical and systematic study in the field.

Outcome

Several outcome studies of FTT—covering from 6 months to over a decade after the onset of FTT—have been conducted over the past 25 years. Unfortunately, findings from these studies are limited by significant methodological problems, including inconsistent definition of FTT, small sample sizes, retrospective designs, absence of control groups and standardized outcome measures, and absence of systematic study of intervention effects (Sturm & Drotar, 1989). For the sake of clarity, findings from these various studies are described here in terms of physical, emotional, behavioral, and intellectual outcomes.

With respect to physical outcome, several follow-up studies have indicated varying degrees of improvement in physical growth 6 months to 11 years following initial "diagnosis" (Elmer et al., 1969; Hufton & Oates, 1977; Shaheen et al., 1968; White, Malcolm, Roper, Westphal, & Smith, 1981). Other investigators have reported poorer physical growth outcomes (Chase & Martin, 1970; Evans et al., 1972; Glaser et al., 1968; Haynes, Cutler, Gray, O'Keefe, & Kempe, 1983; Kristiansson & Fallstrom, 1987; Oates, Peacock, & Forrest, 1985). Weight rather than linear growth has been reported to be especially affected (Mitchell et al., 1980). However, Casey et al. (1984) cautioned that linear growth and behavioral status, rather than weight, are more meaningful predictor variables for long-term prognosis in FTT. In their follow-up study of 59 children aged 3 years who had been hospitalized for FTT during infancy, Sturm and Drotar (1989) found that shorter duration of FTT prior to diagnosis, greater weight gain following initial diagnosis, hospitalization, and time-limited outreach intervention predicted nutritional status at follow-up.

With respect to cognitive and intellectual development and educational performance, controlled and noncontrolled studies have documented a rather grim outcome for FTT children (Chase & Martin, 1970; Elmer et al., 1969; Glaser et al., 1968; Hufton & Oates, 1977; Oates et al., 1985). Drotar, Malone, et al. (1985) emphasize that the later the age of onset of FTT, the better the prognosis for cognitive functioning. However, Mitchell et al. (1980) did not document any statistically significant differences on developmental measures between 12 FTT children and 16 controls, using the McCarthy Scale of Children's Abilities; the authors concluded that social stresses in the families, rather than FTT, were responsible for the developmental deficits seen in both the FTT and control groups.

Chronic malnutrition and growth failure have also been associated with emotional and behavioral problems at school age (Bithoney & Rathbun, 1983; Glaser et al., 1968; Oates et al., 1985). Hufton and Oates (1977) found that half of the 21 FTT children they studied had "abnormal personality" about 6 years after the onset of FTT. In another noncontrolled outcome study of 15 FTT infants from lower socioeconomic background, Elmer et al. (1969) found that only 13% of their 15 FTT children were functioning relatively well 3 to 11 years after the onset of FTT, and that more than half had significant (though unspecified) behavioral problems. In their study comparing 12 FTT and 16 control children, Mitchell et al. (1980) did not find statistically significant differences in the rate of behavioral problems between the two groups, as assessed by an unspecified "behavior problems questionnaire" completed by the "parents." Excessive shyness and enuresis (Glaser et al., 1968; Hufton & Oates, 1977) have been reported. In one controlled study, mothers rated their FTT children as having more speech problems, lying, stealing, temper tantrums, overactivity, attention-seeking behaviors, and encopresis than the immediate younger and older siblings of the FTT children (Hufton & Oates, 1977). In the same controlled study, school teachers rated FTT children as having more "antisocial" and "neurotic" characteristics. However, one noncontrolled study reported that older FTT children did not show consistent patterns of emotional disturbance or personality configuration on projective testing (Glaser et al., 1968).

In summary, there is a wide spectrum of outcomes, including about one-third of FTT children who seem to show no evidence of physical, emotional, or psychological problem on follow-up (Glaser et al., 1968).

FEEDING DISORDERS

Transient feeding difficulties in infancy are common and do not necessarily indicate a feeding disorder. In cases where an infant has both a feeding disorder and FTT, the question of whether the feeding disorder preceded the growth failure or is a result of it is not always easy to answer. Because not all FTT children have a behavioral feeding disorder and not all feeding-disordered children have FTT, it is useful to differentiate FTT from feeding disorder both clinically and conceptually.

The prevalence of feeding disorders is estimated to range from 6% to 35%, with the highest rates in developmentally disabled popula-

tions (Jenkins et al., 1980; Palmer & Horn, 1978; Richman, 1981). Boys and girls seem to be equally affected. In addition, infants born prematurely or requiring artificial methods of feeding for an extended period are at increased risk for developing food refusal or aversion when oral feeding is introduced (Geertsma, Hyams, Pelletier, & Reiter, 1985).

Given the prevalence of feeding disorders in infancy, their detrimental effects on family life, and their association with later behavioral problems (Richman, Stevenson, & Graham, 1982) and eating disorders (Marchi & Cohen, 1990), it is somewhat surprising that no adequate conceptual framework and classification system from which to view these disorders has yet been developed (Dahl & Sundelin, 1986). This problem is reflected in the literature, which is characterized by inconsistencies in diagnostic categories and criteria, and is mostly confined to case series or individual case reports. Many etiological contributors to the development of feeding disorders have been suggested, including prematurity, neuromotor dysfunction, mechanical/anatomical obstructions, nutritional deficiencies, allergies, traumatic oral experiences, inadequacies of the mother–infant relationship, and family dysfunction.

In this section, various feeding disorders are described. The word "feeding" rather than "eating" is used throughout to emphasize the dyadic nature of these problems in infancy. The feeding disorders described below reflect the DSM-III-R (APA, 1987) and ICD-9-CM (WHO, 1978) classification systems. However, other feeding disorders that are not included in these classification systems but that have clinical relevance are also described.

Rumination Disorder (Merycism)

Rumination Disorder is rare (Sheinbein, 1975), and its incidence may be decreasing (Sauvage, Leddet, Hameury, & Barthelemy, 1985). It consists of repeated regurgitation, followed by rechewing and reswallowing partially digested food. The activity is essentially self-induced and purposeful; typically occurs when a child is alone; and is accompanied by a vacant expression, immobility and languor, obliviousness to surroundings, and expressions of extreme relaxation and pleasure. The apparent voluntary and pleasurable nature of the regurgitation differentiates ordinary vomiting and Rumination Disorder. These infants induce rumination by placing their fingers or a piece of cloth in their mouths (Sheinbein, 1975), by using simple tongue thrusts, and at times by no visible means (Sauvage et al., 1985).

The age of onset is typically between 3 and 12 months, and the condition is usually self-limited. However, malnutrition, growth failure, dehydration, and gastric disorders are frequent complications and are believed to be responsible for the 25% mortality rate associated with the condition (APA, 1987; Sajwaj, Libet, & Agras, 1974). DSM-III-R (APA, 1987) reports that both sexes are equally affected. However, in a recent review of 66 cases, Mayes, Humphrey, Handford, and Mitchell (1988) found that the incidence of Rumination Disorder was five times higher in boys than girls.

From the same review of 66 cases, Mayes and her colleagues (1988) concluded that two types of Rumination Disorder can be distinguished. The first type, "psychogenic rumination," is reported to be more common and has its onset in infancy (0.7 to 17.0 months of age). It is often associated with mother–infant relationship disturbances (including neglect and separation experiences), maternal psychiatric disorders, and parental emotional problems (Flanagan, 1977; Menking, Wagnitz, Burton, Coddington, & Solos, 1969; Sheinbein, 1975). Psychogenic rumination is also said to occur primarily in the context of normal development, even though some developmental delays have been noted in some children (Sauvage et al., 1985; Mayes et al., 1988). Krieger (1982) described some of these children as "bright-eyed," hyperactive, and over-stimulated by their parents (Flanagan, 1977). The second type, "self-stimulatory rumination" (Mayes et al., 1988), is associated with mental retardation. Its onset is significantly later than that of the psychogenic type, and can occur any time from infancy through to adulthood. Children in the self-stimulatory group tend to be lethargic and passive and to have a poorer prognosis than those in the psychogenic group (Krieger, 1982).

The differential diagnosis includes distinguishing Rumination Disorder from iatrogenic causes (e.g., nausea-inducing medications), congenital gastrointestinal anomalies (e.g., pyloric stenosis and gastroesophageal reflux), gastrointestinal infections, cerebral palsy, or other neurological conditions affecting muscle tone.

Various treatment methods have been used, including antispasmodic and sedative medications, mechanical devices such as "rumination caps" and nose packing, physical restraints (Menking et al., 1969; Sheinbein, 1975), surgery (Herbst, Friedland, & Zboralske, 1971), behavior therapy using both aversive (e.g., electric shocks and bitter substances) and nonaversive methods (see Winton & Singh, 1983, for a review), and psychotherapy (Menking et al., 1969; Sauvage et al., 1985). In their review of the literature on the treatment of Rumination Disorder, Winton and Singh (1983) underscored the many methodological problems plaguing most intervention studies, making it very difficult to determine which general and behavioral approaches are most effective. Nonetheless, these authors report that the use of aversive procedures (such as electric shocks and bitter substances) produced the most rapid suppression of ruminating behaviors, followed by procedures involving positive reinforcers (such as attention and food).

Pica

As with most types of feeding disorders in infancy, there is lack of agreement on the definition of Pica (Feldman, 1986). Both DSM-III-R (APA, 1987) and ICD-9-CM (WHO, 1978) seem to agree that Pica refers to the persistent ingestion of non-nutritive substances. The definition is sometimes broadened to include compulsive eating of nutritive substances as well (Danford & Huber, 1982; Feldman, 1986). Although many young infants mouth objects (which represents a normal developmental phenomenon), Pica implies that the ingestion of substances is developmentally inappropriate. DSM-III-R (APA, 1987) specifies that the condition must have occurred for at least 1 month in order for the diagnosis to be made, and that it cannot coexist with other mental disorders (such as autism and schizophrenia) or with medical disorders (such as the Klein–Levine syndrome). However, an association between Pica and autism has been documented (Accardo, Whitman, Caul, & Rolfe, 1988).

There are several types of Pica, including geophagia (clay, dirt, sand), which is the most common type in children and pregnant women (Danford, 1982); pagophagia (ice), which is the most common type in iron deficiency states (Rector, Fortuin, & Conley, 1982); lithophagia (gravel, stones); coprophagia (feces); amylophagia (starch); and trichophagia (hair). Other substances can be ingested, including paper, cloth, paint, plaster, insects, metal, needles, pebbles, matches, and many others.

In a survey of 784 infants, Cooper (1957) found that 22% had a history of Pica. Estimates of the prevalence of Pica among institutionalized, mentally retarded individuals range from 10% to 33% (Danford & Huber, 1982; McAlpine & Singh, 1986). However, the incidence of Pica is said to be decreasing because of improved education and nutrition (Feldman, 1986). Children of both sexes are said to be equally affected (APA, 1987), but Kaplan & Sadock (1985) reported an increased occurrence in males. The disorder is usually first apparent between the ages of 12 and 24 months and often remits spontaneously in early childhood, although some cases persist into adulthood (Solyom, Solyom, & Freeman, 1991). Siblings may be affected (Kaplan & Sadock, 1985).

Various theories implicating pharmacological (addictions to pharmacologically active substances), psychological (unmet oral needs, aggression), nutritional (deficiencies), and cultural factors as etiological contributors have been described (Feldman, 1986). Krieger (1982) suggests that Pica is not associated with specific nutritional deficiencies. However, nutritional deficiencies such as iron, calcium, and zinc have been found to be associated with Pica, but the question of whether the deficiencies cause Pica or are caused by it remains unanswered. There is also an association between Pica and cultural factors (Danford, 1982; Forsyth & Benoit, 1989). For instance, in some Southern black subcultures, clay may be fed to infants as a pacifier; in some African cultures, well-being is promoted by the ingestion of soil, which is believed to have magical properties (Danford, 1982). More commonly, Pica is associated with a variety of psychosocial stressors (Singhi, Singhi, & Adwani, 1981), including parental psychopathology, large families, poverty, child maltreatment, suboptimal supervision and stimulation, and family disorganization (Madden, Russo, & Cataldo, 1980; Solyom et al., 1991). However, no single theory seems to explain all types of Pica, and etiological factors may coexist and interact to produce the final clinical picture of a child with Pica (McLoughlin, 1987; Danford, 1982; Feldman, 1986).

Some complications have been described, such as lead poisoning (secondary to ingestion of paint and plaster); intestinal obstructions (secondary to trichobezoars [hairball tumors],

geophagia, or lithophagia); intestinal perforation; infections (toxoplasma or toxocara secondary to the ingestion of feces and dirt); and death from medical complications. Given the lack of consistent definition, and the many methodological problems plaguing research on Pica, the interpretation of available research data remains problematic (Lacey, 1990). However, it must be emphasized that Marchi and Cohen (1990) recently documented a strong relationship between Pica in early childhood and problems with Bulimia Nervosa in adolescence.

The treatment of Pica has focused primarily on correcting medical and surgical complications of the disorder. Aversive and nonaversive behavior therapy (Danford & Huber, 1982), family therapy (Aleksandrowicz & Mares, 1978), and physical restraints (Singh & Bakker, 1984) have all been used with varying success.

Psychosocial Dwarfism

Psychosocial dwarfism is not a separate diagnostic category in DSM-III-R (APA, 1987) or ICD-9-CM (WHO, 1978). Nevertheless, it has been recognized for many decades (Talbot, Sobel, Burke, Lindeman, & Kaufman, 1947) and appears to be quite rare. It has been referred to as "maternal deprivation" (Patton & Gardner, 1963), "emotional deprivation" (Powell et al., 1967), "deprivation dwarfism" (Drash, Greenberg, & Mooney, 1968), "nonorganic FTT" (Hufton & Oates, 1977), "psychosocial short stature" (Tanner, 1973), and "psychosomatic dwarfism" (Ferholt et al., 1985).

Some controversy still exists about the definition of psychosocial dwarfism and about whether or not nonorganic FTT and psychosocial dwarfism are the same entity. Most authors agree that the disorder is characterized by the following:

1. Growth failure (marked linear growth retardation and delayed epiphyseal maturation).

2. Neuroendocrine dysfunction in about 50% of affected children (Ferholt et al., 1983), in particular reversible hypopituitarism (Guilhaume, Benoit, Gourmelen, & Richardet, 1982).

3. History of bizarre eating and drinking behaviors (Money & Wolff, 1974), including (a) polyphagia (e.g., stealing and hoarding food, gorging, eating garbage, emesis, and eating pet food), and (b) polydipsia (e.g., with drinking toilet bowl water, dishwater, and stagnant

water). Other associated problems may include accident proneness, self-mutilation, pain agnosia (Silver & Finkelstein, 1967), encopresis (Hopwood & Becker, 1979), cataplexy (Krieger, 1982), self-induced vomiting, elective mutism, depression, personality disturbances, disturbed interpersonal relationships (Ferholt et al., 1985), unusual patterns of relatedness, impulsivity, aggression, apathy, irritability, withdrawal, and temper tantrums (Green, Campbell, & David, 1984). Sleep disturbances, including abnormality of Stage 4 sleep (Guilhaume et al., 1982) and night roaming while searching for food (Drash et al., 1968), have been reported.

4. Dramatic weight gain and improvement of developmental and behavioral problems, and spontaneous normalization of neuroendocrine function when the child is hospitalized or removed from the home environment (Ferholt et al., 1985; Hopwood & Becker, 1979). When the child returns to the parents, however, any gains made are quickly lost (Ferholt et al., 1985).

Green (1986) and his colleagues (1984) claim that psychosocial dwarfism is classically observed in the absence of malnutrition (as defined by being underweight for height) and overt physical abuse. However, many other investigators believe that malnutrition is responsible for the endocrine abnormalities and the growth failure (Fischoff et al., 1971; Krieger, 1982; Krieger & Mellinger, 1971; Whitten et al., 1969). Others restrict the definition to children above age 2 with severe growth delay, low plasma concentration of human growth hormone, and absence of malnutrition (Blizzard, 1973).

Considerable heterogeneity has been reported in terms of age of onset—this is typically between 18 and 48 months, but may extend to 7 years (Ferholt et al., 1985)—and the presence–absence of developmental delays, malnutrition, and behavioral abnormalities in the child. Specific and global developmental delays have been reported, including borderline intellectual functioning and mental retardation (Barbero & Shaheen, 1967; Drash et al., 1968; Ferholt et al., 1985; Hopwood & Becker, 1979; Silver & Finkelstein, 1967). Some children have histories of FTT or eating problems in infancy (Bowden & Hopwood, 1982), and most children have normal birthweights (Ferholt et al., 1985).

Parental psychopathology (Coleman & Provence, 1957; Ferholt et al., 1985; Fischoff et al., 1971; Hufton & Oates, 1977; Krieger, 1973; Powell et al., 1967; Silver & Finkelstein, 1967)

and physical maltreatment (Drash et al., 1968; Ferholt et al., 1985) have been reported. Indeed, the parents exhibit angry, tense, and rejecting interactions with the child and have globally negative perceptions of the child. Krieger (1973) believes that malnourishment is secondary to personality problems in the parents, who restrict food intake and starve the child. The parents have been described as uncooperative, thus seriously limiting therapeutic work and long-term follow-up (Hopwood & Becker, 1979; Krieger, 1982). Interestingly, siblings are sometimes affected (Hopwood & Becker, 1979).

The differential diagnosis includes distinguishing psychosocial dwarfism from short stature due to hypopituitarism, constitutional short stature, and stress (which has been demonstrated to relate to transient deceleration in the rate of weight gain; Underwood & Van Wyk, 1981).

Long-term complications include short stature and delayed puberty (Money & Wolff, 1974).

Post-Traumatic Eating Disorder

Post-traumatic eating disorder (PTED) is not a DSM-III-R Axis 1 diagnosis (APA, 1987) and is not included in ICD-9-CM (WHO, 1978). The disorder was recently described by Chatoor and her colleagues (Chatoor, Kerzner, et al., 1987; Chatoor, Conley, & Dickson, 1988) as a syndrome of pervasive food refusal secondary to traumatic oral experiences related to medical treatments, such as insertion of endotracheal and nasogastric feeding tubes, vigorous suctioning, and experiences of choking or gagging on food or medicine.

Chatoor, Kerzner, et al. (1987) argue that the incidence of PTED is rising because of the growing number of infants with complex medical problems who survive. Symptoms in older children include intense anticipatory anxiety when thinking about eating, preoccupation with choking (including having nightmares about choking and dying), and panic when forced to eat. Infants exhibit similar anticipatory anxiety and phobic reactions when food is offered (Benoit, 1990).

Chatoor et al. (1988) report that pre-existing psychopathology in the child and the subsequent reaction of the family are critical factors influencing the severity and course of the disorder. They also advocate that the treatment of PTED in an older child should include a combination of nutritional management; behavior modification therapy; and individual and family therapy to address the child's nutritional needs, anticipatory anxiety about eating and choking, developmental conflicts centering around issues of separation and individuation, and the family dysfunction. Behavior therapy has been used successfully with some infants with PTED (Benoit, 1990). However, treatment methods have not been systematically evaluated.

Other Feeding Disorders

Very little has been reported on pathological overfeeding (which may be associated with forced feeding), and even though this problem is seen clinically, it seems relatively rare. Overfeeding has been hypothesized to result when a mother is unable to decipher her infant's cries and offers food in response to every crying episode (Taitz, 1977). The role of pathological overfeeding in the development of obesity remains unclear. The treatment of infant overfeeding has not been studied empirically.

Infantile anorexia nervosa (Chatoor, Egan, et al., 1987; Chatoor, 1989) is considered a developmental disorder of separation and individuation, characterized by FTT, food refusal, or extreme food selectivity. Its onset is between the ages of 6 months and 3 years. Chatoor (1989) believes that the mother's inconsistent and noncontingent responses lead to the lack of somatopsychological differentiation in the infant. Interactions between babies with infantile anorexia nervosa and their mothers are characterized by more dyadic conflict and struggle for control, less dyadic reciprocity and maternal contingency, and more mutual negative affect, compared to those of controls (Chatoor, Egan, et al., 1987). Babies with infantile anorexia nervosa are reportedly willful and provocative toward their mothers, who are intrusive and unresponsive (Chatoor, 1989).

Selective food refusal (pickiness) is a relatively frequent clinical problem, although it has not been systematically studied. Interestingly, picky eating in early childhood has been found to be a protective factor against the development of Bulimia Nervosa, but a risk factor for the development of Anorexia Nervosa, in adolescence (Marchi & Cohen, 1990).

Pervasive food refusal in infants who are fed artificially may not be associated with FTT because the infants' nutritional needs are met. It is not clear whether pervasive food refusal is synonymous with PTED.

The behavioral management of children with a variety of feeding disorders has been described in the form of case series and case reports (Benoit, 1990; Handen, Mandell, & Russo, 1986; Linscheid, Tarnowski, Rasnake, & Brams, 1987; Luiselli & Gleason, 1987). However, no systematic studies comparing various behavioral and other treatment approaches have been conducted.

CONCLUSION

FTT and feeding disorders are generally considered to be complex problems requiring the coordinated expertise of various disciplines, such as pediatrics, psychiatry, psychology, nursing, dietary, social work, speech pathology, occupational therapy, physical therapy; sometimes the services of child protective and other community agencies are needed as well. After over three decades of research in the field, the mechanisms by which various etiological factors interact and contribute to the development and perpetuation of both FTT and feeding disorders in infancy and early childhood remain unclear. The literature on FTT and feeding disorders of infancy and early childhood is limited by inconsistent definitions and methodologies, relatively small sample sizes, and paucity of outcome data. These shortcomings make the available research data difficult to interpret, compare, and generalize. Much work remains to be done to validate existing classification systems; to assess diagnostic and treatment approaches; and to examine the mechanisms by which FTT and feeding disorders lead to later emotional, behavioral, and eating problems.

REFERENCES

Accardo, P., Whitman, B., Caul, J., & Rolfe, U. (1988). Autism and plumbism: A possible association. *Clinical Pediatrics, 27,* 41–44.

Ainsworth, M. D. S., Blehar, M. C., Waters, E., & Wall, S. (1978). *Patterns of attachment: A psychological study of the Strange Situation.* Hillsdale, NJ: Erlbaum.

Aleksandrowicz, M. K., & Mares, A. J. (1978). Trichotillomania and trichobezoar in an infant. *Journal of the American Academy of Child Psychiatry, 17,* 533–539.

Altemeier, W. A., III, O'Connor, S., Sherrod, K. B., Yeager, T. D., & Vietze, P. M. (1985). A strategy for managing nonorganic failure to thrive based on a prospective study of antecedents. In D. Drotar (Ed.), *New directions in failure to thrive: Implications for research and practice* (pp. 211–222). New York: Plenum Press.

American Psychiatric Association (APA). (1987). *Diagnostic and statistical manual of mental disorders* (3rd ed., rev.). Washington, DC: Author.

Barbero, G., & Shaheen, E. (1967). Environmental failure to thrive: A clinical interview. *Journal of Pediatrics, 73,* 690–698.

Bell, L. S., & Woolston, J. L. (1985). The relationship of weight gain and caloric intake in infants with organic and nonorganic failure to thrive syndrome. *Journal of the American Academy of Child Psychiatry, 24*(4), 447–452.

Benoit, D. (1990, October). *Assessment and treatment of infant feeding disorders.* Paper presented at the 37th Annual Meeting of the American Academy of Child and Adolescent Psychiatry, Chicago.

Benoit, D. (1992). *Behavioral assessment and treatment of feeding disorders in infancy.* Unpublished manuscript.

Benoit, D., Zeanah, C. H., & Barton, M. L. (1989). Maternal attachment disturbances in failure to thrive. *Infant Mental Health Journal, 10*(3), 185–202.

Berkowitz, C. D. (1985). Comprehensive pediatric management of failure to thrive: An interdisciplinary approach. In D. Drotar (Ed.), *New directions in failure to thrive: Implications for research and practice* (pp. 193–210). New York: Plenum Press.

Berkowitz, C. D., & Senter, S. A. (1987). Characteristics of mother–infant interactions in nonorganic failure to thrive. *Journal of Family Practice, 25*(4), 377–381.

Berwick, D. M. (1980). Nonorganic failure to thrive. *Pediatrics in Review, 1,* 265–270.

Berwick, D. M., Levy, J. C., & Kleinerman, R. (1982). Failure to thrive: Diagnostic yield of hospitalization. *Archives of Disease in Childhood, 57,* 347–351.

Bithoney, W. G., & Dubowitz, H. (1985). Organic concomitants of nonorganic failure to thrive: Implications for research. In D. Drotar (Ed.), *New directions in failure to thrive: Implications for research and practice* (pp. 47–68). New York: Plenum Press.

Bithoney, W. G., & Rathbun, J. (1983). Failure to thrive. In M. Levine, W. Carey, A. Crocker, & R. Gross (Eds.), *Developmental and behavioral pediatrics* (pp. 557–582). Philadelphia: W. B. Saunders.

Blizzard, R. M. (1973). Discussion in J. L. Van den Brande and M. V. L. DuCaju: Plasma somatomedin activity in children with growth disturbances. In S. Raiti (Ed.), *Advances in human growth hormone research* (DHEW Publication No. NIH 74-612, pp. 124–125). Washington, DC: U.S. Government Printing Office.

Bowden, M. L., & Hopwood, N. J. (1982). Psychosocial dwarfism: Identification, intervention, and planning. *Social Work in Health Care, 7,* 15–36.

Brasel, J. A. (1980). Endocrine adaptation to malnutrition. *Pediatric Research, 14,* 1299–1303.

Caldwell, B. M. (1971). The effects of psychosocial deprivation on human development in infancy. In S. Chess & A. Thomas (Eds.), *Annual progress in child psychiatry and child development* (pp. 3–22). New York: Brunner/Mazel.

Casey, P. H. (1988). Failure-to-thrive: Transitional perspective. *Journal of Developmental and Behavioral Pediatrics, 8,* 37–38.

Casey, P. H., Wortham, B., & Nelson, J. Y. (1984). Management of children with failure to thrive in a rural ambulatory setting: Epidemiology and growth outcome. *Clinical Pediatrics, 23*(6), 325–330.

Chase, H. P., & Martin, H. P. (1970). Undernutrition and child development. *New England Journal of Medicine, 282,* 933–939.

Chatoor, I. (1989). Infantile anorexia nervosa: A developmental disorder of separation and individuation. *Journal of the American Academy of Psychoanalysis, 17,* 43–64.

Chatoor, I., Conley, C., & Dickson, L. (1988). Food refusal after an incident of choking: A posttraumatic eating disorder. *Journal of the American Academy of Child and Adolescent Psychiatry, 27*(1), 105–110.

Chatoor, I., Dickson, L., Schaefer, S., & Egan, J. (1985). A developmental classification of feeding disorders associated with failure to thrive: Diagnosis and treatment. In D. Drotar (Ed.), *New directions in failure to thrive: Implications for research and practice* (pp. 235–258). New York: Plenum Press.

Chatoor, I., & Egan, J. (1983). Nonorganic failure to thrive and dwarfism due to food refusal: A separation disorder. *Journal of the American Academy of Child Psychiatry, 22,* 294–301.

Chatoor, I., & Egan, J. (1987). Etiology and diagnosis of failure to thrive and growth disorders in infants and children. In J. Noshpitz (Ed.), *Basic handbook in child psychiatry* (Vol. 5, pp. 272–279). New York: Basic Books.

Chatoor, I., Egan, J., Getson, P., Menvielle, E., & O'Donnell, R. (1987). Mother–infant interactions in infantile anorexia nervosa. *Journal of the American Academy of Child and Adolescent Psychiatry, 27,* 535–540.

Chatoor, I., Kerzner, B., Menvielle, E., Samango-Sprouse, C., Pesquera, K., Simenson, R., Rankin, J. H., & Lierman, C. (Chairs). (1987). *A multidisciplinary team approach to complex feeding disorders in technology dependent infants.* Symposium presented at the Fifth Biennial National Training Institute, Washington, DC.

Coleman, R. W., & Provence, S. (1957). Environmental retardation (hospitalism) in infants living in families. *Pediatrics, 19,* 285–292.

Cooper, M. (1957). *Pica.* Springfield, IL: Charles C Thomas.

Crittenden, P.M. (1987). Non-organic failure-to-thrive: Deprivation or distortion? *Infant Mental Health Journal, 8*(1), 51–64.

Dahl, M., & Sundelin, C. (1986). Early feeding problems in an affluent society: I. Categories and clinical signs. *Acta Paediatrica Scandinavica, 75,* 370–379.

Danford, D. E. (1982). Pica and nutrition. *Annual Review of Nutrition, 2,* 303–322.

Danford, D. E., & Huber, A. M. (1982). Pica among mentally retarded adults. *American Journal of Mental Deficiency, 87,* 141–146.

Drash, P. W., Greenberg, N. E., & Mooney, J. (1968). Intelligence and personality in four syndromes of dwarfism. In D. B. Cheek (Ed.), *Human growth: Body composition, cell growth, energy, and intelligence* (pp. 568–581). Philadelphia: Lea & Febiger.

Drotar, D. (1985). Failure to thrive and preventive mental health: Diagnostic and therapeutic implications. In D. Drotar (Ed.), *New directions in failure to thrive: Implications for research and practice* (pp. 27–44). New York: Plenum Press.

Drotar, D., & Malone, C. A. (1982). Family-oriented intervention in failure to thrive. In M. Klaus & M. O. Robertson (Eds.), *Birth, interaction and attachment* (Vol. 6, pp. 104–112). Skillman, NJ: Johnson & Johnson Pediatric Round Table.

Drotar, D., Malone, C. A., & Negray, J. (1980). Intellectual assessment of young children with environmentally based failure to thrive. *Child Abuse and Neglect,* 4, 23–31.

Drotar, D., Malone, C. A., Devost, L., Brickell, C., Mantz-Clumpner, C., Negray, J., Wallace, M., Woychik, J., Wyatt, B., Eckerle, D., Bush, M., Finlon, M. A., El-Amin, D., Nowak, M., Satola, J., & Pallotta, J. (1985). Early preventive intervention in failure to thrive: Methods and early outcome. In D. Drotar (Ed.), *New directions in failure to thrive: Implications for research and practice* (pp. 119–138). New York: Plenum Press.

Drotar, D., Woychik, J., Mantz-Clumpner, C., Brickell, C., Negray, J., Wallace, M., & Malone, C. A. (1985). The family context of failure to thrive. In D. Drotar (Ed.), *New directions in failure to thrive: Implications for research and practice* (pp. 295–310). New York: Plenum Press.

Elmer, E., Gregg, G. S., & Ellison, P. (1969). Late results of the "failure to thrive" syndrome. *Clinical Pediatrics,* 8(10), 584–589.

Evans, S. L., Reinhart, J. B., & Succop, R. A. (1972). Failure to thrive: A study of 45 children and their families. *Journal of the American Academy of Child Psychiatry,* 11, 440–457.

Feldman, M. D. (1986). Pica: Current perspectives. *Psychosomatics,* 27, 519–523.

Ferholt, J. B., Rotnem, D. L., Genel, M., Leonard, M., Carey, M., & Hunter, D. E. (1985). A psychodynamic study of psychosocial dwarfism: A syndrome of depression, personality disorder, and impaired growth. *Journal of the American Academy of Child Psychiatry,* 24(1), 49–57.

Finlon, M. A., & Drotar, D. (1983, April). *Social competence and attachment behavior in failure to thrive infants.* Paper presented at the International Conference on Infant Studies, New York.

Fischoff, J., Whitten, C. F., & Pettit, M. (1971). A psychiatric study of mothers of infants with growth failure secondary to maternal deprivation. *Journal of Pediatrics,* 79, 209–215.

Flanagan, C. H. (1977). Rumination in infancy—past and present. *Journal of the American Academy of Child Psychiatry,* 16, 140–149.

Forsyth, C. J., & Benoit, G. M. (1989). "Rare, ole dirty snacks": Some research notes on dirt eating. *Deviant Behavior,* 10, 61–68.

Fosson, A., & Wilson, J. (1987). Family interactions surrounding feedings of infants with nonorganic failure to thrive. *Clinical Pediatrics,* 26, 518–523.

Fraiberg, S., Adelson, E., & Shapiro, V. (1975). Ghosts in the nursery. *Journal of the American Academy of Child Psychiatry,* 14, 387–421.

Frank, D. A. (1985). Biologic risks in "nonorganic" failure to thrive: Diagnostic and therapeutic implications. In D. Drotar (Ed.), *New directions in failure to thrive: Implications for research and practice* (pp. 17–26). New York: Plenum Press.

Frank, D. A., & Zeisel, S. H. (1988). Failure to thrive. *Pediatric Clinics of North America,* 35(6), 1187–1206.

Freud, A. (1946). The psychoanalytic study of infantile feeding disturbances. *Psychoanalytic Study of the Child,* 2, 119–132.

Fryer, G. E. (1988). The efficacy of hospitalization of nonorganic failure-to-thrive children: A meta-analysis. *Child Abuse and Neglect,* 12, 375–381.

Geertsma, M. A., Hyams, J. S., Pelletier, J. M., & Reiter, S. (1985). Feeding resistance after parenteral hyperalimentation. *American Journal of Diseases of Children,* 139, 255–256.

George, C., Kaplan, N., & Main, M. (1985). *Adult Attachment Interview.* Unpublished manuscript, University of California at Berkeley.

Glaser, H. H., Heagarty, M. C., Bullard, D. M., & Pivchik, E. C. (1968). Physical and psychological development of children with early failure to thrive. *Journal of Pediatrics,* 73(5), 690–698.

Gordon, A. H., & Jameson, J. C. (1979). Infant–mother attachment in patients with nonorganic failure to thrive syndrome. *Journal of the American Academy of Child Psychiatry,* 18, 251–259.

Green, W. H. (1986). Psychosocial dwarfism: Psychological and etiological considerations. In B. Lahey & A. Kazdin (Eds.), *Advances in clinical child psychology* (Vol. 9, pp. 245–278). New York: Plenum Press.

Green, W. H., Campbell, M., & David, R. (1984). Psychosocial dwarfism: A critical review of the evidence. *Journal of the American Academy of Child Psychiatry,* 23(1), 39–48.

Guilhaume, A., Benoit, O., Gourmelen, M., & Richardet, J. M. (1982). Relationship between stage IV deficit and reversible HGH deficiency in psychological dwarfism. *Pediatric Research,* 16, 299–303.

Habicht, P., Martorell, R., Yarborough, C., Malina, R. M., & Klein, R. E. (1974). Height and weight standards for preschool children. *Lancet, i,* 611.

Hamill, P. V. V., Drizd, T. A., Johnson, C. L., Reed, R. B., Roche, A. F., & Moore, W. M. (1979). Physical growth: National Center for Health Statistics percentiles. *American Journal of Clinical Nutrition,* 32, 607–629.

Handen, B. L., Mandell, F., & Russo, D. C. (1986). Feeding induction in children who refuse to eat. *American Journal of Diseases of Children,* 140, 52–54.

Hannaway, P. (1976). Failure to thrive. A study of 100 infants and children. *Clinics in Pediatrics,* 9, 69–99.

Haynes, C. F., Cutler, C., Gray, G., O'Keefe, K., & Kempe, R. S. (1983). Nonorganic failure to thrive: Implications of placement through analysis of videotaped interactions. *Child Abuse and Neglect,* 7(3), 321–328.

Herbst, J., Friedland, G. W., & Zboralske, F. F. (1971). Hiatal hernia and "rumination" in infants and children. *Journal of Pediatrics,* 2, 261–265.

Hess, A. K., Hess, K. A., & Hard, H. E. (1977). Intellectual characteristics of mothers of failure-to-thrive syndrome children. *Child: Care, Health, and Development,* 3, 377–387.

Hopwood, N. J., & Becker, D. J. (1979). Psychosocial dwarfism: Detection, evaluation, and management. *Child Abuse and Neglect,* 3, 439–447.

Hufton, I., & Oates, K. (1977). Nonorganic failure to thrive: A long-term follow-up. *Pediatrics,* 59(1), 73–77.

Illingworth, R. S., & Lister, J. (1964). The critical or sensitive period, with special reference to certain feeding problems in infants and children. *Journal of Pediatrics,* 65, 839–848.

Jenkins, S., Bax, M., & Hart, H. (1980). Behaviour problems in pre-school children. *Journal of Child Psychology and Psychiatry,* 21, 5–17.

Kaplan, H. I., & Sadock, B. J. (Eds.). (1985). *Comprehensive textbook of psychiatry* (4th ed.). Baltimore: Williams & Wilkins.

Kerr, M., Bogues, J., & Kerr, D. (1978). Psychosocial functioning of mothers of malnourished children. *Pediatrics, 62,* 778–784.

Kotelchuck, M., & Newberger, E. H. (1983). Failure to thrive: A controlled study of familial characteristics. *Journal of the American Academy of Child Psychiatry, 22*(4), 322–328.

Krieger, I. (1973). Food restriction as a form of child abuse in ten cases of psychosocial deprivation dwarfism. *Clinical Pediatrics, 13,* 127–133.

Krieger, I. (1982). *Pediatric disorders of feeding, nutrition, and metabolism.* New York: Wiley.

Krieger, I., & Mellinger, R. C. (1971). Pituitary function in the deprivation syndrome. *Journal of Pediatrics, 79,* 216–225.

Kristiansson, B., & Fallstrom, S. P. (1987). Growth at the age of 4 years subsequent to early failure to thrive. *Child Abuse and Neglect, 11,* 35–46.

Lacey, E. P. (1990). Broadening the perspective on Pica: Literature review. *Public Health Reports, 105,* 29–35.

Leonard, M. F., Rhymes, J. P., & Solnit, A. J. (1966). Failure to thrive—A family problem. *American Journal of Diseases of Children, 111,* 600–612.

Lieberman, A. F., & Birch, M. (1985). The etiology of failure to thrive: An interactional developmental approach. In D. Drotar (Ed.), *New directions in failure to thrive: Implications for research and practice* (pp. 259–278). New York: Plenum Press.

Linscheid, T. R., & Rasnake, L. K. (1985). Behavioral approaches to the treatment of failure to thrive. In D. Drotar (Ed.), *New directions in failure to thrive: Implications for research and practice* (pp. 279–294). New York: Plenum Press.

Linscheid, T. R., Tarnowski, K. J., Rasnake, L. K., & Brams, J. S. (1987). Behavioral treatment of food refusal in a child with short-gut syndrome. *Journal of Pediatric Psychology, 12*(3), 451–459.

Luiselli, J. K., & Gleason, D. J. (1987). Combining reinforcement and texture fading procedures to overcome chronic food refusal. *Journal of Behavior Therapy and Experimental Psychiatry, 18*(2), 149–155.

Madden, N. A., Russo, D. C., & Cataldo, M. F. (1980). Environmental influences on mouthing in children with lead intoxication. *Journal of Pediatric Psychology, 5,* 207–216.

Marchi, M., & Cohen, P. (1990). Early childhood eating behaviors and adolescent eating disorder. *Journal of the American Academy of Child and Adolescent Psychiatry, 29,* 112–117.

Mayes, S. D., Humphrey, F. J., Handford, H. A., & Mitchell, J. F. (1988). Rumination disorder: Differential diagnosis. *Journal of the American Academy of Child and Adolescent Psychiatry, 27*(3), 300–302.

McAlpine, C., & Singh, N. N. (1986). Pica in institutionalized mentally retarded persons. *Journal of Mental Deficiency Research, 30,* 171–178.

McDonough, S. (1990, October). *Treatment of insensitive caregivers.* Paper presented at the 37th Annual Meeting of the American Academy of Child and Adolescent Psychiatry, Chicago.

McLoughlin, I. J. (1987). The picas. *British Journal of Hospital Medicine, 37,* 286–290.

Menking, M., Wagnitz, J., Burton, J., Coddington, R. D., & Solos, J. (1969). Rumination: A near fatal psychiatric disease of infancy. *New England Journal of Medicine, 280,* 802–804.

Mitchell, W. G., Gorrell, R. W., & Greenberg, R. A. (1980).

Failure-to-thrive: A study in primary care setting—Epidemiology and follow-up. *Pediatrics, 65*(5), 971–977.

Money, J., & Wolff, G. (1974). Late puberty, retarded growth and reversible hyposomatotropinism (psychosocial dwarfism). *Adolescence, 9,* 121–134.

Newberger, E. H., Reed, R. P., Daniel, J. M., Hyde, J., & Kotelchuck, M. (1977). Pediatric social illness: Toward an etiologic classification. *Pediatrics, 60,* 175–185.

Oates, R. K., Peacock, A., & Forrest, D. (1985). Long-term effects of nonorganic failure to thrive. *Pediatrics, 75*(1), 36–40.

Palmer, S., & Horn, S. (1978). Feeding problems in children. In S. Palmer & S. Ekvall (Eds.), *Pediatric nutrition in developmental disorders* (pp. 107–129). Springfield, IL: Charles C Thomas.

Patton, R. G., & Gardner, L. L. (1963). *Growth failure in maternal deprivation.* Springfield, IL: Charles C Thomas.

Polan, H. J., Kaplan, M. D., Kessler, D. B., Shindledecker, M. N., Stern, D. N., & Ward, M. J. (1991). Psychopathology in mothers of children with failure to thrive. *Infant Mental Health Journal, 12*(1), 55–64.

Polan, H. J., Leon, A., Kaplan, M. D., Kessler, D. B., Stern, D. N., & Ward, M. J. (1991). Disturbances of affect expression in failure to thrive. *Journal of the American Academy of Child and Adolescent Psychiatry, 30*(6), 897–903.

Pollitt, E., & Eichler, A. W. (1976). Behavioral disturbances among failure to thrive children. *American Journal of Diseases of Children, 130,* 24–29.

Pollitt, E., Eichler, A. W., & Chan, C. K. (1975). Psychosocial development and behavior of mothers of failure-to-thrive children. *American Journal of Orthopsychiatry, 45,* 525–537.

Powell, G. F., Brasel, J. A., & Blizzard, R. M. (1967). Emotional deprivation and growth retardation simulating idiopathic hypopituitarism: I and II. *New England Journal of Medicine, 276,* 1271–1278, 1279–1283.

Powell, G. F., & Low, J. (1983). Behavior in nonorganic failure to thrive. *Journal of Developmental and Behavioral Pediatrics, 4,* 26–33.

Rathbun, J. M. (1985). Issues in the treatment of emotional and behavioral disturbances in failure to thrive. In D. Drotar (Ed.), *New directions in failure to thrive: Implications for research and practice* (pp. 311–314). New York: Plenum Press.

Rector, W. G., Jr., Fortuin, N. J., & Conley, C. L. (1982). Non-hematologic effects of chronic iron deficiency: A study of patients with polycythemia vera treated solely with venesections. *Medicine, 61,* 382–389.

Richman, N. (1981). A community survey of characteristics of one- to two-year-olds with sleep disturbances. *Journal of the American Academy of Child Psychiatry, 20,* 281–291.

Richman, N., Stevenson, J., & Graham, P. J. (1982). *Preschool to school: A behavioural study.* London: Academic Press.

Rosenn, D. W., Loeb, L. S., & Jura, M. B. (1980). Differentiation of organic from nonorganic failure to thrive syndrome in infancy. *Pediatrics, 66,* 698–704.

Sajwaj, A., Libet, N., & Agras, S. (1974). Lemon juice therapy: The control of life-threatening behavior in a 6–month-old infant. *Journal of Applied Behavioral Analysis, 7,* 557–566.

Sauvage, D., Leddet, I., Hameury, L., & Barthelemy, C.

(1985). Infantile rumination: Diagnosis and follow up study of twenty cases. *Journal of the American Academy of Child Psychiatry, 24*(2), 197–203.

Shaheen, E., Alexander, D., Truskowsky, M., & Barbero, G. J. (1968). Failure to thrive: A retrospective profile. *Clinical Pediatrics, 7*(5), 255–261.

Shapiro, W., Fraiberg, S., & Adelson, E. (1976). Infant–parent psychotherapy on behalf of a child in a critical nutritional state. *Psychoanalanlytic Study of the Child, 31*, 461–491.

Sheinbein, M. (1975). Treatment for the hospitalized infantile ruminator: Programmed brief social behavior reinforcers. *Clinical Pediatrics, 14*, 719–724.

Sherrod, K. B., O'Connor, S., Altemeier, W. A., III, & Vietze, P. (1985). Toward a semispecific, multidimensional, threshold model of maltreatment. In D. Drotar (Ed.), *New directions in failure to thrive: Implications for research and practice* (pp. 89–106). New York: Plenum Press.

Silver, H. K., & Finkelstein, M. (1967). Deprivation dwarfism. *Journal of Pediatrics, 70*, 317–324.

Singer, L. (1986). Long-term hospitalization of failure-to-thrive infants: Developmental outcome at three years. *Child Abuse and Neglect, 10*, 479–486.

Singh, N. N., & Bakker, L. W. (1984). Suppression of pica by overcorrection and physical restraint: A comprehensive analysis. *Journal of Autism and Developmental Disorders, 14*, 331–341.

Singhi, S., Singhi, P., & Adwani, G. B. (1981). Role of psychosocial stress in the cause of pica. *Clinical Pediatrics, 20*(12), 783–785.

Solyom, C., Solyom, L., & Freeman, R. (1991). An unusual case of pica. *Canadian Journal of Psychiatry, 36*, 50–53.

Spitzer, R. L., & Williams, J. B. W. (1986). *Structured Clinical Interview for DSM-III-R: Non-patient version/Personality disorders*. New York: Biometrics Research Department, New York State Psychiatric Institute.

Stewart, R. F. (1973). The family that fails to thrive. In D. P. Hymovich & M. U. Barnard (Eds.), *Family health care* (pp. 341–364). New York: McGraw-Hill.

Sturm, L., & Drotar, D. (1989). Prediction of weight for height following intervention in three-year-old children with early histories of nonorganic failure to thrive. *Child Abuse and Neglect, 13*, 19–28.

Taitz, L. S. (1977). Obesity in pediatric practice: Infantile obesity. *Pediatric Clinics of North America, 24*(1), 107–115.

Talbot, N. B., Sobel, E. H., Burke, B. S., Lindeman, E., & Kaufman, S. B. (1947). Dwarfism in healthy children: Its possible relation to emotional, nutritional, and endocrine disturbances. *New England Journal of Medicine, 236*, 783–793.

Tanner, J. M. (1973). Resistance to exogenous human growth hormone in psychosocial short stature (emotional deprivation) [Letter to the editor]. *Journal of Pediatrics, 82*, 171–172.

Underwood, L. E., & Van Wyk, J. J. (1981). Hormones in normal and aberrant growth. In R. H. Williams (Ed.), *Textbook of endocrinology* (6th ed., pp. 1149–1191). Philadelphia: W. B. Saunders.

Valenzuela, M. (1990). Attachment in chronically underweight young children. *Child Development, 61*, 1984–1996.

Vietze, P. M., Falsey, S., O'Connor, S., Sandler, H., Sherrod, K., & Altemeier, W. A. (1980). Newborn behavioral and interactional characteristics of nonorganic failure to thrive infants. In T. M. Field, S. Goldberg, D. Stern, & A. M. Sostek (Eds.), *High-risk infants and children: Adult and peer interactions* (pp. 5–23). New York: Academic Press.

White, J., Malcolm, R., Roper, K., Westphal, M., & Smith, C. (1981). Psychological and developmental factors in failure to thrive: One- to three-year follow-up. *Journal of Developmental and Behavioral Pediatrics, 2*, 112–114.

Whitten, C. F., Pettit, M. G., & Fischoff, J. (1969). Evidence that growth failure from maternal deprivation is secondary to undereating. *Journal of the American Medical Association, 209*(11), 1675–1682.

Winton, A. S. W., & Singh, N. N. (1983). Rumination in pediatric populations: A behavioral analysis. *Journal of the American Academy of Child Psychiatry, 22*(3), 269–275.

Woolston, J. L. (1983). Eating disorders in infancy and early childhood. *Journal of the American Academy of Child Psychiatry, 22*(2), 114–121.

Woolston, J. L. (1985). Diagnostic classification: The current challenge in failure to thrive syndrome research. In D. Drotar (Ed.), *New directions in failure to thrive: Implications for research and practice* (pp. 225–235). New York: Plenum Press.

World Health Organization (WHO). (1978). *International classification of diseases and its clinical modification* (9th ed.). Geneva: Author.

22

Disorders of Attachment

CHARLES H. ZEANAH, Jr.
OOMMEN K. MAMMEN
ALICIA F. LIEBERMAN

As early as the turn of the century, the medical literature cautioned about the deleterious effects of maternal deprivation on young children. Twelve years after completing an intervention study on the effects of institutionalization on infants, Chapin (1915) asserted:

> The best conditions for an infant require a home and a mother. The further we get away from these vital necessities of life, the greater will be our failure to get adequate results in trying to help the needy infant. Strange to say, these important conditions have often been overlooked or not sufficiently emphasized by those working in the field. (p. 1)

By midcentury, there was also a considerable scientific literature describing the adverse effects of less than adequate caregiving environments on infant development (Goldfarb, 1945; Spitz, 1945, 1946). These included a high mortality rate, poor growth, frequent infections, and delayed and deviant development. These effects occurred even when the infants' physical needs were met, and they could be reversed with individualized care by a mothering figure. The extant studies on the catastrophic effects of maternal deprivation were critically reviewed for the first time by John Bowlby in his monograph entitled *Maternal Care and Mental Health* (Bowlby, 1951). He concluded that maternal care was as vital to mental health as vitamins and other nutrients were to physical health. Ethological observations that primate infants are primed to become attached to their caregivers, and

Harlow and Zimmerman's (1959) experimental evidence that attachment is independent of having physical needs met, led Bowlby to conclude that normal development is contingent on attachment to a mothering figure.

Diagnostic criteria for syndromes of disordered attachment, on the other hand, have appeared only within the last 15 years. Criteria for diagnosing attachment disorders were first provided by the third edition of the *Diagnostic and Statistical Manual of Mental Disorders* (DSM-III; American Psychiatric Association [APA], 1980). Surprisingly, these clinical syndromes have inspired virtually no empirical research. As a result, there are no data on their validity. Zeanah and Emde (in press) have suggested that the criteria appear to have been derived from research on social behavior of maltreated children and infants raised in institutions. They have also observed that the substantially larger body of data on attachment in infancy and childhood, derived from developmental research with normal and high-risk populations, has not yet been integrated into the nosologies. Clearly, data from developmental research bear on issues of qualitative differences in attachment relationships, as well as the question of the point in disturbed parent–child relationships at which an attachment disorder should be designated. In this chapter, we propose diagnostic criteria for five types of clinical disorders of attachment, and use a developmental perspective to add to our understanding of their phenomenology.

THE CONSTRUCT
OF ATTACHMENT

Attachment has proven to be a compelling construct in contemporary developmental research, and in clinical evaluation and treatment of young children. Bowlby's (1969, 1973, 1980) ethological attachment theory has provided a number of testable hypotheses and has stimulated important research paradigms to test them. Controversies have arisen about whether qualitative or quantitative features of attachment are more important, and about whether attachment refers to feelings or behaviors of infants, of caregivers, or of both. Some confusion in the literature is apparent because of the varied ways in which the term has been used. In the contemporary literature, the term "attachment" has been used in the following four ways: "attachment behaviors," "attachment bonds," "attachment system," and "attachment relationships."

"Attachment behaviors" in the infant are signaling behaviors (such as smiling, vocalizing, or crying) and approach behaviors (such as crawling and walking toward the caregiver) that are designed to promote proximity to the caregiver. Although "attachment bonds" can refer to affiliative feelings between individuals in a close relationship, most commonly they refer to the affiliative feelings between parents and infants.

In his outline of attachment theory, Bowlby (1969) used "attachment" to refer to one of four behavior control systems that operate to motivate infant behavior. In addition to the "attachment system," Bowlby described the "exploratory system," responsible for motivating the infant to explore the object world; the "affiliative system," motivating the infant to be with others; and the "fear/wariness system," responsible for monitoring the infant's safety and danger. The attachment system has an external goal of motivating the infant to seek proximity to the attachment figure and an internal goal of motivating the infant to seek felt security. As a behavior control system, attachment involves the infant's use of the attachment figure as a "secure base" from which to explore novel environments (Ainsworth, 1967). At times when the attachment system is activated, the child uses the attachment figure as a "safe haven" to which to return in stressful or dangerous situations (Bretherton, 1980).

Finally, "attachment" is used increasingly to refer to the "attachment relationship," which is the domain of the parent–child relationship involving the caregiver's provision of nurturance and of emotional availability in times of need, as well as the child's seeking of comfort when needed.

DEVELOPMENTAL RESEARCH
ON ATTACHMENT

Development of Attachment

Primate parents and infants are biologically motivated to become attached to each other at birth. The infant is born with a number of characteristics that elicit affiliative responses in adult caregivers. The physical attributes of babyishness are characteristic throughout mammalian species. On the infant's side, the rudiments of attachment are present at birth only through recognition of the mother through auditory and olfactory channels. Infants are born able to distinguish their mothers' voices; in fact, they express a preference for their mothers' voices over other voices, even as newborns (DeCasper & Fifer, 1980). In the olfactory realm, newborns turn preferentially toward their mothers' breast pads instead of toward the pad of another lactating woman (MacFarlane, 1975).

From birth to 3 months, according to Bowlby, the infant is in the phase of limited discrimination of the attachment figure. In fact, social responsiveness is not obvious until after the initial biobehavioral shift at 2 to 3 months.

From 3 to 6 months, the infant is in phase of discriminating social responsiveness. Following the 2- to 3-month biobehavioral shift (Emde, Gaensbauer, & Harmon, 1976), social smiling begins, along with increased visual responsiveness and cooing. Infants as young as 2–3 months of age have been shown to interact differently with their mothers, their fathers, and a stranger. Still, they do not consistently express a preference for a specific attachment figure until after the onset of focused attachment at about 8 months of age.

The third phase of attachment, according to Bowlby, is from 8 months to 3 years. The infant is in the phase of actively seeking proximity and contact. Most of the research on infant attachment concerns itself with this period, when "secure base" and "safe haven" behaviors are most apparent.

In the third year, infants enter the phase of goal-corrected partnership. At this time, infants begin to infer the set goals and plans of their attachment figures and to incorporate the feelings and motives of these others into planning for their own behavior. The essence of this phase is cooperative planning and maintaining plans for attachment-related events, such as proximity and separations. In this phase, the relationship is negotiated by more sophisticated symbolic and communicative abilities, which were not possible for an infant in earlier phases.

Because of the invariance of the sequence of the development of attachment across the vast majority of infants, important differences are more apparent in the qualitative aspects of the organization and representation of attachment. Also, the organization of the attachment system has significantly greater stability and predictive value than do specific attachment behaviors (Sroufe & Waters, 1977; Waters, 1978).

According to Bowlby's theory, the development of infants' organizations of attachment is based on real interactive experiences (as opposed to fantasies) with attachment figures. Those who experience sensitive and emotionally available caregiving, for instance, develop a sense of others as dependably available and supportive, a sense of themselves as worthy of attention and affection, and generally positive expectations of intimate relationships. In contrast, when caregiving is inadequate, the child develops deficiencies in feelings about self and others, and a different set of expectations regarding relationships.

Feelings about the self and expectations of others in intimate relationships are organized by "internal working models." These are large-order memory structures, internal representations that contain all of the processes involved in the individual's subjective experience of others in social relationships (Zeanah & Anders, 1987). They include processes of attention and perception, of affect selection, of memory evocation, and of behavioral responses to others in important relationships (Main, Kaplan, & Cassidy, 1985). Because internal working models evolve from the actual experiences of individuals, they enable the individuals to form expectations of "the other" in relationships and also influence the way the individuals evaluate ongoing interactions in relationships. According to Bowlby (1969), internal working models are constructed during the latter part of the first year of life, based on an infant's experiences of caregiving.

Bowlby's theory, with its careful attention to observable behavior and emphasis on the importance of actual experience in the organization of the child's relationship with his or her caregivers, has stimulated a rich outpouring of empirical research on attachment infancy. In the following section, we review this research briefly.

Attachment Classifications in Developmental Research

By 1 year of age, the infant's attachment behavioral system is well organized, and attachment relationships may be reliably identified and assessed. Developmental research has relied mainly on a laboratory procedure, the Strange Situation procedure (SSP), to assess the organization of attachment in infants (Ainsworth, Blehar, Waters, & Wall, 1978). This moderately stressful laboratory paradigm was designed to evaluate the balance between an infant's attachment and exploratory systems. Inviting toys in a comfortable but unfamiliar environment activate the exploratory system. The procedure relies on separation from the attachment figure in an unfamiliar setting as a means of activating the attachment system. Results from dozens of investigations involving the procedure have generated considerable advances in our understanding of socioemotional development, and no small amount of controversy as well. This research has been reviewed extensively elsewhere (Bretherton & Waters, 1985; Lamb, Thompson, Gardner, & Charnov, 1985; Sroufe, 1988). Before summarizing the major findings with respect to clinical implications, we briefly describe the classification and implications of infant behavior in the SSP.

Infant attachment classifications of "secure," "avoidant," and "resistant" as measured in the SSP have been reliably identified in samples of infants all over the Western world (van Ijzendoorn & Kroonenberg, 1988). Infants classified as secure may or may not cry upon separation, but they approach their caregivers directly or re-establish positive interaction upon reunion. If upset, they are easily comforted on reunion, resuming play and exploration comfortably within a short time. From studies linking sensitive care to the secure pattern and from the infants' reunion behavior (reviewed in Main et al., 1985), we infer that secure infants anticipate that their caregivers will be available for comfort when necessary, and therefore, upon being comforted, the infants resume exploration. Infants classified as avoidant tend not to protest when their caregivers leave the room, and they ignore their caregivers upon reunion and focus instead on the external environment. From a history of caregiving characterized by rejection of the infants' bids for attachment and from the reunion behavior (Ainsworth et al., 1978; Sroufe, 1988), we infer that these infants have learned to suppress the external manifestations of their distress in order not to elicit further rejection (Cassidy & Kobak, 1988). Those infants classified as resistant cry vigorously upon separation and approach their caregivers upon reunion. Nevertheless, they also resist comforting, are not easily soothed, and take a long time to settle down and play with the toys. From a history of inconsistent caregiving (Ainsworth et al., 1978; Sroufe, 1988) and from the pattern of reunion behavior, we infer that these infants have ambivalent feelings about their caregivers as reliable safe havens and secure bases.

The validity of the classifications rests primarily on the demonstrated relationships between them and previous and concurrent patterns of mother–infant interaction. A number of studies have demonstrated that secure attachments are associated with maternal sensitivity prior to and concurrent with the SSP. Ainsworth et al. (1978) suggested that mothers of avoidant infants are more rejecting (turning away the infants' bids for contact and comfort) and that mothers of resistant infants are more inconsistent than mothers of infants later classified as secure. Findings in subsequent investigations have provided modest support for these assertions, although methods of assessment and specific hypotheses have varied across studies (Main & Stadtman, 1981; Belsky, Rovine, & Taylor, 1984; Isabella & Belsky, 1991; Vaughn & Waters, 1990).

Stability of the three major classifications in infants between 12 and 18 months has ranged from 53% (Thompson, Lamb, & Estes, 1982) to 96% (Waters, 1978), and in most investigations it is about 75% (Lamb et al., 1985). Stability is lower in high-risk, low-income samples, and changes from secure to insecure classification have been related to an increase in stressful life events reported by mothers (Vaughn, Egeland, Sroufe, & Waters, 1979). Some long-term stability has been demonstrated, in that infant attachment classifications predicted attachment classifications in 6-year-old children (Main & Cassidy, 1988).

Considerable predictive validity of infant attachment classifications has also been demonstrated.

Insecure attachment in infancy predicts subsequent behavioral problems, impulse control problems, conflicts and struggles with caregivers, low self-esteem, and seriously problematic peer relationships (Lewis, Feiring, McGuffog, & Jaskir, 1984; Erickson, Sroufe, & Egeland, 1985; Easterbrooks & Goldberg, 1990; Sroufe, 1983; Troy & Sroufe, 1987; Cassidy, 1988).

Main & Solomon (1986, 1990) have described a fourth classification of attachment, the "disorganized/disoriented" type. The disorganized classification is made on the basis of the child's demonstrating interrupted, confused, or incomplete strategies for obtaining comfort from the caregiver during the SSP. The conflict behaviors used to classify the infant as disorganized indicate disturbances in the functioning of the attachment system and of the use of the caregiver as a secure base and a safe haven. These behaviors may occur in children whose attachment otherwise could be classified into one of the secure, avoidant, or resistant patterns, or may occur in children whose attachment does not fit one of the other three patterns.

In the Berkeley Longitudinal Study, 14% of a low-risk, middle-class sample of infants were classified as disorganized with one parent, although classifications with each parent were independent (Main & Solomon, 1990). In high-risk samples, the proportion of infants classified as disorganized increases dramatically. The classification is more prevalent in infants whose parents have not successfully resolved losses or traumatic experiences (Main & Goldwyn, in press), parents who have bipolar affective disorder (Radke-Yarrow, Cummings, Kuczynski, & Chapman, 1985), parents who are active alcoholics (O'Connor, Sigman, & Brill, 1987), and parents who are maltreating (Carlson, Cicchetti, Barnett, & Braunwald, 1989; Cicchetti & Barnett, 1991). Recent findings suggest that disorganized attachment in infancy strongly predicts controlling (role-reversed) behavior in middle-class samples (Main & Cassidy, 1988) and behavior problems in impoverished samples (Lyons-Ruth, Repacholi, Alpern, & Connell, 1991).

Perspectives on Attachment Classifications

There are two major hypotheses about what attachment classifications represent. One position is that the classifications reflect infant dispositions of emotional expressiveness. In its extreme form, this formulation holds that attachment classifications are actually temperamental types. Resistant infants (who are not easily soothed upon reunion in the SSP) are most emotionally expressive; avoidant infants (who do not display distress and ignore their caregivers upon reunion in the SSP) are least expressive; and secure infants (who may or may not cry upon separation but are easily soothed) are intermediate between the other two. Evidence supporting this position comes from studies linking early endogenous infant characteristics elicited during the Brazelton Neonatal Behavioral Assessment Scale (NBAS) examination (Brazelton, 1973) to later attachment classifications (Grossman, Grossman, Spangler, Suess, & Unzner, 1985; Lester & Seifer, 1990).

A less extreme form of this argument is that emotional expressiveness determines how aroused the infant becomes during separations, rather than whether the infant is secure or insecure. Evidence supporting this position comes from an investigation in which NBAS autonomic instability predicted amount of arousal in the SSP, but did not predict security versus insecurity (Belsky & Rovine, 1987). Essentially, this position holds that endogenous temperament affects the type of security or insecurity of the infant, rather than security or insecurity per se.

The second major hypothesis is that attachment classifications are not characteristics of the infant, but instead reflect qualitative features of the attachment relationship with the caregiver with whom the infant is assessed. Evidence in support of this assertion come first from studies demonstrating that infants may be classified differently with different caregivers (Belsky, Garduque, & Hrncir, 1984; Belsky & Rovine, 1987; Grossman, Grossman, Huber, & Wartner, 1981; Main & Weston, 1981; Sagi et al., 1985). Relationship specificity of attachment classifications argues against attachment as a within-the-infant characteristic. In a recent investigation, prenatally measured maternal attachment classifications predicted a baby's attachment to the mother but not to the father over a year later, and prenatally measured paternal attachment classifications predicted an infant's attachment to the father but not to the mother over a year later (Steele, Steele, & Fonagy, 1991). These differential antecedents of attachment to mother and to father emphasize the relationship specificity of SSP classifications, although a recent meta-analysis found a modest tendency for classification to one parent to be dependent upon

classification to the other parent (Fox, Kimmerly, & Schafer, 1991).

A growing consensus among investigators considers infant attachment classifications as types of internal representations or internal working models of attachment (Bowlby, 1988; Bretherton, 1985; Cicchetti, Cummings, Greenberg, & Marvin, 1990; Main et al., 1985; Zeanah, in press). Theoretically, these may be affected both by relationship experiences and by endogenous characteristics of the infant.

DISORDERS OF ATTACHMENT

Current Nosologies

Any classification of disorders must meet tests of reliability and validity. Disorders of attachment have not been systematically investigated to address these questions; in fact, we have been unable to identify a single study attempting to validate attachment disorders. Of course, a disorder must be identified and characterized before it can be validated (Rutter, 1965); nevertheless, the lack of research about these disorders raises questions about the adequacy of current criteria.

DSM-IV (APA, 1991) and ICD-10 (World Health Organization [WHO], 1992) designate two major types of attachment disorders of childhood. Both refer to a persistent disturbance in the child's social relatedness beginning before age 5 years that extends across social situations and is distinguished from pervasive developmental disorders. One type of disorder is inhibited, wherein ambivalent, inhibited, or hypervigilant responses are centered on one or more adults. The other type is disinhibited; it includes indiscriminate oversociability, a failure to show selective attachments, a relative lack of selectivity in the persons from whom comfort is sought, and poorly modulated social interactions with unfamiliar persons across a range of social situations.

DSM-IV (APA, 1991) requires that there be evidence of grossly pathogenic caregiving (e.g., frank neglect, harsh treatment) or repeated changes in caregivers. ICD-10 (WHO, 1992) does not include this requirement, although the child must have the capacity for social responsiveness as revealed in interactions with "nondeviant" adults. In contrast, DSM-IV emphasizes that abnormal social behavior ought to be apparent in most social contexts.

These classifications are limited in three ways. First, even though developmental research has clearly demonstrated that attachment may vary across different relationships, DSM-IV and ICD-10 are less emphatic on this point. Second, the criteria appear to be narrowly drawn from maltreatment syndromes, rather than focused specifically on attachment. This also limits the disorder to children in extreme situations; it does not account for children who are in stable, albeit unhealthy, relationships without gross abuse or neglect. Third, our clinical experiences suggest that the disorders as defined do not adequately capture the presentations of disordered attachment.

Below, we propose criteria for Nonattached, Indiscriminate, Inhibited, Aggressive, and Role-Reversed Attachment Disorders. This is preceded by outlining the assumptions, derived from developmental research, that we believe should inform a consideration of disorders of attachment.

Underlying Assumptions for Clinical Disorders

Infants are biologically programmed to develop selective attachments to a relatively small number of caregiving adults. These preferences begin to be clearly expressed at about 7 to 8 months of age. After the age of 1 year, only severe intrinsic abnormalities (such as profound mental retardation or extremely abnormal caregiving environments) are associated with absence of a preferred "attachment figure" in a child. Where the limits of a child's adaptability to large numbers of different caregivers end is unknown.

Attachment is a characteristic of an individual that is differentially expressed toward others. Disorders of attachment represent disorders within the individual that may be manifested differently, depending on the nature of the tie between the child and different adult caregivers. An infant may have a disordered attachment relationship with an important caregiver without manifesting other socially deviant or symptomatic behavior outside the context of that relationship. In our experience, conflicted attachment behavior does generalize beyond the primary caregiving relationship as the child becomes older, but in the first 3 years of life it is most often relationship-specific.

Between the ages of 1 and 3 years, the attachment behavioral system operates to produce a feeling of "felt security" in a child, initially via proximity to the attachment figure. As representational processes mature during the second and third years, literal proximity becomes gradually less necessary. The attachment system and the exploratory system operate in tandem within the child to produce an attachment–exploration balance. Disturbances in this balance represent disturbances in the use of the attachment figure as a secure base from which to explore with confidence, or disturbances in the use of the attachment figure as a safe haven to which to retreat in times of danger.

Disorders of attachment are not synonymous with individual differences in patterns of attachment as measured by the SSP, but instead represent more profound and pervasive disturbances in the child's feelings of safety and security. Attachment classifications derived from the SSP are not diagnoses. It is hardly surprising that a categorical scheme developed for all 1-year-old infants, and including only three or four different types, covers a broad range of adaptations within each type. Sroufe (1988) has emphasized that secure attachment may provide some protection against psychopathology generally, but it does not confer absolute protection. Similarly, he points out that insecure attachments may increase an individual's risk for psychopathology without being linearly related to subsequent psychiatric disorders.

The attachment relationship between the child and a caregiving adult is an unequal partnership in which the adult provides for the child's safety and security, but the child does not provide for the adult's safety and security. Adult–child attachment relationships that invert this pattern to a significant degree, and that are detrimental to the child, represent role reversal.

Caseness and Disorders of Attachment

The problem of "caseness"—that is, the question of when signs and symptoms are severe enough to constitute a case or disorder—is not unique to psychiatry. The answer to the question depends on the purpose intended to be served by making a diagnosis (Rutter & Sandberg, 1985). In infant mental health, this sometimes includes intervening to correct an obviously deviant developmental trajectory, which can be reasonably expected to result in impairment at a later date. DSM-IV defines psychiatric disorders as conditions confined to individuals that cause impairment (distress or disability) or substantially increase the risk of impairment. It does not emphasize abnormalities of relationships or the developmental appropriateness of the presentation at hand. Rutter and Graham (1968) on the other hand, define psychiatric disorders in children as "abnormalities of emotions, behaviors or relationships which are developmentally inappropriate and of sufficient duration and severity to cause persistent suffering or handicap to the child" (p. 563).

Borrowing the emphasis on increased risk for subsequent disorders from DSM-IV, and the emphasis on relationships from Rutter and Graham (1968), we propose that attachment problems become psychiatric disorders for infants when emotions and behaviors displayed in attachment relationships are so disturbed as to indicate, or substantially to increase the risk for, persistent distress or disability in the infants. We are maintaining an emphasis here on defining attachment disorders as disorders within rather than between individuals. Some have argued compellingly that a child's relationship with the primary caregiver is actually the locus of the disorder and the most appropriate focus of intervention (see Sameroff & Emde, 1989), but this position runs counter to long traditions in science and medicine and has not yet been widely accepted. Our point is that it is possible to identify, diagnose, and treat attachment disorders within an individual child, bearing in mind that the child's relationship context will be the focus of intervention for these disorders.

Proposed Types of Attachment Disorders

Following from these assumptions, and drawing on clinical experience and the limited empirical evidence available, we propose five major types of attachment disorders. These are similar to the clinical disorders of attachment described previously by Lieberman and Pawl (1988, 1990). We consider the criteria that follow to be an extension of their work. In fact, the similarities in cases described by two different clinical groups provide preliminary face validity for this typology. The proposed criteria for Nonattached Attachment Disorder, Indiscriminate Attachment Disorder, Inhibited Attachment Disorder, Aggressive Attachment Disorder, and Role-Reversed Attachment Disorder are provided in Table 22.1.

We suggest that these disorders may be diagnosed in children between the ages of 1 and 4–5 years, based on the behavior of the children alone. With the exception of Nonattached Attachment Disorder and a few selected symptoms in the other types, there is no requirement that a child exhibit these behaviors across all significant social relationships; they need only be shown in the presence of at least one attachment figure.

Type I: Nonattached Attachment Disorder

Rather than a disturbance in the attachment–exploration balance, the first type of attachment disorder represents a failure to develop a preferred attachment figure. It is presumably somewhat more common in children who have been institutionalized, those who have experienced extremes of neglect, or those who have experienced multiple changes in primary caregivers. If children with these symptoms and signs do have a history of extreme neglect, they may have significant developmental delays as well. The young twins who inspired the Skeels (1966) longitudinal study are examples of young children who were delayed and unresponsive, but who made significant gains once placed in a more nurturing environment. Other empirical support for this type comes from Tizard and colleagues' longitudinal study of institutionalized children in London (Tizard & Rees, 1974, 1975; Tizard & Hodges, 1978). Of the 26 children who were institutionalized throughout their first 4 years of life, 8 children were observed to be largely detached from everyone, hardly following the staff around and showing little interest in strangers. These children could not be meaningfully engaged by others, and they were perceived by the staff as having no attachments to anyone.

The following case underscores that children with this type of disorder may not lack the capacity to form attachments, but rather may not have had the experiences to facilitate formation of attachments.

Case 1. Mike was a 20-month-old boy referred for evaluation by a pediatrician who felt that he was either depressed or autistic. He had been removed from his biological mother at age 11 months and placed in his current foster family. His foster mother complained that he seemed to be a "vege-

TABLE 22.1. Proposed Types of Attachment Disorders

Type I: Nonattached Attachment Disorder
1. Child fails to demonstrate a preference for a particular adult caregiver, even when hurt, frightened, sick, or in other situations that ordinarily stimulate the attachment behavioral system.
2. Child fails to exhibit separation protest or exhibits indiscriminate separation protest (cries when almost anyone leaves).
3. If the child is social with anyone, he or she is likely to be indiscriminately social.
4) Child has a mental age of at least 8 months.

Type II: Indiscriminate Attachment Disorder
1. Child repeatedly leaves the safety provided by the presence of the attachment figure and wanders off without checking back (e.g., leaves the house and goes into the street or "slips away" in public).
2. Child exhibits a pattern of entering situations that place him or her at risk for physical harm.
3. Child may exhibit socially promiscuous behavior by demonstrating friendly overtures toward or by seeking comfort and nurturance from relatively or completely unfamiliar adults.
4. Symptoms cannot be explained by Attention–Deficit Hyperactivity Disorder.
5. There are two subtypes:
   a. Socially Promiscuous
      (i) Indiscriminate friendliness and shallow social responsiveness are the most prominent features of the child's behavior.
      (ii) Child may seek comfort when distressed, albeit he or she does not express a preference and is often difficult to soothe.
   b. Reckless/Accident-Prone/Risk-Taking
      (i) Child appears to exhibit a pattern of recklessness, accident proneness, and risk-taking behavior that is more than can be explained by a failure to check back with an attachment figure.
      (ii) The child's reckless behavior may have a driven quality to it.

Type III: Inhibited Attachment Disorder
1. Child exhibits an ongoing reluctance to approach, touch, or manipulate inanimate objects such as toys in unfamiliar surroundings, and especially in the presence of unfamiliar people.
2. Child actively avoids or withdraws too readily from social interaction with people other than the attachment figure.

3. Child exhibits a restricted range of affect in social situations, even in the presence of the attachment figure, with predominant mood ranging from sober scrutiny to hypervigilance.
4. There are two subtypes:
   a. Excessive Clinging
      (i) Child appears comfortable in attachment figure's immediate vicinity, but is easily frightened by unfamiliar settings, objects, or individuals. Still, proximity to the attachment figure is anxiety-laden.
      (ii) Separation from the attachment figure is vigorously resisted and leads to severe distress.
   b. Compulsive Compliance
      (i) Child readily complies with directives from the attachment figure, with little or no hesitation or resistance.
      (ii) Child has limited positive affective interchanges with the attachment figure.
      (iii) Child appears frightened of attachment figure.
      (iv) Child may appear less inhibited, frightened, and uninvolved in absence of attachment figure.

Type IV: Aggressive Attachment Disorder
1. Child has a clear preference for an attachment figure, but comfort seeking is often interrupted by the child's aggressive, angry outbursts directed toward the attachment figure or toward the self.
2. Anger (which may be expressed physically, verbally, or both) is a pervasive feature of the attachment relationship and goes well beyond age-appropriate noncompliance and transitory frustrations. N.B.: General noncompliance alone is not sufficient to make the diagnosis, because aggression in the context of the attachment relationship (self-directed or other-directed) is the hallmark of this type.
3. Symptoms of anxiety (separation anxiety, sleep disturbances, etc.) may be apparent but are not a focus of concern because of the prominence of the child's aggression.

Type V: Role-Reversed Attachment Disorder
1. Parent–child relationship is characterized by inversion, so that child assumes roles and responsibilities ordinarily assumed by parent. This is a pervasive pattern in the relationship.
2. Child maintains a nonanxious proximity to the attachment figure in unfamiliar settings.
3. Child is oversolicitous, bossy, overnurturing, or controlling during interactions with the caregiver.
4. Child maintains an unusual degree of scrutiny about caregiver's psychological well-being.

table." She said that he was unresponsive to social interaction except to be aggressive with the other young foster children in her care, including his twin sister. She was especially concerned about his biting himself and others. With regard to exploratory behavior, she said that he tended to remain wherever she put him down, even for hours at a time, and that he would make no effort to reach for toys. She also reported that he seemed to be less responsive than he had been initially, and that the few vocalizations he had originally produced had disappeared. In addition, he seemed interested only in staring at spinning objects.

On evaluation, Mike was initially quite unresponsive and had no discernible reaction to his foster parents' leaving the interview playroom. In general, he seemed more wary than somber. Later, he became interested in a pop-up box and once seemed to have a hint of a smile as the examiner demonstrated it to him. Nevertheless, he was remarkably reticent about interacting. On formal speech and language assessment, he was found to be a passive, reluctant communicator who responded infrequently and inconsistently. His receptive and expressive language were noted to be at a 12-month level, although his wariness and reluctance to interact were felt to be contributory to an extent.

Formal assessment with the Bayley Scales of Infant Development also revealed delays, with overall functioning at approximately 19 months. Mike exhibited early forms of self-directed symbolic play, but he did not use combinatorial play schemes or other-directed symbolic play. Most striking was his reluctance to interact. The degree to which his behavior was the result of developmental impairment or more willfully under his control was not clear.

An intensive outpatient intervention was arranged. Before it could be implemented, however, the foster parents decided to give Mike up. He was placed in a shelter while authorities looked for another foster home for him. Within 2 weeks in the shelter, where he was the youngest and favored child, he improved dramatically. His relatedness blossomed, his expressive language developed at a rapid pace, and he developed a preferred attachment to a particular staff member. Re-evaluation 3 months later confirmed that he had made substantial developmental gains in language, cognitive, and social domains.

Although an Autistic Spectrum Disorder had been suspected, Mike's rapid recovery following placement in a presumably more nurturing environment indicated an attachment disorder.

Type II: Indiscriminate Attachment Disorder

The second type has been recognized implicitly in DSM-IV (APA, 1991) as the "diffuse attachment" criterion of Reactive Attachment Disorder, and explicitly in ICD-10 (WHO, 1992) as Disinhibited Attachment Disorder. In this disorder, the child exhibits an imbalance in the attachment–exploration functions by failing to check back with the caregiver in unfamiliar settings and by failing to retreat to the caregiver as a safe haven when frightened or threatened. Instead, there is an indiscriminate and promiscuous use of others for comfort and nurturance. The major empirical support for the Type II pattern comes from studies of institutionalized children, although clinical experience suggests that it also may be apparent in children with disrupted early attachment histories, such as multiple foster placements.

In their study of institutionalized children independent of physical and emotional deprivation, Tizard and her colleagues (Tizard & Rees, 1974, 1975; Tizard & Hodges, 1978) compared three groups of children who had spent at least their first 2 years in an institution. Of the original 65 children, 24 were adopted between the ages of 2 and 4 years; 15 were restored to their original families between ages 2 and 4 years; and 26 remained in the institution. Of the 26 who remained in the institution, 10 children were described as not having deep attachments, and they were markedly attention-seeking, clingy, and overfriendly with strangers. A minority of adopted and restored institutional children also exhibited overfriendly behavior toward strangers that was a cause of concern for their families. In a comparison group of 65 children of a working-class sample of London families, none of the children exhibited this pattern (Tizard & Hodges, 1978).

Our experience suggests that the Type II disorder may have two subtypes: one with accident proneness and risk-taking behavior as prominent features, and the other limited primarily to children with social promiscuity and indiscriminate comfort seeking.

The following case example illustrates the Reckless/Accident-Prone/Risk-Taking subtype of Indiscriminate Attachment Disorder as it presents in a clinical setting.

Case 2. Robert was referred to an infant mental health clinic when he was 34 months old for evaluation of a variety of behavioral problems, including frequent tantrums, aggressive behavior, running out of his house and into the street, and a willingness to "go with anyone." All of these problems had been apparent since he was about 1½ years old. He had always lived with his mother and a younger sister who was 16 months old at the time of the referral.

There were significant concerns at the time of the referral about Robert's mother's ability to manage him, given that she was already receiving intensive services from the community. These included individual psychotherapy at a community mental health center, a weekly parenting group at another community agency, and an in-home parent aide 2–3 hours a day for 2 or 3 days a week.

During the intake family interview, which included the three family members and the parent aide, Robert seemed initially to ignore his mother and interacted primarily with the parent aide. He showed her toys and sought contact with her. Progressively, his behavior became more unruly and disruptive. He could not sustain an activity, and he was quite provocative with his mother. She seemed uncertain of how to manage him, despite encouragement from the parent aide and the interviewer. As a result, Robert was taken out of the room by the parent aide in order to settle him down and to permit the interviewer to obtain needed history from his mother. He ran around the waiting room, and two adults could not interest him in toys or activities. Suddenly, he bolted into an adjacent room and began pulling a pot of hot coffee off a warmer. He was stopped just before it spilled on him.

Because of his frenetic, out-of-control, and risk-taking behavior at home, and because neither his mother nor the parent aide felt he could be safely managed at home, Robert was hospitalized for a more intensive assessment. In the hospital, he did not pose the behavior problems that were anticipated. Instead, he was quiet and easily engaged by play with toys. What was striking about his behavior was his active seeking of nurturance from total strangers. He greeted adults he had never seen with open arms and requested hugs and kisses from them. It became clear that only during visits with his mother did the risk taking and recklessness become pronounced.

Robert's lack of major impairments in social relatedness, his normal cognitive abilities, and his sophisticated language and pretend play ruled out autistic spectrum disorder, language disorders, and mental retardation. The major consideration for differential diagnosis was a disruptive behavior disorder, especially Attention-Deficit Hyperactivity Disorder. The situational specificity of his disruptive behavior, which was observed and confirmed by more detailed history, made it clear that an attachment disorder explained the problems.

Perhaps a more common presentation of Indiscriminate Attachment Disorder is the subtype we call Socially Promiscuous, which occurs in young children who have had repeated changes in caregivers without the opportunity to develop a preferred attachment figure. In these children, there is no risk-taking behavior, but only indiscriminate sociability.

Case 3. Sarah was a 14-month-old girl who was referred for evaluation by her foster mother, Ms. Glynn, who was concerned that she was depressed. She had been in the foster mother's home for about three months, and the foster mother noticed that she was not like other foster children she had had. Sarah sat by herself for long periods of time, and she rarely smiled or vocalized. Although she did not seek comfort when she was distressed, she was easily settled by anyone when she became upset. This was Sarah's third foster home in 6 months since her removal by child protective services from her mother's home at age 8 months because of neglect.

Sarah was her 16-year-old mother's second child. The mother and her two children had moved out of the maternal grandmother's home because of ongoing conflict when Sarah was 3 months old. Sarah's mother had voluntarily placed the children in a temporary foster home while she entered an inpatient alcohol treatment unit; the children were returned to her upon discharge. Sarah's father was arrested and convicted of assaulting Sarah's mother soon thereafter. When Sarah was 8 months old, she and her brother were placed in separate foster homes. For reasons unrelated to her or her problems, Sarah was moved to another foster home within a month, and 2 months later she was moved into the home of the foster mother who brought her in for evaluation. For 3 months prior to the evaluation, Sarah had had regular supervised visits with her birth mother.

During the initial evaluation session with her foster mother, Sarah seemed comfortable. Nevertheless, she behaved just as familiarly with the interviewer as she did with her foster mother. She tended to wander aimlessly around the playroom, unable to focus on play with toys or social interaction for long. She was a bit clumsy, and when she fell and bumped her head during the session with her foster mother, she cried quietly without looking at her foster mother or reaching out to her. When her foster mother picked her up, Sarah quieted, but her back remained stiff and her expression somewhat blank.

In the subsequent session with her birth mother, Sarah arrived somewhat late. When she entered the playroom, where her mother was waiting for her, she responded to her mother's call and open arms by hesitating before seeming to approach for a few steps. Then she stopped suddenly and busied herself with the toys without ever looking at her mother. This maneuver was not lost on her mother, who cited it as an example of Sarah's aloofness. During this session she also wandered around a bit aimlessly, and again was as willing to sit in the lap of the interviewer as that of her birth mother. Throughout the evaluation, her affective range was a bit constricted, and she did not exhibit toddler exuberance; nevertheless, she seemed more sober than sad. History from both mothers and subsequent home visits confirmed that Sarah had no preferred attachment figure and consistently demonstrated indiscriminate sociability.

Type III: Inhibited Attachment Disorder

At the other end of disturbances in the balance between attachment and exploration are children who are unwilling to venture away from their attachment figures to engage in age-appropriate exploration, at times when it is expectable for them to do so. Two subtypes, Excessive Clinging and Compulsive Compliance, illustrate the different manifestations of this type of attachment disorder.

In the Excessive Clinging subtype, the child may be identified primarily at times when normal exploration is anticipated. The clinging goes well beyond initial shyness or slowness to warm up. In addition to extremes of clinging, the child also exhibits affective constriction, characterized chiefly by an anxious mood at times when around unfamiliar people.

Case 4. Kay was a 28-month-old girl who was referred for evaluation by a child psychiatrist, who had seen her following surgery for a congenital cardiac malformation. The surgery was successful, but it was only one of a large number of operations that Kay had required, and there were more scheduled in the future. The psychiatrist had been consulted because after surgery Kay had appeared extremely frightened and had remained mute for several days. Her mother said about her when she was in the intensive care unit and mute, "You could see the fright in her eyes." Kay was diagnosed

with Post-Traumatic Stress Disorder (PTSD), and her mother was encouraged to seek treatment for her after discharge.

In the initial evaluation session, Kay never once moved from her mother's lap when the interviewer was present. She could not be enticed to interact, even by toys that she eyed longingly, although she played with them eagerly when the interviewer left her alone with her mother and observed them through a one-way mirror. Her mother reported that she had always been inhibited around unfamiliar adults and children.

The mother was not especially concerned about Kay's inhibition, and seemed largely unaware of the effects of her overprotectiveness on Kay. The evaluation made clear that Kay's mother had also been terrified about her—not only in the immediate postoperative period, but also since her initial diagnosis as a newborn. This had led the mother into a much closer (and also a different kind of) relationship with Kay than with Kay's older sister, whom the mother saw as strong and capable.

Further history made clear that there was little to suggest an Overanxious Disorder, as the child did not exhibit generalized anxiety or PTSD, as there were no current symptoms, and as the clinging had preceded the traumatic hospital visit.

The Compulsive Compliance subtype is a manifestation of the child's response to maltreatment or at least excessive punitiveness. The child appears to have learned to comply with the caregiver immediately and unquestioningly, in order to avoid physical abuse. Therefore, symptoms and signs (such as hypervigilance, subdued but wary affect, and lack of spontaneity) are most apparent when the child is in the presence of the attachment figure.

Case 5. George was a 30-month-old boy who was referred for evaluation because of extreme reactions to visitation with his natural mother. He had been removed from her when he was 20 months old and placed in his current foster home. There he was noted to be somewhat boisterous and active, but he was generally easy to care for.

The problem leading to the referral was that George had begun protesting violently when he was picked up by the caseworker for weekly visits with his natural mother. The clinician conducting the evaluation observed George playing in his foster home prior to the pickup. He seemed comfortable and at ease, although he was loud in his play and somewhat noncompliant with his foster mother. When the caseworker arrived and he saw her, George screamed in a terrified manner and attempted to hide. He was carried kicking and screaming into the caseworker's car.

As part of the evaluation, the clinician followed George and the caseworker to his natural mother's house in order to observe him in that setting as well. Although he had cried profusely on the way to his mother's apartment, when he reached the door he stopped crying. He looked soberly at his mother when she opened the door, but he did not greet her in any discernible way. Instead, he walked in silently and stood in her living room. George's 15-month-old brother, who was placed in a different foster home, had arrived a few minutes earlier. The natural mother told George to sit down, and he did so immediately. Although George's brother toddled freely and contently through the apartment, vocalizing often, George did not move from where he sat down initially unless his mother directed him otherwise.

In a 45-minute observation, George never spoke once. He merely nodded or shook his head when asked questions by his mother. He watched her constantly, maintaining a vigilant and anxious expression on his face. He cringed slightly whenever she spoke to him, but he always complied immediately with her directives. A laboratory evaluation session revealed this same pattern of interaction. The relationship specificity of the symptoms made the diagnosis clear.

Type IV: Aggressive Attachment Disorder

Some attachment relationships are suffused with anger and frustration. When anger is a pervasive feature of the relationship, and when the child's aggression toward the attachment figure and/or the self exceeds transitory expressions of frustration, the child may have Aggressive Attachment Disorder. Children begin to use anger instrumentally at about 12 months of age, and this type of attachment disorder becomes more common toward the latter part of the second year and beyond.

Children with Aggressive Attachment Disorder frequently have symptoms of anxiety that may be overlooked by parents, teachers, or treating clinicians because of the prominence or even dangerousness of the aggressive symptoms. Separation anxiety or sleep disturbances, for example, may be interpreted by the parents as defiance.

A child's anger and aggression may not be limited to the attachment relationship, but they should be more apparent in this context than in other contexts. They also clearly exceed age-appropriate expressions of ambivalence. Aggression may be directed toward the self, in the form of head banging or scratching; may be directed toward the attachment figure, verbally ("I hate you") or nonverbally (hitting, kicking, or biting); or may be expressed in the form of severe and prolonged tantrums in response to minor frustrations. The child's world is generally violent: Being a witness and/or a victim of domestic violence is a frequent accompaniment of the child's symptomatology.

Case 6. Dante was a 26-month-old referred for evaluation because he was "out of control." His parents referred to him as a "holy terror." According to his parents, when he was told "no" he threw himself on the floor kicking and screaming, and he hit his mother when she tried to contain him. He also responded to his father's efforts to discipline him by lashing out at him. When he became very upset, he tended to bite himself and banged his head on the floor.

In the initial session of the evaluation, Dante played quietly at first, but became more active and boisterous as the session continued. When his mother attempted to settle him, he hit her and then began to throw a tantrum. A short time later, his mother left the room without saying goodbye to go to the bathroom; Dante cried and banged on the door angrily, trying to follow her. He hit the therapist when she tried to console him, but he calmed down when she told him that he could not hit and that Mommy would be right back.

History revealed considerable violence at home between the parents, which Dante often witnessed. The parents frequently threatened to abandon each other and him. Dante was cared for inconsistently by a large number of family members, friends, and even casual acquaintances. Discipline was inconsistent but usually involved spanking.

Type V: Role-Reversed Attachment Disorder

Although the fifth type of disordered relationship has long been noted by clinicians, empirical support for the construct has become available from attachment research with school-age and preschool-age children (Greenberg, Speltz, DeKlyen, & Endriga, 1992; Main & Cassidy, 1988). Main and Cassidy (1988) described a pattern of reunion behavior that they designated as "controlling" in 6-year-old children separated from their parents for 1 hour in a laboratory paradigm. Two major forms of the controlling pattern have been described: "controlling/caregiving," in which the child is overly nurturant and solicitous toward the caregiver, and "controlling/punitive," in which the child behaves in an overly bossy, punitive, or rejecting manner toward the caregiver (Main & Cassidy, 1988). Home observations of 6-year-olds who exhibit controlling reunion behavior in the laboratory have confirmed that these children and their mothers engage in role-inappropriate behaviors (Solomon, George, & Ivins, 1987).

The controlling pattern has also been described previously in a clinic-referred toddler who was in a role-reversed relationship with his mother (Zeanah & Klitzke, 1991). In this case, the caregiving and punitive forms of controlling behavior were observed to co-occur in the same dyad.

Case 7. Beth was a 24-month-old girl who was referred to an infant mental health clinic for evaluation of a sleep disturbance that had been present for over a year. Her mother reported that she had not slept in her own bed since she was 10 months old, which was about 2 months before she and her husband had separated.

The most striking features of the intake session were Beth's mother's depressed mood, frequent crying, and psychomotor retardation. Although toys were available, Beth played with them only in the first 20 minutes of the interview, when her mother seemed more animated. Her mother looked sadder and began to cry as she described her frustration and hopelessness about a number of stressors. Beth walked over to her and signaled to be picked up. She remained in her mother's lap for almost the entire remainder of the session.

As her mother continued to tell their story tearfully, Beth began to stroke her mother's hair gently. She continued caressing her mother's hair and back intermittently for about 20 minutes. At times, however, she pulled her mother's hair vigorously and provocatively.

In subsequent sessions, this controlling pattern of interaction reappeared. History confirmed that Beth's mother had tended to look to her for comfort and support for a long time, and that Beth bore an excessive amount of the psychological burden of the relationship.

Other Diagnostic Considerations

To be meaningful, a diagnosis must enable the clinician to communicate to others meaningful information about the disorder. The dis-

orders proposed above need to be validated. Even then, other types of disordered attachment may need to be described. For example, the present typology does not address attachments characterized by extremes of avoidance, resistance, and disorganization. If these types of defensive processes and their correlates can be identified in naturalistic settings, then we may have a fuller description of attachment disorders.

Ideally, from a diagnosis one can infer etiology, pathogenesis, prognosis, and treatment. For attachment disorders, as for many disorders, all the relevant data are not yet available. Nevertheless, diagnosing an attachment disorder can enhance the clinician's understanding of the individual, and can also help to focus and direct treatment.

Having to consider attachment disorders in the differential diagnosis can help the clinician make the attachment system an important focus of the assessment of the parent–infant dyad. How the infant uses the caregiver as a safe haven and secure base from which to explore is a useful way of understanding infant behavior during clinical assessments. By analyzing the pattern of the balance between the attachment system and the exploratory system, the clinician may be guided to look at the caregiver–infant relationship in a more informed way. For instance, an infant's showing signs of Nonattached Attachment Disorder (Type I) should suggest an emotionally, if not physically, unavailable caregiver. The Compulsive Compliance subtype of Inhibited Attachment Disorder (Type III) ought to suggest physical abuse or extreme punitiveness in the caregiver–infant relationship. On the other hand, the Excessive Clinging subtype of Type III should guide the clinician into inquiry about the caregiver's feelings about the infant's exploring. In summary, considering a diagnosis of attachment disorder may help to focus the clinician's attention on factors that contributed to the symptoms and signs of disorder in the infant.

Relationship of Attachment Disorders to Other Disorders

Attachment may also contribute to the development of disorders in children other than attachment disorders. Conduct Disorder (Greenberg & Speltz, 1988; Speltz, Greenberg, & DeKlyen, 1990; Greenberg et al., 1992), Major Depression

(Cicchetti & Aber, 1986; Cummings & Cicchetti, 1990), and disorders of social inhibition (Rubin & Lollis, 1988) have been particularly implicated.

Zeanah and Emde (in press) have proposed several possible ways in which insecure attachment may contribute to these disorders. First, insecure attachment may be a necessary but not a sufficient cause of the other disorder. In other words, attachment may make a *specific* and *independent* contribution to the disorder, along with other etiological factors. Second, attachment may *not* make a specific contribution to these disorders; instead the children affected may be deviant on a large number of measures of adaptation, including having insecurely organized attachment. Third, extremely insecure children who have attachment disorders may also have other disorders. Comorbidity is particularly difficult to demonstrate when the disorders in question are not well validated. The task for clinicians is to distinguish between attachment disorders per se and disorders in which insecure attachment is a contributor, specific or nonspecific.

ASSESSMENT

Zeanah and Emde (in press) have delineated several principles of assessment of attachment disorders. First, assessment should focus primarily on a child's relationships with attachment figures, rather than on the child's social behavior in general. It is important to remember that the child's symptoms may vary from one attachment relationship to another. Second, both history and direct observation of the child and the attachment figure(s) should be included in the assessment. Observations of the use of an attachment figure as a secure base in early toddlerhood and of the goal-corrected partnership in later toddlerhood are weighted especially strongly. Third, structured research methods of assessing attachment should be used sparingly if at all to make a diagnosis. The focus of attention should be attachment relationships as they function in naturalistic settings rather than in the laboratory.

The first question for the clinician is whether the child has or is expected to have an attachment to a particular caregiver. For example, a child recently placed in a foster family may be difficult to evaluate for attachment disorders with either her natural or her foster parents. Once the child's attachment relationship has been demonstrated, the child's specific behaviors are of interest in determining whether an attachment relationship is disordered (Table 22.2). These behaviors should be assessed by direct observation whenever possible, with history used to supplement impressions from direct observation.

MANAGEMENT

The question of whether severe early deprivation can be overcome (and, if so, how) has been enormously controversial. Rutter's (1972) suggestion that the degree of reversibility depends on the duration and severity of the privation, the age when the privation ceases, and the completeness of the change of environment is still valid today.

Infants are most likely to become attached to emotionally available, sensitive caregivers. If an infant is deprived of that opportunity, as with repeated changes in foster care, the first effort at intervention should be provision of a stable and consistent caregiving adult who is or is likely to become emotionally invested in the infant. Infants are born with a strong biological propensity to form and to maintain attachments, so that the introduction of an emotionally available attachment figure is the initial treatment of choice.

Perhaps more common problems for clinicians are infants who have disturbed primary attachment relationships rather than no attachment relationships. Although no studies have been conducted attempting to intervene with infants suffering from attachment disorders, several investigations have attempted to intervene with insecurely attached infants in high-risk populations.

Globally supportive interventions with mothers in high-risk samples have not improved infant attachment when SSP classification has been the dependent variable. This has been demonstrated in samples of infants with adolescent mothers (Osofsky, Culp, & Ware, 1988), of preterm infants (Beckwith, 1988), and of infants with socially isolated mothers (Barnard et al., 1988). Several of the investigators speculated that the effects of the intervention might not have become apparent as early as the infants' first birthday. On the other hand, it is clearly possible that these interventions were neither intense nor specific enough to affect infant attachment, at least as reflected in SSP classifications.

TABLE 22.2. Salient Behaviors in the Assessment of Attachment Disorders

Behaviors	Signs of attachment disorders in young children
Showing affection	Lack of warm and affectionate interchanges across a range of interactions; promiscuous affection with relatively unfamiliar adults
Comfort seeking	Lack of comfort seeking when hurt, frightened, or ill, or comfort seeking in odd or ambivalent manner
Reliance for help	Excessive dependence, or inability to seek and use supportive presence of attachment figure when needed
Cooperation	Lack of compliance with caregiver requests and demands by the child as a striking feature of caregiver–child interactions, or compulsive compliance
Exploratory behavior	Failure to check back with caregiver in unfamiliar settings, or exploration limited by child's unwillingness to leave caregiver
Controlling behavior	Oversolicitous and inappropriate caregiving behavior, or excessively bossy and punitive controlling of caregiver by the child
Reunion responses	Failure to re-establish interaction after separations, including ignoring/avoiding behaviors, intense anger, or lack of affection

A more intense intervention that provided demonstrable beneficial effects was conducted with recently immigrated lower-socioeconomic-status women and their infants in San Francisco (Lieberman, Weston, & Pawl, 1991). The clinicians in this investigation were bicultural, bilingual women with master's degrees in psychology or social work, who received special training and ongoing supervision from clinicians experienced in infant–parent psychotherapy (see Lieberman & Pawl, Chapter 28, this volume; Fraiberg, 1980). Pretreatment assessments with the SSP divided the sample into three groups: insecure intervention ($n = 29$), insecure control ($n = 23$), and secure control ($n = 30$).

Sessions lasting 90 minutes each were conducted weekly for 1 year. The focus of the home-based psychotherapy was on the emotional relationship experiences of mothers and their infants. The therapists emphasized the importance and legitimacy of the mothers' needs for protection and safety, both as children and as mothers. They encouraged the mothers to explore their negative feelings of anger and ambivalence toward others. They also addressed the mothers' perceptions and interpretations of their infants. The design of the intervention was to help the mothers use their relationships with their therapists to change their relationships with their infants. In other words, by changing mothers' internal representations, the therapists hoped to changed the mothers' behaviors with their infants, and thereby to change their infants' internal representations of attachment.

Results of the intervention were evaluated when the children were 24 months old in naturalistic and laboratory settings. There were significant increases in more desirable maternal and child interactive behaviors, and an enhanced goal-corrected partnership, in the intervention group as compared to the control groups. Unfortunately, the mothers' own representations of attachment were not assessed in this investigation, leaving the most direct focus of the intervention unassessed. If similar interventions in the future produce similar results, the question for future research will be whether interventions change a parent's perspective on attachment or whether the intervention improves parental behavior without changing the internal representations.

SUMMARY AND CONCLUSIONS

In this chapter we have emphasized the salient role of attachment in the parent–infant relationship. We have summarized some of the literature on the deleterious effects of insecure attachment on child development, and on the relationship of security of attachment to real experiences rather than fantasies. We have noted that disorders of attachment in current nosologies are not fully informed by developmental research on the construct of attachment. We

have outlined the basic assumptions that underlie the classification of attachment disorders
proposed in this chapter. Drawing on the previous reports of Lieberman and Pawl (1988,
1990) and on our own clinical experiences, we
have proposed criteria for five types of attachment disorders. We hope to direct infant mental
health clinicians' attention to the attachment–
exploration balance and to the organization of
the attachment relationship when they are
assessing disturbed parent–infant relationships. Most importantly, we look forward to
attempts to validate disorders of attachment
through critical evaluation of these and other
criteria.

ACKNOWLEDGMENTS

Charles H. Zeanah was supported during the preparation of this chapter by a Research Scientist Development Award from the National Institute of Mental Health (No. MH 00691). We acknowledge the
helpful comments of Marianne Barton about an earlier version of this chapter.

REFERENCES

Ainsworth, M. D. S. (1967). *Infancy in Uganda: Infant care and the growth of love*. Baltimore: Johns Hopkins University Press.

Ainsworth, M. D. S., Blehar, M., Waters, E., & Wall, S. (1978). *Patterns of attachment: A psychological study of the Strange Situation*. Hillsdale, NJ: Erlbaum.

American Psychiatric Association (APA). (1980). *Diagnostic and statistical manual of mental disorders* (3rd ed.). Washington, DC: Author.

American Psychiatric Association (APA). (1991). *DSM-IV options book: Work in Progress*. Washington, DC: Author.

Barnard, K. E., Magyary, D., Sumner, G., Booth, C. L., Mitchell, S. K., & Spieker, S. (1988). Prevention of parenting alterations for women with low social support. *Psychiatry, 51*, 248–253.

Beckwith, L. (1988). Intervention with disadvantaged parents of sick preterm infants. *Psychiatry, 51*, 242–247.

Belsky, J., Garduque, L., & Hrncir, E. (1984). Assessing performance, competence, and executive capacity in infant play: Relations to home environment and security of attachment. *Developmental Psychology, 20*, 406–417.

Belsky, J., & Rovine, M. (1987). Attachment and temperament: An empirical rapprochement. *Child Development, 58*, 787–795.

Belsky, J., Rovine, M., & Taylor, D. G. (1984). The Pennsylvania Infant and Family Development Project, 3: The origins of individual differences in infant–mother attachment: Maternal and infant contributions. *Child Development, 55*, 718–728.

Bowlby, J. (1951). *Maternal care and child health*. Geneva: World Health Organization.

Bowlby, J. (1969). *Attachment and loss: Vol. 1. Attachment*. New York: Basic Books.

Bowlby, J. (1973). *Attachment and loss: Vol. 2. Separation: Anxiety and anger*. New York: Basic Books.

Bowlby, J. (1980). *Attachment and loss: Vol. 3. Loss: Sadness and depression*. New York: Basic Books.

Bowlby, J. (1988). *A secure base*. New York: Basic Books.

Brazelton, T. B. (1973). *Neonatal Behavioral Assessment Scale*. Philadelphia: J. B. Lippincott.

Bretherton, I. (1980). Young children in stressful situations. In G. V. Coelho & P. Ahmed (Eds.), *Uprooting and development*. New York: Plenum Press.

Bretherton, I. (1985). Attachment theory: Retrospect and prospect. In I. Bretherton & E. Waters (Eds.), *Growing points of attachment theory and research*. *Monographs of the Society for Research in Child Development, 50*(1–2, Serial No. 209).

Bretherton, I., & Waters, E. (Eds.). (1985). Growing points of attachment theory and research. *Monographs of the Society for Research in Child Development, 50*(1–2, Serial no. 209).

Carlson, V., Cicchetti, D., Barnett, D., & Braunwald, K. G. (1989). Finding order in disorganization: Lessons for research from maltreated infants' attachments to their caregivers. In D. Cicchetti & V. Carlson (Eds.), *Child maltreatment: Theory and research on the causes and consequences of child abuse and neglect*. Cambridge, England: Cambridge University Press.

Cassidy, J. (1988). Child–mother attachment and the self at age six. *Child Development, 57*, 331–337.

Cassidy, J., & Kobak, R. (1988). Avoidance and its relation to other defensive processes. In J. Belsky & T. Nezworski (Eds.), *Clinical implications of attachment*. Hillsdale, NJ: Erlbaum.

Chapin, H. D. (1915). Are institutions for infants necessary? *Journal of the American Medical Association, 64*, 1–3.

Cicchetti, D., & Aber, J. L. (1986). Early precursors to later depression: An organizational perspective. In L. Lipsitt & C. Rovee-Collier (Eds.), *Advances in infancy* (Vol. 4). Norwood, NJ: Ablex.

Cicchetti, D., & Barnett, D. (1991). Attachment organization in maltreated preschoolers. *Development and Psychopathology, 4*, 397–412.

Cicchetti, D., Cummings, E. M., Greenberg, M. T., & Marvin, R. (1990). An organizational perspective on attachment beyond infancy: Implications for theory, measurement and research. In M. T. Greenberg, D. Cicchetti, & E. M. Cummings (Eds.), *Attachment in the preschool years*. Chicago: University of Chicago Press.

Cummings, E. M., & Cicchetti, D. (1990). Toward a transactional model of relations between attachment and depression. In M. T. Greenberg, D. Cicchetti, & E. M. Cummings (Eds.), *Attachment in the preschool years*. Chicago: University of Chicago Press.

DeCasper, A., & Fifer, W. (1980). Of human bonding: Infants prefer their mothers' voices. *Science, 208*, 1174–1176.

Easterbrooks, A., & Goldberg, W. (1990). Security of toddler–parent attachment: Relation to children's sociopersonality functioning during kindergarten. In M. T. Greenberg, D. Cicchetti, & E. M. Cummings (Eds.), *Attachment in the preschool years*. Chicago: University of Chicago Press.

Emde, R. N., Gaensbauer, T. J., & Harmon, R. J. (1976). *Emotional expression in infancy: A biobehavioral study*. New York: International Universities Press.

Erickson, M. F., Sroufe, L. A., & Egeland, B. (1985). The relationship between quality of attachment and behavior problems in preschool in a high-risk sample. In I. Bretherton & E. Waters (Eds.), Growing points of attachment theory and research. *Monographs of the Society for Research in Child Development, 50*(1–2, Serial No. 209).

Fox, N. A., Kimmerly, N. L., & Schafer, W. D. (1991). Attachment to mother/attachment to father: A meta-analysis. *Child Development, 62,* 210–225.

Fraiberg, S. (Eds.). (1980). *Clinical studies in infant mental health: The first year of life.* New York: Basic Books.

Goldfarb, W. (1945). Effects of psychological deprivation in infancy and subsequent stimulation. *American Journal of Psychiatry, 102,* 18–33.

Greenberg, M. T., & Speltz, M. L. (1988). Attachment and the ontogeny of conduct problems. In J. Belsky & T. Nezworski (Eds.), *Clinical implications of attachment.* Hillsdale, NJ: Erlbaum.

Greenberg, M. T., Speltz, M. L., DeKlyen, M., & Endriga, M. C. (1992). Attachment security in preschoolers with and without externalizing behavior problems: A replication. *Development and Psychopathology, 3,* 413–430.

Grossman, K. E., Grossman, K., Huber, F. & Wartner, U. (1981). German children's behavior towards their mothers at 12 months and their fathers at 18 months in Ainsworth's Strange Situation. *International Journal of Behavioral Development, 4,* 157–181.

Grossman, K., Grossman, K. E., Spangler, G., Suess, G., & Unzner, L. (1985). Maternal sensitivity and newborns' orientation responses as related to quality of attachment in northern Germany. In I. Bretherton & E. Waters (Eds.), Growing points of attachment theory and research. *Monographs of the Society for Research in Child Development, 50*(1–2, Serial No. 209).

Harlow, H. F., & Zimmerman, R. R. (1959). Affectional responses in the infant monkey. *Science, 130,* 421–432.

Isabella, R., & Belsky, J. (1991). Interactional synchrony and the origins of infant–mother attachment: A replication study. *Child Development, 62,* 373–384.

Lamb, M. E., Thompson, R. A., Gardner, W., & Charnov, E. L. (1985). *Infant–mother attachment: The origins and developmental significance of individual differences in the Strange Situation.* Hillsdale, NJ: Erlbaum.

Lester, B., & Seifer, R. (1990). Antecedents of attachment. In T. F. Anders (Chair), *The origins and nature of attachment in infants and mothers.* Symposium presented at the Boston Institute for the Development of Infants and Parents, Pine Manor College, Chestnut Hill, MA.

Lewis, M., Feiring, C., McGuffog, C., & Jaskir, J. (1984). Predicting psychopathology in six-year-olds from early social relations. *Child Development, 55,* 123–136.

Lieberman, A. F., & Pawl, J. H. (1988). Clinical applications of attachment theory. In J. Belsky & T. Nezworski (Eds.), *Clinical implications of attachment.* Hillsdale, NJ: Erlbaum.

Lieberman, A. F., & Pawl, J. H. (1990). Disorders of attachment and secure base behavior in the second year of life: Conceptual issues and clinical intervention. In M. T. Greenberg, D. Cicchetti, & E. M. Cummings (Eds.), *Attachment in the preschool years.* Chicago: University of Chicago Press.

Lieberman, A. F., Weston, D., & Pawl, J. H. (1991). Preventive intervention and outcome with anxiously attached dyads. *Child Development, 62,* 199–209.

Lyons-Ruth, K., Repacholi, B., Alpern, B., & Connell, D. (1991). Disorganized attachment behavior in infancy: Short-term stability, maternal correlates, and the prediction of aggression in kindergarten. In K. Lyons-Ruth (Chair), *Disorganized attachment behavior from infancy to age six: Maternal context, representational processes and child maladaptation.* Symposium presented at the biennial meeting of the Society for Research in Child Development, Seattle.

MacFarlane, J. (1975). Olfaction in the development of social preference in the human newborn. In M. Hofer (Ed.), *Ciba Foundation Symposium: Parent–infant interaction.* Amsterdam: Elsevier.

Main, M., & Cassidy, J. (1988). Categories of response to reunion with the parent at age 6: Predictable from infant attachment classifications and stable over a 1-month period. *Developmental Psychology, 24,* 415–426.

Main, M., & Goldwyn, R. (in press). Interview-based adult attachment classifications: Related to infant–mother and infant–father attachment. *Developmental Psychology.*

Main, M., Kaplan, N., & Cassidy, J. (1985). Security in infancy, childhood and adulthood: A move to the level of representation. In I. Bretherton & E. Waters (Eds.), Growing points of attachment theory and research. *Monographs of the Society for Research in Child Development, 50*(1–2, Serial No. 209).

Main, M., & Solomon, J. (1986). Discovery of an insecure, disorganized/disoriented attachment pattern: Procedures, findings and implications for the classification of behavior. In M. Yogman & T. B. Brazelton (Eds.), *Affective development in infancy.* Norwood, NJ: Ablex.

Main, M., & Solomon, J. (1990). Procedures for identifying infants as disorganized/disoriented during the Ainsworth Strange Situation. In M. T. Greenberg, D. Cicchetti, & E. M. Cummings (Eds.), *Attachment in the preschool years.* Chicago: University of Chicago Press.

Main, M., & Stadtman, J. (1981). Infant responses to rejection of physical contact by the mother. *Journal of the American Academy of Child Psychiatry, 52,* 292–307.

Main, M., & Weston, D. (1981). The quality of the toddler's relationship to mother and to father: Related to conflict behavior and the readiness to establish new relationships. *Child Development, 52,* 932–940.

O'Connor, M. J., Sigman, M., & Brill, N. (1987). Disorganization of attachment in relation to maternal alcohol consumption. *Journal of Consulting and Clinical Psychology, 55,* 831–836.

Osofsky, J., Culp, A. M., & Ware, L. M. (1988). Intervention challenges with adolescent mothers and their infants. *Psychiatry, 51,* 236–241.

Radke-Yarrow, M., Cummings, E. M., Kuczynski, L., & Chapman, N. (1985). Patterns of attachment in two- and three-year olds in normal families and families with parental depression. *Child Development, 56,* 884–893.

Rubin, K. H., & Lollis, S. P. (1988). Origins and consequences of social withdrawal. In J. Belsky & T. Nezworski (Eds.), *Clinical implications of attachment.* Hillsdale, NJ: Erlbaum.

Rutter, M. (1965). Classification and categorization in child psychiatry. *Journal of Child Psychology and Psychiatry, 6,* 71–83.

Rutter, M. (1972). *Maternal deprivation reassessed.* Harmondsworth, England: Penguin.

Rutter, M., & Graham, P. (1968). The reliability and validity of the psychiatric assessment of the child: I. Interview with the child. *British Journal of Psychiatry, 114,* 563–579.

Rutter, M., & Sandberg, S. (1985). Epidemiology of child psychiatric disorders: Methodological issues and some substantive findings. *Child Psychiatry and Human Development, 15,* 209–233.

Sagi, A., Lamb, M. E., Lewcowicz, K. S., Sholam, R., Dvir, R., & Estes, D. (1985). Security of infant–mother, –father, and –metapelet attachments among kibbutz-reared Israeli children. In I. Bretherton & E. Waters (Eds.), Growing points of attachment theory and research. *Monographs of the Society for Research in Child Development, 50*(1–2, Serial No. 209).

Sameroff, A. J., & Emde, R. N. (Eds.). (1989). *Relationship disturbances in early childhood.* New York: Basic Books.

Skeels, H. M. (1966). Adult status of children with contrasting early life experiences. *Monographs of the Society for Research in Child Development, 31*(Serial No. 105).

Solomon, J., George, C., & Ivins, B. (1987). *Mother–child interaction in the home and security of attachment at age six.* Paper presented at the biennial meeting of the Society for Research in Child Development, Baltimore.

Speltz, M., Greenberg, M. T., & Deklyen, M. (1990). The treatment of preschool conduct problems: An integration of behavioral and attachment concepts. In M. T. Greenberg, D. Cicchetti, & E. M. Cummings (Eds.), *Attachment in the preschool years.* Chicago: University of Chicago Press.

Spitz, R. (1945). Hospitalism: An inquiry into the genesis of psychiatric conditions in early childhood. *Psychoanalytic Study of the Child, 1,* 53–74.

Spitz, R. (1946). Anaclitic depression: An inquiry into the genesis of psychiatric conditions in early childhood. *Psychoanalytic Study of the Child, 2,* 53–74.

Sroufe, L. A. (1983). Infant–caregiver attachment and patterns of adaptation in preschool: The roots of maladaptation and competence. In M. Perlmutter (Ed.), *Minnesota Symposium in Child Psychology* (Vol. 16). Hillsdale, NJ: Erlbaum.

Sroufe, L. A. (1988). The role of infant–caregiver attachment in development. In J. Belsky & T. Nezworski (Eds.), *Clinical implications of attachment.* Hillsdale, NJ: Erlbaum.

Sroufe, L. A., & Waters, E. (1977). Attachment as an organizational construct. *Child Development, 48,* 1184–1199.

Steele, H., Steele, M., & Fonagy, P. (1991). *Forecasting security of attachment: Prenatal AAI assessment of parents and subsequent Strange Situation assessments.*

Paper presented at the biennial meeting of the Society for Research in Child Development, Seattle.

Thompson, R. A., Lamb, M. E., & Estes, D. (1982). Stability of infant–mother attachment and its relation to changing life circumstances in an unselected middle class sample. *Child Development, 53,* 144–148.

Tizard, B., & Hodges, J. (1978). The effect of early institutional rearing on the development of eight year old children. *Journal of Child Psychology and Psychiatry, 19,* 99–118.

Tizard, B., & Rees, J. (1974). A comparison of the effects of adoption, restoration to the natural mother, and continued institutionalisation on the cognitive development of four-year-old children. *Journal of Child Psychology and Psychiatry, 16,* 61–73.

Tizard, B., & Rees, J. (1975). The effect of early institutional rearing on the behaviour problems and affectional relationships of four-year-old children. *Journal of Child Psychology and Psychiatry, 16,* 61–73.

Troy, M., & Sroufe, L. A. (1987). Victimization among preschoolers: Role of attachment relationship history. *Journal of the American Academy of Child and Adolescent Psychiatry, 26,* 166–172.

van Ijzendoorn, M., & Kroonenberg, P. M. (1988). Cross-cultural patterns of attachment: A meta-analysis of the Strange Situation. *Child Development, 59,* 147–156.

Vaughn, B., Egeland, B., Sroufe, L. A., & Waters, E. (1979). Individual differences in infant–mother attachment at twelve and eighteen months: Stability and change in families under stress. *Child Development, 50,* 971–975.

Vaughn, B., & Waters, E. (1990). Attachment behavior at home and in the laboratory: Q-sort observations and Strange Situation classifications of one-year-olds. *Child Development, 61,* 1965–1973.

Waters, E. (1978). The reliability and stability of individual differences in infant–mother attachment. *Child Development, 49,* 483–494.

World Health Organization (WHO). (1992). *International classification of diseases: Clinical descriptions and diagnostic guidelines* (10th ed.). Geneva: Author.

Zeanah, C. H. (in press). Subjectivity in parent–infant relationships: Contributions from attachment research. *Adolescent Psychiatry.*

Zeanah, C. H., & Anders, T. F. (1987). Subjectivity in parent–infant relationships: A discussion of internal working models. *Infant Mental Health Journal, 8,* 237–250.

Zeanah, C. H., & Emde, R. N. (in press). Attachment disorders in infants and young children. In M. Rutter, L. Hersov, & E. Taylor (Eds.), *Child and adolescent psychiatry* (3rd ed.). Oxford: Blackwell.

Zeanah, C. H., & Klitzke, M. (1991). Role reversal and the self-effacing solution: Observations from infant–parent psychotherapy. *Psychiatry, 54,* 346–357.

23

Psychosomatic Processes and Physical Illnesses

DAVID A. MRAZEK

Interactions between mind and body are vividly demonstrated by the bodily responses of infants and very young children to their early emotional experiences. Early developmental theorists approached the challenge of probing the inner world of the nonverbal child by first hypothesizing and then trying to demonstrate direct links between early emotional experiences on the one hand, and physiological processes and medical illnesses on the other. From these observations arose the theoretical position that various "psychosomatic" illnesses that may not occur until later in life are actually linked to the ephemeral somatic memories of the first years of life. Furthermore, a conceptualization developed regarding individuals with either temperamental limitations or pathogenic early experiences, who were noted to demonstrate problems with verbal expression of emotions. Such patients were described as "alexithymic" because they struggled to find words (i.e., "alexi-") for feelings (i.e., "-thymia"). During early attempts to conduct psychotherapy with medical patients with psychiatric symptoms, problems in their associational patterns suggested that many were unable to express feelings easily. For them, as for nonverbal infants, it was hypothesized that somatization processes were the product of internal conflicts that could not be resolved verbally. Subsequent "confirmatory" clinical observations provided evidence to support this hypothesized mechanism for the development of disease.

Although such theories have captured the imagination of clinicians for the past century, their explication is beyond the scope of this review. Instead, the objective of this chapter is to examine the empirical evidence that these processes are demonstrated during the first years of life. One conceptual goal is to speculate and to anticipate how new knowledge derived from our greatly expanded understanding of genetic processes can be integrated into a comprehensive theory of developmental psychosomatic psychopathology. After a historical review of the topic, the chapter focuses on current understandings of somatic problems during early childhood. Two clinical conditions, infantile-onset obesity and early-onset asthma, are reviewed in detail; they illustrate both the etiological impact of early stressors on physical conditions and strategies for early intervention.

HISTORICAL EVOLUTION OF CONCEPTUALIZING PSYCHOSOMATIC PROCESSES

In the 1940s, the Chicago school of psychoanalysis became a major center for the conduct of psychosomatic research. Franz Alexander (1950) and his colleagues were pioneers in the creation of the original conceptualization of psychoanalytic psychosomatic processes. Although fascinating individual clinical phenomena were described, the psychoanalytic formulations that were put forward to explain the illness phenomena were never empirically tested in a sufficiently rigorous manner to become widely accepted. Furthermore, historical misconceptions regarding normal physiology led to the suggestion of relatively implausible mechanisms to explain quite complex pathophysiological processes. However, one major contribution of these investigations was to focus attention on the earliest responses of infants to distress. Another major conceptual innovation was the theoretical position that traumatic early emotional experiences are sufficiently potent stressors to create lifelong changes in psychophysiological regulation.

Jean Piaget was a pioneer in the conceptualization of how an infant's mind works. His work has led to a new level of appreciation for the links between cognitive schema and physical processes and actions. His own work was influenced by the empirical studies of Pavlov, who experientally manipulated discrete physiological processes in his classical conditioning experiments. Piaget (1952) appreciated the possibility that physiological processes could become linked to environmental signals, and conceptually expanded a simple reflex theory of relationship to a more complex and interesting set of early associational patterns or schemas that (as he demonstrated) evolve over the first months and years of life. His extremely precise observations provided evidence that infants gradually begin to create quite strong cognitive connections among feelings, ideas, and sensations in an increasingly sophisticated manner. He described the evolution of these schemas in a systematic manner, making the case that these cognitive templates are ultimately used by the child to define reality. To the degree that he considered these learned associational relationships to be incorporated as somatic components during the sensorimotor phase of development, this work provided a phenomenonological description of how a physiological experience (e.g., hunger) actually becomes the signal sensation that can drive a set of behaviors (e.g., crying) designed to achieve a discrete homeostatic state (e.g., satiety). Within this framework, a number of both sensory stimuli (e.g., sight of mother) and motor responses (e.g., sucking on thumb) can become linked to the original signal and to one another. The physiological processes involved in such a process can be measured with increasing sophistication. The behaviors elicited are readily observable. More elusive, however, have been the demonstration of neural processes and the elaboration of control systems that include both the translation of central nervous system processes and the expression of genetic information.

With the advent of increasingly sophisticated understanding of operant conditioning, a more developed theory for the origin of psychosomatic illness became available and was utilized to formulate the process by which physical illness becomes "reinforced" in childhood. For example, work by Creer (1976) in respiratory diseases has provided a greater clarification of the mechanisms by which physiological processes can be manipulated behaviorally. However, little of this work has focused on infancy.

With the evolution of attachment theory, the role that primary attachment relationships play in mediating the emotional experience of children has been highlighted. One specific dimension of a sense of early internal securities that a child develops within the context of the caregiving relationship is the ability to use the relationship as one mechanism for homeostatic control of internal distress. Emde has expanded on both the psychodynamic observations of Spitz (1965) and his own developmental studies designed to chart the early landmarks of normal early development (Emde, Gaensbauer, & Harmon, 1982). Parmalee (1989) has further elaborated on how the experience of supportive relationships can become particularly salient during periods of illness. He has hypothesized that sucessfully adapting to the stressors associated with being ill actually enhances the development of emotional regulation during early childhood.

Sameroff has expanded on his early model of transactional processes (Sameroff & Chandler, 1975) to add a complex dimension to the understanding of how the interactions of multiple risk factors affect physically ill children (Sameroff, 1986). What appears to occur is a process of normal adaptation until a critical threshold is reached, at which point a major perturbation can occur. What is necessary is to develop an interpersonally relevant framework that will enable us to better understand the processes by which infants may begin to gain control of their own emotional homeostasis during periods of internal distress (Sameroff & Emde, 1989).

THE IMPORTANCE OF NATURE IN THE NATURE–NURTURE EQUATION

It has long been conceptualized that a complex interaction exists between the genetic potential of the infant and the environmental experiences provided by the parents. However, the actual relative contributions of these factors, as they relate to the expression of an anticipated phenotype, have rarely been a component of early interventions. This is particularly intriguing, given that clear conceptual models describing possible interactions have existed for more than a generation.

An illustrative example is phenylketonuria (PKU). PKU is an autosomal recessive metabolic disorder that, if left untreated, progresses to produce a dramatic decrease in intelligence. The classic recessive pattern of PKU provided striking evidence that subnormal intelligence could be inherited. The discovery of large quantities of phenylalanine in the blood and urine of these patients led to the search for a single enzyme deficiency that was the result of a problem with the coding of the allele responsible for its production. Eventually, a deficiency of phenylalanine hydroxylase was identified as the problem. As a consequence of this single genetic error, a patient cannot appropriately metabolize phenylalanine, which subsequently accumulates. This observation has led to a therapeutic strategy: Infants identified as having PKU, on the basis of very early elevations in serum phenylalanine, are placed on a diet that contains very low quantities of this amino acid. Instituting this restrictive diet within the first week of life effectively preserves the infants' cognitive abilities. The cost of a screening program for this defective enzyme has been shown to be dramatically cost-effective when the overall cost of caring for mentally retarded children is considered (Hecht, 1987). This approach requires both a biochemical appreciation of the disorder and a dramatic change in feeding behavior.

One striking lesson to be learned from the successful treatment of PKU is that parents are able to follow even complex diets for their children in a dramatically compliant fashion. The most probable reason for this is that the consequences of noncompliance are so ominous. Furthermore, parents have virtually complete control of their infants' eating behavior unless a feeding disorder develops. Given the dramatic success of this approach, it is surprising that so little extension of this effective intervention has occurred with other illnesses.

There are dozens of clinical examples of parents who ignore medical wisdom despite concrete evidence that the prescribed course of action is in the best interests of their own children. A primary reason why some physicians are cautious when considering early interventions is that they are pessimistic about parents' willingness to change their behaviors. For example, they identify that a child is allergic to the family cat, but are told that the parents have decided to keep the cat rather than protect their infant from sensitization, because they feel that the cat is a "part of the family." Similarly, physicians counsel parents of infants at risk for asthma to stop smoking but learn that the nonasthmatic mother of the child has decided to continue to smoke "because she doesn't want to gain weight." A third example is that of an obese father who is counseled that his young son is already in the 99th percentile for weight while being in the 50th percentile for height. The clinical prescription is to place the child on a low fat diet (Epstein, McCurley, Valoski, & Wing, 1990), but the father does not change the infant's feeding routine because he believes that a normal diet would leave his child with a sense of deprivation.

One of the core differences between these examples of noncompliance and the faithful adherence of parents to providing phenylalanine-free diets for their children with PKU is almost inevitably their understanding of the certainty and nature of the negative consequences. For most psychosomatic problems that may arise in infancy, parents can "play the odds" that their children will not suffer if they persist in their preferred behaviors. Because the parents of children with PKU have strong evidence that they will cause immediate, permanent damage to their children's intelligence if they do not alter their behavior, they are willing to make necessary changes.

The genome of a child is fixed at conception; at this time, no new genes can be added. Therefore, change in the environment of the child must be the focus of any intervention. To modify a young child's environment, it is usually necessary to help the family alter either the physical or the emotional experience of the child. What has only recently been appreciated is that while gene *structure* does not change in accordance with environmental events, the *function* of the genes can change. Gene expression can be controlled by a range of other factors, including genetically coded information that regulates gene action and environmental signals that affect the genes themselves. The realization that genetic control is possible through environmental manipulation has led to the development of a new focus of intervention. These treatment strategies can be described as "management of the environmental regulation of gene expression and reactivation" (MERGER). In short, genes can be turned off and on. The exact mechanism by which this happens is only beginning to be understood. Nevertheless, the clinical implications of the management of these processes may be far-reaching. MERGER intervention is discussed in more detail later in this chapter.

INFANTILE ONSET OBESITY

In reviewing psychosomatic processes, there is no more basic consideration than the actual structure and shape of the body itself. A series of new studies has focused on the genetic control of obesity. Studies using large twin samples in which one of the twins has been raised by nonbiological parents have made the importance of the role of genetics in the development of obesity in children more vivid (Stunkard et al., 1986; Price & Gottesman, 1991). Although some studies suggest that heritability may be as high as 80%, in other samples a heritability estimate of closer to 50% has been suggested. Some substantial portion of this heritability, perhaps 25%, may be the result of genetic control of metabolic rate and energy expenditure (Bouchard, Despres, & Tremblay, 1991). What appears to be true is that there is a strong genetically controlled tendency for excessive body weight.

Nevertheless, it is equally critical to consider the role environmental factors play in the development of obesity in children who are genetically at risk. Environmental risk factors such as low socioeconomic status are known to be strong predictors of subsequent obesity. Perhaps the most straightforward and undeniable demonstration of the influence of environmental factors on the expression of obesity can be found in those identical twin pairs in which one individual is strikingly obese and the other twin has maintained his or her weight within normal limits. Their genetic endowment is identical, but their phenotypic expression is dramatically different. Shields (1962) supported this clinical observation in his classic monograph on monozygotic twins, where he reported that two pairs of twins who were reared apart varied in weight by more than three stone (i.e., 42 pounds).

Many obese parents have had a particularly difficult struggle with controlling their own weight. Ironically, this may be one factor that contributes to their "overfeeding" of their own children. This paradoxical behavior is an appropriate area for the infant mental health clinician

to address. Certainly, the risk factors involved with the development of obesity are clear and straightforward. Children should be carefully weighed throughout the first year of life. A discrepancy between the percentile of weight and the percentile of height is an indication of a need to become proactive in monitoring the diet of the child. Since these children do not have problems with consuming food and do not hesitate in becoming active participants in the feeding process, they contrast sharply with children who fail to thrive, and a very different proactive approach is warranted.

How a child becomes obese is not a total mystery. The two primary issues are calorie consumption and energy expenditure. In the first years of life, parents have virtually total control of the diet of their child and a substantial influence on their child's level of activity. The various possibilities for problems in overfeeding are again straightforward. In terms of quantity of food, parents need to be motivated to take active control. Both gradually decreasing the quantities of food consumed at mealtimes and restricting food between meals are reasonable strategies. Yet a key factor in calorie consumption is the choice of foods. The current wisdom is to avoid foods with either high fat or high sugar content, since there is some evidence that these choices tend to lead quickly to the development of strong food preferences, which can contribute to problems in long-term weight management.

Prevention of obesity is a far more effective strategy for eventual weight control than attempts to change the eating pattern of children who have already become obese. Of children at the 95th percentile of weight at birth, 58% are likely to be obese at 7 years of age. Fortunately, 42% will be of normal weight. However, if children who are large at birth are allowed to remain overweight until they are 4 years of age, 98% are still obese 3 years later when they are 7 (Fisch, Bilek, & Ulstrom, 1975).

Despite the importance of early intervention, some parents are resistant. In part, this may reflect how the psychological meaning of eating has evolved for these parents. For example, an obese mother who uses food as a primary method for modulating her own distress often finds it particularly difficult to restrict the child's food intake when the child signals that he or she wants to consume more.

Some parents fear that by restricting the intake of their child, they may in some way do some harm. Currently, the American Academy of Pediatrics advocates restricting the consumption of high levels of fat. Still, until recently, a baby's "chubbiness" was regarded as a sign of "good health." Fortunately, there is now good evidence that appropriate early dieting does not lead to negative outcomes, such as a permanent effect on the ultimate height of a child (Epstein et al., 1990). Yet another anxiety is that focusing too soon on weight control may lead the child to develop an unhealthy preoccupation with eating. The ultimate fear in this regard is that this experience may be associated with the later development of Anorexia Nervosa. Although there has been some suggestion that very intense preoccupation with thinness, particularly between a mother and her daughter during the preadolescent years, can sensitize some girls to developing Anorexia Nervosa, there is no evidence to link early conservative weight control to later problems in this area.

In summary, the problem of obesity in the first 3 years of life illustrates how the emotional needs of parents can interact with a strong hunger drive in an infant to lead the family to ignore warning signs of excessive weight gain. Establishing patterns of overeating early in life can lead to chronic obesity and a wide range of negative medical outcomes associated with excessive weight.

The infant mental health clinician has a fascinating opportunity to assess the complexity of the psychological context in which a child begins to overeat, and to intervene in the process at a very early stage in its development. A collaboration with pediatric practices provides an excellent opportunity to identify children at risk for developing obesity. If pediatric counseling targeted at straightforward methods to maintain the weight of the child at appropriate levels fails, referral to an infant mental health clinician is appropriate. The focus of this intervention requires a strong educational component. However, it must also take into account how the emotional needs of the parents influence the child's emotional experience. Ultimately, it is the pattern of eating and activity that will result in the expression of obesity in those children who are genetically vulnerable.

EARLY-ONSET ASTHMA

Asthma is a "psychosomatic" illness that illustrates many of the clinical issues relevant to the care of young children who have medical problems. All psychosomatic illnesses are "real" diseases that present with tangible signs and symptoms. They are in no way "all in a child's head," as punitive caregivers have historically asserted. However, the onset and course of the illness are influenced by a child's emotional state. Some of the most fascinating questions in medicine focus on how the etiology of illness is influenced by disruptions in homeostasis. These essential questions are focused on defining the "root cause" of both the physical and emotional symptoms, and are based on the premise that there are bidirectional processes involved in symptom expression. As regards the primary or first direction, a set of hypotheses has been developed to explain mechanisms by which early difficult emotional experiences may lead to the expression of physical symptoms and ultimately illness in a genetically vulnerable child. As regards the reverse or second direction, hypotheses have been put forward to illustrate how the illness-specific stressors associated with physical disease may play a role in exacerbating the development of early psychopathological symptoms and ultimately psychiatric illness. Regardless of whether the child's first symptom is one of emotional distress or physical dysfunction, the eventual process very often becomes what is classically described as a "vicious cycle." With increasing emotional disturbance, the somatic symptoms of the infant become acute. Reciprocally, with increasing physical symptoms the emotional state of the child is increasingly compromised, and a wide range of problems in adaptation begin to emerge (Mrazek, 1988).

Asthma is an extremely common pediatric illness, affecting approximately 7% of all children in the United States (Smith, 1988). Consequently, there are more than 4 million children who will develop asthma in the United States alone. Given that nearly three-quarters of these children will develop their first respiratory symptoms in the first 3 years of life, there are nearly 3 million infants and toddlers who will meet the epidemiological criteria necessary to make the diagnosis of asthma. Asthma is normally an illness that is characterized by sudden reversible bronchoconstriction. It usually is accompanied by a high-pitched expiratory wheeze and acute difficulty in breathing, but a young child's cough can be a prominent symptom. It has been increasingly appreciated that inflammatory processes accompany and exacerbate the reactive bronchoconstriction of the child.

Asthma has both a strong genetic component

and a prominent environmental component. However, it is important to realize that there is wide variability in the nature of symptoms among asthmatic children. Their symptoms range from mild chest tightness that occurs in a seasonal pattern at one extreme, to life-threatening bronchoconstriction that can close down a child's airways at the other end of the continuum. Some children have an allergic form of the illness that is triggered by exposure to antigens in the air, which may come from pets, dust, foods, or a variety of other allergens. The asthmatic attacks of other children are triggered primarily through respiratory infections, exercise, or exposure to intense emotional stress, and have no allergic component (Mrazek & Klinnert, 1991).

Psychiatric disturbances occur somewhat more frequently in asthmatic children than in healthy children (Mrazek, Anderson, & Strunk, 1985). However, this is in many ways dependent upon the severity of the asthma. More than half of the children with very serious illness have been reported to demonstrate psychiatric symptoms. Children with very mild illness have rates only slightly exceeding those found in representative epidemiological populations. The severity of illness varies greatly in young infants, and this variation also has considerable implications for their long-term prognosis. Children with very severe early asthma are unlikely to "grow out of it," and have a higher risk for serious episodes later in life (Blair, 1977). In contrast, infants and toddlers who have very mild asthma may be symptom-free after their third or fourth year of life, at a point when their airways have become larger in diameter.

In a classic study conducted in Montreal, key parameters characterizing the interactions between mothers and their infants with mild asthma were examined (Gauthier et al., 1977, 1978). Although subtle differences in the interactions of mothers and their young asthmatic children were noted, these asthmatic children were adapting well overall. This study demonstrated that for children with mild asthma, there was minimal evidence that there were serious problems in the parenting of these infants.

In contrast, another study showed that a sample of 75 preschool children with very severe asthma was doing considerably worse (Mrazek, Anderson, & Strunk, 1983; Mrazek, 1993). These children had experienced multiple previous hospitalizations, and many required steroid medications to control their symptoms. More than half of them were found to have developed a behavioral disturbance when they were systematically assessed using a semistructured maternal report interview methodology. These quite severely asthmatic children had more problems with sleep and depressed mood than a healthy comparison group. In addition, their mothers were found to have difficulty establishing compliance in completing a standardized task when their interactions were assessed by means of a microanalytic interactional coding technique.

If severity of illness were not considered, these two studies of young children with asthma would appear to have yielded contradictory findings. Instead, they provide empirical support for what has become an increasingly central component of our understanding of developmental psychopathology. Risk factors may interact in an additive or synergistic manner, and as these interactions increase, there is an escalation in the probability that there will be a breakdown in a child's adaptation.

Illness-specific risk factors associated with mild asthma are actually quite limited. Although the symptoms associated with mild asthma may place intermittent limitations on a preschooler's activity and contribute to "a sense of being different," the stressors associated with mild disease rarely become an organizing principle in the formation of the identity of the child. In contrast, a child with severe asthma must cope with a number of major stressors. Often respiratory symptoms limit the child's capacity to attend school and develop peer relations. Changes in body image can be dramatic if there is a need to maintain the child on steroid medication. Growth retardation, obesity, and changes in facial appearance can all be disturbing and serve as a constant reminder to these children that they are different. Eventually, many children with severe asthma become sensitized to their symptoms and develop a sense of vulnerability that becomes linked to a growing fearfulness of a severe, life-threatening attack.

Given that the nature of children's emotional difficulties usually reflect the specific aspects of the stressors that they experience, it is not surprising that severely asthmatic children often develop symptoms of anxiety and depression. Furthermore, they are more likely to develop sleep disturbances, in part because they are more likely to experience severe attacks during the night. The primary interactional difficulties noted in the preschool study (Mrazek et al., 1985; Mrazek, 1993) reflected the inability of some of the parents to set limits successfully. Given that asthmatic attacks can occur as a consequence of emotional conflicts, parents sometimes choose to avoid such confrontations even at the cost of "giving in" to their children.

The role that emotional stressors play in the initial expression of symptoms in genetically at-risk asthmatic children has been a controversial area of study. The W. T. Grant Study conducted in Denver focused on a group of 150 infants of asthmatic mothers and a comparison sample. Sixty of the index children also had paternal relatives with asthma. An estimate of the risk for the development of asthma in this sample was about 20% if one parent had asthma and 50% if both parents were affected. A prospective and longitudinal design was used, with all children being identified during pregnancy. Families were usually recruited into the study during the third trimester. Both biological and environmental risk factors were carefully monitored from before the birth of each child. Prominent among them were biological factors, such as the occurrence of frequent each respiratory infections (Frick, German, & Mills, 1979) or high levels of serum immunoglobulin E (IgE). IgE levels from cord blood samples have been shown to statistically predict the onset of asthma and atopic dermatitis in large samples of infants (Michel Bousquet, Greiller, Robinet-Levy, & Coulomb, 1990). However, from a psychiatric perspective, the most interesting hypothesis tested was that early emotional stressors would increase the risk for these children of developing asthma.

All three of these risk factors did, in fact, predict the onset of asthma. Infections were associated with an increased risk of developing asthma by age 2 years, as were elevated levels of IgE (Mrazek et al., 1990). Particularly striking was the finding that ratings of problems in parenting made 3 weeks after the birth of a child were strong predictors of the development of asthma (Mrazek, Klinnert, Mrazek, & Macey, 1991). The natures of these parenting problems were actually quite diverse, but all were clinically judged as capable of causing emotional dysregulation in the child. These parenting problems included maternal depression, overt marital unhappiness, or an insensitivity regarding the emotional needs of the child. These clinical judgments were noted after an hour-long semi-structured interview with each mother and an opportunity to observe the mother interacting with the child in the family home. These judgments were made before the onset of any respiratory symptoms. This latter finding suggests that early disruptions in a child's emotional experience, as mediated through specific caretaking parental practices, may lead to increased vulnerability in the child and to a greater likelihood of the genetic expression of underlying respiratory symptoms. Such a finding supports the development of a program to modulate the expression of these genes.

INTERVENTION STRATEGIES FOR ILLNESSES WITH EARLY EXPRESSION

MERGER intervention, mentioned earlier in this chapter, is a new concept. Until very recently, clinicians viewed the expression of genes as inevitable. Consequently, there was no point in attempting to develop psychosocial interventions for any disease that was believed to be genetically controlled.

Different lines of evidence have made it clear that genes are often expressed at specific points in development or they may never be expressed. Consequently, to the degree that a particular genetic trait has variable "penetrance," which can be understood as a variable probability of expression, both medical and environmental interventions can be tested to determine their influence on the timing or persistence of the expression of the target gene. A simple example of the variable timing of the expression of a gene is male baldness. There is no doubt that this trait is genetically controlled. However, during the first 20 years of a boy's life, there is no physical sign to signal whether he will lose his hair prematurely. For more than 20 years the genes do not express themselves, and if they do produce a gene product, it has no impact on his hair follicles. It is not clear why the genetic switch is suddenly flipped during early adulthood, but it is certain that the genetic message has been latently in place since the initial conception of the individual.

The data related to differential expression of genetically controlled traits in monozygotic twins are of particular interest. Some genes have very powerful penetrance, and at this point in time we have no expectation of being able to influence their expression. It is extremely rare, for example, that identical twin pairs are discordant for eye color. Similarly, if one identical twin develops cystic fibrosis, it is still virtually inevitable that the second twin will eventually develop the symptoms of the disease. This is not to say that in a decade, as we come to understand the precise variability of the different alleles that result in the development of cystic fibrosis, it will not be possible to develop a "gene therapy" that can prevent the expression of this disease. However, it does suggest that environmental interventions are less likely to be successful.

Both infantile-onset obesity and early-onset asthma present attractive models for MERGER intervention. The first necessary strategy is to identify the children at risk. One straightforward method is to use a pedigree analysis. Those children with a high incidence of first- and second-degree relatives who have expressed the phenotype are quantitatively at greater risk. This is equally true for excessive weight or for recurrent wheezing.

In order to be able to mount an effective intervention for a specific child, it is helpful to know whether the child is in fact carrying the gene for the problem. It is highly probable that within a decade, gene sites on the chromosomes that control asthma and obesity will be identified. Furthermore, the sequence of specific alleles should be fully explicated. At that point in time, only children who actually have a known genetic vulnerability will be appropriate candidates for MERGER intervention. However, at this point in time, any child who has a high probability of having an affected gene (as demonstrated by pedigree analysis) is an appropriate candidate for such treatment. This implies that some children who are at no actual genetic risk for the biological expression will be treated; in turn, this necessitates that the intervention have few if any major negative sequelae or side effects.

In the case of obesity, a disproportionate weight-to-height ratio serves as an early warning sign that signals the need for early intervention. For asthma, wheezing during the course of an infectious illness in the first years of life is a good indicator of bronchial hyperactivity and of an increased risk for the development of the disease.

A MERGER intervention has recently been developed for the prevention of asthma, and its effectiveness is currently being assessed. This comprehensive intervention includes three specific treatment components that have each been hypothesized to be effective. None of these interventions has potential negative sequelae. The intervention includes an educational module,

designed to sensitize parents to the known risk factors associated with asthma onset; a hypoallergic module, designed to minimize the exposure of infants to foods known to have high antigenic properties; and a home visiting module, designed to help mothers to respond to their infants more sensitively and to make decisions related to child care and family management that will minimize the exposure of these children to increased emotional distress. One hundred and forty families were originally enrolled in the study, and medical data are available for the entire sample. Although only preliminary findings are available, the low incidence of wheezing and the even lower frequency of the diagnosis of asthma in this sample are striking. These results are preliminary and may represent only a temporary delay in the onset of wheezing symptoms in these genetically at-risk young children, but the overall good health of this cohort is already encouraging.

A parallel MERGER intervention has been conceptualized for obesity; it involves an educational, a dietary, and a parental support component. The obesity program is designed to support families in which obese parents identify an infant who has begun to gain weight excessively.

Infant mental health clinicians will increasingly play a prominent role in the implementation of such interventions. Effecting change in young families requires sensitivity to the developmental needs of infants and toddlers, as well as to the emotional needs of these children and their parents. A multidisciplinary team is usually in the best position to mount such interventions. For such a team to be effective, it must include a clinician who can communicate the key intervention concepts to the parents and, most importantly, help to effect a behavioral change in how the parents relate to their infants. The field of infant mental health has played an instrumental role in providing insights as to how to create these behavioral changes most effectively. However, until recently, the range of families with children who could benefit from such interventions has actually been quite narrow. As the number of illnesses with well-demonstrated genetic bases becomes better documented, the role of environment in the regulation of gene function should become better defined. As more effective strategies to prevent the onset of psychosomatic illnesses are developed and are put into place, the public health implications of such efforts should be substantial.

REFERENCES

Alexander, F. (1950). *Psychosomatic medicine.* New York: Norton.

Blair, H. (1977) Natural history of childhood asthma. Twenty year follow-up. *Archives of Disease in Childhood, 52,* 613–619.

Bouchard, C., Despres, J., & Tremblay, A. (1991). Genetics of obesity and human energy metabolism. *Proceedings of the Nutrition Society, 50,* 139–147.

Creer, T. L. (1976). Behavioral contributions to rehabilitation and childhood asthma. *Rehabilitation Literature, 37,* 226–232.

Emde, R. N., Gaensbauer, T. J., & Harmon, R. J. (1976). *Emotional expression in infancy: A biobehavioral study: Psychological issues.* Volume 10, No. 1. Monograph 37. New York: International Universities Press.

Epstein, L. H., McCurley, J., Valoski, A., & Wing, R. R. (1990). Growth in obese children treated for obesity. *American Journal of Diseases of Children, 144,* 1360–1364.

Fisch, R. O., Bilek, M. K., & Ulstrom, R. (1975). Obesity and leanness at birth and their relationship to body habitus in later childhood. *Pediatrics, 56*(4), 521–528.

Frick, O. L., German, D. F., & Mills, J. (1979). Development of allergy in chidren: I. Association with virus infections. *Journal of Allergy and Clinical Immunology, 63,* 228–241.

Gauthier, Y., Fortin, C., Drapeau, P., Breton, J. J., Gosselin, J., Quintal, L., Weisnagel, J., Tetreault, L., & Pinard, G. (1977). The mother–child relationship and the development of autonomy and self-assertion in young (14–30 months) asthmatic children. *Journal of the American Academy of Child Psychiatry, 16,* 109–131.

Gauthier, Y., Fortin, C., Drapeau, P., Breton, J. J., Gosselin, J., Quintal, L., Weisnagel, J., & Lamarre, A. (1978). Follow-up study of 35 asthmatic preschool children. *Journal of the American Academy of Child Psychiatry, 17,* 679–694.

Hecht, F. (1987). *Genetic diseases in primary pediatric care.* St. Louis: C. V. Mosby.

Michel, F. B., Bousquet, J., Greillier, P., Rabinet-Levy, M., & Coulomb, Y. (1990). Comparison of cord blood immunoglobulin E concentrations and maternal allergy for the prediction of atopic diseases in infancy. *Journal of Allergy and Clinical Immunology, 65,* 422–430.

Mrazek, D. A. (1993). Disturbed emotional development of severely asthmatic children. In A. West & M. J. Christie (Eds.), *Quality of life in childhood asthma.* Chichester, England: Carden.

Mrazek, D. A., Anderson, I., & Strunk, R. (1985). Disturbed emotional development of severely asthmatic preschool children. In J. E. Stevenson (Ed.), *Recent research in developmental psychopathology* (*Journal of Child Psychology and Psychiatry* Book Supplement No. 4, pp. 81–93). Oxford: Pergamon Press.

Mrazek, D. A., & Klinnert, M. (1991). Asthma: Psychoneuroimmunologic considerations. In R. Ader, E. L. Felton, & N. Cohen (Eds.), *Psychoneuroimmunology II* (2nd ed., pp. 1013–1035). Orlando, FL: Academic Press.

Mrazek, D. A., Klinnert, M., Brower, A., & Harbeck, R. J. (1990). Predictive capacity of elevated serum IgE for early onset. *Journal of Allergy and Clinical Immunology, 85,* 194.

Mrazek, D. A., Klinnert, M., Mrazek, P. J., & Macey, T. (1991). Early asthma onset: Consideration of parenting issues. *Journal of the American Academy of Child and Adolescent Psychiatry, 30,* 277–282.

Parmalee, A. H. (1989). The child's physical health and the development of relationships. In A. J. Sameroff & R. N. Emde (Eds.), *Relationship disturbances in early childhood: A developmental approach* (pp. 145–162). New York: Basic Books.

Piaget, J. (1952). *The origins of intelligence in children.* New York: International Universities Press.

Price, R. A., & Gottesman, I. I. (1991). Body fat in identical twins reared apart: Roles of genes and environment. *Behavioral Genetics, 21*(1), 1–7.

Sameroff, A. J. (1986). Environmental context of child development. *Journal of Pediatrics, 109,* 192–200.

Sameroff, A. J., & Chandler, M. J. (1975). Reproductive risk and the continuum of caretaking causality. In F. D. Horowitz, E. M. Hetherington, S. Scarr-Salapatek, & G. Siegel (Eds.), *Review of child development research* (Vol. 4, pp. 187–244). Chicago: University of Chicago Press.

Sameroff, A. J., & Emde, R. N. (Eds.). (1989). *Relationship disturbances in early childhood: A developmental approach.* New York: Basic Books.

Shields, J. (1962). *Monozygotic twins brought up apart and together.* London: Oxford University Press.

Smith, J. M. (1988). Epidemiology and natural history of asthma, allergic rhinitis, and atopic dermatitis (eczema). In E. Middleton, C. E. Reed, & E. F. Ellis (Eds.), *Allergy: Principles and practice* (3rd ed., pp. 891–929). St. Louis: C. V. Mosby.

Spitz, R. (1965). *The first year of life.* New York: International Universities Press.

Stunkard, A. J., Sorensen, T. I. A., Hanis, C., Teasdale, T. W., Chakraborty, R., Schull, W. J., & Schulsinger, F. (1986). An adoption study of human obesity. *New England Journal of Medicine, 314*(4), 193–198.

V

INTERVENTION

This section highlights the means by which our accumulated knowledge about infant disorders and risk conditions can be translated into interventions. Some of the important models for intervention—from the more traditional treatment of particular cases (as illustrated by infant–parent psychotherapy and by interaction guidance) to more broad-based approaches to defined populations at risk (such as early intervention programs, prevention programs, and family support programs)—are described. The most obvious omission in this section is a chapter on family therapy. Of course, all meaningful psychotherapeutic approaches in infancy are family-focused, but the specific assumptions underlying family therapy are not always apparent in the approaches described.

In Chapter 24, Meisels, Dichtelmiller, and Liaw review the literature on early intervention programs for preterm and disabled infants and toddlers. They organize the review around a two-dimensional matrix, with the horizontal axis representing the primacy of intervention with the child and the vertical axis reflecting the primacy of intervention with the parent. Furthermore, they suggest a redirection of research efforts toward more specific and answerable questions, such as which programs are effective for which children and families under which circumstances. Recognizing that diversity in early intervention is mandatory, they advocate the development of highly individualized programs that consider the needs of both children and families as necessary precursors to evaluating effectiveness.

Barnard, Morriset, and Spieker, in Chapter 25, point to the large number of children in the United States who must confront the risk factors delineated in Part II. They call for prevention efforts at the conceptual, program, family, and dyadic levels in order to decrease the number of children born at risk. They organize their review around the traditional divisions of primary, secondary, and tertiary prevention, and they conclude that our capacity to prevent mental and emotional disorders in young children depends upon our ability to support parenting by removing as many impediments as possible.

Weissbourd (Chapter 26) reviews family support programs and the movement they have inspired. Recently, the provision of federal funds to assist states in establishing networks of local family resource and support programs has emphasized the growing recognition of this approach. Weissbourd ascribes the emergence of the family support movement to a combination of changing social conditions and the failure of traditional social service systems to address the needs of families. The movement has also influenced other programs to incorporate some of its most important principles. For example, the emphasis in family support programs on community integration has led other program developers to increase their understanding of communities and how they function and interact with programs. Weissbourd predicts that a comprehensive and effective reform of today's social service system will occur with culturally sensitive, family-focused community services. She calls for government at all levels, in partnership with private community organizations, to develop and expand family support programs.

The last two chapters of the section describe psychotherapeutic approaches to individual infants and families. McDonough (Chapter 27) describes interaction guidance, a brief psychotherapy technique that she has developed to reach difficult-to-engage families of high-risk and symptomatic infants. The technique includes reviewing with the parents videotaped interactions with their infant, in order to highlight positive aspects of family interactions. The emphasis is on enhancing family strengths and competence. The therapeutic relationship in interaction guidance is central to assisting parents in enjoying their child and in developing an enhanced understanding of their child's behavior and development. Case examples illustrate the technique.

In Chapter 28, Lieberman and Pawl describe infant–parent psychotherapy, originated by Selma Fraiberg and her colleagues at the University of Michigan in the 1970s. The goal of this approach is to change how parents perceive and respond to their infant, in order to free the infant from the distortions and displaced affects that result from parents' relationship histories and current stresses. By making the infant–parent relationship the focus of treatment, and by emphasizing the power of the baby's presence, this treatment has been central to the emphasis on infant in context within infant mental health. Again, case examples illustrate the approach.

24

A Multidimensional Analysis of Early Childhood Intervention Programs

SAMUEL J. MEISELS
MARGO DICHTELMILLER
FONG-RUEY LIAW

Early intervention with at-risk and disabled infants and toddlers is burgeoning. Inspired by the passage in 1986 of Public Law (P.L.) 99-457, a renewed recognition of the importance of the early years for positive child development has emerged, and a new alliance of parents, professionals, and policy makers has begun to form. Central to these changes are the compelling beliefs that children who begin life at a disadvantage can be helped; that development is malleable; and that society must assist parents of disabled and developmentally vulnerable children in helping these children reach their potential as fully as possible.

These insights are neither radical nor new. Beginning in the 1960s, psychological research began to delineate previously unknown infant capabilities (Shonkoff & Meisels, 1990). This research underscored the importance of early stimulation for cognitive growth and paved the way for the development of intervention programs to ameliorate developmental disabilities during infancy. Hunt (1961) highlighted the importance of the match between a child's experiences and his or her intellectual level. Moreover, Bloom's (1964) research suggested that proportionately more development occurs early in life during periods of rapid growth, popular-

izing the notion of a "critical period" in human development. Skeels's (1966) follow-up of children institutionalized for mental retardation provided a dramatic demonstration of the effect of environmental intervention upon development. These separate lines of research provided convergent support for the idea of improving children's environments as a means to improve their lives.

The social and political climate of the 1960s, including the War on Poverty that gave rise to Head Start, focused on education as a key to enhancing life circumstances (Zigler & Berman, 1983). Many intervention programs for the disabled were modeled after programs for the disadvantaged. Indeed, civil rights that had begun to be protected by federal legislation of the early 1960s were extended to the disabled in the Education for All Handicapped Children Act (P.L. 94-142) and subsequent legislation. Enacted in 1975, P.L. 94-142 established the right to a free and appropriate public education for all handicapped children of school age. In 1986 this law was amended through P.L. 99-457 in order to strengthen incentives to states to educate preschoolers, and to establish a discretionary program for services to infants and toddlers (Meisels, 1989). This confluence of research findings, political attitudes and forces, and legislative activity over the course of the past 30 years has made possible the wide variety of programs for disabled and developmentally vulnerable infants and their families that exist today.

VARIETIES OF INTERVENTION

This chapter concerns itself with early childhood intervention programs—programs that have been created to promote development during the first 3 years of life by modifying a variety of environmental and/or experiential factors in a child and family's life. In the past 20 to 30 years, numerous intervention programs have been developed, and many reports and studies have been published. For example, the Early Intervention Research Institute at Utah State University identified more than 450 diverse studies of intervention programs for children from birth to 5 years of age (Casto & Mastropieri, 1986; Casto & White, 1985). Needless to say, these studies are by no means equivalent in terms of approach, information provided, research designs, or subjects. Indeed, a distinct literature has emerged that is devoted to reanalysis and meta-analysis of subsets of these studies (see, e.g., Bryant & Ramey, 1987; Casto & Mastropieri, 1986; Dunst, 1986; Dunst & Rheingrover, 1981; Farran, 1990; Ottenbacher & Petersen, 1985; Shonkoff & Hauser-Cram, 1987; Simeonsson, 1985; White, Bush, & Casto, 1985). In one way or another, all of these studies are trying to answer the question, "Is early intervention effective?" However, early intervention programs are extremely heterogeneous. Thus, there is no single answer to this question. Rather, the question should be reframed as follows: "Is early intervention for *these* children, in *this* family situation, located in *these* environmental conditions, using *these* program components, effective?" (see Meisels, 1985). In short, early intervention is a multifaceted phenomenon, and studies of its effectiveness should recognize its inherent diversity.

However varied the universe of early intervention is, it has some clear parameters and regularities. Conventional analyses of early intervention programs have been unidimensional, characterizing programs in terms of the site or location of intervention: home-based, center-based, hospital-based, or a combination of sites. Another one-dimensional approach has focused on the client or target of intervention: child, parent, or family. Such approaches are inadequate, in that programs occurring in the same type of location may differ dramatically in their intervention target and/or strategies. For example, a program that provides intervention in the participant's home may emphasize direct teaching of a curriculum to the infant; another home-based program may focus on teaching the curriculum to the parent. Similarly, although some programs focus primarily on the parent or child, many attend to the needs of children and parents jointly.

Because of the inadequacy of the traditional unidimensional approaches, we propose a two-dimensional model to characterize early intervention programs. The two dimensions are (1) the primacy of intervention with the parent (ranging from high to low), and (2) the primacy of intervention with the child (also ranging from high to low). It is our contention that an adequate analysis of intervention programs requires that the relative amount of attention devoted to both parent and child be addressed. This is not to suggest that all intervention designs are jointly focused on parent and child, because an intensity dimension is also involved. In other words, a specific program may be focused intensely on the parent, while devoting only passing interest to intervening directly with the child. Alternatively, a program may target the child, but may virtually ignore the parent.

On the basis of this scheme, four models of intervention can be differentiated: (1) low-intensity, (2) child-focused, (3) parent-focused, and (4) jointly or dually focused. Figure 24.1 depicts this two-dimensional model, with the horizontal axis representing the primacy of intervention with the child and the vertical axis reflecting the primacy of intervention with the parent.

The lower right quadrant of the figure represents programs that emphasize services to the child. Regardless of the site of intervention, the interventionist works directly with the child. In this model, the role of the parents and family is minimized. Traditional intervention programs usually begin with a thorough assessment of the child's current level of functioning, and proceed to a determination of goals on the basis of developmental appropriateness and usefulness of these goals to the child. These goals are then task-analyzed into smaller teaching objectives that guide the interventionist's work with the child. Generally, the child is considered a pas-

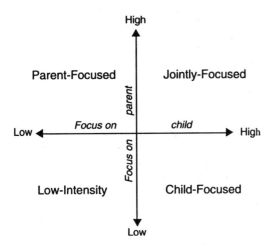

FIGURE 24.1. Two-dimensional model of intervention based on the extent to which the parent and/or the child is the primary focus of the intervention.

sive recipient of instruction, and little prominence is accorded to the child's ability to explore and learn independently. In brief, this model represents programs that directly target the child, with little focus on or contribution from the parent.

The upper left quadrant describes interventions characterized by low child involvement and high parent involvement—the parent-focused models. The target of intervention here is the parent, who is provided with support, information, or training in interactive or teaching techniques. Although the child may be present during intervention activities, the interventionist works directly with the parent. Unlike models that utilize parents solely as teachers, the parent's role exceeds that of a vehicle of instruction or mediator between interventionist and child. Conceptually, the mechanism of change in parent-focused interventions operates in two ways. First, changes in the parent's attitudes and behavior directly affect the child; second, changes in the parent indirectly affect the child through improved parental confidence, decreased stress, or increased social support.

The upper right quadrant of Figure 24.1 represents programs that are jointly focused on children and families. In some respects, these programs combine elements of both the child-focused and the parent-focused models. To the extent that these programs consist of interventions directed at both parents/families and children, through teaching parents to assist their

children and providing direct instruction or enrichment for the children, they are little more than a sum of the other two models. However, in some cases, jointly focused programs go beyond this additive model and transcend the child-focused and parent-focused models. In these jointly focused programs, parents are taught how to read the cues of their children, and to provide intervention for them that is uniquely responsive to their needs. In addition, parents receive support and information that allow them to alter their behavior and perhaps even their style of interaction, in order to further challenge their children to achieve mastery or demonstrate newly acquired abilities. This approach extends the didactic model to one that is comprehensive, systematic, and that focuses on joint participation in intervention activities by children and parents.

The final quadrant in Figure 24.1 is labeled "low-intensity." Low-intensity programs provide either a minimum level of intervention to the parent and/or the child, or require a minimum level of involvement from them. In this model, the chief purposes of intervention programs are to monitor parents/children and to keep track of development. Examples of such programs are found in screening and diagnostic services, and in follow-up programs. The latter are widely utilized with preterm and other children who are biologically at risk. Programs that are strictly diagnostic in purpose are still found in hospital settings and in other service agencies. However, with the provision of increased resources for intervention with very young children, these programs are seen increasingly as only intermediate steps leading to specific intervention programs.

PLAN FOR THIS CHAPTER

The four models presented above form the structure for this chapter. Focusing on two groups of children—preterm infants, and disabled infants and toddlers—we review and discuss intervention programs in terms of these models. Not all intervention studies with preterm and disabled children are covered; before each section, we give the criteria for selecting studies for review. Moreover, this chapter does not primarily constitute a critique of efficacy studies. In a recently published review, Farran (1990) begins by noting,

The last thing the field of early childhood education may need at the moment is another "comprehensive" review of the effects of intervention on children. Surely, among the large number of overviews and meta-analyses, everything that could be said about early intervention has already been said, and firm conclusions are readily obtainable. (p. 501)

Unfortunately, Farran goes on to conclude that this reasonable assumption is unfounded. Her conclusion is that "there are very few studies of intervention efforts with either disabled or disadvantaged children that are scientifically valid enough to summarize" (p. 501).

This stark conclusion does not mean that early intervention efforts are futile—only that many studies of early intervention programs are scientifically wanting. As a result of the inadequacy of the efficacy studies, and the volume of reviews of such studies already published, we do not focus in this chapter specifically on that aspect of intervention. Some of the literature, particularly that dealing with biologically at-risk children, lends itself to a review of studies that have strong research designs. But those programs that have addressed the needs of disabled children are generally not methodologically rigorous. Therefore, while paying close attention to the information that is available concerning the evidence of program effectiveness, we focus primarily on characterizing the actual interventions in use. We begin by discussing interventions with preterm infants, and then we turn to interventions with disabled children.

EARLY INTERVENTION WITH LOW-BIRTHWEIGHT INFANTS

In this section, we review intervention programs that have been implemented for low-birthweight (LBW) infants and/or their parents, based on the two-dimensional matrix proposed above. Our review is restricted to published studies that meet the following four criteria: (1) Subjects were randomly assigned to the intervention or the control group; (2) initial comparability between the intervention and the control children was statistically controlled; (3) the studies were published no earlier than 1980; and (4) substantial deviation from the planned intervention procedures was not reported. Thirteen intervention programs for LBW infants and/or their parents have been identified and are included in this review.

Child-Focused Programs

Neonatal intensive care unit (NICU) stimulation programs that provide appropriate stimulation directly to LBW infants conform to the child-focused model. Traditionally, NICU intervention programs conceptualized LBW infants as sensorily deprived by an understimulating, mechanized NICU environment, and intervention usually involved provision of such extrasensory stimulation as stroking, flexing, rubbing, and handling the infants in order to compensate for the presumed deprivation. However, in the past decade the neonatal intervention paradigm has gradually shifted to view premature infants not as sensorily understimulated or as deficient full-term infants, but as overstimulated and overly stressed by the disruptive effects of the NICU environment and/or by inappropriate caregiving procedures (Als et al., 1986; Meisels, Jones, & Stiefel, 1983). Thus, recent NICU intervention programs are directed at reducing the stress that results from the extensive stimuli of the NICU, regulating infant behaviors, and facilitating social interaction between the infants and their caregivers.

Among the 13 studies of preterm infants selected for review, one provided neonatal intervention directly to the infants in the NICU (Field et al., 1986). Field and her colleagues' (Field et al., 1986; Schanberg & Field, 1987) neonatal sensory stimulation intervention for very-LBW (VLBW) infants (BW < 1500 grams and gestational age [GA] < 36 weeks) consisted of three 15-minute tactile/kinesthetic stimulation episodes per day for 10 days after the infants were admitted to the transitional care nursery. During each stimulation session, the treatment infants (n = 20) received gentle stroking in a prone position and passive movement of the limbs in a supine position by nurses.

Studying the effects of the intervention, Field and her colleagues (Field et al., 1986; Schanberg & Field, 1987) reported that when compared to a group of VLBW control infants (n = 20) at discharge, the intervention infants displayed significantly more weight gain; showed more mature habituation, orientation, motor behavior, and state behavior; spent more time awake and alert; and were discharged 6 days earlier. The positive effects persisted through 12 months, with the intervention infants demonstrating greater weight gain, higher scores on the Mental and Psychomotor scales of the Bayley Scales of Infant Development (Bayley, 1969), fewer neurological "soft signs," and more follow-up clinic attendance. The investigators suggested that the sensory stimulation intervention facilitated the motor activity/alertness of the VLBW infants. The motor activity, then, contributed to weight gain and more organized behavior, which in turn facilitated early parent–infant interactions and contributed to later child development.

Parent-Focused Programs

Parent-focused programs typically recognize the emotional trauma and lack of adequate caretaking experience that often accompany preterm birth, as well as the consequent possibilities of disturbance in the parent–child relationship and delayed child development because of severe biological disadvantage. Thus, in these programs, although the ultimate goal is the amelioration of LBW infants' developmental risk, the primary targets of intervention are the parents.

In the past decade, seven studies and eight programs that meet our criteria concentrated on service delivery to the parents. Four programs focused on increasing social support, decreasing stress, and improving parental confidence and interactive skills (Affleck, Tennen, Rowe, Roscher, & Walker, 1989; Beckwith & Cohen, 1984; Minde, Shosenberg, & Marton, 1982; Rauh, Nurcombe, Ruoff, Jette, & Howell, 1982); three emphasized improving parental caretaking skills and teaching techniques (Barrera, Rosenbaum, & Cunningham's [1986] Developmental Programming intervention; Field, Widmayer, Stringer, & Ignatoff, 1980; Ross, 1984); and one focused on both support and education (Barrera, Rosenbaum, & Cunningham's 1986 Parent–Infant Interaction intervention). We first review the four programs that provided support to parents of LBW infants, and then we discuss the parent training/education programs.

Parent Support Programs

Minde and colleagues (Minde, Shosenberg, & Marton, 1982; Minde, Shosenberg, Thompson, & Marton, 1982) implemented a self-help group intervention to enhance the self-esteem and feelings of autonomy in mothers with VLBW premature infants. During the group meetings, parents shared their feelings about having given birth to premature babies, received information on developmental and medical needs of prema-

ture infants, and later were made familiar with local community resources. By 3 months of age, mothers given this intervention ($n = 28$) visited their infants more frequently in the hospital, and were more responsive to and involved with their infants than were the control mothers ($n = 29$). At 1 year, the intervention mothers also tended to express more realistic perceptions of their infants' development, gave their infants more freedom and independence during play, and vocalized and played more with their infants. Infants of the intervention mothers reciprocated with more social interactions (e.g., sharing of food, playing with and touching their mothers) than did the control infants. Furthermore, intervention mothers reported positive changes in their social and interpersonal relationships and demonstrated autonomy in making decisions.

Beckwith and Cohen (Beckwith, 1988; Beckwith & Cohen, 1980, 1984) investigated the effects of an individualized 13-month home-based, parent-directed intervention for disadvantaged mothers (less than high school education and unskilled or semiskilled occupation; $n = 37$) with premature infants (BW $\leq$ 2000 grams, GA $\leq$ 35 weeks, and in NICU > 3 days). These researchers believed that an emotionally supportive intervenor–parent relationship would enable the disadvantaged mothers to improve their confidence and their interaction patterns, which in turn would facilitate their infants' later cognitive development. No infant curriculum for the children or specific training for the mothers was used.

The effects of the intervention were assessed at 1, 9, 13, and 20 months. The 1- and 9-month assessments showed that the intervention was effective in improving maternal interaction either for those parents who had not received prenatal care or those who had come from more abusive families of origin. At 13 months, the intervention mothers were rated by the home visitors as emotionally more stable and more realistic about their infants' development than the control mothers ($n = 55$), who instead showed more denial and inflexibility in attitudes. No intervention effects were detected on children's mastery motivation, cognitive development, or security of attachment until 20 months, when the intervention children started to outperform the control group on cognitive tasks.

The Vermont Infant Studies Project (Rauh et al., 1982) is a third parent-focused program. This project developed an individualized

Mother–Infant Transaction Project, in which mothers of preterm infants (BW < 2200 grams and GA < 37 weeks) were provided with 11 one-hour sessions of intervention in the hospital and home by a trained pediatric nurse. The intervention sessions emphasized helping mothers to understand their LBW infants' functioning in different domains and to become more sensitive and responsive to their infants' physiological and social cues. The home-based sessions focused on establishing each mother's sensitivity and responsivity in daily caretaking routines, building a repertoire of interactive play experiences with the child, and introducing the mother to the infant's temperamental patterns. The program terminated when the babies were 3 months old.

The investigators followed up their subjects at 6, 12, 24, 36, and 48 months and at 7 years. They reported that at 6 months, mothers given the intervention ($n = 34$) reported significantly higher self-confidence and satisfaction with maternal roles, better child-rearing attitudes, and more positive perceptions of their infants' temperament, when compared with those mothers who did not receive the intervention ($n = 40$) (Nurcombe et al., 1984). No intervention effects were found on cognitive performance (Rauh, Achenbach, Nurcombe, Howell, & Teti, 1988) until the intervention children started to outperform the control group on the McCarthy Scales of Children's Abilities (McCarthy, 1972) at 36 months. At age 4, their cognitive scores were 12.9 points higher than those of the control LBW children, and were equivalent to those of the normal-birthweight children. At age 7, the intervention children's scores were comparable to the normal-birthweight children's on every measure assessed, when the families' socioeconomic status (SES) and maternal education were held constant (Achenbach, Phares, Howell, Rauh, & Nurcombe, 1990).

Affleck et al. (1989) provided an in-home support program for mothers of NICU infants, aiming to aid mothers in making the transition from hospital to home and in coping with a spectrum of potential stresses, as well as to encourage mutually enjoyable mother–infant interactions. The researchers randomly assigned 94 NICU infants (81 were preterm with GA < 36 weeks) to the Transitional Consultation Program intervention ($n = 47$) or to a control group ($n = 47$). The program mothers received transitional consultation from a nurse, beginning a few days before the expected hospital discharge and weekly thereafter for 15 weeks. During each 2-hour home visit, the program consultant encouraged the mothers to choose topics for discussion, and suggested topics only when a mother expressed no specific concerns.

At 6 months, Affleck et al. (1989) reported no main effects of the program, independent of the infants' medical severity or maternal need for support. However, the results indicated that the effects of the program depended primarily on mothers' need for support and, to a lesser extent, the severity of their infants' neonatal medical condition. For mothers needing a high level of support, the program had a positive effect on their responsiveness, perceived personal control, and sense of competence; for mothers with less need of support, the program had a negative effect on these outcomes. In addition, program mothers of infants with a high level of medical severity reported more positive mood; program mothers with healthier infants reported more negative mood. Affleck et al. speculated that program mothers who needed the most support were experiencing greater emotional stress and were using inefficacious coping strategies. They "may have been more receptive to, or made more effective use of, the consultant than did participants who needed little support" (p. 498). In contrast, for mothers who needed little support, the intervention may have disrupted their self-confidence by imparting information to them that they did not seek voluntarily.

Parent Training/Education Programs. This section reviews two programs that trained parents as their child's teacher (Field et al., 1980; Ross, 1984), followed by a description of a pair of programs designed to improve parental interactive and teaching skills (Barrera, Rosenbaum, & Cunningham, 1986).

Field and her colleagues (Field et al., 1980) developed a home-based parent training intervention program specifically for preterm infants (GA < 37 weeks and BW < 2500 grams) of lower-SES, black teenage mothers (age < 19 years). Biweekly half-hour home visits were provided to the mothers after infants' hospital discharge; the visits continued for 8 months. During each home visit the interventionists educated the teenage mothers about developmental milestones and child-rearing practices, taught exercises for stimulating the infants' sensorimotor and cognitive development, and helped facilitate mother–infant communications and interactions.

Field et al. (1980) compared the intervention children ($n = 30$) to the control LBW children ($n = 30$) at 4, 8, and 12 months. They reported that by 4 months of age, the intervention infants had gained more in weight and length measures, and had higher scores on a screening test. The intervention mothers displayed more realistic developmental expectations of and better face-to-face interactions with their infants, more desirable child-rearing attitudes, and more positive ratings of their infants' temperament. These positive effects persisted until the infants were 8 months old. At 12 months, the cognitive gains of the intervention children persisted, but their superiority in motoric development diminished.

Ross (1984) devised a 1-year home-based, mother-focused intervention for 40 low-income families with premature infants (BW < 2200 grams and GA < 36 weeks) in New York. Home visits were provided following discharge from the NICU and continued until 12 months corrected age. During each 45-minute home visit, the parent learned about care and development of premature infants, and was instructed to practice a curriculum of games and exercises with the child for 5 to 10 minutes daily.

Ross reported that at the end of the intervention (i.e., 12 months), the intervention children had significantly higher scores than the control children on the Bayley Mental scale, but not on the Psychomotor scale or on a measure of neurological development. They were also rated by their mothers as more approachable, adaptable, and positive. Although intervention mothers were rated higher on the Home Observation for Measurement of the Environment (HOME) scale (Caldwell & Bradley, 1970) than the control mothers, the intervention mothers did not demonstrate better child-rearing attitudes or knowledge.

Barrera, Rosenbaum, and Cunningham (1986) compared two intervention programs for LBW infants (BW < 2000 grams and GA < 37 weeks) —a Parent–Infant Interaction intervention and a Developmental Programming intervention, each lasting for 1 year. The Developmental Programming intervention focused on instructing parents ($n = 16$) to assess their infants' functioning level and to design and implement an individualized plan of curriculum activities for their children. The Parent–Infant Interaction intervention helped parents ($n = 22$) enhance their observational skills, recognize and respond effectively to their infants' subtle behavioral cues, adjust their own behavior, and improve parent–child responsivity and interactions.

In studying the effects of these two programs, Barrera, Rosenbaum, and Cunningham (1986) reported few intervention effects on the Bayley Mental and Psychomotor scores at 4 and 8 months, when each group of intervention children was compared with 21 LBW children who had received no treatment and 24 full-term children. Yet both Parent–Infant Interaction and Developmental Programming children showed a significant increment in cognitive development from 4 to 16 months. By 16 months, children from both programs demonstrated comparable development to those of full-term controls, had more optimal mental and motoric development, and were engaged in more verbal independent play than their preterm controls. On the HOME scale, intervention mothers from both programs were comparable to the full-term control mothers, and had significantly higher scores than the control preterm mothers when the children were 16 months and 5 years of age (Barrera, Rosenbaum, & Cunningham, 1986; Barrera, Kitching, Cunningham, Doucet, & Rosenbaum, 1990)—findings indicating that the intervention mothers provided a more responsive home environment than the control preterm mothers.

In another study comparing program effects for VLBW children versus relatively heavy LBW children (BW ≥ 1500 grams), Barrera and her colleagues (Barrera, Cunningham, & Rosenbaum, 1986; Barrera et al., 1990) showed that both intervention programs had greater effect for VLBW children and their mothers than for their heavier counterparts on children's Bayley Mental scores and mothers' responsivity at 16 months, as well as on children's visual–motor and social skills, and parent-reported language skills at 5 years.

In summary, the results of the seven parent-focused studies reviewed suggest that this type of intervention is associated with positive parental attitude and perceptions toward the child and toward caretaking, more optimal parent–child interactions, and improved intellectual development in children. In addition, two of the six studies that investigated the home environment (Barrera, Rosenbaum, & Cunningham, 1986; Ross, 1984) reported that the parents given parent-focused intervention provided more stimulating and responsive environments.

Jointly Focused Programs

In this section, three intervention programs for LBW infants and their parents that utilized the jointly focused approach to intervention are reviewed (Als et al., 1986; Infant Health and

Development Program [IHDP], 1990; Resnick, Armstrong, & Carter, 1988). Als et al. (1986) provided individualized and systematic care for VLBW infants (BW < 1250 grams) in the NICU to reduce environmental stress/noise, increase infants' self-regulatory behavior, organize infants' sleep–wake cycle, and facilitate infants' social interactions with their environment. Intervention involved rocking each infant in a hammock, providing specialized positioning, and involving parents in the baby's care. All extraneous stimulations, such as stroking, talking, and frequent position shifts, were removed to avoid overstimulation.

Their sample included 16 VLBW infants born at high risk for the development of bronchopulmonary dysplasia, with the control group ($n = 8$) recruited a year earlier than the experimental group ($n = 8$). The two groups were similar in severity of illness and demographic backgrounds. Compared with the control infants, the intervention infants spent 25 days less on the respirator, 33 days less on oxygen, and 29 days less on tube feeding prior to discharge, and were better modulated and better organized in motor system and self-regulation ability at 1 through 9 months. Intervention infants also had significantly higher Bayley Mental and Psychomotor scores at 3, 6, and 9 months. However, no differences were apparent in weight gain, days in the hospital, or incidence of chronic illness at discharge or in growth measures by 9 months. The assessments of parent–child interactions in a free-play period at 9 months showed that although both intervention and control mothers were invested in making the play successful and enjoyable to the infants, the intervention infants were better organized and more able to understand and accomplish tasks than the control children. The intervention parent–child pairs also demonstrated more turn taking and positive interactions than the control pairs.

Resnick et al. (1988) developed a 1-year intervention program for premature (BW < 1800 grams) infants and their parents in the NICU and at home ($n = 21$). The intervention contained a neonatal infant development program with support for parent–infant interactions and instructions for developmental activities to the parent, and an early childhood education program initiated after infants' discharge from the hospital, consisting of home visits by a pediatric nurse practitioner. During each visit, the home visitor evaluated the child's development, interacted with the child, modeled developmentally appropriate interaction activities, and taught

the parent exercises and activities to use with the infant. Support and counseling were also provided to family members. The control group ($n = 20$) received traditional pediatric care and social services.

Intervention effects were assessed at 6 and 12 months corrected age. Resnick et al. (1988) reported that a significant difference on the Bayley Mental scores emerged at 12 months because of a 14-point drop in the control group's scores. Significant intervention effects were also found in parent–child interactions during a free-play period. On average, intervention dyads engaged in significantly more positive verbal interactions and fewer negative nonverbal interactions than the control dyads. No significant group differences were observed on the children's motoric performance (as assessed via the Bayley Psychomotor scale) at either 6 or 12 months of age.

The IHDP is the most recent and by far the largest intervention study of LBW infants ($n = 985$). The intervention program began when an infant was discharged from the hospital and continued until 36 months corrected age (IHDP, 1990). The intervention included three components: (1) home visits, weekly for the first year and twice monthly for the second and third years; (2) full-time daily child care at a child development center (CDC) in the second and third years of the program; and (3) bimonthly parent support group meetings in the second and third years. During home visits, parents received information on child health and development and learned to use age-appropriate games and activities to enhance development and interaction. At the CDC, the intervention children engaged in the same educational activities as those used at home during home visits. During the support group meetings, parents shared their feelings and obtained support from other parents and from the intervention staff. Infants in both intervention and control groups received high-quality pediatric care service from birth until their third birthday.

Results of the overall effects of the IHDP indicated that the intervention children ($n = 377$) at 36 months corrected age showed significantly more optimal cognitive development as measured by the Stanford–Binet Intelligence Scale (Terman & Merrill, 1972) than the control children ($n = 608$), with heavier treatment infants scoring 13.2 points higher and the lighter treatment infants scoring 6.6 points higher. Significant effects were also found for behavioral competence as assessed via the Child Behavior

Checklist for Ages 2–3 (Achenbach, Edelbrock, & Howell, 1987) and for maternal reported morbidity, with the treatment infants having fewer reported behavioral problems and mothers of treatment infants reporting a higher incidence of minor illnesses. Furthermore, the IHDP intervention had greater effects on the intellectual development of infants of higher birthweight (BW > 2000 grams) and on the behavioral competence of infants of less educated mothers (education ≤ high school).

A series of studies was designed to investigate the association between children's cognitive functioning and behavioral problems at 36 months corrected age and IHDP participation (represented by the sum of the numbers of home visits, parent group meetings attended, and days attended at the CDC). Ramey et al. (1992) reported that children from families that participated more scored significantly higher on the Stanford–Binet IQ test than did children from families that participated less. However, no relationship was found between degree of program participation and children's behavioral competence. Sparling et al. (1991) continued Ramey et al.'s (1992) investigation, but focused on the effect of curriculum implementation, as reflected by two quantity variables: activity episodes per CDC day, and activities per home visit. They found that the CDC activity variable accounted for only 2% of the variance in children's IQ scores at age 3, above and beyond initial status and general participation variables; the home visit activity variable accounted for an additional 6% of the variance. The authors reasoned that the effects of the CDC variables might have been masked by the more powerful and general degree-of-participation variable, which was composed of total numbers of CDC days, home visits, and parent meetings.

Taken together, the results of the three jointly focused studies reviewed are promising. They suggest that this type of intervention is effective in promoting LBW children's cognitive development and social behavior, and in improving parent–child interactions.

Low-Intensity Programs

For LBW infants, the low-intensity model usually takes the form of infant monitoring, follow-up, or observation of the administration/demonstration of appropriate interactive or teaching skills. Two studies included in this review conform to this model (Pfander & Bradley-Johnson, 1990; Widmayer & Field, 1981).

Widmayer and Field (1981) devised a minimal intervention program with black, low-income, teenage mothers of preterm infants. They hoped that if the infants' skills were demonstrated to the mothers, early interactions between mothers and their infants might be more positive, and might ultimately facilitate cognitive development. The infants were randomly assigned to one of three groups: the Neonatal Behavioral Assessment Scale (NBAS)/Mother's Assessment of the Behavior of Her Infant (MABI) group, the MABI group, and the control group. For the NBAS/MABI group, infants were administered the NBAS (Brazelton, 1973) in the presence of their mothers, and their mothers then completed the MABI (Field, Dempsey, Hallock, & Shuman, 1978), an adaptation of the NBAS, at birth and weekly during the first month. The MABI group mothers only completed the MABI at birth and during the first 4 weeks. The control group mothers did not observe the NBAS or complete the MABI.

Widmayer and Field (1981) reported that both the NBAS/MABI and the MABI interventions had significant effects on infant–mother interactions by 4 months, when both groups of mothers and infants displayed better face-to-face interaction than the control group, and had significantly higher scores on the Denver Developmental Screening Test (DDST) adaptability items. At 12 months, only the NBAS/MABI group infants displayed significantly higher scores on the Bayley Mental Development Index (MDI) than the control infants.

Pfander and Bradley-Johnson (1990) investigated the effects of a single parent education class and a follow-up assessment. Thirty-five NICU infants and their parents were randomly assigned to one of three treatment conditions: (1) a parent education class and infant assessment session ($n = 11$); (2) parent education class only ($n = 13$); and (3) infant assessment only ($n = 11$). A control group ($n = 13$) was randomly selected from hospital records of an earlier 6-month period. The parent education class was conducted in the NICU when the infants were between 2 and 6 weeks of age, and addressed infant health and safety, intervention techniques, behavior and emotions, and differences between preterm and full-term infants. The infant assessment session was conducted when each infant was 3 months old, with the parent actively involved in the assessment.

The 6-month cognitive assessments indicated

that infants in both the parent education/assessment and the parent-education-only groups showed significantly higher Bayley MDI scores than the control infants and the assessment-only group. The assessment-only group infants did not differ from the control infants. In addition, infants in all three treatment groups were perceived by the physicians as having been provided with better nutritional care than control group infants. The authors concluded that increasing parental knowledge through a brief form of intervention—a 90-minute parent education class—can be an effective way of enhancing cognitive development for NICU infants.

In summary, the two low-intensity studies reviewed indicate that although intervention was minimal, it was associated with improved parent–child interactions and more optimal child development. However, it is impossible to conclude whether this type of minimal intervention has lasting effects.

EARLY INTERVENTION WITH DISABLED INFANTS

In this section, we review intervention programs for disabled infants that (1) were published no earlier than 1980 and were thoroughly described in the literature; (2) involved at least 12 infants from birth to 3 years of age; and (3) were comprehensive, addressing the children's overall development rather than a limited aspect of development. Intervention programs conducted in institutions, hospitals, and residential treatment programs have been excluded. We have not excluded studies on the basis of methodological considerations, although efficacy research with handicapped infants has been hindered by a paucity of measures standardized on disabled populations, by extremely heterogeneous samples, and by ethical difficulties that preclude random assignment to a no-treatment condition (Greenberg, Calderon, & Kusche, 1984; Guralnick, 1989; Meisels, 1985; Shonkoff, Hauser-Cram, Krauss, & Upshur, 1988; White & Mott, 1987).

Child-Focused Programs

Three programs concentrated principally on service delivery to the child (Bricker, Bruder, & Bailey, 1982; LeLaurin, 1985; Rosen-Morris &

Sitkei, 1981), with the goal of improving cognition, communication, psychomotor development, self-help, and social skills. Although all three programs were primarily center-based, Bricker et al. (1982) provided a home-based component in which the parent adopted the teacher's role as the primary interventionist. The Bricker et al. (1982) and LeLaurin (1985) programs included non-handicapped peers with children whose varied handicaps ranged from mild to severe. Since the Bricker et al. study was designed primarily to study the effects of integrated programming, it is not reviewed here in detail.

The Infant and Toddler Learning Program (LeLaurin, 1985) was designed to ameliorate developmental disabilities by providing child care in a developmentally appropriate learning environment. Although communication with parents occurred regularly, this program was not designed to enhance parents' interactive or teaching style or to modify the home environment. Pre- and posttesting showed significant progress for all handicapped children, with many of the children moving from one diagnostic category to another (e.g., from trainable to educable).

Another less intensive child-focused program for severely/profoundly impaired infants and toddlers (Rosen-Morris & Sitkei, 1981) utilized a specialized curriculum to teach children how to interact with objects. This approach, based on observations of normally developing infants, involved shaping or manual guidance of a child's hands through fine motor activity sequences. Children demonstrated significant progress on both standardized and criterion-referenced assessment instruments from pre- to posttest.

Parent-Focused Programs

At the opposite corner of Figure 24.1 from the child-focused model lie intervention programs that focus attention primarily on the parent. The three programs representing this model (Mahoney & Powell, 1988; Moxley-Haegert & Serbin, 1983; Rosenberg & Robinson, 1985) reflect an ecological approach to child development (Bronfenbrenner, 1975) and demonstrate awareness of the crucial role the family plays in the child's development. These programs acknowledge the importance of the child's primary attachment relationship and build upon it, striving to increase parents' understanding of the relationship between their behavior and their child's behavior. For an infant with chronic medical problems, the parent-focused approach offers the added benefit of fewer adults interacting with a medically vulnerable child.

Rosenberg and Robinson (1985) developed the Teaching Skills Inventory, an instrument designed to assess parental interactive skills and to guide intervention with parents. The optimal ratings on this instrument describe a parent who provides activities matched to the child's interests, level of development, and receptive language skills; requires active responses from the child; and provides positive, enriching, and corrective feedback. The inventory includes items assessing responsivity, verbal clarity, appropriateness of feedback, modification of the task, and effectiveness of guidance and prompts. Using a parent's initial ratings on the inventory as a basis for instruction, a teacher verbally describes and demonstrates interactive techniques, emphasizing the parent's behavior rather than the content of the child's activity. Rosenberg and Robinson found that interactive training based on inventory ratings produced changes in parents' teaching behaviors and in children's interest levels.

The Transactional Intervention Program (Mahoney & Powell, 1988) similarly focused on the parent's interactive style, but advocated a more nondirective maternal style. The children involved functioned in the moderate to severe range of mental impairment; some had additional physical and sensory disabilities. The program was designed to decrease parental directiveness and control and to promote a responsive, child-oriented style of interaction. In particular, trainers focused on two strategies, turn taking and interactive match, in order to modify the parents' overall behavioral style during play, teaching, and caretaking activities with their moderately or severely impaired children. Like Rosenberg and Robinson (1985), Mahoney and Powell found that interactive training modified parents' behavioral style in the expected direction, and that it influenced the children's rate of development.

These two parent-focused interactive studies demonstrated that parents can be taught to change their parenting style in a particular direction, and showed that targeting parental style does result in changes in children's interest level and cognitive status.

Another program provided information to parents rather than specific interactive training. Moxley-Haegert and Serbin's (1983) study compared the effect of three different educational conditions on caregiver implementation of home treatment programs for moderately and severely impaired infants. The experimental group participated in an educational program of assigned readings designed to help parents observe, recognize, and predict developmental progress in their children. Three home visits provided parents with an opportunity to discuss the readings, ask questions about the home treatment program, and receive reinforcement for program activities. The second condition, designed to control the effects of attention, materials, and reinforcement, provided the same methods, readings, and home visits; however, the content emphasized behavior management, rather than the sequence of developmental progress. In the third condition, a no-education control group, participants received three phone calls to encourage their implementation of the home program.

At the termination of the month of intervention, the children in the developmental education group accomplished more objectives of their home treatment program and made greater progress on the Psychomotor scale of the Bayley Scales of Infant Development than the infants in the other two conditions. Similarly, the caregivers in the developmental education condition had higher levels of participation in the assigned home treatment activities than caregivers in the other two conditions. The parents' higher level of implementation in the home treatment programs and the children's progress on the Psychomotor scale were maintained 1 year later.

The three parent-focused programs shared the goal of enriching the infant's environment through direct intervention with the parents. However, they differed in scope, duration, and content. At this point, data are insufficient to permit us to decide whether changing a parent's interactive behavior, increasing parental acceptance of the handicapped child, or providing information about the child's handicap and development will have the most beneficial effects on the child's developmental course.

Jointly Focused Programs

The largest category of programs, located in the upper right quadrant of Figure 24.1, reflects a joint focus on the parent and child. Sixteen programs focused on both parent and child, with the majority utilizing a didactic role for the parent. A smaller number of programs viewed the parent in a broader perspective, and prescribed both teaching and nonteaching roles for the parent.

Didactic Programs

Ten jointly focused programs promulgated a teaching role for the parent that emphasized stimulating and instructing the child (Barna, Bidder, Gray, Clements, & Gardner, 1980; Fitzgerald et al., 1980; Folio & Richey, 1990; Macy, Solomon, Schoen, & Galey, 1983; Oelwein, Fewell, & Pruess, 1985; Piper & Pless, 1980; Rynders & Horrobin, 1980; Sandow, Clarke, Cox, & Stewart, 1981; Turner & Rogers, 1981; Wolery & Dyk, 1985). The major goal of these programs was to increase children's rates of development in cognitive, communication, motor, self-help, and social skills by focusing on both the parents and the children. This group of programs can be subdivided further into two types, home-based and center-based. In the home-based programs, a parent provided direct service to a child at home, even if the parent and child received instruction regarding curriculum activities at a center. In the center-based programs, a child entered a group setting by about 18 months of age, and a parent transferred his or her teaching skills from one-to-one tutoring at home to functioning as a teacher's assistant in a center-based program. Regardless of the site of intervention, the parent's major role was viewed as instructional.

In the home-based didactic model (Barna et al., 1980; Fitzgerald et al., 1980; Folio & Richey, 1990; Piper & Pless, 1980; Rynders & Horrobin, 1980; Sandow et al., 1981), the interventionist's role is to instruct the parent in the best ways to stimulate and teach the child. The parent is mainly a vehicle of instruction or a mediator between the interventionist and the child. Barna et al. (1980), utilizing the Portage Project model (Shearer & Shearer, 1976), provided a clear example of this approach. One of the earliest home-based, parent-mediated approaches, the Portage Project's home teachers visited each family weekly. After an in-depth assessment, the teacher and parent targeted several behavioral objectives. During the visit, the teacher recorded baseline data on the new objectives. It was the teacher's responsibility to task-analyze each objective and only to prescribe goals that could be met within 1 week. The parent then used behavioral methodology to teach

the new behaviors, referring to the home activity chart that had been left by the interventionist as needed, and recording data regarding the child's progress. When the teacher returned, postbaseline data were recorded to document accomplishment of the objectives.

Project EDGE (Expanding Developmental Growth through Education; Rynders & Horrobin, 1980) was an educational program for infants with Down syndrome, based on research in language and conceptual development. The intent of the program was to promote each child's communicative skills through positive interaction with the mother. Project EDGE also acknowledged the mother's unique style of mothering, and avoided dictating narrowly prescribed maternal behaviors. The program provided simple materials; a lesson sheet with descriptions of several short activities; and a list of words, phrases, and sentences designed to develop concepts. Mothers were advised to talk about the materials, but to avoid verbal bombardment or focusing too greatly on labeling. If a child was unable to complete a task, the mother increased her assistance gradually and sequentially, beginning with offering verbal directions and ending with providing gentle manual assistance. To decrease the time burden on the mother, other family members could take over half of the daily hour-long lesson. No significant effects on language abilities were demonstrated at 24 and 60 months; however, significant differences between the intervention and control children were demonstrated on cognitive and motor tests at 60 months.

These two examples contained many essential elements of the jointly focused didactic model, in which the primary goal is the acceleration of the child's development through activities with both child and parent. In these programs, the parent's instructional activities provided the mechanism of change for the child. Instructional methods from the traditional child-focused approach were transferred to parents; however, in contrast to the parent-focused programs, children also participated in other intervention activities.

The center-based didactic intervention programs are best illustrated by the 11 outreach sites of the Model Preschool Program for Children with Down Syndrome and Other Developmental Delays (Oelwein et al., 1985). These sites replicated the program developed by Hayden and her colleagues at the University of Washington (Hayden & Dmitriev, 1975; Hayden &

Haring, 1976, 1977). In this center-based model, parent–infant dyads visited the center once per week; the toddlers' classroom session met for 2 hours, 4 days a week. To insure that the educational program was continued at home, each parent was expected to attend one weekly session with the child. In addition, the educational staff taught the parent to supervise play activities, make materials, and observe and record the child's behaviors. Many conferences and group parent meetings occurred to provide information to the parents, and to foster community involvement and advocacy roles for parents.

The other didactic programs were basically variants of the two basic types, home-based and center-based. Instruction to the parent sometimes occurred in a center, with the expectation that the parent would administer the therapeutic activities daily in the home (Fitzgerald et al., 1980; Oelwein et al., 1985; Piper & Pless, 1980; Wolery & Dyk, 1985). Some programs provided the parents with written plans to take home (Barna et al., 1980; Piper & Pless, 1980); another used televised videotapes accompanied by illustrated activity guides to help parents teach their children (Folio & Richey, 1990). Most frequently, infants were visited at home once (Macy et al., 1983) or twice (Turner & Rogers, 1981) weekly until approximately 18 months of age, when they attended a center program from 1 to 4 days per week (Turner & Rogers, 1981). The parent-as-teacher programs most often employed behavioral instructional methods, with parents keeping records of the children's performance or progress (Fitzgerald et al., 1980; Macy et al., 1983; Oelwein et al., 1985).

In general, didactic programs have found moderate but statistically significant child progress as a result of intervention, with the exception of Piper and Pless's (1980) experiment. The limited intensity and duration of this program resulted in a total of 12 hours of intervention spread over 6 months, and this factor may have been responsible for the lack of significant findings. Whether primarily home- or center-based, the didactic programs consisted of two essential components: direct services to the child (provided in a center or by the parent), and a primary teaching role for the parent.

Comprehensive Programs

Six programs (Bricker & Sheehan, 1981; Connolly, Morgan, & Russell, 1984; Connolly, Morgan, Russell, & Richardson, 1980; Greenberg et al., 1984; Hanson, 1981, 1985; Rose & Calhoun, 1990; Warren, Alpert, & Kaiser, 1986) focused equally on the parent and child, but did not emphasize the parent's didactic role. Although these programs might contain a parent-as-teacher component, they also viewed the parent's role more comprehensively. Four (Bricker & Sheehan, 1981; Connolly et al., 1984; Hanson, 1981, 1985; Warren et al., 1986) used the didactic model with the addition of a formal parent support component. The support groups were conducted most often by social workers and addressed topics determined by the parents. These programs served moderately to severely handicapped infants and used a combination home- and center-based service delivery. Two of these jointly focused programs (Bricker & Sheehan, 1981; Hanson, 1981, 1985) utilized a transdisciplinary approach to service delivery, in which information from the various disciplines was funneled through one person who actually delivered the services. Since the parent-as-teacher model has been described already, only one program (Warren et al., 1986) is reviewed here in detail.

The Optimal Learning Environment program (Warren et al., 1986) exemplifies the didactic model plus formal support. It was designed to maximize the duration of child engagement with people and materials by arranging the environment, schedule, and personnel assignments to minimize management and custodial tasks, and to increase child interest and engagement. After a thorough assessment, each child's individualized functional skills were matched to different activities during the day, so that practice would occur in a logical progression. A well-developed family component, based upon frequent reassessments of needs, included training in instructional techniques and management skills; home visits to help the parent apply newly learned techniques and modify the home environment; and parent support meetings. Unfortunately, no data regarding child cognitive growth or parental effectiveness are available, although a comparison of children's engagement, teacher behavior, and delivery of treatment across time and activities in the model classroom and two other classrooms showed that the program resulted in more actual teaching time and higher levels of child engagement.

Of the other two comprehensive jointly focused programs (Greenberg et al., 1984; Rose & Calhoun, 1990), one addressed the needs of hearing-impaired infants, and the other focused on severely and profoundly mentally impaired infants. The Counseling and Home Training Program for Deaf Children (Greenberg et al., 1984) was designed to facilitate the development of rich, natural communication between deaf children and their families; to support the adaptation of families to the handicap; and to foster the deaf children's sense of competence and self-esteem by facilitating the development of an understanding and secure family environment. To this end, program components included initial counseling and guidance by the program director and optional consultation with a psychiatrist; weekly educational home visits by a teacher of the deaf; group sign language sessions at the center; weekly home visits by a deaf adult for further sign language instruction; and a variety of other parent and family social activities. Both the parents' emotional needs and informational needs were addressed. This program mobilized families to deal with their own reactions to the handicap so that the children's learning would be supported, while also directly addressing the children's communicative needs via a "total communication" approach. Although Greenberg and his colleagues did not find significant child IQ changes as a result of intervention, the experimental children demonstrated more advanced communication skills than the comparison children, and their mothers were less controlling, more reinforcing, and more frequently used sign language during interaction with their children than the comparison mothers. During free play, the intervention dyads interacted for longer periods of time, communicated on a single topic for a longer time, and enjoyed more fantasy play than the comparison dyads.

The Charlotte Circle Project (Calhoun & Rose, 1988; Rose & Calhoun, 1990), utilizing mother–infant interaction research as a foundation, designed a developmental program that concentrated on helping handicapped infants develop a satisfying relationship with their caregivers. The program targeted social reciprocity skills. Unlike interactive programs that focus on the caregivers, the Charlotte Circle Project worked directly with both parents and children to promote improved quality, increased frequency, and longer duration of interactive experiences. Project goals for the children included increasing social responsiveness to primary caregivers and reducing behaviors considered aversive by the parents. Parental goals included participating in mutually satisfying social interactions, increasing responsiveness to their children, increasing competence in caring for their children, and normalizing family life. The project was based on the premise that improved interactive skills would lead to increased stimulation, attention, and support for the children's learning. It resulted in increased cognitive functioning for the children and in improved parental attitudes.

Low-Intensity Programs

The fourth quadrant of Figure 24.1, the low-intensity model of intervention for the child and parent, does not have great relevance for disabled infants and toddlers. An infant with a significant developmental delay or diagnosed disorder who meets special education eligibility criteria usually requires a relatively intense program, rather than participation in a follow-up or monitoring program. Furthermore, because Part H of P.L. 99-457 acknowledges the importance of infant intervention, its passage has accelerated the development of intervention programs for handicapped infants and toddlers. Although intervention programs vary in intensity, low-intensity programs do not exist for this population.

SUMMARY AND DISCUSSION

Many issues are common to intervention programs for premature and disabled infants. To explore these commonalities, we first discuss methodological issues, focusing on research design and measurement difficulties. Then we summarize the outcomes of intervention programs with LBW and disabled infants, followed by a discussion of unanswered research questions. Finally, conceptual issues related to theoretical and programmatic aspects of intervention programs are explored.

Methodological Issues

Methodological adequacy varies greatly among studies of preterm and disabled infants. In general, the quality of research design for the preterm studies is high. For example, random assignment to treatment and control groups was used in all of the preterm intervention studies reviewed in this chapter. In contrast, the feasibility of employing random assignment is a hotly debated issue for intervention studies with handicapped children. Some researchers (Bricker & Sheehan, 1981; Greenberg et al., 1984) state unequivocally that ethical considerations prevent formation of control groups, although others believe that withholding a treatment whose efficacy is unclear does not present insurmountable ethical problems (White & Pezzino, 1986). Of the 22 studies of intervention for handicapped infants reviewed in this chapter, 15 employed single-group pretest–posttest designs; only two used an experimental design (Moxley-Haegert & Serbin, 1983; Piper & Pless, 1980). The one-group pretest–posttest design does not allow for rejection of rival explanations of significant outcomes, and therefore is fundamentally flawed (Dunst & Rheingrover, 1981). Moreover, because the type of design may be significantly associated with the study's results, so that better-designed studies show smaller effects, the significance of positive results reported for interventions with handicapped infants may be artificially inflated.

Measurement considerations add to the difficulty of understanding the effects of infant intervention for both populations. A frequent criticism of intervention research is its over-reliance on IQ scores as the outcome measure of choice (Casto & Mastropieri, 1986; Shonkoff et al., 1988; Zigler & Balla, 1982). Using IQ scores to determine the effects of a program is particularly difficult when the program participants are at-risk or disabled infants. Measuring infant intelligence is complicated by two issues. First, infant test scores do not correlate highly with later childhood test scores (Kopp & McCall, 1982; Lewis, Jaskir, & Enright, 1986). Whether this lack of correlation is related to a change in the nature of intelligence during the early years (from a sensorimotor basis to a more verbal and abstract basis), or whether we have not yet devised instruments sophisticated enough to measure infant intelligence accurately, is unclear. In addition, infants are very difficult subjects to test, since their performance is influenced highly by their affective state and motivational level (Hrncir, Speller, & West, 1985; Meisels, in press; Yarrow & Pederson, 1976). The issue of the usefulness of norm-referenced measurement instruments centers on whether instruments standardized on a normal full-term population provide meaningful information about disabled or premature children (Keogh & Sheehan, 1981). Moreover, because of the irregular and slow growth patterns seen in both LBW and disabled populations, their progress may be obscured by standardized tests that are designed to provide a global summary of performance. The problems inherent in testing these infants make interpreting intervention efficacy data very difficult.

Criterion-referenced instruments, most frequently used in educational programs for handicapped infants, offset some of the problems associated with standardized instruments; however, they do not constitute a solution, since their psychometric properties and content are usually unknown and they do not provide comparability across studies. In addition, gain scores, items passed, and the many change indices and scaling systems (Bagnato & Neisworth, 1980; Meisels, 1987; Simeonsson, Huntington, & Short, 1982; Wolery, 1983) frequently used with criterion-referenced assessment may not reflect progress accurately (Dunst, 1986).

A consensus exists regarding the need for broader-based assessment approaches that include more measures of the child and greater sensitivity to family outcomes (Casto & Mastropieri, 1986; Shonkoff et al., 1988; Zigler & Balla, 1982). In addition, as family-oriented intervention and social systems approaches to intervention become more common, measures of the family's stress, social support, and functioning; parent–child interaction; and parental self-concept should be included in assessment protocols.

Outcomes

Two trends emerge from the studies reviewed in this chapter. One trend pertains to the overall effects of intervention. Tables 24.1 and 24.2 summarize the results of the studies reviewed at the final assessments of their subjects. As might be expected, the child-focused programs measured child development or skill attainment, and the parent-focused programs measured such parental domains as knowledge, attitudes, and interactive style; some programs measured child development or child interest outcomes in addition to parental measures. The jointly focused models were more likely to report measures of both child progress and parental change.

Overall, every program reported positive effects of some type. With the premature populations, the child-focused neonatal programs appeared to produce more optimal growth and

TABLE 24.1 Summary of Results of Interventions for LBW Infants at the Final Assessment

Study	Duration[a]	Age[b]	Outcome measures[c]			
			Child cognitive	Child motor	Parental attitude	Parent–Child interaction
Child-focused model						
Field et al. (1986)	10 days	12 months	+[d]	+	n.a.[e]	n.a.
Parent-focused model						
Affleck et al. (1989)	15 weeks	6 months	n.a.	n.a.	Varied	n.a.
Barrera et al. (1990)	12 months	5 years	−[f]	n.a.	+(VLBW)	+
Beckwith (1988)	13 months	20 months	+	n.a.	−	n.a.
Field et al. (1980)	8 months	12 months	+	−	n.a.	+
Minde, Shosenberg, & Martin (1982)	3 months	12 months	n.a.	n.a.	+	+
Achenbach et al. (1990)	3 months	7 years	+	n.a.	n.a.	n.a.
Ross (1984)	12 months	12 months	+	−	−	+
Jointly focused model						
Als et al. (1986)	Predischarge	9 months	+	+	n.a.	+
Resnick et al. (1988)	12 months	12 months	+	−	n.a.	+
IHDP (1990)	36 months	36 months	+	n.a.	n.a.	n.a.
Low-intensity model						
Widmayer & Field (1981)	1 month	12 months	+	−	n.a.	−
Pfander & Bradley-Johnson (1990)	1 day	6 months	+	n.a.	n.a.	n.a.

[a]"Duration" indicates the length of the intervention.
[b]"Age" indicates the age of the child at the time of the last assessment.
[c]Outcome measures: "Child cognitive" represents the child's performance on cognitive assessments; "Child motor" represents the child's performance on motoric assessments; "Parental attitude" represents the parent's child-rearing attitudes and perceptions of the child; "Parent–child interaction" represents parent–child interactions as measured by HOME scale, interactive style during feeding or free play, the parent's or the child's responsiveness to each other, etc.
[d]A "+" sign indicates significant group differences on the outcome, favoring treatment group.
[e]"n.a." (not applicable) means the study did not include the measure in its final assessments.
[f]"−" indicates no significant group difference between the treatment and the control groups.

sensorimotor scores for the intervention infants by 1 year of age. However, the long-term effects of this type of intervention with LBW infants are unknown, since these studies did not follow their infants at later ages. For the rest of the studies, the majority reported positive effects on children's cognitive development and less consistent effects on children's motoric development. Seven studies assessed effects of the program on parent–child interactions. Among them, four parent-focused programs and two jointly focused programs reported more optimal parent–child interactions and more responsive and stimulating home environments in intervention families, whereas the low-intensity programs reported no intervention effects on this measure. It is important to note that although none of the child-focused or the low-intensity programs reported positive treatment effects on both child outcomes and parent–child interactions, almost one-third (two of seven) of the parent-focused programs and two-thirds (two of three) of the jointly focused programs did.

The interventions for disabled children also showed some positive results in the areas measured for all of the models that were represented. However, many more positive effects were present in the jointly focused didactic programs. Here, with the exception of one highly restricted and time-limited project (Piper & Pless, 1980), all of the programs that provided data reported positive effects for child cognitive and motor development. Surprisingly, very few of the studies in any of the models claimed positive changes in parental attitude or parent–child interaction. However, three of the jointly focused comprehensive programs did indicate positive gains in these areas.

The second trend concerns the long-term effects of intervention. With the exception of the Vermont Infant Studies Project's follow-up to age 7 (Achenbach et al., 1990) and Barrera et al.'s (1990) follow-up to age 5, no studies with LBW children followed their subjects for longer than 3 years. The findings from these two studies suggest that intervention targeting the parent may produce beneficial long-term cognitive and perceptual–motor outcomes. However, the small samples in both studies at the follow-up limit the generalizability of these results, despite their significant findings. Similarly, with studies of handicapped children, very little evidence of long-term effects of intervention exists. Only four studies reported follow-up data after intervention ended.

It can be debated whether evidence of long-term effects is necessary to demonstrate a program's value. Many question whether it is logical to expect long-term changes, given the pervasive shifts in development that take place after

TABLE 24.2 Summary of Results of Interventions for Disabled Infants at the Final Assessment

Study	Age[a]	Length[b]	Child cognitive	Child motor	Parental attitude	Parent–Child interaction
Child-focused model						
Rosen-Morris & Sitkei (1981)	18–72	9	+[d]	+	n.a.[e]	n.a.
Bricker et al. (1982)	10–57	7	+	+	n.a.	n.a.
LeLaurin (1985)	3–31	6–27	+	+	n.a.	n.a.
Parent-focused model						
Moxley-Haegert & Serbin (1983)	M = 21.5	9–15	–[f]	+	+	n.a.
Rosenberg & Robinson (1985)	3–34	3–4	n.a.	n.a.	n.a.	+
Mahoney & Powell (1988)	2–32	M = 11	+	n.a.	n.a.	+
Jointly focused model, didactic						
Barna et al. (1980)	3–48	5–25	+	+	n.a.	n.a.
Fitzgerald et al. (1980)	M = 18.5	M = 29.5	+	+	n.a.	n.a.
Piper & Pless (1980)	M = 9.3	6	–	–	+	–
Rynders & Horrobin (1980)	1–9	60	+	+	–	–
Sandow et al. (1981)	M = 30	36+	+	–	n.a.	n.a.
Turner & Rogers (1981)	0–24	12	+	+	n.a.	n.a.
Macy et al. (1983)	M = 16	M = 14	–	+	n.a.	n.a.
Oelwein et al. (1985)	11–168	8	+	+	n.a.	n.a.
Wolery & Dyk (1985)	17–34	8–12	+	–	n.a.	n.a.
Folio & Richey (1990)	0–36	n.a.	n.a.	n.a.	n.a.	n.a.
Jointly focused model, comprehensive						
Bricker & Sheehan (1981)	5–69	7	+	+	n.a.	n.a.
Connolly et al. (1984)	0–36	48–84	+	–	n.a.	n.a.
Greenberg et al. (1984)	M = 22.2	12	–	n.a.	n.a.	+
		M = 22.8				
Hanson (1985)	1–36	9–18	+	+	+	+
Warren et al. (1986)	0–36	n.a.	n.a.	n.a.	n.a.	n.a.
Rose & Calhoun (1990)	7–33	7.6	+	n.a.	+	n.a.

[a]"Age" indicates the age of the child in months upon entry into the program and final assessment.
[b]"Length" indicates the approximate length of time in months between pretest and the last assessment.
[c]Outcome measures: "Child cognitive" represents the child's performance on cognitive assessments, either standardized or criterion-referenced; "Child motor" represents the child's performance on motoric assessments; "Parental attitude" represents the parent's child-rearing attitudes, perceptions of the child, and program participation; "Parent–child interaction" represents parent–child interactions as measured by the HOME scale, interactive style during feeding or free play, the parent's or the child's responsiveness to each other, etc.
[d]A "+" sign indicates a significant treatment effect.
[e]"n.a." (not applicable) means the study did not include the measure in its final assessments.
[f]"–" indicates no significant treatment effect.

infancy, as well as the uneven quality of later educational environments (Guralnick, 1989; Horowitz & Paden, 1973). Moreover, improving the present lives of children and families is valuable and may in fact set in motion changes that will result in long-term effects (Zigler & Berman, 1983). Regardless of one's opinion regarding the necessity of demonstrating long-term effects, whether or not intervention has persistent effects remains an empirical question that warrants investigation.

Unanswered Questions

Although the research reviewed in this chapter shows that interventions for LBW and disabled infants have had positive results in many areas, a number of issues regarding such interventions remain unresolved. One highly significant issue pertains to how and to what extent the interventions are implemented and experienced (see Emde, 1988). Most of the studies reviewed here simply compared children who received an intervention to children who did not receive it, or to healthy full-term children; it was assumed that the intervention was implemented as designed and/or was received by the subjects in the same manner. This assumption, however, may have been unfounded. Naturally, different infants and families will respond in different ways to an intervention. However, the studies reviewed here rarely examined whether an intervention was differentially efficacious for children of various SES groups, levels of neonatal health status, or severity of handicap. Only 2 of the 13 LBW studies reviewed examined the potentially differential effects of intervention, with one reporting that infants who were lighter (VLBW) improved more (Barrera, Cunningham, & Rosenbaum, 1986), and one reporting that infants who were heavier or born to less educated parents benefited more (IHDP, 1990). The small sample size of the VLBW study, the incomparability of subjects between the two studies, or differences in the intervention approaches may account for the contrasting findings. For studies of disabled children, even less specificity regarding sample differences is available, because of the low incidence of many handicapping conditions and the mix of handicapping conditions found in most programs.

For both disabled and LBW children, other child characteristics (e.g., gender) and family characteristics (e.g., race/ethnicity, SES, single-parent vs. intact families, teenage vs. older mothers) may also affect the intervention participants' receptivity and experience of a program, and subsequently may affect their gains from the program. However, little research has taken these variables into account in work with preterm or disabled children. In order to explore these issues further, we apply the following questions to the research literature: (1) Has an intervention been implemented as planned? (2) What is the relationship between the participants' perceptions and experience of the intervention and the program's effects? (3) How do specific components of an intervention affect outcomes?

Program Implementation

Rarely has an attempt been made to verify the delivery of a planned intervention. Although program implementation has been shown to vary among interventionists (Bissell, 1973) and among participants (Gray & Wandersman, 1980; Hauser-Cram, 1990), as well as to deviate substantially from original plans (Brown et al., 1980; White-Traut & Nelson, 1988), the extent of program implementation has frequently been overlooked and left unmeasured. Difficulty in measuring this variable is heightened when intervention takes place in homes. A home-based intervention with disadvantaged populations found that the home visitor's perception of the events in a visit did not always match a videotaped recording of those same events (Gray & Ruttle, 1980).

A related issue concerns whether a parent actually implements a home program once the visitor has departed. A number of programs have requested that parents keep records, but few have used that information in statistical analyses. An example of variation in participant involvement comes from the Minde, Shosenberg, & Marton (1982) study, which reported that only 75% of their intervention parents attended all or almost all sessions, and the rest attended little more than one-third of the group meetings. In their evaluation of the program, however, the authors did not take this variation into account. Only the IHDP studies with LBW children (Ramey et al., 1992; Sparling et al., 1991) and two studies with handicapped children (Warren et al., 1986; Moxley-Haegert & Serbin, 1983) monitored program implementation and used the data in subsequent statistical analyses. Gray and Wandersman's (1980) warning that the "assumption of a homogeneous treatment is unjustifiable for home-based interventions, which explicitly modify the program to fit the needs of the family, which take place in unique home settings, and which are delivered by a wide range of individuals" (p. 998) must be kept in mind as programs are evaluated.

Experience of the Intervention

As some investigators in early intervention for economically disadvantaged children have suggested, parents' and children's perceptions and experience of an intervention may vary from those intended by the intervention, and researchers should take this into account when assessing the efficacy of a program (Farran, 1990; Heinicke, Beckwith, & Thompson, 1988). An example of the importance of the differences in the experience of intervention comes from the IHDP study. Using these data, Liaw (1991) constructed two variables to reflect the intervention parents' and the LBW children's active involvement in the intervention: (1) a parental interest variable, formed by summing the intervention activities that were presented during home visits in which the parents were highly interested; and (2) a child mastery variable, derived from a sum of the intervention activities taught at the CDC on which the children reached the specified mastery goals. Liaw's analysis indicated that families of different economic status with children of different birthweight status varied in their degree of active involvement in intervention; that high levels of active involvement on the part of both parents and children produced earlier and more pervasive positive effects on LBW children's cognitive and language development; and that low levels of involvement produced fewer or no effects. In short, differential experience may lead to differential outcomes.

Which Components Work?

The manner in which researchers define and specify an intervention limits our understanding of how intervention programs help infants and families. As noted at the outset of this chapter, intervention is often conceptualized dichotomously—an approach that is problematic with such a multidimensional variable as early intervention (Hall & Loucks, 1977). Many programs provide more than one type of intervention (e.g., parent support group, child activity center, informational presentations, classroom sessions), as well as other components that may be provided on an "as-needed" basis. In reality, different families may utilize different components of an intervention program or may use the same components at different intensities. However, if data concerning each subject's involvement (attendance, number of visits, actual length of visits, etc.) with each component are not maintained, it is impossible to know which components at what level of participation are actually responsible or necessary for positive changes to occur.

To date, the only attempts to understand the relative importance of various components have been Moxley-Haegert and Serbin's (1983) study with disabled infants, and Sparling et al.'s (1991) and Pfander and Bradley-Johnson's (1990) projects with LBW infants. Moxley-Haegert and Serbin compared various types of parent-focused interventions, finding that the educational program had a greater effect on children's development than the behavior management program. Sparling et al. compared the parents' exposure to IHDP home visit activities to the children's exposure to the intervention activities at the CDC, and found that the home visit component accounted for more variance in children's 36-month IQ scores than the CDC component. Pfander and Bradley-Johnson (1990) compared the effects of a single parent education session to those of an assessment session, and reported that infants whose mothers attended the parent education session showed more optimal cognitive scores than those whose mothers attended the assessment session. Studies such as these, which examined intervention in a detailed and analytical manner, provide a model for future research.

Given the paucity of research in this area, we do not know whether a certain component must necessarily be present for an intervention to be successful, nor do we know whether individual components have differential impacts on subjects. In other words, we do not know for whom specific components of particular interventions are essential. Thus, in reviewing intervention studies, we should no longer assume full implementation of the intervention, or equal experience of the intervention participants; nor should we neglect the important roles that individual differences in experiencing the intervention play in relation to children's development.

In summary, although the existing research confirms the benefits of intervening with LBW and disabled infants and/or their parents to ameliorate the children's developmental risks, it does not address the issue of *how* intervention is experienced, *what* works, and *on whom* it is best to focus. Because the resources and time that can be used for intervention are usually limited, it is important for researchers to evaluate and determine whether the program is valuable, for whom, and in what ways.

Conceptual Issues Regarding Intervention with Infants

The value of particular approaches to intervention and of particular methods used in intervention programs has received very little research attention. Left largely unexplored have been such issues as the role of parents, their satisfaction with the intervention, and the methods addressed to them. Similarly, teaching techniques employed with infants and optimal characteristics of the staff–family relationship lack empirical support. This section addresses issues related to parents, infants, and intervenors.

Parents: Roles, Demands, Methods

Programs for disabled children most frequently view parents as potential teachers. By means of classroom observation, group informational meetings, and direct individual instruction, parents are trained to provide an educationally enriching environment for their infants. Fewer programs concentrate on fostering a family's emotional adaptation to the birth of a handicapped infant or helping the parents to develop an optimal interactive style. Reviewing early intervention programs for biologically and environmentally at-risk children, Barrera and Rosenbaum (1986) noted that few intervention programs focused on the parent–child relationship, the inherent role of parents as attachment/affectional figures, or the parents' own needs as individuals. Intervention research to date has not provided clear guidance about which parental role should be targeted in the attempt to improve a child's developmental outcome.

A second issue relates to the demanding nature and intrusiveness of high-intensity intervention programs. A parent who is encouraged to learn new teaching techniques, to attend a center-based program with his or her child, to implement a home treatment program, and to participate in informational or support groups may be overwhelmed by the time required for full program participation. Parents may also feel intruded upon by the family assessment procedures necessary to complete an Individualized Family Service Plan (IFSP). Cultural differences between families and intervention staff members may further complicate the intervention process (Hanson, 1985). This is an especially high risk in transdisciplinary programs where information from the various disciplines is funneled through one person who actually delivers the services. It is imperative that programs be individualized and designed to allow each parent significant control over the family's participation. Flexible service delivery options (such as those employed by the Charlotte Circle Project), which provide an array of different ways for a family to participate, should become the norm rather than the exception in program offerings.

Methods with Infants

Although studies of programs usually describe goals and service delivery formats thoroughly, instructional techniques are typically described less fully. Programs with innovative curricula (Rose & Calhoun, 1990; Rosen-Morris & Sitkei, 1981) represent the exception. Other programs seem to use methods originally developed for older or less disabled children (Warren et al., 1986). One unfortunate commonality among many programs is the absence of child-initiated free play and exploration. This underutilization of free play reflects the fact that few programs have developed teaching techniques specifically for infants.

Personnel

Many studies do not report the educational level, training, or certification of program staff members. When staff characteristics are reported, no relationship appears to exist between the focus and methods of a program and the qualifications of the intervenors. Important questions include who should intervene and what combination of education, training, and personality is optimal for successfully intervening with handicapped infants and their families. Are certain staff skills or characteristics necessary, or is success more related to the idiosyncratic match between interventionist and family?

For example, it is frequently mentioned, although usually anecdotally, that parents must deal with their emotional reactions to the birth of a preterm or handicapped infant before they are ready to participate fully in an intervention program (Connolly & Russell, 1976; Fitzgerald et al., 1980; Greenberg et al., 1984; Minde, Shosenberg, Thompson, & Marton, 1982; Warren et al., 1986). This suggests that intervenors must be ready to assist parents who are grappling with emotional issues, and that they must be trained for a therapeutic role that "varies from a teaching to a social work role" (Sandow et al., 1981, p. 141). If educators rather than other clinicians must deal with these issues frequently, then training programs should include skills to help parents confront their emotional reactions to the birth of a handicapped infant.

This issue also raises questions about the optimal relationship between intervenor and parent. In one parent-as-teacher study (Sandow et al., 1981), the relative efficacy of visits every 2 weeks was compared with visits every 2 months. After 1 year, the more frequently visited group showed greater gains. However, after the second year of intervention, the less frequently visited group showed greater progress than the more frequently visited group. Differences between the groups disappeared after the third year. The authors speculated that parents in the more frequently visited group may have become dependent on the intervenor and may have expected the intervenor to take responsibility for the children's educational program; the parents in the less frequently visited group may have developed greater confidence in their ability to work with their children. This study highlights the importance of interventionists' knowing how to gradually transfer skills and responsibilities to the parents as the parents' competence increases, in order to avoid a relationship characterized by dependency.

CONCLUSIONS AND FUTURE DIRECTIONS

This chapter demonstrates that where data are available, positive effects for intervention have been found on some parameters for every study (see Tables 24.1 and 24.2). However, between-study comparisons did not consistently show where these effects were to be found, nor did they particularly follow the emphasis of the models described. Because of the absence of curriculum comparisons and the lack of planned variations in approaches to intervention, the multidimensional model presented in Figure

24.1 cannot formally be tested. Data from Liaw's (1991) study appear to favor the jointly focused model over other alternatives for LBW children. This model also has intuitive appeal for disabled infants and toddlers. However, further empirical evidence is needed before firm conclusions are drawn.

Nevertheless, given the diversity of families' needs and resources, the heterogeneity of disabled and developmentally vulnerable infants and toddlers, and the unpredictable availability of intervention services and providers, it is likely that no single model will be appropriate for all children and families in need. Instead of searching for the "best" intervention model, our attention must shift to a systematic view of the child and family *in situ*. It is critical that we begin to consider the development of highly individualized programs of intervention that consider the needs of both children and families, and that seek to address these needs with the most appropriate theory-driven and empirically substantiated model available. In this respect, the multidimensional analysis that this chapter utilizes provides an approach to maximizing the fit between parent–child needs and intervention resources through careful analysis of program types and intervention emphases.

The various intervention techniques that have been developed and that have been documented in this chapter show us that our attention should not be devoted to model building any more. Today the task is more diagnostic: Using the information that is already available, we must learn how to help specific children and families overcome their problems and begin to realize their full potential.

ACKNOWLEDGMENT

Preparation of this chapter was supported in part by a grant from the National Institute on Disability and Rehabilitation Research.

REFERENCES

Achenbach, T. M., Edelbrock, C. S., & Howell, C. T. (1987). Empirically based assessment of the behavior/emotional problems of 2- and 3-year-old children. *Journal of Abnormal Child Psychology, 15,* 629–650.

Achenbach, T. M., Phares, V., Howell, C. T., Rauh, V. A., & Nurcombe, B. (1990). Seven-year outcome of the Vermont intervention program for low-birthweight infants. *Child Development, 61,* 1672–1681.

Affleck, G., Tennen, H., Rowe, J., Roscher, B., & Walker, L. (1989). Effects of formal support on mothers' adaptation to the hospital-to-home transition of high-risk infants: The benefits and costs of helping. *Child Development, 60,* 488–501.

Als, H., Lawhon, G., Brown, E., Gibes, R., Duffy, F. H., McAnulty, G., & Blickman, J. G. (1986). Individualized behavioral and environmental care for the very low birth weight preterm infant at high risk for bronchopulmonary dysplasia: Neonatal intensive care unit and developmental outcome. *Pediatrics, 78,* 1123–1132.

Bagnato, S. J., & Neisworth, J. T. (1980). The intervention efficiency index: An approach to preschool program accountability. *Exceptional Children, 46,* 264–269.

Barna, S., Bidder, R. T., Gray, O. P., Clements, J., & Gardner, S. (1980). The progress of developmentally delayed pre-school children in a home-training scheme. *Child: Care, Health and Development, 6,* 157–164.

Barrera, M. E., Cunningham, C. C., & Rosenbaum, P. L. (1986). Low birth weight and home intervention strategies: Preterm infants. *Journal of Developmental and Behavioral Pediatrics, 7,* 361–366.

Barrera, M. E., Kitching, K. T., Cunningham, C. C., Doucet, D. A., & Rosenbaum, P. L. (1990). A 3-year early home intervention follow-up study with low birthweight infants and their parents. *Topics in Early Childhood Special Education, 10,* 14–28.

Barrera, M. E., & Rosenbaum, P. (1986). The transactional model of early home intervention. *Journal of Infant Mental Health, 7,* 112–131.

Barrera, M. E., Rosenbaum, P. L., & Cunningham, C. E. (1986). Early home intervention with low-birthweight infants and their parents. *Child Development, 57,* 20–33.

Bayley, N. (1969). *Bayley Scales of Infant Development.* New York: Psychological Corporation.

Beckwith, L. (1988). Intervention with disadvantaged parents of sick preterm infants. *Psychiatry, 51,* 242–247.

Beckwith, L., & Cohen, S. E. (1980). Interaction of preterm infants with their caregivers and test performance at age 2. In T. M. Field, S. Goldberg, Stern, & A. M. Sostek (Eds.), *High-risk infants and children: Adult and children* (pp. 155–178). New York: Academic Press.

Beckwith, L., & Cohen, S. E. (1984). Home environment and cognitive competence in preterm children during the first 5 years. In A. Gottfried (Ed.), *Home environment and early cognitive development* (pp. 235–271). New York: Academic Press.

Bissell, J. S. (1973). Planned variation in Head Start and Follow Through. In J. C. Stanley (Ed.), *Compensatory education for children ages two to five: Recent studies of educational intervention* (pp. 63–107). Baltimore: Johns Hopkins University Press.

Bloom, B. (1964). *Stability and change in human characteristics.* Chichester, England: Wiley.

Brazelton, T. B. (1973). *Neonatal Behavioral Assessment Scale.* Philadelphia: J. B. Lippincott.

Bricker, D., Bruder, M. B., & Bailey, E. (1982). Developmental integration of preschool children. *Analysis and Intervention in Developmental Disabilities, 2,* 207–222.

Bricker, D., & Sheehan, R. (1981). Effectiveness of an early intervention program indexed by measures of child

change. *Journal of the Division of Early Childhood, 4,* 11–27.

Bronfenbrenner, U. (1975). Is early intervention effective? In M. S. Guttentag & E. L. Struening (Eds.), *Handbook of evaluation research* (Vol. 2, pp. 519–603). Beverly Hills, CA: Sage.

Brown, J. V., LaRossa, M. M., Aylward, G. P., Davis, D. J., Rutherford, P. K., & Bakeman, R. B. (1980). Nursery-based intervention with prematurely born babies and their mothers: Are there effects? *Journal of Pediatrics, 97,* 487–491.

Bryant, D. M., & Ramey, C. T. (1987). An analysis of the effectiveness of early intervention programs for environmentally at-risk children. In M. J. Guralnick & F. C. Bennett (Eds.), *The effectiveness of early intervention for at-risk and handicapped children* (pp. 33–78). New York: Academic Press.

Caldwell, B. M., & Bradley, R. H. (1970). *Home Observation for Measurement of the Environment.* Unpublished manuscript, University of Arkansas.

Calhoun, M. L., & Rose, T. L. (1988). Early social reciprocity interventions for infants with severe retardation: Current findings and implications for the future. *Education and Training in Mental Retardation, 23,* 340–343.

Casto, G., & Mastropieri, M. A. (1986). The efficacy of early intervention programs: A meta-analysis. *Exceptional Children, 52,* 417–424.

Casto, G., & White, K. R. (1985). The efficacy of early intervention programs with environmentally at-risk infants. *Journal of Children in Contemporary Society, 17,* 37–50.

Connolly, B. H., Morgan, S., & Russell, F. F. (1984). Evaluation of children with Down syndrome who participated in an early intervention program: Second follow-up study. *Physical Therapy, 64,* 1515–1519.

Connolly, B. H., Morgan, S., Russell, F. F., & Richardson, B. (1980). Early intervention with Down syndrome children: Follow-up report. *Physical Therapy, 60,* 1405–1408.

Connolly, B. H., & Russell, F. (1976). Interdisciplinary early intervention program. *Physical Therapy, 56,* 155–158.

Dunst, C. J. (1986). Overview of the efficacy of early intervention programs: Methodological and conceptual considerations. In L. Bickman & D. Weatherford (Eds.), *Evaluating early intervention programs for severely handicapped children and their families* (pp. 79–147). Austin, TX: Pro-Ed.

Dunst, C. J., & Rheingrover, R. M. (1981). An analysis of the efficacy of infant intervention programs with organically handicapped children. *Evaluation and Program Planning, 4,* 287–323.

Emde, R. N. (1988). Risk, intervention and meaning. *Psychiatry, 51,* 254–259.

Farran, D. (1990). Effects of intervention with disadvantaged and disadvantaged children: A decade review. In S. J. Meisels & J. P. Shonkoff (Eds.), *Handbook of early childhood intervention* (pp. 501–539). New York: Cambridge University Press.

Field, T. M., Dempsey, J. R., Hallock, N., & Shuman, H. H. (1978). Mothers' assessments of the behavior of their infants. *Infant Behavior and Development, 1,* 156–167.

Field, T. M., Schanberg, S. M., Scafidi, F., Bauer, C. R., Vega-Lahr, N., Garcia, R., Nystrom, J., & Kuhn,

C. M. (1986). Tactile/kinesthetic stimulation effects on preterm neonates. *Pediatrics, 77,* 654–658.

Field, T. M., Widmayer, S. M., Stringer, S., & Ignatoff, E. (1980). Teenage, lower-class, black mothers and their preterm infants: An intervention and developmental follow-up. *Child Development, 51,* 426–436.

Fitzgerald, H. E., Brajovic, C., Radicevic, Z., Djurdjevic, M., Djurdjic, S., Novak, J., & Bojanovic, M. (1980). Home-based intervention for infants with developmental disorders. *Infant Mental Health Journal, 1,* 96–107.

Folio, R., & Richey, D. (1990). Public television and video technology for rural families with special needs young children: The ETIPS model. *Topics in Early Childhood Special Education, 10,* 45–55.

Gray, S. W., & Ruttle, K. (1980). The Family-Oriented Home Visiting Program: A longitudinal study. *Genetic Psychology Monographs, 102,* 299–316.

Gray, S. W., & Wandersman, L. P. (1980). The methodology of home-based intervention studies: Problems and promising strategies. *Child Development, 51,* 993–1009.

Greenberg, M. T., Calderon, R., & Kusche, C. (1984). Early intervention using simultaneous communication with deaf infants: The effect on communication development. *Child Development, 55,* 607–616.

Guralnick, M. J. (1989). Recent developments in early intervention efficacy research: Implications for family involvement in P.L. 99-457. *Topics in Early Childhood Special Education, 9,* 1–17.

Hall, G. E., & Loucks, S. F. (1977). A developmental model for determining whether the treatment is actually implemented. *American Educational Research Journal, 14,* 263–276.

Hanson, M. J. (1981). A model for early intervention with culturally diverse single and multiparent families. *Topics in Early Childhood Special Education, 1,* 37–44.

Hanson, M. J. (1985). An analysis of the effects of early intervention services for infants and toddlers with moderate and severe handicaps. *Topics in Early Childhood Special Education, 5,* 36–51.

Hauser-Cram, P. (1990). Designing meaningful evaluation of early intervention services. In S. J. Meisels & J. P. Shonkoff (Eds.), *Handbook of early childhood intervention* (pp. 583–602). New York: Cambridge University Press.

Hayden, A. H., & Dmitriev, V. (1975). The multidisciplinary preschool program for Down's syndrome children at the University of Washington model preschool center. In B. Z. Friedlander, G. M. Sterritt, & G. E. Kirk (Eds.), *Exceptional infant: Vol. 3. Assessment and intervention* (pp. 193–241). New York: Brunner/Mazel.

Hayden, A. H., & Haring, N. G. (1976). Early intervention for high risk infants and young children: Programs for Down's syndrome children. In T. J. Tjossem (Ed.), *Intervention strategies for high risk infants and young children* (pp. 573–607). Baltimore: University Park Press.

Hayden, A. H., & Haring, N. G. (1977). The acceleration and maintenance of developmental gains in Down's syndrome school-age children. In P. Mittler (Ed.), *Research to practice in mental retardation: Vol. 1. Care and intervention* (pp. 129–141). Baltimore: University Park Press.

Heinicke, C., Beckwith, L., & Thompson, A. (1988). Early intervention in the family system: A framework and review. *Infant Mental Health Journal, 9,* 111–141.

Horowitz, F. D., & Paden, L. Y. (1973). The effectiveness of environmental intervention programs. In B. M. Caldwell & H. N. Ricciuti (Eds.), *Review of child development research: Vol. 3. Child development and social policy* (pp. 331–402). Chicago: University of Chicago Press.

Hrncir, E. J., Speller, G. M., & West, M. (1985). What are we testing? *Developmental Psychology, 21,* 226–232.

Hunt, J. M. (1961). *Intelligence and experience.* New York: Ronald Press.

Infant Health and Development Program (IHDP). (1900). Enhancing the outcomes of low-birth-weight, premature infants. *Journal of the American Medical Association, 263*(22), 3035–3042.

Keogh, B. K., & Sheehan, R. (1981). The use of developmental test data for documenting handicapped children's progress: Problems and recommendations. *Journal of the Division for Early Childhood, 3,* 42–47.

Kopp, C. B., & McCall, R. B. (1982). Predicting later mental performance for normal, at-risk, and handicapped infants. In P. B. Baltes & O. G. Brim, Jr. (Eds.), *Lifespan development and behavior* (Vol. 4, pp. 33–61). New York: Academic Press.

LeLaurin, K. (1985). The experimental analysis of the effects of early intervention with normal, at-risk, and handicapped children under three. *Analysis and Intervention in Developmental Disabilities, 5,* 129–150.

Lewis, M., Jaskir, J., & Enright, M. K. (1986). The development of mental abilities in infancy. *Intelligence, 10,* 331–354.

Liaw, F. (1991). *The efficacy of early intervention for low birth weight infants: What works, how, and for whom?* Unpublished doctoral dissertation, University of Michigan.

Macy, D. J., Solomon, G. S., Schoen, M., & Galey, G. S. (1983). The DEBT Project: Early intervention for handicapped children and their parents. *Exceptional Children, 49,* 447–448.

Mahoney, G., & Powell, A. (1988). Modifying parent–child interaction: Enhancing the development of handicapped children. *Journal of Special Education, 22,* 82–96.

McCarthy, D. (1972). *McCarthy Scales of Children's Abilities.* New York: Psychological Corporation.

Meisels, S. J. (1985). The efficacy of early intervention: Why are we still asking this question? *Topics in Early Childhood Special Education, 5,* 1–11.

Meisels, S. J. (1987). Using criterion-referenced assessment data to measure the progress of handicapped children in early intervention programs. In G. Casto, S. Ascione, & M. Salehi (Eds.), *Perspectives in infancy and early childhood* (pp. 59–64). Logan, UT: DCHP Press.

Meisels, S. J. (1989). Meeting the mandate of Public Law 99-457: Early intervention in the nineties. *American Journal of Orthopsychiatry, 59,* 451–460.

Meisels, S. J. (in press). Designing meaningful measurements for early childhood. In B. L. Mallory & R. S. New (Eds.), *Diversity in early childhood education: A call for more inclusive theory, practice, and policy.* New York: Teachers College Press.

Meisels, S. J., Jones, S. N., & Stiefel, G. S. (1983). Neonatal intervention: Problems, purpose, and prospects.

Topics in Early Childhood Special Education, 3(1), 1–13.

Minde, K. K., Shosenberg, N. E., & Marton, P. L. (1982). The effects of self-help groups in a premature nursery on maternal autonomy and caretaking style 1 year later. In L. A. Bond & J. M. Joffe (Eds.), *Facilitating infant and early childhood development* (pp. 240–258). Hanover, NH: University Press of New England.

Minde, K. K., Shosenberg, N. E., Thompson, J., & Marton, P. L. (1982). Self-help groups in a premature nursery: Follow-up at one year. In J. Call, E. Galenson, & R. Tyson (Eds.), *Frontiers of infant psychiatry* (pp. 264–272). New York: Basic Books.

Moxley-Haegert, L., & Serbin, L. A. (1983). Developmental education for parents of delayed infants: Effects on parental motivation and children's development. *Child Development, 54*, 1324–1331.

Nurcombe, B., Howell, C. T., Rauh, V. A., Teti, D. H., Ruoff, P., & Brennan, J. (1984). An intervention program for mothers of low-birthweight infants: Preliminary results. *Journal of the American Academy of Child Psychiatry, 23*, 319–325.

Oelwein, P. L., Fewell, R. R., & Pruess, J. B. (1985). The efficacy of intervention at outreach sites for the program for children with Down syndrome and other developmental delays. *Topics in Early Childhood Special Education, 5*, 78–87.

Ottenbacher, K., & Petersen, P. (1985). The efficacy of early intervention programs for children with organic impairment: A quantitative review. *Evaluation and Program Planning, 8*, 135–146.

Pfander, S., & Bradley-Johnson, S. (1990). Effects of an intervention program and its components on NICU infants. *Children's Health Care, 19*, 140–146.

Piper, M. C., & Pless, I. B. (1980). Early intervention for infants with Down syndrome: A controlled trial. *Pediatrics, 65*, 463–468.

Ramey, C. T., Bryant, D. M., Wasik, B. H., Sparling, J. J., Fendt, K. H., & LaVange, L. M. (1992). The Infant Health and Development Program for low birthweight, premature infants: Program elements, family participation, and child intelligence. *Pediatrics, 89*, 454–465.

Rauh, V. A., Achenbach, T. M., Nurcombe, B., Howell, C. T., & Teti, D. M. (1988). Minimizing adverse effects of low birthweight: Four-year results of an early intervention program. *Child Development, 59*, 544–553.

Rauh, V. A., Nurcombe, B., Ruoff, P., Jette, A., & Howell, C. T. (1982). The Vermont Infant Studies Project: The rationale for a mother–infant transaction program. In L. A. Bond & J. M. Joffe (Eds.), *Facilitating infant and early childhood development* (pp. 259–280). Hanover, NH: University Press of New England.

Resnick, M. B., Armstrong, S., & Carter, R. L. (1988). Developmental intervention program for high-risk premature infants: Effects on development and parent–infant interactions. *Journal of Developmental and Behavioral Pediatrics, 9*, 73–78.

Rose, T. L., & Calhoun, M. L. (1990). The Charlotte Circle Project: A program for infants and toddlers with severe/profound disabilities. *Journal of Early Intervention, 14*, 175–185.

Rosenberg, S. A., & Robinson, C. C. (1985). Enhancement of mothers' interactional skills in an infant education program. *Education and Training of the Mentally Retarded, 20*, 163–169.

Rosen-Morris, D., & Sitkei, E. G. (1981). Strategies for teaching severely/profoundly handicapped infants and young children. *Journal of the Division for Early Childhood, 4*, 81–93.

Ross, G. S. (1984). Home intervention for premature infants of low-income families. *American Journal of Orthopsychiatry, 54*, 263–270.

Rynders, J. E., & Horrobin, J. M. (1980). Educational provisions for young children with Down's syndrome. In J. Gottlieb (Ed.), *Educating mentally retarded persons in the mainstream* (pp. 109–147). Baltimore: University Park Press.

Sandow, S. A., Clarke, A. D. B., Cox, M. V., & Stewart, F. L. (1981). Home intervention with parents of severely subnormal pre-school children: A final report. *Child: Care, Health and Development, 7*, 135–144.

Schanberg, S. M., & Field, T. M. (1987). Sensory deprivation stress and supplemental stimulation in the rat pup and preterm human neonate. *Child Development, 58*, 1431–1447.

Shearer, D. E., & Shearer, M. S. (1976). The Portage Project: A model for early childhood intervention. In T. J. Tjossem (Ed.), *Intervention strategies for high risk infants and young children* (pp. 335–350). Baltimore: University Park Press.

Shonkoff, J. P., & Hauser-Cram, P. (1987). Early intervention for disabled infants and their families: A quantitative analysis. *Pediatrics, 80*, 650–658.

Shonkoff, J. P., Hauser-Cram, P., Krauss, M. W., & Upshur, C. C. (1988). Early intervention efficacy research: What have we learned and where do we go from here? *Topics in Early Childhood Special Education, 8*, 81–93.

Shonkoff, J. P., & Meisels, S. J. (1990). Early childhood intervention: The evolution of a concept. In S. J. Meisels & J. P. Shonkoff (Eds.), *Handbook of early childhood intervention* (pp. 3–31). New York: Cambridge University Press.

Simeonsson, R. J. (1985). Efficacy of early intervention: Issues and evidence. *Early Intervention, 5*, 203–209.

Simeonsson, R. J., Huntington, G. S., & Short, R. J. (1982). Individual differences and goals: An approach to the evaluation of child progress. *Topics in Early Childhood Special Education, 1*, 71–80.

Skeels, H. M. (1966). Adult status of children with contrasting early life experiences. *Monographs of the Society for Research in Child Development, 31*(3, Serial No. 105).

Sparling, J., Lewis, I., Ramey, C. T., Wasik, B. H., Bryant, D. M., & LaVange, L. M. (1991). Partners: A curriculum to help premature, low-birth-weight infants get off to a good start. *Topics in Early Childhood Special Education, 11*, 36–55.

Terman, L. M., & Merrill, M. A. (1972). *Stanford–Binet Intelligence Scale: Manual for the third revision, Form L-M*. Boston: Houghton Mifflin.

Turner, R., & Rogers, A. M. (1981). Project KIDS: Infant education for the handicapped in an urban public school system. *Journal of the Division for Early Childhood, 2*, 40–51.

Warren, S. F., Alpert, C. L., & Kaiser, A. P. (1986). An optimal learning environment for infants and toddlers with severe handicaps. *Focus on Exceptional Children, 18*, 1–11.

White, K. R., Bush, D. W., & Casto, G. (1985). Learning from reviews of early intervention efficacy. *Journal of Special Education, 19,* 417.

White, K. R., & Mott, S. E. (1987). Conducting longitudinal research on the efficacy of early intervention with handicapped children. *Journal of the Division for Early Childhood, 12,* 13–22.

White, K. R., & Pezzino, J. (1986). Ethical, practical, and scientific considerations of randomized experiments in early childhood special education. *Topics in Early Childhood Special Education, 6,* 100–116.

White-Traut, R. C., & Nelson, M. N. (1988). Maternally administered tactile, auditory, visual, and vestibular stimulation: Relationship to later interactions between mothers and premature infants. *Research in Nursing and Health, 11,* 31–39.

Widmayer, S. M., & Field, T. M. (1981). Effects of Brazelton demonstration for mothers on the development of preterm infants. *Pediatrics, 67,* 711–714.

Wolery, M. (1983). Proportional change index: An alternative for comparing child change data. *Exceptional Children, 50,* 167–170.

Wolery, M., & Dyk, L. (1985). The evaluation of two levels of a center based early intervention project. *Topics in Early Childhood Special Education, 5,* 66–77.

Yarrow, L. J., & Pederson, F. A. (1976). The interplay between cognitive and motivation in infancy. In M. Lewis (Ed.) *Origins of intelligence* (pp. 379–399). New York: Plenum Press.

Zigler, E., & Balla, D. (1982). Selecting outcome variables in evaluations of early childhood special education programs. *Topics in Early Childhood Education, 1,* 11–22.

Zigler, E., & Berman, W. (1983). Discerning the future of early childhood intervention. *American Psychologist, 38,* 894–906.

25

Preventive Interventions: Enhancing Parent-Infant Relationships

KATHRYN E. BARNARD
COLLEEN E. MORISSET
SUSAN SPIEKER

THE CHALLENGE: CHILDREN AT RISK

According to a survey of 7,000 kindergarten teachers, 35% of U.S. children are not ready to learn, and these teachers report that the situation is only getting worse (Boyer, 1991). This enormous problem demands our attention. A successful solution will include treatment for families in crisis and preventive programs for those at risk. By the year 2000, it is projected (Chasnoff, Landress, & Barrett, 1990; Center for the Study of Social Policy, 1992; Klerman, 1992; B. Zuckerman, personal communication, 1992) that children in America will have the following characteristics:

- Not wanted (12%)
- Born at low birthweight and/or premature (7%)
- Mothers are substance abusers (11%)
- Parents are alcoholics (10%)
- Mothers are teenagers (10%)
- Mothers are not married (30%)
- Mothers have not completed high school (20%)
- Family income is below the federal poverty line (23%)

These percentages make it evident that a sizable number of children are at risk for their further development. If we want to see that children achieve their potential, we must develop programs that decrease the risk factors for bad outcomes and promote protective factors in their lives. This chapter emphasizes the challenge of carrying out this work, at conceptual, program, family, and dyadic levels. Unless we decrease the number of children born at risk, our capacity to prevent mental and emotional disorders in our nation's children will be seriously diminished.

PREVENTION AS A CONCEPT

Work for children should begin before they are born, should carry them through their greatest hazard which is childbirth, and should be most intensive during their first six years of life. These are the formative years—whether for their bodies, their minds or their loving hearts. (Mary Breckinridge, 1925; quoted in Lubic, 1992, p. 314)

Our conceptual framework comes from the field of public health, in which "prevention" is defined as promoting and maintaining health and as minimizing illness, disability, and suffering. Preventive efforts can be classified by their timing and scope. It is customary to refer to three levels of prevention: "primary," "secondary," and "tertiary." Within each level, some programs address the well-being of entire communities, and others focus on a subset of the community believed to be at increased risk for physical or mental health problems. The terms "primary," "secondary," and "tertiary" are embedded in the medical model of services. Another schema, advanced by Gordon (1983) lends itself to a broader public health model; it uses the categories "universal," "selected," and "indicated," which are largely parallel to the terms from the medical model. The two sets of terms are discussed here in combination.

Primary or universal prevention is distinct from other prevention efforts, in that programs at this level attempt to avert problems before they begin. In epidemiological terms, the goal of this type of prevention is to reduce the incidence of new cases of illness or disability largely by reducing the risk factors. Prenatal care, childhood immunization, and water fluoridation are examples of primary care programs that are universal in scope. Prenatal care is not limited to high-risk women, rubella vaccine only to children likely to encounter the virus, or fluoridated drinking water only to the young. Such programs provide widespread benefit to many and carry risks to few.

Secondary or selected prevention services target individuals whose characteristics place them at increased risk of developing further problems. Like primary prevention, secondary services are provided before problems are evident. For instance, a program that attempts to avert developmental problems attributable to prematurity by providing education to all parents of premature infants is a secondary/selected prevention. Another example is a recent study by our group focusing on interventions for pregnant women in poverty who lacked social and personal resources (Barnard, Magyary, et al., 1988).

Tertiary or indicated programs treat and manage health problems once disease or disability has occurred. This type of intervention can be preventive, insofar as early treatment may prevent the onset of some different disorder at a later time. For example, treatment of Conduct Disorder in the school years may deter subsequent psychopathology in adulthood. In this chapter we review concepts, practices, evidence, and recommended directions for primary/universal prevention programs, as well as for secondary/selected interventions.

PRIMARY/UNIVERSAL INTERVENTION

Prenatal Care

Prevention strategies for infant health and development do exist at the primary or universal level. Prenatal and postpartum health care services are good examples of universal intervention. Well-established rituals of preventive health care during pregnancy define the timing and type of intervention required; outcome studies repeatedly demonstrate a relationship between prenatal care and positive health outcomes for mothers and babies (Miller, 1991).

A recent report from the U.S. Public Health Service (USPHS) Expert Panel on the Content of Prenatal Care (1989) suggested the following objectives of prenatal care:

For the Pregnant Woman
- to increase her well-being before, during, and after pregnancy and to improve her self-image and self-care;
- to reduce maternal mortality and morbidity, fetal loss, and unnecessary pregnancy interventions;
- to reduce the risks to her health prior to subsequent pregnancies and beyond childbearing years; and
- to promote the development of parenting skills.

For the Fetus and Infant:
- to increase well-being;
- to reduce preterm birth, intrauterine growth retardation, congenital anomalies, and failure to thrive;
- to promote health, growth and development, immunization, and health supervision;
- to reduce neurologic, development, and other morbidities; and
- to reduce child abuse and neglect, injuries, preventable acute and chronic illness, and the need for extended hospitalization after birth.

For the Family
- to promote family development and positive parent–infant interaction;
- to reduce unintended pregnancies; and
- to identify for treatment behavior disorders leading to child neglect and family violence. (p. 5)

Problems in Delivery of Prenatal Care

These objectives go beyond the current delivery of prenatal care and emphasize, much more than in the past, objectives for the family. An especially important objective is the reduction of unintended pregnancies. Between 1985 and 1988, 12% of births to women aged 15–44 years were unwanted, and an additional 28% were mistimed. The majority of unwanted births are concentrated in the lowest-socioeconomic status group of women (Klerman, 1992). Harris (1992) has documented the impact of the 1988 Michigan decision to stop Medicaid funding of abortions for poor women who had unintended and unwanted pregnancies. The number of abortions in Michigan state dropped by 20% after that ruling; in that time live births in Michigan increased, and there were increases in low-birthweight infants, in mothers with less than a 12th-grade education, and in infants whose mothers had four or more previous children. Harris contends that these results were largely a result of forcing poor women to bear babies they did not want. He has stated:

> Only when abortion is equally available to poor and non-poor women nationwide will there be a significant reduction in the number of unwanted babies born at high risk; perhaps 300,000 births could be averted if all women had access to safe and affordable reproductive alternatives including contraceptive and abortion services. (p. 22)

An important primary/universal prevention program must be family planning, including abortion services. The number of unintended births has a direct impact on the number of children in need of secondary prevention services. Many of the ecological risk factors for bad child outcomes have to do with family size, stressful lives, low-income and low-education families, and parental attitudes.

Prenatal Care Content to Meet Established Objectives

The USPHS Expert Panel (1989) defined "prenatal care" as health promotion, risk assessment, and intervention linked to the risks and conditions uncovered during risk assessment. Prenatal care is not like an immunization; care activities require the cooperative and coordinated efforts of the woman, her family, her prenatal care providers, and other specialized providers. Health promotion activities recommended by the panel for all mothers include counseling on avoidance of teratogens, safer sex, maternal seat belt use, and signs and symptoms of preterm labor.

The panel concluded that all pregnant women need general knowledge about the physiological and emotional changes of pregnancy; sexu-

ality during pregnancy; fetal growth and development; general health habits; promotion of breast feeding; infant car seat safety; preparation for childbirth and parenting; and family roles and adjustment. For selected persons, the prenatal care needs to include counseling to promote and support healthful behaviors such as good nutrition; smoking cessation; avoidance of alcohol, illicit drugs, and teratogens; and safer sex (USPHS Expert Panel, 1989, p. 45).

The Challenge Before Us: Barriers to Prenatal Care

A challenge not yet met is to provide all women with adequate prenatal care—adequate content, effectively timed. The Institute of Medicine Committee to Study Outreach for Prenatal Care (Brown, 1988) determined that in 1985 only 68.2% of all U.S. women obtained adequate prenatal care. It also found that of all U.S. infants in 1985, 76.2% were born to women who began prenatal care in the first trimester of pregnancy, 18.1% to women who delayed care until the second trimester, 4.0% to women who obtained care only in the third trimester, and 1.7% to mothers who had no prenatal care.

The barriers to the availability of prenatal care are many: poverty; inadequate capacity in the prenatal care system; problems in the organization, practices, and atmosphere of prenatal services; and cultural and personal factors that limit use. For some mothers, such psychological factors as fear, shame, and denial present even more of a bar to care than financial obstacles (Brown, 1988). For these women, the committee report suggested identifying the need for prenatal care through a wide variety of methods, including hotlines; community canvassing by outreach workers or other paraprofessional personnel; and cross-agency referrals, offering social support to encourage continuing prenatal care and services to smooth the transition into parenthood. School-based health clinics are innovations in primary care that have influenced both pregnancy rates and early prenatal care for teenagers.

Innovations in Prenatal Care

Placement of Clinics. School-based clinics, first established in St. Paul, Minnesota, in 1973, had the effect of decreasing pregnancy rates by 50% (Edwards, Steinman, Arnold, & Hakanson,

1980). Now many large cities support school-based clinics, which provide readily available, teen-accepted access to health care. These clinics not only promote family planning, but also support pregnant teens with medical care and training in parenting skills. In order to succeed, clinics must be accessible both geographically and psychologically. Many women delay enrollment in prenatal care because they are conflicted about keeping their pregnancies; until they decide, they hesitate to seek care. We must reach them early to offer family planning and abortion options. Prenatal care that speaks to the objectives proposed by the USPHS Expert Panel (1989) plan must be a national objective for universal/primary care during pregnancy.

Outreach to the Consumer. Many states are increasing their outreach to pregnant women at risk. As an example, the Washington State Plan for Nursing, a collaborative endeavor between the Office of Parent and Child Health of the Washington State Department of Health and the University of Washington School of Nursing, has developed a prenatal care protocol for nursing outreach home visits (Kang, Rolloloazo, Yoshihara, & Thibodeaux, 1989). The state's health districts are implementing these outreach contacts. The protocols outline six home visit contacts beginning as soon as pregnancy is confirmed, to support the initiation or continuance of medical care, to foster health-promoting behaviors, and to focus the mother on mastery of her parenting role. This nurse home visitor outreach is an example of primary/universal prevention moving into secondary/selected intervention for women at risk, such as teenage mothers, poor women, and women with a low motivation for healthful behavior (e.g., with habits of poor nutrition, smoking, or drug or alcohol use). The Washington State Plan for Nurses' Prenatal Protocols was adapted from the nursing care tested in a research project called Clinical Nursing Models (Barnard, Booth, Mitchell, & Telzrow, 1988), to be described later in this chapter.

Child Health Preventive Care

Physical health and emotional well-being are inseparable. In addition to good nutrition and a safe, healthy birth, children need the social and emotional contact that results from loving relationships with others. When children are emotionally supported by caring adults, their prospects for learning are wonderfully enhanced. A caring environment builds emotional maturity and social competence—keys to school readiness. Such an environment is also consequential to cognitive and language development (Boyer, 1991).

Because especially in early childhood physical and emotional health are so closely related, health professionals are frequently in the best position to detect early signs of a variety of troubles, sometimes going beyond those for which the family is seeking help. Health professionals are often more acceptable and less stigmatizing than other sources of support and guidance, especially when physical conditions signal a broader and more complex set of problems.

Content of Child Primary Health Care

The American Academy of Pediatrics Guidelines for Health Supervision establish the content of primary health care for children (Committee on Psychosocial Aspects of Child and Family Health, 1985–1988). The guidelines encourage contact with the parents during pregnancy to allow caregivers and parents to get acquainted, to help the parents feel comfortable about expressing concerns, and then to prepare them for the birth and early child care. During the first 12 months of life, well-child health supervision is recommended at 2–3 weeks of age, and again at 1, 2, 4, 8, 9, and 12 months; it is further recommended during the second year at 15, 18, and 24 months, and then yearly. During these visits physical health is monitored, including height, weight, head circumference, vision, hearing, hematocrit, and follow-up testing of any concerns or historical problems. Developmental and behavioral assessment is also recommended for each health supervision visit. Anticipatory guidance is a critical element of child health supervision. At each visit, developmentally appropriate anticipatory guidance is offered. For example, at 4 months prevention of injury is discussed for a child who will become increasingly mobile; at 6 months stranger anxiety and the infant's increasing interest in toys and games are stressed; and at 12 months injury prevention is again emphasized because of the child's growing ability to get to and get into dangerous situations. Anticipatory guidance also encourages communication and increasing independence.

Challenges in Primary Health Care for Children

The 1988 National Health Interview Survey on Child Health data indicated that 7% of all children under 1 year of age and 5% of 1- and 2-year-olds had no usual place for routine health care; furthermore, 22% of children under 1 year and 16% of 1- and 2-year-olds had no regular provider of sick care (Zill, Moore, Smith, Stief, & Coiro, 1991; Klerman, 1992). Although the majority of U.S. children have contact with primary health care resources, too many children and families do not have adequate child health supervision as defined by the American Academy of Pediatrics. There are many reasons why this universal health supervision is not available, ranging from poverty and inadequate health care facilities in rural and inner-city areas to a lack of incentive to take children for care when they are not sick. Other countries, especially European countries, seem to do a much more acceptable job of providing health care to children and families (Williams & Miller, 1991). Health care would be much more accessible if it was located in the neighborhood. Professor Edward Zigler (personal communication, Bush Center, Yale University, 1991) has proposed that neighborhood schools become the focus for such child services as health care and day care, including before- and after-school care. This plan would require a drastic redistribution of health care resources, but would potentially make access to care more of a reality, especially to low-income families.

Promoting Parenting through Social Relationships

Parenting Challenges

The developmental tasks of the infant and young child provide the context for parenting. During the first months of life, an infant is learning to regulate all body systems. He or she is learning how to process the environment—sights, sounds, textures, smells—as well as how to regulate reactions to the environment. Patterns of sleep and feeding are emerging, as are small, subtle responses to caregiving. Learning to become soothed when comforted is an important developmental milestone. The parent monitors the infant's behavior in response to caregiving. Learning what distinct cries mean, and determining what or how the baby will respond to changes in caregiving routines, are important lessons for the parent (Sander, 1962; Greenspan & Lourie, 1981).

Parents' tasks, during these early months, are to recognize and respond to the cues the baby gives. Knowing the pattern of nonverbal communication cues, sleep–wake organization, the way babies interact with their environment, and the meaning of crying are all important in the first months of life. Physical contact with the baby, such as carrying the baby in a soft infant carrier, promotes immediate responses to the infant's changes in activity. Crying behavior is therefore reduced, and the infant's need for responsive caregiving is addressed.

At about 3–4 months, the baby becomes a very social creature. A social smile is predictable for any adult who acts playful. Games of peek-a-boo and patty-cake show off the baby's human qualities. Babies at this age are learning the give and take of communication. They can provide tremendous positive feedback to their parents by way of long, intent gazing and wide, full-face smiles. Infants need a lot of face-to-face interaction, social games, and talking to. A baby can become the main family entertainment. The adult caregiver is the mediator of the child's environment; without locomotion or efficient hand function, the baby only has contact with what the parent or caregiver facilitates.

At about 7–8 months of age, the infant will start becoming more demanding and want to do things like feeding himself or herself. The baby will also begin pointing with a finger to indicate what he or she wants. Soon the marvelous bursts of language and locomotion will transform the child's world. All during these early months the child has been developing a sense of trust in the environment. The parent has responded first to basic needs of being fed when hungry, comforted when distressed, having fun when ready for exploring the world. With a sense of security the child is ready to explore, to move on all fours and soon to attempt bipedal locomotion, and to use words and phrases to enlarge his or her world. With the ability to communicate and locomote, the child's world expands, and he or she is more involved with eliciting responses from caregivers. After walking begins, parenting improves, even for children in the most high-risk social environment (Barnard et al., 1985).

Primary/Universal Interventions to Promote Parent–Child Relationships

Universal interventions need to start early in order to have the most cost-effective benefits. It is easiest to influence infant–parent/caregiver relationships during the first 3 months of life—a time when the infant is making pronounced biobehavioral changes. One universal approach to a preventive intervention model of effective social partnerships would be to ensure the physical proximity of babies to their caregivers. Several approaches have been used experimentally and have good potential for wider use.

After birth, the ideal course of care would be rooming-in. Although it may not particularly affect high-risk dyads, rooming-in may have a mild facilitating effect for low-risk dyads and does not do harm (O'Connor et al., 1982).

After discharge, every mother should be provided with a soft infant carrier and asked to "wear" the infant for several hours each day. The evidence suggests that the close contact that occurs while the infant carrier is in use ultimately affects the quality of infant–mother relationship. Compared to a control group, more infants whose mothers were given soft infant carriers were securely attached at 1 year in a sample of poor and less well-educated mothers (Anisfeld, Casper, Nozyce, & Cunningham, 1990). We believe this result was achieved not only because proximity and contact were promoted, but also because proximity and contact fostered early communication. The mother could learn to read and respond to her child's cues in the first few months, because she had more opportunity to observe them closely and to experience the results of her responses. Thus, early positive transactions would have had a long-term positive developmental effect.

Parent–Child Communication: A Focus for Universal Intervention

All parents need to learn how to communicate with their new babies. They need to understand the behavioral organization of the infants in regard to sleep and feeding patterns and the infants' capacity to respond. They also need to learn how to read nonverbal communication. Since most births occur in hospitals, parents could be alerted there about what to expect in an infant's behavior in the areas of sleeping, crying/fussiness, nonverbal communication skills, and behavioral organization.

Many studies with full-term and preterm infants suggest that parents who can understand their infants' ways of organizing and communicating are much more likely to enjoy parenting and to respond to the infants in a sensitive and growth-fostering manner. Simple questions to parents about when they think babies hear, see, and are ready to learn reveal that when parents believe babies can engage in the environment, their behavior toward their infants becomes more responsive and growth-enhancing (Snyder, Eyres, & Barnard, 1979).

Instructional materials, called Keys to CaregivinG, have been developed to enhance parents' communication skills; these materials include a set of instructional pamphlets for parents and video modules for health care professionals, particularly nurses (Spietz, Johnson-Crowley, Sumner, & Barnard, 1990). The topics covered include infant state, infant behaviors, infant cues, state modulation, and the feeding interaction. We believe that an important step toward getting the parent–child relationship off to a good start would be for all 4500 hospitals in the United States that deliver newborns to provide parents with exposure to the concepts outlined in Keys to CaregivinG.

Keys to CaregivinG describes the nonverbal behavior of infants, which has positive or negative communication value in terms of social interaction. We have called these cues "engaging" and "disengaging." Engaging cues communicate the need or desire to interact; some familiar engaging cues are smiling at, looking at, and reaching out to another. Disengaging cues signal the need or desire for a break in the interaction; these include crying, turning the head away, and falling asleep. There is often a clustering of these cues to signal hunger (e.g., fussiness, mouthing, clenched fingers and fists over chest and stomach, hand to mouth, sucking movements/sounds, turning to caregiver, flexed arms and legs) or to show satiation or fullness (e.g., falling asleep, extension of arms and legs, decreased sucking, arms straightened along sides). Understanding the language of the newborn is a universal intervention goal that could be implemented. Such understanding would be a great step toward making early caregiving easier for all parents.

Loan (1992) has recently reported that, when the content of Keys to CaregivinG was taught to both nursing staff and new mothers, not only did nurses' knowledge about infants significantly increase; more importantly, the experimental mothers reported that they had received more information while hospitalized. These mothers also showed better parent–infant interaction when measured with the Nursing Child Assessment Satellite Training (NCAST) Feeding Scale (for more discussion of this instrument, see below).

SECONDARY/SELECTED INTERVENTIONS

At the level of secondary or selected interventions, a body of research on interventions with risk groups is directed at reducing risk and/or promoting protective factors. This body of research deals with the risks of infants born prematurely, to adolescent parents, and to parents of low-socioeconomic status. A more limited group of studies focuses on prevention in the instance of child abuse and neglect.

Risk Factors

In spite of the potential to have healthy infants and families, it is estimated that when all the risk factors are added up, 30–50% of newborns are at risk. Parents' emotional distress and lack of interpersonal, educational, and financial resources constitute potent risk factors for their children's intellectual delay, school failure, and psychopathology (Sameroff & Seifer, 1983; Rutter, 1985; Cohen & Beckwith, 1979; Morisset, Barnard, Greenberg, Booth, & Spieker, 1990; Sameroff & Emde, 1990).

In the United States, one-fourth of all children under 6 years of age are growing up in families that cannot afford safe housing, good nutrition, or high-quality health care (Boyer, 1991). Preventive interventions must focus on the fact that mothers and infants in high-social-risk environments experience poverty, inadequate housing, poor health care, and dangerous neighborhoods. These stresses diminish the physical and emotional resources parents need to care appropriately for their infants. In order to survive, the parents must often divert attention to these issues and cannot give the infants the care that they would otherwise be capable of providing.

Infant biological factors such as preterm birth, low birthweight for age, prenatal alcohol or drug exposure, and hypoxia constitute potent risk factors for children's intellectual delay, school failure, and psychopathology (Rutter, 1985; Howard, Beckwith, Rodning, & Kropenske, 1989; Infant Health and Development Program, 1990; Chasnoff, 1991). Selected interventions are needed whenever the basic biological evolution does not have the opportunity to unfold. Papousek and Papousek (1992) sketch four clinical forms that are frequently noted:

1. Missed experiences in initial communication. These include early separation because of premature birth or prenatal complications, as well as adoption of an older baby.
2. Initial discouragement because of infant handicaps. Deviant feedback from the baby may inhibit the emergence of the parent's intuitive behaviors; then, when the infant is capable of being a more responsive social partner, the parents are less effective or have given up.
3. Mismatch between parental and infantile predispositions. Parents may "misread" the fragile status of an infant and fail to provide the level of interactive behavior that is actually needed.
4. Major prolongation in the need for preverbal forms of communication. Retarded children have difficulty acquiring language in the first 3 years of life, when their baby features elicit the type of talk interaction that is most supportive of this development. Slowed, simple language must continue far beyond the time when their baby features no longer exist to elicit it.

Another risk factor is less easily identified: an adult's "working model" of relationships that inhibits the emergence of intuitive parenting. It is our belief that intuitive parenting cannot be taught, but that its elements are absorbed during one's own infancy and childhood. Deprivation and abuse during the early years can affect a parent's working model to the extent that he or she is not able to perceive and act on infant cues in the spontaneous, intuitive way that Papousek and Papousek (1992) describe. In this case, opportunities for stress-free interactions with the infant are not sufficient; therapeutic intervention to alter working models is required. Parents who are likely to have difficulty with the caregiver stage of infancy are individuals who have not been well nurtured themselves. Some of the indicators are lack of high school completion, insufficient income, being under 19 years of age, alcohol or drug use, mental retardation, mental illness (e.g., depression), and lack of support networks. Another predictor of parenting difficulty is the presence of a number of difficult life circumstances, such as trouble with the law, outstanding loans, frequent moving, family arguments, illness in the family, drug or alcohol use in household members, and abusive relationships, to name a few (Tableman & Katzenmeyer, 1985; Barnard, 1989; Mercer, 1990).

It seems obvious that parents whose circumstances are less than ideal need parenting support even more; yet services that exist are not as readily used by women who are unmarried, adolescents, substance abusers, and/or depressed, or who lack resources in general. Prevention strategies must include outreach workers, such as public health nurses, school nurses, teachers, social workers, midwives, and drug counselors. Many in contemporary society have not had the opportunity to learn the parenting role in their own families, since most parents are from families with few children or with the children born close together. Few new parents have observed the parenting of human infants on a daily basis within their families.

Characteristics of Interventions

Interventions differ in a variety of ways. One characteristic is whether the intervention is home- or center-based; another is the training of the intervenor, professional, paraprofessional, or nonprofessional. Timing and duration of the intervention also differ. These many types of interventions are combined with variations in focus and content. All these differences make it difficult to compare interventions. Several recent reviews of interventions (Schorr & Schorr, 1988; Olds & Kitzman, 1990; U.S. General Accounting Office, 1990; Schorr & Both, 1991; Schorr, Both, & Copple, 1991; Infant Health and Development Program, 1990) offer evidence that most early interventions show some positive effect on the parent and/or child; however, most studies have insufficient sample sizes, inadequate design considerations, and too limited follow-up to offer a basis for generalization.

Olds and Kitzman (1990, p. 114) conclude that "efforts to isolate the most important ingredients of successful intervention programs are misdirected, as each appears to play a synergistic role in strengthening the entire program." The authors suggest that prenatal postpartum home visit interventions with the greatest success had three characteristics: (1) an ecological model, wherein systems of material, social, behavioral, and psychological factors interact; (2) nurse home visitors who established a therapeutic alliance with families and who visited frequently and long enough to address the systems of factors directed at outcomes; and (3) the targeting of families at greater risk of mother and child health problems because of their lack of personal and social resources. Patterson and Barnard (1990) concluded from a review of intervention studies with preterm infants and their families that programs including efforts with parents, as opposed to just stimulation of infants, had more positive outcomes. It is impossible at the present time to know how the many factors interrelate or how they ultimately influence infant social and cognitive competence.

Preventive Interventions Focusing on Parent-Child Communication

To advance the field of preventive interventions with high-risk infants and families, we need to understand more fully the mechanisms of problematic development within the context of both the risk and protective factors. At the University of Washington, a group of researchers and clinicians have had the opportunity to work together over several decades and in a number of methodological and intervention studies. We have experienced the complexity of developing children within the context of their unique environments, and we have had the opportunity to try to support and enhance parenting for children at biological risk, environmental risk, or a combination of the two.

We have come to view the process of parent-child interaction, which forms the child's communication environment, as an important window for understanding the process of development and embodying mechanisms for risk as well as protection of the developmental course. We have designed observational scales to evaluate interactions of young children and their parents. The NCAST Feeding and Teaching Scales are used to evaluate the present level of dyadic interaction (Barnard et al., 1989). The resulting scores for the mothers correlate with language-facilitating behavior as scored from actual transcripts of the mothers' interactions with their children. The Feeding and Teaching combined total scores at 1 year correlate ($r = .50$, $p < .01$) with child IQ scores at 5 years (Morisset, 1990).

Theoretical Basis for Emphasizing Social Partnerships for Preventive Interventions

Language and Attachment. The development of language is one of the most impressive accomplishments of early childhood. How such a complex process can occur in a toddler, whose abstract thinking is in many ways very limited, remains a puzzle to developmental researchers. Current theories of language acquisition consider both innate ability and verbal experience to be of the utmost importance for language learning (Newport, Gleitman, & Gleitman, 1977; Hoff-Ginsberg & Shatz, 1982). Previous notions of the human infant as a blank slate, whose development is dependent solely on accumulated learning experiences, have long been abandoned. The remarkable speed and manner in which children master the language of their community leaves little doubt that infants are ready for social interaction from birth (Trevarthen, 1977; Newson, 1977). There is now ample evidence that even very young babies possess an impressive array of perceptual capabilities and behavior patterns, which function to insure the proximity of their caretakers (Ainsworth, Behar, Water, & Wall, 1978; Bowlby, 1969; Schaffer, 1977) and to insure opportunities for communication (Bell, 1973).

Studies of neonatal capabilities reveal an elegant interface between the structural and functional capacities of the newborn and early social experience. For example, within moments after birth, infants demonstrate auditory and visual sensitivity to the stimuli of human interaction. They are perceptually attuned to the range of sounds in the human voice (Eisenberg, 1969), and can discriminate speech sounds on the basis of voicing (e.g., "p" vs. "b"; Eimas, Siqueland, Jusczyk, & Vigorito, 1971) as well as place of articulation (e.g., "d" vs. "t"; Trehub & Rabinovitch, 1972).

Studies demonstrate that infant behavior is organized into patterns of inherent rhythm (Sameroff, 1967). The flow of early dyadic interactions seems to depend largely on mothers' ability to insert themselves into these rhythms. For example, in a study of mothers and infants during feeding, Kaye (1977) showed that mothers tended to interact in precise synchrony with the burst–pause pattern of their infants' sucking. He reported that during bursts of activity, mothers were generally quiet and inactive; during pauses they jiggled, stroked, and talked to the babies, thus taking "turns" as the principal agent in the interaction. This temporal integration of mother and baby has been regarded as a prototype for a great deal of early interaction, and illustrates how, in many ways, the rhythms of even very early exchanges resemble conversational dialogue (Bateson, 1975; Schaffer, 1979).

The match between temporal patterns of preverbal interaction and elements of mature conversation is a common tenet of theories that propose continuity between preverbal interaction and speech. Efforts to identify prelinguistic clues to language acquisition differ, however, in the degree to which affect or cognitive factors are thought to influence infants' early communicative experiences. Theorists who emphasize cognitive factors in the transition from preverbal to verbal states (e.g., Bates, Camaioni, & Volterra, 1975; Bruner, 1975a, 1975b) argue that cognitive achievements, fostered by social and nonsocial experiences alike, lead directly to early word knowledge. In contrast, others (e.g., Thoman, 1981; Eveloff, 1971) claim that communication need not await cognitive competencies. Rather, they suggest that precursors to linguistic expression can be found in the affective forms of communication between mothers and infants.

Thoman (1981) takes an adamant stand for an affect-driven explanation of emerging language. Her argument—that language evolves from social–affective aspects of prelinguistic interaction—rests largely on the assumption that propositional and affective components of language are conceptually and functionally distinct (e.g., Monrad-Krohn, 1947). She speculates that these two constituents of speech develop at different times and at different rates. She cites perceptual (e.g., Stechler & Carpenter, 1967) and neurological evidence to indicate the developmental precedence of a nonpropositional, sensory–affective communication system. Her support includes the work of Lamdella (1977), who speculates that cortical and subcortical structures of the limbic system, instrumental in the regulation of emotion, may also regulate aspects of social and communicative behavior in human and nonhuman primates. Following this reasoning, Thoman claims that human speech could have evolved from a more primitive communication system—one that is primarily affective in nature.

Thoman's assertions are based on her observation that mothers and infants exhibit a wide range of expressive, affective behaviors, even in their earliest interactions. In her view this behavior constitutes communication (albeit unintentional), at least on the infants' part, and functions as an affect-based feedback system to produce a "coupling" of mother and infant behaviors. She proposes affect sharing as the socioemotional process by which mother and infant adapt to each other in the first weeks of life. Thus, the earliest communicative behaviors are those expressions of affect. More ritualized forms of communication are also assumed to serve this same function.

It appears that the quantity and quality of parents' verbal input are highly related. Several studies have shown that mothers who vocalize more are more apt to provide semantically contingent speech (such as the use of expansions and interrogatives), and are more likely to use a lower proportion of imperatives, which function to cut off the children's speaking turn (Olson, Bates, & Bayles, 1984; Barnes, Gutfreund, Satterly, & Wells, 1983; Adams & Ramey, 1980). Extensive longitudinal studies also indicate a strong and enduring relationship between positive linguistic experiences and later child competence (Farran & Ramey, 1980). For example, Clarke-Stewart, VanderStoep, and Killian (1979) reported that in each of five different samples, stimulating and responsive maternal input was predictive of several child outcome measures, including cognition (IQ), language (mean length of utterance [MLU]), and positive interaction with mother. In addition, Wells's (1980) longitudinal study of children from 15 to 60 months revealed that parents' semantically contingent feedback was highly predictive of children's rate of syntactic development. Finally, Elarado and colleagues (Elarado, Bradley, & Caldwell, 1975, 1977; Bradley & Caldwell, 1976) reported that mothers' verbal responsiveness, as measured by the Home Observation for Measurement of the Environment scale, was consistently related to children's performance on standard measures of cognitive and psycholinguistic ability from 6 to 54 months of age.

In contrast to a parental style that facilitates language learning, highly controlling and directive parental input has been shown to have a negative impact on language development (Nelson, 1973; Cross, 1984; Snow, Midkiff-Borunda, Small, & Proctor, 1984). Mothers' functional intent has been shown to differ systematically from a concern with directing the children's behavior to eliciting conversation (McDonald & Pien, 1982). Olsen-Fulero (1982) found individual differences in mothers' controlling versus language-eliciting behavior to be relatively stable, and speculates that maternal style may differentially affect children's language development.

The Interpersonal Context (Internal Representations). Parent–infant interaction and infant attachment influence a child's developmental course. Secure attachment can modify the influence of a high-risk environment on the child's intellectual outcome, language skill, and school performance (Ramey, Farran, & Campbell, 1978; Stroufe, 1983; Greenberg, Cicchetti, & Cummings, 1990; Barnard et al., 1989; Morisset et al., 1990). In contrast, when a mother's mental representation of her infant and herself and of their relationship is insecure (not balanced; Zeanah & Barton, 1989), then the dyad is at risk precisely because the mother's representations are insecure and she recreates that pattern with her own infant. She recreates this insecurity by a complex interaction of emotional and cognitive evaluations and behavioral responses to her infant.

Basically secure mothers in social risk environments need transitional supportive interventions first, and specific skill training next, in a context that acknowledges and builds on their considerable strengths in buffering their infants from greater risk environments. Opportunities for education and employment; high-quality child care; and supportive interaction with partners, peers, and mentors would probably be enough for women with secure attachment models to parent well. It is important to remember that many studies have found that roughly half the women in high-social-risk samples are able to foster a secure attachment relationship with their infants (Spieker & Booth, 1988). This group of mothers, however, has more unstable attachments in the second year of life (Vaughn, Egeland, Waters, & Sroufe, 1979), suggesting that even secure mothers' parenting is vulnerable to the stress associated with social risk.

It is important to remember that a secure, freely autonomous working model does not inoculate one against unhappiness, misfortune, loss, and other vagaries of life. Thus, secure women who are young, have less education, have low incomes, and are isolated benefit from supportive interventions to enhance the cognitive and social outcomes of their children. Similarly, secure mothers in low-social-risk environments with biologically at-risk infants need training in dealing with the specific needs of their infants.

Insecure mothers from more privileged backgrounds may raise children who cope well in the world despite the less secure relationship with their mothers. Insecure infants in these circumstances are usually enabled to grow into individuals whose talents and abilities flower because of the supportive developmental context their families are able to provide. Psychotherapeutic intervention with these dyads may contribute to perceived happiness, but not necessarily to tangible success in terms of functioning in society. Nevertheless, some proportion of these more privileged, insecure infants are also at risk for behavioral problems, and for these families also, the critical component contributing to maladaptive outcomes seems to be family stress (Lewis, Feiring, McGuffog, & Jaskir, 1984). Insecure dyads at social risk ought to be considered at "double risk." Interventions designed at the level of providing support and imparting skills may not "take" sufficiently to effect a change unless attachment issues are addressed as part of the intervention strategy (see Lieberman & Pawl, Chapter 28, this volume).

Exemplars of Secondary Interventions Focusing on Social Relationships with Mothers and Infants

Two interventions we have implemented with at-risk samples are discussed here. The first is the Clinical Nursing Models project (Barnard et al., 1987), which evolved from our prior work (Barnard, Booth, et al., 1988). The second is Nursing Systems Toward Effective Parenting— Premature (NSTEP-P). In both of these intervention programs, a major objective was to influence the parent–child relationship through social interaction and communication. This specific goal related to our general goal of testing preventive intervention within existing community ser-vices (specifically, public health nursing services), to see whether these "real-life" practice settings with specific intervention foci could be effective in lowering the incidence of children from high-risk families with subsequent cognitive and social deficits. Preschool and early school cognitive and social deficits are antecedents for later behavioral disorders (e.g., Patterson, 1982).

The Clinical Nursing Models Project. Prior research (Barnard, Booth et al., 1988) with an intervention focused on providing high-risk families with nursing services during the first 3 months after birth found that 3 months of intervention, averaging 11 hours of nurse home visiting, was not effective with the families who had multiple social problems. Likewise, we found that certain mothers were hesitant to get involved in the intervention process. As we further analyzed the characteristics of these mothers, we found that the women who did not take easily to the nurse intervention were those with few friends, little support, and many problems in their lives. This finding prompted us to conceptualize an intervention that would help us reach the mothers we hypothesized lacked the social skills to make and maintain social relationships.

The intervention we developed and tested was called the Mental Health Model (Barnard et al., 1987). The primary focus of the intervention was on a mother's social skills and relationships with other individuals in her life. We theorized that an individual's capacity to parent a child is based in part on the person's capacity to have satisfying relationships with other adults, since within the adult–adult relationship comes the support necessary to maintain the demanding role of parenting a child. Likewise, we theorized that a parent's capacity to relate to a child is dependent on that parent's life history of previous attachments and interactions.

In addition to the primary intervention focus on social behaviors and relationships of a new mother, we determined that the ideal time to begin the preventive intervention was prior to the birth of the child; therefore, the intervention began in the second trimester of pregnancy and continued until the child's first birthday. We ended the intervention at 1 year primarily for pragmatic reasons of funding; ideally, the intervention would have continued until the child's capabilities of locomotion and language were well established.

What, then, was the specific nature of the Mental Health Model? The nurses providing the intervention had master's-level preparation in parent–child nursing. The four individuals involved developed the intervention objectives and provided ongoing consultation to one another about the implementation of the intervention. A caseload of 25 active families was considered full-time. The nurses were free to set their own context (home, clinic, or elsewhere), schedule, and focus within the framework of objectives for the intervention.

During pregnancy, the major goals of the Mental Health Model were to (1) increase the support of each mother's network; (2) foster decision making about delivery options; (3) deal successfully with situational anxieties and needs; (4) increase the mother's self-image and confidence in parenting; and (5) enhance mother–infant attachment. For each objective there were behavioral outcome criteria. For example, in relation to the goal of enhancing the mother–infant attachment, a nurse assessed maternal–fetal attachment by having the mother complete an inventory and discussing her feelings and preparation for the baby. The nurse helped the mother identify and feel fetal body parts; encouraged the mother to practice communicating with the fetus through massage and talking, and to record fetal movements; and encouraged discussion about parenting values, beliefs, and expectations.

During the intrapartum period, there were three major objectives: (1) insuring the mother's affiliating support; (2) enhancing mother–infant acquaintance; and (3) promoting an environment that enhanced self-regulatory behaviors of the mother and infant. Again, each objective involved behavioral criteria that were monitored by the nurse assigned to the mother. The majority of mothers, for instance, had a support person who would be with them during labor and delivery; in some cases this was the nurse. During the immediate postbirth period (newborn through 3 months), the objectives included maintaining a focus on the mother's support system and were expanded to consider mothering and the baby's adjustment. There was considerable focus on enhancing the mother–infant interaction. The specific behavioral criteria for this objective included developing the mother's awareness of infant cues, as well as encouraging the mother to vocalize to the infant, respond contingently, provide appropriate stimulation, and have appropriate expectations about the infant's capacity to see, hear, show awareness, and learn from the environment.

During the remainder of the first year, the objectives were to (1) maximize the mother's affective involvement with the infant; (2) provide the infant with a variety of stimulation and temporal organization; (3) increase the mother's understanding of reciprocal interaction; (4)

insure the mother's realistic developmental expectations for the child; (5) strengthen the mother's network; (6) increase the sense of trust in mother and child; (7) promote a safe environment; and (8) avoid restrictive caregiving.

The nurses utilized Brammer's "helping relationship" principles (Brammer, 1973) in their work with the mothers; in other words, they viewed their role as working within the framework of the help the mothers wanted. The mothers met 72% of the behavioral criteria established for the intervention objectives, and 80% of the clients stayed in the intervention until their children's first birthday. Although the mothers' psychiatric status was not formally assessed, the nurses reported that many of the women (at least one-third) had significant impairment; one common problem was depression. The nurses were not acting as therapists, and tried to be aware of the psychopathology but not to deal with it in any clinically therapeutic manner. Overall, however, their alliance with the clients could be described as "therapeutic."

The control group for this study was a comparison group receiving nursing follow-up that was typical of public health nursing in the United States during the early 1980s. The nurses providing care for this group were employed by the Seattle–King County Health Department. The model was labeled the Information/Resources Model, to identify that a major objective of public health nurses in serving clients during pregnancy and early parenting is to provide the clients with information and to make them aware of community resources. For this project we developed nurse and client behavioral criteria in keeping with the health department practices of that time. The major differences in the two models were the Mental Health Model's focus on the helping relationship and its emphasis on the mother's social competence with others, including the infant.

Fewer of the mothers in the Information/Resources Model group (53% vs. 80%) completed the intervention. In the Mental Health Model group, there was more client contact; the nurses did more problem-related intervention in contrast to monitoring and referral; and the mothers rated the intervention more positively. The outcomes supported the Mental Health Model's effectiveness in enhancing the mothers' social competencies and interaction with their children (Barnard, Magyary, et al., 1988; Booth, Barnard, Mitchell, & Spieker, 1987).

Preterm Infants: Intervention to Improve Their Capacity to Be Social Partners. A second intervention we designed and tested, the NSTEP-P, was directed at parents with preterm infants. Preterm infants are at higher risk for developmental disabilities than are full-term infants. An early difficulty is the poor quality of parent–child interaction. Three factors are thought to relate to this problem. First, preterm infants are generally more unresponsive and/or irritable; second, parents lack the knowledge to compensate for the infants' lack of organization and responsiveness; and third, some parents lack the resources or are too overwhelmed by the preterm birth to pay close attention to their infants' developmental needs. We designed a specific intervention in which we taught parents about infant state, infant behavior, and infant cues, and then demonstrated how to facilitate the infants' transitions from sleep to wakefulness for feedings and/or interactions. Specifically, parents were taught about infant sleep–wake states of consciousness and the meaning of nonverbal cues. They were taught to alert the infants prior to feeding and to soothe them after feeding. Parents learned the state modulation methods just prior to the infants' discharge and were encouraged to use it at the time of feeding their infants.

Through a series of studies (Barnard et al., 1987; Kang, Barnard, Hammond, & Oshio, 1991; Page, 1992), we have found that when a mother knows the principles of state modulation (variety to alert and repetition to soothe), she engages in more appropriate state modulation during the feeding, the infant accomplishes the feeding more efficiently, and the parent–child interaction is more reciprocal and growth-fostering. In a three-site demonstration of the NSTEP-P intervention, we tested the state modulation component with both a high-education group of mothers and a low-education group. For the high-education mothers, the 90-minute intervention about state modulation given at the time of infant discharge seemed to be enough to set them in the right trajectory. For low-education mothers, a longer-term intervention was necessary to maintain the early positive results. A 6-month, nine-contact follow-up was needed to re-emphasize state modulation and to add foci on parent–child interaction, health and nutrition, stimulation, and support from family and community resources (Kang et al., 1991).

This particular research has made us mindful of the need to learn more about mechanisms associated with bad outcomes. In some cases it is possible to identify the "lack of fit," the "missing link," or the etiology of the problem. Preterm infants have a reduced capacity to be social partners in the early months of life. If we can help parents learn techniques to help infants become more alert and hence to increase their capacity for social interaction, we will have gone a long way in preventive intervention.

CONCLUSIONS

Primary/universal and secondary/selected preventive interventions that match the developmental needs of a child, from the fetus to the toddler, have been discussed in relation to the strategies for providing programs and interventions depending on the risk factors. A straightforward appeal has been made to reduce the number of children at risk by preventing unintended and unwanted pregnancies, which account for approximately 40% of all births. Prenatal care needs to be universally available and started early; care should include the psychological aspects of pregnancy, family relationships, and maternal role development. In addition, all parents need access to child health care that incorporates health and developmental monitoring of the children with assessment and support of the caregivers.

In this chapter we have emphasized the social relationship between parents and children. Encouraging close physical proximity of mothers to their infants is desirable. Helping parents understand the ways and language of infants is a universal responsibility of all health care providers in hospitals, doctors' offices, and community nursing and community education facilities, including television programming.

When a parent or infant is at risk, the need for selected interventions is evident. We have suggested that these interventions deal with the social relationship in the parent–child dyad. Although we have focused on social interactions and relationships, there are many additional aspects to consider. The physical context of families needs to provide a safe environment for parents and children. Children need the unhurried time of parents or other caregivers, as well as responsive caregiving (Zero to Three, National Center for Clinical Infant Programs, 1992). Parents at risk require attention and support from care providers, as well as instruction on specific ways to meet the need of their developing children.

Papousek and Papousek (1992) propose that adults of our species are biologically programmed to provide infants with the intuitive interventions and interactive support that the infants need to make the rapid progress in thought and communication that they do. Parents—indeed, all adults—are the perfect didactic interactive partners for infants because their behavior is a product of coevolution. However, interference can come from many sources, too much rational guidance not the least of them (Bastick, 1982). We cannot teach parents the basics of intuitive parenting; we can only support it. What are needed are sociocultural supports for parenting, "and, particularly, a relaxed, stress-free state of mind" (Papousek & Papousek, 1992, p. 51).

ACKNOWLEDGMENT

The authors acknowledge the support of the John D. and Catherine T. MacArthur Network on the Transition to Early Childhood for providing the intellectual stimulation and the financial means for the authors to explore the issue of risk and prevention during the 1980's.

REFERENCES

Adams, J. L., & Ramey, C. T. (1980). Structural aspects of maternal speech to infants reared in poverty. *Child Development, 51,* 1280–1284.

Ainsworth, M. D. S., Behar, M. C., Waters, E., & Wall, S. (1978). *Patterns of attachment: A psychological study of the Strange Situation.* Hillsdale, NJ: Erlbaum.

Anisfeld, E., Casper, V., Nozyce, M., & Cunningham, N. (1990). Does infant carrying promote attachment? An experimental study of the effects of increased physical contact on the development of attachment. *Child Development, 61,* 1617–1627.

Barnard, K. E. (1989). *Difficult life circumstances manual.* Seattle: NCAST, University of Washington School of Nursing.

Barnard, K. E., Booth, C. L., Mitchell, S. K., & Telzrow, R. W. (1988). Newborn nursing models: A test of early intervention to high-risk infants and families. In E. Hibbs (Ed.), *Children and families: Studies in prevention and intervention.* Madison, CT: International Universities Press.

Barnard, K. E., Hammond, M., Booth, C. L., Bee, H. L., Mitchell, S. K., & Spieker, S. J. (1989). Measurement and meaning of parent–child interaction. In F. J. Morrison, C. E. Lord, & D. P. Keating (Eds.), *Applied developmental psychology* (Vol. 3). New York: Academic Press.

Barnard, K. E., Hammond, M., Mitchell, S. K., Booth, C. L., Spietz, A., Snyder, C., & Elsas, T. (1985). Caring for high-risk infants and their families. In

M. Green (Ed.), *The psychological aspects of the family.* Lexington, MA: Lexington Books.

Barnard, K. E., Hammond, M. A., Sumner, G. A., Kang, R., Johnson-Crowley, N., Snyder, C., Spietz, A., Blackburn, S., Brandt, P., & Magyary, D. (1987). Helping parents with preterm infants: Field test of a protocol. *Early Child Development and Care, 27*(2) 256–290.

Barnard, K. E., Magyary, D., Sumner, G. A., Booth, C. L., Mitchell, S. K., & Spieker, S. (1988). Prevention of parenting alterations for women with low social support. *Psychiatry, 51*(3), 248–253.

Barnes, S., Gutfreund, M., Satterly, D., & Wells, G. (1983). Characteristics of adult speech which predict children's language development. *Journal of Child Language, 10,* 65–84.

Bastick, T. (1982). *Intuition: How we think and act.* New York: Wiley.

Bates, E., Camaioni, L., & Volterra, V. (1975). The acquisition of performatives prior to speech. *Merrill–Palmer Quarterly, 21,* 205–226.

Bateson, M. C. (1975). Mother–infant exchanges: The epigenesis of conversational interaction. *Annals of the New York Academy of Sciences, 263,* 101–113.

Bell, R. Q. (1973). Contributions of human infants to caregiving and social interaction. In M. Lewis & L. A. Rosenblum (Eds.), *The origins of behavior: Vol. 1. The effect of the infant on its caregiver.* New York: Wiley.

Bowlby, J. (1969). *Attachment and loss: Vol. 1. Attachment.* New York: Basic Books.

Booth, C. L., Barnard, K. E., Mitchell, S. K., & Spieker, S. J. (1987). Successful intervention with multi-problem mothers: Effects on mother–infant relationship. *Infant Mental Health Journal, 9,* 288–306.

Boyer, L. E. (1991). *Ready to learn: A mandate for the nation.* Princeton, NJ: Carnegie Foundation for the Advancement of Teaching.

Bradley, R. H., & Caldwell, B. M. (1976). The relation of infants' home environments to mental test performance at fifty-four months: A follow-up study. *Child Development, 47,* 1172–1174.

Brammer, L. M. (1973). *The helping relationship.* Englewood Cliffs, NJ: Prentice-Hall.

Brown, S. S. (Ed.). (1988). *Prenatal care: Reaching mothers, reaching infants.* Washington, DC: Institute of Medicine, National Academy Press.

Bruner, J. S. (1975a). From communication to language—A psychological perspective. *Cognition, 3*(3), 255–287.

Bruner, J. S. (1975b). The ontogenesis of speech acts. *Journal of Child Language, 2,* 1–19.

Center for the Study of Social Policy. (1992). *Kids count data book: State profiles of child well-being.* Greenwich, CT: Annie E. Casey Foundation.

Chasnoff, I. J. (1991). *The perinatal influences of cocaine in the term newborn infant: A current look* (Report of the 100th Ross Conference on Pediatric Research). Columbus, OH: Ross Laboratories.

Chasnoff, I. J., Landress, H. J., & Barrett, M. E. (1990). The prevalence of illicit drug or alcohol use during pregnancy and discrepancies in mandatory reporting in Pinellas County, Florida. *New England Journal of Medicine, 322*(17), 1202–1206.

Clarke-Stewart, K. A., VanderStoep, L. P., & Killian, G. A. (1979). Analysis and replication of mother–child relations at two years of age. *Child Development, 50,* 777–793.

Cohen, S., & Beckwith, L. (1979). Preterm infant interaction with the caregiver in the first year of life and competence at age two. *Child Development, 50,* 767–776.

Committee on Psychosocial Aspects of Child and Family Health. (1985–1988). *Guidelines for health supervision II.* Elk Grove Village, IL: American Academy of Pediatrics.

Cross, T. G. (1984, September). Habilitating the language-impaired child: Ideas from studies of parent–child interaction. *Topics in Language Disorders,* pp. 1–13.

Edwards, L. E., Steinman, M. E., Arnold, K., & Hakanson, E. Y. (1980). Adolescent pregnancy prevention services in high school clinics. *Family Planning Perspectives, 12*(1), 6–14.

Eimas, P. D., Siqueland, E. R., Jusczyk, P., & Vigorito, J. (1971). Speech perception in infants. *Science, 171,* 303–306.

Eisenberg, R. B. (1969). Auditory behavior in the human neonate: Functional properties of sound and their ontogenetic implications. *International Audiology, 8*(1), 34–45.

Elarado, R., Bradley, R., & Caldwell, B. M. (1975). The relation of infants' home environments to mental test performance from six to thirty-six months: A longitudinal analysis. *Child Development, 46,* 71–76.

Elarado, R., Bradley, R., & Caldwell, B. M. (1977). A longitudinal study of the relation of infants' home environments to language development at age three. *Child Development, 48,* 595–603.

Eveloff, H. H. (1971). Some cognitive and affective aspects of early language development. *Child Development, 42,* 1895–1907.

Farran, D., & Ramey, C. (1980). Social class differences in dyadic involvement during infancy. *Child Development, 51,* 254–257.

Gordon, R. (1983). An operational definition of prevention. *Public Health Reports, 98,* 107–109.

Greenberg, M. T., Cicchetti, D., & Cummings, E. M. (Eds.). (1990). *Attachment in the preschool years.* Chicago: University of Chicago Press.

Greenspan, S., & Lourie, R. S. (1981). Developmental structuralist approach to the classification of adaptive and pathologic personality organization: Application to infancy and early childhood. *American Journal of Psychiatry, 138*(6), 725–735.

Harris, I. B. (1992, February 5). *Primary prevention vs. intervention.* Address presented to the Graduate School of Journalism, Columbia University.

Hoff-Ginsberg, E., & Shatz, M. (1982). Linguistic input and the child's acquisition of language. *Psychological Bulletin, 92,* 3–26.

Howard, J., Beckwith, L., Rodning, C., & Kropenske, V. (1989). The development of young children of substance abusing parents: Insights from seven years of intervention and research. *Zero to Three, 9*(5), 8–12.

Infant Health and Development Program. (1990). Enhancing the outcomes of low-birth-weight, premature infants. *Journal of the American Medical Association, 263,* 3035–3042.

Kang, R., Barnard, K. E., Hammond, M., & Oshio, S. (1991). III Preterm Infant Follow-up Project. *NCAST National News, 7*(1), 1–2, 6.

Kang, R., Rolloloazo, M., Yoshihara, K., & Thibodeaux, B. Z. (1989). *Prenatal and postpartum nursing protocols* (Supported by Grant No. MCJ-533462 from the U.S. Public Health Service, Division of Maternal and Child Health, to K. E. Barnard, University of Washington; revision by K. C. Carr). (Available through Washington State Plan for Nursing, DSJS Parent–Child Health Services Contract with the University of Washington School of Nursing, WJ-10, Seattle, WA 98105)

Kaye, K. (1977). Toward the origin of dialogue. In H. R. Schaffer (Ed.), *Studies in mother–infant interaction.* London: Academic Press.

Klerman, L. (1992). *Young children in the United States: Are we meeting their needs?* Briefing paper prepared for the Task Force on Meeting the Needs of Young Children, Carnegie Corporation of New York.

Lamdella, J. T. (1977). The limbic system in human communication. In H. Whitaker & H. A. Whitaker (Eds.), *Studies in neurolinguistics* (Vol. 3). New York: Academic Press.

Lewis, M., Feiring, C., McGuffog, C., & Jaskir, J. (1984). Predicting psychopathology in six-year-olds from early social relations. *Child Development, 55,* 123–136.

Loan, C. (1992). Keys to CaregivinG: Knowledge improves quality of adolescents' interactions with their infants! *NCAST National News, 8*(3), 6–7.

Lubic, R. W. (1992). Prerequisite to midwifery. *Nursing and Health Care, 13*(6), 314–315.

McDonald, L., & Pien, D. (1982). Mother conversational behavior as a function of interactional intent. *Journal of Child Language, 9,* 337–358.

Mercer, R. T. (1990). *Parents at risk.* New York: Springer.

Miller, C. A. (1991). *Maternal health and infant survival.* Arlington, VA: National Center for Clinical Infant Programs.

Monrad-Krohn, G. H. (1947). Dysprosody or altered "melody of language." *Brain, 70,* 405–415.

Morisset, C. (1990). Social influences on language learning. *NCAST National News, 6*(1), 1–2, 6.

Morisset, C., Barnard, K. E., Greenberg, M. T., Booth, C. L., & Spieker, S. J. (1990). Environmental influences on early language development: The context of social risk. *Development and Psychopathology, 2,* 127–149.

Nelson, K. (1973). Structure and strategy in learning to talk. *Monographs of the Society for Research in Child Development, 38*(1–2, Serial No. 149).

Newson, J. (1977). An intersubjective approach to the systematic description of mother–infant interaction. In H. R. Schaffer (Ed.), *Studies in mother–infant interaction.* London: Academic Press.

Newport, E. L., Gleitman, H., & Gleitman, L. R. (1977). Mother, I'd rather do it myself: Some effects and noneffects of maternal speech style. In C. E. Snow & C. A. Ferguson (Eds.), *Talking to children: Language input and acquisition.* Cambridge, England: Cambridge University Press.

O'Connor, S., Vietze, P., Sherrod, K., Sandler, H. M., Gerrity, S., & Altemeier, W. A. (1982). Mother–infant interaction and child development after rooming-in: Comparison of high-risk and low-risk mothers. *Prevention in Human Services, 1,* 25–43.

Olds, D. L., & Kitzman, H. (1990). Can home visitation improve the health of women and children at environmental risk? *Pediatrics, 68*(1), 108–115.

Olsen-Fulero, L. (1982). Style and stability in mother conversational behavior: A study of individual differences. *Journal of Child Language, 9,* 543–564.

Olson, S. L., Bates, J. E., & Bayles, K. (1984). Mother–infant interaction and the development of individual differences in children's cognitive competence. *Developmental Psychology, 20*(1), 166–179.

Page, P. A. (1992). *An investigation of the relationship between maternal–infant patterns of synchrony during feeding, preterm infant state, and a parent administered state modulation treatment.* Unpublished doctoral dissertation, University of Washington School of Nursing.

Papousek, H., & Papousek, M. (1992). Beyond emotional bonding: The role of preverbal communication in mental growth and health. *Infant Mental Health Journal, 13*(1), 43–53.

Patterson, D. M., & Barnard, K. E. (1990). Parenting of low birth weight infants: A review of issues and interventions. *Infant Mental Health Journal, 11,* 37–56.

Patterson, G. R. (1982). *Coercive family process.* Eugene, OR: Castalia.

Ramey, C. T., Farran, D. D., & Campbell, F. (1978). Predicting IQ from mother–infant interaction. *Child Development, 50,* 804–814.

Rutter, M. (1985). Resilience in the face of adversity: Protective factors and resistance to psychiatric disturbance. *British Journal of Psychiatry, 147,* 598–611.

Sameroff, A. J. (1967). Non-nutritive sucking in the newborn visual and auditory stimulation. *Child Development, 38,* 443–452.

Sameroff, A. J., & Emde, R. N. (Eds.). (1989). *Relationship disturbances in early childhood: A developmental approach.* New York: Basic Books.

Sameroff, A. J., & Seifer, R. (1983). Familial risk and child competence. *Child Development, 54,* 1254–1268.

Sander, L. W. (1962). Issues in early mother–child interaction. *Journal of The American Academy of Child Psychiatry, 1*(1), 141–166.

Schaffer, H. R. (1977). Early interactive development. In H. R. Schaffer (Ed.), *Studies in mother–infant interaction.* London: Academic Press.

Schaffer, H. R. (1979). Acquiring the concept of dialogue. In M. H. Bornstein & W. Kessen (Eds.), *Psychological development from infancy: From image to intention.* Hillsdale, NJ: Erlbaum.

Schorr, L. B., & Both, D. (1991). Attributes of effective services for young children: A brief survey of current knowledge and its implications for program and policy development. In L. B. Schorr, D. Both, & C. Copple (Eds.), *Effective services for young children: Report of a workshop by the National Forum on the Future of Children and Families, National Research Council, Institute of Medicine.* Washington, DC: National Academy Press.

Schorr, L. B., Both, D., & Copple, C. (Eds.). (1991). *Effective services for young children: Report of a workshop by the National Forum on the Future of Children and Families, National Research Council, Institute of Medicine.* Washington, DC: National Academy Press.

Schorr, L. B., & Schorr, D. (1988). *Within our reach: Breaking the cycle of disadvantage.* Garden City, NY: Doubleday/Anchor.

Snow, C. E., Midkiff-Borunda, S., Small, A., & Proctor, A. (1984, September). Therapy as social interaction: Analyzing the contexts for language remediation. *Topics in Language Disorders,* pp. 72–84.

Snyder, C., Eyres, S. J., & Barnard, K. E. (1979). New findings about mothers' antenatal expectations and their relationships to infant development. *American Journal of Maternal–Child Nursing, 4,* 354–357.

Spieker, S. J., & Booth, C. L. (1988). Maternal antecedents of attachment quality. In J. Belsky & T. Nezworksi (Eds.), *Clinical implications of attachment.* Hillsdale, NJ: Erlbaum.

Spietz, A., Johnson-Crowley, N., Sumner, G., & Barnard, K. E. (1990). *Keys to CaregivinG: Study guide.* Seattle: NCAST, University of Washington School of Nursing.

Stechler, G., & Carpenter, G. (1967). A viewpoint on early affective development. In J. Hellmuth (Ed.), *Exceptional infant.* New York; Brunner/Mazel.

Stroufe, A. (1983). Infant–caregiver attachment and patterns of adaptation in preshhool: The roots of maladaption and competence. In I. M. Perlmutter (Ed.), *Minnesota Symposium in Child Psychology* (Vol. 16). Hillsdale, NJ: Erlbaum.

Tableman, B., & Katzenmeyer, M. (1985). *Infant mental health services: A newborn screener.* Lansing: Michigan Department of Mental Health.

Thoman, E. B. (1981). Affective communication as the prelude and context for language learning. In R. L. Schiefelbusch & D. Bricker (Eds.), *Early language: Acquisition and intervention.* Baltimore: University Park Press.

Trehub, S. E., & Rabinovitch, M. S. (1972). Auditory linguistic sensitivity in early infancy. *Developmental Psychology, 6,* 74–77.

Trevarthen, C. (1977). Descriptive analyses of infant communication behavior. In H. R. Schaffer (Ed.), *Studies in mother–infant interaction.* London: Academic Press.

U.S. General Accounting Office. (1990). *Home visiting: A promising early intervention strategy for at-risk families.* Washington, DC: U.S. Government Printing Office.

U.S. Public Health Service (USPHS) Expert Panel on the Content of Prenatal Care. (1989). *Caring for our future: The content of prenatal care.* Washington, DC: U.S. Government Printing Office.

Vaughn, B., Egeland, B., Sroufe, L. R., & Waters, E. (1979). Individual differences in infant–mother attachment at twelve and eighteen months: Stability and change in families under stress. *Child Development, 50,* 971–975.

Wells, G. (1980). Apprenticeship in meaning. In K. Nelson (Ed.), *Children's language* (Vol. 2). New York: Gardner Press.

Williams, B. C., & Miller, C. A. (1991). *Preventive health care for young children: Findings from a 10-country study and directions for United States policy.* Arlington, VA: National Center for Clinical Infant Programs.

Zeanah, C. H., & Barton, M. L. (1989). Introduction: Internal representations and parent–infant relationships. *Infant Mental Health Journal, 10*(3), 135–141.

Zero to Three—National Center for Clinical Infant Programs. (1992). *Head start—Emotional foundations for learning.* Arlington, VA: Author.

Zill, N., Moore, K. A., Smith, E. W., Stief, R., & Coiro, M. A. (1991). *The life circumstances and development of children in welfare families: A profile based on national survey data.* Washington, DC: Child Trends.

26

Family Support Programs

BERNICE WEISSBOURD

In 1990, Congress (Public Law [P.L.] 101-501) authorized the first allocation of federal grants to assist states in establishing networks of local family resource and support programs. This action became a milestone, and a fitting climax to a decade in which family support programs evolved from what was initially a collection of independent efforts to what today has been identified as a national movement.

CREATION OF FAMILY RESOURCE AND SUPPORT PROGRAMS

The momentum for the establishment of family resource programs was fueled by the needs that resulted from changing social conditions and the failure of social service systems to respond adequately to those needs. Within only one generation, families in our society have experienced a tremendous amount of change that may be attributed to divorce, remarriage, and single parenthood; a dramatic increase in the number of two-parent working families; and an increase in family mobility that often gives parents intense feelings of isolation. Children, particularly those who live in female single-parent families (where poverty has been estimated to be as high as 60%), have the highest poverty rate of any group in our society.

Although poverty is not synonymous with family dysfunction, it does contribute to a variety of unfavorable patterns and trends in families. Rates of infant mortality, malnutrition, child abuse, ill health, educational disabilities and low achievement, adolescent pregnancy, and alcohol and drug abuse are higher among poor families. Some of these very vulnerable families receive adequate resources and support from the public sector, but most continue to lack the rudiments of a decent income, basic health care, and a quality education. They do not have access to the family-strengthening services that are necessary to reduce the likelihood of experiencing crises. Their lives, therefore, often take on a destructive dimension, as repeated crises become chronic.

The statistics that describe the structure, economic status, and isolation of the family remain alarming. However, some commentators (Bane, 1976; Hareven, 1974) have pointed out the danger of wallowing in a nostalgia for the "world we have lost" (Laslett, 1965), and have emphasized that the family has always had to adapt to changing conditions; trading old stressors for new ones. They suggest that families are adapting to their new context with no more nor less difficulty than usual. Yet there are indications that the stress they are experiencing often overwhelms them. According to the National Commission on Children (1991) report, "Substantial evidence suggests that the quality of life for many of America's children has declined. . . . the fundamental challenge facing us is how to fashion responses that support and strengthen families as the once and future domain for raising children" p. 37.

As new conditions have necessitated new responses in services to families, it has become increasingly clear that the existing systems have failed in their mission. Traditional systems have long dealt with problems as though they are discrete rather than interconnected—treating mental health problems apart from difficulties related to school or housing, or addressing substance abuse and the problems that plague school dropouts separately from parent availability or employment issues, serving only to fragment the individuals they were intending to make more whole. The bureaucratic orientations of agencies often resulted in a focus on just one part of a family's condition, treating family members as adversaries rather than recognizing the family as the constellation most important to the child's development. Those families that most require an integrated program in which agencies work collaboratively are precisely the ones that find themselves to be involved with too many agencies whose efforts, no matter how well-intentioned, are piecemeal, redundant, inefficient, and poorly coordinated.

The result of this fragmented approach is that resources are used to treat existing, well-defined problems, rather than to build the capacity of families to avoid difficulties altogether or deal with them effectively at an early stage. Consequently, the focus of traditional social service systems has all too often been limited to situations in which a family is already judged to be in crisis and intervention is determined to be necessary for the protection of its children. These systems have not responded capably to the totality of changes in family life and to the needs these changes engender.

The combination of changing social conditions and the failure of social service systems to address the needs of families led to parallel lines of development in the family resource movement: first, to the creation of family resource and support programs, and then to the incorporation of program concepts into existing systems.

Across the United States in the middle 1970s, diverse family resource programs emerged. Initiated by both parents and professionals; these programs heralded a different approach to assuring that families would remain strong. Shedding the constraints of impersonal, bureaucratic services, they reflected the deep desire for connectedness and caring relationships that exist in a society where pressures are great and loneliness pervasive. Underlying the diversity of programs lies a shared ideal to enhance the competence of parents by providing a community resource that was responsive to their needs. It was be-

lieved that such programs would better assure healthy child development and that they would increase the capacity of parents to become advocates on their own behalf.

Some family resource and support programs provide direct services to parents; others provide indirect supports such as information. Many programs are comprehensive, providing a range of social, educational, and recreational activities; others offer a single service, such as parent–child classes or telephone support. Many programs are age-specific, serving such populations as parents of adolescents or newborns; others serve families throughout the lifespan. Programs may provide support to families during specific life events such as teenage pregnancy, divorce, family crisis, and relocation. Some are quite adequately funded, but many are not. Some programs are staffed by professionals, others by paraprofessionals or volunteers, and others by all three; others are cooperative groups, organized and led by parents. Some programs are private, nonprofit human services endeavors or part of institutions such as schools or hospitals. Others are free-standing and fully independent.

Within the wide array of family resource and support programs various core services are offered, including social support (peer support groups, parent–child activities, recreational programs, drop-in programs), educational opportunities (informal and structured groups providing information on child development, personal growth, and family relationships), skill-building resources (job training, literacy training), early developmental screening, home visits, community referral, and follow-up.

Out of the rich mosaic of programs varied definitions have emerged; over a dozen can presently be found in the literature. Though the definitions of programs differ from one another, the principles informing them: "share common features that make clear the presuppositions of efforts to support and strengthen family functioning" (Dunst, Trivette, & Thompson, 1991, p. 22).

Although family resource and support programs serve families with children of all ages, the original stimulus for their creation grew out of an orientation toward prevention, represented by the provision of services for families with very young children. The following examples are only a few of the many excellent programs that serve this population (Levine, 1988).

"Parents of Prematures" was founded in Houston, Texas, in 1976 by five mothers of premature babies and a social worker. It has since become a national resource for information on prematures and their families, and provides assistance to others who want to establish similar groups. A by-product of the organization's work can be seen in the fact that a local clothing manufacturer now produces and markets clothes for premature infants.

In Eugene, Oregon, "Birth to Three" works to strengthen families and reduce child abuse and neglect by making support/prevention services available to parents of very young children. Launched with the help of a demonstration grant from the National Center on Child Abuse and Neglect in 1978, this program uses peer support groups to deliver primary prevention services to parents before their problems become habitual or severe.

The "Family Place, Inc." was established in 1981 in Washington, D.C., by the Church of the Saviour. Programs are directed to low-income pregnant women and families with children up to the age of 3, and provide a variety of services (including support groups, referrals, infant development assessments, and emergency food). In addition, the "First Friend" outreach program pairs trained volunteer mothers (the First Friends) with high-risk or first-time pregnant mothers, some of whom are now First Friends.

Established in 1976, "Family Focus" of Chicago, Illinois, serves parents of children from birth through age 3, pregnant and parenting teens, and young teens who are socially and educationally at risk. Family Focus operates drop-in centers in ethnically diverse communities that offer families a range of formal and informal services, including parent discussion groups, child development classes, recreational activities, and skill-building programs. The agency also serves as a program development, training, and resource center, providing technical assistance and consultation to state and local government agencies, child welfare and social service organizations, and community and professional groups interested in establishing family resource and support programs.

These programs, and thousands more like them, have assisted families to function more effectively in their child-rearing roles. The mother in need of help may be having difficulty coping with stressors such as her child's changing needs, unemployment, an apartment without hot water, or insufficient money or food, or may be in less dire straits but feeling so isolated that her capacity to respond to her child is undermined. The downward spiral of stress can sometimes be reversed by the emotional and concrete support that a neighborhood program provides.

THE INCORPORATION OF FAMILY SUPPORT CONCEPTS INTO OTHER SYSTEMS

The enthusiastic response of parents to family support programs and an increasing recognition of their benefits have led increasing numbers of forward-looking social service providers and policy makers to explore the possibilities of incorporating family resource and support principles into state and local government agencies. This increased recognition has come, coincidentally, at a time when the federal budget for social programs has been slashed and decision-making authority has been shifted from the federal to the state level in the form of block grants. As a result, state and local policy makers have found it necessary to take a more active role in planning for and providing education and human services to their constituencies.

Concerned about the ineffectiveness of existing systems, state policy makers found appealing the concept of providing comprehensive, integrated services that would strengthen families and communities, and accomplish that with an orientation toward preventing problems. Thus, in many states, fundamental family resource and support principles became assigned as the basis for reorienting approaches to working with families and children. Particularly significant to state policy and program developers are the principles or concepts described below.

Four Family Support Concepts

The Infant in Context

An understanding basic to family resource and support programs is that to make a difference in the life of a child requires considering the child in the context of the family, and the family in the larger context of community life, social institutions, and government policies. This concept reflects an assumption about the "ecology" of the child's development that, when applied, significantly alters the direction of services (Bronfenbrenner, 1979). The acknowledgment of the connection each child has to his or her social support network makes the notion of "saving" a child from his or her environment appropriate only in extreme circumstances. Additionally, it emphasizes that to serve children well requires a sensitivity to the cultural and social traditions of a community, and an awareness that child-rearing patterns reflect family customs and traditions (Spiegel, 1982). This ecological perspective is bolstered by evidence from Head Start indicating that programs that work with both children *and* parents are more effective than those that work with children alone. It follows that a program that works with the whole family has a greater impact than a program "in which a child attends a center for several hours and then returns to an unchanged home environment for the rest of the day" (Zigler & Black, 1989, p. 12).

Different communities need different services. To succeed in helping families manage and flourish in different community contexts, programs are flexible in terms of locations, goals, and programming. For instance, in a community with a large number of poor, single mothers and families who are likely to need support in obtaining basic services, a health center that is accessible to the mothers might be a suitable site for a family resource program. On the other hand, a community with a greater number of working parents, where there is more concern about the availability of quality child care the community might have a family resource and support program as part of a child care cooperative (Zigler & Black, 1989).

In addition, this perspective stresses interdependence in its acknowledgment that strengthening bonds among people in the community increases the availability of informal support and enriches the community environment for all families (Weiss, 1987). Building strength in one area creates a ripple effect that strengthens a community's collective capacity.

The emphasis on developing an integrated approach to services has its roots in viewing children and families in an ecological context. As previously stated, most public institutions and programs today react rigidly to families' needs by narrowly defining them and responding to each in isolation from other needs. Schools deal with school problems; health agencies treat medical problems; mental health programs counsel on mental health problems. Yet the problems of children and their parents are usually untidy mixtures of interrelated factors. A child doing poorly in school may be hungry or anxious about violence in his family; a par-

ent referred for treatment of depression may be suffering from the fear of impending homelessness. When services are fragmented and narrowly defined, root causes of problems are often overlooked. In contrast, a collaborative approach among service providers holds promise for more positive outcomes.

The Family Self-Sufficiency Model

Families are more capable of supporting themselves when they in turn receive adequate support. It is unfortunate that the myth prevails that families can "do it alone." Social support networks provide for individual and family relationships that are nurturing, build on the capacities of parents to cope with the vicissitudes of daily living, and help them participate in shaping their own futures (Gottlieb, 1981; Henderson, 1977; LaRocca, House, & French, 1980; Telleen, 1983). Although family resource and support programs continually offer parents the kind of experiences that engender a feeling of "belonging," their aim is not to remain permanently in a caretaking role, but rather to increase participants' capabilities and feelings of self-worth.

Supporting families to support themselves is an essential aspect of family resource and support programs. The term "empowerment" is frequently used to describe this, and is often misused, implying the ability of one in authority to bestow empowerment on another. In reality, the program environment is empowering. Opportunities exist through which parents become actively involved in determining program offerings and can share their skills and talents. A major goal is for the program to increase the likelihood that parents will gain the confidence that enables them to become advocates in their personal lives and on behalf of their communities.

Acknowledgment of the importance of self-sufficiency and competency was reflected in changes that were recently made in the national welfare reform law (Family Support Act, P.L. 100–485). The act drastically reorients social service delivery in state-level public welfare systems by requiring family assessments in addition to client assessments, linkages between community-based organizations and state agencies, a procedure for families to set goals, and interagency cooperation and coordination at the state and local levels. Interestingly, evaluations that were made after these changes were instituted in the states of Virginia and Delaware suggest that the self-sufficiency of clients has increased, and that job satisfaction for caseworkers increases when public welfare services are delivered in a manner that supports personal strengths (Mumma, 1989). The satisfaction gained by assisting families through supportive relationships rather than bureaucratic procedures may also help attract highly skilled individuals to the social services field.

Promoting Family Well-Being

Family resource and support programs originated from the concept of prevention, an approach to services whose acceptance has been strengthened by growing evidence of its cost-effectiveness. The prevention orientation, which focuses on hindering, forestalling, or deterring the occurrence of problems or negative functioning, was found to be a significant improvement over the treatment model's emphasis on treating what was viewed as a disorder, disease, disability, or problem. Nevertheless, it became apparent that even this prevention approach was negative, and programs changed their focus to "promoting family well-being." Thus programs moved beyond the concept of avoiding or preventing a problem to one of fostering the most favorable development of all children and families through the enhancement and optimization of positive functioning (Dunst et al., 1991; Weissbourd, 1991).

A commitment to the promotion of family well-being demands that services be available to all, regardless of economic status, race, ethnicity, ability, or disability. It rejects social service programs that are based on a deficit model, and which emphasize negative terms such as "cultural deprivation" or "cultural disadvantage," for such terms imply that the culture of poor or minority people is inferior to that of middle-class or white people, and that, therefore programs should be designed to make up for this "inferiority" (Zigler & Berman, 1983; Zigler & Seitz, 1980).

Family resource and support thinking operates on the assumption that every parent has some strength—interpersonal skills, cognitive or physical capability, or a real connection to their cultural and ethnic identity. Programs place their emphasis upon finding strengths within the family as well as within each of its individual members. By not dwelling on deficits, programs support the dignity and authority of families and enhance their opportunities for change and growth.

Recognizing the Importance of the Early Years

New information about the crucial importance and rapid rate of the cognitive, social, and emotional development that occurs in a child's first 5 years, accompanied by growing concern about the number of children entering kindergarten unable to learn, has spurred the development of programs for early childhood. The expansion of such programs has been stimulated by encouraging evidence of the lasting benefits of early intervention (Lazar, Darlington, Murray, Royce, & Shipper, 1982). Closely linked to the concept of promoting family health and preventing problems early on is the conviction that programs should be available to families from pregnancy throughout the 5 years before formal schooling. Although "getting the right start" does not preclude future problems, it does lay the groundwork for good development.

Changes Based on the Concepts

Increasingly, legislators have realized that tending to the problems of children and families and enriching the communities in which they live requires reshaping standard ways of operating. This means changing the everyday practices of the huge, entrenched public institutions and systems that serve children, so that they are driven not by bureaucratic, legislative, professional, or funding requirements but by the needs of children and families themselves. This also makes it no longer acceptable for a worker to say, "I know what you need, but it's not my job to get it for you."

The principles underlying family resource and support programs have appealed to legislators as vehicles for improving program design and adminstration and for enhancing program effectiveness. As a result of service priorities, political leadership, and funding opportunities, family resource and support concepts are being incorporated in different ways in individual states. In some states, programs are emerging from the social service system; in others they are linked with public health or public welfare services; in still others they are linked with public schools. Statewide programs administered by the department of education exist in Minnesota,

Missouri, and Kentucky, while administration of program in Connecticut, Illinois, Iowa, Maryland, and Oregon lies within their departments of human services. There are some city-wide projects emerging such as the "Healthy Baby Program" in Boston, the "Family Support Center Project" in Seattle, and the "Atlanta Project"; all of which are focused upon reorienting services for children and families. Some of the common elements in state programs are designed to direct service personnel to develop partnerships with program participants/clients, to promote feelings of competence and personal strength, to minimize bureaucratic paperwork, and to view families in the context of the culture and traditions of their communities (Bruner, 1990).

Maryland, Connecticut, and North Dakota are participating in the Annie E. Casey Foundation's Child Welfare Reform Initiative. The goal is to create a service system for families and children that is less categorical and more oriented to early intervention and developmental supports. Each state has identified a substate area in which family support programs and activities will be developed intensively in connection with other services for families in severe crisis (Farrow, Grant, & Meltzer, 1990).

Iowa's Family Development Demonstration grant program, developed as part of its statewide welfare reform initiative, has also incorporated family support principles. The state legislation provides grants for working with Aid to Families with Dependent Children (AFDC) families who are at risk of long-term welfare dependency or family instability. By providing parenting information, day care, employment counseling/skills, and medical assistance, the program hopes to improve the employability of AFDC parents, to reduce the demand for foster care, to improve children's school performance and health, and to generally improve opportunities for the success of these families (Farrow et al., 1990).

Concern for an adequately prepared labor force led to the creation of the "Parent and Child Education" (PACE) program by the Kentucky State Department of Education. This two-generational family literacy program was initiated after Kentucky lost a bid for an automobile plant because the company believed that the state did not have an adequately trained labor force (Weiss, 1989). Preliminary evaluations suggest that PACE is effective. In 1987, at the end of the program's first year, three-fourths of the parents and their children who were initially enrolled had completed the program. Seventy percent of the adult participants had either advanced two grade levels or earned their general equivalency diplomas (Farrow et al., 1990).

In Hawaii, the Family Support Systems' Healthy Start Home Visiting Service which began under a federal demonstration grant in 1975 is now a fully funded program administered through contracts with seven private community agencies by the Hawaii State Maternal and Child Health Branch. Designed to prevent child abuse and neglect, to foster child development in a multicultural/multiethnic environment, and to enhance parent functioning, Healthy Start provides a variety of services: crisis intervention, postpartum screening assessments that screen the hospital charts of all newborns and their families in target service areas, parent training and support services, and a health clinic (American Public Welfare Association, 1990).

The "Community Infant Project" in Boulder County, Colorado, is an example of a program administered by a local government. The project was designed to strengthen family development during the prenatal period and early years of life in order to prevent child abuse and neglect. The county social services, mental health, and public health agencies collaborate to provide in-home visits by parent–infant therapists, nurses, and volunteers who encourage the use of community resources and enhance parents' understanding of children's behavior. Each family is thoroughly evaluated before formal service delivery begins, and an appropriate individual program is designed. The project reports substantial increases in parental confidence, family functioning, and the use of social supports by mothers. Subsequent abuse and neglect reports have not been filed on the families in the program. The cost of serving this category of families in the Colorado State Department of Social Services' traditional child welfare system is dramatically higher (Farrow et al., 1990).

Savings like those achieved in Colorado are not isolated instances. Private family resource programs such as "Homebuilders" in Tacoma, Washington, also save substantial amounts of money. Developed by Catholic Children's Service to prevent the unnecessary removal of children from their families, Homebuilders' services have proven to be less expensive than other options. In 1985, the average cost of the Homebuilders program per family was $2,600, compared to $3,600 per child for foster care, $19,500 for group care, and as much as $67,500 per child for institutional care. At the 1-year follow-up point, 90% of the children involved with Home-builders lived with their families. Given that without Homebuilders' intervention, all those children would have been removed from their families, the savings were calculated to be three to three and a half times the expenditure (Schorr, 1989).

Though these examples represent only a fraction of the programs in which family resource and support principles have influenced changes in state systems, they exemplify the kind of innovative thinking, flexible and comprehensive responses, and long-term planning that can make services become a meaningful part of participants' lives.

ANTECEDENTS, PRINCIPLES, AND PRACTICES

It has been said that the concept and programmatic techniques of family support programs are not new, dating at least from Martin Luther's 16th-century construction of a lifelong, universal education system, with cognitive, emotional, social, and religious dimensions (Braun & Edwards, 1972). The most recent antecedents of family resource programs include self-help groups, parent education, settlement houses, and Head Start. Although family resource and support programs are not identical to any of their forerunners, there are common elements that are derivative, and characteristics of each can be seen in program approaches and components.

Self-help groups, which Pizzo (1987) describes as the mutual provision of support, guidance, and practical services, proliferated in the 1960s, though their origins could be traced to the Friendly Societies that developed in 19th-century England after the Industrial Revolution. These mutual-aid societies gave members useful information for improving their lives, gave direct help to members in the midst of a crisis, and recreated a sense of community (Evans, 1979). Alcoholics Anonymous, founded in 1935 and followed in rapid succession by the American Association for Retarded Children, the United Cerebral Palsy Foundation, and the Mothers' March of Dimes, gave impetus to more structured self-help approaches. It was the creation of hundreds of thousands of self-help groups in the 1960s, however, that alerted the public that membership in such groups could facilitate success in reaching personal goals. Belonging to a group of people who shared a similar interest or problem became an acceptable way of acknowledging interdependence, an important precedent for the peer support emphasis in family resource and support programs.

Parent education, which has a long tradition in this country, was reenergized in the 1960s. Study groups sponsored by maternal associations had begun meeting regularly in 1815 (Schlossman, 1978a), intending to discover the best procedure for "breaking the will of the child." Later, similar programs re-emerged, with a general education component, as a vehicle of choice to redress discrimination against minorities, increase opportunity, and create equality (Schlossman, 1978b; see also Harmon & Zigler, 1980). Concurrently, early childhood efforts (such as Head Start and Parent–Child Development Centers) were shaped to acquaint parents with the principles of child development and strategies for being a good parent. Over the years parent education has expanded from an informal process through which child-rearing information was shared to being an organized association of parents who were seeking understanding and the best ways to raise their children, before it became a key component in early childhood education programs.

Inherent in parent education is the acknowledgment that adults as well as children have a potential for growth. Anthony and Benedek (1970) describe parenthood as a time of re-experiencing the past and of reactivating old conflicts and engendering new hopes. Parenthood viewed in these terms emphasizes possibilities for adult change. "Both parent education and family support, based on the common belief that adults, too, can develop and learn, emphasize the importance of parents having pertinent information" (Weissbourd & Kagan, 1989, p. 23).

Family resource programs are also an outgrowth of the settlement houses that were established to assist newly arrived immigrants living in poor communities. Settlement houses were instrumental in assisting families to gain access to the institutions of the society, to strengthen the communities in which they lived, and to become advocates for the social policies necessary to enhance their family life. These characteristics are reflected in today's family support viewpoint that the family and its fortunes are interrelated with the life of the community (Weissbourd & Kagan, 1989).

As previously noted, Head Start became an important avenue for parent education, but its most significant contribution was that through their programs, parents were given opportunities to be advocates for their families and to gain access to information and resources previously not available to them. Head Start's emphasis on parent involvement validated the vital role that parents play in influencing the educational achievements of their children. The practice of involving parents spread to school and community programs that made efforts to include parents in their processes and to respond to parental concerns. This commitment to parental involvement was an integral part of the War on Poverty's framework of self-administered programs. Their principle of focusing on supporting self-determination rather than dependence upon professionals is central to today's family resource and support systems (Zigler & Freedman, 1987).

Though family resource programs vary widely in the populations they target, the settings in which they exist, and the range of services they provide, they generally share a set of principles and practices that represents a belief system regarding the relationship between family and society. These beliefs are based on a recognition that the well-being of families is the cornerstone of a healthy society, and that dysfunctional families ultimately place our society at risk by jeopardizing the development of future generations. They are also based on an understanding—confirmed in our country by the 1991 report of the National Commission on Children—that parents have primary responsibility for their children, and that it is in society's best interest to support parents in their child-rearing role. The ability of families to fulfill their obligations requires that society, its institutions, communities, and government at all levels must support, not hinder, the capacity of families to raise children.

Basic to family resource and support programs is the emphasis on building trusting and caring relationships between staff and participants, participants and participants, and the program and its surrounding community. This tenet is enunciated in several related principles (Schorr, 1989; Weissbourd, 1991):

1. *Collaboration and shared decision making between professionals and parents.* The quality of staff appears to influence program success more than the particular type of training staff members receive or the roles they play (Florian & Dokecki, 1983). In these programs, participants describe the staff as people they can trust and

people who, in turn, respect and care about them. Staff are perceived as being in "partnership" with participants, as highly committed, and flexible. They are also empathic and have the ability to imbue participants with a sense of their own value, special qualities, and skills.

2. *Cooperative relationships and linkages with community institutions and organizations.* Successful programs work with other agencies to assess community needs and jointly make plans to meet those needs. They foster the awareness that all aspects of the community have the potential for helping or hindering healthy child development and family life. These programs offer services that are coherent, easy to use, ongoing, and open-ended.

3. *Nurturance and facilitation of peer support networks.* Strengthening bonds among families in the community builds informal support networks, thus enabling greater self-sufficiency among families.

4. *Designing programs to meet the needs of parents and to enhance family and individual strengths.* Programs that work do not approach families with bureaucratic or professional "blinders," but respond to their needs in a family and community context. They will circumvent or adapt traditional bureaucratic and professional limitations, often providing services in nontraditional settings and at nontraditional hours. These programs recognize that social and emotional support as well as concrete help, such as food and housing, may have to be provided before a family can utilize other services. The programs try to reduce the barriers of time, money, fragmentation, and psychological and geographic remoteness that often make heavy demands on participants in more traditional social service systems.

5. *Planning programs to insure sensitivity and relevance to the values and culture of the families served.* Program components, staffing, and training are guided by a knowledge of and respect for cultural differences. Program staff members are committed to understanding their own values and ethnicity as a basis for recognizing those of others. Knowledge of the impact of ethnicity and class on the values and child-rearing practices of participants is an essential component of program development.

The responses of participants to programs characterized by these approaches illustrate the qualities that seem to make a difference. A teen parent in one of these programs, who has al-

ready had considerable contact with social service agencies during her 17 years of life, put it
this way to me:

> Here they see you as a person, you know . . . not
> just a big ol' *problem* walking through the door
> . . . They stick with you and see that you get help
> until you get things turned around . . . and then
> they're still there when the good stuff happens, too.

A Hispanic parent expressed relief when acknowledging, "I used to beat my child to make
him behave. Now I know there are better ways
to do that, and it's really better for the whole
family." In a suburban community, a mother
said, "I was so lonely before and so easily frustrated with my child. There should be a family
resource center on every corner."

CHALLENGES

The rapid growth of family resource and support programs, and the hopes invested in their
promise by planners and policy makers, challenge those involved to carefully define, analyze,
and evaluate them in order to assure their quality and effectiveness. One cautionary note is that
the essential characteristics of programs must be
preserved as they are integrated into human service bureaucracies. In order to establish the
"family-friendly" environment required, considerable adjustments will have to be made
in monitoring, record-keeping, and personnel
management practices. Each state that decides
to integrate family resource programs will have
to develop strategies to insure that the components of successful programs are understood at
every level. Attempts to build on the programs
that have been successful in the past must carefully take into account the fact that family resource and support programs evolve from the
needs of those they serve, rather than from the
scope and limits set by the traditional requirements of professionalism and bureaucracies.
This distinction helps to explain why programs
that work for populations at risk are so rare, and
less effective programs so much more common
(Schorr, 1989, p. 259). Moreover, care must be
taken not to dilute successful programs as services are expanded.

Appropriate staffing is another challenging
issue facing family resource and support programs. Presently, staffs consist of professional
and nonprofessional paid staff members, pro-

fessional and nonprofessional volunteers, and
parents who may also be participants. The flexibility of family support programs, while "conceptually sound, is difficult to implement and
necessitates a revised professional role coupled
with different and variegated staffing patterns"
(Weissbourd & Kagan, 1989, p. 25). A major
difference from conventional human services is
that professionals with a heavy sense of their
own authority do not fit in a program where
parents are respected as advocates and as the
most significant influence in their children's
lives. Feelings of competence and independence,
fostered in family support programs, are negated
by a bureaucratic staffing model.

Because these programs are concerned about
working within the culture and context of each
family, many have elected to employ lay workers who may have a greater knowledge of and
familiarity with the cultural traditions, expectations, and child-rearing patterns of the community. Halperin (1990) has identified three assets
of this type of staff: acceptability to families, flexibility and responsiveness, and affiliation with
and knowledge of the community populations.
He has also noted, however, that these workers
have limitations. Lay workers may be more selective in what they observe, tend to take on too
much responsibility, and can have difficulty setting boundaries on their involvement with each
family; families may also be reluctant to divulge
sensitive personal information if lay workers
share similar informal networks.

In addition to ascertaining the most effective
staffing model, care must be taken not to make
a commitment to develop new programs without appropriately preparing personnel at all
levels. Given the increasing impetus to create
programs, attention must be focused on both
preservice and in-service training. There is a
growing interest, particularly in schools of social work, in incorporating family resource and
support principles and practices into graduate
curricula, both as separate courses and as continuing components of sound social work theory.
In the related fields of early childhood education, human development, pediatrics, and nursing, inroads are being made to include family-
oriented approaches as part of professional
training, and there is a continuing need to encourage and expand such efforts.

The importance given to in-service training
can be seen in the constantly increasing number of training materials produced, and the many
and varied training institutes offered. The de-

mand exists for a conceptual framework for training—one that interprets the principles as they relate to practices, defines the skills necessary for implementation, and articulates the knowledge base required to work effectively with both children and their families.

It is a further challenge to professionalize the family resource and support field through defining its role in the social services. We need to identify the elements of high-quality programs (Powell, 1988) and to define guidelines for staff qualifications and program operation. Achieving professional status also requires maintaining an organization that represents the family resource and support constituency, capable of gathering and providing information, acting as a resource for professional development, and advocating on behalf of program interests. The Family Resource Coalition, located in Chicago, Illinois, has served this function for a decade.

An ever-present challenge is that of securing a stable funding base for programs. At this time there is a wide range of funding sources, including local and state governments, corporations, universities, foundations, and nonprofit agencies. Grassroots events such as bake sales, benefits, auctions, and direct mail solicitation, are frequent occurrences; though obviously not major sources of revenue, they do reflect the importance that members of the community attach to these programs.

In addition, the legislative framework for federal funding of family resource and support programs now in place, P.L. 101–501 (1990), includes authorization of the Family Resource and Support Program Grants (Chap. 2, Sect. 933). The grants assist states in planning and establishing new networks of local programs that enhance the ability of families to stay together and thrive. The programs are to be established in communities as a comprehensive approach to helping families, rather than as one more categorical service.

Given both the continuing need to secure a stable funding base for the establishment, maintenance, and expansion of programs, and that the private sector cannot solely maintain family resource programs, we should (1) insure that all preschool education, child care, and welfare reform legislation includes funding for family resource components; and (2) continue to create and support legislation that will directly increase the ability of local communities and states to initiate and maintain programs.

Basic to program development will be efforts to expand and refine the research and evaluation of existing family resource and support programs. Although documentation of key characteristics of successful programs exists, and although it validates our belief that providing social support brings many positive results, further evaluation is needed to detail exactly what works for which participants, under what circumstances, and through what program elements.

Evaluation is another essential ingredient of policy formulation. Though the value of family support seems clear to those working and participating in it, specific data are required to convince others—including potential funders, policy makers, legislators, and the general public—of its efficacy. In addition, good evaluations provide administrators with the information they need to create new programs and alter existing ones. Ironically, programs often find themselves in the frustrating situation of not having the funds to undertake the quality evaluations that would make them more attractive to potential funders and better able to provide the most effective services.

Evaluation must proceed cautiously. We should be careful not to evaluate programs prematurely or to rely on any single piece of information that may be taken out of context. For example, statistics on repeat teenage pregnancies alone may obscure the fact that a particular teenage parent has completed high school, is pursuing college or job training, and has been able to develop a positive, nurturing relationship with her first child. Evaluation should rely on cross-validation, including quantitative and qualitative information, as well as on the opinions of committed practitioners and outside evaluators (Campbell, 1987).

Precisely because of the commitment in family resource and support programs to be community-based, program developers are challenged to increase their understanding of communities and how they function and interact with programs. The approach of family resource and support programs, which are integrated into the community at many levels, must be understood, as well, by legislators, administrators, and providers. Without this knowledge, they will not be able to implement programs that are integral to the community or to support parents adequately in their roles as community advocates. Program administrators and planners must have more intensive knowledge of community organization, of natural community leaders, and of the dynamics of community development. Further study is required as to how programs effect changes in the community, as well as how community resources influence program development.

Finally, the challenge exists to implement changes in government policies that can encourage the spread of family resource and support principles and can maintain the viability of effective programs (Schorr, 1989). Significant changes have been made in government policies to date, as indicated by the changes in federal welfare reform law, passage of a federal bill to assist states in establishing family resource and support programs, and the inclusion of family resource and support principles in state and local government programs. Indeed, future directions based on these concepts have already been identified in studies done by such organizations as the American Public Welfare Association (1990), the Education and Human Services Consortium (Bruner, 1991; Melaville & Blank, 1991; Edelman & Radin, 1991), and the National Commission on Children (1991). In the coming years, the challenge is to maintain a presence at all levels of government decision making and to focus efforts on the arenas where the incorporation of family resource principles will yield the greatest benefits.

CONCLUSION

We know much more than we did 20 years ago about programs that work. We know that strengthening families requires the assistance and support of public policies. We also know that fragmented national strategies, insufficient service resources, and the lack of comprehensive and coherent federal, state, and local interagency coordination conspire to curtail efforts to help families. The knowledge has led to a growing consensus that the comprehensive, effective reform of today's social service system will require culturally sensitive, family-focused community services designed to strengthen families before a crisis occurs. It is interesting to note that among the philosophically and politically diverse members of the National Commission on Children (1991), there was unanimous agreement that federal, state, and local governments, in partnership with private community organizations, should develop and expand community-based family support programs that provide parents with

the knowledge, skills, and support they need to raise their children. To date, these programs have bi-partisan support.

Recognizing the positive benefits of family resource and support programs does not imply that services to assist families in crisis and to protect abused and neglected children are of secondary importance. Nor can family resource and support programs substitute for such fundamental needs as expanded employment opportunities, income assistance programs, and affordable housing. However, integrating family support principles into social service delivery may not only enable us to move from a crisis-driven system to one that prevents problems; it may finally allow us to promote overall family well-being by providing a baseline of good beginnings for all children.

Across the country, there is a driving energy based on hope as new directions are being shaped for programs and services to children and families. The optimism itself raises questions and concerns. How well will programs be planned for and implemented? By what criteria do we measure their effectiveness? What are the vehicles for "changing the landscape" to assure that services—child care, school, health care, child welfare—and communities will be "family-friendly"?

Though there remain questions to be answered, their resolution should reflect a deep commitment to the beliefs that healthy families are essential to a healthy society, and that good programs make a difference in the lives of children and families. Promoting family well-being is perhaps a contemporary version of the vision of our nation's founding fathers to promote the common good.

REFERENCES

American Public Welfare Association. (1990). *The national commission on child welfare and family preservation, a commitment to change: Recommendations* (2nd major draft). Washington, DC: Author.

Anthony, E. J., & Benedek, T. (Eds.). (1970). *Parenthood: Its psychology and psychopathology.* Boston: Little, Brown.

Bane, M. J. (1976). *Here to stay: American families in the twentieth century.* New York: Basic Books.

Braun, S., & Edwards, E. C. (1972). *History and theory of early childhood education.* Belmont, CA: Wadsworth.

Bronfenbrenner, U. (1979). *Ecology of human development.* Cambridge, MA: Harvard University Press.

Bruner, C. (1990). Legislating family support and education: Program development at the state level. In *Helping families grow strong: New directions in public policy* (Papers from the Colloquium on Public Policy and Family Support, pp. 52–76). Washington, DC: The Center for the Study of Social Policy.

Bruner, C. (1991). *Thinking collaboratively: Ten questions and answers to help policy makers improve children's services*. Washington, DC: Education and Human Services Consortium.

Campbell, D. (1987). Problems for the experimenting society in the interface between evaluation and service providers. In S. Kagan, D. Powell, B. Weissbourd, & E. Zigler (Eds.), *America's family support programs* (pp. 345–351). New Haven, CT: Yale University Press.

Dunst, C., Trivette, C., & Thompson, R. (1991). Supporting and strengthening family functioning: Toward a congruence between principles and practice. *Prevention in Human Services, 9*(1), 19–43.

Edelman, P. B., & Radin, B. A. (1991). *Serving children and families effectively: How the past can help chart the future*. Washington, DC: Education and Human Services Consortium.

Evans, G. (1979). *Family Circle guide to self-help*. New York: Ballantine.

Farrow, F., Grant, T., & Meltzer, J. (1990). Challenges and opportunities for public policies on family support and education. *Helping families grow strong: New directions in public policy* (Papers from the Colloquium on Public Policy and Family Support, pp. 4–51).

Florin, P. R., & Dokecki, P. (1983). Changing families through parent and family education. In I. Sigel & L. Laosa (Eds.), *Changing families: Review and analysis* (pp. 23–63). New York: Plenum Press.

Gottlieb, B. H. (Ed.). (1981). *Social networks and social support*. Beverly Hills, CA: Sage.

Halpern, R. (1990). Community-based early intervention. In S. J. Meisels & J. P. Shonkoff (Eds.), *Handbook of early childhood intervention* (pp. 469–498). New York: Cambridge University Press.

Hareven, T. (1974). The family as process: The historical study of the family cycle. *Journal of Social History, 7*, 322–329.

Harmon, C., & Zigler, E. (1980). Parent education in the 1970's: Policy, panacea, or pragmatism. *Merrill–Palmer Quarterly, 26*, 439–451.

Henderson, S. (1977). The social network, support and neuroses. *British Journal of Psychiatry, 131*, 185–191.

LaRocca, J. M., House, J. S., & French, J. R. (1980). Social support, occupational stress and health. *Journal of Health and Social Behavior, 21*, 202–218.

Laslett, P. (1965). *The world we have lost*. London: Methuen.

Lazar, I., & Darlington, R. (1982). Lasting effects of early education: A report from the Consortium for Longitudinal Studies. *Monographs of the Society for Research in Child Development, 47* (Serial No. 2–3, 1–151).

Levine, C. (Ed.). (1988). *Programs to strengthen families* (rev. ed.). Chicago: Family Resource Coalition.

Melaville, A. I., & Blank, M. J. (1991). *What it takes: Structuring interagency partnerships to connect children and families with comprehensive services*. Washington, DC: Education and Human Services Consortium.

Mumma, E. (1989, Spring). Reform at the local level. *Public Welfare*, pp. 15–24.

National Commission on Children. (1991). *Beyond rhetoric: A new American agenda for children and families*. Washington, DC: Author.

Pizzo, P. (1987). Parent-to-parent support groups: Advocates for social change. In S. Kagan, D. Powell, B. Weissbourd, & E. Zigler (Eds.), *America's family support programs* (pp. 228–242). New Haven, CT: Yale University Press.

Powell, D. R. (1988, June). *Seeking dimensions of quality in family support programs*. Paper presented at Dimensions of Quality in Programs for Children and Families: The A. L. Mailman Family Foundation Symposium, White Plains, NY.

Schlossman, S. L. (1978a). Before Home Start—Notes toward a history of parent education in America, 1897–1929. *Harvard Educational Review, 3*, 436–437.

Schlossman, S. L. (1978b). The parent education game: Politics of child psychology in the 1970's. *Teacher's College Record, 79*, 788–808.

Schorr, L. (1989). *Within our reach: Breaking the cycle of disadvantage*. Garden City, NY: Doubleday.

Spiegel, J. (1982). An ecological model of ethnic families. In M. McGoldrick, J. K. Pearce, & J. Giordano (Eds.), *Ethnicity and family therapy* (pp. 31–51). New York: Guilford Press.

Telleen, S. (1983). *The role of social networks and problem solving in a family support program: Introduction to child development staff guide*. Unpublished manuscript, Family Focus, Chicago.

Weiss, H. (1987). Family support and education in early childhood programs. In S. Kagan, D. Powell, B. Weissbourd, & E. Zigler (Eds.), *America's family support programs* (pp. 133–160). New Haven, CT: Yale University Press.

Weiss, H. (1989). State family support and education programs: Lessons from the pioneers. *American Journal of Orthopsychiatry, 59*, 32–48.

Weissbourd, B. (1991). Family resource and support programs: Changes and challenges in human services. *Prevention in Human Services*, 69–85.

Weissbourd, B., & Kagan, S. (1989). Family support programs: Catalysts for change. *American Journal of Orthopsychiatry, 59*, 20–31.

Zigler, E., & Berman, W. (1983). Discerning the future of early childhood intervention. *American Psychologist, 38*, 894–906.

Zigler, E., & Black, K. (1989). American's family support movement: Strengths and limitations. *American Journal of Orthopsychiatry, 59*, 6–18.

Zigler, E., & Freedman, J. (1987). Head Start: A pioneer of family support. In S. Kagan, D. Powell, B. Weissbourd, & E. Zigler (Eds.), *America's family support programs* (pp. 57–76). New Haven, CT: Yale University Press.

Zigler, E., & Seitz, V. (1980). Early childhood intervention programs: A reanalysis. *School Psychology Review, 9*, 354–368.

27

Interaction Guidance: Understanding and Treating Early Infant-Caregiver Relationship Disturbances

SUSAN C. McDONOUGH

The "interaction guidance" (McDonough, 1991, 1992) treatment approach for parent–child relationship disturbances was created specifically to met the needs of infants and their families who had not been engaged successfully in previous treatment or who had refused treatment referral. Many of these families could be described as being "overburdened" by poverty, poor education, family mental illness, substance abuse, inadequate housing, large family size, lack of a parenting partner, and/or lack of adequate social support. In an effort to reach these difficult-to-engage families, the interaction guidance approach was developed to be a brief psychotherapy model that is family-problem-focused. It attempts to enhance individual family strengths and family competence by using video technology to highlight positive aspects of family interactions and to enhance the likelihood of positive therapeutic change within the family. The interaction guidance treatment approach assists family members in gaining enjoyment from their child and in developing an understanding of their child's behavior and development through interactive play experience. The approach also seeks to foster the development of adult family members in their role as their child's parents or primary caregivers. Interven-

tions to modify problematic behavior or to promote healthy patterns of interactional behavior are provided by a therapist who provides guidance but does not undermine the primary caregivers' role. Efforts to intervene with parent–child problems take place within the context of the parent–child relationship, rather than focusing solely on problems in the child or in the parent.

This nonintrusive method of family treatment has proven to be especially successful for infants with failure to thrive (FTT), regulation disorders, and organic problems (Cramer et al., 1990; McDonough, 1992). Parents who are either resistant to participating in other forms of psychotherapy, young or inexperienced, or cognitively limited respond positively to this treatment approach (McDonough, 1991, 1992).

USE OF FAMILY PLAY TO EXAMINE FAMILY INTERACTIONS

The interaction guidance approach attempts to engage families in the therapeutic process by highlighting existing family strengths and competence before attempting to intervene in areas of family concern. One way to begin this process is to focus on pre-existing aspects of high-quality caregiver–infant interaction. Field (1982) presents five characteristics of such high-quality interactions. They include both interactive partners' speaking at the same level, relating to the same thing, taking turns in communicative exchanges, observing each other's signals, and responding contingently. These characteristics are not only essential for good communication, but easily observable in any family play. By observing family members together, the interaction guidance therapist both can draw attention to the pleasurable feelings derived from family interactions and can nurture and coach these behaviors in reluctant or insensitive interactive partners.

In observations of parent–infant interactions, both the structure and style of the interaction can provide important clinical information to the therapist. "Structure" refers to what the dyad or family is doing. Are interactants playing, talking, negotiating, or fighting? "Style" addresses how the family goes about it. For example, when a parent plays with the infant, does the parent follow the infant's lead or try to have the baby do what the parent wants? If the child does not comply, does the parent permit the child to continue playing, make an effort to redirect the activity, or attempt to force or coerce the child to do what the parent wants?

The interaction guidance approach also seeks to nurture the development of adult family members in their role as the child's parents or caregivers. Implicit in that goal is the importance of structural balance as it affects generational and other boundaries (among grandparents, parents, the child, and siblings), parental coalition (e.g., scapegoating, triangulation, parental child), roles and relationships (dysfunctional transactional patterns), and relationship to childhood experience (intergenerational perspective). The interaction guidance approach shares these and other common elements with many family systems therapy treatments, such as structural family therapy (Minuchin, 1974), problem-centered systems therapy of the family (Epstein & Bishop, 1981), and strategic family therapy (Haley, 1976).

Another common aspect among many family-oriented treatments is the focus on working with at least two generations. In interaction guidance treatment, the caregiver is encouraged to invite a parenting copartner into the treatment sessions if he or she so wishes. Treatment "families" can be the child's biological parents and siblings, a single parent and friend, or an adolescent mother and her own mother. The treatment session always includes at least two family generations: caregiver and child. Parents are not seen during the play hour without their children. Although families often bring siblings to the sessions, there are some cases where it is advisable to work initially with the caregiver(s) and a single child. For example, in the case of a monitor-dependent infant who easily becomes overstimulated, it may be more advantageous to work with the parent and child alone until the caregiver is confident of being able to soothe and calm the infant. Gradually, other family members can join the treatment session.

ASSESSMENT OF THE FAMILY AND CAREGIVING ENVIRONMENT

In an effort to understand as vividly as possible the family's experience, the therapeutic process begins with a meeting of family household members at the referral source (i.e., at the hospital, at the human service agency, or in the family home). The child's primary caregiver (often the mother) is asked to invite all family members who assist in the care of the infant to the initial family meeting. The purpose of this household gathering is to gain a clear understanding of how the family views their situation, to describe the interaction guidance program, and to offer the family an opportunity to participate.

During the initial family meeting and/or on subsequent visits to family home, the therapist encourages the family members to tell their own "family story"—that is, the history of their relationship with the infant (Zeanah & McDonough, 1989). The family meeting also permits the therapist to gain an understanding of the family members' perspective on their own child, as well as of their belief system, family rituals, rules, and mores. Because treatment interventions that are sensitive to family and cultural beliefs and practices seem to offer the greatest likelihood of success (Reiss, 1981), the interaction guidance therapist places emphasis on acquiring a clear understanding of the family's view of the problem or situation.

The meetings conclude with the development of family treatment goals that are generated by family members and discussed with the therapist. In contrast to some family interventions that hold the family responsible for treatment success (Bowen, 1971; Minuchin, 1974; Aponte & Van Deusen, 1981), the interaction guidance therapist invites the family members to monitor treatment progress on a weekly basis and to suggest changes in their treatment goals as necessary. The treatment plan is modified according to input from both the family and the therapist. The sharing of responsibility between the family and the therapist for setting treatment goals and monitoring treatment progress reflects the more equitable stance assumed by the interaction guidance approach regarding the relationship between client and therapist.

Throughout the intake period, the therapist works to involve all family members in the treatment planning process. Even if other family members choose not participate in the treatment sessions, their cooperation and support of the child's parents or primary caregivers is necessary to implement and maintain any therapeutic change in family functioning.

INTERACTION GUIDANCE FAMILY TREATMENT

Families generally are seen weekly for hourly treatment sessions. The treatment sessions usually are held in a specially designed playroom equipped with developmentally appropriate toys, a play mat, comfortable chairs or sofa, and a bassinet. A video camera is available to record the play session for viewing by the family and therapist. The room is arranged to be comfortable for the needs of both adults and very young children. Although the therapist usually sits on the floor to encourage more interactive play between the infant and the caregivers, some adults initially choose to sit on a seat and join in the floor play sometime later in the session. Prior to the family's arrival, the therapist selects a variety of toys that the caregivers and infant can use during play. Toys and play materials (e.g., mirror, book, music box) are chosen because they invite use by more than one person. Some of these toys create an unusual display when moved or make a musical sound. For caregivers who seem initially uncomfortable playing with their infant, the toys seem to provide a helpful aid.

Description of a Typical Session

The sequence of activities during each family session remains fairly consistent throughout treatment. Families whose own lives are disorganized and chaotic seem to find this predictable routine comforting. Once a family is welcomed into the playroom, the therapist inquires about what has occurred in the family's life since the last visit. This is an opportunity to learn about the issues and topics with which the family has dealt and how comfortable members are with what has transpired. Early in the treatment process, this is a time of information solicitation and exchange. The family shares stories, offers opinions, and asks questions of the therapist. As the family members display more trust in the therapeutic relationship, they spontaneously share a wider range of affects with the therapist. Members speak of the frustration and disappointment they encounter in their efforts to make changes in their lives or conversely, express the increased enjoyment and satisfaction they receive from their interactions with one another. Consequently, as treatment progresses, the therapist spends more time initially listening to and speaking with the family. In each session, once the therapist judges that the family members appear satisfied that their concerns were heard or addressed, the therapist invites them to play with their infant the way they would if they were home.

While the family members interact with one another, the therapist videotapes approximately 6 minutes of the play sequence. This 6–minute "movie" will be viewed by the family and therapist following family–infant play. In situations where the camera is operated by an assistant, the therapist remains in the treatment room but sits apart from the family and tries not to interact with family members. Whether videotaping or observing the family in the treatment room, the therapist makes particular note of existing positive caregiving behavior and parental sensitivity. The therapist also makes note of behaviors that need to be modified or altered because of their critical importance (e.g., caregivers' failing to adequately provide for infant's safety).

Videotape Viewing and Commentary

To facilitate the parents' understanding of growth and development of their own child, the caregivers are actively involved in observing both the behavior of their infant and their own style of interaction and play with their child. The use of videotape in treatment allows for immediate feedback to the parent(s) or family regarding their own behavior and its effect on the infant's behavior. Through viewing samples of parent–child play interaction, family members become more aware of important interactive behaviors that are positive and need to be reinforced, elaborated, and extended, as well as those interactions that were less enjoyable or inappropriate and require redirection, alteration, or elimination. The use of videotape also provides the parents with the opportunity to listen more carefully to what they say to their child and the manner in which they say it.

After the play interaction session is taped, the videotape is viewed by the family and the therapist. Initially, the clinician attempts to solicit comments from the parent(s) concerning their perception of the session and their thoughts and feelings regarding their infant and their role as parents. A series of systematic probes is posed to the family, such as "Was this play session typical of what happens at home?" or "Were you surprised by anything that happened during the session?" The purpose of these questions is to stimulate discussion among family members and the therapist concerning what the family members saw when they looked at the screen, what it meant to them, how they felt about what they saw, how they thought their child felt, and how they felt about themselves as parents.

Following the caregivers' comments, the therapist then highlights specific examples of positive parenting behavior and parental sensitivity in reading and interpreting their infant's behavior. Focusing on what family and therapist agree is mutually satisfying and enjoyable to all interactive partners seems to convey a sincere sense of caring and concern on the part of the therapist. During these repeated occasions, a family usually begins to realize that the focus of treatment is positive in nature and that the therapist will address family-identified problems through the use of family competence and strength.

Play Session Conclusion

After the videotape is shown and discussed, the therapist continues talking with the family members while they play with their infant. Sometimes issues raised by the family during the video replay are discussed for the remainder of the session. At other times, the conversation expands into other aspects of family life beyond the caregivers' parenting role. The therapist attempts to follow the clients' lead in exploring areas of concern and conflict, but also raises issues the therapist believes are interfering with the growth and development of family members, particularly the infant.

The session concludes with a therapist-led discussion regarding treatment progress or lack of progress. The family is encouraged to comment candidly on the treatment process. The family members are then asked whether they would like to schedule a visit for the coming week. The purpose of offering another appointment to the family, rather than assuming a standing meeting, is to convey the importance of family members' making active decisions concerning their own treatment participation and progress.

Therapeutic Considerations for Video Use

The videotape viewing and feedback aspect of the sessions seems especially meaningful to the family at the beginning of treatment. As family members become more comfortable in spontaneously verbalizing their thoughts and concerns with the therapist, they seem to view the videotape feedback as an opportunity to reflect on what the televised event represents to them in a broader context. For example, some families will use the videotape viewing as a stimulus to discuss events of the past week, while others will reflect on experiences from years past and the feelings that accompany these memories.

Another advantage of videotaping is the opportunity it affords both the family and therapist to review the changes that occur across sessions. In situations where change is subtle and progress is slow, a retrospective viewing of progress over time can often encourage a family's effort at continuing treatment.

At the end of treatment, the clinician prepares an edited videotape documenting the changes that have occurred in parent–child interactions and family transactions over the course of the treatment. This videotape is given to the family members as a record and an example of their sensitive and positive parenting. There are several situations in which offering a copy of the videotape to the family before the completion of treatment may assist in treatment progress. Sometimes a spouse or coparent (friend, relative, household member) is unable or refuses to participate in the treatment sessions. Sharing a "movie" of what happens during a play session often alleviates unspoken concerns or fears by the resistant party about what actually occurs during the treatment hour. Also, having other household members view and hear what is done and said by the therapist often provides a source of validation for the clients in their attempt to restructure or to change previous ways of thinking or behaving. Finally, viewing the videotape is a very concrete way for the family to share the experience with other persons interested and concerned about the infant's well-being and happiness.

THERAPEUTIC APPROACH WITH FAMILIES

The interaction guidance therapist makes certain assumptions when working with families. These beliefs are helpful both in understanding the important role of family members in the infant's life and in working with the family members to broaden their thinking and to change their behavior. Many overburdened families often express feelings of helplessness and rage at their perceived inability to solve very complicated life problems with limited resources.

1. *Embrace the position that parents and other caregivers are doing the best they know how to do.* Although this sounds quite simple, it can be a challenging concept to put into practice. By emphasizing the phrase "the best they know how to do," a therapist is able to keep open the possibility that the parents can acquire new ways of thinking, coping, behaving, and feeling. It also conveys acceptance of and respect for where caregivers are now, without assuming that it is all of which they are capable. Rather, it uses existing positive parental behavior and attitudes to assist in building feelings of self-confidence in the caregivers.

2. *Address what parents believe to be the problem or issue of concern.* As professionals working with multiproblem families, we find it frustrating and often heartbreaking to see parents worry excessively about things that they cannot change or fail to take some direct action that could minimize or alleviate some difficulty. Sometimes what appears to be a critical family need is not identified as an area of concern by the family. The family members may choose to use their resources differently. If a therapist can

acknowledge and accept the family's negative feelings and attributions of child behavior without feeling as if these need to be changed immediately, caregivers may feel heard.

3. *Ask the family what you can do to be helpful.* At the simplest level, the helping process involves two components: (a) A person offers some assistance or aid; and (b) another person accepts what is offered. A professional working with a family can increase the likelihood that the offered help will be accepted by encouraging the family members to decide what, if any, assistance they desire or need, rather than assuming that a clinician-identified problem is the family's source of concern. A therapist should reinforce the role of the parents as decision makers in the family and protectors of the child by deferring to their expertise as the individuals who know their child "best." The therapist should also consider the ramifications of "doing for" (including handling the baby) without being asked to do so. Sometimes "assistance" may be interpreted as the clinician's knowing better, taking over, criticizing, or correcting.

4. *Answer questions posed by the family directly; provide information when asked.* Many families begin treatment with questions they hope to have answered by the therapist. Occasionally the information requested by the family may be unknown or unanswerable, or the material requested may be very technical for family use. Often family members need to have things repeated many times, in many different ways, and sometimes by more than one person before they grasp the meaning of what is being said to them. Even then the family's understanding of the long-term implications of particular circumstances or conditions may change as the family acquires additional information or experiences new insights. Families report that what a professional tells them is not always as important as the manner in which the information is shared. By providing perspective on caregivers' beliefs and feelings, a therapist may be able to convey expertise in a nonjudgmental way.

5. *Jointly decide with the parents the definition of treatment success.* Families who are having difficulties in raising their children or who have already experienced a parenting failure need some reassurance that things are capable of changing. Short-term, problem-focused therapy is one way to begin addressing this concern. Involving a family in an active negotiation of treatment success affords the therapist another opportunity to learn how the family members

attempt to solve problems and to prioritize their goals. For example, is treatment success dependent upon whether the symptoms go away? Do they reflect both on internal changes (feelings, thoughts, beliefs) and behavioral manifestations (the child sleeps through the night)? Or do they reflect only on one? Are these indices of treatment success child-focused, parent-focused, or relational? Responses to questions such as these provide the therapist with insight into how to establish a therapeutic alliance with the family, centered around family-identified treatment goals. Maintaining and strengthening that alliance often occurs when caregivers feel respected and accepted. Consequently, the therapist should make note of caregiver behaviors that he or she wishes to alter or modify, but should address only those that he or she believes to be of critical importance.

6. *Monitor treatment progress weekly with the family.* Involving family members in monitoring their own treatment progress assists the therapist in observing areas of growth and development within the family, as well as issues of resistance and relapse, from the family's point of view. If treatment is proceeding positively, the family can share feelings of achievement and accomplishment. If one party is dissatisfied, those feelings can be explored openly, and changes or a redirection in treatment focus can be suggested. This weekly monitoring appears to be especially helpful in dealing with resistant clients, whose anger often can be addressed and worked through by providing a regular opportunity for them to express their thoughts and feelings about the treatment process. Because one of the principal partners in the relationship (the infant or young child) may not be able to speak in his or her own behalf, the therapist should use his or her own voice to articulate the baby's needs and desires.

INTERACTION GUIDANCE CASE EXAMPLE

The clinical case vignette that follows is used to illustrate the interaction guidance treatment approach for parent–infant relationship problems. The particular treatment issue addressed is that of forming a therapeutic alliance with a resistant family. In this case, it was necessary to work through each parent's resistance to participate in the treatment process before the therapist and family could begin to address perceived

family needs and family treatment goals. The case also provides examples of the intervention strategies employed by an interaction guidance therapist that reflect the characteristics of this treatment approach.

Identifying Information and Referral

Samuel "Sam Jr." was a 4-month-old who was admitted to the hospital for a workup of FTT. This was his second hospitalization; he had previously been admitted at 2 months of age for persistent vomiting. Sam Jr. lived at home with his 21-year-old mother, Lisa; his 20-year-old father, Sam Sr. and his 2.5-year-old half-sister, Jessica. The parents were not married. The mother was on Aid to Families with Dependent Children (AFDC), and the father worked driving a delivery truck between 6 P.M. and 3 A.M.

The parents were described by the referring physicians as "extremely defensive and poor historians." The father was described as "angry, hostile, and threatening." On one occasion, hospital security guards needed to be called when he threatened bodily harm to one of the hospital staff. Lisa, Sam's mother, was described as "withdrawn, depressed, and easily confused." Following the preliminary negative findings of an organic component to the FTT, Sam Jr. and his family were referred for interaction guidance treatment.

Parent–Child Interactions: Hospital and Home

Sam Jr. and his mother were observed interacting on a few occasions, including a feeding, while the baby was hospitalized. For the most part, Lisa interacted very little with Sam Jr.; even when she did, her affect was quite flat and she gave no indication that she enjoyed interacting with her baby. Sam Jr. appeared anxious when interacting with his mother; he avoided eye contact and arched his back regularly. In fact, he appeared more active and alert when interacting with the hospital staff members who came by periodically to check on him.

Sam Sr. rarely visited his son during the baby's hospital stay. When questioned about his visitation, the father replied, "It's Lisa's job to handle the kids." Both parents fed Sam Jr. by placing him in their laps but offering little head or neck support. Each parent expected that the baby could hold an 8-ounce glass bottle without assistance, and both parents became irritated when the nurses offered advice.

The parents described a typical day as follows: Lisa got up at 8 A.M. when the children awoke. She fed both children breakfast, then gave Sam Jr. a bath and dressed him. Lisa left Sam Jr. on the floor with his sister until the next feeding time (12:30 P.M.) while she watched TV. If the baby cried, she put him in a swing or walker and resumed watching TV. The same routine was repeated in the afternoon and evening. As far as feeding was concerned, Lisa prepared Sam Jr.'s formula and then handed him the bottle, which he held himself during the feeding. Lisa either held him during the feeding or gave him the bottle while he was on the floor.

According to the parents, Sam drank 8 ounces of formula at 8 A.M., 12:30 P.M., 2:30 P.M., and 6 P.M. He was put to bed (he shared the parents' bedroom) at 8 P.M. and slept throughout the night. The parents reported that Sam Jr. never awakened for a night feeding. The parents also asserted that he regurgitated mouthfuls of formula and that the vomiting had been going on since birth.

Engaging the Family

In interaction guidance treatment, the therapeutic process begins with a meeting of family household members at the referral source (i.e., at the hospital for Sam Jr.) and/or in the family home. Lisa agreed to meet with the therapist as the spokesperson for the couple. Her message to the therapist was simple: She and "Big Sam" didn't want any outsider telling them what to do for their kid.

As the mother and the interaction guidance therapist sat together in Sam Jr.'s hospital room, Lisa spoke firmly and angrily about how tired she was of "having people telling her what to do." While she spoke, she fed Sam Jr. a bottle. She looked neither at her son nor at the therapist, but rather looked out in space. After the baby finished the bottle, she hoisted him to her shoulder with his face away from hers. Almost immediately, Sam Jr. began spitting up. Each time formula would come up, Lisa would walk over to the paper towel dispenser and wipe off Sam's face with a dry paper towel. Initially, the therapist offered to get a supply of soft cotton diapers or wipes for her to use. She refused the

offer, replying, "I always use these on Sam's face." As they sat together talking about the hospital experience (e.g., tests, examinations, special diets), the therapist shared her belief that it must be very frustrating for Lisa and the baby's father to go through these procedures and interviews and still not have any answer to why their son was vomiting. Lisa nodded and replied sadly, "No one even thinks we're trying." When the therapist told her that she believed that Lisa and the baby's father were doing the best they knew how to do, Lisa brightened and smiled shyly. The therapist used this moment to explain that she had worked with other babies like Sam Jr. after they were discharged from the hospital. She explained her job as helping the parents to keep their baby out of the hospital.

Throughout the time they talked (approximately 1 hour), Sam Jr. continued spitting up. When the therapist felt that she could not tolerate seeing the baby's face wiped again with a dry towel, she offered Lisa purse-size package of tissues for her use. "Oh, don't waste your Kleenex on Sam," Lisa replied. It was then that the therapist appreciated just how little Lisa thought of Sam Jr. and of herself.

As the therapist prepared to leave, she thanked Lisa for taking the time to meet and to talk with her. The therapist reiterated her opinion that the hospital stay must have been very trying for the entire family. She told Lisa how much she had enjoyed getting to know her and Sam Jr., and how she regretted not having the opportunity to get to know the family better. The therapist acknowledged the family's decision not to participate in treatment at this time and offered her assistance if Lisa changed her mind once Sam Jr. was home. Lisa replied, "Oh, I've changed my mind. I think it would be fun to come to your playroom." She invited the therapist to make a visit to the family home the following week to explain and offer the program to Sam Sr.

Reflection on the Engagement Process

During this initial family meeting, the therapist sought to gain a clear understanding of how the family viewed their situation. To do so, she encouraged Lisa to tell her own family story. The therapist listened to gain insights regarding the couple's perspective on Sam and his sister, their belief system about children, and the way in which holidays and family occasions were celebrated. Although both parents were not present for this initial visit, the therapist had an opportunity to listen as Lisa candidly shared her frustration with Sam Jr.'s hospitalizations and the family situation.

Throughout the visit, the therapist embraced the position that the parents were doing "the best they knew how to do." By employing that position, the therapist conveyed her acknowledgment of the hardship the family had endured, while at the same time inviting Lisa to explore alternative ways of viewing the situation.

As planned, the therapist visited in the family home during the following week. The purpose of the second meeting was to invite Sam Sr. to participate in the treatment process. His participation could take a variety of forms. Although the therapist's primary goal was to involve him in the treatment sessions themselves, the therapist anticipated that he might refuse because of his belief that Lisa was the responsible caregiver. Her secondary plan was to gain his support and cooperation for Lisa and the children to attend weekly treatment sessions. Cab transportation could be provided and treatment play sessions would be videotaped, so that he could view them with Lisa or by himself at a later time.

Visit to the Family Home

The home visit was scheduled for the following week in the early evening. On arriving at the family's tenement, the therapist wound her way through the paternal grandmother's flat to a set of steep stairs in the rear of the house. The staircase was not lit; she groped her way up to the third-floor apartment where Sam Jr. and his family lived. As she neared the door, she called out Lisa's name. A door suddenly banged open, and she looked up to see Sam Sr. standing in the doorway.

Initially, Sam Sr. complained that he was being bothered during his rest. The therapist apologized. Then he asserted that the "doctors were stupid idiots who never listened and didn't care." The therapist asked how he came to discover this. Sam Sr. related his own theory of his son's failure to gain weight: "Look, his mother is small, his sister is small, my own mother is small, and we live in this damn small apartment. I think it's the roof of the apartment; there's no room to stand. A person feels trapped!" He recalled that when he had tried to tell this story to a doctor, the physician "looked as if he were

gonna laugh." Sam Sr. responded by threatening to "break the guy's legs"; security was summoned, and Sam Sr. was escorted from his son's hospital floor.

The therapist empathized with his feeling of perceived rejection and frustration. She shared her experience of talking with parents of children like his son—parents who didn't understand why they could not feed their own children. Sam Sr. seemed relieved that there were other parents like himself. Abruptly, he shouted to Lisa, "Are you gonna get her tea or something? It's cold out there!" Sam Sr. invited the therapist into the apartment and suggested she sit on the only stuffed chair available in the apartment. The parents "sat" on the sofa. Actually Sam Sr. had to recline on his side, as the pitch of the roof was so dramatic that a person could sit on one end of the sofa but was unable to do so on the other.

For the next 45 minutes, Sam Sr. demonstrated how he fed his son. Within minutes of finishing his feeding, the therapist and parents watched together as Sam Jr. spit up almost all of the formula. During one particularly poignant moment, Sam Sr. said he wished he had a camera to show the doctors just how much the baby vomited. "That's a good idea," the therapist replied. "We have a camera in the playroom. It would be interesting to film what happens before and after Sam is fed. Maybe we could begin to understand what causes him to become so upset by watching the movie together." Sam Sr. seemed intrigued with the idea. Although he claimed not to have the time to participate in the treatment himself, he thought Lisa and the children should try the program. The interview concluded with the family and therapist's generating some preliminary treatment goals and a plan to monitor treatment progress on a weekly basis. Sam Sr. agreed to participate in regular home visits to evaluate treatment efficacy.

Reflection on the Therapeutic Approach

The family was offered a family treatment program designed specifically to meet the needs of overburdened families who had not been engaged successfully in previous treatment or who had refused treatment referral. After some initial resistance from both parents, the family decided that Lisa would attend the interaction guidance treatment program with the children.

Sam Sr. agreed to participate in periodic home visit sessions to discuss treatment goals and evaluate treatment progress.

The principal family-identified treatment goal focused on Sam Jr.'s inability to gain weight. At the time he began treatment, the baby's weight and height were well below the 3rd percentile on the growth curve. The parents needed assistance in providing Sam Jr. with a more structured and better-regulated environment in order for him to grow and thrive. They also needed parenting skills to ensure that Sam Jr. and his sister would be provided with more than a minimum of care.

In this case, the therapist tried to engage in a supportive, nurturing, and caring interactive style with the entire family. She sought to convey that the family's negative feelings, thoughts, and comments would be heard nonjudgmentally. Within the context of the therapeutic relationship, she hoped the family could explore these emotions and ideas in future family play sessions.

Shared Family History

During the course of the visit to the family home, both parents began speaking about their respective childhoods. They conveyed their mutual desire to protect the children from the hardships they endured as youngsters.

Lisa reported that she was the fourth of six children who grew up in a deprived area of an eastern city. Her father was a manual worker; her mother worked as a waitress. Lisa claimed to remember "nothing" of her childhood, except that she was sexually abused by her father's friend as a youngster. During her teenage years the state department of protective services became involved with the family, and Lisa's two older sisters were removed from the home (a year apart) when the father physically abused them. When Lisa was 17 she became sexually active with a casual male friend; within 2 months she became pregnant. Her boyfriend then left her. At 18, Lisa gave birth to her daughter, Jessica; Jessie's father was not involved in the birth and had not subsequently seen or had contact with his daughter or Lisa. During the first 18 months after Jessie was born, Lisa lived at home with her parents. Her parents cared for the baby while Lisa attempted to finish high school. Lisa described her own parents as Jessie's "real parents" during those early months. Lisa met Sam

Sr. through a friend when Jessie was nearly 2; they moved in together within several months.

Sam Sr. presented himself as being highly knowledgeable and in control of the family. In reality he appeared to be of borderline intelligence. He was very involved with his family of origin and continued spending large portions of his time and money trying to please his widowed mother. Sam Sr. was the second of 12 children. Several of his siblings were intellectually limited; at least one brother was severely retarded; and another brother was in prison. Since the father's death 5 years ago, Sam Sr. had worked at night to help support his younger siblings.

The therapist's impressions of him differed markedly from hospital reports. He presented as a very frightened and vulnerable young man who engaged in a great deal of bravado (e.g., claims of being strong, powerful, and capable of violence) as a way to distance people from him. This posturing quickly changed when his angry claims went unchallenged.

Summary of Treatment Contacts

Lisa and her children were seen 12 times in the playroom over the course of 4 months. In addition to the playroom sessions, three home visits were made at 6-week intervals. Initially, Lisa and Sam Jr. were seen together; after three sessions, Jessie joined the treatment sessions.

When Lisa first entered the playroom, she placed her son on the floor and went to sit on the sofa. The therapist invited Lisa to select toys or activities that her son might enjoy. Lisa shrugged her shoulders, but neither spoke nor made any selections. When encouraged by the therapist to join her son on the floor, Lisa sat behind her son and presented Sam with one toy after another. With the exception of a brief interactive sequence of approximately 20 seconds, Sam Jr. showed only momentary regard to any of the objects placed before him. Lisa appeared oblivious to his apparent lack of interest and continued mechanically to present each toy. Several minutes into the filming of the play session, Sam Jr. began whimpering and fussing; his behavior quickly escalated to loud crying. Lisa made no attempt to pick him up or otherwise to comfort him. Rather, she continued placing toys in front of him.

During the video viewing and feedback session, Lisa sat transfixed watching the images on the screen. The therapist attempted to explore

Lisa's thoughts and feelings about the televised play activity: Did she enjoy the experience? Was this play session typical of what happens at home? Did she believe that Sam Jr. enjoyed himself? Lisa responded by shrugging or nodding. The therapist then reviewed the videotape with Lisa, pointing out an interactive sequence early in the session when Lisa appeared to be imitating Sam's vocalizations. The therapist highlighted the reciprocity in the exchange and the perceived shared positive affect that mother and child enjoyed. Lisa smiled broadly and began speaking about her belief that Sam Jr. was oblivious to her: "I just don't seem to matter to him. No one does." The therapist rewound the videotape to review the interactional sequence again. She paused the tape on a scene in which Sam Jr. had a wide grin on his face, and then said, "You certainly know your boy better than I do, but it seems to me that he thoroughly enjoys your attention. Look at the way his face brightens when he sees you!" With this guidance, Lisa acknowledged that she could see what the therapist saw: "Sam's really smiling!"

During the following visit, Lisa said that Sam Jr. preferred playing games such as peek-a-boo and tickling. She volunteered to show the therapist their family games. During the peek-a-boo game, Lisa, with her hands covering her face, lunged at Sam Jr. as he lay on his back. She repeatedly exclaimed "Peek-a-boo! Peek-a-boo! Peek-a-boo!" without pausing to note his reaction. Sam Jr. lay staring wide-eyed and looking somewhat frightened. Lisa looked up at the therapist and said disappointedly, "I guess he's not going to do it for me today." The therapist observed that although Sam Jr. appeared to be watching his mother intently, he almost seemed too startled to react. The therapist coached Lisa in playing the game once again, but this time Lisa was to pause when she said "Peek-a-boo" and to look at Sam Jr.'s face before continuing the game. Lisa tried again, waiting for her son's response before continuing. Sam Jr. cooperated by kicking his legs vigorously. Lisa tried the game again. This time the baby's response included waving his arms and kicking his legs. Lisa smiled broadly and repeated the game several more times. As Sam Jr.'s interest waned, Lisa again became more intrusive. The therapist suggested that the lack of responsiveness might be his way of telling Lisa that he wished to play something else. As Lisa sat back, Sam Jr.'s body relaxed, and he made eye contact with his mother and smiled.

Subsequent visits to the playroom elaborated and extended many of the themes presented in the first sessions (i.e., caregiver responsivity, sensitivity and reciprocity, reading infant behavioral cues, and affective attunement). One of the most dramatic documented differences between the first treatment session and later visits had to do with the amount and quality of face-to-face contact between Lisa and Sam Jr. Lisa often referenced the first time she saw herself and her son playing together. This young woman's caregiving had been so impoverished as to leave her unable to recognize signs of her infant's affective engagement with her. She needed to be nurtured and cared for herself before she was able to separate her own unmet needs from the those of her baby.

Reflection on Treatment Efficacy

Several areas of concern were speculated to be related to Sam Jr.'s symptoms. They included his parents' unresolved loss, trauma, and conflicts (the paternal grandfather's death, Lisa's history of sexual and physical abuse, and the couple's conflict over the extended family).

Visiting the home was a sobering experience. Living in the home and looking out over the surrounding areas must have been very depressing for a young woman with virtually no outside supports.

In the early stage of treatment, Lisa would enter the playroom each week speaking about how nice it was to finally get out of the house. The trip to the playroom permitted Lisa and her children some respite from the confined area of their apartment. She often remarked that attending the treatment session was the only time she and the children left their apartment during the week. Several months into treatment, Lisa no longer waited for a cab to be sent for her. She had taught herself how to use public transportation and reported that she felt "free" for the first time.

As Sam Jr.'s parents became better able to read their son's signals and cues, they began to experience more success and enjoyment in feeding their son. His weight increased markedly. Within several weeks, Sam Jr.'s enhanced energy made him a far more enjoyable interactive play partner. The treatment goals then broadened to include assisting the family to find a child care program for Jessie and exploring the possibility of Lisa joining a survivors' treatment group.

Lisa independently pursued a referral to Head Start for Jessie, which included gathering documentation from a variety of different public welfare offices. Sam Sr. participated in periodic home visits but resisted any effort to involve him in the weekly treatment sessions. However, he frequently asked Lisa to bring home a videotape of the play session. Lisa reported that Sam Sr. began to be more responsive to her request that he spend more time at home with her and the children, rather than visiting his mother and siblings. At the conclusion of treatment, however, she saw this situation as a source of continuing conflict.

When discussing treatment efficacy with overburdened families, it seems important to clearly define what is meant by "treatment success." Unfortunately, the vast majority of these families will never be free from the problems caused by poverty, lack of education, a family history of mental illness or substance abuse, large family size, inadequate social support, or lack of a life partner or a coparent. However, many of these families use their relationship with their therapist to help make meaningful changes in their lives (McDonough, 1991). In many cases, the families are able to reallocate their limited resources more effectively to meet their infants' needs. Other instances call for the therapist to help the caregivers redefine their own mental health issues in a way that permits the infant to grow and develop along a more appropriate developmental course (McDonough, 1992).

In this case, several areas remained unresolved when the family left treatment. The first area concerned the unresolved trauma that Lisa experienced as a result of sexual abuse by her father's friend and suspected severe physical abuse from her father. Lisa resisted joining a survivors' support group, although she did make an introductory phone call and gather information about the group and its purpose. Another area concerned Sam Sr.'s unresolved feelings of loss resulting from his father's death. Whereas the therapist felt some hope that Lisa might eventually seek out further therapy, she did not have that same optimism regarding Sam Sr. The final area of concern related to the perceived structural imbalance within this family. Even at termination, the couple was dominated by an intrusive paternal grandmother and "obligations" to the paternal family.

Despite these unresolved issues, there was cause for optimism and enthusiasm regarding successful aspects of the treatment. When the family left treatment, Sam Jr. was at the 60th percentile in weight and height. He had become a happy and interactive play partner. Perhaps most importantly, his mother was proud to have effected this positive change in his behavior.

EVALUATION OF THE INTERACTION GUIDANCE APPROACH

The interaction guidance treatment approach is currently being implemented in a variety of sites in the United States and abroad. Because the approach was developed to meet the needs of overburdened families who had not been previously engaged successfully in treatment, efforts have been made from the onset to collect systematic data on each participating family. Depending upon what aspect of the therapeutic process has been examined, various measures have been implemented. However, across all studies, individual families' participation in treatment and overall program progress are assessed in several ways. In studies conducted in our own clinical setting (McDonough, 1991, 1992), several measures and scales are employed to assess pre- and posttreatment differences. The Home Observation for Measurement of the Environment (HOME) inventory for families of infants and toddlers (Caldwell & Bradley, 1984), the Family Resource Scale (Leet & Dunst, 1986), and the NET Help Scale (Boukydis, 1990) are used during the initial family home interview for treatment planning purposes. The HOME scale and the NET Help Scale are also completed at the 3-month posttreatment home visit to assess the short-term changes in the family environment and social support system.

Once treatment begins, parent–child play is assessed weekly on the Parent–Infant Interaction Scale (Clark & Seifer, 1985). This scale allows the clinician and/or external evaluator to rate the quality of the parent–child interaction along 10 dimensions. The first part of the scale examines parental interaction behavior along a hierarchy from least to most sensitive. The second section assesses parent and child social referencing abilities. The last portion evaluates the quality of reciprocity and parent affect. The scale has proven to be a sound clinical instrument and research tool in similar clinical intervention programs (Clark & Seifer, 1983, 1985).

Because each treatment session is videotaped, additional measures can be employed to examine treatment efficacy by impartial evaluators. In current studies, for example, parent–infant communication, caregiver sensitivity, and occurrence of child maltreatment are being examined across treatment sessions (Flanagan, Fimble-Coppa, Riggs, & McDonough, 1991). The most objective source of information regarding the treatment progress are the videotapes. Perhaps the most clinically meaningful sources of information concerning treatment efficacy are the family exit interviews completed at the conclusion of the follow-up home visits.

SUMMARY AND CONCLUSION

Although the interaction guidance approach shows promise as a treatment for parent–infant relationship disturbances, it is important to reiterate that the treatment efficacy data are still being gathered both in the United States and abroad (Cramer et al., 1990; McDonough, 1992). The interaction guidance treatment approach was designed to offer an alternative to dynamically oriented psychotherapies (Cramer & Stern, 1988; Fraiberg, Adelson, & Shapiro, 1975), a behavioral pediatrics orientation (Brazelton, Yogman, Als, & Tronick, 1979; Brazelton, 1984), an interaction coaching model (Field, 1982; Clark & Seifer, 1983), or behaviorally oriented approaches (Patterson, 1982) to family change. (Stern-Bruschweiler & Stern, 1989, provide an excellent review of treatment approaches for parent–child relationship disturbances in their model for conceptualizing the representational world of the primary caregiver in mother–infant therapies.) Clearly, the interaction guidance approach incorporates some of the same principles that underlie these and other successful therapeutic treatments. Interaction guidance makes no effort to supplant other therapeutic efforts to intervene in the lives of families in distress and crisis. Rather, it is designed to supplement existing infant–parent interventions and therapies.

During the last several decades, major changes have occurred in our understanding of the relationship between parents and children. Before this period, there was a clear belief that parents raised their children. Following this, more attention was paid to how children raise their parents. Finally, we have reached integration in the form of a unified theory about how infants develop and how their caregivers facilitate or hinder this developmental process (Sameroff &

Emde, 1989). In this more recent view, neither the caregiver's behavior nor the infant's behavior determine how the relationship will develop; the perspectives and behaviors of both partners must be accounted for.

Unfortunately, some parents and infants experience relationship disturbances that seriously compromise the growth and development of each interactive partner. Improving the relationship often reduces an infant's regulation difficulties by increasing the mutual satisfaction both caregiver and child obtain from their interactions. The interaction guidance treatment approach addresses family relationship problems by observing ongoing parent–infant interactive behavior and by providing guidance to caregivers in their effort to gain a more complete understanding of their infants', and of their own, feelings, thoughts, and actions. In doing so, the interaction guidance therapist facilitates the growth and development of each family member.

REFERENCES

Aponte, H. J., & Van Deusen, J. M. (1981). Structural family therapy. In A. S. Gurman & D. P. Kniskern (Eds.), *Handbook of family therapy*. New York: Brunner Mazel.

Boukydis, C. F. Z. (1990). *NET Help Scale*. Unpublished manuscript.

Bowen, M. (1971). The use of family theory in clinical practice. In J. Haley (Ed.), *Changing families*. New York: Grune & Stratton.

Brazelton, T. B. (1984). *To listen to a child*. Reading, MA: Addison-Wesley.

Brazelton, T. B., Yogman, M., Als, H., & Tronick, E. (1979). Joint regulation of neonate–parent behavior. In E. Tronick (Ed.), *Social interchange in infancy* (pp. 7–22). Baltimore: University Park Press.

Caldwell, B. M., & Bradley, R. H. (1984). *Home Observation for Measurement of the Environment*. Little Rock: University of Arkansas.

Clark, G. N., & Seifer, R. (1983). Facilitating mother–infant communication:A treatment model for high-risk and developmentally delayed infants. *Infant Mental Health Journal, 4*, 67–82.

Clark, G. N., & Seifer, R. (1985). Assessment of parents' interactions with theirdevelopmentally-delayed infants. *Infant Mental Health Journal, 6*, 214–225.

Cramer, B., Robert-Tissot, C., Stern, D. N., Serpa-Rusconi, S., DeMuralt, M., Besson, G., Palacio-Espasa, F., Bachmann, J., Knauer, D., Berney, C., & D'Arcis, U. (1990). Outcome evaluation in brief mother–infant psychotherapy: A preliminary report. *Infant Mental Health Journal, 11*(3), 278–300.

Cramer, B., & Stern, D. N. (1988). Evaluation of changes in mother–infant brief psychotherapy. *Infant Mental Health Journal, 9*, 20–45.

Epstein, N. B., & Bishop, D. S. (1981). Problem-centered

systems therapy of the family. In A.S. Gurman & D.P. Kniskern (Eds.), *Handbook of family therapy.* New York: Brunner/Mazel.

Field, T. (1982). Interaction coaching for high-risk infants and their parents. In H. A. Moss, R. Hess, & C. Swift (Eds.), *Prevention in human services: Vol. 1, Section 4. Early intervention programs for infants* (pp. 5–24). New York: Haworth Press.

Flanagan, P., Fimble-Coppa, D., Riggs, S., & McDonough, S. C. (1991). *Parenting intervention for young teenage mothers at high risk for child maltreatment.* Children's Trust Fund Grant proposal.

Fraiberg, S. H., Adelson, E., & Shapiro, V. (1975). Ghosts in the nursery: A psychoanalytic approach to the problem of impaired infant–mother relationships. *Journal of the American Academy of Child Psychiatry, 14,* 387–422.

Haley, J. (1976). *Problem-solving therapy.* San Francisco: Jossey-Bass.

Leet, H. E., & Dunst, C. J. (1986). Family Resource Scale. In C. J. Dunst, C. M. Trivette, & A. G. Deal (Eds.), *Enabling and empowering families: Principles and guidelines for practice.* Cambridge, MA: Broadline Books.

McDonough, S. C. (1991). Interaction guidance: A technique for treating early relationship disturbances in parents and children. In J. Gomes-Pedro (Ed.), *Bebe XXI.* Lisbon, Portugal: Condor Press.

McDonough, S. C. (1992). Treating early relationship disturbances with interaction guidance. In G. Fava-Vizziello & D.N. Stern (Eds.), *Models and techniques of psychotherapeutic intervention in the first years of life.* Milan: Raffaello Cortina Editore.

Minuchin, S. (1974). *Families and family therapy.* Cambridge, MA: Harvard University Press.

Patterson, G. (1982). *Coercive family process.* Eugene, Oregon: Castalia.

Reiss, D. (1981). *The family construction of reality.* Cambridge, MA: Harvard University Press.

Sameroff, A. J., & Emde, R. (Eds.). (1989). *Relationship disturbances in early childhood: A developmental approach.* New York: Basic Books.

Stern-Bruschweiler, N., & Stern, D. N. (1989). A model for conceptualizing the role of the mother's representational world in various mother–infant therapies. *Infant Mental Health Journal, 10*(3), 142–156.

Zeanah, C.H., & McDonough, S.C. (1989). Clinical approaches to families in early intervention. *Seminars in Perinatology, 13,* 513–522.

28

Infant-Parent Psychotherapy

ALICIA F. LIEBERMAN
JEREE H. PAWL

The goal of infant–parent psychotherapy is to assist the infant or toddler under age 3 to achieve satisfactory socioemotional functioning through improvement in the parent–child relationship. As a rule, therapeutic sessions are conducted jointly with parent(s) and child, although variations of this basic format may be introduced, depending on the age of the child, family composition, and other factors.

The basic idea underlying this approach is that the particular context of working together with the parents and young child offers unique access to a richer range of observation, immediate experience, comment, and reflection than individual sessions with either the parents or the child. The hope is that a developmental trajectory that leans toward an unpromising outcome can be redirected toward an outcome holding much greater promise for parents and child. It was with this in mind that in 1973 Selma Fraiberg began her seminal program for the treatment of parent–infant dyads and triads. Her aim, as she described it, was to free infants from the distortions and displaced affects engulfing them in parental conflict (Fraiberg, 1980, p. 70). Her legacy continues to inspire many individuals and agencies in their efforts to work with the parent–child relationship in infancy and toddlerhood.

WHO IS THE PATIENT?

Beginning practitioners of infant–parent psychotherapy often find themselves grappling with the question: Who are we treating, the parent or the baby? The briefest answer is this: Both.

This is by no means self-evident. When the relationship between infant and parent is in difficulty, there is an inclination to focus on the parent as the primary patient. This is particularly the case if the parent seems significantly disturbed. However, even as we conceptualize infant–parent psychotherapy as the effort to free the baby from parental conflict, we must ask: What baby? What kind of baby? What particular baby?

It needs to be remembered that Fraiberg's inspiration for this form of intervention originated in her successful work with blind infants and their parents, where the problems stemmed directly from the infants' disability. Fraiberg recognized that the absence of essential cues and reactions from a blind infant affected the parent's ability to create the needed empathic resonance with the child. Nevertheless, the parents' individual responses and reactions to the child were used as an essential ingredient in understanding what might be needed and how the therapist might help in each particular case. In spite of the clearly transactional beginnings of infant–parent psychotherapy, intervention has often focused relatively little on the child's role in situations where the parent was identified as having a mental disorder or being disturbed in other ways.

The specific contribution of infants is being increasingly highlighted in the current social context of *in utero* exposure to drugs and other intrauterine assaults. But infants do not need to be physiologically at risk to affect the relationship. Their idiosyncratic impact on their parents is, in fact, *always* an issue in any work with infants and parents. With this in mind, Stanley Greenspan's early program of intervention with multiproblem families included separate work directly with each infant as a compensation for what the child might fail to provide of the necessary nutrients to a thriving relationship (Greenspan et al., 1987). Berry Brazelton, writing from a developmental pediatrics perspective, shows how an infant may "bring a parent along"— clearly underlining the infant's ability to affect and foster the development of the parent (Brazelton, Koslowski, & Main, 1974).

These considerations are relevant to an understanding of who is being treated and why. Neither the parent nor the infant is the sole and ultimate focus of intervention. The focus is rather on their relationship, which is created through the interactional expression of each of their unique characteristics. It is important, then, to be as respectful of the specific infant's contribution (and adaptation) as of the specific parent's contribution (and adaptation). This means that the therapist must hold fast in his or her mind the uniqueness and relevance of the parent's and child's mutual influences as they affect and respond to each other. Although the external ebb and flow of the work responds to evolving clinical needs and possibilities, the *internal* focus in the mind of the therapist must be steadfastly maintained on the parent–child relationship.

THE PROCESS OF EVALUATION

Every treatment begins with an extended period of evaluation, which may last between 4 and 6 weeks and is designed for two major and interrelated purposes. One objective is to ascertain whether a therapeutic alliance conducive to useful work can be formed. The second purpose is to gather the information needed to determine whether infant–parent psychotherapy is appropriate and necessary, and, if so, to decide on the clinical priorities and optimal treatment format.

Parental Motivations and Expectations

Families are referred from many different sources, and parents vary greatly in their motivation to meet with a therapist. At one end of the continuum are parents mandated by the courts to make use of infant mental health services; at the other extreme we find parents who are worried about their feelings toward their baby or about the baby's behavior. Between these two extremes lie most of the patients with whom the infant–parent psychotherapist works: neither clearly and overtly coerced to seek services, nor approaching the therapist purely on their own initiative. This referral pattern applies particularly to community programs serving families who cannot afford private professional fees and whose situations may appear particularly worrisome to the referring agencies.

The parents' source of motivation and their willingness to use services are important facilitators or impediments in the process of forming a therapeutic relationship. These factors also affect the extent to which a therapist may assume agreement with a parent as to the nature of the work. For example, a young teenage mother who is rough and impatient with her 3-month-old baby may follow the suggestion of a day care provider to call an intervention program whose staff members are "people who know a lot about mothers and babies." The mother's motivation to call can range from intrinsic eagerness to receive help to reluctant compliance with a suggestion that she perceives as an actual mandate or even as an implicit threat. Her specific attitude and expectations are not only crucial to the relationship between therapist and patient; they speak as well to the permission she may give to the therapist to conduct an evaluation, let alone therapy.

Although in some sense parental "permission" may evolve implicitly as parent and therapist continue to meet, its initial presence or absence should be clearly understood by the therapist as an issue that is initially wholly unresolved and needs to receive careful attention. In many cases, uninformed, grudging consent is the best way to describe the parent's initial agreement to meet with the therapist. This may be true not only of the single adolescent mother, but also of the affluent young couple whose fear of alienating their pediatrician leads them to "comply" with his or her suggestion to consult with an infant mental health program.

How the parents have arrived in the therapist's office (or how the therapist was allowed into their home) is, then, an important aspect of the initial evaluation phase. The therapist's responsiveness to the parents' experience is a crucial first step. This involves acknowledging all the feelings available—including anger, relief, reluctance, and hope. The therapist needs to remember that the parents are bound to experience a considerable amount of institutional transference about who the therapist "is" and how the therapist may treat them. It is crucial to address these transferences, which are almost always readily available if the therapist is willing to look for them.

The following excerpt from an initial session illustrates how the therapist's thoughtful handling of this mother's negative expectations made it possible to begin a productive collaboration. Mrs. Scott was referred by the local department of social services after four of her five children had been returned following foster home placement. Her oldest son, aged 10, had been recently discharged from a residential treatment program and was also living at home. Mrs. Scott had frequent and severe epileptic seizures, and her IQ score placed her in the 30th percentile. Her social worker considered her "unworkable" because of her aggressiveness toward the authorities. She was referred to our program for work with her 15-month-old boy, who was developmentally delayed.

The first session was described as follows by the therapist:

When I entered the Scotts' apartment, Martine was sitting on the sofa with five active children around her. The TV was on and the volume was high. The floor all around was cluttered with small objects and pieces of paper. I asked, "Martine Scott?" She looked at me angrily and said, "Yes?" I introduced myself, and Martine "evacuated" the children from the big couch in the living room; I could feel that she was trying hard to treat me well. She said, "You can talk." So I talked. I told her about the program. She had doubts about "programs." While talking she began collecting the mess from the floor. She stood on the other side of the living room; the loud TV was between us as we talked. It was clear that this expressed her attitude toward both me and "programs." I respected her doubts, and told her that we (she and I) might find that the program would not be useful for her. She told me about her experiences with social workers, who always told her that her children were not OK. She told me that they took her children from her. I said that she was telling me that "programs are problems." She smiled at me.

. . . After a few minutes of my being there, one of the children, the 5-year-old, who has a speech disability (so Martine told me), said something to me that I could not understand. I asked Martine what he said, and Martine told me that he said something like "You ain't nobody's friend."

. . . During the hour she said a few times that she was not sure about the program, and I emphasized that it would be her decision to work with me or not. She told me that only a few days ago the court "let her loose." Whenever social workers came to her house, they told her that she was "not doing good." It all began when Shawnee (aged 2½) had a bruise that was caused, so she said, by some allergic reaction. She looked worried as she spoke. I understood that she was thinking that I would tell the court if I saw something wrong, and then her children would be taken from her again. I said that I promised her that if I saw a problem I would first talk with her about it and try to solve the problem with her. She seemed to be relieved, and lowered the volume of the TV.

Martine then described her relationship with the social work system. I could gradually feel and sympathize with the hurt and helplessness she experienced. When she talked bitterly about the system's taking children from their mother, I said to her that I knew that their mother is the most important thing children might have, more important than a million dollars. Martine responded by telling me about her own mother raising her children with this spirit. She said she was not sure about programs because she did not want to "spread her life around." I asked her about this, and she told me that the social workers talked about her behind her back. Whatever she said, they told everybody. I said that it must be very humiliating, and I, like her, thought that personal matters should be kept as much as possible between her and the person she spoke with. I said that even if I talked with [her social worker], I would not tell him personal things she told me. She stopped and said, "You are a therapist, right?"

. . . She went to her bag and took out a paper that Shawnee brought her the same day from day care, and showed it to me. There were stars on the page, and at the bottom of the paper was written the word "superstar." Shawnee got enough stars that day to be a superstar. I agreed with her about the importance of that paper and Shawnee's being proud of it. Martine told me that Shawnee had recently been moved from a preschool where the teachers said he was not smart. Now he was doing much better. I said that maybe she felt like Shawnee when she was dealing with the social workers who told her that she was bad. Maybe when she heard that, it made it difficult to be as good as she wanted. She had a strong emotional response, smiled, seemed to be thoughtful, and said, "Yeah, it might be."

. . . Toward the end of the session, she talked about her difficulties raising five children and especially about her difficulties walking each of them to their different schools. She always takes all of them with her because she has no place to leave them. She mentioned the father, who is not with them any more, saying that he was good for the children but not at all good for her. She seemed pained when she said that. After a little bit more than an hour, I left after we scheduled a meeting for next week.

This description of the session has been quoted in detail because it shows how the mother's response evolved from a hostile, guarded stance to active participation, including the disclosure of some painful aspects of her personal life. This change was made possible by the therapist's consistent respect for her reluctance to accept his offer of treatment, his legitimizing the appropriateness of her emotional experience, and his ability to address directly her worries about him.

Of course, the initial session cannot clarify how a parent's institutional transference mixes and matches with expectations formed earlier in his or her history. That is the subject of much further work. But as the excerpt above shows, dealing with the initial transference serves both parent and therapist well.

Therapist–Parent Relationship

The basic stance of the therapist with a parent begins at the beginning. During the period of evaluation, one must exercise the firm habit of thinking of the parents as full partners in whatever course the evaluation and possible treatment will take. The therapist must genuinely conceptualize the effort as doing something *with* someone and not *to* someone. This respect for the wishes and capacities of a parent must be a defining factor of the therapeutic relationship.

The therapist's attitude mirrors those attributes he or she seeks to foster in the parent–child relationship. This parallel process between the therapeutic relationship and the parent–child relationship becomes the foundation for further work. Certainly the therapist does not deny or play down his or her expertise on developmental issues, but the way in which this expertise is delivered becomes an essential aspect of the

work. In fact, how the therapist conveys specialized knowledge may well determine whether or not he or she gets a chance to use the rest of this expertise—in other words, whether the parent agrees to continued therapeutic contact.

The quality of the relationship between therapist and parent is perhaps more crucial in infant–parent psychotherapy than in any other form of treatment, because it is intended to be a mutative factor in the parent's relationship with his or her child. The parameters of respect, concern, accommodation and steady, basic positive regard become crucial as the containers of the entire process of treatment.

Only within this context can the parent's negative transference to child and therapist be usefully discerned. The more disturbed the parent, the more crucial does this reliable emotional context become. Many initial qualities of the therapist–patient relationship will change with time (and one would hope for such change), but the parameters of respect and mutuality must remain in order to withstand the misunderstandings, the distortions, and the transference and countertransference assaults it will need to weather throughout treatment.

This aspect of the therapeutic relationship can be seen as providing the parent with a "corrective attachment experience," which contrasts with the parent's conscious or unconscious expectations of abandonment, punishment, criticism, or ridicule as the normative responses from past or present attachment figures (Lieberman, 1991). The therapist's behavior fails to confirm these expectations and exposes the parent to a more nurturing and reciprocal experience of relationships. In the course of treatment, this new adaptive experience becomes gradually internalized and incorporated into the parent's internal representations of himself or herself and of the child.

Therapist–Child Relationship

The relationships that develop between therapist and child in this model are as varied and multilayered as the therapist–parent relationships. The older the child becomes, the truer this is. The 2-month-old infant is less likely than the 2-year-old child to need or want a separate personal relationship with the therapist. The therapist has a responsibility to understand how his or her relationship with the parent affects the child and how his or her relationship with the child affects the parent. Issues of competition, jealousy, and displacement in relation to the therapist are live ones for both parent and child, and must be sensitively evaluated and monitored. The relationship between therapist and child must be characterized by the same qualities of mutuality and respect that inform the therapist–parent relationship, and which are also gradually internalized by the child as a component of his or her sense of self and of relationships. Within that basic framework, the nature of the relationship will vary as understanding and the evolution of the work dictate. The presence of the baby or toddler in the sessions, however, creates its own special countertransference and identification challenges, which must be carefully monitored so that the therapist–child process complements rather than undermines the therapist–parent endeavor.

The Therapist's Experience

The evaluation period is also the time when the therapist begins to assess his or her own threshold for accommodation and his or her tolerance for dependency needs in relation to this particular patient.

Many patients routinely referred to community agencies are parents who in their own childhood have suffered extreme deprivation. They need a great deal of care, attention and concrete assistance, and they demand in one way or another that those needs be met. To some degree they really must be met. Gratification of needs is not always inappropriate or dangerous; neither does it lead automatically to some dreadful degree of unsurmountable regressive dependency. Consciously modulated gratification of needs can, in fact, lay the groundwork for much effective therapeutic work.

For this to be the case, the therapist must ascertain his or her own tolerance for being needed, and must become aware of the inadvertent or erroneous promises that may be conveyed through specific actions or verbalizations. The real issue is to learn early in each specific therapeutic endeavor where one's tolerances are. Therapists differ dramatically in their willingness to be available outside the sessions, or to provide concrete assistance with everyday problems. Within reasonable limits, different therapists may be more or less forthcoming and still be effective, but they need to know just how forthcoming they can be and at what cost. Angry,

resentful therapists do very poor work or burden others with the costs of their largesse. Optimally, one's initial generosity should be held in check until reality can weigh in.

On the other hand, some threshold of willingness to be available is essential for a therapist to work effectively with very deprived parents. Being below that threshold is not a moral failing unless the imbalance between therapist availability and parent need is not recognized. The evaluation period is the time to begin recognizing it. Issues of availability and flexibility may not be as important with less disturbed parents, although countertransference issues always necessitate careful monitoring in the work with infants and families.

Gathering Information

A main goal of the evaluation is to learn as much as possible about the child's and parent's functioning and their relationship, and to decide together how the therapist can be useful. This is equally true whether the meeting is mandated by the courts or freely chosen by the parent. There needs to be some acknowledged joint agenda, however tentative and however fuzzy, and even if this lack of clarity persists for some time.

Procedures vary as to how the therapist seeks information in the process of developing a joint agenda. There are virtue and efficacy in letting the parent choose the topics and experience their attendant affects spontaneously. This fluidity is extremely useful in understanding the parent's tolerance for painful affect, his or her habitual coping and defensive mechanisms, and, most importantly, how the parent wants to be seen and understood. When the therapist wishes to gather specific information, it is usually best to introduce topics or ask questions as they flow naturally from the conversation. Clearly the parents know that they are seeing the therapist "because" of the baby, and the therapist may feel free to make the child a part of the conversation as this seems to fit where the parent is leading. Simultaneously, the therapist observes how the parent experiences the child, how the child is functioning developmentally and affectively, and what the qualities of their exchanges are. In addition, direct questions and probings are used to begin testing the limits of the parent's tolerance for self-examination.

Developmental testing of the child can be a very useful component of the evaluation process. A parent's anxiety about the child's performance can be considerably alleviated if the test is presented as an opportunity to observe the child's preferred modes of learning, his or her responses when an item is too easy or too difficult, and how he or she compares with other children of similar age. When the testing is videotaped, portions of the tape can be reviewed with the parent in order to elicit impressions and lay the foundation for further work.

Gathering information includes also the people and settings playing a major role in the child's life. This may involve, depending on the situation, the child's day care or child care provider, social workers, pediatricians, and infant specialists in programs for developmentally delayed children. Grandparents, the parent's boyfriends or girlfriends, foster parents, and other significant people may also be interviewed if clinically appropriate and necessary to understand the parent's and child's experiences in greater depth. Infant–parent psychotherapy tends to sprawl, but not without good reason. Careful liaison with those who matter in the lives of parent and child is considered an integral part of the effort to bring about beneficial change.

The Role and Usefulness of Diagnosis

Diagnosing Parents

Diagnostic thinking shapes and is shaped by the course of evaluation and treatment. This is a complex process, because in infant–parent psychotherapy the diagnostic categorization of the parents presents special challenges in anticipating the course of treatment and predicting outcome. Parents with such serious diagnoses as schizophrenia in some form, Borderline Personality Disorder, or Bipolar Disorder may use treatment well and become adequate parents, while others with much less severe psychiatric disorders may remain mired in their anger and rejection of their children. This clinical experience is consonant with research findings that psychiatric diagnosis is not a good predictor of disturbances in parenting (Sameroff, Seifer, & Zax, 1982).

This is not surprising. Parents' emotional investment in their infants cuts across diagnostic categories; so does their motivation to make use of treatment on behalf of their child. As a result, infant–parent psychotherapy can be used effec-

tively with parents who are unlikely candidates for conventional insight-oriented psychotherapy, including those with Narcissistic, Antisocial, and Borderline Personality Disorders (Fraiberg, 1980). Other factors that usually conspire against successful involvement in individual therapy, such as low educational level, social marginality, and inability to introspect, also do not interfere unduly with the progress of infant–parent psychotherapy.

The clinical usefulness of diagnosis is also related to the nature of the population served. When parents enjoy relatively stable circumstances, accurate diagnoses may be relatively uncomplicated to make. The picture becomes considerably more complex when parents live in abject socioeconomic conditions, subjected to the daily degradations and violence increasingly associated with urban poverty (Kotlowitz, 1991). This is even truer if they have also been physically or sexually abused as children and/or as adults.

In these circumstances it is difficult to make informed diagnostic decisions. Is a young mother suffering from Post-Traumatic Stress Disorder as a result of repeated experiences of violence, or does she have Borderline Personality Disorder, perhaps with early trauma as a significant etiological factor? Does a father suffer from an organic brain syndrome, or is he exhibiting transitory symptoms of drug abuse? Does another parent have Schizoid Personality Disorder, or is he or she exhibiting a complex transference reaction of avoidance and withdrawal based on previous experiences with mental health professionals?

Questions of differential diagnosis are often difficult to elucidate in any mental health setting, but they are particularly elusive in the context of infant–parent psychotherapy. Most often we are quite appropriately presented to the parents as professionals who "help parents in their relationship with their babies." This is not the kind of introduction that leads gracefully to a formal psychiatric evaluation. Moreover, such an evaluation only accentuates the already implicit asymmetry of power between the parents and therapist, detracting from the model of reciprocity and receptiveness that needs to be established.

This is not to say that psychiatric diagnosis has no role in infant–parent psychotherapy. In the course of the initial evaluation, observations and trial interventions are aimed in part at acquiring an accurate diagnostic impression of the parents, leading to the assignment of a *Diagnostic* and *Statistical Manual of Mental Disorders* (DSM) diagnosis. This is not a purely academic exercise. It helps the infant–parent psychotherapist decide whether to refer the parent for individual psychiatric treatment in conjunction with infant–parent psychotherapy, and, if so, how that referral should be made. In addition, thinking systematically about the strengths and vulnerabilities of the parent within an objective diagnostic framework helps the therapist to anticipate some of the likely upheavals in the course of treatment, to reflect on the specific nature of the distortions in the parent's perception of the baby, and to better understand impasses in both evaluation and treatment.

These processes, in turn, inform clinical decisions on issues of focus and timing. For example, mothers with serious Narcissistic Personality Disorder are often unable to tolerate a therapist's attention to their babies, which they may experience as abandonment or rejection. They also tend to perceive any comment about their child rearing as a wounding criticism on their mothering. In this context, the appropriate therapeutic response is to focus on such a mother and to provide her with the attention she needs. This therapeutic stance may be adopted throughout the evaluation and into treatment, and it may continue for many months. Until the mother's sense of herself is sufficiently strengthened, there may be only a modest place for occasional, carefully timed, and tactfully phrased reflections on the baby's experience. For this mother, improvement in her psychological functioning and in her relationship with her baby may not come from an exploration of conflict, but primarily from changes in her sense of self as a result of her therapist's initial and continuing empathic availability.

Parents with concrete thinking styles and impoverished egos may need expressions of empathy and support conveyed through actions rather than words. Identifying concrete needs and offering assistance—such as driving them to an appointment, helping them to fill out forms, or interceding on their behalf during bureaucratic transactions—make real for them the therapist's more abstract offers of help. This is not only because such actions help to build trust in the parents that a therapist can see things from their point of view, or because advocating for them gives them some flickering hope that the therapist might be capable of helping after all. Even more importantly, the therapist's availability in concrete and emotionally supportive

ways often represents for the parents a first encounter with the notion that relationships can be rewarding and helpful rather than burdensome, disappointing, or abusive. Parents with severely impoverished egos often do not perceive themselves as people who can be likable or deserving of care and attention. Discovering that the therapist thinks highly enough of them that he or she is willing to make concrete efforts on their behalf can become the first step in enhancing the parents' sense of their own worth. This, in turn, is an important condition in enabling parents to become more positively invested in their babies. The psychological growth resulting from this approach is often astounding. One mother expressed her new sense of herself in these words: "Isn't it interesting how something that begins outside ends up inside of you, like being alone and not fitting in? That's why what I do with my baby is so important, because it's going to end up inside of her."

Parents with a diagnosis of Antisocial Personality Disorder, many of whom engage in criminal activities (which they may either boast about or confess sheepishly to the therapist), are often relieved when the therapist conveys a realistic concern about the consequences of these activities for the parents and their babies. In such a case, neither empathy nor interpretation is sufficient. Rather, the therapist needs to build a framework that emphasizes acceptance of the parent coupled with urgent concern about protection from danger. The therapist needs to find a nonthreatening way of conveying to the parent his or her worry that the activities involved can lead to harm—for example, parental incarceration and foster placement for the child. Only such an approach carries some hope of encouraging self-exploration and behavioral change, with the therapist as an ally in instituting difficult changes in lifestyle.

For parents with a sturdier sense of self and with a more painfully acute awareness of inner conflict about their babies, the approaches described above may not be appropriate. The more strictly psychodynamic model of freeing the baby from engulfment in the parent's unresolved childhood conflicts (Fraiberg, 1980) is most readily and immediately applicable in these situations, where the parent is willing and able to explore the past in order to understand its links with present parenting difficulties.

Without exception, however, a continuing awareness and sensitive monitoring of the quality of the relationship between the therapist and the parent remain at the forefront of the treatment. Often, linking conflicts in parenting with childhood experiences represents the culmination of a long therapeutic process that may begin with the painstaking and unswerving appreciation for the parent's subjective experience outlined in earlier paragraphs.

Diagnosing Infants

The diagnostic classification of infants and toddlers presents even thornier problems than that of adults (see Emde, Bingham, & Harmon, Chapter 14, this volume). As mentioned earlier, the extraordinary individuality of babies in the first days of life is now well recognized, as is the impact of a baby's attributes on a parent's pleasure and self-confidence as the caregiver. The available evidence indicates that parents and babies engage in subtle transactional interactions from the time they set eyes on each other; that they adapt to each other's idiosyncrasies; and that babies' expectations about the rhythms of everyday life are affectively colored by the nature of these adaptations. (See Stern, 1985, for a review of this literature.)

If the relational context in which an infant or toddler is assessed is so inextricably linked to the behaviors we observe, how can we tease apart diagnosable psychopathology in the baby from costly but highly specific adaptations to situational demands? Winnicott's (1960/1965) ineffable quip that "there is no such thing as a baby" is an appropriate organizing core for pondering this question. By implication, it is equally true that "there is no such a thing as a parent." Whole volumes have been written to explicate the interactional process so aptly implied in Winnicott's pithy remark (e.g., Sameroff & Emde, 1989).

The rapid rate of development in infancy adds yet another dimension to the difficulty of early diagnosis. For example, do we think of a fussy, inconsolable, overly reactive 2-month-old as having a regulatory disorder (see Greenspan & Wieder, Chapter 18, this volume), or do we postulate that he or she suffers from that trying but time-limited affliction of infancy known as colic (Lester, Boukydis, Garcia Coll, & Hole, 1990)? Or is colic an early and reversible form of regulatory disorder? Perhaps only time can tell. The puzzles of developmental continuities and discontinuities are still being unraveled, and the answers, as they emerge, will undoubtedly shed much light on the diagnostic issues of early infancy.

In spite of the difficulties inherent in early diagnosis, it is clear that a comprehensive classification system for infants and toddlers is much needed at this stage in the development of infant mental health as an autonomous field. Such a system can legitimize the existence of mental health disturbances in infancy and toddlerhood. It can provide a uniform vocabulary to facilitate communication among professionals and enhance the collaboration between researchers and clinicians. It can also enrich the practitioner's repertoire by raising alternative clinical hypotheses that might not emerge spontaneously in the course of assessment and treatment, partly as a result of the clinician's own biases and preferred modes of thinking about etiological factors. Given the current state of the art in this area, diagnostic categories for infants and toddlers can be used as if they were descriptive statements that summarize (more or less accurately) many hours of detailed observation. Although the DSM categories are useful for charting purposes, an important effort to develop a new taxonomy is now being conducted by the Diagnostic Task Force of Zero to Three, National Center for Clinical Infant Programs, chaired by Stanley Greenspan. This comprehensive classification system promises to become a useful tool for a more uniform description of early disturbances, which can enhance communication among infant mental health professionals both within and between subdisciplines.

THE TREATMENT PROCESS

The intent of the evaluation process is to make the transition to treatment relatively seamless, except as it is acknowledged and agreed to by the parents. In this sense, treatment partakes of many of the features characterizing the evaluation, but the therapist now has explicit parental permission to explore and intervene.

Treatment Formats

The classic format of infant–parent psychotherapy consists of joint meetings of the therapist with the parent(s) and baby. This setting works best when the infant is preverbal and when his or her own input and demands can be incorporated more or less smoothly into the therapeutic work with the parents. The process then moves back and forth between past and present, feelings and behavior, following the flow of parental associations and interactions between parent and child.

As a baby becomes a toddler, his or her own demands may be so imperiously asserted that therapist and parent can hardly exchange a few words, let alone explore in depth the parent's feelings about the situation. It may also happen that a parent speaks in the child's presence about life events, feelings, and experiences that are quite frightening for the child or that directly affect the child's sense of self in relation to the parent. In some cases, marital discord plays a major role in the parents' experience of the child and needs to be addressed out of the child's hearing.

In all these circumstances, the treatment format may consist of alternating joint parent–child sessions with sessions where the therapist meets with the parent(s) alone, or adding weekly sessions for the same purpose. Flexibility in this regard is a major virtue in finding the right arrangement to support the therapeutic work.

The evaluation process may uncover particular vulnerabilities in the child that are shaping a parent's responses in major ways. Direct treatment of the child, intermixed with focused work on the parent–child relationship, is then the method of choice. Didactic guidance may be offered to the parent in the context of ongoing exploration of his or her initial and current feelings toward the child. Sessions with the parent(s) alone can alternate with joint parent–child sessions. The joint sessions may focus on trying out different approaches to the child and offering the parent fairly didactic "practice" in handling the child's difficult behavior, while also exploring the impediments the parent may encounter in these attempts. The individual sessions may be used to explore in greater depth the parent's experience of what transpires during the joint sessions and in the course of daily life with the child.

Parents' active input is an essential ingredient in choosing the treatment format. The parents need to experience the setting and composition of the sessions as compatible with their needs in order to have useful work take place.

The Content of Treatment

The content of treatment varies depending on the circumstances, both between cases and in the evolution of the work within a case, as the following vignette illustrates.

Antonio, 22 months old, was referred by his pediatrician because of intractable tantrums, recklessness, and accident proneness. His mother was furious at him, called him a "monster," and threatened to leave him. His father spoke about the need for patience and understanding, but seemed depressed and ineffective. Both parents reported that they screamed at each other, threatened each other with divorce, and occasionally scuffled with each other. With the parents' input, treatment was arranged to include weekly individual sessions with the mother, weekly sessions with parents and child, and monthly sessions with the couple.

The joint sessions with the child were used to speak to the child's feelings of need for protection and of anger and anxiety when the parents did not recognize these needs. Tantrums as they occurred were traced to their immediate antecedent causes, and the parents' and child's different perceptions of these causes were explored in emotionally supportive ways and in a simple language addressed to the feeling experience of parents and child.

For example, Antonio climbed on his father's back, obviously enjoying this. The father went along with him for a while and then abruptly put the child down with rough movements. Antonio was startled at first, then cried bitterly. The therapist asked the father how he understood what just happened. After the father spoke, the therapist translated the experience to Antonio: "You were having such a good time, and then your daddy's back started to hurt and he put you down. You got scared." Feeling supported by the therapist, the father was able to take over and told Antonio, "Come sit on my lap." Antonio sulked and did not move. The therapist said, "I think Antonio's feelings are still hurt." The father laughed, picked up Antonio, and cuddled him. The therapist said, "I have the impression that when Antonio is rough on your back, you kind of get angry with him without meaning to." The father thought for a minute and said, "Maybe. I'm scared my back will go out and I won't be able to work." The therapist asked whether the father found it hard to tell Antonio he couldn't climb on his back. The father answered, "I don't want to be a weakling." He told Antonio, "I'm sorry I scared you." Antonio cuddled against him. In the marital sessions, the therapist had a chance to explore what "being a weakling" meant for this father.

The individual sessions with the mother focused initially on her experience of Antonio as a demanding child who could never be satisfied and who cried "for hours" when she withdrew the breast after nursing him. Gradually she began to describe her planned but unwanted pregnancy, which she perceived as forced on her by her husband's wish to have a child; her wish to "make it" in the corporate world without being tied down by her husband's demands for companionship and her son's demands for constant attention; and her disappointment at her husband, who in her words *was* a "weakling," easily daunted by the challenges of life. As she described her feelings, Mrs. Mendes showed no awareness of or empathy for either her husband's or her son's experiences, and dismissed with impatience the therapist's cautious attempts to explore this area. After many months of the therapist's consistent mirroring of her experiences, Mrs. Mendes began to describe her own mother's dislike of being a mother and the older woman's contempt both for her husband and for Mrs. Mendes, both of whom she predicted would "never be anybody." Mrs. Mendes's identification with her mother's contemptuous attitude toward mothering and her simultaneous effort to prove her wrong by "becoming someone important" then became clearer. As this conflict was explored, the therapist asked, "How does Antonio fit in all this?" Mrs. Mendes said, "He keeps me down!" Surprised by her outbursts, she went on to reflect, "Oh, my God, I guess I blame *him* because I feel so stuck. But it's not his fault, poor devil." For the first time, she could experience some empathy for her child, although still embedded in much anger. A long process proved necessary to untangle the complex web of identifications, projections, and projective identifications that had evolved between Mrs. Mendes and her child. Antonio's difficult temperament was thoroughly explored as a contributing factor to Mrs. Mendes's distress. Her responses to Antonio during the joint sessions were examined whenever appropriate in the individual work, and this proved extremely useful in freeing Antonio from his mother's enduring and pervasive intrapsychic conflicts and enhancing her understanding for her child's difficulties.

The marital sessions were focused on supporting the legitimacy of each of the parent's longings and ambitions, acknowledging sympathetically the conflicts and misunderstanding that inevitably arose, helping them to identify the early warning signs that an explosive confrontation was brewing, and helping them to practice together new forms of communication. As the therapist helped them to remember their feelings when their own parents fought, they were also able to empathize more with

Antonio's terror and to tone down their arguments when he was present.

Clearly, no single case can represent the whole range of cases where infant–parent psychotherapy can be the treatment of choice. However, the case chosen for illustration here is a useful example of the kind of work necessary when the child, the parents, and the marital relationship are all contributing powerfully to the disturbance prompting the referral.

Boundary Issues

The question of professional boundaries is rampant in infant–parent psychotherapy, because the intervention may occur in many different contexts and it may involve communication with many different agencies and significant people. The therapist may drive a parent to the pediatrician's office or intercede on the family's behalf with the housing authorities; he or she may discuss with the child welfare worker the details of a reunification plan or argue against (or in favor of) the child's removal from the home. The therapist may also walk into a family fight when he or she arrives for the home visit, or may find the mother's new lover sneaking out when he or she rings the bell.

Boundary issues are complex and cannot be determined by fiat once and for all. Each specific situation involves important clinical issues and demands thoughtful consideration. Whether, for example, the therapist attends the high school graduation of a parent who had been demoralized and suicidal at the beginning of treatment 2 years earlier cannot be answered as an abstract question, but is an issue for this particular treatment; the decision needs to be shared by parent and therapist. It is important to learn to share with the parent some aspects of the therapist's thinking on the issues, so that making the decision becomes a genuine experience of mutual trust.

COMMON
THERAPEUTIC MISTAKES

Infant–parent psychotherapy is often a bewildering endeavor. The dilemmas of focus and timing frequently encountered in individual psychotherapy become magnified when a needy baby and a needy parent (or two) are clamoring, each in his or her own way, for the therapist's attention. Some of the more frequent therapeutic mistakes that occur in this context are described below.

1. *The therapist becomes so involved in the parental experience that he or she forgets to include the baby in the evolving understanding of the situation.* Sometimes the parent's account of past experiences or present circumstances is so compelling that the therapist becomes unwittingly drawn into a form of intervention that would be indistinguishable from individual psychotherapy were it not for the physical presence of the baby. When this happens, the therapist listens to the parent's story only in its individual dimension, without asking herself how what he or she is hearing might reflect on the parent's feelings toward the baby. Valuable opportunities to understand the parent–infant relationship in greater depth and to intervene if appropriate are missed in this way.

The infant–parent psychotherapist needs to listen to the parents not only with a "third ear" (Reik, 1948), but also with a "fourth ear." The fourth one is reserved for the baby's experience and for ascertaining how it may fit in the ongoing parental narrative. Knowledge gained in this process need not be spoken about at the moment (or perhaps ever), but it should become an integral part of the therapist's *attitude* toward the family, permeating those interventions she does choose to make. Optimally, every therapeutic intervention should be made with an awareness of how it may affect the baby and with the intent to bring a beneficial component into the parent–child relationship.

2. *The therapist is too timid in introducing the baby's experience into the therapeutic process.* Sometimes the therapist is keenly aware of how the baby fits into the content of the session, but fails to introduce this topic because he or she feels awkward about interrupting the parent's flow of associations, worries about antagonizing the parent, is unsure about timing, or is influenced by a variety of other considerations.

A major factor in this hesitation is a therapist's lack of experience in infant–parent psychotherapy. This form of intervention, although rooted in traditional psychodynamically oriented psychotherapy, calls for a special flexibility of focus in moving back and forth between the parent's and the baby's experience, between concrete events and feeling states, and between the past and the present.

This flexibility of focus calls also for a therapeutic vocabulary that can encompass simultaneously the separate though intertwined subjective experiences of the parent and the baby. Like all therapeutic outlooks and vocabularies, those of infant–parent psychotherapy are acquired slowly and painstakingly in the course of many hours of work and many trials and errors, as the therapist finds his or her own style and seeks "goodness of fit" with each of many different parents and babies. This job is made more difficult by the fact that the baby cannot articulate his or her feelings. Even experienced therapists who are at ease practicing individual, marital, or family psychotherapy find themselves daunted by the task of remaining constantly attuned to the unspoken signals of a baby in need, interpreting those signals, and incorporating this understanding into the work with the parents.

Sometimes the therapist's timidity in speaking for the baby is not attributable to inexperience. The work of infant–parent psychotherapy can evoke powerful countertransference feelings, including intense identification with a neglected baby, rage at abusing parents, fear of violence, or a myriad of other hidden emotions that may render the therapist mute or at least tongue-tied. When this situation lasts over many sessions, it seriously compromises the work of infant–parent psychotherapy because it effectively shuts the infant off from the therapeutic process. Consultation with a colleague or supervisor is indicated when the therapist's efforts to overcome this impasse through his or her own efforts are not successful.

3. *The therapist colludes with the parent in the maltreatment of the child.* Sometimes the therapist's reluctance to address the infant's experience is so pervasive a stance, or extends to such severe or chronic instances of abuse and neglect, that it becomes a collusion with the parent's maltreatment of the child.

The therapist may consciously believe that it is only a matter of choosing the right timing, or that the therapeutic alliance is not yet strong enough to withstand a direct focus on the infant. These may be valid considerations, but there are occasions when the seriousness of the maltreatment should lead the therapist to ask: "How long until I find the right timing? Can a genuine therapeutic alliance be built on a foundation of silence about parental cruelty? What is the effect on the child of this essential complicity?"

Not addressing maltreatment legitimizes it. If a therapist introduces himself or herself as a specialist in the parent–child relationship but witnesses its excesses without intervening, a parent may well assume that there is nothing wrong with his or her actions—that the therapist is not objecting because no objection is warranted. This conclusion can only strengthen the parent's acted-out conviction that relationships with children are based on control rather than reciprocity. If parents were themselves psychologically or physically abused (as is most often the case), the unconscious inference is that they "deserved what they got" when they were children, just as their own children now deserve the punishment received. The therapist's stance legitimizes their own early maltreatment.

As we have said repeatedly throughout this chapter, the infant–parent psychotherapist seeks to incorporate a child's physical presence and emotional experience into the therapeutic process in a way that helps both the parent and the child. Ultimately, colluding with a parent in the child's maltreatment betrays the parent as well as the child, because the therapist's silence and inaction rob the parent of the opportunity to change his or her inner experience in ways that increase the pleasure and self-esteem derived from the relationship with the child.

4. *The therapist is so identified with the infant that he or she cannot be empathically attuned to the parent's experience.* It is difficult to watch a baby suffer from maltreatment without blaming the parent. The therapist may witness situations where an infant or toddler is ignored, misunderstood, yelled at, slapped, or punished harshly and arbitrarily. The therapist may also listen to parental diatribes against the child ("He's a monster," "She hates me," "She has the temperament of a drug addict," "He'll become a mass murderer") while also being horrified by the infant's predicament as a target of parental projections. There are also situations in which less volatile parents consistently reject, ignore, or misinterpret their children's needs and behaviors in equally distressing ways.

Anger at a parent, rescue fantasies, and guilt for being unable to instantly remedy a child's plight are common responses in these situations. When the therapist is unaware of the countertransference nature of such emotions, he or she may speak with passionate eloquence on behalf of the baby while remaining totally oblivious to the parent's intense and unmet emotional needs. Worse, the therapist may find himself or

herself lecturing or even recriminating against the parent. The parent, in turn, may recoil in silence, lash out in anger, or pretend to comply while withdrawing inwardly from further exchanges. The therapeutic dialogue is broken, at least for the moment.

In responding in this manner, the therapist is in effect failing with the parent in the same way that the parent is failing with the baby, although in a more controlled and articulate form, and ostensibly for a just cause—the protection of the child. While the parent blames the baby, the therapist blames the parent. In this therapeutically damaging parallel process, parent and therapist both forget that the situation at hand is only the most immediate and concrete representation of a tormented emotional landscape where both parent and baby are being victimized. Blame does not help. Only understanding holds hope for a way out of this re-enactment.

A therapist who feels himself or herself about to be overpowered by strong wishes to recriminate against the parent or save the child will do well instead to remain silent until these intense emotions abate. These few minutes can be used to struggle for inner balance in whatever way works best for the individual therapist—for example, by reviewing what he or she knows about the parent's past and present experiences that may restore empathy; by staying with his or her emotional reaction as a vehicle for gauging more accurately the emotional forces at work; or by reminding himself or herself (as many times as necessary) that anger and identification with one victim are poor guides to immediate therapeutic intervention with a dyad.

The therapist may emerge from this process with the right attitude to explore the situation in a way that simultaneously supports the parent and the child. Alternatively, the therapist may find that he or she is still in the grip of intense emotions. He or she may muster the presence of mind to underline to the parent the need to reflect on what just happened, but more extensive intervention may need to be postponed until the therapist gains a better hold on these strong feelings. Opportunities to intervene when it is appropriate will always continue to present themselves. In any event, the experience may serve to enrich the therapist's commitment and skill in working *with* the parent as the primary therapeutic stance, and considering unilateral action as the last resort in protecting the child from serious and immediate harm.

CONTRAINDICATIONS TO INFANT-PARENT PSYCHOTHERAPY

There are situations where infant–parent psychotherapy is not the treatment of choice, in spite of marked disturbances in the parent–child relationship. This is particularly the case when a parent has no control over the source of the problem, or no motivation to try to exercise control over it. One such circumstance is when a parent is involved in such severe drug abuse that the habit has become his or her major priority and the parent cannot mobilize inner resources on behalf of the child. Another situation is when a parent's psychosis, thought disorder, or mental retardation is pervasive and not amenable to treatment, affecting his or her judgment and hence the safety of the child.

Multiproblem families whose difficulties are chronic and severe may not benefit from infant–parent psychotherapy alone. In this situation, a careful evaluation is necessary to determine the range and kinds of supportive services that can provide necessary adjuncts, as well as the ways in which such services can best be integrated. Such things as respite care, day care, job training, parent support groups, parent education, and drop-in centers may well serve to enhance the infant–parent psychotherapy, or it may be clear that until there is sufficient improvement in parental functioning such referrals will prove fruitless and possibly undermining. Unless the family chaos or the nature of a parent's psychiatric disturbance makes any regularity of meeting impossible, or the major difficulties are not expressed within the parent–child relationship, an extended evaluation period will provide the testing ground for parent and therapist to determine the potential usefulness of the work. Improvement of any kind in the developmental environment of a young child is sufficient reason to pursue the effort, as long as the goals are reasonable and realistic.

OTHER APPLICATIONS OF INFANT-PARENT PSYCHOTHERAPY

The conception of infant mental health underlying infant–parent psychotherapy goes well beyond the clinical setting of intervention with infants and parents. It extends to consultation to child care centers and child protection agencies, and to efforts to influence the legal system through consultation with private attorneys and the city attorney's office as well as testimony in the domestic and juvenile courts.

The importance of respecting and working to enhance a child's primary emotional relationship is at the center of all these endeavors. In day care settings, this attitude translates into an explicit focus on the relationship between the child and the day care provider (Pawl, 1990). In consultation with child protection agencies and legal institutions, the effort is to help social workers, attorneys, referees, judges, and all those with the power to shape decisions to work together in developing the plan that is most likely to protect the child in the long run, regardless of personal values and opinions about the biological parents' lifestyle or the foster parents' idiosyncrasies. When a collaborative outcome is not possible, court testimony is used to speak for the emotional experiences of the child.

Just as the therapist's relationship with the parent is a major mutative factor in infant–parent psychotherapy, the working relationship with the representatives of the different agencies needs to be at the core of consultation activities. Expertise cannot be imposed by fiat, no matter how persuasive the arguments. Understanding the specific outlook, viewpoint, concerns, and responsibilities of the other professionals is essential in fostering a dialogue that may lead to interagency cooperation on behalf of the child, and hence to a more comprehensive and viable long-term plan.

THE EFFECTIVENESS OF INFANT-PARENT PSYCHOTHERAPY: RESEARCH EVIDENCE

The practice of infant–parent psychotherapy has been marked by consistent efforts to determine its efficacy via objective methods of evaluation. Two major research projects provide strong evidence that infant–parent psychotherapy is indeed useful in alleviating distortions in a parent's perception of the baby, ameliorating conflicts in the parent–infant relationship, and enhancing the child's socioemotional functioning.

An early study (Fraiberg, Lieberman, Pekarsky, & Pawl, 1981a, 1981b) assessed the effectiveness of treatment by focusing on each parent–infant dyad before and after the intervention. This involved an $n = 1$ method, with each infant serving as his or her own control. The sample consisted of 50 infants in the age range of 0–3 years and their parents, referred for treatment because of impairments in their infant–parent relationships. Clinical rating scales were developed for five assessment categories: infant health, affective–social functioning, adaptive modes, cognitive–motor performance, and quality of parenting. The score for quality of parenting included adequacy of physical caregiving, ability to read the baby's signals, and emotional availability. Each scale had 6 points, from adequate (1) to gravely impaired (6).

Each baby and parent were rated on the basis of data collected during two assessment periods, one at the beginning and one at the end of treatment. After treatment, between 89% and 96% of the babies improved by at least 1 rating point over their pretreatment performance in the various assessment categories. The percentage of infants who recovered completely and were rated as fully adequate (1) in their functioning after treatment ranged from 59.2% for adaptive modes to 61.5% in the affective–social area. Similarly, 86% of the parents improved relative to their pretreatment scores, and 62.5% were rated as providing fully adequate care after treatment.

A more recent evaluation of the effectiveness of infant–parent psychotherapy used a systematic research design with random assignment of mother–infant dyads to intervention and control groups (Lieberman, Weston, & Pawl, 1991). The central hypothesis was that after the termination of treatment the intervention group would perform significantly better than controls in measures of maternal empathy, infant security of attachment, and mother–child partnership.

The hallmark of this study was the integration of the clinical methods of infant–parent psychotherapy with the well-validated research methodology developed to study individual differences in the quality of attachment (Ainsworth, Blehar, Waters, & Wall, 1978). Conceptually, infant–parent psychotherapy is eminently compatible with attachment theory, because both systems share the theoretical tenet that the emotional quality of the mother–child relationship is both an index of and a contributor to the infant's mental health. From this common core, attachment theory has spearheaded a rich tradition of research to operationalize the socioemotional implications of this position, whereas infant–parent psychotherapy has focused on the creation of clinical methods of intervention to ameliorate the consequences of early attachment disturbances. It follows that a systematic evaluation of the effectiveness of parent–infant psychotherapy can be greatly enhanced by the research methodology derived from attachment theory (Lieberman, 1991).

Anxious attachment as assessed in the Strange Situation (Ainsworth et al., 1978) was used as the operational criterion for clinical intervention. The sample comprised 100 low-socioeconomic-status, Spanish-speaking 12-month-old infants and their mothers. Anxiously attached dyads were randomly assigned to an intervention or a control group. Securely attached dyads comprised a second control group. Clinical intervention (infant–parent psychotherapy) began immediately after experimental group assignment and lasted 1 year, until each baby's second birthday. The outcome evaluation at 24 months was modeled after the Strange Situation; however, it lasted 1½ hours and included 20-minute episodes of free play with the mother and with a stranger, as well as one 10-minute separation episode.

The infant–parent psychotherapy sessions consisted of weekly visits with each mother and baby, which lasted 1½ hours and took place at the home or in our office playroom, as preferred by the mother. Each dyad had one intervenor during the entire intervention period. There were four intervenors, all of them bilingual, bicultural women with master's degrees in psychology or social work.

The therapeutic goals were operationally defined as an increase in the mother's empathic responsiveness to the child's signals and in her active engagement in interaction with the child; an enhancement of the reciprocal partnership between mother and child in negotiating the ubiquitous disagreements of toddlerhood; and a decrease in the child's avoidance, resistance, and angry behaviors directed at the mother. Taken together, these outcome measures were considered to comprise the major behavioral manifestations of a secure mother–child relationship that could protect and promote the toddler's mental health.

The results of the statistical analyses showed that the treatment goals were largely achieved. The intervention group performed significantly better than the anxious controls in the outcome measures and was essentially indistinguishable from the secure control group.

Optimally, intervention research ought to elucidate not only *whether* a treatment method is effective, but also *how* it is effective. In order to shed some light on this very complex question, we assessed each treatment group mother on three parameters that might contribute to treatment outcome: regularity of attendance, mother's relationship with the intervenor, and level of therapeutic process attained. Each of these measures involves a rating scale where every anchor point is extensively described (Greenspan & Wieder, 1987). Scoring was done by the therapist and Lieberman after the termination of treatment.

The results showed that regularity of attendance was not significantly correlated with any of the outcome measures. The mother's emotional relationship with the therapist was significantly correlated to only two outcome measures: Mothers who formed a strong positive relationship with the intervenor tended to be more empathic to their infants at outcome, and their children in turn tended to show less avoidance on reunion. The most influential treatment variable was the level of therapeutic process attained by a mother—in other words, her ability to use infant–parent psychotherapy to explore her feelings toward herself and toward her child. This measure was significantly correlated in the predicted directions with most outcome measures. Mothers who used the treatment for psychological exploration were more empathic and more actively engaged with their toddlers at outcome. Their children showed less anger and avoidance, more security of attachment, and more reciprocal partnership in the negotiation of mother–child conflict.

This well-differentiated pattern of findings emerged in spite of the predictably high intercorrelation among the three measures of therapeutic process. Such a clear picture suggests that treatment attendance by itself is not conducive to therapeutic change. In other words, the mere act of attending treatment is not associated with improved socioemotional functioning in either infant or mother—a finding that negates the hypothesis that the social component of treatment may by itself lead to change.

A good relationship between mother and intervenor was associated with increased maternal empathy and decreased infant avoidance, suggesting that the human quality of the therapeutic relationship has significant repercussions on both mother and child behavior. By itself, however, this emotional connection seemed to be a less powerful vehicle for change than when it was used by the mother for the explicit purposes of self-exploration. These findings provide support for a psychodynamic view of therapeutic change as based on the emotional self-knowledge that can be achieved through a nurturing and supportive therapeutic relationship (Wallerstein, 1986).

These research findings are clinically rewarding, because they support the stance of infant–parent psychotherapy that the subjective experience of mother and infant rather than their behavior is the proper focus of treatment (Fraiberg, 1980; Lieberman & Pawl, 1990). Our research results indicate that making subjective experience rather than behavior the focus of treatment actually leads to significant behavioral change in both mother and child.

CONCLUSION

Infant–parent psychotherapy is a multifaceted method of intervention that uses joint work with parents and infants under 3 years of age with the ultimate goal of improving parent–infant relationships and the children's socioemotional functioning. The therapist strives to create a therapeutic relationship characterized by flexibility and receptiveness to the parent's and child's needs. This therapeutic relationship with the parent is a basic catalyst for change, and it becomes the vehicle for utilizing a combination of intervention modalities that include insight-oriented psychotherapy, unstructured developmental guidance, emotional support, and concrete assistance. The underlying assumption is that the corrective experience of the therapeutic relationship, generated through the therapist's stance in regard to the parent, coalesces with the new knowledge and self-understanding fostered by the different therapeutic modalities. It is these processes, created by therapist and parent, that can lead to enduring changes in the parent's and child's experience of each other, the quality of their relationship, and their sense of themselves.

REFERENCES

Ainsworth, M. D. S., Blehar, M. C., Waters, E., & Wall, S. (1978). *Patterns of attachment: A psychological study of the Strange Situation.* Hillsdale, NJ: Erlbaum.
Brazelton, T. B., Koslowski, B., & Main, M. (1974). The

origins of reciprocity: The early mother–infant inter-action. In M. Lewis & L. Rosenblum (Eds.), *The effect of the infant on its caregiver* (pp. 49–76). New York: Wiley.

Fraiberg, S. (Ed.). (1980). *Clinical studies in infant mental health.* New York: Basic Books.

Fraiberg, S., Lieberman, A. F., Pekarsky, J. H., & Pawl, J. H. (1981a). Treatment and outcome in an infant psychiatry program: Part I. *Journal of Preventive Psychiatry, 1,* 89–111.

Fraiberg, S., Lieberman, A. F., Pekarsky, J. H., & Pawl, J. H. (1981b). Treatment and outcome in an infant psychiatry program: Part II. *Journal of Preventive Psychiatry, 1*(2), 143–167.

Greenspan, S. I., Wieder, S., Lieberman, A. F., Nover, R., Lourie, R., & Robinson, M. (Eds.). (1987). *Infants in multirisk families.* Madison, CT: International Universities Press.

Greenspan, S. I., & Wieder, S. (1987). Dimensions and levels of the therapeutic process. In S. Greenspan, S. Wieder, A. F. Lieberman, R. Nover, R. Lourie, & M. Robinson (Eds.), *Infants in multirisk families* (pp. 391–430). Madison, CT: International Universities Press.

Kotlowitz, A. (1991). *There are no children here.* Garden City, NY: Doubleday.

Lester, B. M., Boukydis, C. F. Z., Garcia Coll, C. T., & Hole, W. T. (1990). Colic for developmentalists. *Infant Mental Health Journal, 11*(4), 321–331.

Lieberman, A. F. (1991). Attachment theory and infant–parent psychotherapy: Some conceptual, clinical and research considerations. In D. Cicchetti & S. Toth (Eds.), *Models and Integrations Rochester Symposium on Developmental Psychopathology* (Vol. 3, 261–288). Hillsdale, NJ: Erlbaum.

Lieberman, A. F., & Pawl, J. H. (1990). Disorders of attachment and secure base behavior in the second year of life: Conceptual issues and clinical intervention. In M. T. Greenberg, D. Cicchetti, & E. M. Cummings (Eds.), *Attachment in the preschool years* (pp. 375–398). Chicago: University of Chicago Press.

Lieberman, A. F., Weston, D. R., & Pawl, J. H. (1991). Preventive intervention and outcome with anxiously attached dyads. *Child Development, 62,* 199–209.

Pawl, J. H. (1990). Infants in day care: Reflections on experiences, expectations and relationships. *Zero to Three: Bulletin of the National Center for Clinical Infant Programs, 10*(3), 1–6.

Reik, T. (1948). *Listening with the third ear.* New York: Farrar, Straus.

Sameroff, A. J., & Emde, R. N. (Eds.). (1989). *Relationship disturbances in early childhood.* New York: Basic Books.

Sameroff, A. J., Seifer, R., & Zax, M. (1982). Early development of children at risk for emotional disorders. *Monographs of the Society for Research in Child Development, 47*(7, Serial No. 199).

Stern, D. (1985). *The interpersonal world of the infant.* New York: Basic Books.

Wallerstein, R. S. (1986). *Forty-two lives in treatment: A study of psychoanalysis and psychotherapy.* New York: Guilford Press.

Winnicott, D. W. (1965). The theory of the parent–infant relationship. In D. W. Winnicott, *The maturational processes and the facilitating environment* (pp. 37–55). New York: International Universities Press. (Original work published 1960)

VI

SOCIAL APPLICATIONS OF
INFANT MENTAL HEALTH

Beyond the particular infant and family in need of assistance are larger issues of concern to millions of other infants. In this arena, the knowledge we have acquired about the development of normal, high-risk, and disordered infants may be applied to broader questions of social policy. Zero to Three, a national advocacy group, has taken a leading role in the United States in advocating on behalf of infants and their families.

To begin Part VI, Barton and Williams (Chapter 29) review research on infant day care, including the current controversies over out-of-home care in the first year of life. They caution against a simplistic reduction of the issues to questions of good versus bad, and call for answers to more specific questions in future research. Pointing out that current debates derive as much from what we do not know as from what we do know, the authors also recommend more careful specification of the dimensions of social development to be assessed in future studies, as well as more careful specification of most aspects of high-quality care. Finally, they grapple with the issues of what parents and policy makers are to do in the period before more definitive answers become available.

In Chapter 30, Horner and Guyer review the complex problems confronted by infant mental health professionals who are asked to assist in the determination of custody and visitation issues involving infants. They consider the role of expert witnesses, as well as the problems created by large gaps in our knowledge base. They also consider expert bias—in paticular, the ways in which personal belief and folk wisdom can find their way into expert opinions. They distinguish between cognate expertise (i.e., an expert's refined knowledge concerning various domains of infancy and early childhood) and technical expertise (i.e., an expert's specialized skills for infant observation or parent interviewing, for purposes of eliciting and clarifying relevant information). They also provide guidelines for court-ordered clinical evaluations concerning infant custody.

The final chapter, by Zigler, Hopper, and Hall, provides a broad overview of social policy issues relevant to infant mental health. Unlike many previous authors in this volume, they do not call for more research and caution us about how little we know. Instead, they emphasize the knowledge we have accumulated already and the best ways to translate it into improvements in the lives of infants and families. Pointing out the interrelatedness of the family, school, health, and child care systems comprising the context of infant mental health, they review a number of policy-related problems facing infants and their families, and provide suggestions for implementing solutions. They conclude optimistically, citing a growing consensus among parents, policy makers and business leaders that infant mental health is too crucial to everyone to be left to chance.

29

Infant Day Care

MARIANNE BARTON
MARTHA WILLIAMS

The past 15 years have witnessed dramatic changes in the caretaking experience of U.S. infants. In 1972, 24% of mothers of infants under the age of 1 year were employed; by 1987 that figure had risen to 51%, and the increase is expected to continue (Bureau of Labor Statistics, 1988, cited in Hayes, Palmer, & Zaslow, 1990). As a result, more than half of U.S. infants are cared for by persons other than their parents. Policy makers and parents alike have turned to social scientists to assess the possible impact of these enormous social changes. The issue obviously speaks to important practical decisions for parents, but also to theoretical questions related to our belief in the importance of early experience, and to political issues regarding the changing role of women in U.S. society. For all of these reasons, the question of possible effects of early day care on infant mental health has been hotly debated in the scientific literature and the popular press. Unfortunately, despite heated debate, very little consensus has emerged.

Review of the literature on early nonmaternal care reveals a confusing array of data, which lends itself equally well to markedly divergent conclusions. In the minds of some researchers, day care is viewed as a risk factor associated with disturbances in infant–parent attachment in infancy and atypical social development later on (Belsky, 1988; Sroufe, 1988). Other researchers reviewing the same data argue that these conclusions are overstated, and that at present the data are insufficient to enable us to conclude

that early substitute care is related to negative developmental outcomes (Phillips, McCartney, & Scarr, 1987; Thompson, 1988; Clarke-Stewart, 1988, 1989). In some measure this confusion can be attributed to the difficulties involved in conducting methodologically sound research in this area. Equally important, however, are serious conceptual difficulties that have limited the questions asked of the data and led to oversimplification of a very complex issue.

We begin this chapter with a discussion of these conceptual concerns, in an effort to establish some perspective on the data to follow. We then review the data relating nonmaternal care in the first year of life to insecure parent–infant attachment and later social maladjustment. We propose alternative models both for understanding the data and for framing research questions. The chapter closes with a look to the future and suggestions for policy and further study.

THE CONCEPTUAL PROBLEM

As Richters and Zahn-Waxler (1988) point out, the primary question asked of day care researchers has been this: Is infant day care bad for children's social and emotional development? The question seems straightforward enough, but in fact it is based on a series of untenable assumptions. First, it assumes that the experience of nonmaternal care can be isolated from a host of other influences on a child's development. In fact, the decision to place an infant in substitute care may be viewed as the final expression of any number of variables related to family functioning. These may include marital functioning; financial status; attitudes toward parenting and career; desire for motherhood; and many other antecedent variables that could, in and of themselves, explain differences observed between children in maternal care and those in substitute care. Researchers almost invariably note this problem in outlining limitations to the conclusions they draw from their data, but it has yet to be carefully investigated as an alternative theoretical model. Those researchers who have looked at family variables (see Belsky & Rovine, 1988) have tended to view them as moderator variables that may mediate the presumed "effects" of substitute care, rather than as alternate explanations for those "effects."

Second, a focus on the search for "effects" of substitute care implies that nonmaternal care is a unitary construct. Clearly, it is not. Infant care arrangements vary dramatically, both in the settings chosen (center vs. family day care vs. at-home sitter) and in the quality of care provided. In what has been described as a second wave of child care research (Hayes et al., 1990), investigators are beginning to look at variations in child care environments and their relationship to children's development. Increasingly, the data suggest that measurable aspects of child care environments are indeed related to child outcome assessments (see Ruopp, Travers, Glantz, & Coelen, 1979), and that the selection of child care settings may be related to family characteristics (Howes, Rodning, Galluzo, & Myers, 1988). Hayes et al. (1990) suggest that a third wave of child care research may be emerging, which will focus on the mutual influence of home and child care environments on children and families. Given these complexities, the question of any general effects of nonmaternal care seems increasingly misleading.

In addition, it seems reasonable to expect that substitute care of any sort will have a different meaning for different children. Some children may adapt easily to substitute care and do very well; other children may find the experience much more disruptive. Although researchers are beginning to explore the effects of such variables as sex and temperament on children's presumed response to substitute care, very little is known to date about which children flourish in nonmaternal care and which children do not.

Finally, the question of whether substitute care is bad for children is troubling for reasons other than the conceptual confusion it creates. It is also pragmatically useless and politically inflammatory. Demographic data suggest that mothers of children under 1 year of age constitute the fastest-growing segment of the labor force (U.S. Bureau of the Census, 1986). Substitute care for infants is a reality of U.S. life in the 1990s. The critical issue for social scientists is how to make that care most positive for infants and their families.

It would seem that an early focus on a rather simple theoretical model in the face of an extremely complex reality has primed us for simple answers that are confusing and unsatisfying, and that fuel the emotional debate surrounding the issue. Richters and Zahn-Waxler (1988) suggest that a more fruitful question might be this: Under what conditions are what outcomes associated with what patterns of early nonmaternal care, to what extent, and why? Framing the question in such a manner is likely to mean that child care research to date can offer only tentative and carefully qualified answers. Given the many familial, social, and cultural factors that influence child development, this seems a much more reasonable perspective from which to understand the effects of one of those many potent influences: nonmaternal care in infancy.

NONMATERNAL CARE AND COGNITIVE DEVELOPMENT

Day care researchers agree that early substitute care has neither positive nor negative effects on long-term cognitive development among middle-class children (Belsky, 1988; Clarke-Stewart, 1988, 1989). Children from economically impoverished homes, however, appear to benefit from exposure to high-quality substitute care. Among these children, participation in day care appears to prevent, or at least to delay, the declines in cognitive functioning frequently observed in the preschool years (Belsky, 1988; Clarke-Stewart, 1988, 1989).

NONMATERNAL CARE AND ATTACHMENT

The most significant controversy surrounding research on infant day care concerns the relationship between nonmaternal care and the infants' attachment to their mothers. Numerous early studies demonstrated that infants of working mothers are clearly attached to their mothers and prefer them to their caregivers (Clarke-Stewart, 1989; Clarke-Stewart & Fein, 1983). What is in question is the *quality* of an infant's attachment to his or her mother.

John Bowlby's ethological model of attachment theory describes an infant's attachment to his or her mother as a specific component of the mother–infant relationship that develops in the first year of life (Bowlby, 1969). Bowlby posited that as a result of the many interactive sequences that occur in the course of caregiving, the infant develops an internal model of the mother or attachment figure, and of the self in relation to that figure. This internal construct, or working model, informs the infant's subsequent interaction with the mother (and, as development proceeds, with others). Over time, it contributes to the development of a sense of self (Sroufe & Fleeson, 1986).

As described in Ainsworth and Wittig (1969), Mary Ainsworth and her colleagues designed a laboratory paradigm, the Strange Situation, to measure infants' internal models of a specific attachment relationship. On the basis of an infant's response to two separations from and reunions with his or her mother, the infant is classified as securely attached or as falling into one of two categories of insecure attachment: insecure/avoidant or insecure/resistant. (A fourth attachment classification has been developed recently, but it has not been used in child care research as yet and is not considered here.) Infants classified as secure seek proximity to their mothers on reunion and are soothed by the reestablishment of parent–child contact. Infants classified as insecure/avoidant may avoid contact with their caregivers on reunion and may treat a stranger employed in the assessment much as they do their caregivers. Infants classified as insecure/resistant seem ambivalent upon reunion with their caregivers and both seek and resist contact with them.

The Strange Situation has been studied extensively in an effort to relate infant attachment classifications both to antecedents in mother–infant interaction and to subsequent developmental outcomes. Early studies by Ainsworth and her colleagues revealed marked differences in mother–child interaction in the home, which were related to subsequent infant attachment classifications. Mothers of secure infants were observed to be sensitive and responsive to their infants; mothers of infants classified as avoidant were more rejecting in their interaction; and mothers of infants classified as resistant were less consistent, less sensitive to infant signals, and more inept (Ainsworth, Blehar, Waters, & Wall, 1978). Subsequent studies have continued to find differences in mother–child interaction related to infant attachment classifications, but these have not been completely consistent. In addition, there are considerable questions regarding the relationship between variations of maternal behavior in the normal range and infant attachment classifications (see Campos, Barrett, Lamb, Goldsmith, & Steinberg, 1983, and Lamb, Thompson, Gardner, Charnov, & Estes, 1984, for reviews.) Egeland and Farber (1984) completed a careful review of the data relative to the antecedents of secure attachment classification. They concluded that the data relating attachment security to variations in maternal–child interaction are relatively weak, and that maternal affective personality variables may be better predictors of infant attachment classification than maternal caregiving behaviors.

The data relating infant attachment classification at 1 year to subsequent developmental outcome are much more impressive. Children classified as securely attached at 1 year have been found to be more compliant and cooperative as preschoolers (Matas, Arend, & Sroufe, 1978; Sroufe, 1983) and more effective in problem-solving tasks as preschoolers (Matas et al., 1978). Increasingly, security of attachment at 1 year is viewed as one protective factor in promoting adaptive personality development.

At least some attachment researchers have argued that early use of nonmaternal care may disrupt the attachment relationship. They propose that infants who experience repeated separations from their mothers may view their mothers as inaccessible and seek to minimize their dependency upon them. As a result, they may develop internal models of attachment characterized by insecurity and specifically by avoidance (Barglow, Vaughn, & Molitor, 1987). Sroufe (1988) points out that full-time working mothers' diminished contact with their infants may deprive them of opportunities to fine-tune their relationship, potentially contributing to less comfortable and possibly less secure parent–infant relationships. These theoretical predictors have led to a series of studies investigating the relationship between the use of substitute care in infancy and security of attachment at 1 year.

Mother-Infant Attachment

Early studies investigating the relationship between nonmaternal care and attachment yielded little evidence that substitute care was related to insecurity of attachment (Doyle & Somers, 1978; Brookhart & Hock, 1976; Hock, 1980; Kagan, Kearsley, & Zelazo, 1978). These studies have been strongly criticized on methodological grounds: They typically employed small samples, used ratings of attachment-related behavior rather than overall attachment classifications, and studied infants in very-high-quality group care settings (see Belsky, 1988, for a review). As a result of these shortcomings, the data have largely been supplanted by a second wave of research efforts.

Over the last several years, investigators have studied large samples of infants, mostly from intact, middle-class families, who have received substitute care in a variety of settings in largely stable circumstances. The overall pattern of results suggests that extensive (more than 20 hours per week) use of nonmaternal care in the first year of life is associated with an increased incidence of insecure attachment classifications (Jacobson & Wille, 1984; Belsky & Rovine, 1988) and perhaps with an increased incidence of avoidant attachment classifications in particular (Barglow et al., 1987). The data are not completely consistent, however, since several studies have also reported no differences in mother–infant attachment classifications related to the use of substitute care (Easterbrooks & Goldberg, 1985; Chase-Lansdale & Owen, 1987).

In a recent review, Clarke-Stewart (1989) tabulated the results of 17 studies that assessed the relationship between nonmaternal care and mother–infant attachment, using infant attachment in the Strange Situation as the dependent variable. She concluded that in this combined sample of 1247 infants, 36% of the infants of full-time working mothers were classified as insecurely attached, while only 29% of the infants of nonemployed or part-time working mothers were so classified. She noted that although differences in individual studies did not always reach statistical significance, the difference in her combined sample was highly significant ($\chi^2 = 6.21$, $p < .01$). Clarke-Stewart did not present data relative to the incidence of avoidant attachment classification, presumably because many of the available studies lacked sufficient subjects to permit an analysis of differences between insecure attachment classifications.

Lamb, Sternberg, and Prodromidis (1992) recently reported on their reanalysis of 13 studies of nonmaternal care and security of attachment. These authors used log-linear analyses to develop statistical models that best explained the data set they assembled. On the basis of their analyses of 897 subjects, they concluded that there was a significant association between early nonmaternal care and insecure attachment classification. Furthermore, among infants in nonmaternal care who were classified as insecure, there was an increased incidence of insecure/ avoidant classification. These analyses suggest an increase in insecure attachment classification among infants who experienced more than 5 hours per week of substitute care, with no consistent increase in the incidence of insecure attachment as the extent of substitute care use increased.

Father-Infant Attachment

To date, only two studies have examined the relationship between nonmaternal care and infant–father attachment. In both studies, boys but not girls who were enrolled in substitute care for more than 35 hours per week were more likely to be classified as insecurely attached to their fathers (Chase-Lansdale & Owen, 1987; Belsky & Rovine, 1988). In the first study, boys were more likely to be classified as insecure/resistant; in the second study they were more likely to be classified as insecure/avoidant.

Clearly, there is an impressive and increasingly incontrovertible body of data suggesting that nonmaternal care in the first year of life is associated with infants' classification as insecurely attached, and perhaps specifically with the insecure/avoidant classification. Although there seems little doubt about the veracity of these conclusions, there continues to be enormous controversy about their meaning. Before we discuss the various theoretical explanations proposed, it seems critical to consider significant methodological issues that have been raised as threats to the validity of the data.

The Question of Measurement

The first critical issue in assessing the import of the available literature concerns the Strange Situation itself and its ecological validity for children in nonmaternal care. The Strange Situation was designed to create a stressful situation for a 1-year-old infant and to induce him or her to exhibit attachment-related behaviors. As Clarke-Stewart (1988) notes, children in substitute care experience regular separations from their attachment figures, and probably become accustomed to them to a much greater degree than children whose mothers are at home. Thus the children in substitute care may be less stressed by the procedure, or may behave in a more independent fashion, which is then erroneously interpreted as avoidance. Researchers have begun to evaluate this possibility, but the data are inconsistent.

Some studies report that day care children are less likely to seek proximity to their mothers (Hock, 1980; Goosens, 1987) and are more likely to play comfortably with toys in their mothers' absence (Doyle & Somers, 1978); these reports suggest at least greater independence, if not diminished distress. Data from Lamb et al.'s (1992) reanalysis of the available studies lend some support to this view. Lamb et al. found a significant association between a child's age at assessment and security of attachment, such that infants assessed in the Strange Situation at age 16 months or older were more likely to be classified as insecurely attached, regardless of their child care history. Since children do grow more independent with age (Clarke-Stewart & Hevey, 1981), Lamb et al.'s data may suggest that for older infants at least, independent behavior may be confused with behaviors indicative of insecure attachment.

Belsky and Braungart (1991) recently attempted to address this issue directly by comparing the behavior of insecure/avoidant infants who had experienced extensive nonmaternal care with a sample of insecure/avoidant infants who had not experienced such care. They reasoned that if the Strange Situation is less stressful for infants in substitute care, or if those infants show precocious independence, they should be less distressed and more involved in exploratory play than infants in maternal care. The data revealed the opposite results: Infants in nonmaternal care were more distressed and less involved in exploratory play during the two reunion episodes of the Strange Situation than were those infants cared for by their mothers. These data are based on a very small sample ($n = 20$) of infants who were 12 months old at the time of assessment. Nonetheless, they suggest that for 12-month-olds in substitute care, the Strange Situation is indeed stressful.

Another approach to the question of the validity of the Strange Situation for infants in substitute care would be to use other measures of the attachment construct as dependent variables (Clarke-Stewart, 1989). Recently, researchers have employed a Q-sort technique in which mothers, teachers, or observers rate infants' attachment quality, but again the results are inconsistent. Several studies have reported no differences between groups based on Q-sort ratings of attachment (Belsky, 1988; Howes et al., 1988). At least one study, however, did find differences between two groups of children who had or had not experienced nonmaternal care in the first year, with the nonmaternal care group more likely to be rated as insecure at age 3 (Silverman, 1990). Clearly, the question of the validity of the Strange Situation for infants experiencing nonmaternal care, and particularly for those over the age of 15 months, is far from settled. Nonetheless, it seems unlikely that the findings of insecure attachment associated with substitute care can be attributed solely to measurement artifact.

The Magnitude of the Differences

If one accepts the data relating nonmaternal care and insecurity of attachment as valid, one must next question the magnitude of the differences observed between the two groups. One way of doing so is to examine mean scores on ratings of avoidance. Lamb et al. (1992) reported that while infants in nonmaternal care received significantly higher avoidance scores, the mean difference between the two groups was less than 0.5 point on a 7-point scale. Furthermore, the average scores attained by infants in substitute care fell in the range described by Ainsworth et al. (1978) as only slightly avoidant. Thus, the differences between the groups, though statistically significant, appear to be quite small (Clarke-Stewart, 1988, 1989).

A second way of assessing the magnitude of between-group differences, suggested by Clarke-Stewart (1989), involves comparison of the distribution of attachment classifications. Distributions of attachment classifications in normal samples can vary significantly; however, in most studies of middle-class infants approximately 66% are classified as securely attached, 22% are classified as insecure/avoidant, and 12% are classified as insecure/resistant (Ainsworth et al., 1978; Thompson, 1988). Although some studies of children in substitute care report higher-than-average rates of insecure classification,

Clarke-Stewart's tabulation of the data across studies revealed that the distribution of insecure attachment classifications among the children of working mothers (22% avoidant, 15% resistant), while different from a comparison group of maternal care children, was not markedly different from the distribution in the larger population. Furthermore, Thompson (1988) points out that the comparison groups in the Belsky and Rovine (1988) and Barglow et al. (1987) studies had a higher-than-expected proportion of securely attached infants. When Thompson compared rates of insecure attachment classification in Belsky and Rovine's and Barglow et al.'s substitute care groups with broader distribution patterns, he failed to find significant differences between the two groups. These data are helpful in placing the potential risk of insecure attachment associated with substitute care in some perspective. They also raise important questions regarding the interpretation of that "risk."

The Meaning of the Data

Attachment researchers (Belsky, 1988; Barglow et al., 1987; Sroufe, 1988) argue that the insecure attachment observed in some children in substitute care occurs because they experience the daily separations from their mothers as inaccessibility and perhaps even as rejection. It may be that in fact this is the case. At present, however, we simply do not know whether that is the mechanism by which an increased incidence of insecure attachment occurs among day care children. In fact, there is some evidence to suggest that alternative explanations are at least as plausible.

First, if daily separations from the mother are implicated as causal factors here, those separations disrupt the mother–child bond only for a small portion of children who experience them. The majority of infants in substitute care (65%) are securely attached to their mothers. Furthermore, attachment theory would not predict that repeated separations of infants from their mothers would result in an increased incidence of insecure infant–father attachments. Indeed, one might expect the opposite trend, since infants whose mothers work spend more time with their fathers than do the infants of nonworking mothers (Clarke-Stewart, 1988). The fact that insecure infant–father attachment classification is also associated with the use of substitute care in the

first year suggests that potential causative factors may lie in antecedent family variables, which influence the choice of care arrangements as well as the infants' subsequent attachment classification. Research on family variables related to substitute care is only beginning, but to date it has focused on three areas: patterns of behavioral interaction in infant–parent dyads; psychological or attitudinal variables in parents; and factors related to the experience of full-time employment for mothers.

Parent-Child Interaction

Investigations of interactive behavior in employed mothers and nonemployed mothers have revealed few differences between the two groups on dimensions of physical contact, responsiveness, or sensitivity (Clarke-Stewart, 1989) or overall quality of interaction (Hock, 1980; Schubert, Bradley-Johnson, & Nuttal, 1980). Stith and Davis (1984) observed naturally occurring interactions between 5- to 6-month-old infants and their mothers, and reported no differences in the quality of such interactions between infants in day care and infants not in day care. Caruso (1990) obtained ratings of parent–child interaction during a structured teaching task completed in the home, and reported that mothers of 1-year-old infants who had extensive day care experience demonstrated higher-quality interaction patterns than did mothers of infants in exclusive home care. Specifically, mothers of day care infants were viewed as more sensitive to infant cues than were mothers of home care infants. Some studies suggest that working mothers are more physically affectionate than nonworking mothers (Schwarz, 1983), and more interactive in the early evening (Pederson, Cain, Zaslow, & Anderson, 1982). Although a few studies have revealed discrepant findings (e.g., that working mothers play less with objects with their infants than do nonworking mothers; Zaslow, Pederson, Suwalsky, & Rabinovich, 1983), in general the literature reveals few differences in interactive behavior between employed and nonemployed mothers.

Maternal Psychological Variables

Hock, Morgan, and Hock (1985) looked at a group of mothers who intended to remain at home after the birth of their children. In their sample, mothers who changed their plans and returned to work reported less positive feelings about motherhood and more difficulty tolerating infant fussiness. Farber and Egeland (1982) found that working mothers of insecure infants reported less prenatal desire for motherhood than did working mothers of secure infants. A study of 30 middle-class working mothers revealed that maternal integration, a composite variable rated from interviews with mothers, was significantly associated with security of attachment. In addition, when the variance associated with the maternal integration variable was controlled, neither ratings of maternal acceptance nor ratings of sensitivity were significantly associated with security of attachment (Benn, 1986). Belsky and Rovine (1988) reported that working mothers of insecure infants in their sample received lower scores on interpersonal sensitivity and empathy, and were less happily married, than mothers of secure infants. These data lend support to the notion advanced by Egeland and Farber (1984) that maternal affective and personality variables may be better predictors of infant attachment classification in general than maternal caregiving behaviors. This seems as likely to be true for infants in substitute care as for those in exclusive maternal care.

Recently, attachment researchers have begun to focus their search for important components of parental psychological functioning on the assessment of internal organizational models specific to attachment. Main and Goldwyn (in press) have developed an interview measure of adults' state of mind with respect to attachment that is consistently and strongly related to infant attachment classification (Main, Kaplan, & Cassidy, 1985). To date, researchers have not looked systematically at parental working models of attachment in samples of parents who do and do not use early substitute care. It may well be that parents with less adaptive models of attachment relationships—perhaps specifically parents who minimize or dismiss the import of attachment-related concerns—are overrepresented among families who elect to use early substitute care, or at least in the subset of early child care users whose infants are insecurely attached.

Factors Associated with Maternal Employment

Numerous studies have documented that working mothers frequently feel stressed, tired, and overburdened (Clarke-Stewart, 1989). The pos-

sibility that those factors might contribute to their diminished accessibility to their infants, and potentially to their partners' decreased availability as well, is real. Thus it may be that infants of working mothers are more likely to be classified as insecure not because they are too often separated from their mothers, but because at least some mothers have inadequate physical or emotional energy left after juggling the demands of work and home to be focused affectively on their infants. Owen and Cox (1988) reported that mothers in their sample who worked more than 40 hours per week were more anxious and dissatisfied than those who worked fewer hours. Anxious mothers in this study were less sensitive, animated, and reciprocal in interaction with their infants, and their infants were more likely to be classified as insecurely attached.

Taken together, these studies suggest that there are wide variations in attitudes, internal psychological functioning, and life experience among the mothers of infants in nonmaternal care. Just as these variables help to determine infant attachment classification in infants in exclusive maternal care, they may explain variations in attachment quality among infants in substitute care. Thus familial factors must be viewed not as mediators of any presumed effects of substitute care, but rather as alternate and equally plausible explanations for the association between nonmaternal care and insecure attachment.

Attachment and the Quality of Substitute Care

There is very little evidence to date suggesting a relationship between quality of care and attachment classification. In large measure, this is because the major studies investigating attachment security and substitute care have offered little information regarding the quality of care provided. Elevated rates of insecure attachment have been reported in studies of children in varying care settings, including center care (Belsky & Rovine, 1988) and at-home sitter care (Barglow et al., 1987). Lamb et al. (1992), however, have suggested that infants in center care may have a slightly elevated risk of insecure attachment, although the authors caution that their conclusions are based on small cell sizes. In her review of the substitute care literature, Clarke-Stewart (1988) argues that there is little reason to expect quality of care to affect attachment classification, since Strange Situation classifications are measures of a specific relationship. This is an important point, but it does not mean that quality of care is unrelated to the eventual outcome of children on attachment-related dimensions. One might expect quality of care to exert an indirect rather than a direct influence on attachment relationships, and indeed, the data suggest that this is the case. For example, infants who are insecurely attached to both parents are at greater risk for subsequent social–emotional difficulties than are infants securely attached to one parent and insecurely attached to the other (Belsky, Garduque, & Hrncir, 1984; Main & Weston, 1981). Similarly, recent evidence suggests that infants classified as insecurely attached to their mothers, but securely attached to substitute caregivers, appear more socially competent than infants classified as insecurely attached to both mothers and caregivers. Moreover, children were more likely to form secure attachments with caregivers in settings characterized by smaller child-to-adult ratios and more responsive care (Howes et al., 1988). These data suggest that for some children at least, substitute care in a high-quality setting may help ameliorate the long-term consequences of insecure infant–mother relationships. Howes et al. (1988) also report that infants who were insecurely attached to their mothers were more likely to be placed in poor-quality care arrangements, suggesting complex interactions between family characteristics and the selection of substitute care settings.

Child Characteristics

Researchers have recently begun to address the problem of identifying which children in substitute care are most likely to be classified as insecurely attached by assessing child characteristics that might distinguish between the two groups. Once again, however, the data are far too limited to permit the drawing of consistent conclusions. Belsky (1988) suggests that boys may be more vulnerable to insecure attachment classification as a function of care experience. Two studies of independent samples have addressed this issue directly; in both cases, boys in substitute care were more likely to be insecurely attached to their fathers, but there were no differences as a function of sex in maternal–infant attachment classification (Belsky & Rovine, 1988;

Chase-Lansdale & Owen, 1987). Belsky (1988) also suggests that temperament may be an important moderator variable, with difficult infants in substitute care more likely to be insecurely attached. Data from his own research support this view (Belsky & Rovine, 1988), but it is important to note that temperament was assessed by maternal report, making it difficult to know whether infant variables or maternal perceptions were at issue. To date, no other data relating infant temperament and heightened vulnerability to substitute care are available.

Age at Enrollment

Data from the few studies that have looked at age of enrollment suggest that infants enrolled in substitute care during the first half of the first year of life are less vulnerable to disturbances in the attachment relationship than infants enrolled in substitute care during the second half of the first year. Benn (1986) reports that in her sample, mothers of securely attached sons returned to work earlier in the first year than did the mothers of insecurely attached sons. Chase-Lansdale and Owen (1987) studied only mothers who returned to work before their infants were 8 months old, and they reported no differences in maternal–infant attachment classification related to substitute care. Finally, Lamb et al. (1992) have found support in their meta-analysis for the notion that substitute care initiated early in the first year is less likely to be related to insecure attachment than is substitute care initiated between 6 and 12 months. Explanations for these data are not intuitively obvious. Some writers (see Lamb et al., 1992) suggest that interruptions to the parent–infant relationship prior to the firm establishment of specific attachments are less disruptive than are parent–child separations occurring after the attachment bond has been formed. Such a prediction does not necessarily follow from attachment theory. Indeed, it could be argued that parent–infant separations in the first 6 months of life should be more disruptive, because they interfere with the consolidation of secure attachment relationships. The data cited above are extremely tentative and might be explained by any number of variables unrelated to a child's age. For example, it may be that mothers who return to work early are different in some way from mothers who return to work later. Perhaps early-returning working mothers are less ambivalent or less anxious regarding their decision, and can be more comfortable and less distracted in interaction with their infants, thereby promoting more comfortable attachment relationships. At present such notions are purely speculative. We simply do not know whether or how variations in age of enrollment in substitute care within the first year of life affect attachment classification.

Summary

Upon careful review of the literature, it seems clear that substitute care in infancy is associated with elevated rates of insecure attachment classification at 1 year. What is much less certain is what these data mean. Although there is a need for more than one measure of attachment in young children, it seems unlikely that excessive reliance on the Strange Situation fully explains the findings just reviewed. At the same time, the assertion that the increased incidence of insecure attachment classification among children in early substitute care can be attributed to the children's daily separation from their mothers seems premature at best. In fact, the data suggest that family variables antedating the use of substitute care may be at least as important as the use of substitute care itself and are deserving of much more careful investigation.

Finally, not all or even most infants enrolled in substitute care demonstrate disturbed attachment relationships. It is unclear how those infants classified as insecurely attached differ from their securely attached counterparts, and how such factors as age at enrollment and quality of care contribute to infant outcome. Finally, it is unclear what implications these data have for infants' long-term development. That question is considered in the next section.

NONMATERNAL CARE AND SOCIAL ADJUSTMENT

A second area of investigation in the search for potential "effects" of early nonmaternal care is social–emotional development. Some researchers (Belsky, 1988) have argued that nonmaternal care in the first year of life is related to subsequent social maladjustment, and particularly to an increased incidence of aggression and noncompliant behavior. This argument, if supported by the data, is a compelling one, because aggression and noncompliance in preschoolers are exactly the behaviors associated with the long-term outcome of insecure and particularly avoidant attachment classification in infancy (Sroufe, 1988). Unfortunately, the data at present are far too limited and inconsistent to permit any statement of a clear relationship between early nonmaternal care and social–emotional maladjustment. Moreover, the available data are beset by a host of methodological difficulties, which limit the generalizability of findings. Before we proceed to a review of the data, it seems useful to consider these limitations.

Methodological Considerations

Studies relating early substitute care and attachment have been appropriately criticized for excessive reliance on a single outcome measure, the Strange Situation. Studies in the area of social development suffer from the opposite problem: Researchers have employed a wide variety of tools to assess social behavior. As a result, it is not possible to combine data across studies to yield some estimate of the consistency of findings or the size of effects. More significantly, definitions of the construct being assessed vary greatly from study to study, making clear interpretation of the data across studies almost impossible. It is difficult to know, for example, what a finding of "increased noncompliant behavior" means.

Second, most studies relating early substitute care to behavioral difficulties have focused on infants in group care settings. In one study that revealed increased anxiety among children in group care, no differences were found between children in sitter care and those in exclusive maternal care (McCartney, Scarr, Phillips, Grajek, & Schwarz, 1982). The data therefore have limited generalizability, since only a small proportion of infants in substitute care are in group care settings (Phillips, 1987). Moreover, it may be that the effects described in these studies are related to aspects of group care experience rather than to nonmaternal care more generally.

Finally, although a number of studies suggest an association between early day care experience and difficult social behavior, other studies support the opposite finding—that infants in substitute care in fact show precocious social–emotional development.

Taken together, these factors suggest that the data relating substitute care experience to later social development must be interpreted with considerable caution. As we shall see, the data are riddled with sufficient inconsistency to make interpretation difficult at best.

Social Development

A number of studies have reported enhanced social development among day care children. Although the particular traits identified are variable, the results are all in the direction of more positive development. Early studies identified trends among day care children toward more frequent interaction and greater cooperation with peers than their home-reared counterparts (Lay & Meyer, 1972; McCrae & Herbert-Jackson, 1975; Schwarz, Strickland, & Krolick, 1973). Rubenstein and Howes (1979) compared the quality of social interaction and play behavior among toddlers in day care and those in maternal care, and observed more frequent exchanges of positive affect between day care children and adults. They also noted more advanced play among day care children. McCartney et al. (1982) reported that along with advanced language development, day care children exhibited greater considerateness. In their 1986 study, Howes and Olenick found that day care children were more likely to exhibit self-regulatory behavior. Andersson (1989) discerned a tendency among day care children in Sweden, particularly those who entered care as early as 6 months of age, to be more persistent and independent as well as more socially confident.

An equal number of studies reveal an association between early day care experience and negative social–emotional development, particularly increased aggressive or noncompliant behavior. As with studies of positive social behavior, it is difficult to summarize this data because of the use of widely varying measurement tools. Nonetheless, several studies have suggested that children who experience group care in the first year of life exhibit increased physical and verbal aggressiveness toward peers (Schwarz, Strickland, & Krolick, 1974; Haskins, 1985; McCartney et al., 1982; Barton & Schwarz, 1981), as well as increased verbal and behavioral noncompliance with adults (Rubenstein & Howes, 1983).

If one accepts the possibility that early day care experience is related to increased levels of aggression or noncompliance, it becomes critical to assess the duration and magnitude of these effects. In several studies that reported increased aggression and noncompliance among day care

children, the negative behaviors disappeared over time (McCartney et al., 1982; Schwarz et al., 1974) or dissipated appreciably (Haskins, 1985). Similarly, in a retrospective study of 8-year-olds from the Bermuda public school system, Schwartz (1983) found no relationship between early day care experience and six dimensions of emotional functioning, including task orientation, distractibility, hostility, considerateness, introversion, and extroversion.

In contrast to these studies, Barton and Schwarz (1981) found evidence of more enduring differences between day care children and those in maternal care among the middle-class 8- to 10-year-olds they studied. In their retrospective study, day care children were rated as more aggressive and more socially isolated by their peers. These children were not rated differently on either dimension by their teachers. Although there are several possible explanations for the differences in peer versus teacher ratings, the fact that teachers did not identify day care children as more aggressive or more withdrawn suggests that the magnitude of the effect was limited.

Two studies have directly addressed the question of the magnitude of differences observed between day care children and those in maternal care. Rubenstein, Howes, and Boyle (1981) found that day care children were rated as more active, fearful, aggressive, and noncompliant than peers without day care experience. They also found, however, that the two groups of children were indistinguishable on a measure of behavior problems. In a recent study, Howes (1990) observed that children who entered low-quality day care in the first year of life showed a profile of social maladjustment as preschoolers, as defined by difficulties with peers, distractibility, diminished task orientation, and diminished consideration for peers. Further assessment revealed, however, that only 4% of these children had behavior problem scores within the pathological range.

Haskins's (1985) study comparing children in a cognitively oriented day care program with children in other combinations of home and center care is particularly interesting with regard to both the magnitude and duration of the presumed effects. Elevated aggression occurred only in the group of youngsters who attended a cognitively oriented program, and the ratings of aggression for these children were greater on every variable than for children enrolled in day care for longer periods of time. Some of the children in the cognitively oriented center had to be eliminated from the study after an additional treatment component was added to their program to reduce the very high levels of aggression observed. Although these results suggest an effect of significant magnitude, they also suggest that a program-specific variable may have been at issue here.

The duration of effects in this study was assessed 2 and 3 years after the children entered school. At the 2-year follow-up, ratings of aggression were significantly higher for the experimental group (the children who had attended the cognitively oriented center) than the control groups. The 3-year ratings of aggression declined on all measures, although teacher ratings revealed that children in the experimental group continued to be more aggressive than those in the control groups. Teacher ratings also revealed, however, that children in the experimental group were not considered more difficult to manage or less likable than their peers in the control groups. In this particular study, then, there appeared to be a strong correlation between early group care experience and increased aggression, but only for children in one of several group care settings. Although the levels of aggression observed in children from the cognitively oriented program dissipated over time, they did not disappear completely. At the same time, higher levels of aggression appeared not to be particularly significant in these children's overall social adjustment.

In summary, then, it appears that early use of substitute care in group care settings is related to findings of increased aggression toward peers and increased noncompliance toward adults. It is much less clear that these behaviors should be labeled "social maladjustment," and in fact the evidence suggests that they may fall within the limits of normal, nonpathological variation.

In any case, in the absence of longitudinal data, we cannot conclude that increased aggression and noncompliance are the long-term sequelae of insecure attachment among day care graduates. This is a possibility, but at present we simply do not know. To date, only one study has presented a longitudinal follow-up of children in differing care arrangements. In 1980, Vaughn, Gove, and Egeland reported an increased incidence of insecure/avoidant attachment classification (but not an increased incidence of insecure attachment overall) among a sample of high-risk infants whose mothers had returned to work or school in their first year of life. In a follow-up of these children, Vaughn,

Deane, and Waters (1985) found that while children previously classified as insecure appeared least competent on a problem-solving task, infants with substitute care experience who had previously been classified as securely attached were indistinguishable from their insecurely attached agemates. These data have been interpreted to mean that early substitute care experience may exert negative effects even for these children classified as securely attached (Belsky, 1988; Sroufe, 1988). It is important to note, however, that families who used substitute care were distinguished from nonusers by increased levels of stress and less stable adult relationships, and that the substitute care arrangements provided were extremely unstable. Thus the data are suggestive only of some association between early use of substitute care and long-term adjustment.

It is also possible that increased aggression and noncompliance are related not to maternal–child separation, but to the experience of group care per se. Some writers have suggested that as a result of increased peer exposure, children in group care orient more strongly toward peers and less strongly toward adults (Clarke-Stewart & Fein, 1983; Belsky, 1984), and that this peer orientation has both positive and negative results (Hayes et al., 1990). It may be that children with early group care experience are more independent and less likely to comply with adults' arbitrary rules (Clarke-Stewart, 1989). There are simply insufficient data at present to enable us to choose among these differing interpretations.

Finally, it is possible that increased aggression and noncompliance are related to the experience of certain kinds of group care in infancy. Indeed, it can be argued that the most significant finding to emerge from investigations of substitute care and social development is the suggestion that program-specific variables (e.g., cognitive orientation) or aspects of the environment (e.g., group size) are predictive of positive and negative outcomes. It is to these data that we now turn.

QUALITY OF CARE

Characteristics of High-Quality Care

Researchers seeking links between variations in substitute care experiences and subsequent social development have defined the independent variable "quality of care" in several ways. Early researchers used broad measures of quality based on a composite of many factors (e.g., group size, caregiver training) or a general measure of the child care environment. Review of these data reveals that quality of care is indeed associated with variations in children's social development, and that poor-quality care is particularly associated with the negative behavioral patterns ascribed to substitute care more generally. Moreover, a small number of studies suggest that effects associated with poor-quality care persist at least into the early school years (Hayes et al., 1990). In McCartney et al.'s (1982) study of Bermudan children enrolled in a variety of day care settings, children in low-quality settings performed poorly on measures of sociability and considerateness. An overall measure of quality was also related to the Bermudan children's language development, with higher-quality care associated with improved language skills. Howes and Olenick (1986) reported that children in high-quality day care centers were more compliant, less resistant, and better able to regulate their behavior than children in low-quality centers. In a longitudinal follow-up of day care graduates, Howes (1990) found that quality of care in infancy predicted social development in kindergarten. Children who had experienced lower-quality care as infants were rated by their teachers as more hostile and less task-oriented than children who had experienced higher-quality care. Children who had entered low-quality care settings in the first year of life were rated least positively by their kindergarten teachers on dimensions of considerateness and distractibility.

These studies are helpful in validating the common-sense assumption that high-quality care is better for children than low-quality care. They are less helpful in enabling us to ascertain which components of substitute care environments contribute most significantly to differences in children's behavior.

The second approach to measuring quality of care has focused on specific, measurable, and potentially regulatable aspects of child care environments, as these occur in community-based settings. The National Day Care Study (Ruopp et al., 1979), a large-scale study of community day care centers initiated by the federal government, revealed that group size, child-to-staff ratios, and caregiver training were significant predictors of both caregiver behavior and child outcome. For infants and toddlers, group size appeared to exert the most powerful effect. Larger group sizes and higher child-to-staff

ratios were associated with more restrictive and management-focused staff behavior, with diminished social interaction and language stimulation between staff and children, and with increased apathy and overt distress among infants.

Subsequent studies have revealed that smaller group size is associated with more positive caregiver behavior both in centers (Howes, 1983) and in family day care settings (Stith & Davis, 1984). In addition, children in smaller group settings have been described as more talkative (Howes & Rubenstein, 1985), more positive in their affect, and less avoidant upon entering their child care settings (Cummings & Beagles-Ross, 1983). Low child-to-staff ratios are associated with more nurturant and nonrestrictive caregiver behavior (Howes, 1983) and with increased talk and play behavior in toddlers (Howes & Rubenstein, 1985). Recently, lower ratios have also been associated with a higher incidence of secure attachment to caregivers among toddlers (Howes et al., 1988).

The National Day Care Study also identified caregiver education as an important determinant of high-quality substitute care, although the research regarding the nature of appropriate training is somewhat mixed. For infants and toddlers, overall educational level, rather than specific training in child development, was associated with increased social interaction and language stimulation and with decreased apathy (Ruopp et al., 1979). In one study, children who had caregivers with higher levels of education appeared more competent socially, while children cared for by individuals with more child-related training appeared less competent (Clarke-Stewart, 1987). Other studies suggest that specific training in child development may be critical. For example, caregivers with more child-related training spend more time engaged in teaching, helping, or interactive activities in family day care homes than do untrained caregivers (Stallings & Porter, 1980; Fosberg et al., 1980). Similarly, trained caregivers have been found to be more responsive and more socially stimulating than untrained caregivers (Howes, 1983) and more positive and less punitive in their interactions with children (Arnett, 1987). Several factors may explain the variability in the data, including the age of the children and the range of caregiver training assessed in various studies (Hayes et al., 1990). In addition, little is known about the specific nature of training received by caregivers. Clarke-Stewart (1989) suggests that some kinds of caregiver training may encourage behavior supportive of intellectual growth at the expense of social development. Clearly, much more research is needed on the nature of appropriate training for caregivers. Even so, it seems clear that more education and perhaps more child-related training for caregivers are generally related to more positive outcomes for children.

The question of caregiver training seems closely related to the structure and content of substitute care environments. Although some evidence suggests that more structured child care programs are related to improved cognitive skills (e.g., McCartney et al., 1982; Ruopp et al., 1979), few data are available regarding any relationship between the structure of a day care environment and children's social development. The Haskins (1985) study cited earlier would seem to suggest that some types of programmatic emphases may be related to differences in social behavior, but this possibility has yet to be investigated systematically in infants. Among preschoolers, data from the High Scope Preschool Study (Schweinhart et al., 1986, cited in Hayes et al., 1990) suggest that children in heavily structured, teacher-directed settings evidence less adequate social adjustment than do children in settings characterized by child-initiated learning activities in a supervised setting. Taken together, the data from these two studies offer provocative clues regarding the ways in which substitute care environments may influence social development, but they remain highly speculative at present.

Caregiver experience appears not to be consistently related to either staff behavior or child development. Howes (1983) reported that experienced caregivers were more responsive to children's bids for attention, but Ruopp et al. (1979) described less social interaction and cognitive stimulation of infants among more experienced caregivers. Kontos and Feine (1987) found no relationship between caregiver experience and child outcome. Clearly, experience is a complex issue. Day care staff members are generally poorly paid and suffer a turnover rate of approximately 41% (Hayes et al., 1990). Although long-term experience in a stable environment under adequate working conditions may indeed augment caregiver skills, it seems likely that long-term experience in less adequate settings may lead to frustration and diminished investment in child care activities.

While caregiver experience seems unreliable as a yardstick of quality, caregiver stability has emerged repeatedly in recent studies as an important component of good-quality care. Early studies revealed that infants interacted more with more stable caregivers (Rubenstein & Howes, 1979) and evidenced less distress and more positive affect when left by their mothers with more stable caregivers (Cummings, 1980). More recently, several studies have related caregiver stability to positive social development (Phillips et al., 1987; Clarke-Stewart, 1987; Howes, 1987; Howes & Stewart, 1987). These data are not surprising; it seems clear that the ability to establish a consistent relationship with one or two predictable caregivers over time should augment an infant's sense of security and well-being. Although caregiver stability is obviously not regulatable per se, the high turnover rate among substitute care providers seems closely related to the very low pay scale and other difficult working conditions (e.g., long hours, isolation). At least some of these factors are regulatable.

In summary, considerable evidence now exists that substitute care environments are highly variable in their quality, and that this variation is systematically related to differences in children's social and cognitive development. It seems clear that high-quality care for infants and toddlers is characterized by small group size, low child-to-staff ratios, the use of a small number of trained and stable caregivers, and the provision of moderate amounts of structure without being exclusively adult-directed. In such settings, children's daily experience is more likely to include interactions with consistent adults that are characterized by frequent caregiver speech to children, more caregiver time spent in play and interaction than in limit setting or management, more nurturant caregiver behavior, and a less punitive and restrictive approach to discipline. Children who experience these more positive substitute care arrangements appear less likely to exhibit the negative social behaviors associated with early substitute care.

Family Characteristics and the Quality of Care

In keeping with a broader, more complex focus on the interaction between familial characteristics and substitute care in the day care literature more generally, research on quality of care has also begun to include greater emphasis on familial factors. Several studies have revealed a positive relationship between socioeconomic status (SES) and quality of care (Kontos & Feine, 1987; Goelman & Pence, 1987), although this relationship may be mediated by the availability of subsidized day care to low-SES families (Hayes et al., 1990). Much more striking, however, is recent evidence of a relationship between other family characteristics and quality of care. Howes and Olenick (1986) reported that families whose lives were more complicated (e.g., families in which spouses lived separately, worked long hours, or worked split shifts), and therefore presumably more stressful, were more likely to use low-quality center care. In a second study, Howes and Stewart (1987) found that families viewed as stressed or restrictive used lower-quality child care, whereas families described as nurturing and well supported used higher-quality child care.

In addition, several studies have reported that child-rearing attitudes and parental involvement distinguish users of high- and low-quality care. In the Howes and Olenick (1986) study, both parents and caregivers of youngsters in low-quality settings were less involved in interaction and less invested in eliciting child compliance with requests. Similarly, in the Bermudan study, parents of children in high-quality centers placed greater value on social skills and less value on conformity than did parents of children in poor-quality centers (McCartney, 1984; Phillips et al., 1987). Kontos and Feine (1987) reported similar findings in their assessment of center quality in 10 Pennsylvania day care centers: Families who valued prosocial behavior chose day care centers of higher quality.

These data are significant because they reveal yet another pathway through which familial characteristics influence the development of children in substitute care. Equally important, they suggest that those children most in need of highly supportive child care environments are those least likely to be placed in such settings. For these children, substitute care may constitute a true developmental risk, and one they can ill afford.

FUTURE DIRECTIONS

The present review of the literature on substitute care clearly reveals that the issue cannot be reduced to a simple question of good versus bad. Moreover, the judicious reader must conclude that while concerns with the extensive use of nonmaternal care in infancy are real, they are based, as Sroufe (1988) points out, as much on what we do not know as on what we know.

Thus a focus on the future must begin with the ubiquitous call for more research. Clearly, we need to fine-tune much of what we have learned. We need a broader range of measures of attachment in young children, as well as more careful specification of the dimensions of social development under scrutiny. Long-term follow-up of substitute care graduates is also critical to an understanding of the data linking substitute care and insecure attachment. Furthermore, we need much more careful specification of most aspects of quality. For example, how large can child care groups become before a child's experience is compromised? We must identify how caregivers are best trained and what kinds of environments best support positive caregiver–child relationships. And obviously, we must refine our thinking and our tools for measuring family characteristics, particularly psychological factors related to parenting. But, perhaps most importantly, researchers must move beyond a simple cause-and-effect model toward more complex conceptual frameworks that permit the investigation of multiple pathways of influence and bidirectional interactions. McCartney and Galanopoulos (1988), as well as Richters and Zahn-Waxler (1988), suggest the use of ecological models that permit the specification and integration of many sources of influence on child development. Such strategies are difficult, time-consuming, and expensive, but they reflect the realities of children's experience much more faithfully.

Unfortunately, parents and policy makers cannot await an improved research base before making critical decisions regarding early child care. Some researchers have argued that, given the current state of knowledge, increased investment in group care for infants is unwarranted (Sroufe, 1988). Certainly, given the concerns with attachment security, increased reliance on options that would permit parents to spend more time at home with their infants (such as parental leave, job sharing, and flexible schedules) seems critical. But demographic data suggest that the numbers of working parents of infants are increasing, as is the use of group care settings (Hofferth & Phillips, 1987). In the absence of more flexible parental leave provisions, policy makers must focus on improving the quality of substitute care available. Despite relative consensus on what constitutes high-quality care, state regulations for infant care do not generally reflect research findings. For example, although most states regulate staff-to-child ratios, some states permit caretakers to care for up to seven infants, despite the 1:4 ratio advocated by researchers and professional groups. Similarly, a minority of states regulate group size in day care centers, and only slightly more than half require specified training for caregivers (Hayes et al., 1990). The situation regarding family day care is even more troubling. Despite evidence that regulated family day care settings provide a higher quality of care than unregulated settings (e.g., Fosberg et al., 1980), experts estimate that 60% of family day care homes are unregulated. Finally, at-home sitter care is completely unregulated and largely unstudied. Obviously, our inability to allocate resources to improve substitute care for young children threatens to shortchange our children's development, even as our understanding of how to facilitate development grows.

Finally, social scientists must think carefully about the answers they frame to parents who ask for guidance in making agonizing decisions about child care. Alan Sroufe (1988) argues that perhaps parents should be told the "whole story, how development at one phase builds from earlier development, how the infant–caregiver relationship evolves from a history of shared time and interaction" (p. 290). Obviously, parents must be told about the data regarding security of attachment and about the limitations of the data. They should understand the importance of stable, high-quality care, and should learn how they can identify such care. But perhaps equally importantly, parents should be told that the decision to use substitute care represents the formation of partnership for parenting, not an abdication of parenting. Regardless of whether or not they use substitute care, parents remain the most significant influence on their developing children. Their ongoing relationship with their children, their choice of child care settings, and their own involvement and collaboration with caregivers will heavily determine their children's experience. In the flurry of debate over substitute care, neither scientists nor consumers can afford to lose sight of that fact.

REFERENCES

Ainsworth, M. D. S., Blehar, M., Waters, E., & Wall, S. (1978). *Patterns of attachment: A psychological study of the Strange Situation.* Hillsdale, NJ: Erlbaum.

Ainsworth, M. D. S., & Wittig, B. A. (1969). Attachment and exploratory behavior of one-year-olds in a strange situation. In B. M. Foss (Ed.), *Determinants of infant behavior* (Vol. 4, pp. 113–136). London: Methuen.

Andersson, B. E. (1989). Effects of public day-care: A longitudinal study. *Child Development, 60,* 857–866.

Arnett, J. (1987, April). *Training for caregivers in day care centers.* Paper presented at the biennial meeting of the Society for Research in Child Development, Baltimore.

Barglow, P., Vaughn, B., & Molitor, N. (1987). Effects of maternal absence due to employment on the quality of mother–infant attachment in a low risk sample. *Child Development, 58,* 945–954.

Barton, M., & Schwarz, J. (1981, August). *Day care in the middle class: Effects in elementary school.* Paper presented at the annual meeting of the American Psychological Association, Los Angeles.

Belsky, J. (1984). Two waves of day-care research: Developmental effects and conditions of quality. In R. Ainslie (Ed.), *The child and the day-care setting* (pp. 1–34). New York: Praeger.

Belsky, J. (1988). The 'effects' of infant daycare reconsidered. *Early Childhood Research Quarterly, 3,* 235–272.

Belsky, J., & Braungart, J. (1991). Are insecure–avoidant infants with extensive day care experience less stressed by and more independent in the Strange Situation? *Child Development, 62,* 567–571.

Belsky, J., Garduque, L., & Hrncir, E. (1984). Assessing performance, competence and executive capacity in infant play: Relations to home environment and security of attachment. *Developmental Psychology, 20,* 406–417.

Belsky, J., & Rovine, M. (1988). Non-maternal care in the first year of life and attachment security. *Child Development, 59,* 157–167.

Benn, R. (1986). Factors promoting secure attachment between employed mothers and their sons. *Child Development, 57,* 1224–1231.

Bowlby, J. (1969). *Attachment and loss: Vol. 1. Attachment.* New York: Basic Books.

Brookhart, J., & Hock, E. (1976). The effects of experimental context and experiential background on infants' behavior toward their mothers and a stranger. *Child Development, 47,* 333–340.

Caruso, D. (1990). Infant day care and the concept of developmental risk. *Infant Mental Health Journal, 11,* 358–364.

Campos, J. J., Barrett, K. C., Lamb, M. E., Goldsmith, H. H., & Steinberg, C. (1983). Socioemotional Development. In M. M. Haith & J. J. Campos (Vol. Eds.), *Handbook of child psychology* (4th ed.): *Vol. 2. Infancy and developmental psychobiology* (pp. 783–915). New York: Wiley.

Chase-Lansdale, P. L., & Owen, M. T. (1987). Maternal employment in a family context: Effects on infant–mother and infant–father attachments. *Child Development, 58,* 1505–1512.

Clarke-Stewart, K. A. (1987). Predicting child development from day care forms and features: The Chicago study. In D. A. Phillips (Ed.), *Quality in child care: What does the research tell us?* (pp. 21–42). Washington, DC: National Association for the Education of Young Children.

Clarke-Stewart, K. A. (1988). The 'effects' of infant day care reconsidered: Risks for parents, children, and researchers. *Early Childhood Research Quarterly, 3,* 293–318.

Clarke-Stewart, K. A. (1989). Infant day care: Maligned or malignant? *American Psychologist, 44,* 266–273.

Clarke-Stewart, K. A., & Fein, G. G. (1983). Early childhood programs. In M. M. Haith & J. J. Campos (Vol. Eds.), *Handbook of child psychology* (4th ed.): *Vol. 2. Infancy and developmental psychobiology* (pp. 917–1000). New York: Wiley.

Clarke-Stewart, K. A., & Hevey, C. M. (1981). Longitudinal relations in repeated observations of mother–child interaction from 1 to 2½ years. *Developmental Psychology, 17,* 127–145.

Cummings, E. M. (1980). Caregiver stability and day care. *Developmental Psychology, 16,* 31–37.

Cummings, E. M., & Beagles-Ross, J. (1983). Towards a model of infant daycare: Studies of factors influencing responding to separation in daycare. In R. C. Ainslie (Ed.), *Quality of variations in daycare* (pp. 159–182). New York: Praeger.

Doyle, A., & Somers, K. (1978). The effects of group and family day care on infant attachment behaviours. *Canadian Journal of Infant Behavioural Science, 10,* 38–45.

Easterbrooks, M. A., & Goldberg, W. (1985). Effects of early maternal employment on toddlers, mothers and fathers. *Developmental Psychology, 21,* 774–783.

Egeland, B., & Farber, E. A. (1984). Mother–infant attachment: Factors related to its development and changes over time. *Child Development, 55,* 753–771.

Farber, E. A., & Egeland, B. (1982). Developmental consequences of out-of-home care for infants in a low-income population. In E. F. Zigler & E. W. Gordon (Eds.), *Day care: Scientific and social policy issues* (pp. 102–125). Boston: Auburn House.

Fosberg, S., Hawkins, P. D., Singer, J. D., Goodson, B. D., Smith, J. M., & Brush, L. R. (1980). *National Day Care Home Study* (Contract No. HEW 105-77-1051). Cambridge, MA: Abt Associates.

Goelman, H., & Pence, A. R. (1987). Effects of child care, family, and individual characteristics on children's language development: The Victoria Day Care Research Project. In D. A. Phillips (Ed.), *Quality in child care: What does the research tell us?* (pp. 89–104). Washington, DC: National Association for the Education of Young Children.

Goosens, F. A. (1987). Maternal employment and day care: Effects on attachment. In L. W. C. Tavecchio & M. H. van Ijzendoorn (Eds.), *Attachment in social networks* (pp. 135–183). Amsterdam: North-Holland.

Haskins, R. (1985). Public school aggression among children with varying day care experience. *Child Development, 56,* 689–703.

Hayes, C. D., Palmer, J. L., & Zaslow, M. I. (1990). *Who cares for America's children?* Washington, DC: National Academy Press.

Hock, E. (1980). Working and non-working mothers and their infants: A comparative study of maternal caregiving characteristics and infants' social behavior. *Merrill–Palmer Quarterly, 46,* 79–101.

Hock, E., Morgan, K. C., & Hock, M. (1980). Employment decisions made by mothers of infants. *Psychology of Women Quarterly, 9,* 383–402.

Hofferth, S., & Phillips, D. (1987). Child care in the United States, 1975–1995. *Journal of Marriage and the Family, 49,* 559–571.

Howes, C. (1983). Caregiver behavior in center and family day care. *Journal of Applied Developmental Psychology, 1,* 99–107.

Howes, C. (1987). Quality indicators in infant and toddler child care: The Los Angeles study. In D. A. Phillips (Ed.), *Quality in child care: What does the research tell us?* (pp. 81–88). Washington, DC: National Association for the Education of Young Children.

Howes, C. (1990). Can age of entry into child care predict adjustment in kindergarten? *Developmental Psychology, 26,* 292–303.

Howes, C., & Olenick, M. (1986). Family and child influences on toddlers' compliance. *Child Development, 57,* 202–216.

Howes, C., Rodning, C., Galluzo, D., & Myers, L. (1988). Attachment and child care: Relations with mother and caregiver. *Early Childhood Research Quarterly, 3,* 403–416.

Howes, C., & Rubenstein, J. (1985). Determinants of toddlers' experience in day care: Age of entry and quality of setting. *Child Care Quarterly, 14,* 140–151.

Howes, C., & Stewart, P. (1987). Child's play with adults, toys, and peers: An examination of family and child-care influences. *Developmental Psychology, 23,* 423–430.

Jacobson, I., & Wille, D. (1984). Influence of attachment and separation experience on separation distress at 18 months. *Developmental Psychology, 20,* 477–484.

Kagan, J., Kearsley, R. B., & Zelazo, P. R. (1978). *Infancy: Its place in human development.* Cambridge, MA: Harvard University Press.

Kontos, S., & Feine, R. (1987). Child care quality, compliance with regulations, and children's development: The Pennsylvania study. In D.A. Phillips (Ed.), *Quality in child care: What does the research tell us?* (pp. 57–80). Washington, DC: National Association for the Education of Young Children.

Lamb, M. E., Sternberg, K. T., & Prodromidis, M. (1992). Non-maternal care and the security of infant–mother attachment: A reanalysis of the data. *Infant Behavior and Development, 15*(1), 71–83.

Lamb, M. E., Thompson, R. A., Gardner, P., Charnov, E. L., & Estes, D. (1984). Security of infantile attachment as assessed in the 'Strange Situation': Its study and biological interpretation. *Behavioral and Brain Sciences, 7,* 127–171.

Lay, M. Z., & Meyer, W. J. (1972). *Effects of early day care experience on subsequent observed program behaviors* (Final report to the Office of Education, Subcontract No. 70-007). Syracuse, NY: Syracuse University.

Main, M., & Goldwyn, R. (in press). Attachment classification related to infant–mother and infant–father attachment. *Developmental Psychology.*

Main, M., Kaplan, K., & Cassidy, J. (1985). Security in infancy, childhood and adulthood: A move to the level of representation. In I. Bretherton & E. Waters (Eds.), Growing points of attachment theory and research. *Monographs of the Society for Research in Child Development, 58*(1–2, Serial No. 209), 66–104.

Main, M., & Weston, D. (1981). The quality of the toddler's relationship to mother and to father: Related to conflict behavior and the readiness to establish new relationships. *Child Development, 52,* 932–940.

Matas, L., Arend, R. A., & Sroufe, L. A. (1978). Continuity of adaptation in the second year: The relationship between quality of attachment and later competence. *Child Development, 49,* 547–556.

McCartney, K. (1984). The effect of quality of day care environment upon children's language development. *Developmental Psychology, 20,* 244–260.

McCartney, K., & Galanopoulos, A. (1988). Child care and attachment: A new frontier the second time around. *American Journal of Orthopsychiatry, 58*(1), 16–24.

McCartney, K., Scarr, S., Phillips, D. A., Grajek, S., & Schwarz, J. C. (1982). Environmental differences among day care centers and their effects on children's development. In E. F. Zigler & E. W. Gordon (Eds.), *Day care: Scientific and social policy issues* (pp. 126–151). Boston: Auburn House.

McCrae, J. W., & Herbert-Jackson, E. (1975). Are behavioral effects of infant day care program specific? *Developmental Psychology, 12,* 269–270.

Owen, M., & Cox, M. (1988). Maternal employment and the transition to parenthood. In A. E. Gottfried (Ed.), *Maternal employment and children's development: Longitudinal research* (pp. 85–119). New York: Plenum Press.

Pederson, F., Cain, R., Zaslow, M., & Anderson, B. J. (1982). Variation in infant experience associated with alternative family roles. In M. Laosa & I. Sigel (Eds.), *Families as learning environments for children* (pp. 203–222). New York: Plenum Press.

Phillips, D. A. (1987). Indicators of quality in child care: Review of research. In D. A. Phillips (Ed.), *Quality in child care: What does the research tell us?* (pp. 1–20). Washington, DC: National Association for the Education of Young Children.

Phillips, D. A., McCartney, K., & Scarr, S. (1987). Selective review of infant day care research: A cause for concern! *Zero to Three: Bulletin of the National Center for Clinical Infant Programs, 7*(3), 18–21.

Richters, J. E., & Zahn-Waxler, C. (1988). The infant day care controversy: Current status and future directions. *Early Childhood Research Quarterly, 3,* 319–336.

Rubenstein, I., & Howes, C. (1979). Caregiving and infant behavior in day care and in homes. *Developmental Psychology, 15,* 1–24.

Rubenstein, I., & Howes, C. (1983). Socio-emotional development of toddlers in daycare: The role of peers and of individual differences. In S. Kilmer (Ed.), *Early education and daycare* (Vol. 3, pp. 21–45). Greenwich, CT: JAI Press.

Rubenstein, J. L., Howes, C., & Boyle, P. (1981). A two-year follow-up of infants in community-based day care. *Journal of Psychology and Psychiatry, 22,* 209–218.

Ruopp, R., Travers, J., Glantz, F., & Coelen, C. (1979). *Children at the center: Final results of the National Day Care Study.* Cambridge, MA: Abt Associates.

Schubert, J. B., Bradley-Johnson, S., & Nuttal, J. (1980). Mother–infant communication and employment. *Child Development, 51,* 246–249.

Schwartz, P. (1983). Length of day care attendance and attachment behavior in 18 month old infants. *Child Development, 54,* 1073–1078.

Schwarz, J. C. (1983, April). *Infant day care: Effects at 2, 4, and 8 years.* Paper presented at the meeting of the Society for Research in Child Development, Detroit.

Schwarz, J. C., Strickland, R. G., & Krolick, G. (1973). Effects of early day care experience on adjustment to a new environment. *American Journal of Orthopsychiatry, 43,* 340–346.

Schwarz, J. C., Strickland, R. G., & Krolick, G. (1974). Infant day care: Behavioral effects at preschool age. *Developmental Psychology, 10,* 502–506.

Silverman, N. (1990). *Attachment, maternal behavior and preschool competence at age three.* Unpublished doctoral dissertation, Boston University.

Sroufe, L. A. (1983). Infant caregiver attachment and patterns of adaptation in preschool: The roots of maladaption and competence. In M. Perlmutter (Ed.), *Minnesota Symposium on Child Psychology: Vol. 16. Development and policy concerning children with special needs* (pp. 41–81). Hillsdale, NJ: Erlbaum.

Sroufe, L. A. (1988). A developmental perspective on day care. *Early Childhood Research Quarterly, 3,* 283–291.

Sroufe, L. A., & Fleeson, J. (1986). Attachment and the construction of relationships. In W. Hartrup & Z. Rubin (Eds.), *Relationships and development.* Hillsdale, NJ: Erlbaum.

Stallings, J., & Porter, A. (1980). *National Daycare Home Study.* Palo Alto, CA: SRI International.

Stith, S. M., & Davis, A. J. (1984). Employed mothers and family day care: A comparative analysis of infant care. *Child Development, 55,* 1340–1348.

Thompson, R. (1988). The effects of infant daycare through the prism of attachment theory: A critical appraisal. *Early Childhood Research Quarterly, 3,* 273–282.

U.S. Bureau of the Census. (1986). *Estimates of the population of the U.S. by age, sex and race, 1980–1985* (Current Population Reports, Series P-25, No. 985). Washington, DC: U.S. Government Printing Office.

Vaughn, B. E., Deane, K. E., & Waters, E. (1985). The impact of out-of-home care on child–mother attachment quality: Another look at some enduring questions. In I. Bretherton and E. Waters (Eds.), Growing points of attachment theory and research in child development. *Monographs of the Society for Research in Child Development, 50*(1–2, 110–123).

Vaughn, B. E., Gove, F. L., & Egeland, B. (1980). The relationship between out-of-home care and the quality of infant–mother attachment in an economically disadvantaged population. *Child Development, 51,* 1203–1214.

Zaslow, M. J., Pederson, F. A., Suwalsky, J. T. D., & Rabinovich, B. A. (1983, April). *Maternal employment and parent–infant interaction.* Paper presented at the biennial meeting of the Society for Research in Child Development, Detroit.

30

Infant Placement and Custody

THOMAS M. HORNER
MELVIN J. GUYER

The subject of infant placement and custody turns on five conditions of disrupted caregiving: (1) parental death or catastrophic displacement (e.g., as a consequence of war or natural disaster; (2) voluntary abandonment; (3) contractual or oblatory exchanges (e.g., legalized adoptions); (4) marital dissolutions requiring dispositions of property and minor children; and (5) state findings of parental unfitness, which may stem from neglect, abuse, or both. Different eras and societies have had particular ways of dealing with infant placement and custody under each of these conditions. In this chapter we focus on infant custody and placement under the fourth condition.

Infant custody cases are rare, as parents and courts alike seem to share the view that mothers ought to have primary care of the very youngest children. But the number of infant custody litigations, as well as visitation litigations, seems to be increasing: Fathers are asserting, for various reasons (in most instances having to do with genuine wishes to preserve contact and involvement in their young children's lives), their interests in either having custody of their infants or assuring more than token contact with them.

SOCIAL AND LEGAL FOUNDATIONS OF JUDICIAL DETERMINATIONS OF CHILD CUSTODY

Historically, the regulation of family life has belonged to the individual states in accordance with provisions made by the U.S. Constitution (see specifically the Ninth and Tenth Amendments). But in recent decades Congress and the federal judiciary have been prominent in the sphere of defining and regulating family life (see Melton & Wilcox, 1989). Thus, the right of married partners to use contraceptives (*Griswold v. Connecticut*, 1965), the right of persons of different races to marry (*Loving v. Virginia*, 1967), and the right of religious groups to educate their children in accordance with religious practices when the latter conflict with statutes governing the education of children (*Wisconsin v. Yoder*, 1972) all represent areas where federal courts have overruled states in matters affecting family life. The federalization of child support payment enforcement, the federal defining of adoptive parent rights in custody disputes (*Stanley v. Illinois*, 1972), and the Parent Kidnapping Prevention Act are further examples of the expanding role of the federal government in dealing with family law.

Changes have occurred in how children's interests are defined and promoted by the states as well as by the federal government and courts. Many of these changes have entailed extensions of rights and interests traditionally enjoyed by adults to children. Thus, criminal defendant rights have been expanded to include juveniles (*In re Gault*, 1947; *In re Winship*, 1970; *Pee v. United States*, 1959; *Kent v. United States*, 1966), as have certain rights (extended within the penumbra of *Roe v. Wade*, 1973) to seek abortions (*Bellotti v. Baird*, 1983). The findings of *In re Gault*, *Pee v. United States*, and *Kent v. United States* have provided the legal buttresses for appointments of guardians *ad litem* in child custody cases (see Inker & Peretta, 1971, as well as Davidson & Gerlach, 1984). Children's rights to sue either physicians (or, theoretically, their parents) on the basis of wrongful life, though largely unsuccessful, have been upheld in several courts (*Curlender v. Bioscience Laboratories*, 1980; *Harbeson v. Parke-Davis*, 1983; see also Horowitz & Hunter, 1984; Peters, 1980; Weir, 1984).

Various public interest proponents have sought to extricate children from many historically rooted parental child-rearing prerogatives (see, e.g., Foster & Freed, 1972; Gross & Gross, 1977; Hart, 1991; Horowitz & Davidson, 1984; Wilcox & Naimark, 1991). Probably the most energetic of these efforts have been in the area of child abuse and neglect. Congressional enactment of the Model Federal Reporting Law has resulted in its adoption in one or another close version by all 50 states, and in the rapid creation of a vast and penetrating infrastructure of investigative, evaluative, and treating agents who, through a combination of powerful incentives and deterrents, have in essence been deputized to report suspicions of child abuse and neglect.

Parallel forces acting upon and within the judiciary have achieved for children certain exemptions from having to give testimony in the presence of criminal defendants on the basis of the harm it might cause them (*Maryland v. Craig*, 1990). This has pitted, squarely within the domain of the Sixth Amendment's provision for a defendant's right to confront witnesses in trials, the putative interests of a child (in *Maryland v. Craig*, the child's "right" not to undergo the stress of courtroom interrogation) versus the established interests of adult parents (i.e., the right to confront and cross-examine witnesses) accused of abusing or neglecting a child.

CONTESTED CHILD CUSTODY AND CHILD-PARENT CONTACT

Approximately 75% of the 1.1 million divorces that are now occurring each year involve dispositions concerning minor children (Glick, 1988). An uncounted proportion of these children are below the age of 4. When child custody and contact are contested by divorcing parents, their central conflicts generally focus on who shall exert primary proximal (i.e., day-to-day) and ultimate (i.e., life course) decision making in relation to a child. Within the context of contested custody, each parent can be expected to assert that he or she is acting on behalf of the child's interests.

Courts are generally reluctant to interfere with traditionally held and legally protected parental prerogatives concerning child rearing. Thus, when divorcing parents agree as to how custody and child–parent contact is to be distributed, courts are likely to concur. When divorcing parents disagree, courts must then make decisions concerning both custody and the distribution of respective child–parent contacts. If custody is not to be jointly held by the parents, then one must be designated as having sole custody, and conditions must be set as to when the noncustodial parent shall have contact with the child.

Courts are sufficiently cognizant of general principles of child development and adjustment that they are generally able to avoid decisions whose effects would be harmful to a child. Yet, when one parent alleges that the other is unfit to have custody of (or contact with) a specific child, courts are given the problem of determining the factualness of the allegation. Although courts recognize that many allegations by parents are made in order to gain advantage in one or more collateral issues (such as property settlement and child support payment determinations), or to carry on hostilities originating within the marriage or divorce proceedings, they also recognize that allegations of relative or absolute unfitness often have validity. In these circumstances, courts have come increasingly to seek both facts and guidance from persons presumed to be skilled at doing such things—persons widely termed child mental health and development "experts."

The putative interests of children in custody cases have been articulated by most state legislatures and courts under the familiar rubric of "best interests," a phrase whose judicial interpretation is almost limitless (see Katz, 1974, p. 1). (For a thorough discussion of the definitional problems of the "best interests" principle, see Chambers, 1984. For an overview of the "best interests" provisions in the 50 states, see Freed & Walker, 1988, pp. 506–513.) Many states have codified these interests. Thus, Michigan has elaborated 11 factors to be considered when determining child custody (Mich. Comp Laws Ann. § 722.23, 1987), the last of which, proving Katz, refers to "any other factor considered by the court to be relevant to a particular child custody dispute."

THE USE OF EXPERTISE

Goldstein, Freud, and Solnit's publication of *Beyond the Best Interests of the Child* (1973) crystallized for the present era a view of clinical expertise that emphasized experts' essential role in serving the interests of children. Despite a far from uniform reception within the legal community (Crouch, 1979), many courts have become increasingly reliant on mental health and child development specialists in matters of contested child custody and of parent fitness determination.

Yet experienced consultants have come to understand that, with exceptions, referrals from courts are motivated by the courts' wishes to dislodge intractable parents from steadfastly opposed positions. Sometimes courts simply wish to have an external rationale for making one or another disposition. Some parents seek their own consultations and then seek to have the court receive recommendations from the evaluators who have provided the consultations. Such a consultation is unfortunately often one-sided, in that the evaluator fails to make contact with the other parent. For this reason, most courts seek the consultation of an expert who will see both parents as well as their child(ren), and who will insist on a waiver of client privileges of confidentiality. We strongly recommend that evaluations be inclusive of both parents, as well as of other family members who might be relevant to the development and care of the targeted child(ren).

Experts in the social and behavioral sciences are rarely as impartial as they typically try to appear (see Diamond, 1959), and the potential for activism on the part of experts in cases affecting children in relation to either their parents or the state is significant (Guyer & Horner, 1990). It is a rare case of contested child custody that cannot stir as much controversy between experts as between litigants (Guyer & Ash, 1987). In fact, whether studied individually or systematically, experts are as likely to disagree as to agree (Horner, Guyer, & Kalter, 1992)—with respect to findings as well as recommendations—when they are confronted with the same case material. This is largely the consequence, we believe, of the fact that social scientists and child mental health clinicians in general have been unable to fill significantly the large gaps that exist in knowledge concerning early childhood experience and outcome. In an exhaustive survey of the social-scientific literature, Lakin (1991) has pointed out the inadequacy of social-scientific research with respect to the major legal questions concerning divorce and child custody determination. Goldstein, Freud, and Solnit (1987) have come to caution experts to recognize (and thereby not to try to go beyond) their genuine limitations in this regard. This includes, of course, the impossibility of predicting with any greater accuracy than that of the court itself outcomes from an array of specific decision-making possibilities.

Nevertheless, mental health and child development experts continue to constitute an extremely powerful force in child custody/contact decision making when parents contest custody. With an 85% concordance between expert recommendations and judicial outcomes, experts' recommendations to courts effectively close off further court-situated conflict in a significant majority of cases, by virtue of the experts' either successfully mediating an "agreement" between the parents, or adding a highly weighted bargaining chip to the adversarial process (Ash & Guyer, 1986).

Most mental health professionals have come to view themselves as uniquely qualified to provide information and recommendations to courts concerning appropriate decisions to be made when parents dispute the custody of their children or the distribution of child–parent contact (see, e.g., Black & Cantor, 1989). Some professional organizations have sought to establish guidelines for its members who conduct child custody evaluations (e.g., American Academy of Child and Adolescent Psychiatry, 1988; Joint

Committee of Children's Charter of the Courts of Michigan, Inc., and the Michigan Association for Infant Mental Health, 1985)—largely in response to a perceived need to reduce trends toward indiscriminate practices by experts and indiscriminate uses of experts by courts.

The principal role of the expert is to offer courts bases for making decisions concerning child placement. When several options exist, the expert's role is often to rank-order the desirability of each option. These roles are defined by the court's implicit desire to maximize the likelihood of a *positive* outcome in a child's life, and, correlatively, to minimize the likelihood of any *negative* outcomes, such as Goldstein et al.'s (1973) principle of the "least detrimental alternative." Virtually all uses of experts by courts turn on their jointly held belief that experts can make genuine contributions toward *predicting* certain outcomes, which is also to say toward *preventing* certain undesirable outcomes. Experts giving testimony in infant custody cases frame their recommendations almost universally in terms of either prevention or amelioration. They thereby imply that they possess abilities to predict outcomes relative to specific custody/contact options, although this is questionable in our view.

The opportunities for child mental health experts to inject personal bias and/or folk wisdom into their recommendations are proportionately great. Several social and clinical scientists have raised serious precautions concerning the validity of clinical experts within judicial proceedings (e.g., Guyer & Horner, 1990, 1991; Kotelchuck, 1982; Meehl, 1971, 1973; Melton & Limber, 1989; Melton & Wilcox, 1989; see also Weithorn, 1987; in the legal literature, see Cohen, 1985; Gass, 1979; Gross, 1990; Levy, 1989; and McCord, 1986, 1987). Moreover, along the lines of perceived bias, courts often detect in expert testimony what one jurist has characterized as "an ease with which [clinical experts are] willing to suspect the worst rather than the best about a person, even when the best has been a person's whole life."

Still, genuine expertise exists, and we categorize its elements as "cognate" and "technical" (Guyer & Horner, 1991; Horner et al., 1992).

Cognate Expertise

Cognate expertise consists of an expert's refined knowledge concerning various domains of in-

fancy and early childhood. These domains include (1) development and maturation, including behavioral and affective dynamics associated with various ages; (2) physical health; (3) familiar or predictable patterns of vulnerability and resiliency (e.g., extremely premature birth) or characteristics (e.g., physical handicaps, extreme temperament); (4) categories of normative as well as clinically relevant adjustment and their associations (or lack thereof) with specific outcomes; and (5) the normative extent and variety of caregiving and caretaking contexts that can be or are *predictably* associated with specific outcomes.

Infant mental health experts must be critical and discerning consumers of what their field currently has to offer in the way of *facts* as opposed to *theories* concerning development, vulnerability–resilience, adjustment, and the various experiential and contextual factors influencing infants and very young children. Infant mental health consultants providing cognate expertise to courts should be able to cite not only areas of consensus-based fact relative to individual infants, but areas of significant controversy as well. To the extent that consensus-based facts concerning infants and toddlers exist—whether these facts refer to development and maturation or to clinically relevant vulnerabilities in relation to various caretaking circumstances that might befall children consequent to one or another judicial action (and here one must also acknowledge "negative facts," or facts concerning what is not necessarily the case when one is considering infancy from its several perspectives)—experts should strive to let the court take notice of such facts (see Melton, 1987).

Technical Expertise

Technical expertise encompasses an expert's specialized skills in eliciting and clarifying information that is relevant to any of several cognate areas. Interviewing a parent for relevant details of the infant's individual and familial history, physical health, adjustment, and the like is of obvious importance in any claim to technical expertise in infant mental health. Similarly, the ability to observe infants for their characteristic behavioral and communicative dynamics is essential to any claim to technical expertise. Infant mental health consultations should routinely include contacts with the infant and each parent under conditions that allow the consultant to form opinions concerning not only parental competence and disposition, but also the infant's disposition and behavioral dynamics toward and with that parent. The observation/assessment paradigm of Gaensbauer and Harmon (1981) is prototypical of paradigms that are commonly used by infant mental health practitioners, and that may be effective in obtaining valid observations of infant and infant–parent dynamics.

An ability to assess formally the maturational organization and dynamics of the infant relative to normative expectations is important. Although it is not as critical to the ordinary custody/contact consultation as interviewing and observation are, developmental testing may be useful as a rapport-building device with infants, as a context for observing parental dynamics concerning achievement or compliance (see Pawl & Bennett, 1980), or in a case when questions of special programming for the infant have been prompted. The expert making use of such testing should, of course, bear in mind the psychometric limitations of quantitative assessments (e.g., Horner, 1988).

The origins of both cognate and technical expertise in infant mental health are both formal (e.g., specialized training and education) and experiential, but it should be obvious that most of what constitutes formal education and training in contemporary child psychiatry, psychology, and social work excludes the requisite knowledge and technical instruction that would be appropriate and necessary to providing a court with anything that is probative beyond what the court is already likely to know or understand. Courts are becoming increasingly cognizant of not only the limits of expertise, but the shortcomings of curricula vitae and other professional resumés in reliably attesting to given professionals' actual expertise (Guyer & Horner, 1991).

FAMILIAL DISSOLUTION AND READJUSTMENT

The infant/toddler status of many children in custodial/contact disputes is typically raised both by parents and by clinical authorities as an external standard for judicial decision making. Unfortunately, many mental health consultants, even ones with infant mental health experience and qualifications, reach recommendations concerning infant custody and parent contact on the basis of the most perfunctory considerations, and therefore fail to take into account the range of individual differences among infants and toddlers with respect to coping with change. The latter includes not only change associated with ordinary maturation and environment, but also change unique to divorce (i.e., altered parental moods, behavior, and presence).

Continuity of Care and Parent-Infant Contact

One of the principles frequently advanced by infant mental health specialists who undertake custody evaluations is that there should be continuity of care and contact with the primary attachment figure. This principle underlies a number of common recommendations by professional consultants to courts, including (1) that an infant should be in the sole custody of one parent; (2) that an infant should not have overnight contacts with the noncustodial parent; and (3) that no change of custody should occur following establishment of a "permanent" custodial environment.

The principle of continuity, once used to advocate against nonparental child care outside the home, has become a basis of judging the adequacy of such caretaking. The possibility of being exposed to poor day care notwithstanding, parents and children have come to accept ample (and in many instances high) proportions of nonparental child care during infancy and the preschool years as an adequate if not effective means of adjusting to the realities of the economic conditions underlying their lives. Infants and toddlers within such caretaking circumstances successfully nap, eat, toilet, play, and cope with the distresses of minor injuries and mundane frustrations while away from their parents.

Continuity of infant care is a supraordinate principle that overarches many kinds of distributed care, including one in which two divorced parents continue to have contact with their child(ren) following divorce. If the principle offers any specific guide to the court, it is that if fathers and mothers are to maintain and deepen meaningful emotional relationships with their infants and toddlers, it must be within a supraordinately defined context of frequent, fairly regular, and realistic opportunities to be together—not only to have the pleasure of each other's company, but also to work out the details of managing frustrations, defining limits, and building a history of genuine relationship with each other as against a history simply of contacts.

One assumption underlying the principle of continuity of care and contact is that infants cannot easily tolerate multiplicity of people or locales in their care, and that transitions, rather than being occasions (admittedly sometimes difficult ones) for adaptation, are inherently and inevitably "traumatic." This assumption is reinforced by the understanding, built upon observations in developmental research as well as upon conventional wisdom, that infants' cognitive and emotional capacities are limited as means of coping with change (see Gean, 1984; Goldstein et al., 1973). The assumption is also reinforced by the understanding, again built on the foundations of both research and conventional wisdom, that having developed focal attachments to their caregivers, infants pose certain restrictions with respect to how they receive, tolerate, and use the soothing and nurturing actions of a parent.

Often the term "traumatic" is applied to events or conditions that are alleged to predict a harmful outcome. Thus, when an expert informs the court that to shift custody of a particular child at this time would be potentially traumatic, this may refer not so much to its immediate effects as to the long-term possibilities of the child's becoming severely maladjusted.

Yet the present era of day care, driven largely both by economic necessity and by changing societal attitudes concerning effective distributions of extrafamilial child care, has taught us that a child can thrive under multiple caretaking conditions so long as each is stable, emotionally available, coherent, and sensitive to the child's developmental and personal needs, and so long as each is comfortable for the various caretakers involved (including, of course, the parents). Moreover, although in an ordinary two-parent family it is often possible to identify in an infant a primary attachment relationship with one or the other parent, we are past ignoring that the infant may also have deep and positive attachments to other figures as well, such that when the primary attachment figure is absent the infant effectively uses the capacity of the nonprimary attachment figure to act as a secure base of exploration or haven of safety.

Experience in consulting with day care centers and in-home care providers, combined with centuries of accumulated familiarity with conditions in which nannies have functioned, therefore rebut claims made on general or external grounds alone that infants are better off under the sole or exclusive care of one person rather than more than one. Enter, then, the contemporary father who seeks to have contact with his infant child more than the weekly hour or two that is perfunctorily decreed by many courts. He expresses not only his desire to have more than an occasional contact with his son or daughter, but also to be available in ways that promote and deepen, rather than dilute, that child's attachment to him. He believes that the widely spaced, disconnected contacts that constitute the familiar staple of the courts are insufficient to both his own and his child's needs.

In cases such as these, the infant mental health specialist may assure the court that as much as it is the one parent's (again, let us say the father's) burden to demonstrate that the infant can tolerate the amount of separation from the mother that would be needed to allow the father–infant relationship to deepen, it is the mother's burden to demonstrate that separations from her in degrees that would be effective toward preserving the father–infant relationship are harmful (as against being comparable to the kind of separations that would occur if the child were in day care). Obviously, when parents are in significant conflict over the specific care of the infant, the specialist must advise the court as to measures that might effectively reduce either the conflict or its effects (see, e.g., Johnston & Campbell, 1988). Obvious, too, is the need to protect the infant from intractable parental natures, which in more cases than traditional presumptions concerning the needs of infants would predict will not always favor the mother.

In our work with courts and parents, we have become accustomed to addressing not only each parent's rights for meaningful and relationship-deepening contacts with an infant or toddler, but the infant's or toddler's rights to such contacts as well. To be sure, providing for these rights may require considerable effort on the part of the parents, and perhaps one can say that effort is required on the part of the infant as well. Of course, the nature of the effort for the infant and the parents will be quite different. As mediators and other professional specialists in postdivorce counseling have learned over the years, the termination of a marriage in no way alters the necessity of parents' working constructively and jointly to achieve continuity and security in their children's lives. This applies to infants and very young children as well.

The issues, therefore, of selecting day care, preschool, and other extraparental care facilities, and of creating a framework of caregiving that promotes and deepens an infant's relationship with each parent, require courts and parents alike to be more considerate of joint or shared custodial arrangements than they often are with respect to their youngest wards. Courts need to be mindful of an infant's needs to have frequent and extended contacts with each parent, including opportunities to adjust to the respective (and sometimes different) ministrations of those parents, if the infant is to establish more than superficial or perfunctory ties to each parent. The question naturally arises as to what provisions should be made in the face of various gradations of interparental conflict.

Custody

The most common issues raised by the parent seeking to dismantle the relationship between his or her young child and the other parent are those of custody alternatives; the nature and extent of the contact between the child and each parent; and the significance of maintained versus disrupted sibships.

Custody Alternatives

The term and concept of "custody" are rooted historically in the practice of allocating children in conjunction with the presumed or arbitrated proprietary rights of parents. Unfortunately, the conflict-engendering dynamics of this historical artifact permeate nearly every contested custody/contact case, such that in the minds of the protagonists, the issue of to whom the child rightfully "belongs" occludes the issue of how the responsibilities of child rearing will be distributed once the parents no longer live in the same dwelling.

The principal legal alternatives in child custody cases are "single-parent custody," in which one parent bears/enjoys the bulk of decision making with regard to the child while the other parent bears/enjoys less or none, and "joint custody," in which the court recognizes the joint decision-making privileges/obligations of the divorced parents. In the case of infants and toddlers, the choice of these alternatives has been traditionally decided on the basis of presump-

tions concerning what children of that age require in order to continue thriving. The "tender years" doctrine has until recent years ruled, and in most judicial quarters still reigns, when it comes to infants and preschool-age children.

Some students of joint custody have suggested on the basis of observation and experience that there are unique challenges to the adjustment of young children facing divided parenting (e.g., Gean, 1984; Steinman, 1981). It is evident, even when parents are ostensibly cooperative and supportive of a joint custody arrangement, that some young children seem to react adversely to divided parenting (e.g., Steinman, 1981). Yet, as Clingempeel and Repucci (1982) and McKinnon and Wallerstein (1986) have separately concluded, there are presently no secure bases for predicting which children will do well and which not under joint custodial conditions (see also the exhaustive review of shared parenting/joint custody studies by Lakin, 1991). Certainly, as McKinnon and Wallerstein (1986, p. 183) have averred, there is no present basis for *presuming* that joint custody constitutes a preferred alternative to single-parent custody; this admission also, it seems, concedes tacitly that single-parent custody as well begs no presumption of preferability.

Studies of the long-term effects of divorce have been consistent in their demonstrations that divorce can have lasting effects in children's lives, and that many of these effects are negative (see, e.g., Wallerstein, 1991; see also Levitin, 1979). Yet, since many of the outcomes described by investigators of long-term effects are those that might be associated with a number of experiential backgrounds not including divorce, clinicians and courts dealing with individual instances must be wary about making decisions based on these studies alone.

Our experience, as well as that reported by others (e.g., McKinnon & Wallerstein, 1986), has been that when parents are able to minimize discordant tones and duplicitous acts with regard to the day-to-day life of a young child, many very young children, no matter how young (except, perhaps, most newborns), can cope favorably even when transient symptoms of distress are evident (see below). Symptoms of child distress that are sometimes encountered are traceable to problems in other settings (e.g., day care, preschool) or to developmental disturbances wrought by conflicts between the child and one of the parents—disturbances that could well have been manifested without parental divorce. Not surprisingly, when parents are discordant and duplicitous, children are likely to be deleteriously affected, much as children who live in homes filled with domestic turmoil are also frequently affected.

Although joint custody levels the legal playing field somewhat between parents as they enter the conflict-steeped waters of divorce and its aftermath, it presents very few if any inherent opportunities for eliminating the effects of chronic parental quarreling. In those cases in which the parents arrive at effective means of dealing with the day-to-day matters of raising their children under the conditions of separated parenting, the issue of joint custody is, from the standpoint of practical purposes, usually moot.

Although individual case instances can always be recruited in support of routinely advocating one or the other custodial option, in our work with infants/toddlers and their divorced/divorcing parents we have formed no general impression that single-parent custody inherently eliminates the problems that arise in the aftermath of divorce, or that joint custody insures greater communication and support in divorce's aftermath. Joint custody ought, it would seem, to constitute the option of choice when all things are close to being equal and the parents have a demonstrated commitment to making that option work—if only because it consecrates the benefit that accrues to individuals and society when, married or not, parents act nonadversarially in their child-rearing efforts and practices.

Nature of Child-Parent Contact

Whether one is raised by married or divorced parents, one's childhood status requires recognition by parents of age-correlated needs, requirements, and challenges. The developmental lines described by Anna Freud (1965), which include attainments in eating, bowel and bladder control, play and imagination, formations of peer relationships, and the like, are as applicable to infants and toddlers living in the aftermath of divorce as they are to children living in intact families. Although more recent, largely theoretical elaborations of the tasks and dynamics of early development have been made since Freud's delineations (see, e.g., Greenspan, 1981, 1989, 1991), and although highly valuable theoretical departures from classical formulations of the infant and toddler as perilously tucked between the poles of separation and dependency

have been made (e.g., Stern, 1985), Freud's basic focus on venues of early childhood development and socialization remains an effective orienting beacon for the infant mental health specialist.

The issue of custody (except where a parent has been determined to be unfit) is less important, it would seem, than the nature of the contacts a young child has with each parent, particularly when viewed against the array of developmental tasks and attainments expected of children during infancy and toddlerhood. Even so, as we have already commented, the proportions of children who cope effectively under single-parent and joint custodial arrangements, where the parents are working positively together, allow for no secure generalizations to be made as to which custody option is *a priori* more favorable. There are, though, a number of issues that recur across cases, and some comment can be made about these.

Frequency of Contact. Whether custody is joint or in the possession of one parent, the frequency of contact between infants and their divorced parents is an issue that must be addressed. In spite of evidence that early precursors of attachment exist in the first several months of life, early homeostatic adjustments required of a newborn strongly favor contact plans that subordinate the frequency and extent of contact between the infant and the noncustodial parent to the eating and sleep–wake cycle of the infant. When breast feeding is undertaken by the mother, the schedule of contacts must be left entirely in her hands, even if the court perceives one of her motives for breast feeding to be that of controlling contacts between the newborn and the father.

In such a case, the infant's access to the father should be spaced so as to preserve the foundations for later bonding with the father. This means that the infant and father must have opportunities to experience each other in more than token ways, even as concessions are made to the aforesaid homeostatic and specific necessities. Strong evidence exists to suggest that children of divorce may reasonably expect to lose meaningful contact with their birth fathers during their childhoods ($p > .40$) (Furstenberg & Nord, 1985; Furstenberg, Morgan, & Allison, 1987). The roots of these losses are probably many, but certainly one of them is the contact imbalance that often accrues when insufficient incentives are in place for fathers to fulfill their children's contact needs; this lack of incentives is often associated with insufficient opportunity to develop and deepen the child–parent relationship, as against merely spending time together in order to honor a right or decree.

If the security of emotional and interpersonal bonds with specific others is rooted in early contacts with emotionally significant others, then the recommendation that must come forth to courts from members of the infant mental health community is one of encouraging and supporting contacts with noncustodial—or, in joint custodial circumstances, *both*—parents.

Overnight Contact. Any infant mental health clinician who has dealt with infants with sleeping irregularities knows the importance of consistency and routinization of before-bedtime activity in helping parents improve troublesome sleep patterns in infancy (Ferber, 1985). If the clinical population of infants with sleep disturbances were used as the benchmark for judicial decision making concerning overnight contact between infants and noncustodial parents, then one could certainly and reasonably argue that an infant's sleeping ought to be limited to one site only. Yet when one surveys a larger population of infants (including even those who are yet waking at least once briefly in the night), one encounters a variety of sleep onset dynamics that defy any presumption as to whether given infants ought or ought not to sleep in more than one setting.

Again, experience with day care has shown that many infants, once acclimated to the alternate setting, tolerate multiple sleeping sites. Added to this is our experience that very many infants in divorced parental circumstances can tolerate alternate sleeping circumstances once they are acclimated to them. Exceptions occur, of course, as when an infant wakes specifically to be breast-fed. In these cases, sleeping should be confined to the mother's home until weaning has occurred.

Day Care versus Parent Care. In an era in which (except for the materially advantaged) most mothers as well as fathers must work outside the home in order to maintain economic security, the task of seeking nonparental child care is common. The day is past when courts could presume that a mother, by virtue of child care payments made by the father or by virtue of tradition-bound child care practices, would remain in the home to care for her children. With over 50% of mothers in the work force at

least part-time, it is pointless to presume that in the aftermath of divorce a mother of even very young children is not going to work outside the home either as an economic necessity or as a respite from child care duties, even when she benefits from regular and punctual financial support from the father. Nowadays, if it is difficult to make ends meet within marriage, it is much more difficult to so so as a single divorced parent.

Courts are increasingly dealing with postdivorce conditions that include day care provisions. In many instances, either the commencement of nonparental day care or an expansion of already established nonparental day care will be required. Infant mental health professionals must therefore make themselves aware of the day care status of their consultees, so that recommendations acknowledge and build upon, rather than subvert, its potentially positive effects in a young child's adjustment to parental divorce.

Yet, when the alternative of either parent's caring for the infant exists in relation to ongoing day care, it generally makes little sense to restrict the contact that that parent can have with the infant in favor of having the infant in day care. Nor, in most cases, does it make much sense to restrict the contact of relatives who are familiar with the infant (e.g., grandparents) when reasonable caretaking experiences are characteristic.

Sibships

In an era that has begun to emphasize the elemental importance of sibling bonds (Dunn, 1988), many child custody experts have come to recommend on principle alone that siblings should not be divided between divorced parents. They argue, with some justification, that even as child–parent bonds are broken, sibling bonds should be left intact.

The key term in this consideration is the term "broken." We prefer the term "changed." Just as the changed circumstances and routines of child–parent contact following divorce need not be defined as losses in any absolute sense, changed circumstances and routines in relation to siblings following divorce need not be characterized as absolute losses. An infant's specific or decreed needs to have his or her principal contacts be with one parent ought not to be used as the determining factor when one or more older siblings' custody and contact with the divorcing parents are also at stake. The use of child–parent contact schedules that maximize sibling contact can compensate for divisions in sibships that may be prompted by circumstances that would make it reasonable or preferable to divide them. Thus, the court can alternate its customary weekend contact schedules, such that every weekend the siblings are permitted to be together in either the custodial or the non-custodial parent's home. The court can also arrange contacts during the week to occur so that siblings join each other.

INFANT DISTRESS IN THE CONTEXT OF PARENTAL CONFLICT REGARDING CUSTODY/CONTACT

Like many of their divorcing parents, many children react adversely—in other words, symptomatically—during parental divorce. Authorities are divided on the specific lasting effects of divorce, although it seems safe to say that the risk of long-term effects of one kind or another following divorce is probably augmented by divorce itself (see Wallerstein, 1991). In individual cases, however, the predictive capacities of experts are so weak as to be negligible. Some authorities point to the broad range of individual differences in children's adjustments to divorce, and point as well to what seem to be a main determining force of children's adjustments to divorce—namely, parental adjustment following divorce (Kalter, 1990). Divorce itself is less a specifically injurious event than it is a marker of forces that, as they continue to exert themselves in the psychic life of the child, impinge upon (sometimes to the point of threatening) the child's capacities to grow and adapt.

Evaluating Infants' Reactions: The Need for Caution

The age at which the forces of family dissolution occur, as well as the duration of their uniquely deleterious effects, no doubt influences how children cope with and eventually adapt to it. Infants and toddlers are obviously unique with regard to a number of variables linked to age, not the least of which, of course, is their stark inability to comprehend what is happening and why. Like older children, infants and toddlers react to altered circumstances, and muster coping capacities as conditions of subjective distress arise. Yet, unlike many older children, they lack capacities to influence (or at least to try to influence) outcomes. A question courts frequently pose to experts concerns what to do about adverse reactions when they occur, and, implicitly, how to prevent or minimize them.

Frequently, an infant's or toddler's reactions to parental discord and distress are taken by one parent to be a sign of the other parent's deleterious effects on the child, and sometimes the child's reactions are made to serve the personal need or interest of the parent interpreting the symptom. For example, when a toddler has difficulty falling asleep or is easily irritated following a stay with one parent, the other parent (and an expert as well) may be quick to conclude that the stay with the first parent has resulted in the child's state of mind or behavior. Rarely, in our experience, the possibility raised that the *return* to the second parent's care is at the foundation of the child's irritable or sensitive condition, even when the first parent communicates that things have gone well during the just-completed stay. Yet this latter possibility, which is hardly a remote or negligible one in our experience, must be considered by the court consultant who is informed by a parent of such conditions.

Another reaction often encountered in a toddler is a protest against going with the parent who has come to pick the toddler up for a designated time. Many parents and experts rush to the inference that such a child wishes not to be with the parent picking him or her up. They rarely consider the alternative possibility that such protests are not indictments of the approaching parent's care, but rather the direct expressions of the child's understandable wish not to leave the parent with whom he or she has been for the past several days or so. Yet, again, the latter possibility must be actively considered.

On occasions such as the foregoing, parents may, instead of defining themselves as they do in other areas of the child's life—namely, as agents to help the child cope with the distresses of parental estrangement—seek to dislodge each other on the basis of the child's manifest distress. It is characteristic of many infant expressions and reactions that they confirm what the observer already believes about the situations in which they occur (in this regard, see Condry & Condry, 1976). Many times, the task of the infant mental health specialist is to help one parent and the court see that a given child's seemingly negative expresssions do not mean that the child holds the same attitudes toward the other parent that the one parent himself or herself holds.

Many of the conditions seen in infants undergoing family dissolution are similar to conditions one might see in reasonably well-adjusted marital contexts. They include alterations in the patterning of organismic rhythms, such as appetite and sleep–wake cycling; alterations in mood and emotional expressivity; alterations in social-interactive and adjustment dynamics; and alterations in the course of maturation and/or social development.

Many conditions, of course, while similar to those encountered in nondissolving families, are so proximal to an actual event in the dissolution process (e.g., one of the parents' departing the family home) that they seem reactive rather than spontaneous. Certainly, cause-and-effect determinations are among the more difficult distinctions to make even under ordinary clinical evaluative circumstances, where the onset of a problem may not be accurately recounted by the parents, where the actual precipitants of the symptomatic condition are not specific (and therefore not discernible) as etiological agents per se, or where the proximity of symptomatic expression and specific events bear no actual causal relationship.

To be sure, the dissolution of the parental system is inherently stressful for parents and children. Yet the ranges of intensity and duration of infant distress reactions are so broad, and so dependent upon a complex array of variables, that one cannot offer general or uniform advice in matters of postdivorce adjustment and care. Individual cases must be carefully studied; this is greatly preferable to any exercise of a uniform policy based on external criteria.

Sources of Distress

Variables that influence the expression of distress reactions in infancy and toddlerhood may be broadly categorized as "parent-stimulated" or "infant-stimulated."

Parent-Stimulated Distress Variables

A parent undergoing marital dissolution is typically distracted by the vicissitudes of impending change, preoccupied with the coping requirements of drastically altered relationships and routines, and affectively stimulated in ways that may intrude upon the well-being of the caregiving relationship. Familiar interactive and behavioral routines are altered, sometimes dramatically, sometimes disastrously. Each parent typically changes both subtly and dramatically from the perspective of the experiencing infant or toddler.

One should not presume that the changes brought about by the physical separation of the parents are either the most significant or the most crucial for the infant. The preseparation climate of family functioning is a very important factor as well, and some physical separations may actually bring improvements in the emotional climate each parent creates with and for the infant.

Probably the most economical way to characterize the array of parent-stimulated stressors is in terms of the parent's capacity to continue functioning effectively in the capacity of an auxiliary ego (Spitz & Cobliner, 1965), which is also to say in an emotionally available manner (Emde & Sorce, 1983). Certainly, under the circumstances of relational deterioration and dissolution, one cannot expect that these capacities will be optimally distributed or patterned within each parent during his or her immediate and surrounding moments, although some parents indeed seem to be particularly artful at maintaining these capacities. Nor would one expect that these capacities will be equally distributed between the parents at any given time. Fortunately, most infants are highly resilient in this respect.

Infant-Stimulated Distress Variables

On the infant side, two principal sets of variables are important to consider. One relates to temperament; the other relates to experience.

The temperamental characteristics of infants and children, though still a matter of strong debate (see Bates, 1987), are widely acknowledged by clinicians to play powerful roles both in reactions to stressful events and as shapers of parental behavior (Chess & Thomas, 1987, 1991). Clinical consultants must account for temperamental proclivities in infants and toddlers that may affect observed or reported adjustments during or following parental divorce and custody/contact determination. The intensity, duration, or recovery dynamics of young children reacting to (or simply dealing with) specific events, or even general conditions, are not reliable indices of how inherently stressful such events or conditions are. Thus, events and conditions alleged by one parent or the other to be inherently detrimental to the infant need to be evaluated not only for what appear manifestly to be their stressful properties, but also for how much the dynamics of child temperament may be influencing a perception of intrinsic severity. This is not to state that an infant's manifest reactions and expressions should not be given consideration or credence. Yet, in listening to the voice of the infant, the expert must assure himself or herself and the court that it is indeed the infant's voice and not the voice of the parent's or expert's preconceptions that is being heard.

Experiential variables are, of course, highly related to the age of the infant, which means as well the cognitive and self-psychological status of the infant. Adults tend to interpret infant states and communications in highly adult-centric ways, insuring that what is observed in infants fits their conceptions of what infancy must be like phenomenologically. Although it is appropriate to focus on what Stern (1985) has termed, in contrast to the "observed" (and therefore objectified) infant, the "experiencing" (and therefore subjective) infant, the exact nature of infant experiences of specific events or conditions remains an elusive area for courts and infant clinicians alike when they are employing frank preconceptions concerning the nature of infancy itself. Even though empathic modes of perception and inference are brought to bear on the subject of a given infant's apparent distress, the task of interpreting that experience to the court is at times arduous. Infant specialists seem generally to understand that one cannot construct the "general" infant from particular instances, because so much of what one observes concerning an infant or toddler may vary from occasion to occasion. This understanding constitutes the best case for multiple contacts with an infant with each parent before drawing general inferences on which recommendations may be based.

GUIDELINES FOR COURT-ORDERED CLINICAL EVALUATIONS CONCERNING INFANT CUSTODY

The essentials of comprehensive infant assessment have been well articulated (e.g., Greenspan, 1991; Minde & Minde, 1986; Hirshberg, Chapter 11, this volume; Clark, Paulson, & Conlin, Chapter 12, this volume), and therefore need not be elaborated here. In this section we outline what we believe to be the appropriate methods and structures for undertaking court-consultative evaluations and assessments of infants exposed to their parents' separations and divorces. Although individual circumstances may stimulate the consultant to vary his or her evaluative procedures, we believe that the framework presented here is sufficiently general to apply broadly to the challenges posed by cases of contested infant/toddler custody.

With rare exceptions, court-ordered child custody evaluations are difficult cases from the outset. Courts and disputing parties are not particularly disposed to extend the length of a postdivorce proceeding beyond what the parties themselves limit by virtue of their coming to agreements concerning their property and minor children. Thus, like almost all child custody/contact cases that end up in one's consulting office as the result of a court order, one may expect in most cases to encounter a condition of near or outright intractability. Unusual situations, and the personalities who create them, do not permit the usual assumptions about human nature to be maintained, and it is wisest in all custody/contact cases to divest oneself of them.

Aims of an Infant Custody Evaluation

The aims of an infant custody evaluation are twofold. One aim is to inform the court of general considerations that apply to the infant or toddler at hand, as described above under "Cognate Expertise." Such considerations should include the general characteristics and needs of children of comparable age, gender, ethnicity, and social class, and should include reference to the span of parenting practices and philosophies surrounding such children. The second aim is to inform the court of characteristics and needs of the specific infant or toddler at hand. Such considerations should include aspects of the infant's relationship with each parent, including its observed and reported dynamics; aspects of the infant's temperament; and notable specific needs such as those pertaining to established medical or developmental conditions, including those diagnosable using standard nomenclature (i.e., the *Diagnostic and Statistical Manual of Mental Disorders* or the *International Classification of Diseases*).

General Information

Obviously, one cannot provide a complete discourse on infancy within the format of a report made to a court concerning a particular infant undergoing his or her parents' custody dispute. Reports of treatise proportion are definitely aversive to a court that is solely in need of relevant information and bases for its decision making. Nevertheless, being aware that certain general facts and principles are applicable to particular situations and in specific cases, the consultant will find courts generally receptive and appreciative when he or she is briefly didactic on one or several of the matters raised by the custody dispute itself. Brief, focused presentations of the general, impartially held knowledge or thinking in the field of infant development and mental health should be made when necessary in relation to specific points concerning the infant that have been raised in the report, or in relation to positions adopted by one or the other parent on behalf of the child. Such presentations can be very helpful to a court that is unsure of itself on such matters.

In areas where controversy or divided thinking is known to exist concerning the nature of infants or toddlers at particular stages of development or maturation, or where divided opinions exist concerning the conditions in which infants and young children thrive optimally, the consultant should state for the court the range of studied opinions rather than simply stating the one he or she prefers. Expressions of preferred opinions by the consultant should occur within the larger context of varying points of view concerning infancy. The consultant should assiduously avoid presenting theoretical positions as matters of demonstrated fact, even when he or she believes that a particular theoretical position has great explanatory power. Moreover, the absence of a firm factual basis for a particular opinion should be acknowledged, and factual voids should not be filled with theory.

Specific Information

Specific information relayed to the court should encompass the facts of the infant's condition as encountered during the evaluation. This should routinely include the infant's history of care by each parent (separately as well as jointly), the infant's history of wellness and illness, the infant's trajectories of maturational and developmental milestones, and unique aspects of the infant's temperament. Special needs, such as those relating to established disorders (e.g., Pervasive Developmental Disorders), should be defined. These should include, of course, programmatic needs insofar as special therapies are concerned. Each parent's observed characteristics and attitudes also belong to the realm of specific information to be provided to the court.

Scope and Conduct of an Infant Custody Evaluation

The infant custody/contact evaluation has three major components: parent contacts and interviews; infant observations and assessments; and collateral contacts, such as those that may occur with parental relatives (e.g., grandparents) or significant day care personnel. It is the court's mandate to gather information upon which to base its decision making concerning the placement and custody of children. It is the infant mental health consultant's role to conduct a state-of-the-art evaluation of the infant and parents, for purposes of providing the court with information and guidelines concerning this particular case. Thus, the court has the more comprehensive role to play vis-à-vis the eventual disposition of the infant. It is not the consultant's role to duplicate the court's established procedures for gathering and weighing facts in the process of custody/contact decision making.

This point is less critical in routine custody consultations, but it is extremely critical in cases in which specific allegations are made by one party against the other concerning parental fitness. We have seen a number of instances in which the evaluator has converted his or her evaluative/consultative task into becoming private investigator, prosecutor, jury, and judge rolled into one. Such evaluators lose sight of the fact that theirs is but one part of a larger fact-finding process.

Parent Interviews

In most cases, the consultant's general and specific aims will be served if he or she conducts a brief series of interviews with each of the parents in order to obtain background information as well as information concerning the present circumstances. The latter should include, of course, the respective views of each parent as to the impasses that preclude their deciding distributions of custody and contact for themselves.

Given the purpose and nature of child custody evaluations, the evaluator cannot—and should not—offer the privilege of confidentiality to any party to an evaluation that will influence a custody/contact outcome. The absence of such a privilege should be made an explicit part of the clinician's introduction of the parents to the evaluative task.

Many evaluators find it helpful to begin their evaluations with a conjoint interview, the obvious rationale for this being that if the parents cannot be in each other's presence in order at least to discuss their differences, the prognosis for joint custody is made more definite than any evaluative effort based on individual interviews alone would make it. Yet few courts request evaluations in cases where the parents have already demonstrated capacities (even minimal ones) for conjoint if not cooperative communications. Thus, in commencing a court-ordered infant custody/contact evaluation with a conjoint interview, the evaluator should expect that separate interviews will also be needed.

Aside from obtaining the sort of information that is routinely gathered in such interviews, it is useful, once basic rapport is established, to invite each parent to "predict" what the evaluator will see and experience when he or she arrives at the point of observing the infant in the presence of each parent. This allows the evaluator to weigh the parents' respective capacities for being objective, and for holding relative as opposed to absolute views concerning the infant and the other parent.

It is important that the evaluator be specific in his or her approach to each parent's views of the other's fitness (or, as is often the case in court-ordered evaluations, each parent's views of the other's liabilities). It is easy to stop at a parent's general ascriptions of the other parent's being too strict, or too negligent, or whatever. Inquiries as to how the parent came by those opinions, and as to the literal events that have occurred to lead to them, are essential.

Many clinicians are inclined to recommend clinical services beyond the evaluative contacts they have had with parents. Some raise with individual parents the possiblity of parent guidance or child psychotherapy as a means of assessing the genuineness of their concern for the child, and of assessing what is widely termed their "psychological-mindedness." There is no evidence that either the desire or willingness to enter a therapeutic relationship focused on the child's adjustment is indicative of greater concern or care on the part of a parent, or that it is indicative of a greater capacity to parent. Given the high degrees of impression management parents exhibit during court-ordered assessments, it is impossible to distinguish genuine desires for therapeutic guidance from simple compliance or impression management in the statements they may make concerning their willingness or desire for treatment. In our experience, parents rarely follow up on stated intentions to seek guidance or help following the court's determination of child custody.

In general, recommendations for treatment should be avoided, either as an incentive or as a deterrent to one or another recommended outcome. Treatment, which may take the form of parent guidance or parent–infant psychotherapy, ought, when raised by the consultant, to be described simply as a process that can be helpful to some individuals who are motivated to seek solutions through the guidance that knowledgeable and caring others in the mental health or pastoral professions can offer.

Infant Observations and Assessments

Infants evaluated in custody cases should be observed in the presence of each parent, and often more than one observation per parent will be indicated. Infants' reactions to novel settings certainly justify the utilization of contacts in the infant's own dwelling (or dwellings, if the parents live separately). Yet, useful as they are, home contacts are impractical for many clinicians. Given established methods for helping infants adjust to the novelty of the evaluator's observation setting, and given ways therefore to account for setting reactions as against more trait-determined reactions (e.g., see Gaensbauer & Harmon, 1981; Solyom, Horner, & Hoffman, 1983), the use of a comfortable clinic setting need not be avoided.

Formal developmental testing is generally not necessary or useful in custody cases, except insofar as it is undertaken to answer specific questions concerning the developmental status of an infant or toddler. When such testing is carried out, attention must be paid to the variable nature of the quantitative findings obtained (which cannot be readily attributed to familiarity effects), so as not to convey false impressions of the infant's actual capacities (see Horner, 1980, 1988; see also McCall, 1979; Kopp &

McCall, 1982). Observations made during such testing or interviews should never be used by clinicians to make either postdictive or predictive statements concerning (1) specific events that are alleged by one parent or the other to have occurred, or (2) outcomes that may be associated with the several custody/contact options available to the court. Nor should the clinician imply to courts that such devices are reliable—or even valid—toward making such statements. Direct observations of the child interacting with each parent under both child-led and parent-led conditions are far preferable as bases for drawing inferences concerning the nature of the child–parent relationship. Even under these conditions, the clinician must refrain from specifically postdictive or predictive statements that cannot be supported beyond opinion or guess alone.

Collateral Contacts

Although custody/contact disputes are essentially disputes between the parents of an affected child, it is sometimes useful to seek input from individuals outside the family who are emotionally salient or significant to the child. These may include grandparents or, as has been implied earlier in the chapter, regular day care providers. Although the subjects of which parent (in the collateral figures' opinion) should have custody, and of how contact between the infant and each parent should be distributed, inevitably arise in such contacts, the primary benefit of these contacts is in the observational material they can provide with respect to the infant or toddler's individual dynamics and patterns of development and adjustment.

Sometimes parents have been in marital counseling or individual therapy, and request that the evaluator contact the therapist as a means toward furthering their case. Sometimes as well, upon hearing that another mental health care provider has knowledge concerning one or both parents, the evaluator considers contacting the provider. Experience has taught that with some exceptions (none that are predictable), such contacts add little that is genuinely useful to the evaluative process, and simply expand the scope of what is already discernible in the direct interview/observation circumstances of the evaluation itself. We are disinclined to seek input from other mental health providers unless there are specific questions or verifications of fact that these providers can address.

The Infant Custody Report

Courts are benefited most by reports that contain factual information and reasonable recommendations. The more clearly an evaluator can present the facts and issues as they relate to an infant's particular developmental and situational characteristics, the more readily the court can reach its own conclusions as to the nature of child custody and child–parent contact in this case. Naturally, reports can be written so as to lead the court to the conclusions that would be those of the evaluator himself or herself. Courts generally rely on reports to obtain a sense of what the expert's testimony would be if he or she were summoned. In actual practice, clinicians are infrequently summoned.

In states where the legislature or judiciary has set forth factors to be considered in determining custody and child–parent contact, some experts, surrogating themselves as judges, choose to address each of the factors individually. In essence, they presume that their evaluations, which constitute only one part of the judicial process of fact finding and decision making, nevertheless serve effectively as the whole of fact finding and decision making. We believe that although the practice of addressing factors individually may demonstrate erudition on the part of an evaluator, it does little to convey what is generally asked by a court of a clinician— namely, a clinical appraisal of the parents and infant/toddler, as well as advice on the developmental and psychological needs of a child undergoing familial dissolution.

CONCLUDING REMARKS

The "best interests" standard, according to Rodham (1973), is not a standard but a rationalization used by decision makers to justify their judgments about children's futures: In this view, a child is "an empty vessel into which adult perceptions and prejudices are poured" (p. 513). Seductively implying that there is a verifiably *best* alternative for children, it prevents both decision makers and those to whom they are accountable from carefully weighing the possible negative impact of any recommendation that might be made (see again Rodham, 1973, p. 513). Although the "best interests" principle has for some time now provided a haven of conceptual safety for mental health specialists engaged in court-initiated consultations concerning child custody and child–parent access, the failure thus far to find within the bodies of knowledge and techniques specific to the mental health professions a secure base for decision- and recommendation-making principles has resulted in continuing quandaries concerning the "best interests" of infants and young children.

Custody consultations are never easy or pleasant, and seem to afford very few opportunities for infant mental health practitioners to apply the skills that make them feel effective in other domains of activity. Yet, apart from the knowledge and technical skill clinicians bring to situations involving infants and parents in the throes of family dissolution, the most powerful tools they have in these cases are those that serve them effectively in the wider realms of infant mental health—namely, the caring and supportive attitudes they bring to the turmoils of infancy, and their willingness to consider the various points of view particular infants might have when their families divide. The expert who is cognizant of his or her limits as an expert is the one who is best prepared to assist courts and families in their efforts to select from arrays of reasonable alternatives and opportunities for treading life's many possible paths.

REFERENCES

American Academy of Child and Adolescent Psychiatry. (1988). Guidelines for the clinical evaluation of child and adolescent sexual abuse. *Journal of the American Academy of Child and Adolescent Psychiatry, 25*, 655–657.

Ash, P., & Guyer, M. J. (1986). Child custody and the law: The functions of psychiatric evaluation in contested child custody and visitation cases. *Journal of the American Academy of Child and Adolescent Psychiatry, 25*, 554–561.

Bates, J. E. (1987). Temperament in infancy. In J. D. Osofsky (Ed.), *Handbook of infant development* (2nd ed., pp. 1101–1149). New York: Wiley.

Bellotti v. Baird, 443 U.S. 622 (1983).

Black, J. C., & Cantor, D. J. (1989). *Child custody*. New York: Columbia University Press.

Chambers, D. L. (1984). Rethinking the substantive rules for custody disputes in divorce. *Michigan Law Review, 83*, 477–569.

Chess, S., & Thomas, A. (1987). *Origins and evolution of behavior disorders from infancy to adult life.* Cambridge, MA: Harvard University Press.

Chess, S., & Thomas, A. (1991). Temperament. In M. Lewis (Ed.), *Child and adolescent psychiatry: A comprehensive textbook* (pp. 145–159). Baltimore: Williams & Wilkins.

Clingempeel, W. G., & Repucci, N. D. (1982). Joint custody after divorce: Major issues and goals for research. *Psychological Bulletin, 91*, 102–127.

Cohen, A. (1985). The unreliability of expert testimony on the typical characteristics of sexual abuse victims. *Georgetown Law Review, 74*, 429–456.

Condry, J., & Condry, S. (1976). Sex differences: A study of the eye of the beholder. *Child Development, 47*, 812–829.

Crouch, R. E. (1979). An essay on the critical and judicial reception of *Beyond the best interests of the child. Family Law Quarterly, 13*, 49–103.

Curlender v. Bioscience Laboratories, 106 Cal. App. 3rd 811, 165 Cal. Rptr. 477 (1980).

Davidson, H. A., & Gerlach, K. (1984). Child custody disputes: The child's perspective. In R. M. Horowitz & H. A. Davidson (Eds.), *Legal rights of children* (pp. 232–261). New York: McGraw-Hill.

Diamond, B. L. (1959). The fallacy of the impartial expert. *Archives of Criminal Psychodynamics, 3*, 221–236.

Dunn, J. (1988). Annotation: Sibling influences on childhood development. *Journal of Child Psychology and Psychiatry, 29*, 119–127.

Emde, R. N., & Sorce, J. (1983). The rewards of infancy: Emotional availability and maternal referencing. In J. D. Call, E. Galenson, & R. L. Tyson (Eds.), *Frontiers of infant psychiatry* (Vol. 1, pp 17–30). New York: Basic Books.

Ferber, R. (1985). *Solve your child's sleep problems.* New York: Simon & Schuster.

Foster, H. H., & Freed, D. J. (1972). A Bill of Rights for children. *Family Law Quarterly, 6*, 344–375.

Freed, D. J., & Walker, T. B. (1988). Family law in the fifty states: An overview. *Family Law Quarterly, 21*, 417–571.

Freud, A. (1965). *The writings of Anna Freud: Vol 6. Normality and pathology in childhood: Assessments of development.* New York: International Universities Press.

Furstenberg, F. F., Morgan, S. S., & Allison, P. D. (1987). Paternal participation and children's well-being after marital dissolution. *American Sociological Review, 52*, 695–701.

Furstenberg, F. F., & Nord, C. W. (1985). Parenting apart. *Journal of Marriage and the Family, 47*, 893–904.

Gaensbauer, T. G., & Harmon, R. J. (1981). Clinical assessment in infancy utilizing structured playroom situations. *Journal of the American Academy of Child Psychiatry, 20*, 264–280.

Gass, R. S. (1979). Comment. The psychologist as expert witness: Science in the courtroom? *Maryland Law Review, 38*, 539–621.

Gean, M. P. (1984). Psychiatric aspects of placement and visitation of children under three years of change. In J. D. Call, E. Galenson, & R. L. Tyson (Eds.), *Frontiers of infant psychiatry* (Vol. 2, pp. 495–501). New York: Basic Books.

Glick, P. C. (1988). The role of divorce in the changing family structure: Trends and variations. In S. A. Wolchik & P. Karoly (Eds.), *Children of divorce: Empirical perspectives on adjustment* (pp. 3–33). New York: Gardner Press.

Goldstein, J., Freud, A., & Solnit, A. J. (1973). *Beyond the best interests of the child.* New York: Free Press.

Goldstein, J., Freud, A., & Solnit, A. J. (1987). *Before the best interests of the child.* New York: Free Press.

Greenspan, S. I. (1981). *Psychopathology and adaptation in infancy and early childhood.* New York: International Universities Press.

Greenspan, S. I. (1989). *The development of the ego: Im-*

plications for personality theory, psychopathology, and the psychotherapeutic process. Madison, CT: International Universities Press.

Greenspan, S. I. (1991). Clinical assessment in infancy and early childhood. In J. M. Wiener (Ed.), *Textbook of child and adolescent psychiatry* (pp. 53–64). Washington, DC: American Psychiatric Press.

Griswold v. Connecticut, 381 U.S. 479 (1965).

Gross, B., & Gross, R. (1977). *The children's rights movement.* Garden City, NY: Doubleday/Anchor.

Gross, G. (1990). *Expert evidence.* Unpublished manuscript, University of Michigan School of Law.

Guyer, M. J., & Ash, P. (1987, October). *Expert v. expert: Opinions in the courtroom.* Paper presented at the meeting of the American Academy of Child and Adolescent Psychiatry, Washington, DC.

Guyer, M. J., & Horner, T. M. (1990). The activist expert in custody cases: A challenge to psychiatry. *Proceedings of the American Academy of Child and Adolescent Psychiatry, 6,* 22.

Guyer, M. J., & Horner, T. M. (1991, May). *The fallibility of experts.* Paper presented at the Advanced Criminal Defense Practice Conference, Criminal Defense Attorneys of Michigan, Southfield, MI.

Harbeson v. Parke-Davis, 98 Wash. 2d 460, 656 P.2d 483 (1983).

Hart, S. N. (1991). From property to person status: Historical perspective on children's rights. *American Psychologist, 46,* 53–59.

Horner, T. M. (1980). Test–retest and home–clinic characteristics of the Bayley Scales of Infant Development. *Child Development, 51,* 751–758.

Horner, T. M. (1988). Single versus repeated assessments of infant abilities using the Bayley Scales of Infant Development. *Infant Mental Health Journal, 9,* 209–217.

Horner, T. M., Guyer, M. J., & Kalter, N. M. (1992). Prediction, prevention and clinical expertise in cases of child custody in which allegations of child sexual abuse have been made: III. Studies of expert opinion formation. *Family Law Quarterly, 26,* 141–170.

Horowitz, R. M., & Davidson, H. A. (Eds.). (1984). *Legal rights of children.* New York: McGraw-Hill.

Horowitz, R. M., & Hunter, B. G. (1984). The child litigant. In R. M. Horowitz & H. A. Davidson (Eds.), *Legal rights of children* (pp. 72–113). New York: McGraw-Hill.

Inker, M. L., & Perretta, C. A. (1971). A child's right to counsel in custody cases. *Family Law Quarterly, 5,* 108–120.

In re Gault, 387 U.S. 1 (1947).

In re Winship, 397 U.S. 358 (1970).

Johnston, J. R., & Campbell, L. E. G. (1988). *Impasses of divorce.* New York: Free Press.

Joint Committee of Children's Charter of the Courts of Michigan, Inc., and the Michigan Association for Infant Mental Health. (1985). *Guidelines for assessing parenting capabilities in child abuse and neglect cases.* (Available from either Children's Charter of the Courts of Michigan, Inc., 115 West Allegan, Suite 500, Lansing, MI 48933, or the Michigan Association for Infant Mental Health, Department of Psychology, Michigan State University, East Lansing, MI 48924-1117)

Kalter, N. (1990). *Growing up with divorce.* New York: Free Press.

Katz, S. N. (1974). Introduction. In S. N. Katz (Ed.), *The

youngest minority* (Vol. 1, pp. 1–24). Chicago: American Bar Association Press.

Kent v. United States, 383 U.S. 541 (1966).

Kopp, C. B., & McCall, R. M. (1982). Predicting later mental performance of normal, at-risk, and handicapped infants. In P. B. Baltes & O. G. Brim (Eds.), *Life-span development and behavior* (Vol. 4). New York: Academic Press.

Kotelchuck, M. (1982). Childhood and neglect: Prediction and misclassification. In R. H. Starr, Jr. (Ed.), *Child abuse prediction: Policy implications* (pp. 67–104). Cambridge, MA: Ballinger.

Lakin, M. (1991). *The place of joint custody within the context of alternative post-divorce custodial arrangements: Psychological effects on children and adolescents.* Unpublished manuscript, University of Michigan.

Levitin, T. E. (Ed.). (1979). Children of divorce. *Journal of Social Issues, 35,* 1–186.

Levy, R. J. (1989). Using "scientific" testimony to prove child sexual abuse. *Family Law Quarterly, 23,* 383–409.

Loving v. Virginia, 388 U.S. 1 (1967).

Maryland v. Craig, 110 U.S. 3157 (1990).

McCall, R. M. (1979). The development of intellectual functioning in infancy and the prediction of later I.Q. In J. D. Osofsky (Ed.), *Handbook of infant development* (1st ed., pp. 707–741). New York: Wiley.

McCord, J. (1986). Expert psychological testimony about complaints in sexual abuse prosecutions: A foray into the admissibility of novel psychological evidence. *Journal of Criminal Law and Criminology, 77,* 1–66.

McCord, J. (1987). Syndromes, profiles and other medical exotica: A new approach to the admissibility of nontraditional psychological evidence in criminal cases. *Oregon Law Review, 66,* 19–76

McKinnon, R., & Wallerstein, J. S. (1986). Joint custody and the preschool child. *Behavioral Sciences and the Law, 4,* 169–183.

Meehl, P. E. (1971). Law and the fireside inductions: Some reflections of a clinical psychologist. *Journal of Social Issues, 27,* 65–100.

Meehl, P. E. (1973). *Psychodiagnosis: Selected papers.* New York: Norton.

Melton, G. B. (1987). Judicial notice of "facts" about child development. In G. B. Melton (Ed.), *Reforming the law: Impact of child development research* (pp. 232–249). New York: Guilford Press.

Melton, G. B., & Limber, S. (1989). Psychologists' involvement in cases of child maltreatment. *American Psychologist, 44,* 1225–1233.

Melton, G. B., & Wilcox, B. L. (1989). Changes in family law and family life. *American Psychologist, 44,* 1213–1216.

Mich. Comp. Laws Ann. § 722.23 (West Supp. 1987).

Minde, K., & Minde, R. (1986). *Infant psychiatry: An introductory textbook.* Beverly Hills, CA: Sage.

Pawl, J., & Bennett, J. W. (1980). Martha: A focussed clinical use of the Bayley in consultation. In S. Fraiberg (Ed.), *Clinical studies in infant mental health: The first year of life* (pp. 260–269). New York: Basic Books.

Pee v. United States, 274 F.2d 556 (D.C. Cir. 1959).

Peters, R. (1980). Wrongful life: Recognizing the defective child's right to a cause of action. *Duquesne Law Review, 18,* 859–901.

Rodham, H. (1973). Children under the law. *Harvard Educational Review, 43,* 487–514.

Roe v. Wade, 410 U.S. 113 (1973).

Solyom, A., Horner, T. M., & Hoffman, P. (1983). Infant clinical assessment procedure: A tool for diagnosis and intervention in the second and third year. *Infant Mental Health Journal, 4,* 104–115.

Spitz, R., & Cobliner, W. (1965). *The first year of life.* New York: International Universities Press.

Stanley v. Illinois, 405 U.S. 645 (1972).

Steinman, S. (1981). The experience of children in a joint custody arrangement: A report of a study. *American Journal of Orthopsychiatry, 51,* 403–414.

Stern, D. N. (1985). *The interpersonal world of the infant.* New York: Basic Books.

Wallerstein, J. S. (1991). The long-term effects of divorce on children: A review. *Journal of the American Academy of Child and Adolescent Psychiatry, 30,* 349–360.

Weir, R. F. (1984). *Selective nontreatment of handicapped newborns.* New York: Oxford University Press.

Weithorn, L. A. (1987). *Psychology and child custody determinations: Knowledge, roles and expertise.* Lincoln: University of Nebraska Press.

Wilcox, B. L., & Naimark, H. (1991). The rights of the child: Progress toward human dignity. *American Psychologist, 46,* 49.

Wisconsin v. Yoder, 406 U.S. 205 (1972).

31

Infant Mental Health and Social Policy

EDWARD ZIGLER
PAULINE HOPPER
NANCY W. HALL

Families today are struggling to cope with rapid and startling social change. The demographic status of the United States has changed so profoundly during the past three decades that even the very definition of "family" is under debate. Economic shifts, changes in the makeup of the labor force, and changes in childbearing patterns have had a marked influence on the lives of U.S. citizens in general, and on U.S. infants and children in particular. Moreover, there is a growing discrepancy between the image of the United States as a family-oriented nation and the harsh reality of the failure of our social policies to keep pace with the new realities of family life. Critical needs of infants and families are going unmet; although the full impact of this situation cannot yet be assessed, it is clear that our youngest citizens are already suffering the most serious repercussions.

Infants and young children, especially those who live in poverty, are the logical focus of prevention efforts directed toward enhancing mental health. Obstacles to successful growth and adaptation appear early in life, even before birth. Eliminating those obstacles, or reducing their impact, is the aim of primary prevention. And directing prevention efforts toward children means helping families and communities as well. A child's natural development does not unfold in isolation, but is shaped within the context of the family, child care, community, and society

at large. Conditions in these environments can influence an individual child's development profoundly for better or worse.

It is not that we don't know how to support families, or what infants and children need to achieve healthy growth and optimal development. Research findings relevant to these issues are readily available, and point clearly to the most cost-effective ways to address the unmet needs of infants and their families. Instead, the nation's failure has been in neglecting or ignoring those findings when developing policy and allocating funding. A closer look at the changes affecting families today, coupled with a brief review of what we have learned from the history of early childhood intervention, may put us in a better position to translate the lessons of scholarship into policies that will benefit children and families.

THE NEW U.S. FAMILY

The experience of growing up in the United States has changed for a large number of our nation's children. The most striking change stems from the increase of women in the out-of-home workforce—a change attributable in part to the economic need for two incomes in most families, and in part to the rise of single-parent households, the vast majority of which

480

are headed by women. One-quarter of all children in the United States are being raised in single-parent homes; among black children that figure is greater than 50% (Select Committee on Children, Youth, and Families [Select Committee], 1987). Of children born in 1980, it is estimated that 70% will spend at least a part of their childhoods in single-parent families (Hofferth & Phillips, 1987).

Approximately 51% of the mothers of infants are now in the U.S. labor force (Bureau of Labor Statistics, 1987). This figure is expected to rise by 1995 to at least 66%. Since 1960, the time mothers have to spend with their infants has dropped by 10 to 12 hours per week (*Newsweek*, 1990). One major study estimates that 88% of the women in the workforce will become pregnant at least once during their working years, but that fewer than 40% of these will have access to maternity benefits (Gamble & Zigler, 1986; Schroeder, 1988). Almost half of the working women with children under 3 are their families' sole breadwinners (Kamerman, Kahn, & Kingston, 1983)—a statistic owing at least in part to the nation's high rate of divorce, which has leveled off in recent years at about 50% (*Newsweek*, 1990).

The rate of pregnancy to teenage parents is equally disturbing. Since 1960, the proportion of teen births occurring outside marriage has risen from 15% to 61%. Approximately one out of every six babies is born to a teenager; this totals about 500,000 to 600,000 each year (Select Committee, 1987). When children give birth to their own children, both mothers and infants are at increased risk of attenuated educational achievement, poverty, inadequate prenatal care, poor health care, and inadequate nutrition, and infants are at risk for low birthweight. Teenagers are also less likely than older mothers to space subsequent deliveries adequately, resulting in heightened medical and economic risk (Edelman, 1991). Of these pregnancies, it has been reported that 80% are unplanned and unwanted; however, 96% of teen mothers choose to keep their babies (Osofsky, 1990).

There is a tendency to believe that the problems represented by these mind-boggling statistics are so immense that there is little that can be done to alleviate them—whether they reflect the ravages of crack, crime, or abuse, or simply the dull and insidious deprivation inherent in continually experiencing inadequate child care.

What we would like to do in this chapter is dispel the notion that the problems facing children in the United States are insurmountable. They are not, and we have at our immediate disposal the tools needed to begin crafting practical solutions for these problems. Social policy development in the United States today lags pitifully far behind the sweeping demographic changes that have challenged our very definition of the family. As a result, some of the most basic needs of contemporary U.S. children and families are going unmet. The political *Zeitgeist* of the 1980s reflected a pervasive lack of interest in effectively addressing those needs, and the fallout from such uninterest is proving to be genuinely catastrophic here in the 1990s. Our children are its immediate victims, but in the long run the entire nation will suffer the effects of such widespread legislative and economic neglect.

Yet the situation can be remedied. We know what works. Lessons from the history of early childhood intervention and child and family policy have reliably demonstrated which factors in a child's environment work to enhance development and lead to improved outcomes. Throughout the past three decades, we have swung widely from optimism to pessimism and back again in our beliefs about effecting positive changes in the lives of children. Yet certain conclusions consistently emerge: Early intervention programs involving the family as a unit are far more effective than those treating the child in isolation. In addition, enhancing a child's health status, motivation, and general social competence tends to improve the quality of a family's life more than simply raising the child's IQ scores (Provence & Naylor, 1983; Seitz, 1990; Schweinhart, 1988; Zigler & Berman, 1983).

Decades of study have revealed the interrelatedness of the systems comprising the context of child development: family, school, health, and child care (Belsky, 1981; Bronfenbrenner, 1979; Zigler, 1970; Zigler & Gilman, 1990; Zigler & Trickett, 1978). Our imperative now is to translate this knowledge into a shield to protect parents and children from the detrimental effects of overwhelming social change. Toward that end, we offer a look at some of the major policy-related problems facing infants and their families, and some suggestions for implementing solutions.

INFANTS IN POVERTY

General causes of the impoverishment of increasing numbers of families in the United States include a high national debt; diversion of funds from social programs to defense and other budgetary items; the high cost of the recent Persian Gulf war; and redistribution of federal funds to state and local governments, which have their own budgetary problems (Fulginiti, 1991). The net result is that the poor as a proportion of our population are growing faster than the nation as a whole. Infants and young children are among the most vulnerable and immediate victims of national demographic changes. Thirty-seven million U.S. children live in poverty (Maurer, 1991). Approximately one child in five in this nation lives below the poverty level; more than one-third of the children in families headed by persons younger than 30 are poor (Children's Defense Fund, 1990). One-third of all urban children and one-fourth of all rural children live in poverty (Chan & Momparler, 1991), and among black children the figure rises above 50% in some geographic regions (Children's Defense Fund, 1990).

In spite of the Reagan and Bush administrations' campaign commitments to shore up the crumbling foundations of child and family services, budgetary cuts and changes in policy regarding children and families have left infants more vulnerable than ever to the ravages of inadequate health care, poor nutrition, chronic illness, and high rates of infant mortality. The deaths of more than 10,000 young children each year can be linked to the poverty in which they live; this is greater than the number of children who die from traffic accidents and suicide combined (Chan & Momparler, 1991; Children's Defense Fund, 1990; Wright, 1991).

Homelessness

Although reliable figures on homelessness in the United States are difficult to obtain, estimates are that one out of four homeless people is a young child. A growing body of research on the effects of homelessness on infants and children points out the grossly inadequate nutrition, poor health care, lack of immunizations, and increased susceptibility to chronic disease experienced by this population (Acker, Fierman, & Dreyer, 1987; Miller & Lin, 1988; Parker et al., 1991). Research on maternal depression and homelessness has revealed that of the homeless women with young children tested with the Beck Depression Inventory, over half scored in the

depressed range (Parker et al., 1991). Whether the mechanism involves the mediating factor of maternal depression—long known to be devastating to the social development and attachment status of infants and toddlers (Klaus, Leger, & Trause, 1982; Minde & Minde, 1986; Redding, Harmon, & Morgan, 1990)—or whether children are simply responding to the transience, insecurity, dangers, and frequent parent–child separations experienced by homeless families, it is clear that children's mental health is being compromised. Research by Bassuk and her colleagues (Bassuk, Rubin, & Lauriat, 1986) reveals that homeless children living in shelters are more likely than housed children to be depressed, shy, anxious, withdrawn, or demanding. A family's homelessness is also often given as a rationale for foster care placement of its young children (Children's Defense Fund, 1990).

Access to Health Care

Lack of adequate housing is not the only crisis facing poor young children. Seventy nations worldwide provide medical care and financial assistance to all pregnant women. Sixty-one countries provide basic medical care to all workers and their dependents. The United States, which spends more money per capita on health care than any other nation on earth (approximately 11% of our gross national product), does neither (Cleveland, 1991). In our two-tiered system of health care, medical benefits are for all practical purposes denied to many. Over 10 million children in the United States have no health insurance (Fulginiti, 1991).

Again, poor infants and young children pay the price. Among industrialized nations, the United States ranks 21st in its performance in preventing infant mortality, with about 10.1 of every 1,000 babies and approximately 20 of every 1,000 black infants dying in the first year of life (National Center for Health Statistics, 1989). We rank 28th in the prevention of mortality among black infants, 29th in the prevention of low birthweight, and 15th in protecting infants with polio vaccines. Between 1988 and 1989 there was a fivefold increase in cases of measles in the United States, most of it occurring among preschool children. By 1989, recorded cases of measles were 10 times higher than the record low number of cases recorded in 1983. Only 50% of black children (as compared with 80% of whites) are fully immunized against measles, mumps, and rubella by age 2 (Children's Defense Fund, 1990).

Breaking the Cycle

We have the knowledge to solve these problems. Social policy analysts, pediatricians, and child advocates uniformly advocate a prevention-oriented approach (Cleveland, 1991; Harris, 1987; Schorr, 1989; Wright, 1991). Harris (1987) recommends breaking the cycle of poverty through early intervention programs instituted in infancy or early childhood, focused on preparing a child to succeed in school and later in life—not through increasing IQ scores, but through enhancing socialization, motivation, parent involvement, and community ties to educational arenas. Such programs have been tried and found to be highly effective in improving academic successes, in curbing juvenile delinquency, in helping families to gain control over the spacing of their children, in minimizing child abuse and neglect, and in enhancing the general quality of life for participants (Harris, 1987; Seitz, Rosenbaum, & Apfel, 1985; Zigler & Hall, 1987).

One such comprehensive family support model, the Yale Child Welfare Research Program, has proved to be highly successful in helping young disadvantaged mothers to support the development of their children and to improve the quality of family life (Provence, Naylor, & Patterson, 1977). The intervention focused attention primarily on mothers, with the expectation that if parents' own lives could be improved, a host of problems that typically affect poor children might be prevented. Mothers who were expecting their first child were invited to enroll in the program prior to delivery, and services (delivered by a multidisciplinary team) were continued until 30 months postpartum. Each dyad received postpartum pediatric visits in the hospital, regular well-baby care, and developmental evaluations, with a focus on discussions of child health and development between the mother and the pediatrician. Although the goal of these evaluations was not to teach the parent directly about child development, care was taken to respond to the mother's own interests and questions, and to give her an opportunity to observe the examiner's techniques for

handling difficult behavior. Home visitors provided not only moral support, but practical assistance to these mothers in obtaining housing, nutritional education, and support, and further empowered these families to help themselves by linking them as needed to additional community resources. Mothers were also given a chance to use center-based day care, in which each infant was assigned a primary caregiver who focused on the infant's social and emotional development, and on working with the mother to instill a sense of continuity between day care and home.

When the program ended at 30 months postpartum for each dyad, significant gains for each infant were restricted to enhanced language development (Rescorla, Provence, & Naylor, 1982). A 10-year follow-up, however, revealed broad differences between intervention and control children (Seitz et al., 1985). The intervention children demonstrated better adjustment to school and higher school attendance. Positive effects accruing to intervention mothers included higher rates of employment and self-support, higher educational attainments, lower birth rates, closer observance of their children's school performance, and a greater sense of enjoyment in parenting. The Yale program and its longitudinal follow-up teach two important lessons: that services to the whole family can bring significant, cost-effective, long-term social benefits to children; and that such services must be sustained and comprehensive in order to achieve long-lasting effectiveness. Significantly, this program addresses all four of the systems basic to a child's opportunities for optimal growth: family, health, day care, and school.

A new wave of intervention programs that hold promise for improving the quality of life for infants and families focus not just on infancy, but on infants and parents (usually mothers) simultaneously (Smith, 1991). Often tied into the Jobs Opportunities and Basic Skills (JOBS) program mandated by the 1988 Family Support Act, these programs target welfare-dependent young mothers and their children, with the goals of ameliorating both the short- and long-term sequelae of poverty. The Family Support Act provides funding for basic skills education for public assistance recipients, as well as employment training, child care, and other services to support these families; while not all two-generation programs are directly linked to the JOBS program, some of the most promising are. One of these, the Expanded Child Care Options program, provides high-quality child care to enable women eligible for support through the JOBS program to take advantage of educational and vocational programs offered.

Another JOBS-related intervention currently being mounted links the JOBS program with Head Start. The reauthorization of Head Start by the 101st Congress (Children's Defense Fund, 1991) provides for funding aimed at making Head Start accessible to all eligible children by 1994 (currently, only 27% of the potential recipients are actually served). The Head Start–JOBS link has three goals. First, the collaboration would provide extended day care to Head Start children, to enable parents to attend school or vocational programs. Second, comprehensive case management addressing family needs and child development would be implemented. Finally, Head Start centers themselves would serve as on-the-job training sites for participants interested in working in early childhood fields.

The Comprehensive Child Development Program provides a broad, family-based range of services to both infants and mothers (Abt Associates, 1990). Poor families with children under 1 year of age, recruited at 24 sites nationwide, are given access to a wide range of support services for 5 years. These include health screening, immunizations, child care, developmentally appropriate early childhood programs, and nutritional services. The children's mothers are also offered prenatal care; parent education classes; and assistance and referrals to help them find appropriate housing, educational services, and job training. A planned evaluation component will include a matched comparison group.

Smith (1991), in her review of the two-generation intervention model, notes that early childhood intervention programs will not on their own solve the problems of poor children. Nor will job training programs aid mothers if child care and other family-based services are unavailable. She recommends an expanded commitment to programs of this type; the establishment of an interdisciplinary research network to assess their impact; and the collaboration, support, and guidance of a variety of federal agencies.

Along with a commitment to early intervention, we must change our national orientation and priorities as a demonstration of our willingness to take responsibility for supporting children and families. Such groups as the American Academy of Pediatrics demonstrate their commitment in their legislative lobbying efforts on behalf of families (Fulginiti, 1991). Moreover, Medicaid and insurance reforms, along with the passage of a national health care bill such as Senator Edward Kennedy's Better Health for All Americans Act (Cleveland, 1991), would guarantee appropriate, affordable, accessible health care to all infants and children, regardless of their socioeconomic status. Until we provide all infants with the basic necessities of health care, nutrition, and housing, we cannot possibly hope to expect the youth of this nation to flourish, let alone mature into even minimally healthy and productive adults.

CHILD ABUSE

Although the lack of consensus on the definition of child abuse, coupled with failures to detect and report many cases, hinders our efforts to calculate its incidence with complete accuracy, it is clear that its prevalence and its devastating effects on children and on society now constitute a national emergency (Giovannoni, 1989; Krugman, 1991; Zigler & Hall, 1989). The Children's Defense Fund (1990) estimates that at least 2.2 million children are abused each year—a figure that represents a 225% increase from the 1976 figures, and a 48% increase in the last 5 years alone. Homicide is now the leading cause of injury-related deaths among children younger than 1 year in the United States (Children's Defense Fund, 1990). Infants have always represented a disproportionately large percentage of abused children. Kempe, Silverman, Steele, Droegmueller, and Silver (1962) found that children under 3 years of age were overrepresented, and Gil (1970) found that 25% of reported child abuse cases involved children under 2 years. There is considerable evidence that stresses related to parenting an infant can contribute to child abuse: Premature and/or low-birthweight infants (Gil, 1970; Klein & Stern, 1971; Parke & Collmer, 1975) and irritable or colicky infants (Frodi, 1981; Lester, 1984) appear to be particularly vulnerable.

Considerable controversy has arisen in the past decade over the predictability of child abuse. The belief in the intergenerational transmission of child abuse is perpetuated in both the scholarly and the popular presses, with some authors reporting that up to 90% of all abused children will themselves become abusive parents. As Kaufman and Zigler (1987, 1989) point out, however, there is a striking lack of empirical support for this belief. These authors suggest that the intergenerational transmission of abusive parenting occurs in perhaps 25–40% of all cases. Although this is still a significant rate of child abuse, the perpetuation of the intergenerational myth can lead us into three traps.

First, unquestioning adherence to the intergenerational hypothesis blinds us to the role played by mediating variables in determining *whether* an abused child will grow up to be an abusing parent. Instead of asking, "Do abused children become abusive parents?" we should be asking, "Under what circumstances is the transmission of abuse most likely to occur?" Second, failure to apply correctly the lessons of our research, as we continue to rely on popular (and, in this case, apocryphal) notions of child development and family interaction, leads us astray. Our true task should be to determine what factors can break the "cycle of abuse" (to the extent that there is such a cycle), and to contribute this understanding toward the development of programs and policies aimed at curbing child abuse. Finally, reliance on unfounded methods of identifying those whom we believe to be at risk of committing violence against children puts *us* at risk of abusing the civil liberties of those who have not yet transgressed, and may never transgress, against a child. Identification of infants believed to be at risk of child maltreatment (Leventhal, Garber, & Brady, 1989), without the provision of supportive services (not penalties) aimed at ameliorating that risk, aids no one (Kaufman & Zigler, 1989; Solnit, 1980).

Although we cannot predict with any certainty which parents will abuse their children, we do know that there is a strong link between family stress and child abuse (Garbarino, 1982; Gil, 1970; Kaufman & Zigler, 1989; Newberger, 1982; Olds & Henderson, 1989; Zigler, 1980). Basic to the social stress model of child abuse is the idea that social stresses, working in interaction with certain aspects of the cultural milieu and with family dynamics, build up until they result in an outbreak of aggression—in this case, against a child. The logical treatment model in this case involves supportive family interventions; in fact, such interventions are highly effective in improving the quality of life for infants and families in general, and specifically in lowering the incidence of child abuse in the target populations.

We know that 70% of all cases of child abuse begin with inappropriate or overly severe discipline. Furthermore, abusive parents often hold unreasonable expectations for their children's behavior, and as a result may punish inappropriately or strike out in anger at what is actually a normal behavior for a child of a given age (Zigler & Hall, 1989). The Missouri-based Parents as Teachers (PAT) program mounted an intervention in 1985 consisting of home visits to parents beginning in the last trimester of pregnancy and continuing throughout infancy. Parents who participated in this program were found to be significantly more knowledgeable than comparison group parents about child development and about discipline.

Another promising program that has resulted in sharp decreases in the rates of child abuse is the Prenatal/Early Infancy Project (PEIP; Olds & Henderson, 1989). Low-income, first-time mothers in a semirural community near Elmira, New York were assigned at random to one of four treatment groups. Children in the comparison group received only infant developmental screenings at 1 and 2 years of age, and the other families received an increasingly broad range of services; these included free transportation to prenatal care and well-child care appointments, developmental screenings, and frequent visits by a home visitor whose goal was the overall promotion of the health and well-being of the infants and mothers. At the end of 2 years, not only did the home-visited women in the PEIP express a greater sense of life satisfaction and control over their own lives, but the incidence of child abuse was far less than in the control group (4% as opposed to 19%). Furthermore, home-visited women were observed to scold, restrict, punish, yell at, spank, or hit their children less frequently than comparison group women (Olds, Henderson, Tutelbaum, & Chamberlin, 1986; Olds & Henderson, 1989).

Clearly, early intervention programs offering a broad range of support services aimed at helping parents to care for their children are effective tools in the prevention of child maltreatment. In order for such programs to be made economically and practically possible, however, money, commitment, and knowledge about the needs of children and families must all come together. Toward that end, the U.S. Advisory Board on Child Abuse and Neglect has recommended 31 critical steps it feels are essential if we are to control the rising incidence of child abuse (Krugman, 1991, p. 514). These steps can be grouped under eight headings:

- Recognition at a national level of this emergency.
- Provision of leadership at the presidential, gubernatorial, and mayoral levels in the fight against child abuse, and the demonstration of a commitment to rebuilding our nation's family support infrastructure.
- Coordination of leadership.
- Generation of further knowledge about child abuse.
- Dissemination of that knowledge.
- An increase in the human resources necessary to address the crisis.
- Provision of new programs and improvement of existing programs.
- Planning for the future.

As Schorr (1989) has emphasized, a reliance on the knowledge base we have, and a dedication to channel resources to effective interventions such as the PAT and PEIP projects, have put the control of child abuse within our reach. Only with the nationwide commitment of government at all levels, however, can this goal be achieved.

CHILD CARE

Given that approximately 60% of the mothers of preschool children now work outside the home (Bureau of Labor Statistics, 1987), largely out of economic necessity, it is essential that we devise a system of high-quality child care. Assessing the factors that make up adequate nonparental care is not simply a matter of asking whether child care is good or bad for children. Two decades of intensive research in this area have led us to understand that the question involves a host of variables that interact to determine the outcome of substitute care on individual children—variables such as family makeup, type of child care, child temperament, and even the individual child's gender.

Expert opinion on the specific effects of nonmaternal care for infants varies widely (see, e.g., Belsky, 1986, 1987; Phillips, McCartney, Scarr, & Howes, 1987; and Scarr, Phillips, & McCartney, 1990). A conference convened in 1987 by the National Center for Clinical Infant Programs, the National Academy of Sciences, and the Institute of Medicine was attended by a panel of experts on the effects of substitute care during early childhood. In spite of significant variation in their beliefs and the research findings presented at the conference, the participants were able to reach a consensus quickly on two points. The first was that the quality of the child care environment is directly related to measurable child development outcomes; below a certain threshold of quality, we are compromising our children's development. The second was that much research remains to be done (National Center for Clinical Infant Programs, 1988).

These points of agreement are echoed in the results of a meta-analysis on the effects of nonmaternal care on infant and toddler attachment to the mother, assessed via the Strange Situation paradigm (Lamb, Sternberg, & Prodromidis, 1992). Lamb and his colleagues found that although children who had experienced exclusively maternal care were significantly more likely to be securely attached than infants who had been in substitute care for more than 5 hours a week, the rate of secure attachments in both groups was high—71% and 65%, respectively. They point out, however, that this effect is likely to be mediated by quality of care, as all of the families were middle-class, two-parent families that were able to afford good-quality child care.

The components of high-quality child care have been known for years. Good-quality settings are characterized by low child–staff ratios, low staff turnover, decent wages, appropriate staff training, and relatively small classroom size (Ontario Ministry of Community and Social Services, 1991; Phillips & Howes, 1987; Ruopp, Travers, Glantz, & Coelen, 1979; Whitebook, Howes & Phillips, 1989). Efforts represented by the Federal Interagency Day Care Requirements (1980), along with requirements suggested by the Child Welfare League of America (1984) and the National Association for the Education of Young Children (Bredekamp, 1987), are strikingly similar in their recommended standards for the basics of child care quality (for a complete review of the child care standards issue, see Phillips & Zigler, 1987).

Unfortunately, the current low status and training level of American child care workers may render them ill equipped to provide the kind of care children need. The National Child Care Staffing Study (Whitebook et al., 1989) found that child care staffers provided more "sensitive and appropriate caregiving" when they received more formal education (including work in early childhood education), when they received higher wages, and when they worked in centers committing a higher budgetary percentage to teaching personnel. In 1988, the average hourly wage of child care workers providing center care was $5.35. Over half of the sample earned less than $5.00 per hour. The annual compensation for workers in this study was below the poverty level for families of three (the average family size of the respondents) for that year. It is not surprising, then, that staff turnover in 1988 was at an all-time high of 41% per year, or that 93% of all child care centers experienced some turnover in staff (Whitebook et al., 1989). High-quality child care is indistinguishable from developmentally appropriate early childhood education; we should therefore train and compensate child care staffers as befits their important role in the lives of our children.

Yet the federal government has largely abdicated its responsibility to children with respect to this concern. Child development experts agreed over 20 years ago that an appropriate child–caregiver ratio for infant care should be no greater than 3:1, yet only three states presently meet this requirement. In some states, ratios of 6:1 or even 8:1 are permitted by law (Young & Zigler, 1986). Policies such as this one institutionalize child neglect, since one person cannot provide even basic safeguards for eight infants at a time—let alone provide the warmth and stimulation essential for their optimal development. Standards provide minimum but valuable insurance that children will not be subjected to care that jeopardizes their growth and development. Nevertheless, special-interest groups have lobbied against the enactment of adequate child care standards. These groups include large, for-profit child care centers; small "mom and pop" centers; and, most surprisingly, the State Governors' Association.

In order to insure even minimally adequate environments for our children in out-of-home care, uniform child care standards meeting known developmental requirements should be enacted. But an additional obstacle to a family's ability to obtain high-quality care has been cost, which has risen to approximately $3000 per year for preschool care of even moderate quality. Twice as much may be needed for infant care (Children's Defense Fund, 1990). Clearly, most families would need assistance in purchasing such care. Under recent federal legislation, Child Care and Development Block Grants are avail-

able to the states to assist families in paying for child care and related programs, with priority given to economically marginal families (Budget Reconciliation Act of 1990). Potential funding is also available under Title XX, although these funds are not designated specifically for child care. In addition, a promising new avenue for funding an integrated programmatic model lies in the Human Services Reauthorization Act of 1990, which allocates funds for the purpose of developing a network of family resources and support programs within communities.

In our design of these programs, we have the capacity for meeting all of the family's primary support needs within one physical plant located in the community: the neighborhood school.

THE SCHOOL OF THE 21ST CENTURY

The most effective solutions for children and families will be those that are broadly based, that provide a wide range of services, and that fulfill long-term goals. Among these are universal preschool education beginning at 3 years of age, preventive health screening during the first 3 years of life, access to family support and child care resources, and ready availability of education for parenthood. One comprehensive model for achieving those goals is The School of the 21st Century (Zigler, 1989; Zigler & Lang, 1991), a proposal that sets the neighborhood school at the center of a network of child care and family support services. In this model, two on-site programs would provide child care—one meeting the needs of school-age children who require before- and after-school and vacation child care, and the other filling the need for year-round, developmentally appropriate all-day care for 3- to 5-year-olds. Children eligible for kindergarten would attend school for half a day and the child care program, as needed, for the other half.

The 21st-Century Model addresses the four systems that determine growth and development in childhood. These are health, family, education, and child care. In the 21st-Century School, a health module would screen children for potential problems that may impair their development and success in school. Similarly, a resource and referral network would provide families with ready access to supportive services within the community. The school experience would be enhanced by a high degree of home-to-school continuity and parental involvement, which are essential components of successful early childhood programs (Seitz, 1990; Provence & Naylor, 1983). Good-quality child care would also be made available to parents, to be used according to family requirements.

Child care for children 0 to 3 years of age—by far the most difficult and expensive to obtain—would also be integrated into The School of the 21st Century. The first of three additional programs for children in this age group would incorporate the tenets of the Missouri-based PAT program by giving home-based family support and parent education beginning in the third trimester of pregnancy and continuing for the first 3 years of the child's life (Zigler & Hall, 1991).

In addition to a PAT component, infant and toddler services would be available to these families through a network of licensed or registered neighborhood family day care providers—a group that is at present highly heterogeneous. These would become more uniform in quality through the use of the school as a hub for training, monitoring, and general support. Finally, a resource and referral service would be provided through the network to help locate appropriate child care for children with special needs or for children of parents who work unusual hours.

All of the components of The School of the 21st Century would be available to parents on a voluntary basis. Although the components are interdependent, each community could implement various aspects of the proposal according to community need, with the goal of providing appropriate, affordable, developmentally based care to all children who need it (for a complete discussion of The School of the 21st Century, see Zigler & Lang, 1991). Funding for implementing the plan, currently being piloted in several states, is achieved through a variety of individualized approaches. In Connecticut, for example, start-up funds for three demonstration projects were appropriated through the state legislature, and the projects are administered by the state department of human resources. In Missouri and Kansas, local school boards administer the programs, which are funded through modest parental fees. In Colorado, the program receives funds from a wide base of supporters, including the state department of education, the department of social services, handicapped education programs, and local businesses.

Although the school of the 21st century would act as a hub for family day care for children 0 to 3 years of age, a comprehensive family support program should make other options available for parents who may not wish to place their young infants in out-of-home care. Parental leave and a child care allowance on a national basis would assist parents in caring for their very young children.

PARENTAL CARE LEAVE

Experts in child development disagree as to how children are affected by placement in full-time, nonparental care during the first year of life (Belsky, 1986; Phillips et al., 1987). We are now seeing children placed in out-of-home care as early as 2 weeks after birth ("Human Services Reauthorization," 1988). There is growing concern that placing a child in substitute care at this age may be detrimental to both child and parents. The first weeks in the life of an infant represent a sensitive period for the development of reciprocal relationships (Bronfenbrenner, 1988; Hopper & Zigler, 1988). The child's development of a sense that the world is a stable, predictable place depends largely on the sense of continuity and responsiveness provided by the child's caregiver. We cannot as yet predict with certainty what the effect of multiple caregivers on children so young will be (Hopper & Zigler, 1988).

The transition to parenthood, no matter how joyful, is one of the most stressful experiences in a person's life (Belsky, Spanier, & Rovine, 1983). It takes time for a mutually satisfying parent–infant relationship to emerge, and adequate social supports are essential for the healthy development of this relationship. But instead of finding supports commensurate with the stresses of this important period, parents are often forced to select from a severely limited range of less than optimal alternatives: One parent, usually the mother, must stay home, often at the risk of the family's economic stability; or parents must place their infant in substitute care long before they feel ready to do so. Women who must return to employment outside the home before they feel ready report feeling stressed, guilty, and cheated out of an important experience (Farber, Alejandro-Wright, & Muenchow, 1988).

The United States and South Africa are the only industrialized nations in the world with no national paid parental leave policy. Seventy-five other nations offer such a benefit, which includes, on the average, a 4- to 5-month leave with replacement of 60–90% of a woman's wages. Current disability-based maternity leaves, for which fathers and adoptive parents are ineligible, do not address the needs of the family during this period. In 1985 the Yale Bush Center in Child Development and Social Policy convened a panel of experts from the fields of child development, business, labor relations, and social policy to study this problem. This advisory committee of the Infant Care Leave Project ultimately recommended that the United States implement a national infant care leave law that would enable a new parent to take a 6-month job-protected leave (3 months with partial income and 3 months without compensation) following the birth or adoption of a child (Zigler & Frank, 1988). Nevertheless, Congress was able to pass only a 12-week unpaid leave during its last session of 1992; even this minimal leave was vetoed by President Bush. Clearly, a 12-week unpaid leave is not a solution to the infant care problem among families who need a double income to survive financially. To support parents in a meaningful way, we need both job-protected leave and a child allowance that will help parents through the first year of their child's life.

CHILD ALLOWANCE TRUST FUND

Good-quality infant care is the most difficult and expensive to obtain, costing more than $200 a week in some cities (Children's Defense Fund, 1990). Again, parents are faced with a range of poor choices: They must sacrifice necessary income to stay at home and care for the new baby; add the precariously high cost of good-quality infant care to the family budget-balancing act; or compromise quality (and possibly the child's development) by settling for a less costly, but perhaps also less appropriate, care setting. In the end, having such a poor range of choices is often tantamount to having no choice at all.

Parents in some 67 other industrialized nations have another alternative. These nations provide a family allowance, or child allowance, directly to families for each child in the home. This is typically a flat amount for each child, although in some countries the allowance varies with age, birth order, and the number of children in the family. We propose that such an allowance be made available in the United States by expanding the Social Security system to pro-

vide an annual stipend of approximately $5,000 to families for a child's first year. At present, when two parents are working, 7.65% of a family's income goes into the Social Security fund for use at some future date. Through the child allowance, we would simply be making some of these funds available when they are needed for the transition to parenthood. In so doing, we would restore to parents the right to raise their infants and toddlers according to the dictates of their own ideals, not the limitations of their pocketbooks.

This plan would be consistent in spirit with President Bush's child care tax credit proposal, but would differ from his plan in three ways. First, the family allowance would be made available to families regardless of income; any family who had contributed to the Social Security system would be eligible to receive funds under the plan. Second, the Bush plan came with a $1,000 cap—hardly enough to provide realistic help to families who may have to pay six times that amount each year for infant day care. Finally, the child allowance trust fund would not discriminate against parents who wish to leave the out-of-home workforce to care for their children themselves; the funds could be used to replace income for such families, as well as to finance good-quality day care for those wishing to work outside the home.

Funding mechanisms for such an allowance vary from country to country. In France, where the policy was originally implemented as a pronatalist effort (though those who would oppose such a plan for the United States on these grounds should be aware that it was not successful in this regard), the child allowance is part of a comprehensive family policy that also supports a range of child care options. The child allowance is available to all French families for 9 months, beginning in the fifth month of pregnancy. Following that, an additional allowance is available for the first 3 years of the child's life on a means-tested basis; 80% of all French families are eligible for this support.

Similar arrangements are made in other nations. The Canadian government provides a modest allowance for all children under 18, though this stipend is taxed as income. The Austrian government provides an allowance for each child equaling 15% of the average female wage, and a plan implemented in West Germany in 1986 provides for a universal allowance from birth to 6 months, followed by a stipend available according to financial need. Sweden gives a tax-free allowance for each child under 18 and a paid parental leave, among other family support benefits.

The U.S. plan proposed here would be consonant with Jule Sugarman's proposal for increasing federal child and family program funding levels through a Social Security add-on. However, the children's allowance proposal is less costly than the Sugarman plan and is focused specifically on the problem of securing care for children in the first year of life. In the child allowance trust fund plan proposed by Zigler and Lang (1991), funds would be released on a yearly basis directly to parents, to be used at their discretion. The plan is thus consistent with the administration's emphasis on choice in family support planning: A parent can elect either to care for a child at home or to purchase infant care. These funds could be realized through either a flat or a graduated Social Security tax increase.

The ideological basis for the child allowance is a conservative, family-oriented one. Moreover, the proposed funding mechanism is entirely consistent with the original goal of the Social Security system—to relieve families of the economic burdens of caring for family members. The goal of such a plan is to give families a real choice by offering a wider range of realistic child care alternatives.

LOOKING TOWARD THE FUTURE

None of these solutions will be achieved without effort and commitment, and they cannot be achieved at all under an ideology unwilling to prepare for the future. We are optimistic, however, that they *will* be achieved—both because of a growing insistence on the part of parents that the government be held accountable for meeting the needs of families, and because the businesses and decision makers responsible for the implementation of family support programs are becoming more willing to invest in human capital (Committee for Economic Development, 1991). Evidence is mounting that people are eager to integrate such family-oriented supports into our educational, child care, and business systems. Members of the National Education Association and the Parents and Teachers Association have looked with favor on the "school of the 21st century," and have contributed to the development and implementation of the 21st-century concept.

Parents are beginning to make their elected officials aware of their needs. A recent national survey presented to President Bush by parents reveals that 75% of respondents believe that the federal government should take responsibility for developing policies to make child care more affordable and accessible. The same survey revealed that quality of child care was of even greater concern to these parents than cost (Zinsser, 1989). Parents are a busy, beleaguered constituency, but they are a powerful one, and they will not tolerate for much longer the lack of real monetary or political commitment to families.

American employers are feeling pressure from parents who realize that they can neither be effective workers themselves nor raise a new generation of productive citizens when the basic needs of their families remain unmet. Commitment to the needs of children and families is far from a sentimental leaning; attending to family concerns is good science, good business, and good politics.

REFERENCES

Abt Associates. (1990, June). [Project summary of the Comprehensive Child Development Program impact evaluation prepared for the Two Generation Research Network Meeting sponsored by the Foundation for Child Development, New York, held June 8, 1990 in Washington, DC]. Cambridge, MA: Author.

Acker, P. J., Fierman, A. H., & Dreyer, B. P. (1987). An assessment of parameters of health care and nutrition in homeless children. *American Journal of Diseases of Children, 141,* 388–391.

Bassuk, E. L., Rubin, L., & Lauriat, A. S. (1986). Characteristics of sheltered homeless families. *American Journal of Public Health, 76,* 1097–1101.

Belsky, J. (1981). Early human experience: A family perspective. *Developmental Psychology, 17,* 3–23.

Belsky, J. (1986). Infant day care: A cause for concern? *Zero to Three, 6,* 1–9.

Belsky, J. (1987). Risks remain. *Zero to Three, 7,* 22–24.

Belsky, J., Spanier, G. B., & Rovine, M. (1983). Stability and change across the transition to parenthood. *Journal of Marriage and the Family, 45,* 567–577.

Bredekamp, S. (Ed.). (1987). *Accreditation criteria and procedures.* Washington, DC: National Association for the Education of Young Children.

Bronfenbrenner, U. (1979). *The ecology of human development.* Cambridge, MA: Harvard University Press.

Bronfenbrenner, U. (1988). Strengthening family systems. In E. Zigler & M. Frank (Eds.), *The parental leave crisis: Toward a national policy.* New Haven, CT: Yale University Press.

Budget Reconciliation Act of 1990.

Bureau of Labor Statistics. (1987). *Employee perspectives: Women in the labor force* (4th quarter, Report No. 749). Washington, DC: U.S. Government Printing Office.

Chan, V., & Momparler, M. (1991, May). George Bush's report card. *Mother Jones*, pp. 44–45.

Child Welfare League of America. (1984). *Standards for day care.* New York: Author.

Children's Defense Fund. (1990). *S.O.S. America! A Children's Defense Fund budget.* Washington, DC: Author.

Children's Defense Fund. (1991). *The state of America's children 1991.* Washington, DC: Author.

Cleveland, W. W. (1991). Redoing the health care quilt: Whole cloth or patches? *American Journal of Diseases of Children, 145,* 449–504.

Committee for Economic Development. (1991). *The unfinished agenda: A new vision for child development and education.* New York: Author.

Edelman, M. W. (1991, May). Kids first. *Mother Jones*, pp. 31–32, 76–77.

Farber, E., Alejandro-Wright, M., & Muenchow, S. (1988). Managing work and family: Hopes and realities. In E. Zigler & M. Frank (Eds.), *The parental leave crisis: Toward a national policy.* New Haven, CT: Yale University Press.

Federal Interagency Day Care Requirements. (1980, March 19). *Federal Register*, Part V, *45*(55), 17870, 17885.

Frodi, A. (1981). Contribution of infant characteristics to child abuse. *American Journal of Mental Deficiency, 85,* 341–349.

Fulginiti, V. A. (1991). Far from the ideal: The plight of poor children in the United States. *American Journal of Mental Deficiency, 145,* 489–490.

Gamble, T. J., & Zigler, E. (1986). Effects of infant day care: Another look at the evidence. *American Journal of Orthopsychiatry, 56,* 26–42.

Garbarino, J. (1982). Healing the wounds of social isolation. In E. H. Newberger (Ed.), *Child abuse.* Boston: Little, Brown.

Gil, D. (1970). *Violence against children: Physical child abuse in the United States.* Cambridge, MA: Harvard University Press.

Giovannoni, J. (1989). Definitional issues in child maltreatment. In D. Cicchetti & V. Carlson (Eds.), *Child maltreatment.* New York: Cambridge University Press.

Harris, I. B. (1987, March 24). *What can we do to prevent the cycle of poverty?* Clifford Beers Lecture presented at the Child Study Center, Yale University, New Haven, CT.

Hofferth, S. L., & Phillips, D. A. (1987). Child care in the United States: 1970–1995. *Journal of Marriage and the Family, 49,* 559–571.

Hopper, P., & Zigler, E. (1988). The medical and social science basis for a national infant care leave policy. *American Journal of Orthopsychiatry, 58,* 324–338.

Human Services Reauthorization Act of 1990, P.L. 101-501. (1988). Infant day care [Special issue]. *Early Childhood Research Quarterly, 3*(3).

Kamerman, S., Kahn, A. J., & Kingston, P. (1983). *Maternity policies and working women.* New York: Columbia University Press.

Kaufman, J., & Zigler, E. (1987). Do abused children become abusive parents? *American Journal of Orthopsychiatry, 57,* 186–192.

Kaufman, J., & Zigler, E. (1989). The intergenerational transmission of child abuse. In D. Cicchetti & V. Carlson (Eds.), *Child maltreatment.* New York: Cambridge University Press.

Kempe, C., Silverman, F., Steele, B., Droegmueller, W., & Silver, H. (1962). The battered child syndrome. *Journal of the American Medical Association, 181,* 17–24.

Klaus, M. H., Leger, T., & Trause, M. A. (1982). *Maternal attachment and mothering disorders.* Skillman, NJ: Johnson & Johnson.

Klein, M., & Stern, L. (1971). Low birth weight and the battered child syndrome. *American Journal of Diseases of Children, 122,* 15–18.

Krugman, R. D. (1991). Child abuse and neglect: Critical first steps in response to a national emergency: The report of the U.S. Advisory Board on Child Abuse and Neglect. *American Journal of Diseases of Children, 145,* 513–515.

Lamb, M. E., Sternberg, K. T., & Prodromidis, M. (1992). Non-maternal care and the security of infant–mother attachment: A reanalysis of the data. *Infant Behavior and Development, 15*(1), 71–83.

Leventhal, J. M., Garber, R. B., & Brady, C. A. (1989). Identification during the postpartum period of infants who are at high risk of child maltreatment. *Journal of Pediatrics, 114,* 481–487.

Lester, B. M. (1984). A bisocial model of infant crying. In L. Lipsitt & C. Collier (Eds.), *Advances in infancy research: Monographs in infancy* (Vol. 3). New York: Academic Press.

Maurer, H. M. (1991). The growing neglect of American children. *American Journal of Diseases of Children, 145,* 540–541.

Miller, D. S., & Lin, E. (1988). Children in sheltered homeless families: Reported health status and use of health services. *Pediatrics, 81,* 668–673.

Minde, K., & Minde, R. (1986). *Infant psychiatry: An introductory textbook.* Beverly Hills, CA: Sage.

National Center for Health Statistics. (1989). *Vital statistics of the United States, 1987: vol. 2. Mortality. Part A.* Washington, DC: U.S. Government Printing Office.

National Center for Clinical Infant Programs. (1988). *Infants, families and child care. Toward a research agenda.* Washington, DC: Author.

Newberger, C. M. (1982). Psychology and child abuse. In E. H. Newberger (Ed.), *Child abuse.* Boston: Little, Brown.

Newsweek. (1990, Winter–Spring). The 21st century family [Special edition].

Olds, D. L., & Henderson, C. R., Jr. (1989). The prevention of maltreatment. In D. Cicchetti & V. Carlson (Eds.), *Child maltreatment.* New York: Cambridge University Press.

Olds, D. L., Henderson, C. R., Jr., Tutelbaum, R., & Chamberlin, R. (1986). Improving the delivery of prenatal care and outcomes of pregnancy: A randomized trial of nurse home visitation. *Pediatrics, 86,* 16–28.

Ontario Ministry of Community and Social Services. (1991). *Factors related to quality in child care: A review of the literature.* Toronto: Author.

Osofsky, J. D. (1990, Winter). Risk and protective factors for teenage mothers and their infants. *SRCD Newsletter.*

Parke, R. D., & Collmer, C. (1975). Child abuse: An interdisciplinary analysis. In E. M. Hetherington (Ed.),

Review of child development research (Vol. 5). Chicago: University of Chicago Press.

Parker, R. M., Rescorla, L. A., Finkelstein, J. A., Barnes, N., Holmes, J. H., & Stolley, P. D. (1991). A survey of the health of homeless children in Philadelphia shelters. *American Journal of Diseases of Children, 145,* 520–526.

Phillips, D., & Howes, C. (1987). Indicators of quality in child care: Review of the research. In D. Phillips (Ed.), *Quality in child care: What does the research tell us?* Washington, DC: National Association for the Education of Young Children.

Phillips, D., McCartney, K., Scarr, S., & Howes, C. (1987). Selective review of infant care: A cause for concern. *Zero to Three, 6*(6), 18–24.

Phillips, D., & Zigler, E. (1987). The checkered history of federal child care regulations. In E. Z. Rothkopf (Ed.), *Review of research in education* (Vol. 14). Washington, DC: American Educational Research Association.

Provence, S., & Naylor, A. (1983). *Working with disadvantaged parents and children: Scientific and practical issues.* New Haven, CT: Yale University Press.

Provence, S., Naylor, A., & Patterson, J. (1977). *The challenge of daycare.* New Haven, CT: Yale University Press.

Redding, R. E., Harmon, R. J., & Morgan, G. A. (1990). Relationships between maternal depression and infants' mastery behavior. *Infant Behavior and Development, 13,* 391–395.

Rescorla, L. A., Provence, S., & Naylor, A. (1982). The Yale Child Welfare Research Program: Description and results. In E. Zigler & E. W. Gordon (Eds.), *Day care: Scientific and social policy issues.* Boston: Auburn House.

Ruopp, R., Travers, J., Glantz, F., & Coelen, C. (1979). *Children at the center.* Cambridge, MA: Abt Associates.

Scarr, S., Phillips, D., & McCartney, K. (1990). Facts, fantasies, and the future of child care in the United States. *Psychological Science, 1,* 26–35.

Schorr, L. B. (1989). *Within our reach: Breaking the cycle of disadvantage.* New York: Doubleday.

Schroeder, P. (1988). Parental leave: The need for a federal policy. In E. Zigler & M. Frank (Eds.), *The parental leave crisis: Toward a national policy.* New Haven, CT: Yale University Press.

Schweinhart, L. J. (1988). *A school administrator's guide to early childhood programs.* Ypsilanti, MI: High/Scope Educational Research Foundation.

Seitz, V. (1990). Intervention programs for impoverished children: A comparison of educational and family support models. *Annals of Child Development, 7,* 73–103.

Seitz, V., Rosenbaum, L., & Apfel, N. H. (1985). Effects of family support intervention: A ten-year follow up. *Child Development, 56,* 376–391.

Select Committee on Children, Youth, and Families, U.S. House of Representatives. (1987). *U.S. children and*

their families: Current conditions and recent trends, 1987. Washington, DC: U.S. Government Printing Office.

Smith, S. (1991). Two-generation program models: A new intervention strategy. *Social Policy Report, 5*(1), 1–15.

Solnit, A. J. (1980). Too much reporting, too little service: Roots and prevention of child abuse. In G. Gerbner, C. Ross, & E. Zigler (Eds.), *Child abuse.* New York: Oxford University Press.

Whitebook, M., Howes, C., & Phillips, D. (1989). *Who cares? Child care teachers and the quality of care in America: Final report, National Child Care Staffing Study.* Oakland, CA: Child Care Employee Project.

Wright, J. D. (1991). Children in and of the streets: Health, social policy, and the homeless young. *American Journal of Diseases of Children, 145,* 520–526.

Young, K. T., & Zigler, E. (1986). Infant and toddler day care: Regulations and policy implications. *American Journal of Orthopsychiatry, 56,* 43–55.

Zigler, E. (1970). The environmental mystique: Training the intellect versus development of the child. *Childhood Education, 46,* 402–414.

Zigler, E. (1980). Controlling child abuse: Have we the knowledge and/or the will? In G. Gerbner, C. Ross, & E. Zigler (Eds.), *Child abuse: An agenda for action.* New York: Oxford University Press.

Zigler, E. (1989). Addressing the nation's child care crisis: The school of the twenty-first century. *American Journal of Orthopsychiatry, 59,* 484–491.

Zigler, E., & Berman, W. (1983). Discerning the future of early childhood intervention. *American Psychologist, 38,* 894–906.

Zigler, E., & Frank, M. (Eds.). (1988). *The parental leave crisis: Toward a national policy.* New Haven, CT: Yale University Press.

Zigler, E., & Gilman, E. P. (1990). An agenda for the 1990s: Supporting families. In D. Blankenhorn, S. Bayme, & J. Bethke-Elshtain (Eds.), *Rebuilding the nest.* Milwaukee, WI: Family Service America.

Zigler, E., & Hall, N. (1987). Preventing juvenile delinquency. In E. Aronowitz & R. Sussman (Eds.), *Issues in community mental health: Youth.* Canton, MA: Prodist.

Zigler, E., & Hall, N. W. (1989). Physical child abuse in America: Past, present and future. In D. Cicchetti & V. Carlson (Eds.), *Child maltreatment.* New York: Cambridge University Press.

Zigler, E., & Hall, N. W. (1991, May). Early intervention and family support: Where we have been, where we are going. *Parents as Teachers Newsletter.*

Zigler, E., & Lang, M. (1991). *Child care choices: Balancing the needs of children, families, and society.* New York: Free Press.

Zigler, E., & Trickett, P. (1978). IQ, social competence, and evaluation of early childhood intervention programs. *American Psychologist, 33,* 789–798.

Zinsser, C. (1989, July). Special survey results: Your message to the President on child care. *Working Mother,* p. 36.

Index

Abortion services, 388
Abused infants, 166
Acculturation, 61
Active–aggressive type, regulatory disorders, 283, 286–288
Active person and active environment, 4
Addiction, 148
Adjustment disorders, 230
  case example, 232–233
Adolescent fathers, 114–115
Adolescent mothers
  and grandmothers, 48
  inventions, 115–116
Adolescent parents, 106–116, 481
  biological risks, 109
  child development, 110
  depressed mothers, 109
  individual differences affecting outcomes, 111
  mental health risks, 108–109
  parenting risks, 109–111
  poverty, 108
  protective factors, 112–114
  psychodynamic framework, 106–108
  risk factors, 108
Adolescent pregnancies, 10
Adult Attachment Interview, 218
Affect attunement model, 134–135
Affect communication, 30
Affective development in primary caregiving relationship, 14–31
Affect regulation, 21
African–American families, 60
African parents, 58
Age of children
  day care, 452–453
  parental mental illness, 123–124
Aggressive attachment disorder, 343
Alcohol abuse, 151–153
Ambivalent attachment, 25, 166
Anger expression, 22
Angry expression, 166
Anorexia nervosa, 327, 354

Anxiety–provoking in interview process, 179–181
Asian–American parents, 64
Asian families, 60
Asperger Syndrome, 238
Assessment, 191–207
  attachment disorders, 345
  of family and caregiving environment
    interaction guidance, 415–416
  of risk factors
    maltreatment, 167
  sleep disorders, 306–307
  as therapeutic process
    case example, 204–206
Asthma, 354–356
At-risk children, 199
Attachment disorders, 332–347
  aggressive, 343
  assessment, 345
  caseness, 337–338
  construct, 333
  disinhibited, 336
  indiscriminate, 340–341
  inhibited, 336, 342–343
  management, 345–346
  nonattached, 338–340
  relationship to other disorders, 344–345
  role-reversed, 343–344
  socially promiscuous, 341–342
  types, 338–344
Attachment relationships, 333
  information gathering for interviews, 182–183
  parental mental illness, 127–128
  parents, 17
Attachment system, 23–26
Attachment theory, 20
  behaviors, 21, 333
  classifications, 334–336
  developmental research, 58, 333–334
  fathers, 41–42

intergenerational context, 16
internal working models, 334
of maltreated infants, 166
and separation
  siblings, 50
Atypical Pervasive Developmental Disorders, 238
Autism
  categorical definitions, 242–243
  clinical assessment, 243–245
  clinical description, 238–342
  cognitive development, 240–241
  communicative development, 240
  course and prognosis, 242
  diagnosis, 237, 242–243
  dimensional definitions, 243
  early development, 238–239
  epidemiology, 241
  interventions, 245–247
  neurobiological studies, 241
  psychopathy, 238
  psychosocial factors, 241–242
  social development, 239–240
Autistic-like behaviors, 245
Autonomy and regulation
  fathers, 42–43
Avoidant attachment, 24, 334

Background information on infant and family in interview process, 177–178
Bayley Mental Development Index, 51
Bayley Scales of Infant Development, 165, 194, 197
Beck Depression Inventory, 126
Behavioral regulation, 263
Behavioral risk factors
  prematurity, 89
Behavioral techniques
  sleep disorders, 312–313
Behavior Problem Checklist, 89
Behavorial inhibition, 18–19
Berkeley Guidance Study archives, 15

Best interests standard in child custody, 476–477
Bicultural, 61
Biological conditions, communication disorders, 264, 265–266
Biological regulation, 20
Biological risks, adolescent parenthood, 109
Biological systems in development, 9
"Birth to Three," 404
Black communities, grandmothers, 48
Brain dysfunction, 90
Brazelton Neonatal Behavioral Assessment Scale (NBAS), 146, 150, 196–197, 212, 336
Breast-fed infants, 96–97

Canalization, 9
Caregiver–child therapy, 274–275
Caregivers
    communication disorders, 274–275
    educational programs
        communication disorders, 275
Caseness of attachment disorders, 337–338
Central nervous system (CNS)
    cocaine effect, 145
    prenatal influences, 143–144
Cerebral infarction, 146
Cerebral palsy, 88
Charlotte Circle Project, 374
Child abuse, 484–486
    communication disorders, 266–267
    controlling, 485–486
Child allowance trust fund, 489–490
Child care, 486–487. See also Day care
Child characteristics, day care, 452
Child development
    adolescent parenthood, 110
Child development models
    early childhood education, 5
    environmental context, 5
    stability in, 4–5
Child-focused
    early intervention, 362–363, 364–365, 370
Child health preventive care
    primary/universal intervention, 389–390
Childhood adversity
    poor infants family life, 80–81
Childhood Disintegrative Disorder, 237–338
Childhood family patterns on parenting behavior, 16
Childhood psychosis, 236
Child–parent contact
    custody of infants, 463–464
Children born of parental mental illness, 124–133
Chlorpromazine, 150
Chowchilla study, 292
Chronosystem, 57
Classification, 225–234
    attachment, 334–336
    communication disorders, 262

etiologic factors, 226
failure to thrive (FTT), 318–319
purposes, 227–228
schemes, 228–231
Clinical description
    autism, 238–242
Clinical implications
    sociocultural context of infant development, 60–66
    substance abuse, 154
Clinical nursing models project secondary/selected interventions, 396–397
Clinical problem-solving procedure, 216–217
Clinical relational matrix
    interview process, 174–175
Cocaine, 145–148
    substance abuse, 145–148
Cognated expertise
    custody of infants, 465
Cognitive development
    autism, 240–241
    red flags, 255
Coherence of mind, 17
Collateral contacts
    court-ordered clinical evaluations in custody, 476
Collectivist sense of self, 58
Comfort seeking, 23–26
Common sleep problems, 307–309
Communication
    behaviors, 270
    first year, 263
    purposes, 263
    second year, 264
Communication disorders, 259–276
    adjusting language and social input, 274
    biological conditions, 264, 265–266
    caregiver–child therapy, 274–275
    caregivers, 274–275
    child abuse/neglect, 266–267
    classification, 262
    communicative bids, 273
    congenital factors, 265
    contingent responding, 274
    domains of assessment, 269–272
    educational programs, 275
    environmental conditions, 264, 266–267
    exaggerated intonation, 274
    expressive language and communication, 269–270
    facilitative versus directive style, 273–274
    genetic and metabolic disorders, 265
    interactional disturbances, 266
    interactive strategies, 273–274
    intervention principles, 272–273
    language-related cognitive abilities, 271
    mental health professional implications, 275–276
    postnatal factors, 266
    poverty, 266
    prevalence, 262

receptive language and communication, 270–271
risk factors, 264–267
simple vocabulary and reduced sentence length, 274
social–affective behavior, 271
speech production, 271
Communicative bids, 273
Communicative development
    autism, 240
Communicative partners, 271–272
Community frame, 107
"Community Infant Project," 407
Comparative paradigms, 61
Competence, 26
Comprehensive Child Development Program, 484
Conflict in interactions
    parental mental illness, 129
Congenital abnormalities, 89, 146
Congenital factors
    communication disorders, 265
Connecticut Infant–Toddler Developmental Assessment Program, 194, 200
Consequences for infant development
    parental mental illness, 121–124
Construct
    attachment disorders, 333
Contested custody of infants, 463–464
Contingent responding
    communication disorders, 274
Continuity of care
    custody of infants, 466
Co-occurring forms of
    maltreatment and infant development, 162
Correlation between early and later performance of children, 8
Cosleeping, 310, 312
Counseling and Home Training Program for Deaf Children, 374
Course and prognosis
    autism, 242
Court-ordered clinical evaluations in custody, 473–476
    collateral contacts, 476
    infant custody report, 476
Cuento therapy, 64
Cultural code, 57
    environtype, 10
Culturally competent clinician, 66–67
Cultural mistrust, 66
Cultural variant, 60
Custody
    alternatives, 468–469
    best interests standard, 476–477
    day care versus parent care, 470
    infant distress regarding, 471–473
    nature of child–parent contact, 469–470
    overnight child–parent contact, 470
    report, 476
    sibling bonds, 470–471
Custody of infants, 462–477
    child–parent contact, 463–464
    cognated expertise, 465

contested, 463–464
continuity of care, 466
familial dissolution and readjustment, 466–471
judicial determinations, 462–463
legal issues, 462–463
parent–infant contact, 466
technical expertise, 465–466
trauma, 467
use of experts, 464–466

Day care, 445–459, 446
age at enrollment, 452–453
child characteristics, 452
conceptual problem, 445–446
family characteristics, 457–458
father–infant attachment, 448
high-quality care, 455–457
maternal employment, 451
maternal psychological variables, 450–451
measurement, 448–449
nonmaternal care
and attachment, 446–453
and social adjustment, 453–455
versus parent care custody, 470
quality of care, 455–458
Death
from child maltreatment, 160
Definition of self, 58
Demographics
poverty and infant development, 74
Dependency, 148
Depressed infants, 166
Depressed mothers, 21, 29
adolescent parenthood, 109
Depression, parental mental illness, 123, 126, 127
Deterministic constitutional model of development, 5
Deterministic environmental model of development, 5
Development
active versus passive views, 4
parental psychopathology, 11
Developmental aspects of sleep–wake organization, 305–306
Developmental assessment, 194
Developmental blockage, 83
Developmental considerations
failure to thrive (FTT), 317–318
Post-Traumatic Stress Disorder (PTSD), 292–295
Developmentally and affectively retarded, 166
Developmental models, 3, 5–9
Developmental orientation, 225
Developmental Quotient (DQ), 7
parental mental illness, 125
Developmental research
attachment, 333–334
Developmental screening tools, 196
Developmental sequelae
prematurity, 88–98
Developmental status evaluation, 193

Development areas, consistency in, 58
Devreux Adolescent Behavior Rating Scale, 90
Diagnosis, 225–234
autism, 242–243
parental mental illness, 121
process, 233–234
role and usefulness, 432–434
Diazepam, 150
Difficult infant temperament, 18, 163
Difficult-to-care-for infants, 81
Digo culture, 10
Disabled infants, 199, 370–374
Disinhibited attachment disorder, 336
Disorders of Affects, 229–230
Disorders of Social Development and Communication, 229
Disorganized/disoriented attachment, 25, 166, 335
Distress–relief interactions, parental mental illness, 126
Diurnal organization, 305–306
Divorce effects, 468–469
Domains of assessment, communication disorder, 269–272
Drowning and near-drowning, 161
Dyadic interaction, parental mental illness, 125–129

Early childhood education child development model, 5
Early Coping Inventory, 199
Early intervention, 98
child-focused, 362–363, 364–365, 370
didactic programs, 372–373
disabled infants, 370–374
experience of, 379
four models, 362
jointly-focused, 363, 367–369, 371–374
low-birthweight infants, 364–370
low-intensity, 363, 369–370, 374
methodological issues, 374–375
methods with infants, 380
outcomes, 375–378
parent-focused, 363, 365, 370–371
parents, 380
parent support programs, 365–366
parent training/education programs, 366–367
personnel, 380–381
program implementation, 378–379
programs, 361–381
two-dimensional model, 362
varieties, 362–363
East African cultures, 10
Easy infants, 18
Economic conditions
poverty and infant development, 75–76
Emergency admissions, 97
Emotional support of fathers, 40
Emotion regulation, 19–23
Environmental factors

communication disorders, 264, 266–267
continuity, 8
effects of child on, 5–6
failure to thrive (FTT), 318
parental mental illness, 122
Environtype, 9–12
cultural code, 10
family code, 10–11
individual code, 11
regulation and development, 11–12
subsystems, 10
Epidemiology
autism, 241
mental retardation, 250–251
Ethnic populations, 59–60
guidelines for psychological services, 66
match in intervention, 65
Evaluation
gathering information, 431–432
infant distress regarding custody, 471–472
infant–parent psychotherapy, 428–434
interaction guidance, 424–425
mental retardation, 254–256
therapist's experience, 431
Exaggerated intonation, communication disorder, 274
Exosystem, 57, 98
Expert use, custody of infants, 464–466
Exploratory motivation, 26
Expressed emotion, 129
Expressive language and communication, communication disorder, 269–270

Face-to-face interaction
parental mental illness, 126
play, 21
procedure, 212–213
Facial displays, 22
Facilitative versus directive style, communication disorder, 273–274
Failure to bond, 163
Failure to thrive (FTT), 317–323
classification, 318–319
defined, 318
developmental considerations, 317–318
environmental factors, 318
family characteristics, 320–322
family situation, 321
individual differences, 318
infant characteristics, 319–320
maltreatment and infant development, 161
maternal characteristics, 320
mother–infant relationship, 320–321
normal growth and eating patterns, 317–318
organic versus nonorganic, 318–319
outcome, 322–323
physiological factors, 317

Failure to thrive (*continued*)
   siblings characteristics, 321–322
   treatment, 322
Families
   in communities, 15
   dissolution and readjustment cus-
      tody of infants, 466–471
   failure to thrive (FTT), 320–322
   family-centered care, 63
   life in poverty, 76–81
   self-sufficiency model, 405–406
   in which fathers were absent, 38
Family Administered Neonatal Activities, 200–201
Family code
   environtype, 10–11
Family context
   infant contributions, 17–19
   of infant mental health, 14–31
   measurement issues, 17–19
   mental retardation, 256
   model, 15, 16
   parental mental illness, 130–133
   temperament models, 17–19
"Family Focus," 404
Family interview, 173
"Family Place, Inc," 404
Family play interaction guidance, 414–
   415
Family Rating Scale, 90
Family relationships
   father's role, 39–45
   grandparents' role, 45–50
   infant–caregiver, 38–39
   siblings, 50–52
Family support, 402–412
   early years importance, 406
   evaluation, 411
   incorporation with other systems,
      404–408
   infant in context, 404–405
   parent education, 408
   self-help groups, 408
   self-sufficiency model, 405–406
   well-being of family, 406
Family system theory, 107
Family treatment
   interaction guidance, 416–418
   play session conclusion, 417
   typical session, 416
   videotape viewing and commentary,
      416–418
Fathers
   attachment, 41–42
   attachment in day care, 448
   autonomy and regulation, 42–43
   care in absence of mothers, 42
   direct effects, 41–45
   experience of caring alters behavior
      of father, 44
   impact on maternal mental health,
      42
   indirect effects, 40–41
   interaction with infants, 39–40
   in neonatal intensive care unit,
      95
   physical play, 43–44

play, 39
   role in family relationships, 39–45
   role of marriage, 41
   rough-and-tumble play, 43
   social support, 40–41
Feeding disorders, 323–327
   anorexia nervosa, 327
   merycism, 323–324
   overfeeding, 327
   pica, 324–325
   post-traumatic eating disorder, 326–
      327
   prevalence, 323
   psychosocial dwarfism, 325–326
   rumination disorder, 323–324
Fetal abuse, 161–162
Fetal alcohol syndrome, 151–152
Financial resources, lack, 162
Folktale therapy, 64
Formulation in interviews, 188–189

Gender differences, 59
Genes in development, 9
Genetic and metabolic disorders, 265
Genotype, 11
Goal-corrected attachment behavioral
   system, 24
Goodness-of-fit model, 19
   parental mental illness, 133–134
Grandfathers, 49
Grandmothers, 112
   as babysitters, 45
   in black communities, 48
   infant development, 45–48
Grandparents
   direct effects, 46–50
   indirect effects, 45–46
   as primary caregivers, 48
   role in family relationships, 45–50
   as socialization agents, 47
Greenspan–Lieberman Observation
   System for Assessment of
   Caregiver–Infant Interaction
   during Semi-Structured Play,
   202
Griffiths Mental Development Scales,
   197–198
Gussi infants, 50

Handicapped children, 200, 370–374
Harvard Child Maltreatment Project,
   166
Head Start programs, 361, 408–409,
   484
Health care access for infants, 482–483
Heroin, 149
High-risk method, parental mental ill-
   ness, 120
Hispanic families, 60, 64
Holding environment, 23, 192
Homelessness, 76, 482
Home Observation for Measurement
   of the Environment, 201–202
Hospitalized infants, 91–92
   breast-fed infants, 96–97

emergency admissions, 97
   process studies, 96
Hospitals
   mental health worker influencing
      ecology, 98–100
   school-age children's experiences, 91
Human development models, 57
Hypersensitive type, regulatory disorder, 282–283, 284–286

Identification of disorders, parental
   mental illness, 123
Imitation and interaction, siblings, 51–
   52
Impact on maternal mental health
   fathers, 42
Inattentive parenting, 81
Indiscriminate attachment disorder,
   340–341
Individual code, environtype, 11
Individual differences
   affecting outcomes
      adolescent parenthood, 111
      failure to thrive (FTT), 318
Individualized Family Service Plan
   (IFSP), 60
Individual state and developmental
   regulation
   parental mental illness, 125–126
Individuals who overcome biological
   adversity, 3
Infant and Toddler Learning Program,
   370
Infant assessment
   measures, 196–200
   parent–infant interaction/relation-
      ship measures, 200–204
   process, 192–194
   reliability and validity, 194–196
   therapeutic process, 204–206
Infant–caregiver
   family relationships, 38–39
Infant characteristics
   failure to thrive (FTT), 319–320
Infant day care, 445–459
Infant distress regarding custody, 471–
   473
   evaluating reactions, 471–472
   infant-stimulated distress variables,
      472–473
   parent-stimulated distress variables,
      472
Infant Health and Development Program, 368
Infant in context
   family support concepts, 404–405
Infant mental health workers, 98–102
   case examples, 99–100, 101, 102
   consultation and support, 100–101
   influencing hospital ecology, 98–100
   providing direct treatment, 101–102
Infant Mullen Scales of Early Learning,
   194, 198–199
Infant–parent psychotherapy, 427–441
   contraindications, 439
   effectiveness, 439–441

evaluation process, 428–434
other applications, 439
patients, 427–428
therapeutic mistakes, 436–438
treatment process, 434–436
Infants
input to relationship
information gathering for interviews, 185–186
research procedures in clinical assessment, 212–213
status symbol for adolescents, 80
temperament, 17
Infant-stimulated distress variables
infant distress regarding custody, 472–473
Information gathering for interviews, 181–188
attachment relationship, 182–183
parent–infant interaction and relationship, 181–182
physiological regulation, 183–184
play, 184
power and control, 184–185
regulation of emotion, 185
safety and protection of infant, 183
specific precipitant, 188
teaching and learning, 184
what the infant brings to relationships, 185–186
what parents bring to relationships, 186–188
Inhibited attachment disorder, 336, 342–343
Integration, parental mental illness, 133–136
Interactional disturbances
communication disorders, 266
Interaction guidance, 414–425
assessment of family and caregiving environment, 415–416
case example, 419–424
evaluation, 424–425
family play, 414–415
family treatment, 416–418
therapeutic approach, 418–419
Interactionist model of development, 5, 8
Interaction style
parental mental illness, 126–127
Interactive processes, 20
Interactive strategies
communication disorders, 273–274
Intergenerational context of parent–infant relationships, 14, 15–19
parental contributions, 15–17
Intergenerational transmission
maltreatment, 162
parental mental illness, 122
Internal working models, 16, 17, 80
attachment, 334
Interpersonal context, secondary/selected interventions, 395–396
Intervention
autism, 245–247
communication disorders, 272–273
sleep disorders, 311–313

transactional model of child development, 7
who should implement, 64–66
Interviews
anxiety-provoking, 179–181
background information on infant and family, 177–178
clinical relational matrix, 174–175
formulation, 188–189
goal, 174
with infants and families, 173–189
Information gathering, 181–188
termination, 188–189
transference, 175–177
IQ scores, parental mental illness, 125
parental mental illness, 125

Job Opportunities and Basic Skills (JOBS), 483–484
Joint attention, 192, 263
Joint custody, 468–469
Jointly-focused early intervention, 363, 367–369, 371–374
Judicial determinations, custody of infants, 462–463

Kauai Longitudinal Study, 164
Keller, Helen, 3
Kids Count, 159
Kikuyu infants, 10, 50

Language adjustment, communication disorder, 274
Language and attachment
secondary/selected interventions, 394–395
Language and communication development, 262–264
Language and communication disorders
sequelae of early childhood, 267–268
Language-related cognitive abilities
communication disorders, 271
Languages, 27
Learning contexts, 271–272
Legal issues, custody of infants, 462–463
Lifespan developmental approach, 107
Longitudinal designs, parental mental illness, 124
Love withdrawal, 28–29
Low-birthweight infants, early intervention, 364–370
Low intelligence, 162
Low-intensity, early intervention, 363, 369–370, 374
Low socioeconomic status, 162
underweight infants study, 7

Malignancies, 89
Maltreatment
assessment of risk factors, 167

co-occurring forms of, 162
death from, 160
drowning and near-drowning, 161
failure to thrive, 161
fetal abuse, 161–162
history of, 162
and infant development, 159–168
Munchausen syndrome by proxy, 161
nature and scope of problem, 159–160
physical abuse, 160
primary prevention, 167–168
protective factors, 164
risk factors, 162–163
sequelae, 164–167
sexual abuse, 161
statistics, 159–160
treatment, 168
Management, attachment disorders, 345–346
Marijuana abuse, 153–154
Marital dissatisfaction, 131–132
Marital quality
before birth of child, 15
parental mental illness, 131–132
Marital satisfaction, 41
Mastery motivation in relational context
mutual regulatory processes, 26–27
Matched states, 21
Maternal characteristics
failure to thrive (FTT), 320
Maternal diagnosis
parental mental illness, 122–123
Maternal employment
day care, 451
Maternal grandmothers, 45
Maternal psychological variables
day care, 450–451
Maternal psychopathology, 129
Maternal substance abuse, 143–155
Measurement
day care, 448–449
family context, 17–19
infant assessment, 196–200
Medication
sleep disorders, 311
Mental health risks
adolescent parenthood, 108–109
Mental retardation, 250–258
epidemiology, 250–251
evaluation and differential diagnosis, 254–256
family context, 256
natural history, 252–254
pathogenesis, 251–252
perinatal difficulties, 252
prenatal causes, 252
presenting signs and symptoms, 254
risk factors, 253
treatment, 257–258
MERGER intervention, 352–353, 356–357
Merycism, feeding disorders, 323–324
Mesosystem, 57, 98
Methadone, 149

Microsystem, 98
Middle-of-the-night insomnia, 309
Minnesota Mother–Child Project, 167
Misidentification of children, 61
Mixed type regulatory disorders, 283–284
Model of illness, 63
Models of transmission
    parental mental illness, 121–122
Montreal Children's Hospital, 88
Moral emotions, 27–28
Mother–infant relationship
    facial affects, 21
    failure to thrive (FTT), 320–321
    in poverty, 82
    secondary/selected interventions, 396
    transactional model of child development, 6
Mothers
    attentiveness to poor infants, 78
    mood swings, 78–79
Multidisciplinary, 225
Multigenerational, 225
Multiple admissions, 91
Multiple caregivers
    in poverty, 82
Multiple-risk models
    parental mental illness, 136
Munchausen syndrome by proxy
    maltreatment and infant development, 161
Mutual regulation model
    parental mental illness, 135
Mutual regulatory processes, 19–30
    emotion regulation, 19–23
    between infant and caregiver, 14
    mastery motivation in relational context, 26–27
    regulation of evaluative standards and affects, 27–30

National Center for Clinical Infant Programs, 229
Nation Child Care Staffing Study, 486
Natural history
    mental retardation, 252–254
Nature and nurture significance, 4
Nature of child–parent contact
    custody, 469–470
Near-drowning, 161
Negative maternal attitude toward pregnancy, 162
Neonatal Abstinence Scale (NAS), 146
Neonatal intensive care unit, 94
    fathers in, 95
    siblings in, 95
Neurobiological studies
    autism, 241
Night waking problems, 307–308
No-illness control groups
    parental mental illness, 124
Nonattached attachment disorders, 338–340
Nonautistic Pervasive Developmental Disorders, 237–238

Nonmaternal care
    and attachment in day care, 446–453
    and cognitive development in day care, 446
    and social adjustment in day care, 453–455
Non-normative development, 12
Normal growth and eating patterns
    failure to thrive (FTT), 317–318
Nursing Child Assessment Satellite Training Teaching and Feeding Scales, 201
Nutritional factors
    poor, 147
    of poor infants, 75
    sleep disorders, 309

Obesity, 353–354
Object relations point of view, 107
Older infants and toddlers
    research procedures in clinical assessment, 213–218
Opiates, 148–151
Opium, 150
Optimal Learning Environment program, 373
Organic versus nonorganic
    failure to thrive (FTT), 318–319
Organizational perspective
    of social interaction, 19–20
Other-directed behaviors, 21
Outcome
    early intervention, 375–378
    failure to thrive (FTT), 322–223
    Post–Traumatic Stress Disorder (PTSD), 295
    prematurity, 89–92
Overfeeding, 353–354
    feeding disorders, 327
Overnight child–parent contact
    custody, 470

Parasomnias, 313–314
Paregoric, 150
Parental Acceptance Procedure, 217–218
Parental care leave, 488–489
Parental contributions
    intergenerational context of parent–infant relationships, 15–17
Parental drug abuse, 75
Parental goals hierarchy, 57
Parental mental illness, 120–136
    affect attunement model, 134–135
    age of children, 123–124
    attachment relationships, 127–128
    beyond dyad, 129–130
    children born of, 124–133
    conflict in interactions, 129
    consequences for infant development, 121–124
    depression, 123, 126
    diagnoses, 121
    distress–relief interactions, 126

DQ scores, 125
dyadic interaction, 125–129
environmental models, 122
face-to-face interaction, 126
family context, 130–133
goodness-of-fit model, 133–134
high-risk method, 120
identification of disorders, 123
individual functioning, 124–125
individual state and developmental regulation, 125–126
integration, 133–136
interaction style, 126–127
intergenerational transmission, 122
IQ scores, 125
longitudinal designs, 124
marital quality, 131–132
maternal diagnosis, 122–123
methodological issues, 123–124
models of transmission, 121–122
multiple-risk models, 136
mutual regulation model, 135
no-illness control groups, 124
parenting perceptions and beliefs, 128–129
postpartum depression, 132–133
psychosocial stress, 133
schizophrenia, 123, 125–126, 130
transactional model, 135–136
"Parent and Child Education," 407
Parent Behavior Progression, 202–203
Parent–child communication
    secondary/selected interventions, 393–398
Parent–Child Early Relational Assessment, 203–204, 215–216
Parent–child relationships
    primary/universal intervention, 391
Parent-focused
    early intervention, 363, 365, 370–371
Parent–infant contact
    custody of infants, 466
Parent–Infant Development Program and Clinic, 204
Parent–infant interaction/relationship
    infant assessment measures, 200–204
    information gathering for interviews, 181–182
Parent–Infant Relationship Global Assessment Scale, 230
Parents
    attachment relationships, 17
    criminal record, 162
    early intervention, 380
    education
        family support, 408
    input to relationships
        information gathering for interviews, 186–188
    perceptions and beliefs
        parental mental illness, 128–129
    psychopathology development, 11
    research procedures in clinical assessment, 218
    responsiveness to infant signals, 19

social relationships
  primary/universal intervention, 390–392
"Parents of Prematures," 403
Parent-stimulated distress variables
  infant distress regarding custody, 472
Parent support programs
  early intervention, 365–366
Parent training/education programs
  early intervention, 366–367
Passive person, 4
Passive person–active environment, 5
Passive person–passive environment, 4
Paternity blues, 133
Pathogenesis
  mental retardation, 251–252
Pathological model of family adaptation, 256
Patients
  infant–parent psychotherapy, 427–428
Pattern of early care
  poor infants family life, 76–78
Peer relationships, 268
Perinatal difficulties
  mental retardation, 252
Personnel
  early intervention, 380–381
Pervasive Developmental Disorders, 236–247
Phenobarbital, 150
Phenotype, 11
Phenylketonuria (PKU), 352
Physical abuse
  maltreatment and infant development, 160
Physical play
  fathers, 43–44
Physiological factors
  failure to thrive (FTT), 317
Physiological regulation
  information gathering for interviews, 183–184
Piaget, Jean, 351
Pica, feeding disorders, 324–325
Placement of infants, 462–477
Play therapy, 64
  behaviors, 21
  information gathering for interviews, 184
  session conclusion, 417
Postnatal factors
  communication disorders, 266
  substance abuse, 144–145
Postpartum depression
  parental mental illness, 132–133
Post-traumatic eating disorder
  feeding disorders, 326–327
Post-Traumatic Stress Disorder (PTSD), 291–303
  case examples, 296–300
  developmental considerations, 292–295
  historical overview, 291–292
  outcome, 295
  remembering experience, 293

symptoms, 293
  treatment, 300–302
Poverty
  adolescent parenthood, 108
  childhood adversity, 80–81
  communication disorders, 266
  demographics, 74
  economic conditions, 75–76
  family life, 76–81
  health and social risks, 74–75
  implications for well-being, 83–85
  and infant development, 73–85
  of infants, 481–484
  pattern of early care, 76–78
  poor families, 75–76
  quality of early parenting, 78–80
  relationships, 81–83
  urban neighborhoods, 76
Power and control
  information gathering for interviews, 184–185
Practicing family, 14
Premature infants, 89–91
  poor, 79
  secondary/selected interventions, 398
  stereotypes, 93
Prematurity, 87–103
  behavioral risk factors, 89
  biological risk factors, 88–89
  developmental sequelae, 88–98
  outcome studies, 89–92
  prevalence, 87–88
  process studies, 92–98
  survival, 87–88
Prenatal care
  clinics, 388–389
  delivery problems, 387–388
  primary/universal intervention, 387–389
Prenatal causes of mental retardation, 252
Prenatal/Early Infancy Project, 485
Prenatal influences, substance abuse, 143–144
Preoccupied attachment, 25
Preschool Behavior Questionnaire, 90
Presenting signs and symptoms, mental retardation, 254
Pressed-lips expression in infants, 24
Prevention-oriented, 225
Preventive interventions, 386–399
  primary/universal, 387–392
  secondary/selected, 387, 392–398
  tertiary/indicated, 387
Primary caregivers
  affective development in primary caregiving relationship, 14–31
  grandparents as, 48
Primary intersubjectivity, 22
Primary language disorders, 262
Primary prevention
  maltreatment and infant development, 167–168
Primary regulatory-based eating disorder
  regulatory disorders, 284

Primary regulatory-based sleep disorder
  regulatory disorders, 284
Primary/universal intervention
  abortion services, 388
  child health preventive care, 389–390
  delivery problems, 387–388
  parent–child relationships, 391
  parenting through social relationships, 390–392
  prenatal care, 387–389
Process-orientation, 20
Process studies
  hospitalized non-premature infants, 96
  prematurity, 92–98
Project EDGE, 372
Protective factors
  adolescent parenthood, 112–114
  maltreatment and infant development, 164
Protolanguage, 23
Psychic Trauma Disorders, 229
  case example, 231
Psychosocial dwarfism, 164
  feeding disorders, 325–326
Psychosocial factors
  autism, 241–242
Psychosocial stress
  parental mental illness, 133
Psychosocial stressors, 230
Psychosomatic processes
  early-onset asthma, 354–356
  historical evolution, 350–351
  infantile onset obesity, 353–354
  intervention, 356–357
  nature–nurture equation, 351–353
Psychosomatic processes and physical illnesses, 350–357
Psychotherapy, 427–441
Public Law 99-457, 60, 194, 361
Puerto Rican families, 58

Quality of care
  day care, 455–458
Quality of early parenting
  poor infants family life, 78–80

Racial status, 163
Receptive language and communication
  communication disorders, 270–271
Reciprocal interactionist model of development, 6
Recording devices, sleep disorders, 307
Regulation and development
  environtype, 11–12
Regulation of emotion
  information gathering for interviews, 185
Regulation of evaluative standards and affects
  mutual regulatory processes, 27–30
Regulatory behaviors, 21

Regulatory disorders, 229, 280–290
    active–aggressive type, 283, 286–288
    case example, 231–232
    hypersensitive type, 282–283, 284–286
    mixed type, 283–284
    new construct, 280–282
    primary regulatory-based eating disorder, 284
    primary regulatory-based sleep disorder, 284
    therapeutic approaches, 284–290
    therapeutic principles, 289–290
    types, 282–284
    underreactive type, 283, 288–289
Regulatory systems in development, 9
Relational stability, 30
Relationship to other disorders
    attachment disorders, 344–345
Reliability and validity
    infant assessment, 194–196
Remembering experience
    Post-Traumatic Stress Disorder (PTSD), 293
REM-NREM cycle
    sleep disorders, 306
Reparative sequences, 21
Represented family, 14
Research procedures in clinical assessment, 210–219
    procedures for older infants and toddlers, 213–218
    procedures for parents, 218
    procedures for young infants, 212–213
    specific structured assessments, 211–219
Resiliency, 112
Rett Syndrome, 238
Richman–Graham Behavior Questionnaire, 90
Risk factors
    adolescent parenthood, 108
    communication disorders, 264–267
    maltreatment and infant development, 162–163
    mental retardation, 253
    secondary/selected interventions, 392–393
Rochester Longitudinal Study (RLS), 8
Role of marriage
    fathers, 41
Role-reversed
    attachment disorders, 343–344
Rough-and-tumble play
    fathers, 43
Rumination disorder
    feeding disorders, 323–324
Rutter Child Scale, 90

Safety of infant
    information gathering for interviews, 183
Scaffolding, 192
Schizophrenia, parental mental illness, 123, 125–126, 130

The School of the 21st Century, 487–488
Secondary intersubjectivity, 23
Secondary language disorders, 262
Secondary/selected interventions
    clinical nursing models project, 396–397
    interpersonal context, 395–396
    language and attachment, 394–395
    mothers and infants, 396
    parent–child communication, 393–398
    preterm infants, 398
    risk factors, 392–393
Secure attachment, 24, 334
Security of attachment, 20
Self-conscious emotions, 27
Self-directed behaviors, 21
Self-esteem, 113
Self-help groups
    family support, 408
Self-regulation of distress, 23–26
Serious medical illness, 87–103
Sexual abuse, 161
Shell shock, 291
Shyness, 18–19
Siblings
    attachment and separation, 50
    caretaking, 50–51
    characteristics
        failure to thrive (FTT), 321–322
        imitation and interaction, 51–52
    indirect effects, 50
    influences on infant development, 50–52
    in neonatal intensive care unit, 95
    role in family relationships, 50–52
    sibships, 470–471
    turn taking, 51
Sibships, 470–471
Simple vocabulary, communication disorder, 274
Single-parent custody, 468
Sleep apnea syndrome, 314
Sleep disorders, 305–315
    assessment of sleep, 306–307
    behavioral techniques, 312–313
    common sleep problems, 307–309
    developmental aspects of sleep–wake organization, 305–306
    diurnal organization, 305–306
    intervention, 311–313
    medication, 311
    middle-of-the-night insomnia, 309
    night waking problems, 307–308
    nutritional factors, 309
    origins, 309–311
    parasomnias, 313–314
    persistance, 311
    recording devices, 307
    REM-NREM cycle, 306
    sleep apnea syndrome, 314
    sleep onset insomnia, 308–309
    sleep–wake cycle, 305–306
    ultradian organization, 306
Sleep–wake cycle

sleep disorders, 305–306
Slow-to-warm-up infants, 18
Social–affective behavior
    communication disorders, 271
Social–anthropological models, 56
Social comprehensive, 113
Social development
    autism, 239–240
Social–ecological perspective, 107
Social input adjustment, communication disorder, 274
Social interaction, 263
    organizational perspective, 19–20
Social-interactive behaviors, 166
Socially promiscuous
    attachment disorders, 341–342
Social policy, 480–490
    new U.S. family, 480–481
Social referencing, 22–23, 130
Social regulatory systems in development, 8, 9
Social stress, 162
Sociocultural aspects of care, 60
Sociocultural context of infant development
    clinical implications, 60–66
    empirical evidence, 57–59
    ethnic groups in U.S., 59–60
    implications for mental health care providers, 66–67
    problem definition, 61–62
    theoretical models, 56–57
    what can be done, 63–64
    who can help with problem, 64–66
    why is there a problem, 62–63
Socioemotional factors, 90
Specific precipitant, information gathering for interviews, 188
Specific structured assessments
    research procedures in clinical assessment, 211–219
Speech production
    communication disorders, 271
Stability and organization in relationships, 30
Stanford–Binet Intelligence Test, 194, 198
Starvation, 161
Still-face procedure, 21
The Strange Situation, 50, 213–214, 334
Structural damage by drug abuse, 143
The Structured Playroom, 214–215
Structured research procedures in clinical assessment, 210–219
Substance abuse, 163
    alcohol, 151–153
    clinical implications, 154
    cocaine, 145–148
    marijuana, 153–154
    opiates, 148–151
    postnatal influences, 144–145
    prenatal influences, 143–144
Sudden infant death syndrome (SIDS), 310
Symptoms, Post-Traumatic Stress Disorder (PTSD), 293

Synaction, 93
System of relationships complexity, 14

Teaching, information gathering for interviews, 184
Teaching Skills Inventory, 371
Technical expertise, custody of infants, 465–466
Temperament, 113–114
  affect focus, 19
  biological differences, 18
  dimensions, 17
  as inherited personality, 18
  models of family context, 17–19
  theories, 17–19
Termination
  interviews, 188–189
Terrible twos, 27
Tertiary/indicated preventive intervention, 387
Theoretical models, sociocultural context of infant development, 56–57
Theory of mind, 23
Therapeutic approaches
  regulatory disorders, 284–290
Therapeutic mistakes
  infant–parent psychotherapy, 436–438
Therapeutic principles
  case examples, 284–289
  regulatory disorders, 289–290

Therapeutic process
  infant assessment, 204–206
Therapist–child relationship, 430–431
Therapist–parent relationship, 430
Tool use procedure, 26–27
Tool use task, 216
Transactional Intervention Program, 371
Transactional model, 57
  of child development, 6–8
  intervention program, 7
  mother–infant interaction, 6
  parental mental illness, 135–136
  premature infants, 92–96
  twins study, 7
Transdisciplinary Play-Based Assessment, 199
Transference, interview process, 175–177
Trauma, custody of infants, 467
Traumatic neurosis, 291
Treatment
  failure to thrive (FTT), 322
  maltreatment and infant development, 168
  mental retardation, 257–258
  Post-Traumatic Stress Disorder (PTSD), 300–302
Treatment process
  boundary issues, 436
  content, 435–436
  formats, 434–435
  infant–parent psychotherapy, 434–436
Turn taking
  sibling, 51

Twins study
  transactional model of child development, 7

Ultradian organization sleep disorders, 306
Underreactive type regulatory disorder, 283, 288–289
Unmatched states, 21
Unwed fathers of poor infants, 77
Urban neighborhoods, poor families in, 76

Vagal reactivity, 18
Vagal tone, 18
Vermont Infant Studies Project, 365
Videotape viewing and commentary, family treatment, 416–418
Visual co-orientation, 130

Way stations, 92
Wechsler Intelligence Scale for Children, 198
Welfare families, 74
Withdrawal symptoms, 149–150
Within-the-person construct, 19
Women in out-of-home workforce, 480–481
Working Model of the Child Interview, 218

Yale Child Welfare Research Program, 483